Mystery Women: An Encyclopedia of Leading Women Characters in Mystery Fiction

Vol. III (1990-2000) Revised

Colleen Barnett

Poisoned Pen Press

Revised Edition

10 9 8 7 6 5 4 3 2

Library of Congress Catalog Card Number: 2001086357

ISBN: 978-1-59058-422-4

Poisoned Pen Press
6962 E. First Ave. Ste 103
Scottsdale, AZ 85251
www.poisonedpenpress.com
info@poisonedpenpress.com

Printed in the United States of America

Dedication

This book is dedicated to mystery fans, beginning with the 6th, 7th, and 8th graders at St. Joseph's Academy in Green Bay, Wisconsin (where I attended grade school and high school) who shared my passion for Nancy Drew and Judy Bolton. The series has been written to share my discoveries. I hope that readers will correct my flaws (in a kindly fashion) and make me aware of new authors and new sleuths.

What fun reading can be!

...and to the additions to our family, Jean and Lucee, Trina, Joshua and Ainslee, Metsu and Abebu. What joy they have brought.

In Memoriam
John E. Barnett
(1923-2004)

New Table of Contents

Characteristics of the Female Sleuth in the 1990s and Beyond

Like other fictional characters, female sleuths may live in the past or the future. They may represent current times with some level of reality or shape their settings to suit an agenda. There are audiences for both realism and escapism in the mystery novel. It is interesting, however, to compare the fictional world of the mystery sleuth with the world in which readers live. Of course, mystery readers do not share one simplistic world. They live in urban, suburban, and rural areas, as do the female heroines in the books they read. They may choose a book because it has a familiar background or because it takes them to places they long to visit. Readers may be rich or poor; young or old; conservative or liberal. So are the heroines. What incredible choices there are today in mystery series! This three-volume encyclopedia of women characters in the mystery novel is like a gigantic menu. Like a menu, the descriptions of the items that are provided are subjective.

Volume 3 of *Mystery Women* as currently updated adds an additional 42 sleuths to the 500 plus who were covered in the initial Volume 3. These are more recently discovered sleuths who were introduced during the period from January 1, 1990 to December 31, 1999. This total almost doubles the number of sleuths introduced in the 1980s (298 of whom were covered in Volume 2) and easily exceeded the 347 series (and some outstanding individuals) described in Volume 1, which covered a 130-year period from 1860-1979. It also includes updates on those individuals covered in the first edition; changes in status, short reviews of books published since the first edition through December 31, 2008.

There are discernable reasons for the explosion in mystery series with female sleuths. The mystery novel has gone beyond the puzzle aspect to embrace issues that directly affect the lives of contemporary women. Many, but not all of the narratives, have serious themes such as the pressures faced by career women with children and/or spouses; the environmental consequences of industrial expansion; and the evils of child abuse, incest, and spousal abuse that were always there, but of which we are now more aware. Not everyone wants to be educated when they pick up a mystery novel, but if well done, the social message can be delivered as part of an exciting investigation. Many women readers have turned from the traditional novel to the mystery novel to explore their own feelings about the world they live in.

Women buy more mysteries than men; read more mysteries than men; and female sleuths dominate the world of the mystery author. Some male writers have written excellent series featuring women under their own names; others use initials or pseudonyms. Frank King has had four such series; one, Sally Tepper under his own name; three as Lydia Adamson; i.e. Alice Nestleton, Deirdre Quinn Nightingale, and Lucy Wayles. Other male authors have both female and male sleuth series and utilize the female in supporting roles in books identified as featuring the male.

The traditional mystery still exists. The puzzle mystery (see Cora Felton and Sherry Carter by Parnell Hall) and the cozies proliferate. Familiar genres like the police procedural and the hard-boiled private detective are there, but now the primary character, or at least a significant member of the ensemble, will be a woman. She may have talents and skills that complement those of the traditional male detective. Andy Sipowicz of *NYPD Blue* would meet his match in Jane Tennison.

The number of females with major roles in police procedurals exceeds 75 in this decade. That could not have been realistic before the full impact of the Equal Employment Opportunity Act of the 1960s. Add in others who work in association with police departments (forensic specialists, bloodhound trainers, bail skip tracers and parole officers); and well over one hundred private investigators. The number of female attorneys is not at all unrealistic. Most current law school classes have close to 50 percent women students.

However, the menu includes many sub-genres tailored for women readers. The antique dealers, the caterers, operators of hotels and bed & breakfasts, quilters and crafters each have their own constituency. Their popularity may reflect the trend back to more traditional female roles as explored by Karine Moe and Dianna Shandy in *Glass Ceilings and 100-Hour Couples* and by Gail Collins in *America's Women* and *When Everything Changed.* All three of these books combined statistical material and personal interviews indicating that some women chose to "opt-out" of full-time, high energy careers to place a greater emphasis on family. These changes included: part-time work when the employer agreed (although it may have meant reduced salaries); early retirement, and perhaps a change in occupation to managing a shop, a Bed and Breakfast, or some similar business which allowed more flexibility as to schedules and hours worked.

The changes in style of many female sleuths also reflect legal, political, and economic changes. Females, according to Collins, (1) now own one-third of U. S. businesses; (2) women are earning 55% of all college degrees including more than half recently granted in dental and veterinary schools; close to that amount in medical and law schools; and provide 47% of the current workforce. Those numbers may well be changed by the profound recession of 2008-2009 and later. The occupations dominated by men, such as construction, have suffered more seriously than those in which women have secured parity. This has lead to an increase in marriages where the wife is either the primary breadwinner or, at least for a time, the only one.

Marriage and Children

A simple overview of the sleuths covered in Volume 3 indicated that the majority were women in mid-life, the thirties and forties. Those are years when members of the general female population are trying to make it to their son's or daughter's basketball games, attending band concerts, and preparing for summer camp, school graduations and weddings. This is a great change from the early days of the mystery novel that focused on the elderly spinster and the young unmarried woman.

Many of the current sleuths disdain marriage or consider it a short-term contract, voidable at will. The number of those sleuths identified as "single with lover" exceeds that of those termed merely "single." There are happily married couples, to be sure, but usually they are to be found among those for whom murders are not a professional interest. The pressures upon police officers as shown in the high divorce rate makes that understandable.

A small number of sleuths proclaimed themselves as disliking children, not wanting their bodies damaged by pregnancy, or their lives complicated by families. Jane Tennison, Mary diNunzio, Skip Langdon, and Munch Mancini had abortions. At least two-dozen sleuths were unwed mothers or pregnant outside of marriage when their narratives ended. Several chose not to inform the father of the child (Molly Bearpaw and Dr. Amy Prescott). The motives for the decisions not to marry or to have children were a facet of the need for independence, and the fear of making a commitment. That may sound fascinating at age twenty-one, but can be viewed differently at forty, fifty, even sixty when the grandchildren are coming to visit—the reader's perspective changes over time. The free spirited adventuress who appealed to a reader in her/his youth may seem shallow, even barren, as the decades past.

Some of the sleuths covered herein are identified as single moms (unwed, divorced or widowed) for at least part of the series. Quite a few married again. Whether single mom or married couple, where both parents worked there were childcare problems. Some children felt neglected or ignored. Solutions included help from relatives, au pairs, live-in help, and childcare facilities. What was even more controversial were the risks taken by mothers of minor children; those who were married, but more particularly those who were the sole parent.

For the older sleuth, there were fewer problems. The children were adults, had lives of their own. Biggie Weatherford, whose deceased son was an alcoholic, had a second chance. She took her grandson, J.R., into her home. This is a not unusual situation. Many grandparents in the real world fill that role when their children have drug or alcohol problems.

One way in which childless sleuths show concern, even a nurturing spirit, is in special attention to nieces (Kay Scarpetta, Nikki Trakos, and Glynis Tryon), or for the children of their husband's first marriage (Meg Gillis, Simona Griffo, and Laura Principal).

Parents and Siblings

Having spouses, children or pets was more or less a voluntary decision. Having parents was a biological necessity. Fathers deserted their families (Allison O'Neill, Dr. Sylvia Strange, Vicky Bauer and others), died young (Mandy Dyer, Caroline Canfield, and Rachel Alexander), were alcoholics (Kay Williams, Dr. Michael Stone, Nan Robinson, Angela Gennaro and others), or rejected their daughters (Helen Black, Sarah Decker Brandt, Lucie Wilton Archer, and Tory Travers). A few were abusers (Fey Croaker, Eve Dallas, Anna Turnipseed).

Mothers abandoned their daughters, too (Anne Vernon and Fran Varaday), or were alcoholics (Vicky Bauer, China Bayles, Lily Connor, and others). Mothers were more likely to be rejected because they interfered (Midge Cohen, and April Woo), or were too critical. A few female sleuths lost both parents as children and were cared for by relatives. Aunts scored low as parental substitutes. They were stuffy and restrictive (Cassandra Swann), or cruel (Mary Russell and Ursula Blanchard). Grandfathers came off well (Laura Fleming, Casey Jones, Jennifer Gray). Grandmothers varied from kindly (Kate Shugak, Benni Harper, Jimi Plain, and Molly Bearpaw) to rigid (Emily Silver) or mean (Jackie Kaminsky). Parents could be problematic in other ways. Some sleuths made noble efforts to care for senile or chronically mentally ill parents (Anne Hardaway, Judith Thornton, and Benny Rosato).

Siblings frequently became the focus of investigations by female sleuths. Brothers were accused of pederasty (Karen Perry-Mondori and Phoebe Siegel), or were killed in Vietnam or on duty as police officers (Maggie MacGowen, and Claire Breslinky). Brothers, sisters, fathers and mothers were occasionally accused of crimes and proven innocent by the female sleuths. Lest we forget, most relatives were supportive and loving.

Widows were no longer beyond romance. For one thing, some widows were young women whose husbands were killed in accidents, or murdered. Beyond that, age forty is no longer the end of life. Widows and divorcees meet men in the investigations, leading to affairs or a second marriage.

Pets and Cars as Substitutes

One aspect of the need to have controlled associations with another living creature is the acquisition of pets. The sleuths of the Nineties frequently have a dog (usually a named breed, but more frequently recently a mutt). The dogs range from Brenda Midnight's tiny Yorkie to Great Danes (Dr. Haley McAlister) and Scottish Deerhounds (Teal Stewart). Some of the dogs serve useful purposes as guard dogs or show dogs. Connor Westphal has a signal dog, a Siberian Husky, to help with her hearing problems. Dogs create problems; they have to be walked, groomed, licensed, and kept quiet so as not to annoy the neighbors. They're not quite as difficult as children, but still! Cats are different. They are more independent, needing less attention. At least 60 female sleuths in Volume 3 had acquired cats. They too ranged in size from Magdalena Yoder's kitten (which she carried around in her bra!) to Irene Kelly's twenty-pounder. Cats on a few occasions became co-protagonists—Harry Haristeen had to share the limelight with Mrs. Murphy and a Welsh Corgi named Tee Tucker. They carried on conversations (in italics) and led Harry to solutions and out of danger. Penelope Warren had Big Mike and Temple Barr had to deal with Midnight Louie. Even castration didn't settle Midnight Louie down. There were stranger pets: Stella the Stargazer a.k.a. Jane Smith had a lizard that laid an egg. Chicago Nordejoong had an eight-foot boa constrictor. Things could get tight around her! Hannah Malloy and Kiki Goldstein shared a Vietnamese pig. Charlie Plato had a Netherland dwarf rabbit. Charlotte Carter had no problems with her stuffed rabbit. All were evidence of some level of nurturing in the sleuth.

Some sleuths personified their vehicles, even giving them names. Fran Vierling had an old Blue Jaguar named Ralph. Other sleuths retained cars belonging to their deceased fathers, brothers, husbands and lovers in order to hold on to memories. There was a sense that having an old car evidenced a lack of conformity—Sutton McPhee had her Beetle; Haley McAlister had a 1960 Corvette convertible; Adele Monsarrat had a 1978 Pontiac station wagon. Claire Rawlings drove an old brown Mercedes; Molly Piper had a 1986 Honda Civic. Matty Madrid drove her "Red Menace", an elderly Toyota. Finances entered into the picture. Harriet Bushrow, an octogenarian, drove her old car until someone blew it up. Liz Sullivan lived in her 1969 Volkswagen bus for a while. Taylor Morgan's Suzuki Sidekick enabled her to reach her isolated Alaskan home in the winters. Robin Light drove a yellow Checker cab. Connor Westphal had a 1957 Chevrolet, but usually rode her mountain bike to work. Sophie Rivers had no car.

Villains

The villains have changed too. The end of the Cold War diminished the espionage novel or at least refocused it on individuals or small groups as opposed to evil empires. The headlines have promoted the serial killer who, motivated by a displaced anger that arises from the past, murders individuals with whom he or she had limited personal contact. Agatha Christie and her contemporaries had rules about not having servants, mentally ill persons, or those not introduced early in the narrative turn out to be killers. (Agatha on occasion broke such rules.) Now, a large percentage of killers are perceived as mentally ill.

There were still the basic motivations of greed, jealousy and revenge, which operated in the more intimate circles of the victim's lives. Plotlines often contrasted the official police determination that the killer was a burglar, or a serial-or drive-by-murderer, with the insistence of the sleuth that the motivation lay within the family, the workplace, or the past. As in prior decades, sleuths sometimes did not share their findings, allowing criminals to go unpunished when the motivation for the crime seemed justifiable.

Major influences on the mystery novel:

Malice Domestic® promotes mysteries that have controlled sexuality and violence with their Agatha Awards. However, many of the highly promoted narratives exploit sexuality and violence, as do movies and television programs.

Religion plays a relatively small role in mystery narratives. Clerical sleuths include Sister Agnes Bourdillion; Sr. Cecile Buddenbrooks, Rev. Theodora Braithwaite and Mother Lavinia Grey. There are also series published by fundamentalist religious houses in which religion has a considerable impact on characters such as Danielle Ross, Beth Marie Cartwright, and Beth Seibelli (Cole). Catholics take a hard rap. At least eighteen sleuths present themselves as having rejected Catholicism. On the other hand, several Jewish sleuths found joy in reviving their religious life (Mary Russell and Jessica Drake). Tess Monaghan, Rachel O'Connor, and Phoebe Siegel each had one Jewish parent and one Irish Catholic parent. Patricia Sprinkle has an excellent series featuring MacLaren Yarbrough, a happily married woman with religious principles.

Politics remained important but without the Sixties fervor. Most sleuths were too young to have taken part in the anti-authority rebellions. There were conservatives such as Shirley McClintoch, Lilly Bennett, and Baroness Jack Troutbeck. Devon MacDonald, Marti Hirsch, Hannah Wolfe, and Francesca Miles were more radical in their viewpoints. To some degree this represents the changes in the role of women. Many of the achievements sought by the earlier feminists; i.e. equal pay, equal opportunity in employment, adequate parental leave, relief from sexual harassment had been, at least partially, achieved through legislation. They were, to the annoyance of early feminists, taken for granted. (Again see the books cited above by Collins).

The historical feminist viewpoints were well expressed through the mysteries by Nell Bray, a British Suffragette, Glynis Tryon, who was in Seneca Falls for the Woman's Convention, Hester Latterly, a British nurse who served in the Crimean War, and Magdalene La Bâtarde, a brothel keeper who had been abused by her husband. There was something both educational and comforting about the historical mysteries. They dealt with problems that had already been settled or at least alleviated. Catherine Levendeur's family suffered from anti-Semitism in the Twelfth century, but it has not disappeared. From the wildly wicked Claudia Seferius in Augustinian Rome to Eve Dallas in the 2040s, there were interesting women in interesting times.

Ethnic and Gender Sub-Genres

The lesbian mystery has become a significant sub-genre. Like mysteries with heterosexual heroines, they explore the problems of their existence: acceptance in the work place, rejection by families, and for a few, the desire to have children and/or to have their relationship given status by a marriage ceremony. Earlier lesbian mysteries came out of Naiad, New Victoria, or other feminist publishing houses. Now general publishers are releasing some. For one reason, established authors who have series with heterosexual sleuths may have a second one with a lesbian. Other signs of an acceptance of homosexuals are by their involvement with sleuths as relatives, neighbors, friends, helpers, and employees. (Sophie Greenway; Kay Scarpetta, Cat Caliban, Savannah Reid; Abby Timberlake, and Catherine Wilde). The acceptance of lesbian mysteries by a general readership may depend upon the explicitness of the sexual relationship or the anti-male stance of the sleuth.

Race and ethnicity were also explored in the mystery novels, some of which were written by African-American or Native American authors. African-American sleuths were far from the stereotyped servant role (except for devious Blanche White). They included police officers and private investigators, a stockbroker and a college professor.

Hispanic sleuths usually came from less affluent backgrounds, except for the Florida based Cuban community (Britt Montero and Lupe Solano). Matty Madrid, one of the recently discovered sleuths, had her roots in the Northern part of New Mexico and its Hispanic population.

Native Americans were almost always portrayed against the background of their reservations. They often projected their own spiritualism into the narratives (Molly Bearpaw, Ella Clah, and Daisy Perika). The protagonists were distinguished by their tribes (Vicky Holden, an Arapaho attorney; ex-convict Angela Biwaban, an Anishinabe from Minnesota; Vicky Bauer, a Canadian Indian teacher; and the best known Kate Shugak, an Aleut in Alaska. Some were of mixed parentage. Anna Turnipseed was part Modoc and part Japanese; Jane Whitefield's father was a Seneca; her mother was Irish-American.

There was a smaller contingent of Asian sleuths. None were played for laughs like Charlie Chan. They included Chinese Americans April Woo and Lydia Chin. Rei Shimura who was one-half Japanese and one-half American, and the devious Holly-Jean Ho, who wrestled the Triads. She was part Hakka Chinese, and part English.

Among the sleuths, at least nine had interracial affairs: Emily "Blue McCarren, Judy Best, Starletta Duvall, Robin Light, Meredyth Sanger, Dr. Amy Prescott, Liz Broward, April Woo, and Jane Tennison.

Handicaps and Skills

The sleuths included remarkably ingenious and courageous women. Among those with physical disabilities were:

- Callahan Garrity, Hannah Malloy, and Hannah Ives, who survived breast cancer;
- Haley McAlister, who spent her teenage years in seclusion because of leukemia;
- Connor Westphal and Annabelle Hardy-Maratos, who were deaf;
- Lauren Crowder, who coped with multiple sclerosis and managed a pregnancy;
- Amelia Sachs, who had arthritis;
- Kate Shugak, who had her throat slashed in subduing a child molester;
- Maddy Phillips, who was blind and paraplegic;
- Kay Farrow, who was a colorblind photographer;
- Bo Bradley, who was manic-depressive and Natalie Gold, who feared it because of her dad;
- Peaches Dann, who had memory problems; Ariel Gold, who had amnesia;
- Nora Callum, whose knee cap was blown away by gunshot;
- Filomena Buscarsela, whose lungs were damaged by toxic chemicals; and
- Jo Fuller, Torie O'Shea and Savannah Reid, who coped with weight problems.

The following were five-feet tall or under: Allie Babcock, Sunny Childs, Molly Piper, Kate Shugak, and Aurora Teagarden.

The following were six-feet tall or more: Starletta Duvall, Lark Dailey Dodge, Laura Ireland, Shirley McClintock, Dr. Evelyn Sutcliffe, and Nikki Trakos.

A dozen or more sleuths had problems with alcohol: Vicky Bauer, Anna Pigeon, Olivia Brown, Helen Black, Cora Felton, Nanette Hayes, and Jessica James. Others successfully used Alcoholics Anonymous or similar programs to stay sober: C. C. Scott, Blaine Stewart, Tyler Jones, and Lorraine Page. Claudia Seferius was addicted to gambling.

Women who endured the death of one or more children included: Harriet Bushrow, Kate Harrod, Devon MacDonald, Shirley McClintock (2), Lee Squires, Dr. Michael Stone, Lucie Wilton Archer, Hannah Trevor (3), and Catherine Wilde. Matty Madrid was the sole parent of a profoundly disabled daughter.

Some were unable to bear children and felt that loss: Smokey Brandon, Rosalie Cairns, Rachel Crowne, Tory Bauer, and Veronica Pace.

Both Helen Sorby and Magdalena Yoder were fooled into marrying bigamists.

Some of the women who killed in self-defense or in the line of duty suffered depression and guilt. Those who had been abused by fathers or spouses had long-term problems.

All in all, a gutsy group. There were a few who admitted that they were addicted to risk-taking (Kate Banning, Carrie Carlin, Molly DeWitt, Jennifer Marsh, and even Ginger Barnes). Several of them had spouses and children to consider. Others had prison records or ought to have them: Angela Biwaban, Lily Bard, Casey Jones, Liz Sullivan, and Catherine Wilde (who never got caught).

Among those with special skills:

- Maggie Maguire learned mesmerism, tumbling, and card tricks;
- Venus Diamond could lip read;
- A dozen or more spoke several languages—Fizz Fitzgerald, Simona Griffo, Matilda Haycastle, Jane Perry, and Cassandra Reilly;
- Ariel Gold had a terrific aural memory;
- Cassandra Swann a strong visual memory;
- Emma Rhodes had an IQ of 165; and
- Becky Belski, Ruby Rothman, Julie Blake, Anneke Haagen, Lorelei Muldoon, and others were skilled with computers.

Education

Leaving the historical series out of the equation, the female sleuths in the 90's and beyond were well educated. Fewer than a dozen indicated they had less than a high school degree. In addition to those who had completed high school, there were those who had several years of college, and a hundred or more who had bachelor's degrees. The sleuths included those with M.B.A., Ph.D., and medical, pharmacy, veterinary or law degrees. The named schools were heavy on the prestigious institutions: Stanford, UCLA, USC, and UC Berkeley on the West Coast, and Wellesley, Barnard, Sarah Lawrence, Harvard, Dartmouth, Cornell, Columbia, and Johns Hopkins on the East Coast. Among the Ph.D. degrees were those in geology, zoology, microbiology, and chemistry. However, not all their skills came from formal education.

Hollis Ball communicated with her deceased husband. Sarah Booth Delaney communicated with a maid who had attended her family for generations. Nuala McGrail and her infant daughter were fey. Several of the Native American sleuths possessed spiritual powers. Jo Hughes was an astrologer; Karen Hightower, a white witch.

Jordan Myles had been a top ranked tennis player; Eva Wylie was a wrestler; Cheryl Crane was a professional bicyclist; Robin Vaughn competed in dressage. Others were adept in martial arts and used those skills to save their lives. Perdita Halley and Leslie Frost were professional musicians.

Settings

Not surprisingly, the two states that had the largest number of resident sleuths were California and New York. The southern and southwestern states were particularly well represented in this decade. Outside of the United States, Great Britain was, as it has always been, a major source of female sleuths, followed by Canada. Sleuths were to be found in Botswana, Russia, China, ancient Macedonia, seventeenth century Japan, Belgium, Israel, Australia, and New Zealand.

Some sleuths were peripatetic and rootless. Cassandra Reilly preferred it that way. Others moved frequently because of their occupations—espionage agents, diplomats, professional athletes, and government employees in the Fish and Wildlife Service or the National Parks.

Innovations

Computers, DNA, and cell phones added to the resources of police, private detectives, and unofficial sleuths. Specialized networks made it possible for the police to obtain information about the suspects in a case. Other sleuths found their way to the same material by hacking into systems or having a friend at the police department who would share. Access to a cell phone made it possible for the reckless or negligent sleuth to summon help when faced with an unsuspected killer. This was a reality check from the world around the fiction.

The Real World of the 1990s and the 2000s

In the real world of the 1990s, women were taking their places in the military. Their service in the Gulf War, and more recently in Afghanistan and Iraq, resulted in deaths, capture, injuries, exposure to fumes from burning oil fields, and chemical weapons. They sought broader opportunities to serve, and were closer to combat than before. The military academies accepted women routinely, but headlines exposed abusive treatment by their fellow cadets at the Air Force Academy, and by their fellow officers in the Tailhook scandal. Even a private military school such as the Virginia Military Institute could be forced to accept women if public money was used in its administration. Entry into the military services at a command level was one thing; being accepted on a personal level was another

Female doctors were actively recruited for positions throughout hospitals—including the operating rooms and emergency services—not just into the specialties to which they had previously been shunted. Medical, dental, and veterinary schools noted huge increases in the number of female students, approaching or exceeding fifty percent of the class in some cases.

Women had moved beyond acceptance in law schools, and into partnerships in major law firms. They were competitive in elections for appeal courts, and appointed to the U.S. Supreme Court (most recently Sonia Sotomayor and Elena Kagan).

Major corporations made serious efforts to include females in top management and on their boards of directors. This was accomplished with considerable success because women were perceived as less likely to be corrupt. When scandals occurred in industry, women were often the whistle blowers.

The Church of England agreed to ordain women. Many Protestant denominations had done so for decades, although in some cases that has aroused considerable dissent. The Roman Catholic Vatican resisted both a female clergy and married priests, even as parishes closed and the average age of current priests climbed and entries into the priesthood deceased.

Recent presidential teams included highly competent women as top advisors and members of the Cabinet. The Clinton cabinet included the first female Secretary of State, Madeleine Albright. President Bill Clinton shared a virtual co-presidency with his talented wife, Hillary when he ran for office. She became a candidate for the Democratic nomination for president and has served as Secretary of State for President Obama. President George W. Bush relied heavily on Karen Hughes and Condoleezza Rice. The numbers of women in both houses of Congress and in state legislatures increased accordingly. This increase was not only in numbers but in influence. Nancy Pelosi is Speaker of the House; Republican Senator Olympia Snow has used her position on the Senate Finance Committee to move the Democratic health care bill.

The most recent phenomenon in the advancement of women in politics has come from the right wing of the Republican Party. When Senator John McCain made an impulsive decision to select Sarah Palin as his running mate, he had no idea what he was unleashing. Sarah's homespun, socially conservative stance has energized a surprising number of young and old voters who had tired of the traditional politicians. These all followed in the footsteps of Eleanor Roosevelt who used her influence and her power to advance both women's rights and the civil rights of minorities.

This does not mean that the United States political system offered economic or political equality to women candidates or appointees. Other democratic governments such Great Britain, Ireland, and New Zealand had female prime ministers or presidents while the United States backed off after the Geraldine Ferraro nomination in the 1984 election and Sarah Palin did not improve John McCain's campaign. The legal structure, primarily through the Civil Rights Act of 1964 and its amendments, had established the right to a discrimination-free work environment, although individuals often failed to find justice. Public services, factories, and businesses took note of frequent lawsuits to gain equality and adjusted their hiring policies.

High schools and universities opened opportunities for women in fields previously dominated by men. The sports programs were carefully monitored to provide substantially equal athletic resources for female students. Did this provoke a backlash? Of course. Still, the United States participation in recent Olympics showed not only a token acceptance of equality, but produced well-trained teams in new fields; i.e. women's soccer.

The economic downturn during the first decade of the Twenty-first century has affected women differently than in prior depressions and recessions. Usually women suffered disproportionally as did racial minorities. Women are no longer a minority. They get paid less but that makes it easier to retain them and discharge men. They own their own businesses. They are employed in fields that are less affected by the downturn. Men, particularly those in construction and factory work, have been heavily affected. In two wage-earner families, the wife may be the surviving employee. This can be good in a good marriage, but hard on a fragile one. (I have assimilated much of this information, not only from sources listed in the Reference Section, the daily newspapers and weekly newsmagazines, but also from personal observations within my circle of family and friends.)

Feminism as a political cause has seriously diminished in its impact. Young and even middle aged women have little or no sense of the limitations placed upon females in prior generations. Those days are ancient history to them. They can get credit cards, obtain mortgages, serve on juries, have taken part in high school classes and athletics that were denied to females in the past. Young girls who decades ago had few role models for success in politics can look at Hilary Clinton, Nancy Pelosi, Michelle Obama, and Sarah Palin.

The failure of the Equal Rights Amendment to gain ratification no longer resonates. Many of the indignities and restrictions it sought to alleviate have been dealt with by legislation, most recently the 2009 Fair Pay Act signed by Obama.

Publishing

The expansion in the Eighties of the market for books written by women about female investigators, frequently dealing with issues of concern to women, continued well into the Nineties. The sleuths' politics tended to be liberal, occasionally tied to earlier anti-war or feminist activities. More conservative viewpoints emerged in the 1990s reflecting a national trend.

Increasingly, the mystery explored the dynamics of gender, family relationships, and the struggle of women to balance a professional and personal life.

As they turned their hands to mysteries, women writers were more likely to have experience within the systems they explored as:

- Journalists—Edna Buchanan, Peg Tyre, Celestine Sibley and sportswriter Alison Gordon;
- Attorneys—Lia Matera, Carolyn Wheat, Linda Fairstein, and Sarah Caudwell;
- Computer experts or medical personnel—Patricia Cornwell and Sally Chapman; and
- Former policewomen (Lee Martin).

Writers from Spain, Canada, and Australia enriched the bookshelves. American sleuths had less traditional backgrounds—African-Americans from inner cities, Native Americans on reservations, and Asians entering the mainstream.

Mysteries with female sleuths became sexually explicit, exploring interracial, heterosexual and homosexual relationships. They were increasingly violent, often concentrating on crimes against women. The earliest mysteries featuring women characterized them as victims or villains. They were written by men. Now women write mysteries which feature hired female killers, thieves, and corrupt officials.

Women mystery readers on the go gained access to books on tape. Paperback reprints remained a standby (even a necessity considering the prices), but paperback originals often served as minor league experience for new writers who moved on to hardcover. Kindle and E-books have advantages beyond books on tape, but they may turn out to be harmful to publishers. If that occurs, the number of books accepted for publication may decline and limit opportunities for authors.

The multiple mergers within the publishing industry had extensive negative impacts, but stimulated an increase in small presses. The big names were to be found in the major publishing houses. Mid-level authors had shorter stays there, but were often picked up by smaller publishers and/or reduced to paperback status. The higher costs of both hardcover and paperback books spawned a large number of used bookstores with major mystery sections.

Whereas, a century before, a single female sleuth (Amelia Butterworth) emerged in a three book series over a decade, now, several series with women investigators were introduced each month. Not all of the expansion was worth reading. Popularity bred duplication and imitation. Although the best were very good, there was a considerable amount of mediocrity.

What of the Future?

Although the 1990s and the first decade of the Twenty-first century set new heights for the introduction of series featuring women sleuths there was some concern about the future of books in general and mysteries in particular. Children and teenagers are offered other methods of learning information and are attracted to television, video games, and the Internet for entertainment. The high cost of books, particularly hardcovers, may be good for libraries, but weaken sales generally.

New books featuring sleuths covered in Volume 3, which were not reviewed because they were published after December 31, 2008, are listed at the end of the biographies and in the appendices. They will continue to provide entertainment for their fans.

Authors whose sleuths were covered in Volume One (1860-1979) or Volume Two (1980-1989) continue their series including the following:

- Marcia Muller's Sharon McCone;
- Ellen Hart's Jane Lawless;
- Jill Churchill's Jane Jeffry;
- Robert Tanenbaum's Marlene Ciampi;
- Hazel Holt's Mrs. Malory;
- Linda Barnes's Carlotta Carlyle
- Sue Grafton is only up to U for Kinsey Millhone;
- Carolyn Hart's Annie Laurance Darling
- Joan Hess's Claire Malloy and Arly Hanks;
- Jill McGown's Judy Hill
- Anne Perry's Charlotte and Thomas Pitt;
- Gwen Moffat's Melinda Pink;
- Elizabeth Peter's Amanda Peabody Emerson;
- Valerie Wolzien's Susan Henshaw;
- Dorothy Cannell's Ellie Haskell; and
- the endless Jessica Fletcher series by Donald Bain.

Several authors have segued from their original sleuths to one introduced as a character in earlier books. Miriam Monfredo has put Glynis Tryon aside to concentrate on her two nieces, Kathryn and Bronwyn; Faye Kellerman has kept Rina Lazarus home while focusing on her step-daughter, Cindy Decker; Talba Wallis who appeared in the Skip Langdon series by Julie Smith has her own series. This should not be taken to mean that Glynis, Rina, and Skip will not reappear.

Established authors who have had one or more successful series have created new sleuths.

- Donna Andrews introduced Turning Hopper, an Artificial Intelligence Personality;
- Nancy Bell with Judge Jackson Craig;
- Claudia Bishop, under her real name, Mary Stanton, with Bree Winston-Beaufort;
- Simon Brett with Carole Seddon and Jude;
- Rita Mae Brown with Jane Arnold, the seventy-one-year-old Master of the Hunt;
- Taffy Cannon with detective Joanna Davis and under the name Emily Toll, travel director Lynn Montgomery;
- Margaret Coel with reporter Catherine McLeod;
- Judith Cutler with Det. Chief Inspector Fran Harman;
- Catherine Dain with Faith Cassidy;
- Margaret Duffy's Ingrid Langley Gilliard;
- Sophie Dunbar with Ave and Frank Bernstein;
- Ann Granger with Lizzie Martin;
- Carolyn Hart who added ghostly Bailey Ruth Raeburn;
- Charlaine Harris with Sookie Stackhouse and vampires;
- Nancy Baker Jacobs with arson investigator Susan Delaney;
- H. R. F. Keating with Harriet Martens;
- Christine Green with D.I. Thomas Rydell and Denise Caldicote;
- Marne Davis Kellogg with Kick Keswick;
- Susan Kelly with Chief Inspector Megan Davies;
- Kate Kingsbury with Elizabeth Hartley Compton;
- Rochelle Krich with true crime writer Molly Blume;
- Priscilla Masters with Dr. Megan Barnesto;
- Robert Tanenbaum's Butch Karp and Marlene Ciampi;
- Mary Jane Maffini with Charlotte Adams;
- Mabel Maney with Jane Bond;
- Peter May with Enzo MacLeod;
- Lise McClendon with Dorie Lennox;
- Claire McNab with intelligence agent Denise Cleever;
- Marlys Millhiser with Lennora Poole;
- Marcia Muller with deputy sheriff, Rhoda Swift;

- Denise Osborne with interior decorator Salome Waterhouse;
- Anne Perry with members of the Reavley family during World War I;
- Thomas Perry, with Jack Till, who also helps people disappear;
- Nancy Pickard with true crime writer Marie Lightfoot;
- Aimee and David Thurlo with Sister Agatha and a vampire cop Lee Nez;
- Judith Van Gieson with Claire Reynier; and
- Elaine Viets with Helen Hawthorne in the Dead End Job Series.

And many more who are listed under the original sleuths' entries.

Organizations and Conferences

A major factor in the success of the female mystery series has been the support provided by such groups as Mystery Writers of America, Inc., Sisters in Crime, and Malice Domestic®. They promote reviews, provide advice, and give grants to novice writers. Their conventions are a great place to learn from successful authors and meet other aspiring writers. There are many more annual conferences available, which welcome fans as well as authors. They may be based upon a sub-genre, a regional setting, or all of the above.

Resources and Credits

Because of the time frame in which this volume was written, there was less use of non-fiction involved, although I have added to my resource list at the end of the book. Personal reading of newspapers and magazines provided information as to political, religious, and economic changes. Standards such as *People in the News* by David Brownstone and Irene M. Franck (Macmillan) and *The Timetables of American History*, Laurence Urdang, editor, (Simon and Schuster, 2001) filled in gaps.

I wish to express gratitude for the works of Allen J. Hubin and Willetta L. Heising. They are treasures. They have alerted me to new female characters, pseudonyms, and alternate titles. I don't know how I would have managed without the Internet. Amazon.com; Barnes and Noble.com, Bookfinder.com, and library catalogues helped me with alternative titles for books, new publications, and dates, and corrected my spelling when my handwriting was illegible.

Booksellers such as Mary Helen Becker and subsequent staff at Booked for Murder in Madison, Wisconsin, Jeff Hatfield of Uncle Edgar's, Pat and Gary of Once Upon a Crime in Minneapolis were generous. I have ordered many books from Canada and Australia through dealers located by means of Bookfinder.com.

Robert Rosenwald of the Poisoned Pen Press took on this series knowing that it would not be a moneymaker. Editors Joe, and later his wife Lisa, Liddy brought their skills and good humor to the project. The librarians at the Boscobel Public Library have been unfailingly kind and competent in providing me with access to books from outside of the local area while I lived in Wisconsin. I have found the libraries in St. Paul to be equally supportive.

As always my family has been my greatest resource. My children (particularly my son Andrew, a librarian and author and my daughter-in-law Vonne Meussling Barnett) have located and, in several cases, reviewed books to which I lacked access. My daughter, Cathie Wilson, has acted as my chauffer to meetings, has shared her books and her discoveries of new series.

In Conclusion

As always I must plead guilty to errors and omissions. There are series I have failed to locate, new books I have not listed, and new sleuths I have not identified. I am a good speller but a lousy typist and have terrible handwriting so I have surely misspelled names and miscopied dates. Given all the wonderful resources and help from others, I accept responsibility for all errors.

Now it is time for me to close the books and return to reading for pleasure. I have taken great delight in identifying authors who deserved more credit and exposure than they received. My background in political science and law have enabled me to contrast historical periods with the way women were portrayed in mysteries during that time.

When this update is published, I will have celebrated my eighty-fifth birthday.

I have neither the capacity nor the interest in writing a Volume Four, which would cover the female series sleuths introduced between 2000-2009. I began my research on the development of the female sleuth in 1975. Thirty-five years is enough. I wish someone would continue the project, but it has been time-consuming and can be expensive. There were many rewards including the opportunity for me to read many excellent books, to meet with mystery writers and fans who shared my enthusiasm for mysteries and female sleuths, and to work with the staff at Poisoned Pen Press.

Biographies of Sleuths, Introduced Between 1990 Through 1999

Laura Ackroyd

Author: Patricia Hall (pseudonym for Maureen O'Connor)

While fellow reporters abandoned the *Bardfield Gazette* for London or other urban newspapers, Laura Ackroyd remained as feature editor, although irritated by her irascible editor and frustrated by the lack of opportunity. Grandmother Joyce, retired from active politics and living in a deteriorating public housing project (the Heights), needed her support. Laura's parents had sold their profitable business and retired to Portugal. Her former lover, Vince Newsom, had moved on, leaving Laura bruised by his defection. Even with a career, sometimes she envied her best friend Vicky Mendelson, a former classmate now expecting her third child. At thirty, Laura was described as a green-eyed redhead. She had studied social sciences at the local university but also worked on the student newspaper. Her politics were impacted at different times by her grandmother's radical/labor stance and her father's conservatism.

Politics was the focus in *Death by Election* (St. Martin, 1994), when a campaign to "out" closet homosexuals occurred during a parliamentary election. Inspector Michael Thackeray, a recovering alcoholic, needed Laura's contacts among university faculty and students to solve two murders and a suicide.

Despite a spark between Laura and Michael Thackeray, he had made no effort to see her again when *Dying Fall* (St. Martin, 1995) began. Grandma Joyce watched with dismay as the "Heights" deteriorated under poverty, drugs, and delinquency. Someone was organizing the young people into car theft and drug dealing, but the residents did not trust the police enough to work with them. Laura and Thackeray represented different viewpoints on the conviction of a teenage boy for the sexual abuse and murder of a young girl, but worked together to rectify an error.

Laura, who was uncomfortable with her current editor, accepted an assignment to monitor the *Armadale Observer* during *The Dead of Winter* (St.

Martin, 1997). The publishing company that owned both the Observer and the Barfield Gazette was dissatisfied with the passive stance that the Observer was taking on local controversy. Instilled with the leftist viewpoint of her grandmother, Laura enjoyed challenging the local power structure. Thackeray loathed Armadale, his native area, but had never shared the reasons for his feelings. As he and Laura "assisted" the local police when a local activist was murdered, she learned more about the man she loved.

In *Perils of the Night* (St. Martin, 1999), Laura reluctantly agreed to go undercover as a hooker for a newspaper article on the clash between the street trade and local vigilantes. Her disguise was too good. The murder of a young prostitute led Laura to a broader picture of the vulnerable young women—some sexually abused as children—who were as much victims as criminals.

Conflict was inevitable when Thackeray interrogated aging movie star John Blake about a decades old death and more recent murders in *The Italian Girl* (Constable, 1998). At the same time, Laura was not only interviewing Blake in her capacity as a freelance writer, but had encouraged his advances. He was in the area to open a cinema museum but was also giving consideration to filming a new movie in the area. Thackeray used the tension aroused by Laura's connection to Blake to reveal a secret that affected their relationship.

Laura and Thackeray were separated as *Dead on Arrival* (Constable, 1999) began, both geographically and personally. Unable to accept that he had concealed a major secret of his life, Laura went to London to interview for a short-term assignment. While there, she witnessed the murder of a Somali youth but was disappointed by the response from the Dockside police inspector in charge of the case. Laura's advocacy for the victim's brother created another conflict of interest for Thackeray. He was investigating the disappearance of a young Pakistani girl in a case that paralleled hers.

Thackeray was the focus of *Skeleton at the Feast* (Allison & Busby, 2001). He had been sent to St. Frideswide's College, Oxford (where he had studied as a young man) to attend a criminal justice training session. Part of the reason for this assignment was to have him elsewhere while internal affairs reviewed his involvement in an ill-fated police action during which a female officer had been killed. He was equally uncomfortable at Oxford, which he had entered from a state school, having few of the graces so prized among the upper class students. Recently appointed Master of the College Hugh Greenway, who had been Thackeray's tutor and friend, convinced him to investigate privately the disappearance of a well-known professor. Meanwhile Laura assisted Sergeant Kevin Mower, still unstable and mourning, in a case involving an attack on a teenage girl who needed protection in her own household.

The shot that killed thirteen-year-old Dana Smith as she walked out of an abortion clinic in *Deep Freeze* a.k.a. *Deep Waters* (Allison & Busby, 2001) was assumed by many to be the act of a pro-life adherent The community was deeply divided on the issue as were Laura and Thackeray, who still mourned the death of his only child. Thackeray's sergeant, Kevin Mower, was drinking heavily at a time when his skills were needed. Together they followed rumors that the surgeon who performed the abortion had a personal motive for taking late term cases.

Laura and Thackeray were thwarted in their efforts to probe the expansion of drug activity in the community during *Death in Dark Waters* (Alison & Busby, 2002). She had been summoned to the Heights by her feisty but aging grandmother. Joyce wanted Laura to publicize the heroin trade among the low-income youth that had led to a series of deaths. She was also concerned about what she perceived as misguided efforts to gentrify the area. Not surprisingly, Ted Grant, Laura's editor, supported the developers. He had never liked Laura anyway. Thackeray had been ordered to focus his attention on sales of Ecstasy to upper class youths, limiting the time he could give to locate a missing mother and her twin daughters.

The death of Simon Earnshaw threw the future of Earnshaw Mills into doubt in *Dead Reckoning* (Allison & Busby, 2003). The market for English wool was miniscule, but closing the plant would put workers, many of them Asians, on the streets. Simon's heirs and their relative shares in the business were pivotal as to alternative uses for the facility. The Asian community was divided by hostility between the right wing British Patriotic Party and the conservative family values of the Pakistanis. On a personal level, although Laura and Thackeray were deeply in love, there was a problem. She desperately wanted children.

The death of a mother and two of her children in *Sins of the Father* (Allison & Busby, 2005) followed by the disappearance of the father, Gordon Christie, might have been written off as a domestic tragedy. The subsequent death of a third unidentified child and the discovery of a corpse in Gordon's car, convinced Thackeray and Laura that there was more going on. A personal family loss had left him depressed to the point that his job and their relationship were at risk.

It was not the right time for Laura and her grandmother Joyce to interfere in a police investigation; particularly, as in *False Witness* (Allison & Busby, 2005), when the officer in charge was DCI "Len" Hutton from the Armedale station. Joyce, a member of the board of Woodlands School for troubled youth, believed that Hutton had made a biased and hasty arrest in the murder of headmaster Peter Graves. Stevie Fletcher, a black teenager whom Graves had expelled that day, was charged with the crime. Thackeray had not handled the case because he was out-of-town on assignment. He had other issues with Hutton that might be exacerbated if he interfered. His ability to deal with these issues came at a time when he was preoccupied by the news that his long institutionalized wife Aileen was close to death. He was racked with guilt over his response to his son's death and Aileen's attempted suicide. This is a powerful narrative in which Laura and Thackeray struggled to maintain their relationship.

Author Patricia Hall developed interesting subordinate characters while expanding on the background of her protagonists. Plotting was more than adequate. The books were subtitled *A Yorkshire Mystery*. *Devil's Game* (Allison &

Busby) was published in 2009. *By Death Divided* and *Death in a Far Country* (both Allison & Busby, 2009) are now available in paperback.

Irene Adler

Author: Carole Nelson Douglas

English detective Sherlock Holmes was touched, and then outwitted, by only one woman, opera singer Irene Adler. Irene now has a series of her own. Penelope Huxleigh, an orphaned minister's daughter whom Irene had rescued and made a member of her household, narrated Irene's adventures. Penelope, later "Nell," moved from naiveté to independence under the tutelage of the worldly Irene. Over the years, their household acquired a menagerie: parrot, cat, mongoose, and snakes. Irene claimed to have worked as Merlinda the Mermaid in an underwater carnival act during which she perfected her ability to hold her breath, a valuable skill to her as an opera singer. She had been a Pinkerton agent before she left America. The narratives were presented as a collection of information gained by Fiona Witherspoon, Ph.D., a modern day researcher.

In *Good Night, Mr. Holmes* (TOR, 1990), jeweler Charles Tiffany hired Irene to recover antique gems. After placing Nell as the secretary of solicitor Godfrey Norton, Irene toured Europe where she met Prince William of Bohemia, who was captivated by her chestnut hair, tiger-brown eyes, and spirit. Unacceptable as a wife, unwilling to be a mistress, Irene returned to England. The Prince hired Holmes to retrieve a picture linking him to Irene. Norton, who had fallen in love with Irene, helped her find the jewels and resolve the Prince's problem. Norton and Irene married but reputedly died in Europe.

Actually, together with Nell, they were alive and well in a Parisian suburb, as *Good Morning, Irene* (TOR, 1991) began. This book has been re-released as *The Adventuress* (2003). After Irene, Godfrey, and Nell temporarily rescued a suicidal heiress, the young woman's trail led to Monte Carlo. Irene moved in the intersection of the nobility with the theatrical world, unbound by convention. The narratives glittered with glimpses of Bram Stoker, Oscar Wilde, Anton Dvorak, and Sarah Bernhardt.

Holmes and Dr. Watson returned in *Irene at Large* (TOR, 1992) reissued as *A Soul of Steel (2006)*. An unjustly accused English officer re-entered Nell's life, providing the restless Irene with a new challenge. Dr. Watson, then serving in the British Army, had rescued Quentin Stanhope, a British spy named Cobra. Now Stanhope believes that Watson is in danger. Unable to return publicly to England, Irene sent Nell and Norton to unmask the real traitor, but joined in surreptitiously. Nell, who eventually remembered Stanhope from her work as a governess, had a personal interest in his survival and vindication.

Irene's Last Waltz (TOR/Forge, 1994), recently released as *Another Scandal in Bohemia,* renewed Irene's connection to Crown Prince Wilhelm in a story reminiscent of *The Prisoner of Zenda*. She had returned to Prague after learning that Wilhelm was treating Clotilde, his new bride, with disdain. Their marriage had not even been consummated. This did not sound like the William that Irene remembered. Sherlock Holmes and Watson, Quentin Stanhope (the British intelligence agent whom Nell favored), and Tatyana, a seductive female spy (who will return in later narratives) added to the confusion.

Chapel Noir (Forge, 2001) ended with both Nell and Godfrey in danger. Irene had been called to Paris from her Neuilly home to investigate the brutal deaths of two women in a brothel. Inspector Francois le Villard requested her presence. Behind him were the powerful figures of Baron Alphonse de Rothschild and the Prince of Wales, currently visiting in Paris where a World Exposition was being held. On a sometimes parallel but increasingly intersecting level was an investigation by Sherlock Holmes. Irene and Nell, joined by a mysterious American woman who had been an occupant of the brothel, followed a long and torturous trail through Paris. The book ended with a cliffhanger, suitable for daytime serials but hardly appropriate for a hardcover book.

Castle Rouge (Forge, 2002) picked up where the prior book ended. Given that the total number of pages in the two books exceeded 950 pages, not every mystery reader will approve. Nevertheless, fans of the series can follow Irene in crisis. She needed the resources of Pink (better known as Nellie Bly), Bram Stoker, Quentin Stanhope and other big name friends when both Nell and Godfrey disappeared. They paralleled Holmes and Watson's continued search for the identity of Jack the Ripper, while seeking to rescue the two most important people in Irene's life from a personal enemy.

In *Femme Fatale* (Forge, 2003), Irene and Nell were lured to New York City by Nellie Bly. According to Nellie, the mother whom Irene had never known was in danger from a serial killer. Their search revealed Irene's childhood among lower class entertainers. The victims in the serial killings were individuals whom Irene vaguely remembered. Having been a child performer close to prior victims, it was possible that Irene would be a target. Nellie also induced Holmes to visit New York where he played a role in the outcome.

Irene and Nell stayed on in New York City during *Spider Dance* (Forge, 2004, another extremely long narrative) in the hope that Irene could trace her mother. Was she the Eliza Gilbert who had been buried in the Green-Wood Cemetery? Was Eliza really Lola Montez, a theatrical adventuress, both praised and vilified in the past? Holmes eventually enlisted Irene's help when Willie Vanderbilt, not only had a crucified corpse in his pool room, but a missing teenage daughter.

The series, initially so promising, drowned in repetitiousness as each narrative relied on prior books for plots. Nelson is also the author of the Midnight Louie series.

Cherry Aimless and Nancy Clue

Author: Mabel Maney

Nancy Drew and Cherry Ames inspired young girls of the 1920s-1940s to consider themselves more independent, more courageous, and more resourceful. That impact may seem irrelevant to those who found their inspiration in more recent heroines. Each generation suffers from an inability to understand the past beyond the statistics and the history books. Mabel Maney's send ups of Cherry Ames and Nancy Drew will offend some not only because their updated counterparts were lesbians, but also because they show no sense of what the originals meant to a prior generation.

Cherry Aimless, a young woman in her twenties, was a probationary nurse at Seattle General hospital in *The Case of the Not-So-Nice Nurse* (Cleis, 1993). Raised by a critical mother and a moody father, she grew up to be extremely conventional. Her twin brother Charles, an interior decorator in New York City, was gay. Her sense of deference to authority caused Cherry to put aside her concerns about a missing patient before she left on vacation. By the end of that vacation, she had taken a female lover, and created substantial but necessary changes in a religious facility.

As Cherry and her role model, Nancy Clue, progressed through their adventures they built up a crew of lesbian victims and/or helpers. During *The Case of the Good-for-Nothing Girlfriend* (Cleis, 1994), Nancy and Cherry et al traveled from California to Illinois. Nancy intended to prove that the family housekeeper Hannah Gruel had not killed her father, attorney Carter Clue. There were complications en route. Once in River Depths, Nancy realized who was determined to convict Hannah and to conceal Carter Clue's evil tendencies.

In *A Ghost in the Closet* (Cleis, 1995), Cherry, Nancy and their gang joined up with the Hardly boys, Joe and Frank. Disclosures relating to the boys' father and Nancy's mother caused life changes. Gay and lesbian characters mated and matched. The only heterosexual couple was villainous.

Rachel Kaminsky Alexander

Author: Carol Lea Benjamin

The sudden death of Rachel Kaminsky's father when she was a child affected her profoundly. She worked as a dog trainer before her marriage to dentist Jack Alexander. Since their divorce, she and her pit bull, Dash, lived and worked in a cottage on the grounds of a town house in New York City. Although now a private investigator, she supplemented her income by acting as caretaker. Rachel capitalized on her innate curiosity, which caused her to "pick at things" until she understood them. She regularly took Dash to visit nursing home residents and AIDS patients in a hospice as a volunteer activity. Rachel attributed her need to take risks to a rejection of her overly cautious mother. She found acceptance and understanding from her friendly therapist Ida Berkowitz. Rachel's sister, Lili, was more like her mother; married with children and content to remain in the home.

As *This Dog for Hire* (Walker, 1996) opened, Dennis Keaton, an illustrator of children's books, hired Rachel to find Magritte, a Basenji. The dog was co-owned with painter Clifford Cole, who had been killed when struck by a car. The police treated Cole's murder as gay bashing. Rachel connected it with his paintings featuring Magritte. Cole's paintings increased in value, but Rachel found them more helpful in detecting a killer. There were interesting scenes at the Westminster Dog Show.

Rachel's Aunt Ceil who lived in a gated community near Coney Island had often provided summer vacations for Lili and Rachel. When she asked Rachel to help her friends, David and Marsha Jacobs, in *The Dog Who Knew Too Much* (Walker, 1997), Rachel could not refuse. It helped that the Jacobs were willing to pay whatever was necessary to discover why their only child had killed herself. Rachel moved into Lisa Jacobs' apartment, wore her clothes, introduced herself to Lisa's friends as a cousin, and became convinced that the death was not a suicide.

Although Rachel had ended her work as a dog trainer at the time of her marriage, it was an excellent cover for her participation in a training seminar in *A Hell of a Dog* (Walker, 1998). The organizer, Samantha Lewis, anticipated problems among the trainers due to their methodologies and egos. Rachel was to prevent violence, but she failed; then persisted long enough to trap a wary killer.

During an insightful narrative in *Lady Vanishes* (Walker, 1999), Rachel related her investigation of murder and mayhem at a group home for autistic and developmentally disabled adults. There were touches of long awaited love and creative care for the residents, mixed with the greed of those who added dog-napping to their crimes.

The Wrong Dog (Walker, 2000) was a powerful narrative exploring canine and human cloning. Sophie Gordon, the epileptic owner of a seizure alert dog (Blanche) did not refuse when asked to allow Blanche to be cloned. The promised puppy was delivered, but, after Sophie hired Rachel to find the cloners, she was murdered.

Rachel's dark side was explored in *The Long Good Boy* (Walker, 2001). She did undercover work in an area of New York populated by transvestite hookers and meat packing companies. There was a connection between the two. A trio of transvestites employed Rachel to find the murderer of Rosalina who plied her/his trade on the street and in a meat packing plant. Rachel depended on a pair of hookers and her faithful Dash for backup.

Rachel had a vague recollection of police detective Tim O'Fallon as *Fall Guy* (Morrow, 2004) began. He had been a silent presence at group therapy sessions for law enforcement officers after 9/11. Rachel and Dash had participated in the program. So it came as a surprise that she had been named the executor of his estate. His death was presumed to be suicide because his own gun had been used. Tim's sister, Maggie, filled in the blanks as to Tim's life; i.e. their crisis filled teenage years which included two family suicides and a series of "accidents". Rachel's exploration gave her understanding of Tim's efforts to rehabilitate alcohol and drug abusers.

Dogs figured into *Without a Word* (Morrow, 2005) but there was so much more. Leon Spector hired Rachel to locate his wife Sally, who had left their home five years before. Their daughter Madison, already afflicted with facial tics, had become mute when Sally left. Personally aware of the impact of losing a parent, Rachel took on the responsibility of (1) finding Sally, but (2) also discovering the murderer of a doctor who had been treating Madison's disorder. Fascinating characterizations.

The Hard Way (Morrow, 2006) was another example of Benjamin's increasing skills. She uses the mystery to explore the time and the place we live in. Rachel was hired to find out who had pushed Gardner Redstone in front of a subway train. Her client, his daughter Eleanor, shared the statements made by witnesses. Gardner and Eleanor owned and managed a small but very lucrative chain of designer leather goods stores (GR Leathers). The first assumption based on the witness statements was that a tall, thin, white haired vagrant was the killer. Finding him was the first step. Rachel accomplished that, with the help of a brain-damaged young Iraq war veteran, by posing as Eunice, a befuddled street person. This was just the beginning. There was another layer to the search, for a killer who was not mentally ill, but had good reason to want Gardner dead. A thoughtful look at why some people go without while others indulge in conspicuous consumption.

As in several other series, Dash (short for Dashiell) played a role in the mysteries, calling Rachel's attention to "suspicious items." The allocation of human qualities to an animal plus gratuitous crudity may diminish the appeal of the series for some readers and enhance it for others.

Carol Lea Benjamin is also the author of non-fiction books on the raising and training of dogs.

Angelina "Angie" Amalfi

Author: Joanne Pence

Angelina Amalfi was the petite food critic and food editor for a San Francisco Bay area shopper. As one of five daughters of a rich immigrant, she could afford to live comfortably on a small salary. A single Vassar graduate in her mid-twenties, she had traveled extensively. In her spare time, she was writing a book, tutoring Hispanic children and teaching San Francisco history to adults. Needless to say, Angelina was determined to be a success.

In *Something's Cooking* (Harper, 1993), Angelina found a bomb on her doorstep shortly after disreputable Sammy the Blade was murdered. Because

Sammy had been a contributor to Angie's food column, Inspector Paavo Smith wondered if there had been hidden messages in his recipe ingredients.

When that job ended, Angelina talked Chef Henri into hiring her to screen the calls during his culinary program at station KYME during *Too Many Cooks* (Harper, 1994). The death of several San Francisco restaurateurs connected with Chef Henri brought Paavo back into Angelina's life. Their romantic ups and downs competed for attention with the mystery aspects of the narratives.

In *Cooking Up Trouble* (Harper, 1995), Angie accepted a position as dietary advisor at an isolated vegetarian inn, only to have her employer disappear. Angie had been appalled to learn that the only guests at the inn (terrible food might be responsible) were investors in the hostelry. Someone seemed to want the project to fail as accidents plagued the inn. By the time Paavo arrived to spend a week with her, a murder and another disappearance kept him too busy to enjoy her company.

Angie was more victim than sleuth in *Cooking Most Deadly* (Harper, 1996), a mélange of plots: (1)An impoverished exile who wanted to reclaim her lost Faberge egg; (2) three elderly thieves who used a restaurant to front their planned jewel robbery; and (3) Angie's search for advice on whether or not she should marry Paavo.

As the series progressed, Pence's skills developed to create a balance among her light humorous touch, the romance between Paavo and Angie, his professional involvement in the murders, and Angie's lesser contributions.

Paavo's career was seriously undermined in *Cook's Night Out* (Harper, 1998) by rumors and evidence that he was cooperating with the numbers racket. Angie's latest project, the creation of a new candy, engendered leftovers. She donated them to the Random Acts of Kindness Mission, which had close ties to Klaw, a villain whom Paavo had reason to detest. A very sticky situation.

Angie was granted two of her wishes in *Cooks Overboard* (Harper, 1998). Paavo agreed to accompany her on a freight line cruise; then, he resigned from the police force. When she realized that Paavo, the civilian, was not the man she admired, Angie had a convenient solution. The vacation included missing formulas, murderous spies, and a quartet of bumbling former secret agents.

A new financial venture drew Angie's attention to UFO enthusiasts in *A Cook in Time* (Harper, 1999). She had no idea of the complexities and rivalries involved. Two groups (one headed by her former beau, Derrick Holton) vied for public attention. A series of sadistic deaths investigated by Paavo was solved partly through Angie's involvement.

To Catch a Cook (Avon, 2000) was the best so far of the series, going beyond the gimmicks of Angie's search for a career. The narrative focused on why Paavo and his sister Jessica had been abandoned by his mother, and left to be raised by her friend Aulis Kokkonen. An antique brooch given by Paavo to Angie triggered reactions from the Russian Mafia, a treacherous government agent, and a woman who had not ended her quest for revenge. Angie's latest career plan (videotaping restaurant reviews) was ended by four lawsuits.

Elements of horror were blended into *Bell, Cook, and Candle* (Avon, 2002) as the police department, including Paavo, investigated ritual killings. Angie was preoccupied with a new venture, Comical Cakes. Ominous figures of the Goths including their leader, Baron Severus, and his assistant Wilbur Fieldren loomed over Angie and her friend, Connie Rogers.

If Cooks Could Kill (Avon, 2003) kept Angie and Connie busy. Angie was so excited about her engagement to Paavo that she seemed to have lost her common sense, always in short supply. She showered Paavo with expensive and embarrassing gifts, ignored offers of interesting jobs, and indulged in matchmaking among her friends and acquaintances. One such venture matched Connie with Dennis, a defensive end for the San Francisco 49'ers. He never appeared for the first date, but his pal, Max, did. That was the lesser of Connie's problems. She was being pursued by a woman recently released from prison. This was one of the weaker stories.

Angie had been a devoted fan of the television serial, *Eagle Crest,* so in *Two Cooks A-Killing* (Avon, 2003), she jumped at the chance to prepare the Christmas dinner planned for a reunion of the cast after ten years. Angie's parents were close friends of the Waterfield family whose estate was the set for the show. The unseen presence at the gathering was that of young Brittany Keegan who died mysteriously before the series ended. Angie came to believe that Brittany had been murdered and that the killer was attending the reunion.

Courting Disaster (Avon, 2003) is probably as good as it gets with Angie and her problems. She had made a deal with her strong-minded mother, Serafina. If Serafina would stay out of the wedding plans, she could put on the engagement party. However Serafina, somewhat miffed, refused to share her plans, even the site of the party. Angie was diverted into helping her neighbor Stan Bonnette and Hannah, the young pregnant woman he had befriended. Paavo became professionally involved with the young couple, but also had to deal with Angie's father.

Paavo and Angie used vacation time to visit his old friends Doc Griggs and Ned Paulson in Jackpot, Arizona during *Red Hot Murder* (Avon, 2006) Aulis Kokkonen had made Paavo aware that Griggs had been upset by the disappearance and subsequent death of Hal Edwards, an elderly patient. When Ned failed to appear to meet Paavo and Angie, they feared he had suffered a similar fate. Local law enforcement was a joke; but then so were inedible family recipes, Angie's search for a deceased chef's cookbook, and her efforts to ride horseback and drive a cook wagon. Edwards had been a very wealthy man. Was there a will or would his former wife and estranged son inherit?

This time it was Angie's sister, Caterina aka Cat, who involved her in an international chase during *The Da Vinci Cook* (Avon, 2007), which showed continued improvement. Cat, accused by her supervisor at Moldwell/ Renker (sound familiar?) of having stolen a religious relic, went to the home of the owner, old friend Marcello Piccoletti, to confront him. There was a man's corpse on the floor, the relic (chain of St. Peter) was gone, and a man she believed to be Marcello's brother Marco was fleeing the scene. Angie and Cat flew to Italy to locate both Marcello and Marco in order to prove that Cat was not a murderer. Paavo and Charles (Cat's under appreciated husband) were left behind. Paavo had to cope with the four remaining Amalfi women while trying to solve the case.

The series focused on the romantic complexities of the heroine, her lover, and her family. Coincidences were a frequent ingredient. A considerable number of the earlier books have been reprinted recently as mass-market paperbacks.

Gabrielle "Gabe" Amato

Author: Paul Patti

Gabrielle "Gabe" Amato and her husband Andy were police officers. A tall, dark-haired woman of French-Greek descent married to an Italian, Gabe was the technician while Andy worked by instinct and experience. They ran together, worked together, and shared everything.

In *Silhouettes* (St. Martin, 1990), the couple transferred from the Miami police department to West Palm Beach, hoping to start a family. The victim in their first murder case was in a witness protection program, forcing Andy to fight the FBI's intervention. His search for the killer took Gabe into danger.

During *Death Mate* (St. Martin, 1992), Andy insisted that the pregnant Gabe share his investigation of the murder of a female vice officer. Her confrontation with a serial killer had a tragic ending. Gabe never achieved equal status, although she took more than her share of risks.

Mali Anderson

Author: Grace F. Edwards

Mali was a no nonsense African-American who, after being terminated by the New York City Police Department, sued for damages and won. Her dismissal had come after she punched a fellow officer who sexually harassed her. Mali had no intention of returning to NYPD. Instead she focused on finishing her Masters thesis and earning a Ph.D. Mali was one of two daughters of widower Jeffrey Anderson, a music teacher and blues and jazz player. Her mother had been a dancer with Katherine Dunham. Although she had no children, Mali was raising her eleven-year-old nephew, Alvin, orphaned when his parents were killed in an airplane crash. They shared their household with Ruffin, a Great Dane. When in Harlem, Mali introduced herself as "the bass player's daughter" as her father Jeffrey was well regarded.

When *If I Should Die* (Doubleday, 1997) opened, Mali was a witness in the death of Erskin Harding, tour director of the Uptown Children's chorus, of which Alvin was a member. Initially the incident seemed to be an attempted kidnapping in which Erskin had intervened. On investigation Mali discovered other motives for murder. Help from Detective Tad Honeywell gave promise of a serious relationship for Mali.

The death of Thea, a young barmaid at the Half-Moon, involved Mali during *A Toast Before Dying* (Doubleday, 1998). The most obvious suspect was Kendrick Owen, brother of Mali's friend Bertha "Bert." Owen. The motive for Thea's death did not emerge until after additional murders and a hard look at Thea's past, her sexual partners and her parentage.

No Time to Die (Doubleday, 1999) pitted Mali against a tortured serial killer who struck at her neighborhood, her friends, and, finally, at Mali herself. Edwards took the reader to the streets of Harlem, a once proud community where music and fellowship had made poverty tolerable, but had changed. Mali had a personal decision to make. The police department had offered to reinstate her if she dropped her lawsuit. Her reluctance to return had to be balanced against the possibility that she would lose in the judicial system.

In *Do or Die* (Doubleday, 2000), the community had less hope, and more drugs. The death of Starr Hendrix, daughter of family friend Ozzie, thrust Mali into the world of pimps and hookers. She shared recollections of the good days in the community as she probed for a double killer.

The series resonated with great settings; the Harlem of today flavored with reminiscences of the musical greats who had populated it a generation ago. CBS television had announced a new mystery series, *Mali Anderson,* scheduled to be shot in 2003. Queen Latifah was projected to play the leading role, but the deal must have fallen through.

Although no further books in the Mali Anderson series were located, Edwards continued to write novels depicting life within the African-American community.

Margit Andersson

Author: Tiina Nunnally

Margit Andersson, a translator for Koivisto Translation Agency who specialized in highly technical material, was essentially an independent contractor. Liise, her employer at Koivisto, was a demanding perfectionist, who placed great stress on Margit.

She had grown up in St. Paul, Minnesota where her father, an émigré from Sweden, taught at a private high school. Margit earned Bachelor and Master degrees, but dropped out of a Ph.D. program. Her personal life was compartmentalized: a long distance relationship with sculptor Joe Niehoff, who lived in New Mexico where he had a female mentor for his work. Margit shared her Seattle home with a cat, Gregor; and spent free time with Renny Latham, an African-American waitress and painter. For entertainment, Margit attended poetry nights at the Cedar Café. For relaxation, she ironed. Except for an occasional fish dish, she was a vegetarian. Although this seemed a placid life, Margit had terrifying nightmares.

In *Runemaker* (Fjord Press, 1996), Margit befriended Soren Rasmussen, an elderly fisherman whom she met while working as a translator at a local hospital. While she was visiting Joe in New Mexico, Soren left a message on her answering machine. On her return, she stopped by his home, only to find him dead. His violent death sent her on the trail of ancient Danish treasure...with a killer on her heels. One new element in Margit's life was Detective Alex Tristano.

Another facet of Margit's work as a translator was explored in *Fate of Ravens* (Fjord, 1998) when, while working for Star Airlines, she saw an elderly tourist fall down the escalator and die. The death seemed to be a heart attack, brought on by fright. Once a freedom fighter in the Second World War, Rosa Norgaard had been terrified by an image of the past—a traitor whom she believed to be dead. Alex Tristano, who had not been in touch, resuscitated their earlier romance, and was available when she needed help against a killer. In the process of her investigation, Margit's father made her aware of her Danish mother's wartime experiences.

The insertions of background material on Scandinavian history, customs and language were rather clumsy. Although no additional books featuring Margit Andersson were located, Nunnally has become a significant literary figure through her translations, including that of *Smila's Sense of Snow.*

Lady Aoi

Author: Ann Woodward

Eleventh century Japan is itself a mystery to most readers, but Woodward provided a commendable opening via the Lady Aoi series to those who are interested. The woman referred to as "Lady Aoi" (which means "blue") had a personal name, which was never used. She served as a "lady in waiting" to a Princess, but had strong connections with the Emperor himself to whom she provided medical expertise.

Her father, who had been a royal tutor, had taught her to read, a skill that few Japanese women possessed at that time. Lady Aoi could read not only Japanese but also Chinese and therefore had access to their remedies. She had a collection of scrolls, which embodied considerable medical knowledge from China and Japan. No information was provided as to marriage or children, but she seemed very close to the powerful Minister of the Right, advisor to the Emperor and father of the Princess.

In *The Exile Way* (Avon, 1996), the first inkling that someone sought to use Lady Aoi as a wedge to undermine the Minister of the Right came when the medication used by Aoi to ameliorate the pain and distress of the Emperor's eye problems was stolen. There were powerful forces in the capital that sought to replace the Emperor with his more easily influenced son. When the Minister of the Right was sent into exile and probable death, Aoi was determined to save his life. Her adversaries included two men, who, as boys, had suffered emotional distress when removed from their family homes.

The Princess, who had reconciled her differences with her powerful husband, was facing her first pregnancy as *Of Death and Black Rivers* (Avon 1998) began. Lady Saisho, a young naïve attendant, developed an unusual relationship with the visiting Governor of Mutsu. The Governor was reputed to be a violent man, acceptable when he was fighting against the Ezo tribes on his border, but less so when he refused central government demands or kidnapped young women. As one of the senior ladies in waiting, Lady Aoi felt responsible for the younger staff members. She was assisted, even rescued, by the Prince and his unstable associate, the Combmaker.

Belle Appleman

Author: Dorothy and Sidney Rosen

Few readers will remember the way of life that existed for Americans during the 1930's. The Rosens in their depiction of Belle provide a glimpse of what it was to be a factory worker in New York City at a time when labor unions lacked power. Female workers had an additional handicap in that traditional craft unions did not accept women workers. Belle was fortunate in that trade unions were more open to change. She was a Jewish immigrant in her thirties, who ate kosher at home, but not in restaurants. Her deceased husband, Daniel, had been a pharmacist. She was ambitious, working hard to improve her language skills by attending night classes. The authors frequently described characters by reference to movie stars of the period: a "Bette Davis stare", a "prim Loretta Young look". Men were compared to Gary Cooper, Basil Rathbone, and others.

During her first two weeks at Classic Clothing Company, Belle learned about the union-management strife and the romantic intrigues among the workers as *Death and Blintzes* (Walker, 1985) began. The union had been accepted by boss Victor Gordon, but deeply resented by his partner, Marvin Karsh. Jeanette Laval, union shop steward, was unpopular with the female workers because she fraternized with management staff. They weren't too pleased with her man-hunting either. When first Jeanette, then Marvin was murdered, Belle took on a second job, amateur detective.

Although the time frame, mid 1930's, had not changed in *Death and Strudel* (Academy Chicago, 2000; i.e. 15 years later), Belle's life had. She had left her job at Classic Clothing, which disappointed her friend and co-worker Nate Becker. She was now employed at the drug store where Daniel had been a pharmacist. The death of a young woman following a botched abortion drew Belle into the personal lives of her co-workers, her boss, and the doctors who patronized the pharmacy. The death of the abortionist who may have been a blackmailer widened the pool of suspects. This time she worked with Irish cop, Jim Connors.

Sprightly narratives. Although the first in the series came out in 1985, it did not qualify as a series until the second book in 2000.

Lady Susanna Appleton

Author: Kathy Lynn Emerson

Queen Elizabeth I had taken the throne of England upon the death of her Catholic half-sister, Queen Mary. Young Susanna Leigh, who had married Sir Robert Appleton, had always been a Protestant sympathizer. She easily aligned herself with the new Queen. After the death of both parents, she had become the ward of a powerful nobleman in whose household Robert had lived. A marriage between them had been deemed suitable. Robert, whose religious beliefs were second to his political and national interests, was active on Queen Elizabeth's behalf in negotiating with her potential allies in Europe. He had not been faithful to Susanna; in fact he had a mistress, Constance Crane in Dover. Jennet, maid to Susanna, was an important figure in several of the narratives.

As *Face Down in the Marrow-bone Pie* (St. Martin, 1997) opened, Sir Robert was unavailable to deal with a crisis at Appleton Manor, the family home that he had avoided for years. He and Susanna lived instead at Leigh Abbey, a property that had belonged to her family but was his as a result of the marriage. Susanna not only managed Leigh Abbey's business affairs, but also was well known for her expertise in herbs and, to a lesser extent, poisons, having authored two serious tomes on the efficacy and dangers of plants. The steward at Appleton Manor, John Bexwith, had died upon eating a marrow-bone pie. Rumors that a ghost had attended the death caused the servants to abandon the manor. In Robert's absence, it fell to Susanna to deal with the matter.

Whether it was Susanna's knowledge of herbals or her skill in solving mysteries that caused Queen Elizabeth to order her to Madderly Castle, was questionable in *Face Down Upon an Herbal* (St. Martin, 1998). Sir Robert believed it was to provide a rationale for his presence during which he investigated rumors of forgery and counterfeiting. During this experience, Walter Pennington, Robert's friend and Queen Elizabeth's advisor, came to admire Susanna. Young Catherine, Robert's illegitimate sister, found a worthy spouse.

Susanna's status in life changed in *Face Down Among the Winchester Geese* (St. Martin, 1999) as a result of her investigation into the death of a young woman during Queen Mary's reign and subsequent deaths upon the same date each year. Although she was able to prove that Robert was not the killer, his escape from England made it unlikely that he would or could return. It suited Susanna to be treated as a widow. Their marriage had not been a happy one. She had never wanted children. Before he left, Robert had signed over the profits from Leigh Abbey.

A letter from Robert, now legally declared dead, summoned Susanna to London in *Face Down Beneath the Eleanor Cross* (St. Martin, 2000). She carried the gold he demanded, but Robert had been murdered before she arrived. Susanna was charged with his death, an offense punishable by a fiery death. She refused to escape the country; instead, fought vigorously to prove her innocence by identifying the real killer. In the process she learned whom she could trust.

With Robert dead, Susanna was free to remarry. In *Face Down Under the Wych Elm* (St. Martin, 2000), she rejected the proposal of her lover, wealthy ship owner and neighbor Nick Baldwin. She was however willing to travel abroad with him as his mistress. In Maidstone, she learned that Constance Crane, once Robert's mistress, and an elderly cousin were to be tried for witchcraft and murder. She had not forgotten her own experience when she had been unjustly accused. Who would kill two men and frame two women for their deaths?

She would not risk her independence by marriage, but in *Face Down Before Rebel Hooves* (St. Martin, 2001) Susanna risked her freedom and her life to spy on rebels seeking to place Mary, Queen of Scots, on the English throne. Wily Sir Walter Pendennis learned that Eleanor, his badly injured wife, had conspired with the rebels. He convinced Susanna to assume the role of Eleanor and insinuate herself into the insurgent group of nobles.

The legends of St. Brendan and King Arthur were among the materials studied by a group of academics visiting Sir Walter's isolated Cornwall estate in *Face Down Across the Western Sea* (St. Martin, 2002). Queen Elizabeth had placed Lady Susanna in charge of the group although her role was not fully accepted by them. The unexpected arrival of Eleanor, Sir Walter's estranged wife and Rosamund, her daughter, added complications. The murder of scholar Martin Calthorpe raised fears of Spanish intervention in Queen Elizabeth's goal of proving a prior English claim to North America.

The possibility that Queen Elizabeth might visit Leigh Abbey created consternation in *Face Down Below the Banqueting House* (Perseverance Press, 2005). A huge retinue could be expected to accompany the Queen. Exploratory visits by yeoman Brian Tymberley did nothing to relieve Susanna and Nick's tension. Tymberley and his servant Miles Carter seemed unduly interested in ferreting out damaging information about the Appleton and Baldwin families and members of their households. In his role as justice of the peace, Nick characterized Carter's deadly fall as an accident. A second death made that less likely.

Rosamund, the pre-teen daughter of Susanna's deceased husband, sent out a call for help in *Face Down Beside St. Anne's Well* (Perseverance, 2006). The message did not go to Susanna, but to Rob, Jennet's son. When Jennet learned of it, she reported to Susanna. Rosamund had undertaken to investigate the death of her French tutor, Louise Poitier. Rosamund had been placed under the guidance of Lady Bridget Hawley at Bawkenstone Manor. The Manor was close enough to the residence where Queen Mary of Scotland had been placed to create concern that an attempt might be made to rescue Mary and take her to France. The multiple viewpoints (Susanna, Eleanor, Rosamund, Jennet, and mysterious Annabel MacReynolds) added to the complexity of the narrative.

Susanna's affection and a sense of responsibility for her deceased husband's half-sister Catherine and her children sent her to Scotland in *Face Down*

O'er the Border (Perseverance, 2007). Catherine, also a widow, had been staying at the home of her mother-in-law Jean, (Lady Russell) in order to be near her eight-year-old son, Gavin (Lord Glenelg), whom the Court assigned as ward to Sir Lachlan Dunbar. When Jean was murdered, Catherine's friend Annabel MacReynolds convinced her to flee, as she would be a suspect. Susanna and Nick Baldwin, apprised of the circumstances, needed to locate Catherine in order to help her and her children.

Emerson was also the editor of *Murders and Other Confusions* (Crippen & Landru, 2004) which included short stories re Nick Baldwin; Jennet, a younger Susanna and Rosamund. Her third series, set in Denver in the late Nineteenth century, features intrepid female reporter, Diana Spaulding. She has a new series, writing as Kathryn Dunnett, featuring Lisa McCrimmin.

Lucie D'Arby Wilton Archer

Author: Candace Robb

See: Lucie D'Arby Wilton, page 870.

Kathryn "Kate" Ardleigh

Authors: Robin Paige, joint pseudonym for Susan Wittig Albert and William J. Albert

Kate Ardleigh's parents had come from different realms of society, a factor of importance during the Victorian era. Her father, who died before she was born, was the dispossessed son of a wealthy English family. Her mother, an impecunious young Irishwoman died five years later, leaving Kate to be raised by her Uncle Sean O'Malley, a New York City policeman. Redheaded Kate, who had worked as a typist and a tutor, finally found a career that met her personal needs, writing. She used the pseudonym, Beryl Bardwell, to write exciting serials printed in a popular monthly magazine.

As *Death at Bishop's Keep* (Avon, 1994) opened, Kate visited her wealthy Aunt Sabrina in England. Aunt Sabrina shared with Kate her involvement in the mysterious Order of the Golden Dawn where she met such notables as Sir Arthur Conan Doyle and Oscar Wilde. Kate's interest in the unidentified corpse found at a nearby archeological dig brought her into contact with Sir Charles Sheridan, who was impervious to the charms of more docile women. Checking out the corpse, the archeological site, and possible suspects seemed a good way to get material for her next book.

Kate went from murder suspect to heiress, and, by *Death at Gallows Green* (Avon, 1995), was an accepted member of local society. She reached out to shy young Beatrix Potter, who worked with Kate to solve the murder of young police sergeant Arthur Oliver. His dead body had been found by two servants during a entertainment for the staff. Sir Charles had been a childhood friend of

Oliver so he took a strong role in the investigation. His other goal was to persuade Kate to marry him.

An historic country estate, at which both were guests, presented an ideal time and place for Charles and Kate to break through their reserves and declare their love in *Death at Daisy's Folly* (Berkley, 1997). Unfortunately this had to be accomplished amidst the furor when a political zealot framed their hostess, a royal mistress, for murder.

During *Death at Devil's Bridge* (Berkley, 1998) and within a few short months of their marriage, Sir Charles and Kate were inveigled into hosting a motorcar exhibition and race by their neighbor Bradford Marsden. The highlight of the event was to be the release of a balloon, which would be pursued across the terrain by motorcars. The participant first reaching the point of descent would be the winner. There were those who disapproved of the race and enmities among the contenders. Wilhelm Albrecht, a German driver, was killed when someone tampered with the brakes on his vehicle. Kate's deductive skills and Sir Charles's use of fingerprints identified the killer.

Death at Rottingdean (Berkley, 1999) found Kate and Charles in enhanced roles as the Baron and Baroness of Somersworth, but with little time to spend together. They rented a small home at Rottingdean, hoping to enjoy the companionship of Rudyard Kipling and his militant aunt, Lady Georgianna Burne-Jones. Rottingdean and its residents hid a secret, ostensibly a harmless one. Charles, Kate, and Kipling with the help of eleven-year old Patrick discovered hidden depths to the conspiracy. There were hints that Patrick was a prototype for Kipling's *Kim*.

Blackmail, upstairs and downstairs, permeated *Death at Whitechapel* (Berkley, 2000). The plot centered on the events of the prior decade—the mutilation killings by Jack the Ripper. Jennie Jerome Churchill, Winston's mother, drew Kate and Charles into the controversy. Her blackmailer claimed proof that Jennie's husband, Lord Randolph, had been the Ripper. Years of deceit by powerful forces within the government could not withstand the Sheridans' search for the truth. Less admirable aspects of young Winston's character were explored.

Patrick's disappearance from the boarding school where he had been sent by Kate and Charles was only one subplot in *Death at Epsom Downs* (Berkley, 2001). The use of drugs to affect the performance of racehorses had not yet been banned in England. The death of a jockey, a runaway horse, and the impact on race results caused the Jockey Club to ask Lord Charles to investigate. Meanwhile Lillie Langtry, former mistress of the Prince of Wales, urged Kate, to rewrite one of her books as a play in which Lillie would star.

Charles had two items on his agenda when, in *Death at Dartmoor* (Berkley, 2002) he and Kate journeyed to Princetown near the Dartmoor prison: (1) to fingerprint all inmates, and (2) to use fingerprints to prove that Dr. Samuel Spencer, a confessed killer, had not murdered his wife, Elizabeth. Through their friend Arthur Conan Doyle, the Sheridans were invited to the home of Sir Edgar Duncan where Lady Duncan had arranged for medium Nigel Westcott to conduct a séance. Kate also had a double agenda: to gather insights and atmosphere for her next Beryl Bardwell book and to meet her long time friend Patsy Marsden, now a world traveler and photographer. Their agendas blended skillfully into a narrative of escape, murder and betrayal. Arthur Conan Doyle's detective skills were far outpaced by those of Charles and Kate. Great research.

Death at Glamis Castle (Berkley, 2003) weaved a fascinating story from the time Bonny Prince Charlie spent in Scotland, blending it with the possible plight of Prince Albert Edward, the unstable eldest son of King Edward VII. "Eddy" as he was familiarly referred to was confined in Glamis Castle. His disappearance caused consternation because the public had been led to believe that he had died previously. A state funeral had been held by the royal family to that end. Because the death of his personal maid was reminiscent of the Jack the Ripper murders, having Eddy out of the picture was desirable. Sir Charles was asked by the King to take charge of the search with the help of the Household Guard. Kate, who was looking for background for a new Gothic novel, was even more help.

The bomb that young anarchist Yuri Messenko thought would make him a hero in *Death in Hyde Park* (Berkley, 2004) killed him when it blew up in Hyde Park. His co-workers at the *Clarion*, an anarchist publication, Ivan Kopinski and Pierre Mouffetard, came under scrutiny by Inspector Earnest Ashcraft, and were eventually arrested for complicity. As was union representative Adam Gould, who had only been at the *Clarion* building to take editor Charlotte Conway out for dinner. Charlotte escaped via a window, observed by visiting author Jack London, and sought refuge with her friend, actress Nellie Lovelace. Nellie, whose career had been jumpstarted by Kate Sheridan, took Charlotte to Bishop's Keep in the hope that Kate could help Charlotte. This proved to be of mutual benefit because Lord Charles had been asked to conduct an investigation of the Hyde Park incident. He thought his knowledge of fingerprints might prove useful in the case.

Kate's interest in Rosamund Clifford and her affair with King Henry II prompted an invitation to Blenheim Palace, the home of the Duke and Duchess of Marlborough in *Death at Blenheim Palace* (Berkley, 2005). Before they arrived, Charles was aware of a series of burglaries at noble homes over weekends when there were many guests. He was alert to the possibility that servants might be involved. The Duke's guests noted his attentions to flirtatious Gladys Deacon, and so did his wife, Consuela, whose family fortunes had rescued the Duke and Blenheim. Within 24 hours of the Sheridan's arrival, housemaid Kitty Drake and Gladys had disappeared. Charles enlisted the help of Winston Churchill and young Ned Lawrence (later to be known as Lawrence of Arabia), but Kate and Consuela did some detecting on their own. The interactions between Kate and her author persona Beryl Bardwell were disconcerting.

Friend Bradford Marsden, who had made substantial investments in Guglielmo Marconi's new wireless telegraph, requested help from Charles in *Death on the Lizard* (Berkley, 2006). A series of incidents had occurred at wireless stations, possibly including murder at Poldhu in Cornwall. Coincidentally Bradford's dauntless sister, Patsy Marsden, was determined that Kate should join her on a visit to Jenna, Lady Loveday in that area. Jenna was in mourning for the deaths of her husband and her ten-year-old daughter Harriet coupled with guilt that she might have been responsible for the child's death. Other guests in the neighborhood included a mysterious sailor, an enthusiastic golfer, a titled spiritualist, and a spy on vacation.

Jessie Arnold

Author: Sue Henry

Jessie Arnold was described as a honey blonde who had been born in Minnesota, but fell in love with Alaska when her dad was stationed there while in the Air Force. Her parents and sister moved back to Minnesota, but Jessie stayed on. She supported herself as a racer, dog trainer and breeder, having forty or more dogs under her care. Jessie had never recovered from the disappearance of a younger sister, blaming herself (as did some others). Her older sister eventually moved to Ohio.

The series was initially identified as "Alex Jensen's" and the heroine was probably Alaska itself. Nevertheless, Jessie Arnold played a significant role in *Murder on the Iditarod Trail* (Atlantic Monthly Press, 1991) as a determined woman who placed second in this famous dogsled race from Anchorage to Nome. There had been several "accidents" during the race, and Sergeant Alex Jensen, Alaska State Trooper, was investigating them when he met Jessie. She had been a potential victim when her rifle was stolen shortly before an angry moose was herded into the path of her sled. Other mushers initially did not welcome female participants.

Alex Jensen and Jessie became lovers. During the next two books, *Termination Dust* (Morrow, 1995) in which she assisted Alex by reviewing the journal left behind by a gold rush miner; and *Sleeping Lady* (Morrow, 1996) in which Jensen sought a missing husband and was tempted by his wife, Jessie had no significant role. She provided a home base and companionship for Jensen, but little else.

In *Death Takes Passage* (Avon, 1997), Jessie and Alex traveled together on a ship recreating the 1897 transportation of two tons of gold from Skagway to Seattle. Fellow passengers included descendants of early gold miners and confederates of thieves who later boarded the ship. Jessie took part in Alex's action to retake control of the "Spirit of '98" from the potential thieves.

Deadfall (Avon, 1998) focused on Jessie's travails when an unknown stalker threatened her reputation and her life. Convinced by Alex to leave town, Jessie chose an isolated island off the Alaskan coast as her refuge. While

Alex and his friends sought to identify the person who was using Jessie to manipulate others, the stalker joined her on the island.

The series took a defining turn in *Murder on the Yukon Quest* (Avon, 1999) when Alex returned to Idaho to deal with a family crisis and Jessie became the primary sleuth. The Yukon Quest was an extended dogsled race that placed a high premium on endurance. Jessie entered for the first time, but sacrificed her own chance to win to help an injured racer. She made two choices: one, whether to keep a secret or seek help in a kidnapping; the other, whether to continue her relationship with Alex or stay without him in her beloved Alaska.

In *Beneath the Ashes* (Morrow, 2000), her friends on the police force gave Jessie the benefit of the doubt when she was implicated in arson and murder. Someone was setting Jessie up, paying off old scores. That could be the obsessed arson investigator, the badly scarred wife, or the husband from whom the woman was fleeing.

In a scenic drive up the Alaskan highway during *Dead North* (Morrow, 2001), Jessie transported a 31-foot Winnebago RV from Idaho to Alaska. Scenery notwithstanding, it was a hellish trip as she and sexagenarian widow Maxie McNabb befriended young Patrick Cutler. Patrick had fled Cody, Wyoming after the murder of his mother. Although he was at risk of being accused of matricide, his real danger was from the killer who pursued him. New and old friends assisted Jessie, Maxie and Patrick as they journeyed north. Maxie McNabb became the protagonist in a later series of her own.

During *Cold Company* (Morrow, 2002) Jessie focused on the new log cabin that Vic Prentice's crew was building for her until a skeleton was discovered in the cellar cavity. More recent murders of young women were connected to roses delivered to them shortly before their deaths. When roses were sent to Jessie, she resisted the advice of her friends. A serious injury forced her to evaluate her need for independence based in part on a youthful tragedy. Fellow musher Lynn Ehlers alleviated her sense of loss due to Alex's absence. NB: As a collector (seventy years ago) of Nelson Eddy records, I wish to clarify that he, not Mario Lanza, made *Stout Hearted Men* popular.

Jessie was more victim than sleuth in *Death Trap* (Morrow, 2003). She "just happened to be in the wrong place at the wrong time." But she had three men who cared enough about her to help out. Alex had returned to Alaska. Phil Becker and Lynn Ehlers were always available. Maxie McNabb had reappeared in Jesssie's life. Both Maxie and eight-year-old Danny Tabor were on the run, which kept both the police and the criminals busy.

Jessie had spent most of her Alaskan time inland so the invitation in *Murder at Five Finger Light* (New American Library, 2005) to join a group rehabbing the Five Finger lighthouse sounded great. Laurie Trevino and Jim Beal, who had appeared in prior books, had purchased the entire island. Alex had taken up residence with Jessie, but could not join her because of a professional conference. En route Karen Emerson asked Jessie for help, describing herself as an abused woman fleeing a stalker. This was not a request that Jessie could ignore so she invited Karen to join the group on Five Finger Island. Everything went downhill from there. Although Alex and Jessie saved the day and their relationship, the reader may find the connections among the villains murky and inadequately explained.

Even with her knee still in recovery and no snow, Jessie had been running her dogs with a four-wheeled cart in preparation for races as *Degrees of Separation* (Obsidian, 2008) began. On one such trip they discovered a corpse on the path. Knowing that Jessie was depressed by the death of a favorite dog, Alex urged her to stay out of the investigation. Although she ignored his advice, the narrative was primarily a police procedural. Maxie McNabb visited, staying long enough to give Alex some good advice on how to handle the tangled mix of clues in the case.

Those seeking another Alaskan heroine might also enjoy Kate Shugak by Dana Stabenow.

Although there were at least two intervening mysteries featuring senior sleuth Maxie McNabb and her dachshund, Stretch, Henry returned to Jessie Arnold in *Cold As Ice* (2010).

Kristin Ashe

Author: Jennifer L. Jordan

Kristin Ashe was one of five children, four daughters and a son. Her brother David, who had suffered from epilepsy since childhood, lived in a home for chronically mentally ill residents. Her oldest sister, Ann, was employed as art director in Kristin's business. Two other sisters, Gail and Jill, had moved to California. There was no indication of their marital status. Kristin perceived their mother, Carolyn, as passive and emotionally abusive. The children had come in quick succession, which may have contributed, to her bouts of depression. As a child, Kristin remembered coming home from school, wondering if her mother was still in bed. Her father Bill was initially recalled as being a loving father although he had a problem with alcohol. Since her parent's divorce, Bill had remarried happily. There had been no personal contact between Kristin and her mother for almost two years. As an adult, Kristin had nightmares, difficulty with relationships and negative feelings about men in general. Her warmest family contact was with her paternal grandmother, whom she visited regularly, took shopping, and joined in card games. She also had a close and affectionate relationship with the children of her friend, Peggy—Jessica (4) and Zeb (7). Kristin described herself as "lean," with brown hair cut short. Her usual attire consisted of a button down shirt, jeans, and Topsiders without socks.

Kristin's primary occupation was as the head of a marketing and graphics art business (Marketing Consultants) in Denver Colorado. Her secondary roles were as an investigator for vulnerable women and as a volunteer at the Denver Rape Crisis Center. Later she closed down the marketing business and went full time in the investigation agency. Fran Green gradually eased her way into a partnership. She was a former nun, lesbian in her 60's, who was borderline promiscuous. Fran was often played for laughs, coming up with new lines of business that ventured into the unsavory.

Destiny Greaves, current lover of Kristin's best friend Michelle, sought help locating her birth family in *A Safe Place to Sleep* (Our Power Press, 1992). She was unable to remember anything about her life before she was adopted at age four by Ben and Liz Greaves. Her unsatisfactory relationship with Liz led her to seek for her "real" mother. Kristin was deeply affected by the request. She too had no recollection of her early childhood. In researching Destiny's background, Kristin released her own repressed memories. She and Destiny supported one another as the facts emerged— information that each found difficult to handle.

In *Existing Solutions* (Our Power Press, 1993), Kristin was asked by Destiny Greaves to find the man who had raped and impregnated her mother. Kristin made the connection to a prominent businessman, who was also the executive director of a religiously oriented rape crisis center. She was disturbed to find that his charm influenced Destiny to accept his version of the relationship. Kristin was less gullible, her hostility fueled by her need to confront her own father. A very angry book with a conclusion that might satisfy Kristin and Destiny but disturb others.

Even though Kristin had made a commitment to Patrice Elliott to discover why her sister, Lauren Fairchild, had killed herself in *Commitment to Die* (Bean Pole, 2004), she was juggling two major personal problems at the time. Her brother David had been found in a coma and was hospitalized. Kristin's relationship with Destiny Greaves was endangered by Kristin's reluctance to move into Destiny's elaborate home. Even then, her need to understand Lauren and her affection for Ashley, Patrice's handicapped daughter, made it impossible for Kristin to stop until she knew why Lauren died.

Kristin's lucrative marketing business was on vacation for the holidays in *Unbearable Losses* (Spinsters Ink, 2006), but she had plenty to keep her busy, e.g. personal matters like the breakup of her friend Fran Green's lesbian relationship. Fran had become an ally in many of Kristin's investigations. She pitched in to help when Kristin was hired to investigate thefts of the Crumpler sisters' over-elaborate Christmas decorations. Her big case was that of Lori Parks, director of top rated Children's Academy. Lori had been receiving threats of violence which not only targeted her but her daughter. Lori's reluctance to share information complicated matters.

Kristin did not distinguish herself professionally in *Disorderly Attachments* (Spinsters Ink, 2006) by accepting $10,000 to investigate Destiny for Dr. Carolyn O'Keefe, superintendent of the Denver Metro Public Schools. O'Keefe had made it clear that the reason for the probe was to further her flirtation with Destiny. At that point Kristin could have opted out, but didn't, nor did she make Destiny aware of this assignment. In her role as head of the Lesbian

Community Center, Destiny was actively seeking contacts with school principals to protect high-school-aged gays and lesbians. O'Keefe had capitalized on this connection to see her frequently. Fran Green, now Kristin's business partner, sought to handle this matter while Kristin investigated the possibility that a deteriorating mansion owned by Hazel Middleton might be haunted. Kristin carried out that assignment but was unable to avoid involvement in O'Keefe's case. More about relationships and ghosts than mystery.

Selective Memory (Spinsters Ink, 2007) can be classified as a mystery only in that the narrative gradually revealed the character of Alex Madigen. Kristin had been recommended by Alex's case manager at Sinclair Rehabilitation Center to assist Alex in recovering her past. A one-car accident months before had left Alex with multiple injuries, including serious brain damage which affected both short-term and long-term memory. The plan was that Kristin would learn "who" Alex was by interviewing friends, but the narrative dwelt heavily on Alex's thoughts which often varied from what she told Kristin and others. The important people in Alex's life were Stacey, who until recently had been her lover, and Clarissa, a woman from her past whom she could not forget. Alex had been a child musical prodigy who quit Julliard just before graduation and ended up writing advertising jingles. Her relationships were compared to those of Clara and Robert Schumann and Johannes Brahms. The book might well have been classified as romance.

If No One Is Looking (Spinsters Ink, 2008) involved Kristin, Fran, and Destiny in two delicate situations. When three-year-old Kayla Martin, the child of lesbians Gwen Martin and Tracey Reid, disappeared, Destiny took the lead in organizing volunteers to search for the child and in raising funds which might be needed if Gwen and/or Tracey were held responsible. Fran took time from the search for Kayla to check out charges that a female high school coach had improper contacts with her students. Kristin's approach to both of these cases did not necessarily agree with those of Destiny or Fran, but she was determined to find Kayla. One of the better books in the series.

Billie August

Author: Gillian Roberts pseudonym for Judith Greber

The pairing of the old-timer and the new kid on the block is an established narrative device in fiction. Emma Howe and Billie August brought their own perspective to the roles. Tough unemotional Emma ran an investigative agency in Marin County, California. She was a short, stocky widow in her fifties with two adult children: Nathaniel and Caroline. Some of Emma's cynicism was well earned. Husband Harry had been a frequently unemployed gambler who died in another woman's bed. When George, her current lover, proposed, she was unwilling to make a commitment. A sense that Nathaniel was the favored child had led to Caroline's belief that she was not important to her mother.

Billie's youth, her physical appearance (tall and slim), and her background (East Coast college degree in music and drama) all stood in contrast. Billie's parents had divorced. She had custody of her son, Jesse, but lived in fear that her former husband, Cameron Smith, might abduct him again. He had done so when Jesse was two, but she traced them down and retrieved the boy. Ivan, a Russian college student, provided childcare services in exchange for his room and board. Billie's employment with Emma was similar. She exchanged her youth, enthusiasm, and inexperience for a chance to work for a rigid and demanding, but savvy, investigator.

Although she had always employed males before, Emma was sufficiently impressed by Billie's dogged pursuit of Cameron to hire her in *Time and Trouble* (St. Martin, 1998). Billie proved her mettle in what began as a simple case. Sophia Redmond's claim for physical disability was suspect, but there were other problems in the Redmond family. Daughter Penny had found evidence of a triple homicide but was unwilling to approach the police. When Penny disappeared, Sophie hired the agency to find her.

In *Where's the Harm?* (Five Star, an anthology of short stories, 1999), Emma appeared in H*eart Break* during which her inattention to a meandering conversation by old friend Vivian Carter almost desensitized her to a question about murder.

Emma, aware of her own flawed relationship with daughter Caroline, agreed in *Whatever Doesn't Kill You* (St. Martin, 2001) to help Heather Wilson find her birth mother. To lighten her load, she assigned Billie to uncover exculpatory material that might help Gavin Riddock prove that he had not killed his dearest friend, Tracy Lester. Both investigators struggled through their misunderstandings. In the climax, Billie saved the day. Emma learned more about herself and about the need for truth between parent and child. Sometimes it was necessary, sometimes, cruel. Billie provided a tempering impact on Emma's rigidity.

Roberts is also the author of the Amanda Pepper series covered in Volume 2.

Cat Austen

Author: Jane Rubino

Allegrezza Caterina Fortunati Austen or "Cat," was a young widow living in the Atlantic City area with two small children. She was provided with a supporting cast of six brothers—five in law enforcement and one in the priesthood. Cat worked as a freelance reporter, barely scraping by on her deceased husband Chris' pension (no Social Security?). She also rented part of the Ocean City house she had inherited from an aunt to Ellice, an African-American who later married Cat's youngest brother, Freddy. The shortage of funds was Cat's justification for her determination to "get the story" and sell it. At times that meant leaving sick children in the care of a friend, and taking risks that might leave her children parentless. She did not hesitate to break and enter, steal documents, or withhold information from the police, including Lt. Victor Cardenas with whom she was having a chaste relationship.

Just before he was gunned down in *Death of a D.J.* (Write Way, 1994), obnoxious right-wing disk jockey Jerry Dudek chose Cat as his confidante. She became convinced that the motive for his death lay in an exposé of prominent individuals planned for his radio show. Cardenas passed the scrutiny of Cat's family as a possible suitor for her affections. She was beginning to realize that her life had to go on without Chris.

Fruitcake (Write Way, 1997) was filled with extended family involvement and expanded by overly detailed characters in subplots. Then, it segued into a police procedural (Lt. Victor Cardenas and staff) and mixed it with Cat's work as a freelance reporter. References to events in the prior book could complicate the narrative for those who had not read it. Cat stumbled over another corpse, which sent her on a parallel investigation to that headed by Lt. Cardenas.

Although Cat and Victor had planned a Caribbean tour, it was postponed as *Cheat the Devil* (Write Way, 1998) opened. Cat had a sense of relief because she was not ready for what such a joint trip entailed. Her joy was short-lived. She learned that Victor had cancelled because of a series of murders tied to St. Agnes' parish where her brother, Dominic was pastor. Dominic became a suspect based on connections between his church and repentant women with criminal histories. At least this time she didn't need Cardenas to save her from a killer.

Cop Watch, a television production company, reenacting real life dramas, was shooting a film based on the death of disk jockey Jerry Dudek as *Plot Twist* (Write Way, 2000) began. A drawing card for the film would be the appearance of beautiful and talented actress, Tammi Ann Butler. Crime reporter Ron Spivak had made it known that he had access to information that would damage Tammi Ann's career. His death while playing a part in the production caused Cat Austen and Victor Cardenas to keep secrets from one another. This would be more difficult to understand if the prior books had not explained their relationship.

While Lt. Victor Cardenas huddled with other investigators in a dining room at the Sterling Phoenix Hotel and Casino in *Cake Job* (Worldwide, 2003, one of a collection of four novellas in *Deadly Morsels*) Cat blithely wandered around the wedding vendor show in the Great Hall. Victor and the others were concerned with the safety of state's witness Paulie Forgione and members of his family. Paulie was to testify against corrupt union leader Cholly Mackenzie who reputedly had arranged for the murders of Paulie's two children. It was Cat who, by her close attention to others in the ballroom, was plunged into a mildly humorous concoction of abduction, murder, and romance.

Raise the Dead (Lumina Press, 2004) may be the best in the series. It contains human pathos, tension and a terrific conclusion. Cat had received phone calls offering information on her husband Chris's death but ignored them. When television reporter Whitney Rocap suggested a meeting including Cat and the unknown caller, Cat declined. Whitney's murder, an attack on Cat when she surprised an intruder, and the connection with State of the Art, the fertility clinic where Cat and Chris had received help, will keep the reader spellbound. This was a winner. Rubino packed more excitement into 235 pages than most do in 400.

The narratives had multiple subplots that connected up eventually often through coincidences. All cases sent to Cardenas' desk seemed to involve Cat, her family, her childhood and high school chums. The narratives improved over the course of the series.

Jane Austen

Author: Stephanie Barron, pseudonym for Francine Mathews.

Some disparate elements work surprisingly well together: strawberries dipped in melted chocolate, Laurel and Hardy, history and mystery. Some work better than others. Jane Austen, the English clergyman's daughter whose writings have frequently been the subject of television programs and movies, appeared as the sleuth in this mystery series. The narrative material was purportedly based upon information discovered in her journals and letters. Jane's close ties to her five siblings, particularly her only sister, Cassandra, and her progress from a Hampshire rectory to Bath were significant aspects in the narrative.

In *Jane and the Unpleasantness at Scargrave Manor* (Bantam, 1996), she was a guest at the home of her friend, Isabel, now Countess of Scargrave, when the Earl died of gastric distress. Jane was aware that Isabel had married Frederick to protect her own financial interests. A letter accusing Isabel of conspiring with Fitzroy, Frederick's nephew, to kill the older man was sent to the local magistrate. Jane described the reactions and interactions of other members of the household in letters to her sister Cassandra as evidence accumulated against Isabel and Fitzroy. She set herself to prove them innocent.

During *Jane and the Man of the Cloth* (Bantam, 1997) Jane, Cassandra and their parents visited on the Dorset Coast. En route to their destination, Cassandra was injured in an accident, causing them to accept hospitality from Geoffrey Sidmouth until their carriage could be repaired. Even though Sidmouth was not accepted in the community, Jane found him attractive. He was suspected of being "the Reverend", head of the local smugglers and a killer. Even though Jane shared this suspicion, she took an active role in checking out the French connections of others in the community, aided by Lord Harold Trowbridge. The adventure portrayed Jane as more adventurous and physically active than a reader of the Austen novels would expect.

The social season in Bath, a location preferred by Jane's aging father, included masked balls. In *Jane and the Wandering Eye* (Bantam, 1998), she attended such a gathering at the home of the Dowager Duchess of Wilborough, whose son, Lord Harold, had assisted Jane in the prior investigation. Lord Harold, concerned about his niece's social activities, asked Jane to observe the young woman's friends. Among those present at the ball were members of a theatrical troupe, one of whom was murdered that evening. The arrest of Lord Harold's nephew for the crime spurred him and Jane into investigating the lives of other suspects.

Jane and the Genius of the Place (Bantam, 1999) was set within Jane's small social circle during a visit to her affluent brother Neddie in Kent. The group, however, was large enough to contain the seeds of murder, financial skullduggery, and espionage. She and Neddie pursued a killer whose motive had an element of patriotism, but whose genius was wasted.

Charles Danforth had suffered great personal tragedies in the past year—the deaths of his wife and four of his children. In *Jane and the Stillroom Maid* (Bantam, 2000), he was perceived by the locals as cursed. This perception increased upon the death of Tess, a maid in his household. The Devonshire society in which Charles lived and which Jane visited abounded with social intrigue. Lord Harold (the man to whom Jane had given her affections without hope of a proposal) worked with Jane to go beyond the confusion to a sly killer.

Jane moved from affairs of the heart to matters of national importance in *Jane and the Prisoner of Wool House* (Bantam, 2001) The plight of Captain Tom Seagrave, accused of murdering a French prisoner, aroused both sympathy and support from Jane and her seagoing brother, Frank. Frank used his official position at some damage to his own reputation. Jane risked greater physical danger by tending to the needs of French prisoners at Wool House. Spurred on, she ventured into depraved sections of Southampton in search of a prostitute, and risked personal injury rescuing a French gentleman from a burning ship. She was getting more adventurous as the series progressed.

Jane had never forgotten Lord Harold; so in *Jane and the Ghosts of Netley* (Bantam, 2003), she could not refuse to help him. In Lord Harold's viewpoint, wealthy Sophia Challoner had left Portugal for England only to serve as a spy for Napoleon Bonaparte. Jane had mixed feelings for Sophia, a warm and generous woman. She found it difficult to see her as a Papist traitor. One phase of Jane's life was forever changed in the outcome.

When *Jane and his Lordship's Legacy*(Bantam, 2005) opened, it was just ten months since Lord Harold Trowbridge had died. Jane and her mother were moving into Chawton Cottage when a solicitor delivered a chest containing Lord Harold's personal memorabilia. His intention was that she write his biography, a publication which might embarrass important personages. Chawton Cottage was part of the manor inherited by Jane's brother Edward who had been adopted by a childless couple. Austens were not welcomed in the village, even less so when a corpse was discovered in the cottage cellar. Jane was painfully aware that the material now in her possession made her vulnerable to theft, even to murder.

In *Jane and the Barque of Frailty* (Bantam, 2006), Jane visited with her brother Henry and his wife Eliza at their London home. Henry was underwriting the cost of publishing Jane's first book, to be called *Sense and Sensibility*, and she wished to be available to deal with the publisher. Both Henry and Eliza had aspirations to move in high society (the Ton). Eliza's eagerness to please a titled acquaintance placed her and Jane in serious trouble. They had possession of jewels belonging to the Russian Princess Evgenia Tascholikova, who had been discovered dead on the steps of the home of Lord Castlereagh, rumored to be the object of her affection. With Eliza's help and that of young solicitor Sylvester Chizzlewit, Jane had a crash course in the iniquities of the upper class. The "Barque" referred to seventeen-year-old Julia Radcliffe, once the daughter of a prominent family, now a courtesan with her own salon. There were just too many footnotes; informative but disruptive of the narrative.

As Francine Matthews, Barron authored the Merry Folger series, also covered in this volume.

After a lull, Stephanie Barron resumed the Jane Austen series with *Jane and the Madness of Lord Byron* (2010).

Kate Austen

Author: Jonnie Jacobs

Kate Austen, who already had a daughter, Anna, was pregnant with a second child when her husband Andy left their California home to "find himself" in Europe. The family dog, Max, part Airedale, was a comfort. For a while Kate worked part-time in an art gallery, owned by her best friend Daria Wilkens. She pulled herself together, and reached out to others rather than nursing her own grievances. That kindness on occasion led to trouble.

During *Murder Among Neighbors* (Kensington, 1994), Kate volunteered to care for Kimberly, whose mother, Pepper Livingston, had been murdered. Pepper had been a beautiful, wealthy woman, a friendly neighbor who often carpooled with Kate. Robert, Pepper's bereaved husband, was grateful for the support. Lt. Michael Stone asked Kate, as a close friend to look over Pepper's room for changes, and she provided him with insights as to the relationship between Pepper and Robert.

When her friend Mona Sterling's death was deemed a possible suicide during *Murder Among Friends* (Kensington, 1995), Kate took in Libby, the woman's teenage daughter. The conflicting evidence that Kate brought to Lt. Stone's attention set the police on the track to her killer. As in the prior book, the killer was too close for comfort. Excellent plotting. Although Andy had not signed the divorce papers, Michael Stone convinced Kate (and Anna and Libby) to accompany him on a vacation.

Initially the death of Kate's promising art student, Julie Harmon, seemed to be the work of a serial killer in *Murder Among Us* (Kensington, 1998). Kate's live-in lover Michael moved out of the house temporarily while Faye, Kate's mother-in-law, visited. Her divorce from Andy was in process but Faye had not accepted the end of the marriage. Libby, who still lived with Kate, felt guilty because she had not befriended Julie. Kate's own sense of guilt over failing to respond to a needy student drove her to investigate. Unlike many other female sleuths, she shared her clues with the police department to their annoyance.

Murder Among Strangers (Kensington, 2000) had a quick start. A pair of escaping criminals kidnapped Kate when she stopped to offer assistance on the highway. She had seen Sheryl Ann Martin sitting alone in a car late in the evening and was unable to control her charitable impulse. Once she saw the corpse in the trunk, it was too late. Kate was expected to keep him company.

Jacobs has a second series, featuring attorney Kali O'Brien. (see later in this volume)

Allida "Allie" Babcock

Author: Leslie O'Kane

Allida Babcock (Allie only to her close friends) made it clear that she was neither a dog trainer (although she had been) nor a veterinarian. She was a pet therapist, offering services to owners whose dogs did not respond to training. After college, Allie had worked as a technical writer in Chicago while training dogs on the side. At age thirty-two, she returned to her home state, Colorado, to concentrate on dog therapy. With limited funds, Allie rented a portion of Russell Greene's business quarters. He was a shy electrical engineer who was determined to go beyond their professional relationship. What made that a real possibility was that he was short; Allie being slightly less than five feet in height. This had not deterred her from being a star basketball guard in high school.

Allie's father had been a pilot who was killed in an automobile accident. Her mother, Marilyn, rose to the occasion, went back to work and raised two children. She still gave flying lessons. When Allie had large dogs to work with, they were housed at Marilyn's. Eventually she moved back in with her mother, while looking for an affordable place of her own. Allie's brother was a pilot for United Airlines. She had resisted the pressure to become a pilot, pleading vertigo.

Allie's pet therapy business increased after she was interviewed on Tracy Truett's local radio program in *Play Dead* (Fawcett, 1998). Tracy, who had been intoxicated at the time, highlighted Allie's theory that vegetarian businesswoman Hannah Jones might have been murdered. Hannah had a serious illness and a gun, but those who knew her doubted that she would have killed herself without making provision for her pet, Sage. The subsequent death of Beth Gleason, the young woman caring for Hannah's collie, was an obvious connection to Allie, but not to the police. The best clues came from the collie

An assignment to choose the better placement for a Silky Terrier in a dog custody case in *Ruff Way to Go* (Fawcett, 2000) was just the start for Allie. Shogun, the dog in the custody dispute disappeared, When Allie located him, she was perceived as taking sides by her placement. Suds, a husky with a litter of pups, was being fostered by Cassandra, Allie's neighbor, while the owner was in a halfway house. When Cassandra was murdered, Allie took Suds and her pups, but that brought more trouble. Marilyn, Allie's mom, ended up with a half-dozen dogs and newborn pups in her home. The bizarre ending gave faithful Russell Greene a chance to be a hero. Entertaining but with loose ends.

Allie was not at all certain that she should take on Ken Culberson and his unruly golden retriever, Maggie, as clients in *Give the Dog a Bone* (Fawcett, 2002). Ken, a naïve television repairman, had struck it rich with the invention of a new form of circuitry. Still he lived in a trailer with Maggie as his only companion in the belief that his dead wife's spirit inhabited the dog's body. Shortly before Ken was murdered, he wrote a codicil to his will which entrusted Maggie, his heiress, to Allie's care until she found a suitable home. Not surprisingly there were several applicants for the position.

O'Kane has a second longer series featuring Molly Masters, a wife and mother who gets very involved in the schools attended by her children while working part-time designing faxable greeting cards (covered in this volume).

Johnelle "Johnnie" Baker

Author: John Miles, pseudonym for John Bickham, but first book initially credited to Arthur Williams

Johnnie Baker returned to Tenoclock, Colorado for refuge and a new start. A tall blonde who had hoped for a career as an actress, she had failed to find steady work in either New York City or California. After her marriage collapsed, she fled to the rundown farmette bequeathed by her parents. She began work as a deputy. Her appointment as sheriff was more of a public relations move than a tribute to her ability. Tenoclock had poised itself to become the next Vail, a Mecca for tourists.

Big Jim Way was sheriff when *Missing at Tenoclock* (Walker, 1994) began. It would have been easy for Johnnie to write his death off as a drunken accident, but there were too many connections with the disappearance of a teenage waitress and her father. The remnants of the sheriff's department were sadly incompetent to handle murder investigations, so Johnnie hired her mentor Butt Peabody as deputy.

During *Tenoclock Scholar* (Walker, 1995), the community reeled under a series of crimes and disturbances (which were interpreted by some as the fulfillment of an Anasazi curse). Johnnie and Peabody believed that the local Indians were being framed for the murders of Richard Tomlinson, who ran a nearby salvage yard, and two subsequent deaths (1) arson at the courthouse annex where records were stored causing the janitor's death (2) the violent death of Ute Billy Kickingbird. These were crucial cases for Johnnie as she had only been sheriff for seven months. Noah Webster, a naive scholar in search of archeological and genealogical information, was part of the problem and part of the solution.

These were entertaining with interesting regional touches.

Hollis Ball

Author: Helen Chappell

Sam Wescott had a significant impact on the life of Hollis Ball as a young woman. He was a member of the distinguished Wescott family of Santimoke County, Maryland, even if he was considered the "black sheep." She was a Beddoe's Island girl, a member of a socially isolated community that lived by its own rules and regulations. Falling in love was out of the question. Getting married would be foolish. Still they did. Sent ashore to pick up supplies for their honeymoon voyage on Sam's boat, Hollis returned to the dock only to see him sailing off without her. Sam did not return for ten years, existing as a remittance man in far off places where he could do no further harm to the Wescott family reputation.

In the meantime, Holly built a life. She earned a college degree, took a low paying job as reporter for the *Watertown Gazette*, subjecting herself to an incompetent editor and an absentee owner. Quality reporting was not a goal for the *Gazette*. Keeping the advertisers happy was.

At age thirty-five, she shared a Spartan rental house on the mainland with Venus, an even more independent cat. Her parents (Herk and Dolly) and her brother Robbie hoped that she would settle down, marry again and have a family. Her dad and brother were watermen who fished what was left in Chesapeake Bay, guided hunting parties, and fought against the economic oppression of the canneries and fish companies. Hollis had smoked until an exposure to chemical fumes damaged her lungs, and still had a cigarette when stressed. Reese's Peanut Butter Cups were another comfort indulgence. State Police Sgt. Ormond Friendly played an increasingly important role in her life over the series.

Sam Wescott returned to Hollis' life during *Slow Dancing with the Angel of Death* (Fawcett, 1996) although not in human form because the boat on which he arrived exploded. He appeared as a ghost that materialized only to a select few. Toby Russell, bar owner and Hollis' cousin, maintained that he and Hollis had the "gift" of second sight from a grandmother. Sam needed to make amends for his life. At his funeral, Hollis learned of the Wescott family plan to develop wetlands. Political pressure had removed restrictions on building in the area. Within days she had become a fugitive from the law, assisted by her family and watched over by Sam, whom she had spent ten years trying to forget.

Even though Herk, Hollis' father, was a duck decoy collector, she knew little of their value as antiques or art works until *Dead Duck* (Fawcett, 1997). During preparations for the Annual Decoy Jamboree, unpopular Judge Findlay Finch was murdered. State Police Sgt. Ormand Friendly, who had dealt with Hollis before, thought she might be of some assistance in his investigation. Although Sam helped Hollis escape death; neither he nor she were primarily responsible for identifying the killer. There are lots of folksy details on the extended Beddoe's Island family and the denizens of Watertown.

Jennifer Clinton, a childhood friend of Hollis, returned to Santimoke County in *Ghost of a Chance* (Dell, 1998) when her mother's skeleton was discovered in a submerged car. For decades Jennifer, now a television soap opera star, had feared that Renata had abandoned her. Now she believed that her mother had been murdered and pressured Hollis to investigate. Sam fleshed out his presence by doing some of the narration. Other spectral figures appeared: Edgar Allan Poe and Renata Clinton, Jennifer's mother.

For those who are not and never were Elvis Presley fans, a strong dose of "the King" and his emulators may be too much in *Giving Up the Ghost* (Dell, 1999). Albie Lydekker, Hollis' cousin and godfather, had earned her childhood affection by his kindness. When Bang-Bang Devine, Albie's partner in an Elvis contest, was murdered, Hollis took it upon herself to defend Albie from suspicion as his killer. Sgt. Friendly, although a closet Elvis fan, disagreed. Sam took leave of Hollis after a quarrel, but returned when she realized how much she had come to depend on him.

If you thought the Ball family was eccentric, wait till you read about their inbred cousins, the Fotneys in *A Fright of Ghosts* (Tidewater, 2006). Sluggo started the action when he convinced Hollis's brother, Robbie, an expectant father, to come to Shellpile Island and help him catch eels. The next thing Hollis heard, Robbie had been arrested for Sluggo's murder. She and cousin Toby headed off to the rescue, but Sam's father, wealthy H.P. Wescott and a dazzling defense attorney were already there. Hollis stayed on to prove Robbie's innocence, but had to deal with a town full of Fotneys, including three of Sluggo's wives. Her best allies were ghosts; i.e. Sam and an ancient pirate Shecky Johnson. A short humorous read.

Under the name Leslie Trevor, Chappell did the book versions of the television show *Policewoman,* featuring Pepper Anderson. See Volume 1

Sophia "Sophy" Bancroft

Author: Karla Hocker

Although originally named Sophia Bancroft, the young governess preferred to be called Sophy. That was not all she was called. She was frequently referred to as "impetuous," "incorrigible," and "impertinent." Moving into a home in the ambiguous position of governess was not easy for a young woman who had been raised in a noble family. Unfortunately her father, Baron Wingfield, produced only daughters, so at his death his title, estates, and many debts went to a collateral relative Jonathan Bancroft. Jonathan did not expect that attaining the title would require him to provide for his predecessor's three daughters. His suggested remedy for the girls' plight was marriages arranged with his dissolute friends. Sophy preferred to be a governess. She used her meager earnings to send her sister Linnet to boarding school. The youngest daughter, Caroline remained at Rose Manor, the family estate. Sophy knew that she could rely on

Susannah, Jonathan's wife, to care for Caroline. Susannah had also provided dubious references for Sophy's qualifications as governess.

In *The Impertinent Miss Bancroft* (Walker, 1991), by the time Sophy was hired by Lucian, Lord Northrup, she had been fired from seven positions over the past two years. Her responsibilities were to teach the nephews and niece who had been left in Northrop's care while their parents were on an extended journey. That became a sideline when Sophy learned that thefts in the household had cast doubt on an elderly member of the family. She not only flaunted her experiences as a "thief-taker," but also continued to investigate even after murder was done. Another man might have dismissed Sophy, but Lucian fell in love.

With the nieces and nephews away for the summer, Sophy's continued presence in Lucian's home raised questions of propriety in *The Incorrigible Sophia* (Walker, 1992). Lucian rejected her cousin Jonathan's demand that she return to his estate. He reconsidered when she became embroiled in matters of state security. Andrew, Lucian's brother, was arrested for murder and treason. Sophy felt it was up to her to save the family name of the man she loved.

The series, set in London, was referred to by Walker as a Regency Romance, and is a blend of gothic romance and mystery. Hocker has written other standalone romance novels of that period.

Kate Banning

Author: Cecilia Tishy

Kate Banning made a mid-life career change, moving from Boston, where she had been an investigative reporter, to a position as a coordinating editor in Nashville, Tennessee. Her new employer, Fleetwood Publications, contracted to provide magazines and public relations materials for industries, many of which had previously used in-house staffs. Kate edited articles that she had commissioned freelance authors to write. Her new boss, Hughes Amberson, was pleased with her work.

The move was not without complications. Kelly, the thirteen-year-old daughter of Kate's marriage to a medical student, found it difficult to be accepted in her new school. Sam Powers, a charter airline pilot, juggled his schedule to find time to be with them. Kate missed having friends in whom she could confide. Kate's parents had died when she was very young. The grandmother who raised her had been dead for sixteen years. There were no aunts, uncles, or cousins to provide emotional support. In her late thirties, still dark blonde, Kate placed a high importance on being independent. She was unwilling to accept Sam's financial help or his proposals. Considering that Kate's former husband had no contact with his daughter, Kate had a tendency to be reckless. Her investigations in Boston had provided her with helpful contacts in the criminal justice system. In Tennessee she had no such allies.

It got nasty in Nashville when rising country music star Brandi Burns was killed in a car wreck during *Jealous Heart* (Dowling, 1997). Brandi's sister

Bobbie had learned that Kate was an investigator so urged her to look into the case. Their efforts were stymied. There were threats, arson, and an attempt at murder before Kate got the key to the killer.

Kate came to realize by *Cryin' Time* (Dowling, 1998) that she needed the excitement that came with her investigations. She agreed to do a background check on Tory Blackfeather. UpShot Records wanted the information before they signed him to a major contract. Only when Shay Labrand, the woman in Troy's life, disappeared did Kate realize that she and Troy were the only ones concerned about Shay's welfare. The recording company argued that she would either return or he would be better off without her. Kate had to go it alone against violent opposition.

A new line of business for Fleetwood, handling communications between entertainers and their fans, emerged in *Fall to Pieces* (Dowling, 2000). Country music legend LilyAnn Page was a potential client. Page's manager, Dottie Skipworth, insisted that Kate be assigned to the project. Her sub-agenda was that Kate would investigate recent accidents involving LilyAnn. There were multiple motives within LilyAnn's household and staff for wanting the singer dead or incapacitated.

Tishy has moved on to another series featuring psychic sleuth Regina Cutter, who found a new occupation after her divorce, as a psychic working with the Boston Police Department.

Lily Bard

Author: Charlaine Harris

Lily Bard, a National Merit Scholar who graduated from college with a 3.9 average (out of 4.0), ran a "cleaning and errand running service" in Shakespeare, Arkansas. Her potential, the ties to her birth family in Bartley, Arkansas, and her engagement had been casualties when she was convicted of killing one of the men who gang-raped her. Now in her thirties, she put the past behind by immersing herself in physical work, learning to defend herself, and walking the streets at night when she could not sleep. Inevitably during her cleaning chores she learned a lot about her clients.

While walking early one morning during *Shakespeare's Landlord* (St. Martin, 1996) Lily became aware that someone was moving her garbage cart. Investigating, she discovered the corpse of Pardon Albee, the elderly man from whom she had purchased her home. Given her record, she was reluctant to contact the authorities, but made an anonymous call to friendly police officer Claude Friedrich. Lily could not avoid involvement in the investigation, but she learned she had friends in Shakespeare.

Arriving early at the Body Time gym in *Shakespeare's Champion* (St. Martin, 1997), Lily discovered bodybuilder Del Packard dead in what might be an accident or murder. She did not need more involvement in crime. Her rescue of African-American Darnell Glass from bullies may have contributed to his subsequent death. These incidents sensitized Lily to the existence of a right wing extremist group, and provided her with a romantic interest when private investigator Jack Leeds became her lover.

For all of her prickliness, Lily could be endearing and credible. *Shakespeare's Christmas* (St. Martin, 1999) was the gripping account of how Lily and Jack Leeds searched her hometown (Bartley, Arkansas) for a missing child. It had not been easy for Lily to return to Bartley. There were too many memories, but she was a bridesmaid for her sister Varenna's wedding. The interplay among Jack, Varenna, Lily and her parents was engrossing.

It was bad luck for Lily to be the one who discovered the brutalized corpse of Deedra Dean, the "black sheep" of a prominent family, in *Shakespeare's Trollop* (St. Martin, 2000). Deedra, one of Lily's clients, was notably promiscuous. Lily's rescue of Deedra's wealthy great-grandfather from a house fire did nothing to allay the suspicions of Lt. Jump Farraclough. Lily and Jack Leeds came to realize during the investigation just how much they needed one another.

Frightened by a violent nightmare in *Shakespeare's Counselor* (St. Martin, 2001), Lily attended a therapy group for victims of rape. Tamsin Lynd, the group counselor, had been the victim of a vicious stalker. Escalating cruelties upset the group. They were followed by murders centered on Tamsin and her husband, Cliff Egger. Both Tamsin and Cliff had an intimate enemy who could not accept defeat. Lily and Jack's relationship progressed, providing her with confidence that she might have a healthy marriage and a family. Lily was working part-time with Jack to earn her license as a private investigator, but continued to provide housekeeping services for a few clients.

Intriguing. Lily was such a distinctive character, but Harris has diversified. Very prolific, she has three other series: (1) Aurora Teagarden, see elsewhere in this volume); (2) the Sookie Stackhouse vampire series; and (3) Harper Connelly, who has a talent for locating corpses. I miss Lily.

Holly Barker

Author: Stuart Woods

Holly Barker was in her late thirties as the series began. An army brat, she had enlisted in the ranks at age seventeen, where she was assigned to the military police. She secured her bachelor's degree through the University of Maryland, which has an educational component at military facilities. As a result she was chosen for officer's training. She had reached the rank of major and headed a military police company when her career in the service came to an end. Holly joined a younger female officer in pressing sexual harassment charges against a superior officer. The military court found the charges unfounded, leaving both women in a vulnerable position.

In *Orchid Beach* (HarperCollins, 1998), Police Chief Chet Marley, a friend and former comrade of Holly's father, Master Sergeant Ham Barker, offered Holly a position as his deputy in a small Florida town. Chet warned

Holly in advance that there would be problems, both in Orchid Beach and within his department. Chet's mortal injuries occurred within hours of Holly's arrival, leaving her with limited credibility in local circles. Unsure of whom she could trust within the police department, she received help from her father, from criminal defense attorney Jackson Oxenhandler, and eventually from the FBI. The problem in Orchid Beach had impact far beyond the city limits.

Holly was devastated by a personal loss as *Orchid Blues* (Putnam's, 2001) began. She pulled herself together when confronted by a sinister right wing cult that robbed banks to finance their goals. She called upon her ally, FBI agent Harry Crisp, and a new friend Stone Barrington (from Wood's other series), but the real action was left to Ham Barker, restless in his retirement. Holly provided support to Ham when he went undercover in the phantom group and was there when needed.

Holly was ready for a new man in her life as *Blood Orchid* (Putnam, 2002) began. FBI undercover agent Grant Early seemed an unlikely prospect; Moreover, he declined to explain the purpose of his move into the area. Palmetto Gardens, formerly used by drug dealers, was purchased from the U.S. General Services Administration by retired real estate developer Ed Shine. However corpses appeared regularly. Ed and Holly almost joined them. Unable to get cooperation from the Miami FBI office, Holly had to wing it.

Reckless Abandon (Signet, 2004) was subtitled, *A Stone Barrington Novel* but Holly had a significant role. Enraged that, after she had captured Trini Rodriguez, the FBI took control and put him in a Witness Protection Program, she made up her mind to retrieve him. He had murdered twelve persons in her jurisdiction! Arriving in New York City where Trini was located, she contacted Stone, who invited her to share his home. His connections helped Holly to locate Trini, but they were stymied by the FBI, Italian-American gangs, and Arab terrorists. Lance Cabot, whom Stone had dealt with in his past book, wanted to recruit Holly for the CIA. She considered it very seriously.

Although *Iron Orchid* (Putnam 2005) was subtitled "A Holly Barker Novel", she was part of an ensemble of Stuart Woods characters involved in a government technical force. Their task was to capture Teddy Fay, rogue CIA technical expert who used his skills to kill people with whom he disagreed politically. Fay and U. S. President Will Lee appeared earlier in Woods other series, *Capital Crimes*. Holly's involvement as a brand new barely trained CIA operative was unrealistic. After a faked death, Fay continued to eliminate international terrorists until Woods stashed him wherever he keeps his characters between books. Disappointing for Holly Barker fans. Holly appeared only by reference in *Two Dollar Bill.*(Putnam's, 2005), a Stone Barrington novel.

Holly's character as a small town Florida police chief had ended by *Dark Harbor* (Putnam's, 2006). She had become a secondary character in the Stone Barrington series. This came about partly because she was now working with Lance Cabot. Cabot and Holly were CIA employees who questioned Stone Barrington's involvement in the death of his cousin, Dick Stone. She was able to provide technical expertise, but was more a victim than an investigator. Woods may not be aware that Holly Barker fans and Stone Barrington fans are not necessarily the same.

Shoot Him If He Runs (Putnam, 2008) sent the ensemble to St. Matt's in the Caribbean on the trail of assassin Teddy Fay. President Will Lee (see Volume 2) and his closest associates were aware that Fay had survived an accident, but the public and most of Congress believed otherwise. CIA consultant Stone Barrington (the primary), his cop buddy Dino Bachetti who brought along his lady friend, and Holly were sent to locate him, and notify Will Lee as to his whereabouts. Holly, at this point a CIA employee, was aware that they were carrying out a personal mission for the president. St. Matt's was controlled by the dictatorial regime of Sir Winston Sutherland, who felt no need to cooperate with the United States' government. Holly's role was subordinate to Barrington's but she had opportunities to show her special skills.

She is no longer a primary sleuth. Too bad. She had some interesting aspects as a small town police chief. Maybe things will get better in *Hothouse Orchid* (2009) Woods also has a series with Attorney Ed Eagle.

Janet O'Hara Barkin

Author: Ellen Godfrey

Author Ellen Godfrey should be congratulated for developing a mystery series designed to be read by adults who have recently become literate. There has been for decades an effort in both the United States and Canada to have volunteers and school systems teach reading to persons whose needs were not met initially. A problem has been finding recreational literature on which they can improve their skills.

At age twenty-four, Janet Barkin had a record of failure. She had recently been fired from her job at Thrifty Foods and divorced by her husband Pat, an undercover police officer. Her ability to find work was limited by her lack of a high school diploma. She had left high school at sixteen because she was not doing well. Now she wanted to earn her G.E.D. She currently lived in Evanston, Illinois, an upper class suburb.

Janet and her best friend, Sally Lee, had only one reason to feel good about themselves, as *Murder on the Loose* (Contemporary Books, 1998) began, but it was a big one. Janet, with the assistance of her German Shepherd (Leah), had picked the right numbers in the lottery. Both women had been mistreated by the men in their lives. They were aroused to action by their empathy for immigrant women smuggled into the country for cheap household labor. They were aware that some had been murdered when they rebelled against the system. Subsidized by the lottery money, Janet set up the Women's Rescue Company. With the help of Mrs. Gretsky, her septuagenarian landlady, and Porsha Moore, a teenage African-American, they not only saved a potential victim but also trapped the killers.

Janet's good feelings did not last. In *Murder on the Lovers' Bridge* (Contemporary Books, 1998), Roach Roads, whom she had helped to convict, was out on bail pending an appeal. Pat, her former husband who still believed they would get back together, was belligerent when he saw her with Lt. Larry Keegan. Close friend Nina Montez was being stalked by her rejected ex-lover, Paul Moro. When first Nina, then Paul, were killed with the same gun, the evidence pointed to Janet.

In *Murder in the Shadows* (Contemporary Books, 1999), Janet and her staff became involved when "Sink" their popular alderman was accused of sexually harassing his female employees. The attorney handling this and other sexual harassment suits in the community was Dennis O'Hara, Janet's estranged brother. Two women employees at "Sink's" office were murdered. Although Larry Keegan was active in the cases, he and Janet withheld information from one another until they had nowhere else to turn.

These were subtitled "Thumbprint Series". Godfrey has written two other series with female sleuths: Rebecca Rosenthal, a Canadian Jewish widow who was covered in Volume 1 and Jane Tregar, another Canadian who reorganized her life after divorce, covered in Volume 2.

Hannah Barlow

Author: Carroll Lachnit

Hannah was adrift, estranged from her brother Michael, a priest who blamed her for the death of their unstable mother. Their father, a retired police officer, had remarried. She had a sense of guilt because Janie Meister, a child for whom she had some responsibility, was believed to have been killed by an abusive father. As a result Hannah left the police force, and entered law school. She was a hard working redhead, older than her fellow students.

In *Murder in Brief* (Berkley, 1995), Hannah was accused of plagiarism in the preparation of a student trial brief. It got worse when her brief partner, Brad Cogburn, was murdered. The documents supporting the research done by Hannah had been in Brad's possession. They disappeared. A vagrant who had Brad's credit card was arrested for the murder, but Hannah believed he had been killed by someone he knew. Her search uncovered several motives for killing Cogburn.

By Hannah's appearance in *A Blessed Death* (Berkley, 1996) she had graduated from law school and was working for a large firm in Orange County, California. A casual assignment thrust her into a religious scandal. Father Raymond Kostka, a priest accused of pederasty, had disappeared with a young boy. The boy had reputedly received a miraculous cure through prayers to Maria Luz Duran, a potential saint. Hannah no longer practiced her faith but she was concerned not only with the child, but also with the death of Maria Luz Duran. Was she a martyr killed for her faith, or the victim of lust and corruption? The answer was painful.

Hannah and former classmate Bobby Terry purchased a law practice in *Akin to Death* (Berkley, 1998). Among the cases included in the acquisition was the adoption of young Matthew by Stephen and Rebecca Drummond. The final hearing had ended only hours before the appearance of Kurt Sundstrom, a putative father who had not been included in the process. It fell to Hannah to sift through the lies and equivocations of Laura Benson, Matthew's birth mother. A difficult task when Laura was murdered.

Hannah had been deeply affected by the disappearance and presumed death of incest victim Janie Meister. In *Janie's Law* (Berkley, 1999), she faced a conflict of interest. Should she investigate a series of murders in which the victims were child molesters, or join her rage with those who sought vengeance? Given a second opportunity to save Janie from a life of misery, Hannah did not hesitate. Women who are themselves mothers may find this a painful read.

Still shy of forty, Hannah had driven her lover Guillermo away by her reluctance to marry and have a family of her own.

Thea Barlow

Author: Carol Caverly

Thea Barlow, originally from Chicago, was determined to make a success of her second career on *Western True Adventures* magazine. As *All the Old Lions* (Write Way, 1994) began, she was working on a series concerning early whorehouses in the West. Intrigued by writer Minnie Darrow's references to Halfway Halt, a bordello run by Jersey Roo, she drove to Wyoming. On her arrival in Hijax, Thea was harassed after she mentioned Minnie. There was more to this story than what could be found in Jersey Roo's diary. The real story was the death by lynching of an innocent man. On the positive side she met an attractive geologist Max Holman.

Thea was combining business with pleasure when she visited Rawhide, Wyoming in *Frogskin and Muttonfat* (Write Way, 1996) to interview Kid Corcoran. The Kid termed himself "the last of the Old Time Bandits," and was a potential subject for a magazine article. Of equal interest was the fact that Max Holman was working a nearby oil claim. Although Corcoran had a terrible reputation in Rawhide, he resembled Thea's grandfather so she ignored the rumors. Unfortunately for both Thea and the Kid there were New Time Bandits in Rawhide.

Thea had barely arrived in Garnet Pass when, in *Dead in Hog Heaven* (Write Way, 2000), she was suspected of killing two women with whom she was only slightly acquainted. Thea's plan to write an article about Hog Heaven, a haven for aging but active Western prostitutes, had attracted her to the town. The area was in need of renovation and several citizens had major plans for drawing tourists. Fortunately the deputy sheriff was a pal of Max, providing him and Thea with time to uncover a murderous scam.

A quirky series.

Danielle Barnea

Author: Jon Land

Constant tension existed between protagonists, Danielle Barnea, a chief inspector in the Israeli National Police and the man she loved, Ben Kamal, a Palestinian detective. Danielle had grown up in Israel, where her father was a general in the Army. Her two brothers had died in the service of their country. Her mother had died shortly after the death of her older son. Her father died during the series. Danielle's work consumed her.

Ben, whose family had moved to the United States after the Six Days War (1967), had not only been educated in America but was a Christian. His father had returned to Palestine, only to be killed. His mother and brother Sayeed remained in Michigan. Sayeed was involved in the Palestinian movement. Ben went a step further. He had been a detective on the Detroit Police Department and accepted an assignment to build up the Palestinian Security Force. He needed to get away. A serial killer had assassinated his wife and two small children. This damaged his belief in a beneficent Creator. Ben had an uneasy relationship with fellow members of the Palestine police force. Both he and Danielle were protected to some degree by the achievements of their fathers and her brothers.

She and Ben met in *The Walls of Jericho* (Forge, 1997) when they worked together to identify a serial killer who mutilated his victims. Eventually both realized that they were being manipulated by the security forces of their countries. They went beyond their mission to capture "the Wolf," following the trail of a copycat killer who was responsible for three of the murders. They bonded based on their hopes for peace. A friendly soldier of fortune saved both their lives.

Danielle was aware that every Israeli woman was expected to bear a child. Her attempt to do so had failed. Ben had lost children to a vicious killer. Both were drawn into an investigation of child smuggling during *The Pillars of Solomon* (Forge, 1999). The interference by officials in the Israeli and Palestinian governments caused Danielle to be suspended and forced Ben to exceed his authority. Each sensed that the cover-up related to a decades old secret from a time when there seemed no hope for a peaceful solution to the hostilities between their countries.

Walk in the Darkness (Forge, 2000) described Ben's journey from the point when he lost his faith in God to a personal miracle. For Danielle, it was a time of choices. She knew that her career in the Israeli police force would end if she and Ben married. She was not ready to make him aware of changes in her life. Ben's nephew Dawud's corpse was one of a dozen bodies found at an archeological site on the West Bank. It was unclear whether the scene of the crime was under the jurisdiction of the Palestinian or Israeli government. The Israelis took charge. A third component to the dispute was a rogue group of Swiss Guards (Vatican Police) who were interested in scrolls that might provide evidence to events following the crucifixion of Jesus Christ. This was a fantastic narrative.

During *Keepers of the Gate* (Forge, 2001), Land skillfully wove together a trio of plots: (1) teenagers who used computers for blackmail, (2) an underground group seeking to kill former Nazis who had assumed the personas of Jewish survivors, and (3) the discovery of a medical innovation which might eradicate major diseases and genetic abnormalities. Danielle had a personal reason for hoping the discovery was valid. She and Ben worked jointly and individually through one crisis after another, accepting that their two countries were no longer moving towards peace.

The estrangement between Ben and Danielle ended in *Blood Diamonds* (Forge, 2002) when Ben learned that she was in an Israeli jail. She had been charged with the murder of Commander Moshe Baruch, who had ousted her from her job in the National Police. She and Ben had been caught up in a massive scheme to exchange munitions for diamonds. However, this went beyond the routine guns and explosives of the past, to include a secret weapon designed during the Cold War that could destroy much of humanity. General Latisse Matabu, leader of the Revolutionary United Front in Sierra Leone, was motivated as much by the need for personal revenge as for the welfare of her people.

After a flawed raid on the compound of the People's Brigade in Idaho as *The Blue Widows* (Forge, 2003) began, Danielle returned to Israel to become the head of the National Police. The Brigade was a violent right wing organization headed by Hollis Buchert. Ben stayed on working with John Narajan in Security Concepts. State Department official Alan Lowenthall hired Security Concepts, but most specifically Ben, to investigate the activities of Mohammed Latif, a Saudi whose entry into the U. S. had been sponsored by Sayeed, Ben's brother. Terrorist attacks on a U.S. technical facility where smallpox toxins were stored did not initially seem to connect with the murder of an elderly Israeli/Arab woman in Israel. By the time they did, Ben and Danielle were caught up in a layered conspiracy that forced them both to work outside the protections of their governments, enmeshed in U.S. efforts to trap terrorists, an Israeli plan to infiltrate Saudi Arabia, and the efforts of an obsessed woman to destroy America. As before family and history were vital to the narrative.

Danielle and Ben were each coming off assignments for the United Nations Safety and Security Service when in *The Last Prophecy* (Tor, 2004). They were sent to investigate a massacre in a small Palestinian town. There were layers of deceit as to the motive for the attack and the nationality of the attackers. Danielle's questions caused her to be re-assigned elsewhere by Peruvian Alexis Arguayo, head of the UN S&SS. Meanwhile Ben remained in Palestine initially but along with his former supervisor Colonel al Asi traveled to Baghdad, and France. Danielle was not to be shunted aside so easily so she set off on her own to investigate a strange document discovered at the end of World War II by a medical evacuation unit. It contained coded prophecies by Nostradamus, which predicted terrible attacks on the United States.

Land has a new series featuring Texas Ranger Caitlin Strong.

Ginger Barnes

Author: Donna Huston Murray

Ginger Barnes was a throwback to the Fifties—a housewife with two children, married to a Philadelphia prep school headmaster. She was unpretentious, working hard at promoting her husband (Robert Ripley Barnes better known as Rip) and his employer, Bryn Derwyn Academy. Redheaded Ginger was a "fixer," a talent learned from her deceased father who had been a football coach. She made herself available to scrub floors, make curtains or carry out minor plumbing repairs at the Barnes home or the Academy. The Barnes family barely managed on Rip's salary. With her children in school, Ginger became obsessed with investigations.

The status of Bryn Derwyn, a newcomer in local private education, was at risk in *The Main Line Is Murder* (St. Martin, 1995). Attorney Richard Wharton had been killed on the premises. The police arrested Randy Webb, the school's development director. Ginger, who had discovered Wharton's body, confronted a major donor with mob connections in her quest for the murderer.

Except for minor vandalism, school problems were left behind in *Final Arrangements* (St. Martin, 1996). Ginger intervened in the death of flower arranger "Iffy" Bigelow, a high school friend of her mother, Cynthia. Lt. George Mills, assigned to the downtown Philadelphia case, remembering Ginger's kindness to him in elementary school, tolerated her interference. The murder motive will be obvious early in the narrative to seasoned mystery fans.

A series of increasingly violent incidents had occurred in Barnes' pleasant neighborhood as *School of Hard Knocks* (St. Martin, 1997) began. Ginger had more personal problems. Her husband, Rip had become preoccupied and secretive. Her dear friend Liz Kelman was disinterested in Ginger's concerns. The neighbors were annoyed with elderly Letty McNair whose property was in disrepair. Ginger agreed to negotiate with Letty, but refocused when Liz was killed and Letty seriously injured.

Ginger was off-campus in *A Score to Settle* (St. Martin, 1999) when she helped her pregnant cousin Michelle Turner whose quarterback husband Doug was a murder suspect. Ginger's knowledge of football, gained from her father, was a significant factor in identifying the real killer.

Ginger admitted that nothing since the births of her children had provided the high she felt from solving murders. Still, there was no good reason for her to go out of her way to help dog trainer Linda Arden in *No Bones About It* (St. Martin, 1998). Linda, who had treated Ginger badly during their high school years, was accused of training a dog to kill her former husband. Ginger came to the rescue, if only for the dog's sake.

Actress Jan Fairchild contacted Ginger, a former classmate, in *Farewell Performance* (St. Martin, 2000). She planned to combine business and pleasure by returning to her hometown, Ludwig, Pennsylvania, to publicize her forthcoming film, *Going Home Again*. Ginger arranged for Jan to stay with mutual friend Didi Martin. At times, Jan's flair for publicity was annoying, but that was no reason to murder her. Ginger didn't want the killer to be one of her old friends, but who else was there?

It was only by chance that Ginger wandered into the federal courtroom where Charlie Finnemeyer was on trial for fraud in *Lie Like a Rug* (St. Martin, 2001). It was providential for Charlie and his wife Birdie who had been babysitters for Ginger in her childhood. Ginger did not believe Charlie capable of passing off an artificially aged Oriental rug as a 300-year antique. Even less could she believe that he or Birdie had killed a prosecution witness and the victim of the fraud.

A pleasant series with warm touches and intimate crimes.

Temple Barr

Author: Carole Nelson Douglas

Some people claim an affinity between female sleuths and cats. The Barr series went a step further with a male feline protagonist, Midnight Louie, sharing the spotlight with tiny Las Vegas public relations advisor Temple Barr. Midnight Louie had appeared solo in books, published by Five Star: *The Cat and the King of Clubs; The Cat and the Queen of Hearts; The Cat and the Jill of Diamonds; Catnap,* and *The Cat and the Jack of Spades.*

Redheaded Temple made her debut in *Catnap* (Tor, 1992) when she discovered the body of foulmouthed Chester Royal at the Bookseller's Convention. She and Louie confounded Lt. C.R. Molina (a 5' 10" female policewoman) connecting Royal's death to events in his past.

Temple had not recovered from her abandonment by magician Max Kinsella in *Pussyfoot* (Tor 1993). He was on her mind, on Molina's list of murder suspects, and on the hit list of local gangsters. The death of several strippers during a contest sensitized Temple to their lifestyle, and to the fact that they were often victims of child abuse.

During *Cat on a Blue Monday* (Forge, 1994), Temple was shocked at revelations about the two men most important in her life: Kinsella, and handsome but reticent Matt Devine, who manned a hotline for persons in trouble. Cat haters were on the loose, and so was a killer who never forgot his rejection.

In the overloaded *Cat in a Crimson Haze* (Forge, 1995), Matt Devine dealt with post-clerical celibacy and rumors of child molestation by the local priest. Temple promoted the Crystal Phoenix casino as a vacation spot for families, not easy when corpses tumbled from the ceiling. Cute, but not terminally so.

The alphabetical parade continued with *Cat in a Diamond Dazzle* (Forge, 1996) during which Max Kinsella returned, rivaling Matt for Temple's attentions. While they postured, she mixed with romance writers at a local conference. Temple searched for a missing shoe while solving the murders of two handsome hunks who posed for book covers. The narratives were getting longer.

Cat with an Emerald Eye (Forge, 1996) failed to resolve Temple's relationships with Max and Matt or Matt's search for his stepfather. The narrative explored Max's escapades in Ireland. Temple and Louie were present at a séance during which prominent mediums and psychics sought to contact Harry Houdini. When a male participant was murdered, Temple and Max investigated. The final conclusion, as final as anything was in this series, depended on knowledge of classic movies.

During *Cat in a Flamingo Fedora* (Forge, 1997), someone tried to sabotage Midnight Louie's career as a television commercial star. Add the unexplained death of Darren Cooke, a lecherous comedian, Matt Devlin's regular crisis line calls from a compulsive womanizer, and Domingo, a performance artist who wanted Temple's help to "flood Las Vegas with pink flamingoes." There's a mystery in there somewhere.

An opportunity to enhance Midnight Louie's advertising career sent Temple and the cat to New York City in *Cat in a Golden Garland* (Forge, 1997) where they visited her outspoken aunt, Kit Carlson. Temple and Louie competed against Savannah Ashleigh and her cat, Solange. Down at the heels Santa Claus Rudy Lasko, was murdered while playing the jolly old gentleman at the agency Christmas party. Unabashed by her visitor status, Temple took on the case. Max Kinsella offered to share his perilous future with Temple—but on his terms.

Temple's relationship with Max had been formalized when she accepted a ring with no assurances for the future as *Cat on a Hyacinth Hunt* (Forge, 1998) began. On her return from New York City, she was accosted by Matt's abusive stepfather, Cliff Effinger. When Effinger was murdered, Matt became a suspect. A new nemesis arrived in Las Vegas to tempt Matt, to harass Temple, and, if possible, to destroy Max.

During *Cat in an Indigo Mood* (Forge, 1999), the tangled plot lines twisted and twirled. The reader learned more (possibly more than they want to know) about the post-clerical woes of Matt Devlin and his fellow ex-priests. New characters crowded in: a drug sniffing Maltese, an embittered former police officer, and three corpses. The personal life of Los Vegas police Lieutenant Carmen Molina became a subject for concern.

Cat in a Jeweled Jumpsuit (Forge, 1999), featured the Elvis legend. A new Las Vegas attraction, the Kingdome based upon Presley, opened with one hundred impersonators vying for a prize to be awarded by a pseudo-Priscilla. There were young Elvises, old Elvises, and, finally, dead Elvises. Matt's radio career was temporarily enhanced by phone calls from a convincing Elvis.

Only a reader familiar with prior books in the series will make sense of *A Cat in a Kiwi Con* (Forge, 2000). The serial deaths of stripper Cher Smith, magician's assistant Gloria Fuentes, and college professor Jeff Mengel were tied together by prior incidents. Temple, Matt, Max, and Lt. Molina participated in the investigation at various levels. Kitty O'Connor who had a history with Max and Rafi Nadir, whose connection with Carmen Molina was of a personal nature, played significant roles.

By *Cat in a Leopard Spot* (Forge, 2001) not much had changed. Kitty O'Connor was still stalking Matt to add his chastity to her belt. The killer of stripper Cher Smith and perpetrator of other assaults on women had not been arrested. Cyrus Von Burkleo, the proprietor of a ranch where wannabe hunters killed aging or domesticated exotic animals, died in a bizarre fashion. Among the suspects was Osiris, a leopard kidnapped from a magician. Only the death of the ranch owner was resolved. The other cases were left dangling. There were moments of tenderness when Matt returned to Chicago to visit his mother. Louie, active as always, added two Yorkies as allies in the rescue of vulnerable animals.

Same old, same old in *Cat in a Midnight Choir* (Forge, 2002): Matt Devine trying to decide which is the lesser of two evils as presented by Kitty the Cutter; Max working to protect the Cloaked Crusader, an aged magician, from Snyth (a group of second rate rivals); Midnight Louie, his mother and his daughter slinking in and out of the picture. Temple defended Max when he was suspected as a serial killer. As before, that single issue was cleared up, but others left for the next narrative.

This time it was Matt who was Molina's prime suspect in *Cat in a Neon Nightmare* (Forge, 2003). Vassar, the high price call girl hired on Molina's advice, had fallen or been pushed to her death. Not that Max didn't have problems too. He had infiltrated Snyth with remarkable results. Another death. More guilt. Molina failed to disclose her conflict of interest in these matters. One villain deleted. A new one entered the scene.

What's new in *Cat in an Orange Twist* (Forge, 2004). Quite a bit. Temple has signed on as public relations person for the new Maylord's Furniture Outlet. Rafi Nadir, former Los Angeles cop is on their security force. Max and his mentor Gandolph (purportedly dead) are still infiltrating Snyth. What's old? Too many references to prior unsolved cases. With Max too busy, Temple relied on Matt for help when the grand opening at the store was marred by quarrels among the employees, which ended with everyone in the dark and someone shooting. No one killed then, but at a subsequent "blessing" with orange peel liquid, the body of decorator Simon Foster was discovered.

Fear that her thirteen-year-old daughter Mariah might be in danger sent Lt. Molina to Temple for help in *Cat in a Hot Pink Pursuit* (Forge, 2005). Without the lieutenant's knowledge, Mariah had entered and become a finalist in a teenage reality show. Solution: had Temple enter posing as a late teenager contestant to watch over Mariah. In exchange Molina would lay off Max Kinsella. Using the name Zoe Chloe Ozone, Temple changed her appearance, hopefully enough to fool her Aunt Kit who was one of the judges and her rival public relations specialist Crawford Buchanan. Bigger problems i.e. there was a killer, maybe two, involved in the reality production. Midnight Louie, as usual, shared the spotlight, prowling through the secret corridors of the ancient mansion where the contestants and staff were lodged. This was an interesting spoof of reality shows featuring sexual exploitation of teenage contestants.

In this 18th book of the series, *Cat on a Quicksilver Caper* (Forge, 2006), some of the on-going plotlines came closer to finality. Temple's assignment as public relations manager for a major Russian Art Exhibit to be held at The New Millennium was on a collision course with Max's plan to win entry into SNYTH by stealing Czar Alexander's priceless scepter. The art exhibit was to take place in conjunction with a daring aerial/magic display by the Cloaked Conjuror and his new assistant Shangri-La. She had made major problems for Temple by abducting her and stealing the engagement ring Max had given her. Matt was ardently pursuing her; in fact, considerable space was devoted to the religious aspect of their relationship as he rejected celibacy for the love of Temple. Max had to deal with Lt. Carmen Molina, who fixated on him as the source of all evil.

Max had gone, either undercover or into the great hereafter, but in *Cat in a Red Hot Rage* (Forge, 2007) he had made it clear that Temple should turn to Matt Devine, as a more reliable prospect for a long term relationship. That was fine with Matt and worked well for Temple so they went at it with gusto. Their bliss was interrupted by a frantic phone call from landlady Electra Lark. A member of a local chapter of the Red Hat Society, she had been found standing over the strangled corpse of another attendee at the national convention. That might not have been enough except that the victim, Oleta Lark was the woman who enticed Elmore, Electra's third husband, away. The Crystal Phoenix and the city of Las Vegas were flooded with mature women with red hats and purple garments. They were followed by a smaller group, the Black Hatted Brotherhood who resented the womens' activities. Lots of cat conversation. C. R. Molina continued to focus on the missing Max which got her into a lot of trouble.

The traditional bachelor's party before the wedding of Temple's Aunt Kit's to Aldo Fontana took an unusual turn in *Cat in a Sapphire Slipper* (Forge, 2008). The bridesmaids, each the girlfriend of one of Aldo's bachelor brothers, decided to hijack the group and take them to Sapphire Slipper, a registered brothel in rural Nevada. That plan didn't work because one of the regulars at the brothel was murdered during the visit. Temple, Van von Rhine, Aunt Kit and Electra were summoned to find the killer before the police became involved. Louie, as always, had a significant role. Max, amnesiac and disabled in Switzerland, had his own problems. There's always something dangling at the end of the books in this series.

Matt's introspective reminiscences and Louie's soliloquies and sexual ardors (even though he had been surgically sterilized) may be endearing to some and annoying to others, but the series has a popular following. Next: *Cat in a Topaz Tango* (2009), *Cat in an Ultramarine Scheme* (2010).

Douglas, like several other established authors, has added another series, featuring paranormal investigator Delilah Street.

Bel Barrett

Author: Jane Isenberg

After graduation from Vassar, Bel had married handsome Leonard Barrett. Although the marriage had produced two children (Mark and Rebecca), it did not survive. Her frantic need to be over-involved may be attributed not only to her physical condition but also to a lifetime of activism. Lenny had purportedly decided upon divorce when she spent their wedding anniversary chained to a California redwood.

Bel, whose birth name Sybil was used only by her widowed mother Sadie, worked as a professor at River Edge Community College, New Jersey. Graying, menopausal, and fifty, she was ABD (all but dissertation) at Eleanor Roosevelt University, working on the dissertation while teaching English. Her final degree would be in applied linguistics. Bel was a non-observant Jew, possibly as a result of her father's influence. Ike had been an atheist and a communist. Bel enjoyed classical music, a glass or two of sherry, and collected miniature china shoes.

Bel developed a supportive circle of intimates and friends: her "domestic partner", retired economics professor Sol Hecht; her college roommate Sandi Golden; Sarah Wolfe, who eventually became managing editor of the *Jersey City Herald;* private investigator Illuminada Gutierrez; and Betty Ramsey, assistant to the college president. Sol and Bel shared their home with cats (Virginia Woolf and Emily Bronte). Bel's efforts to deal with her menopausal symptoms included estrogen patches and taking part in an internet support group.

Bel had aroused the students when there was a cutback in library hours and worked to unionize the faculty at River Edge Community College. She went a step further in *The "M" Word* (Avon, 1999). The death by poison of Dr. Altagracia Garcia, a progressive administrator, had been attributed to an aggrieved student. Bel mobilized Illuminada and Betty who agreed that Ozzie Beckman was innocent of the charge. Together they uncovered a murder plot by those who resisted change.

Sol's extended absence on business presented a problem for Bel in *Death in a Hot Flash* (Avon, 2000). Should she make him aware that she was involved in another murder investigation? She had personal problems to deal with: (1) daughter Rebecca's traffic accident, (2) the news of her father Ike's death; and (3) the decision to have her mother move in with her, at least temporarily. Sadie was living in a past when Ike was still alive and Bel was married to Lenny. Solving a murder barely made the top three of Bel's concerns. Once she got beyond the more obvious motives for undertaker Vinny Vallone's death, she and her accomplices zeroed in on the killer.

Frank Sinatra's impact on Hoboken (his hometown) played a major role in *Mood Swings to Murder* (Avon, 2000). You could hardly walk down the street or enter a bar without hearing a Sinatra tune. An offshoot of the singer's popularity was the competition among Sinatra impersonators. When Louie

Palumbo, who strongly resembled Sinatra but was a second rate singer, was murdered, Bel and Sol found his body. She was currently overwhelmed by son Mark's extended visit, by the revelation that her daughter Rebecca was pregnant and planning an unconventional wedding ceremony, and by her work at the community college. Still she made time to investigate Louie's death.

Estrogen patch or not, Bel was really "off the wall" in *Midlife Can Be Murder* (Avon, 2001). Sandi Golden, recently returned from California, convinced Bel to attend an adult bat mitzvah class. There, Bel met Ashley Solomon, whom she may have wronged in the past. As a form of mitzvah (good deed), Bel investigated the death of Chris Johansen, a young "market analyst" (read that as an industrial spy) in the computer business. With the aid of her new Torah knowledge, extra-curricular work as a cleaning woman, and her ensemble of helpers, Bel uncovered a modern tragedy, replicating that of King David and Bathsheba.

Bel had gone out of her way to help dyslexic student Belinda Judd in *Out of Hormone's Way* (Avon, 2002). When Bel substituted for her officemate Wendy O'Connor as faculty advisor for the student kayaking club, she came to know Belinda better and to share her joy in a new job as a security officer at the Mall. When Belinda disappeared; then, was found murdered, Bel involved Betty and Illuminada in a personal investigation. Even though Illuminada was dealing with the after effects of treatment for breast cancer, she provided what help she could.

It was a surprise to Bel that Eunice Goodson, the new adjunct lecturer in anatomy at River's Edge Community College, supplemented her income as an exotic dancer at Big Apple Peel in *Hot and Bothered* (Avon, 2003). It was a shock to learn that Eunice had been strangled on her way home from work. It was a blessing when RECC President Ron Woodman, now on tranquilizers, asked Bel to investigate the murder. She had intended to do so anyway, because she liked Eunice, had helped her find a home and get integrated into the Park Avenue neighborhood. Sol was unlikely to participate. He had been crossing the river on a ferryboat when the World Trade Center was attacked on 9/11 and suffered from PTSD. He wanted to leave Hoboken! Isenberg explored the lives of several exotic dancers in a sympathetic manner.

Sol, Bel's live-in lover and fiancé, had given up on keeping Bel out of murder cases, but in *Hot on the Trail* (Avon, 2004) he set a conditions: she could investigate the death of Dom Tomaselli, but she had to start moving on their wedding plans. Dom had been a racing pigeon enthusiast since childhood. He used his skills in a special unit during World War II and continued the hobby after he married and had children. His daughter Flora, a middle-aged RECC student, did not believe her father fell or jumped from the rooftop of her building into the snow where he froze to death. Bel knew Dom as a member of a class she was teaching for senior citizens. She utilized the memoir/journals written by Dom and the other students to understand the past and its impact on Dom's death.

Bel was really "wired" in *Hot Wired* (Avon, 2005). She had reason to be concerned because Naftali Thompson, a former student, was broadcasting rap during which he accused her of racism and sexism. Because she had given him a low grade for his class work, he had been unable to transfer into a larger college. Rather than continue and improve his record, Naftali joined the army, lost an arm in Iraq. He blamed this injury on Bel. When Naftali was murdered, the police focused on Bel as the killer. Her determination to prove her innocence was hampered by her over-active imagination. She was concerned that her daughter's marriage was failing. The scenes in which she investigated the rap scene were well done even though it was foreign territory to her. (and would be to some readers.)

Witty and charming. Bel appeared in a short story, *The Proof Is in the Patch* in the anthology, *Motherhood Is Murder* (Avon, 2003)

Connie Bartholomew

Author: Sally Gunning, nee Carlson

Connie, a tall lean blonde, came to Nashtoba, Cape Hook in New England to work as a high school teacher. That changed when she met Peter Bartholomew and began working in Factotem, his jack-of-all-trades business. There was always a market for Pete's services because the population swelled during the summer months. Short-term residents needed someone to manage their property. Although he had gone to college, Nashtoba was all the world that Pete wanted, a fact that was not clear to Connie until after they married. She was easygoing to some extent, but grew restless. An overnight infidelity while she was drunk caused Connie to leave the island. Pete made no effort to restore their relationship, got a divorce, and continued with his life in Nashtoba. Connie's return was unexpected, and it took time to work things out. Pete was always the primary. Connie served as suspect, then assistant. Polly, Pete's moody sister, played similar roles. An older client, Sarah Abrew provided sage advice. Willy McOwat, a big city export who became the local police chief, worked with Pete and aspired to marry Polly.

Hot Water (Pocket Books, 1990) began when Pete found a client dead in the bathtub. Although Edna Hitchcock had both alcohol and Seconal in her system, there were suspicious circumstances. Years before, Edna's sister Lizzie had died a similar death. Pete investigated, keeping at arm's-length from Connie even though she had important information to convey.

As *Under Water* (Pocket, 1992) began, Pete found the body of Bentley Brown, a seventeen-year-old girl who had worked at Factotum. Bentley had been the quiet subdued twin, while her sister, Carlisle was very popular. The post-mortem showed that the victim had been pregnant. A class ring found near the body provided a clue that Connie pursued. She subbed as a teacher at the high school, and, while Pete was in the hospital, stepped in and ran his business.

Bait shop owner Newby Dillingham had just kissed Connie under the mistletoe at a Christmas party in *Ice Water* (Pocket, 1993) when someone shot him in the head. This was more than a lack of holiday spirit. Newby's refusal to sell his bait shop had forestalled plans for a major real estate development in Nashtoba. That might have been the motivation for this and two subsequent murders. Pete was inclined to look elsewhere. Although he and Connie were literally seeing a lot of one another, he retained a residue of anger about her betrayal.

In *Troubled Water* (Pocket, 1993), the deaths within hours of two elderly sisters were deemed natural by the local doctor. Pete couldn't settle for that conclusion. Not only had Connie inherited the sisters' property, but there were suspicious circumstances surrounding both deaths.

Connie was living in the house she had inherited in *Rough Water* (Pocket, 1994) when Pete invited her to accompany him on a whale-watching tour. This was not a casual trip. Sister Polly convinced Pete to join her and her intended husband, knowing that Pete would not approve of Jackson Bears or his overbearing manner. Pete was not the only one. Someone killed the potential bridegroom.

By *Still Water* (Pocket, 1995), Connie and Pete were lovers, but remained in their own households. Pete was preoccupied with the "accidents" to new bride, Claire Simmons. However, it was Claire's adoring husband who was killed. Pete kept an eye on the suspects, but until Connie gave him a hint, he was looking in the wrong direction.

Connie was out of town taking care of her ill mother during *Deep Water* (Pocket, 1996) when Cobie Small, a boozing beachcomber, was murdered. Pete's sister Polly joined him in a hunt for a killer and hidden treasure, but Connie returned to finish the job.

Weddings were the focus in *Muddy Water* (Pocket, 1997) when bridegroom Walt Westerman was accused of killing his bride-to-be before the ceremony. Connie was convinced of Walt's innocence, driving Pete to investigate other suspects. Pete and Connie's personal plans to remarry barely survived.

Hurricane Charlotte threatened Nashtoba in *Dirty Water* (Pocket, 1998). Pete and Connie's honeymoon ended abruptly with the news that eighty-eight-year-old almost blind Sarah Abrew had confessed to murder. Sarah may have been guilty of something, but it surely wasn't murder.

Five-year-old Lucy Suggs found a skull near the creek bed in *Fire Water* (Pocket, 1999), thereby unearthing a chapter in Pete and Connie's lives that brought them insights into their relationship. Connie had a miscarriage in an earlier episode, but found a way to meet her maternal needs. A pleasant series during which Connie decided that Pete's innate goodness was something that she could not live without.

Seemingly, this series ended when author Sally Gunning turned to writing historical mysteries.

Miriam Bartimaeus

Author: Anna Apostolou (a pseudonym), possibly for P. C. Doherty

Miriam Bartimaeus was twenty years old in 326 B.C., a slim young woman with black hair and a medium build. She and her twin brother Simon were Jewish. They had been joined together at the elbow at birth, but were successfully separated. After their mother died, the twins were sold as slaves to King Philip of Macedon. He allowed them to be educated by Aristotle who tutored Alexander, his heir. Simon and Miriam also entertained the court with two-person shows, telling stories from the Old Testament. They lived at King Philip's court where Simon worked as a scribe, and, of necessity, became involved in the intrigues that flourished there. King Philip had divorced his wife, Olympias. Alexander (to become "the Great") was her son and presumably Philip's. There were those who chose to believe otherwise and aligned themselves with Caranus, the son of Philip's second marriage. Miriam was a confidante and close friend to Alexander.

As *A Murder in Macedon* (St. Martin, 1997) began, King Philip had gathered his friends and enemies to celebrate his coronation as captain general of the armies of Greece. He did not survive the night, murdered by Pausanias, the captain of his guard. Pausanias was killed shortly afterwards. Alexander's position as heir was in jeopardy. After he gained temporary control of the situation, he asked for assistance from Miriam and Simon in learning what caused loyal Pausanias to turn against him.

An uprising in Thebes threatened Alexander's empire. In *A Murder in Thebes* (St. Martin, 1998), he hurried to relieve his surrounded garrison and to retrieve the crown of Oedipus, which would prove him to be a "pure" man. Clever, yes. Cruel, yes. Hardly pure. Alexander used his friends, including Miriam, to recover the missing crown and identify the Persian spy who incited the uprising.

Miriam tolerated Alexander's brutality of which she was well aware because she witnessed his massacres. She had few feminine virtues, and was perceived by some as masculine in her nature.

Laurel Bartlett

Author: Lee Roddy

Laurel had served as a Union Spy during the Civil War. A tiny woman with dark hair, she had begun these activities when only 18, motivated by her soldier brother's death. She did not make the rest of her family aware of what she was doing, lest they believe she was promiscuous. Her widowed father was a firm judgmental man who had made a fortune producing wheels for railroad cars. At times she used blackface to pass as a slave, and developed a Southern accent to be used in polite Confederate society.

The war had ended by *Days of Deception* (David C. Cook Publishing, 1998), but there was no going back to home life for Laurel. She had become addicted to excitement and danger. She convinced Pinkerton, with whom she had worked during the war to let her continue for his agency, traveling south again to investigate possible thefts by railroad employees. Laurel had her own agenda. She had been engaged to Claude Duncan, a Union soldier who had been seen in the area to which she would travel. En route she met Confederate Captain Ridge Grainger (spelled without the "i" elsewhere). He was returning from a charitable mission to deliver a message from a dying Union soldier, but traveled as a guard for gold bullion on the train. Laurel's faith in God was restored by what she learned about both Claude and Ridge.

Although Laurel and Ridge were strongly attracted to one another in *Yesterday's Shadows* (Chariot Victor, 1999), there were obstacles. Ridge's fiancé Varena had married an older, richer man while he was in the service. Now a land-poor widow, she was determined to win him back. After spending some time in Virginia, accompanied by her Aunt Agnes, Laurel realized that she would never fit in there. She accepted two assignments that would take her to California: one, from Pinkerton to assess the opposition to the transcontinental railroad; the other, from the Chicago Globe to locate the witness to a murder. The narrative covered both Ridge's dilemma and Laurel's adventures in the same time period.

The final book in what was called the *Pinkerton Lady Chronicles* series was *Tomorrow's Promise* (Cook Communication Ministries, 2000). Laurel was devastated when she and Ridge discovered the body of her dear friend, Sarah Perkins. Laurel was convinced that Sarah had been murdered because of the work they had shared during the Civil War. She withheld information from the authorities until she realized that she might be the next victim.

These were Christian mysteries that will appeal to many readers. Those interested in the period should check out the series by Miriam Monfredo covering women spies during the Civil War.

This was a difficult series to locate, available to me only in large print by Thorndike. However, the earlier publications in paperback are used to identify the date and original publishers.

Alma Bashears

Author: Tess Collins

Alma Bashears had no intention of ever returning to Contrary, Kentucky. Her father Esau, a coal miner who had been urged out of town for his union activities, left for Detroit when she was a young girl. The plan had been that he would earn Christmas money for the family in an automobile factory, but Esau never returned. A humiliating gang rape by sons of upper class families in Contrary had one positive side effect. Under pressure by her mother, money was found to subsidize Alma's college education. She left town without looking back, leaving behind her wild but loyal brother Vernon and more placid sister, Sue. There was no place to go but up. A law degree, an internship with the state Supreme Court, and years of hard work at a corporate law firm found Alma comfortable financially and professionally. A relationship with State Supreme Court Justice Jordan McFedries met her personal needs.

Yet, when in *The Law of Revenge* (Ivy, Ballantine, 1997), Alma received a message that Vernon had been charged with murder, she went home. Some things remained the same: the condescension of the "downtowners" towards the people from the hollows, the rigid social structure, the power of the good old boys and sometimes the good old girls. These presented obstacles to defending Vernon for the murder of businessman Bill Littlefield. Alma remembered that Vernon had been there for her when she was assaulted. She persisted but sometimes her emotions overwhelmed her legal expertise.

Alma surprised herself and everyone else by deciding to stay in Contrary as law partner to old friend Jefferson Bingham. The arrangement was short term. The emotional tension between Jefferson and Alma made it impossible for them to work together. By *The Law of the Dead* (Ivy, 1999), Alma had successfully run for State Attorney against her former adversary, Walter Gentry. The pressure of family versus professional responsibilities did not abate. Pregnant Kitty Sloat, Alma's cousin, was mutilated and murdered. Kitty's teenage son Danny disappeared making him a potential suspect. At the end a question left unanswered will make readers hope for another in the series.

Three vindictive women stood between Alma and her dream of finding her father in *The Law of Betrayal* (Port Town Publishing, 2003). On her deathbed Charlotte Gentry, a long time enemy of Alma, had made her aware that the Gentry family had something to do with his disappearance. Jefferson Bingham and Grady Forester, both of whom, loved Alma, reluctantly agreed to help her investigate. After Grady's death, wealthy Elaine Bartholomew who loved him, accused Alma of the murder. Ambitious special prosecutor Judith Drake was determined to prove Alma guilty. Walter Gentry, Jr, Charlotte' son, argued that he could save her. Some will find the mystical aspects of the narrative, relating to the Melungeons, hard to swallow.

Author Tess Collins deserves to be added to Sharyn McCrumb and Margaret Maron as depicters of the rural South.

Bast a.k.a. Karen Hightower

Author: Rosemary Edghill, pseudonym for Eluki Bes Shahar

See: Karen Hightower, page 346.

Tory Bauer

Author: Kathleen Taylor

Tory Bauer, a farm girl in a small town with precise social striations, had married Nicky, the first man she fell in love with, tolerated his infidelity, and coped with his death and her inability to bear children. After Nicky's death in a car accident, Tory moved in with his nymphomaniac cousin, Del Bauer and her son, Presley. The boy, a young teenager, filled an empty place in Tory's life.

She may seem an unlikely heroine, but this was South Dakota, a land of temperature extremes, insularity and independence. These characteristics were displayed, perhaps to extremes, in Delphi, a small town just off a major highway. Like her setting, Tory had physical limitations. She was overweight (at least in her own estimation), in her forties, and self-educated, but she was a survivor. Her career was waiting on tables at the Delphi Café, where unpleasant tourists were offered the local water. Tory's mom, Fernice Atwood, still lived on the family farm where she cared for her aging and "loony" mother, Nillie. Fernice had married a bigamist, kept his name and their child, but little else after he disappeared. She supported herself and Nillie as a writer of lurid romances under a pseudonym. Only Tory was aware of Fernice's secrets.

Tory, who had never quite fit in, enjoyed good music (including James Taylor), drank Black Russians, devoured books, especially mysteries, and was disdainful of some of Delphi's rituals (Delphi Daze, homecoming football games, etc), but she had no desire to live anywhere else. Her heart was set on married feed dealer Stuart McKee. Even though she had a comforting friendship with wealthy Neil Pascoe, he failed to make a dent in her passion for Stuart. Del, Tory, and young part-time college student Rhonda Saunders initially worked for Aphrodite Ferguson at the café where much of the action took place.

The first published book of the series, *Sex and Salmonella* (Avon, 1996), centered on Delphi Daze, a local promotion that featured an amateur show and traveling carnival, and introduced many of the characters. A young carnie, Lily Mitchell, died under unusual circumstances. Tory, who found the body, overcame her initial errors of judgment and resolved the issues surrounding Lily Mitchell's birth, life, and death.

Stuart McKee and Tory publicly acknowledged that they were dating in *The Hotel South Dakota* (Avon, 1997), but not that they had been sleeping together for months before his wife Renee left him. Both they and the town were engrossed in the all-year high school alumni homecoming. The celebrity guest, movie star J. Ross Nelson, had disappeared from Delphi after a riverside keg party at the 1969 homecoming. A member of the football squad drowned that night. Most of the survivors of the party were present for the reunion as events reminiscent of the 1969 incidents occurred: a death and a disappearance. Tory had played a role in the earlier fiasco. This time she persisted until she understood what had happened.

Those who read the series by chronological publication dates will be surprised by *Funeral Food* (Avon, 1998; a contributor to Amazon.com stated that it had been published earlier by University Editions under the title *The Missionary Position).* As the author explained, this narrative predated the two published earlier. It amplified and explored the characterizations. Readers might be advised to read it first. It explored Tory's passion for Stuart McKee and Neil Pascoe's gentle help as he watched her from the sidelines; the revelation of secrets in the lives of Tory's mother, father, and grandmother. There were murders: the death by bludgeoning of a young Mormon missionary, and another corpse buried deep but not deep enough. This was a poignant story.

Tory gracefully admitted that she jumped to early and erroneous conclusions at times, but in *Mourning Shift*, (Avon, 1998) she couldn't be blamed. Within a few days, she learned that Aphrodite, Tory's employer, was preparing to divorce her husband, Gus Ferguson. Then Gus's corpse was discovered in the restaurant bathroom. Gus's daughter, Alanna Luna, showed up with her son Brian. Aphrodite never enjoyed her newfound freedom. She was blown to smithereens by a car bomb. It got worse; Renee McKee returned pregnant. Was it Stu's child?

It was only New Year's Eve but cabin fever was running rampant in Delphi during *Cold Front* (Avon, 2000). Gina Adler was driven wild by her husband Ron's infidelity. Tory accepted a ride from Stu McKee in an emergency, only to be stuck overnight with him in a snowdrift. No one, not even Neil, believed that they had not been intimate. The frozen body of Ian O'Hara, Del Bauer's pen-pal dream man, was discovered in the back of Stu's pickup.

Perhaps Tory had become too blasé about corpses by *Foreign Body* (Avon, 2001). A member of the Traveling European Lutheran Youth Choir died, leaving behind a note that could destroy Rev. Clay Deibert's career. While inching cautiously closer to a commitment, Tory and Neil juggled Swedish translations, youthful sexual escapades, and mysterious numbers. Her mother Fernice's future had not been dealt with, leaving a hook to make readers hope for another book in the series.

The language was explicit and coarse at times. Readers may or may not admire Tory, but if they read the series, they will not forget her. The narratives fit somewhere between Joan Hess' Maggody series and William Inge's plays, with a touch of the movie *Fargo*.

Vicky Bauer

Author: Leona Gom

Vicky O'Rourke had an unsettled childhood. Her Irish-Canadian father had abandoned her and her Native American mother, who subsequently became an alcoholic. It had been no better at school. Determined to prove that she was the equal of the white students, she had excelled initially. Depressed at her lack of resources, she planned to drop out during her senior year. Teacher Conrad Bauer had intervened, offering to have her live in his home, performing casual work, but without any sexual involvement. The death of Vicky's mother and pressure from the school led to a marriage between Vicky and Conrad. They often spent time apart. He remained at his school while she went off to college. Later they went to Germany, where Conrad had been born.

After-Image (Second Story, 1996) took place while the Bauers were in Germany. He was a civilian employee of the Canadian Army in occupation. Vicky, an insecure woman who relied on alcohol for comfort, had embarrassed Conrad by public drunkenness and outbursts. She had no credibility when she reported that she had seen a man kill a woman when she was in the forest taking pictures. When military authorities returned to the site with her, the body had disappeared. The developed pictures that might have verified her story went missing. Someone wanted Vicky to believe she had been delusional. There was another problem. Vicky was scheduled to return to Edmonton to begin her Ph.D. program. Conrad did not intend to accompany her.

When he finally returned to Canada, Conrad gave up teaching to accept work as a translator in Vancouver. Vicky put aside her plans for a Ph.D. in film studies. The only work available to her was as a substitute teacher. Hiring part-Canadian Indian teachers from central Canada was not a priority in the small town where the Bauers lived. After being informed that Conrad had been seriously injured, she lost control and her job. Conrad remained in institutional care in a coma from which he might never recover while Vicky subsisted on occasional stints as a substitute.

She was surprised in *Double Negative* (Second Story Press, 1998) to be called to substitute at Farrar Secondary School where she had been in trouble. Already burdened by daily visits to Conrad, and the return of her putative father, Arthur O' Rourke, Vicky was unable to handle the impact of a relationship with her new neighbor, Richard Menard. He had one too many children to suit Vicky. Conrad's untimely death, just when it appeared that he was coming out of the coma, solved Vicky's financial problems but left her emotionally adrift. Her only friend, Amanda, had helped her to supplement her income by tutoring. This was something she could handle.

Vicky, lonely since Conrad's death, opened her home and heart to Rachel Mandaro in *Freeze Frame* (Second Story Press, 1999). She invited Rachel to move into a basement room in her home, and encouraged her to divorce her abusive husband Dennis. Rachel was subsequently killed by a hit and run driver. Vicky's probe into Rachel's life: a rigid father, teenage pregnancy, and an office seduction revealed a different victim and a different killer than Vicky had originally constructed.

This was a difficult series, partly because Vicky was unlikable in the first book. Although she became less dependent on alcohol, she continued to be unstable and needy in the later books.

China Bayles

Author: Susan Wittig Albert

Former corporate attorney China Bayles opened an herb store in Pecan Springs, Texas after fifteen years in a career chosen to please her father. A brown-haired woman in her early forties, she retained the logical mind and knowledge of the law that figured in her investigations. Her need for control made her uncomfortable with long-term commitments or intimacy. China had difficulty forgiving her mother Leatha, now a recovering alcoholic and happily remarried, until late in the series. Her tenant, Ruby Wilcox, who ran a New Age occult shop, often shared her investigations.

As *Thyme of Death* (Scribners, 1992) opened, China had settled into the small college town and made friends. The death of Jo Gilbert, an environmental activist and member of NOW (National Organization of Women), was considered a suicide because of her breast cancer. China and Ruby disagreed and carried out their own investigation, leaving former police officer Mike McQuaid out of the loop.

China's personal life was still "on hold" in *Witches' Bane* (Scribners, 1993). Although Mike had proposed marriage, she hesitated, worked on her herbal cookbook, and attended a Tarot course taught by Ruby. After the class held a joint meeting with white witches on Halloween, Sybil Rand, the owner of a "poison garden", was found murdered. Photographer Andrew Drake, the man in Ruby's life, was an obvious suspect, but she believed him innocent. China did not want children and was glad that Mike McQuaid had no expectations for them in a marriage. He gained custody of his son Brian eventually and that met both their needs.

China's thriving business needed additional space in *Hangman's Root* (Scribners, 1994), but she was wary of Mike's solution, the joint lease of a lovely country home. Dottie Riddle, an elderly collector of stray cats, had been accused of the murder of animal researcher Miles Harwick. Her protests against his current project had been met with threats against her life. The number two suspect was Ruby's daughter Amy Roth, given up for adoption after birth. Amy had sought Ruby out, announcing that she was her child.

Local accountant Rosemary Robbins, who was a "China look-alike", was driving McQuaid's truck when she was killed in *Rosemary Remembered* (Berkley, 1995). McQuaid was convinced that paroled convict Jake Jacoby had committed the murder after mistakenly thinking the victim was China. She solved the crime, mended fences with Brian, McQuaid's son, and peppered the vengeful ex-convict.

China was in a mental funk as *Rueful Death* (Berkley, 1996) began. She had left her legal practice partly because it consumed her life. Then she poured the same manic activity into her herb shop, denying herself the expected relaxed living style. Friend Maggie Garrett, a local restaurateur and ex-nun, suggested a retreat at her former convent. Although China left personal and business decisions behind, she found a new set at St. Angela's; i.e. Tom Rowan, Jr. a former lover seeking to renew their relationship, and sibling rivalry among the "sisters." She tackled these complications with her usual determination.

China's attitude towards marriage had changed during the retreat. However, her plan to accept the next time McQuaid proposed marriage ran into difficulty during *Love Lies Bleeding* (Berkley, 1997). He had become preoccupied, unreceptive to her charms, and was given to unexplained absences while working on a research project involving former Texas Rangers. A former law school classmate, Justine Wyzinski, asked China and Ruby to help her in a case. It turned out to be the murder of Roy Adcock, a former Ranger and the husband of Dolores who helped in China's garden. Her path crossed with those of McQuaid and the new woman in his life.

The tragic incident that left McQuaid paralyzed and receiving therapy in a nursing home initially ended their wedding plans in *Chile Death* (Berkley, 1998). His stint as a chili tasting judge, and the death of libidinous insurance agent Jerry Jeff Cody after tasting a contestant's chili drew China and McQuaid together. It was Ruby Wilcox, China's tenant and new partner, who saved the day.

Potential suspects in the murder of real estate developer Edgar Coleman were as plentiful as weeds in *Lavender Lies* (Berkley, 1999). Coleman had bribed or blackmailed the mayor and members of the Pecan Springs city council to approve his annexation plans. While McQuaid, now the temporary chief of police, concentrated on the obvious suspects, China took time from her wedding preparations to look elsewhere. She had all the usual accomplices: Ruby, college security director Sheila Dawson, and her mother, Leatha.

Carl Swenson, supplier of mistletoe to China's Thyme and Seasons business, died in a hit and run accident just as the holiday season began in *Mistletoe Man* (Berkley, 2000). China knew that Swenson had been harassing the Fletcher sisters who had purchased land from him. She took her responsibility to McQuaid and her role as an "officer of the court" seriously enough to share this information with the authorities. However, she valued her friendship with the Fletchers enough to seek the real killer.

China had rejected her maternal relatives who resided in and around Jordan's Crossing, Mississippi, not because of personal antipathy but from her distaste for the traditional South and its history of slavery. She could not, however, reject her mother Leatha's cry for help in *Bloodroot* (Berkley, 2001). Leatha had returned to Jordan's Crossing to assist Great Aunt Tullie, but found it beyond her strength. Tullie, who had raised Leatha, was not only in danger from failing health, but might at any moment be charged with murder. The sexual escapades of the past had resulted in a series of tragedies. China and Leatha faced the most serious problem either had ever encountered.

An Unthymely Death (Berkley, 2003) was a collection of short stories by Albert. China, Mike and Ruby featured in many of them. The background consisted of local rituals; i. e. county fairs, maypole dancers, etc., and the prevalence of rampant gossip in the community.

The town of Indigo had been dying for years, but in *Indigo Dying* (Berkley, 2003), a group of determined business owners (some newcomers) were determined to extend its life. They did so by investing money in buildings which they leased from Casey Ford, and by holding special events such as the Indigo Arts and Crafts Fair. China and Ruby came to town (a) to work with friend Allie Selby in dyeing workshops, and (b) to sell their products at a fair booth. Casey Ford was Allie's uncle. She had leased her farm from him and was devastated when Ford announced his intention of selling the mineral rights under all of his land to a strip mining company. His subsequent death sent China, Mike, and Ruby into a complex investigation. A little too much explanatory material about indigo, the art of dyeing cloths, and the need to use mordants to fix the dye. When the technical material eased, the plot took off.

There were lots of surprises in store for China in *A Dilly of a Death* (Berkley, 2004). She was trying to focus on plans for the upcoming Pecan Springs Picklefest, but was distracted when Amy, her friend Ruby's daughter, came by. Amy, who had been given up for adoption had a strained relationship with Ruby, so it was from China that she sought help. She was pregnant, wanted to stay with China and Mike until she could set up her own place. Mike had a surprise for China, too. He had tired of teaching at the local college, wanted to return to detective work as a private investigator. Phoebe Morgan, wealthy owner of Morgan Pickles and chairman of the Picklefest, disappeared. Albert did a masterful job of tying this all together, with a sense of humor and pickle jokes.

Aunt Velda's discovery of treasure in a hillside cave was the springboard for *Dead Man's Bones* (Berkley, 2005) because further exploration revealed the skeleton of a murdered man. China became involved because her stepson Brian (now 14) found the remains. Ruby was not only in the throes of a new romance, but played a strong role in the latest production of the Pecan Springs Community Theatre Association. The organization had accepted the conditional gift of a new site for their production. In exchange they had agreed that their next show would be a "hagiographic" (worshipful) play extolling the contributions of the donor Jane Obermann and her father, the author. Albert skillfully blended the two story lines.

What began as a favor for high school principal Lisa Simon in *Bleeding Hearts* (Berkley, 2006) escalated into a series of shocking disclosures. Lisa asked China to check into the possibility that successful high school coach Tim Duffy had behaved inappropriately with students. Since the information received by Lisa was anonymous, China had to be very cautious in checking the matter out. The death of college student Angela Lopez had been ruled a suicide, but her mother had read the girl's diary which created suspicion that she might have been murdered. Leatha, China's mother, had gained possession of intimate letters written by her husband Robert, which disclosed surprising information. A final incident, the theft of a prize entry from the first annual show of the local quilting group, had to be dealt with carefully. This kept China busy and personally involved.

China spent very little time at her shop during *Spanish Dagger* (Berkley, 2007). She had too many other problems to deal with. Her newly discovered half-brother Miles hired Mike McQuaid (China's husband, now a private detective) to check out the death of their father, Robert. That line of investigation was shunted aside temporarily to be dealt with in a future book. Ruby

Wilcox, who was trying to cope with her mother, now a victim of Alzheimer's, suffered another blow when local businessman Colin Fowler was murdered. She was seriously in love with Colin, knew that he had a mysterious past, and that lately they had drifted apart. Her insistence that China investigate pitted her against not only DEA agents, but her good friend, Chief of Police Sheila Dawson.

Nightshade (Berkley, 2008) finished the trilogy within the China Bayles series that dealt with her father's secret life. Miles Danforth, her half-brother believed that their father, attorney Bob Bayles, had been murdered. China had always resented the limited attention her father gave her, so she had no enthusiasm about pursuing the matter. Her husband, Mike McQuaid, restless in his new career as a private investigator, was more than willing to work with Miles. That changed when Miles was murdered. Now it was personal. China was determined to learn who was behind the vendetta on her family, and then put it all behind her. Very well developed characters with a taut plot.

Next: *Wormwood* (2009), *Holly Blues* (2010)

Author Susan Wittig Albert and her husband Bill also write the Kate Ardleigh series under the name Robin Paige. On her own, Susan has a separate series, based on Beatrix Potter.

Madeline Bean

Author: Jerrilyn Farmer

Madeline Bean grew up in the Midwest but relocated to California. After attending the Culinary Institute in San Francisco, she worked as a pastry chef at a Berkeley restaurant. Later, Madeline and coworker Wesley Westcott moved to Los Angeles where they became partners in a catering business. Madeline was, by then, an attractive red-blonde in her thirties. As the business prospered she and Wes added staff including Holly Atkins, who eventually rose to partner. Madeline was dependent on Diet Coke to keep her going. An early romance had ended when the man she loved left her. She talked occasionally about marriage and babies but couldn't fit them into her lifestyle. Her relationship with Wes was platonic, unlike that with erratic sitcom producer Arlo Zar. She and Arlo were so involved in their careers that they barely noticed how little they shared. The purchase of the former home of a silent film comedian solved both business and personal problems for Madeline. The downstairs was the headquarters for her business. She lived in the upstairs.

Madeline was thrilled in *Sympathy for the Devil* (Avon, 1998) when penurious producer Bruno Huntley chose her firm for a major dinner at his home. Huntley, thrice wed, had two adult sons (Graydon and Bruno, Jr) whom he treated with contempt, and four-year old Lewis from his current marriage to a much younger woman. Madeline pulled her staff together to win new customers by her firm's performance for Bruno. Unfortunately, he dropped dead during the proceedings, which had a negative impact. She stirred the brew of suspects until the murderer boiled over.

Having sold the catering business, Wes and Madeline created a new corporation: Mad Bean Events. The firm scored a coup in *Immaculate Reception* (Avon, 1999) when it was chosen to serve breakfast to 2,000 guests during a Papal visit to Los Angeles. Xavier Jones, the fiancé who left Madeline ten years before to become a Jesuit brother, was the advance man for such arrangements. Murder, romantic explorations including one with Detective Chuck Honnett, and revelations about a suppressed encyclical enlivened the Papal visit.

Madeline gave no serious consideration to purchasing Vivian Duncan's successful wedding consultant business in *Killer Wedding* (Avon, 2000), although Vivian was determined to sell it to her. The corporation that had purchased the catering business from Madeline and Wes brought a law suit on the grounds that Mad Bean Events was a violation of the non-competition clause in the sale. Until the matter was settled, MBE was shut down. In the interim Wes, Holly, and Madeline were happy to attend the Sara Silver/ Brent Bell wedding as managed by Vivian. When Madeline and Chuck Honnett discovered Vivian's corpse, she needed no urging to find the killer.

It all began with a game, a mah-jongg box that Wes had found while remodeling a house, but in *Dim Sum Dead* (Avon, 2001), there were heavy losers. Inside the rosewood box was the diary of Dickey McBride, a deceased movie star. Within the book were references to past misdeeds and affairs that seriously affected women who were still alive. Madeline's conscience would not allow her to stop until she discovered which one was willing to kill for the box.

Mumbo Gumbo (Morrow, 2003) is an incredible concoction for Madeline who took on a short term assignment as a writer for *Food Freak*, a culinary game show. The narrative blended the disappearance of head writer Tim Stock, a secret room, Berry-Blue dyed wool, and deliberately confused recipes into an incredible yarn. The subsequent arson and murder brought Madeline back into Lt. Chuck Honnett's arms. Best enjoyed by dyed in the wool fans.

The black-white design for the food, decorations, and attire at the Mad Bean catered Jazz Ball was a tremendous success in *Perfect Sax* (Morrow, 2004). From there on, things went down hill. The final item in the charity auction was an exceptional tenor saxophone. Winner Bill Knight who purchased the sax for $100,000 claimed that it was stolen. Madeline returned home exhausted, only to find her house surrounded by police vehicles. A redheaded corpse had been found in her bedroom. Honnett had hurried to the scene, fearing that Madeline was dead. She wasn't but someone was willing to keep trying.

Holly, the third partner in the catering business was to marry screenwriter Donald Lake in two weeks, so in *The Flaming Luau of Death* (Morrow, 2005) she arranged a wild weekend in Hawaii for the female members of the bridal party. Those invited included Holly's four younger sisters and her best friend, Liz Mooney. Before they left, Holly shared a concern with Madeline. Years before on an alcohol fueled trip to Los Vegas after her high school prom, Holly had married Marvin Dubinsky. She had only gone to the prom with him to be kind, but that was ridiculous. However there had been no divorce, no annulment, and no contact in the succeeding years. She had a second concern, actually. She was getting threatening E-mail sent to her married name, demanding access to Marvin. Some vacation that turned out to be.

Desperately Seeking Sushi (2009) plus *Murder at the Academy Awards* (2009) co-authored with Joan Rivers!

Goldy Bear (Schulz)

Author: Diane Mott Davidson

For those who enjoy good food and good books, Goldy Bear is a find. Bruised by her marriage and divorce from abusive John Richard Korman, she supported herself with a catering business. A short, plump blonde in her early thirties, she was the mother of eleven-year-old Arch. Her divorce settlement had subsidized her Aspen Meadows, Colorado business, but she had a running battle to keep Korman current on his child support.

In *Catering to Nobody* (St. Martin's, 1990), Goldy was providing lunch after the funeral of Arch's teacher Laura Smiley, when Dr. Fritz Korman, John's father, became ill from poisoned coffee. He survived, but Goldy's business was seriously damaged. This prompted her investigation into the possibility that Laura had not committed suicide. Detective Tom Schulz offered the stability needed when the solution hit close to home.

John Richard Korman used Arch's visitation time to undermine Goldy in *Dying for Chocolate,* (Bantam, 1992). She was working as a live-in cook for General Bo and Adele Farquhar, but managed to juggle investigating the murder of her friend Dr. Philip Miller. This meshed with her plans to get Arch admitted to exclusive Elk Park Prep.

Arch made it into Elk Park Prep in *The Cereal Murders* (Bantam, 1993), but at some cost. Goldy agreed to provide food for a variety of school events, assisted by Julian Teller, a part-Navajo student and a "big brother" to Arch. Someone was making Arch miserable; even more seriously, someone was killing the top students in the senior class. When Goldy accepted the proposal of Tom Schulz her personal problems came closer to solution.

However, in *The Last Suppers* (Bantam, 1994), the wedding had to be postponed. Tom disappeared at the scene of a crime—the murder of Rev. "Ted" Olson, the Episcopalian priest who was to have married them. Tortured by fears for his safety and a lingering doubt that he might have left her at the altar, Goldy could not settle for the police investigation. She probed a theological dispute to find Tom and his abductor.

During *Killer Pancake* (Bantam, 1995), Goldy catered a meal for Mignon Cosmetics. In the process, she witnessed the hit and run death of Claire Satterfield, beloved of her assistant, Julian Teller. Her efforts led to the exposure of unacceptable experiments by cosmetic companies. A killer cooked up a way to escape Goldy.

In *The Main Corpse* (Bantam, 1996), Goldy was determined to prove her friend Marla Korman was innocent of murder. She created a conflict of interest with Tom's job by organizing a jailbreak and risking anaphylactic shock for Marla. Less appropriately, she involved Arch as an accessory. Goldy must have been hitting the cooking sherry in this one.

Much as she detested her former husband with some justification, Goldy could not abandon him in *The Grilling Season* (Bantam, 1997). John Richard was still Arch's father. Suz Craig, calculating executive vice president of the health maintenance organization for which John Richard worked, had been murdered. Although he had a cozy personal relationship with Suz, it had curdled under professional pressures. He had been the last person known to be on the scene. To preserve her relationship with Arch, Goldy had to get him off the grill.

Goldy and Tom were besieged from all sides in *Prime Cut* (Bantam, 1998). He had been suspended for insubordination on a crime scene where Goldy found a body. She was being undercut and undermined by a rival caterer. Old friend and mentor Andre Hibbard hired Goldy as an assistant for meals served on location for an advertising agency. She, Tom, and Archie had missed Julian, now studying at an Eastern College. His return not only as an assistant, but also as a family member reinvigorated Goldy.

With her kitchen needing major repairs before it could be reopened for business, Goldy grasped at a six-week stint on a television cooking show in *Tough Cookie* (Bantam, 2000). The setting was the Summit Bistro at Killdeer Ski Resort owned by Goldy's friend, Eileen Druckman. A business meeting with former beau Doug Portman ended in his murder. In order to clear her name, Goldy had to solve two prior deaths. The killer knew she was on his trail and was prepared to deal with her.

The opportunity to serve English delicacies at a renovated castle sent Goldy scurrying to her cookbooks in *Sticks & Scones* (Bantam, 2001). She and Arch took residence at the castle when their home became dangerous. An injury forced Tom to join them. The hijacking of a Federal Express truck carrying some rare postage stamps complicated preparing meals for Eliot and Sukie Hyde, the eccentric castle owners. Poor Arch tried to balance his affection for his father with the realization that he was a deeply flawed man.

Some people never grow up, Goldy learned in *Chopping Spree* (Bantam, 2002). Her stint catering an elaborate brunch at Westside Mall for women with too much time and too much money was a disaster. An argument between a husband and wife about expensive purchases, and the expulsion of a teenage kleptomaniac were bad enough, but an attempt on the life of Barry Dean, mall manager and a college friend of Goldy was over the top. Barry had been helping her unload her van in the parking lot. A second attempt on his life was successful. Goldy had to prove that no one on her staff was responsible.

Goldy and Marla were upset to learn that John Richard's prison sentence had been commuted and he was back in Boulder as *Double Shot* (HarperCollins, 2004) began. Was it he who ravaged Goldy's new catering facility and knocked her out just before a major event at which she was to serve the meal? He was at the memorial luncheon, brandishing a new younger woman on his arm, and demanding that Goldy bring Arch to his elegant leased home for their weekly golf game at 4P.M. They barely made it but John Richard was not to be found until Goldy located him shot to death in his garaged car. The presence of Goldy's pistol, which she kept locked in her glove compartment, made problems for her and for Tom, who was taken off the case because of a conflict of interest. Lots of culinary details slowed down the action, but the plotting was good.

Dusty Routt was not only a neighbor but was employed at Hanrahan and Jule law firm in *Dark Tort* (Morrow, 2006). Goldy who had been retained to cater breakfast and snacks for the firm, had been giving Dusty lessons in food preparation on Thursday evenings at the office. As the narrative began, Goldy tripped over Dusty's corpse when she entered the building. Dusty, whose family lived in a Habitat for Humanity home, was ambitious to improve herself; maybe, too ambitious. Her mother, Sally, had no faith in the legal system with some justification, so she begged Goldy to discover Dusty's killer. That meant getting on a more personal level with the attorneys, their families and support staff. There were several villains. This was warm and fuzzy, but had good plotting.

The rich imperious ladies who lunched and dined in Aspen Meadow during *Sweet Revenge* (Morrow, 2007) made Goldy painfully aware that she had overbooked for the Holiday season. Even if things had gone well there would have been problems, but they didn't. During preparation for a breakfast for staff and volunteers at the Aspen Meadows Library, someone killed former district attorney Drew Wellington. Goldy's impression that she had seen murderess Sandee Brisbane, who had disappeared into a fiery forest, made no impression on Tom. Motivations for killing Drew presented several possibilities. After being defeated for re-election, he had become an antique map dealer. He was not only a ladies' man but reputedly attracted to underage females. His former wife and current fiancée were among the difficult females who plagued Goldy. Everyone should have a forgiving friend like Marla Korman.

Fatally Flaky (2009)

Possible other series by Davidson featured Toni Underwood; i.e. *Deadly Rendezvous and Deadly Gamble.*

Molly Bearpaw

Author: Jean Hager

Molly Bearpaw, although exposed to the indignities suffered by members of her race, worked within the system as an investigator for the Native American Advocacy league in Oklahoma.

She was a Cherokee, raised by her grandmother after her father deserted the family and her mother committed suicide. Tall and thin with black hair and dark brown eyes, she had earned a degree in psychology with a minor in anthropology.

In *Ravenmocker* (Mysterious Press, 1992), while investigating the death of Abner Mouse at the local nursing home, Molly was reintroduced to the tribal beliefs of the Ravenmocker, an evil spirit. The attending physician said Abner died as a result of a stroke, but his son Woodrow sought Molly's help. The autopsy indicated food poisoning, but no such substance was located in the facility. Mercer Vaughn, who had been Abner's roommate, contacted Molly after a similar death in the unit, Molly and Deputy Sheriff D.J. Kennedy checked recent visitors to the facility.

Molly, vulnerable after an affair with a married man, showed an interest in Kennedy.

The Redbird's Cry (Mysterious Press, 1994) was less successful in integrating background material about the Cherokee Nation and its political rivalries and mythology into the narrative. After a blowgun dart killed Tom Battle, attorney for the Nation, and valuable wampum was stolen from a museum exhibit, Molly and Kennedy sought the connection. She may have been preoccupied; Kennedy wanted a commitment that she was not ready to give.

Seven Black Stones (Mysterious, 1995) explored the conflict between Indian tradition and the expansion of gambling on reservations. Zebediah Smoke, an elderly Indian who opposed the construction of a nearby bingo hall, was suspected of using magic to kill two construction workers. Black stones symbolic of a Native American curse had been left in the vicinity of the deaths. Although only one of the two men had been currently employed at the construction site, the stones aroused the suspicions of lazy county sheriff Dave Highsmith. Personal aspects of the victims' lives were uncovered by Molly, leading to a solution. The narrative flowed smoothly, and expanded on Molly's character.

When Molly's initial grant ended, the tribal council hired her as investigator of major crimes on the reservation. During *The Spirit Caller* (Mysterious, 1997), she investigated the hanging death of Talia Wind, a dropout from the Eagle Rock religious community, only to learn that her long absent father was a primary suspect. Molly had no place in her life for a repentant parent; least of all, one in jail for murder, but she realized that Rob Bearpaw might not be guilty of desertion or homicide.

A well-constructed and interesting series.

Read about Jean Hager's other books featuring Tess Darcy (The Iris House Bed and Breakfast series to be found later in this volume.) She has a second Native American series based on Mitch Bushyhead.

Karen Crist Becker

Author: David Wiltse

See: Karen Crist, page 188.

Grace Beckmann

Author: Jackie Lewin

Although she was married to Dr. Albert Beckmann, head of Internal Medicine at a Colorado university and had twin seventeen-year-old sons (Spence and Paul), Grace worked as a free lance writer. She had attended graduate school in English, but her work experience was part-time as a wedding consultant in a department store. Albert was a pilot and she often accompanied him on his trips although she was a nervous passenger. She was a trim dark haired woman in her forties, active in a tennis club and an excellent horseback rider, as the series began. One of her assets was an exceptional memory for numbers. One of her problems was that her widowed mother was extremely dependent upon her. Spence shared his mother's interest in detection, and lacked interest in college although he graduated high school with a 4.0. Paul was a bookworm.

Albert who could well afford a private plane, was careful with money so in *Murder Flies Left Seat* (Avalon, 1998) he arranged to share ownership of one with businessman Parker LeMay. On the morning when Albert and a reluctant Grace were to take off for a weekend trip in the Piper, they arrived to learn that the plane was gone. Jann, LeMay's Vietnamese wife, had flown off without a preflight check or notification to the tower. Mechanic Jack Potts had noticed that she was carrying a substantial package. The plane crashed, killing Jann. Detective Morrisey made Albert and Grace aware that the motor had been tampered with. Concerned that they might have been the targets, Grace and Albert did some investigating on their own, enough to make them targets. Well plotted.

James Delacroix, owner of the Copper Creek (FBO) airport, seemed to be well fixed financially although the small airport had little business. He was a casual acquaintance of Albert and Grace as *Death Flies on Final* (Avalon, 1999) began. They had met him at his daughter Arlene's wedding. She was Albert's head nurse. En route to Carlsbad Caverns in Albert's plane, they stopped at Cross Creek Airport to refuel. Before they left, Grace overheard James hang up on a phone call; subsequently he gave Albert an envelope to take to Arlene. On their return trip, they stopped by again out of concern, only to find him dead. A valuable ring that they had noticed on his finger was missing. This was really none of their business, but Arlene asked Grace to investigate. When a good friend was arrested for the murder, the whole family pitched in.

There was a gap in the series, the next book, *Fear of Dying* was published in 2004 by Five Star. Grace's interest in why Wendy Pace was murdered stemmed not so much from an innate curiosity but rather a feeling that she might have saved the young pregnant woman. All of a sudden motherhood, birth and adoption became important. Millie, the family housekeeper who had been there for Grace as a child, wanted information for a friend. Tennis partner Sarah Jane was considering adoption. Paige Passerelli, son Paul's girlfriend, asked Grace to find a missing friend. Someone else wanted her to mind her own business.

This was a very interesting series with an intelligent heroine in a successful marriage, too bad it ended here.

Jane Bee

Author: C. C. Benison, pseudonym for Douglas Whiteway

Just entering her twenties, Jane Bee left college and her native Canada to tour Europe. Her father, a member of the Royal Canadian Mounted Police, and her mother, a journalist, had separated. Two older sisters remained in Canada; one a doctor, the other married to a potato farmer. Jane's travels ended when her money did, so she visited Great Aunt Grace in England.

Jane's response to a blind ad in a London newspaper led to a position as maid at Buckingham Palace and an acquaintanceship with Queen Elizabeth II during *Death at Buckingham Palace* (Bantam, 1996). Influenced by the unexplained presence of gum on the carpet, Jane believed that Robin Tukes, a young Canadian footman, had been murdered. Was Robin killed because he was the heir to an earldom, even one tainted by rumors that a prior Earl had been Jack the Ripper? Was his death connected to the theft of King Edward VII's diary? Queen Elizabeth decided what action should be taken, based on information provided by Jane.

Jane was among the servants to accompany the royal family on Christmas vacation in *Death at Sandringham House* (Bantam, 1997). While helping out at the Dersingham village hall, a royal footman discovered the corpse of a local actress dressed to resemble the Queen. The tiara worn by the victim may have been one possessed by the Duchess of Windsor, but stolen after World War II. Jane's father, experienced as a member of the Royal Canadian Mounted Police, was on hand to assist in the investigation, but again it was the Queen who called the suspects together for the final denouement.

Queen Elizabeth and her entourage moved to Windsor Castle for their semi-annual visit, highlighted by the selection of new members of the Order of the Garter and by the Royal Ascot Races as *Death at Windsor Castle* (Bantam, 1998) began. Queen Elizabeth was sitting for her portrait, when artist Victor Fabiana confessed to murdering Roger Pettibon, assistant curator of her art collection. Jane Bee uncovered multiple suspects and a single overwhelming motive.

Mildly entertaining.

Becky Belski

Author: C. A. Haddad

When Becky Belski was five-years-old, her mother was convicted of murder and sent to prison. Unable to care for her child, she put Becky up for adoption. Kindly Winnie McKennah raised Becky in Sioux Bluffs, Iowa. When she attended the University of Illinois, Becky met and married Yuri Belski, a Russian Jew who had been her teaching assistant. After she graduated with a degree in computer science, they moved to California and somehow fell out of love.

After the divorce, Becky returned to Evanston, where she was employed by Resources, a slightly illegal computer hacking business. Winnie had died recently and Becky had no living mother. She married again. Her second husband, divorce attorney Michael Rosen, had too much mother to Becky's way of thinking. His family did not approve of Michael's marriage to a gentile. This made the holiday season difficult as Michael felt the pressure of family obligations. Becky had been made to feel unwelcome so she preferred to remain at home. In her thirties, Becky wanted to begin a family, but Michael felt they should wait.

During *Caught in the Shadows* (St. Martin's 1992), Becky researched the financial and personal affairs of Lionel and Daryl Aberdeen under the guidance of Daryl's skilled divorce attorney Bellini Reese. She had no expectation that she would be uncovering her own past. The need to know was so overwhelming that Becky took a leave of absence to discover why her mother had accepted an unfavorable plea bargain and why her stepfather's estate had supported Becky during her student years.

In *Root Canal* (Severn House, 1994), Becky earned the gratitude of her sister-in-law Debee. She was the one and only suspect in the eyes of the Highland Park Police Department when her dentist husband, Barney Rogov was found dead at the office. Becky rallied the staff at her office to investigate who else might have benefited from Barney's death. Her probing really touched a nerve with local, national, and international police forces. A pregnancy may limit Becky's further involvement in violent crime.

Claire Breslinsky Benedetto

Author: Mary Anne Kelly

See: Claire Breslinsky, page 116.

Christine Bennett

Author: Lee Harris, pseudonym for Syrell Rogovin Leahy

As a fourteen-year-old orphan, Christine Bennett, initially cared for by her Aunt Meg, was placed in a convent because the care of her disabled son, Gene, was all that Aunt Meg could handle. Eventually Christine joined the religious order as Sister Edward Francis. When the convent no longer met her needs, she returned to secular life, and a home bequeathed to her by Aunt Meg. Christine had earned a master's degree while a nun, which she put to use teaching part-time at a college near New York City.

In *The Good Friday Murder* (Fawcett, 1992), Christine met James Talley, a resident of Greenwillow Home. Talley and his twin brother Robert, idiot savants, had been confined to institutions after being found guilty of their mother's brutal murder. When James' presence at Greenwillow created controversy, Christine reinvestigated the mother's death, alerting the killer. On a more positive note, she became acquainted with detective Jack Brooks.

Christine moved into a physical relationship with Brooks in *The Yom Kippur Murder* (Fawcett, 1992). She was a volunteer visitor to three elderly apartment residents, one of whom was murdered. Christine's assistance to Nathan Herskovitz's heirs drew her into his underground activities during World War II.

By *The Christening Day Murder* (Fawcett, 1993), Christine had not reconciled her extra-marital relationship with her religious faith. When present at an abandoned church for a baptismal ceremony, she discovered a skeleton in the basement. Many of the town's former residents had skeletons in their own closets and resented Christine's investigation.

Christine and Jack celebrated with his fellow police officers in *The St. Patrick's Day Murder* (Fawcett, 1994). When detective Scotty McVeigh was shot down in a parking lot, the murder investigation uncovered a Scotty they had never known. Jack, overwhelmed by disclosures about his friends, asked Christine to investigate.

Jack was attending night law school by *The Christmas Night Murder* (Fawcett, 1994). When he and Christine visited her former convent, she learned of the disappearance of Fr. Henry "Hudson" McCormick, priest to Native American reservations. Christine remained to evaluate the charges of sexual misconduct against the priest, find his kidnapper, and the real abuser.

Christine and Jack had been married for six months by *The Thanksgiving Day Murder* (Fawcett, 1995). Her interest in the disappearance of young wife Natalie at the Thanksgiving Parade was motivated in part by her recollection of attending parades with her father. Natalie had left her husband to go after a balloon-man, but never returned. Christine needed to find Natalie or her killer. On another track, she wanted to identify a woman who had met her father surreptitiously. In so doing, she helped to heal a family breach.

The Passover Murder (Fawcett, 1996) involved Christine in the Seder ritual of friend Melanie Gross' family. During a Passover sixteen years before, Melanie's Aunt Iris had disappeared. Her body was discovered several days later. At Melanie's request, Christine inquired into the family's past to find a killer. Melanie's dad, Abe Grodnick, who had terminal cancer, would die easier if he knew what had happened to his sister. Christine agreed to investigate.

There was much that the Grodnick family had not known about Iris: i.e. a marriage, a divorce, problems at the office. There was also something Abe knew but hesitated to reveal.

By *The Valentine's Day Murder* (Fawcett, 1997), Jack and Christine were expecting their first child. She had no intention of getting involved when acquaintance Carlotta French asked for help in finding her missing husband, Val. But when the bodies of Val Krassky's two best friends, who had been his companions on the night of his disappearance, emerged from Lake Erie, finding Val took on a new dimension. The reasons for the deaths and the disappearance had to lie in the background of the three young men, but they seemed to have no past.

A casual encounter at a New Year's Day party made Christine and Jack aware of the disappearance of Susan Stark in *The New Year's Eve Murder* (Fawcett, 1997). Even though Christine was still nursing baby Eddie, she looked for Susan. Instead she found another, yet unidentified, young woman dead. She was unsure if Susan was a killer, a victim, or a frightened witness. By now Christine had built up an ensemble of helpers, including Attorney Arnold Gold and Sr. Joseph, head of St. Stephen's convent where Christine had grown up.

An opportunity for a free vacation on Fire Island was too good for Chris and Jack to pass up in *The Labor Day Murder* (Fawcett, 1998). Blue Harbor residents had concealed a secret for fifteen years. When local fire chief Ken Buckley's murdered body was found in the remains of a burned building, questions were raised as to a similar fire 15-16 years before. The need of two persons to know the details of the earlier fire caused two unnecessary deaths.

Some series decline in quality. *The Father's Day Murder* (Fawcett, 1999) surpassed prior narratives. Although Christine's involvement in the affairs of the "Morris Avenue boys" was strained, the characterizations and the gradual disclosures that identified the killer of novelist Art Wien were absorbing. Art had been the lecherous member of the group born and raised in the Bronx, each of whom distinguished himself in a profession or business. Whom had he threatened?

Sister Joseph of St. Stephen's Convent had played a large role in Christine's life as teacher, confidante, and advisor, but, in *The Mother's Day Murder* (Fawcett, 2000), Christine investigated her past. She had been shocked by the appearance at her home of a young woman, presenting herself as a novice at St. Stephen's; then claiming to be Sister Joseph's daughter. When "Tina" was found dead in a nearby yard, Christine invaded Joseph's privacy because the police considered her a suspect in the murder.

During *The April Fools' Day Murder* (Fawcett, 2001), Christine came across as intruding into the lives of people who had a right to their privacy. Although husband Jack was still employed by the New York City Police Department, the death of businessman Willard Platt occurred in a different jurisdiction. Christine had come upon what initially seemed to be Platt's corpse, but was an April Fool's Day prank. Then she learned that he had been murdered hours later. Christine took it upon herself to interview family members and other suspects, asking intimate questions. Not only did Jack not discourage her behavior, he sought official reports to bolster her investigation. The information she gathered was withheld from the appropriate police until the killer was identified.

An open basement window, a heavy rain, and sodden boxes left behind by Aunt Meg sent Christine on a trail in *The Happy Birthday Murder* (Fawcett, 2002). Christine believed that the death of young developmentally disabled Darby Maxwell while visiting in Connecticut was connected to the apparent suicide of reputable businessman Larry Filmore in New York state. Four-year-old Eddie, Christine and Jack's son, had become ill at a birthday party, but it didn't end there. Not up to the quality of earlier books.

Coincidentally Jack and Christine were sent to Israel so that Jack could liaise with Israeli police during *The Bar Mitzvah Murder* (Fawcett, 2004), while their friends Mel and Hal Gross were there. The Grosses were attending an adult bar mitzvah for Hal's wealthy cousin, Gabe. Gabe was abducted, then killed while in Jerusalem, but Jack and Christine came to believe that the roots of the crime were in the United States. As she had previously, Christine withheld significant information from her husband. Too much of a travelogue.

A phone call from an unknown woman who mentioned her 25th wedding anniversary alerted Chris to a double murder in *The Silver Anniversary Murder* (Fawcett, 2005). She involved the police immediately and shared some of what she knew with her husband, Jack, now a private investigator. Detective Joe Fox, with whom Chris had worked before, shared any reports and information he garnered on the case. When Ariana Brinker, daughter of the two victims, surfaced, she and Chris followed an extended trail to discover why her parents had been on the run for over two decades.

An invitation to join Sr. Joseph on a professional trip to Arizona in *The Cinco de Mayo Murder* (Fawcett, 2006) awakened a memory for Christine. With the help of former classmate Mandy, she brought to mind the death of fellow high school student Heinz Gruner. During a summer vacation while a student at Rimson College, Heinz had fallen to his death while hiking in Arizona. Motivated by Heinz's mother's grief and sense of guilt, Christine investigated, hoping to prove that he had not killed himself. He had not been alone on the mountainside.

At least one of the earlier Christine Bennett books is being republished as authored by Syrell Leahy. Author Lee Harris has recently begun a new series, featuring Detective Jane Bauer.

Lilly Bennett

Author: Marne Davis Kellogg

After Lilly Bennett finished her debutante years, she had to choose between marriage to a proper suitor or a job. She entered an unlikely profession for a person of her social class—police work. When that became a bore, she combined her years of experience as chief of detectives in Santa Bianca, California with her family's financial and social clout in her hometown of Roundup, Wyoming to set up her own investigative agency. Lilly was an unregenerate right-winger, proud of her Western heritage, resentful of big government, and intolerant of those less fortunate. The status of her "international security agency" was bolstered by a rigged appointment as a U.S. Marshall. A single woman in her forties, she was strikingly attractive with chestnut hair and turquoise eyes. She captured the attention of Richard Jerome, the most eligible man in Roundup and a New York City transplant who managed the local opera. That's right! There was opera in Roundup, Wyoming; a clue that reality was not essential to the background of the narrative. Country girl, maybe, but Lilly could appraise the cost of a guest's attire with a single glance.

As *Bad Manners* (Warner, 1995) began, Lilly attended a party at the home of wealthy publisher Walter Butterfield during which he was murdered. His ambitious daughter Ellen was holding the gun when Lilly entered, but her docile twin sister Christine confessed. Roundup not only had grand opera, but soap opera as the suspects' sexual peccadilloes were revealed.

Lilly's loyalty to childhood friend, Fancy French, was tested in *Curtsey* (Warner, 1996). Fancy fell off the wagon, only to find herself a suspect in the murder of Rita, Baroness von Sigen und Mengen. The Baron, also a suspect, hired Lilly to prove otherwise. She did so with her usual supercilious competence.

Lilly was not used to waiting for anything that she wanted, but in *Tramp* (Doubleday, 1997), Richard Jerome could not get her attention long enough to propose. She was embroiled in the affairs of the Roundup Repertory Company, and the death in her presence of its primary backer, Cyrus Vaile. Recently appointed to the Repertory Company's board of directors, and bolstered by her expertise in toxicology, Lilly insisted on an autopsy. The investigation included highly dramatic suspects, a treasure hunt, and a doomed romance for Lilly's brother, Elias. (Minor error in the text: Laurence Olivier did not play Rochester in *Jane Eyre.* That was Orson Welles. Olivier was Heathcliff in *Wuthering Heights*.)

Although she and Richard were to be married in a week, Lilly could not resist a double fee to find the killer of rich and ruthless oil heiress, Alma Rutherford Gilhooly in *Nothing but Gossip* (Doubleday, 1999). The Rutherford family corporation was involved in major renegotiations, which pitted Alma against her half-sister, Mercedes. A frightened killer made four unsuccessful attempts at murder before Lilly cuffed him. The wedding was as elegant as even Lilly's mother could have hoped.

The greed of land developers, the abusive treatment of women and dysfunctional families provided multiple motives in *Birthday Party* (Doubleday, 2000). Members of a prominent Wyoming family were systematically murdered. With help from a Mafia don and support from U.S. Attorney General

Janet Reno and FBI Director Louis Freeh, Lilly and her merry band first identified the killers, then the motive.

Lilly was different, and enjoyed it. Many readers will, too.

Author Marne Davis Kellogg has a new series with Kick Keswick as the protagonist.

Mildred Bennett

Author: Susanna Hofmann McShea

Mildred Bennett was one of a quartet of Connecticut retirees who defied stereotypes. A silver haired woman, almost sixty when her husband left her for his secretary, Mildred returned to Raven's Wing to sell her family home. Her only son had died at twenty-two in a car accident and she was estranged from her daughter. Retired police chief Forrest Haggarty, eccentric nurse Irene Purdy, and Dr. Trevor Bradford became her family.

In *Hometown Heroes* (St. Martin, 1990), Haggarty connected a recent murder to disappearances stretching back to 1944. He injured his back while investigating the woods near Mildred's home. He remained as her guest with medical assistance from Irene and Dr. Bradford. There were those who considered Forrest's suspicions to be signs of senility. His friends rallied to prove otherwise, although the solution was hard to accept.

By *The Pumpkin Shell Wife* (St. Martin, 1992), Forrest and Irene were living together. His back problems had subsided and her need for isolation had ended. They joined with Mildred to discover why Esther Maine, a local mother of four children, would go to a deteriorating New York City hotel, only to be killed. Trevor's return from retirement in California enriched Mildred's life. The quartet moved into the home Mildred owned in New York, gathering information that changed their perceptions of the victim, her husband and other members of her family.

Mildred wanted no more contact with murder, but, in *Ladybug, Ladybug* (St. Martin, 1994), she could not resist the plea of a mother who, like herself, had lost a son. Seminary student Kevin Cannivan had died in what was termed autoerotic asphyxia, but what his mother called murder. The final solution was a bitter revelation, but identified a killer who took vengeance into his own hands. This was the most engrossing narrative in an improving series. Sadly, at that point, it ended.

Dr. Kate Berman

Author: William Appel

Kate Berman was a psychologist working with the New York City Police Department. She dropped out of her role as a criminologist, but continued her work at the Summerfield Institute in Rhinebeck. Kate's husband Josh had formerly been a Medical Examiner in New York City. When they moved to the countryside, he took a position as medical examiner for Duchess County. There were no children from the marriage, but the Bermans had adopted Kate's orphaned niece, Jenny, who was now in college.

Whisper... He Might Hear You (Donald I. Fine, 1991) employed many of the familiar devices in current novels featuring a female criminologist: (1) media attention which makes a serial killer aware that she may pose a danger; (2) threats against members of her family; and (3) the capacity to invade the mind of the killer, thus being able to predict the next move. Kate, Josh, and Police Chief Bill Casey gradually built a profile of a rich deviant, abused as a child, who sought victims that sounded like his abuser. That could be Jenny, so there was no time to be spared.

A killer with a split personality was revealed at the beginning of *Widowmaker* (Walker, 1994). Police Chief Bill Casey, a widower for six years, was ruining his chances with Nora Cassidy by his excessive drinking. He asked Josh and Kate for help in this case. Their cooperation and media coverage made them vulnerable to the personal attention of the killer.

Eleanor "Ellie" Bernstein

Author: Denise Dietz

Where there was food, there were calories. Auburn haired Ellie Bernstein joined the fight against weight as a group leader for Weight Winners in Colorado Springs, Colorado. Her weight had been a problem since high school, and probably influenced the break-up of her marriage. She was in her forties, financially secure, obsessed with reruns of *M*A*S*H*, mystery stories, and the Denver Broncos football team. Ellie was the mother of Michael from her marriage to Tony, a real estate broker.

In *Throw Darts at a Cheesecake* (Walker, 1992), Ellie reluctantly accepted that not only were the deaths of successful members of her weight reduction group not accidents, but that she was being stalked. Alone except for her cat, "Jackie Robinson," since her son, Michael had entered college, Ellie formed personal and professional ties with the investigating officer, Lt. Peter Miller.

In *Beat Up a Cookie* (Walker, 1994), remnants of a group that attended a *M*A*S*H* costume party eleven years before were suspects and later, possible victims in the murder of Ginny Whitley, aka "Hot Lips". Individual members of the group dressed as and assumed the personas of characters in the television series. Although the premises were novel, the dialogue was forced.

Ellie re-surfaced in 2005 in *Chain a Lamb Chop to the Bed* (Five Star). Painter Garrett Holliday and his redheaded wife Heather had been friends of Ellie for years. When portraits of Heather were slashed and left behind in the homes of purchasers who had been murdered, Ellie became involved. After all she too had modeled for Garrett. Her preoccupation with these cases had to be put aside because Lt. Peter Miller needed time off and wanted to spend it with her at Lonesome Pines Ranch near Aspen. He didn't realize that among the other guests and staff members were several closely connected to the Holliday family.

Ellie and Peter Miller reappear in *Strangle a Loaf of Italian Bread* (2009).

Constable Judy Best

Author: Stephen Cook

Judy Best, a lean blonde Englishwoman, had spent four years working in a bank before she decided on a career as a police officer. The male-dominated atmosphere in the Rotherhite Village area was problem enough, but her romance with Clinton Pink, a black telephone installer, created hostility. Her color blindness was an asset when she was assigned to patrol racially mixed Chaucer Estates.

During *Dead Fit* (St. Martin, 1992), Judy's membership in the Docklands Squash and Weights Club led to harassment by financier Duncan Stock. Stock's murder was solved quickly by the arrest of two layabouts, a solution unacceptable to Judy. At this point even Clinton let her down, suggesting that they "cool it". Winston Leggit and Wayne White, the jailed suspects, knew Judy from her time on the beat and trusted her. She did not let them down, even though she had to work things out without support from fellow officers.

Enterprising real estate developer Derek Kingswood joined with local Tory leader John Bullock during *One Dead Tory* (Foul Play, 1994) to condemn city property for commercial development. More aware of public sentiment, Bullock backed out of the deal. When he was found dead, more than his financial escapades were revealed. Judy and her devout partner, Colin Borden, felt the influence of the Masonic Order in political and police circles. She paid a price when she pursued another suspect after the police made an easy arrest.

By *Rotten Apple* (Macmillan, 1996), Judy had been promoted to Detective Inspector. She did not relish her assignment to investigate Brian Ruddock, a sadistic fellow police officer who had been accused of harassing a bank robbery suspect's wife and a young police recruit, and of possible involvement in robberies. Although Judy supported Ruddock's claim that a suspect gun had been planted in his home, she became persona non grata on the squad for her activities, as well as the target of a hit man. It did not help that Ruddock's attorney was Phil Masters, Judy's discarded lover. Another grim police procedural.

These were dark narratives with realistically crude dialogue. Author Stephen Cook offered more than puzzle solutions. He was concerned about discrimination, favoritism in public office, and police brutality.

Petronella "Petey" Biggers

Authors: Crabbe Evers, pseudonym for William Brashler and Reinder Van Til

The inclusion of a helpful niece, "Petey" Biggers, to the baseball mystery series featuring retired sportswriter Duffy House, helped. Duffy's jargon and interminable reminiscences cried out for relief. "Petey" began as a supporting character, but moved up to equal status.

Duffy's retirement was cut short by appeals from Baseball Commissioner, "Grand" Granville Chambliss, to solve murders. "Petey," a Phi Beta Kappa from Oberlin who had planned to attend Northwestern Law School, convinced Uncle Duffy to let her help. She was the classic redhead with green eyes, a prototype for adventuresome young women. Each book focused on a different team and ballpark.

Murder in Wrigley Field (Bantam, 1991) was set in Chicago, Duffy's hometown. The victim was young and promising Cubs pitcher, "Dream" Weaver who had been shot outside the team dressing room. "Petey" went undercover as a groupie; dated several of the players, and cozied up to the club manager's wife. Meanwhile Duffy, using more conventional methods to investigate, needed Petey to go to bat for him.

Murderer's Row (Bantam, 1991) took Duffy to New York and to Rupert Huston, the obnoxious, interfering manager of the New York Yankees. Huston was killed on hallowed ground, the center field monuments at Yankee Stadium. This prompted Petey to join Uncle Duffy in New York. She was fascinated by the combination of baseball and murder. She and Duffy worked on parallel tracks but both came to the same unhappy conclusion about the killer. Lots of name dropping, but good background on the sport.

Bleeding Dodger Blue (Bantam, 1991) sent Duffy to Los Angeles seeking background for his memoirs. He witnessed the murder of Dodger's manager Jack Remsen, purportedly by the notorious Sunset Slasher. At Chambliss' suggestion, Petey joined the investigation. She saved Duffy's life again. It took more time to find the "copycat" who killed Remsen.

Fear in Fenway (Morrow, 1993) found rival factions competing to purchase the Red Sox from widow Patsy Dougherty. Duffy, who had been invited to attend an Old Timers Celebration, brought Petey as his guest. A series of murders might be connected to the possible sale. Duffy was distracted by the magnetic Patsy, so Petey did much of the footwork, using the Commissioner's name to open doors, even at the police department.

Cries of anguish from Detroit Tigers fans about the owner's plan to move the team from Tiger Stadium prompted Duffy to assess the situation in *Tiger's Burning* (Morrow, 1994). Duffy's pal, Jimmy Casey, who had been the announcer for Tiger games for 35 years, contacted him. He had been fired because he knew of corruption in the plan to get a new ball park. Duffy went to Detroit arriving there on the "Night of the Hawk", annual rioting and burning. The torching of the stadium and the death of Kit Gleason, a dedicated fan whose body was found on the premises, kept both Duffy and Petey busy.

Lots more baseball teams and parks but the series ended.

Elizabeth "Lisbee" Billings

Author: Loretta Scott Miller

Lisbee, who graduated with a degree in computer science and a minor in criminal justice, had a job waiting for her. Her father, T.J. Billings and her great-uncle Beau had opened Anadarko Grace Investigations in a former church. Both T. J. and Beau were licensed private investigators. Lisbee was very close to her father; Amelia, her mother, having died from cancer when she was ten. T. J. had his problems too. Uncle Beau had raised him He hadn't done well in school, but finally found a job with his father-in-law as an investigator. When he was ready to go out on his own, Beau a retired Oklahoma oil man joined him in the Santa Cruz, California area. The name Andarko had been T. J.'s hometown in Oklahoma. Lisbee who had suffered nightmares since her mother's death, still used a night light to sleep. She dressed provocatively, and had casual sex.

The initial book, *A Ride on the Trojan Horse* (E-Book, 1st Book Library, 1997), featured the trio in a pair of investigations. T.J. had no choice. He was shot by a sniper en route home from a tryst with a divorced woman. His rescuer, Willa Kelley, had a problem of her own. She was being sexually harassed by Murdock Jones, her handyman. Lisbee, who had agreed to check computer security for Jeremy Boal of the Evergreen Institute, realized that Jeremy had withheld significant information from her. Meanwhile Beau checked on a car that might have belonged to the sniper that injured T.J. There were multiple subplots but they were well blended.

The second book, *Cypher,* was published in 2000; then reprinted in 2006 by Shannon Road Press. The narrative had a complex background, the black-market in corporate software and the discovery by retired professor Dean Deutch of a program (*Hole in the Dike*) that could bypass existing computer security systems, threatening the future of local Pan Global Inc. All three of the Billings had connections to those involved. T.J. had promised his old friend Harley Sullivan to investigate the death of his grandson, Chipper who worked for Pan Global. The quid pro quo was Harley's gift to T.J. of a trawler, the "Emily T." Great Uncle Beau had been hired to check the welfare of developmentally disabled Camellia Teng, whose protective brother Rudy was involved in a scheme originated by Chipper. Lisbee had studied higher math with Professor Deutch, became personally involved with Deputy Justin Highstreet, and had provided counsel on security to Pan Global. There was a considerable amount of technical material woven into the narrative.

Verity "Birdie" Birdwood

Author: Jennifer Rowe

At first it was unclear whether Verity "Birdie" Birdwood or her old school friend Kate Delaney was intended to be the primary sleuth in this Australian series. Succeeding books gave the advantage to Birdie. She was a strange creature, moving in and out of the novels and short stories. Trained as a solicitor, Birdie chose not to practice law, instead did research for the Australian Broadcasting Corporation. Her inherited wealth made work an option, not a necessity. Kate, a book editor, remained a continuing character, often triggering Birdie's involvement with murder. Birdie's name was appropriate. She was tiny with frizzy brown hair, an insatiable appetite for adventure and puzzles, but emotionally detached.

Tension abounded in *Grim Pickings* (Bantam, 1991) when Kate, her husband Jeremy Darcy, and their daughter attended the annual apple picking at her Aunt Alice's rural home. Alice lived within a colony of relatives who competed for control and wealth. Betsy Tender, Alice's controlling niece, who meant well and was well-organized insisted that Alice move to town. She had no tolerance for members of the family who did not meet her standards. The death of Damien Treloar, an estranged in-law, caused hidden resentments to surface and exposed an unexpected motive for murder.

In *Murder by the Book* (Bantam, 1992), Kate made Birdie aware of the conflicts among four distinguished Australian writers who were being honored by publishers Berry & Michaels. Before Birdie took a hand, eminent author Sir Saul Murdoch and royalties manager Sylvia De Groot were murdered to protect a reputation. The question was : whose reputation?

In *Death in Store* (Doubleday, 1993), Birdie worked with Kate and Detective Dan Toby in short stories that expanded upon the characters of Birdie, who solved her first mystery at fourteen, Jeremy and his romantic past; and Kate, who fooled everyone but Birdie.

Author Jennifer Rowe staged a traditional gathering of suspects at an isolated beauty spa in *The Makeover Murders* (Doubleday, 1993). Birdie, an unlikely candidate for a beauty spa, was researching Deepdene, but concealed her identity. When it became apparent that the murder of spa manager Margot Bell was connected to prior deaths, Dan Toby and Birdie probed the past to learn who killed, and would kill again.

Birdie's past surfaced in *Stranglehold* (Bantam, 1995) when her probe into the murder of her father's close friend, radio raconteur Max Tully, included as suspects family members with whom she had played as a child.

In *Lamb to the Slaughter* (Bantam, 1996), Jude Gregorian, an idealistic attorney who had been very close to Birdie during her law school years, was instrumental in the release of a convicted killer. Jude and Birdie accompanied Trevor Lamb when he returned to the scene of his wife Daphne's death, taunting and laughing, until someone silenced him. This was a painful experience for Birdie.

The introspective Birdie was balanced by hot-blooded characters and dramatic interactions.

Jennifer Rowe has a second series featuring Tessa Vance.

Angela "Angie" Biwaban

Author: J. F. Trainor

Native American sleuth Angela Biwaban combined criminal activities with her investigations. She described herself as 5' 4", slim with dark eyes, hair, and skin, and twenty-eight years old. A member of the Minnesota Anishinabe tribe (Chippewa), Angela had a Master's degree in accounting from Montana State University, which she misused to embezzle money for her mother's medical care. During her sentence in a South Dakota women's prison, she learned a new set of skills. Angie's father had died when she was in junior high and her mother died from cancer while she was in prison. Her grandfather Charlie Blackbear remained a stable element in her life and shared in her adventures.

Target for Murder (Zebra, 1993) introduced Angie as a fugitive from probation officer Paul Holbrook. Her old friend Mary Beth Tolliver, widowed, pregnant, and penniless, needed help to resettle. Angie had a broader agenda: to restore the Tolliver fortune, and punish Jim Tolliver's killer.

As *Dynamite Pass* (Zebra, 1993) opened, Angie had expanded her furlough to visit family in Utah and conduct her own investigation of the "accidental" death of her cousin Bill, an employee of the National Forest Service. Assuming an identity as speculator Sara Soyazhe, Angie insinuated herself into the circle of local businessmen who would benefit from Bill's death. She made a profit doing so.

In *Whiskey Jack* (Zebra, 1994), former ally Mick Grantz had been jailed in Port Wyoochee, Washington for the murder of his ex-wife. Angela followed the pattern of false identity and a scam to entice local profiteers. She had to be more careful. The FBI was searching for "Pocahontas," based on her prior activities. She left the villain and her false identity in the quicksand.

In *Corona Blue* (Kensington, 1994), Angie was relegated to farm work as part of her probation. Shots fired at the combine machine she was driving, a disappearing corpse, and family secrets brought her to the attention of the authorities. Assuming another identity, Angie conned local banker Sam Covington into providing mortgage money for her farmer friends. Bankers were fair game for Angela.

In *High Country Murder* (Kensington, 1995), Angie pulled her "drop game" to bail out the Rooley family mortgage. This was an unlikely gesture. Sarah Rooley Sutton had made Angie's life miserable at her most recent work placement. However someone had almost run Angie down while she was wearing Sarah's clothes. That made it personal and in the process, she was able to set aside some valuables for her future.

The Biwaban adventures will appeal to those who like a touch of larceny in their heroine, and a good read at paperback prices. Later books, beginning with *Corona Blue*, went hardcover but they were worth it.

Helen Black

Author: Pat Welch

Helen Black, in a partially humorous vein, referred to her cat, Boobella, as having lasted longer than her girlfriends. She had been raised in a Southern community dominated by fundamentalist religion. Her Uncle Loy and Aunt Edna had helped Helen when her father rejected her after he saw her kissing a girl.

Although initially a police officer, Helen became a private investigator in Berkeley, California by the time *Murder by the Book* (Naiad, 1990) began. After a bank robbery that included murder, she was hired by Donna Forsythe to prove that Donna's lesbian lover Marita was not involved. Police Officer Manny Dominguez, Helen's former partner, provided her with inside information on the bank staff, the security measures, and possible suspects. Vignettes about employees were interspersed with Helen's investigation. Helen's lover during the series was Frieda, an artist, who did not approve of Helen's occupation.

In *Still Waters* (Naiad, 1991), Helen investigated the death of former mentor Jill Gallagher, a newspaper reporter who had been working her way back from alcoholism. Frieda insisted on accompanying her. Their relationship did not survive the tensions and the personal jealousy that resulted.

During *A Proper Burial* (Naiad, 1993), Frieda brought Cecily Bennett, her new lover, to Helen for assistance when the young woman questioned the death of her Aunt Elizabeth. Helen worked her way through the murky problems of the politically powerful Bennett family and reunited with Frieda.

Open House (Naiad, 1995) brought Helen back to her Mississippi roots, when she inherited a home from an elderly aunt. She rekindled a relationship with Beth, a youthful lover now a police officer. Helen unearthed a scandal involving local gentry, including a member of her own family.

At the request of Dr. Jill Mason, now Frieda's partner, Helen went undercover in the Pro-Life movement during *Smoke and Mirrors* (Naiad, 1996). Members of Dr. Howard Logan's fundamentalist church were picketing the Linville Memorial Clinic in Lafayette, California. When accountant Melinda Wright was killed on clinic property, the first assumption was that the protestors were responsible. The second premise was that Jill Mason was the killer. Helen found a new love from among the clinic volunteers, and some compassion for Dr. Logan, even through she disagreed with his beliefs. She described her own position on abortion as support for a woman's right to choose, rather than for abortion itself.

Helen, in need of money, took on a hopeless case. She was hired to prove that young female executive Leslie Merrick had not committed suicide in *Fallen from Grace* (Naiad, 1998). She had been fired from her position at Centurion Sportswear, but jumping out of an 8th story window seemed extreme, Although Helen was beaten, bruised and almost killed, she battled a major corporation and a frightened killer. Saving Vicky Young, the mother of her current lover Alison, was a bonus.

Helen was in bad shape physically, emotionally, and financially in *Snake Eyes* (Naiad, 1999). Unable to go back to her agency, she took a minimum wage job as a security guard at a factory. Then came the invitation for Helen and Alison to join her beloved Aunt Edna and Uncle Loy at a Nevada hotel where they had won a Thanksgiving weekend vacation. Romie's Catfish Restaurants, now managed by Carmen Kittrick, who was enmeshed in family problems, had sponsored the contest. This was a fine kettle of fish, but it brought back Helen's urge to investigate when Carmen was murdered.

The dismal descent of Helen continued in *Moving Targets* (Bella Books, 2001), when she returned to Tupelo, Mississippi for her Uncle Loy's funeral. She had planned to stay only to comfort Aunt Edna and her developmentally disabled son, Bobby. Helen, suffering from depression, could not resist her need for alcohol. Revelations as to Uncle Loy's involvement with another woman led to a series of deaths. There had been a cover-up in Tupelo. This time Helen's efforts to expose the guilty brought her to disaster.

There was nowhere for Helen to go but up in *A Day Too Long* (Bella, 2003c). Released on parole from prison, she settled in Tynedale, Mississippi where her Aunt Edna and Cousin Bobby lived. Her prison sentence was based on a conviction for negligent homicide. Once settled with a job at Smart Save warehouse, Helen moved into Mrs. Mapple's boarding house. The disappearance of nine-year-old Sissy Greene, who resided there with her mother, now in the process of a divorce, was the start of more trouble for Helen. She had found the child's corpse in a park.

Out of prison and back in California in *A Time to Cast Away* (Bella, 2005), Helen had little hope for the future. With her prison record, she would be unable to get a private investigator's license. She coped with temporary jobs arranged by an agency. A single act of kindness, giving a drunken Alice Harmon a ride home, brought change. Concerned about Alice's welfare, Helen returned. She and the apartment building supervisor found her body. The responding police officer was Helen's former cop partner Manny Hernandez, but he cut her no slack. Only the kindness of lesbian minister Maggie Evans brought hope to Helen as she sought Alice's killer.

The narratives included explicit sexual passages.

Elizabeth Blair

Author: Lizbie Brown pseudonym for Mary Marriott

Elizabeth left her native Virginia after her husband Jim died in an accident caused by a drunken driver. She selected Bath, England as a location for her shop, "Martha Washington," which featured such distinctly American craftwork as quilts. The book titles were the names of quilt patterns. Elizabeth had three sons and a daughter, who were dismayed by her decision to move to

England, but did not oppose it. Kate, the eldest was a New York City newspaper reporter; Jim, Jr was married with a family; the twins, Ed, a doctor, and Holly, a nurse, lived near one another in Michigan. Elizabeth's interest in England stemmed from genealogical research into an ancestor, Robert Lightfoot, who immigrated to America in 1744. Her shop was located beneath the detective agency run by young Max Shepard, who involved her in his investigations.

As Elizabeth settled gently into Bath in *Broken Star* (St. Martin, 1992), another newcomer was less accommodating. Television star Larry Aitken irritated the locals with his demands. When Dr. Charles Wetherall, a critic of Aitken's was poisoned under suspicious circumstances, Aitken hired Max to find the killer, which he did with Elizabeth's assistance.

Max was helping Helen Weston, a recently divorced woman, search for her kidnapped children in *Turkey Tracks* (St. Martin, 1995). While he was busy, Elizabeth took on a case of her own. Joanna Drew, the sister of the curator of the Wetherburn Museum, had been shot. Elizabeth was asked to substitute for her at the museum. She saw that as an opportunity to learn more about the Drew/Maddock families and to verify a connection with ALF (Animal Liberation Front) which had targeted her shop.

Elizabeth spent far less time in her quilt shop as she became more involved in Max Shepard's detective agency in *Shoo-Fly* (Hodder & Stoughton, 1998). An ailing Hubert Neville wanted to know who killed his charming son, Julian, and why he was killed. The multiple suspects were fellow workers and their spouses who had suffered humiliation and rejection from the careless Julian. On the happier side, Max divested himself of a faithless lover, finding a satisfactory replacement on hand.

Groom Johnny Mullligan's pregnant former lover Kat Gregg, who disrupted the wedding in *Double Wedding Ring* (Hodder & Stoughton, 1998), was found murdered later that night. Not surprisingly, Mulligan was most likely to be suspected. His mother Rose, a cleaning woman, hired the Shepard Agency to prove Johnny's innocence. The subsequent death of antique dealer Marcus Finney who had discovered the corpse widened the circle of suspects. Elizabeth focused her attention only after she found the pattern.

In *Jacob's Ladder* (Hodder & Stoughton, 2000), Elizabeth was overwhelmed by the flu and by the anniversaries of her husband's death and of a regretted miscarriage early in her marriage. Her sense of depression deepened when an unwanted infant was deposited at the front door of Rev. Philip Fletcher, the philandering local vicar. Max set her to work on the mysterious death of famous explorer Connor Bartram, a man so obsessed with his career than he had nothing left for his children or their mothers. Every member of his family had a motive to kill Bartram but until that circle widened, Elizabeth could not identify the killer. These incidents caused Elizabeth to reflect on her relationships with her own children.

Elizabeth's contact with actress Flora Messel while sharing a train compartment had been brief and unpleasant in *Cat's Cradle* (Hodder & Stoughton,

2001). Still, she was one of the last to see Flora alive and might identify fellow passengers. A contact by the police department launched Elizabeth and Max into a parallel investigation. Flora's complex family relationships and her professional contacts were replete with suspects. Two subsequent deaths raised the stakes for a killer. Max's indolence almost cost Elizabeth her life.

The series will appeal to readers of cozies. Her doggedness, her awareness of patterns, and the connections between historical quilt patterns and current events distinguished Elizabeth.

Sonora Blair

Author: Lynn S. Hightower

Sonora Blair accepted her widowhood with grace. Her husband had been unfaithful. Her work as a homicide specialist with the Cincinnati, Ohio police department kept her busy. She was a tiny blonde in her thirties with two children: Tim, a teenager, and Heather, age seven.

"Flash," a serial killer who utilized fire to murder white males, felt an affinity to Sonora in *Flashpoint* (HarperCollins, 1995). Sonora could not ignore the fact that Flash knew intimate details of her parents' lives and her mother's death. The pressure escalated when Flash killed in what was perceived to be a favor to Sonora.

As *Eyeshot* (HarperCollins, 1996) began, Sonora and Detective Sam Delarosa were skeptical when Butch Winchell identified body parts to be those of his missing and unfaithful wife. Evidence in Julia Winchell's luggage and in messages indicated otherwise. While at a Cincinnati conference she had identified a man whom she had seen commit a murder eight years before. But the man she recognized was a popular official who would use every tool to discredit Sam and Sonora.

Too many things went wrong at once in *No Good Deed* (Delacorte, 1998). Fifteen-year-old Joelle Chauncey and the horse she had been riding were missing. Stable owner Donna Delaney had been maimed, but was unwilling to discuss her injury. Sonora and her unit focused on the child until her body was discovered buried in a manure pile. There were possible connections among the incidents that had to be investigated. Sonora's role was complicated by the presence of a federal agent whom Sonora found personally attractive but professionally annoying. She had decided who the killer was early on, as will some readers, but needed a motive.

Sonora was barely managing financially as *The Debt Collector* (Hodder & Stoughton, 2000) began. She and Sam Delarosa were horrified when they investigated a home invasion in which four of five members of the Stinnet family were killed. She felt no sense of closure when two of the killers were assassinated. There had been a third man involved whom she intended to identify. On a personal level, Sonora had ended an unhappy relationship and was sharing her life with Mark Gillane, an emergency room doctor. She also needed to evaluate her role as a mother. Was her career eating up time that her children deserved?

Sonora was vulnerable—an intimate relationship with a potential victim during a murder case damaged her professional reputation. Hightower has a second series featuring Lena Padgett, a private investigator. Lena's first appearance in *Satan's' Lambs* in 1993 was not followed up until after 20001, but she has since made at least two appearances.

Eliza Blake

Author: Mary Jane Clark

As the series began, Eliza Blake was a widow. Her husband John had died of cancer when Eliza was pregnant with their daughter Janie. Eliza had grown up in Newport, Rhode Island where she attended the University of Rhode Island. Now she juggled her career at television station KEY with her responsibilities to four-year-old Janie. Eliza initially worked for a KEY affiliate in Providence, but so impressed the New York office that she was invited to become the co-anchor for their morning news program, *KEY to America.* Bill Kendall, anchorman on the evening news had become her dear friend and mentor. At thirty- four, she was a tall woman with brown hair, and had recovered from a breakdown that occurred after John's death. Unfortunately Eliza did not have a rewarding relationship with her overprotective mother.

Bill Kendall's death and the subsequent revelation that he was HIV positive in *Do You Want to Know a Secret?* (St. Martin, 1998) created havoc among his survivors: a divorced wife, a handicapped son, and the married woman who had been his lover. Although Eliza provided short-term relief on the evening news, KEY News president, Yelena Gregory, chose ambitious Pete Carlson as the permanent replacement. Planted material in the tabloids inferred that Eliza's breakdown and subsequent counseling were the result of drug abuse, Eliza probed the deaths of Bill and her therapist until she uncovered political skullduggery.

Eliza had a few lines in *Let Me Whisper in Your Ear* (St. Martin, 2000) and appeared by references in *Do You Promise Not to Tell* (St. Martin's, 2000) as a fellow staff member at KEY News, but had no personal impact on the plots.

Eliza's experience with a treacherous housekeeper in the big city prompted her move to Ho-Ho-Kus, New Jersey in *Close to You* (St. Martin, 2001). The problems of being a television newscaster followed her and her five-year-old daughter Janie even as they sought refuge. Stalkers, admirers, and hopeful aspirants for her personal affection all became suspects when threatening messages, phone calls, and a burglary caused the network to provide protection. The precautions were ineffective against a wily fanatic, but Eliza had learned to protect herself.

Whatever family atmosphere existed among staff at KEY evaporated quickly during *When Day Breaks* (Morrow, 2007). Constance Young, who had replaced Eliza in the morning news program, defected to a rival network.

Executive producer Linus Nazareth was aware that a significant segment of the show's audience would follow Constance to her new position. He selected his current romantic interest, Lauren Adams, to replace her. Eliza, now anchor for the KEY evening news, was caught between Constance and Lauren and their staffs. When Constance's body was discovered, she had possession of a valuable Arthurian piece of jewelry which had disappeared from the Cloisters Museum. Clues emerged slowly but the Sunrise Suspense Society, consisting of producer Annabelle Murphy, cameraman B.J. D'Elia, and Dr. Margo Gonzalez, worked with Eliza to a successful conclusion.

What could be more horrifying for Eliza than to have her only child, Jane, abducted along with her housekeeper, Carmen Garcia, in *It Only Takes a Moment* (Morrow, 2008)? Once it was established that Jane had been lured away from Camp Musquapsink, Eliza called on every resource: her close friends, local police and the FBI. Frustrated by a series of false leads, Eliza even sought help from a psychic.

Clark's series really is based on an ensemble. Next: *Dying for Mercy* (2009).

Josephine Blake

Author: Janet Harward

The series could be described as a police procedural with personal overtones. In her early forties, Josephine Blake was a blonde but graying detective inspector in Devon, England. Armed with a college degree, she had worked her way up the ranks from WPC (woman police constable). Even then, she encountered gender discrimination on the job from supervisors, co-workers and those whom she supervised. Her marriage to Tom had suffered from Josephine's dedication to her career, eventually causing him to leave, and then divorce her. Their daughter, Jessica, a teenager preparing for University, had a considerable amount of unsupervised time.

In *The Teddy Bear Murders* (O'Neill, 1996), Josephine was assigned to serial murders. In each incident the killer had left a teddy bear at the scene of the crime. The circle of suspects included men and women who frequented the Blue Forest, a club for single, divorced and separated persons. Procedure eventually solved the crimes, but there were avenues left unexplored early in the case that will annoy experienced mystery readers.

In Memory of Murder (O'Neill, 1997) had more intricate plotting. Vicious attacks on teenage girls were interwoven with a series of what seemed to be accidents and suicides. With Jessica away at college and Tom working out of town, Josephine could concentrate on the investigation. An attack of conscience by a conspirator prevented a final murder and identified a remorseless killer.

Echoes of Death (O'Neill, 1998) showed continued improvement, but again featured a serial killer. The criminal who fashioned his activities on those of Jack the Ripper had a personal fascination with Josephine. She was intended to be his final victim. The leap of deduction made by Josephine in tying current cases to the Ripper was a stretch. The divorce from Tom freed Josephine for an affair with forensic psychologist, Dr. Andrew Blythe.

Josephine was plagued by both her physical injuries and the emotional trauma from the attack by a copycat Jack the Ripper as *Death Is the Issue* (O'Neill, 1999) began. After an initial recovery, she requested a six-month secondment to Birmingham, her hometown. "Brim" had changed. It was larger. There were more crimes, traffic hazards. The landmarks of her youth had been replaced. Because of Josephine's reputation, her new supervisor, DCI Robert Lyle demanded a quick solution to several deaths and mutilations occurring along the city canals. Jo seemed abrasive and humorless.

Julie Blake

Author: Sally Chapman

Having already developed an ulcer earning success as an executive in the computer industry, Julie did not need a murder. After a Stanford University MBA and experience in the field, she had become the head of a major research project in Silicon Valley. A tiny brunette and former air force brat, Julie at thirty-four was engaged to Charles Stafford, a handsome fellow executive at ICI Computer, Inc. She ate out even for breakfast and gulped Maalox.

The murder of co-worker Ronald Gershbein in *Raw Data* (St. Martin, 1991) sidetracked both Julie's professional and personal goals. Gershbein had been working at the office on a restricted defense project. Because of high security, no outsider could have committed the crime. Julie's computer skills meshed with those of Vic Paoli of the National Security Agency to trap a killer. The experience convinced her to abandon her current job to join Paoli in detecting computer fraud. Her engagement having ended, she and Paoli became lovers.

Business came slowly to the new firm, Data 9000 Investigators. In *Love Bytes* (St. Martin, 1994), they were hired to locate Arnie Lufkin, an accused computer thief who had disappeared while released on bail. Julie, recognizing that Lufkin, a specialist in virtual reality, would be a formidable adversary, risked her own safety and that of her best friend, "Max" La Costa.

Sex intertwined with technology in *Cyberkiss* (St. Martin, 1996). Short on clients and cash, Julie convinced Paoli that they should find "Night Dancer," the anonymous correspondent on ErotikNet, who was threatening Bernie Kowolsky, a Biotech manager. For a while it was unclear if Bernie had indeed been murdered or merely injured. After his remains were found and his girlfriend, Gloria Reynolds was murdered, they realized that Night Dancer was someone very close to Bernie.

By *Hardwired* (St. Martin, 1997) Julie, Vic Paoli, and their dog Cosmos had settled into a comfortable home and office lifestyle. Margo Miller, Vic's ex-girlfriend, approached him with an offer. NASA Mission Control in Houston was having computer problems. They wanted an outside agency to clear them up before the next astronaut team was launched. Strange experiences on a prior flight were somehow connected to this phenomenon. Battling against interference from Houston's temporary director Lisa Foster and her own jealousy of Margo, Julie, with Vic's help, tracked a secret satellite and mercenary scientists.

Technical enough to fascinate some but bore others.

Dr. Joanna Blalock

Author: Leonard Goldberg

Female sleuths operating as forensic pathologists have been very popular since Patricia Cornwall's Kay Scarpetta. Joanne Blalock, a tall slender blonde in her thirties, worked at a Los Angeles hospital complex. She had a distinguished education and career, but her personal life had been incomplete since her divorce. Her widowed mother, suffering from Alzheimer's, died before the second narrative. Her father had died earlier in a plane crash. Her only sibling was a sister, Kate.

Joanna's friend, nurse Karen Rhodes, contacted her for help in *Deadly Medicine* (Signet, 1992), but was dead before they could meet. Karen's father, an U.S. Senator, rejecting the initial diagnosis of suicide, allowed Joanna to do the autopsy. Lieutenant Jake Sinclair, who became her live-in lover, attributed the death to a serial killer while Joanna focused on Karen's connection with recent brain research.

Hospitals did not provide a safe place for professional staff in *A Deadly Practice* (Signet, 1994). Members of a surgical team were not only sued, but murdered. Joanna, whose pathology decisions had been challenged in malpractice proceedings regarding a patient, became the sole surviving defendant in the lawsuit. The anesthesiologist and gynecologist had been murdered. She emerged with her life and reputation intact. These narratives contained segments during which the anonymous killer's viewpoint was expressed.

Deadly Care (Dutton, 1996) found Joanna overburdened at work and angry about her relationship with Jake, who had traveled to Greece for his ex-wife Eleni's funeral. At the hospital she sought (1) the identity of a female corpse whose face had been battered and fingertips removed, and (2) the pattern in the deaths of patients, which threatened the viability of the hospital transplant programs and the reputation of a major medical supplier.

Joanna and Jake had ended their relationship as *Deadly Harvest* (Dutton, 1997) began. She had a personal interest in transplanted organs because her sister, Kate, an archeologist, who became ill while working in Guatemala, might need one. Professionally, she was concerned by deterioration in transplanted livers, one of which was in the corpse of a murdered man. Jake Sinclair was working the murder case. It was his generosity and kindness to Kate that brought them back together. Scientific intrigue and raw greed did not show up in biopsies, but Jake and Joanna found them.

Deadly Exposure (Dutton, 1998) was referred to as a "novel of medical suspense", and was indeed novel. Joanna had been detached from her regular duties to investigate possible toxins which might have been brought to earth by an asteroid which fell 65 years ago. The government agency in charge was ETOX (Extraterrestrial Toxic Agent Team, originally set up to monitor materials returned from trips to the moon.) This investigation was the result of deaths, which occurred in Alaskan waters. Joanne's role was to autopsy the body of a dead Coast Guardsman. In the process she determined why a young boy with asthma had survived the toxin.

Right wing terrorists seeking revenge on the federal government targeted Joanna in *Lethal Measures* (Dutton, 2000). She and Jake traced evidence from a series of bombings and murders to the Ten Righteous, threatening the group's plan for a symbolic act on April 19th. Joanna was heavily guarded but vulnerable when members of her family were threatened. Joanna lost a relationship that she treasured, but rediscovered one that would last.

The third person narrative in *Fatal Care* (Signet, 2001) split into strands: (1) the medical investigation by Joanna and her team as to the incidence of rare cancers among patients who had received an experimental artery cleansing; (2) the police procedural featuring Jake Sinclair who probed the deaths of a distinguished researcher, the financial backer of a genetics laboratory; and a burly Russian immigrant, and (3) the interactions among the villains.

Karen Crandall's unique combination of doctoral level training in physics and her medical degree in neurology made her a brilliant scientist and inventor, but in *Brainwaves* (Signet, 2002), it earned her the enmity of her co-workers at the Brain Research Institute of Memorial Hospital. Her death, badly disguised as suicide, did not fool Jake Sinclair or Joanna Blalock. Brain surgeon Dr. Christopher Moran, a member of the BRI staff, had problems of his own. Two recent surgical patients had died. Simon Murdoch, hospital administrator and Moran maintained that there was no evidence of malpractice. Joanna was more skeptical. Goldberg wound these two strands into his narrative, but the medical technology was awesome and the future prospects, frightening.

Joanna was already experiencing burn-out as *Fever Cell* (Signet, 2003) began. She had come to believe that there was no future for her with Jake Sinclair. Then the FBI called her to do the autopsy on terrorist Mohammed Malik, only to learn that Jake was her local contact with FBI investigator William Kitt. She and Jake were in touch, but worked separately; he, out in the field; she in the more dangerous infectious disease unit. Each had to contend with confusion caused by the CIA and FBI agents who had agendas of their own. This was a post 9/11 novel which raised chilling questions about biological warfare.

A well plotted series.

Ursula Blanchard

Author: Fiona Buckley

Ursula Blanchard grew up during the period following the death of Henry VIII of England. She was aware of the bloody pogroms carried out by his Catholic daughter, Mary, and by the turbulent Protestant reign of Elizabeth.

Ursula's mother Anna had been an attendant to Ann Boleyn, whom Henry executed. Anna's unwed pregnancy caused her to be sent home from the palace to an unforgiving family. She died while still a teenager. Care of Ursula was transferred to her Uncle Herbert and Aunt Tabitha who were adherents of the Catholic faith. Ursula escaped their control when she ran off to marry Gerald Blanchard, scion of a prominent family. The young couple lived in Holland where Gerald served Sir Thomas Graham, representative of the Queen. Among Gerald's duties were those connected to espionage, but his premature death came from a case of smallpox.

Remembering Anna's devotion to Ann Boleyn and Gerald's services to herself, Elizabeth granted Ursula a place at court. Their daughter Meg was farmed out to friends, Rob Henderson and his wife. Over time a special relationship developed between Ursula and the Queen.

By *To Shield the Queen* (Scribners, 1997) a.k.a. *The Robsart Mystery*, Ursula had made powerful friends at Court. Sir William Cecil, advisor to Elizabeth, recruited her to watch over Amy Robsart, the seriously ill wife of Sir Robert Dudley. Amy's death placed suspicion on Dudley who had remained at Court to romance the Queen. Ursula became friendly with Matthew de la Roche, widowed son of a French father and English mother, who had returned to England to manage family estates. Elizabeth had Ursula's loyalty but she loved Matthew, a Catholic.

Matthew and Ursula had married, but parted by *The Doublet Affair* (Scribners, 1998). He had been exiled to France after Ursula uncovered a Catholic plot. She was still in the Queen's service, sent this time to spy upon the Masons, a Catholic family that had come under suspicion. Aided by faithful servants, Ursula used recently acquired lock picking skills to identify the disloyal and dishonest killers.

Ursula agreed to accompany Luke Blanchard, her former father-in-law, to France in *Queen's Ransom* (Scribners, 2000). She would not only serve as an escort to bring Helene, Luke's niece, to England but would carry a message to the French Queen Regent. Ursula had a third reason for going to France, the hope that she might be with Matthew again. There were other agendas of which she was initially unaware.

An unfortunate loss prompted Ursula's husband Matthew to arrange for Meg to join her mother in France as *To Ruin a Queen* (Scribners, 2000) began. When Meg disappeared, Ursula returned to England in a panic, only to learn that she had been lured there to serve again as Queen Elizabeth's spy. Her task was to uncover a plot that might challenge Elizabeth's claim to the throne.

Ursula traded her comfortable home at Withysham for a job in a Cambridge pie shop during *Queen of Ambition* (Pocket Star, 2002). She had been biding her time at her country estate waiting to join her husband Matthew in France as soon as the plague subsided. Ursula and Rob Henderson were sent to Cambridge where Queen Elizabeth would soon visit. A playlet planned by college students to welcome the Queen had a hidden agenda. There were a lot of things hidden: a wife, coded messages, and secret rooms. The death of student Thomas Shawe aroused Ursula's suspicions but created a rift between her and a close comrade.

Although neither Aunt Tabitha nor Uncle Herbert Faldene had any claim to Ursula's loyalty, in *A Pawn for a Queen* (Scribners, 2002) she agreed to locate their son Edward who was en route to Scotland with an updated list of Queen Mary of Scotland's supporters. She went without the knowledge or approval of Queen Elizabeth or Sir William Cecil, but she had Elizabeth's best interest in her heart. She planned to get the list and turn it over to Elizabeth. Postponing her desire for a more peaceful life, she felt the call of excitement. Her Scottish welcome included a sad death and a lawless suitor.

Ursula had enjoyed a respite from intrigue as *The Fugitive Queen* (Scribners, 2003) began. Her new husband, Hugh Stannard was unlikely to get her pregnant but a competent lover. Out of kindness Ursula agreed to be guardian to Penelope Mason, even obtaining a place for the nineteen-year-old at Court. When Penelope disgraced herself by her attentions to a married man, Ursula was instructed to escort her to a gifted estate in Yorkshire where she could meet a suitable but rare husband i.e. a Catholic but supportive of Elizabeth. There were other items on her agenda: to warn Queen Mary to stay out of the enquiry as to Darnley's death and to learn what she could about Mary and her second husband, the Earl of Bothwell.

The placid life which Ursula envisioned as Hugh Stannard's wife, ended abruptly in *The Siren Queen* (Scribners, 2004). At the request of the Duke of Norfolk, Hugh, Ursula, and Meg visited him in London, to consider his secretary Edmund Dean as a suitor for Meg. In the process they became aware that Norfolk was plotting to marry Mary Stuart and see her restored as Queen of Scotland and heir to the English crown. Cecil arranged for Ursula to insert herself into the household of Italian banker Roberto Ridolfi to learn more about the plot. Unfortunately, Gladys Morgan, Ursula's elderly servant, was accused of witchcraft. By this time both Ursula and Queen Elizabeth realize that they have a special connection.

Well written and documented, covering a period in which two Christian religions displayed little tolerance for one another.

Kathryn Bogert

Author: Diane Petit

Kathryn Bogert, who planned a career as an artist, won a scholarship for a Bachelor in Fine Arts degree. It did not work out. She gave up and returned to her hometown just outside of Chicago. She attributed her failure to lack of encouragement from her father, Harry, and her lover, Gary. Kathryn had, at least subconsciously, blamed a lot of her childhood problems on Harry. He was an alcoholic who placed great stress on both Kathryn and her mother. After her mother was killed by a drunken driver, Harry took control of his drinking.

Kathryn was a tall thin blonde, who had parlayed her height (5' 10") into a star role on the high school volleyball team. During the series, she found herself pitted against a former rival, detective "Phil" Panozzo. She moved back into the family home in Landview, Illinois and created a new career. Kathryn set up a company called "Good Buys" to manage estate sales; i.e. the dispersal and sale of personal items left by a deceased. This provided a convenient setting for being in homes after a death had occurred. She and her former home economics teacher, Jewel Johnson, collaborated on a book, *The Garage Sale Handbook.* Eventually Jewel became an important part of Harry Bogert's life, although he disclaimed any intention of marrying her. While cruising garage sales and working estate sales, Kathryn acquired an unusual wardrobe. Jewel, an expert seamstress, remodeled men's suits for her to wear. Rather than a purse, Kathryn depended on a backpack.

The most important acquisition Kathryn made in *Goodbye, Charli* (Avalon, 1998) was Charli himself, a Brittany Spaniel with above average intelligence. She and Charli met when Kathryn contracted for the sale of Herb Pawlicki's personal belongings. In his lifetime, Herb had been notorious for his practical jokes, comedic style and magical tricks. Not everyone approved. In return a killer played a fatal joke on Herb. Charli joined the Bogert household.

Kathryn's friendship with Frolic Galbreath led to a contract to handle her Aunt Ella's estate sale in *Goodbye, Charli-Take Two* (Avalon, 1998). Aunt Ella had left a large assortment of quilted and crocheted handiwork, household goods, and movie memorabilia. Frolic's Aunt Ruby interfered until someone murdered her. A bonus was an attractive male detective who focused on Kathryn as a suspect. Ella's finest work, an afghan, inspired Kathryn to pick up her brush and paint again, this time to please herself.

Gertrude Trent chose to have her estate sale while she was still alive in *Goodbye, Charli-Third Time Lucky* (Avalon, 1998). Kathryn became aware that Gertrude had lived an exciting but hidden life. When Kathryn found the corpse of author Guy Tortelli in a basement freezer, she and Gertrude worked together to find a killer. During the narrative, Kathryn had her first art show in four years, a stunning success.

The last book in the series (due to the death of the author), *Goodbye, Charli-Fourth Edition* (Avalon, 1999), was more imaginative, but less credible. After the hit-and-run death of her former high school teacher Gene Waite, Kathryn was put in charge of his estate goods. He had become a vendor of marked down, used, and overstocked items. Among his possessions there had been a valuable Fuzzy Wuzzy, a successor to the Beanie Baby. A fire destroyed the sales goods. However Kathryn achieved two goals: she settled long term problems with her father and rekindled a romance.

The narratives had good minor characters and plots but would have been improved by more careful editing.

Mariah Bolt

Author: Taylor Smith (Maureen G. Smith)

Mariah Bolt didn't have a lot going for her as a child. Her poet/novelist father left the home suddenly, running off with a wealthy heiress. He died penniless in Paris, reputedly of natural causes. Her mother Andrea was pregnant with younger sister Katie at the time of the abandonment. Andrea worked two jobs to provide for her children. She never said an unkind word about Ben and always assumed he would return to them. Katie died in an accident at age twelve when Mariah was away at school. Her first thought was to move home and be a support to her mother. She was told to take her things and leave, only later did she realize this was a real sacrifice on her mother's part. After her mother died, Mariah had no sense of family. Her maternal grandparents had disowned their daughter for marrying Benjamin Bolt. His parents were dead. As a result she focused on her education with no thought of marriage until she met David Tardiff, a PhD candidate in nuclear physics at the University of California-Berkeley. Their relationship became serious, but did not survive his move to the nuclear facility at Los Alamos. Mariah's feelings about nuclear weapons caused her to leave. She was recruited by Frank Tucker, who became her mentor at the CIA. Frank and Mariah worked in the analysis branch of the agency, but took occasional assignments in the operations branch. An accident which caused the death of a co-worker/friend at Los Alamos motivated David to leave and brought them back together. They married and within a short time she was pregnant. David's affiliation with the International Atomic Energy Agency required a move to Vienna. The CIA accommodated Mariah by placing her undercover at the U. S. Embassy.

Tragedy struck the family as *Guilt by Silence* (MIRA, 1995) began. David had volunteered to pick daughter Lindsay (now 13) up at school, a task that usually fell to Mariah. A truck crashed into their car, leaving David brain-damaged and paralyzed and Lindsay with a serious injury to her left leg. A move back to the Washington area facilitated care for both of them, although David had to be placed in a convalescent care home in McLean, VA. It was CBN television reporter Paul Chaney who directed Mariah's attention to the possibility that the accident was planned and that she might have been the intended victim, perhaps because of her involvement in operation CHAUCER. Mariah's efforts to investigate were balked by her superiors at the CIA. Even her mentor Frank Tucker was withholding information. A stalker made her aware that she and Lindsay were still in danger. A lengthy but engrossing narrative.

Still recovering from David's death, Mariah and Lindsay planned a summer vacation in California as *The Innocents Club* (MIRA. 2000) began. Jack Geist, deputy director of CIA operations, created a problem. He insisted that Mariah attend a formal USSR-USA exhibition at the Arlen Hunter Museum in Los Angeles. Her mission was to approach and try to recruit Yuri Belenko. Belenko, who had shown a personal interest in Mariah, was the assistant to Foreign Minister Valery Zakharov. On another level Agent Chap Korman had possession of a recently discovered manuscript by Ben Bolt, Mariah's father. There was some question as to its authenticity and as to whether or not Ben had been murdered. Heavy reading.

Smith switched over to standalones and a series featuring Hannah Nicks, a former police officer who served in a private security force in Iraq.

Nora Bonesteel

Author: Sharyn McCrumb

Author Sharyn McCrumb's strong sense of place and skillful character development blossomed in her "Appalachian Ballad" novels. Although Sheriff Spencer Arrowood dominated the series, Nora made significant appearances in many of the books. A septuagenarian, she lived in an isolated valley under primitive conditions, but people in trouble found their way to her door. Nora had always had the "sight," a gift respected by Appalachians of Scotch-Irish heritage. She was not involved in the first of the series, *If Ever I Return, Pretty Peggy-O* (Scribners, 1990). Both she and Arrowood made minute appearances in *Ghost Riders* (Dutton, 2003) an historical novel.

In *The Hangman's Beautiful Daughter* (Scribners, 1992), Nora's quilting foretold tragedies in the valley. Her knitting of a too large sweater for a deceased infant foretold that the mother would take care of an older child. Although Nora rarely left her home, the impact of her special gifts spread through the valley.

During *She Walks These Hills* (Scribners, 1994), Nora recognized the apparition of young Katie Wyler as she made her fall journey down the Appalachian Trail. Katie had made this pilgrimage ever since her real life flight from the Shawnees who had killed her family and captured her in 1789. Nora became a resource to young Jeremy Cobb who followed Katie's annual journey. Jeremy needed more than guidance. He was in danger. This was a lyric narrative.

More of Nora's past was revealed in *The Rosewood Casket* (Dutton, 1996), which centered on the gathering of the four Stargill sons, as their father Randall lay dying. He wanted to be buried in a rosewood casket built by his sons. Nora had loved Randall, but he could not cope with her mystical powers.

McCrumb put her considerable skills into the fictional reconstruction of an actual crime in *The Ballad of Frankie Silver* (Dutton, 1998). Spencer Arrowood convalesced from a bullet wound in his mountainside home. As he rested, Spencer reassessed his role in a similar crime twenty years before. Then Deputy Arrowood had been a witness against Fate Harkryder charged with murdering two young college students. Now Fate was scheduled to be executed. Spencer reviewed not only Harkryder's case, but also the legendary killing of Charlie

Silver by his young wife Frankie in 1833. He noted the pattern that explained Fate's involvement in murder. Would there be time and the will to rectify an error? Nora's role was minimal.

McCrumb wove segments of her personal family history into *The Songcatcher* (Dutton, 2001). Three factors influenced the lives of successive generations of the McCourry family: (1) The reclusive, even anti-social, nature of family members; (2) the curse that in each generation the oldest child would be rejected by the father; and (3) the attachment to a somber folk song. Country singer Lark McCourry had reconciled herself to her father's contempt, but returned to her hometown when he became ill. She hoped that during the visit she could capture the lost melody and words to the folk song. Nora Bonesteel and Spencer Arrowood were called upon to help.

Nora's appearance in *Ghost Riders* (Dutton, 2003) was as a minor character in what was an historical novel, not a mystery. She did have an impact on the conclusion, but the focus of the narrative was on McCrumb's account of how the Civil War impacted on three residents of western North Carolina. The Appalachian area was not fertile ground for large plantations or slave owners. Zebulon Vance, an ambitious lawyer, held no brief for slavery, but he went along with local resistance to what they considered unwelcome interference by the Northern states. Vance served briefly in the Confederate army but spent most of the war as the Confederate Governor of North Carolina. During his army service he met young Malinda Blalock, who had cut her hair, bound her breasts, and donned men's clothing to join her husband in the Confederate army. Keith Blalock had signed up, seeking an opportunity to desert and join the Union forces. When this seemed unlikely to happen, the Blalocks managed to return to the hills and carry on in an irregular force of Yankee sympathizers. McCrumb described the intimacy of the hatreds in the community as a result of the collision of the Southerners who supported and those who opposed the war.

Contemporary characters included Nora, Sheriff Spencer Arrowood (who researched a possible connection to the last casualty east of the Mississippi), and Rattler (an elderly man who shared "the sight" with Nora. Rattler and Nora were concerned that the exercises of Civil War re-enactors of the Battle of Zollicoffer might re-awaken the "Ghost Riders".

McCrumb developed into a haunting writer with disquieting plots and excellent characterizations. Her first series had featured Elizabeth MacPherson (see Volume 2); after ending the Arrowood/Bonesteel books, she focused on NASCAR narratives.

Sister Agnes Bourdillon

Author: Alison Joseph

After more than a decade in a cloistered convent, Sister Agnes ventured out into the secular world. She had been the child of wealthy parents who encouraged her to marry worldly French businessman Hugo Bourdillon. Agnes, battered physically and emotionally by his abuse, had been rescued by a kindly curate, Father Julius. He found her refuge in an English convent. Although Agnes spent many happy and dedicated years in the convent, she never forgot the more exciting aspects of her prior life. On her release from the cloister, she served (still as a nun) in a teenage refuge mission run by Father Julius. She drank whiskey, spent free time with mildly disreputable friends, and danced with men as she moved into general society.

By *The Hour of Our Death* (Headline, 1995), Agnes had transferred to a less restrictive religious order that emphasized good works in the world. She was allowed to remain at the shelter while taking part in the local religious community life. The secular world still held its attraction for Agnes; as did men, such as painter Alex Jeffes. Jeffes was painting the portrait of a professor at the medical complex where Agnes was substituting as a religious counselor. She did not accept that a member of the hospital staff died a natural death.

In *Sacred Hearts* (St. Martin, 1996), Father Julius made Agnes aware that Hugo was the primary suspect in the death of his second wife, Philippa. Although she had never discounted his cruelty, Agnes did not believe Hugo capable of murder. Putting aside her responsibilities to the shelter, Agnes investigated Philippa's "business" activities, and made a drinking buddy of Hugo's latest mistress, Athena. The conclusion was startling, short of a miracle, but Agnes was no saint.

Sister Agnes investigated the death of a young runaway, Becky in *The Quick and the Dead* (Headline, 1996). In the process she associated herself with protestors against the destruction of a wood lot to make way for highway construction. Her intense involvement in their cause disturbed Agnes' religious beliefs. Faith was a struggle for her as she encountered evil.

During *A Dark and Sinful Death* (Headline, 1997), Agnes wrestled with her conscience. She had been assigned as a French teacher at St. Catherine's school for girls. Among her students were several who needed a confidante and supporter, but Agnes was more interested in solving the murder of young gardener Mark Snaith, followed by a second mysterious death. She was tempted by what seemed a charitable act, to accompany a dying friend to France. The complex plotting had Agnes dealing with industrial takeovers, unhappy lovers, and a vengeful killer.

Agnes next assignment was in the chaplain's office at Silworth Prison for Women during *The Dying Light* (Headline, 1999). While absorbing herself in the problems of two female prisoners Agnes avoided coming to grips with her mother's fatal illness. Revelations from the past forced Agnes to see her mother (and herself) with new insights. The plot was flawed by an abundance of coincidences.

Agnes was unprepared to make choices as *The Night Watch* (Headline, 2000) opened. Should she take her final vows as a religious? The inheritance of a home in Provencal provided an alternative. Father Julius had his own crisis, the re-entry of the Kavanaugh family in his life. Agnes who had always depended upon Julius for solutions found him distant and unavailable. She had to rise above her need and provide him with support. On another level she had to resolve her own crisis of faith.

It was D-Day coming up for Agnes in *The Darkening Sky* (Allison & Busy, 2004). She had to decide whether or not to take her final vows in the religious order. Any possessions she owned, including her family home in Provence, would be transferred to the religious community. She had come to enjoy the privacy of her small apartment, evenings in a wine bar with her unorthodox friend, Athena, and personal freedom as she worked at S. Christopher's House, a facility for alcohol and drug dependent individuals. The death of a Falkland Islands veteran, Andy "Walker" McFadden, a resident at St. Christopher's, brought her to crisis point. A close working relationship with Alisdair Brogran, a sort of "brother" to Walker, was tempting. They investigated whether or not Walker's death was the result of a random street fight or a planned assassination. When it all worked itself out, including a serious illness for her confidante Father Julius, Agnes knew what she wanted.

Agnes chafed under the obedience required of her after her final vows in *Shadow of Death* (Allison & Busby, 2007). She was assigned to work with Shirley, a lay librarian at Collyer House, an ancient building which had once housed an unhappy married couple, but later became the joint property of the Order and of the National Health Service. As a result she became involved with the personal lives of psychiatrist Philip Sayer and his wife; with the murder of a disturbed young mother, and the determination of who should gain custody of her child. On the premises might be found the journal of Alice Hawker, a seventeenth century figure who may also have left behind a "magical" crystal ball, coveted by several individuals. Agnes suffered from spiritual doubts and the problems in Athena's love life.

Agnes returns in *A Violent Act* (2009).

Victoria "Vic" Bowering

Author: Dorian Yeager

Actresses who double as female sleuths need to have time on their hands. Victoria "Vic" Bowering was on the fringes of professional success, therefore frequently at leisure. Her relative luxury during her marriage to attorney Barry Laskin had ended with their divorce. Now she and her cats shared a tiny New York City apartment. They were not always alone. She had two suitors: newscaster Brad Sinclair and police sergeant Dan Duchinski. Vic was a tall redhead, a New Hampshire Episcopalian. She found no inconsistency between her religion and her belief that she was clairvoyant. Her confidante and mentor was Jewel La Fleur, an obese ex-stripper who occupied an apartment in the same building.

In *Cancellation by Death* (St. Martin, 1992), Barry invited Vic to a party for television actor Kendall James during which James was murdered. Vic worked with her tarot cards, telepathy, and the chaste Duchinski to clear Barry of embezzlement and murder charges.

Vic was on the verge of a nervous breakdown during *Eviction by Death* (St. Martin, 1993). As president of the Tenant's Union, she opposed lecherous and vengeful landlord Harvey Wood. Jewel's tenancy was endangered so when Wood was murdered, Vic and former landlord Ben Feldstein protected her rights.

The opportunity to replace an actress who might have been murdered occurred in *Ovation by Death* (St. Martin, 1996). Vic enjoyed the role of Miss Mona in *The Best Little Whorehouse in Texas* and the amorous attentions of Nick Jacobs, her "drop dead handsome" costar. Complications came when her two current beaus visited while Vic investigated efforts to sabotage the production.

Libation by Death (St. Martin, 1998) was disappointing. Stretched to 224 pages by generous spacing, it was a series of vignettes strung together by a weak plot. Bartending, while "at liberty," Vic became enmeshed in what seemed to be an IRA plot. She solved no mystery; uncovered no secrets; merely impeded a serious investigation. Not worthy of the series.

Yeager has a second series covered in this volume featuring Elizabeth Will.

Barbara "Bo" Bradley

Author: Abigail Padgett

Barbara "Bo" Bradley, a manic-depressive, chose a stressful occupation for a vulnerable woman—child welfare worker. Her work exposed her to the abuse and neglect of children, a burden hard to leave at the office. She was haunted by her sister Laurie's suicide. Bo had ended her own marriage to Mark Bradley because she would not bring a child into the world fearing it might share her disability. Bo shared her San Diego beach cottage with an aging fox terrier named Mildred. Painting was her emotional outlet. With silver-red hair and green eyes, she was attractive at forty, but fighting weight-gain, a side effect of her medication. At times her manic-depressive swings enhanced her social work skills, making her more sensitive to the moods of others. In other situations, empathy with victims added to her burdens. The child of a violinist and a research scientist, she had an Irish grandmother who insisted that Bo had "the sight." Bo consulted regularly with Dr. Eva Broussard, a psychiatrist of French Canadian/American Indian heritage.

In *Child of Silence* (Mysterious Press, 1993), Bo was assigned to Weppo, a four-year-old abandoned child, initially considered to be developmentally disabled. Only Bo recognized that the boy was hearing-impaired. By her challenges to the system on Weppo's behalf, Bo attracted the attention, and then the affection, of pediatrician Andrew La Marche. Medical attention was not enough to solve Weppo's problems. Someone wanted him dead.

During *Strawgirl* (Mysterious Press, 1994), Bo discontinued her lithium in order to lose weight even though she risked the M-D roller coaster. When sent East to retrieve eight-year-old Hannah, the sister of a victim of child sexual abuse, Bo kept the girl hidden. Even as she slid into a manic phase, Bo had allies who protected Hannah, and Bo herself.

When her office-mate Estrella's pregnancy made her unavailable in *Turtle Baby* (Mysterious, 1995), Bo covered her caseload. She investigated the poisoning of Acito, an eight-month-old Mayan child, whose mother had placed him with friends. Bo was reluctant to declare Chac, Acito's mother, guilty of child abuse, even more so when Chac was murdered, and Acito's convict "father" was killed.

Moonbird Boy (Mysterious, 1996) began with Bo deep in a depression caused by the death of her dog, Mildred, who represented the last ties to her married life. She recuperated at Ghost Flower Lodge, where Native American philosophy and tradition were used as therapy. The murder of comedian Mort Wagman, a fellow patient who had supported Bo in her recovery, drew her into a complex plot involving a small child and corporate takeovers. The resolution was contrived but even a weak Bo Bradley is a good read.

The reluctance of Bo's supervisor Madge Alderhoven to assign Bo to supervise a catatonic foster child was initially unexplainable in *The Dollmaker's Daughters* (Mysterious, 1997). Madge had no tolerance for personal involvement by workers, a problem for Bo. Young Janny Malcolm's obsessive need for a scruffy but elaborate doll connected with a dream that had haunted Bo recently.

The narratives were deeply moving, and Bo was endearing as she struggled to maintain herself between euphoria and despair.

Author Abigail Padgett began a different series featuring Emily "Blue" McCarron. (also covered in Volume 3). I miss Bo.

Helen Bradley

Author: Patricia H. Rushford

Helen Bradley had been widowed by the death of her first husband, Ian McGrady, a State Department employee who died in Lebanon. Their son Jason worked for the Portland, Oregon police department. His twin sister, Kate was married with children. Helen's second husband, J.B., an FBI agent, was a long time family friend. The Bradleys continued to live in the Portland, Oregon, area although J.B. frequently worked out of town. Helen, a former police officer, felt comfortable on her own. Even in her new job as a travel writer, she kept her service revolver handy. She had conservative viewpoints (strongly pro-life, disapproved of euthanasia). She not only attended St. Matthew's Church, but also was a deacon.

In *Now I Lay Me Down To Sleep* (Bethany House, 1997), while J.B. was away on an assignment, Helen was contacted by Irene Kincaid. Irene insisted that the death of her husband, Dr. Andrew Kincaid, had been improperly designated a natural death. Irene's stepson Paul, a doctor claimed she was suffering from Alzheimer's, and fiercely defended his father's diagnosis. When Irene died unexpectedly while a resident of Edgewood Manor, a senior citizen's complex,

Helen moved into the facility to investigate with help from Jason and his daughter, Jennie.

J.B. was restless after he retired from with the agency. He drove Helen crazy around the house as *Red Sky in Mourning* (Bethany House, 1997) began. They made arrangements to work on separate projects. He would evaluate using his cabin cruiser to start a charter business. She would visit the Long Beach Peninsula to complete a travel book begun by Isabelle Dupont who had died under mysterious circumstances. After J.B.'s heart attack, Helen searched among her new friends for a smuggler, a polluter, and a killer.

Except for an unrealistic emphasis on murder by a ghost, *A Haunting Refrain* (Bethany House, 1998) was a competent closed circle mystery. Rich "Uncle Paddy" summoned Helen and other family members to an isolated island off the Northwest Coast. The old man had been plagued by suspicious "accidents," which he wanted Helen to investigate. Helen's dad had died when she was ten. Paddy had been a devoted father figure.

Helen wasn't the only anxious wife in *When Shadows Fall* (Bethany House, 2000). After a later night phone call, J. B. had packed his bag and left without explanation. The next day, wealthy Eleanor Crane called Helen. Her husband, the acting mayor of Bay Villages, was also missing. Alex Jordan, a new employee, was sent by contractor Chuck Daniel's wife, to fix a leaky roof in the addition recently added by the Bradleys. Chuck hadn't come home the night before either. Initially interested only in J.B.'s absence, Helen had to change focus when she discovered a corpse on the beach.

This was an earnest series, responding to social issues such as Oregon's current assisted suicide law. Author Patricia Rushford has a juvenile series (also issued by Bethany House) that features Jennie, Helen's granddaughter and two other adult series: one featuring Angel Delaney, and the other focused on detective "Mac" Mc Allister. She has also written non-fiction books relating to management of children, adult parents, and general family issues.

Joanna Brady

Author: J. A. Jance (Judith Ann)

Joanna had a short but happy marriage to Andy Brady. They had a daughter, Jenny, when the series began with *Desert Heat* (Avon, 1993). The family was excited by Andy's campaign to unseat Sheriff Walter McFadden, whom he had served as a deputy. When Andy failed to return home for an anniversary celebration, Joanna found him dead in his car. His fellow officers called it suicide. Joanna, although her loyalty was shaken at times, knew it was murder. She was determined to find the killer. One result of Joanna's successful probe into Andy's death was her decision to run for sheriff of Cochise County, Arizona. Her daughter Jenny, who had supported the decision at first, grew anxious at the thought that Joanna would be in danger. Joanna's mother, who had always resented her daughter's close attachment to her father, a former sheriff, developed into a generous campaigner. The sheriff's department was stunned when Joanna won the election. A young ex-hooker who wanted a new start helped Joanna's successful investigation.

In *Tombstone Courage* (Morrow, 1994), Joanna had two murders to solve before her term of office began. Harold Peterson, an elderly rancher, who had been accused by his runaway daughter of having sexually abused her in her childhood, was found dead. Below his corpse was a skeleton, whose provenance solved two mysteries.

Joanna realized that election did not make her a qualified sheriff so in *Shoot, Don't Shoot* (Morrow, 1995), she enrolled in the Arizona Police Officer's Training Course in Peoria, Arizona. The atmosphere at the training session was misogynistic, placing Joanne and fellow policewoman Serena Grijalva under additional pressure. When Serena was murdered, Joanna battled the authorities to prove that the death was the work of a serial killer. On a personal level, Joanne had mixed feelings when her mother brought an unexpected guest to Thanksgiving dinner.

Joanna was introspective in *Dead to Rights* (Avon, 1996), comparing her difficult relationship with her widowed mother to problems with her own daughter, Jenny. Joanna had been aware that Amos Buckwalter, the local veterinarian, had killed a young woman while driving under the influence of alcohol. The connection between that tragedy, and Buckwalter's subsequent murder, brought back memories of her own loss. New friend, Butch Dixon, came along on his motorcycle just when Joanna needed help.

Butch was still in the picture during *Skeleton Canyon* (Avon, 1997), but Joanna was preoccupied with the murder of Bree O'Brien, daughter of a wealthy valley family. There was an obvious suspect, Nacio Ybarra, the young Mexican-American whom Bree was secretly meeting. Bree's bigoted father and guilt-ridden mother were of little help when Joanna probed for a less personal motive for the crime.

Perhaps it was a good thing that eleven-year-old Jenny Brady was away visiting relatives with her grandparents during *Rattlesnake Crossing* (Avon, 1998). Her absence made it possible for Joanna to devote her attention to a series of killings in the community. Not every bit of her time because Butch Dixon had sold his supper club and moved to Bisbee to court Joanna. Joanna needed Jenny safe and Butch close by.

The personal and professional crises in Joanna's life merged in *Outlaw Mountain* (Avon, 1999). She had an interfering mother, an eager lover, and a daughter who needed more of her time...and that was before she got to the office. Once there, Joanna dealt with the murder of elderly Alice Rogers, serious drug traffic, and the tensions between developers and environmentalists. Plans for Joanna and Butch's wedding became difficult because Joanna's mother wanted a big ceremony.

During *Devil's Claw* (Morrow, 2000), her elderly friend and neighbor, Clayton Rhodes, died suddenly, bequeathing his adjacent land to Joanna. Reba

Singleton, Clayton's daughter, accused Joanna of causing his death. At work, Joanna concentrated on finding Lucy Ridder, a teenager, who could be either a witness to her mother's death, or the killer. Joanna was maturing in her job, becoming more tolerant of the young people with whom she dealt.

Newly married, Joanna had a decision to make as *Paradise Lost* (Morrow, 2001) began. Should she run for re-election as sheriff? She measured her job's impact on Butch and on her daughter, Jenny. Multiple murders, including one of thirteen-year-old Dora Matthews, pushed Joanna and her detective squad to their limits. The fear that Jenny might be a target affected Joanna deeply. What she learned about motherhood during her investigation did too. Well-done.

Joanna and Washington State investigator, J. P. Beaumont (Jance's other sleuth) met during *Partner in Crime* (Morrow, 2002) but with evident mistrust on both sides. The murder of reclusive artist Rochelle Baxter might have been written off as a domestic matter, had Joanna not learned that "Rochelle" was in a protected witness program, placed there by the state's attorney in Washington. Her real name was Latisha Wall. As the reader learned about Latisha's background, there was also considerable introductory material about J. P and his domestic problems

Joanna updated her priorities in *Exit Wounds* (Morrow, 2003). More than one friend and relative had urged her to abandon her workaholic ways, even though she faced opposition for re-election from former deputy Ken Galloway. It wasn't easy because of her physical condition (a result of injuries in prior book), but she tried to spend more time with Jenny and Butch. That became virtually impossible when reclusive Carol Mossman was shot to death in her overheated trailer home. Joanna was shocked at the public response, disproportionate concern about the seventeen dogs who had perished along with Carol. Whether the voters liked it or not, Joanna focused on the reason for Carol's death and those of two independent film producers who were determined to expose scandalous abuse. Excellent plotting.

Joanne was almost at the end of her pregnancy in *Dead Wrong* (Morrow 2006) when the body of an unknown man was discovered by a Border Patrol officer. A visit from Ted Chapman, head of the county jail ministry, produced an identification. The victim was Brad Evans who had pleaded guilty to the death of his pregnant wife, Lisa Marie, even though her body had never been found. While incarcerated, Evans had been a model prisoner, and had dedicated his life after prison to helping other men change. Joanna's father had been involved in the Evans case. Her research exposed a conspiracy that spanned three generations. This was an exceptionally good narrative from a fine writer.

It never rains but it pours and it did pour in Cochise County, Arizona in *Damage Control* (Morrow, 2008), literally and figuratively. The washes between Joanna's house and her office flooded. Cell phones were affected. Tired by her job, Joanna depended on Butch, Jenny, and surprisingly her mother, Eleanor to help out with four-month-old Dennis. Eleanor and her husband, medical examiner Dr. George Winfield were at odds about his long work hours, often side by side with Joanna. Butch needed quiet to meet a deadline on his mystery novel. Meanwhile Joanna dealt with (1) a possible suicide pact, (2) discovery of a recent skeleton stuffed in black plastic bags; (3) the shooting of an intruder by homeowner Lauren Dyson; and (4) fire at a mobile home which left physically disabled Lenny Sunderson dead, his wife and two grandsons homeless. All over one weekend.

These were excellent narratives written by an author who richly described her setting. Next: *Fire and Ice* (2009). Jance has introduced a new female sleuth, TV anchorwoman Ali Reynolds and continues with her J. P. Beaumont series.

Theodora Braithwaite

Author: D. M. Greenwood

Theodora Braithwaite was at least the fourth generation in her family to be called to serve the church. Among her ancestors were men of great prominence in the Church of England, who provided her with credentials not to be ignored even by those who were leery of female clerics. She had attended Cheltenham Ladies College and was a graduate of Oxford University. Her decision to remain a deacon rather than to be priested was described as "an effort to remain in conformance with the universal Catholic Church." She was a tall athletic woman who enjoyed horseback riding.

Theodora appeared in a supporting role during *Clerical Errors* (St. Martin, 1992). When cleaning woman Mrs. Thrigg discovered the head of Rev. Paul Gray, Theodora and lay assistant Ian Caretaker emerged from the suspects to find a solution.

In *Unholy Ghosts* (St. Martin, 1991), Theodora investigated when Hereward Marr, an inept rural pastor, was murdered. She stayed at the home of Bishop Charles Julian and his wife, while they were in Italy, and was a temporary neighbor to St. Benet Oldfield Church, where Marr had been posted. Having recognized a possible suspect, she found it difficult to leave the matter to the local police. The killer revealed himself in a low-key narrative during which only Theodora and the religious sidelights brought any spark to the story.

Theodora was devoted to her religious vocation. Her hobby was scholarly research into the life of Thomas Henry Newcome, founder of the Order of St. Sylvester. Ambitious Dean Vincent Stream had been sent to Bow St. Aeffric to initiate change in *Idol Bones* (St. Martin, 1993). He was critical of female priests, but Theodora, the descendant of generations of clergy, could not be easily dismissed. Someone else did not tolerate the Dean's aggressive policies because he was found dead at the base of a pagan idol.

Holy Terrors (Headline, 1994) had Theodora teaching at St. Veep's, the exclusive London girl's school, once attended by her grandmother. She concluded that the abduction of Jessica Stephanopolous, whose father was a Greek military attaché was connected to the death of Paul Kostas, a "holy terror" male student at a nearby comprehensive school. Researching Greek and Turkish religious and political history, she found the missing girl and restored a triptych to its rightful owners.

In *Every Deadly Sin* (Headline, 1995), Theodora's unhappiness about her pastor Geoffrey Brighouse's choice of a spouse sent her off to recuperate at St. Sylvan's Well. St. Sylvan's purported to offer a rustic retreat for those in need of spiritual rejuvenation. Theodora found only dissension among the staff and guests. When Ruth Swallow, the cook, was murdered, both the quality of the meals and the level of contentment plummeted.

A reader unfamiliar with the hierarchy of the Church of England will benefit from the explanation contained in *Mortal Spoils* (Headline, 1996). The narrative was a slow moving account of how Theodora and Tom Logg, a lay employee of the religious bureaucracy, coped with the disappearing corpse of a foreign religious leader. Seeking to avoid problems, Logg had moved the body, thought about it some more, but by the time he and Theodora sought to return it, the body was gone. On a personal level Geoffrey Brighouse had married, making it impossible for Theodora to reside in the basement at St. Sylvester's parsonage. She had her first apartment in a decrepit building in a disreputable neighborhood.

Continued research for the biography of Cleric Thomas Newcome took Theodora to the seminary in *Heavenly Vices* (Headline, 1997). Her arrival came at a time when the faculty and staff, as well as his family, were reeling from the recent death of Warden Conrad Duff. In the process of assessing Newcome's personal papers and those of his delightful wife Esther, Theodora discovered the motive to kill Duff.

Theodora found a kindred soul in *A Grave Disturbance* (Headline, 1998) when she went to a rural Cathedral town. It was not her hostess, Susan Tye, whose primary concern was that her husband Reginald, provost of the Cathedral, was being blackmailed, but Lionel Comfit, an iconoclastic assistant Diocesan secretary. They worked together to solve two murder cases in which religious and profane motives clouded title to valuable land. Not very Christian, but very human.

Theodora had accepted the invitation to a clerical conference during *Foolish Ways* (Headline, 1999) because it had been issued by a family friend, Father Raymond Sentinel. She was aware that her speech on the role of women in the Church of England would be controversial. She saw women as preserving the religious heritage of the Church, rather than aspiring to prestige and power. The death of another presenter, Joshua Makepeace a.k.a. Josh the Jester, skewed the conference agenda. Theodora's insights were solicited by Superintendent Spruce, with whom she had worked before. She came to realize that her intervention might benefit members of her family. There were revelations of a male only religious group, the humanitarian mission of which might have been subverted by greedy members.

Several of the Braithwaite mysteries have recently been re-released as paperback editions.

Smokey Brandon

Author: Noreen Ayres

Career choices had been a problem for Smokey Brandon. A mid-sized blonde with a good figure, she began as a stripper under the name Dusty Rose Shannon. The fringe benefits were limited and the lifetime expectancy short. Smokey joined the police force, marrying a fellow officer. When she was injured on duty and Bill, her husband, died of hepatitis, she resigned. Further education made it possible for her to move into the technical side of law enforcement as an Orange County, California police lab technician. Smokey and Bill never had children because her mother's use of DES, a synthetic version of estrogen, during the pregnancy caused Smokey to have a hysterectomy to avoid potential cancer. She had a pet guinea pig (Motorboat), was active in environmental causes, and very knowledgeable about bird life.

As *A World the Color of Salt* (Morrow, 1992) began, Smokey worked a case that she could not ignore. She had known Jerry Dwyer, the victim, and she feared that Patricia, her best friend, a real estate broker, was headed for serious trouble.

In *Carcass Trade* (Morrow, 1994), Smokey lightened up a little. She had an off-again, on-again relationship with investigator Joe Sanders that helped. As before, her arrival at a death scene involved someone she might have known. If the burned corpse was Miranda, her former sister-in-law, could her brother Nathan be the killer? If not, who died with Miranda's car and where is she now?

Smokey re-emerged six years later in *The Juan Doe Murders* (Five Star, 2000), during which her loyalties were divided. She had evidence regarding serial murders of illegal aliens from Mexico. However her source was David Sanders, college age son of Joe Sanders, now her lover and partner. Joe had been hospitalized after a serious heart attack. She had to make a decision because lives were at stake.

Smokey was reckless on the job, treading on the territory of the police officers. She succeeded well enough to get support, even when she stepped on another agency's investigation.

Sarah Decker Brandt

Author: Victoria Thompson

Sarah Decker had grown up within the privileged society of early Twentieth century New York City. She was a descendant of one of the resolute Dutch families who had controlled the city from its beginnings. Her father, Felix Decker, was wealthy and powerful, deeply concerned about the social position of his family. Sarah's older sister Maggie showed her rebellious nature, first by complaining about the conditions at her father's shipyards; then by falling in love with a clerk. Felix fired young Peter, hoping to end the matter there. Instead Maggie became pregnant and married Peter, but died in childbirth. Her parents had offered no help to the young couple.

Traumatized by her sister's death, Sarah scandalized her father by becoming a midwife and marrying young doctor Tom Brandt. Initially, although she lived only a few miles from her parents, she was cut off from them emotionally and financially. Tom was murdered in a case that had not been solved. Sarah persisted in her work as a midwife, caring for poor women who could not afford a doctor. She lived in a low-income neighborhood and watched her pennies. Over the series the ties between Sarah and her parents, particularly her mother, became closer.

Sarah and Sergeant Frank Malloy were at odds with one another from the moment they met in *Murder on Astor Place* (Berkley, 1999). The death in a boarding house of young Alicia Van Damm, the pregnant daughter of a prominent family, brought them together. Sarah viewed police officers as corrupt although new Police Commissioner Theodore Roosevelt was conducting a reorganization. Malloy had equal contempt for midwives because his wife had bled to death under a midwife's care, leaving him to raise a seriously disabled son. Their involvement in Alicia Van Damm's case matched Sarah's upper class connections and her acceptance in less exalted circles with Malloy's police work. A good start.

While calling on Agnes Otto, one of her midwife cases, in *Murder on St. Mark's Place* (Berkley, 2000), Sarah learned of Gerda Reinhard's savage death. Gerda was one of the many teenage factory workers who frequented dance halls where they met young men. From Gerda's friends, Sarah became aware that other girls had met similar fates. She and Frank shared concerns, information, and a day at Coney Island in following up on the murders. Sarah reconciled with her father in order to check out a young man from a prominent family who amused himself with shop girls. As their alliance took on an emotional quality, Frank looked into Tom's death, which had been given little attention by the police.

Frank had no intention of involving Sarah in an investigation during *Murder on Gramercy Park* (Berkley, 2001). Still he needed her help for the very pregnant Letitia who had just discovered the corpse of her husband, Dr. Edmund Blackwell, a magnetic healer. What had seemed a suicide was a murder. What had seemed a simple childbirth brought unexpected complications. Having Sarah in close proximity was both a professional and personal achievement for Frank.

Mrs. Ellsworth may have been an overly imaginative neighbor but she had saved Sarah's life in a prior episode, so in *Murder in Washington Square* (Berkley, 2002) Sarah agreed to meet with her son, Nelson, a young bank employee. His sad story of Anna Blake, who had aroused his sympathy, accepted his charity, and now claims that he is the father of her expected child, was disturbing. Nelson, a naive man, had offered to marry Anna, but she was not interested. When Anna's corpse was discovered in Washington Square park, Nelson was arrested as a murder suspect. Even though this case had not been assigned to him, Frank Malloy helped Nelson get released and worked with Sarah on finding an alternative suspect. They were each vaguely aware of their mutual attraction. At the end Frank had to make a major decision concerning Sarah.

Widower Richard Dennis seemed a blessing to Sarah's parents in *Murder on Mulberry Bend* (Berkley, 2003) as a potential son-in-law. Instead he involved Sarah in the Prodigal Son Mission where his deceased wife, Hazel, had done volunteer work. When a young mission resident wearing clothes donated by Sarah was murdered, Frank Malloy needed her to identify the girl. He feared, with some justification, that she would get over involved. She did so in a very personal way, acquiring a new member to her household. On his own time, Frank was still investigating Tom Brandt's death.

Frank was surprised when he was personally selected by Police Commissioner Teddy Roosevelt to investigate the bombing that killed businessman Gregory Van Dyke in *Murder on Marble Row* (Berkley 2004). Members of the Van Dyke family were intimate friends of Sarah's parents, Felix and Elizabeth Decker. There was no way Frank could keep her out of the case even though he feared future bombings. The focus on anarchists came because Gregory's oldest son, Creighton had left home to live with radicals. Sarah, who received surprising help from her mother, provided nursing service to two family members and friends, who may have had reasons to want Gregory dead.

Sarah was called upon by Wilfred and Claire Linton, in *Murder on Lenox Hill* (Berkley, 2005) to determine whether or not their seventeen-year-old developmentally disabled daughter, Grace, might be pregnant. It seemed unlikely because the Lintons were very protective of Grace. She went out only to supervised activities at the Church of the Good Shepherd and to accompany her mother on visits to friends. There was no professional role for Frank in this matter, but Sarah pulled him in. He had jurisdiction later when Rev. Oliver Upchurch, charismatic leader of the Church, was poisoned during services.

The Italians and the Irish did not get along well in New York City at the turn of the century so, in *Murder in Little Italy* (Berkley, 2006), it was not surprising that the Ruocco family, headed by matriarch, Patrizia, did not welcome an Irish daughter-in-law. Nainsi was a teenager, pregnant at the time of a secret marriage, and the bride of Antonio, the youngest of three brothers. Sarah assisted at the birth of the baby, obviously full term, and probably not sired by Antonio. Patrizia was ready to throw both Nainsi and the infant out of the house. When Sarah made her follow-up visit the next morning, Nainsi was dead of causes not immediately apparent. Mrs. O'Hara, Nainsi's mother, who arrived to meet her new grandson, fled the building screaming "Police, Murder". This situation had the potential for serious public disturbances.

Police Commissioner Teddy Roosevelt assigned Frank Malloy to solve the case quickly. Frank vainly hoped that Sarah would stay on the sidelines.

The trouble that Sarah and Frank Malloy had with the Italians was trumped in *Murder in Chinatown* (Berkley, 2007) by the murder of Angel Lee. Angel's father Charlie was a prosperous Chinese businessman but her mother Minnie was an Irish immigrant. The Irish looked down on the hard-working Chinese. In return the Chinese considered Irishmen to be lazy drunken louts. Charlie had arranged for Angel, only 15, to marry an older man. Instead she ran away, married her Irish boyfriend, Quinn O'Neal. Her subsequent death placed both the Lee and O'Neal families under suspicion. Sarah, who had recently delivered a child to Quinn's sister-in-law at the apartment where they all lived, couldn't stay out of it. Frank reluctantly joined her. At some point, he reminded her that she had responsibilities now, as the guardian for five-year-old mute Catherine whom she had taken into her home.

Sarah must have taken that to heart because she played a lesser role in *Murder on Bank Street* (Berkley, 2008). Frank Malloy continued his quest to identify Tom Brandt's killer, but with assistance from new sources. Danny, the street boy who had led Tom to a fatal meeting, described his killer as an older, upper class man with a silver headed cane, probably the murder weapon. Felix Decker, Sarah's father, subsidized the cost of two Pinkerton agents to help Malloy. His third assistant was a volunteer whose involvement caused Sarah serious concern.

The series, subtitled *A Gaslight Mystery*, had obvious parallels to Anne Perry's Thomas and Charlotte Pitt narratives: the upper class young woman paired with a lower class detective, the geographical titles, and the exploration of women's roles in an earlier society. The plots were well drawn and the characters, diverse. Those who enjoy Pitt's series should find this one very interesting for its sense of time and place.

Next book in this series: *Murder on Waverly Place* (2009); *Murder on Lexington Avenue* (2010)

Kate Brannigan

Author: Val McDermid

Kate Brannigan, an auburn-haired former law student, was the minority partner in Mortenson and Brannigan, private investigators in Manchester, England. The daughter of a factory foreman and a housewife, she had an unconventional lover, rock music reviewer Richard Barclay, but, conventionally, she did his ironing. They did not live together, first having apartments in the same building; later owning adjacent houses joined by a conservatory. A small woman in her late twenties, she upgraded her physical skills with Thai "boxing," and her technical skills by regular use of a computer.

In *Dead Beat* (St. Martin, 1993), Kate and Richard attended a party hosted by rock star Jett, whose biography Richard hoped to write. Instead Kate was hired to locate Jett's former collaborator/lover Moira Pollock. Too late. She had been murdered and her female lover Maggie Rossiter was the primary suspect. Upon investigation Kate learned that the competitive entourage around Jett provided multiple motives for murder.

Kickback (St. Martin, 1993) drew Kate into a more prosaic setting, construction sites. Builder Ted Barlow's access to credit had dried up. The conservatories he built disappeared. Kate's friends, crime reporter Alexis Lee and her architect lover Chris, broadened the investigation when they were defrauded in a real estate transaction.

During *Crack Down* (St. Martin, 1994), Richard worked with Kate on an investigation of fraud by car dealers. He was arrested under suspicion of car theft, drug peddling, and possible child pornography. Calling in her network of friends, Kate proved Richard's innocence while acting as surrogate parent for his visiting son Davy. She had no interest in having her own children but enjoyed Davy.

Richard was deeply troubled by his experience, so, in *Clean Break* (Scribners, 1995), his relationship with Kate was fragile. Her attention was focused on two new cases: art thefts, that might involve old friend, Dennis O'Brien, and product tampering which definitely involved murder.

Kate put her extensive network of feminist friends to work in *Blue Genes* (Scribners, 1996). Her primary task was to discover the killer of a female gynecologist who offered totally female conception to lesbians who wanted a child. While juggling the scientific data, Kate challenged criminal elements in the music industry, uncovered scams by tombstone merchants, and restructured her private investigation agency. Her partner Bill Mortenson planned to marry and move to Australia. He wanted to sell out his interest, which could create problems for Kate.

Kate did not hire out as a bodyguard unless, as in *Star Struck* (HarperCollins, London 1998), she needed money. Her client was soap opera star, Gloria Kendal. However the murder victim was not Gloria, but Dorothea Dawson, pet psychic of the *Northerners* television show.

The dialogue and Kate's musings were catchy and irreverent. McDermid is a versatile writer. She has at least two other series: one featuring reporter Lindsay Gordon; the other, pairing Tony Hill and Carol Jordan which has been the basis for a television series. She also contributes short stories to anthologies

Dr. Celeste Braun, PhD

Author: B. B. Jordan (Frances Brodsky)

Celeste, although she had achieved remarkable success in her career as a molecular biologist, was less fortunate in her personal life. Her relationship with her parents was weak. Probably her closest relative was Great-Aunt Ada Cohen. She had no personal interest in the Jewish religion, rather resented her distinctive nose and remarks comparing her appearance to that of Virginia Wolff. She drove a 1978 MGB convertible, one of the last made. In her thirties she was single, but sexually active. Celeste had earned her PhD at Oxford and spent time in South America. She had limited respect for any form of government although much of her work was subsidized by grants. She was the principal Investigator in the Virology Department at Bay Area University in San Francisco. Other duties included supervising virology residents. Before she came to Bay Area, Celeste had worked in scientist Jane Stanley's lab at Harvard. Another close friend was Harry Fleming, an on again/off again lover, who had given up his career as a scientist to become a reporter.

Celeste was working hard to get tenure at Bay Area in *Principal Investigation* (Berkley, 1997). She also served as a consultant to Fukuda Pharmacology, the Japanese firm that produced Protex. Protex had been developed by Celeste's mentor, Dr. Jane Stanley in her Harvard laboratory. Vicious personal attacks on Jane and her work on Protex enraged Celeste. They originated from Dr. Simon Phillipson, a virologist who promoted his own company's product, Bazuran. Dr. Toshima Matsumoto, vice-president of Fukuda, sought Celeste's advice as to whether or not Fukuda should acquire the production rights to Bazuran. Working with Harry Fleming and attractive virology student Mac Macmillan, Celeste uncovered surprising information. A half dozen charts explained the conclusions. Even then the scientific data will overwhelm many readers. (including me)

The basic premise of *Secondary Immunization* (Berkley, 1999) was so unlikely that it provided a frail vehicle to sustain the plot. Celeste discovered the corpse of an FBI agent in a San Juan catacomb while taking part in a professional conference. She had been recruited by FBI agent Jack Minot to infiltrate certain clinics by using her Fukuda connections. The concern was that American patients in these clinics were being used, probably without their knowledge, to convey information of value to the Mafia. Celeste's focus on her assignment was distracted by her love affair with "Stash", purportedly a former CIA agent and now the director of a scientific conference center. At a standstill, a second avenue of investigation opened up when Celeste's great-aunt, Ada Cohen nee Audrey Rubinstein was diagnosed with cancer. She was a legitimate patient for entry into the suspect system. Good old Harry Fleming turned up to provide first aid for Celeste.

Triplet Code (Berkley, 2001) involved a change in focus. There were no diagrams. The academic politics involved were as virulent as any disease. Most interesting was the improved plotting. Celeste and her lab staff had made a major scientific advancement in immunology. It was a good time for her because she was up for a tenure hearing for promotion to associate professor. John "Mac" Macmillan re-entered her life and rekindled their relationship. All this occurred at a time when three male virologists died under suspicious circumstances.

Nell Bray

Author: Gillian Linscott

The aggressive behavior of early English feminists caused them to be arrested and force-fed, but eventually acknowledged. Nell Bray worked initially in the Women's Social and Political Union under the leadership of Emmeline Pankhurst. Her father had been a politically active doctor although not that successful professionally. After he died, her mother remarried. Her brother Stuart, also a doctor, inherited Whinmoor, the family estate when other male relatives died. She supported herself by translating documents from French and German supplemented by 150 pounds yearly from her father's estate. She had attended Somerville College at Oxford.

Nell played a very active role in protests for Women's Rights. She was sent to Holloway Prison for throwing a brick at #10 Downing Street. As a result she became active in prison reform. She was not only a feminist, but also a pacifist.

In *Sister Beneath the Sheet* (St. Martin, 1991), she was chosen to collect a bequest of £50,000 from notorious courtesan Topaz Brown whose "suicide" had taken place in France. The fastidious Topaz had died dressed in tawdry clothing after drinking cheap wine laced with laudanum. Nell solved the murder, while saving a young suffragette from a misguided fanatic.

During *Hanging on the Wire* (St. Martin, 1993), Nell was as committed to pacifism as to woman suffrage. She distanced herself from feminists who supported the British war effort. Nell visited a hospital in Wales for shell-shocked servicemen, who were perceived by some as cowards because they broke down under battle conditions. Someone meant to kill one or more of the patients, including Nell's former beau.

Although still active in the woman suffrage movement in *Stage Fright* (St. Martin, 1993), Nell protected American Bella Flanagan, unhappily married to the impecunious Lord Penwardine. Bella's decision to star in a George Bernard Shaw play, which ridiculed marriages such as her own, was bound to incite controversy, even murder.

Angry at the inactivity of the British Parliament, Nell spent her savings on a trip to the French Alps in *An Easy Day for a Lady* (St. Martin, 1995) a.k.a. *Widow's Peak.* Shortly after the discovery of the corpse of Arthur Mordiford frozen in the glacier for thirty years, Nell was hired by the Mordiford family to have the body returned to England. Her work expanded when a current murder cast a new light on the decades old tragedy.

Nell's rapport with the Pankhursts had diminished, but in *Crown Witness* (St. Martin, 1995) she headed the stewards on a women's march in London, paralleling the Coronation celebration. She was jailed when a cart loaded with dynamite attached itself to the parade, and the driver was murdered.

As *Dead Man's Sweetheart* (St. Martin, 1996) a.k.a. *Dead Man's Music* began Nell was reluctant to admit she had "burned out." The inducement of a week at Whinmoor, the country home where she had spent so many glorious vacations, sent her there to visit her physician brother Stuart. He and his wife, Pauline, were delighted to have Nell and recently unemployed teacher Rose Mills as their guests. Stuart, however, did not want her involved in the murder of neighbor Osbert Newbiggin. The accused killer was due to be hanged in two weeks, but a stalwart few, believing him to be innocent, convinced Nell and Rose to join their cause.

The arrest of Emmeline Pankhurst and other suffragettes in *Dance on Blood* (St. Martin, 1998) convinced Nell that there was a spy in their group. MP David Lloyd George (not yet the Prime Minister) had similar concerns. Letters from a high cabinet official to a woman contained significant information that would be of value to Germany. The death of young Laurence Gilbey, who had gone undercover to investigate, left a vacuum. George made a deal with Nell. She would replace Gilbey. He would drop charges against her, but politicians don't always keep their promises.

During *Absent Friends* (St. Martin, 1999), Nell went to a rural area in northwestern England. She was looking for a constituency in which she might run for Parliament as part of the first election in which women over the age of thirty could vote. Not one, but two of her former lovers (Simon Whittern, previously assumed to have died overseas, and Bill Musgrave) assisted in the campaign which was complicated by attacks on candidates for office. One of Nell's supporters believed that her husband had been murdered. Even a loss can be a victory to a feminist.

Verona North, daughter of Nell's cousin, Commander Ben North, had been a credit to her parents. Then why, in *The Perfect Daughter* (Virago, 2000), had she hung herself in the boathouse? Verona had left her family behind to attend art school in London. Ben, and more particularly his wife, Alexandra, had asked Nell to "keep an eye" on the girl. Nell's infrequent contacts with Verona provided no answers to Verona's pregnancy, her suicide, or the presence of morphine in her body.

It seemed a daring attack on social conventions, when in *Dead Man Riding* (St. Martin's 2003), Nell, then an Oxford student, spent vacation time with a study group of mixed gender. Nell, two girlfriends, three male students and a young don traveled to the stud farm of James Benton. His great-nephew, Alan was one of the male students and very attentive to Nell's friend, Imogen. James Benton, who was pro-Boer, was attacked by local youths. He responded by firing into the group. Arthur Mowbray one of the attackers disappeared, leading the community to believe that James had killed him.

Nell not only did not receive the real Boucher painting bequeathed to the cause of suffragism by Philomena Venn in *Blood on the Wood* (Virago, 2003) but it took her a while to figure out what was going on in the Venn household. Oliver, a dedicated Fabian, had allowed an extremist element of the society to camp on his estate. He was unwilling to admit that he had substituted a copy for Boucher's *Odalesque*. When Nell tried to retrieve the original, she discovered a corpse in the Venn household.

These were witty and compassionate views of a critical time for Englishwomen and society in general.

Dr. Temperance "Tempe" Brennan

Author: Kathy Reichs

Dr. Temperance Brennan divided her time between the Laboratoire de Sciences Judiciares et de la Medecine Legale in Quebec and her position at the University of North Carolina-Charlotte. Her usual procedure was to spend summers in Quebec except for emergencies, and the rest of the year in North Carolina. The demands on her time filled the gap when her marriage of twenty years to Peter, an attorney, ended in a separation., Tempe remained celibate for long periods of time. The first man who became a serious attraction was Lt. Andrew Ryan of the Quebec Sûreté. He had a troubled past with drugs and alcohol. Temperance detested smoking, feared guns, and had successfully dealt with her own alcohol problem.

Her initial field of study had been historic anthropology at Northwestern University in Evanston, Illinois, but she was drawn to forensic work. She had extensive experience in Africa, Puerto Rico, and the U.S. coastal islands. Her daughter Katy was now in college. Temperance had a close relationship with nephew Kit, who was neglected by his divorced parents. Her only ongoing companion was a male cat, Birdie.

Although the bulky narrative may contain more forensic details than some readers will enjoy, *Déjà Dead* (Scribner, 1997) offered a well-constructed plot. During a yearlong stay in Quebec, Temperance noted similarities in the mutilation deaths of women ranging in age from sixteen to forty-seven. In many cases their bodies had been dismembered. Initially the Canadian detectives assigned to the most recent cases were skeptical, even resentful, of her theory. Tempe amassed physical evidence and outside opinions typing the cases together. She personally located another buried body. The death of close friend ethnologist Gabrielle Macauley and danger to daughter Katy stirred Tempe into direct action, making her the next target of a killer.

In *Death du Jour* (Scribners, 1999), Tempe's anthropological skills and the fact that she had connections both in the South and in the Montreal area made it possible for her to connect a variety of cruel deaths. Evidence of murder and brutality was found in the ruins of a burned house, on a college campus, and on an island refuge for Rhesus monkeys. The cult of killers' final destination, an isolated location outside of Montreal, had to be found in time to save Tempe's flighty sister, Harry. Another strand of the narrative concerned the origins of a Nineteenth century "religeuse" who was a candidate for beatification by the Catholic Church.

Forensic anthropology was not a dainty profession, but, as in *Deadly Decisions* (Scribners, 2000), it was toughest when Temperance worked on the bodies of children and teenagers. Montreal was wracked by a biker war over drug territories. They were killing one another, which suited some citizens just fine. Temperance was drawn into the struggle on a personal level. Her lover, Andy Ryan, had been dismissed from the Sûreté on suspicion of ties with drug smugglers. Visiting nephew Kit spent his time hanging around with the motorcycle gangs, and became a potential victim of the internecine war.

Tempe's journey to Knoxville, Tennessee was interrupted during *Fatal Voyage* (Scribners, 2001) by a call sending her to the site of a plane crash in which all passengers and crew had been killed. Multiple federal, state, and local officials were involved in the probe. The problem for Tempe was not too many investigators but too many bones, bones that could not be tied to the crash victims. Her personal concern for this anomaly led to a disciplinary action that threatened Tempe's career and precipitated another death. Tempe realized that she was not contending with a single criminal. There was something very distasteful going on. Tempe, female sheriff Lucy Crowe, homicide detective Andrew Ryan, and FBI agent Brian McMahon cooperated to unearth a conspiracy. The specifics of her work may be distasteful to some readers.

Temp's visit to Guatemala in *Grave Secrets* (Scribner, 2002) initially focused on the recovery and identification of the bodies of 23 persons killed by right wing government forces in the small village of Chupan Ya. Some of those involved in the atrocities that took place between 1962-1996 went unpunished and currently held positions of authority in the government. Tempe's risks multiplied when she agreed to assist Special Crimes Investigator Bartolome Galiano in his search for four missing young women, one of whom was the daughter of a Canadian diplomat. Initially balked by Guatemalan officials, Tempe rallied support to identify a Jane Doe, who might be one of the four. Galiano gave Ryan competition for Tempe's attention.

Temperance had it all planned as *Bare Bones* (Scribners, 2003) began, a vacation with Quebec detective Andrew Ryan to test their relationship. Her job intervened, thanks to a chow dog named Boyd who saddled her with bear bones, bird bones, and human bones. This was followed by a dead newborn and a crashed airplane on a drug smuggling route. Temperance used her remarkable skills but was sidetracked by unusual syndromes and species.

Within days after Temperance came to Montreal in midwinter to testify in a murder case, she became involved in a horrifying investigation as narrated in *Monday Mourning* (Simon & Schuster, 2004). The skeletons of three young females had been discovered in the basement of a pizza parlor. Detective Luc Claudel wanted to write the bones off as "historic". Temperance's instinct told her they were comparatively recent and evidence of murder. There were problems on a personal level with Andrew Ryan. Was she just the most recent of his conquests?

The death of Orthodox Jew Avram Ferris in *Cross Bones* (Scribners, 2005) was ghastly enough so that Temperance was called in to determine whether it was suicide or murder. Later she was approached by a man who provided a photo indicating that the skeleton pictured therein was the cause of Ferris's death. She, Andrew Ryan, and biblical archeologist Jake Drum traced the skeleton, then traveled to Israel to seek answers to the broader questions involved. The truth might have serious implications for both Jews and/or Christians. Not everyone will be comfortable with the premises explored.

It was Temperance's close friendship with Charleston County Coroner Emma Rousseau that pulled her into the investigation of mysterious deaths in *Break No Bones* (Simon & Schuster, 2006). Sheriff Junius Gullet was not ready to label the incidents murder. The victims had been bound, hung from a tree and stuffed into an oil barrel, which was then submerged. There seemed to be no pattern among the victims. Temp's work involved a conflict of interest because her estranged husband, Peter was involved in one of the cases. Their proximity did not sit well with Andrew Ryan. Only her commitment to help Emma kept Temperance on track.

Bones to Ashes (Scribners, 2007) began with Temperance's poignant memories of summers on the beach with her friend Evangeline Landry. They ended when Evangeline and her younger sister Obeline no longer visited her relatives in the area. Decades later, those memories reawakened when cold case squad Sgt. Hippo Gallant sought Temp's help in identifying the bones of a teenage girl from Acadia, the victim of a strange disease. She made time for this even though her schedule was packed. Lt. Ryan, who continued to have professional contacts with Temp even though their personal relationship had floundered, was struggling with a series of disappearances and unidentified bodies of young women which might be connected to a serial killer. Harry, Temp's younger sister, shared her interest in finding Evangeline and Obeline.

Temp was in no condition to take on three investigations into the deaths of juveniles in *Devil Bones* (Simon & Schuster, 2008). Daughter Katy was bored in her new job, complaining constantly. Pete, her estranged husband, finally asked for a divorce to marry 29-year-old Summer. Ryan had left Temp hanging while he returned to Lutecia, the mother of his drug addicted daughter, Lily. Within a short time, Temp was summoned to three crime scenes: (1) a cellar possibly used by practitioners of Santeria where a female skull was found, (2) the headless body of a twelve-year-old boy found in the river, and (3) a second headless torso found on the shores of a local lake. Right-wing politician Bryce Lingo tied these events together, heralding a crusade against Satanism and incompetent legal procedures to mete out punishment. As always Temp can handle it.

Author Kathy Reichs, who is a forensic anthropologist, provided competent background for the series. Fox television network purchased the rights to the Temperance Brennan series for a show called *Bones*. *206 Bones* will be released in 2009, and *Spider Bones* in 2010.

Lucy Trimble Brenner

Author: Eric Wright

See: Lucy Trimble, page 820.

Claire Breslinsky (Benedetto)

Author: Mary Anne Kelly

One of the more volatile families in mystery fiction must be the Polish-Irish Breslinsky clan of Queens, New York. Claire had never dealt with the death of her twin brother, Michael, a police officer. Younger sister Zinnie coped by joining the police force; older sister, Carmela, by her work as a gossip columnist. Claire left home and wandered the globe, seeking some personal understanding. The Breslinsky sisters were highly competitive where men were concerned, yet they survived as a family, partly because of mother Rose and father Stan.

When Claire found no answers abroad, she returned to the family home in *Park Lane South, Queens* (St. Martin, 1990). The Breslinskys, now including Michaelaen, Zinnie's son from an unsuccessful marriage, had almost absorbed Claire when the neighborhood was traumatized by the sexual abuse and murder of a small boy. Claire became an important source for Detective Johnny Benedetto's investigation. The solution came from her memories of childhood, from English bulldog Mayor's warning of danger, and from a glance into a neighbor's garbage can.

By *Foxglove,* (St. Martin, 1992), Claire had married Johnny, borne a son (Anthony), and moved into a large home. She hoped to renew her friendships with neighbor "Tree" Dover, Tree's demanding husband Andrew, and seven-year-old daughter, Dharma. Tree was dead before they could get together. Although the distractions were chaotic, Claire absorbed Dharma into her own family, and solved Tree's murder.

The Benedetto marriage was in trouble as *Keeper of the Mill* (St. Martin, 1995) began. Claire visited her old haunts in Germany to take part in the wedding of dear friend, Isolde Donnerwetter. She had a second agenda for her visit to St. Hildegarde's Mill—a treasure trove left behind by Jewish refugee Iris von Lillienfeld. Claire, away from home and family, was tempted by Temple Fortune, an attractive British film producer.

In *Jenny Rose* (St. Martin, 1999), Claire became the family representative by default at an Irish funeral. When the family was informed that her mother's sister Deirdre had died in an explosion, Claire had reasons of her own to make the trip. She had lost faith in her marriage and Temple Fortune was in Ireland. She had not seen him in five years but she could not forget him. Mary, Claire's mother, revealed one family secret just before Claire boarded the plane, but she did not tell all she knew. There were many surprises awaiting Claire at the Cashin family complex in rural Cork, not the least of which was murder.

A new Claire Breslinsky novel is always welcome and *The Cordelia Squad* (Thomas Dunne, St. Martin's, 2003) exceeded expectations. In the interval Claire had divorced Johnny, and returned to her family home in Queens. This time she intended to put down roots for herself and the two children, beginning with the purchase of the rundown Witzig mansion that she planned to make into a bed and breakfast. Her children, parents, and siblings were aghast but pitched in. Claire needed help. There was an arsonist in the neighborhood, perhaps with a personal interest in Claire. Fortunately there was also a fireman who found her attractive. There were terrific characterizations as always. The interactions within Claire's family were sensitive and provocative.

Pack Up the Moon (Thomas Dunne, St. Martin, 2006) eschewed the mystery format although Claire was the primary character. It was a prologue to the earlier books, set in Germany and India during the period of time when Claire wandered the globe trying to make sense of her twin brother Michael's death.

This was an excellent series with a complex heroine and intricate plots. Author Mary Ann Kelly is a lyrical writer with a sense of place. I wish she had been kinder to Johnny Benedetto though.

Lily Brewster

Author: Jill Churchill, pseudonym for Janice Brooks

Lily Brewster and her brother Robert had grown accustomed to the good life of the Roaring Twenties. When the Great Depression hit, their father made a quick departure...jumping from the window of his office building. By 1931, Lily was employed at Chase Memorial Bank. Robert had even fewer skills so he took short-term jobs as a bartender and maître d', supplemented by acting as an escort to elderly ladies. This was no kind of a life.

A surprising opportunity presented itself in *Anything Goes* (Avon, 1999) when Great Uncle Horatio was murdered while yachting on the Hudson River. The siblings were provided with an inheritance dependent upon their residence in his now vacant mansion. A stipend would be provided for the upkeep of the house. More importantly if they remained there for ten years, there would be a substantial bequest at their disposal. Lily and Robert wanted to be accepted in Voorburg-on-Hudson, but they had to explain the presence of another corpse in the "Grace and Favor" cottage.

What seemed an ingenious way to relieve Robert's boredom in Voorburg-on-Hudson and add to their income during *In the Still of the Night* (Avon, 2000) had unfortunate repercussions. They invited literary giant Julian West to be their celebrity guest and recruited six other paying attendees for a weekend. Tensions among the group led to murder and theft. Lightly handled, the narrative touched on the impact of World War I, the Depression, and the emergence of Franklin D. Roosevelt.

Robert and Lily exposed their financial status to the locals during *Someone to Watch Over Me* (HarperCollins, 2001). Everyone had assumed they were still wealthy and in charge of the mansion in which they were living. While tearing down an old icehouse to salvage the lumber, Robert found a male corpse, initially unidentified. Meanwhile, Lily became involved in the death of her friend Roxanne Anderson's brutal husband, Donald. The local newspaper editor Jack Summers traveled to Washington, D.C. to report on the Veteran's Bonus March. Through each of these encounters, the trio became more aware of the poverty under which their neighbors lived. Lily provided the vital clue to discover the killer of the unknown victim Robert had discovered. Robert solved the mystery of Donald Anderson's death. A fair exchange.

Neither Lily nor Robert was the primary sleuth in *Love for Sale* (Morrow, 2003) although Lily put one and one together in time to solve the case. Brother Luke Goodheart, a radio preacher, rented several rooms at Grace and Favor for a conference with his employees. Only after he was murdered in the bathtub, did Chief of Police Howard Walker learn that Goodheart aka Charles Pottinger had been misusing money meant for the poor and abused women on his staff. The narrative made good use of historical background and had endearing touches as to minor characters.

The prospect of working in a nursing home didn't suit either Robert or Lily in *It Had To Be You* (Morrow, 2004) but they needed the money. Their new employer made it clear that Lily would be scrubbing floors and Robert would be lugging huge baskets of laundry up and down two flights of stairs. They had no idea that they would be drawn into another of Police Chief Howard Walker's murder investigations. The victim, resident Sean Connor, had been rude and difficult to care for but he was expected to die a natural death within hours when the murder occurred. Lily's special skills with female suspects proved valuable. There was more interesting historical material re the inauguration of Franklin Delano Roosevelt, which Robert attended.

Robert and Lily had further diminished roles in *Who's Sorry Now?* (Morrow, 2005). Lily acquired an interest in anthropology when the remains of a young Native American female were discovered in their backyard. The terms of the trust made it impossible for her to take college courses. Robert impressed his fellow citizens by solving the need for a safe place for mail delivery now that the local post office was closed. But when Edwin McBride, the impoverished railroad porter who had been expected to manage the mail service was murdered and an émigré from Berlin master tailor Kurtz was harassed, it was police chief Howard Walker and his new deputy Ron Parker who did the detecting.

This was a lighthearted series, reminiscent of the Golden Ages of the mystery novel. The book titles are the names of songs popular during that period.

Kat Bronsky

Author: John J. Nance

There was limited exploration of Kat's character or background in the two-book series. She was an attractive woman in her thirties, sporting chestnut brown hair. After working several years as a psychologist, she had entered the FBI training school and planned to work as a hostage negotiator. While stationed in the Salt Lake City, Utah FBI office, she was supervised by Clark Roberts. Her unorthodox methods placed stress on Roberts, because she violated established rules of the FBI, the headquarters in Washington, D.C. did not appreciate her independence, nor did other FBI agents.

Although just a rookie, Kat played a significant role in *The Last Hostage* (Doubleday, 1998) but the narrative focused on pilot Ken Wolfe. Widower Wolfe had suffered when his nine-year-old daughter Melinda, disappeared, then her ravaged body was discovered. When Bradley Lumin prosecuted for the crimes was released on a technicality. Although the possibility of federal charges existed, none were brought. Two years later Rudolph Bostich, the federal attorney who had failed to bring charges, was a passenger of Wolfe's flight 90 for AirBridge airlines. Wolfe, fearful that Lumin would continue to be a danger to young girls, grasped the opportunity to put pressure on, not only Bostich, but the legal system. In so doing he endangered the lives of all the other passengers and the crew on Flight 90. Kat was assigned to negotiate with Wolfe. Nance's exploration of the courageous and cowardly reactions of those whose lives were endangered was very well done. Hard to put down.

An unplanned meeting with Pulitzer Prize reporter Robert MacCabe in Hong Kong set Kat on the trail of possible terrorists in *Blackout* (Putnam's, 2000). MacCabe had been contacted by a friend who had significant information about the recent destruction of a U. S. airplane. Before they could meet, Warren Pierce had been killed in what authorities chose to consider a suicide. Kat and Robert made reservations to return to the United State to investigate, but she was diverted by a request to solve a problem at the American Consulate. The plane which MacCabe boarded without her was attacked, followed by continued efforts to shoot it down. MacCabe realized after several incidents that he was the primary target. Again Nance did a fine job of establishing the characters of several others on the flight: a fourteen-year-old boy who had worked with his dad on simulators; a resourceful African-American woman who played video games; a doctor and his new wife, a nurse, who came to the rescue of the injured and a stewardess who put the interests of her passengers ahead of her own. Meanwhile Kat investigated the source of these attacks: Cuban government; foreign terrorists; or a problem closer to home. She continued with Robert's help to resolve this issue, even though she was not certain whom she could trust.

Nance, a pilot himself, wrote other aeronautical mysteries, but they were standalones.

Dr. Liz Broward

Author: Fay Zachary

Tall, blonde, self-assured Dr. Liz Broward was the daughter of Paul Broward, a domineering defense attorney. Against his wishes, she entered the state university, then medical school where she became a hematologist. Once in practice in Phoenix, she shared an affair with Zach James, a Native American graphic artist whose wife she had treated during a terminal illness.

During *Blood Work* (Berkley, 1994), Dr. Liz and Zach became involved through his illness and her concern for Agnes Schultz, a woman suffering from porphyria—a blood defect that creates a craving for human blood. A mentally ill man determined to "cure" porphyria victims by killing them selected Liz as his next target.

By *A Poison in the Blood* (Berkley, 1994), Liz had borne Zach's child and planned to marry him. Hester Jones, daughter of a severely handicapped diabetic, had never forgiven Paul Broward for his part in limiting her father's award in a lawsuit. She embarked upon a disastrous vendetta against Liz and those she loved.

This was a depressing series.

Olivia Brown

Author: Annette Meyers

Olivia Brown was determinedly up to date...for the 1920s. Her fiancé, Franklin Prince, had been killed during World War I. Since then, disdaining marriage, she had serial lovers, both male and female. After the early death of both of her parents, bachelor Jonas Avery, a family friend, had cared for Olivia. Her tutor, Sarah Parkman, a Vassar graduate, had inspired Olivia to write poetry. Her idol was poetess Edna St. Vincent Millay. After Avery's death, Mattie Timmons, his housekeeper, became Olivia's live-in companion providing some stability in her hectic life. Her hair had been bobbed and she preferred to be called Oliver.

She discovered that she had been left a house in Greenwich Village and the money to maintain it by her lesbian Great-Aunt Evangeline Brown. Harry Melville, a reclusive private investigator, had a lifetime tenancy in Aunt Evangeline's house and they became great friends. She joined the Provincetown Players, who produced the works of controversial authors such as Eugene O'Neill. After play practices and performances, the cast went to speakeasies and partied until dawn. She was not sleep deprived. She slept most of the daylight hours. Poetry was her great love. Her poems had some success but they were not a major source of income. Money was not a problem for Olivia; alcohol, particularly gin, was and so was murder.

Olivia, the object of desire for a stable of unstable young men, in *Free Love* (Mysterious Press, 1999) not only denied them her exclusive attentions but seemed to bring nothing but death to her acquaintances. One after another members of her Greenwich Village circle were murdered, their throats slashed. Detective Gerry Brophy was kind (and attentive to Mattie Timmons). His partner Charlie Walz was contemptuous of the lifestyle adopted by Olivia and the Greenwich Village community. Olivia almost became the final victim of a killer whom she failed to fear. Her safety was enhanced by the goodwill of the Hudson Dusters, an Irish street gang.

Olivia's life continued to be narcissistic and frenetic in *Murder Me Now* (Mysterious Press, 2001) Her stable of beaus included Monk Eastman, a Jewish mobster and killer. Attendance at a rural house party drew Olivia and

Harry Melville into a convoluted series of murders, which pitted government agencies against the Black Hand (forerunner of the Mafia). The ranks of Olivia's beaus were depleted by the end of the narrative, but she was already eyeing replacements.

The poetry was good. Readers will have to decide for themselves about Olivia.

Meyers is also the author of the Xenia Smith/Leslie Wetzon series covered in Volume 2.

Sister Cecile Buddenbrooks

Author: Winona Sullivan

Whatever limitations life in the convent might have created for Sr. Cecile Buddenbrooks, poverty was not a problem. Her atheist father had left her a fortune. Under the terms of his will, Sr. Cecile could not use the money to advance religion. The manager of Jerry Buddenbrooks' trust was Paul Dorys, Cecile's long time friend and the one significant man in her life. He had been the son of the Buddenbrooks' family cook. Jerry had subsidized Paul's education through law school. Paul remained a bachelor, never giving up hope that Cecile would leave the convent and marry him.

Her order of nuns was the fictional Notre Dame de Bon Conseil located in Boston. Rather deviously Cecile manipulated the provisions of the trust. She did not spend his money on religion. She used it to finance her private investigation agency; then, turned that income over to the convent. An attractive redhead, she had a private investigator's license and was fluent in several languages. Cecile's life was enriched when Leonie Drail became her ward. Helene, Leonie's mother, had attended school in Switzerland with Cecile. After Helene's death, her husband Dennis asked Cecile to serve as the girl's guardian. Because Dennis spent time overseas in his work for the CIA, this meant having her as part of the convent household on occasion.

During *A Sudden Death at the Norfolk Cafe* (St. Martin, 1993), Jane, the pregnant daughter of prominent politician Abe Hersey, hired Sr. Cecile. Jane had stolen a briefcase filled with blackmailing information from her lover, Martin Moon. Realizing that Jane was in danger, Cecile spirited her to the motherhouse in Paris. She could remain there until the child was born. Martin wanted his briefcase and revenge.

Bradley Locke, an unwise CIA agent, allowed himself to be kidnapped in Florida during *Dead South* (St. Martin, 1996). The agency recalled that young Cecile Buddenbrooks had served them in the past. They recruited her to find Locke. Assisted by doughty Sister Raphael and twelve-year-old Leonie Drail, Sister Cecile ventured into the slums of Miami Beach and the surrounding swamps.

Cecile, like other nuns at Concilia Retirement Community in Miami, worked outside of the convent to earn money. She was the provincial director of her order in the area and resided with the other religious and some lay boarders in a remodeled motel. As *Death's a Beach* (Ivy, 1998) began, Leonie was living with them while Dennis was in Europe. Cecile had developed a maternal affection for the independent girl. That responsibility created a conflict of interest when Leonie became entangled in a murder case that Cecile had been hired to solve. Sister Raphael and kindly Native American police officer Jim Cypress joined forces with Cecile.

Leonie played an even more dangerous role in *Saving Death* (Fawcett, 2000). She had been present when livestock breeder John Cruz hired Cecile to prove that Juan Caldo, an escaped convict, had been innocent of the murder of lecherous Victor Torres twenty years before. Caldo had a motive to kill Torres, but so did his women, their husbands and fathers. Cecile's efforts to develop an alternative suspect were stymied when a hit man was hired to kill her. Leonie inserted herself into the action with a bang.

Ingenious plots.

Caley Burke

Author: Bridget McKenna

A redhead in her early thirties, Caley Burke was a novice private investigator. After her divorce from reporter Michael Carlson, she was uncertain about what she wanted to do with the rest of her life, except to stay in California. Her parents had moved from one community to another, causing her to change schools frequently. Caley had grown up without roots. She and Michael had tried to start a family, but stopped after two stillborn children.

As *Murder Beach* (Diamond, 1993) began, Valerie Hayden urged Caley to come back to Murado Beach for their class reunion. There were memories that made that difficult. Rob Cameron, now a police sergeant, had dumped Caley for the homecoming queen but she never forgot him. Was that good news or bad news?. The death of local developer Chandler Stone tested Caley's loyalties. Valerie wanted Caley to find other suspects if disfigured artist Tony Garcia was charged with the murder. There were motives available but Caley didn't always look in the right place.

During *Dead Ahead* (Berkley, 1994), Caley attended the funeral of old friend Cassandra Lowry. She learned that a rightist organization, American Rescue Coalition, had caused divisions within the community of Cedar Ridge, California. Cass had died in a car crash, but her friends believed that her opposition to ARC was behind the accident. Caley's fear that she might be unable to protect herself proved to be groundless.

Caley's experiences in Cedar Ridge had left her so distraught that in *Caught Dead* (Berkley, 1995), her employer insisted that she take time off and see a psychiatrist. Even on sick leave, Caley could not avoid trouble. Her sympathies were aroused when teenager Sam Holland hired her to identify his father. His mother Annie, a waitress at the local hotel, would not tell him who the man had been. She had problems of her own. Annie was arrested for the murder of her wealthy and prominent sister.

Maxey Burnell

Author: Carol Cail a.k.a. Kara Galloway

Maxey Burnell, the only child of a single mother, began life in a small Ohio town. In search of change, she moved to the more stimulating community of Boulder, Colorado. Maxey had experience as a bookkeeper and reporter, when she applied at *Blatant Regard*, one of two local papers. Jim Donavan hired Maxey as an advice columnist, but she gradually took on other responsibilities. One she later regretted was marriage to fellow staffer Reece Macy. After the divorce, Maxey and Reece worked together, but there was no reconciliation.

Rita Stamp, who felt the police had bungled her husband's disappearance, contacted Maxey for help in *Private Lies* (Harper Paperbacks, 1993). Maxey, burdened with extra work after Donavan was killed by a car bomb, chose not to get involved. Later, when Rita was murdered, Maxey discovered the connection to Donavan's death. The pluses were a relationship with Detective Sam Russell and the news that she and Reece had inherited *Blatant Regard.* Somewhat less important was her acquisition of Donovan's cat, Moe.

Reece and Maxey managed their joint ownership of the newspaper during *Unsafe Keeping* (St. Martin, 1995) better than she and Sam did their personal relationship. Maxey found another beau, Calen Taylor, investigator for the Boulder Fire Department, when a series of runaway vehicles, that were presumed to be juvenile pranks, turned into arson and murder. The physical details in the narrative were unlikely, but interesting.

Reece's decision to sell his interest in the paper to the publisher of a sadomasochistic literary magazine appalled Maxey as *If Two of Them Are Dead* (St. Martin, 1996) opened. She used paid vacation time to visit her mother's sister, Janet. and the site of her murdered mother's grave in Nebraska. Once there, she had another shock. Not only was her father still alive, but, according to Janet, he was the killer. There was no way that Maxey could return to Boulder without meeting her father, and clearing his name.

Maxey insisted upon information and independence in *Who Was Sylvia?* (Deadly Alibi, 2000). She wanted to know more about Sylvia Wellman, the deceased packrat who had wandered through the stores in Maxey's neighborhood, and about Basil Underwood, a ne'er do well who died in a recent fire. When her inquiries caused Maxey to be targeted as victim #3, she refused to move in with her lover, arson inspector Calen Taylor. All her questions were finally answered but she had to depend on a man to save her life. Perhaps she learned something.

Maxey was interviewing Betty Allbright, a candidate for city council, in *Death Kindly Stopped* (Deadly Alibi, 2003) when Lonnie Coffey, a driver for

Kenn Limousines arrived. She had been sent to invite Ruey, Betty's daughter, to share a night on the town with her former husband Georgie Nickles. When Lonnie returned to her vehicle, Georgie was dead, knifed. Even when there were subsequent murders that might be connected, Maxey held back, remembering risks she had taken in the past. It didn't help that Sam Russell was the investigating detective. Scotty Springer, Maxey's partner, plans to retire. She had to get active or get out. A literary puzzle aided in the solution.

Dr. Clare Burtonall

Author: Jonathan Gash

Author Jonathan Gash, creator of the lovable rogue Lovejoy, was responsible for this series featuring Clare Burtonall, a competent English doctor but a deeply disturbed human being. Her parents were described as "rigid," but it had not rubbed off on Clare. She married Clifford Burtonall, a crooked and manipulative real estate developer, who provided her with even less emotional support than her parents. Because she did not work well with authority figures, Clare practiced medicine as a locum, taking short-term assignments in established practices although she had been trained as a cardiologist.

She was in her late twenties as *Different Women Dancing* (Viking, 1997) began. During a short term assignment she witnessed an "accident" which led to the theft of files. She realized that Clifford was working with a group seeking to take over Pleases, Inc, the local prostitution agency. Driven by her physical needs, she entered into a paid relationship with Bonn, a male hooker whom she met casually in a park. Bonn, an ex-seminarian who had lost both faith and hope, was being groomed to takeover Pleases. The current owner, Posser, wanted Bonn to marry his daughter Martina who managed the business. Violence was an on-going way of dealing with competitors and unsatisfactory employees.

Clare continued her unhappy marriage and her destructive affair with Bonn during *Prey Dancing* (Viking, 1998). When she tried to carry out the request made to her by Marie Cullokin, an HIV-infected drug addict, she became enmeshed in Martina's organization. There seemed to be no potential happiness for any of these dark characters.

By *Die Dancing* (Macmillan, 2000), Clare was working in an inner city clinic. She belatedly recognized that the clinic was primarily concerned with the health of male and female prostitutes. She was still obsessed with Bonn who was incapable of returning her feelings or Martina's. The focus was on the machinations within Martina's organization, Bonn's struggles to understand women (he came across as rather dim), and a vendetta with local politicians. The text was degrading to both sexes.

Nevertheless, next book in this series: *Bone Dancing* (2002) was even worse. Bonn and Clare were instrumental in helping a young boy who was being abused while in a religious orphanage, but there was little in which to take satisfaction. They tolerated the use of teenage prostitutes by Pleases, Inc, which employed them both. Clerical sexual perversion, the local development of dangerous drugs, murder as a cover-up saturated the narrative.

Blood Dancing (Allison & Busby, 2006) returned readers to the sex trade in Manchester, England. Why they would choose to go there is unclear. Bonn continued to ply his trade for Pleases. Clare was no longer associated with the organization, having an independent practice. Bonn, Clare, and Pleases "girls" are concerned about a savage attack that left a fourteen-year-old on life support. The pederast who was responsible was released from jail on a technicality. Clare was one of several hospital staff members who had to decide whether or not to disconnect the victim's life support. Bonn did not approve of having fourteen-year-old hookers on the street. There were others who saw a simple solution to the miscarriage of justice. Kill the pederast. It didn't stop there, the doctors who had to make the decision of life or death were also potential targets. Bonn and Clare were not in accord as to what action to take.

A loathsome series.

Filomena "Fil" Buscarsela

Author: k. j. a. Wishnia

Filomena Buscarsela had been born and educated in Ecuador. Her native country became an unsafe place because of her rebellious activities while a student at the State University in Guayaquil. After she became an American citizen, Filomena was hired by the New York City police force. She was still a rebel. Her brother had been brutally killed by CIA operatives in Ecuador. Her departure from the police department was due in part to problems with drugs and alcohol. She had a sense of the religious faith into which she was born, but confessed to God rather than a priest. She attended Mass but questioned church tenets and practiced Brujeria on occasion. In addition to her other skills, Fil spoke English, Spanish, and Quichua, an Ecuadorian dialect. After some unstable living arrangements she settled down with an orange tabby cat, Puchungo. A daughter, Antonia, joined the household during the series. Antonia's father Raul was a loafer, a lecher, and slow pay.

In *23 Shades of Black* (Imaginary Press 1997), Filomena was a police officer. There were inherent difficulties in her employment. Her enforcement responsibilities put her at odds with the Hispanic community. Within the department she had few allies, and more than a few who not only harassed her but also put her at risk, or set her up for trouble with superior officers. An assignment to check out a toxic leak at a food stamp office drew her into a personal crusade against industrial pollution in factories owned by Samuel Morse. Her sense of justice drove Filomena beyond the boundaries of her cases. Her hard work was counteracted by her susceptibility to alcohol and the system's treatment of females and minorities. This was a bitter narrative that at times portrayed Filomena as the only one who cared.

Filomena worked at the non-profit Environmental Action Foundation during *Soft Money* (Dutton, 1999). Information discovered on the job provided her with a chance to damage Samuel Morse who had almost killed her. Enraged by the murder of friendly shopkeeper Lazaro Perez, and to some degree ignoring her responsibilities to her child, Filomena took serious risks. In order to get the cooperation of the Dominican mob to bring Lazaro's killers to justice, Filomena participated in a cover-up.

The Glass Factory (Dutton, 2000) will leave Filomena's fans breathless with the first chapter. Her exposure to toxic chemicals at the hands of Samuel Morse led to a diagnosis of terminal lung cancer. Filomena needed to live for Antonia, now four, but if she must die, she would spend her remaining months destroying Morse and his "evil empire." Hard up for money, she found unexpected allies in the Long Island home of Columba, Raul's sister, who was initially hostile but came to love Antonia.

Filomena was an angry woman, disappointed to realize that justice and equality were not guaranteed even in the United States. In *Red House* (St. Martin, 2001), her cynicism was justified by greedy landlords, neo-Nazi bullies, and corrupt police. She had completed six months of the two years required for a private investigator's license as an employee of the Davis and Brown Agency. She worked the system to help vulnerable but unprofitable clients such as unstable Sonny Tesoro, an occupant of a renovated factory that might be toxic. She was stirred to action by the death of Manny Morales, a housing advocate and therapist for autistic teenagers. Manny was one of the good guys and Filomena was determined that his killer be found.

Filomena took Antonia (now 13) to Ecuador to visit family and friends in *Blood Lake* (St. Martin's Minotaur, 2002). The country was in ferment due to the upcoming elections. She gave little thought to seeing her former love, Juanito, believing him to have died. The government police thought otherwise. She sought out Father Samuel Campos, who had once saved her life, and now put his own at risk by opposing government use of paramilitary organizations. After he was murdered, Filomena was determined to punish his killer. This had to be done outside the law. Stan, a doctor who had come to care for Filomena, visited Ecuador to see her, but she sent him away. It was too dangerous.

This was a highly praised series, heavy on polemics.

Harriet Bushrow

Author: Graham Landrum (Final book completed posthumously by son Robert Graham Landrum.)

At eighty-eight years of age, Harriet Bushrow found herself alone. Her husband, Lucius Quintus Cincinatus Lamar Bushrow, and their only son (just plain Lamar) died. With no children or grandchildren, Harriet immersed herself in community affairs in Borderville, located on the Virginia/Tennessee line. Her primary ally was Helen Delaporte, an ex-Yankee who lived just across that border. Other members of the Daughters of the American Revolution (D.A.R.) joined in during the narratives.

The Famous D.A.R. Murder Mystery (St. Martin, 1992) was a "collaborative report" from members of the D.A.R. Harriet and her cohorts found a fresh corpse while searching an obscure cemetery for the grave of a Revolutionary War veteran. Sheriff Butch Gilroy showed little interest in the death of an unknown vagrant, but Harriet persisted until she could present her case to the authorities.

In *The Rotary Club Murder Mystery* (St. Martin, 1993), the Rotarians learned that their luncheon speaker and district governor Charles Hollonbrook had died suspiciously in his locked hotel room. Deciding that this was a case for Harriet, the club subsidized her trip to North Carolina to learn more about the victim. Harriet used her Baptist connections and old friends to probe the past. She touched a nerve, because someone bombed her aged De Soto. After Harriet did her locked room exposé, all the police had to do was make an arrest.

Harriet (now ninety) and Helen took it upon themselves during *The Sensational Music Club Mystery* (St. Martin, 1994) to learn who killed Monica Gaulton. Monica had left Borderville in her youth, returning to serve first as housekeeper, then as wife to wealthy Douglas Gauton. His potential heirs resented Monica, but it took an Ouija board to point out a killer.

In *The Historical Society Murder Mystery* (St. Martin, 1996), Helen's position as chairman of the Ambrose County Historical Society made her aware of the theft of a valuable portrait bequeathed to the Society. Harriet was in a nursing home recuperating from a broken hip, but she played a major role in the investigation, tying the murder of local dilettante Randal Hartwell to an art theft ring.

Rita Claymore was killed in her garden during *The Garden Club Mystery* (St. Martin, 1998). When African-American teenager Slater Walls was accused of committing the murder during a burglary, Harriet intervened. Suspicions then focused on individual members of the Buena Vista Garden Club who had clashed with the judgmental and officious Rita over the past months. Harriet rallied her allies to discover clues unnoticed or ignored by the legal authorities.

Very low-keyed.

Rosalie Cairns

Author: Betsy Struthers

Rosalie Cairns had put aside her work on a Ph.D. in literature and employment as a librarian in Toronto to move to a small North Ontario town with her husband Will. Will, formerly a government employee, sought change. Woodworking had been his hobby, but now it became a career. His competence and artistic sense were gradually making him a success. Rosalie worked part-time at a bookstore owned by a Toronto gynecologist. The Cairns had no children, a matter of deep concern and divided opinions. Repeated efforts and medical intervention had brought no results. Will wanted to adopt, but Rosalie was unwilling even through she was reaching the end of her childbearing years. Her now deceased mother had left her with the impression that her father, George Cook, had abandoned them both.

The Cairns' lives were changed when, in *Found: A Body* (Simon & Pierre, 1992), she did just that while walking her dog Sadie along the riverbank. The victim, Toronto attorney Jennifer Rumble, had connections to Will, to Rosalie's employer, and to a former beau of Rosalie's. Even if she wanted to stay out of it, she couldn't because a diary was missing and someone was certain that Rosalie had it.

As *Grave Deeds* (Simon & Pierre, 1994) began, Rosalie was finishing her Ph.D. at York University in Toronto. She accomplished this by spending the weekdays in Toronto and sharing weekends with Will. Beatrice Baker, a great-aunt of whom she had no knowledge, invited Rosalie to visit. The elderly woman was dead when Rosalie kept their appointment. The fact that Beatrice had bequeathed valuable vacation area property to Rosalie aroused resentment from collateral relatives. By the time Rosalie had established her claim and Beatrice's killer was identified, she did not know if she wanted the property.

A Studied Death (Simon & Pierre, 1995) was the most ambitious of the series. Rosalie had accepted a temporary appointment as a professor at the university in her hometown. The death of Sophia Demetrius, a student whom she was advising, affected her deeply. Sophia left behind an undernourished and badly cared for infant whose paternity was in question. There was a possibility that Sophia's death was connected to two fatal "accidents" to females on campus. There had been protests concerning violence to women students.

An otherwise interesting series was marred by the use of mentally disturbed villains in all three novels. Struthers, a poet, concentrated on poetry in at least five subsequent books.

Catherine "Cat" Caliban

Author: D. B. Borton, pseudonym for Lynette Carpenter

Catherine "Cat" Caliban established her Cincinnati investigative agency during the 1980s after her 38-year marriage to Fred ended with his death. They had three children—stockbroker Sharon, perpetual student Franny, and multi-married business executive Jason. A tiny pepper-pot with a rough tongue and rude vocabulary, Cat created a second family out of the tenants in her building, the Catatonia Arms: gay bartender Kevin O'Neill; artist Melanie Carter and attorney Alice Rosenberg, a lesbian couple; African-American Moses Fogg, a retired police detective; three cats; and a beagle. She was free of gender or racial prejudice. Cat compared herself at times to movie actresses; e.g. Lana Turner and Margaret Rutherford who were not in the least bit alike. It is significant that this series is set in the 1980's.

In *One for the Money* (Diamond, 1993), Melanie and Alice's tour of Cat's building ended when the decaying corpse of a mentally ill street-woman was discovered in a vacant apartment. Cat honed her investigative skills by researching the origins of Betty Bags and her missing friend, Lucille Skelton, climaxing in a clue to hidden treasure.

In *Two Points for Murder* (Berkley, 1993; republished in 2005 as *Two-Shot Foul*), Cat helped A. J. McManniss, Jr., a small boy, recover his cat, which had been taken off with material for the local Goodwill. In her search for the cat, she had come upon a notebook. Information in the notebook consisted primarily of numbers and had belonged to Juky Kay, a talented basketball player who had recently been murdered. At the request of his family Cat investigated, but she also copied the material for the benefit of the police. There had been assorted health problems on the team which might be connected.

During *Three Is a Crowd* (Berkley, 1994), Cat coped with the return of Franny, her highly educated but non-functional daughter, hoping that the influence of her new friends would straighten her out. Other problems soon took her mind in another direction. The Central American Coalition to which Franny belonged sponsored a rally during which Steve Sanders, a former Rochester NY, Vietnam era anti-war protestor, was murdered. Subsequently Curtis, a street person, brought Steel, a Vietnam veteran who had gone to school with Sanders, to Cat's house. Steel feared that he would be suspected of the murder, and he was right. Cat used research to help identify the killer. Who else had been members of AWOS (Anti War at Ohio State)? Who went to prison? Had there been a mole in the group?

In *Four Elements of Murder* (Berkley, 1995), Cat added teenage computer freak, Delbert Sweet, to her household when his visiting parents left him behind. He came in handy when Cat accompanied her pal Louella Simmons to Tennessee to investigate the mysterious death of environmental activist Red McIntyre. Red, who was Louella's uncle, had been concerned about pollution in his home state and in Ohio. His car had gone off the road, killing him. Red had left a message. Powerful local forces aligned themselves against Cat's interest in chemical waste.

Cat and her friends enjoyed a course in ceramics at the local activity center during *Five Alarm Fire* (Berkley, 1996) until someone used the kiln to dispose of a corpse. With only ash and bones to work from, identification took considerable time. A line of enquiry emerged based upon the presence of Rockwood Goldstone pottery. Cat might not have artistic skill, but she wove her way through an intricate family structure to find a killer who could not accept his heritage.

During *Six Feet Under* (Berkley, 1997), Cat was drawn into Rocky Zacharias' life and that of her entire family by her friend and tenant, Moses Fogg. She had urged the former police officer to obtain a private investigator's license under which she could work. Rocky was not a paying client. She was a recently released convict whose three children were living with their great-aunt. There were complications as to fellow prisoners whose medical needs had gone unmet in prison, and had died mysteriously. Moses and Cat were the only hope she had left. The narrative had scathing revelations as to the quality of care, medical treatment, education and training received by women in correctional institutions.

Gussie Baer wanted to know who killed her grandson Peter in *Seventh Deadly Sin* (Hilliard Harris, 2004). His throttled corpse had been discovered in the river. Police were stymied. Peter was well liked, an "All –American boy". His parents wanted nothing to do with her investigation so Cat sought out his friends at school. Help came from Peter's ten-year-old sister, Monica, who smuggled out personal papers belonging to Peter. From them, Cat and Moses (now legally private investigators, discovered the fate of three other teenagers and the connections to Peter. Very sad story.

Although the narrative format (frequent changes in time periods) was confusing at times, *Eight Miles High* (Hilliard Harris, 2007) was a fascinating story, one that needed to be told. Toots Magruder, who had served in the Women's Airforce Service Pilots (WASPS), hired Cat and Moses to investigate the deaths of two comrades from World War II and an attempt to sabotage a plane she had been flying. The pattern that emerged combined the personal tragedy of a killer and his victims with the larger tragedy, the failure to recognize the achievements of the WASPS (who unlike other women's service units) had been denied any military benefits until 1977 because of opposition, primarily by veterans' organizations.

Borton also wrote the Gilda Liberty series, covered in this volume.

Sister Rose Callahan

Author: Deborah Woodworth

The North Homage Shaker Village near Langour, Kentucky had taken in Rose Callahan when she was three years old. She left the village at age eighteen to test the world. During her year on the outside, Rose met and had an affair with Seth Pike. She returned to chastity and the Village a year later. Seth had a problem with the Shakers. Not only had Rose ended their romance to return there, but his mother Elsa abandoned him and her husband to become a Shaker. Rose was a tall, thirty-five-year-old redhead by the year 1936 when the series began, and had become trustee for North Homage, handling all business matters.

There was hostility to the Shaker Village in the town of Langour. The austerity and hard work of the Shakers provided a secure living at a time when the Depression had put many locals out of work, leaving some hungry and homeless.

To understand the series it is necessary to understand Shakers. The membership was composed of adult men and women who were both pacifists and celibate, even if they had been married before signing the covenant. Children entered the Village as orphans or family members of adult Shakers. They were raised communally, not under the guidance of individual parents. Men and women avoided even a casual touch from members of the opposite sex, using different doors to buildings, eating and meeting at opposite sides of rooms or halls. This particular Shakers group, which had diminished in membership, had as their spiritual leaders, Eldress Agatha Vendenberg and Elder Wilhelm Lundel. Agatha, then eighty-five and in poor health, had been unable to deter Wilhelm from returning the dress, language, and practices of North Homage to those of an earlier period when the movement had flourished. The Eldress guided the females; the Elder, the males, but Wilhelm was inclined to go beyond his authority.

The death of an itinerant who sought sustenance with the Shakers was explored in *Death of a Winter Shaker* (Avon, 1997). Johann Frederick had come to North Homage at a time of turmoil. Eldress Agatha, dangerously near to death, wanted Rose to succeed her. Wilhelm had selected a more malleable candidate, Sister Elsa Pike, as the replacement. As the Langour villagers' hostility to the Shakers erupted in violence, Rose sought Frederick's killer. With sorrow, she accepted the decision of her protégée Gennie Malone to leave the village at age eighteen and reside in Langour.

The hostility in the village against the Shakers was inflamed again during *A Deadly Shaker Spring* (Avon, 1998) by incidents reminiscent of those that had occurred twenty-five years before. Rose was aware of banker Richard Worthington's enmity, but sought more information on apostates (former members) who might be in the area. She searched the journal of Eldress Agatha for clues. Rose had to simultaneously solve a twenty-five-year-old murder and a more recent killing before a mob attacked North Homage Village.

A small band of Believers (covenanted Shakers) from the Mt. Lebanon headquarters of the movement accompanied Andrew Clark when he replaced Rose as trustee in *Sins of a Shaker Summer* (Avon, 1999). Clark placed more emphasis on developing and selling medicinal herbs than on those used in cooking. The newcomers brought dissension. The illness of children in the community might be a side effect of the new herbal products. Rose's former protégée Gennie, a skilled herbalist, agreed to work with the Medicinal Herb Group testing the efficacy of their products.The deaths of Brother Hugo and Sister Patience made it clear that a killer was within the community.

Danger came to North Homage during *A Simple Shaker Murder* (Avon, 2000) through a group of New Owenites, headed by Gilbert Owen Griffiths. Gilbert claimed to be a descendant of Robert Owens whose communal society had been short lived. Rose came to realize that Wilhelm was determined to convert and absorb the New Owenites, a non-religious group that did not practice celibacy. Gilbert had his own designs upon the prosperous Shaker village. Rose's personal concern was for eleven-year-old Mairin, a neglected child who might have witnessed a murder by hanging.

During *Killing Gifts* (Avon, 2001), Rose, accompanied by her former protégée Gennie Malone, responded to a call for help from the Hancock, Massachusetts Shakers. Julia, a promiscuous young woman hired to work in the Shakers' Fancy Goods Shop, had been murdered. Rose and Gennie learned the backgrounds of the full Shakers, the new novices, and the hired help. Rose reached out to help young Dulcie, Julia's sister, but came to wonder if she might have precipitated a disaster by her advice and questions. Gennie, who was engaged to Sheriff Grady O'Neal, played a significant role in the investigation.

The Shakers were diminishing in number, so in *Dancing Dead* (Avon, 2002) Andrew Clark and Rose convinced Wilhelm to let them turn a vacant building into a guest hostel. Andrew alerted Rose to strange interactions among their guests. Could they be connected to mysterious sightings of a ghost that carried a lantern and danced in front of windows in Shaker buildings? The murders of a guest and a member of the Shaker brotherhood brought Grady O'Neal on the scene. Gennie had left him, returning to North Homage while she made a decision about her future.

A charming series!

Nora Callum

Author: Thomas McCall

Police Lieutenant Nora Callum was a determined woman, who let nothing stop her advancement in the Chicago police department. Not the prosthetic she had to wear after her left knee was destroyed by a shotgun blast. Not the desertion of Richard, her ne'er-do-well husband, or her responsibilities to their seven-year-old daughter, Megan. Not even the vigorous opposition of her superior officer, Deputy Chief Raymond Melchior, to women in general, handicapped women more specifically, and Nora in particular. A tall blonde, whose father wanted her to pursue a classical education, Nora dropped out of Loyola to join the police force after his death, and rose from the ranks. She had been fortunate in her partners: Jack Flaherty until he died of an aneurysm, and then African-American police lieutenant Art Campbell.

Nora was thirty-three when *A Wide and Capable Revenge* (Hyperion, 1993) began. The shooting of Eva Ramirez, a young Hispanic housewife, which took place in church and that of Semyon Lugotov, an obscure European printer, were traced to historic hatreds that struck close to Nora's personal relationships. Lugotov had come to the police department indicating that he knew something about the shooting, but was given inadequate attention. Nora took risks and responsibilities that threatened her professional status, but with Campbell's help avoided Melchior's retaliation. She did not always bother with the procedures, so some problems could be expected.

In *Beyond Ice, Beyond Death* (Hyperion, 1995), Nora and Art investigated the death of Edward Boyes, a NASA scientist who had been teaching at Loyola. His body had been hidden in the woods for months. No one had reported a similar person missing. Nora's investigation, hampered by political pressure for a quick solution, spread to a cooperative space mission between the United States and the Soviet Union.

The series ended even though it had showed promise.

Claire Camden

Author: Audrey Peterson

Claire Camden was an American divorcee in her forties with a grown daughter, Sally. Her academic career had been put on hold for a sabbatical in England. A commuter marriage to Miles Camden ended when he preferred his male lover. As part of the divorce judgment, Claire was awarded their flat in Belford Square, London. She spent her time writing a biography of Victorian female mystery writer M. L. Talbot.

Dartmoor Burial (Pocket, 1992) blended Claire's investigation of the recent murder of pregnant Darla Brown with her research on M. L. Talbot, and Talbot's novel, *The Specimen.* In *The Specimen,* eighteen-year-old Emily Spalding, after rejecting her father's choice for her husband, also died suspiciously while pregnant. The parallels were ingenious but difficult to follow. The investigation brought Claire into contact with the investigator, Neil Padgett, whom she had met and liked earlier.

During *Death Too Soon* (Pocket, 1994), Claire's stint as house sitter in Dartmoor enabled her to spend more time with Superintendent Neil Padgett, who had become important in her life and who attended a nearby university. The placement also provided access to papers involving M. L. Talbot. The disappearance and death of Cheryl Bailey, Sally's African-American housemate, was followed by that of Freida Nolan, wife of a prominent professor. Both women had the initial "C" carved between their breasts. Again Claire received insights from a book written by Talbot. Tensions arose between Padgett and Claire in the course of the investigation.

Neil dealt with the situation by taking a sabbatical in Australia, so in *Shroud for a Scholar* (Pocket, 1995), Claire invited old friend and fellow academic, Iris Franklin, to stay overnight. There was trouble when Claire returned to her apartment to find Iris' battered corpse, and herself on the suspect list. Claire's efforts to clear her name became entangled with historical documents that contained a potential literary scandal and an unsuspected murder.

Complex plotting requiring an attentive reader, but, once begun, the series is absorbing.

Letty Campbell

Author: Alma Fritchley

Leaving behind a humdrum stint as an insurance clerk, Letty Campbell used an inheritance to become a chicken farmer. There were chickens, a strutting rooster named Erik, and a vegetable garden. Fortunately for her, Aunt Cynthia not only left her a home and acreage in West Yorkshire, but investment income that took the risks out of the venture. Letty's lesbian identity was no shock to the locals because Aunt Cynthia had spoken of it regularly. Letty brought her current lover, classic car dealer Julia Rossi, along with her. Julia did not adapt to rural life so returned to Manchester after six months. Letty's mother, a strong-willed woman who worked for a solicitor, was supportive of her daughter's lifestyle. Letty was notable for her short hair, her vegan diet, and her devotion to an elderly Citroën 2CV car now stored in her barn.

During *Chicken Run* (The Women's Press, 1997), Letty leased part of her holding for a classic car auction. Unbeknown to her and Julia, the event was arranged to facilitate an illegal transaction involving drugs and plutonium. The mystery aspects of the narrative were submerged under the lesbian romances, breakups, and realignments. During one of the switches, Letty met and aligned herself with librarian and budding author Anne Marple.

Anne (and her niece AnnaMaria) had moved onto the farm by *Chicken Feed* (Women's Press, 1998). Anne's book on the ancient Babylonians had brought media attention and the opportunity to tour the United States. Letty had little time to be lonely. Laura, Anne's younger sister, arrived from Australia with a five-year-old motherless girl in tow. Julia's new romance, Member of Parliament Sita Joshi, disappeared leaving a bloody car behind and causing the authorities to put Julia in jail. Again the relationships among the women dominated, and sometimes who was with whom became confusing.

Anne's success as an author broadened her world so that she broke off her ties to Letty in *Chicken Out* (The Women's Press, 1999). AnnaMaria and Liam, her 18-month-old son, remained part of Letty's household. The death of George Eversham, Letty's friend and neighbor, brought complications—information about Aunt Cynthia, who had bequeathed the farm to Letty, and the woman Cynthia loved, a Czech refugee who had smuggled artwork into England to conceal it from the Nazis.

George had bequeathed his property to Letty. Its sale value and the announcement that Margaret, Letty's mother, was to marry her wealthy employer, Col. Harry Thompson would have been enough excitement for Letty in *Chicken Shack* (The Women's Press, 2000). However, a jealous former wife, a resentful daughter, escaped bank robbers, and a salacious chef added to the complications. Letty loved and lost, at least temporarily.

The books ambled along, then ended with chaotic finishes. They were set in an almost totally female world. Violence was limited to attacks that did not necessarily involve murder. But they were funny.

Margaret Campbell

Author:Peter May

Forensic pathologist Margaret Campbell had a temporary placement at the University of Public Security in Beijing, China. A graduate of the University of Chicago, she had previously been employed in the Cook County Medical Examiner's Office. Her mother, a cold and distant woman, was of German heritage. Margaret always felt that her mother blamed her when her brother drowned. She also felt some guilt for the tragic end to her marriage. Working in a Chinese social structure was different for her. She was naturally no nonsense, even brusque in her dealings with others. It was necessary, but not easy, for her to realize that "saving face" was important and that the three most important words were "Patience, patience, patience".

Depressed by the emptiness of her personal life in the United States, Margaret had welcomed the invitation to present a six-weeks course at the Beijing Police University but things did not turn out as expected in *The Firemaker* (Coronet, 1999). A meeting in the United States with Police Chief Chen Anming had led to the assignment. Li Yan, a detective and recently appointed supervisor in Chen's department, began his acquaintance with Margaret during an unfortunate traffic accident. They met again when Chen recommended her to perform an autopsy of an unidentified man who had burned to death. His death was initially connected to two others that occurred the same night. Not only did Li resent her appointment but it got worse when her findings contradicted the theory held by the police. It took the interference of Li's highly regarded Old Yihu, to convince Li to work with Margaret. Hostility became respect; then, something more. This is a tense and absorbing narrative as Margaret and Li faced personal danger and professional calamity from powerful authorities.

Detective Li Van was assigned to go to Shanghai and direct the investigation that followed the discovery of more than twenty unidentified corpses at a building site in *The Killing Room* (Hodder and Stoughton, 2000). At that time Margaret was in Chicago attending her father's funeral. Li Van insisted that on her return, she be hired as pathologist on the investigation. Beijing police officials were not necessarily welcome in Shanghai nor were female pathologists, but that did not account for all the obstacles placed in the way of the investigation. Margaret's autopsies disclosed the pattern that connected the victims to one another and to a powerful Chinese Communist party member. The relationship between Margaret and Li Van was at risk because she resented his closeness to Nien Mei Ling, his attractive opposite number in Shanghai. When Xinxin, Li Van's six-year-old niece became a potential victim, they worked together.

The close relationship between Margaret and Li deteriorated in *The Fourth Sacrifice* (Coronet, Hodder& Stoughton, 2000) under the pressure of his job. His promise to contact her did not survive his dedication to his career. He had been told to stay away from Margaret and did so. Margaret had already made reservations to fly back to the United States when the fourth in a series of beheadings occurred. This victim was an American citizen so both the American Embassy and Chinese officials insisted that Margaret remain in China and take part in the investigation. Handsome archeologist Michael Zimmerman provided Margaret with an alternative romance. He was working on a reenactment of the opening of an historic tomb and preparing to escort Terracotta Warriors to the United States for an exhibition. Margaret's conclusion after she performed an autopsy was that there were two separate killers. Aspects of archeology, Chinese history and physical descriptions enhanced the narrative.

As *Snakehead* (Hodder and Stoughton, 2002) opened, Margaret had known for almost a year that Li Yan had been assigned to the Chinese Consulate in Washington, D. C. as the criminal justice liaison. Yet he had never contacted her. She would not have been difficult to locate in her current job, teaching at a Criminal Justice Center and at Sam Houston State University in Texas. The discovery of dozens of dead illegal Chinese immigrants in her jurisdiction brought the INS, FBI, and Li Yan to Houston. Forensic results from body tissues made the authorities aware that the immigrants had brought with them the seeds of a major disaster. Chinese who had been smuggled in earlier had to be located and isolated to avoid an epidemic. However the efforts of the task force were consistently thwarted by a possible leak to terrorists.

Li and Margaret were planning their betrothal party and marriage as *The Runner* (Hodder & Stoughton, 2003) began. None too soon because their baby was due in a month. Jean, Margaret's mother, was coming to China to be present. Li's estranged father surprised everyone by announcing that he would be there. All of these concerns had to be set aside when Li and Margaret were drawn into an investigation of the unexplained deaths of six Chinese Olympic athletes. Although the technical language was sometimes difficult to absorb, this was a fascinating narrative.

The bureaucracy of China still controlled Margaret and Li's lives in *Chinese Whispers* (Hodder & Stoughton, 2004). They had not married although, along with their son Li-Jon, they had moved into an official apartment. Their arrangement was simply ignored by the government at this point. Li, in fact, was the first recipient of an award for superior police work but within a few weeks was a pariah. Margaret, still recovering from her Caesarian, was a stay-at-home mother, seriously bored by her inactivity. All of this changed when the fourth victim of a serial killer was discovered. Section One, in charge of the investigation, was under pressure for quick results. Even when it became evident that the killer was following the methods of Jack the Ripper, the only clue to his identity was a personal hostility to Li.

Although the personal relationships were unusual, the plots were reminiscent of Michael Crichton's novels. The books were originally published in England, but now are being released in the United States by Poisoned Pen Press.

Jane Candiotti

Author: Clyde Phillips

Jane Candiotti had made her family and her work the focus of her adult life. Tall, dark-haired, and just short of forty she was an inspector in the Homicide Unit of the San Francisco Police Department. Inspector Kenny Marks remained her partner and a friend even though their affair had ended. She wanted a family; he, a few years younger, preferred to wait. The other place that Jane felt at home was with her extended Italian-American family. Her mother had died when Jane was only twelve and she had become mother to her younger brother, Timmy. Jane's anchor was her beloved father, "Poppy" who wanted to see her married and to have grandchildren. Her closeness to her family did not extend to their religion. She had ceased to consider herself a Catholic years before.

Fall From Grace (Morrow, 1998), a stunning and complex narrative, found Jane assigned to the murder of Jenna Perry. Jane fell desperately in love with David Perry, Jenna's widower. She was well aware that the couple had separated before the murder occurred, that David would inherit a fortune, and that he was deeply attached to Libby, his teenage daughter. Not only Jane but also Inspector Kenny Marks and Lt. Ben Spielman recognized the conflict of interest. All that mattered to Jane was to find Jenna's killer before David was harmed. That might not be enough.

The successive deaths of a former police officer, two active duty coworkers, and an undercover cop in *Blindsided* (Morrow, 2000) left no doubt that these were the acts of a serial killer. Jane and Kenny, by then living together, headed the task force with the responsibility for identifying, then capturing the killer. Jane drew attention to herself by publicly describing him as "an animal." As they worked the case, Jane and Kenny coped with stresses in the own relationship; then, had to reassess their evaluations of fellow officers.

Jane Candiotti had a strength and a vulnerability similar to Jane Tennison in PBS's *Prime Suspect.* Both were displayed in *Sacrifice* (Morrow, 2003). In one evening, two murders occurred in San Francisco's 19th precinct. The first was that of benevolent businessman Philip Iverson which took place in a hotel parking ramp; the second, the discovery on a San Francisco Bay pier of the body of African-American street person Willie Temple. Subsequent deaths piled up. Jane and Kenny, were under terrific pressure, both personal and professional, to find Iverson's killer. Jane was motivated to solve the Temple case as other victims had also been homeless. The narrative dealt with the police department's need to give priority to the murder of an important businessman.

Caroline Canfield

Author: Jacqueline Fiedler

After Caroline Canfield's father died of a heart attack, her mother, a cabaret singer, became the sole support of the family. This meant leaving Caroline and her younger sister with their maternal grandmother while she was on the road.

Caroline worked for famed muralist Tony Chirico when she finished art school. After a nasty fall from scaffolding, she knew that was not how she wanted to spend her life. Tony had taught her a great deal about painting, given her a sense of shapes and colors, showed her how he placed subliminal messages in his works, and had been a mentor and father figure. Caroline had always enjoyed the outdoors and wild animals, so she opened a studio as a wildlife artist in Fox Valley, Illinois. At thirty-one, Caroline had not recovered from an unhappy relationship.

She had vowed never to paint a mural again, but in *Tiger's Palette* (Packet Books, 1998) she made an exception She agreed to finish the mural at the Fox Valley Zoo, left incomplete when Tony Chirico died in a fall. The circumstances of his plunge from a scaffold, plus the messages she detected in the completed portion of the new Asian Center, made this more than a job. A failure to have the Center finished by a given date might cause the loss of a major bequest. Engrossing.

Depressed by the results of her investigation into Tony's death, Jane turned her attention to a chat room on wolves during *Sketches with Wolves* (Pocket Books, 2001) The interchange among persons known only by nicknames culminated in a weekend at the privately owned Wolf Prairie Preserve near Spoon River, Illinois. Heavy snowstorms isolated the group that included a large number of eminently disagreeable individuals, plus one attractive male. On her first day at camp, she came upon a corpse, which she took to be that of Rebecca, a young waitress, that subsequently disappeared. The others—except the killer—were convinced she was either mentally ill, an alcoholic, or a drug addict.

Carrie Carlin

Author: Nancy Tesler

Carrie Carlin's divorce from Rich Burnham had left her devastated. They had been married for eighteen years when he opted out; only then did she learn that he had been unfaithful for most of that time. Rich must have had a good lawyer. He ended up with the big house and swimming pool; she, with two children and a home in a less sumptuous location. A graduate of Cornell University, Carrie was capable of surviving with generous child support and some alimony plus her earnings as a biofeedback clinician. She had previously worked for a major pain clinic, but chose to go independent. Carrie, twelve-year-old Allie, and ten-year-old Matt lived in Norwood, New Jersey. Her office was in nearby Piermont, New York. Her father had remarried (mother died when Carrie was three) to Eve, who had fussed over him since his bypass surgery. The Carlin (she returned to her maiden name in private life) household included three Siamese cats (Plácido, Domingo, and José) and a large crossbred dog (Horton). Given so many dependents, Carrie was reckless, and addicted to the excitement of murder investigations.

Carrie's first encounter with the police department came in *Pink Balloons and Other Deadly Things* (Dell, 1997). Erica Vogel, the woman who had caused her divorce, was murdered. Carrie had spied upon Erica from a neighbor's yard shortly before the killing. Because she realized that her presence and quick exit made her look suspicious, Carrie investigated other potential suspects. Her professional clients were an integral part of the narrative, as were italicized segments of her dreams, recollections, and innermost thoughts. She received courteous even affectionate treatment from Lt. Ted Brodsky.

A call from Carrie's best friend, Meg Reilly, revealing that Meg's husband, Kevin, was missing and her brother-in-law, Peter, dead from a boating accident, sent Carrie to Key West in *Sharks, Jellyfish and Other Deadly Things* (Dell, 1998). Ted Brodsky warned her in advance that there was something fishy about Kevin's disappearance. Meg was certain that he was still alive although he had not contacted her. Hostile police, suspicious FBI agents, and too-good-to-be-true marine biologist Jonathan Olsen created red herrings galore. Even, at a snail's pace, Carrie and Meg found solutions.

Swept along by the action in *Shooting Stars and Other Deadly Things* (Dell, 1999) readers will probably ignore the overload of coincidences in the plotting. Lt. Ted Brodsky, who was working the murder of travel agent Helena Forester, was unable to keep Carrie from interfering, even to the extent of risking serious injury. At one point she gave thought to what would happen to her children if she lost custody or were killed. Meg Reilly counseled Carrie that she was punishing Ted for Rich's infidelity. She invited him to move in.

Ted's presence in the household became a logistical problem in *Golden Eggs and Other Deadly Things* (Dell, 2000) when Eve, Carrie's stepmother, made a surprise visit. While Carrie struggled with a multiple personality client at the office, she saw several different aspects of Eve at home. Eve had been disdainful of Carrie's involvement in murders; now she wanted her help when she was suspected of having killed a blackmailer. Eve's past had elements that she had never disclosed, but could no longer ignore. Poor Allie and Matt put up with the confusion by spending a lot of time with Meg Reilly, their mother's best friend.

The presence of eminent researcher Dr. Hubert Fruendlich was one of the reasons Carrie attended a major bio-feedback conference in *Slippery Slopes and Other Deadly Things* (Perseverance, 2003). His new techniques might be something she could use in her work. However she had no use for his predatory sexual techniques. The conference was held at a Vermont ski resort, offering thrills on the slopes. Not so for attractive research assistant Charlie Anders however, whose murder put Carrie in a difficult situation. She was trying to control her risk taking behavior, but what's a woman going to do when she's a suspect?

Hollis Carpenter

Author: Deborah Powell

Hollis Carpenter, a lesbian newspaper reporter for the *Houston Times* during the 1930s, was a rough-talking woman in her thirties, who narrated her stories with an ironic humor, typical of the hard-boiled detectives of the time.

She was ready to quit when assigned to cover a society gathering in *Bayou City Secrets* (Naiad, 1991). However the party began a new affair for Hollis, and provided a great story about guns smuggled from the local police department to Bolivia, then at war with Paraguay.

Houston Town (Naiad, 1992) began when her friend Charlotte sought Hollis' help. She had returned from a tryst to find a dead man in her bed. Hollis had no faith in the police, so hid Charlotte before calling them. There were few whom she could trust. The police, local politicians, a female evangelist, and the dead man's family, all had something to hide.

The narratives improvised lesbian themes on a Thirties "private eye" model—a tough investigator taking on the evils of the community single-handed.

Bel Carson

Author: Annie Ross

Bel Carson was orphaned at age nine, and placed in an institution, which fortunately allowed her to attend an excellent school. Bel's kindness to Rosa Collins, a chronically mentally ill child, brought her to the attention of Rosa's guardian, Great Aunt Jenny. Jenny's age prevented her from adopting Bel, but she arranged to serve as her foster mother and treated her with great affection. In her twenties, Bel married Jamie whose lingering death at age twenty-eight left her a widow. By this time she was a news director at RTV, a regional British television station. During the years when she nursed Jamie, she lost touch with Rosa, but still thought of her as a younger sister.

In *Moving Image* (Headline, 1995), Bel was consulted by solicitor Jack Doulton who served as Rosa's trustee. She learned that Rosa had not cashed her trust checks for months and was nowhere to be found. Bel's dogged insistence on finding the woman that Rosa had become, and those who had destroyed her, made her dangerous. RTV was currently understaffed, investigating a series of bombings, when recently fired employee Archie O'Reilly was killed in an explosion. A compelling narrative.

It would have been opportune if things had settled down at RTV in *Shot in the Dark* (Headline, 1996). Trevor Gates, a recently hired but unqualified news editor, set everyone, and particularly Bel's friend, Mags, on edge. Mags and Bel were taken off the regular news reporting and assigned to follow police coverage of the rape murder of sixty-five-year-old nun, Sister Kate. Mags suffered pain, disgrace and humiliation before Bel could put the pieces of the puzzle together. In addition to good friends at work, Bel had a new accomplice—nine-year-old George.

Bel, Mags, hotshot cameraman Joe Bolton and neophyte researcher Amanda Green were sent to Kansas in *Double Vision* (Headline, 1997). British farmer Malcolm Laurie had been accused of murdering his wealthy young American wife, Lenie. Bel's team was to produce a documentary of Laurie's trial. Within weeks, Amanda had been accused of a second murder. Operating outside of her usual support system, Bel tied these two deaths to a third killing. She met Dr. Carl Scott who made her realize that it was time to move on from her mourning.

Wilhelmina "Willa" Carson

Author: M. Diane Vogt

When introduced, Willa was a U. S. District Court judge located in Tampa, Florida. She and her husband George lived upstairs in a mansion located on Plant Island. George, who had been a banker in Detroit, Michigan, had decided with Willa's approval, to leave the Michigan winters behind and relocate there. The first floor of the elegant building had been converted into a restaurant, Minaret (named after the towers), which became very popular and lucrative. Willa, who had earned a law degree from prestigious University of Michigan and practiced in a good firm, was nominated and approved as a federal judge. This may have been partly due to George's strong connections with the Republican party. She was low on the judicial totem pole, the only one whose office suite had not been transferred into the new federal building. Her relationship with Chief Justice Osgood Richardson was prickly at best and featured in several of the narratives. George and Willa were childless, but had two Labs, named Bess and Harry after the Trumans. She had auburn hair, was tall (5'11") and athletic, loved golf, jogged regularly. She named her elegant Mercedes convertible "Greta" while George drove a Bentley. They were obviously living well. Willa had no need to cook because she could eat downstairs at the restaurant or have food sent up to their living quarters. She dressed very casually for work, covering jeans and t-shirts with her black robes; sometimes, this created problems when she had to make appearances without changing. Neither she nor George were interested in local society except as its members used the Minaret for exclusive and elegant dining.

George who was conservative, relentlessly honest, and pragmatic provided a good balance for Willa's sometimes erratic decisions. Willa's childhood had been equally erratic. Her mother Grace, an early widow, had studied nursing while she and Willa lived with good friend Kate Austen and her family. She supported Willa on her own until she met and married insurance broker, James Harper. From age 5 to 16 (when Grace died) Harper had been the only father she had known. When, after a difficult year in which cancer gradually depleted Grace's health, she died, Harper unable to cope with his own grief, returned Willa to Kate Austen who became a second mother. Willa had been devoted to her mother, a loss she never quite recovered from. Kate's children became like siblings to her.

That may explain why in *Silicon Solution* (Sterling House, 1999), Carly, Kate's daughter, came to Willa when she was in trouble. She did this in spite of the fact that she had always been jealous of the relationship between Kate and Willa. Carly, like her two brothers, was an attorney, currently working for MedPro, a corporation heavily invested in breast implants. The murder of Dr. Michael Morgan, one of the three original owners of MedPro, brought Carly, Kate and other friends of George and Willa under suspicion. On occasions Willa's strong commitment to family caused her to stretch the ethical strictures of her position. Jason, one of Kate's two sons who became attorneys, was in continuing contact with Willa and George. He had political ambitions and served as an assistant to Florida's senior U. S. Senator Sheldon Warwick. Both Jason and Warwick also played roles in later narratives.

Although he was a war hero and former Army chief of Staff, political insiders were shocked when General "Andy" Andrews was nominated for a vacancy on the U. S. Supreme Court in *Justice Denied* (Writer's Showcase, 2000; republished as *Marital Privilege* in 2004 by New Millennium). President Benson, a Democrat, offered no explanation for the nomination made without the usual consultation with top staff and Senate leaders. Upon his arrival at the Senate, Andrews was preceded out of the car by his assistant, John Hamilton, who was shot and killed. Undaunted Andrews, who had a law degree but had never practiced, met with the Judiciary committee headed by Senator Warwick. Unfortunately after an acrimonious exchange, both the Andrews family and Senator and Mrs. Warwick came to Minaret for dinner that night. Their hostility escalated until Willa was injured and George told them all to leave and never return. Andrews's death, considering his personality, was only briefly considered a suicide. When the murder weapon, a .38, was traced to George, he was charged with murder. Willa was determined to prove his innocence before he could be indicted. Kate Austen convinced Willa to use a journal to marshal her thoughts and what she had learned.

Willa was overwhelmed with surprises during *Gasparilla Gold* (Mystery and Suspense Press, 2002) not the least being her stepfather James Harper's visit with his new bride, Suzanne. There had been little contact between them over the years, although she had cared about him a great deal at one time. Add to that, the body of ALS victim Ron Wheaton had been discovered by Suzanne on the Minaret terrace during festivities connected to Tampa's Gasparilla Pirate Fest. ALS (a deadly disease) had reduced Ron to a wheelchair with death inevitable as it progressed. His wife, Margaret, was not only a friend of Willa's but her legal secretary. Willa was not content to let Tampa Police Chief Ben Hathaway decide whether or not Margaret was a mercy killer or if she had another more insidious motive. Excellent plotting with some minor inconsistencies and an inexplicable failure to immediately share a clue with Hathaway.

Just as the prior book ended, Willa had another shock. Recently remarried Kate Austen Colombo had been like a mother to her; that made it difficult in *Six Bills* (New Millennium Press, 2003) for her to accept her decades younger husband, Leonardo. Her discomfort did not keep Willa from agreeing to meet with their friend Harris Steam. Harris had been only two when his mother Billie Joe Steam was convicted and sentenced to life imprisonment for the murder of his father, Trey Steam. Over three decades later, Harris still believed in Billie Joe's innocence although no appeals of the verdict had been successful. At the least he hoped that she might be paroled so that she could spend her last days with her grandchildren. She was dying of cancer, a fact which had not been officially verified. This, like the appeals, had been vigorously opposed by Trey's influential family. In 1972, Billie Joe had been the only female in a musical sextet, Six Bills, in which Trey was the lead singer. Before she had finished Willa had met, researched, and interviewed the other four members of the group and Trey's family. The results were traumatic.

Charlotte Carter

Author: Rebecca Tinsley

Charlotte Carter's parents had set their hearts on her becoming a barrister. Her dad was a solicitor; her mother, a magistrate. She chose instead to go into journalism, becoming the business reporter for National News Network. Her parents did not realize how much their ambitious daughter was like them in her concentration on her career. She lived alone in an impersonal West London flat; not even a pet, just a stuffed rabbit named Alfred for comfort. At twenty-eight, Charlotte did not lack a personal life, but it had little stability. The men she wanted (those with goals similar to her own) preferred more pliable women. She sought physical involvement from men, but was unable to get the emotional commitment she had hoped for. Charlotte shied away from heavy drinking, although she knew her wines. Her weakness was food. Her occasional binges were on chocolate.

In *Settlement Day* (Headline, 1994), material sent anonymously alerted Charlotte to a strategic error made by top officials of the Brodie-McClean Bank. She interviewed bank officials and businessmen. As a result, Charlotte became the bank's negotiator with Global Technology, an American firm that had developed a nerve gas that could damage American interests in Latin America. Charlotte's persistence cost her the job at National News Network and her gullibility about men put her in personal danger.

Charlotte seemed content with her job at the BBC, but she moved on in *The Judas File* (Headline, 1995). She was assigned to shadow Michael Fitzgerald, the new Minister of State for Northern Ireland. Charlotte was instrumental in unmasking purported supporters of Fitzgerald who were tied to the Loyal Unionists. The Judas File was a list of terrorists who would provide Army Intelligence with information and a blueprint for assassination. Charlotte obtained evidence, which forced the authorities to open up the process to families of victims.

These were complex thrillers, requiring close reading. Tinsley had experience in the business and financial worlds that provided authenticity, but not always clarity.

Sherry Carter

Author: Parnell Hall

See: Cora Felton, page 258.

Beth Marie Cartwright

Author: Virginia Stem Owens

As the series began, Beth Marie Cartwright was a rather repressed and naïve woman in her thirties living in a small Texas town. She had spent two years at the nearby state college, but dropped out when her mother became ill.

Miss Mineola Magill had gradually bought up available farmland in Watson County but at age ninety-four, she had become capricious. In *At Point Blank* (Baker Book House, 1992), her death was followed by a prison escape. The escapee, Finney Blalock, the son of a Baptist minister, had a reputation as a "bad boy." He was shot, seemingly in self-defense in Beth Marie's presence. Her role as a witness brought Beth Marie to the attention of Norton, a handsome new deputy, but also made her a potential victim.

St. Barnabas' Episcopalian Church reeled with the news that (1) their buildings had been sold and (2) that the deaths of Rector Arlen Canby's two children and hospitalization of his wife, Cassie, were being treated as a murder/attempted suicide. As *Congregation* (Baker, 1992) began, plans were made for Father Dan Kamowski to conduct the children's funeral and then shut down the parish. Instead he was drawn into a private investigation by a letter written by Cassie. Beth Marie had only a minor role. She was now working as a reporter on the Somerville Courier and had Norton as her suitor.

Still, as *A Multitude of Sins* (Baker, 1993) began, Beth Marie was restless and dissatisfied. A chance to work with big city reporter Geoff Granger seemed to meet her personal and professional needs. At that point, Ignacio Macarenas, a deranged young man seeking to clear his deceased mother's name, abducted Beth Marie. Father Dan, Norton, and Geoff joined the search for Beth Marie, each with his own motivation.

Sgt. Samantha Casey

Author: S. D. Tooley

As introduced in *When the Dead Speak* (Full Moon, 1999) Samantha Casey was a sergeant in the Chasen Heights police department. But much of what formed her character gradually emerged in that narrative. Her mother, Abby Two Eagles, had been befriended by reporter Samuel Casey and his wife Melinda as a young woman fleeing the reservation. Abby lived in the Casey home as a housekeeper and friend. When the Caseys realized that Melinda could never bear a child, they asked Abby to be a surrogate mother. This comfortable relationship ended when Sam and Melinda were killed. Abby took Samantha (then only five) back to the Lakota reservation. Years later they both returned to the luxurious home that she had inherited. Her career after graduation from the Police Academy had been enhanced by her godfather, Police Chief Don Connelley. "Sam", as she preferred to be called, attributed her psychic powers to her Native American heritage. Her great grandmother and Abby were both medicine women. One aspect of her power was that by touching the dead or items they had handled, she received visions as to how the death had occurred.

The discovery of the body of Hap Wilson, a Korean veteran who had been declared AWOL, changed the course of Sam's life. The corpse had emerged when a truck crashed into a pillar of the overpass on Bishop Ford Freeway. Sam had extracurricular activities, assignments unconnected to her police duties during which she and her unconventional friend, Jackie Delaney, went undercover. Former FBI agent Jake Mitchell had witnessed one such adventure and recognized Sam when they both worked on the Wilson murder. What emerged was a connection between Hap Wilson's death, the death of her parents and a secret of the Korean War. Sam married Jake Mitchell, according to tribal rules, in order to have someone to care for her mother Abby, and was expecting a child by the second book. The formality of Sam signing a marriage license was necessary before the marriage became formally legal, but after a head injury she was not certain whether she had signed it or not. Sam's position in Chasen Heights, a Chicago suburb, was threatened at times by superior officers.

Nothing Else Matters (Full Moon Press, 2000) was based on events which took place in the prior book, beginning with the death of Sam's father and culminating in the deaths of Stu Richards, a young police officer, and that of police Chief Don Connelly, Sam's godfather. The fact that Stu had been killed with Sam's gun was grounds for suspension when she returned to duty after extensive hospitalization. Jake Mitchell, who was given Sam's position, was perceived by her as an enemy, even though he tried to protect her. These factors were superimposed upon the story of Sparrow, a hit man who came to Chasen Heights to kill, only to learn that he was being set up. An interesting effort that failed from overload.

Sam was drawn to a forest area where Catherine De Marco, a pregnant teenager, had been savagely murdered seventeen years before in *Restless Spirit* (Full Moon, 2002). The discovery of an initialed button and the word spoken by Catherine in Sam's vision became clues in identifying the killer. There was no time to waste because fellow teenager Jimmy Taggart had been convicted of the crime and was due to be executed. Sam's powers were a factor again when she linked Catherine's death to a subsequent murder. Jake Mitchell and Sam had personal decisions to make, but they had good news about her suspension hearing. Even then she considered leaving the police force to work as a private investigator.

Abby, Sam's mother, and activist Alex Red Cloud had been across the street when, in *Echoes from the Grave* (Full Moon, 2007) a backhoe unearthed bones and Native American artifacts. They made it impossible for property owner and real estate developer Elton Breyton III to cover up the discovery. Because the bones included a human skull, Jake Mitchell and his partner Frank Travis were sent to the site. By this time, a busload of Native Americans had joined Red Cloud in the pit, leaving only when they had taken much of the unearthed material. Sam and Jake had to be careful to avoid conflicts of interest, particularly when it became apparent that the bones and skull were not centuries old. Sam's visions kept her focused on the victims, while Jake and Frank worked within the system to make connections.

There were excellent characterizations, but the series will be most interesting to those who accept Sam's powers as realistic.

Next, *What Lies Within* (2010)

Brooke Cassidy (Devlin)

Author: Mary Kruger

Brooke Cassidy never left her humble origins behind. Her father, Police Officer Mike Cassidy had married a young woman from the Social Register. After her death, Mike provided for their child, Brooke. After Mike's death, Brooke became part of her Aunt Winifred's elegant household in Newport, Rhode Island. She retained fond memories of young Matt Devlin, whose family had offered her a home. This was the "Gilded Age," the 1890s with the nation at peace, and wealth concentrated in the hands of bankers and industrialists.

Matt and Brooke became reacquainted in *Death on the Cliff Walk* (Kensington, 1994). She identified the corpse of Rosalind Sinclair, daughter of a privileged family, in a setting where several servant girls had been murdered. The community had tolerated the earlier murders. The local citizens wanted Rosalind's death solved without involving suspects of her own class. Clues left by the bodies, unfortunately made this impossible. Even though Matt was officially taken off the case, they worked together to find the killer and then decided to marry. Matt and Brooke relocated to New York City where he found work with the police department.

Aunt Winifred had provided a European honeymoon as her wedding gift, when *No Honeymoon for Death* (Kensington, 1995) opened. Their presence on an expensive ship, dressed fashionably, and mixing with the first class passengers made Matt uncomfortable. When prominent financier Julius Hoffman disappeared, Matt took charge at the captain's request. He and Brooke worked together to reveal the real victim at sea.

The Devlins' return to New York City in *Masterpiece of Murder* (Kensington, 1996) explored the problems of an early Twentieth century police officer with a wealthy wife who wanted to dabble in his cases. Brooke had access to information about the suspects in the theft of lost masterpieces and the death of curator Joseph Warren. However, her involvement in Matt's investigation created difficulties between him and fellow officers.

The relationships were reminiscent of those in Ann Perry's Thomas and Charlotte Pitt series, but the narratives lacked their depth.

Kruger subsequently wrote a series identified as the "knitting mysteries" featuring shopowner Ariadne Evans.

Molly Cates

Author: Mary Willis Walker

Molly Cates' childhood and youth had been disturbed by the early death of her mother and the mysterious death by drowning of her father. As a seventeen-year-old school dropout, she had married Grady Traynor, a rookie police officer in West Texas. The marriage did not survive. Both Grady and Molly were devoted to their daughter Jo Beth as she grew to womanhood and became a law school graduate.

Molly's next two marriages ended in divorce. Her professional life was more rewarding. At forty she had a successful career as a crime reporter and freelanced as a non-fiction writer. Molly had made her big impact with an account of the murder of Mrs. "Tiny" McFarland, a Texas socialite. The confessed killer Louis Bronk, having exhausted his appeals, was due to be executed. He still protested his innocence. In *The Red Scream* (Doubleday, 1994), Molly reinvestigated when Georgina, the second wife of Tiny's widower, was murdered. Two-time widower Charlie McFarland's resemblance to Molly's own father impeded her investigation. Grady, once convinced she was on the right track, helped Molly and they rekindled their youthful romance.

The beginning of *Under the Beetle's Cellar* (Doubleday, 1995) was so intense that it might deflect some readers. The character development and plot were exceptional. A Doomsday cult had kidnapped eleven first-born children and school bus driver Walter Demming, not for ransom, but for its own fanatical purposes. Molly's prior connection with cult leader Samuel Mordecai, who had a "direct line to the Almighty," made her an insider on the case. The problem that she, Grady, and the FBI had was to rescue the children before they were harmed.

Molly had never let go of her belief that Vernon Cates, her father, had been murdered. In *All the Dead Lie Down* (Doubleday, 1998), she made another attempt to learn how he died. Grady, incredibly tolerant considering her infidelity, asked her to let it go. She was not to be deterred. Molly emerged from this obsession with the help of several homeless people in time to avert a catastrophe. She found answers to her questions. Not the ones she wanted, but the ones she would live with from now on.

These were above average narratives.

Kate Cavanaugh

Author: Cathie John, pseudonym for Cathie and John Celestri

Working with chapters, resembling a journal, the authors fashioned a reader-friendly sleuth suitable for lazy days. Kate Cavanaugh was tall, single and extremely wealthy. She took advantage of all these factors. At some time in her future she would become the CEO of Crown Chili (52 stores with headquarters in Cincinnati, Ohio). Earlier, she had traveled Europe, the Middle East, and Asia, developing a broad array of exotic recipes. Cherry Jablonski and Jasmine Woods, who shared her travels, remained friends, visited, and took part in her murder investigations. For the present she indulged herself as the owner and manager of Round the World Catering. Her social and economic position provided access to the best families and corporations in the community. The high quality of her services brought repeat business.

Home to Kate was "Trail's End," a hideaway that she shared with her dog, a terrier named Boo Kat. Her household included an industrial level kitchen where she and her staff, headed by Tony Zampella, worked, and the family kitchen, presided over by housekeeper Phoebe Jo Boone whose husband Robert was the groundskeeper and handyman. Her maternal uncle, attorney Clifford T. Vashermann, and a board of directors on which her mother played a significant role managed Crown Chili. Patricia ("Tink") Cavanaugh, Kate's widowed mother, was portrayed as superficial and obsessed with Kate's marital prospects.

Preston Schneider, local food and fine arts critic, considered Kate one of his few friends. Kate learned in *Add One Dead Critic* (Journeybook, 1997) that Preston had earned his enemies. The police, in the form of Officer Matt Skinner arrested the church choir director Terry Poole for Preston's murder. Not only had Terry and his wife, Marilyn, been supportive of Kate during her bout with cancer, but she considered him incapable of murder. An assignment to cater the wake dinner provided Kate with access to Preston's home and eventually to his secret computer files. Cherry Jablonski became a houseguest and accomplice along with Julie Ann Boone, the teenage daughter of Phoebe Jo and Robert.

Former fellow traveler, Jaz Woods, now divorced but still deep into spiritual pursuits, showed up at Trail's End Farm in *Beat a Rotten Egg to the Punch* (Journeybook, 1998). Jaz linked Kate to the Circle of Light community, which was having a convocation at the nearby Golden Valley Spiritual Center. Kate discovered the body of local artist Brad Holtman, who was connected to the Circle, while walking Boo Kat. She believed his death to be part of a power struggle within the cult. Kate still had her eye on Matt Skinner but progress was slow.

Having achieved undisputed success as a caterer bored Kate. In *Carve a Witness to Shreds* (Journey Press, 1999), she was approached by socialite Charlotte Oakley to investigate Eric Lloyd, her prospective son-in-law. Far more interesting than the young suitor was his father. Developer Victor Lloyd planned to bring back the good old days in Newport, KY across the river from Cincinnati. Not everyone agreed that those were good days, remembering the gambling halls, the brothels, and the reputed connections with organized crime. Victor's death prompted his uncle, Peppino Guiliani, to seek Kate's services to find the killer. He had a powerful incentive to get her cooperation—secret information about her family.

Lindsay Chamberlain

Author: Beverly Connor

At age twenty-seven, Lindsay Chamberlain had reached many of her parent's expectations. The daughter of a professor of English literature (her father) and a breeder of Arabian horses (her mother), she had earned a Ph.D. in anthropology and served on the faculty of the University of Georgia. Her particular field of interest was the early Native American society of the area and the impact of the Spanish Conquistadors. Her summers were spent on archeological/anthropological digs. During the academic year, she lived in a log cabin on a 36-acre spread where she kept her horse, Mandrake. Not all of Lindsay's interests were scientific. She and Derrick Bellamy, a college friend and fellow professional, were an amateur ballroom dance team.

In *A Rumor of Bones* (Cumberland House, 1996), Lindsay was asked to examine bones from a rural excavation to determine whether they were recent victims of a serial killer of small girls. Lindsay found it traumatic to tell parents that their missing daughters had been brutally murdered. The further discovery of an adult body, a woman whose death had taken place decades before, complicated the investigation. During the summer, Lindsay became romantically involved with Derrick Bellamy, a change from their platonic relationship.

Questionable Remains (Cumberland House, 1997) offered Lindsay a valuable glimpse into the past when she visited a dig in the Northern Georgia/Tennessee area. Utilizing excavated bones, she recreated the interaction of early Native Americans and Spanish explorers. She had recently testified at a trial against Denny Ferguson, who was at large and seeking vengeance. The suspicious death of college student Gil Harris in a major cave located in a national forest preserve was connected to other recent deaths. Lindsay challenged local authorities to find the real victims and the motives for their deaths.

Dressed to Die (Cumberland House, 1998) found Lindsay in a vulnerable position. Boxes stored by her grandfather contained not only stolen artifacts but also a human skeleton. When the artifacts disappeared, both Lindsay and her brother Sinjin were accused of theft. This occurred at a time when the University of Georgia was considering a proposal to combine the archeology and anthropology departments, thus cutting down on staff. Continuing accusations that members of the Chamberlain family were stealing material from the University harmed Lindsay's prospects of attaining tenure. She might even lose her job. However she continued to assist the authorities in locating the body of Shirley Foster, a textile expert who had been missing for four years. At the time of her disappearance, Shirley had withdrawn a considerable amount of money, which had never been found. The narrative wove together four semi-connected mysteries (theft of the artifacts; death of the man whose skeleton had been found with the artifacts; Shirley's death; and the death of chemistry student Gloria Rankin, that initially seemed to be an accident). Required concentrated reading.

Readers will be both educated and entertained by *Skeleton Crew* (Cumberland House, 1999), during which two plotlines blended in fascinating interplay: (1) the 1585 voyage of a Spanish vessel which culminated in murder and a wreck, and (2) the archeological reconstruction of the Spanish vessel by the University of Georgia. The reconstruction depended for much of its authenticity on a diary written by a survivor. Lindsay and construction company executive John West played significant roles in the discovery of a treasure ship and the identification of an ambitious killer. They were attracted to one another although they had clashed before about the appropriateness of excavating Native American artifacts.

A terrifying episode during which Lindsay was abducted and temporarily buried alive in *Airtight Case* (Cumberland House, 2000) left her amnesiac and unsure of herself. Her director Francisco Lewis had described her assignment at a Great Smoky Mountains, Tennessee site as a "vacation" but he had a hidden agenda. Workers at the project were suspected of theft and murder. Lindsay used her research and technical skills to solve historical mysteries and current skullduggery. Longer than usual, but absorbing.

Connor more recently introduced a new female sleuth, forensic anthropologist Diane Fallon

Paris Chandler

Author: Diane K. Shah

Paris Chandler, an attractive green-eyed blonde, was assisting Hollywood gossip columnist Etta Rice of the Hearst papers, when *As Crime Goes By* (Bantam, 1990) began. Paris was a widow whose husband, a member of the Chandler newspaper family, died in World War II. Her parents were Irene, a B-grade movie actress, and Paul Masterson, a screenwriter. Paris fought the Chandler family for her widow's portion of the estate. She ended up with a Bentley she couldn't drive and little else. Alcoholic reporter Walt Ainsley motivated Paris to be more than a gossip gopher. She accomplished this by scooping the police department on the death of a mysterious woman who had presented herself as Mrs. Helen Seeberg, wife of movie director Jack Seeberg. Helen had sought publicity as to an affair she was having.

By *Dying Cheek to Cheek* (Doubleday, 1992) Paris had become a television personality. Her former lover Jim St. Clair was murdered while working on a political exposé. Paris investigated with the help of a newly sober Ainsley, her pseudonymous chauffeur Nick, and ex-hooker Tee Jones.

The Paris Chandler series would have benefited from judicious editing. Under the glitter and name-dropping, there were plots deserving a clearer focus.

Olivia Chapman

Author: Margaret Logan

Olivia Chapman had every reason to be tense and claustrophobic. Her father had died while serving in Korea; her mother, from cancer. Her husband Philip was in a vegetative state at a nursing home as a result of a motorcycle accident, leaving her to raise two teenage sons. Fortunately her interior decorating business kept her focused on the future. She and the boys, when not away at boarding school or at summer jobs, lived in an apartment above Chapman Interiors of Boston. She was described as a tall, slender woman in her early forties. Olivia's son Ryland had problems at school because he preferred drama to sports. He was concerned that he would be labeled "gay." Olivia's tenant, Dee Quintero, was homosexual.

Olivia's first contact with murder came in *The End of an Altruist* (St. Martin, 1994) when she appraised antiques at the home of Nobel Prizewinner Dr. Jonathan Grissom, a notorious womanizer. Grissom was researching a chemical blocker, which would do for cocaine what methadone had done for heroin. His murder and a subsequent attack on his wife cast suspicion on Olivia. Her husband Philip, released from artificial support, died peacefully.

Olivia, who had a problem saying "no," encouraged battered wife Lori Lutz to move in with her in *Never Let a Stranger in Your House* (St. Martin, 1995). Lori and her friend, "Boy" Lyman involved Olivia with a housing project opposed by the neighbors. Lori's abuse of her hospitality and confidence alienated Olivia, who had been dating attractive Assistant District Attorney James Warriner. When Lori's husband was murdered, Olivia's insights into the husband's diaries made her a target for his killer. Above average plotting.

Emily Charters

Author: Fred Hunter

Chicago police officer Jeremy Ransom, the protagonist of the series, was a hard-bitten, hard-drinking loner when he met elderly widow, Emily Charters. His first impression of her as a dithery elderly woman gave way to affection and respect. Emily and Jeremy filled a need for one another. He painted her house; she provided him with Sunday dinner but more importantly each contributed a sense of belonging to the other.

In *Presence of Mind* (Walker, 1994), Ransom was stalled on the murder of prominent attorney Lawrence Watson. On her own, Emily connected his death with those of young Barbara Landis and elderly theatergoer Meg Ferguson. Meg was a personal friend. Emily and the victims were members of a sparse audience that had attended a play. With Emily as the tethered goat and the potential suspects dwindling by further murders, Ransom made his case.

Emily continued to be supportive in *Ransom for an Angel* (Walker, 1995). She was someone with whom Jeremy could discuss his cases and gain an occasional insight, often based on her literary quotations. The very attractive Angela Stephens announced to Jeremy that she was going to be murdered by someone who resembled her husband Frank. She had been consulting Melina, a tarot-reading seer. Angela's subsequent murder proved that, while she may have been an angelic wife and sister, she was easily manipulated, a fatal flaw.

Emily had heart bypass surgery in *Ransom for Our Sins* (Walker, 1996), distracting Ransom. He pursued a religious fanatic who may have had faith, but little hope or charity. Ransom identified the killer just in time to prevent another crucifixion.

Emily's health remained a concern for Jeremy as *Ransom for a Holiday* (St. Martin, 1997) began. His solution was a Christmas vacation at a Michigan guesthouse. The inn, owned by Sara Bartlett, had been recommended by Lynn Francis, whom he employed to clean Emily's house. Lynn had failed to mention that a murder had occurred on the premises two years before, and that Sara, although not tried in a court, had been judged guilty by the residents of LeFavre. Bored by the rural calm, Emily and Jeremy rescued Sara from disgrace and death.

Emily quoted Shakespeare and noted cryptic remarks on television but *Ransom for a Killing* (St. Martin, 1998) was a straight police procedural featuring Jeremy and his partner, Gerald White. After nine years in prison, African-American Ben Harvey had been released. His DNA test proved he had not raped a white high school classmate. If not Ben, then who was the rapist and had he added murder to his crimes?

Abigail Pearson was suspected of having Alzheimer's because she saw her missing husband Phillip in the house during *Ransom Unpaid* (St. Martin, 1999). Emily was outraged. People were too quick to label the elderly as senile for events that would be ignored or explained away for a younger person. She intervened, offering herself as a short-term companion for Abigail. She evaluated those who might benefit if Abigail were to die or be removed from her home. As always, Jeremy was there for back up.

A successful new opera company from Santa Marta, California was engaged to present *Carmen* as the first performance at the Sheridan Center in *Ransom at the Opera* (St. Martin, 2000) The two principals, Maria Cortez and Ricardo Nuevo, had promising careers projected for them. They were expected to provide the Santa Marta Company with a great future. Unfortunately, first Maria was indisposed; then Ricardo was poisoned on their opening night. Emily was in the audience but it was Jeremy's continued questioning of witnesses that uncovered a remorseless killer.

Louie Dolores, a ruthless real estate developer, sought to garner public approval in *The Mummy's Ransom* (St. Martin, 2002) by subsidizing an exhibition of Chilean mummies. He was harassed by Samantha Campbell of the Historical Preservation Society who knew that he was contemplating the demolishment of another historic factory. Even some of Dolores's business associates thought he was pushing the envelope. A "mummy" appeared on several occasions at the exhibition hall. Hector Gonzalez, of the Chilean Museum that had loaned out the mummies, felt this was a message from their ancestors. When Dolores was murdered, the case was assigned to Ransom, who called on Emily to assist in interviews of witnesses and suspects.

Ransom was "at sea" only figuratively because it was Emily and her housekeeper, Lynn Francis who went on a four day Great Lakes cruise in *Ransom at Sea* (St. Martin, 2003). Lynn struck up a friendship with Rebecca Bremmer who was escorting her unstable Aunt Marcella Hemsley. Marcella's behavior, due to Alzheimer's was well known on board as was the stress under which Rebecca was living. Marcella's murder while the ship was docked at a rural port led to Rebecca's arrest, primarily because no one else on board seemed to have a connection to Marcella.

Although Emily played a limited role in some of the outcomes, she added a cozy touch to a police procedural. Hunter's next series featured gay Alex Reynolds.

Dr. Elizabeth Chase

Author: Martha C. Lawrence aka M. K. Lorens

Her parents (neurologist father and securities analyst mother) and her education (some premedical training at Stanford and two Ph.D.'s) had given Elizabeth Chase great promise for the future. She was thoroughly grounded in science, but she was also a strong believer in extra-sensory powers, ghosts and out of body experiences (OBE). She had worked as a psychotherapist but found it too stressful. Elizabeth shared her home with Nero (a Rhodesian Ridgeback) and Whitman (a Himalayan cat). Her loyalty to the Packer football team was suspect because she called them the Wisconsin, rather than Green Bay, Packers.

As the series began she was in her early thirties, living in a home/ office in a restored farmhouse in Escondido, California. She had never married; had ended a yearlong relationship with a man because she did not feel "right" about marrying him. Her current career was as a private investigator, often assisting the police department.

As *Murder in Scorpio* (St. Martin, 1995) opened, one glance at a photo was all Elizabeth needed to know that Janice Freeman was dead. Police Sgt. Thomas McGowan, who had known Freeman since high school, wanted more. He was so convinced that the accident in which she died was murder that he subsidized Elizabeth's investigation privately. McGowan, too, had extra sensory perception, and was there for Elizabeth when she was in danger.

A series of rapes reported on the television in *The Cold Heart of Capricorn* (St. Martin, 1997) prompted Elizabeth's dream, foretelling a murder yet to occur. When the setting she had described to the authorities became a murder site, Elizabeth was accepted as part of the police unit investigating the crime.

Visions, and clues in her dreams and in those of the victims enabled Elizabeth to identify a killer and trace his escape route.

As *Aquarius Descending* (St. Martin, 1999) began, Elizabeth renounced her vow to never become involved with cults again. She succumbed to attorney Vince Shaffer's plea to find his daughter, Jen. No matter that Jen had been Tom MacGowan's lover. Elizabeth's courage and psychic powers were not enough to avoid a calamity that would change her life forever.

Still in mourning, Elizabeth planned to let her investigator's license expire.

In *Pisces Rising* (St. Martin, 2000), her good friend Scott Chatfield urged Elizabeth to take part in the defense of compulsive gambler Bill Hurston. After a failed attempt at suicide in a hotel room, Hurston had been found with the scalped body of his friend Dan Aguillo, manager of the Mystic Mesa Casino. There were undercurrents of tribal enmities, gambling syndicates, and politics to muddy the waters. A Native American shaman helped Elizabeth see the investigation through and restored her belief.

In *Ashes of Aries* (St. Martin, 2001), a kidnapper/arsonist sought vengeance on Frank Fielding, his wife, and their four-year-old son Matthew. Elizabeth, who had been hired to find the boy, was certain that his abduction and the fire that killed his parents were connected. Her success in locating Matthew drew the attention of the arsonist to Elizabeth and her family. On the personal level, Elizabeth met an engaging television reporter, but was not ready for another relationship.

Fascinating, particularly for those who do not require logical deduction in their mysteries.

Nikki Chase

Author: Pamela Thomas-Graham

African-American Professor Nikki Chase had worked too hard to become the only female member of the Harvard University Department of Economics to take lightly rumors that Dean of Students Rozella Fisher had received unfair promotions. Rozella, also an African-American, did not have a college degree, usually a job requirement for administrative positions at Harvard. Nikki's devotion to her work was reflected in the name of her cat, John Maynard Keynes. After her initial Harvard degree, Nikki had worked on Wall Street, then returned to Harvard for her MBA and LLD. She had worked for four years in the Economics Department as the series began.

Rozella Fisher was murdered in *A Darker Shade of Crimson* (Simon & Schuster, 1998). Nikki's assignment to an important faculty committee provided access to Rozella's records, to the impact she had on co-workers and her former husband Isaiah Fisher, and to financial manipulations within the department.

Nikki's loyalty to Harvard did not keep her from checking out the murder of conservative Amanda Ingersol Fox in New Haven during *Blue Blood* (Simon & Schuster, 1999). She was contacted by Amanda's husband Dean Gary Fox who was a friend and a suspect. Nikki's experience at Yale taught Nikki that old friends couldn't always be trusted; that conservatives can be warm and generous human beings, and that she, too, was guilty of stereotyping.

Nikki came to realize how different Princeton was from Harvard and Yale in *Orange Crushed* (Simon & Schuster, 2004); more intimate, less diverse, and smaller. The opportunity to attend a conference there coincided with a chance to attend a party for her mentor, Prof. Earl Stokes, and to visit her brother, Eric. Rumors surfaced that Stokes would accept a position at Harvard, leaving behind a considerable legacy and a new Afro-American Studies building. Stokes' murder occurred the same night as the building was torched. Nikki stayed on, learning more about the man he had become, personally and academically.

Excellent characters and background.

The series was dubbed as "Ivy League Mysteries"

Laura Chastain

Author: Lelia Kelly

Certain professions, by their very nature, attract highly competitive, even arrogant, individuals. Criminal lawyers, surgeons, and war correspondents frequently fall into this category. These fields have been less accessible to women. The characteristics they demand are not those society has fostered in females in the past. Laura Chastain, a daughter of the South, initially planned to practice corporate law within the upscale Atlanta firm of Prendergrast and Crawley. It was understood by senior partners that when valuable clients or members of their families encountered problems with the criminal justice system, it might be necessary for the firm to provide services. Such assignments would be routed to younger members of the staff. Laura was not only successful in such instances but she enjoyed them. After five years at P&C, she pressured to have a criminal justice unit within the firm, and to have her competence rewarded by a partnership. Single at thirty, Laura's personal life was enriched by an affair with Tom Bailey, her mentor and the chief litigator at P&C.

As *Presumption of Guilt* (Kensington, 1998) opened, her relish for the courtroom was tested. She had just successfully defended Alex Hunnicutt, Jr., the son of an important client, charged with rape. Her new client was police detective Jeff Williams charged with killing Corey Taylor, a suspect in a juvenile rape investigation. Since Taylor had been in custody at the time of his death, someone in the sex crime unit was responsible. Her relationship with Bailey, her status within the firm, and her rapport with the police were all endangered by the corruption she encountered.

Although her surroundings were far less opulent at the District Attorney's office, Laura encountered problems similar to those in private practice during

False Witness (Kensington, 2000). Seeking proof that James Stanley had conspired in the murder of his wealthy wife Christie, she took a calculated risk by granting transactional (total) immunity to a witness. When the strategy backfired, Laura compromised her ethics to achieve the result she wanted. She found comfort in her friendship with police lieutenant Amos Kowalski, head of the sex crime unit and her adversary in the prior narrative.

Within a few pages of *Officer of the Court* (Pinnacle/Kensington, 2001) Laura's well-ordered life fell apart. Her relationship with Kowalski was jeopardized by his loyalty to fellow officers. Her new position as deputy prosecutor under Meredith Gaffney, head of major crime cases in the District Attorney's office, lost its appeal. She was prosecuting Roland Jervis, a man whom she not only believed to be badly represented, but also believed to be innocent. Jervis had been stopped while driving Lawrence Belew's car with Belew 's corpse in the trunk. Nevertheless, Laura's sense of justice forced her to take steps, which jeopardized her future.

Sunny Childs

Author: Ruth Birmingham

After earning a degree in philosophy and spending two years as a stock analyst, Sunny Childs spent ten years at Peachtree Investigations in Atlanta. In that time she acquired a financial interest in the business, as well as a heavy share of the responsibilities. Gunnar Brushwood, the public face for the agency, had established himself as a take-charge guy, big game hunter, and world traveler. Unfortunately that left him little time to train his operatives, handle the finances, and take a personal role in investigations. Sunny, who prided herself on telling the truth, was reduced to forging Gunnar's signature, giving false information to potential clients, and coping with those who wanted Gunnar's personal attention.

Sunny was initially unaware that Gunnar had served with her father, Captain John Childs. Since John's reported death, Sunny's mother Miranda had married four times, buried three elderly but well-to-do husbands, and was now living happily with number five, Dr Harry Wineberg. Sunny had never married. Her attraction to unsuitable men may have been a protective technique to avoid real involvement. Walter, Sunny's brother, aspired to be a musician when he was young, but was diverted by Miranda into law school, ending up in a large Atlanta firm. A half-sister, Sue emerged later in Sunny's life. Sunny was a tiny brown-haired woman (5' 0", less than one hundred pounds), but skilled in the martial arts. She lived in a loft, located in the Fairlie-Poplar area of Atlanta.

Reliance Insurance wanted Gunnar to take personal charge of recovering a stolen painting by Childe Hassam in *Atlanta Graves* (Berkley, 1998). He was off on another of his jaunts, leaving no address. It was up to Sunny to save the day. Actually she had five days because they were overdrawn at the bank. There were corpses along the way. At the end she was unsure whether the real villain had been arrested.

Sunny and her mother emerged from their stereotypes in *Fulton County Blues* (Berkley, 1999), a poignant narrative. The death of Jerry Reynolds, a Vietnam veteran who had served as John Childs' sergeant, awakened Sunny's interest in her father, a matter that Miranda refused to discuss. She took time off from Peachtree Investigations to seek the truth and to clear her father's name. As she had been warned, the disclosures were painful. At one point her irrational response may have sensitized Sunny as to how people react under continued stress.

Sweet Georgia (Berkley, 2000) returned to a more conventional, yet well-plotted private investigator mystery format. Peachtree was hired to find and bring back alive country singer Georgia Burnett. Gunnar and Sunny believed the abduction to be a public relations gimmick. He continued the case and was adjudged a hero for his rescue of Georgia. Sunny refused to take part in the ransom process and was fired. Two months later, Georgia was murdered and Gunnar was indicted for murder. His attorney hired Sunny to find the real killer. She began an affair with Barrington Cherry, an African-American FBI agent.

Blue Plate Special (Berkley, 2001) was a classic narrative, reminiscent of the Twenties. Instead of an island or isolated mansion, the setting was a Cabbagetown diner. The suspects included a dozen patrons who were present when nineteen-year-old Keith Trice held up the cashier while shooting his pistol several times to intimidate those present. During a short interval when the lights were out, real estate broker Phyllis McClint, was murdered. Trice denied firing the final shot, but held them all as hostages, demanding money and a getaway plane. He settled for having Sunny interview all of those present to reveal who the killer was. It wasn't that simple. The treatment of the residents of Cabbagetown who saw their lifestyles being eradicated by gentrification was sympathetic, but realistic.

When Sunny changed her vacation plans to investigate a murder at Hellespont Lodge in *Cold Trail* (Berkley, 2002) she realized that Jennifer Treadway's death had already been investigated by the Georgia Bureau of Investigation. GBI agent Wayne Allgood made her aware that his efforts to work the case had been sabotaged. The Lodge belonged to a group of married women who hunted game, but also had been successful in bagging wealthy husbands. Jennifer and Sunny's mother, Miranda, were both members of the group. Miranda had not participated in the decision to hire Sunny. Martha Herrington, who became the next victim, had done so.

Birmingham packed a tremendous amount of background, tension and a touch of humor into 250 page *Feet of Clay* (St. Martin's Minotaur, 2006) at a time when many mystery novels were bloated to 400-500 pages. Sunny's ditzy cousin, Lee Lee Edwards, had a new project, a documentary on convict Dale Weedlow, due to be executed for the murder of two young women. Lee Lee managed to stir up such a fuss that the local good ole boys had her arrested on trumped up charges. Walter, Sunny's attorney brother, was assigned to handle her case. Meanwhile Sunny became convinced that Dale had been framed, and did something about it.

Birmingham on several occasions had a double-dipped ending in which the case seemed to be solved, only to reveal another level of deception. Sunny focused on her personal sense of justice rather than the legal issues. She falsified evidence and allowed murderers to escape formal punishment.

Lydia Chin

Author: S. J. Rozan

Lydia Chin, a Chinese-American living in New York City, chose an unusual occupation for a woman of her background—private investigation. Only 5' 1" and 110 pounds, she was able to take care of herself, and was working on a black belt in karate. Frequently, she worked with Bill Smith, a divorced solo investigator who sought a more personal relationship. Neither Lydia's widowed mother nor her four brothers would approve such an alliance. She dated Chinese-American suitors, but admitted serious feelings for Smith. Mrs. Chin and the brothers—Elliot, Ted, Andrew and Tim—appeared in the series. Mr. Chin, a cook, had died when Lydia was thirteen. Her name in Chinese, used for effect when she dealt with elders in the community, was Chin Ling Wan-ju. The series changed focus with each book, as the Lydia and Bill alternated as narrators and primaries.

In *China Trade* (St. Martin, 1994), narrated by Lydia, a distinguished committee of Chinatown business and professional citizens hired her to locate two stolen crates of priceless porcelains. Bill joined in the investigation, which pitted them against two Chinese-American gangs fighting over the protection racket and the reluctance of a widow to have her husband's reputation damaged.

Concourse (St. Martin, 1995), a lovely read with lyric descriptions narrated by Bill Smith, relegated Lydia to a supportive role. Old friend Bobby Moran sought Bill's services when his nephew, Mike Downey, a security guard, was killed. Bill went undercover at the nursing home where Mike had worked. He needed help so Lydia handled the outside investigation.

She played a more significant role during *Mandarin Plaid* (St. Martin, 1996). Her brother Andrew introduced Lydia to Genna Jing, whose fashion designs were being held for ransom. Lydia and Bill were to broker the exchange, but became targets instead. Lydia, a risk taker by inclination, went undercover as a wannabe model. Even after she was fired from the case, her primary suspect murdered, and Bill tossed in a police cell, Lydia persisted.

When Bill went undercover as a mason on a major construction site in *No Colder Place* (St. Martin, 1997), he needed an ally in the business office to investigate the problems, including murder, that plagued the building. Lydia resented what she considered a subordinate assignment, but agreed to go along with his plan. They cut through the layers of deception between financial backers and the men working to meet a deadline. The title reflected the sense of achievement that construction men have when what they built takes on a life of its own.

A Bitter Feast (St. Martin, 1998) was a Lydia book. It explored the struggles between the established Chinese families and the ambitious newcomers to New York City's Chinatown. Lydia agreed to help her friend Peter Lee locate four immigrant waiters whose disappearance might have been connected to pro-union activity.

Stone Quarry (St. Martin, 1999) focused on Bill, who regularly took off by himself to a remote cabin in upstate New York. He had friends there: young Jimmy Antonelli, whose older brother Tony ran a local bar. Bill had been there for Jimmy when as a youngster he got into trouble. Bill also had powerful enemies. Lydia followed up on clues in New York City after the theft of valuable paintings from wealthy widow Eva Colgate. Lydia joined Bill in time for a short but eventful visit. He had a need to be alone. He loved classical music, and played the piano but only for himself.

The underpinnings of Chinese society were familiar to Lydia: family unity, a sense of history, and debts of honor. They were significant in *Reflecting the Sky* (St. Martin, 2001). Grandfather Gao, a major figure in New York City's Chinatown, commissioned Lydia and Bill Smith to courier items from the estate of his dear friend Wei Yao-Shi to family members in Hong Kong. Lydia knew Gao would not have insisted on Bill's presence had there not been danger involved.

Lydia had always known that Bill had hidden demons. They emerged in *Winter and Night* (St. Martin, 2002) when his nephew, Gary Russell, was picked up by the New York Police. Gary asked them to contact Bill, not his father, Scott. Gary had left his home in small-town Warrenstown, New Jersey to carry out a mission. Bill and Lydia came to realize how high school sports in Warrenstown had become an obsession with renegade jocks. Traditionally their criminal actions went unpunished. Lydia and Bill tied the recent death of Tory Wesley to the rape of Beth Victor 23 years before. Lydia learned what made Bill the man he had become and helped him avert a tragedy.

The series showed improvement with each book. There were two different narrative styles. Those featuring Bill were more "hard-boiled." The Lydia books placed more emphasis on relationships.

For a time the Bill Smith/Lydia Chin series was put on hold as Rozan produced two excellent standalones. New Lydia Chin/Bill Smith in 2009: *The Shanghai Moon*

Wyanet "Wy" Chouinard

Author: Dana Stabenow

Wyanet Chouinard was initially merely a subsidiary character in the second Stabenow series featuring Alaska State Trooper Liam Campbell. Wyanet and

Liam had a personal history. Their affair ended when she could no longer deal with the fact that he was married and a father. Wyanet had attended the University of Alaska at Fairbanks, where she studied to be a teacher. She took time out to backpack through Europe, even taking a cooking class in Paris. When she realized that teaching was her adoptive parents' goal, not her own, she found a new career. She became the owner of the Nushagak Air Taxi Service. Wyanet's own lineage included Yupik, an Alaskan people. She had spent some time in a foster home. Both her father and grandfather had abandoned their families. During the series, she sought to adopt twelve-year-old Tim whose alcoholic mother had abused him.

Liam had loved his wife Jenny enough to marry her, but the passion he felt for Wy went beyond anything he had experienced. They met again in *Fire and Ice* (Dutton, 1998). Liam was in disgrace for failure to properly supervise his subordinates and mourning the death of his son. His wife Jenny barely existed in a coma. These problems led to a demotion and reassignment to Newenham, a remote fishing town. Wy was the first person he saw when he exited the plane. She was standing over the mangled body of Bob DeCreft who assisted her in spotting schools of herring for the fishermen. Her role in the narrative was subsidiary to Liam's investigation of DeCreft's death and the subsequent murder of a brutal fishing magnate. She figured as a love interest, but also as a suspect.

There were heroics enough to go around in *So Sure of Death* (Dutton, 1999). Liam conquered his fear of airplanes. Wy measured up by using her Tai Chi to disable a killer. They wrestled with their personal problems: relationships with parents and their own tangled past in an excellent narrative.

Wyanet provided Liam with valuable information and made remarkable landings during *Nothing Gold Can Stay* (Dutton, 2000). The narrative covered several storylines—an abused young wife, an insane killer, an urban woman who endured Alaska's solitude as long as she could because she loved her husband, old lovers and young lovers. All superimposed on the background of the Alaska story: huge spaces, undependable weather, and indomitable residents.

Liam, who had been sent out to Newenham as a punishment, had a chance to return to the Anchorage office in *Better to Rest* (Signet, 2003). Now with Wy and Tim in his life, he wasn't sure he wanted to leave. Would they come with him? Would she marry him? These thoughts had to be set aside when hunters discovered the wreck of a World War II C-47 on the face of a glacier. The next day the body of popular widow Lydia Tompkins was discovered in her home. Liam pursued the case with exceptional vigor because he liked Lydia. He and his assistant, Diana Prince, did the police procedural aspects, but there were complications. The Air Force sent a representative, Liam's father, Col Charles Campbell who was determined to reach the wreck. Wy re-discovered a member of her family, became aware of a special gift, and clued Liam in on a possible motive for both murders.

The narratives were primarily police procedurals. Wyanet added a second dimension.

Stabenow has a longer, better known series featuring Kate Shugak, covered elsewhere in this volume.

Ella Clah

Authors: Aimee and David Thurlo

For Ella Clah, a member of the Navajo tribe, becoming an FBI agent was an achievement. When her husband Ernest was killed in an accident during his army service, she finished her education and separated herself from her family and culture. Her father had been a Christian preacher. Through her mother Rose, Ella had inherited special powers of observation and spirituality, which she suppressed. The family legend was that a female ancestor broke a taboo by having an unacceptable sexual relationship. Rejected by her own clan, the ancestor had allied herself with witches, gaining powers that she could pass down through the female line. This legacy came to haunt Ella later. The expectation was that each family unit should have two children. If one were evil, the other could create balance and overcome the evil.

Ella had eight years of FBI experience, mostly recently in the Los Angeles office, when she learned her father had been murdered, as *Blackening Song* (Forge, 1995) opened. The case was not in her territory and the family connection would create a conflict of interest. Nevertheless, Ella took leave, convinced that only a Navajo could solve the murder. She had become an outsider to her people, now torn between the younger traditionalists and the elderly who had become complacent by years of dependence. FBI agent Dwayne Blalock who had been assigned to the case had no time for Ella, and little understanding of tribal ways. Ella utilized her mystical powers to achieve her purpose. The narrative showed promise.

During *Death Walker* (Forge, 1996), Ella moved in with her mother, and made efforts to assimilate into the tribe located in New Mexico. Someone was killing tribal members who were the repositories of tradition, ancient skills, and history. Some blamed Ella's family for the bad luck that had fallen on the tribe. Peterson Yazzie, Ella's nemesis currently confined in a mental institution, claimed that his powers as head of the Skinwalkers caused the disasters. With the assistance of tribal officer Justine Goodluck who was Ella's cousin, Ella separated the Skinwalker malevolence from a copycat killer.

The insidious powers of Ella's father-in-law, Randall Clah, haunted her even after his death in *Bad Medicine* (Forge, 1997). Angelina, the risk-taking daughter of Senator James Yellowhair, died in an automobile accident. Ella and her friend, Dr. Carolyn Roanhorse, decided that the young woman's death was caused by poison that affected her driving ability. Senator Yellowhair found that unacceptable. He set out to destroy Carolyn's credibility, forcing Ella into a conflict of interest. She knew Carolyn was right, but her championship of a suspect created problems for the Navajo police department.

Enemy Way (Forge, 1998) found Ella beset by problems and enemies. Two reservation youth gangs terrorized neighborhoods and battled one another. The Brotherhood, an Anglo group, sought money to fund a hit man to kill Ella. Lisa Aspass, the fiancée of Ella's friend Wilson Joe, was murdered, provoking a series of killings by Skinwalkers. On a personal level, Rose, Ella's mother, was seriously injured by a drunken driver. The complications were an overload. Ella sought her brother Clifford's help to combat their mutual enemies, the Skinwalkers. The Skinwalkers and their association with the family of her deceased husband, Eugene Clah, had become an ongoing narrative device. Time to move on.

The news that she was pregnant was not necessarily an unpleasant surprise for Ella in *Shooting Chant* (Forge, 2000). Defense attorney Kevin Tolino was the father, but she had no wish to marry him. Her more pressing problems were professional: the increased hostility between liberal members of the Navajo tribe and the Traditionalists and the death of a researcher at a plant located on reservation land. Aware that she had a new life to protect and that her brother Clifford was involved with the aggressive Fierce Ones Society, Ella still had a duty to carry out. Her child was female, an heiress to the special powers of the maternal line.

No matter what Ella had accomplished, she could not overcome the hostility of the Bitter Water clan, the vitriol of commentator George Branch, or the legend that predicted evil in each generation of her family. In *Red Mesa* (Forge, 2001), all these factors worked against Ella when she was accused of killing her assistant and cousin, Justine Goodluck. Ella was under attack, but good friends stepped in when she needed them most. Fortunately Justine surprised them all.

Ella, her mother, and her daughter Dawn showed courage in *Changing Woman* (Forge, 2002). When the reservation was plagued by vandals and the tribe plagued by drought and unemployment, some proposed gambling casinos as a remedy. The reservation police department was understaffed but still blamed for the vandalism. Kevin Tolino, Dawn's father, sought a referendum on the gambling, while Rose, a traditionalist, feared that casinos would destroy tribal values. Outsiders combined with the pro-gambling group to create a crisis situation. An escaped convict had a personal goal, to kill Ella.

Rose Destea, Ella's mother had a book of her own, *Plant Them Deep* (Forge, 2002?) in which she was appointed by the tribal council to investigate the disappearance of wild plants that had religious significance. Ella pitched in near the end to help her mom, as did Herman Cloud and other members of the Plant Watchers.

The death of police officer Jason Franklin in *Tracking Bear* (Forge, 2003) occurred when the tribal police force was understaffed and badly supplied. The latest controversy was whether or not a uranium mine should be opened on tribal land and a nuclear power plant set up. This project was to be Navajo Electrical Energy Development (NEED). Who would control such a project?

Outsiders or the tribe? A series of murders targeted those who opposed NEED. The narrative rambled, diverting into Kevin's role as Dawn's father, Rose's ascendance as a tribal leader; Justine's hesitance about a long term commitment;. Nobody was focusing on the main plotline. Disappointing.

Ella's miraculous recovery from serious injuries incurred during a fall in *Wind Spirit* (Forge, 2004) brought her nothing but trouble. Not only had the incident been interpreted as linking her to Chindi (the evil left behind by the deceased) but she'd fallen into a skinwalker's cave. Rose and Dawn were feared and shunned. A cure was possible through a particular Sing available only through one man, currently off on a personal quest. Ella had a job to do meantime. Councilman Lewis Hunt's proposal for gun registration led to the destruction of his home and the death of his wife. Ella had to straighten out her personal life and establish her priorities.

The disappearance of novice FBI agent Andrew Thomas on the reservation put Ella in a difficult position during *White Thunder* (Forge, 2005). Thomas had intruded on a Sing, a serious breach of tribal custom. Had he been harmed by an enraged participant at the ceremony, the authorities would get little cooperation from those involved. Gregory Simmons, Thomas's FBI supervisor, threatened to flood the area with officers if Thomas wasn't located quickly. A short cell phone message set Ella on his trail, but she had to find him before a killer did.

Ella's personal life was in ferment during *Mourning Dove* (Forge, 2006). Rose who provided care for Dawn, planned to marry her long time beau, Herman Cloud, and move into his home. Kevin, Dawn's father, wanted more time with her. Returned National Guardsman Jimmy Blacksheep, had been murdered during what might have been a carjacking. Both the tribal police and the local officers, including Jimmy's brother Samuel, were on the case. After receiving an enigmatic message, Ella was convinced that the motive for Jimmy's murder stemmed from his time in Iraq. The murder of Valerie Tso had personal ramifications for Ella in *Turquoise Girl* (Forge, 2007). Valerie was the daughter of Lena Clani, Rose's best friend. She was also the mother of Boots who provided after school care for Ella's daughter, Dawn. There were religious aspects to the killing that harkened back to the time when Ella's deceased father, Raymond Desai was pastor of the Divine Word Church. All this became complicated when Lena, frustrated by delays, sought help from the Fierce Ones

The discovery of dying George Charley by Ella and Justine was just the beginning of a difficult investigation in *Coyote's Wife* (Forge, 2008). George had been driving Ervin Benally's vehicle. Benally, George's employer, had been called back to his office just as the two men were going to cut wood. Benally, owner of StarTalk Communications, sought permission to provide the reservation with wide access to telephones. Not everyone wanted the service although it could be a lifesaver to the isolated and those in poor health. StarTalk was subsidized by Abigail Yellowhair, prominent businesswoman and widow of a state senator. Abigail's daughter Barbara handled the business aspects of StarTalk while Ervin promoted its acceptance. He was being harassed, by the newly emerged Fierce Ones (traditionalist vigilantes) and by Skinwalkers. Abigail demanded instant results but others were to die before matters were brought to a conclusion. A rival for Kevin's affections made life difficult for Ella.

Thurlos have two other series, one featuring Sister Agatha, who serves as one of two extern nuns in a cloistered community; the other, Lee Nez who is both a state patrol officer and a vampire! New Clah book, *Earthway* (2009); *Never-ending-snake* (2010).

Claire Jenner Claiborne

Author: Sophie Dunbar

See: Claire Jenner, page 401

Denise Cleever

Author: Claire McNab

Denise was an intelligence agent for ASIO, Australian Security Intelligence Organization. Among her skills was the ability to speak both Indonesian and Japanese.

The Aylmer family, under the leadership of mother, Noreen, was suspected of a half-dozen crimes in *Murder Undercover* (Naiad, 1999). Denise was sent to their family owned island, posing as a waitress/bartender at the resort hotel. Brothers Quint and Harry Alymer demanded a highly disciplined workforce. Staff were not allowed to mix with guests. When a second guest died unexpectedly, tensions increased. Denise had a problem of her own, the start of an affair with Roanna Alymer, Noreen's daughter.

The Hiddwing Institute, a right wing foundation dedicated to ending immigration and to the promotion of a Caucasian Australia, intrigued Denise's superior officers in *Death Understood* (Naiad, 2000). She was sent undercover; first, at the Melbourne office; then, at the headquarters in Brisbane, Queensland. Denise attracted the attention of Rhys Hiddwing, head of the family since his father and his Aunt Clara disappeared into the desert. Rhys' sister Becky found Denise appealing on another level.

ASIO concerns about Edification, a terrorist group in Australia, came at the right time for Denise in *Out of Sight* (Naiad, 2001). Well known terrorist sympathizer Dana Wright, who was being followed by British agents, fell while rock climbing. With Dana in a coma, it was convenient for Denise to assume her identity, fly to Australia, and infiltrate the group. She became part of a student group to be trained by Edification at a secluded camp in Northwest Australia. The final exercise was to be a real assassination. Explicit sexual intimacies were included in the final chapter.

Because she was the only intelligence agent able to recognize master terrorist Red Wolf, Denise was "loaned" by ASIO to the United States Homeland Security Agency in *Recognition Factor* (Bella, 2002). Using the persona Diana Loring, a right-wing terrorist who had operated in East Asia, Denise gained admittance to the Safe Homes Organization. Her assignment was to identify Red Wolf and pass that information on to Security, but it wasn't that simple. She was under close observation by her terrorist host and hostess. Fortunately a familiar ally was there to lend a hand.

A series of suicide bombings directed the attention of ASIO and the CIA in *Death by Death* (Bella Books, 2003) to Easehaven, a private mental hospital, and its director Graeme Thorwell, PhD. Thornwell's patroness, wealthy Fenella von Berg, had subsidized Graeme's transformation into a handsome man and underwritten the three clinics he now supervised. Two of the suicide killers had been patients at one of the clinics. Denise, undercover as psychotherapist Dr. Constance Sommers, joined the Easehaven staff after intensive coaching. Although she became convinced that the mysterious Sanctuary Project at Easehaven was connected to the murders, Denise was unsure which staff members were involved.

Denise's next assignment in *Murder at Random* (Bella, 2006) was to go undercover as Ann Meadows, a straight-laced terrorist expert who took early retirement from Australia's Defense Intelligence Organization in order to care for her dying husband. Now a widow, Ann had been recommended as a resource to sensationalist newspaper, *The Trumpeter* whose publisher Jason Benton had a right wing agenda. Australia was in shock after a series of terrorist attacks. Benton and Emmaline Partlow, heads of the Supremity Church, promoted Rafe Thorne and his Right Way Party as the answer to the current government's ineptitude in ending the terrorism. "Ann" was to explore these connections, serving on a committee at *The Trumpeter*. Her role as a conservative heterosexual was at risk because her former lover Roanna Aylmer was aligned with Benton.

The Carol Ashton series by McNab was covered in Volume 2

Clare Cliveley (Murdoch); Miranda Cliveley

Author: Ann Crowleigh, pseudonym for Barbara Cummings and JoAnn Power

During the series set in England's Victorian era, Mirinda Cliveley aka Indy shared her love with Grand Duke Gustav von Frey, a married German diplomat. She was considered eccentric, rode a bicycle, worked as a professional photographer, and turned her inheritance into a business. When she and her twin sister Clare inherited Scarborough House, they partitioned it, each keeping a portion for a personal residence. On the surrounding land, they tore down outbuildings to erect rental town houses.

Clare Cliveley Murdoch, widow of a British army officer, had no children, but considered her stepson Ian as her own. She had premonitions and the twins communicated with one another without words.

During the demolition of the old carriage house in *Dead As Dead Can Be* (Zebra, 1993) an infant corpse was uncovered, causing concern in the extended family as to its parentage. Because not much was expected of the local police, the twins and Ian solved the mystery on their own.

Although "Indy" played the stronger role in the first book, Clare came into her own in *Wait for the Dark* (Zebra, 1993). Among their tenants was Eurasian widow Lee Davenport. The death of a Chinese man on the premises of Cliveley Close on the night of the twins' birthday party was connected in Clare's mind to Mrs. Davenport's pregnant guest, a "distant cousin" named Yi-an. Her knowledge of antiquities, Chinese history and culture enabled Clare to find the killer at considerable risk.

Nancy Clue

Author: Mabel Maney

See Cherry Aimless, page 6.

Midge Cohen

Author: Toni Brill, pseudonym for Anthony and Martha Olcott

After earning a Ph.D. from Cornell and teaching Russian at Ithaca College, Midge Cohen decided upon a second career, writing children's books. She was a divorcee whose Jewish mother, Pearl, was determined that Midge should marry again and have children. Although Pearl lived on Fifth Avenue, Midge had inherited a three-room Brooklyn apartment that, together with alimony, subsidized her career as an author. She had left Paul, her veterinarian husband, because he bored her. Ithaca College bored her. Teaching undergraduates bored her.

Pearl was on the alert for prospective sons-in-law. In *Date with a Dead Doctor* (St. Martin, 1991), her candidate, Dr. Leon Skripnik, needed a translator for letters written in Russian by his cousin, Shmuel. By the time Midge had prepared the translation, Skripnik was dead, leaving her to worry about blind cousin Shmuel and a possible Chagall.

A short-term romance with Police Lt. Mike Russo washed out on a Sicilian beach, as *Date with a Plummeting Publisher* (St. Martin, 1993) opened. The trip left Midge thinner and trimmer but alone. When Pearl learned that Simon Brent-Waterhouse needed a Russian speaking date for a dinner party, she volunteered her daughter. Simon exited an upstairs window leaving the suspicion that Midge had possession of an important publishing contract. Russo saved her life, even though he no longer wanted to be a part of it.

Witty, but superficial.

Beth Seibelli Cole

Author: Ed Stewart

See: Beth Seibelli, page 732.

Kathryn "Casey" Collins

Author: Diana Deverell

Kathryn "Casey" Collins had earned a reputation for non-conformity in the conservative U.S. State Department. She remained on staff because of her undeniable expertise in terrorism. They accepted her limitations. She accepted the fact that she would probably be denied promotion. Her mother had died when she was young. The relationship between Casey and her father Victor was very close. His descent into Alzheimer's was difficult for her. The significant other in her life was Stefan Krajewski, whose undercover assignments for Denmark and loyalties to Poland complicated their relationship. She also had a close working arrangement with Holger Sorensen of the Danish Defense Intelligence Service. She was described as having blond hair. Her pet was a German Shepherd called Blondie that she had inherited from a man who sought to take her prisoner.

Stefan and Casey had met when she was assigned to the U.S. Embassy in Poland. He was hired to teach Polish to the employees, but, unknown to the embassy, he was affiliated with the Polish Communist intelligence agency. Neither the embassy nor the Polish communists knew that he was a double agent, working for Holger Sorensen of Danish Intelligence. Information as to the activities of Middle Eastern terrorists groups was passed from Stefan to Casey to American and Danish authorities. Even after this assignment and Casey's return to the United States, she and Stefan kept in touch and met secretly.

An explosion aboard an American plane carrying several members of the State Department's intelligence unit cast suspicion on Casey during *12 Drummers Drumming* (Avon, 1998). Stefan was suspected of soliciting information from Casey and passing it along. He had not revealed everything about his family to her. Frantic because she believed that Stefan might have been a passenger on the downed plane, Casey left the U.S. surreptitiously. She worked with a disparate group under the general direction of Holger to prevent wholesale slaughter. She balanced her love for her father and for Stefan against her obligations to her job and her country.

Casey had divided loyalties again in *Night on Fire* (Avon, 1999). Currently located in Denmark, she was pleased to be assigned to the terrorism task force investigating a plane crash in Bangor, Maine. Gerry Davis, a CIA operative in Denmark who had been like a brother to her, needed help to locate guided missiles which may have been diverted to unfriendly hands. En route to the Maine assignment, the choice was taken out of her hands. A corpse had been found in her apartment. The Danish police would not let her leave the country. Casey's personal loyalty to a boy dying of leukemia was pitted against her love for a daring adventurer.

Author Diana Deverell had background in the U.S. Foreign Service, which was reflected in the narratives.

Henrietta "Henrie" O'Dwyer Collins

Author: Carolyn Hart

To her friends, Henrietta O'Dwyer Collins was "Henrie O'," and, at age sixty after a full life, she had many friends. Her son, Bobby, had been killed at age 12 in a car accident. She still had a daughter, Emily. Besides her extended career as a reporter, she had published several novels.

Recent widow of Richard Collins, Henrie O', a lean silver-haired woman, was reexamining her life as *Dead Man's Island* (Bantam, 1993) began. In her youth she had loved Chase Prescott deeply. Their relationship ended when she recognized that he was too ruthless and ambitious. When they parted she did not tell Chase she was pregnant. Their daughter never knew that Richard was not her father. When Chase, now a media magnate, urged Henrie O' to visit his isolated island home, she could not resist the chance to see him again. After his murder, she had to discover the killer.

There was no sensible reason for Henrie O' to get involved in the murder of Patty Kay Matthews in *Scandal in Fair Haven* (Bantam, 1994). Patty's second husband Craig, the obvious suspect, was a weak man who took refuge in his aunt's cabin at a time when Henrie O' was occupying it. This was supposed to be a vacation for Henrie O' but Aunt Margaret was a good friend so she assumed the role of aunt to clear Craig's name.

Henrie O' was on the faculty of Thorndyke University in Missouri during *Death in Lovers' Lane* (Avon, 1997). It was not only her sense of professionalism but also her distaste for student Maggie Winslow that prompted Henrie O' to urge the young woman to dig into three unsolved murder cases. That assignment ended in Maggie's death. Henrie O' had no choice but to probe the crimes to mitigate her sense of guilt. She was aware that the college administration disapproved of her involvement. Henrie O' exercised her right to use the information she gained according to her personal sense of justice.

Henrie O's husband Richard had been visiting at Pulitzer Prize winner Belle Ericcson's Kauai estate at the time of his death. Henrie had always believed he died in an accident. In *Death in Paradise* (Avon, 1998), an anonymous message implied that he had been murdered. Unable to deal with the uncertainty of his relationship with Belle and the possibility of murder, Henrie O' retraced his final weeks. He had helped Belle when her daughter, CeeCee had been kidnapped and killed several years before; then returned when a witness wanted to share previously unknown information. Henrie O' realized that she would have to solve CeeCee's death to find Richard's killer.

An inheritance left by Chase Prescott had enabled their daughter Emily and her husband to purchase a small Texas newspaper. While helping out on the paper, Henrie O' received a frantic call from her dearest friend, Gina Wilson, who had lost contact with her granddaughter, Iris. Since Santa Fe, Iris' current location, was within driving distance, Henrie O' was more than willing to help. In *Death on the River Walk* (Avon, 1999), she insinuated herself into the business and personal affairs of the Garza family who ran a distinguished antiques firm and inn. Henrie O' not only needed to find Iris, an employee at the store, but to identify a killer among the family members.

Henrie O' was unsure what her role would be when she attended the wedding of her former son-in-law Lloyd Drake to Connor Bailey in *Resort to Murder* (Morrow, 2001). Her daughter Emily, formerly married to Lloyd, convinced Henrie O' that she could help her grandchildren deal with the occasion. Both Lloyd's and Connor's families opposed the wedding. Someone set out, first to terrify Connor, then to kill her.

Although Henrie O' had turned down Jimmy Lennox's proposal when, in *Set Sail for Murder* (Morrow, 2007), Jimmy asked a favor, she couldn't refuse. She had come to realize that she might have made a mistake in not marrying him. The request, that came after Jimmy had married documentary producer Sophia Montgomery, was that Henrie O' accompany his new family on a Baltic Cruise. He paid for her passage, but she was to meet him "accidentally" as an old friend. Jimmy believed that one of Sophia's stepchildren from a prior marriage to Frank Riordan planned to kill her. Frank's will had placed Sophia as trustee over legacies to the four adult children. Soon she had to decide whether to distribute the funds, extend the length of the trust, or even cease payments to the stepchildren out of the trust funds. Excellent characterizations and an enticing plot.

Henrie O' seemed a warmer, more personal heroine than Hart's other sleuth, Annie Laurence Darling. The supporting characterizations developed gradually, holding the reader's interest.

Her third sleuth, Bailey Ruth Raeburn, returned to earth after her death to help others in trouble.

Gail Connor

Author: Barbara Parker

Gail Connor, a corporate attorney with a major Miami firm, had preserved her marriage to David out of love for Karen, their eleven-year-old daughter. She and David had met at the University of Florida. When they divorced, Gail received custody of Karen and the house. David was awarded their yacht, which he traded for down payment on a restaurant.

Gail's legal training did not prepare her for the problems she encountered in *Suspicion of Innocence* (Dutton, 1994). The pregnant body of her younger sister Renee had been discovered in the Everglades. The immediate assumption was suicide. Irene, their disconsolate mother, insisted on a thorough investigation.

Suspicion focused on Gail, who not only inherited Renee's share in a family trust, but might also have resented her relationship with David. Gail hired attractive criminal attorney, Anthony Luis Quintana, to look out for her interests and protect her from those she trusted.

Karen's dislike for Quintana presented problems in *Suspicion of Guilt* (Dutton, 1995). Irene, Gail's mother, played cards regularly with a group, which included wealthy Althea Tillett. When Althea's fall down her staircase was determined to be murder, Patrick Norris, Althea's nephew and Gail's former lover, was the prime suspect. Gail's efforts on Patrick's behalf put her in jeopardy in her law firm, aroused anger on the part of a powerful non-profit organization, and pitted her against Althea's stepchildren. At the conclusion, Gail left the firm and set up in private practice with her mentor, Larry Black.

Problems between Gail and Quintana continued in *Suspicion of Deceit* (Dutton, 1998). Tom Nolan, lead singer in the Miami Opera's presentation of *Don Giovanni,* was suspected of collaborating with the Castro regime. As general counsel for the opera company, Gail investigated the charges. The probe opened questions about an earlier period in Quintana's life when he joined with Castro sympathizers in Nicaragua. The death of Emily Davis, a member of the group, had been covered up. More recent murders made it necessary to expose the part that Quintana and others played in Emily's murder.

In a comparatively short period of time, Gail's life changed drastically. She had used client's funds to pay her own bills (grounds for loss or suspension of her law license in most, if not all, states). She had escaped from a husband with too little sense of responsibility into the arms of a fiancé who was domineering and jealous. During *Suspicion of Betrayal* (Dutton, 1999), Gail became over-involved in a divorce case. The wife, whom she represented, needed to discover her husband's assets. Anthony, whose client was the husband, sought to limit that discovery to increase the husband's bargaining power in the property settlement. David, Gail's former husband, disturbed by Anthony's influence, sought primary physical placement of their daughter, Karen. Gail struggled to balance her own needs against those of Anthony and Karen.

Gail was convinced that she never wanted to see Anthony again, not even to make him aware that she was pregnant with his child. Yet, in *Suspicion of Malice* (Dutton, 2000), she allowed herself to be drawn into the investigation of Roger Creswell's murder and the complexities of the Creswell family. Anthony was protecting the interests of a peripheral member of the family, unaware that his daughter Angie was involved. Temperamentally unsuited to one another, Gail and Anthony were too deeply in love to maintain their distance.

Gail seemed irrational in *Suspicion of Vengeance* (Dutton, 2001) when, lacking any criminal appellate experience she represented the grandson of a family friend. Kenny Clark, after twelve years of appeals, was reaching the end of his tenure on Florida's death row. First Gail, then Anthony, fought quixotically to prove that Clark was innocent. They worked within time constraints against a resistant legal system. Gail's resources were exhausted. Fortunately Anthony persisted with the help of a less conscientious ally.

Anthony had successfully defended young Billy Fadden from a charge of arson, so in *Suspicion of Madness* (Dutton, 2003), he was contacted by family when Billy was accused of killing waitress Sandra McCoy. The call was made by Billy's mother, Teri, and her second husband, resort owner Martin Greenwald. Gail accompanied Anthony on what was expected to be a two-day trip to Lindeman Key where Martin's Buttonwood Inn was located. Their neighbor, Joan Lindeman Sinclair, a reclusive former movie star, had helped Billy when he was depressed. He was in a lot more trouble than his mother realized. So was Joan. The mood was set by the isolation of the island and a threatening storm.

Readers may gain insight into life in Cuba from *Suspicion of Rage* (Dutton, 2005). Anthony and Gail planned a post wedding trip there, taking both children and Gail's mother. Due to restrictions, they traveled through Cancun, Mexico. Anthony's niece in Cuba would be celebrating her 15th birthday. Even before they left, U. S. officials suggested that Anthony urge his brother-in-law General Ramio Vega to defect. He had conflicts of interest. His grandfather, who lived in Miami, was anti-Castro. His father lived in Havana in a home for Cuban war veterans. He had friends active in the underground in Cuba. This didn't sound like much of a vacation to Gail, all she wanted was to get her family safely home.

Parker has a new sleuth: Attorney C J. Dunn

Rev. Lily Connor

Author: Michelle Blake

The character of Lily Connor was as complex as the narratives in which she appeared. A former Catholic, she became an Episcopalian priest though she was never quite comfortable in the role. Like St. Paul, she was considered a "tentmaker," making her living outside the church. Lily worked as a member of ecumenical organizations, as co-director of the local Women's' Center, and also received money from a fixed income source. Her financial security and profession did not affect her appearance. She regularly wore Texas garb: jeans and boots along with a parka to accommodate the Boston weather, and her clerical collar.

Lily had no interest in a permanent parish assignment. She filled in short term for regular pastors at the request of her African-American bishop, Lamont Spencer. Her priesthood did not inhibit her love affair with Catholic police photographer Tom Casey, but she refused to move in with him or to marry him. She showed no interest in children or pets. Her closest friend was Charlie Cooper, whom she had met in the seminary, and who resided in a nearby Anglican monastery. It was Charlie to whom she could disclose her dreams and moments of illumination without embarrassment.

Lily, who had been raised in Benton, Texas, had a miserable childhood. Her mother, who belonged to a wealthy family, had problems with alcohol. She left the family home, seeing Lily only during summer visits. Lily had no current connection with members of her mother's family. When Lily's father became terminally ill, she took a leave of absence to nurse him until he died. Lily's Boston connection came with her education, first in a Catholic college, and later in an Episcopalian seminary. Like her mother, she has had a problem with alcohol. She handled it with abstinence, but occasionally binged.

Her assignment as interim pastor to a wealthy upper class church in *The Tentmaker* (Putnam, 1999) made the parishioners uncomfortable. The death of her predecessor Rev. Frederick Barnes, a diabetic, had suspicious aspects that Lily could not (or would not) ignore. There was the possibility that he had been murdered and there had been insinuations that he had sexually abused the son of a prominent parish official.

Given her Texas roots, Lily was liberal in her outlook and her choice of friends. Theologian Anna Banieka, a childhood survivor of Auschwitz, had been more than a friend. She was a mentor to Lily. When, in *Earth Has No Sorrow* (Putnam, 2001), Anna disappeared, Lily had to find not only the physical Anna, but also the sense of who she really was. Ignoring her responsibilities at the Women's Center, this search became an obsession. A second objective was the need to prove young Andrew Hatcher innocent of murdering Anna. Lily questioned her faith and her place in the church. At some point the introspection became wearisome. She finally agreed to return to Alcoholics Anonymous and consider counseling.

A stint as the replacement Episcopalian priest at Tate University brought Lily into contact with Samantha Henderson, a former theology classmate in *Book of Light* (Putnam's, 2003). Their relationship had been more important to Samantha than to Lily who was reluctantly drawn into Samantha's dilemma. She had access to an early source for the Gospels. Even the photos of the script had an impact on Lily, strengthening her faith, opening her up to greater tolerance. There were those who would steal or kill to withhold public knowledge of the *Book of Light.*

These are thoughtful reads, above and beyond the average mystery novel.

Nancy Cook

Author: D. J. H. Jones, a pseudonym

Nancy Cook, a non-tenured assistant professor at Yale University, had excellent credentials (Ph.D. in English from Princeton). She attended the annual meeting of the Modern Language Association (MLA) to check out potential job openings. Single and in her early thirties, Nancy wanted security in her life. She was hostile to the concept of "publish or perish" which dominated the selection of tenure, believing instead that teachers who could "teach" should be recognized for their value. She even considered seeking work in another field.

In *Murder at the MLA* (University of Georgia Press, 1993), Nancy attended the MLA convention in Chicago during the Christmas holidays.

Susan Engleton, the leader of the Wellesley group interviewing job applicants, was poisoned by coffee. Her death occurred on the same day as the "fall" of Professor Michael Alcott from an upstairs balcony. Detective Boaz Dixon had reason to believe that there was a serial killer at work. He recruited Nancy for her entrée into the world of academia.

The special relationship between Nancy and Boaz continued in *Murder in the New Age* (University of Georgia Press, 1997). After Nancy returned from a vacation in Scandinavia, she sublet a room in Santa Fe where she hoped to find the solitude necessary to complete her book on Chaucer. Its publication would give her the recognition needed after her contract at Yale ended. The other occupants of Nancy's boarding house were diverse characters, into virtual reality, channeling, vegetarianism, peyote, and eventually murder. Fortunately Boaz had an errand to run in Santa Fe. He helped the local police by using Nancy to tempt a killer.

Alexandra Cooper

Author: Linda Fairstein

Looking back from her current position as Assistant District Attorney, Alexandra Cooper could review the twists of fate that had shaped her life. Her father Benjamin, a retired cardiologist, was the descendant of Russian Jews. Her mother, Maude, a Scandinavian from New England, had been a nurse. Maude, a Finnish Christian, had converted to the Jewish faith and Alexandra was raised as a Reform Jew. She was the only daughter of four children. Although she had accepted that her skills were not at a professional level, Alexandra loved ballet and continued to take lessons. While in high school, she had been on the swim team, which came in handy in one of the narratives. After graduation from Wellesley, she attended law school at the University of Virginia in Charlottesville. Her plan to marry medical student Adam Nyman ended when he was killed in a highway accident. Disinterested in homemaking, Alexandra existed primarily on carryout food; often eaten while watching *Jeopardy!*, a passion she shared with Detective Mercer Wallace and homicide investigator Mike Chapman. She had never married and never had a live in lover.

Alexandra's primary focus as litigator for the Sex Crimes Unit of the New York Police Department during *Final Jeopardy* (Scribner's, 1996) was gathering evidence against William Montvale, an alleged serial rapist. She worked with Wallace, Chapman, and her neighbor, Dr. David Mitchell. Alexandra was stunned to learn that actress Isabella Lascar to whom she had loaned her vacation home at Martha's Vineyard had been found dead in the driveway. Lascar, who had fled from a stalker, was in a car rented in Alexandra's name so the first assumption had been that Alexandra was dead. District Attorney Paul Battaglia was concerned that she might have been the intended victim.

Alexandra needed time to recuperate after the Lascar case. In *Likely to Die* (Scribner's, 1997), she was assigned to the murder and presumed rape of Prof.

Gemma Dogen, a prominent surgeon killed within a major hospital/university complex. There was a diverse supply of suspects: vagrants who frequented the premises, fellow professionals, disgruntled patients and their families. Alexandra and her staff sifted through a variety of motives before the climax in which she ran for her life.

The rape/murder of former beauty queen Denise Caxton was assigned to Alexandra's unit in *Cold Hit* (Scribner's, 1999). Suspicions arose that it was connected to the unsolved theft of art works from the Isabella Stewart Gardner Museum in Boston. A deliberate misrepresentation in a local newspaper made Alexandra the target of vicious killers and brought Mercer close to death.

The Deadhouse (Scribner's, 2001) was evidence of author Linda Fairstein's narrative skills. She blended intricate historical references about Blackwell's Island (located in the East River between Manhattan and Queens) with her usual legal thriller. The death of King's College professor Lola Dakota could have been blamed on Ivan, her rejected husband. He had stalked Lola but had a solid alibi. Alexandra, Mike and, to a lesser degree, Mercer followed a trail that combined academia with murder, history with buried treasure and glimpses into the private lives of the sleuths. Absolutely engrossing.

Alexandra and Mike Chapman had spent many happy childhood hours in Manhattan's Metropolitan Museum of Arts and the American Museum of Natural History, but in *The Bone Vault* (Scribner's, 2003), they were there on business. The body of a young South African researcher Katrina Grooten, had been discovered in a sarcophagus being shipped abroad. The trail led back to secret vaults passionately guarded by the museum authorities. Lots of interesting background material on the changing roles of museums and their conflict with the ethnicities whose antiquities had been collected for study and display.

The Kills (Scribner, 2004) was exciting enough to be a page-turner, but the reader had better slow down or get lost in the maze of connections. Alexandra was prosecuting former military intelligence agent Andrew Tripping for the rape of investment banker Paige Vallis and the abuse of his own son, Dulles. Paige's murder and the intervention of attorney Graham Hoy who sought to adopt Dulles changed the equation and expanded the circle of suspects. Along the way the Secret Service, the CIA and King Farouk entered the narrative. Queenie Ransome, an elderly dancer with a prestigious resume, was also murdered. Alexandra, Mercer, and Mike needed all the help they could get.

The personal and professional lives of Mercer, Mike, and Alexandra blended in *Entombed* (Scribner, 2005). Vicious attacks by a serial rapists had resumed after five years, creating panic in the high rent areas of Manhattan. When the Poe House (where Edgar Allan Poe lived for a short time), was in the process of demolition, the skeleton of a young woman was found. She had been walled up to die, naked and alone. The Poe connection segued into the death of a second woman connected to the Jane Doe. Alexandra, following up on the Poe angle, was attacked. Mike's devastation at a personal loss made him unavailable for police work. Additional attacks and concerns about possible witnesses made solving this case a priority.

Getting involved in the disappearance of Ballerina Natalya Galinova in *Death Dance* (Scribner, 2006) seemed one way for Mercer and Alexandra to reconnect to Mike. Although he had returned to work, he was still unable to deal with the death of his fiancée. The discovery of Natalya's body at the Metropolitan Opera under circumstances that could include the possibility of attempted rape, gave Alexandra official standing. There were literally thousands of individuals who had access to the backstage area, requiring hours of interrogations by lesser personnel. Mike and Alexandra focused on close associates. Behind the glitter, the narrative exposed the bitter professional rivalries, the shifting allegiances and the arrogance of the powerful. The ending was over the top though.

Bringing a murder charge against Brendan Quillian for the death of his wife Amanda in *Bad Blood* (Scribner, 2007) had risks. Brendan had an airtight alibi and a top defense attorney. The charge was actually murder for hire. It looked like a losing case until an explosion killed Brendan's older brother in Water Tunnel #3. Mike Chapman disagreed with the quick response that blamed terrorists. The narrative contained a fascinating tale of the families who had worked underground to build the tunnels that provided water to New York City.

Killer Heat (Doubleday, 2008) was lighter than usual in courtroom drama, providing a heavy dose of geography and history with regard to the islands off the New York coast. Detective Mike Chapman involved Alexandra into a series of brutal killings of young women connected by their modus operandi. The corpses were found close to historic New York forts, islands, and batteries. They were looking for a serial killer, who might have been released under the current New York State law as to the detention of sexual perverts.

The technical backgrounds of the narratives reflect Fairstein's experience as a prosecutor and her knowledge of New York City. Next: *Lethal Legacy* (2009); *Hell Gate* (2010).

Dr. Jessica Coran

Author: Robert W. Walker

The combination of medical examiners, serial killers, and mutilation murders has been in vogue since Patricia Cornwell's Kay Scarpetta was introduced. Dr. Jessica Coran, a redheaded medical examiner at the FBI laboratory in Quantico, Virginia, was the forensic expert on a team headed by her mentor, Otto Boutine. Aware that she was a potential target, she carried a Smith & Wesson .44, and was an excellent shot.

In *Killer Instinct* (Diamond, 1992), Jessica's first experience with a bloodthirsty killer was the death of Annie Copeland, a Wisconsin prostitute left hanging in an abandoned cabin. Maddened by Jessica's public comments, the killer made a personal contact. The police were fooled into believing that the killer was already dead so she had to become the next victim. She almost did.

During *Fatal Instinct* (Diamond, 1993), Mad Matthew Matisak, a prisoner at the Federal Penitentiary for Criminally Insane, wanted to share in Jessica's investigations. There was a serial killer in the news, "The Claw," who had galvanized the politically sensitive police bureaucracy into premature action. Jessica believed that the deaths were the work of more than one man. A tip from Mad Matthew put Jessica on track for a highly improbable solution.

In *Primal Instinct* (Diamond, 1994), Jessica took a Hawaiian vacation while recovering from her wounds. The local FBI recruited her to find the Trade Winds Killer. The reader was quickly made aware of his identity and motivation for killing young women, often prostitutes. It took much longer for Jessica and Inspector James Parry to reach that point. At the end, local justice prevailed.

In *Pure Instinct* (Jove, 1995), Jessica had reason to be concerned. When Mad Matthew escaped, intending to subdue and consume her, the FBI kept her in the headquarters laboratory under guard. Unable to handle the restrictions, Jessica negotiated a role in the investigation of the "Queen of Hearts" deaths in New Orleans. The introduction of a secondary psychic investigator, Dr. Kim Desinor, expanded the potential for success in identifying the deranged killer. Desinor also appeared in Walker's other series (see Meredyth Sanger).

Darkest Instinct (Jove. 1996) changed the location to Florida, the serial killer to a mother-hating Englishman, but the format was constant. Jessica continued to attract virtually every male with whom she came into contact. She patched up her relationship with Jim Parry, who was threatened by her reluctance to give up her current job and join him in Hawaii. A bloated 498 pages will turn some readers off.

After Jessica and Jim enjoyed a vacation together, each returned to their own homes as *Extreme Instinct* (Jove, 1997) began. Don't even begin the narrative unless you are ready to believe that Jessica has again become the personal prey of a serial killer. This time a deeply disturbed young man decided to lead Jessica on a chase among the national parks, intending to make her his ninth victim.

The series continued in *Blind Instinct* (Berkley, 2000) during which Jessica was loaned to Scotland Yard to help solve a series of crucifixion murders. The narrative contained guidebook level material and definitions of English colloquialisms. Jessica, with all her education and experience, was as naïve as a 1920s "Had I But Known" heroine, exposing herself to unnecessary danger. Her six-year affair with James Parry having died of neglect, Jessica enjoyed a new romance with Scotland Yard inspector Richard Sharpe

Credibility for the skills of Jessica and Kim Desinor suffered a blow in *Bitter Instinct* (Berkley, 2001). Kim convinced Jessica to accept an assignment that would involve working with her former lover, James Parry, now assigned to the Philadelphia office. The case involved a series of bizarre killings, deaths induced by poison in the pen of a murderer who carved poems on the victim's bare backs. This was done seemingly with the consent of the victims. They were young and innocent individuals, who took part in a recent fad of displaying their bodywork at clubs primarily located in the 2nd Street area. The suspects, and there were many, were routinely weird. Jessica used warrantless entries to gather information. Kim conjured up clues that eventually connected.

A reader would need a masochistic streak to keep reading of Jessica's latest adventure in *Unnatural Instinct* (Berkley, 2002). Maureen De Campe, a strict but well regarded appellate judge in Washington D. C., had been abducted. No ransom had been demanded so it was assumed to be a crime of vengeance. DeCampe's records, not only in her current position but when she presided over criminal cases in Texas, had to be reviewed. Jessica had been enjoying time off with Richard Sharpe who had retired and moved to Virginia. She was called back to work, and Richard, who had ties as a consultant to the FBI, joined in the investigation. Not only was there a time limit on how long the judge might survive the gruesome treatment she was enduring, but her death could affect the future of Kim Desinor. There were transitional aspects to the book as Meredyth Sanger and Lucas Stonecoat handled aspects of the Texas research. They have their own series.

There must be a market for thrillers like *Grave Instinct* (Berkley, 2003). Walker scraped the bottom on this one. Lurid and explicit depictions of the removal of the brain of young females while they were alive are distasteful. Jessica was assigned to the case by her supervisor Eriq Santiva when the third corpse was discovered. Daryl Cahil, recently released from an institution for the criminally insane, had desecrated graves to obtain brain tissue for food. Santiva was certain that he was the current "Skull Digger". Jessica used deception and persistence in searching for a copycat whose appetite demanded living victims; then a third fanatic; then a fourth. Yuck!

The reader of *Absolute Instinct* (Berkley, 2004) will be aware from the start that artist Giles Gahran has been a sadistic killer since his youth. His handiwork, the removal of a victim's spinal column, did not come to FBI attention until the death of Louisa Childs in Milwaukee. African- American FBI agent Darwin Reynolds requested Jessica's involvement, hoping to convince her that this was the work of a serial killer. Robert Towne, also African-American, was due to be executed for the murder in Oregon with a similar modus operandi. They sought a delay in his execution.

The narratives contained high levels of explicit violence and sexual perversion, which will not appeal to some readers. Walker frequently displayed his contempt for legal niceties and judges who recognize defendant's rights.

In addition to the Meredyth Sanger/ Lucas Stonecoat "Edge" series, Walker has introduced a third protagonist, Inspector Alastair Ransom.

Candi Covington
Simone Covington

Author: Nora DeLoach

This series featuring an African-American mother/daughter team had titles referring only to Mama Candi Covington; however, daughter Simone Covington was a prominent figure in the books. As a paralegal to Atlanta attorney Sydney Jacoby, Simone had some knowledge of the law. Candi, whose husband James was a retired military man, was employed in the local welfare office. She was on excellent terms with the local police chief, a white man. Candi and James had a strong marriage. Simone and her attorney boyfriend Cliff Roberts initially had no immediate plans. Simone was very close to her parents who lived in Otis, a small town in South Carolina. Her two brothers, both of whom were in the Army, rarely visited their parents.

In the initial book, *Mama Solves a Murder* (Holloway House, 1994), Simone blended two cases: (1) her assignment to help Jacoby find a reasonable defense for her former college roommate, Cheryl La Flamme who was charged with killing a man who had molested her, and (2) closer to home, the search for the killer of welfare caseworker Rita Ginn and of elderly Aunt Aggie Nelson. Rita was Candi's cousin. Both Rita and Aggie had been inquiring about possible child abuse in the neighborhood. Candi's "hunches" and reasoning provided solutions in both situations with help from Simone.

Murder came too close for comfort in *Mama Traps a Killer* (Holloway, 1995). Young Danny Jones, in whom James had shown an interest, was murdered. Simone questioned not only whether he was James' son, but also whether James was involved in the murder. A parallel case, which Candi solved for Attorney Jacoby was less credible. As a result of his involvement, Cliff became accepted as part of the Covington family.

Simone was shocked during *Mama Stands Accused* (Holloway, 1997). Her Uncle Ben had asked her help in purchasing a home for a woman who was not his wife. Ben was not a widower—at least not when the story began. When his mean-spirited wife Agnes was struck down with an axe, he became an obvious suspect. Simone returned to the family home in Otis to work with Candi in finding an alternate killer. Candi had problems of her own. She had been accused of stealing food stamps from a client whom she had investigated for child neglect.

During *Mama Saves a Victim* (Holloway, 1997), Simone was depressed because Cliff was always too busy for their planned vacation. She and Candi, while driving along the highway, struck and injured a young woman who seemed to be running away. The victim, when taken to the hospital, provided no identification; then, was abducted by a gunman. Simone connected Jane Doe to her brother Will. Candi connected the incident to a prior abduction and a possible impersonation.

Simone was needed at home as *Mama Stalks the Past* (Bantam, 1997) began. Candi was concerned about James' drinking. Secondly, the son of elderly reclusive neighbor Hannah Nixon accused Candi of taking advantage of his mother, who had named her as trustee for valuable land. Hannah, who had a series of marriages ending in her husbands' deaths, had been poisoned. Finally, the Covington family had been squabbling about a trust in land from Josiah Covington. The senior family member, 99 year old Uncle Chester, died mysteriously in the hospital.

In *Mama Rocks the Empty* Cradle (Bantam, 1998). Simone returned to Otis, Georgia to care for Candi while she was recuperating from bunion surgery. She couldn't keep her mother down when they learned of the savage murder of welfare mother Cricket Childs and the abduction of her infant daughter, Morgan. Cricket was on Candi's caseload so she had to take a hand. Simone came to understand her own feelings about motherhood during the investigation.

Sarah Jenkins was a local gossip and therefore one of Candi's best resources. She could not collect on the insurance policy she'd taken out on her goddaughter, Ruby Spikes. The young woman's death had been labeled suicide. In *Mama Pursues Murderous Shadows* (Bantam, 2000), Sarah begged Candi to prove otherwise. When Ruby's death was followed by that of an important witness, Candi was well on her way to solving the case. She incurred risks that left James wondering if they would make it to the big 35th wedding anniversary party Simone had planned.

Candi Covington realized that she had been disarmed by the seeming innocence of a callous killer in *Mama Cracks a Mask of Innocence* (Bantam, 2001). Yet she persisted in her personal investigation of the death of righteous high school senior, Brenda Long. Simone, who returned to Otis for community volunteer work, helped her mother, but it was James' dog that saved the day. This was less than a triumph for Candi. She had withheld valuable information because she disliked the investigator on the case.

These were comparatively short novels with interesting characterizations and plots. Simone, unlike many other young female characters, had an endearing relationship with her mother. The series ended with Nora DeLoach's death.

Dr. Kate Coyle

Author: Desmond Cory, pseudonym for Sean McCarthy

Dr. Kate Coyle was a secondary character in author Desmond Cory's John Dobie series, set in England. She was a general practitioner who did pathology for the police department in Cardiff, Wales. Her professional background was top quality. The daughter of a physician, she had studied medicine at Guy's Hospital in London. Although raised as an Irish Catholic, she did not practice her faith. Her marital status was unclear. Dobie was a professor of mathematics at Cardiff University. His approach to all problems was on a highly theoretical level. She provided a leavening touch to their investigations.

John Dobie's abstract thinking had contributed to his success as a mathematician. During *The Strange Attractor* (Macmillan, 1991) a.k.a. *The Catalyst* (St. Martin, 1991), it did nothing to endear him to the local police. Dobie's story of being drugged and tied up, of seeing first a friend's wife dead on his bed, and later, his wife Jenny dead on the same bed, fell flat. Fortunately Dr. Kate Coyle was on hand to provide Dobie with an alibi and sympathy until he could deduce the killer's identity. The strange attractor was a mathematical factor that distorted an original, and otherwise valid, equation; i.e. "pulls particles out of the pattern."

Dobie was unsettled by the death of his wife Jenny and his status as a suspect during *The Mask of Zeus* (St. Martin, 1993). With the blessings of his department head, he accepted a stint as a visiting professor in Cypress. Within days he was drawn into a case with similarities to his own, a husband (Adrian Seymour) accused of having killed his Cypriot wife (Derya Tuner, once a student of Dobie's). Hampered by his ignorance of local politics, Greek mythology and literature, he used mathematical thinking and computer expertise to unearth a mystery and then leave it buried. Kate, left behind, provided bits of information but little else.

As *The Dobie Paradox* (St. Martin, 1994) began, Kate and Dobie were en route to the Tongwynlais Rehabilitation Center where Adrian Seymour was being treated. It was Kate who discovered the body of Beverly Sutro, a young, reckless student from nearby Dame Margaret's School for Girls. Among the complexities in the case were the site of the murder, the weapon used, and the identity of the killer. Dobie brought his theoretical skills into play but at some cost. His Paradox, a theory he developed some years before which had received limited acknowledgement was now given international recognition.

These were not easy to read, but witty and erudite, a treat for the discriminating reader.

Tempe Crabtree

Author: Marilyn Meredith

Life had not always been easy for Tempe. Her first husband, Milt, a California Highway Patrol officer, died while on duty when their son Blair was two years old. Although she was partly Yanduchi, initially she had little sense of her Indian heritage. Her second husband, Joseph "Hutch" Hutchinson, the pastor of the Bear Creek Community Church in California, had strong feelings when in later life, Tempe became fascinated by the spiritual rituals of the Yanduchi. This developed into a sense that she had spiritual powers that she could tap into in her work. Hutch was also concerned when her job as deputy sheriff intruded upon their time together and her responsibilities as a pastor's wife. As the series began, Blair was a teenager, active as a volunteer with the local fire department, and eager to join when he became eighteen.

Tempe's Yanduchi heritage influenced her supervisor, Sgt Jerome Guthrie, to assign her to provide security at the Pow Wow at the Dennison Fairgrounds in *Deadly Omen* (Golden Eagle, 1999). With her limited background, Tempe was fascinated by the big turnout, colorful costumes, jewelry and the general participation in the dances. She quickly became aware of Katherine Davelos's determination that her daughter Linda should defeat Marella, daughter of Violet Celso, for the title of "Princess". She heard the quarrel between Marella and her boyfriend, Cody Endrezza. She already knew that rancher Grant Whitcomb detested all Indians, and Jake Celso, Marella's father, in particular. Marella's disappearance led to the discovery of her body by Tempe. It wasn't her case but the Dennison police had quickly focused on the wrong suspect.

A pattern of religious division between Tempe and Hutch had developed by *Unequally Yoked* (Golden Eagle, 2000). When three-year-old Vicky Leaphorn disappeared from the campground where her itinerant family occupied a tent and a van, Tempe was put in charge of the search. At this point she was operating within her job description. After an arrest had been made, Tempe was empowered by the spiritual revelation she achieved, and investigated independently.

In 2001, Meredith released *Deadly Trail* (Hard Shell Word Factory), a prequel to *Deadly Omen*. This narrative may well have been written earlier. The narrative established the deep love between Tempe and Hutch, but also hinted at potential problems for their marriage. Nick Two John worked at the Bear Creek Inn owned by his boss, Andre Donato. He was having an affair with Andre's wife, Claudia, but also had an influence on Tempe, scolding her for failing to learn about the Yanduchi traditions. He was sure that she had special powers. She needed all the help she could get when Nick was accused of murdering Andre.

Hutch's plan for a restful vacation at the isolated Tapper Lodge was scuttled in *Intervention* (Golden Eagle, 2002). First of all, Oscar winning script writer Mallory Benoit had invited several guests to the Lodge so she could present a new script in which they might be interested. Within her select group of guests there were tensions and rivalries. They included her former husband and an actor against whom she had a grudge. A tremendous snowstorm isolated the group, leaving Tempe to handle the investigation when Mallory was murdered.

The local narcotics force sought Tempe's help in *Wingbeat* (Golden Eagle, 2005) in discovering the possible site for a marijuana farm in her territory. Joe Seberry, a garrulous retired deputy sheriff, suggested that Tempe investigate the "old Wasserman place" now occupied by strangers. When she visited the long neglected farm, she met Sue and Lorenzo Montelongo, Earl and Peggy Postma. She recognized Sue as a woman she had recently stopped for speeding. Later Tempe recognized Sue as the corpse dumped in someone else's grave. Tempe had a far greater personal concern. The description of a redheaded man, driving a blue and white pickup exposing himself to school children, bore a strong resemblance to her husband, Hutch.

The on-going crisis between Tempe's dabbling in Native American spiritualism and Hutch's Christian beliefs survived a test in *Calling the Dead* (Mundania, 2006). Tempe had gone beyond her authority in two cases. Doreen, (her last name was given in one place in the narrative as "Felton"; in another, as "Shelton") died as the result of a fall from a bridge. Doreen had been sexually abused as a child. Her attacker had possibly already finished his prison sentence. There was a question as to whether this should be treated as a suicide or a murder. On another level, Hutch, who had often opposed her involvement in criminal cases to which she was not assigned, sought Tempe's help. Felicity Pence, a member of the local Volunteer Sheriff's Patrol, had called him early in the morning, worried about her older husband, Arthur. After Arthur's death, Hutch and Tempe noted Felicity's search for comfort from elderly veterinarian, Dr. Barry Northcott.

Domestic disturbances are among the most dangerous calls for deputies and police officers, so in *Judgment Fire* (Mundania, 2007) Tempe was careful when she entered the home of Tom and Jackie Cannata, a well-known local couple. Subsequent calls to the Cannatas ended when Jackie was seriously injured and Tom arrested. Sgt. Guthrie instructed Tempe to make on-going calls to check on Jackie when Tom was bailed out. It wasn't enough. Jackie was murdered; the house set on fire. Aided by insights gained through a Native American ceremony, Tempe went beyond the obvious, using her own memories to widen the circle of suspects.

When forest fires raged through the Bear Creek area in *Kindred Spirits* (Mundania, 2008), Tempe went up and down the safe roads checking on local residents. Divorced artist Vanessa Ainsworth did not seem to be around; only later did Fire Chief Pete Rountree notify Tempe that her body had been found, dead not from the fire, but murdered. Tempe had only met Vanessa once when she visited the house on a domestic violence call, but Detectives Morrison and Richards insisted that because both she and Vanessa had a Native American heritage, she could be an asset to their investigation. She was sent to Crescent City on the Oregon/California border to interview Vanessa's cousin, activist Abigail Jacoby. She may not have developed any clues from the contact but she learned a lot about the abuses perpetrated on members of the Tolowa tribe over a period of 150 years. When Vanessa's spirit appeared to Tempe, she took risks to identify the killer. Hutch's assistance helped to heal the gulf that had grown between them.

There was considerable value to this series, but it would have benefited from more careful editing. The narratives were short but simplistic.

Melissa Craig

Author: Betty Rowlands

Melissa Craig was nineteen, pregnant, and unmarried when Guy, her child's father, was killed. After her own parents rejected her, Guy's mother and father offered to share their home and family name. She always referred to herself as a widow.

She was forty-four and her son Simon was employed in the Texas oil fields, when Melissa appeared in *A Little Gentle Sleuthing* (Walker, 1991). She had achieved professional success as a mystery novelist and college lecturer, and moved to the English countryside. Together with artist Iris Ash and local reporter Bruce Ingram, Melissa developed a sideline as an investigator. Her interest, piqued by anonymous phone calls intended for "Babs", crystallized when Babs Carter's corpse was found on property belonging to Banbury Estates.

In *Finishing Touch* (Walker, 1992), flirtatious Angelica Caroli, an employee at the college, was found with her throat slashed. Angie's manipulations had created bad feeling among several of her admirers. Melissa's more than friendly interest in a male suspect kept her focused until the killer was discovered.

Melissa and Iris visited France during *Over the Edge* (Walker, 1993), but retained the cozy flavor of the series. Iris, who owned a second home in France, had been hired to teach an art course in Roziac. Melissa accompanied her to gain background for a new novel. Her investigation was aided by a dream that connected events. The plot reached into World War II and the French Resistance for motivation. A local cavern had been used to house a variety of refugees, some of whom had been betrayed. Melissa's use of revelations gained in her dreams struck a false note.

Romance became a serious possibility for Melissa in *Exhaustive Enquiries* (Walker, 1994), when she reached a new level in her relationship with Chief Inspector Ken Harris. She had agreed to write a pantomime to be performed by a local theatre group with wealthy Richard Mitchell subsidizing the production. His murder derailed the production, but Melissa went underground for a solution.

Melissa felt a need for time away from Ken in *Malice Poetic* (Hodder & Stoughton, 1995). She became a guest at the Uphanger Learning Center where she could work on a book. New acquaintance Ben Strickland had been a prominent reporter until the death of his wife turned him into a drunk. When their host Stewart Haughan, a rude bully, was murdered leaving few to mourn him, Ken Harris was assigned to the case. Melissa did not share her suspicions with him until after a second murder.

When author Leonora Jewell was murdered in her isolated cottage during *Deadly Legacy* (Hodder & Stoughton, 1995), it was assumed that the murder occurred during a burglary. Joe Martin, Melissa's literary agent, also represented Leonora. He commissioned Melissa to finish the novel that Leonora had almost completed. Melissa discovered that Leonora had developed a new ending for her book, a criminal modus operandi that was currently in use. Is that why she was murdered? And why Melissa was in danger?

After a party, Ken Harris and Melissa stopped to check on elderly friend Martha Willis, only to find her dead in *Smiling at Death* (Hodder & Stoughton, 1996). Her face had been painted into a bizarre clown's grin, a distinguishing characteristic of a serial killer in a nearby village. The death of another victim in Upper Benbury, also smiling at death, produced suspects who had alibis for the earlier deaths. Melissa's casual glance at a drawing revealed a startling connection between a vamp and vengeance.

As *The Cherry Pickers* (Hodder & Stoughton, 1998) began, Melissa was unsure as to whether or not she could be happy with such a protective, even domineering, man as Ken Harris. Iris, who was leaving the area to marry, had her house up for sale. Ken was considering purchasing the property and, if Melissa agreed, connecting it to her home. He had left the police to become a private investigator. The murder of Hilda Rice, a wayward gypsy girl, had aroused the men in her clan who were prepared to find their own justice. Before that could happen, Melissa and Bruce Ingram cooperated to identify the killer.

Sexually precocious teenage girls and men susceptible to such attractions triggered death and speculation in *The Man in the Window* (Hodder & Stoughton, 2000). Graham Shipley, Melissa's shy new neighbor, became the target of local gossip after Cissie, a teenage girl, was found dead. Graham was questioned and held by the police department; then, fired. Melissa persisted in investigating other local males who indulged in "unnatural practices."

Melissa's parents had ceased to be a part of her life. They had rejected her when she became pregnant. Almost thirty years later in *The Fourth Suspect* (Hodder & Stoughton, 2001), she was informed that Frank Ross, her cold and judgmental father, had been murdered. Her mother Sylvia, a fragile woman dominated by her husband, was the primary suspect. Joe Martin, Melissa's literary agent, accompanied her on a visit. If, as Sylvia claimed, she was innocent, then someone else was guilty. With no support from the police department, Melissa investigated her father's personal and professional activities. There were at least four other suspects. The episode made Melissa aware of how important Joe was in her life. He had been waiting a long time.

Sylvia, Melissa's mother, had developed a sense of independence by *No Laughing Matter* (Hodder & Stoughton, 2003). While temporarily living at Framleigh House, a retirement home, she was very interested in her fellow residents, including unpopular Flavia Selwyn-Tuck and her annoying dog. When both Flavia and the pet were murdered, Melissa cautioned Sylvia not to get too involved. To be sure that she didn't, Melissa consulted with both Det. Sgt. Matt Waters and reporter Bruce Ingram. Both women attracted the attention of the killer.

Melissa, now married to Joe, was writing novels, rather than mysteries by *Sweet Venom* (Hodder and Stoughton, 2004), but that didn't stop her need to get involved when murder occurred. The death of retired barrister Aidan Cresney by a swarm of his own bees shocked those who knew of his proficiency with the insects, but provided relief to some. He had dominated the double household he shared with his wife, Caroline, and the attached dwelling in which his brother Quentin and sister-in-law Sarah lived. Sarah's subsequent death under similar circumstances was too much of a coincidence. When the local gossips focused on Caroline, she turned to Melissa for help.

A cozy series with interesting twists. Rowlands has a second series featuring Sukey Reynolds. (Covered elsewhere in this volume).

Cheryl Crane

Author: Greg Moody

Cheryl Crane, formerly CharLouise Cangliosi, had grown up in Michigan, the younger sister of Raymond, a promising cyclist. In his youth, Will Ross had become close to the Cangliosi family. Stewart Kenally, the owner of Two Wheels, a serious bike shop, mentored Will, Raymond and eventually Cheryl. Raymond's early death on the track had ruptured the relationships. Will's decision to avoid the Cangliosi family had saddened Raymond's mother Rose and angered Cheryl. She became a serious mountain bike racer. After an injury requiring considerable healing time, she took a position on the Haven Pharmaceutical cycling team in Europe. She functioned as a soigneur (trainer, physical therapist and gofer). By this time Will was a divorced man in his early thirties. Cheryl did not disclose their prior connection. She described herself as tough, i.e. "Don't anybody f—— with me. I'm from Detroit."

Their reunion came about during *Two Wheels* (Velo, 1995) when a vacancy occurred on the Haven team as a result of the death of Jean-Pierre Colgan, the lead rider. Will, whose career was on the downside, was a strange choice for a replacement. Teammates assumed that his former wife, Kim Grady Ross, a manager with Haven Pharmaceuticals, had arranged it. Gradually Kim's reason for adding an under motivated second-rate rider to the squad emerged. Will increasingly relied on Cheryl as others failed him. There was excellent background on European cycling.

At thirty-two, Will wanted one more season during *Perfect Circles* (Velo, 1998). It meant a place on the Haven team during the Tour de France (a classic to be compared with the World Series or the Super Bowl). Manager Carl Deeds and new owner Henri Bergalis convinced the team to use "vitamin enhancers" manufactured by Haven Pharmaceuticals. While some team members showed dramatic improvements, Will's performance declined. There had to be a reason why he was affected differently. Cheryl made it known that she would return to the United States to ride on a team coached by Stewart Kenally. She and Will were lovers so this was more than a professional decision. Moody included another touch of whimsy: a man in a brown suit, seen only by or near the dying.

Will and Cheryl were in Vail, Colorado during *Derailleur* (Velo, 1999). Now Cheryl was a participant (as team leader and captain of the Two Circles mountain bike team sponsored by Haven). Will was depressed by serious leg injuries that kept him on the sidelines. Except for mechanic Hooty Bosco, neither was made welcome by the team. Leonard Romanowski, who had been Will's agent, deposited a stolen fortune in Will's room. Stan and Ollie (not to be confused with Laurel and Hardy) had been hired by the mobster from whom the money had been stolen. Their potential for violence terrified Cheryl who knew them. They were the Detroit based uncles from whom she had fled.

Will's luck seemed boundless in *Deadroll* (Velo, 2001). Fired from Bosco Bikes, a job he had come to hate, he achieved hero status and a position as a sports reporter at Channel 6 television station. Cheryl, almost eight months pregnant, did not take part in Will's joust with a terrorist. The series continued without her in *Dead Air* (2002).

Mary Alice Tate Sullivan Nachman Crane

Author: Anne George

See: The Tate Sisters, page 790.

Ruby Crane

Author: Jo Dereske

Tragedy brought Ruby Crane back to the timberlands of Northern (not Upper) Michigan from the San Francisco area. She and her husband Stan had been divorced for six years when he was killed in a one-car accident. Their teenage daughter, Jesse had been in the car with her father, but was thrown or pushed out of the vehicle before the crash. She suffered severe neurological damage, which reduced her to a semi-comatose condition at first. Ruby hoped that the serenity and privacy of her cabin near Sable, Michigan would allow Jesse to recover. The property included a fifteen-acre stand of timber. Although Jesse gradually regained the ability to feed herself, walk, speak, and read, she was a different child. Her spontaneity had been replaced by a need for careful planning and organization. She was alive and still recovering. That was success in Ruby's eyes. At thirty-seven, Ruby was an attractive woman, cautious about relationships, and needing privacy for her own recovery.

Although Sable was Ruby's hometown, she had moved to an inherited cabin by the riverside. Her father, whose abusive behavior had driven Ruby away before she could complete high school, lived in town. He had aged, even mellowed, but Ruby found it difficult to accept him back into her life. Jesse and her grandfather became friends. Ruby's older sister Phyllis, an engineer living in New Mexico, had remained close to their father. Phyllis tried to stay in contact with Ruby and Jesse, but her overtures had been rebuffed. In the last book, Ruby revealed that she had kept in regular contact with their mother.

Ruby's education had been haphazard. While living near the Stanford campus, she had attended classes without registering as a student. She came to love books, seeking them in garage sales and used bookstores. After her divorce, private detective Ron Kilgore hired Ruby as a receptionist. Kilgore, who noticed Ruby's fascination with handwriting, subsidized her training as a document examiner. She brought her equipment and she continued to work with Kilgore via the mail. That was not enough money to provide for Jesse's needs. Fortunately nursing assistant DeEtta Greenstone needed a job as badly as Ruby needed help. She was willing to provide day care for Jesse in exchange for food and the space to park her trailer to escape an abusive husband. DeEtta was able to push Jesse farther towards independence than her protective mother could. The first place Ruby applied for work was the studio of photographer Mabel Parker. Mabel went beyond portraits to do excellent nature photography. She was less interested in her financial affairs, an area in which Ruby had developed expertise. Things were working out.

The move to Michigan was intended to be an escape from stress. During *Savage Cut* (Dell, 1996), Ruby accepted that local problems created a different kind of stress. Sable depended upon timber and tourists for survival. Most government land was now unavailable to loggers. Competition for private timber acreage was fierce. Ruby responded to the dear friend of her childhood, Mina Turmowski when she called for help. The deaths of Mina's husband Corbin, then of Mina herself did not receive the vigorous investigation that Ruby felt was necessary. She jeopardized herself, and eventually Jesse, when she used her forensic skills to unearth secrets that the Sable community preferred to ignore. Her allies were DeEtta, timber consultant Hank Holliday, and mildly confused Mrs. Pink.

Hank had become more than a friend by *Cut and Dry* (Dell, 1997). Unfortunately he was absent much of the time while Ruby investigated the death of beautician Alice Rolley. Jesse had been a beneficiary of Alice's personal generosity. She had raised and heavily contributed to a fund for Jesse's tutoring and therapy. The probe into her death by methodical sheriff Carly Joyce did not satisfy the local citizens, jeopardizing his chances for reelection. Ruby was encouraged to run a parallel investigation but cooperated with Carly. A new neighbor, terminally ill police detective Johnny Boyd, found a reason to prolong his life, helping Ruby turn over secrets in the seemingly tranquil city of Sable.

Ruby had sensed that her sister Phyllis was in trouble. She did not realize how bad it was until *Short Cut* (Dell, 1998). A section of a project designed by Phyllis had collapsed sending Eddie Peppermill, a teenage trespasser, to his death. Eddie's parents began a lawsuit. Phyllis contended that her design had been altered. Ruby's expertise with documents was her only hope. Ruby and Jesse flew to New Mexico, meeting Phyllis' coworkers; some friendly, others hostile. Two other deaths occurred before the killer took his last desperate gamble endangering both Phyllis and Jesse.

Ruby gradually lost some of her anger and resentment towards her father and sister. Dereske has a second series featuring librarian Helma Zukas (covered in this volume)

Karen Crist (Becker)

Author: David Wiltse

John Becker was a semi-retired FBI agent, who remained on call for special assignments as a "hit man." He had suffered abuse as a child, and feared that he might be capable of abusing others. He had extra sensory perception when it came to killers, partly because of the potentially cruel element in his own behavior. Karen Crist, a divorcee in her thirties and the deputy director of the FBI unit concerned with kidnapping, came closer to understanding Becker than anyone else. She had suffered abuse in her childhood and married a man who abused both her and their son, Jack.

In *Close to the Bone* (Putnam, 1992), John Becker was just a familiar name to Karen. She was currently assigned to the fingerprints unit and looking for some field action. Her expertise enabled the agency to pinpoint a hired killer through his fingerprints at the Canadian entry point. Becker was able to connect with the killer he hunted so closely that he could sense his thoughts. John and Karen became lovers. There had been a prior Becker story, *Prayer for the Dead* in which Karen did not appear.

When *The Edge of Sleep* (Putnam, 1993) began, it had been years since Karen and John worked together. She recruited him to find abductors, who kidnapped young boys to meet the needs of a woman who lost her only child. Karen's son Jack, of whom Becker was very fond, was at risk of being the next victim.

Karen and John were living together as *Into the Fire* (Putnam, 1994) began. Their relationship forced him into another bizarre and brutal investigation of serial murders. His supervisor threatened to assign the cases to Karen if Becker turned them down. There were explicit scenes of homosexual activity in prison.

By *Bone Deep* (Putnam, 1995), marriage to Karen had made John Becker a happier, more relaxed person at a time when he needed all of his intensity to recognize a serial killer who had insinuated himself into their community. The killer, who held a responsible position and was married, sought the companionship of John and Karen. Her role advanced the plot only as victim, even though she remained Becker's titular supervisor as Associate Deputy Director in charge of Serial Killings for the FBI.

Karen's injuries sidelined her in *Blown Away* (Putnam, 1996). Becker continued to work, but with Pegeen Haddad as his assistant. There was a time when she was more than that. Karen's condition led to serious consideration as to whether or not she would ever return to her job. Becker's concern about Karen was a distraction from his job. After a discouraging investigation for the "mad bomber" known as Spring, during which Becker was obstructed by his new supervisor who was prone to taking credit for what went well and blaming his subordinates for any failure. Becker was ready to quit. Karen, on the other hand, wanted to return to work.

Author David Wiltse devoted a large part of his narratives to the killers and kidnappers, focusing on their symbiotic relationships with one another and their pursuers. He had a second series featuring Deputy Billy Tree

Fey Croaker

Author: Paul Bishop

Fey Croaker may be excused by the physical and sexual abuse done to her by her father, but she was a confrontational, contentious person to work with and a terror to oppose. As supervisor of the homicide unit at West Los Angeles, others perceived Fey as an affirmative action appointee. She recognized that there was some truth in this perception. She also felt she deserved the promotion. Her personal life had been disappointing. None of her three marriages had been successful. She had lovers, but was fiercely independent. Her relationship with her brother Tommy had faltered when his drug addiction led him into crime. Fey had protected him as a child, but that ended when he robbed her house. She saw to it that he was charged, convicted, and sent to jail. Fey, though not a good supervisor generally, had an interesting unit which functioned well. Detective Arch Hammersmith and Rhonda Lawless were referred to as "Hammer" and "Nails".

Fey's home was tasteful, set on several acres of land that included a stable for her two horses. She also acquired a white cat, which she named Brentwood after the neighborhood in which he had been abandoned by the death of his owner. A second cat, Marvella, joined the household later. Fey's last two divorce settlements had provided her with ample assets. Later she became a substantial donor to a children's hospital.

As *Kill Me Again* (Avon, 1994) began, Fey's unit was under pressure. There had been too many unsolved cases since she became supervisor. The first big case of the New Year involved the death of Miranda Goodwinter, a woman who had multiple identities in the past. In one of those identities, her husband Isaac had been found guilty of her murder. Disloyalty within Fey's unit was counterbalanced by the good professional contacts she had made over the years.

Relentless defense attorney Devon Wyatt, whose son Darcy had been charged with rapes, made Fey's life miserable in *Twice Dead* (Avon, 1996). Vicious murders of young male prostitutes in the Los Angeles area were attributable to a serial killer. That meant that the central homicide/robbery unit should handle them, but Fey fought to keep control of the case. Even after it was transferred, she and FBI agent Ash believed the current defendant was incapable of the crime. Fey, who had been seeing a therapist, was mortified and criticized when a tape of her sessions was publicly released. Her comments affected the outcome of a case involving Jo Jo Cullen, a basketball star represented by Devon Wyatt. She could use more therapy by the time she and Ash solved the cases.

Although the series was essentially a police procedural, *Chalk Whispers* (Scribners, 2000) explored Fey's character. As a result of sexual abuse by her now deceased father, police officer Garth Croaker, she was determined to protect vulnerable children. She had this opportunity when, as a lieutenant, she and her unit were transferred to the Robbery-Homicide unit at Headquarters. Their first case was the death of activist Bianca Flynn. Flynn had been connected in the past to Garth Croaker.

The Los Angeles Police Department had been under fire since the Rodney King arrest. In *Tequila Mockingbird* (Scribners, 2001), the shots were coming from within. The shooting of Detective Alex Waverly by his pregnant wife April seemed a simple domestic murder. The fact that Waverly was already dead at the time made a difference. Fey was a pawn in the struggle between established members of the department and the new chief. She was given access to a slush fund, which allowed her to hire private security forces. Fey took both physical and professional risks to expose an ambitious administrator.

Pattern of Behavior (Five Star, 2000), a collection of short stories and novellas by Bishop, included a novella of the same name as the title and a short story featuring Fey which had a lighter than usual tone.

Author Paul Bishop had a professional police background, which provided realism to the narratives, but his heroine was difficult to like.

Victoria Cross

Author: Penny Sumner

Victoria Cross, a tall brown-haired woman in her thirties, had been born and educated in England. Her father had died before her birth, earning the Victoria Cross for his gallantry. She combined her talent as an archivist with credentials as a document analyst certified by Scotland Yard. For five years she worked for an investigative agency in London owned by her lesbian lover, Alicia. When their relationship ended, Victoria moved to New York City where there were opportunities for her to work.

The American respite ended in *The End of April* (Naiad, 1992) when Victoria's great aunt Rosemary Myers, also a lesbian, needed her help. Rosemary, an Oxford Don, found a temporary University position for Victoria. She probed threatening letters sent to April Tate, an activist law student. While April was visiting her sick child, a friend who occupied her apartment was murdered. Victoria, who had become enamored of April, considered several different motives for the threats and violence before finding the correct one.

Victoria stayed on in England, but moved to London in *Crosswords* (Naiad, 1995) where she investigated gangs of the Sixties to find a man who had disappeared twenty-five years earlier. The man was the key to the discovery of a missing Chinese vase, more valuable now that the other one of a pair was available. Victoria's lover did not approve of her investigations because of the danger.

The first person narratives were effusive; the attitude, anti-male.

Lauren Crowder

Author: Stephen White

Clinical psychologist Alan Gregory was the male series protagonist, the narrator of all but two books, and the dominant sleuth. His difficult and independent lover (later wife) Lauren Crowder was worthy of more attention than she received, eventually appearing only by reference or without real participation. Lauren grew up in Washington, where she earned her bachelor's degree. She transferred to Stanford, earning a law degree at Boalt Law School, and then became a deputy district attorney in Boulder, Colorado. Lauren, who had a prickly personality, had divorced Jacob Crowder. He remarried and practiced law in Denver. Despite the fact that she suffered from multiple sclerosis, Lauren played an aggressive game of softball in a woman's league, was a brilliant billiards player, and skied. Her illness was partially controlled by medication, but she had periods of great fatigue, vertigo, and blindness. After her second marriage, she gave birth to a daughter, Grace.

Lauren met Alan Gregory in *Privileged Information* (Viking, 1991). His determination not to reveal client-therapist information to the police department wavered under suspicion that a patient was a serial killer. When his career was threatened by unfounded rumors, he used confidential information to defend himself. Although his divorce had not been finalized, he and Lauren became close. The knowledge of her disability did not cause Alan to turn away, as other men had done.

During *Private Practices* (Viking, 1994), battered wife Claire Draper was killed by her husband Harlan in the office of Diane Estevez, Alan's partner. Subsequently, he and Lauren witnessed an explosion that took the life of Larry Templeton, a prospective witness before the grand jury. Their roles had changed. Now it was Lauren who could not reveal confidential information. Their relationship was complicated by the return of Meredith, Alan's wife who sought a father for her unborn child.

Lauren was a major figure in *Higher Authority* (Viking, 1994), which took place in Utah. Her sister, Teresa had a habit of running when under pressure, but she stood her ground when sexually harassed by Blythe Oaks, a female supervisor at the Utah Women's Symposium. Blythe's strong connections to a U.S. Supreme Court justice and the Mormon Church made a difficult combination to oppose. Lauren worked on the case, recruiting civil rights litigator Robin Torr, a former law school classmate, and their close friend, Detective Sam Purdy. When Blythe was murdered, there were added complications. Teresa took off, making her a prime suspect.

Alan and Lauren had married by *Harm's Way* (Viking, 1996), but still experienced difficulties between their professional responsibilities. When friend and neighbor Peter Arvin was murdered, Alan and Sam Purdy investigated his past to find the motive. Lauren's role was limited.

Remote Control (Viking, 1997) began with Lauren shooting her gun in the vicinity of a murder, leading to her arrest and imprisonment. Her illness caused a transfer to the hospital, leaving Alan and Sam Purdy to exonerate her and identify the killer.

Lauren had gone to Washington, DC because her mother had a suspected heart attack and played no role in *Critical Conditions* (Dutton, 1998)

During *Manner of Death* (Dutton, 1999), two former FBI agents warned Alan and Lauren that a killer was systematically murdering individuals who had been staff members of Orange Unit at the University of Colorado Hospital, Denver in 1982. Alan had never shared with Lauren the powerful feelings he had then for Dr. Sawyer Sackett when they had worked there. Lauren dealt with two fears—that she and Alan might be the next target, and that Sawyer might threaten their marriage. There was a clever insertion of the D. B. Cooper story.

Cold Case (Dutton, 2000) was one of the best of the series, although Lauren played a minor role. Members of the Locard Society, a group devoted to reopening unsolved murder cases, approached Lauren and Alan. They were not members of the group but consented to affiliate themselves on a local case involving the deaths of two high school students. One victim, Mariko Hamamoto had been a patient of a psychologist who was now a member of Congress. Congressman Dr. Raymond Wells had been married to Gloria Welle, sister of Lauren's former husband. Gloria's kidnapping and death were attributed to a disturbed patient of Dr. Welle. The two cases became "hot" and so did the action. Lauren's pregnancy had ameliorated her multiple sclerosis, but made it important that both she and Alan avoid risks. He found it impossible.

Author Stephen White kept getting better. As *The Program* (Doubleday, 2001) began, Lauren was still pregnant. Alan was filling in temporarily as therapist to individuals in the Witness Protection Program. The central figure, however, was New Orleans Assistant District Attorney Kirsten Lord. When a man whom she had sent to prison targeted her, Kirsten entered the Witness Protection Program. Her husband was assassinated and an attempt was made to kidnap her nine-year-old daughter. Kirsten (real name Peyton) formed a strange alliance with Carl, a former hit man. Lauren's role as a legal advisor to Peyton exposed her and her unborn child to danger. White explored the ethics of killing, the moral implications of self-defense and murder to protect another human being.

Even with baby Grace to care for and signs that her MS symptoms were returning, Lauren wanted to return to the practice of law in *Warning Signs* (Delacorte, 2002). Not as an assistant prosecutor, but in the defense of police detective Lucy Tanner. Top defense attorney Cozier Maitlin, who had been retained by Lucy, asked Lauren to assist. Lucy, Sam Purdy's partner, was arrested in the death of District Attorney Roy Peterson. Alan was in the midst of a personal crisis. He measured his responsibility to confidentiality of patient information (a mother's concern about her son's activities) against the need to protect lives. The son, Paul, was spending time with RAMP, fantasizing about revenge against those who had failed to convict criminals who had injured family members.

The diminution of Lauren's role continued. Although she was working full time as prosecutor for Boulder County, she had no meaningful role in *The Best Revenge* (Delacorte, 2003) except in providing her husband with emotional support. Alan had provided therapy for both Tom Clone, an ex-convict, and FBI Kelda James, who had produced the evidence to get him released. This was not a good time for Alan. He was burned out and making mistakes. An intriguing premise.

Alan's problem in *Blinded* (Delacorte, 2004) was initially out of Lauren's jurisdiction. His patient, attractive Gibbs Storey, had not only told Alan that she believed her husband, Sterling, was a murderer but she requested that he inform the authorities. Lauren needed heavy doses of steroids to function. She felt guilty about burdening Alan.

Count Lauren among the missing in *Missing Persons* (Dutton, 2005). Not that she's in any personal trouble, but that she played no significant role in the narrative. Alan and his partner, Diane Estevez, discovered the body of her friend, clinical social worker Hannah Grant. Hannah had been consulted by fourteen-year-old Mallory Miller, now missing. Alan, who tried to stay out of it, had counseled Mallory's parents. When Diane disappeared, Alan had no choice but to intervene. Wordy and slow.

Kill Me (Dutton, 2006) had little space for either Lauren or Alan. His role was as therapist and eventually as a target. Lauren did not appear. The main focus was on X, a wealthy man, who learned late in life that he had fathered a son. X had made a deal to have Death's Angels kill him quickly, but changed his mind.

At a time when Alan needed a clear mind in *Dry Ice* (Dutton, 2007), he was extraordinarily introspective. Michael McClelland, a killer who had been placed in a mental health facility rather than prison, partly due to Alan's influence, escaped. Both Lauren and Alan were aware that McClelland sought revenge against them and Sam Purdy. McClelland had spent much of his time doing Internet research. Alan, Lauren, and Sam all had secrets that, if exposed, would cause damage. Some interesting plotting but depressing.

Lauren and Grace were in Europe during *Dead Time* (Dutton, 2008) on her personal quest to locate the child she had given up for adoption. Alan was drawn into the problems experienced by his former wife, Meredith, a New York City television producer. She desperately wanted a child, so together with her intended husband Eric arranged for Lisa, a surrogate mother, to bear their offspring. After Lisa disappeared, Meredith asked Alan and Sam Purdy to find her, a task made more difficult by events occurring decades before in the Grand Canyon.

Next, *The Last Lie* (2010).

Rachel Crowne

Author: Ellen Rawlings

Even after two failed marriages freelance investigative reporter Rachel Crowne was drawn to risk-taking. At thirty-five, she had been deeply affected by her inability to bear children. Not only had it been the cause of her first divorce, but she also had a strong maternal instinct. This warmth had attracted her second husband (Ray) but his needs for mothering went beyond her capacity. She was seriously considering adoption or foster parenting when the series began. Rachel had attended religious education classes as a child but her attachment to Judaism was more ethnic than religious. Leaving things unfinished had become a habit. She gave up on her Ph.D. in English without doing her dissertation.

Her strongest ties were to her brother, David, who taught chemistry at the University of Tel Aviv in Israel, to her best friend, magazine publisher Nancy Martin, and to her neighbor, police detective Tom Brant. They lived in Fairfield, Maryland, between Washington, D.C. and Baltimore. Brant was an occasional source of information but more frequently advised her to stay out of police business. Their regular racquetball matches gained in tension as Rachel's skills improved. She worked out regularly at an athletic club, and rode her mountain bike.

Rachel's mother had died when she was nine. Her father and three older brothers were very protective so Rachel avoided them when she got in trouble. She described herself as short with light brown hair.

Rachel was indignant in *The Murder Lover* (Fawcett Gold Medal, 1997) when she attended the funeral of Elspeth Goldman, the granddaughter of an elderly friend. Elspeth's death was the first in a series of attacks and murders on Jewish women who had recently become engaged. An assignment for Nancy Martin's magazine, *The Howard County Target,* sent Rachel to interview neo-Nazi Mark Michaels. His bigotry, added to Rachel's recent visit to the Holocaust Museum in D.C., deeply affected her. She served as a tethered goat for the police department, faking an engagement to draw out the killer. She did not intend to be another Jewish victim.

Elspeth Goldman's former husband Jordan had become Rachel's lover but he backed away in *Deadly Harvest* (Fawcett, 1997). His children came first. Rachel was too given to recklessness. She had embroiled herself in the death of Dilly Friedman, an inner city schoolteacher whom she had intended to highlight in a magazine article. Dilly's brother convinced Rachel to follow through on the project, hoping that she would find the killer. Rachel was fascinated by Dilly's story: a sociable young college student who spent most of her personal time with five male fellow students, but after graduation led a very restricted social life. Her investigation did not so much lead Rachel to the killer, as it did lead the killer to Rachel.

It was interesting that unlike many males connected to high-powered female sleuths, Jordan gave serious thought to the negative aspects of risk-taking and opted out for the sake of his children and his own mental health.

Edwina Crusoe

Author: Mary Kittredge

Edwina Crusoe worked in a traditional female occupation, nursing, but with the independence provided by wealth and education. A petite woman with dark hair and eyes, she rode horseback, enjoyed skin diving, changed her own tires, and drove fast but competently. Her deceased father had been an industrialist and a diplomat. Her mother was a successful romance writer.

During *Fatal Diagnosis* (St. Martin, 1990), Edwina held a staff position at Chelsea Memorial Hospital, New Haven, Connecticut. Two couples disputed the parentage of the surviving child in a possible baby switch. Young Hallie Dietz had lived all her life with Margaret and Oliver. The Dietz's claim to Hallie was contested by Bill and Jane Claymore whose child had purportedly died of liver disease. Edwina went undercover at the rural hospital where young Hallie Dietz had been born to discover the motive for two murders. Police detective Martin McIntyre assisted her.

Edwina became a nurse-consultant, but in *Rigor Mortis* (St. Martin, 1991) returned to Chelsea Hospital to investigate a series of "mercy " killings. Millie Clemens believed that her husband Walt had been murdered. Janet Bennington claimed that she saw someone "slip" something into her aunt's medication shortly before she died. Other bodies were exhumed. Edwina had to overcome her distaste for the primary suspect before she could identify the killer.

Cadaver (St. Martin, 1992) portrayed Edwina as more detective than nurse. The narrative was stacked with plots: a religious fanatic roaming the hospital corridors, the possible suicide of a staff member, questionable research into baldness, and McIntyre's abduction. An overload bent on shock value.

Walking Dead Man (St. Martin, 1992) began with what seemed to be impossibility., a young woman stalked by a man whom she had killed. Edwina would have dismissed the claim except that Theresa Whitlock was murdered shortly after she asked for help. After their marriage, Edwina and Martin had moved to the countryside, where she was lonely, restless, and terrorized by threats.

Edwina was a forty-year-old expectant mother as *Desperate Remedy* (St. Martin, 1993) began, and in no condition to investigate attacks on Dr. Victor Grace and his wife, Renata, newcomers seemingly without a past. After saving the police from charging the wrong man, she learned she was expecting twins.

Francis and Jonathan were two-years-old when *Kill or Cure* (St. Martin, 1995) began, time enough for Edwina to develop cabin fever. She returned to duty as an investigator when William Granger, a successful young doctor, entered the emergency room at Chelsea Hospital, then shot and killed a security guard and his own wife. Edwina was hired to find evidence that would support a defense based on mental illness. In a secondary investigation, Edwina agreed to help Marion Bailey, another nurse, whose son Gerry had witnessed the shooting, but was unable to repeat what Granger had said to him.

Interesting plots.

Regan Culver

Author: Audrey Stallsmith

Mystery series with a Christian background and a female sleuth are few and far between. (See *Mystery Women:* Volume 1 for Margo Franklin and Volume 2 for Jennifer Grey, both characters created by Jerry Jenkins.) Regan Culver was the child of her father's second marriage, much younger than her half-sisters. Alden Culver had been a distinguished naturopath and Rosemary, Regan's mother, had been a gardening columnist. This series, subtitled "Thyme Will Tell Mysteries," combined religion and gardening. Regan was a college-educated horticulturist.

During *Rosemary for Remembrance* (Waterbrook Press, 1998), Regan was the primary beneficiary in her father's will but Alden had been murdered. She was regarded with suspicion by the police and with hostility by her own family. Police Chief Matt Olin took the "socially deprived" chip off his shoulder when Regan met him more than half way to romance. When Regan confronted the real killer, she was fortunate that friends, family, and Matt Olin intervened.

Regan and Matt's engagement was not working out by *Marigolds for Mourning* (Waterbrook Press, 1998). She was busy managing the family herb farm, but made time to investigate the forty-year-old murder/suicide involving Jack Hargrove's grandfather and grandmother and the more recent attempted murder of Jack in what was perceived as a heroin overdose. Local adults were quick to accuse young Jack and his African-American football buddy, Gabe, of being involved with drugs. Other students knew them better. Gabe and Lucerne, an eccentric new student, helped Regan and Matt to unmask a killer and restore a reputation.

Matt and Regan did not settle their differences in *Roses for Regret* (Waterbrook Press, 1999). However, she was instrumental in uniting two other couples. Problems on the Board of Directors of NORA (a rose growers association) sent Regan to a small town in Pennsylvania. She met wildlife rescuer Damia Day and Bram Falco, the director of a fertilizer factory, who were at odds with one another about pollution. Their ill feeling went back two decades to an accident that involved their parents. The denouement lacked credibility.

Christian messages of forgiveness were part of the solutions to all problems except those of Matt and Regan.

Lark Dailey (Dodge)

Author: Sheila Simonson

Although she owned a bookstore, six-foot-tall Lark Dailey had a secondary interest. The "jock" in a family that prided itself on intellectual brilliance, Lark had played Big Ten women's basketball at Ohio State. Lark would have been in the Olympics had the United States not withdrawn that year. Now she coached the team at a nearby California junior college. Her mother, a poet, had been an ardent pacifist during the Vietnam War. Her father, although no longer a Quaker, had been a conscientious objector in World War II who served overseas with the AFSI. He had a career as a college professor, but had taken emeritus status. Her only brother was a stockbroker.

In *Larkspur* (St. Martin, 1990), Lark and her lover, police officer Jay Dodge, visited the mountain lodge of gay poet Dai Llewellyn in time for his death. Lark's mother had been named as Dai's literary executor, but no one expected the position to be open so soon. Several murders later, Lark still had not identified the killer, but should not be faulted because the murderer had the weakest motive of the suspects.

In *Skylark* (St. Martin, 1992), Lark attended a bookseller's convention in London, to be followed by husband Jay en route to a police conference. Meantime she shared a London apartment with Ann Veryan, who received a package containing material written in Czech. Further complications came from a mysterious attack on Czech poet Milos Vlacek, an eviction notice, and the murder of their elderly landlady. Lark, Jay and the English police separated international intrigue from homegrown greed.

Starting a family was Lark's primary concern in *Mudlark* (St. Martin, 1993). She was nesting at their new home in Washington, while Jay taught police administration at the local college. Having sold her California bookstore, Lark opened a new one in Shoalwater. With financial help from her parents, she purchased a building with several units and located the store on the first floor. The community seemed friendly but within days, Lark and her friend Bonnie Bell found Cleo Cabot Hagen's corpse, a nearby house was torched, and an attacker entered the Dodge home. Many of the locals, formerly employed in logging or fishing, resented the influx of well-to-do Californians, but that's no motive for murder. What was?

Meadowlark (St. Martin, 1996) introduced Lark to Bianca Fiedler, a vehement and wealthy environmentalist with an organic farm. Bianca, a manipulative woman, induced Lark to manage a writer's workshop. She was less supportive when Lark investigated the murder of master gardener Hugo Groth on the premises. The solution was weak, dependent upon an unlikely confession.

A miscarriage left Lark unhappy and restless as *Malarkey* (St. Martin, 1997) opened. She sought relief in a trip to Ireland. Her ailing father occupied a guesthouse on the estate of Alex Stein. Although Alex and his wife Barbara disapproved of amateur "war games," they had allowed them on the Stanyon Hall property where Alex based his software enterprises. While walking the grounds, Lark discovered the body of Slade Wheeler, business manager of the corporation and participant in the "war games." Lark was reluctant to tell Jay that she was involved in another murder case. He joined her in time to be kidnapped. Ireland's mythical history included a special "magic" that brought great joy to the Dailey/Dodge household.

Inconsistent quality, but the better ones are well above average. Simonson has a new sleuth, librarian Meg McLean

Lt. Eve Dallas

Author: J. D. Robb, pseudonym for romance novelist Nora Roberts

Eve Dallas had suppressed the memories of the first eight years of her life. Found homeless, physically and sexually abused in Dallas, Texas when she was eight, the "brandy-eyed" dark-haired child was placed in foster care. She found her first real home in the New York City Police Department. Real peace came from her marriage to Roarke, a powerful businessman who had been active in Irish terrorism. On the surface, Eve was a controlled, competent investigator who rose to the rank of lieutenant. At night, she was tortured with dreams, in which she experienced sexual abuse by her father. She rejected the use of hypnosis to deal with her latent fears, and only reluctantly made the departmental psychiatrist aware of her problems. Until her marriage, Eve had shared her home with a cat, Galahad. Her best friend was Mavis Freestar, a raunchy nightclub singer whom she had arrested when Mavis was a juvenile. All of this took place in the fourth decade of the Twenty-first century.

Naked in Death (Berkley, 1995) was a composite of mystery and science fiction with romance tossed in. Eve was entitled to time off after an incident in which she killed with justification; still, she went right back to work. She handled a sensitive murder in which Sharon DeBless, the socially prominent victim, had chosen to make her living as a "licensed companion" (Twenty-first century nomenclature for "hooker"). Eve became sexually involved with the primary suspect, Roarke, an Irish billionaire.

Roarke had become an important part of Eve's life by *Glory in Death* (Berkley, 1995), but had links to several women who were killed with a common method. The victims, all outspoken professional women, had their throats slashed. Eve's efforts to draw out the killer, using herself as bait, failed. Only at the cost of another life, did she discover the man who needed to silence women.

Immortal in Death (Berkley, 1996) followed Eve as she prepared for marriage. She was sidetracked when Mavis was arrested for the murder of beautiful model Pandora. No police officer would be given charge of a case in which she was so personally involved but credibility was not a major factor in this series.

Eve and Roarke's honeymoon was distracted by the presumed suicide of Drew Matthias in *Rapture in Death* (Berkley, 1996). Only after two other deaths had been called to her attention, did Eve identify the pattern and the intent to ruin Roarke.

Ceremony in Death (Berkley, 1997) placed Eve in an unenviable position, investigating the death of veteran police officer Det. Sgt. Frank Wojinski. This meant bypassing Captain Feeney, the man who had trained her and become a surrogate father. Wojinski had carried out an unauthorized investigation of a satanic cult to which his naive granddaughter Alice Lingstrom belonged. When both Wojinski and Alice died under suspicious circumstances, Eve pitted herself against the powerful forces of evil, which sought to make her a victim.

A religious fanatic tantalized Eve with riddles and hints as he killed Irish-Americans in *Vengeance in Death* (Berkley, 1997). Roarke concealed his role in the incident that led to the murder spree. One of the better narratives in the series.

Christmas and Santa Claus had no meaning in Eve's childhood and youth but the celebrations were important to Roarke in *Holiday in Death* (Berkley, 1998). Eve selected a few gifts but her primary concern was a serial killer who utilized the twelve days of Christmas to dramatize his vicious murders. As part of the conclusion Eve learned whether or not she would go beyond duty and kill a perpetrator.

Eve was pitted against a powerful antagonist in *Conspiracy in Death* (Berkley, 1999) when she investigated the collection of diseased organs from elderly street people and vagrants. Because artificial substitutes for body parts were widely available in the year 2056, Eve suspected prominent surgeons and researchers were conducting experiments in the regeneration of organ tissues. When physical threats failed to stop Eve, she was attacked professionally.

Loyalty, usually a positive quality, led a daughter to seek revenge (and a considerable amount of money from New York City) in *Loyalty in Death* (Berkley, 1999). Eve and Roarke were targeted because they represented wealth and power. On a more personal level young and naïve Luke Peabody, brother of Eve's assistant, was drawn into the conspirator's devious schemes. Eve's skeptical nature and Roarke's vast resources avoided a major catastrophe.

Although there were plentiful electronic gimmicks for the science fiction fan and passionate passages for the romantics, *Judgment in Death* (Berkley, 2000) also provided the best action of the Dallas series. Her investigation of cop-killers was paralleled by a duel with criminal Max Ricker, once an associate of Roarke's. The methodology and motivation were well handled, although place name spellings were faulty: Utumwa, Iowa; Juno, Alaska! Get an atlas please!

The renovated Old Globe Theatre belonged to Roarke who financed the revival of the classic Agatha Christie play *Witness for the Prosecution*. In *Witness in Death* (Berkley, 2000), when murder occurred on stage during opening night, the investigation belonged to Eve Dallas. The victim, Richard Draco, for all his brilliance was as vicious as the character he played in the drama. Among members of the cast were several who had suffered from his behavior. Author J. D. Robb made intelligent use of the similarities between characters in the play and those involved in the murder investigation, one of her better narratives.

Hitman Sylvester Yost had beaten, raped and murdered associates of Roarke. Identifying him during *Betrayal in Death* (Berkley, 2001) was merely the first step for Eve. Capturing and convicting Yost was more difficult. Considering that Roarke felt guilty that the victims died to injure him, she allowed him to take part in the investigation. Success in his quest demanded a price from Roarke.

The sadistic young killers of *Seduction in Death* (Berkley, 2001) would give Twentieth century Leopold and Loeb a run for their money. Eve, whose childhood memories were revived by the cases, was determined to bring them down. Unlike Leopold and Loeb, the Twenty-first century murderers had expertise in chemicals that would trigger sexual responses and computer skills that enabled them to find victims on the Internet. With Roarke's resources, legal or illegal, Eve would do whatever was necessary to end their reign of terror.

A series of mysterious deaths during *Purity in Death* (Berkley, 2002) rallied all of Eve's resources from Roarke down to 17-year-old Jamie Lindstrom. A vigilante group, known as "Purity Seekers" had devised a computer virus that would kill pederasts, drug dealers and blackmailers, but also killed or injured innocent parties. The group included powerful and disaffected individuals, many of whom had suffered when the legal system failed to bring predators to justice.

By now Nora Roberts' name was superimposed on the J. D. Robb books. She did herself proud in *Reunion in Death* (Berkley, 2002). The hatred that ex-convict Juliana Dunne felt for Eve was based on the fact that it was Eve's investigation that put her in prison for the murder of her third husband. A conwoman as well as a killer, she used her early release to get revenge. Even when Roarke and Eve realized that Juliana was responsible for subsequent deaths, she remained elusive. Eve, with Roarke's help, confronted her own demons, often in steamy sex.

It was obvious early on in *Portrait in Death* (Berkley, 2003) that the killer of young innocent victims, beginning with college student Rachel Howard, was mentally ill. The young women, all of whom had a special "glow", had been photographed by Dirk Hastings, but Eve did not believe he was the killer. Photos sent with a message to reporter Nadine Furst had emanated from "Make My Scene", a data club frequented by young adults. Eve rallied Peabody, McNab, Feeney, and some new allies, including rookie policeman Trueheart. Roarke was otherwise occupied. He had received startling news about his birth mother, a poignant segment of the narrative that Eve shared. Mavis Freestone's continued pregnancy brought something of comic relief.

Even Eve Dallas was shocked by the vicious murder of licensed companion Jacie Wooton in *Imitation of Death* (Berkley, 2003). It had been carried out in a method reminiscent of Jack the Ripper. Jacie was not the first victim and would not be the last. Eve who was taunted by messages left within the corpses addressed to her, was not going to quit. The notepaper limited the number of suspects, some very well known. Eve, Peabody and Roarke narrowed that number to one.

Remember When (Putnam, 2003) is a worthy effort by Nora Roberts as herself and as J.D. Robb. In Part One, Laine Tavish, daughter of Big Jack O'Hara, a professional conman and thief, had made a life for herself. She changed her name, earned a college degree and set up an antique business in Angel's Gap, Maryland. Her mother, who had left no trail behind when she and Elaine departed, eventually found happiness in a second marriage and lived in New Mexico. Everything changed for Laine when Uncle Willy, Jack's partner, entered the antique shop, left but was killed in a car accident within minutes. This minor connection brought Laine to the attention of two men: Max Gannon, a former cop now working for an insurance company, and Alex Crew, who together with Willy and Jack had carried out a major jewel theft. Part Two began when Samantha Gannon, granddaughter of Max and Laine wrote a book, based upon their recollections, focusing on what happened to the 25% of the diamonds never recovered. Samantha's house was burglarized while she was on a book tour; her friend Andrea who was housesitting was murdered. Eve Dallas, who was assigned the case, quickly picked up on the connection to the missing diamonds as a motive.

Eve still fought her demons in *Visions in Death* (Putnam, 2004) but she was making headway. She was more open to friendships, and shared her trauma with Delia Peabody. At work, she remained a tireless tyrant. It may sound repetitions (it is). A serial killer was raping, murdering, and mutilating women, several in city parks. Celina Sanchez, a psychic who had envisioned the attacks as they occurred, wanted to work with the police. Overcoming her doubts, Eve agreed. She and Peabody went on television taunting the killer with devastating results.

Eve and Roarke took on a formidable enemy in *Divided in Death* (Putnam, 2004), the HSO, a national security agency that had been set up during a period of civil disturbance. They made the choice to do so at a time when their own relationship was vulnerable. Both Reva Ewing and her mother, Caro, were valuable employees of Roarke's security business. Reva was suspected of murder when her unfaithful husband and his lover were murdered.

Origin in Death (Putnam, 2005) may be the best of the Eve Dallas series because it provided a horrifying glimpse of the future where science challenged God. Eve learned of the death of Nobel Prize winner Dr. Wilfred Icove, when she was at the hospital on business. He and his son, Will, ran a center for reconstructive and cosmetic surgery. Icove's death opened a door through which Eve and Roarke saw a future that frightened them. Someone else felt the same way.

The novella *Midnight in Death* (Berkley, 2005) had been published earlier in the anthology *Silent Night*, The plotting was linear. Serial killer, David Palmer, had escaped from a life term in a unit for mental defectives. His agenda was well in place. He intended to kill slowly, recording the reactions of the victims, those who were responsible for his detention. The list was prominently displayed on the corpse of Judge Harold Wainger who had tried his case. When called to the scene Eve quickly identified the victim, the killer, and the fact that her name was on the list.

When Eve discovered nine-year-old Nixie Swisher, the only survivor of a mass murder, in *Survivor in Death* (Berkley, 2005) the last thing on her mind was taking a personal interest in the child. Peabody made it happen. Nixie had clung to Eve, her rescuer. She was the only witness to the deaths of her parents, brother and other occupants of the family home. Professional killers were taking no chances so Nixie was a target and so was anyone else who got in their way. The deaths of two fellow officers motivated not only Eve but the entire homicide unit. Eve's vulnerabilities were well explored. She didn't let Nixie down.

It only took a few minutes in Trudy Lombard's presence, as *Memory in Death* (Putnam, 2006) began, to change Eve from a competent professional to a terrified child. Trudy struck when she tried to blackmail Roarke. She may have had a back-up plan but the next time Eve and Roarke saw her, she was dead. Only her son Bobby, who had been kind to Eve as a child, mourned Trudy. Investigating her death was a conflict of interest for Eve so she gathered evidence quickly to clear herself and Roarke in case they should be suspected.

Roarke and Eve had met Tandy Willoughby when they attended birthing classes with Mavis in *Born in Death* (Berkley, 2006). Mavis and Tandy, a young Englishwoman, had become great friends. When she disappeared, Mavis begged Eve to take on the case. Eve's resources were already strained by the murders of Natalie Copperfield and Bick Byson, both employees of Sloan, Myers, and Kraus Accounting. Eve was confident that Natalie had encountered improprieties in an international account handled by the firm, and shared her concerns with Bick, her fiancé. The involvement of Roarke and Eve in the birth of Mavis's child was played for humor.

Another novella, *Interlude in Death* (Berkley, 2006) from the anthology *Out of this World* found Eve in an uncomfortable position. She had been sent off Earth by her supervisor to take part in an Interplanetary Law Enforcement Security Conference held on Olympus. Roarke who owned most of Olympus, accompanied her. They were both targets of a plot to destroy their reputations, perhaps leading to criminal charges by a man who could never forget.

Author Roberts is undoubtedly creative. *Innocent in Death* (Berkley, 2007) has improbable but fascinating plotting tied into a potential breach between Eve and Roarke. When popular teacher Craig Foster was poisoned while at Sarah Child Academy, Eve struggled to find a motive for his death. His recent marriage was loving. His students and co-workers professed admiration for him. A second faculty murder added complexity. Normally Roarke would have been Eve's major resource; not so, this time. "Maggie" Percell, a rich and beautiful woman, had a professional and personal interest in Roarke. Her manipulations drove Eve into erratic behavior.

Creation in Death (Putnam's, 2007) may turn off readers who do not enjoy a mixture of sadistic torture and torrid sex in their mysteries. A serial killer whom Eve and Feeney had failed to identify had resurfaced in New York City. They were aware that he was still active, but out of their jurisdiction. He abducted, viciously tortured, and finally killed young women. The three new victims were all employees of one of Roarke's business interests, which made it personal. A fourth young woman had been abducted putting the police under pressure to find her before she was murdered.

Thomas and Ava Anders seemed a devoted couple, so when he was murdered while she was on a trip with friends in *Strangers in Death* (Putnam, 2008) Ava seemed more victim than suspect. Thomas's death had aspects of prostitution and kinky sex that just might have been staged. Eve had her suspect picked out early, but lacked any evidence to support her belief. Solid police procedure and Roarke's recollection of an Alfred Hitchcock movie made a surprising connection.

The death of a popular Spanish Harlem priest while officiating at a funeral mass in *Salvation in Death* (Putnam, 2008), was only the first shocker. Eve, called to the scene, learned first that the victim had been poisoned by tainted communion wine, and later, that he was an imposter. Within a short time, a second similar death, that of evangelist Jimmy Jay Jenkins raised the question: was this second death a copy-cat murder or were they dealing with a serial killer. In the first case, Eve focused not on the background of Father Miguel Flores, but on that of the imposter. There was an interesting dialogue as to how justice was to be best served.

The prose was dramatic, the sex steamy, and the science fiction at the gimmick level. Still, they roll out to eager readers. *Promises in Death* (2009), *Kindred in Death* (2009) but surely there will be more.

Lots more! Short stories in *Three in Death* (2008); *Indulgence in Death* (2010); even *Treachery in Death,* already scheduled for 2011!

Daisy Dalrymple

Author: Carola Dunn

The fortunes of Daisy Dalrymple's family had declined since the death of her father and only brother. Under English law in the 1920s, the title and land holdings descended only to a male heir. Her mother, Lady Maud, was allowed to live in the Dower House. Daisy, still recovering from the death of her fiancé (a conscientious objector who drove an ambulance during World War I), moved to a London apartment. She found work as a reporter. Her skills included photography and shorthand. Daisy was comfortably plump with honey brown hair, blue eyes, and a facial mole.

During *Death at Wentwater Court* (St. Martin, 1994), set in the Twenties, Daisy developed a magazine series on the great homes of England. The death of lecherous Lord Stephen Astwick by drowning in a frozen pond at Wentwater fascinated Daisy, then a guest. She had taken photos of the scene and was available to transcribe the interviews for Scotland Yard Inspector Alec Fletcher.

Daisy continued her series for *Town and Country* magazine in *The Winter Garden Mystery* (St. Martin, 1995). The Parslow family, with the exception of Lady Valeria, made her welcome. While viewing the garden accompanied by the Welsh assistant gardener Owen Morgan, she discovered the partially decomposed body of Owen's fiancée, Gracie. The pregnant Gracie had been a danger to someone but Daisy did not believe it was Owen.

Daisy was still balancing the widowed Fletcher and more traditional suitor Phillip Petrie, who had been a friend of her deceased brother, as *Requiem for a Mezzo* (St. Martin, 1996) opened. Her neighbors included soprano Bettina Abernathy, Bettina's husband Roger, a music teacher, and Bettina's sister, Muriel Westlea. When Bettina died on stage from poison, family members and fellow singers had a multiplicity of motives. Alec and Daisy carried on parallel investigations, which coalesced.

In *Murder on the Flying Scotsman* (St. Martin, 1997), Daisy traveled by train en route to view a Scottish castle for her next assignment. Her acquaintance with former classmate Amelia Desmond drew Daisy into the intrigues of the McGowan family, the senior member of which had let his heirs know that death was imminent. However, it was not Alistair who was murdered, but his younger twin brother Albert, a passenger on the Flying Scotsman. Daisy insisted the death was murder, drawing Alec into the investigation. Phillip Petrie had routinely proposed to Daisy, but he was smitten upon meeting American heiress Gloria Arbuckle.

Daisy, happily released Phillip from any obligation as *Damsel in Distress* (St. Martin, 1997) began. When Gloria was abducted, she assisted in the search. Caleb Arbuckle, Gloria's father, insisted that the police be kept out of the case. Phillip and Daisy recruited a coterie of upper class volunteers to scour the countryside for Cockney kidnappers. Alec risked professional reprimand by joining in the rescue.

British traditions—the Henley Regatta and weekends in the country—were juxtaposed with British class distinctions in *Dead in the Water* (St. Martin, 1998). Daisy and Alec visited her aunt Lady Cynthia Cheringham near the site of the annual races. Among their fellow guests were the Ambrose College crewmembers who reflected the disparity in social position that led to murder.

In *Styx and Stones* (St. Martin, 1999), Daisy found murder mixed with gossip, narrow mindedness, and class snobbery in a small rural village. She was visiting to help Lord John Frobisher, her brother-in-law, who had been receiving poison pen letters. She almost destroyed her relationship with Alec by her reckless behavior.

Daisy had not been a devotee of the natural sciences, but in *Rattle His Bones* (St. Martin, 2000), she frequented the British Museum to gather material for articles requested by both American and English magazines. Not surprisingly it was she who found the corpse of quarrelsome Dr. Pettigrew amidst a pile of bones. The discovery that valuable gems had been replaced by paste replicas provided a motive for murder. Which of the cantankerous curators was the culprit? Less interesting than prior books, because the supporting characters were drier than the bones.

In *To Davey Jones Below* (St. Martin, 2001), American millionaire Caleb Arbuckle used his influence to arrange that, after their honeymoon, Alec would be assigned as a liaison to new FBI director, J. Edgar Hoover. Alec and Daisy were to travel by ocean liner in the company of Arbuckle, Phillip Petrie, and Gloria. Other passengers included British steel man Jethro Gotobed and his new bride Wanda whom Arbuckle considered a "gold digger." Not even the gale-like weather could explain a series of deaths by "falling overboard." Alec with Daisy's assistance soothed the troubled waters with an explanation of the incidents and of Wanda's subsequent death.

While Alec was liaising with J. Edgar Hoover in Washington, Daisy remained at the Hotel Chelsea in New York City during *The Case of the Murdered Muckraker* (Kensington, 2002). Even with an FBI agent hovering over her, Daisy involved herself in the murder of fellow hotel guest Otis Cardmody. Daisy had witnessed Carmody's fall down an elevator shaft after he had been shot. While the Tammany Hall tinged police focused on political adversaries and marital discord, Daisy and Alec looked elsewhere.

Daisy combined business with pleasure when she wangled an invitation for her, Alec, and his daughter Belinda to spend Christmas at Brockdene Manor in *Mistletoe and Murder* (St. Martin's Minotaur, 2002). Lord Westmoor, owner of the property, had settled some shirttail relatives at Brockdene. During the visit the possibility arose that the mixed-blood relative, looked down upon by the others, might be the true heir to the Earldom. Of course, murder ensued.

Daisy (now Daisy Dalrymple Fletcher) could avoid the dentist no longer. Her toothache was unbearable so in *Die Laughing* (Kensington, 2003) she kept her appointment with Raymond Talmadge. The waiting room was empty. She, nurse Brenda Hensted and Raymond's wife, Daphne, entered the treatment room, only to find him dead in the dental chair. The police officer who responded might have dismissed the case as accidental or suicide, but Daisy noted signs of murder. The Talmadges were members of the Fletcher's social circle. Gossip provided multiple suspects and brought about a second death.

When, in *A Mourning Wedding* (St. Martin's Minotaur, 2004), Daisy's best friend, Lucy Fotheringay invited her to visit Haverhill where her wedding was to take place, Lucy warned Daisy that her relatives were "murderous". That may have been the most sensible remark Lucy made as she dithered about whether or not to go through with the ceremony. That became a moot question when Great-Aunt Eva, a collector of unpleasant facts and rumors, was throttled. Haverhill was the home of Lucy's wealthy grandfather, Nicholas the Earl of Haverhill, who supported many members of his extended family. The next death was that of gentle Lord Aubrey Fotheringay, the heir to the earldom.

Nicholas and Daisy agreed that Alec should be summoned. He insisted that Daisy, now pregnant, stay out of it. This one is difficult to understand, without reference to a genealogical chart.

Daisy had taken her stepdaughter, Belinda and a young friend, Deva Prasad, to a seaside guesthouse in *Fall of a Philanderer* (St. Martin, 2005). Soon after Alec joined them, they witnessed a quarrel between the lecherous bartender George Enderby and young Peter Anstruther who had just returned from Naval service. Peter's wife, Cecelia, had spent the time with George. The discovery of George's battered corpse cast suspicion on Peter. This was highly patterned, seemed to drag on.

Daisy was six months pregnant when she accompanied her friend Gwen Tyndall to her family home in *Gunpowder Plot* (St. Martin, 2006). Daisy had been unaware of the dynamics of the family. Lady Tyndall and the four children had never challenged Sir Harold, keeping him unaware of problems because of his temper. That changed when son and heir Jack brought engineer Martin Miller as a guest. Miller, a commoner, had not only offered Jack a job in his firm, but showed an interest in Gwen. Sir Harold expected Jack, on graduation, to return to Edge Manor and accept his responsibilities. Jack's casual invitation to Australians Jimmy and Ellie Gooch to attend the family viewing of the Guy Fawkes display created havoc.

A series of magazine articles on the Tower of London seemed a strange assignment for Daisy in *The Bloody Tower* (St. Martin's Minotaur, 2007). After her visits there as a child, she had suffered from nightmares, and now she had two-month-old twin babies. Daisy was restless however and Nanny rigidly limited Daisy's and Alec's visits to the nursery. Mel Germond, Daisy's friend, knew the Resident Governor of the Tower, Major General Arthur Carradine and members of his household. She was able to arrange that Daisy would cap off her series by staying overnight as Carradine's guest to watch the historic ceremony of the Keys. That placed Daisy on site when Chief Yeoman Warder Crabtree was murdered, perhaps by mistake for another member of the unit. Alec was not pleased to learn that Daisy found another body, but he valued her insights of the potential suspects.

The bequest to Alec of a lovely spacious home in Hampstead came at a time when the family needed more room in *Black Ship* (St. Martin's Minotaur, 2008). Once settled in, they were eager to make friends in the neighborhood. Daisy was particularly drawn to young Audrey Jessup and her mother-in-law Moira who lived next door. The discovery of a dead man in the common garden area, forced Alec to assume his professional role. Daisy sought to protect her friends from unfair assumptions. Black ships carried liquor from England to the United States during Prohibition.

Interesting cozies initially published in paperback, later in hardcover. *Sheer Folly* (2009). Dunn also has a new sleuth, Eleanor Trewynn.

Abigail Danforth

Author: Marian J. A. Jackson, pseudonym for Marian Rogers

Abigail Danforth was a liberated woman in the late 1890s. Her mother had died when she was born. Her rich and over-protective father had Abigail educated at home. Nevertheless she was infected with the Sherlock Holmes virus and determined to be a female detective. Dressed in male clothing, she traveled alone at night into places where no female would be safe. She rode, shot, and took laudanum to sleep at night. Abigail's slightly older companion Maude Cunningham, who still wore mourning for her husband's death, had been considered a wise choice to watch over Abigail. However she proved to be equally unconventional.

In *The Punjat's Ruby* (Pinnacle, 1990), Lord Frederick, Abigail's shy English suitor, was taken advantage of by scurrilous friends. His hospitality was outraged when a valuable jewel belonging to a guest was stolen. Following Holmes's modus operandi, Abigail recruited street urchins headed by Molly O'Brien, to assist in her enquiries. Maude became Watson to Abigail's Holmes

On their return to the United States, Abigail and Maude set out on a cross-country train trip in *The Arabian Pearl* (Pinnacle, 1990). When Abigail's horse, Crosspatches, and a beautiful stallion belonging to Charles Osgood were stolen, they cut short their journey to recover them. Osgood was murdered in the process. At one point in her pursuit of the thieves, Abigail resorted to violence which later appalled her.

On arrival in San Francisco during *The Cat's Eye* (Pinnacle, 1991), Abigail helped Maude discover the killer of Charles Everet Davenport III, Maude's husband and father of the child she had miscarried. Charley had been disinherited by his wealthy father, who was less than honorable himself. In order to gain information, Abigail dressed as a young man, went out at night to unwholesome places of business. She met celebrities e.g.; Jack London, Ambrose Bierce. Abigail's cruel deception by handsome Jason Aldrich caused her to reject romance and dedicate her life to detection.

Even a trip to the lush Hawaiian Islands in *Diamond Head* (Walker, 1992) did not relieve Abigail's depression. Her manservant Kinkade confessed to the murder of Lilliana, a beautiful island princess. Matthew Tarkington, a young sugar planter who feared he might have leprosy, sought Abigail's help. She solved both problems and, leaving Kinkade behind, moved on to new adventures.

In *The Sunken Treasure* (Walker, 1994), Abigail, Maude and her maid Jacqueline joined a private yacht party. Their host was Malcolm Tibault, a womanizer who ignored the needs of his younger, most recent wife, Ariadne, to dance attention on Maude. Other guests and a mysterious stowaway had their own agendas, the discovery of Napoleonic treasure in the Caribbean. Another famous encounter, the illusionist Houdini.

Camp and fun at times, weird at others.

Judah Daniel

Author: Ann McMillan

See: Narcissa Powers, page 660.

Peaches Dann

Author: Elizabeth Daniels Squire

If there were just one word for Peaches Dann, she would forget it unless she wrote it down. She did not gradually lose her memory. She never had one that functioned well. Over the years she developed a series of mnemonic strategies to cope. She worked these strategies into a book for fellow sufferers and shared some of her experience in the narratives. Peaches and her husband Roger had run a small craft shop, but after his death she sold out. Her only child Eve was in the import/export business in Singapore. Her widowed father had become senile but still dominated an extended family of aunts, uncles, and cousins. After Roger's death, Peaches spent leisure time with Ted Halloran, a widowed college professor who found her handicap charming.

During *Who Killed What's-Her-Name?* (Berkley, 1994), Peaches discovered the body of her Aunt Nancy in the pond at her father's home. The fact that Nancy was wearing a dress similar to one owned by Peaches and several subsequent accidents made her wary. If, as her father had hinted, Peaches knew something about the killer, she could not remember what it was. The "Hansel and Gretel" trail saved her life and Ted's.

In *Remember the Alibi* (Berkley, 1994), Peaches and Ted, now married, became aware of a series of deaths of elderly persons that had been classified as suicides. The deaths were scattered over time and a large geographical area. Ted and Peaches used library and newspaper resources to trail the killer, who had Peaches' father in North Carolina on his list.

Memory Can Be Murder (Berkley, 1995) focused around Peaches' cousin, Anne Newman. Anne had recently moved into the area with her artist husband Sam to live on the estate of former actress Revonda Roland. Revonda's wealth came not from her career, but from marriage to a prosperous elderly man. The death of Revonda's son Paul, a devotee of magic and the occult, put the Newmans first on the list of suspects. Peaches helped Cousin Anne to realize that her problems were the result of dyslexia.

Family genealogy charts should be a help to the reader of *Whose Death Is It, Anyway?* (Berkley, 1997). When Kim, the adopted daughter of Peaches' cousin Mary, disappeared, her mother asked for help. After the murder of a young girl, eventually identified as Kim's twin who had been adopted by a different family, Kim was considered vulnerable. So was Peaches as she researched the family lines to learn who would want the girls dead. This was more than a little confusing. Author Squires compared it to "I'm My Own Grandpa."

Pops (Harwood Smith) went to Tennessee to remarry at age 86 in *Is There a Dead Man in the House?* (Berkley, 1998), drawing Peaches into another family mystery. While working to renovate a family home, the new bride Azalea was injured in a fall from a ladder. Her claim to an inheritance may depend upon proving that an ancestor was not a killer. More current crimes motivated Peaches and Ted to visit Tennessee to solve the old murder.

Gradually Peaches was extending her circle of investigations beyond her own family. In *Where There's a Will* (Berkley, 1999), old friend Marietta Anderson convinced Peaches to verify whether or not her brother Wingate's death was an accident. Marietta and seven other members of her family had recently inherited $15 million apiece from Uncle Hiram. Other beneficiaries were killed or attacked over a period of time. Peaches joined the frightened survivors on a luxury cruise, which included the killer as a passenger.

Peaches, who had taken a position on the local weekly newspaper in Monroe County, added new tools to her repertoire in *Forget About Murder* (Berkley, 2000), a handheld electric memory device and a Polaroid camera. They were helpful when Belle, a childhood friend, was suspected of killing Isaiah Hubbel, a reclusive Vietnam veteran. Belle had blamed Hubbel for her husband's death from lung cancer. The memory enhancer proved to be a double-edged sword.

Cute, with some excellent hints for those—including me and maybe you—who have memory problems.

The series ended with Elizabeth Daniel Squire's death in 2001.

Meg (Margaret Ann) Darcy

Author: Jean Marcy, pseudonym for Jean Hutchinson and Marcy Jacobs

Meg Darcy had been fatherless since she was a small child. She had a younger sister, Nicole, and a brother Brian, who was married to Cheryl. Her family was aware of her sexual orientation and accepted it.

When her dad abandoned the family, Walter Miller, a step-uncle had taken an interest in Meg. After her service in the Military Police, Walter offered Meg a job at his Security Agency in St. Louis. She had a personal friendship with Patrick Healy, a gay bookstore worker who had an adjacent apartment and shared the care of Meg's cat, "Harvey Milk." Her earlier affair with a fellow soldier had ended badly. There had been only meaningless short-term relationships until she met police detective Sarah Lindstrom.

Meg and Ann Yates had been friends, nothing more. In *Cemetery Murders* (New Victoria, 1997), Ann's Aunt Mary Margaret was the most recent victim of a killer who preyed on elderly women. Ann hired Meg to act as liaison with the police department in finding the killer. This provided an opportunity for Meg to spend time with aloof detective Sarah Lindstrom.

Meg's initial encounters with Sarah had been intense but without an emotional component. In *Dead and Blonde* (New Victoria, 1998), Meg was the person Sarah turned to when she was in trouble. Sarah had taken in attorney Vivian Rudder, her former lover, when Vivian fled the abuses of a subsequent partner. Returning home late one evening, Sarah found Vivian dead. The most obvious suspects were connected by sexual relationships. The focus changed when Meg realized that Sarah had been the intended victim of the attack and remained in danger.

Patrick, Meg, and Sarah were recovering from injuries as *Mommy Deadest* (New Victoria, 2000) opened. Meg became involved in a case because she could not turn down a friend. Nina Ripley's nephew Kyle, a student at alternative Scott Joplin High School, had been arrested for the murder of popular principal Maureen O'Malley. The police were not looking for other suspects. Meg's intervention seemed pointless at first because Kyle was unresponsive. Meg focused on other reasons why O'Malley would be murdered. They were there and Meg found them.

Miller Security did not handle domestic cases, but in *A Cold Case of Murder* (New Victoria, 2003) Meg made an exception. Diane Mann planned to leave her abusive cop husband Doug, taking their adopted daughter with her. First, she needed to know who Jessica's real mother was. Working with Colleen, the agency receptionist, Meg focused on 17-year-old Teresa Rushing, who had been murdered shortly after she gave birth. Meg's interest was in making a connection. Her lover, Det. Sarah Lindstrom, now relegated to the Cold Case Squad, wanted to solve Teresa's murder, a very cold case. Other issues with Lindstrom played a large role in the narrative.

Tess Darcy

Author: Jean Hager

Tess Darcy transformed a small town Missouri home bequeathed to her by a spinster aunt into a bed and breakfast operation called Iris House. Her father had remarried after the death of Tess' mother and was stationed overseas by the State Department. Frank and his second wife Zelda had two children, Maddy and Curt. Over the series Tess developed a close relationship with Luke Fredrik, a wealthy investment counselor.

A major project for Tess' new business was to provide lodgings for officers of the local garden club, which was hosting a four-state conference. In *Blooming Murder* (Avon, 1994), the officers of the Victoria Springs Garden Club and their spouses were a discordant group. Sexual jealousy and infighting for power marred the preparations for the conference, and eventually led to the murder of gardening expert Lana Morrison. Tess had her Aunt Dahlia and the faithful servants of Aunt Iris to help her cope with the crisis.

Former rivalries and relationships surfaced when graduates of the local high school returned for a reunion in *Dead and Buried* (Avon, 1995). Fortunately, most of them stayed at Iris House. Tess observed their reactions when Francine Alexander, a fading author, disclosed that she was writing a roman a clef about their years together. When Francine was poisoned, the suspects were conveniently close.

Not only had Tess developed an interest in quilt making, but several professional quilters stayed at Iris House during *Death on the Drunkard's Path* (Avon, 1996) for a major quilt show. Tess' conviction that mournful Mary Frank was a target for murder left her confused when Cassie Terhune, a top rated quilter, was killed. The solutions to the mysterious events were simplistic.

The decision to hire a paid professional to direct the Victoria Springs Christmas pageant in *The Last Noël* (Avon, 1997) brought havoc into the lives of three couples. The new director Sherwood Draper, aroused hostility by a flirtation that angered his wife Mavis and Denny Brookside, the husband of flirtatious Lily, the woman involved. Draper's death focused suspicion on Mavis, but Tess followed up on the man's dying words to prove otherwise. She also reestablished her priorities as to Luke and Iris House.

Business was slow after the holidays, so in *Sew Deadly* (Avon, 1998), Tess helped out of the local senior citizen center. She was aware of Edwina Riley's reputation as a troublemaker, causing several fellow group members to have a motive for murder. It was more difficult to deduct how Edwina had been killed. A subsequent murder, that of Jenny Vercourt, co-owner and manager of the Senior Center along with her husband Willis, changed the focus. Learning more about Edwina who lived a life of hypocrisy, was the road to follow. Luke and Tess found a solution to the problem as to where they would live after their wedding.

Tess was overwhelmed by her forthcoming marriage to Luke and the construction of an addition to Iris House in *Weigh Dead* (Avon, 1999). She had agreed to turn the facility over for two weeks to Lida Darnell's diet retreat. The participants included an author of diet books with a weight problem; an overweight businessman whose model wife finagled him into the program; a pair of quarreling sisters, and an investigative reporter. Out of that mix came murder. Tess feared that the police would concentrate on the most likely suspect.

Not even the plans for her wedding and honeymoon would deter Tess from interfering in a police investigation during *Bride and Doom* (Avon, 2000). Her cook and friend Gertie Bogart had been accused of murder. Chef Julian Walker had alienated his pregnant wife Raylene and coworkers, but the police focused on Gertie. She had discovered Walker's body. She had blood on her hands. She had vowed revenge when Walker had used treachery to defeat her in a cooking contest. Based on information gained listening to private conversations, local gossip, and insights provided by her visiting father, Tess sorted it out in time to prevent another murder.

Readers who enjoyed the series should also read the series featuring Molly Bearpaw, also by author Jean Hager, covered in this volume.

Ruby Dark

Author: Bruce W. Most

This series by author Bruce Most, featuring Ruby Dark, a skip chaser in the bail bonding business, is darker than that of Janet Evanovich's portrayal of Stephanie Plum. Ruby, still flaunting her red hair at fifty, was a widow who had taken control of the business when her husband Al was murdered. She had been born of an alcoholic mother and a father who had abandoned his first family. Ruby disappeared from sight at age sixteen, then reappeared in Denver, forty-years-old and married to Al. The rumors as to where and how she had spent the intervening years were such that her half-brother Jack wanted nothing to do with Ruby. That did not stop Jack's son, David Piszek, from looking Ruby up when he needed a job to help finance his legal education.

Ruby was kind to strays. She owned Collateral, an old English Mastiff, whose owner never redeemed her, and Alabaster, a black Persian cat who wandered in. David found Ruby to be fascinating and scary. She was optimistic, confrontational, and even vengeful. She made decisions on her "gut feeling" rather than a defendant's reputation and financial worth. Unlike most bondsmen, Ruby was not reinsured for financial loss. Her solution was to find the skip. To do so she would lie, break and enter, pose as a police officer, and whatever else it took. She enjoyed jazz, hot chili peppers, strong coffee and an elderly Lamborghini that she drove when off-duty. Her business car was equipped to handle reluctant passengers. Detective Morgan Reed, a widower who worked for the Denver Police Department, endangered his own career by helping Ruby, whom he loved.

Ruby's lack of reinsurance put her at risk in *Bonded for Murder* (St. Martin's Paperbacks, 1996). The lucrative fee for bonding media executive Barry Gibson was too good to pass up, particularly when rival bondsman Cadillac Johnson inferred that she wasn't up to it. Gibson was in custody for the murder of obnoxious radio talk show host Royce Kray. Kray had been killed in Gibson's penthouse with Gibson's gun. When Gibson disappeared, Ruby and David had a limited time to produce him for the court. Ruby's best ally, Big Jim Baird, was murdered during the search. No way was Ruby going to sacrifice money and loyalty and let this one go.

David and the reader learned more about Ruby's past in *Missing Bonds* (St. Martin's Paperbacks, 1997). He accompanied her in the search for Bullet Joe, a potential three-time loser who had skipped his bond. Bullet Joe, or Earl as his parents called him, might have been a thief, but he was not a killer. Yet his fingerprints were discovered in the bloody living room of Sean Powell who had co-signed the bail bond. After learning that there was no Sean Powell, Ruby focused, not on Bullet Joe's disappearance, but on Powell's identity and the possibility that the U.S. Government had abandoned missing servicemen in order to meet other goals.

Gritty with touches of humor.

Jane da Silva

Author: K. K. Beck, pseudonym for Katherine Marris

Jane da Silva was described as 5' 6", slim with brown hair and "pewter" eyes. A native of Seattle, she had traveled to Europe for her college "junior year abroad," and rarely returned to America. Marriage to a European racing car driver ended with his fatal accident. Jane survived by her marginal skills as a chanteuse in undistinguished bistros. Over the years she worked as a governess, translator, hand model, editor of a tourist guide, and businesswoman, but never settled down. Jane was almost forty when Great Uncle Harold Mortensen bequeathed his fortune to her in trust, on the condition that she would inherit only if she returned to Seattle and solved "hopeless cases." While she sought to qualify, the trustees allowed Jane expense money and the use of Uncle Harold's home.

In *A Hopeless Case* (Mysterious Press, 1992), attorney Calvin Mason introduced Jane to teenage pianist Leonora Martin. Leonora's plans to enter Julliard were doomed when her mother willed the family funds to a Sixties religious cult. Jane followed the Fellowship of the Flame to its Flamemaster, but also tracked the academic frauds who had siphoned off Leonora's inheritance.

Jane, who was considered to have "failed" in her first case, returned in *Amateur Night* (Mysterious, 1993). Kevin Shea had been convicted of murdering workaholic pharmacist Betty Cox from whom he sought drugs with a fake prescription. The trail of a missing witness, possibly named Brenda, led Jane to Vancouver, British Columbia where she realized that she was being followed, and that "Brenda" was in danger.

In *Electric City* (Mysterious, 1994), when Irene March, an employee of a clipping service, disappeared, her fellow employees came to Jane for help. Irene's interest in the lives of persons whose problems were described in the newspapers coupled with her appearance on the television show *Jeopardy!* put her at risk of murder. Jane needed her friend Bob Manalatu's muscle to get through this case.

Still unable to qualify for the inheritance by *Cold Smoked* (Mysterious, 1995), Jane sang at a second rate hotel bar to survive. On the night of her finale (she had been fired), Jane became involved in the death of Marcia, a skimpily dressed dancer. Motivated by the victim's parents, she signed on with a seafood magazine to cover the industry's public relations campaigns, monitoring the hostilities between the deep-sea fishermen and those who raised farmed salmon. Even if her investigation did not merit attention from Uncle Harold's trustees, she earned a reward.

Interesting premise with an offbeat sleuth. Sorry that there weren't more books.

K. K. Beck also wrote the Iris Cooper series covered in Volume.

Queenie Davilov

Author: Denise Osborne

Queenie Davilov had memorable characteristics. She and her two brothers, Rex and Raj, had been named after her mother's favorite horses. Her mother, an orphan who claimed aristocratic origins, had accumulated her children from different fathers without benefit of matrimony. L. J. (Lillian Jeanette) Davilov raised her family on a ranch near Norman, Oklahoma. Queenie went on to college, and over a period of time worked as a reporter, private investigator, and script supervisor for movie productions, aspiring to become a scriptwriter. She was a tall woman with "sapphire blue" eyes and long black hair worn in a braid. She was athletic (had played rugby in college), rolled her own cigarettes, liked Jack Daniels whiskey, and carried a satchel containing a knife, pistol, and lock picks. Although interested in neighbor Dick Takahashi, she remained single. Her religious interest was in a goddess, represented by a golden icon, but she carried a lucky Jim Rice baseball card for protection when flying.

As *Murder Offscreen* (Holt, 1994) opened, Queenie was at a meeting. Well-known Hollywood agent Eric Diamond was considering her script for production. Instead she was summoned by her boss, Burke Lymon. He was preparing for the premiere of his latest horror movie, but his two stars (Nessa and L. D. Barth) had disappeared. When Burke was killed, Queenie dusted off her investigative skills and traveled east to research the man behind Burke Lymon.

In *Cut to: Murder* (Holt, 1995), Queenie traveled to Barcelona and rural Catalonia to develop a script on the Spanish Civil War. She was hired, not only to replace a prior writer, but also to investigate the betrayal of producer Fernando "Freddie" Frazier's mother during the Civil War. The narrative used secret passages, clues in a children's book, and sibling rivalries for an interesting conclusion.

The series showed promise, but ended there. Osborne has begun a new series featuring interior decorator Salome Waterhouse.

Angie DaVito

Author: Louise Shaffer

Angie DaVito and her more talented sister, Connie, had entered show business as children, "The Singing DaVito Sisters." Connie dropped out, choosing the life of wife and mother, but Angie persisted. She had always considered herself less attractive than Connie, but was drawn to the entertainment world. After an unsuccessful try at acting in New York City, she was steered to the technical side of daytime television by her friend and mentor, Jesse Southland. When Jesse was written out of *Bright Tomorrow*, Angie quit her job as producer for the show and walked. This impetuous action damaged her professional reputation, but, five years later, the vice-president of American Broadcasting Network in charge of daytime television, Gregg Whithall, lured her back.

The show was in trouble as *All My Suspects* (Putnam, 1994) began. Later Gregg, was murdered. With the help of widowed detective Teresa O'Hanlon, Angie looked beyond the current dissension on the set to an old and painful motive. On a positive note, she met Teresa's brother Patrick who had developed Mother Maggie's Bakery.

Although Angie preferred the soaps, she was not in a position to turn down offers. In *Talked to Death* (Putnam, 1995), she hired on as Cee Gee Jones' producer. Cee Gee and her entourage had been together for years, building an extremely popular talk show. Then Grace Shipley, the head producer, was fired. Shortly after Angie took over, Grace was murdered. Teresa O'Hanlon shared her investigation into the ties that bound Cee Gee to her old friends.

Readers who watch daytime television may enjoy this series.

Jane Day

Authors: Ron Nessen and Johanna Neuman

Jane Day, a liberal reporter for the *Washington Post*, formed an uneasy alliance and relationship with right wing radio show host, Jerry Knight. A single woman in her thirties who shared a District of Columbia apartment with a cat named Bloomsbury, Jane was prepared to dislike three times married and divorced Knight. She was distinguished by her "carrot" colored hair and green eyes; he, by his rude and critical mouth. Part of the reason Jane enjoyed Washington was that it put her a continent away from her controlling mother, Mavis.

Knight & Day (Forge, 1995) was set in Washington, D.C. Jerry's and Jane's lives converged when Jane exposed the irregularities of Republican presidential candidate Senator Barton Jacobson. Her source, Curtis Davies Davenport, an environmental activist, was murdered shortly after an appearance on Knight's talk show. Both felt some responsibility. Guilt made it easier for them to work together. The rapport (bristly as it was) between Knight and Day was based on mutual respect for (a) commitment, (b) intelligence, (c) a sense of humor, and (d) enjoyment of the exploration of ideas and concepts. Equally endearing was their friend, African-American detective A. L. Jones, who spent his time with facts and people, not ideas. Jones accepted much of what Day and Knight argued about. They talked the talk. He walked the walk, spending his free time making a difference in the life of a motherless boy, La Troy.

The murder of CNN reporter Dan McLean at a banquet during *Press Corpse* (Forge, 1997) raised the question as to whether the deadly poison he imbibed had been meant for him or for the President of the United States. While Knight and Day sparred and stirred the waters, Jones quietly went about his job, identifying not only the intended victim, but also the killer and his motive.

When Jane accompanied Jerry to the Kennedy Center where he would take part in the Honors Ceremony during *Death With Honors* (Forge, 1998), she used the opportunity to interview semi-retired actress Carla Caldwell.

Caldwell, an advocate for left wing causes, created a stir when she insulted the President and hinted at her own liaison with a Washington celebrity. It was Jane who discovered the dying Carla in her dressing room. In the end, it was not what Carla had done that caused her death, but what she had failed to do. Jane's article on Congressman Revell Gates' conversion to liberalism after his four-year-old daughter died of cancer brought Jane an offer to come to Hollywood to do a screenplay based on the incident. It would mean leaving, at least temporarily, her job on the *Post* and her developing relationship with Jerry. At the end she went to Hollywood. She hasn't been heard from since.

Patricia Delaney

Author: Sharon Gwyn Short

Patricia Delaney had turned her back on her conservative Irish-Catholic family. She rejected the musical career her father had urged upon her. Instead she worked in a topless nightclub, Poppy's Parrot. When the dancing became distasteful, she convinced the proprietor to give her a job as a bouncer by tossing him. She never lost her feeling for music, loved opera and played drums and fiddle in attorney Jay Bell's Queen River Band in her spare time. Patricia eventually took a job in Adams Security and Investigations in downtown Cincinnati. After some experience, she established her own agency. She was down to earth, drove a pickup, had a parrot tattoo on a buttock, and owned a beagle, Sammie. A tall, athletic woman, she lifted weights and swam to keep in shape, but ran a modern business using her computer effectively.

Elsa Kauffman sought Patricia's help in *Angel's Bidding* (Fawcett, 1994). Andy Lawson, an employee in her father's extensive real estate business, had disappeared. Her semi-retired but still domineering father, Friedrich Kauffman, was receiving threats accompanied by Victorian hatpins, which had once belonged to her grandmother. Not only was Lawson found dead, but there was no sign of the $100,000 that had disappeared at the same time.

In *Past Pretense* (Fawcett, 1994), Patricia initially failed to recognize Gigi Lafferty, a former topless dancer, who had saved her life ten years before. Gigi asked Patricia to research her life, as she would if her husband Neil were the client. Only after a tragedy occurred did Patricia pay her debt.

She had an unexpected guest in *The Death We Share* (Fawcett, 1995). Her father (Joseph)arrived, having left her mother (Margaret) back in Maine. Dad, an opera buff, helped when ex-diva Carlotta Moses denied rumors that she had abandoned her child, only to have the claimant killed.

These were interesting, well-plotted mysteries.

Sarah Booth Delaney

Author: Carolyn Haines

Sarah Booth Delaney was the last in her family line, the Delaneys. From her mother, a Peace Corps worker and Socialist, Sarah Booth (both names always, please) had developed the strength and inclinations that made her different than the other Mississippi Delta "Daddy's Girls". They were characterized by their feminine gifts, the goal of a good marriage and continued dependence on males. She attended the right school—"Ole Miss." Still, she disdained sororities, chose the most unlikely beaus, and dabbled at being an actress for a decade in New York City. Her devoted parents had died together in a traffic accident. She had no siblings or cousins. She returned to Zinnia, Mississippi at age thirty-three, only to learn that Dahlia House, home of generations of Delaneys, was heavily mortgaged and subject to foreclosure. Real estate developers were eager to purchase it, tear down the house, and build a mall. The house was still occupied by the ghostly apparition of Jitty, who had served the family during the Civil War and continued to monitor its existence and Sarah's.

At her age, she could postpone bearing a child who would carry on the family traditions. In *Them Bones* (Bantam, 1999), she could not lose Dahlia House. Her solution was to betray her long time friend, Tinkie Richmond, by kidnapping her dog and holding poor Chablis for ransom. She also involved herself in the affairs of the notorious Garrett family. Handsome Hamilton Garrett had moved to Europe after both of his parents died in mysterious accidents. Sarah Booth was hired to discover whether or not he had killed his mother. Sarah Booth was uncertain as to his guilt, but he had her thinking seriously about marriage and babies. She had reluctantly accepted an engagement ring from her more staid suitor, Harold Erkwell.

Sarah Booth's second case in *Buried Bones* (Bantam, 2000) revolved about the anticipated memoirs of reclusive author Lawrence Ambrose. Ambrose had received acclaim as a writer, sculptor, artist, activist in the French Resistance during World War II, and as mentor to aspirants in the arts. His taunting as to personal revelations to be made in the book presented a motive for his subsequent death. Ambrose had contracted to have former model Brianna Rathbone to be the titular author of the narrative, hoping to revive both his career and hers. At the request of a woman who had loved Lawrence but never married, Sarah Booth followed a trail back to a special summer in the 1940s that changed many lives and led to his murder. New hope for her romance with Hamilton Garrett completed the narrative, and offered the possibility that Jitty might get her wish—another generation to haunt.

Splintered Bones (Delacorte, 2002) initially had too much of everything except murder. When brutal husband Kemper Fuquar was killed, his wife Lee, a long time friend of Sarah's, asked her to take care of their daughter Kip (age 14, going on 20). Kemper, Lee, and Kip were members of the "horsey" set. Lee bred and trained thoroughbreds at their Swift Level property. Sarah was not content to have Lee languish in prison even though she confessed to Kemper's murder. The narrative was overloaded with murderous suspects, dreams, and visits from Jitty. There were intimations that Sheriff Coleman Peters was personally interested in Sarah.

When African-American blues pianist Ivory Keys was murdered in *Crossed Bones* (Delacorte, 2003), the most likely suspect was white guitarist Scott Hampton. Hampton, who had befriended Keys when both were in prison, was working at Key's blues club. Ida Mae, Ivory's wife, not only believed Scott was innocent, but hired Sarah Booth to prove it. It wasn't easy because Sunflower County, Mississippi was being torn apart by racial feelings, unseen since the 1960's. Sarah's emotions were raw. One relationship had ended and there was nothing on the horizon.

Hopefully Sarah Booth was charging by the hour when she agreed in *Hallowed Bones* (Delacorte, 2004) to prove that faith healer Doreen Mallory had not killed her disabled daughter, Rebekah. New Orleans detective Arnold Le Mont had made no effort to consider alternative suspects such as the child's father. Sarah had personal conflicts. Sheriff Coleman Peters, her former beau, was tied to his unstable and pregnant wife. Hamilton Garrett urged Sarah Booth to return to Paris with him.

News of Quentin Mc Gee's savage murder struck Tinkie Richmand, Sarah Booth's partner in an investigation agency, as an opportunity in *Bones To Pick* (Kensington, 2006). All they needed was a client, but one appeared quickly. When Allison Tatum, Quentin's lesbian lover, was arrested, her brother Humphrey, hired the Delancey Agency to prove that Allison was innocent. Other suspects were connected to Quentin's expose of sexual misbehavior, nefarious businesses practices and inter-racial blood lines in Zinnia. Tinkie used her psychic friend Madame Tomeeka, as a resource.

Just when Sarah Booth was ready to let the past be bygones in *Ham Bones* (Kensington, 2007), her old enemy Renata Trovaioli made it impossible. It was Renata who arranged for the stage production of *Cat on a Hot Tin Roof* to appear in Zinnia when the intended New Orleans theater was unavailable. Her co-star Graf Milieu had been Sarah Booth's lover during the years when she was in New York City and working as Renata's understudy. Renata's death, during the intermission of the first performance of the show, gave Sarah Booth a chance to shine, but it also made her a prime suspect in the murder. Her current relationship with Sheriff Coleman Peters was no help. He arrested her. Tinkie and Cece, Sarah Booth's best pals, never wavered in their support, nor did Graf who wanted Sarah Booth to be his co-star in a future Hollywood production.

Sarah Booth bid a sad farewell to Zinnia as *Wishbones* (St. Martin's Minotaur, 2008) began. She and move actor Graf Milieu headed for Hollywood to be screen-tested for parts in Federico Marquez's remake of *Body Heat*. Fueled by their personal attraction for one another, they wowed Marquez. Early scenes were filmed in Hollywood, but the cast and crew flew to Petaluma, Costa Rica for the remainder. They occupied, over the objections of Marquez's daughter Estella, the mansion once owned (and rumored to be haunted) by Carlita, Marquez's deceased wife. It was no ghost who killed actress Suzy Dutton or who continued to wreak havoc in Petaluma. Not only three of Sarah Delaney's Zinnia pals, but Jitty came to visit and help out.

These were well-plotted mysteries with good characterizations that might have been even better without some of the distractions. Next: *Greedy Bones* (2009)*; Bone Appetit* (2010)

Robyn Devara

Author: Karen Dudley

Like author Karen Dudley, Robyn Devara was a Canadian field biologist. Animals and the outdoors had always been an important part of Robyn's life. However, when she chose a field of specialization she decided upon birds. Her adventures as a staff member at Woodrow Consultants blended ornithology, environmental concerns, and murder. Her base office was in Calgary, but assignments took her throughout Northwestern Canada. At age thirty-three, Robyn had other interests: classical music, a cat named Guido after a faithless boyfriend, and a growing interest in small animal biologist Kelt Roberson. Her family ties were fragile. Both she and her younger brother Jack, a musician, had always felt that their parents doted upon her older brother Neil, a gay dentist.

As *Hoot to Kill* (Ravenstone, 1998) began, the Wilderness Association hired Woodrow Consultants to investigate a claim that there were spotted owls in the forests of Marten Valley, British Columbia. Robyn planned to avert local hostility by conducting a low-level search, but that became impossible when she discovered the corpse of contentious foreman, Bill Reddecop. Bill, like a large percentage of the residents, was an employee of Seidlin Lumber. His wife, Lori had been the female who ended Robyn's romance with boyfriend Guido when they were in college. Assisted by Kelt, who joined her on the job, and some local allies, Robyn uncovered duplicity by Seidlin Lumber, but she was naïve about one of her new friends and paid a price.

During *The Red Heron* (Ravenstone, 1999), Robyn went to her friend June McVea's bed and breakfast in Holbrook, Alberta to recuperate from injuries. It was a coincidence that Woodrow Consultants had a contract to clean up a contaminated local factory site. Both her health and a warning from the local RCMP were deterrents to Robyn getting involved when the corpse of environmentalist Richard DeSantis was found in the woods. That didn't stop her because the Woodrow site work was being sabotaged, peripatetic gnomes were bringing ominous messages, and her hostess was a possible suspect.

Macaws of Death (Ravenstone, 2002) would be worth reading for the depiction of the Costa Rican jungles and its inhabitants, but there was so much more. The discovery of dead smuggled birds at the Calgary airport gave hope of a new species of macaw. Leaving her relationship with Kelt unresolved, Robyn headed for Costa Rica as part of a team to explore that possibility. It was not only the snakes and insects that received her with hostility. There were poachers eager to merchandise the rare birds. One after another, members of the group camped in Corcovado National Park were being eliminated by what might have been accidents. Robyn had tolerated the in-group tensions but did not intend to be a victim.

Robyn found herself desperately lonely for Kelt in *Ptarmageddon* (Ravenstone, 2006) when he traveled to Northern Alaska to study the climatic impact on pikas (small members of the rabbit family). Her decision to join him was based on the news that ornithologist Selena Barry had been savagely murdered, leaving behind extensive field notes on ptarmigans. She had left instructions that the field notes were to go to Robyn who had never met her. Her arrival at Willow Creek introduced Robyn to several emotionally damaged individuals who had reasons to harm Selena. Robyn used what she learned from the field notes to follow Serena's trail into the wilderness.

This was an earnest series with a message applicable not only to Canadians but to environmentalists in the northwestern sector of the continent. Bird lovers will find interesting information embedded in the narrative. The plotting was good and the physical descriptions were terrific.

Brooke Cassidy Devlin

Author: Mary Kruger

See: Brooke Cassidy, page 146.

Betsy Devonshire

Author: Monica Ferris, a pseudonym for Mary Monica Pulver Kuhfeld

Betsy Devonshire grew up in Milwaukee, Wisconsin where her father worked in a factory. She went to college after four and a half years in the U.S. Navy and an unsuccessful early marriage. Hal, one of her professors, became her second husband. After eighteen years of marriage to Betsy, Hal started a divorce action in order to marry a nubile student. When other students came forward to seek vengeance or recompense for Hal's sexual peccadilloes, he lost his job and his fiancée. That had left Betsy, her brown hair going gray at fifty-five, unsure of her own future.

In *Crewel World* (Berkley, 1999), she visited her sister Margot in Excelsior, Minnesota, without any plan as to whether it was to be a short or extended stay. Within days of her arrival, her decision was made. Margot provided comfort, a home, a part-time job at her needlecraft shop, and entrée into her circle of friends. Betsy needed all the friends she could get when Margot was cruelly murdered. The local police dismissed her death as a burglary gone wrong which spurred Betsy into her own investigation. Margot's generous bequests solved Betsy's financial problems, providing security and acceptance in Excelsior.

By *Framed in Lace* (Berkley, 1999), Betsy had adapted to the slower pace of life. That did not mean she had decided that Excelsior was where she wanted to spend the rest of her life. She had successfully challenged landlord Joe Mickels' efforts to break Margot's lease on the shop. The part-time workers (gay Godwin du Lac, and Shelly Donohue) had rallied to help her learn about needlecraft, payroll, and ordering supplies. Best of all, she and police officer Jill Cross (later Larson) had become close friends. Seventy-four-year-old Martha Winters, a member of the Monday Club which gathered at the shop each week, was accused of murder. She had allegedly killed her husband Carl who had disappeared decades before and Trudie Koch, a young woman whose skeleton was found on a submerged boat. Betsy reluctantly agreed to conduct her own investigation.

The discovery of an old tapestry sent church ladies into a renovation project that almost cost Betsy her life in *A Stitch in Time* (Berkley, 2000) Several attempts to kill Betsy failed, leaving her confused as to why she had become a target. Hal, visiting Excelsior, in hopes of a reconciliation that would ease his financial problems, was one prospect. It could be Joe Mickels whose plans for real estate development had been thwarted by Betsy...or someone with a hidden secret.

An unhappy side effect of her success in solving murders was a series of nightmares during *Unraveled Sleeve* (Berkley, 2001). Her personal life was not faring well. Her plans to purchase the building had fallen through. Seeking quiet and isolation, she and police officer Jill Cross attended a "stitch-in" at a lodge near Lake Superior during the winter months. No television, no personal telephones, but, unfortunately, murder. Betsy discovered a body that subsequently disappeared. She not only had to convince Jill and a sheriff, but herself, that it had not been another nightmare.

The focus in *A Murderous Yarn* (Berkley, 2002) was on Lars Larson's latest hobby, antique cars. His purchase of a 1911 Stanley Steamer propelled him, Jill and Betsy into the activities of the Minnesota Antique Car Club. When manufacturer Bill Birmingham was murdered during a group run, Betsey provided the alibi for his wife, Charlotte, a logical suspect. Betsy learned a lot (as will the reader) about antique cars, but her knowledge of "orts" (cross stitching) solved the case.

The plotting and modus operandi in *Hanging by a Thread* (Berkley, 2003) had merit but they were submerged under layers of chitchat, ghost stories, poltergeists, and Godwin's romantic problems. Local contractor Foster Johns had been shunned for years because he was believed to have murdered his mistress Angela Schmitt and her husband Paul. He asked Betsy to clear his name. She focused on the characters: Foster, a man deeply in love; Paul, a controlling husband; and Angela, a frightened wife. It took a while to unravel the evidence piled up against Foster.

Blame it on the Christmas rush, but *Crewel Yule* (Berkley, 2003) was not up to the series standards. Betsy and Godwin drove through the stormy weather to attend the International Needlework Retailers Market in Nashville, Tennessee. Coincidentally, Jill Cross Larson was in town for a police seminar, held at a different hotel. Bad weather made in necessary for Jill to stay overnight at the Consulate with Betsy. That put her on scene, and temporarily in control, when Milwaukee storeowner Belle Hammermill pitched from a ninth floor balcony to the atrium below. Three potential suspects emerged quickly. They had to use the process of elimination.

The division between arts and crafts made Betsy's next case in *Cutwork* (Berkley, 2004) more difficult. Over the last few years, she had developed expertise in crafts, but when the family of surly teenager Mickey Sinclair asked for her help, she was a rank amateur. Carver Rob McFey had been murdered at the Art Fair where Betsy worked as a volunteer. It seemed clear that Mickey had stolen cash from McFey's booth. Again Betsy relied on her sense of character to focus on which of the other suspects was guilty of murder. McFey had used his carving skills to lampoon others.

Godwin DuLac turned to Betsy in *Embroidered Truth* (Berkley, 2005) when his lover, attorney John Nye, threw him out. Efforts to console Godwin became useless when first they discovered John's dead body; then, Godwin was arrested for the crime. The Monday Bunch pitched in making donations for his attorney fees and filling in at Crewel World so Betsy could detect.

It seemed just a coincidence initially, in *Sins and Needles* (Berkley, 2006), that Jan Henderson and newcomer Lucille Jones had so much in common. Over time it became evident that Lucille, who had learned she was adopted, had relocated from Houston to find her birth mother. Jan's mother quashed that possibility. She'd never had twins nor another baby girl. This all took a sinister turn when Jan discovered her great aunt Edyth dead in bed, and according to the funeral director, murdered! Edyth's substantial estate had some interesting provisions.

An accident while riding horseback put Betsy on the sidelines in *Knitting Bones* (Berkley, 2007). When Allie Germaine, head of the Embroider's Guild asked for help, Betsy wanted to say "no". Allie's husband, Bob, who was to have accepted a $24,000 check on behalf of the National Heart Coalition, had disappeared. Police considered Bob a thief. Allie wanted Betsy to prove them wrong. She played the "Nero Wolfe" role while Godwin DuLac did the fieldwork. Still it took a crow for the final touch.

Monday Brunch Club member Doris Valentine had an eager audience waiting for her when she returned from a trip to Thailand in *Thai Die* (Berkley, 2008). She shared the contents of a suitcase filled with lovely silks, brocades, saris, a statue of Ganesha, and jewelry. Then she opened a box she was supposed to deliver to antique dealer Oscar Fitzwilliam that contained a Buddha sweltered in an old rag. Readers and Betsy were aware that Doris had smuggled the package into the United States. When Oscar Fitzwilliam was murdered and other violence continued, Betsy became personally involved. Doris was after all, a tenant in her building. Doris surprised everyone, including her boyfriend Phil Galvin, with her special skills.

Nest in the series: *Blackwork* (2009); *Sew For, Sew Good* (2009); *Buttons and Bones* (2010)

Above average. Pulver has also written/co-written two other series: One featuring Sister Frevisse, co-authored under the name Margaret Frazer with Gail Bacon, and the Kori and Peter Brichter series, written as Mary Monica Pulver.

Molly DeWitt

Author: Sherryl Woods

Molly DeWitt was a divorced mother who left a stultifying marriage to work as a public relations specialist in the Miami/Dade County film office. On the negative side, she encouraged her son Brian's's mistrust, even dislike, for his father, Hal. Molly worked at her job only when pushed to do so by her boss, Vincent Gates. Her love of excitement led her to take risks for herself and Brian. The series showed the difficulty in presenting a mystery heroine with a full time job and primary responsibility for a child.

Molly had positive qualities. She did not jump into bed with the first police officer or private investigator she encountered, not even multilingual detective Michael O'Hara. She was loyal to her friends, and eager to be involved in their problems. She loved Brian, and eventually recognized that Hal did too.

In *Hot Property* (Dell, 1992), Molly questioned residents and staff when Allan Winecroft, the unpopular president of the condo association, was murdered. Despite phone calls threatening both Molly and Brian, she persisted. Molly found a killer, but ended up in the hospital. O'Hara, also Brian's soccer coach, was supportive of the boy, but tentative in his relationship with Molly.

In *Hot Secrets* (Dell, 1992), Molly's work took her to a movie set. Director Greg Kinsey's employment of aging alcoholic actress Veronica Weston proved unwise. Their quarrels made Veronica a suspect when Kinsey was shot. Molly used her position to have O'Hara assigned to the case but continued her own investigation.

In *Hot Money* (Dell, 1993), Molly's friend Liza Hastings involved both Molly and O'Hara in her environmental fundraising. By the time the body of fundraiser Tessa Rafferty was discovered dead in the water, Molly was hooked on detecting. The resolution of the crime lacked credibility.

Hot Schemes (Dell, 1994) focused on a timely topic, the ambitions of Florida based Cubans to overthrow the Castro government. O'Hara, whose mother had remained behind in Cuba, was raised by relatives in Florida. When his uncle Tio Miguel Garcia disappeared, Mike placed family loyalties above job responsibilities, but needed Molly's help to find the traitor among the Cuban refugees.

Venus Diamond

Author: Skye Kathleen Moody

The daughter of a famous beauty, movie star Lady Bella Winsome-Diamond, Venus Diamond chose to spend her life in a far different atmosphere than her mother's London home. Bella, a devout opponent of birth control, provided Venus with four siblings possessing assorted idiosyncrasies. Unlike her flamboyant mother, Venus was a tiny topaz-haired woman. She had been devoted to her quiet father, a spaceship designer, who died of a heart attack when she was five. Her studies at Oxford concentrated on Shakespeare and lepidoptera. Her original goal had been to work for NASA. Among her less recognized skills was the ability to lip-read. She became an agent for the Federal Fish and Wildlife Agency of the Department of the Interior. The last three of her eight years service had been spent in Asia. She eventually married Richard Winters, a Seattle businessman.

Wracked by periodic bouts of malaria and dumped by a former admirer, Venus was in no mood for a transfer back to the United States in *Rain Dance* (St. Martin, 1996), much less to an isolated Washington state area, Ozone Beach. Given inadequate background and limited official support, Venus was expected to solve the murder of wealthy widow Madge Leroux. Ozone Beach had no police force to combat an unhealthy strain of corruption and evil.

The battle for control of coastal mountain meadows dominated *Blue Poppy* (St. Martin, 1997), pitting commercial interests against local environmentalists. Venus and the regional Fish and Wildlife Agency resisted pressure to sell virgin land that had the potential to nurture an almost extinct variety of butterflies. The murders of a biologist, a model, a chef and an elderly environmentalist were motivated by jealousy and greed rather that the wider concerns. Venus, as always, paid a physical price for her involvement. A jealous rival for her affections derailed Venus' engagement to Richard.

As *Wildcrafters* (St. Martin, 1998), began Venus and Richard were preparing for their honeymoon in Hawaii. She was recalled to work by FWA because of her knowledge of the Olympic Peninsula of Washington State. A child, one of a pair of twins, had disappeared. The speculation included several possibilities—kidnapped, eaten by animals, or taken by an unknown spirit. The disappearance led to turmoil in two marriages: that of the parents (a) Winn Nighteagle, the suddenly rich father fighting addiction, and Theresa, the single minded mother who believed her child was still alive and, (b) to a lesser degree, the recent marriage of Venus and Richard. He did not fight Venus' loyalty to the agency; instead, went undercover to help her.

Habitat (St. Martin, 1999) was cluttered by assorted points of view, multiple characters and subplots. Venus, who was coming off as a cross between Peter O'Donnell's Modesty Blaise and Nevada Barr's Anna Pigeon, needed a clear identity of her own. She found herself in a malaise at the end of a year's marriage to Richard during which she had taken leave from her job. When

Richard was called to an overseas assignment, Venus cut her hair, donned her black leather jacket and took on a special assignment. Renowned scientist Dr. Hannah Strindberg had been murdered, putting her experiments to save endangered species at risk. Venus' love of the chase invigorated her as she battled international conspiracy and achieved a dream of her own.

Legislation to breach dams along the Columbia River to facilitate the movement of spawning salmon was unacceptable to a small group of anarchists in *K Falls* (St. Martin, 2001). The Fish and Wildlife Service was one of many agencies poised to deter violence by this group. Venus remained on desk duty by her supervisor's orders until coworker and friend Louis Song disappeared. Alienated from Richard, Venus went undercover among a motley group of terrorists. Farce mingled with force and Indian legends.

Medusa (St. Martin, 2003) should be read with gloves and hip boots. When Venus took French leave of her required rehabilitation for Post Traumatic Stress Disorder, she was highly motivated. Tim, her twelve-year-old adopted brother, had been accused of murdering a playmate. After Venus arrived at her mother Belle's home, problems multiplied as car smuggling, child abuse, pornography, and the development of a dangerous virus were added. The casualties correspondingly multiplied. Although engrossing the narrative was implausible at times.

The Good Diamond (St. Martin's Minotaur, 2004) provided background on ultra-conservative militia, diamond mines and smuggling. Venus was mistakenly arrested by the RCMP. She ignored common sense rules about backup and shot her way out of traps when she traced the killers of undercover agent Buzz Radke. She uncovered the facts about a huge uncut diamond, but somehow Venus got lost among the assorted characters in the complex plot.

Poppy Dillworth

Author: Dorothy Tell

Poppy (Papillon Audubon) Dillworth was a Southwestern senior citizen and private investigator. Her dialogue and italicized thoughts were peppered with comments delivered in a dialect reminiscent of actor Gabby Hayes. She was the daughter of a preacher, raised in poverty, who loved the outdoors. As a young girl, she had hunted to provide food for herself and her mother, and was an excellent "fisherperson." That was the way she would state it. Before becoming an investigator, Poppy had spent forty years in the Caliche County, Texas Sheriff's department. She was a serially monogamous lesbian. Her current lover Belle Stoner was a mother and grandmother.

Although Poppy appeared first in *Wilderness Trek* (Naiad, 1990), it did not qualify as a mystery.

Poppy immersed herself in lesbian groups and culture during *Murder at Red Rock Ranch* (Naiad, 1990) where Nan Hightower, owner and operator of a 6,000-acre Texas ranch, was killed in what the authorities called suicide. Poppy and her heterosexual assistant, Marcie, began their careers with this investigation. The eventual ownership of the valuable property provided motives for women who worked there as manager or business manager, and for Nan's relatives and lesbian lovers. The mystery plot was interspersed with the relationships among the women.

During *The Hallelujah Murders* (Naiad, 1991), Poppy and Belle vacationed at the Hallelujah Bend Camp, a lesbian resort. Poppy's former partner had died, and her relationship with Belle was a recent one. Chris Janner, an opponent of dam construction on the Hermosa River, died mysteriously. Using a video camera to supplement her failing memory, Poppy set out to find the young woman's killer.

Mary DiNunzio

Author: Lisa Scottoline

Although her twin sister Angie had become a nun and her parents were religious, Mary DiNunzio no longer practiced the Catholic faith. Both parents were hardworking Italian-Americans. Seventy-five-year-old Matthew was a retired tile setter. Vita, who was nearly blind, had done piecework sewing. A hit-and-run driver had killed Mary's husband, Mike. There had been no children, although she had had an abortion. She shared her home with a cat named "Alice."

As *Everywhere That Mary Went* (HarperCollins, 1993) began, Mary was getting anonymous phone calls, seemingly from someone who knew when she would be home and when she would be at the office. She was employed in litigation at Stalling & Webb, a corporate practice, waiting to see if she made partner. Incidents continued to plague her. Someone entered her apartment in her absence. Her gay secretary Brent Polk was killed by a hit-and-run driver after they went out for dinner. She went to confession and visited her sister Angie at the convent, looking for some rationale for what was happening to her. Mary discovered the man who had killed both Mike and Brent. Although both she and her best friend, Judy Carrier, made partner, they declined the honor and left the firm.

Mary and Judy eventually became members of Benny Rosato's all-female law firm in Philadelphia. She played supporting roles in some of the Bennie Rosato narratives,(Under Rosato, see *Courting Trouble, Vendetta Defense)* but carried a primary role in at least three books.

In *Moment of Truth* (HarperCollins, 2000), Mary was not even sure she wanted to be an attorney anymore. She had almost no criminal law experience, but client Jack Newlin considered that a bonus. He had confessed to killing his wife because he wanted to protect his daughter, and preferred inadequate representation. Fortunately for all concerned, Mary was aware of his motivation. Together with one of the arresting officers, she fought City Hall to be heard, risking her life for a man she had come to love. Bennie was on a month-long vacation during the narrative.

Killer Smile (HarperCollins, 2004) explored a little known segment of U. S. history; i.e. that after Pearl Harbor 600,000 Italian residents of the United States, who were not naturalized citizens were required to register as "enemy aliens" and 10,000 of them were interned in camps far from their homes. Mary Di Nunzio became obsessed with the case of Amadeo Brandolini. His files had disappeared. He was long dead, found hung from a tree in the Missoula, Montana internment camp. His estate sought reparation for the loss of his fishing board. It soon became apparent that there was much more at stake. Mary's unusually reckless, sometimes foolish, behavior placed her in danger.

It was great to have Mary and the Rosato legal firm back in *Lady Killer* (Harper, 2008). Trish Gambone and her three "Mean Girl" pals had harassed Mary during her years at St. Maria Goretti High School. Mary was surprised when Trish turned up at Rosato and Associates, looking for help. Bobby Mancuso, with whom Trish had been living for seven years, might propose in the near future. That was a step Trish didn't want to take because not only was Bobby working with the Mob, he was physically abusive. She feared he would kill her. Mary had her own, more loving, memories of Bobby, but she gave Trish the best legal advice available. Trish had no interest in temporary restraining orders or leaving the area, and berated Mary as being "no help at all". When Trish disappeared, the three "Mean Girls" and Mrs. Gambone held Mary responsible. Consequently so did "the Neighborhood". Bobby's murder only made things worse. Mary had to find Trish at any cost. She gained a new ally, handsome Anthony Rotunno who had reputation problems of his own. This was a very moving narrative.

This became an ensemble series, featuring individual members of the all-female Rosato law firm. See Benedetta "Bennie" Rosato, elsewhere in this volume.

Next: *Think Twice* (2010)

Flavia Di Stefano

Author: Iain Pears

Flavia Di Stefano, a fair-haired Northern Italian, used her art degree from the University at Turin to work with the National Art Theft Squad, which was connected with the Polizia. She and academic/art expert Jonathan Argyll were introduced to American readers in *The Raphael Affair* (Harcourt, 1992). Flavia met Jonathan when he was under arrest for vagrancy in Italy. He instituted and then complicated the search for a hidden Raphael. His speculations caused panic in museum authorities and the police department. The alleged Raphael was destroyed by fire before it could be authenticated. Jonathan and Flavia identified the master criminal only through the devious schemes of her supervisor, General Taddeo Bottando.

Bottando's fiscal and turf protection problems surfaced in *The Titian Committee* (Harcourt, 1993). When American art historian Louise Mary

Masterson was murdered in Venice, Flavia was ordered to go through the motions of an investigation without irritating the Venetian police She could not ignore a second death and layers of artistic intrigue.

During *The Bernini Bust* (Harcourt, 1994), Jonathan, then employed by a well-known London art gallery, transported a Titian purchased by the Moresby Museum in Los Angeles. Arthur Moresby, the museum grantor who had ordered the Titian and a smuggled Bernini bust, was murdered. The smuggling prompted Flavia's intervention, which brought about a change in her relationship with Jonathan from friend to lover.

As *Giotto's Hand* (HarperCollins, 1994) opened, Dottore Corrado Argan, an ambitious rival within the bureaucracy, challenged Bottando. He needed a coup to bolster his reputation. The detection of Giotto, a thief who over three decades had stolen uncataloged masterpieces in personal collections, would be appropriate. Flavia and Jonathan followed Giotto's trail through Italy and England, false trails and two murders, to reach a conclusion that met Bottando's needs, but perhaps not those of justice.

Bottando, who had been reassigned to an international posting, gave Flavia two choices as *Death and Restoration* (HarperCollins, 1996) began. She could accept a transfer with him or take over as head of the Italian art theft agency. Jonathan, now her fiancé, wanted her to cut back on her activities so they could spend more time together. However, the reappearance of old adversary Mary Verney in Rome was too intriguing to ignore. Mary had been noticed at a time when Father Xavier Munster, an aging monk, had been attacked and an obscure Madonna icon stolen from a monastery church.

In *The Last Judgement* (Scribners, 1996), Jonathan's gullibility led him into disaster when he delivered *The Death of Socrates* by painter Jean Floret to Mullins, the prospective buyer in Rome. Unfortunately, Mullins no longer wanted the painting. Jonathan agreed to resell it. When Mullins was brutally murdered, investigating officer Giulio Fabriano, a former lover of Flavia, was disposed to consider Jonathan a suspect. The painting held clues disclosing the identity of a World War II traitor. By this time Flavia was acting director of the Art Theft Squad and had married Jonathan.

Art and artifice blended in *The Immaculate Deception* (Scribners, 2000). Political pressures forced Flavia, still only acting-director of the Museum, into a no-win situation when a painting on loan from the Louvre was stolen. Bottando was considering retirement. Flavia had lost her zest for advancement in the Art Theft Squad. Jonathan had a mission of his own, determining the provenance of a Madonna owned by Bottando. Jonathan, Flavia, Bottando, and the elusive Mary Verney showed surprising aspects of their characters against a background of art history and mythology.

The books combined the mystery of murder and the deceptions of art with heavy dollops of Italian and art history. Meant to be savored, leaving a wondrous aftertaste and an appetite for more. Pears has continued to write extraordinarily fine novels, but not in this series, most commonly designated " The Jonathan Argyll series"

Lark Dailey Dodge

Author: Sheila Simonson

See: Lark Dailey, page 197.

Matty Donahue

Author: Pat Freider

Matty, who for all her Irish name had both Native American and Spanish ancestors, practiced law in Santa Fe, New Mexico. She had a troubled past. Four years before the series began, she had convinced a judge to award custody of Tommy, a seriously troubled teenager, to his father. She was engaged to the father, so when Tommy killed both himself and his dad, she felt tremendous remorse. This fiasco brought her a short-term revocation of her license to practice law. Even when reinstated she was close to unemployable but as *Signature Murder* (Bantam, 1998) opened, she had obtained low level legal work at Frederick and Danforth. Joe Danforth, one of the partners, had employed Matty's mother as a paralegal so gave her a break. The horrifying death of Isadora Stanton, an elderly eccentric client, thrust Matty back into a sense of guilt. She had arranged for Teddy Bellisandro to be hired by Isadora as a chauffeur when her driving shills faded. Teddy became Isadora's confidante and dear friend. Now he was suspected of killing her because of the similarity to a murder in his past. Matty was obsessed with proving Teddy's innocence at any cost, and there was a cost.

Matty may not have a commitment to an attorney's responsibility to act as an "officer of the court", but in *Privileged Communications* (Bantam, 2000) she knew the technicalities needed to save her client, Jimmie Abita, from disclosure of his medical records. When scurrilous investment counselor Alan Prather and his psychologist wife Denise died in an explosion, the initial determination was murder/suicide. Denise was in last stage Huntington's Chorea. However Det. Daniel Baca believed they had been murdered and sought tapes Denise had made of therapy sessions, including Jimmie's. His wife, Angie was rehabilitating the main house on Matty's property, causing Matty to spend a lot of time with their young son, Sam. He became very important to her, important enough so that she would risk her law license and her life to protect the boy. Highly imaginative plotting.

Brigid Donovan

Author: Karen Saum

Brigid Donovan, a former Roman Catholic nun, held a variety of post-convent jobs: true crime writer, waitress, cleaning woman, and, most recently, was an investigative journalist in New England. By age fifty-two, she had recovered from alcoholism, married twice, had two sons, and discovered her lesbian orientation.

In *Murder Is Relative* (Naiad, 1990), Brigid was hired by Claire Du Lac, a wealthy Canadian dowager, to investigate the death of her son-in-law, David Thorne. His daughter, Sister Genevieve, had become a nun. The suspects and informants were blackmailing nuns, illegitimate children, rapists, and drug dealers.

Murder Is Germane (Naiad, 1991) reunited Brigid with a nun after whom she had "lusted." This involved her in the affairs of a quasi-religious group that hosted Latin American refugees. A steady flow of erotic glances, hints of incest and illegitimacy overwhelmed the mystery elements of the plot.

As *Murder Is Material* (New Victoria, 1994) opened, Brigid viewed with skepticism the stigmatic wounds on the hands of young Julie. Should this same doubt be attributed to Julie's claims that her grandmother, the respectable director of a charitable organization, intended to murder her. Murder, kidnapping, and a return to alcohol occurred before Brigid got things under control.

Delilah Doolittle

Author: Patricia Guiver

Delilah Doolittle and her friend Eve left England to make a home in the United States when they were in their twenties. Their friendship began when Delilah was a scholarship student at an exclusive preparatory school. The series gave limited information as to how the two women spent the next two decades, but Eve, a fashionable beauty from a wealthy family, eventually married a prosperous Texan. It was Eve and her husband Howard Cavendish who had introduced Delilah to Roger, the man she married at age fifty. Unfortunately, she expected Roger to be a solid citizen, not a gambler. He expected her to be wealthy. The not altogether happy marriage ended when Roger was killed in an accident; at least, so it was perceived at the time.

Delilah was in her mid-fifties as the series began, a tiny woman who dyed her gray hair to resemble her original chestnut locks. She settled in San Diego in the one asset Roger had left, a family home. Delilah developed her own profession: pet detective. Over a period of time, she added pets to her childless household: a Doberman (Watson), a three-legged cat (Hobo), and a cockatiel (Dolly). Her days were spent in search of missing animals or in finding the owners of pets confined in municipal kennels. She toured shelters, read and placed newspaper ads, and spent leisure time at Dog Beach, a stretch of ocean side where pets were allowed. Although Delilah frequently expressed her intention of remaining single, over the series she and Detective Jack Mallory moved closer to a personal relationship.

Delilah's first encounter with the authorities came in *Delilah Doolittle and the Purloined Pooch* (Berkley, 1997). She discovered a corpse in a client's doghouse. The dog, Jessie Lomax' prize German Shepherd Herbie, had disappeared. For some reason it was extremely important to locate Herbie before the control officer did. Both Jack Mallory and "Tiptoe Tony" Tipton, a friend of Roger's were introduced.

When park biologist Bill Jackson was murdered in *Delilah Doolittle and the Motley Mutts* (Berkley, 1998) the assumption was that the murder was connected to the Surf City battle over wetlands. This assumption was reinforced when activist Mabel Redpath, a collector of stray dogs, was found dead. While searching for a missing Puli, Delilah found a triple killer just in time to escape herself. She acquired Hobo here.

Delilah Doolittle and the Careless Coyote (Berkley, 1998) was the least credible of the series (none of the books should be taken too seriously). It was weakened by coincidences and a convenient confession. The search for Mavis Byrde's prize Abyssinian cat led to Delilah's discovery of Lizzie Walker's corpse. Lizzie, an aging eccentric, had been killed because of her dedication to cats. Detective Mallory alternated between warning Delilah to stay out of his cases and being concerned when she didn't get involved.

Cats and dogs had been Delilah's line of work, but in *Delilah Doolittle and the Missing Macaw* (Berkley, 2000), she expanded her practice to include birds. She (and Watson) discovered the corpse of Jose Martinez, who was suspected of smuggling exotics from Mexico. Her friend Beryl Handley's parrot had been stolen. A new friend, Vance De Vayne, suffered the loss of a pair of breeding macaws. Finding out what was going on would be a feather in Delilah's cap. She proved that she could still ride a Harley, just not safely.

The events surrounding Roger's death had never been clear to Delilah. In *Delilah Doolittle and the Canine Chorus* (Berkley, 2001), she connected them to a burglary at her home. The discovery of a deed hidden there by Roger drew her back to Las Vegas where Roger had been killed. Although Delilah had difficulty in distinguishing her friends from enemies, she could always depend on Tony, Eve, and most definitely Jack Mallory.

Delilah was induced to meet her pal, Evie Cavendish at Hilda Dorsett-Bragg's dude ranch in *The Beastly Bloodline* (Perseverance, 2003).The Duke of Paddington, Hilda's prize stud, had died unexpectedly, possibly of poison. Hilda had already decided who was guilty, but she hired Delilah to prove her right. When the tragic death of ranch manager Hank Carpenter was initially deemed to be suicide, Delilah took on a bigger challenge. The addition of detective Jack Mallory as a homicide expert to the beautiful local sheriff, Anna Banning, provided a personal note to the narration.

Although one of Delilah's cases predominated in each book, she often achieved success in several other searches.

Jessica Drake

Author: Rochelle Krich

Jessica Drake, a slim dark-haired Los Angeles police officer in her thirties, had thirteen years experience on the force. She was currently assigned to Homicide. Her parents, a retired doctor and a socially ambitious housewife, had never approved of her career choice. Gary, her former husband, blamed Jessica's miscarriage on the dangers she encountered at work. She had her own fear: heights, particularly driving in the mountains. Over the series she had an increasing sense of her Jewish heritage, and began eating kosher in her own home. Her mother Frances Claypool, a child of German Jews during the Holocaust, had been left with an abusive Polish woman, and never saw her parents again, accounting to some degree for her inability to relate to her daughter.

As *Fair Game* (Mysterious Press, 1993) opened, there was a random killer in the Los Angeles area. The goal for Jessica and her partner Phil Okum was to find the pattern that tied the serial deaths together (young/old; black/white; pregnant/emigrant). Jessica found the key factor. Tipped off by the media as to her role, the killer targeted her as a victim. While this was going on Jessica had company. Her sister Helen and Matthew, her eight-year-old nephew, had moved in because of marital problems. Very well done.

During *Angel of Death* (Mysterious, 1994), Jessica investigated threats to Jewish attorney Barry Lewis, who represented the White Alliance in their fight for a parade permit through a primarily Jewish neighborhood. The harassment led to a series of murders. Much of the interest in the narrative came from Jessie's increased awareness of anti-Semitism, personalized when she learned that she had a Jewish heritage through her abusive mother.

Jessica's interest in Judaism was further stimulated in *Blood Money* (Avon, 1999). She was assigned to the death of an unknown man whose holocaust tattoo had been obscured. Norman Pomerantz had come to Los Angeles for an event that "would change his life." Unfortunately his plans clashed with those of a greedy killer. Jessica and Gary (her former husband) worked at repairing their relationship. She uncovered a lifetime of deceit and a scam that preyed upon Holocaust survivors.

Jessica's friendship with therapist Renee Altman had begun in their childhood. It had been put on hold as Renee's call-in radio program became popular. So Renee's unannounced visit to Jessica in *Dead Air* (Avon, 2000) came as a surprise. Renee believed she was being stalked but could not provide the proof necessary for Jessica to take official action. The situation changed when Renee's daughter Molly was kidnapped and Blanca, her housekeeper, murdered. The first suspect was Barry, Renee's husband who was seeking sole custody of the child. The more likely candidate was an unknown male caller to Renee's program who blamed her for the problems in his marriage. As the reconciliation with Gary faltered, Jessica turned to her religious faith for comfort.

The massacre of plastic surgeon Ronald Bushnell, his nurse, and receptionist led in a half dozen different directions during *Shadows of Sin* (Morrow, 2001). Assorted information incriminated a dissatisfied patient, an estranged foster son, the boy's father, members of Bushnell's family and the nurse with whom he had an affair. Jessica investigated each possibility, intrigued by the relevance of the Torah on the sins of parents and children.

An intriguing series.

Eve Duncan

Author: Iris Johansen

Eve Duncan had begun life as the illegitimate child of a teenage mother who succumbed to drug addiction. She grew up in the toughest part of Atlanta, Georgia, but was determined from the first to make something of her life. That plan was diverted when, as a teenager, she also bore an illegitimate child whose father had no interest in either marriage or parenthood. Declining the option of abortion, Eve had two goals: the care of her daughter Bonnie, and financial independence. She obtained a degree in Fine Arts at Georgia State that led to a career as a forensic sculptor, Eve's life was brutally changed when Bonnie disappeared. Bonnie's body was never found. Her abductor was believed to be a serial killer named Fraser who confessed to the crime, was tried and sentenced to death. Eve reunited with her mother, Sandra, now a drug free court reporter. She concentrated on her career, but each child's skull that she reconstructed was one more step in her search for Bonnie's remains. There were two significant men in Eve's life: billionaire John Logan, who whisked her off to his South Sea island when she was depressed, and former FBI agent Joe Quinn, who met Eve when he investigated Bonnie's disappearance. Joe's wife Diane had always resented his closeness to Eve. They continued to work together, which contributed to the end of Joe's marriage.

Eve had clearly set out the dimensions of her work: the skeletal remains of children, but in *The Face of Deception* (Bantam, 1998), she had a challenge she could not refuse. Billionaire John Logan would make a huge donation to the Adam Fund for Missing and Runaway Children in exchange for her reconstruction of an adult skull that he would provide. Logan felt guilty that Eve would be unaware of the dangers involved, but there was a greater danger in knowing. Engrossing.

Even after Fraser's execution, Bonnie's death remained an obsession for Eve as *The Killing Game* (Bantam, 1999) began. Joe Quinn contacted her on Logan's island, to reveal the discovery of a skull that could be Bonnie's. He did not know that both their lives would be thrown into chaos by a killer who wanted to add Eve to his list of victims.

The Search (Bantam, 2000) had only a sideline role for Eve. Yes, she had been wealthy John Logan's lover, but that was over. She was married to Joe. True, John had pressured Sarah Patrick and her golden retriever into helping to locate Bonnie's burial site. Indeed John and Sarah met again when Eve buried Bonnie appropriately. From then on, except for minor appearances, Eve focused on her own problems, building a new level of integration with her adopted daughter, Jane McGuire. Logan had a new and dangerous assignment for Sarah, which would take them to Colombia, the search for an abducted employee at one of his research facilities. He knew the kidnapper, Martin Rudzak, a man he had thought would never get out of prison. He had, determined to get revenge not only for his imprisonment, but also for the years of separation from the woman he loved, Chen Li, who had married Logan. Sarah and John, an unlikely pair, eventually became compatible while thwarting Rudzak's maniacal plans.

The knowledge that the skeleton she had buried as Bonnie's was not that of her daughter, caused Eve to leave Joe Quinn, and her adopted daughter Jane McGuire behind in *Body of Lies* (Bantam, 2002). She accepted an assignment from U. S. Senator Kendall Melton to reconstructed a skull possibly that of Melton's opponent in the last election. Only after attempts to murder Jane, Eve's mother, Sandra, and Eve herself did she become aware that she was a pawn in the struggle between a cabal of powerful men and a victim who became a killer. Bonnie still appeared to Eve in dreams.

Jane MacGuire had become tremendously important to Eve so the fact that she was threatened by Aldo Manza, an obsessed man, in *Blind Alley* (Bantam, 2004) devastated Eve. She could not bear to lose "another child". Jane, however, was a street wise seventeen-year-old, confident that she could cope with the help of Joe Quinn, Eve and charming Scotland Yard detective Mark Trevor. For all of the dramatic tension engendered by Aldo's obsession, it seemed contrived. Jane and Trevor played the primary roles, not Eve and Joe.

Jane, who had been with Eve and Joe since she was ten years old, was a Harvard University student as *Countdown* (Bantam, 2005) began. Eve, as readers of the series are aware, knew of Jane's resemblance to Cira, an actress who fled from the volcanic explosion of Mount Vesuvius 2000 years ago. But Eve and Joe were relegated to background roles while Jane was targeted by those who thought she could lead them to gold, purportedly hidden by Cira. Mark Trevor surfaced when an attempt was made to kidnap Jane, but he had his own agenda.

There can be too much of a good thing. The hope that gunrunner Luis Montalvo could find Bonnie's grave and her killer sent Eve to Colombia in *Stalemate* (Bantam, 2007). She had been urged to reconstruct a skull for Montalvo by the CIA because he had agreed to release one of their agents if she came. Joe was adamantly opposed to the venture and followed her when she left. Montalvo had been a young soldier in the rebel army of Antonio Armandariz when he met and married Antonio's daughter, Nalia. She uncovered evidence that powerful drug dealer Ramon Diaz was double-crossing her father, but was murdered by him. Her father allowed Diaz to convince him that Nalia had fled to Australia with stolen money. Now a wealthy man, Montalvo had discovered the whereabouts of Nalia's skeleton. Eve by reconstructing the skull would provide the evidence he needed. A great adventure, which exposed the depths of Eve's obsession to a man who was equally obsessed.

As *Quicksand* (St. Martin, 2008) began, Luis Montalvo (see priors) had presented Eve and Atlanta police officer Joe Quinn with the names of three men who had claimed to have killed Bonnie. Henry Kistle was on the list. Quinn, Eve, Montalvo, Jane McGuire (Eve's adopted daughter) and young Miguel Vicente headed to Clayborne Forest where Kistle had last been seen. A former Army ranger, Kistle roamed the woods, killing police officers who searched for him. Because Kistle was suspected of the recent death of a local boy, county officers were in charge but the CIA brought Dr. Megan Blair, a reluctant psychic, into the woods to locate the corpse of young Bobby Joe Windlaw. Action shifted back to the Atlanta area, but Kistle kept in contact with Eve, luring her on to seek him out, hinting that his current captive would be buried near Bonnie's grave. This quest for Bonnie's grave had become obsessive, too many others died in Kistle's games.

Next: *Blood Game* (2009); *Eight Days to Live* (2010)

Lady Alix Dunraven

Author: James Brady

Author James Brady, who lived in the Hamptons and has spent his working years among the rich and the famous, knew his setting well enough to develop credible characters and plot within a light hearted framework. The narrator of the series was reporter Beecher Stowe who returned to the family estate after heroic action in Algiers. His new assignments for *Parade* magazine were frequently based on his home turf.

In the first of the series, *Further Lane* (St. Martin, 1997), self-made multi-millionaire Hannah Cutting was murdered on a nearby beach. Beecher was responsible for the background story on her life, in which lay the seeds of her death. Competition arrived in Lady Alix Dunraven, an emissary of Random House for whom Hannah had been writing a "tell all" book. For all of his foreign travel, Beecher had remained rather naïve. Alix moved into his home and his life. Their professional cooperation solved the mystery, but no promises were made.

Alix (Alixandre after a distant cousin, the deceased Czarina of Russia) was the twenty-six-year-old daughter of an Earl when she met Beecher. After a double first at Oxford where she coxed the winning crew, Alix was employed by HarperCollins in London. Her work there as an editor won her an award, which entitled her to a one-year detachment to Random House in New York City. Her literary skills were matched by encyclopedic knowledge. A tall slim brown-haired woman, she was distinguished by a husky voice which melted Beecher down. This was hard on Beecher as Alix was frequently rumored to be engaged to assorted scions of the British nobility, sports stars, and foreign princes. She explained to Beecher that he should not worry. She would never get engaged to him because he would take it seriously. Alix's role models included Clare Boothe Luce, Pamela Harriman, and Isabella Stewart Gardner, all Americans. Inconsistently, her favorite author was John Buchan of the Richard Hannay adventure series.

There were secrets and mayhem in *Gin Lane* (St. Martin, 1998) but it was less of a murder mystery than a novel of manners. Beecher combined vacation time with a story on the Baymen (the commercial fishermen). Alix was there for the wedding of her former suitor, Fruity Metcalfe. Crude radio entertainer Leicester "Cowboy" Dils and his entourage occupied an estate on exclusive Gin Lane. Cowboy was subject to considerable ridicule by the community, but, before he left Southampton, his credentials as a gentleman were clear to Beecher. Brady had fun with the overreactions of secret service agents in preparation for an appearance by the President and First Lady (the Clintons) at the wedding. Alix was bright and sexy, but without any significant impact except on poor Beecher. He really ought to get himself a life.

The House That Ate the Hamptons (St. Martin, 1999) blended fact, fiction and humor. Beecher's father (generally referred to as "The Admiral") had publicly retired from his position as Chief of Naval Intelligence, but he frequently carried out secret assignments for the government. One such task interacted with local opposition to a huge home, ostensibly built by a Texas oilman, but intended for Prince Fatoosh the Malevolent. Alix added her talents to those of real life (Bill Cohen of the Defense Department) and imaginary characters (Howard Roark. the creation of Ayn Rand) in an effort to secure peace in the Middle East. Name-dropping was rampant (George Plimpton, Ben Bradlee and Sally Quinn, Martha Stewart). Alix returned to London after another memorable episode.

Beecher worried that Alix would be bored when she arrived for *A Hamptons Christmas* (St. Martin, 2000). Instead, she was charmed. She became emotionally attracted to Susannah aka Emma, a neglected ten-year-old girl. Alix, the Admiral, Beecher and the regulars made the holiday memorable, and the narrative endearing. The ridicule and the tensions among Old Money and New Money, the assorted Native American tribes, the blue-collar workers and small business owners who populate the Hamptons were still there. Still, there was a strain of sweetness in this narrative. Emma, the child whose parents did not know how to love her, found friends who did.

Very light reading, but fun.

Starletta Duvall

Author: Judith Smith-Levin

Starletta Duvall, a six-foot tall, shorthaired African-American woman, would have attracted attention under any conditions. As a police lieutenant in Brookport, Massachusetts, she could be downright scary to a suspect. Her physical skills were impressive and her language as scatological and sexually explicit as any found in the men's locker room. Although they were effective for fictional purposes, Star's ventures into undercover work were unrealistic for her rank and professional responsibilities.

Her mother, originally from Chicago, had died when Starletta was twelve-years-old. Her father Lenny, a police officer who had been born in New Orleans, was killed in action. The incident was something that Star never forgot. Lenny, then out of uniform, had been in pursuit of a criminal when another police officer, assuming that a black man with a gun in his hand must be the perpetrator, shot him.

Not everyone on the police force in Brookport was tolerant of Star's gender and race, but she had some excellent connections. Her Italian-American sergeant, Dominic Paresi, not only became a friend, but eventually settled down with Star's best friend, Venetia (Vee) Spencer-Martin, also an African-American. The captain in charge of the unit, Arthur Lewis, had been Len Duvall's partner on the force. He was careful not to show any favoritism for Star as she worked her way up through the ranks, but she could count on his support when needed. The most significant person in Star's personal life became Dr. Mitchell Grant, a wealthy white forensic scientist. Grant's wife had found his career choice unacceptable for her desired social standing. They had divorced. Neither she nor their daughter Robin could tolerate Star as Grant's lover. That was not the primary reason that Star refused to move in with Grant. She placed a high value on her independence. He lived on a different social and economic level. Star was just as happy with Hershey's Kisses as with gourmet chocolates. She and Vee had fun together, hunting antiques, hitting up singles bars and ice cream parlors. Jake, Star's cat, was even more anti-social than she was.

During *Do Not Go Gently* (Harper Paperbacks, 1996), Star became obsessed with finding the man who was killing successful African-American women. This prompted her to go undercover to entice the current suspect. Unfortunately, she almost succumbed to his "maleness." Although the rationale for the killer to set Star up for failure and death was credible, the convoluted way he went about it was not. The reader may feel deceived by the first person interludes of a suspect.

When popular religious leader Desmond St. John was murdered in *The Hoodoo Man* (Ballantine, 1998) the modus operandi was reminiscent of a multiple killing by then teenager Carlyle Biggs, Jr. A victim of physical abuse, Biggs had killed both his parents and two younger brothers. He had served his time, and was currently working in Worcester, Massachusetts. Because the earlier deaths had taken place in New York, NYPD Sergeant Lisel Werner joined the task force. She was protective of Carlyle, seductive to Dr. Mitchell Grant, and obnoxious to Star. There were more corpses, including that of an eviscerated infant, before Star put it all together.

Except for token scholarship students, Bromleigh Academy was patronized by upper class rich or wannabe parents. It became obvious in *Green Money* (Fawcett, 2000) that affluence did not meet all the needs of some students. A series of vicious murders in nearby St. Francis Park mirrored a popular computer game. Although headmaster Marshall Butterworth was in total denial, Star and Paresi persisted till they uncovered the killers.

"Corporate raider" Dan Rayner had been Dr. Mitchell Grant's college roommate. In *Reckless Eyeballin'* (Fawcett, 2001), Grant was loath to believe that Dan could be involved in his wife Cynthia's murder. The other suspect in the vicious killing was Cynthia's lover, African-American Judge Harlan Robinson (also married), the probable father of her unborn child. Both men had alibis, but another death produced a third suspect.

Robin (Grant's daughter) moved into her father's apartment where Star had been spending much of her time. That firmed her decision to end the racially mixed relationship. The narrative had a strange teasing conclusion. X (a convict who, under a prison employment contract, made the reservations for Vee and Star's coming vacation) expected to be there when they arrived in Hawaii, but there was no sign of a forthcoming book.

Mandy Dyer

Author: Dolores Johnson

Mandy Dyer's father died when she was one-year-old. Since then divorce had been the problem in her family. Even before the end of Mandy's marriage to Larry Landry, her mother Cecelia had racked up five more marriages. Mandy had hoped for a career as an artist, but dropped out of school to subsidize Larry's law school education. She subsequently supported herself through a Denver dry cleaning business inherited from her Uncle Chet. It was a substantial operation with up to 18 employees and a high degree of computerized efficiency. Nevertheless she put in long hours trying to pay off the mortgage that resulted from the improvements.

At thirty-five she was self-sufficient, sharing her third floor apartment in a Victorian house with Spot, an ill-tempered yellow cat. Her closest friend was investigative reporter Nat Wilcox. They frequently had different agendas in the narratives, but they never forgot their history of mutual support.

Betty the Bag Lady was a frequent visitor at Dyer's Cleaners, regularly sharing their morning snacks. In *Taken to the Cleaners* (Dell, 1997), Betty presented herself with a Dyer's laundry bag containing a bloody man's suit. Within hours the suit had been connected to the murder of attorney Harrison Van Dyke. Attractive detective Stan Foster listened to Mandy's theories, but he did not provide the level of protection for Betty that Mandy considered necessary. Betty had glimpsed the man who put the suit in a refuse container. Mandy carried out a parallel investigation until things were ironed out. (Sorry, but author Johnson was given to puns).

From the time that rival dry cleaner Farley Mills moved to Denver in *Hung Up to Die* (Dell, 1997) he set out to destroy Mandy's business. Eventually she came to realize that the harmful incidents that had occurred in the past few months, and perhaps Farley Mill's murder, could not have occurred unless one of her employees was involved. Several of them, including her top worker and dear friend Mack Rivers, were serious suspects.

Mandy's friend Kate Bosworth, owner of an antique dress shop, brought vintage clothing to be cleaned at Dyer's. The antique Fortuny gown she had purchased for a pittance in *A Dress to Die For* (Dell, 1998) was extremely valuable. Only after Kate had been murdered did Mandy ferret out that the value was not just in the garment itself, but in its connection to criminal activity. In the process she learned more about Detective Stan Foster and Betty the Bag Lady (now sober and looking for a job).

Mandy had a problem saying "no" to her friends. Although she and Stan Foster had not seen one another in months, she couldn't turn him down in *Wash, Fold, and Die* (Dell, 1999). This was nothing personal. He wanted her to identify a recent murder victim by means of a laundry mark on his shirt. Mandy knew the victim, artist Jeremiah Atkins. She knew his widow, Rosalie, who wanted help finding Jeremiah's family. Even after prior scary experiences, Mandy ventured into dangerous situations without providing backup. She and Stan decided to try dating again. He was worried about marriage. Based on her mother's multiple weddings, Mandy had no interest in getting married.

When Mandy accepted the challenge of cleaning and remodeling a three-generation wedding dress in *Homicide and Old Lace* (Dell, 2000) she was unaware of the groom's identity. By the time she learned he was Larry Landry, her former husband, she was committed to the work. By the time she found Larry standing over the corpse of his intended bride Olivia Torkelson, Mandy had only one choice. Find the killer, whether Stan Foster liked it or not.

Thelma Cadwick's bequest to Mandy of a bag of worn dresses made no sense in *Buttons and Foes* (St. Martin's, 2002). The discovery of multiple buttons sewed on the dresses led to an exploration of the value of buttons based on age, decoration, and scarcity. With Stan Foster out of her personal life and not much of a resource, Mandy turned to private investigator Travis Kincaid. They had known one another during their high school days when he was considered a "wild one". Thelma had left word clues for Mandy to follow.

Photographer Laura Donnelly, who was not only a friend of Mandy's but was her mother (Cecelia's) step-niece, had a problem in *Taking the Wrap* (St. Martin's 2004). While taking photos at a mountainside restaurant, there had been a mix-up in outerwear. Someone had left a red coat behind and taken Laura's tan car coat. Only clue was a nondescript dry cleaner's tag. It might have ended there except that when Laura left Mandy's shop, she was struck down by a hit and run driver. Mandy learned that another guest at the Rendezvous restaurant that night had died in a car accident. A third party, Carol Jennings who had an apt in Lauren's building, had disappeared. Even Mandy took her lumps, but Betty the Bag Lady, Stan Foster, and Travis Kincaid all pitched in to help.

Mandy had noticed from the items that Ardith Brewster sent to be dry cleaned in *Pressed to Kill* (St. Martin, 2007) that she had spruced up her wardrobe. Although Ardith would not identify her new suitor, she mentioned his unusual wardrobe, that she'd met him at the Dyer's Cleaner Open House the prior March, and that they were spending the weekend together. Ardith's subsequent death by strangulation connected to several similar attacks on women. One victim, Lorraine Lovell, had also been a customer. Mandy vacillated between sharing her information, and withholding what she considered confidential. When she needed the police, she expected them, including Travis Kincaid, to be available. Humor was provided by Cece, Mandy's mom, and her meddling in Nat Wilcox and his bride's wedding plans.

A cozy series with a likeable heroine, interesting cleaning tips, and a pleasant Denver, Colorado setting.

Tracy Eaton

Author: Kris Neri

Tracy's family had ill-equipped her for a normal life. Her mother, actress Martha Collins, and her father, Alec Grainger had married, divorced, remarried, divorced, married others, divorced. Her childhood had been erratic. She had been independent most of her life, earning a living as the author of a mystery series, featuring Tessa Graham. She brought all of this to her marriage to conventional attorney, Andrew "Drew" Eaton. The marriage did not end the contacts with her parents, who frequently called upon her to mediate their personal difficulties. Fortunately they spent much of their time abroad. Over a period of time the Eatons added a dog, Buddy, and a cat, Harriet Houdini.

Tracy considered her family dysfunctional, but in *Revenge of the Gypsy Queen* (Rainbow, 1999), she learned that her new in-laws were also flawed. However both she and Drew were fond of his younger sister, Marina so they flew to New York City to take part in her wedding. Marina and her fiancé, Tony Lora, had developed a successful restaurant and bar, The Gypsy Princess. Their hard work was put at risk when Marina was kidnapped. The ransom was to be the sale of The Gypsy Princess to billionaire real estate developer Lord Hunt. When Marina's unconventional Uncle Philly also disappeared, no one seemed concerned.

As *Dem Bones' Revenge* (Rainbow, 2000) began, Tracy was an attractive woman in her thirties who bore a considerable resemblance to Martha. Some of her childhood memories had filtered their way into Tracy's latest book, *Deadly Shadows* which she was having trouble finishing in time to suit her publisher. While under considerable personal stress, Tracy learned that her mother was a murder suspect. The victim, Vince Sperry, had played a role in both Martha and Alec's past. While Martha was under suspicion, Alec was nowhere to be found. Uncle Philly, who had developed a serious crush on Martha, was there to help, but Tracy called in a lot of favors among members of the Hollywood set before she had the full picture. Well plotted.

Tracy's subsequent adventures provided her with good background material for the next book. However, Kris Neri, who runs the Well Red Coyote Bookstore in Sedona, Arizona, was still looking for a publisher when last contacted. Too bad because the first two read very well. Neri has a new book out however, *High Crimes on the Magical Plane (2009,)* featuring Samantha Brennan and Annabelle Haggerty.

Good news! After a delay, the third book in the series "Revenge for Old Times' Sake" is now available

Catherine Edison

Author: Margaret Haffner

Catherine Edison remained close to her childhood friends, a tight knit group which banded together in Kingsport, Canada. Her husband Paul had not been a member. He virtually gave up his law practice to assist Calvin Parker in his political career. Paul and Catherine had a teenage daughter, Morgan. Catherine, a Ph.D. in plant pathology, was able to support the family even with Paul banking everything on a government career when Calvin reached higher office.

In *A Murder of Crows* (HarperCollins, 1992), one after another of Catherine's intimates was struck by tragedy. Certain that the reason for this attrition was somewhere in their past, and alerted to danger by a tarot card reader, Catherine found a tragic answer.

Kingsport became untenable for Catherine, so she took a short-term assignment to an agricultural chemical facility in *A Killing Frost* (HarperCollins, 1994). Her experience with publicity made her reluctant to befriend garage owner Ed Royce, who had been acquitted of murder. Her daughter Morgan became friendly with Royce's son. Everyone in Atawan treated Royce like a killer except the Edisons, who were renting the house formerly occupied by murder victim Tracy Tomachuk. Royce convinced Catherine to help prove his innocence.

Another good import from Canada.

Louise Eldridge

Author: Ann Ripley

Unlike many female sleuths, Louise Eldridge lived within a comfortable marriage. She and Bill, who was employed by the Foreign Service and the CIA, had two daughters: Janie was at home and Martha was a student attending Northwestern University. Louise was a tall dark-haired woman, who had never utilized her college degree except in volunteer work until her family was grown. The family had moved frequently due to Bill's assignments, but handled it well. Louise's primary outlet was her passion for gardening. When she sought a job, she found one writing a gardening column for a local paper.

As *Mulch* (St. Martin, 1994) began, the Eldridge family had settled in a close knit community in Northern Virginia, and been included in group activities. Eager to get her yard in shape, Louise had gathered garbage bags from neighbors filled with their leaves and lawn clippings. When the Eldridges opened the bags to fill in a low spot in their yard, they found a female torso, later identified. Although the police were suspicious that Bill might be connected with the murder, Louise and her daughter Janie proved otherwise.

Louise's recovery from the emotional and physical scars in her prior investigation was aided by an opportunity to co-host a television program on organic gardening in *Death of a Garden Pest* (St. Martin, 1996). She received personal satisfaction from her independence, but Louise realized that her relationship with Bill and Janie suffered from her inattention. When she became a primary suspect in the murder of Madeleine Doering, whom she had replaced on the program, Louise needed Janie and Bill's help to prove the case against a fairly obvious killer.

Environmentalists had a stake in a forthcoming Congressional election in *Death of a Political Plant* (Bantam, 1998). With the girls off visiting, Louise took something of a risk, inviting activist Jay McCormick whom she had dated in her college days to stay at the Eldridge home. He was active in a special quest and needed a place to hide. This had to be short-term because Louise was expecting three top gardeners from the Perennial Plant Society. She found another accommodation for Jay to ease the situation. Later he was discovered dead in the Koi fish pond. His computer was missing, but some of his notes could be on the premises. Several people were intent on finding them before they could become public. A verbal clue led Louise to significant evidence. She had a problem sharing her information with the authorities.

In *The Garden Tour Affair* (Bantam, 1999), Louise and her family traveled to Connecticut where she was to film local gardens and historic houses. Their fellow guests at the Litchfield Falls Inn were a volatile mix of married couples (including newlyweds), business rivals, and a suspected killer. Louise's close attention to detail was, as in prior narratives, a factor in identifying killers.

Louise needed different skills when she went to Lyons, Colorado to film western episodes for their television series in *The Perennial Killer* (Bantam, 2000). Her husband Bill was undercover in the area, monitoring a possible threat to the decommissioning nuclear facility, Stony Flats. Daughter Janie was at an Estes Park summer camp. Two murders in the Porter family, owners of the property on which Louise was filming, added to a series of tragedies they had experienced. Louise felt strangely separated from her family. She was drawn into a possible relationship with a man who might be the killer. She faced down a mountain lion, but it took a domineering domestic cat to save her from a possible indiscretion. The outcome helped Louise to set her priorities as her career and Bill's took separate routes.

On her regular dog-walking excursions, Louise had come to know and enjoy the company of ethnobotanist Peter Whiting. During *Harvest of Murder*

(Kensington, 2001), less pleasant aspects of his personality surfaced. She had been impressed by his devotion to the Brazilian forests, his scorn for predators who abused the land and its residents. He bragged that he and his younger wife Polly had discovered a beverage that prolonged not only life, but also vigor. The commercial potential of such a product was tremendous, enough to cause his murder.

The Christmas Garden Affair (Kensington, 2002) began slowly, introducing multiple characters and considerable technical material, but picked up speed with the murder of Bunny Bainfield, an entrepreneur in the field of garden marketing. Even Louise's television program had suffered from Bunny's competition. At the invitation of Maud Anderson, wife of the president-elect, academics, authors, government official and commercial nursery interest gathered in Alexandria to explore the future of native American plants. Louise's cooperation with the police caused old and new friends to shun her. She learned a lesson that contributed to a peaceful Christmas within her own family.

Garden club members had a lightweight public image, but in *Death at the Spring Plant Sale* (Kensington, 2003) Louise convinced her producer to highlight the Old Georgetown Garden Club Plant Sale. She would combine the taping with a visit at the home of Emily Holley, a former college friend. Louise was surprised at the change in Emily, passive even subservient to her domineering husband, Alex. That changed when Catherine Freeman, wife of prominent economist Walter Freeman, was murdered. Emily, Louise and pregnant Laura Alice Shea combined to find Catherine's killer.

If Louise had been disappointed that her former neighbor Peter Hoffman had avoided the penal system for killing Kristine Weere by successfully pleading insanity, she was incensed by *Summer Garden Murder* (Kensington, 2005). Released from a mental hospital after four years, he returned to the old neighborhood, intruded on a private party, and set himself up for murder. Unfortunately he also set Louise up as his probable killer.

Producer Marty Corbin should have realized there would be fireworks when he took *Gardening with Nature*, the television show starring Louise and John Batchelder to the island of Kauai in *Death in the Orchid Garden* (Kensington, 2006).One projected episode would feature three botanists with wildly divergent views on the discovery of obscure species of plants and their introduction into a new area. First, Louise discovered the body of explorer Matthew Flynn at the base of a cliff. Later, a second even more prominent botanist was murdered and John, injured. John had stated publicly that he and Louise were investigating. He had been, but she wasn't until she had to in order to protect herself.

These were short, interesting books with a likeable heroine. Author Ann Ripley has a wonderful sense of place in her narratives. Her descriptions of settings and characters are vivid and revelatory

Elizabeth I, Queen of England

Author: Karen Harper

Elizabeth I, Queen of England, daughter of Henry VIII and Anne Boleyn (whom he executed), survived a tumultuous childhood. She was aware that English Catholics considered her parents' marriage bigamous and that her half-brother, Edward VI and her half-sister, Mary I, had prior claims to the throne. Elizabeth spent most of her early years in isolation from the seat of power. At twenty-five, she became queen. Her time had not been wasted. She could read Latin, Italian, Greek, French and Spanish. She was physically active and adventurous. Her interests extended to science. Although she had limited experience in world affairs, she became an adroit stateswoman leading England to a position of international might. Domestically, she was always aware of manipulation, particularly by males seeking to share or use her power. That fear made her unwilling to marry; thereby, denying her country the Tudor heir that it needed for stability.

While Queen Mary I reigned, Princess Elizabeth had been kept under close surveillance. During *The Poyson Garden* (Delacorte, 1999), she assembled a band of loyal followers in exile: actor Ned Topside; herbalist Meg Milligrew; her faithful former governess Kat Ashley, later to become first lady of the Bedchamber; and Stephen Jenks, then her stableman, but later her bodyguard. All of these accompanied her when she ascended to the throne. She could depend upon the support of Sir William Cecil, who acted as executor over the properties left to Elizabeth by her father, Henry VIII. An unknown woman was determined to kill Elizabeth in revenge for injuries to her own family. The plotter was connected to Queen Mary, a fact that caused Elizabeth to wonder whether her half-sister approved of the attempts on her life. Interspersed with Elizabeth's portion of the narrative are the musings of "She" a.k.a. " The Lady of the White Peacock," the woman who not only intended to kill the Princess, but to poison thousands of her Kentish supporters. Queen Mary's death solved many problems, but there were more to come.

Even as Elizabeth rode to her coronation in *The Tidal Poole* (Delacorte, 2000), her enemies schemed to replace her with her cousin, Mary of Scotland. Each execution to secure her government left survivors filled with hate. Elizabeth and her privy plot council (an unofficial body which included trusted servants and Sir William Cecil) investigated the murder of Penelope Whyte, a wanton young woman, initially unaware that the death was part of a scheme to assassinate Elizabeth. Cecil was as loyal a follower as she had despite his personal ambitions and his jealousy of her other favorites. The favorites had included Sir Robert Dudley, lieutenant of Windsor Castle who sought her hand even when married; John and Bella Harrington who had stood by Elizabeth before her accession to the throne.

By the end of *The Twylight Tower* (Delacorte, 2001), Elizabeth had come to suspect the loyalty of most of these intimates. The deaths, by unexplained falls, of a musician, a serving man, and Amy Robsart Dudley, Robert's wife, gave Elizabeth good reason for suspicion. Perhaps none of them had caused these deaths directly, but several had withheld information or conspired against their queen. Elizabeth took an active role in detection using devices contrived by Dr. John Dee, a young scientist. They included a rig to transport her through the air, mirrors to send messages, and spyglasses to see long distances.

Plots to discredit Elizabeth and restore a Catholic monarchy kept her in a state of agitation in *The Queene's Cure* (Delacorte, 2002). Not only had a pock-marked effigy been placed in her royal coach, but a dead disfigured woman was dumped in the palace pond. Smallpox, an on-going threat in England, had always horrified Elizabeth. The schemers sought access to Elizabeth through mute fourteen-year-old Gil Sharpe who did sketches for her. Meg Milligrew had fallen into disrepute with Elizabeth and was included among those suspected of trying to terrify Elizabeth

Elizabeth flaunted her father's law of decorous behavior during the holidays in *The Queen's Christmas* (St. Martin, 2003) by declaring a 12-day feast. This horrified the local clergy. Elizabeth had done it partly to provide her dying friend Kat Ashley with a good time. Someone used the festivities to humiliate and endanger Elizabeth. When Ned Topside became a serious suspect, Meg's actions on his behalf could jeopardize her betrothal to Stephen Jenks, Elizabeth's bodyguard.

It was not the grand plots of her Papist relatives that plagued Elizabeth in *The Thorne Maze* (St. Martin's Minotaur, 2003), but the fear of smallpox and Kat's bouts of dementia. Elizabeth had left London behind to escape the ravages of the disease, traveling to Hampton Court, Hatfield House, and finally the area where Lord William Cecil was planning a luxurious home. Members of Elizabeth's retinue were murdered on the grounds of her residences. Both Elizabeth and Cecil feared that the killer might be someone they loved.

As *The Fyre Mirror* (St. Martin's Minotaur, 2005) began, Elizabeth was in need of a respite so she moved her court to Nonesuch Palace, a remarkable edifice built by Henry VIII who had torn down a manor house and wiped out a village for a proper setting. There was no rest for Elizabeth there. One of the three artists competing to paint her official portrait was killed in a mysterious fire. Gil Sharpe who had returned from studies abroad was suspected, as were Dr. John Dee and his frivolous young wife, Katherine. Two more fires followed. At this point, Elizabeth took the offensive, even going undercover to identify the killer/arsonist.

Starched accessories (cuffs and ruffs) were all the rage in England as *The Fatal Fashione* (St. Martin, 2006) began. Elizabeth was not only criticized by members of Parliament and the House of Lords for her failure to marry and provide an heir, but by a Puritan minister for her "foolish fashions". All this seemed trivial when the murder of Hannah von Hoven, a Flemish starcher, occurred. There were mysterious connections between Hannah and Thomas Gresham, one of Elizabeth's top advisors. After further deaths, Elizabeth rallied her Privy Plot Council. She served not only as leader of the group but took action when the others were at risk.

Despite Sir Williams Cecil's advice that she should stay in London during *The Hooded Hawke* (St. Martin, 2007), Elizabeth set out on an extended tour of Sussex and Hampshire, accompanied by an entourage of 200 attendants. Ned and Meg were included in this group, both mourning the death of their son. Meg was inconsolable. A series of attacks on Elizabeth during which others were injured or killed did not deter her. Nor did the fact that among her hosts were devout Catholics. Also within her retinue were her disloyal cousin, Thomas Howard, the Duke of Norfolk and an unidentified archer, the Hooded Hawke. She had a new champion, much resented by Robert Dudley, Sir Frances Drake

Greater information as to Elizabeth is available elsewhere but author Karen Harper smoothly inserted factual material with the elements of the mystery novel. Readers may be interested in *The Queen's Governess* (2010) by Harper which goes into more detail about the importance of Kat Ashley.

Elizabeth Elliot

Author: Irene Allen, pseudonym for Kirsten Peters

Elizabeth Elliot was a slightly overweight woman in her late sixties, who served as Clerk of the Meeting in the Boston Quaker assembly. A graduate of Wellesley, she found her volunteer activity challenging. The widowed Elizabeth exemplified the charitable and tolerant beliefs of her religion. Her two sons were adults and did not appear in the narratives.

In *Quaker Silence* (Villard, 1992), Elizabeth was concerned about the limited response in her Quaker assembly to the needs of the homeless, about their attitudes towards homosexuals, and the propriety of argument during meeting time. When wealthy Quaker businessman John Hoffman was murdered, the police focused on Tim Schouweiler, a young vagrant who had quarreled with Hoffman. Elizabeth pursued other motives for his death, and influenced the killer to admit his guilt. She also found herself attracted to Neil Stevenson, an attractive older man who attended the Quaker meetings.

In *Quaker Witness* (Villard, 1993), Janet Stevens, a Harvard graduate assistant, spoke with anguish when college officials dismissed her claim of sexual harassment by Professor Paul Chadwick. Elizabeth contacted Prof. Joel Timmermann, a Quaker faculty member, but found him no more understanding than his colleagues. When Chadwick was murdered, and Janet suspected, Elizabeth set a trap for the killer, hoping that he would confess to the police. Although he declined to do so, she taped his admissions.

Quaker Testimony (St. Martin, 1996) placed Elizabeth's tenure as Clerk of the Meeting at risk. She was a suspect in the death of Hope Laughton, a young mother who protested the United States participation in the Gulf War by refusing to pay income tax. Elizabeth not only proved her own innocence but that of the victim's husband, Sheldon.

Although a devout pacifist, Elizabeth did not intend her visit to former college friend, Reba Nichols, to involve breaking and entering a nuclear facility in *Quaker Indictment* (St. Martin, 1997). Reba owned considerable land near the Hanford, Washington nuclear testing site. When she was denied information by government agencies, Reba was reluctant to sell or bequeath property that might be contaminated. Reluctantly Elizabeth accompanied Reba to the borders of the site, and waited for her return, only to witness her detention by security forces. Reba was found later that night in her home, dead. Reba had a core group of environmentalists who were eager to help Elizabeth find the killer.

Like other religious mysteries, the Elliot series had the extra dimension of enlightening the reader about a particular faith. Low key.

Eve Elliott

Author: Barbara Lee

Eve Elliott had left her position in a New York City advertising agency to visit her widowed aunt in Pines on Magothy, Anne Arundel County, Maryland. (A reader should not confuse this locale with Maggody, Arkansas. The only resemblance was that neither Magothy nor Maggody easily absorbed outsiders). Eve was childless and in the process of divorce from her husband, Ben. Her prior work had provided no comfort. She had taken no pride in promoting the sales of cigarettes. Aunt Lillian, an established real estate broker, urged Eve to make her visit into a permanent move.

As *Death in Still Waters* (St. Martin, 1994) began, Lillian's business was in dire straits, partly due to Uncle Max's death. Dogs were important in Anne Arundel County. Ray Tilghman would only sell his property to a purchaser who would care for his two dogs. Lillian would like to broker that sale. When she and Eve arrived to discuss their services, Ray was dead. While taking a real estate course, Eve lived at the Tilghman house to take care of the dogs. The motives for Ray's death evolved from decades old violence, but Eve risked probing into them.

Fortunately Eve's subsequent training as a real estate agent included self-defense, because in *Final Closing* (St. Martin, 1997) there had been a series of assaults on female saleswomen. The police connected the murders with sexually threatening phone calls. Two of the victims had been employees of Mitch Gaylin, a rival real estate broker who was personally interested in Eve. When she began receiving the phone calls, she had to find some answers or risk her life.

The morality of selling fragile Maryland seashore to developers was a problem for Eve in *Dead Man's Fingers* (St. Martin, 1999). Landowners were hostile to any government limitations on their rights to build or sell. Environmentalist Lauren DeWitt was uncompromising in her demands for regulation and enforcement. Eve and Lillian were greeted with hostility by former friends who disagreed with their stance on the issue. Lauren De Witt was murdered.

Given that Lauren had been checking into land and building permits, she might have uncovered dangerous information.

These were intelligently written narratives with a mature cozy, heroine. The locale was important. The series was subtitled *A Chesapeake Bay Mystery.*

Trade Ellis

Author: Sinclair Browning

Trade (that's female) was a rancher and a private investigator in the Tucson area. She had attended the police academy but dropped out. Not for lack of intelligence. She just missed being high school valedictorian and had a college degree in English literature. She seemed to be unattached, and made her life around her ranch, the animals, and her work. Her racial heritage was partly Scots; with one Apache grandmother, who still lived on the reservation. Her uncle, Charles Borden was a deputy sheriff in Pima County. His children were Bea and Top Dog (tri-athelete and member of Apache firefighters featured in the narratives). Her home was shared with Blue (an Australian cattle dog), Mrs. Fierce (a Cock-a-Schnauzer), and Petunia (a potbellied pig); Her two special horses were Gray and Dream. Even her Dodge pickup had a name, "Priscilla". She ran Brahma cattle on her ranch. Had a problem with claustrophobia. The human closest to her was her foreman, Martin Ortiz.

Trade had been a part-time investigator for eight years as *The Last Song Dogs* (Bantam, 1999) opened but had never before worked a murder investigation. Charlene Williams and Buff Patania, former cheerleaders at Tucson's Hegelian High School hired Trade to find out who had killed four of the eight cheerleaders, nicknamed "The Song Dogs". Trade hadn't socialized with this group during high school but she learned a lot about them in a short time.

Trade managed to get herself into a lot of trouble during *The Sporting Club* (Bantam, 2000), but she earned some of it. She had made real progress in verifying the formerly repressed memories of romance author Victoria Carpenter. Veronica had hazy recollections of a black man and his two young sons being beaten by members of her father's "Sporting Club". Trade's mistake was in sharing the information she gathered with her primary suspects. The narrative featured lovely descriptions of Arizona. Fortunately she had help from her ex-beau Assistant District Attorney Abel Messenger.

The marriage of 36-year-old bull rider J. B. Calendar to 68-year-old heiress Abigail von Theissen was treated initially as a mercenary move in *Rode Hard, Put Away Dead* (Bantam, 2001). Any laughter ended when Abby was murdered during a camping trip. J. B. was arrested. Trade knew both Abby and J.B. slightly as they had purchased a nearby ranch. She helped J.B. get a good defense attorney. Finding other suspects wasn't as easy. Martin Ortiz, who often helped her, was pre-occupied by threats to Cori Elena, his former mistress and mother to his daughter. Cori Elena may have incurred the wrath of the Mexican Mafia. An extended read with good basic plotting.

Trade was reluctant to help elderly Lourdes Escamilla find her grandson, Eddy, in *Crack Shot* (Bantam, 2002). He and two friends had escaped from Los Hijos, a private semi-military juvenile detention facility. Josh Bowen, who had escaped with Eddy, was "run over" by the Los Hijos van driven by staff member Sgt. Loren Mitchell, at least that was the initial determination. Josh was the stepson of recently widowed Congressman Clayton Bowen. Trade did agree to escort Lourdes to a meeting with Col. Roger Fuller, ex USMC, current director of Los Hijos, after which she decided that Eddy and his surviving pal, Tony Bernini, needed help.

The series took a kinky turn in *Traggedy Ann* (Bantam, 2003). Not only did Trade hide herself in a cave to watch the activities of KIVA, a sex cult, but the experience was so devastating that she required an Apache spiritual cleansing. Some readers may be turned off by the explicit details. The death of Cordelia Jones, symphony cellist, was connected to the cult. When Terez Montiel, television reporter on the case, disappeared, her sister hired Trade to find Terez, which she proceeded to do without regard to investigations by the Tucson police or the DEA. Not up to Browning's usual standards. She does a masterful job of describing her setting, but the narrative would benefit from editing out extraneous material.

Kay Engels

Author: Triss Stein

Growing up poor in Falls City, New York gave Kay Engels no incentive for returning to her twentieth class reunion. She had never been a part of the "in" crowd; probably few members of the class would even remember her. Even less would they associate her with the successful journalist that she had become. Kay's father had been a foreman at a local factory. Her mother worked as a saleslady at a department store. They had modest aspirations for their only child, but supported her choices. They never told her that she had been adopted. She won a full scholarship to Radcliffe, while working as a campus correspondent for the *Boston Globe*. Five years of overseas assignments for the *Times* had been more than enough so she returned to New York City.

Kay found employment with *Now* magazine, described as a cross between *Time* and *Life*. She had been less successful in her personal life, a short marriage ended in divorce. She realized that her total dedication to her career might have been a factor in the failure of her marriage. Her parents moved to Florida, but had died by the time the series began.

Kay was in her late thirties in *Murder at the Class Reunion* (Walker, 1993). She had convinced herself she would attend the event as a professional assignment, to observe the progress in the community over the past two decades. There had been few positive changes, but a resurgence was anticipated because the low status military base was being activated full time. This meant an influx of 30,000 military personnel into a county with a population of only 58,000.

Kay's focus changed when her predatory classmate Terry Campbell was murdered at the reunion dinner/dance. She could accept that the killer was probably one of their classmates, but hopefully not handsome Tony Campbell, Terry's cousin. Kay refused to sanitize her coverage of the investigation, even when offered information as to her own birth and adoption.

In *Digging Up Death* (Walker, 1998), Kay's college roommate Vera Contas, now an archaeologist, was excavating a site fifty feet off Wall Street. Her project was delaying a major construction project of Elkan Properties, a major real estate developer. The delays were extended by Vera's discovery of artifacts tying the site to a Seventeenth century tavern frequented by Captain Kidd, and then, by the murder of Kevin Conley, a young construction worker. Vera had become a suspect because of her personal relationship with Kevin, but Kay assumed she was being framed. During the narrative, Kay sought and located her birth mother who was instrumental in saving Kay's life.

Modest but interesting.

Lynn Evans

Author: Claudia McKay

Lynn Evans' parents were cold and business oriented, very active in community affairs, but not remembered as affectionate. Part of her heritage was Native American. Her two sisters were older and, after she left South Dakota, she had little contact with either of them. Lynn became an investigative reporter for the *Hartfield Chronicle.*

As *The Kali Connection* (New Victoria, 1994) began, Lynn was recovering from the end of her relationship with her partner, Shirl. While investigating the death of Sam Jenson, a member of the Kalimaya Society, Lynn became attracted to Marta, a dedicated member. Her concern that the group, or at least some members, might be carrying out illegal activities was intensified when Marta left for Nepal. Lynn followed, but did not receive the welcome she had envisioned.

By *Twist of Lime* (New Victoria, 1997), Lynn turned up in Belize. She had volunteered her services at an archeological site managed by old friend, Dr. Sarah Donovan. False identities, "Ugly Americans," ruthless drug dealers, and DEA agents made her vacation into a chore. She gathered information but did not contribute to the solution of the crimes. Lynn had focused on the wrong suspects.

Faith Sibley Fairchild

Author: Katherine Hall Page

Faith Sibley was a blue-eyed blonde from New York City who had been educated in fine private schools but also became accomplished at jiu jitsu. She had no intention of marrying a minister, as had her socially prominent mother, Jane. Still, when she met Tom Fairchild, she closed down her Manhattan catering. Faith was not, nor did Tom expect her to be, the typical minister's wife involved in parish activities. Instead, she found bodies and resumed catering at a lower level.

In *The Body in the Belfry* (St. Martin, 1990), Faith seemed discontented and intolerant of the small Massachusetts town in which they lived. Her comforts, besides her husband, were their infant son Benjamin and her good friend Pix Miller, wife of Sam, a local attorney. Faith cleared Dave Swenson, a young man accused of murdering Cindy Shepherd, his blackmailing girlfriend, persisting even after she was threatened.

Faith's character mellowed in *The Body in the Kelp* (St. Martin, 1991).She and Benjamin vacationed on a Maine island while Tom attended a clerical summer camp. Pix, a summer inhabitant of the island, helped Faith to decipher the puzzle in a quilt top, find the "treasure," and reveal who had murdered Matilda Prescott and Roger Barnett. Faith, responding to the hospitality of the islanders, learned that there are cuisines other than French.

In *The Body in the Boullion* (St. Martin, 1991), Faith still missed New York City and preferred espresso, but had learned to drink the local coffee. Her contempt for local soups made her vulnerable when Farley Bowditch dropped dead with his face in her bouillon. Bowditch, a parishioner of Tom's, resided in a nearby nursing home. Faith's visits led to a volunteer stint in their kitchen, isolation by a snowstorm, a visit by a corpse, and a trio of killers.

The Fairchild family received a change of scenery in *The Body in the Vestibule* (St. Martin, 1992) prompted when Tom took a sabbatical in Lyons, France. The opportunity to be in a metropolitan area, to sample French cuisine seemed splendid to Faith...until she found the body of a vagrant in the vestibule. By the time the "flics" arrived, the corpse had disappeared and the incident was considered an aberration of her pregnancy. Faith proved to herself and Tom that she was not hallucinating. She survived a kidnapping and a personal attack to give birth to daughter Amy.

The Body in the Cast (St. Martin, 1993) returned the Fairchild family to Aleford, Massachusetts. Her catering business was enhanced by a food contract for the cast and crew of a movie version of *The Scarlet Letter* directed by Max Reed. Faith solved the murder of cast member Sandra Wilson to protect her professional reputation and influence a local election. The investigation was complex because Sandra might not have been the intended victim.

Faith sat on the sidelines in *The Body in the Basement* (St. Martin, 1994), during which her friend Pix Miller served as the sleuth. Pix strengthened her bonds with teenage daughter Samantha and her independent but ailing mother Ursula, while summering on Sanpere Island. Her knowledge of quilt patterns exonerated young Duncan Cowley accused of murder.

The battle between conservationists and developers formed the background for *The Body in the Bog* (Morrow, 1996). Faith's friend, Millicent Revere McKinley, had organized P. O. W. (Protect Our Wetlands) to fight the powerful Deane family. Blackmailing and murder cooled the activism. The narrative was slow to develop but offered interesting touches of local enthusiasm for the reenactment of Revolutionary War battles and the power of citizen involvement in small town government.

Pix Miller was the focus of *The Body in the Fjord* (Morrow, 1997), when she and her mother, Ursula Rowe, traveled to Norway. They made the trip to help Marit Hansen a friend whose granddaughter Kari was not only missing, but was suspected of murder.

Faith, in one of the pastoral duties she enjoyed, visited retired librarian Sarah Winslow in *Body in the Bookcase* (Morrow, 1998) only to find her dying amidst evidence of a robbery. Faith, busy catering a major wedding, returned to her home the next day, to find that it too had been burgled. Feeling vulnerable, Faith gathered the victims of other burglaries to seek a pattern, and discovered that antiquities, not electronics, had been targeted.

The Body in the Big Apple (Morrow, 1999) was a prequel. As the narrative began, Faith was twenty-three and the possessor of a bachelor's degree in English. She was the daughter of Rev. Lawrence Sibley and his wife, Jane Lennox, a real estate attorney. Putting aside her college degree, she studied cooking at the New School. Subsidized by a trust fund from her grandfather, Faith opened Have Faith, a catering service. Her long friendship with shy Emma Stanstead led to her first criminal investigation. A blackmailer threatened Emma's husband Michael's campaign for political office. Within Emma's family there were secrets which if revealed could damage not only his political aspirations, but also his work as an attorney. The murder of Nathan Fox, a Sixties radical, raised the stakes even higher.

The first body in *The Body in the Moonlight* (Morrow, 2001) was found inside Ballou House at a mystery dinner catered by Faith to raise funds for church renovation. It was a public relations setback for her catering service and a disservice to her marriage. Tom had been close to Gwen Lord, the victim. His church members had agreed on the need to raise funds, but were divided as to which project should have priority. Faith took an active role in questioning possible suspects, but the denouement fell short in credibility. However, as a by-product of her probe she ended a vicious slander against elementary school principal George Hammond.

Faith and Tom were not looking forward to their children's teenage years, so why, in *The Body in the Bonfire* (Morrow, 2002) would she agreed to teach a between semesters cooking class at exclusive Mansfield Academy? Probably because she couldn't refuse her friend, African- American attorney Patsy Avery who had a hidden agenda for wanting Faith on campus. African-American scholarship student Daryl Martin was being harassed and threatened by a person or persons unknown. It got more serious when Daryl was accused of murder. The Fairchilds had personal problems. Tom's parents, after all these years, were getting a divorce. The series continued to improve.

Faith had been eager to return for the summer to Sanpere Island, Maine as *The Body in the Lighthouse (Morrow, 2003)* began. Work was progressing on the remodeling of their cottage and Tom was eager to be involved. With Ben and Amy enrolled in day camp, Faith anticipated a restful vacation. It was not to be. Skunks forced the Fairchilds out of their unfinished cottage. Ursula Rowe, owner of a larger vacation home and Pix Miller's mother, was eager to take them in until their place was habitable. Ursula was concerned by vandalism, a long-term feud between two local families over lobster fishing rights, and a sense of foreboding that the commercialization of development was changing the island she loved. Although Faith had plenty to keep her busy (she had agreed to help with an amateur production of *Romeo and* Juliet), she managed to find two corpses near a legendary lighthouse.

Just when Faith accepted Aleford as her home and the parish and community accepted her, Tom decided that he needed a change as *The Body in the Attic* (Morrow, 2004) opened. The physical move from the modest parsonage to an historic mansion in Cambridge created a sense of unease for Faith. This was augmented by a distancing from Tom, who was now a lecturer at Harvard's School of Divinity. In Faith's volunteer work, she encountered a former beau, Richard Morgan, one of the "vagrants" or was he? They met at expensive restaurants, a fact that she did not share with Tom. A journal written by Dora, an abused and ultimately pregnant farm girl who had worked at an inn, was discovered in the mansion's attic. Over the engrossing narrative, the reader is exposed to several men who were not what they seemed to be, and one, Tom, who was.

Coming from a two-child family, Faith always felt overwhelmed by the male-dominated Fairchilds, but in *The Body in the Snowdrift* (Morrow, 2005) she couldn't turn down the invitation from her father –in-law Dick for a weeklong visit to Pine Slopes, Vermont on his 70th birthday. The sibling rivalry, marital discontent and parental problems with grandchildren made it almost a relief for Faith to substitute for John Forster, the missing chef at the resort's French restaurant. Repeated accidents made it clear that the resort was in real trouble, and before she was through, so was Faith.

The Body in the Ivy (Morrow, 2006) might be characterized as a tribute to Agatha Christie's *And Then There Were None,* because the setting and context were reminiscent, but it is more than that. Faith accepted an offer to spend a week on Bishop's Island as a caterer and guest. The hostess was the reclusive author Barbara Bailey Bishop. Faith was the only guest who had not been lured there by false pretenses. Seven graduates of Pelham College arrived with heavy baggage and something of a shared history, the death of manipulative fellow student, Helene "Prin" Prince. Three decades later, hostess Barbara Bishop, Prin's twin sister, wanted to know if one of her guests might have been responsible. Excellent characterizations. Very interesting author's note at the end.

Faith's willingness to help her friend, Patsy, check out the possibility of art forgery in *The Body in the Gallery* (Morrow, 2008) had unexpected results. Once Patsy verified her suspicions, she came up with a plan that had advantages to them both. Patsy, chairman of the Board of Trustees of the Ganely Art Museum, would hire Faith to takeover the dismal gallery cafeteria. This worked for Faith because her catering business was negatively affected by economic conditions. Finding a body had become routine for Faith, this time a naked young woman. Her husband, Tom, who had lost his patience, accused Faith of neglecting their children for her jobs. Their son, Ben, was in trouble and needed closer supervision. As usual Faith pulled it off with a happy ending, but had to weigh the conflicts between her job and her maternal responsibility. Both Faith and author Page showed considerable knowledge about food, art, literature, and clothing.

This has been an intelligently written low-key series with a heroine who developed, becoming more endearing as the narratives progressed. Next: *The Body in the Sleigh* (2009)

Phoebe Fairfax

Author: Suzanne North

Phoebe Fairfax worked two or three days a week as a "cameraperson" for Calgary television program *A Day in the Lifestyle*. Her real vocation was as producer/photographer for nature documentaries. The paid employment subsidized her films, which were well recognized, if not remunerative. Phoebe's parents, a retired banker and his wife, spent summers in Canada, but traveled to warmer climates during the other three seasons. Phoebe lived on a forty acre spread outside of Calgary, Alberta that she had inherited from her Uncle Andrew. Andrew's male lover, Cyrrie Vaughn, a retired stockbroker, remained close to Phoebe. He provided refuge and consolation when she was in trouble. Phoebe's marriage to Gavin had failed.

The German Shepherd Gavin left behind had been just "the dog" to Phoebe. He earned his name "Bertie" for courage in defending her household. She had two horses on the ranch, one of which she intended to breed. Phoebe's other great interest was in music. Uncle Andrew had also bequeathed her his grand piano. She practiced both classical and popular music, but rarely displayed this talent to others.

During *Healthy, Wealthy, and Dead* (NeWest Press, Canada, 1994), Phoebe, her exacting producer Ella Baxter, and interviewer Candi Sinclair visited a Canadian ranch for a *Lifestyle* segment. An international corporation had converted the ranch into a health/recreation facility. There was dissension among the managers as to how the property should be merchandised. When

Phil Reilly, the business manager, was murdered, Phoebe recalled a prior death at the ranch that had been termed an accident. Her investigation went beyond the economic rivalries among staff to uncover an obsessive killer.

In *Seeing Is Deceiving* (McClelland & Stewart, 1996), producer Ella Baxter, a recent mother, was on leave. Phoebe and Candi carried on with an assignment to film interesting aspects of a Psychic Exposition and Symposium held in a small community near Calgary. Candi's affection for her old friend, Tracy McMurty, now living in an abusive situation, drew Phoebe into another murder investigation. Tracy was the primary suspect when Jonathan Webster, her live-in lover was poisoned. Another above average plot with interesting side characters.

With the Royal Tyrrell Museum of Alberta as a background in *Bones To Pick* (McClelland & Stewart, 2002) paleontologist Dr. Graham Maxwell announced his newest and greatest discovery, "Homo Musica", three skeletons which he declared to be a new hominid species, capable of making music. An elaborate reception included Phoebe, Candi, and Ella, who were doing an hour-long program on Maxwell, several old college friends, staff and anti-Darwin protestors. Maxwell's corpse was discovered by Phoebe and Candi the next morning when they arrived to conclude their interview.

Casey Farrel

Author: Patricia Matthews with the assistance of Clayton Matthews

Casey Farrel, a dark-haired mixture of Irish and Hopi Indian heritage worked as a private investigator in Arizona. She had been educated at Northern Arizona University, then moved to Los Angeles. She did clerical work and occasional investigations for a detective agency until the son of the owner took over. He had a short-term relationship with Casey, which caused a pregnancy, then a miscarriage, and the end of their affair. She returned to Arizona without definite plans.

As *The Scent of Fear* (Severn House, 1992) began, Casey was sleeping in her car, having been ejected from her apartment because of unpaid rent. Both she and Donnie, a small boy looking for his dog, were on scene when a corpse was deposited in a dumpster. Realizing that she had probably caught a glimpse of the notorious "Dumpster Killer," Casey contacted the police. Sergeant Josh Whitney offered Casey support, even a place to live, at some risk to his job. Aware that young Donnie Patterson was also vulnerable, Casey hid him on the Hopi Reservation until the killer emerged.

By *Vision of Death* (Severn House, 1993), temporary custody of Donnie had been awarded to Casey. She now held a responsible position on the Arizona Governor's Task Force on Crime. Her assignment to investigate the deaths of Mexican "wetback" laborers placed her in conflict with powerful ranch families, desperate to protect their businesses and reputations.

Donnie had been legally adopted by *Taste of Evil* (Severn House, 1993) when he and Casey vacationed in Prescott. The victim of murder at the rodeo grounds turned out to be a long lost relative of Casey. The family insisted that she solve the crime. After muddling through red herrings and a premature arrest by the local police, Casey found a killer who had announced his motive early in the narrative.

Casey was unwilling to formalize her relationship with Sgt. Josh Whitney, as *Sound of Murder* (Severn House, 1994) began. They were friends, companions, and even lovers. Circumstances forced them to work as a team when they witnessed the murder of Billy Joe Baker, a country and western singer at a local dance hall.

With Donnie safely lodged with Uncle Daniel, Casey investigated the deaths of successful businessmen and women in the idyllic atmosphere of Sedona during *Touch of Terror* (Severn House, 1995). She risked her life by infiltrating a cult that had turned from worship to murder.

Casey was a pleasant protagonist in a regional mystery that was weak on technical details. Author Patricia Matthews has also written a large number of romance novels.

Kay Farrow

Author: David Hunt, pseudonym for William Bayer

Kay Farrow, color-blind from birth, chose photography and specifically art photography as a career. The word color-blind did not adequately express her condition. Unlike the typical red-green color-blindness, the abnormality from which Kay suffered was a total inability to see colors. She was an achromat (a person with autosomal recessive achromatopsia). Bright lights blinded her. During the daylight hours she wore dark red glasses. In the evening, her vision was excellent. Her hearing was exceptionally sharp. Kay, initially considered sculpture when she enrolled in the San Francisco Art Institute, but became hooked on photography. She finally achieved a black belt in aikido, a pleasure that had become her spiritual goal.

Despite her handicap, Kay, a tiny dark haired woman in her mid-thirties, had worked for a San Francisco alternative newspaper. She then became an independent fine arts photographer. Her first book, *Transgressions,* portrayed battered women, showing not only their wounds, but also their fight to survive.

Kay's widowed father Jack had retired from the police force under pressure. He had always enjoyed baking, opened up a shop and achieved some recognition for the quality of his breads. Carlotta, her mother, a music teacher in the school system, became agoraphobic. When Kay was twenty, Carlotta used Jack's pistol to kill herself. Kay kept in touch with former friends on the *Bay News*: Pulitzer Prize winning reporter Joel Glickman, a former hippie now in his fifties; and her mentor, Maddy Yamada who had reported on the war in

Vietnam. Although single, Kay eventually had a casual long-term relationship with Dr. Sasha Patel. One advantage, she saw colors when they were having sex.

Kay's original intent in her second book, *Exposures,* was to portray the transactions between adult males and young male prostitutes. The death of teenager Tim Lovsey in *The Magician's Tale* (Putnam's, 1997) changed her focus. Tim, a Gulch district hooker, had become personally important to Kay. He was saving enough money to move to Mexico where he had already purchased a home. The ghastly manner of Tim's death was reminiscent of a series of mutilation murders on which Jack Farrow had worked. Kay's determination to find Tim's killer had to be balanced against the need to protect her father. There were powerful men and a woman who could not allow Kay to focus on Tim's killer or the previous cover-up. She met Patel in an emergency room after she was savagely beaten.

Old friend Maddy Yamada, a fearless photojournalist now in her seventies, had been a substitute mother as well as a mentor. Maddy's death in a hit and run accident in *Trick of Light* (Putnam, 1998, a.k.a. *Trick Shot)* was mysterious. It occurred in a sleazy part of town, an unlikely destination for an elderly woman at night. Kay became curious about a nearby apartment where prominent citizens took part in orgies. Kay reviewed Maddy's past and possible motives for her death.

These were well written narratives with style, adding an esoteric quality to Kay's musings and deductions. Author David Hunt was remarkably proficient in portraying Kay's obsessions with an older lover and with the mystery in her father's past.

Jo Farewell

Author: Andrew Puckett

Jo was a registered nurse aka "Sister" in the West Midlands, England who appeared in at least two of the series featuring Tom Jones, married investigator for the Department of Health. Jo initially worked at the Birmingham Hospital after she was accredited. Deciding that she preferred to be in a small hospital, she returned to her hometown, Latchvale, a cathedral city. Her parents were alive, still lived in Latchvale, but they were not close to Jo. They had been older when she was born which may have been a contributing factor to the distance.

Jo was the supervising nurse at the Intensive Treatment Unit at St. Chad's Hospital so it was not surprising in *The Ladies of the Vale* (Collins, 1994) that she noted the high number of deaths occurring over a six-weeks period. Moreover the victims had all been recovering; then died. She ignored the orders of her superiors to forget the matter, notified Det. Insp. Colin Anslow of her suspicions. That contact brought in investigator Tom Jones of the Department of Health. Jones went undercover as a fiscal analyst. Racketeer Len Sutton whose wife had been a victim, was determined that her death would be avenged. Even after Jones and Jo identified the pattern, they still had multiple suspects. The end to the relationship that had developed between Jones and Farewell left her adrift.

It was finances not her desire to be reunited with Tom Jones that motivated Jo to agree to work with him again in *The Gift* (Severn House, 2000). Tom's boss, Marcus Evans, recruited Jo to pose as Tom's wife in order to investigate alleged improprieties (which might include murder) at Colcott Manor Fertility Clinic. They were to go into residence there, ostensibly seeking to improve their chances of conceiving a child. Even the heavy fee that Jo charged for her participation wasn't worth what Jo suffered. It was her story, which she narrated.

Cora Felton

Author: Parnell Hall

Cora Felton was a fraud. To help her niece Sherry Carter she had agreed to take on the persona of The Puzzle Lady. Her sweet appearance was the gimmick that helped Sherry's crossword puzzle column sell to 250 newspapers across the country. Cora was multi-married and divorced from Jerry, Arthur, Frank, Henry, and Melvin in that order. She had an eye open (most of the time) for husband number six. She was a serious drinker and smoker, although she moderated her drinking later in the series. Her pattern was to rise in the morning, straighten herself out with a single Bloody Mary; then, go on the wagon until dinnertime. In the evenings she drank until she was incoherent or comatose. Under stress, she just drank from morning until collapse. On the highway she was a disaster. Unfortunately she was also licensed to carry a gun. Cora had absolutely no interest in crossword puzzles, but she was an avid mystery fan and, when sober, had a deductive mind and became proficient at Sudoko.

Sherry Carter, who had an honors degree from Dartmouth, also had an abusive husband, Dennis Pride, an itinerant musician. She and Cora moved into small town Bakerhaven, Connecticut to avoid Dennis. His brutality had caused her to miscarry their child. Sherry drank decaf coffee, diet coke, and on rare occasions had a mild alcoholic beverage. Besides constructing the puzzles, her job was to preserve the illusion that Cora was the Puzzle Lady. On occasion she filled in as a substitute teacher at a preschool. Dennis remained a threatening factor in Sherry's life.

A puzzling clue, left in the hand of a young unidentified murder victim, led Bakerhaven Chief of Police Dale Harper to Cora in *A Clue for the Puzzle Lady* (Bantam, 1999). Cora, who faked her way out of exposing her ignorance of crossword puzzles, was fascinated at being involved in a murder case. She and Sherry each solved a crime, not by puzzles, but by deduction and persistence. Sherry met Aaron Grant, an attractive young reporter who quickly realized she was the Puzzle Lady.

Voracious relatives gathered to hear the reading of wealthy Emma Hurley's will in *Last Puzzle and Testament* (Bantam, 2000). They learned that the primary beneficiary would be the one who first solved a puzzle. Cora was named as the ultimate judge of the contest. Cora, a fake herself, knew a fake puzzle when she saw one. She realized that the puzzle actually did not deal with crosswords, but this insight came only after a killer began eliminating beneficiaries.

Harvey Beerbaum, a rival crossword constructor, finagled Cora into co-hosting a charity crossword puzzle tournament in *Puzzled to Death* (Bantam, 2001). Cora was far more interested in the murder of Judy Vale, the "town tart". When accused of her death, Judy's husband Joey produced a strong alibi. No one seemed to know who had been Judy's most recent lover, but he might have been one of those now participating in the contest. Initially Police Chief Harper warned Cora to stay out of his investigation, but he sought her help when puzzles were found at crime scenes. Cora not only survived the tournament without exposure, but also identified the killer, becoming eligible for a reward. Sherry's role was minimal in this narrative, as she was more frequently in subsequent books.

Acrostic puzzles accompanied mysterious deaths and murder attempts in *A Puzzle in a Pear Tree* (Bantam, 2002). Cora, Sherry, attorney Becky Baldwin and Aaron Grant were among the participants in a twelve days of Christmas pageant. Sherry was also one of several females to portray the Blessed Mother in a living maternity scene. She became the official murder suspect when high school student Dorrie Taggart, another pageant participant, was killed by a poisoned dart. Is that wacky enough? Add in feuding families, double adultery, an obsessed play director and a Scotland Yard detective. Neither the plot nor the characterizations can withstand scrutiny but Hall likes it zany.

It's best not to read *With This Puzzle I Thee Kill* (Bantam, 2004) too carefully. Cora Felton was ready to marry again, although Sherry did not approve of Raymond Harstein, III, the prospective groom. Still she agreed to be matron of honor. She was less agreeable when asked to serve in the same capacity for her college roommate, Brenda Wallenstein's wedding to Dennis Pride, her former husband. Someone else was upset because Raymond was murdered before the ceremony could take place and Dennis was arrested.

Will wonders never cease? Attorney Becky Baldwin, hostile to Sherry who had replaced her in Aaron Grant's affections, hired Cora to reinvestigate the death of teenager Anita Dryer in *And a Puzzle to Die On* (Bantam, 2004). Anita's sister hired Becky to review the case. Darryl Daigue has been in prison for twenty years on a life sentence for Anita's death. When Cora interviewed Darryl at the prison, he looked like a killer to her. Her presence at the prison irritated Warden Prufrock, motivating Cora to continue. The man whom Darryl suspected of the murder, Ricky Gleason, was already dead so he could hardly defend himself. Two other murders followed adding to the suspicion that no one wanted the truth to emerge.

Cora, now that she's regularly sober, is still a smart mouth and totally unable to solve a puzzle, but in *Stalking the Puzzle Lady* (Bantam, 2005), she showed her investigative skills. Cora had been about to end the deception as to who was the Puzzle Lady when she learned that her investments had decreased in value. So she agreed to take part in a promotion campaign for a major sponsor, Granville Grains. This meant that she and Sherry would tour the area visiting small grocery stores, meeting with children and parents. The narrative contained (in italics) insights into a man who proposed to win Cora or kill her.

The title, *You Have the Right to Remain Puzzled* (Bantam, 2006), is apt. Many readers may stay puzzled even after the denouement. Cora's attempt to help Mimi Dillinger, a young wife, by an apology in the form of a crossword puzzle, was a disaster. Cora's career as the "Puzzle Lady" and the comfortable income she and Sherry shared were jeopardized. Benny Southstreet whose puzzle Sherry had "adapted" sued for plagiarism. Restless, Cora also accepted a challenge by Chief Dale Harper, to find missing chairs for Wilbur, an antique dealer.

The Sudoko Puzzle Murders (St. Martin's Minotaur, 2008) capitalized on the recent popularity of Sudoko puzzles. Cora, who had no idea how to solve a crossword puzzle, had natural skills for the numerical sudoko. A casual meeting with Japanese publisher Hideki Takiyama elicited an offer for Cora to write a Puzzle Lady Sudoko book. Long time rival publisher Aoki Yoshiaki, fooled Sherry into signing with him. Some of the antipathy between the two men was personal, relating to Aoki's wife, Reiko. The subsequent murders were those of two New York City private investigators, but both Sudoko and conventional crossword puzzles were conveniently left as clues. Good dialogue, but limited character development.

Next: *Dead Man's Puzzle* (2009); *The Puzzle Lady vs. The Sudoku Lady* (2010)

Not only for those who enjoy puzzles.

Jane Ferguson
Hillary Scarborough

Author: Paula Carter (A possible pseudonym)

Jane Ferguson had supported her husband Jim Ed through law school, thereby postponing her own law degree. After he earned his, he dumped her. Under the divorce decree she was required to reside in Alabama so that their daughter Sarah would have regular access to her father. The prospect of continuing to live in Prosper (pop: 50,000) was all right with Jane. She had come to love the area and the people who lived there.

She needed a job very quickly because the divorce decree provided meager child support payments. Her resume was equally meager, boasting only of clerical level work at a radio station. When she applied for a position at Elégance du Sud, she was well aware of her personal limitations for the job. Elégance du Sud was the corporate name for Hillary Scarborough's multiple enterprises, featuring catering, party planning, and interior decoration. Hillary's television show touted her as the "Martha Stewart of the South."

Jane had no domestic skills. She seemed less responsible at times than her precocious daughter Sarah. Hillary, a dark-haired woman in her forties, was married to the elusive Billy. He appeared by reference in all of the narratives but rarely in person. Billy was a local power whose influence frequently rescued the duo when they were in trouble. Jane had a champion of her own: Buddy Fletcher, a scruffy burglar, who had been rescued from a prison sentence by Jim Ed. Divorced or not, Buddy felt he had an obligation to watch over Jane and Sarah ("Jim Ed's little girl").

Author Paula Carter set up the disparate characters of her sleuths in *Leading an Elegant Death* (Berkley, 1999). Jane's initial interview with Hillary occurred during a visit to the home of rival telecaster Sylvia Davis. Sylvia's confrontational public affairs program on another channel had cut deeply into Hillary's audience. It seemed strange that she would hire Hillary to redecorate her home. The discovery of Sylvia's corpse by Hillary and Jane, coupled with the rivalry, caused detective Beau Jackson to focus on Hillary as the killer. He focused on Jane but with a more personal agenda. She dodged one attack after another as she earned her wages by proving Hillary's innocence. Hillary enjoyed the excitement and kept Jane on the payroll.

In *Deathday Party* (Berkley, 1999), both Hillary and Jane came across as flighty, even hysterical, during an unplanned stay at the isolated Bean family home. Their visit was intended as a preliminary contact to arrange for a party in honor of ghostly ancestor America Elizabeth. On arrival they were informed of the death of Cassandra Bean, author of the local horoscope column who had contacted them about the party. Her relatives had no qualms about carrying out plans for the celebration. Even as the corpses piled up, Hillary and Jane were prevented from leaving by damage to a nearby bridge. The suspects, all members of the Bean family, were so eccentric that the sheriff was unwilling to take Jane's calls seriously. He and Beau Jackson were preoccupied with the search for an escaped convict.

When Hillary and Jane journeyed to the south of France to attend a cooking school operated by Madam Hulot in *Red Wine Goes with Murder* (Berkley, 2000), they were accompanied by seven other residents of Prosper: Sarah and her friend Shakura, Beau and Buddy, the elusive Billy, and a local couple, Henry and Lola McEdwards. Hillary noted that they were being followed by Paul Hayes, a banker from Prosper. When he was found floating in a wine vat at their rental, the French police became involved. Another murder, two arrests, and the abduction of three members of the group caused them to feel unwelcome. However Hillary and Jane had no intention of returning home until the killer/kidnappers were identified. Most readers will find it less difficult than they did.

Sister Fidelma

Author: Peter Tremayne, pseudonym for Peter Ellis

Sister Fidelma was an Irish religious at a time when the Church of Rome was extending its authority over diverse forms of Catholicism. During the Seventh century, Irishwomen had equality at a level not found elsewhere. Fidelma, the daughter of a King of Munster, received an extensive education that qualified her to serve as a "dalaigh," a prosecutor or defender in the courts of Ireland. Ireland had religious houses, which not only included both genders, but also permitted marriages among those of the lower orders. While studying at the bardic school, Fidelma had fallen deeply in love with Brother Cian, a fellow student. He dropped her when a more advantageous marriage became available.

There was considerable cultural shock for Sr. Fidelma when she attended a major religious conclave in England during *Absolution by Murder* (Headline, 1994). Oswy, King of Northumbria presided over the gathering, at the end of which he was to decide whether his kingdom would accept the rule of the Church of Rome. The death of Abbess Etain of Kildare, the major voice for the Irish church, a woman who had been Fidelma's mentor, was murder. The potential for political chaos led Oswy to appoint Fidelma and Brother Eadulf, a handsome young adherent of the Roman Church, to find the killer.

Shroud for the Archbishop (Headline, 1995) took place in Rome where Fidelma had been sent to meet with the Pope, carrying the Rule of her Order for approval. Eadulf's employer, Wighard, the Archbishop Designate of Cambridge, was strangled and his chest of gifts to the Pope plundered. Eadulf and Fidelma were assigned to prove that the killer had been Ronan, an Irish monk. There were political ramifications to the murder of a Saxon bishop by an Irish monk. Fidelma took the inquiry on condition that she and Eadulf have full authority. Neither politics nor religion was the motive for the death.

On her return from Rome, her brother Colgu, heir apparent to the throne of Muman, summoned Fidelma. As *Suffer Little Children* (Headline, 1995; St. Martin, 1997) began, Muman was accused of failing to protect Dacan, a famous scholar who was studying within its borders. Fidelma was charged to discover the killer to avoid paying the blood price. A major portion of the narrative was devoted to the historical and cultural aspects of the period in Ireland. Her quest included punishing marauders who searched for youthful claimants to the throne of a sub-kingdom. She missed Brother Eadulf.

Fidelma's original mission in *The Subtle Serpent* (St. Martin, 1996) was to discover the killer who was responsible for the decapitation of a young woman at a convent. She was met with disdain and hostility by both the local civil authority and Abbess Draigen, the sister superior of the religious house. It became more difficult for Fidelma to concentrate on the murder. She found a leather-bound missal on board an abandoned ship from Gaul. This was the missal she had given to Brother Eadulf when they parted. Fidelma could no longer deny the importance that he held in her life.

When Fidelma severed her ties with the Order of St. Brigid at Kildare, she returned to Cashel where her brother Colgu ruled as King of what is now Munster. In *Valley of the Shadow* (Headline, 1998), aware of her skills and needing a representative whom he could trust, he asked Fidelma to carry out a dangerous mission. She was to travel to Gleann Geis where, under the authority of Chief Laisre, teachers and ministers of Christian belief were hounded and killed. Fidelma had Eadulf as her companion. Soon he and Fidelma realized that Laisre was not the only adversary they must challenge. Fidelma's freedom and safety were threatened when she was accused of murder. She was not permitted to defend herself, but Eadulf could.

The isolated kingdom of Araglin had become rich and prosperous, but, as Sister Fidelma learned in *The Spider's Web* (St. Martin, 1999), greed had become a byproduct. The lascivious king Eber of the Araglin had been murdered and Fidelma was appointed to judge Moen, his purported assassin, a severely handicapped young man. Others would die before she could gather evidence against a fanatic killer. Eadulf came close to death during the investigation.

King Colgu, Fidelma's brother, was at risk of losing his authority in *The Monk Who Vanished* (Headline, 1999). An attack on Donennach, Prince of the Ui Fidgente, a visiting dignitary imperiled a peace treaty. Religious relics of political significance had been stolen and Brother Mochta, their guardian, was missing. The outcome might incite the greedy forces of Northern Ireland. Fidelma with Eadulf's help investigated the crimes to enable the matter to be settled peacefully. Her uncertainty about Eadulf's place in her life motivated Fidelma to go on a Spanish pilgrimage.

Fellow passengers on the pilgrim ship during *Act of Mercy* (Headline, 1999) included Brother Cian, the former suitor who had betrayed Fidelma. A series of murders, pursuit by Saxon raiders, and bad weather taxed the captain's seamanship and Fidelma's investigatory skills. In the course of the trip, Fidelma was challenged by an internal question. Was she more of a dalaigh than a religeuse? Had she lost sight of her commitment to her faith?

Informed that Eadulf had been charged with murder, Fidelma ended the pilgrimage and returned to Ireland in *Our Lady of Darkness* (Headline, 2000). He had been imprisoned in the kingdom of Laigin, tried, sentenced, and was to be hung. Her efforts to prove Eadulf's innocence were opposed by Fianamail, a young and inexperienced king, her archenemy Judge /Bishop Forbassach, and ambitious Abbess Fainder.

Fifteen of Fidelma's exploits were combined in *Hemlock at Vespers* (St. Martin, 2000). Although each had considerable merit when read singly, the collection was heavy with repetition. The shorter formats included a multiplicity of personal and tribal names, which were difficult to distinguish one from another. Of particular interest was the title short story in which a visitor at Fidelma's motherhouse was poisoned before he could return to his chieftain with important news. Fidelma wrestled with her respect for the past and her awareness that change was necessary. She did not expose the killer but she ended her ties to the religious order.

Turbulent winds sent the ship carrying Fidelma and Eadulf to Porth Clais on the English coast in *Smoke in the Wind* (Headline, 2001). They were forced to disembark because Eadulf had been injured. While waiting for transport to Canterbury, they accepted an assignment from King Gwlyddien. They were to investigate Llanpadern Abbey from which all humans and stable animals had disappeared as if by magic. They were guided by Brother Muerig who had legal status equivalent to that of Fidelma. He was to preside over charges of rape and murder against Idwal, a slow-witted shepherd boy. After Meurig's murder, it was up to Fidelma and Eadulf to tie the incidents together.

Fidelma had agreed to accompany Eadulf to Seaxmund's Ham, his birthplace, as *The Haunted Abbot* (Headline, 2002) began. A letter from childhood friend Brother Butolf motivated Eadulf to visit Aldred's Abbey en route. The meeting with Butolf never took place. He had been murdered. They encountered hostility from Cild, a rigid abbot, and became involved in a plot to depose the current King of East Anglia. This was not a pleasant time for Fidelma. She was ill. Females were not accorded equality in Britain. At the end she had great news for Eadulf

The marriage entered into between Fidelma and Eadulf in *Badger's Moon* (Headline, 2003) was one of several types permitted by the Irish church in the Seventh century; i.e. a trial marriage of one year. The birth of their son Alchu added impetus to a decision. The challenge of investigating serial murders of young maidens in the land of the Cine na Aeda energized Fidelma. Strangers, black religious from Africa who were guests of the local monastery, became the preferred suspects. The identity of the killer took considerable time due to a difficulty in determining the time of deaths. En route home, they had bad news. This is not the first time Tremayne has indulged in last minute cliffhangers for the following book. Annoying.

On their return from Rath Raithlen, Fidelma and Eadulf were greeted by terrifying news in *The Leper's Bell* (Headline, 2004). Their son Alchu had been abducted. His nursemaid Sarat had taken the child with her to visit her sister, Gobnat. Sarat was found savagely beaten to death, but there was no sign of Alchu. The cause for these events was complicated by a ransom demand from the Ui Figenti, seeking the release of prisoners. Fidelma and Eadulf's capability to deal with this crisis was diminished by the discord between them as to the future for their trial marriage.

Although Fidelma was as adventurous and intelligent as always in *Master of Souls* (Headline, 2005) she had become a less attractive character. Against Eadulf's wishes, she had accepted an assignment from King Colgu that would take them into the lands of the conquered Ui Fidgente. Abbess Faife and six nuns from Ard Fhearta had been intercepted on a pilgrimage. The Abbess had been murdered; the other sisters, abducted. By the time Fidelma, Eadulf, and Conri, warlord of the Ui Fidgenti and a nephew of the abbess, arrived, there had been a second murder, that of the Venerable Cinaed. Fidelma took on both cases, opposed by local forces who resented the dominance of Cashel.

Because of the prestige of Fidelma and her brother King Colgu of Muman, the elite of Eire's five kingdoms were invited to attend her wedding to Eadulf in *A Prayer for the Damned* (Headline, 2006). Individual guests had their own agendas. Pro-Rome Abbot Ultan planned to protest the marriage based on his belief in clerical celibacy. Others, for assorted reasons, wanted Ultan dead. His murder caused the wedding to be postponed. King Muirchertach, the principle suspect, requested that Fidelma serve as his advocate. This took place during a time when the Roman Catholic church sought to control the religion in the Five Kingdoms, where many Irish preferred more liberal interpretations of the Bible.

Fidelma had such a fine reputation in Tara that, in *Dancing with Demons* (St. Martin's Minotaur, 2008) when the High King was murdered by Dubh Duin, chief of the Cinel Cairpre, she and Aedulf were requested to head the investigation. Duin had killed himself, but had he acted alone? What was the motivation for this crime? Fidelma had anticipated an early resolution, but there were layers of guilt to be uncovered; religious, political, and personal. The technical question as to how the assassin had gained access to the castle during the night led to answers that raised more questions.

Next: *The Council of the Cursed* (2009); *The Dove of Death* (2010)

These were not easy reading. The unfamiliar personal and place names, and the theological climate of the period required close attention, but there were human mysteries there for the serious reader. At times Fidelma came across as arrogant and pretentious.

Suze Figueroa

Author: Barbara D'Amato

Suze Figueroa, who combined Irish and Hispanic in her heritage, was a Chicago policewoman. The Catholicism inherent in both ethnic groups had not taken with Suze, although she had received religious education. During the series, her sister Sheryl, wife of Robert Birch and mother of two children, became physically and cognitively damaged by a car crash. Suze moved in with the Birch family, bringing her seven-year-old son, J. J. Her police partner was African-American Norm Bennis to whom she was fiercely loyal.

In *Killer.app* (Forge, 1996), one mistaken stroke on her computer keyboard at SJR Data Systems had permitted Sheryl Birch to enter into confidential corporate files. She made her sister Suze aware that she suspected SJR's project "cutworm" was accessing important information from computers that they had installed in business and government offices. Initially Suze did not connect this matter to the murder of Chicago police officer Don Frieswyk, or to the death during surgery of computer analyst Kiro Ogata. The extent of a cyber conspiracy gradually emerged in a taut narrative, which even the computer handicapped will enjoy.

Suze's standing among her fellow officers, especially those who hung around after work at the Furlough Bar, was seriously damaged in *Good Cop, Bad Cop* (Forge, 1998). The Bertolucci brothers had vastly different careers in the police force. As a young officer, Nick had taken part in a badly handled raid on a purported Black Panther hideout. No blame had been assigned to him for the death of young Shana Boyd. He had risen to management level and was well respected. His younger brother Aldo, who spent his youth being brutalized by their father, became a lazy, dysfunctional patrol cop. When Aldo's partner was killed in an accident, Suze followed through on her suspicions with a conclusion that rocked the precinct.

As *Authorized Personnel Only* (Forge, 2000) began, Suze was unaware that escaped robber Harold Valentine was hiding out in the home she shared with her son and her sister Sheryl's family. His continued presence went undetected during a week when Suze and Norm Bennis, working as acting detectives, identified and arrested a serial killer. Suze and Sheryl combined their strengths to overcome the intruder.

Colleen Fitzgerald

Author: Barbara Johnson

Colleen Fitzgerald put her degree in police science to work as an employee of Sampson & Rhoades, Investigators. She was aware of her sexual orientation, had female lovers, but had never discussed the matter with her parents or grandparents. Both her brother William and sister Meagan were married and had families. Only Meagan seemed aware that Colleen was a lesbian. She had no live-in lover, sharing her household with Smokey, the cat.

When *The Beach Affair* (Naiad, 1995) began, Colleen had been celibate for a year and was very tense. The "Beach" was Rehoboth, Delaware, a popular spot for gay and lesbian tourists and residents. When body builder/ gym owner Candy Emerson was found dead, a barbell on her neck, the insurance company hired Sampson & Rhoades to investigate. New on the job, low on the totem pole, Colleen was assigned the case. Her first focus was on the beneficiaries of Candy's insurance policy, but there were other motives to be explored. Colleen almost died trying.

During *Bad Moon Rising* (Naiad, 1998), Colleen was assigned to investigate the death by drug overdose of Amber Rose, a star in porno videos. Colleen's personal preference would have been to connect sleazy producer Jackson Ramses to the death. Revelations about Amber's personal life, and the disclosure of an earlier and difficult identity led to other suspects. The interplay among Colleen, her current lover Gillian who had gone to school with Amber, and a new acquaintance, feminist attorney Jenna Bolden, played a strong role in the narration.

Fizz Fitzpatrick

Author: Joyce Holms

Independence was of vital importance to Fizz Fitzpatrick. A tiny blonde in her late twenties, she and her older brother Colin had been raised by a grandfather after their parents were killed. Gramps regularly compared Fizz unfavorably to Colin who had become a successful wild life photographer in South Africa. This experience caused her to focus on her own needs, rather than to rely on others. She described herself as not "doing lonely." She had attended art school, but broke that off to travel the world at age eighteen. During her seven wandering years, she had cooked, waited on tables, harvested melons and held other low level, poor paying jobs. Along the way she became fluent in three languages with some skill in two more. Her current goal was to become an attorney as her father had been. He and her mother had died in an avalanche.

To that end she was employed in the Edinburgh office of solicitor Tam (Thomas) Buchanan while continuing her studies. Fizz's education ate up most of her income, causing her to be not only frugal, but downright cheap. She ate best when someone else paid the check. She did not own a car, and walked rather than take public transportation. This emphasis on the ultimate goal caused Fizz to bend the rules—break and enter homes when information was needed, and use information to put pressure on adversaries. This stood in contrast to Tam's rigid ethical principles.

Only the fact that he was desperate for clerical help in *Payment Deferred* (Headline, 1996) motivated Tam Buchanan to accept Fizz as his assistant at the legal advice clinic of an Edinburgh community center. He had no intention of involving her in an investigation, particularly one relating to child molestation by Murray Kingston, a man he had once considered a friend. Fizz had her own agenda, an internship in Tam's law firm while she completed her degree. Widower Kingston had been convicted of the molestation and served his sentence. Now he wanted to regain custody of the daughter whom he had allegedly abused.

Tam's need for recuperation after gallbladder surgery fit right into Fizz's agenda in *Foreign Body* (Headline, 1997). She had been deeply upset by the disappearance of her old friend Bessie Anderson. Unable to work the case herself because she could not leave Edinburgh, Fizz convinced Tam to occupy a cottage in Am Bealach on land owned by her disapproving grandfather. While in the woods, Fizz and Tam discovered an unoccupied tent. Concerned that a camper was at risk, local volunteers made a search, leading to the discovery of a battered corpse. Fizz was determined to prove a connection between this murder and Bessie's disappearance.

Fizz was barely surviving financially as *Bad Vibes* (Headline, 1998) began. As the prior narrative ended, Tam had fired her from a part-time job at the family law firm. His father talked him into changing his mind. She worked nights at the Royal Park Hotel and eagerly accepted an offer from Tam's new and lecherous partner Dennis Whittaker to help with real estate work. While on duty at the hotel, she responded to the discovery of a dead guest, Herr Bernd Kerfeld. He had that same day purchased a valuable painting, which was not to be found. Coincidence was not a word in Fizz's dictionary. His sister hired Fizz to recover the painting, which meant learning its provenance. Tam was becoming protective of Fizz. He kissed her and wrote it off as "brotherly." Whom was he kidding?

A rather bawdy joke by Fizz at a party held in the Buchanan family home in *Thin Ice* (Headline, 1999) caused Tam to leave early. That forced him to listen to his cousin Mark's problem. Hazel Tarrant, the young woman whom Mark had come to love, did not go to the police when her son Robin was abducted from a childcare facility. She was convinced that her former husband Barnaby had taken the boy. Tam agreed to locate Barnaby and arrange for Robin's return, but hoped to keep Fizz out of it. Not likely.

Fizz, while professing disdain for Tam's conservative approach, constantly interfered with his love affairs in *Mr. Big* (Headline, 2000). She manipulated Gramps into moving to Greenfield House, a retirement home for members of the theatrical profession. This suited her current agenda: learning who at Greenfield was in touch with Chick Mathieson, a murdered drug dealer. Tam went along with her plans because the arrested suspect in Mathieson's killing was Freddie McAuslan, a recently released convict whom his father had represented in court. Neither Tam nor his father believed that Freddie was capable of murder.

Tam Buchanan was probating Vanessa Grassick's will. Her death in *Bitter End* (Headline, 2001) was none of his concern. That is, until Fizz got on the case. Vanessa and neighbor Jamie Ford, presumed to be her lover, had died as a result of a gas explosion at the Grassick's country home. What was more disturbing was the disappearance of Poppy, Jamie's widow. Fizz let the cat out of the bag, placing herself and Tam in danger again.

The instinctive rescue of elderly alcoholic Scott McKenzie from a car crash in *Hot Potato* (Allison & Busby, 2002) was consistent with Tam's innate goodness. What neither he nor Fizz realized at the time was they had taken on responsibility for a man wanted by the police in connection with robbery and murder. Even less were they aware that McKenzie was on the run from rival gangs. With their professional reputations at stake, Fizz and Tam cavorted through a market, brothel, and a series of smuggler's trucks. Tam just can't understand why he is drawn to this innocuous but frequently dangerous female.

When Tam and Fizz returned in *Hidden Depths* (Allison & Busby, 2006) they had still not coped with their attraction for one another. Irene Lloyd and her partner Kerr Gilgillan had been friends of Fizz since they attended art school. When Irene disappeared, Kerr went to Fizz for help. Irene had achieved success in cataloging and restoring artworks. She was employed by Sir Douglas Fergusson and his spinster sister Marjory to catalog the paintings in their home. Kerr, who was the estate manager for Abbeyfield House, and Irene shared a dwelling on the estate. Because the couple had openly quarreled, the police were disinterested until a valuable Rubens painting disappeared. Then suspicion focused on Irene as a thief, something neither Fizz nor Kerr could accept. They needed Tam's steady hand to guide them through the investigation. By this time, Fizz had qualified as a solicitor and was working at the law office formerly headed by Tam's father. However, Tam had left the firm, and joined a group of barristers to become an advocate.

Mrs. Sullivan's request that Fizz and Tam prove that she, not Terence Lamb, had killed Amanda Montrose in *Missing Link* (Allison & Busby, 2006) was so ridiculous that they were reluctant to get involved. The police had written her off as unstable, but she was so appealing that Fizz and Tam agreed to check out her story. This didn't happen fast because so many other potential suspects had secrets in their past: Amanda's husband Ewan, Terence Lamb, the local reporter Chloe Mills. Even the killer knew that Tam and Fizz belonged together. Isn't it about time they caught on? They have each seen positive changes in the other due to their current relationship.

Good plotting and well-drawn characters.

Dixie Flannigan

Author: Chris Rogers

Dixie Flannigan scorned her birth name, Desiree Alexandra, as she did almost everything else from the first twelve years of her life. Her birth mother, Carla Jean, had been a promiscuous hard drinking single woman. Dixie considered Barney and Kathleen Flannigan to be her parents. They had adopted her from a halfway house for teenagers, a placement necessary when she was molested by one of Carla Jean's men. Barney and Kathleen made her feel wanted, as did their daughter Amy, just three years older than Dixie. Nurtured by loving adoptive parents, provided with an excellent education, Dixie still retained scars from her early years.

After law school Dixie spent ten years as an assistant district attorney in Houston, Texas. The inadequacies of the legal system turned her enthusiasm into despair. She quit her job, but retained personal friendships in the legal system. Her substitute career, expected to be short term, was as a bounty hunter, sometimes bodyguard, working for attorneys who were aware of her skills. Along the way she adopted a Doberman mix, MUD (Mean Ugly Dog) who lived with her at the home she had inherited from the Flannigans. The decision that the pecan farm would go to Dixie while Amy inherited the family's summer home in New England had been mutually agreed upon. Amy was married to businessman Carson Royal. Their son Ryan (twelve as the series began) was very close to Dixie. Dixie and her friend from childhood, assistant district attorney Brenda Benson, taught a martial arts class to women and to the students at Ryan's private school.

So close to Christmas, Dixie was reluctant to take on a new case as *Bitch Factor* (Bantam, 1998) began. Her friend, defense attorney Belle Richards, convinced her to keep an eye on Parker Dann who had been indicted for vehicular manslaughter and leaving the scene of a crime. Because Dann, a talented and successful salesman, had drifted about the United States and Canada, Belle feared he would leave the state. He had been drunk that evening with poor recollections as to how he got home, but his car had been used in the accident. A $10,000 fee was the final inducement for Dixie to take the case. She earned every cent of it finding, transporting, and watching over Dann until the court reconvened after the holidays.

After testifying in a rape case that resulted in an acquittal, Dixie took what seemed to be a cream puff assignment in *Rage Factor* (Bantam, 1999). Dixie had strong feelings about Lawrence Coombs, the rapist who had been found not guilty. His charm and family connections seemed to render him untouchable. Nevertheless she found the tactics of the "Avenging Angels," a vigilante group who abducted and punished, even killed, individuals who had escaped justice under the law, unacceptable.

Edna Pine had been a dear friend and neighbor of Barney and Kathleen Flannigan. When Dixie witnessed a slimmer, trimmer Edna robbing a bank in *Chill Factor* (Bantam 2000), she had to know why. Edna was the third older woman to rob a local bank. She and Lucy Ames had disposed of the loot before they were shot down by police officers. A right wing underground group, "The People," avenged the deaths of Edna and Lucy and threatened to kill local politicians. Dixie was vulnerable, bringing her close to danger before she recognized it.

The villains created by author Chris Rogers were monsters. Her narratives included enough sub-plots and strains to keep the reader off balance, but made for an exciting read.

Laura Fleming

Author: Toni L. P. Kelner

Even after years away from the South, Laura Fleming had deep feelings for her family and former neighbors. She had been "different;" i.e., ambitious and restless, in a small North Carolina town. Her decisions to go North for her education, to marry Richard, a college professor at Boston College, and to make only rare visits home had not been a rejection of her family.

Her dearest relative was the grandfather who had raised her, so when he was mysteriously injured at the local mill in *Down Home Murder* (Zebra, 1993) Laura returned home. She was the only one who saw a connection between "Paw's" accident and the rape and murder of college student Melanie Wilson (which the locals preferred to blame on young African-Americans). Laura and Richard with the help of her cousin Thaddeous risked rejection to find the truth.

Dead Ringer (Zebra, 1994) returned Laura to Byerly where she had inherited property from "Paw." The death of Richmond architect Leonard Cooper in the offices of Walters' Mill caused several local secrets to be uncovered, secrets that had led to blackmail, and one of which had motivated murder.

In *Trouble Looking for a Place to Happen* (Kensington, 1995), Laura and Richard visited Byerly to attend the fifth wedding of Aunt Ruby Lee (to Roger who had been her third husband). Seventeen-year-old cousin Ilene had found an undesirable mentor, Tom Honeywell, who was murdered during a local music festival. Laura had no choice. Family came first. She had to find the killer, or the wedding might be postponed.

In *Country Come to Town* (Kensington, 1996), the balance tilted north. While Richard was in England, Laura utilized cousin Thaddeous in the investigation of murder among her college friends. She went undercover in a computer software company founded by seven of her ex-MIT classmates to discover who had killed Philip Dennis, her former lover. There was reverse culture shock for Thaddeous, but some of Laura's mystique was missing in Bean Town. Better not to take the girl out of the country.

Laura's next visit home did not presage a murder. It had already occurred, as *Tight as a Tick* (Kensington, 1998) began. Aunt Maggie, Richard and Laura's hostess, put them to work on the case right away. Carney Alexander, vindictive knife seller at the Tight as a Tick flea market, had multiple suspects for the knife in his back. He had been figuratively stabbing fellow exhibitors in the back for several years.

By now the citizens of Byerly, North Carolina must have viewed visits by Laura and her Yankee husband with some concern. *Death of a Damn Yankee* (Kensington, 1999) did nothing to dispel their apprehensions. The local workforce was divided as to the potential sale of Walters' Mill to a Northern firm. Arson, industrial espionage and finally murder upset Laura's family and Byerly.

Laura, pregnant with their first child, would have preferred a quiet Christmas in Boston during *Mad as the Dickens* (Kensington, 2001). Aware as she was that her husband Richard had always wanted to direct a play, she should have been suspicious of the opportunity offered by her manipulative cousin, Vasti. Certainly, Dickens' *A Christmas Carol* was challenging. Richard had to work with an amateur cast in a second rate auditorium, with only one-week to prepare for the performance. It didn't enhance the chance for success when Seth Murdstone, who played Scrooge, was murdered. Circumstances indicated that a member of the cast or crew was probably the killer. Even the reckless Laura considered the welfare of her unborn child as she encountered not only the present danger, but had to plan a future in which she might need to curtail her activities.

By *Wed and Buried*(Kensington, 2003), infant Alice had joined the family, but that did not deter Laura and Richard from returning to Byerly for a wedding reception. Aunt Maggie Burnette, who had never married, had eloped with Big Bill Walters, owner of the mill (where Maggie had worked), the bank, and more. Laura and Richard exchanged vows that they would not do anything to endanger Alice or themselves when Bill and Maggie made them aware that there had been several attempts on his life. A fourth attempt during the reception was foiled by Laura (or as she is known locally "Laurie Anne"). There was no turning back. Laura had six great-aunts all eager to care for Alice while her parents checked out the large number of people who had reason to resent Big Bill.

Touches of the rural South enriched the narratives. The plots were interesting, but the culprits often discernible by a well-read mystery fan.

Caz Flood

Author: Alex Keegan

Caz Flood had abandoned her birth name, Katherine, which no longer fit her casual lifestyle—Levi 501's, T-shirts, Asics trainers, and a leather jacket. Her parents had divorced when she was six. Initially her mother had primary custody. At her death, eleven-year-old Caz moved in with her father, a police officer. Caz took a degree in psychology at a red brick university, but followed her father, now retired, into the Brighton police force, beginning as a constable. She combined an ability to make her presence felt (she carried a riding crop up her sleeve) with computer expertise, intuition, a skill at assuming accents, and an awareness of body language. Caz kept fit by running every morning, but for work purposes drove an elderly MGB GT, named Fredericka, until it was destroyed. She was a dedicated feminist who had little time for small talk, which did not make her universally popular on the local force. She responded to crude remarks by male coworkers with her own invectives However, Detective Inspector Tom MacInnes offered her support and affection.

Caz needed that support in *Cuckoo* (Headline, 1994), when fellow tenant George Burnely was viciously murdered in what seemed a homosexual assignation. Her gut feeling was that George was not gay. Similar murders had an unusual characteristic; all victims had recently received £1,000 cash payments. Caz's investigation was initially deflected by her attraction to a possible suspect and by official pressure. The solution had an original motive and an "up in the air" ending.

Her job was all-important to Caz. In *Kingfisher* (Headline, 1995), she proved her loyalty to the force repeatedly: (1) covering up for fellow officer who made a mistake; (2) following up on a missing person case on her own time because she knew the victim, Claire Cook; and (3) overcoming her well-founded claustrophobia to save a young woman's life. The entry of Valerie Thomas (a man) into her life made her aware that she had other priorities than her work.

Vulture (Headline, 1995) picked up with Caz returning gingerly to work after injuries. No easy re-entry. She was assigned to the case of a serial rapist.

Victims were unknown to one another, although all showed some interest in competitive running. With major resources diverted elsewhere, Caz and two other female officers bore primary responsibility for the cases, until one ended in murder. Caz's computer skills were put to good use, as were the records of race entries and photographs of the finishers.

MacInnes ordered Caz to take time off to recover from injuries as *Razorbill* (Headline, 1996) began. A sports club that attracted runners in the Canary Islands seemed ideal. Massage, baths, and careful exercise brought Caz to a physical level she hadn't enjoyed for years. Others weren't so lucky. Guests were drowned, fell over cliffs or off roofs. Once back in England, Caz convinced MacInnes to let her return as a disaffected police officer seeking a part-time job. She went seriously over the top on this case.

Reading *A Wild Justice* (Piatkus, 1997) is not for the faint of heart or emotionally fragile. Caz's role in the investigation of a mutation murder came at a time of personal burnout and conflict in her relationship with Val. A transfer to the Criminal Protection Service was meant to provide relief. Instead CPS cases of child abuse, particularly sexual abuse, added to Caz's tension. Two more brutal deaths of adult males and their connections to a child abuse sex ring drove Caz to seek a solution outside the boundaries of the legal system. She was ready to commit to marriage...and perhaps a family.

Possible other: *Robin* but no copy or listing was found.

Judith Grover McMonigle Flynn

Author: Mary Daheim

See: Judith Grover McMonigle, page 551.

Merry Folger

Author: Francine Mathews a.k.a. Stephanie Barron

Merry Folger paid a price for accepting a position as detective on the Nantucket Police force. She had credentials: a college degree and graduation from the Massachusetts Police Academy. Still, there were those who implied that she won the job because her father was the police chief. In reality, John Folger bent over backwards not only to make Merry earn her position, but also to keep her out of potential danger. Merry's mother, an artist, had committed suicide shortly after the death of her son in Vietnam. Since then, Merry had lived with her father and grandfather, the retired police chief of Nantucket. A tall, slim blonde in her thirties, she had never married, but was courted by wealthy cranberry grower Peter Mason. Her feeling that they came from incompatible social and economic backgrounds inhibited their romance.

In *Death in the Off-Season* (Morrow, 1994), Peter was suspected of murdering his brother Rusty, who had fled to Brazil ten years before to escape indictment for securities fraud. The motive for murder was buried in the dysfunctional Mason family, but did not surface until a rare flower pointed the way.

Merry's friendships with restaurant owner Tess Starbuck and her fiancé Rafe influenced her actions in *Death in Rough Water* (Morrow, 1995). While investigating the death of fisherman Joe Duarte, Merry convinced Rafe to help Joe's daughter stay in the business. When the town pier burned, the body of pier manager Mitch Davis was discovered. He had been shot. It became clear that more than ownership of a boat or the parentage of a child was involved. Through it all, Merry's relationship with Peter deepened.

She felt the need to separate herself from her father and grandfather as *Death in a Mood Indigo* (Bantam, 1997) began. With Peter and Rafe's help, she moved to an apartment over a garage as the tourist season approached in Nantucket. Merry questioned two frightened children who had discovered a skeleton partly buried on the seashore. The medical examination indicated that death had occurred as a result of strangulation. Assorted government agencies sent representatives to the site, assessing whether or not this was another casualty of a serial killer already in custody. Merry's involvement became personal when the killer sent her a lock of hair from a victim, but she refused to retire from the case. Turf protection among the agencies led to additional deaths and delayed identification of a thief and more than one killer. Excellent characterizations in a convoluted plot.

A call to return to Nantucket Island to investigate young Jay Santorski's death ended Merry's plans to vacation with her fiancé Peter Mason in *Death in a Cold Hard Light* (Bantam, 1998). Merry realized that she had placed her loyalty to her father, Chief of Police John Folger, above that to Peter. Peter was not unaware of the implications. She missed Peter and still felt ostracized by fellow police officers because of perceived nepotism. Merry explored Jay's connections to drug addicted Margot St. John, to obsessed marine biologist Hannah Moore, and to missing police detective Matt Bailey. She knew that her father held missing pieces in the puzzle and perhaps some responsibility for Margot's subsequent death, but she persisted at a personal cost. On the positive side, John Folger's failures permitted Merry to accept her own humanity.

Author Mathews turned her own experience as a former CIA analyst into narratives featuring agent Caroline Carmichael. She also writes the Jane Austen series under the pseudonym Stephanie Barron. Multi-talented.

Margo Fortier

Author: Tony Fennelly

Anyone searching for an unconventional sleuth, need go no further. Margo Fortier, then known as "Cherry," had been an exotic dancer in a disreputable New Orleans nightclub, Madame Julie's, during the 1970s. When the opportunity came to marry Julian Fortier, a homosexual from an impecunious but highly reputable family, Margo didn't hesitate. She and Julian lived well together, accepting casual infidelities without reproach. Julian became a moderately successful publisher. Eventually Margo's job as a society columnist supplemented his income. An Irish-American from Boonton, New Jersey, Margo had broadened her limited education over the years by reading. As a result she could handle herself at any level of society with help from *Miss Georgia's Guide to Charm.* Margo's best friend was an elderly German expatriate, Baroness Gaby Schindler, with whom she shared her feelings. Margo's convictions after fifteen years of respectability were remarkably conservative. She had changed, not to fit in, but as a reflection of what she had learned along the way. She no longer drank alcohol, was anti-war, anti-abortion, against the legalization of marijuana, and disdainful of telephone or computer sex.

As *The Hippie in the Wall* (St. Martin, 1994) began, Madame Julie's had disappeared, but the building was being reconstructed for a new enterprise. When workmen found a skeleton behind a wall, they contacted the police. Lt. Frank Washington, an African-American officer who had frequented the facility as a young man to watch the dancers, contacted Margo to learn where the other employees had gone. She recognized the remains, and ran a parallel investigation to find out why a young man, excited about being a father and ready to marry, had to die.

In *1-900-DEAD* (St. Martin, 1997), one of the less conservative of Margo's interests was her study of astrology, which assisted her in getting an assignment to report on the death of Mystic Delphine, a fortune teller. Actually Frieda Harris, a.k.a. Delphine had several scams going. Her staff members were potential suspects as were those whom she had bilked. Margo, using her Irish immigrant grandmother as model for a former life, replaced Delphine as a channeler. It takes one to know one.

The roots of Margo's hair were graying and her waistline had thickened, but in *Don't Blame the Snake* (Top Publications, 2000), she had retained her sharp mind, and even sharper tongue. She joined Julian on the Riverside Crimewriter's cruise on the Mississippi only to get away from the New Orleans heat. Her fellow passengers included a herpetologist, a reformed burglar, two mid-rank authors, and a desperate publisher. Lt. Frank Washington, her old friend and a lecturer on the cruise, connected several of the passengers to a murder he had been investigating. A subsequent murder, using a poisonous snake, made it likely that they had a killer on board. The narrative provided a caustic look at the publishing business.

Witty dialogue and an eccentric heroine made the series entertaining. Fennelly's more recent series features gay former Assistant District Attorney Matthew Sinclair. After a nine-year hiatus, Margo returns in *Home Dead for Christmas* (2009)

Jill Francis

Author: Andrew Taylor

An affair with a married man who lacked compassion when she miscarried left Jill Francis vulnerable. She exchanged an excellent position as a London political columnist for temporary quarters in Lydmouth and employment on a second rate rural newspaper, edited by Philip Wemyss-Brown. Phillip had known and loved Jill. Charlotte, his wife, although she was aware of the tie between them, overcame her jealousy, hovering over Jill with good intentions and unwelcome suggestions. It should be noted that the series was set in the 1950s.

As *An Air That Kills* (St. Martin, 1995) began, England was only ten years past the end of World War II. The demolition of an aged inn disclosed the bones of a child, which triggered an investigation by recently arrived Inspector Richard Thornhill. Around this discovery were woven the anger of a young woman forced to care for a father she had reason to hate, a series of robberies, and the tendency to blame it all on local "bad boy" Charlie Meague. The connection between Jill and Thornhill was electric, but both were too prudent to act on it.

While Thornhill was coping with his ambitious supervisor in *The Mortal Sickness* (St. Martin, 1996), Jill came upon a corpse in the church. Father Alex Sutton, the new Episcopalian priest, had received complaints about his "popishness." It got worse when there were rumors that he dallied with female parishioners and stole a valuable chalice to finance his amorous activities. Thornhill and Jill worked simultaneously, but not in tandem, to relieve the cleric of suspicion.

By *The Lover of the Grave* (Hodder & Stoughton, 1997), Jill had settled into her own home, Church Cottage, which she shared with a cat named Alice. The return of expatriate movie actor Lawrence Jordan caused limited excitement in the village. The locals were preoccupied with a window peeper and the death of local schoolmaster Mervyn Carrick. The narrative explored the spousal abuse, nativism, and attempts to cover-up sexual indiscretions to be found in rural communities. Thornhill and Jill, thrown together by their investigations, found temptation too strong to ignore.

In *The Suffocating Night* (Hodder & Stoughton, 1998), Jill's connections to former lover Oliver Yateley, now a member of Parliament, and to Richard Thornhill, both married men, were skillfully woven into the local fabric. Two cases, (1) the prior disappearance of teenager Heather Parry, and (2) the recent death of Cameron Rouse, a sleazy freelance London journalist, at the local inn were the focus of attention. The police and community concentrated consecutively on four different suspects, including Philip Wemyss-Brown, Jill's employer. The narrative reflected the anti-Communist fervor during the Korean War, in which England played a role, and the continuing social stratification of British society when it came to the dispensation of justice.

Jill and Richard's affair could not remain a secret in Lydmouth. Charlotte Wemyss-Brown made her disapproval known to both parties.

She and Richard realized how dangerous their alliance might be during *Where Roses Fade* (Hodder & Stoughton, 2000). The death by drowning of a local waitress revealed secrets in several local households. What had seemed innocent was shown to be vicious. At the conclusion, Jill and Richard realized that they could not live without regard for the future. He had a family and a career. She had risked everything for his love, even a possible pregnancy.

Author Andrew Taylor explained in his preface that *Death's Own Door* (Hodder & Stoughton, 2001) was Edith Thornhill's story. She was the vital but unexplored person in Jill's affair with her husband, Richard. Edith had a life before Richard, one which she had never revealed—a summer visiting her Gran in nearby Trenalt, and participation in a play written by Hugh Hudnall whom she loved but could never have. All the loves and hatreds, and the betrayals and misunderstandings of the summer of 1938 resurfaced when Rufus Moorcraft killed himself. The outcome forced each member of the triangle to make decisions: Richard to take a new job; Jill, to move away; Edith, to reject the past.

When Jill agreed to return to Lydmouth in *Call the Dying* (Hodder and Stoughton, 2004), she was aware of the problems she'd face. Philip Wemyss-Brown, the Gazette editor, was gravely ill. Charlotte, his wife who bankrolled the paper, lacked the funds to compete with a new rival, *The Evening Post*, owned by a media chain (Champion Group). The most difficult part was seeing Richard again. He had never contacted her in the three years since she left Lydmouth, their love affair ended. Richard shared her dismay but he had problems of his own: a "pisser" who urinated through mail slots, and an assault on the former assistant editor of the Gazette. These incidents continued after Jill's arrival, even escalated. The murder of retired Dr. Bayswater and the disappearance of visiting engineer Paul Frederick were somehow tied together by a pair of gloves. Even with multiple viewpoints and assorted crimes, Taylor kept the tension high and provided a startling conclusion.

Although they did not usually work together, Thornhill and Jill shared the focus of the books. The tension between them made further adventures something to be eagerly awaited. The books were subtitled "A Lydmouth series." Taylor is also the author of the Roth Trilogy and a series featuring William Dougal and Celia Prentisse (see Volume 2)

Lucy Freers

Author: Lindsay Maracotta, a pseudonym

Lucy, a thirty-seven-year-old redhead and producer of animated short subjects, was married to Kit Freers, a promising young director. Initially, they lived modestly in their Los Angeles area home with their daughter Chloe, who attended Windermere, a progressive elementary school. Lucy maintained a downtown office where she conducted business. She volunteered, as did many of the parents whose children attended Windermere School, teaching animation as part of the art course.

Her mother had been killed in an accident when Lucy was twelve. Her father, who had remarried, lived in Six Elms, the small Minnesota town where Lucy was raised. She was still a Midwesterner, unimpressed by Hollywood, who collected vintage clothes, Fiesta ware, and costume jewelry. Lucy was aware that Kit was more eager to adapt to the California lifestyle than she was.

It did nothing for the sale of the Freers' home, when Lucy and prospective purchasers found a dead body in the family pool as *The Dead Hollywood Moms' Society* (Morrow, 1996).

Lucy and Kit were interrupted "pre coitus" in *The Dead Celeb* (Morrow, 1997) by a call from production assistant Cheryl Wade. She had just discovered director Jeremy Lord's corpse in her bathroom. This was not good news. Lord and Kit are at odds about the picture being filmed on location in Northern New Mexico. The good news was that the local police tabbed it a natural death so Lucy set off for Los Angeles, leaving Kit to deal with what could be done to complete the film. That didn't work either because as Lucy drove home, Cheryl confessed to having accidentally murdered Lord. Could they just let it go? Not really because Cheryl was discovered in a coma the next day, purportedly suicide. Did that solve matters? Not really because someone thinks it necessary to kill Lucy.

It wasn't chocolate or pickles that pregnant Lucy craved in *Playing Dead* (Morrow, 1999). She craved daughter Chloe's male nanny, Brandon McKenna who had been her first lover. Ostensibly he had taken the job to be able to finish a book. His murder involved Lucy in the world of talented child actors and their ambitious parents.

Sister Frevisse

Author: Margaret Frazer, pseudonym for Mary Monica Pulver and Gail Frazer; after the first six books, Gail became the sole author and Pulver began the Betsy Devonshire series as Monica Ferris.

Seventeenth century Sister Frevisse, the great-niece of Geoffrey Chaucer, had been appointed hostler (hostess) for the convent of St. Frideswide, but she turned out to be far more. Her cousin, Thomas Chaucer, had been an important influence in Frevisse's early life, encouraging her desire for education.

As *The Novice's Tale* (Jove, 1992) began, Lady Ermentrude and her entourage visited the convent, hoping to convince young and ultra-pious novice Thomasine to leave. The sisters were appalled when Lady Ermentrude, who had left on a side trip, returned drunken and boisterous. Her subsequent death, preceded by that of Martha, a greedy servant, was believed to be a poisoning.

The Servant's Tale (Jove, 1993) gave a grim picture of the lives of the poor, particularly women without a male provider. Barnaby Shene, a local drunkard died at the Priory after an accident from which he had been expected to recover. The traveling players who had brought his injured body to the convent for nursing were suspected of this and subsequent deaths. Frevisse, who had traveled extensively with her family, felt empathy for the acting group and wanted to clear them.

The Outlaw's Tale (Jove, 1994) took Frevisse out of the convent to accompany Sister Emma to a family wedding. En route, the nuns were kidnapped by a band of outlaws led by Frevisse's cousin Nicholas, who sought her help and that of Thomas Chaucer in obtaining a pardon. The captivity was spent in a private home where Oliver Payne, an unwilling host, was murdered for his sins.

As *The Bishop's Tale* (Berkley Prime Crime, 1994) opened, Thomas Chaucer was dying. He had a message sent to the convent and entrusted his dearest friend, Bishop Henry of Beaufort, with a gift for Frevisse. Frevisse's role, when she arrived after the death, was to comfort the immediate family and assist in the elaborate funeral ceremonials. However, when Sir Clement Sharpe, an unpleasant guest, died mysteriously at the formal dinner, Beaufort utilized her as an investigator. Her companion Sister Perpetua's research skills in the Chaucer library provided a significant clue.

Thomas Chaucer died, so, in *The Boy's Tale* (Berkley, 1995), Frevisse contacted his daughter Lady Alice, the Countess of Suffolk, whose husband was a confidante of young King Henry, when the convent gave shelter to Jasper and Henry, two endangered children. Subsequent deaths of travelers increased the nuns' concern for the children.

A new mother superior, Domina Alys, brought change to St. Frideswide's convent; more than Sister Frevisse could handle in *The Murderer's Tale* (Berkley, 1996). The opportunity to make a pilgrimage to Oxford was a relief. Sr. Frevisse and infirmarian Dame Claire stopped en route at Minster Lovell where Lionel Knyvet, a handicapped nobleman, fought prejudice, ambition, and an accusation of murder.

Frevisse found her vows of obedience particularly onerous, when Domina Alys was selected prioress of St. Frideswide in *The Prioress' Tale* (Berkley, 1997). Not only did Alys encourage freeloading by her relatives who depleted the priory's store of food for the winter, but also she involved the nuns in a feud between two powerful families.

The need for a replacement prioress was utilized by Sister Frevisse's Benedictine supervisors for their own agenda in *The Maiden's Tale* (Berkley, 1998). They sent her off to London ostensibly to escort Dame Elizabeth to St. Frideswide where she would become the mother superior. While in London, Frevisse's family relationship with Alice, Countess of Suffolk, drew her into intrigues of romance (not for her, however) and international politics.

A rumor that Master Roger Naylor, steward for the convent, was not freeborn brought new challenges to Frevisse in *The Reeve's Tale* (Berkley, 1999).Not only was she in charge of the business and agricultural affairs of the convent; she also served in a judicial capacity along with the village reeve, Simon Perryn. The entry of Master Montfort, the King's crowner, into the investigation of two local deaths pressured Frevisse into action. Two innocent men might be punished for crimes committed by others with much to conceal. Her mission accomplished, she was content to return to the convent.

Robert Fenner, a landless younger son, had become the third husband of wealthy Lady Blaunche, because he saw no alternative for his future. By *The Squire's Tale* (Berkley, 2000) he had developed affection for his wife and deep love for their children. He was shocked by his attraction to Katherine, a young woman in the household for whom his wife had plans. Sisters Claire and Frevisse were on hand to care for the pregnant Blaunche, at a time when she was engaged in a land contest. Blaunche had arranged a marriage between Katherine and Benedict, her son from a prior marriage. Robert was the most obvious suspect when Benedict was murdered, but Frevisse's attention to details led to the killer who conveniently disclosed his unexpected motive.

The death of Morys Montfort, former crowner, would have been of minor interest to Fresvisse at any other time, but in *The Clerk's Tale* (Berkley, 2002) she was thrust into action. Frevisse had accompanied her superior, Domina Elizabeth, to St. Mary's convent, arriving shortly after Montfort's corpse had been discovered on the grounds. While crowner, Montfort had made many enemies, but his death came about while he, as newly appointed escheator, was to rule on a sizeable inheritance. Powerful lords had a vested interest in the outcome, but so did the families involved.

A request that Frevisse travel to Bury St.Edmunds to assist her cousin Alice became a command in *The Bastard's Tale* (Berkley, 2003). The quid pro quo was a valuable gift to St. Frideswide. Alice would accompany her husband, the Marquis of Suffolk, to a meeting of the Parliament to which all members had been summoned by King Henry VI. Humphrey, Duke of Gloucester and uncle to the King, had been lured from his Welsh lair with a hint that his wife, Eleanor, might then be released from prison. Gloucester had to be careful because his influence on the King had been diminished. Henry VI was now surrounded by a new generation of nobles, including Suffolk, all greedy for power. Frevisse, lowly Bishop Pecock, Joliffe the actor who later became a spy, and young Arteys, illegitimate son of Gloucester, joined Alice in an attempt to curb violence

The need to control, even to bully his wife and grown children had persisted even after Sir Ralph Woderove was murdered in *The Hunter's Tale* (Berkley, 2004). His detailed will limited his wife's right to remarry, the marital choices of his children and left residual power to Sir William Trensal, his son-in-law and neighbor. No one mourned Sir Ralph but each wondered who among them had caused his death. Frevisse came on scene as escort for his teen-age daughter Ursula who attended school at the convent. She ultimately served as counselor for the entire family.

When Laurence Helyngton escorted a bedraggled Christiana, the widow of his cousin Edward to St. Frideswide's in *The Widow's Tale* (Berkley, 2005),

Domina Elizabeth accepted her as a penitent, not a guest. Neither she nor Frevisse was aware that Laurence and his avaricious sister, Milicent lied in order to obtain custody of Christiana's two daughters, heirs to Edward's lands. When Laurence and Milicent learned that a dying Edward had empowered Christiana and her brother Sir Gerneys to take possession of a document that would expose treachery on the part of the Duke of Suffolk, husband of Frevisse's cousin, Lady Alice, their plans changed. Domina Elizabeth and Frevisse came to Christiana's rescue.

Only her desire to repair her relationship with Cousin Alice, the Countess of Suffolk, motivated Frevisse to agree in *The Sempster's Tale* (Berkley, 2006) to travel to London with a hidden agenda. The stated purpose was to make arrangements for a donation of vestments. However semptress Anne Blakhall and mercer Raulyn Grene had a precious cargo for Frevisse to transport to Alice. This was not a healthy time to be in London. Jack Cade's rebels were camped outside the city, prepared to enter in protest against King Henry VI. Brother Michael, who formerly worked with the Inquisition in France, preached publicly against the Lollards and the Jews. Anne and her lover, Jewish merchant Daved Weir, had been threatened. This was a serious exploration of the treatment of Jews in England and the involvement of the Catholic Church.

There was a role for Frevisse in *The Traitor's Tale* (Berkley, 2007) but it was diminished. She functioned as a hand holder and representative for her cousin, Lady Alice while Joliffe, a spy in the employ of Richard, Duke of York, had most of the action. The Duke of Suffolk, Alice's deceased husband, had been reviled and murdered for his manipulations after the breach of treaty in Normandy. Alice feared for her son's future. Joliffe had wider concerns. Someone close to the throne sought to blame the Duke of York for Jake Cade's Rebellion. As part of the campaign this person had ordered the deaths of members of the Suffolk household. The emphasis in the series had moved away from Frevisse and the plotting had become more historically complex.

The initial chapters of *The Apostate's Tale* (Berkley, 2008) dwelt upon the reception that apostate sister Cecely received when she returned to the convent she had abandoned. Cecely had fallen in love with Guy Rowcliffe, a visitor in St. Frideswide's guest house. When he left, she did too. When she returned after Guy's death, she was accompanied by their son, Edward. Members of Guy's family arrived shortly afterwards, seeking the boy, but also possessions that Cecely might have appropriated. As complications arose, Frevisse noticed that Domina Elisabeth was overwhelmed, so she took matters into her own hands.

Joliffe became the protagonist in his own series.

Leslie Frost

Author: Janice Weber

Leslie Frost's origins may have been far more conventional than those of Modesty Blaise and other undercover agents of the Sixties, but her series was as good or better. She had grown up in East Berlin, the daughter of a diplomat. She had been educated first at a Berlin technical school, then at the Massachusetts Institute of Technology, finally at Julliard. There had always been a reckless streak in Leslie. She had already achieved fame as a concert violinist when she married Hugo Lange, only to be widowed in two months. At that point, Leslie used the skills often found together: mathematics and musical ability as a member of a small U.S. intelligence unit composed of seven women each code-named after an exclusive U.S. woman's college. Leslie was "Smith." Maxine, a fellow motorcyclist, had recruited her into the group. Maxine, a singer, was the lover of Leslie's brother Ronald who ran a Berlin nightclub.

Over the eight years since Leslie became active in the group, five of her fellow operatives had either died or disappeared. Leslie lived near the Grunewald in Germany with her black butler/manager Curtis, one of the few who were aware of her dual roles.

As *Frost the Fiddler* (St. Martin, 1992) began, Leslie witnessed the murder of a police officer while on tour in Leipzig. She followed up on the incident out of curiosity, but fell deeply in love with "Burberry," a suave German intelligence agent. In reality, he was Emil Flick, the Deputy Chief of the International Trade Fair, but also an amateur violinist who admired Leslie's professional skills. The narrative involved deadly computers, and a resurgence of German nationalism. One death after another claimed Leslie's adversaries, leaving her bereft.

Hot Ticket (Warner Books, 1998) returned an older Leslie, still at the top of her form as a violinist, but depressed. After an appearance at a White House concert, she was to meet with "Barnard," the other survivor of the Sisters. She found Barnard dead. The only clues were a ticket to Belize and tickets to a play at Ford's Theater. Other attendees at the theater were Bobby Marvel, the lecherous president, his wife Paula, and members of his inner circle. It got crazy, mixing in Leslie's strong attachment to egg-shaped musician Fausto Kiss, the imprisonment of noted ethnobotanist Dr. Louis Bailey, who was the brother of the dying vice-president, and Leslie's unnerving trips to Belize.

The books were throwbacks to the spy thrillers of the Sixties featuring characters with odd names: Fausto Kiss; Krikor Tunalian; Tanqueray Tougan; and extended casts that will send the reader backtracking to figure out who they are and with whom they are allied. Not quite Modesty Blaise, but then she couldn't play the violin.

Josephine "Jo" Fuller

Author: Lynne Murray

Josephine "Jo" Fuller was a woman of size (5' 8" and over 200 pounds) who had accepted her condition as genetic and no longer apologized or felt guilty about it. Her marriage of six years to Griffin, ended due to his infidelity. Her degree in psychology provided no easy route to employment so she responded to a newspaper ad seeking someone to take on special assignments for the "advancement of women." Alicia Madrone, a wealthy widow confined to a wheelchair, assigned Jo to evaluate organizations to which Mrs. Madrone was considering substantial donations. This proved to be a satisfactory arrangement for both parties. Jo had credibility in some circles because her widowed father had worked in a government intelligence agency. She had traveled with him as he moved from one country to another.

In *Larger Than Death* (Orloff Press, 1997), Jo felt guilty when her friend and mentor, Nina West, a Seattle businesswoman, was murdered. Nina had contacted Jo for help at a time when she was unavailable. The modus operandi of Nina's death connected it to those by a serial killer, "Captain Ahab" who targeted large women. Jo learned that she and Nina's illegitimate son, Bill, had inherited an eight-unit apartment building. She investigated the secret lives of Nina and her tenants. Along with the apartment she inherited Raoul, Nina's gray Persian.

Jo was still recuperating from Nina's death and an unexpected attraction to Nina's lover, Thor Mulligan, in *Large Target* (St. Martin, 2000). She was sent to San Diego by Alicia Madrone who was concerned about Amy Russo, her dear friend Sally Rhymer's daughter. Jo's probe of a charitable group to which Amy belonged was the springboard to a broader investigation when Sally's husband, Ron was kidnapped. Mulligan visited Jo in San Diego but after a brief encounter, returned to Seattle.

Jo and her former husband Griffin had parted when he and Francesca Benedict had an affair. At the time, Fran's husband Teddy and Jo had consoled one another. When she and Teddy met next in *At Large* (St. Martin, 2001) he wanted help. His new girlfriend, Lucille, who had recently dieted down from 300 to 150 pounds, was angry because his divorce was still pending. That problem was solved when someone killed Fran. Griffin, Jo, and Teddy made the top three in suspects, followed by several members of the Benedict family. Mulligan was still holding off from a relationship with Jo, but hung around.

No problem with overweight ladies in *A Ton of Trouble* (St. Martin, 2002). A matter of taste (to some bad taste), that producer Wolf Lambert chose to make porno films featuring buxom babes. So what if Thelma (aka Mandy Hanson) formerly Wolf's bookkeeper, mistress and porn star has branched out on her own. When, at Wolf's invitation, Jo visited his Sonoma Valley vineyard, she found a corpse stuffed into a wine barrel. Not Wolf, he's out of it because of an alcohol/drug mixture. Jo's interest in watching porno videos and learning how they are made was distasteful to her beau, Mulligan. Confusing.

Nell Fury

Author: Elizabeth Pincus

Nell Fury, a San Francisco private investigator, started her own agency after working for Continent West. She, her brother Harry, and sister Grace were raised in Cleveland, but had moved away. Their parents were dead. Nell had a fifteen-year-old daughter, Pinky, co-parented with Caroline, an older lesbian lover. Pinky spent her summers in San Francisco with Nell, but returned to school in London where Caroline lived.

The Two-Bit Tango (Spinsters, 1992) put Nell in a dilemma. She was hired by Olive Jones to find her lesbian twin sister Cate, lost somewhere in the San Francisco area. Nell had to not only rescue Cate from kidnappers, but also prove her client was not a murderer.

In *The Solitary Twist* (Spinsters, 1993), Nell's interest was piqued when Christa Lovett "picked her up" during an airplane trip. Christa hired Nell to investigate Philip Gold, fiancé of Christa's former lover, Ellen Norway. Gold's murder, the abduction of Ellen Norway, and the disappearance of Christa added complications. The narrative included lesbian relationships, Sixties radicals, and the murky parentage of a child hostage.

Nell returned again in *The Hangdog Hustle* (Spinsters, 1995) during which she investigated the death of Kent Kishida, a Chicano-Japanese homosexual who had been recruited to go undercover for a government agency.

The sex was explicit.

Jan Gallagher

Author: Jo Bailey, pseudonym for Joseph Bailey

Although the mysteries were subtitled "General Jack" referring to Jackson County General Hospital, Jan Gallagher was the focus of the series. Jan never had it easy. Twice married and twice divorced with four children, she worked as security supervisor at the hospital. She had challenged her employer in a sexual discrimination suit for a promotion, and won the case. Jan's victory created hostility with her supervisor and the hospital administrator. Coworker Gavin Larsen, who also sought the job, held a grudge. Things were not much better at home. Jan's irregular hours often sent her home exhausted. Her mother Claire, now sixty-seven and showing signs of senility, was responsible for the children during the day.

In *Bagged* (St. Martin, 1991), Dr. Jonathan Croft, the chief of neurology was killed. His body had been deposited in a bag on the hospital premises. The corpse went undiscovered for several days, but when found, management placed pressure on Jan to solve the case. With the help of homely Detective Frank White, she found the killer but scored no points with the hospital.

In *Recycled* (St. Martin, 1993), the administration recalled Jan to her position as security supervisor. They had relegated her to updating old manuals. A rocket launcher had downed a medical helicopter. Carmen Romero-Muehlen, a dangerously ill drug dealer awaiting a transplant, had to be protected. Romero-Muehlen was expected to provide evidence against her former allies. Although the FBI had an ulterior motive for selecting Jan to assist them, she survived and achieved their purpose.

In *Erased* (St. Martin, 1996), Jan experienced the frustration of being a well-meaning member of a racial majority. When a gang melee threatened the hospital, Lyle Brown, an African-American security officer, was taken hostage to be exchanged for Rainy Penshorn, a criminal currently a patient. While the FBI and local authorities handled the negotiations, Jan dealt with the hostage's girlfriend Felicia Smith, a social worker on staff. She found herself drawn into the treachery of the process, overwhelmed with guilt at the death of a woman whom she wanted to befriend. A downbeat ending.

The narratives were gloomy and the heroine harried.

Theresa Galloway

Author: Terris McMahan Grimes

Theresa Galloway was a college graduate who worked as personnel officer for the Department of Environmental Equity in Sacramento. As an African-American professional woman with a hard working husband (Temp) and two children (Aisha and Shawn), she did not need to involve herself in murder investigations. What she needed was to be able to say "no" to her widowed mother, Lorraine Barkley, who called on Theresa whenever she was concerned about a friend or neighbor. Temp, a law school graduate who managed his own contracting business, resented Lorraine's predawn calls. After the death of Carolyn, an older daughter, from leukemia and the marriage of son Jimmy to a German woman while stationed overseas, Lorraine became increasingly dependent on Theresa.

During *Somebody Else's Child* (Onyx, 1996) Lorraine intervened to help Louise, an elderly friend then caring for two grandchildren whose mother had a drug problem. When Louise was killed and one of the grandchildren ran off to search for his mother, Theresa took on all their problems.

She was having difficulties at the office and had promised Temp to "mind her own business." It wasn't possible in *Blood Will Tell* (Signet, 1997). Raymond, who claimed to be her deceased husband's child, had visited Lorraine. Temp, already under financial stress, was furious when Theresa utilized bail bondsman Bailey Howard, a former beau, to check out Raymond's background. Raymond's murder alerted Theresa to an unexpected family treasure, but she had to find a killer first. This was a convoluted plot with some questions left unanswered.

Maggie Garrett

Author: Jean Taylor

Maggie Garrett was a tall redheaded private investigator in San Francisco who limited her clientele to gays and fellow lesbians. She had no permanent relationships, but did have a series of lovers. Although she had grown up on a family farm in Iowa, there was no life for Maggie there so she moved to California. Her working partner had died, leaving her the sole proprietor of the detective agency, assisted only by a computer literate high school student. Maggie shared her Noe Valley home with a pug dog and her two cats (Pod and Fearless).

The homosexual community in San Francisco was shocked when a gay newspaper accused the Pride Lesbian and Gay Democratic Club of financial irregularities connected to public officials. Maggie investigated the charges and a subsequent murder during *We Know Where You Live* (Seal, 1995). The ensuing probe split the supporters of gay rights, and endangered Maggie's life.

In *The Last of Her Lies* (Seal, 1996), a friend made Maggie aware of a possible breach of professional ethics by psychotherapist Moira Ericson. According to a journal, Ericson had seduced Kelly, the client whom she was treating for depression. The Ericson family hired Maggie to find Kelly and investigate the charges. Moira could think of no reason why Kelly would have defamed her, but then she did not know the real Kelly.

Julia "Callahan" Garrity

Author: Kathy Hogan Trocheck

Julia "Callahan" Garrity had earned a master's degree in criminology from Georgia State. She had worked her way up (and down) the scale from police officer to private investigator to operator of an Atlanta cleaning service. Callahan was single in her late thirties, but had shared relationships with men over the years. Her mother Edna, a sometime beautician, was her partner in the "House Mouse" cleaning business, which employed a hard-working group of disabled, elderly, and low functioning individuals. Callahan had two brothers, Keith and Brian, and a sister, Maureen.

In *Every Crooked Nanny* (HarperCollins, 1992), Callahan added a client when her staff was busy. The customer was former sorority sister Lilah Rose (Ledbetter) Beemish. Dust was the least of Lilah Rose's problems. The body of Kristee, her children's nanny (and her husband's lover) appeared in the storage facility where Lilah Rose kept her furs. Even though dismissed as cleaner and investigator, Callahan persisted. The good news was that Callahan had a new man in her life, Andrew McAuliffe of the Atlanta Regional Commission. The bad news—she had a malignant lump in her breast.

McAuliffe wanted more than sleepovers at the house Callahan shared with Edna Mae in *To Live and Die in Dixie* (HarperCollins, 1993), but Callahan rejected a move to his country home. Rather than continue the standard post-radiation cancer treatments, Callahan chose to take tamoxifen. The House Mouses (or Mice) cleaned Eagle's Keep, a mansion owned by antique dealer and Civil War buff Elliot Littlefield, who had been recently released from a murder charge on a technicality. When they discovered the corpse of Bridget Dougherty, his seventeen-year-old assistant, her sister Jocelyn hired Callahan to investigate.

Callahan's mother had always been supportive of her detecting, but in *Homemade Sin* (HarperCollins, 1994), Edna drew the line. Not family! The victim, killed with only her disabled son Dylan as a witness, was Callahan's cousin, Patti. Against the wishes of Patti's husband Bruce McNair, the police, and even McAuliffe, Callahan persisted until she solved this murder.

Vonette Hunsecker, a former member of the VelvetTeens, had never been friendly with Callahan, but in *Happy Never After* (HarperCollins, 1995) she needed help. Dolores Carter, another woman in the famous singing group of the Sixties, was missing, just when there was the possibility of a comeback. Callahan found Rita Fontaine, the last of the trio, standing over a dead body. The victim was Stuart Hightower, the record producer who had made the VelvetTeens famous and then dropped them. That's show biz.

Although Callahan's cancer was in remission, Edna's health problems shook the House Mice in *Heart Trouble* (HarperCollins, 1996). Adrift since the relationship with McAuliffe ended, at odds with her sister Maureen, and with dissension among the "Mice," Callahan diverted her attention to finding the killer of Whitney Dobbs, a woman Atlanta hated. Whitney had hit and killed eight-year-old Faneeta Mayes while driving intoxicated. Her punishment had been minimal which enraged the African-American community. The narrative was cluttered, the ending untidy, but Mac and Callahan agreed to give their relationship a second chance.

A dreaded hurricane promised extra cleaning chores for the House Mice in *Strange Brew* (HarperCollins, 1997). When Callahan explored the area looking for Mac's Labrador Retriever, she discovered the corpse of Jackson Poole. Callahan had met Poole. He was the developer of a microbrewery to be located in a building formerly occupied by Wuvvy, one of the characters of Little Five Points. Wuvvy, who had disappeared, had motive and opportunity to kill Jackson, but Callahan did not believe Wuvvy was a killer.

Family humor blended with tragedy in *Midnight Clear* (HarperCollins, 1998). Brian, Callahan's unreliable younger brother, deposited his three-year-old daughter Maura with Edna. Callahan had given up on Brian, but his mother had not. She was determined to keep Maura from her sluttish mother, Shay. That became more complicated when Shay was murdered and Brian became a suspect.

Callahan had never been a fan of the professional Irish so she was less than enthusiastic about accompanying her ex-partner, Bucky Deaver, to a Shamrock Club dance in *Irish Eyes* (HarperCollins, 2000). Bucky was mortally injured during a stop-off at a liquor store on their ride home. Callahan did not want it to be true, but she connected recent burglaries to bent cops, many of them wearing the green. Her obsession in finding Bucky's attacker left no time for Mac who was considering a move to Nashville.

Callahan was depicted as capable and enterprising in a series with fast action and memorable characters. What a shame that the series ended! Trocheck has a new series focused on retired reporter, Truman Kicklighter.

Anneke Haagen Genesko

Author: Susan Holtzer

See: Anneke Haagen, page 318.

Angela Gennaro

Author: Dennis Lehane

Patrick Kenzie was the primary private investigator in the series, but he could not manage professionally or personally without Angie, the granddaughter of a Mafia don. Her alcoholic father Jimmy died young, "disappearing in a mob hit," and leaving his wife to care for two small daughters. Patrick had loved Angie as long as he could remember, but she married his best friend, Phil. Phil's alcoholism and lack of success led to domestic abuse, which Patrick could not help but notice. His one effort to "teach Phil a lesson" failed; Angie had a worse beating. She loved both men, but was loyal to her husband. Patrick and Angie worked out of an office in the bell tower of St. Bart's Catholic Church in Boston, specializing in lost persons. Their responsibilities on one case went far afield. They killed a drug dealer; then had to live with the knowledge that a witness to their crime existed and might use the information to make a deal with the police.

Their assignment in *A Drink Before the War* (Harcourt Brace, 1994) was to find Jenna Angeline, an African-American cleaning woman who might have taken confidential material from political offices. The investigation was hampered because Jenna's family was involved in a crack dealing gang. Angie reached her limit with Phil, using a stun gun to protect herself.

As *Darkness, Take My Hand* (William Morrow, 1996) opened, Angie was sharing her freedom with assorted men while Patrick concentrated on a lovely surgeon. Their lives were thrown into turmoil by a request to protect young Jason Warner. After Jason was killed, Patrick struggled with a deranged killer whose potential victims came from the neighborhood where Angie, Phil, and Patrick had grown up.

Angie and Patrick took on a formidable foe in *Sacred* (Morrow, 1997), when dying tycoon Trevor Stone employed them to find his missing daughter, Desiree. Desiree may have been an innocent victim of "Grief Relief," an organization that preyed upon the vulnerable, but there were layers of deceit here. Angie and Patrick risked their own lives and pitted two greedy conspirators against one another. In the process, they put their past behind them and established a personal relationship. It was easier to begin than to maintain.

Patrick and Angie were united in their determination to find Amanda, the neglected daughter of Helene, an alcoholic, during *Gone, Baby, Gone* (Morrow, 1998). They had been asked to intervene by Lionel McCready, Helene's brother. However, their standards of justice diverged. Angie's concern was the welfare of Amanda to the exclusion of other interests. Both she and Patrick had risked their lives to save not only Amanda, but also other children. They risked much more in returning Amanda to Helene. They separated again, physically and in spirit.

In *Prayers for Rain* (Morrow, 1999), Patrick brought Angie back into his life. She had nothing to do with her grandfather, but her connections with the Mafia came in handy. Patrick had failed an innocent client, Karen Nichols. Karen had been driven to her death by a cruel manipulator determined to destroy her family. Patrick engaged in a duel of wits with first one, then another adversary.

This was a dark but compelling series with complex plotting, interesting characterizations, and above average writing. Recently listening to three of the books on cassettes while driving, I became aware of the profanity, which is easy to ignore while reading. While appropriate in that setting, it may offend some listeners. Lehane is a terrific writer, best known for standalone *Mystic River* that was made into an excellent movie.

Announced for 2010, a new Kenzie/Gennaro book, *Moonlight Mile.*

Carole Ann Gibson

Author: Penny Mickelbury

Carole Ann Gibson had grown up in Jacaranda Estates in California, where her mother Grayce still lived. Her father had been killed during the Vietnam War. Carole's first employment after graduation from law school was with a large firm, which assigned her to criminal defense work. This was an enviable position for a young African-American female just out of school. Although successful, she found the assignments distasteful. Eventually she joined with former police office Jake Graham in an international security-consulting firm in Washington, D.C. She still took occasional work as an attorney to keep current with the law.

In *One Must Wait* (Simon & Schuster, 1998), just as Carole resolved to drop out of criminal cases for the firm in which she practiced, she learned that her husband, Al was equally unhappy with his job. Having shared their discomfort, they decided to resign. Carole would do so at once. Al, an attorney, had matters to deal with in a case regarding Parish Petroleum in Louisiana. He was murdered. After a period of intense mourning, Carole became aware that Al's death might have been connected to his work. Gathering her resources for backup, Carole created a new identity to work undercover until she could identify Al's killer. That accomplished, she opened a solo practice in Washington, D.C. The Louisiana trip had given Carole a sense of purpose. The descriptions of family and kinship among African-Americans in the South were warm and revealing.

As *Where to Choose* (Simon & Schuster, 1999) began, the past weighed heavily on Carole. She had been unsuccessful in defending Ricky Ball who had recently escaped from a halfway house. He was vindictive against Carole and against Gloria Jenkins, a lesbian with two children who had testified against him. Gloria and her family had been placed in a Witness Protection Program. With pressure building, Carole almost welcomed her mother's plea for help. Returning to the Jacaranda Estates, she was appalled at the changes: frightened elderly residents whose complaints had been shrugged off by the police department. When the residents took the law in their own hands, Carole recognized the evil that permeated the once proud project.

GGI (Carole and Jake Graham's corporation) took on two major cases in *The Step Between* (Simon & Schuster, 2000): (1) the disappearance of Annabelle Islington who left her powerful father just twenty years after her mother had; and (2) an investigation of Seaboard Shipping and Containers' bid to take over OnShore Manufacturing. They were forced to drop the second assignment when Grace, Jake's wife was kidnapped. The two cases were entwined in a complex, and at times confusing narrative. When Carole needed someone to lean on as she confronted her fears, Warren Forchetti, New Orleans attorney was there to help.

Jake and Carole saw the contract to install security system in Isle de Paix, a Caribbean island, as a golden opportunity in *Paradise Interrupted* (Simon & Schuster, 2001). Each had visited the unspoiled island in the past. Now with the former dictator Henri Le Roi gone, they could assist in restoring an atmosphere that would foster the tourist trade. Within weeks, Carole learned that a granting agency was withholding funds because of suspected drug activity, that a murder attempt had been made on the current president Philippe Collette, and that suspected drug dealer and killer Denis St. Almain had fled to the island. A stranger to the mixed family alliances in Isle de Paix, Carole gathered the agency resources and new allies, despite a serious conflict of interest.

Mickelbury has a second series featuring lesbian Police Lieutenant Gianna Maglione.

Meg (Mary Margaret) Gillis

Author: C. J. Songer

Mary Margaret "Meg" Gillis was the youthful widow of Charlie Gillis, a policeman killed in action. She had been a police officer herself. Suspicions that Meg and fellow police officer Mike Johnson had been involved in Charlie's death were never proven, but led to their temporary suspensions. Uncomfortable with the results, Meg and Mike resigned and took a cash settlement, which they used to open a security agency called John Gill Security Corporation. Their business was primarily installing security systems in businesses and homes in the Beverly Hills area. Mike was the salesman; Meg, the administrator and manager. He occasionally took on other jobs without consulting or even informing her. She enjoyed baseball and, when particularly agitated, got in her car and drove the freeways.

Meg had difficulty with human relationships. Even her cat remained nameless. One exception had been Josh, Charlie's twelve-year-old son who lived with his mother, Caroline. Meg voluntarily agreed to pay child support in exchange for visitation rights.

Her meeting with Sgt. Joe Reilly in *Bait* (Scribners, 1998) was contentious. A call from a man whose son was missing, claiming to be a client of Mike's, caused Meg to seek police support. The call turned out to be bogus. When Meg left the police station, her car had been stolen. It was found soon enough but with bloodstains inside. Mike had disappeared. There were serious problems within the Beverly Hills and nearby Burbank Police Departments, complicated by arguments between the police and the DEA (Drug Enforcement Agency). Meg and Mike looked like handy scapegoats.

Meg came to trust and care for Joe Reilly, but she had not reached the point where she could be totally honest with him. This surfaced in *Hook* (Scribners, 1999) when Mike requested that Meg serve divorce papers on behalf of Sylvia, a battered wife. Her plan was to meet Rudolfo de la Pena dressed as a hooker. Then it got complicated. When Rudolfo was found dead, a presumed suicide, Meg was less certain as to who was the victim. Highly complex personal relationships among Sylvia, Rudolfo and other members of the Free Argentina organization complicated Meg's investigation.

These were gritty, urban narratives with a prickly heroine whose need for independence crippled her ability to share.

Susan Given

Author: Margaret Barrett, pseudonym for Anne Beane Rudman, and Charles Dennis

Susan Given was an assistant district attorney in New York, assigned to the Asset Forfeiture Unit. That meant that she stripped adjudged criminals of assets, which made her no friends among the local crime bosses. Her immediate supervisor, deputy district attorney Lydia Culberg, detested Susan. Dr. Hugh Carver, a television therapist and Susan's husband, sought custody of their two adopted children in a pending divorce. Polly (14) and Ivy (10) had been adopted during the nineteen-year marriage. They were currently in Susan's custody but had regular contacts with their father. He did not approve of Susan's affair with actor/writer Michael Roth, but had a pseudo-Swedish lover of his own. Susan did not need any more problems, yet she seemed to look for them. She was described as still blond in her mid-forties.

Given the Crime (Pocket Books, 1998) presented Susan with crises that struck at both her professional and personal lives. The Tesla family controlled the garbage business in New York. A rival company run by Tom Patterson from Oklahoma had placed lower bids but received no contracts. Junior, the vicious son of Nick Tesla, carried out a personal vendetta against the Pattersons. This came to Susan's attention because young Nellie Patterson attended school with Polly and Ivy. While pursuing the assets of drug dealer Vinh Ho Chi, Susan took on the Tesla family. The narrative was complex, involving a variety of characters and agendas.

Junior Tesla haunted Susan's dreams in *Given the Evidence* (Pocket Books, 1998). Her divorce proceedings, now into their third year, dragged on. Her relationship with Michael had ended. Susan had to step up to the plate when she was assigned to prosecute prominent banker Dwight Pelham. Pelham had been accused of participating in money laundering as a tactical maneuver requested by federal authorities. This was not the time for a trip to the Caribbean, which merely added to her problems. As did a visit from her niece Brandy who had unrealistic expectations of a television career. The narrative descended into clutter and coincidence.

Some printings may list the authors as Anne Beane Rudman and Charles Dennis and other references may list them as Margaret Barrett and Charles Dennis.

Ariel Gold

Author: Judy Mercer

Ariel Gold had a tragic history, which unfolded during the narratives. Providing too much of the background at this point would damage the suspense. She had a photographic and aural memory that was exceptional, and a protective German Shepherd, Jessie. Henry Heller, Ariel's supervising producer on *Open File* (a weekly television program), tried to be helpful. He was cautious about relationships because he had been married three times, divorced three times, and had a teenage son, Sam who needed him.

In *Fast Forward* (Pocket, 1995), Ariel had awakened one morning in a Los Angeles home that she gradually realized was her own but without any knowledge as to her name, family members, or occupation. The presence of bloody clothing and a gun made her reluctant to seek help from the authorities. The persistent Henry Heller provided some basic information. He then pushed her into a world with which she was ill equipped to deal. Ariel was aware that, amnesiac or not, she was a danger to someone. In the process she became a different person from the pre-amnesiac Ariel. Intricate, but credible.

In *Double Take* (Pocket, 1997), what was to have been a relaxing visit to the South Carolina home of B. F. Coulter, Ariel's newly discovered grandfather, escalated into a two-generation murder investigation. Meanwhile Henry Heller wrestled with a moral problem. Richard Cummings, a producer on his staff had dropped an unsolved death case, resigned, and suddenly became affluent. The credibility of *Open File* was important to Henry. Increasingly, so was Ariel. A pattern had developed in the series: two cases, both with the potential to become projects for *Open File*, and at least one with personal ramifications for Ariel.

Henry and Ariel seemed on their way to a stable and loving relationship in *Split Image* (Pocket, 1998). Then Jack Spurling reentered her life. Jack, whose earlier trial for murdering his wife Eve had ended in a hung jury, attracted Ariel as a prospect for a great program. Reopening the file, which she had begun before the amnesia, might end the uncertainty for Jack. He would prefer to begin a new life with Ariel. Henry was dejected and deeply suspicious that Spurling would bring her unhappiness.

Laya, Ariel's yoga teacher and friend, was blinded within days of witnessing a murder. In *Blind Spot* (Pocket Books, 2000), Ariel had two projects: (1) to assist Laya in either having surgery to restore her sight, or in making an adjustment as a blind person; and (2) to discover who had placed acid in her friend's eye drops. Ariel endangered herself and Laya by choosing the wrong confidantes, suspecting the wrong person.

These were engrossing. They will be most enjoyable if read in order, but perhaps with other books in between, as they were frequently downbeat.

Natalie Gold

Author: Jody Jaffe

Horses were the most important part of Natalie Gold's life. The narrative played heavily on the incongruity of a petite redheaded Jewish-American from Philadelphia, currently living in the rural South. Her father, a wastrel whom her mother had divorced, had played only a minor role in Natalie's life. She made her peace with him eventually. David, her deceased stepfather, had filled the void. Her brother Larry, a married attorney, played an occasional role in her investigations. There was a tendency towards manic-depression in the Gold family. Natalie rarely drank alcohol or strayed from her vegetarian diet. At thirty-six, she was a reporter on the *Charlotte Commercial Appeal*. Although she was disorganized, she was a good worker, wrote well and had exceptional interviewing skills. Dissatisfied with her current assignments, she sought an opportunity to prove she could handle topical news.

Her chance came in *Horse of a Different Killer* (Fawcett Columbine, 1995) when a champion stud was found savaged in the stable, close to the body of trainer Wally Hempstead. Natalie used her equine expertise to accompany divorced crime reporter Henry Goode to the murder scene and to disprove the theory that the horse had killed the trainer. Natalie and Henry worked together, weighing the motives of those who had reason to fear Wally.

Chestnut mares were considered unreliable, but that was not enough to explain the death of Josane Leigh Ashmore, an ambitious former beauty queen, in *Chestnut Mare, Beware* (Fawcett Columbine, 1996). Trainer Charlie Laconte was aware that the horse, Nobody's Fool, had already sent three good riders to the hospital. Still, when Josane insisted, he sold her the horse. As Natalie researched a feature story on Compassionate Friends, parents who mourned the death of children, she and Henry uncovered a list of potential murder victims.

In Colt Blood (Fawcett Columbine, 1998), ambitiously combined a variety of themes and characters. Natalie's father, Lou who suffered from bi-polar disorder, became closely involved with Sarah Jane Lowell, a horse whisperer. Lou and Sarah Jane disappeared shortly after the murder of alcoholic stable owner Fuzzy McMahon, leading to suspicions that Sarah Jane was involved. When Natalie was certain that Sarah Jane was innocent at least as to murder, she had concerns about Fuzzy's husband Bobby, a lecherous blacksmith, and their teenage daughter Ashlee. There were changes at the newspaper, which threatened Natalie's status until she became so valuable an asset that her future was secured.

Of general interest but appealing particularly to those who enjoy horses.

Jaffe is also the author of the Robin Vaugn series, covered in this volume.

Kiki Goldstein

Author: Annie Griffin, pseudonym for Sally Chapman

See: Hannah Malloy, page 508.

Augusta Goodnight

Author: Mignon F. Ballard

Angels have been popularized on television as problem solvers. Why not a crime solving angel? In this series, angel Augusta Goodnight has been the continuing character. Perhaps because of her difficulty in adjusting to current times, she had no permanent assignment to a human. She just filled in when the primary angel was indisposed. In her angel capacity she could appear and disappear at will, a considerable aid during an investigation. The previous time

Augusta had made a personal appearance on earth was during World War II so initially she was confused by the lack of rationing, surprised but delighted by the stylish shoes and clothes, but definitely preferred the music of the 1940s. She not only solved crimes—she cooked, baked, made curtains, cleaned house, and advised on romantic matters.

Mary George Murphy had made three unsuccessful attempts at suicide when Augusta entered her life in *Angel at Troublesome Creek* (St. Martin, 1999). She informed Mary George that she obviously did not want to commit suicide or she would not have been so inept. She then made it clear that the fiancé who had dumped Mary George hadn't been worth keeping. Finally, she moved on to a more serious matter: the recent death of Mary George's beloved adoptive mother, Aunt Caroline who had rescued eight-year-old Mary George from an orphanage. Augusta agreed that the death had not been a natural one. Aunt Caroline had been pushed down the attic stairs.

Prentice Dobson needed help when Augusta appeared in *An Angel to Die For* (Berkley, 2001). The magazine, *Martha's Journal*, where she had worked, was defunct. Her lover, Rob McCullough had left for England, encouraging her to follow but without making the commitment she anticipated. She returned to Smokerise, her family home, to mourn the recent death of her wayward sister, Maggie. Although there was trouble enough at Smokerise (two murders), Prentice's primary concern was finding Maggie's son and keeping him safe. Augusta guided her along the way.

Minda Hobbs, a recent widow, returned to Angel Heights, South Carolina in *Shadow of an Angel* (St. Martin's Minotaur, 2002) where she'd grown up living with her grandmother, Vesta Maxwell. The big family home seemed empty and cheerless until Augusta joined her there. Augusta had unfinished business in Angel Heights. She protected and guided Minda as she and her family put together the pieces of an historic quilt. Augusta had been part of the Westbrook family's past and her responsibilities towards a long dead woman had not ended

Kate McBride, estranged from her husband, Ned, took Josie, her ten-year-old daughter, to a family reunion in Bishop's Ridge, North Carolina during *The Angel Whispered Danger* (St. Martin's Minotaur, 2003). Old memories disturbed her: the dead body that she, cousin Grady, and her best friend Beverly had found twenty years before; the disappearance of Great-Uncle Ernest's young wife forty years ago; and the purported drowning of two young hippies. Fortunately Augusta and her trainee angel Penelope, were on hand as current tragedies occurred: Uncle Ernest's housekeeper killed; his lady friend attacked by bees; and Josie lost in the woods. Revelations from the past explained more recent motivations for violence.

Widowed Lucy Nan Pilgrim got more visitors than expected in *Too Late for Angels* (St. Martin's Minotaur, 2005). First, an elderly woman came to the house seeking her mother. "Shirley" knew the names of the prior owners and gave Lucy Nan enough information that she suspected that the disturbed woman was really Florence Calhoun who had disappeared from Stone's Throw over sixty years ago. She would be a cousin of Ellis Saxon, (Lucy Nan's best pal). The next guest was Augusta on one of her fill-in assignments. The next time "Shirley/Florence" appeared she was dead, found in the church parking lot. That was the second unexplained death in days for Stone's Throw. Calpernia Hemphill, prominent but annoying local leader, had died from a fall. In the process, Lucy Nan acquired a suitor, Ben Maxwell.

Even with Augusta's help, Lucy Nan Pilgrim had a lot of trouble putting the pieces together in *The Angel and the Jabberwocky Murder* (St. Martin's Minotaur, 2006) The recent disappearance, then murder of college student D.C. Hunter, connected to prior deaths over the last decade. All occurred to young people, three of whom were students at local Sarah Bedford College. The victims seemed to have no connections with one another...except messages they received, containing quotations from Lewis Carroll's *Through the Looking Glass.* The narrative included interesting segments, during which college students learned skills used generations before; i.e. making lye soap, cooking over open fires, weaving.

Lucy Nan had become a regular in the series by *Hark! The Herald Angel Screamed* (St. Martin's Minotaur, 2008) Strange things were happening at Willowbrook, ancestral home of Lucy Nan's family. No one was currently resident in the deteriorating manor, but custodian Preacher Dave Tansey and his family lived in a cottage on the ground. While searching for a Christmas tree in the Willowbrook woods, Lucy Nan, Augusta, and friends came upon the body of an unknown man who had fallen from an upstairs balcony. Augusta was practically a member of the Thursday Club by now, although Lucy Nan and Ellis Saxon were the only ones who could see and hear her. She caroled with the group, made wonderful desserts, decorated Lucy Nan's house, and helped solve two murders. The big clue was a locket presented to Thursday Club member, Idonia Mae Culpepper, by a new beau.

Augusta was a background character in each narrative, coming on scene when needed, adding touches of humor with her changes of attire, and difficulties with current language, music, and styles.

Hester Gorse

Author: Donald Harstad

The primary in this realistic Midwestern police procedural was Deputy Sheriff Carl Houseman, but he frequently depended upon Hester Gorse's special training and laboratory skills. As an employee of the Iowa State Department of Criminal Investigation, she had been trained in the FBI Criminal Profiling School. Hester had gone undercover in narcotics investigations, and was generally available to local units. She enjoyed Snickers, and acquired a small beagle, "Big Ears"

Eleven Days (Doubleday, 1998) was a chronological account of the impact on a rural Iowa town when members of a satanic cult were slaughtered. More than a few had taken part in the killing but the leader could not be identified until he was cornered in a church. Terse prose based on author Donald Harstad's experience as a law officer may be too graphic for some readers.

Gun battles between county deputies and unknown assailants brought state and federal agencies into Nation County, Iowa during *Known Dead* (The Fourth Estate, 1999). Carl, who was in temporary charge of the sheriff's office, used any means available to protect local interests, yet find the killers. Hester worked with him during interviews, withholding information from federal agents who had their own agenda.

Hester provided suggestions and played a heroic role in the roundup of Gabriel, head of a right wing terrorist group, during *The Big Thaw* (Doubleday, 2000). A burglary investigation expanded to a double murder case and ended as a major incident involving the FBI. A plot to seize the profits of a river gambling boat was foiled by cooperation among different levels of government.

When a routine window-peeper call developed into a multiple murder in *Code 61* (Doubleday, 2002) Carl called the State Criminal Investigation Agency, requesting Hester's presence in Nation County. The most recent victim had been Edie Younger, the niece of Sheriff Ridgeway. Her body had been discovered in a bathtub at the Manor, a refuge for depressed young adults. Murder was bad enough, but by a vampire, in Iowa! Hester's role was subordinate as Carl and his staff operated in a professional manner. She did disclose details of her own period of depression which affected her attitude towards the owner of the Manor.

Hester and Carl responded to a shooting on a county road in *A Long December* (Rugged Land, 2003) with no expectation that it would eventually become a nationwide investigation. A second death in Iowa plus more in New York City raised a terrorist alarm and brought a dozen state and federal agencies into the case. Hester's role was limited, partly because of an on-duty injury and the perplexities of dealing with budget issues. The switching back and forth in time sequences detracted from the paced of the narrative.

I was informed by an E-Mail from author Harstad that *The Heartland Experiment* was the working title for *A Long December*, not a separate book.

Senator Eleanor "Norie" Gorzack

Authors: Barbara Mikulski and Marylouise Oates

Eleanor "Norie" Gorzack's appointment as United States Senator from Pennsylvania was perceived by many as a tribute to her as the widow of a Vietnam War hero. She had qualifications of her own. A registered nurse, she had served as Pennsylvania Public Health Director. She was being used as a "placeholder," occupying the position while other politicians planned to run for the office.

However, encouraged by her circle of close friends and supporters, she seriously considered making a run for a full term at the next election. Norie was described as a short, graying blonde in her forties.

As *Capitol Offense* (Dutton, 1996) began, Norie was adjusting to life in the District of Columbia. Her staff, primarily holdovers from the previous senator, worked to bring her up to date on current legislation. Her particular interests included health and veteran's affairs. John Browning, a veteran who sought her help as she boarded the subway between her office building and the Capitol was killed. This thrust her into an investigation of murder, smuggling, and the fate of MIAs.

Once she learned that her husband Jack had indeed died in Vietnam, Eleanor made a decision to run for a full term. During *Capitol Venture* (Dutton, 1998), a tourist area in Pennsylvania was seriously damaged by flooding. The Keystone Militia, a right wing group, sought to take advantage of the calamity. After Eleanor was injured and the local congressman Bob Bercolini was murdered, she realized that other forces sought to avoid an investigation into mysterious deaths in the Jericho area.

Co-author Barbara Mikulski, a United States Senator, was well able to provide the background and color for a political mystery.

Belle Graham

Author: Nero Blanc. Pseudonym for Cordelia Frances Biddle and Steve Zettler, a married couple.

Belle, a tall, blonde self-contained woman, was the daughter of two college professors. Her mother had died; her father moved to Florida. At one time she had aspired to a career as a poet, but realized her talents in that field were inadequate. When the series began, she was divorced from Garret, an Egyptologist, and had a relationship with private investigator Rosco Polycrates. She continued to live in the home she and Garret had shared, although he had taken most of the furniture. She rarely cooked, considered deviled eggs to be her specialty. She was employed as the crossword editor for the Massachusetts based *Evening Crier.* It didn't hurt her in her sub-specialty, detection, that she had a fabulous memory, retained almost everything she heard or read.

The death by strangulation of the Herald's crossword editor, Thompson Briephs, brought Belle and Rosco together in *The Crossword Murder* (Berkley, 1999). Briephs had been found dead at his home on Windward Island. His mother, Sara, had called the Coast Guard to check on him. Dissatisfied with the police response, she hired Rosco to investigate. Rosco's first move was to contact his former police partner, Lt. Al Lever, who revealed sordid aspects of Briephs' life. He had been blackmailed and left clues as to the identity of the blackmailer in the form of crossword puzzles. Belle was a perfect ally.

Former actress Genie Pepper and television star Jamaica Nevisson went back a long way, but as *Two Down* (Berkley, 2000) opened, Genie had abandoned her career plans for a happy marriage to investment banker Tom Pepper. It was to the Pepper home that Jamaica went for refuge when she was overwhelmed by notoriety. The two women disappeared when they went for a sail down the coast, although the boat and dinghy were found. Based upon mysterious crossword puzzles sent to her in the mail, Bella was sure they were alive. Rosco, who had been hired by Tom Pepper, was more skeptical.

Belle wanted to focus on her wedding to Rosco, to take place in eight days, but events in *Crossword Connection* (Berkley, 2001) made that impossible. She had trouble with the enthusiastic interference of her elderly friend Sara Briephs and Cleo (Rosco's sister). Her own father, who did not approve of Rosco, made it known that he would not be in attendance at the wedding. When two murder victims were discovered with crossword puzzles from a Boston newspaper under their bodies, Belle wanted no part in the investigation. Subsequent events changed her mind.

Belle had more or less written her father, Ted, off when he failed to appear at the wedding but in *A Crossword to Die For* (Berkley, 2002) he made an overture, a healing visit. She waited in vain at the railroad depot for his arrival, only to learn that he had died of a heart attack. Later while gathering up her dad's possessions in Florida and preparing to sell his Sanibel condo, Belle learned about a Ted Graham drastically different from her recollections. She met Debbie Hurley, Ted's adoring young assistant, learned that Ted had recently purchased a $97,000 fishing boat and had made three unexplained visits to Belize. Furthermore, on his trip from Florida to visit Belle, Ted had stopped over in New Jersey. These anomalies added up to the possibility that he had been murdered As usual crossword clues figured into the solution.

A Crossworder's Holiday (Berkley, 2002) was a collection of short stories/novellas: (a) While visiting in Nantucket, Belle was approached by an antiquarian who needed her help in a contest, rating ability to distinguish between fake and authentic literary materials; (b) while visiting Sara Briephs in Vermont, they found themselves isolated at a murder site. They dithered with a crossword recipe but police solved the crime: (c) Roscoe went alone to visit a friend in Pennsylvania, but kept in touch with Belle by phone when his friend's potential inheritance was at stake; (d) an FBI agent needed Belle and Roscoe when he was given advance warning that a crime would occur during the Mummers' Parade in Philadelphia; and (e) off in the Cotswold's visiting friends, a ghostly presence left puzzles in Belle's room re a series of disappearances. These are best if you really enjoy puzzles.

The locals in Taneysville, MA were not pleased when industrialist Alex Gordon purchased the vacant Quigley home and proceeded with a major addition in *Corpus de Crossword* (Berkley, 2003). Not only did the machinery shake the foundations of the adjacent Episcopalian church, but also all workers were brought in from outside. Work ceased when the bulldozer unearthed a human skeleton. Congressional candidate Milt Hoffmeyer III hired Rosco to investigate when the local police force tabled it a "cold case". Belle was drawn into the investigation by a series of crossword puzzles that hinted at the identity of the victim. Intricate plotting and a startling conclusion.

A Crossworder's Gift (Berkley, 2003) was a lighthearted collection of five short stories, during four of which Rosco and Belle traveled to the Caribbean, Canada, Las Vegas, and the Grant Canyon.

Wrapped Up in Crosswords (Berkley, 2004) was one of three mysteries capitalizing on the Christmas season, short and cozy. There were three ex-convicts on the loose, wearing Santa Claus suits. Unfortunately Lt. Al Lever, Rosco, and forensic scientist Abe Jones were also attired as Santas as they called on merchants to collect toys for needy children. The wrapping toys party held each year at wealthy Sara Briephs home included a secret Santa gift exchange with romantic overtones. That was tolerable, but talking dogs!

Scriptwriter Chick Darlessen sold producer Lew Groslin a screenplay of Belle and Rosco's last big cases in *Anatomy of a Crossword* (Berkley, 2004) First Belle, then Rosco, and finally Sara Briephs all flew to Los Angeles. It wasn't a happy setting. Chick was murdered. Cast members were injured or threatened. Belle's crosswords were less significant than a connection to a television crossword quiz show.

While taking part in the Holiday Decoration Contest at the Paul Revere Inn during *A Crossworder's Delight* (Berkeley, 2005) Belle discovered an original collection of dessert recipes designed by a mother for her daughter. The recipes were in crossword form, making it necessary to fill in the blanks before starting to cook. When a signed copy of Longfellow's poem on Paul Revere disappeared, Rosco was hired to retrieve the item. Its return did not solve the problem. Twelve-year-old E. T. Whitman teamed with Rosco and Belle, earning a happy home.

Another Word for Murder (Berkley, 2005) tied together a hit-and-run death, a kidnapping-murder, the theft of 22 foreign cars, and a series of crossword puzzles sent to Belle. Her new friend, Karen Tacete, initially sought Belle's help when her husband Dan, an oral surgeon, disappeared. When a kidnapper contacted Karen, she asked Belle and Rosco to back off and refused to involve the police. However there was no way to keep Lt. Al Lever out of it when a badly burned corpse was identified as Dan. Rosco had two cases going: the hit-and-run death of the "Snyder kid" and the car thefts. The cryptic crosswords sent to Belle were a literary device that seemed contrived.

It was Roscoe who was sought to handle the insurance claim for a fire at Todd Collins' horse farm and to locate a mysterious young woman in *Death on the Diagonal* (Berkley, 2006) but Belle's puzzling skills were significant in the solution. The Collins clan and staff lived under stress on an estate containing various homes and cottages. There had been fires attributed to arson. On a separate track wealthy Walter Gudgeon was concerned about the disappearance of Dawn Davis, a young woman he had befriended. Sara and Belle helped to tie the cases together.

Cordelia Frances Biddle turned to a different setting for a subsequent historical series featuring wealthy young Martha Beale.

Charlotte Graham

Author: Stefanie Matteson

Charlotte Graham, an aging Oscar winning actress, carried overtones of the Bette Davis-Katharine Hepburn personas, sharing their pride in a New England heritage. In her sixties and seventies, she had some professional opportunities but was usually "at leisure" during her investigations. She retained black hair with some help, gray eyes, and a soft husky voice. Charlotte had married four times, but only her second marriage to Will, who died, had been successful. Two others ended in divorce, and the fourth was deteriorating. A number of her deductions came as the result of dreams.

During *Murder at the Spa* (Diamond, 1990), cosmetic queen Paulina Langenberg invited Charlotte to visit her High Rock Springs beauty spa. Paulina, a canny Hungarian who parlayed her mother's homemade skin cream into a fortune, believed someone was sabotaging the Spa's reputation.

In *Murder at Teatime* (Diamond, 1991), Charlotte visited Stan and Kitty Saunders at their Maine island home. Neighbor J. Franklin Thorndike shocked everyone with his plans to remarry. His subsequent death brought police who unaccountably welcomed Charlotte's assistance.

United States/Japanese history framed *Murder on the Cliff* (Diamond, 1991) set in Newport, Rhode Island. Charlotte witnessed the Black Ships Festival commemorating the U.S. entry into Japan. Famous geisha Okichi-Mago, a young Japanese descendant of Townsend Harris, the first U.S Counsel to Japan, fell off a cliff. Her lover Shawn Hendrickson, an American sumo wrestler, was stabbed to death while meditating. Charlotte did not accept simple solutions, not surprising considering the tensions among the guests at the Saunders home. Excellent background material.

Charlotte returned to Maine for *Murder on the Silk Road* (Diamond, 1992) but only to prepare for a trip by plane, train, and bus to an anthropological site in China where paleontologists and geologists squabbled over what killed the dinosaurs. Charlotte was more concerned about who killed members of the expedition and stole Chinese statuary and manuscripts. Again credible background.

Murder at the Falls (Berkley, 1993) revealed more than a reader might need to know about the vanishing "diner." Charlotte had often accompanied real crime writer Tom Plummer on searches for the old, working class restaurants. Murder was on the menu in Paterson, New Jersey. Her fourth husband Jack Lundstrom, who had failed to lure her to Minneapolis society, came on scene to help trap a killer, but also to make Charlotte aware that he wanted a divorce.

Chastened, Charlotte returned to Maine in *Murder on High* (Berkley, 1994). Working on her biography offered relief, but entangled her in the death of former screenwriter Iris O'Connor. Charlotte's investigation recalled the "black" period in her life, a time when her lover, western star Linc Crawford, died and no one in Hollywood wanted to hire Charlotte.

Charlotte had handled aging well, but in *Murder Among the Angels* (Berkley, 1996), she considered plastic surgery. Her visit to Dr. Victor Lauria, a highly recommended practitioner, at his home in Zion Hill led her into a bizarre investigation of serial murders. The victims bore a startling resemblance to one another. In the course of the narrative, Matteson explored the history and beliefs of the Swedenborgian religion.

Charlotte was entranced by an Addison Mizner designed home in Palm Beach when she attended a formal dinner in *Murder Under the Palms* (Berkley, 1997). She had agreed to model clothing designed by her goddaughter Marianne Montgomery at a charity event to aid the local Historic Preservation Society. She did not anticipate that prominent local jeweler Paul Feder would be murdered or that she would be reunited with a great love of her life, bandleader Eddie Norwood. They had met when she was a young starlet traveling on the *Normandie*. The *Normandie* and its tragic ending in an act of espionage was the background for this well researched mystery.

Mystery paperback originals are long past the time when they were lurid and inept. This series moved up to hardcover, had varied locales and credible technical material from the start.

Inspector Liz Graham

Author: Jo Bannister

Inspector Liz Graham worked regularly with her mentor, Chief Inspector Frank Shapiro, and morose Sgt. Cal Donovan. A tall fair-haired Englishwoman, Liz was married to Brian, an art teacher. She found her relaxation in horseback riding. On the job, she performed diligently, but her greatest successes came with hunches based upon solid information.

When Liz was assigned temporarily to Castlemere in *A Bleeding of Innocents* (St. Martin, 1993), it was to replace Inspector Alan Clarke, killed in a hit and run. Sgt. Donovan, who had also been injured, was convinced that they had been targeted. Liz and Donovan worked together to find the pattern in a series of seemingly unrelated murders. Liz's decision to accept a permanent position in Castlemere required a considerable sacrifice on Brian's part. He left a comfortable situation as head of the art department, and accepted a lesser post in a new setting.

As *Charisma* (St. Martin, 1994 apa *Sins of the Heart*) opened, Liz worked late hours and weekends on serial murders of young women She became vulnerable to the charismatic presence of handicapped Welsh evangelist Rev. Michael Davey. While Brian unpacked dishes and scrambled to make meals,

Liz and Donovan struggled with a drug investigation that confused their murder probe.

During *A Taste for Burning* (St. Martin, 1995), Liz and Donovan fought their own suspicions to prove that Shapiro had not suppressed evidence to send suspect Trevor Foot to prison. Shapiro's son Robin had been suspected of being the pyromaniac at loose in Castlemere. While Shapiro was on suspension, Liz and Donovan worked the cases.

The relationship between Liz and Shapiro was shaky as *No Birds Sing* (Macmillan, 1996) began. Liz wanted and received his support when she was raped in her own backyard. Her need to be independent made her insensitive as to how her tragedy affected Brian. Donovan had most of the action, going undercover in a gang of sadistic robbers. He and Liz helped one another cope with their injuries.

In *Broken Lines* (Macmillan, 1998), Donovan was the victim of a false accusation, that he had brutally beaten young criminal Mikey Dickens, son of Roly, head of a powerful crime family. Earlier, after interrupting a robbery, Donovan had pursued Mikey's car, and rescued him after an accident. With Donovan first suspended, then kidnapped by Roly Dickens, Liz and Frank Shapiro had little time to identify the real attacker. Interesting premises.

The roles of the police, the prostitute Lara, and the professional assassin, all for hire, were explored in *The Hireling's Tale* (Macmillan, 1999). Frank Shapiro had been wounded by a killer's bullet. Liz suffered under the stress of a replacement supervisor. Most significantly Donavan wrestled with fears, guilt and frustration with police bureaucracy.

Both of the men in Liz's life were at risk during *Changelings* (St. Martin, 2000). Brian, her husband was within the group of suspects in a blackmailing scheme. Cal Donovan was stricken with pneumonia while traversing the canals during his sick leave. His rescuers included criminals who had mixed intentions about letting him survive.

Bannister wrote well with a sharp eye for the peccadilloes of the powerful. This was a British ensemble police procedural. Bannister had an earlier series featuring Clio Rees Marsh (see Volume 2), and a later one featuring Brodie Farrell.

Lindy Graham-Haggerty

Author: Shelley Freydont

Although she had been a dancer in the past, Lindy's career went on the back-burner when she married businessman Glen Haggerty and raised their two children. Glen's professional responsibilities required frequent and extended trips to Europe. Son Cliff, a college student, was always busy with friends during vacations, and seventeen-year-old Annie, a cellist, attended a professional music high school in Switzerland. Glen had been a workaholic, but grew calmer over the years. The household was reduced to Lindy, Glen, and an Irish setter (Bruno! What a name for an Irish breed) This prompted Lindy to return to modern dance, but at a different level. She became the rehearsal director for Jeremy Ash Dance Company. Some of her co-workers were also former dancers and friends. Her best friend, Biddy McFee, frequently played an important role in the series, as did costumer Rose Laughton, and Rebo (no last name) one of the dancers. The younger dancers (referred to as "kids") were a motley group, in which gay and straight males were outnumbered by females. Although she retained the family home in New Jersey, the dance company was based in New York City. Lindy was in her early forties as the series began; described as 5'5" tall, a trifle heavier than she had been in her dancing days with brown hair worn short.

In *Backstage Murder* (Kensington, 1999). Biddy McFee, the usual rehearsal director, now on crutches, convinced Lindy to substitute for her. Lindy knew most of the staff, but the dancers were new to her, except for primary Carlotta Devine. Carlotta, making what might be her final appearance, was resentful of her understudy, Andrea Martin. Given the tensions among the cast and staff, it was no surprise that Carlotta was murdered. Fighting off the temptation to quit, Lindy worked hard, lost weight, regained her agility. Good thing, she needed it.

Rock producer Cameron Tyler had recruited a half-dozen musical acts to perform on the maiden voyage of his luxury cruiser, *The Maestro,* as *High Seas Murder* (Kensington, 2000) began. The Jeremy Ash Dance Company and the other professionals were to mix freely with the passengers who would attend lectures, rehearsals and performances. The mixture of opera stars, ballet and modern dancers, cabaret acts, and a string quartet contained volatile ingredients. Several of the performers shared a past that led to murder. Lindy (on her own because Glen was in Paris) linked up with Biddy, Rose, Rebo and his pals, plus emotionally fragile rock star David Beck to sort things out.

Wealthy patroness Marguerite Easton invited JADC to the 50th anniversary of the Arts Retreat held at her upper New York estate in *Midsummer Murder* (Kensington, 2001). Jeremy Ash, who had been a scholarship student at the retreat in his youth, had great affection for Marguerite. The death of one student and the disappearance of another was treated with prejudice by the local sheriff. Byron Grappel had a grudge to pay off against a member of Marguerite's staff. His insinuations about sexual misconduct between staff and students brought damaging publicity to the Retreat. Lindy could not keep out of the investigation even though her daughter Annie was visiting her. She called upon her friend Bill Brandecker, a former police detective now teaching at John Jay College of Criminal Justice. Theirs was a delicate relationship. Both were on guard about letting it become too important.

It was Lindy's participation in her home town's Mischief Night Marathon, to raise money for a teen center, that led to her involvement in murder during *Halloween Murder* (Kensington, 2002). While chasing after Bruno, her son Cliff's dog, she discovered a corpse in the water. The body was later identified as that of private investigator Earl Koopes. One aspect of the Marathon was a production of *The Crucible* by a group of high school students who were identified as "troubled". Janey Horowitz, who had taught the class, was dying of cancer. Her replacement Melanie Grant had come to town with Fallon, the mentally disturbed daughter of prominent attorney Howard Porter, and her manipulative boyfriend, Derrick Justine. Were these newcomers responsible for the increase in drug traffic? And murder?

Jeremy and Biddy had no idea what they were getting the Jeremy Ash Dance Company into when, in *A Merry Little Murder* (Kensington, 2003), they agreed to take part in the International Ballroom Competition in Atlantic City. Costumer Rose Laughton was enthusiastic about a reunion with her friend, dance studio owner Dawn Gilpatrick. Dawn needed a friend. Her former husband, "Junie" Baker, had set up a rival studio. Dawn's protégée, dancer Katja Andrejewski, had just learned that her partner and lover, Shane Corbett, was leaving her and Dawn's entourage. When Shane was murdered under contrived circumstances, the plot deteriorated. Lindy tried to help but the Atlantic vacation that she had hoped to share with Bill Brandecker took some strange twists.

Freydont has a new series starring Katie McDonald, a Sudoku detective.

Jennifer Gray

Author: Georgette Livingston

Many aspects of this series suggest that it might be meant for an older teen or young adult readership. The narratives were relatively short and simplistic. The format provided wide spaces on pages. Jennifer Grey seemed naïve and guileless. A resident of Calico, Nebraska, she lived with her grandfather, a Protestant minister, and his housekeeper, Emma Morrison, who had innocent aspirations to a larger role in Wesley Gray's life. Jennifer had been a rebellious child who resented the move to Rev. Wesley Gray's home after her parents were killed. When she was brought back from an attempt to join a traveling circus, Wes and Emma relaxed their discipline. The situation improved. After graduation from the veterinary school at Michigan State, Jennifer was offered employment by Dr. Ben Copeland, DVM, and subsequently made a partner in his business.

Had I read *The Unlucky Collie Caper* (Avalon, 1995) first, I might have realized the series was meant for younger readers. However it was the last one to be located. The poisoned collie that Dr. Ben had successfully treated was shot by his owner, rancher Richard Aldrich. At that point Jennifer took seriously Pam Aldrich's ascertain she had been the target of the poison. After all Pam was Richard's fourth wife., the others had died young. Jennifer researched the earlier deaths.

An aging St. Bernard—Elvis—helped Jennifer rescue two mischievous brothers in *The Dog Named Elvis Caper* (Avalon, 1995). A bonus was the assistance by her grandfather, helping the children and their parents work out their problems.

Jennifer's enthusiasm for detection led her on a false trail in *The Deadly Dog-Bone Caper* (Avalon, 1996). Her discovery that a bone she had removed from a dog's throat was of human origin led to the unearthing of two skeletons. She was certain that the culprit was shady businessman Elmer Dodd, but learned otherwise. For all her piety, Jennifer did not hesitate to lie to the press and the owner of the property where the bones were found. She utilized stolen dental records in her investigation.

Local gym teacher Sabina Rider fit the profile of a cat burglar in *The Black Cat Caper* (Avalon, 1996), but Jennifer and Wes believed her to be innocent. The citywide Halloween costume party had been cancelled because of a rash of robberies. The identity of the real criminal came to Jennifer just in time.

In *The Precocious Parrot Caper* (Avalon, 1996), Jennifer was surprised to learn that her grandfather and Emma had been close early in their lives. She had rejected him then but never married. He was now a widower, sharing a home with her and Jennifer. As to the parrot, several people who disliked birds wanted custody of Scamp, a bird left behind in a boarding house. When Jennifer was granted custody, she learned that the bird might hold the key to buried treasure.

The gimmick in *The Telltale Turkey Caper* (Avalon, 1996) was a diamond necklace found in the cavity of a frozen turkey purchased for the Gray Thanksgiving dinner. The culprit was soon identified but he disappeared. When Jennifer and Wes located him, a friendly bowler saved the day.

In *The Mischievous Monkey Caper* (Avalon, 1996), the Cannon family circus came to Calico to recoup from a series of accidents. Not only was Wes an old friend of the owner, but Jennifer's skills were needed to save an undernourished lion cub. They could not resist involvement in the circus' problems, which included a drunken camel, a high-wired tiger, and a pilfering monkey.

Flooding and the threat of continued rain sent the residents of Calico into shelters as *The Tenacious Terrier Caper* (Avalon, 1997) began. Wes' church welcomed a variety of volunteers and homeless. Jennifer was forced to revise her opinion of reporter Ken Hering and shed her prior beau, attorney Willy Ashton. Continuing characters, the bootlegging Cromwell sisters, assisted in the preparation of foods to Emma's dismay as Jennifer discovered how a jeweled brooch found its way into a Yorkie's stomach.

The Labor Day weekend was the occasion for a major fair in Calico during *The White Elephant Caper* (Avalon, 1997). A white elephant sale designed to raise money for city expenses after the flood was a highlight. Jennifer was bowled over by a handsome stranger, but he was more interested in money. A casual purchase by Jennifer at the sale saved the Cromwell sisters from eviction in a picturesque manner.

The plot in *The Potbellied Pig Caper* (Avalon, 1997) was more ambitious and more confusing. An old girlfriend of Willy Ashton returned to Calico to settle her mother's estate. Although Willy, now the local mayor, welcomed her attentions, Jennifer thought she meant trouble. A potbellied pig, confusion as to identities, and a recent murder kept her busy.

Emma surprised her fellow students at a writing class with a mystery story about a woman who had killed and buried five husbands in *The Pink Rabbit Caper* (Avalon, 1998). The citizens of Calico took notice, including an anonymous writer who suggested that there might actually have been unauthorized burials in their complacent community.

In *The Chattering Chimp Caper* (Avalon, 1998), the newly rich Cromwell sisters doted on their pet chimpanzee, Peaches. They brought her to Dr. Jennifer Gray when she seemed moody and agitated. Perhaps Peaches was reacting to discord arising from suitors to the mature twins. When Peaches was kidnapped, the nature of the ransom led to the greedy abductor.

Dr. P.J. (Penelope Jennifer) Gray

Author: Shirley Kennett aka Morgan Avery

P. J. (as she preferred to be called) Gray reacted emotionally and decisively when her architect husband, Steve sought a divorce to marry a younger woman. She was nearing forty, comfortably settled in a Denver advertising agency where she used her Ph.D. in psychology for marketing research. Giving up her job, home and marriage, she hustled Tommy, their ten-year-old son, into an ancient VW and headed for St. Louis. Without any investigative experience, she accepted a position as director of CHIP (Computerized Homicide Investigations Project), an understaffed, under-funded, unproven unit in the St. Louis Police Department. She worked with overweight, foul-mouthed, and excessively belligerent detective Leo Schultz. He resented a female boss, was initially unimpressed by her use of computerized virtual reality scenarios, and had family concerns of his own.

P. J. made a dramatic entry into the department in *Gray Matter* (Pinnacle, 1997). She was assigned to investigate a decapitation case before she had found a place to live. P. J. and Leo reached an accommodation gradually and added detectives Anita Collings and Dave Whitmore to the unit. They needed all the help they could get, including some from FBI agent Ted Malmacher, to tie the immediate murder to a series killer who added P. J. to his list.

As *Fire Cracker* (Kensington, 1997) began, the man called "Cracker" was introduced. As a small child he had misinterpreted a sexual interaction between his father and stepmother. CHIP was initially assigned to investigate a hospital death caused by tampering with computerized information. Continuing incidents focused on the patients of Dr. Eleanor Graham. Leo and P. J. had a formidable adversary, even more capable at the computer than she was. Cracker had money to hire killers and arsonists, and was connected with drug dealers. They brought several criminals (a mercy killer, a money launderer, and a greedy doctor) to justice, but Leo and P. J. displayed remarkable tolerance for Cracker's misguided vendetta.

P. J. enjoyed her work and gradually found the meaning that her consumer research had never provided. In *Chameleon* (Kensington, 1998), the violence came close to home. Teachers at Thomas' junior high school were being brutally murdered. Only when she could no longer ignore the truth, did she recognize that Thomas might be involved with the killer. A vacation seemed the answer for P. J. and their son, but merely provided another setting for terror.

Act of Betrayal (Kensington, 2000) was attributed to Morgan Avery, but it's the Kennett series. Leo, now divorced had become more than a member of P. J.'s unit, but neither one of them wanted to deal with it. The savage murder of Rick, Leo's son who had just been released from prison, devastated him. However, P. J. did not believe that Leo would get drunk, run down a four-year-old child, drive away from the accident and leave town. So what really did happen?

Although P. J. was hired by the St. Louis Police Department because of her expertise in creating virtual reality set-ups, in *Time of Death* (Five Star, 2005) they provided only minimal help in solving what became a series of brutal murders. The remains of Arlan Merrett's disfigured body had been found on the banks of the Mississippi river. Focus was on his wife; then on his brother-in-law, as suspects, but as additional murders, which bore some similarity, occurred, no discernable pattern of motive emerged. Continued questioning by P. J. and Leo into the Arlan's family background, that of his wife, Jean, and her estranged sister, May, brought more significant information. There was a side story concerning P. J.'s son Thomas who was drawn into real life danger by his involvement in an Internet game. Leo solidified his role in P. J. and Thomas/s lives by taking charge of family safety.

Narratives frequently focused on a serial killer whose behavior and motivation began in childhood.

Gale Grayson

Author: Teri Holbrook

The suicide of her poet husband Tom haunted Gale Grayson. Still she stayed on in the model English rural community in which he had grown up. Tom had aligned himself with terrorists; then, shot himself in the local church before the police could apprehend him. The fact that these events had left her pregnant and far from her own family in the United States did not garner Gale support among the villagers. She was a competent professional historian with a special interest in the English support for the Confederacy during the American Civil War. Her great comforts were her daughter Kathleen Prudence (Katie Pru) and the soothing repetition of weaving.

When Gale's child minder, young Lisa Stillwell, was murdered en route to the Grayson home in *A Far and Deadly Cry* (Bantam Prime Crime, 1995), the investigating officers were those who had come to Fetherbridge to arrest Tom. Inspector Daniel Halford, who had never forgotten the bereaved young woman, fought off the local prejudice against Gale until she was released from suspicion by another tragedy.

Gale returned to her native Georgia in The *Grass Widow* (Bantam, 1996). There she encountered narrow-mindedness among the residents of Statlers Cross, where her family had lived for several generations. The community had elevated the long past death of Linnie Glynn Cane into a folk story, bolstered by "sightings" of the woman, who had been found hanging from the tree in her yard. Fighting to protect Katie Pru from the impacts of Tom's suicide and other family deaths, Gale investigated Linnie's life. Meanwhile Sheriff Alby Truitt probed the more recent death of Martin Cane, Linnie's grandson and Gale's cousin.

The past and present were intertwined in *Sad Water* (Bantam, 1999). In both eras, the issues of trust and betrayal, responsibility to family, acceptance of and resistance to change were crucial. The historical aspect covered Luddite resistance to machinery in the production of cloth. It had led some workers to use terrorist tactics against the mill owners. An arts council grant enabled Gale and her protégée, photographer Nadianna Jesup, to travel to the English village of Mayley. They explored the connection between the former Yates Mill in England and its successor in Statlers Cross, Georgia through photographs and text. Nadianna's discovery of a torso led to involvement in a series of murders and suicides, where trust, betrayal, and sibling loyalty were explored.

Gale's return to Statlers Cross in *The Mother Tongue* (Bantam, 2001) contrasted the hostility expressed against her in England as a foreigner with a similar lack of acceptance in Statlers Cross where Gale's grandmother Ella Alden was revered. The Nguyen family, three generations of women from Vietnam, aroused the anger of the locals by painting their home a bright blue color. The discovery of the corpse of a male member of the Nguyen family along side those of two local men unleashed violence against foreigners. Ella Alden, even though mourning one of the two local men, feared a cycle of violence. Chief Inspector Daniel Halford, who visited Statlers Cross to be with Gale, Sheriff Alby Truitt, Gale and Ella marshaled opposition to the discrimination. A stranger in town revealed to Gale the reason behind her husband's suicide and restored her faith in his love, allowing her to love again.

Author Teri Holbrook has a wonderful sense of place, drawing upon the parochialism of the sequestered community whether in Georgia or England. Gale was more victim than sleuth in many aspects but developed well over the narratives.

Charlie Greene

Author: Marlys Millhiser

Charlie Greene, the single mother of fourteen-year-old Libby, had fared better than many pregnant teenagers. Her adoptive father Howard died just before the child was born. Her mother, Edwina, a biology professor at a Boulder, Colorado college, did not force Charlie into an ill-advised marriage. Instead she supported Charlie until she was able to care for herself and Libby. Edwina was providing short term child-care for Libby as the series began. Charlie had a responsible career as a literary agent, first in New York and then with Congdon & Morse in Los Angeles.

Charlie was in her thirties when she set off to interview Oregon author Jack Monroe in *Murder at Moot Point* (Doubleday, 1992). On arrival, she was accused of killing seventy-eight-year-old Georgette Glick in a hit-and-run accident. It turned out that Georgette had been shot first. The local sheriff impounded Charlie's car and placed her in protective custody in a local motel. Maybe Charlie had been working with too many science fiction writers. She used "out of body experiences" to find the killer.

In *Death of the Office Witch* (Penzler, 1993), the staff at Congdon & Morse were complacent when receptionist Gloria Tuschman disappeared only to be found dead in the alley. There were obvious motives, but Charlie delved deeper under the influence of the deceased Gloria's voice and the encouragement of police lieutenant David Dalrymple. Her probing placed her and Libby in serious danger.

Murder in a Hot Flash (Penzler, 1995) found Charlie monitoring her mother's behavior. Edwina, an advisor on a documentary being filmed in Utah, was accused of being unstable and disruptive. Charlie, leaving her job behind, traveled to the set. Mysterious clouds and strange behavior on the part of animals were attributed to the filming of a horror movie by another company. That she could ignore, but not the arrest of Edwina for murdering Gordon Cabot, the director of the horror film.

Edwina continued to play a major role in Charlie's life during *It's Murder Going Home* (St. Martin, 1996). So did Mitch Hilsten, the handsome actor with whom she shared a romance while in Utah. Edwina's breast cancer brought Charlie and Libby back to Boulder, the college town where Charlie had changed her own life, and created Libby's. The neighborhood had changed. Someone wanted it to change even more. There were fires, wandering mountain lions, satanic rituals, and murder. Libby met the man who had fathered her, but found him wanting.

Nobody Dies in a Casino (St. Martin, 1999) was cluttered. There were conversations with Charlie's inner voice, science fiction pyrotechnics, astrologers, right wing former military men, and robbery at a Las Vegas gambling casino. All of this took place while Charlie was ostensibly on vacation. She was connected to a half-dozen plus murders within the first five days. An undisciplined narrative.

The first mistake for Charlie was to spend her vacation at home as *Killer Commute* (St. Martin, 2000) began. Next was to get blood all over her sweatshirt when she found neighbor Jeremy Fiedler dead in his car. The narrative became bizarre: messages from the dead, recurring deafness for Charlie, multiple identities, and a stubborn detective who had focused on Charlie as a killer. Reality far outweighed by emphasis on humor.

The Rampant Reaper (St. Martin, 2002) was murky and confusing. Edwina had convinced Charlie to accompany her to Myrtle, Iowa for the funeral of Great Aunt Gertie. The town had no school aged children. The adults were caretakers for their parents and grandparents, many of whom lived at Gentle Oaks Health Care Center. At times two generations in a family were residents there. The social construct of Myrtle placed heavy responsibilities on the females in a family. They were to sacrifice themselves to care for older relatives. Edwina felt considerable pressure which is why she had taken Charlie along for moral support. Someone else had another solution. Elderly residents at Gentle Oaks were dying under suspicious circumstances. When a staff member was murdered, the police and media became involved. Should not be read by anyone over forty.

The series resurfaced in 2005 with *Voices in the Wardrobe* (Severn House). Although Millhiser's wit and ingenuity have saved some otherwise mediocre narratives, this one was seriously confusing. Out of friendship, Charlie combined attendance at a San Diego conference with escorting Maggie Stutzman to the Sea Spa at Marina del Sol. Maggie was in bad shape, coming off medical drug interactions. Charlie flitted back and forth as, one after another, corpses appeared and were connected to Maggie. Charlie had at least five allies in her efforts to prove Maggie innocent, one of which was her now emancipated daughter, Libby. They played hide and seek as the body count increased.

The touches of extra-sensory perception were distracting in what had the potential to be a good series. Some will enjoy the mixture. Author Marlys Millhiser has a second series featuring Lennora Poole.

Sophie Greenway

Author: Ellen Hart, pseudonym for Patricia Boehnhardt

Sophie Greenway had separated herself from her parents, well-to-do hoteliers in St. Paul, Minnesota. At seventeen, she joined a rigid religious group, the Church of the First-Born. She attended the church's Bible College in California; then, married Norman Greenway, a young minister. The church eschewed modern medicine, believing in the restoration of good health by prayer. Sophie rebelled against this concept when her six-year-old son Rudy was desperately ill. When she left Norman, he fought for custody and won. Disheartened, Sophie returned to the Twin City area, and her parents, Henry and Pearl

Tahtinen. She built a new life for herself, first as a food critic; then, as editor of *Squire's Magazine*, a local publication. She married Bram Baldric, local radio talk show host and budding author. Rudy avoided contact with his mother until he was eighteen.

As *This Little Piggy Went to Murder* (Ballantine, 1994) began, Sophie and Bram were in Duluth, visiting old friends, Amanda and Luther Jorenson, en route to Northern Minnesota. Several murders tied to the business owned by Amanda's father and the senatorial campaign of her brother, Jack, delayed their vacation and tested Sophie's loyalty to old friends. When Rudy asked if he could come to the Twin Cities, to live with Sophie, and attend the University of Minnesota, Sophie and Bram were delighted.

During *For Every Evil* (Ballantine, 1995), Bram, Sophie, and Rudy frequented the Minneapolis art world. Hale Micklenberg, a vitriolic art critic, was suspected of threats against his wife Ivy, but it was Hale who was found dead in their home. Among the suspects, there were several with secrets, with motives for murder, and with a sense of guilt. Rudy, accepting his own homosexuality, was relieved by Sophie and Bram's understanding.

Ministers, adherents, and apostates of the Church of the First-Born descended upon Minneapolis and the Maxfield Plaza Hotel during *The Oldest Sin* (Ballantine, 1996). Sophie's parents, owners of the hostelry, had deeded it over to her and Bram before leaving on an extended vacation. Among her first guests were four women who had shared an apartment with Sophie during her years at Bible School. Absent, was the sixth occupant, Ginger Pomejay, whose early death still haunted the others. They wondered if she had been murdered.

Author Ellen Hart interspersed the contemporary narration in *Murder in the Air* (Ballantine, 1997) with letters written in the past by youthful reporter Justin Bloom to his mother, Heda. Justin had fled to Europe when accused of murdering Kay Collins, the woman he loved. He may have inadvertently caused Kay's death, but he had not killed her. Heda, a wealthy businesswoman and new owner of the radio station where Bram worked, authorized the revival of a long abandoned radio serial, *Dallas Lane, P.I.* The initial plot featured a case similar to Kay's death and postulated that Justin had been framed. Bram worked closely with the project and eventually involved Sophie and Rudy.

In what may be the best yet of her Greenway series, *Slice and Dice* (Ballantine, 2000), Hart blended third person narration with a journal and interviews by an investigative reporter. Marie Demontraville had undertaken an unauthorized biography of eminent culinary expert, Connie Buckridge. Nathan, Connie's son, had been Sophie's first lover. She was also connected as the newly appointed restaurant reviewer for the local newspaper. George Gildenmeister, the prior reviewer who had become increasing vindictive in recent reviews, was murdered. Marie, befriended by Bram; Connie, who had spent her life concealing the truth; and Sophie, who fought Nathan's desire to resume their relationship, kept the action flowing to a startling conclusion.

Sophie and her coworker, Bernice Washburn had just finished a radio interview in *Dial M for Meat Loaf* (Fawcett, 2001) when Bernice was notified that her father was gravely ill. Sophie offered transportation to rural Rose Hill She had not realized that the harsh Minnesota weather and the problems of the Washburn family would necessitate a longer stay. John Washburn, a prominent businessman with a mysterious past, had confessed to the murder of blackmailing handyman Kirby Runbeck. Certain that he was protecting someone, Sophie examined those whom John loved enough to shelter from punishment. The first clue was in her own memory. She had known John under a different name years before.

Death on a Silver Platter (Fawcett, 2003) had the familial complexities of a daytime serial. Sophie and her parents had been close to the wealthy Veelund family for years. Although Sophie and Elaine Veeland had been pals since childhood, there was a great deal of family history of which neither was aware. The murders of Elaine's mother Millie and Elaine's teenage daughter Tracy opened Pandora's box. A box containing a journal written by Pearl, Sophie's mom, was equally explosive.

Bram and Sophie became involved in the personal affairs of two other couples in *No Reservations Required* (Fawcett, 2005). Newspaper publisher (and Sophie's boss) Bob Fabian had become depressed. His beloved wife Valerie had been killed in a car accident, partly caused by Ken Loy. When Ken was murdered on the anniversary of her death, the unidentified killer bragged to Bob about what he had done. Bob's efforts to call 911 ended when he was shot, but the operator heard a vague reference to "brother." Whose brother? Valerie's brother, Phil Banks who during the narrative married young Chris Parillo or Bob's half-brother, Andy Gladstone who inherited the Minneapolis Times Register? The ending may be distasteful to some readers.

Author Ellen Hart, who also writes the Jane Lawless series, presented an interesting setting, a different heroine, and more than competent plots.

Liz Gresham

Author: Carol Dawber

It has been a long time since a New Zealand woman was generally recognized as a mystery writer. Ngaio Marsh, one of the Golden Age authors, included New Zealand locales in several of her books featuring Inspector Roderick Alleyn and his wife, Troy.

Liz Gresham and Inspector Doug Fisher rented units in the same building and had become acquainted over a period of time. She was older, a widow; he, a divorced man with children. They enjoyed one another's company but it did not amount to an affair. Liz, who had grown up on a farm in the South Canterbury area, was attuned to the pleasures of New Zealand's natural resources, but well adapted to city life. She was still active as a librarian, using her skills to access information needed by Doug. Her spare time was spent sketching and painting, work that had received recognition and provided her with supplemental income. She was fit and enjoyed swimming and kayaking.

Liz and her friend Bridget Armstrong anticipated some hardships in *Backtrack* (River Press, 1992) as they "tramped" the Heaphy Track, South Island, N.Z. They joined hikers proceeding along the track, stopping for overnights at huts maintained by the park rangers. A quartet of college students, a married German couple, a divorced man with his nine-year old son, an American businessman, and two locals filled out the group. By the time Liz and Bridget discovered the body of young Nina Weller (wife in the German couple) off the beaten track, the weather had deteriorated. Fortunately Inspector Doug Fisher arrived before they became totally isolated. Someone in their midst was a killer and would kill again.

Dawber's New Zealand reflected a common problem, the stresses between burgeoning industry and the need to protect natural resources. Set in Nelson, a picturesque South Island community, *Earthwork* (River Press, New Zealand, 1993) portrayed the death of Kirsten Colby, a commercial model who had ties to an environmental group. Inspector Doug Fisher of Wellington was assigned temporarily to replace a retiring officer. He needed help acclimating to the community and meeting individual suspects. Some of that help came from Constable Jan Rycroft, who had a conflict of interest in the case. The rest came from Liz Gresham, who visited Nelson on a vacation. Her low-key approach and a friend within the Earthworks artistic group alerted Liz to possible motivations among the suspects in time to keep Doug from arresting the wrong person.

Sounds Easy (River Press, 1994) had three narrative strains, of which Liz's was the least significant. She was still working at the library, but had agreed to provide the illustrations for a children's book by widower Oliver Loomes. She visited him at his secluded home regularly to compare notes, filling a gap in his life. She was always aware that he was dying of leukemia. On her trips, she noted an attractive blonde whom she saw on the ferryboat, and overheard while kayaking. Liz's sketch of the woman helped Doug. He was following a suspected murderer and drug dealer who connected up with the blonde. She, who was known by a variety of names, had become an obsession to an unhappily married carpenter.

Mother Lavinia Grey

Author: Kate Gallison

Mother Lavinia Grey, who preferred to be called "Mother Vinny" was the vicar of St. Bede's, a rundown Episcopalian parish slated for absorption into a more prosperous church in a nearby town. A tiny slim widow, who had entered the church after the death of her husband Stephen, Lavinia became comfortable in Fisherville, New Jersey. She played her cello with other baroque music lovers, tended to her minuscule congregation, and sponsored projects for less fortunate members of the community. Although she had initially accepted that St. Bede's was terminal, she fought the hierarchy for its survival.

In *Bury the Bishop* (Dell, 1995), Mother Lavinia and three active members of her congregation attended a clerical/laity meeting, during which the bishop was murdered. There were clues that indicated that a member of her delegation was the killer. Since the bishop had sought to close down St. Bede's, Lavinia was a suspect. While trying to prove otherwise, Lavinia absorbed first, a pedigreed dog; then, Saraleigh, an abused mother and her children, into the vicarage. The motive for the bishop's death lay in his family relationships, and that was where Lavinia and detective David Dogg found the answer.

Community support provided St. Bede's with a reprieve, but in *Devil's Workshop* (Dell, 1996) Lavinia had a host of new problems. There were rumors of Satanism in the community, religious objects had been stolen from St. Bede's and Rex, Saraleigh's former husband, returned. He had appeared on the eve of her marriage to Ralph, a disabled member of Lavinia's community. When Ralph was arrested for murder, these problems coalesced, keeping David and Lavinia busy. David returned to his former wife, although they did not remarry.

As *Unholy Angels* (Dell, 1996) began, Mother Vinny found a new escort in Mac Barrow, an African-American retired baseball player, who offered to renovate and play the parish organ. Members of Lavinia's congregation were among those aggrieved by the sale of the Little League baseball grounds to land developer Bunker Todd. When he was murdered, she probed not only the athletic implications of the death, but also Todd's sexual activities.

A few days of contemplation and rest from the worries of St. Bede's was Lavinia's goal in *Hasty Retreat* (Delacorte, 1997). She and Deacon Deedee Gilchrist led a group to St. Hugh's Monastery in upper New York State. Trouble was already there in the persons of Rev. Rupert Bingley (who wanted to shut St. Bede's down) and politician Rodman Sedgewick. While she kept her eye on both of them, aged missionary Brother Basil was murdered, and Sedgewick's loving wife Ouida was poisoned. Lavinia had to take a second look at the situation, but from a difficult position.

A casual encounter in the cemetery brought Lavinia into the lives of Shannon Smith and her father Mark in *Grave Misgivings* (Delacorte, 1998). The Smiths had come from Phoenix, Arizona with the ashes of Mark's mother, Mary Agnes Fitzroy Smith. They intended to bury her ashes beside the grave of his father, James W. Smith, who may have died during the 1955 flood. No such grave was to be found. The search for a live James W. Smith was fraught with danger for both the Smiths and Lavinia, but she received an unexpected reward.

A quirky series that sought to strike a balance between humor and awareness of human suffering.

Dr. Mackenzie "Mac" Griffin

Author: Jeanne McCafferty

Money and social position had never been important in the Griffin family. Their financial needs had been met over generations by prudent investments and trust provisions. Mackenzie Griffin's parents were professors at Riverside University in Registon, Connecticut. She often thought they were totally immersed in their fields of study (Elizabeth in Classics and Walker in American History). Then she would be surprised at how aware they were of the lives led by their three children. During their formative years most matters dealing with the children had been left to Stella, the family housekeeper. In her early teens, Mac had taken on parental responsibilities for her two younger siblings, Chad and Whitney. Rather than attend Riverside, Mac earned her bachelors degree at Connecticut College; then changed to New York University, ending up with a Ph.D. in Criminal Justice. Chad and Whitney kept up the family tradition, taking their degrees at Riverside.

At age thirty-one, Mac lived comfortably in a four-room apartment in New York City. She chose the location because it provided her with a small garden area in her backyard. Her social life was limited. Her best friend continued to be Sylvie Morgan, a friend from college days who was still waiting for her big break in the theatre. An ardent suitor had been dropped instantly when Mac learned he had inquired as to the state of her trust funds. That left her very cautious as to romance.

Mac taught at John Jay College of Criminal Justice at CCNY. Initially she specialized in crimes relating to stalkers, but gradually branched out into more general applications. Over a period of years, her work providing seminars for the New York City Police Department had led to consultancies on cases where stalkers were suspected.

Lt. Mario Buratti had no money in the budget for a psychological consultant in *Star Gazer* (St. Martin, 1994), but he knew Mac would be intrigued by his latest murder case. Video editor Martin Jury had been found dead in a studio, lying in a pose reminiscent of Peter Rosellini's latest video. A second murder patterned on a subsequent Rosellini video convinced both Mac and Mario that a serial killer was obsessed with the pop star. With dozens of suspects to sift through, they were under pressure. One problem was solved. Peter Rosellini was very interested in Mac, and had more money and prestige than she did.

Mac's psychological skills were less important in *Artist Unknown* (Headline, 1995). She visited her parents in Registon where brother Chad had recently purchased an art gallery. The death of the prior owner set Mac and Chad on the trail of art thieves. Mario Buratti entered the case when Mac was assaulted in New York City. One surprising accomplice was Walter, Mac's father who aided and abetted the search of a suspect's home.

A subway bombing in *Finales and Overtures* (Headline, 1996) was treated as a seminal event, one that would be remembered as had been the murders of the Kennedy brothers and Martin Luther King. The incident might seem minor to a current reader in comparison with the Twin Towers and Pentagon attacks. The narrative used the bombing to highlight the impact on police officers, parole officers, social workers, and emergency responders. Mac had been nearby when the explosion occurred, so was an appropriate therapist to work with a group of police officers. She had taken a sabbatical from John Jay to work on PEPSI, a project that evaluated the emotional price paid by persons in the criminal justice system. She was simultaneously involved with a murder on the stage of the new Century Theatre. Sylvie had her first big break in musical theatre in *Reunion.* Her public disagreement with director Gil Richardson weighed against her when she was discovered standing over his corpse with a knife.

Simona Griffo

Author: Trella Crespi, pseudonym for Camilla Trinchieri

The fulsomely described Simona was in her thirties, physically "well endowed," with brown hair like "whole wheat fettuccini." She had attended Barnard College and was an accomplished linguist. The daughter of a retired Italian diplomat, Simona was a divorced resident alien working in New York as an art buyer when the series began.

During *The Trouble with a Small Raise* (Zebra, 1991), Simona investigated the poisoning of Fred Critelli, creative director at Harland, Heffer, and Higgins. As a fellow employee, she was a suspect, bringing her into contact with handsome detective Stan Greenhouse.

Simona's contacts in the movie world emerged during *The Trouble with Moonlighting* (Zebra, 1991). She spent vacation time as a dialect coach on an Italian film in New York. The death of aging actress Johanna Gayle added to stress on the location. Johanna and director Sara Varni had been in constant conflict, but Johanna also had a romantic rival. A third suspect emerged.

The romance with Greenhouse was on hold when Simona went to a Caribbean island in *The Trouble with Too Much Sun* (Zebra, 1992). A stint as volunteer sitter for "Lundi", an endearing two-year-old boy, involved Simona in his promiscuous mother's murder. There were witchcraft and cocaine addictions among the suspects.

During *The Trouble with Thin Ice* (HarperCollins, 1993), Simona vacationed with Stan and his fourteen-year-old son Willy. Simona and Willy worked together to clear Kesho Larson, an African-American friend whose inheritance of a Frank Lloyd Wright home and plans for an interracial marriage, made her a suspect in murder.

Simona became more endearing when viewed in her native Italy during *The Trouble with Going Home* (HarperCollins, 1995). Her trip was precipitated by the news that her mother had left the family home and moved in with friend Mirella Monti, director of an art school. Simona was barely off the plane when the robbery and murder of Tamar Deaton was tied to the Monti family. She managed to solve the case, reunite her parents, and successfully end her ties to Carlo, her former husband.

Simona's decision to move in with Stan brought objections from Willy's mother, Irene, in *The Trouble with a Bad Fit* (HarperCollins, 1996). Simona juggled problems at home and at work when a major advertising account was jeopardized by the death of model Phyllis Striker. Roberta Riddle, a designer seeking a comeback, had mysterious ties to Phyllis who was killed in her office building. The risks that Simona took in investigating the connections among Roberta's employees and friends endangered her safety.

A week on Long Island with Stan and Willie was not enough for Simona in *The Trouble with a Hot Summer* (HarperCollins, 1997). Advertising executive Bud Warren hired Simona and her friend Dmitri to investigate the death of his wife, Polly. The police considered Bud the most likely suspect in Polly's drowning. They perceived his subsequent disappearance and death as suicide. Laurie, their vulnerable daughter, wracked first by her parents' divorce, then their deaths, asked Simona and Dmitri to continue their investigation. Trust was the significant factor for Simona. Whom did Bud trust enough to remove his life jacket when he was at sea in his kayak?

The pattern was similar to that in many series where the female sleuth was involved with a police officer, who would prefer she left the investigating to him, but benefited from her detecting.

Anneke Haagen

Author: Susan Holtzer

Anneke Haagen's connection to the authorities was opportune when she found corpses. She provided services as a computer consultant to the Ann Arbor, Michigan police department. A silvery haired woman in her forties, Anneke was divorced from her husband Tom. Their two daughters were grown. When not working, she kept busy with her collection of art deco. Karl Genesko, whom she eventually married, had a distinguished football career at the University of Michigan and in the National Football League before he became a police officer.

It was while antique hunting at garage sales that Anneke discovered Joanna Westlake dying in her car, as *Something to Kill For* (St. Martin, 1994) opened. Young Ellen Nakamura, a competitor of Joanna's, was a potential suspect so mutual friends convinced Anneke to investigate. Lt. Karl Genesko not only did not disdain her help, but became interested in her as a woman. Greed among collectors was the obvious motive, but it was shared by so many.

The destruction of her home by fire had left Anneke prone to anxiety, as *Curly Smoke* (St. Martin, 1995) began. She rented a small cottage in an urban enclosure, where her neighbors were under pressure to sell to developers. The killer of James Kenneally, a homosexual who opposed the project, had to be a resident as the area had been cut off by a storm. Anneke found historic reasons for protecting the area, but nearly lost her life when she found a secondary use for dental floss. Karl Genesko made it clear that he wanted a commitment.

Karl was encouraged to participate in alumni activities during Homecoming in *Bleeding Maize and Blue* (St. Martin, 1996). The threat of a recruitment scandal at the University of Michigan galvanized the athletic department into action. One result was the death of NCAA investigator Alvin Greeneway, also a Michigan alum. Anneke worked with Karl and Zoe Kaplan, an ambitious campus reporter, utilizing her considerable computer expertise to uncover information.

In her next mystery, *Black Diamond* (St. Martin, 1997), Holtzer combined an interesting glance at the history of Northern Lower Michigan with murder. Anneke and Karl played substantial roles in the investigation of Gerald Swann's death, but Zoe Kaplan and Swann's daughter Clare provided most of the action. Clare, who had not seen her father in twenty years, was fortunate to have Zoe as an alibi when he was found dead in her room. Cautious of any conflict of interest with her role as reporter, Zoe probed the history of the Swann family as hinted at in letters written a century before. An absorbing novel.

The Silly Season (St. Martin, 1999) again focused on Zoe Kaplan. UFO's revisited the University of Michigan campus and expert Thomas Edison Stempel was killed. Anneke and Karl clarified the issues, but it was Zoe's book. This one was for laughs.

Readers may be leery initially of *The Wedding Game* (St. Martin, 2000), which has a heavy Internet component. Read on. Anneke's involvement in a chat room restricted to computer game developers and fans took a serious turn when confrontational participant Vince Mattus was murdered. She had sufficient pressures in her life at that point with the wedding plans. Being a suspect added to the stress. Zoe and Karl pitched in to help.

San Francisco was an ideal honeymoon location for Anneke and Karl during *Better Than Sex* (St. Martin, 2001). They eagerly accepted an invitation to watch the University of Michigan football game at their friend Richard Killian's sports bar, Maize and Blue. Karl wasn't the only one who took UM football seriously. Anneke was annoyed by the intrusive and provocative questions asked by doctoral candidate Lindsay Summers as to individual food choices. Lindsay was silenced by poison in her no-salt tomato juice. The murder had implications beyond the bar room; Karl and Anneke called on Zoe Kaplan to investigate in Ann Arbor.

Marina Haines

Author: Dawn Stewardson

Marina Haines worked as an investigator for Sherwin McNee Indemnity of California in their Auto Claims Division, until she was transferred to Special Claims. A dark-haired young woman in her late twenties, she was guided in her personal, and sometimes professional, life by messages from Princess Amonit, a 3,000-year-old presence. The mummy beads worn by Marina conveyed the messages. Her over-protective mother was deeply concerned about Marina's activities. I don't blame her.

Until *The Mummy Case* (Harlequin, 1994), Marina's claims insurance experience had been with vehicle liability. Within a few weeks of her transfer to the Special Claims Division, she was assigned to discover how the mummy case holding the 3,000-year-old body of Princess Amonit had disappeared while on loan to a San Francisco museum. The substitution of a replica required a high level of skill. Not only did Marina closely resemble the Princess, but mummy beads given her by a suspect emanated messages from Amonit. Revington York was first a suspect, then, a partner in detection.

Marina had mourned Revington as dead. She was almost as angry as she was relieved to learn in *The Mummy Beads* (Harlequin, 1994), that he was alive and well in Boston. Even after his explanation that he was in a Witness Protection Program, Marina was unwilling to accept that their relationship had ended. Under the direction of Princess Amonit, she negotiated with gang leader Chucky Cochrane, currently in jail, who had a contract out on Revington. In return, she promised to rescue Angie his kidnapped wife, and identify her abductors. The Princess wanted relief too: the recovery of her mummy so she could rejoin it.

Very light fare. Stewardson is better known for her romance novels.

Perdita Halley

Author: Sarah Smith

The pre-World War I trilogy featuring biochemist Alexander von Reisden and almost blind pianist Perdita Halley should be read sequentially to be best enjoyed. Alexander, whose identity was the focus of *The Vanished Child* (Ballantine, 1992), had been raised under the name von Reisden. He had been left homeless after the Boer War. As Alexander von Reisden he became a well-known chemist, but appeared as Richard Knight, the missing heir to an American fortune. As Richard, he met young Perdita, a virginal musician destined to marry Harry Boulding, a rival heir. The question was who had killed William Knight, Richard's brutal grandfather. Perdita was torn not only between her affection for Harry and her deeper love for Alexander/Richard, but between her need to be a performing musician and marriage. At this time it would have been unseemly for a married woman to have a musical career.

The Knowledge of Water (Ballantine, 1996) found both Perdita and Alexander in Paris. Although they met on occasion, she was dedicated to her career. He operated a facility for the treatment of the chronically mentally ill. Multiple plot lines intersected. New paintings by French Impressionist Claude Mallais, an artist believed to be dead, had surfaced. Perdita was exposed to women for whom marriage had meant the end of their creative lives. Paris experienced a devastating flood. Alexander wanted a wife; Perdita could not attend the conservatory if she were married. He was also preoccupied by the death of "Mona Lisa", a mentally ill street beggar. Perdita's decision not to marry became more difficult.

A Citizen of the Country (Ballantine, 2000) was set in 1910. The threat of war between France and Germany loomed on the horizon. Alexander encountered difficulty in getting a major army contract because of his Germanic (von Reisden) background. On a grander scale, Maurice Cyron's plan to thwart a quick German entry into France was endangered by his family members. Alexander balanced his love for Perdita (now his wife), their son Toby, and, increasingly, his Uncle Gilbert Knight against a professional responsibility for his patient, mentally ill playwright and theater owner Andre du Monde, and his devotion to Paris.

An astounding series, complex but rewarding.

Peaches Dann Halloran

Author: Elizabeth Daniels Squire

See: Peaches Dann, page 208.

Elizabeth Halperin

Author: Nancy Goldstone

After her separation from author Howard Hack, Elizabeth Halperin turned her back on urban life and moved with her infant daughter, Emily, to Lenox, Massachusetts. Howard and Elizabeth had an unusual marriage. She was employed as a commodity trader in New York City, supporting him while he worked on a novel. The huge success of his books and the birth of their first child threatened that balance. Elizabeth's determination to be a stay-home mother, and the presence of an infant, horrified Howard. He needed isolation for his literary efforts and preferred that Elizabeth continue her employment. His one million-dollar advance enabled him to move out and begin divorce proceedings. Her recent bonus and the rent for the Manhattan apartment were initially her only source of income.

As *Mommy and the Murder* (HarperCollins, 1995) began, Howard's naked corpse was discovered at the home of Margaux Chase. Both Howard and Elizabeth had been present for a masquerade party. There had been an affair between Margaux and Howard. The divorce papers had never been signed; so Elizabeth was now a wealthy widow, and the primary suspect. Members of the children's play group to which Elizabeth belonged rallied round to prove her innocence.

Local police chief Ned Rudge remained suspicious of Elizabeth, so, in *Mommy and the Money* (HarperCollins, 1997), he had no hesitation in considering her as a killer when a man she had been dating was murdered. Developer Jonathan Nichols had been attentive to Elizabeth but there had been no sexual involvement. However, he had boasted about their relationship, giving the illusion that she might know where he had hidden his ill-gotten gains.

Some clever gimmicks in a mildly entertaining but unrealistic series.

Judy Hammer and Virginia West

Author: Patricia Daniels Cornwell

Judy Hammer was introduced as the unhappily married chief of police in Charleston, South Carolina. She had been born in Arkansas. Her rise to this position was only briefly described. She had earned Phi Beta Kappa at Boston University in Criminal Justice. As a young police officer she had met Seth Hammer, an attractive city official, who not only tolerated her assertiveness but welcomed it. As Judy worked her way up the ladder, Seth became obese. He watched endless television shows, and lost any interest in his work. The couple had two sons—Jude was content in his chosen life as a jazz player; Randy was a wannabe actor. Neither had married although they had significant others and had presented the Hammers with four grandchildren.

Deputy Chief Virginia West, then in her forties, had never married. She had risen from the ranks, although some college education was mentioned. At least one more deputy chief (Jeannie Goode, traffic) was also a female. Virginia's household included an Abyssinian cat (Niles) but she wanted something more. She had always been competitive. Virginia formed a strange attachment to reporter/volunteer police officer Andy Brazil. Only twenty-two, Brazil, whose mother was an alcoholic, was attracted to older dominant women.

The trio emerged in *Hornet's Nest* (Putnam, 1997) while investigating a serial killer who targeted businesswomen. The narrative was frequently interrupted by episodic diversions as West, under Hammer's orders, took Brazil along as she cruised the streets in a patrol car.

The setting changed to Richmond, Virginia in *Southern Cross* (Putnam, 1998). Hammer had been widowed and acquired a Boston Terrier (Popeye). West and Brazil were estranged. After leaving Charleston, Hammer accepted a short-term assignment to reorganize the Richmond Police Department under a National Institute of Justice grant. She imposed a New York control system, which immediately created local resistance. Like a NFL football coach, she took her assistants with her when she moved. Brazil was no longer a reporter, but a technical assistant in charge of "research, public information and building a Web site." There was a murder, but the narrative was an undisciplined romp that raised doubts as to whether Hammer and/or West were capable at their jobs.

By *Isle of Dogs* (Putnam's, 2001), Hammer was superintendent of the Virginia State Police. Protégée Andy Brazil was still on her staff. Virginia West had been dropped. Brazil took advantage of Hammer's patronage by setting up a Web site as Trooper Truth in which he rambled on about Virginia history. He also used the Internet to get information as to the murder of lesbian government employee Trish Thrash, and the whereabouts of Hammer's Boston Terrier. The narrative contained bizarre characters— inbred residents of an offshore island, duplicitous dentists, incompetent government employees, and vicious young criminals. Brazil carried the major portion of the action while Hammer dealt with the impact of his essays. Cornwell turned her talents from forensics to farce in this one.

Cornwell is better known for her series featuring Kay Scarpetta.

Emily "Em" Hansen

Author: Sarah Andrews

Author Sarah Andrews' love of the outdoors shone in her narratives. The character of Emily "Em" Hansen emerged more slowly. She was a shy young geologist, unsure of her abilities or her impression on others. Emily's mother Leila, a proper Bostonian, had cast aside tradition to marry Clyde Hansen, a young Westerner attending college in the East. When their love did not survive the move to Wyoming, she became an alcoholic. Em's maternal grandmother, who was still an influence to be reckoned with, had insisted that Em attend an Eastern prep school. There, she was no more comfortable than her mother was in Chugwater. Em's special achievement and great joy was riding quarter horses in the barrel races at rodeos. Her affection for her mother diminished over the years. She visited home only to see her dad.

Em took underemployment as a mud-logger with Blackfeet Oil Company as *Tensleep* (Signet, 1994) opened. She mourned the death of her mentor Bill Kretzmer at the Bar Diamond oil site. Em did not believe his death was an accident. She could have left the matter to the police department, stifling her suspicions that Bill had uncovered criminal activity at the site, but did not.

Em's investigation may have prompted her promotion to the company headquarters. In *A Fall in Denver* (Scribners, 1995), she received no welcome from her fellow employees. Scott Dinsmore, who had shared her concerns that something was wrong with production levels at Lost Coyote Field, leaped from the sixteenth floor of the building. Em renewed acquaintances with former prep school classmates, and made a treacherous new alliance.

The loss of Em's job as the oil industry fell into hard times hit her economically, but it was the death of her beloved father that devastated her as *Mother Nature* (St. Martin, 1997) began. When U.S. Senator Pinchon hired Em to investigate the murder of his daughter Janet, she assumed he wanted the killer found. That was her first mistake. Em almost became Janet, also a geologist, wearing her clothes, driving her truck, working for her former employer to discover what Janet had learned to make her so dangerous. In uncovering family secrets, weary and confused Em brought back memories of her own childhood and the death of her older brother, hidden too long, now exposed so that she had to deal with them.

J. C. Mencken's request that she get involved in the death of his wife Miriam, which had left his daughter Cecelia amnesiac, in *Only Flesh and Bones* (St. Martin, 1998) was coupled with an offer to find Em a job. Even that wasn't enough to motivate Em. What did was her former friendship with Cecelia, currently being treated by therapist Dr. Melanie Steen. Miriam and Cecelia had been living at a rented ranch in Wyoming. Cecelia was competent enough when she discovered her mother dead in bed to call 911, but later the night and most of the following week disappeared from her memory. Access to Miriam's journal, which she had left with her friend Cindey, provided answers, causing Em to feel considerable sympathy for Miriam. Another, more loyal friend, Julia, provided a second journal by Miriam.

Em must have had rocks in her head when she accepted an unverified request to speak at a paleontologist's conference in *Bone Hunter* (St. Martin, 1999). Within hours of her arrival in Salt Lake City, her host George Dishey had been murdered and she was in handcuffs. The local police department provided Officer "Ray" Thomas Brigham Raymond, a handsome escort and confederate for finding the real killer, but her life was in danger. Em's belief system (agnosticism) was challenged by her love for Ray, a devout Mormon.

Pocketed within *An Eye for Gold* (St. Martin, 2000) were heavy layers of Western history, metallurgy, and environmental concerns. The plot was viewed by an assortment of characters. Tom Latimer, a top FBI agent, was too valuable to be sent West on a minor fraud case. Kyle Christie, a second-rate geologist for a mining company, envied his missing partner Don McCallum's "eye for gold." Laurel Dietz's ambition outran her skills. Em's role was to follow up on the reports left by dead biologist Pat Gilmore and verify that there were no endangered species that would justify withholding permits to mine a collection of old gold claims. Em was distracted by Ray's marriage proposal, unsure that she could be a Mormon wife—and mother. Danger clarified her decision.

Em had moved to Salt Lake City because of Ray, but in *Fault Line* (St. Martin, 2002), neither mother nature nor Ray's family cooperated. A moderate earthquake caused structural damage in the city, casting doubt on the construction work in facilities which would be used during the 2002 Olympics. Ray's family and particularly his manipulative sister Katie made it clear that Em would be an unsuitable wife and mother. Without steady income and still working on a graduate degree, Em became involved in the FBI investigation of the deaths of whistleblower Dr. Sidney Smeeth, a state geologist. There were other complications, a few too many: the unplanned pregnancy of wealthy young Faye Carter; the connections between the Raymond family and the firms responsible for construction.

However rational Em had been in her past investigations, she "lost it" completely in *Killer Dust* (St. Martin's, 2003). She and FBI agent Jack Sampler had made a commitment but within hours he'd left her behind to respond to another woman's needs. She realized how little she knew of Jack's life, yet tried to believe in him. She took off for Florida where Jack had gone with Faye Carter and Tom Latimer at her side. That's where it got complex, mixing in terrorists, space shuttles and the disappearance of microbiologist Cal Wheat.

Em's primary employment in *Earth Colors* (St. Martin's, 2004) was as live-in babysitter for Faye Carter's daughter. An offer from art gallery owner Tert Krehbeil seemed providential. Using her knowledge of minerals, Em was to verify the authenticity of a Frederick Remington painting owned by Tert's family for three generations. Faye's role was to act as an air courier. Em saw the project as a potential thesis topic needed to complete her master's degree. Her growing knowledge of the toxic potential of early pigments led Em to believe there was a killer in the Krehbeil family.

Although her romance with Detective Raymond had ended, he called on Em's expertise in *Dead Dry* (St. Martin, 2005) when a mutilated corpse was uncovered on the floor of a quarry. Em not only provided professional information but identified the victim, Afton McWain. Em had known Afton and his wife Julia for years, but there had been changes. Afton, who had become wealthy, left Julia and the children, moving to a ranch with a younger woman, Gilda who claimed to be his common-law wife. He had abandoned his materialism and was living a primitive lifestyle. His beliefs caused Alton to challenge local real estate developers (including a real estate agent, representative of a savings and loan, and a real estate attorney). Ray's personal problems were interspersed in Em's investigation during which she worked with a rookie detective, Michele Aldrich.

Lovely sense of place.

Anne Danielle Hardaway

Author: Beth Sherman

Anne Danielle Hardaway was presented as a redheaded ghostwriter in her thirties, who lived at Oceanside Heights, New Jersey. Her commitment to the area was very strong. When her primary employer, Triple Star Publishing, moved, she arranged to work out of her home. Work for Anne was ghostwriting how-to books and autobiographies. She gained a storehouse of second hand knowledge on household care, building repair, cooking, exercise, and even mental health. Her work tended to be methodical, beginning with a list, then an outline, drafting and redrafting from scraps of material gained by interviews, tapes or notes from the acknowledged author. Nevertheless, she had problems with her own procrastination and the lack of cooperation from the titular authors. Her life was disciplined. She ran three miles four to five times a week. She had almost a mystical relationship with the sea. She drove a red 1968 Mustang that attracted considerable attention.

Even romance could not pull Anne away from her family home. Not all of her memories of Oceanside Heights had been happy ones. Her mother Evelyn had been an early victim of Alzheimer's. Evelyn's bizarre behavior, even in public, had been a great source of embarrassment to Anne. Her father left the family to get a divorce but contributed financially. Anne stayed with Evelyn until she had to be institutionalized. Then she occupied the house alone except for an adopted cat, one-eyed Harry. She had friends: librarian Delia Graustark, bank loan officer Helen Passellbessy, and African-American detective Mark Trasker.

Anne felt an affinity with Tigger Mills as *Dead Man's Float* (Avon, 1998) began. She had been ostracized by her mother's illness. Tigger left Oceanside Heights after little Ruthie Klemperer died in a fire for which he had been blamed. His return twenty years later led to his death. Jack Mills, Tigger's younger brother, joined Anne in probing not only Tigger's death, but the earlier arson.

Mallory Loving had survived two husbands, drug and alcohol abuse, and a stint in porno films. As *Death at High Tide* (Avon, 1999) began, she had a new husband and a revived movie career. Background scenes from her forthcoming film, *Dark Horizon* were being shot in Oceanside Heights, near Landsdowne Park where Mallory and her twin sister Sheila had grown up. This was convenient for Anne who was ghostwriting Mallory's autobiography. The complications of working with Mallory deepened when she disappeared and was presumed dead.

Hurricane force winds swept across the New Jersey coast in *Death's a Beach* (Avon, 2000). Damage to Anne's Victorian cottage included needed repairs to the cellar floor. A skeleton, at first unknown and then shown to be hypnotherapist Steven Hillyard who had treated Anne's mother, was discovered in the process. Anne's personal investigation expanded to cover a series of deaths at the local nursing home.

In *The Devil and the Deep Blue Sea* (Avon, 2001), teenage witches surfaced in Oceanside Heights. The death of one of the young women and the disappearance of another would normally not have concerned Anne; however, the granddaughter of her dear friend Delia Graustark, was involved. Her association with Detective Mark Trasker took on a personal component as they worked together.

Anne must have been naïve to think that gathering her mother's family together in Oceanside Heights would go smoothly in *Murder Down the Shore* (Avon, 2002). Great Aunt Hannah who continued to maintain a home there, although she lived in Boston, was as demanding and tight-fisted as ever. She, her son Henry, and four of Anne's cousins were the only ones who attended. Hannah's murder was predictable, as she had ignored pleas for financial assistance from several relatives. Greed did not explain the savagery of the attack, however. Well aware that she was a prime suspect, Anne, assisted by Detective Mark Trasker, rose to the occasion.

Chapter headings in the series included information as to personal care, household hints and other excerpts from the books Anne was ghosting.

Annabelle Hardy-Maratos

Author: Hialeah Jackson, pseudonym for Polly Whitney

Annabelle Hardy-Maratos, who had an Ivy League Ph.D. in English, had enjoyed teaching. She had resigned because her deafness was gradually increasing. Taking over Hardy Security, the Miami business built up by her father Jacob, seemed the best available alternative. Jacob, a widowed former police officer, could spend his time fishing, except for occasional visits to the office. Annabelle, also a widow, needed to keep busy. Her successful marriage had ended after only two years when her husband Nikki Maratos died. They had met when Nikki was at the Yale Law School and Annabelle was working on her Ph.D. Seven years had passed since his death. Only in the second narrative did Annabelle seriously consider another man.

An only child, Annabelle had no children, sharing her home with two cats (Running Shoes and Ahoy Matey), and collecting first editions. She functioned well through signing and reading lips. Dave the Monkeyman (Jorge Enamorado), the son of Cuban emigrants, was her assistant. Dave's character was overdrawn. His language was abusive even to Annabelle. His ridicule of religion, of persons and objects held sacred by others was excessive and distasteful. He wore gaudy clothes and facial make-up, and carried a pet parrot around with him. He was intelligent enough to handle the financial aspects of the agency, and had a photographic memory for documents and movies. He loved Annabelle, and showed loyalty and affection in his own way. Whatever his mental age, he operated emotionally somewhere in the teens.

Shortly after assuming control of the agency, Annabelle and Dave investigated the death of nuclear physicist Rolando Ruiz de Castillo in *The Alligator's Farewell* (Dell, 1999). "Rollie" had plunged—or was pushed— into a nuclear pool, carrying with him a deadly secret. Hardy Security was hired by the University of the Keys to prevent further mishaps and to protect its reputation.

Milady (Millie) de Vargas, a Key West attorney, acted as primary caretaker for the Ernest Hemingway Museum in *Farewell, Conch Republic* (Dell, 1999). After her body was found in the barred Hemingway studio, the police arrested Gabriel Perez, a guard provided by Hardy Security. Annabelle and Dave flew to Key West to protect Gabriel and their own interests.

Polly Whitney has a second series featuring Mary "Ike" Tygart and Abby Abagnarro

Mary Minor "Harry" Haristeen

Author: Rita Mae Brown and her cat, Sneaky Pie

Who was the series sleuth? Mary Minor "Harry" Haristeen or, as the subtitles would have you believe, "Mrs. Murphy," her striped cat? These were difficult times for Harry. Her mother and father had died within the past four years. Her ten-year marriage to veterinarian Pharamond "Fair" Haristeen had ended. Fair had lived up to his name with $1,000 a month in maintenance; but was slow to pay. Harry coped in small town Crozet, Virginia because she had inherited a 120-acre farm. She earned pocket money as postmistress, a position that made little use of her art history degree from Smith College. Harry found social life difficult, because the friends that she and Fair had shared as a couple were choosing sides. Widow Miranda Hogendobber, who was a major resource for Harry, never faltered in her loyalty. Harry's post-divorce household included Mrs. Murphy, a Welsh corgi named Tee Tucker and two horses. A second cat, Pewter, joined them later. Harry's employment and her relationship with Fair changed over the extended series.

In *Wish You Were Here* (Bantam, 1990), while at work, Harry kept an interested eye on incoming mail; even at times sharing this information with her best (human) pal, Susan. With assistance from the menagerie (whose communications appeared in italics), Harry and Susan connected a series of deaths with postcards and copies of the letters of Claudius Crozet, for whom the town had been named.

During *Rest in Pieces* (Bantam, 1992), once she had decided that her marriage had ended, and that Fair loved widow Olivia "BoomBoom" Craycroft, Harry re-emerged into the town's social life. Handsome Blair Bainbridge, a professional model who had purchased Foxden Estate, was the popular choice to meet her needs. Folks needed something new to gossip about. Something turned out to be the dismembered body of a vagrant, briefly seen in the bank and around town.

During Blair's absence in *Murder at Monticello* (Bantam, 1994), the relationship between Harry and Fair improved to the point where they were dating. Fair attended her family events and assisted her in an investigation of murder, human bloodlines, and inheritance at the former home of President Thomas Jefferson. Of course, so did Mrs. Murphy.

Another historical home of Virginia, this time James Monroe's Ash Lawn, featured in *Pay Dirt* (Bantam, 1995). Turmoil arose when the financial stability of the local bank was threatened. Out-of-town biker Michael Huckstep and two bank officers were murdered. Kerry McCray, a sympathetic young woman, had been framed for the crimes.

Tee Tucker, Harry's Welsh corgi, shared the spotlight with Mrs. Murphy in *Murder, She Meowed, or Death at Montpelier* (Bantam, 1996). They saved Harry from a crazed murderer. Someone was killing steeplechase jockeys. The animal network knew where major evidence was hidden but the humans were slower to figure it out.

Roscoe Fletcher, headmaster at St. Elizabeth's high school, a man of questionable morals, did not seek publicity, but, in *Murder on the Prowl* (Bantam, 1998), he received some when his obituary was prematurely published in the local paper. Harry was interested because Brooke Tucker, Susan's daughter, was unhappy at her current school and wanted to transfer to St. Elizabeth's. A second false obituary of a friend of Roscoe's followed. These obits weren't just wishful thinking. Someone killed Roscoe as he went through the local car wash.

Cat on the Scent (Bantam, 1999) called for a major suspension of belief. Wealthy local citizens suborned a politician to advance their plan to meet water needs. When members of the group were shot, only the animals were privy to the killers' identities. Their heroic rescue of a suspect stretched even Harry's credulity. The cast of characters expanded with each narrative.

Shortly before the 20th annual Crozet high school class reunion in *Pawing Through the Past* (Bantam, 2000), former graduates each received a cryptic message, "You'll never grow old." The death of arrogant ladies man Charlie Ashcroft, followed by two other deaths, made it murder. By the time the Homecoming dinner and dance took place, the pets were working hard to find the killer before Harry was endangered. The narrative provided a strong message about the cruelty of teenagers against those who are different.

The investigation of three deaths connected to the Crozet Hospital in *Claws and Effect* (Bantam, 2001) proceeded on different levels. Sheriff Rick Shaw headed the official case. His deputy, Cynthia Cooper, joined with Harry on an independent investigation. The clinching clues, however, came from the pets who discovered a secret room in the facility; then had to lead the humans to the site.

The annual Hogwood Festival and the Wrecker's Ball brought all the locals and their guests together in *Catch As Catch Can* (Bantam, 2002). One guest, handsome foreign diplomat Diego Aybar, gave Fair some competition for Harry's time and attention. The mystery began low key with the theft of Minerva Hogendobber's hubcaps, but escalated when Dwayne Fuqua, the thief, was hanged; salvage car operator Sean O'Bannon was poisoned; and taxidermist Don Clatterbuck was shot. This was too much. In the end Harry had a ball.

The residents of Crozet who sat in a cluster at the University of Virginia womens' basketball games during *The Tail of the Tip-Off* (Bantam, 2003) took sports seriously. The mysterious death of contractor H. H. Donaldson at a game yielded several suspects from personal and business relationships. The pets had the modus operandi figured out far earlier than Fair and Harry did. Harry and BoomBoom put on an athletic performance when necessary.

Rabies is a diagnosis that strikes the heart with fear, but in *Whisker of Evil* (Bantam, 2004), the ensuing panic was an over-reaction. Yes, Barry Monteith's brain showed evidence of the rabies virus, but that was not what killed him. When Barry's partner Sugar Thierry did die of rabies, Harry and her ensemble looked beyond the silver-haired bat, back to 1974.

Cat's Eyewitness (Bantam, 2005) was talky. Oh, there was a murder, two in fact. Brother Thomas had been killed and left in the cold in front of a statue of the Virgin Mary at Mt. Carmel Monastery. The statue had gained notoriety because it seemed to be producing tears of blood. Local newscaster Nordy Elliott made the most of the events until he was killed. Susan and Harry took an interest because Brother Thomas was Susan's great-uncle. The narrative focused on several relationships: Susan and her husband Ned; Harry and Fair; Rev. Herb Jones who was considering a second wife, and BoomBoom with a surprising new romance

After a slow start, *Sour Puss* (Bantam, 2006) took off with the disappearance of grape and fungus expert Vincent Forland. He had been in Crozet before, warning of the dangers of mycotoxins and visiting individual small vineyards including Harry's. She no longer worked at the post office. Under new rules in a new site, she would not have been allowed to bring her pets to work. She and Fair had remarried. There were lots of suspects, another murder, and Fair became a suspect. There were also digressions by Brown on leather boots, global warming and combustion engines.

During *Puss 'n Cahoots* (Bantam, 2007) Fair and Harry took time off to attend the Saddlebred Competition in Dennison, Kentucky. They visited old friends, horse-breeder Joan Hamilton and her husband, trainer Larry Hodge. The competition that Larry and his horse faced in the five-gait matches included rival trainers Booty Pollard and Charly Trackwell. Booty and Charly may cooperate on some projects but where horses are concerned, it's a life or death rivalry. The pets led Harry to a solution but had to overcome a nasty monkey belonging to Booty.

Gynecologist Will Wylde was well known and liked in Albermarle County so why was he shot down in his parking lot as *The Purrfect Murder* (Bantam, 2008) began? Possibly because he regularly performed what he referred to as "terminations", but others called abortions. A pro-life advocate confessed to the crime. A second murder was not so easily solved even though the police arrested architect Tazio Chappars when she was discovered standing over Carla Paulsen's body with a knife.

In *Santa Clawed* (Bantam, 2008) the monks from the monastery of the Brothers of Love included men who had in their past led lives of sin and illegality. Now they reached out by running a hospice for hard-to-place patients; i.e. Alzheimer's, AIDS, etc. Lower down the hill they raised and sold Christmas trees. It was there that Fair and Harry discovered the corpse of Brother

Christopher, his throat slashed. There was no way Sheriff Rick Shaw and Deputy Cynthia Cooper could keep Harry out of their case as the death toll mounted.

Author Rita Mae Brown showed a light touch that will be appreciated even by those allergic to cats. Brown has a second series featuring Jane Arnold, master of the Jefferson Hunt Club, an aficionado of fox hunting. Coming in 2010 *Cat of the Century*

Benni (Albenia) Harper

Author: Earlene Fowler

Albenia "Benni" Harper had never dealt with her husband Jack's death. Their parting when he left the ranch for drinks at the local bar had been strained. They had met in high school, both children of local ranchers. Left alone at the ranch in her thirties, Benni moved to town. Her father provided a home for Dove, the grandmother who had raised six-year-old Benni after her mother died of cancer. Benni was tiny with red-blond hair frequently worn in a braid down her back. Her degree in American history and her interest in handcrafted objects qualified her for the position of curator of the Josiah Sinclair Folk Art Museum in San Celina, California, sponsored and dominated by the wealthy Constance Sinclair.

As *Fool's Puzzle* (Berkley, 1994) began, Benni was preparing for a quilt show to feature products of the local artist's cooperative. Because young Eric Griffin, the sponsor's appointed custodian, was behind schedule on hanging the quilts, Benni returned to the museum late in the evening, only to discover the corpse of potter Marla Chenier. Fearing that her cousin Rita, who roomed with Marla, might be involved, Benni withheld information from police chief Gabe Ortiz. The revelation that the murder might be tied to Jack's death spurred her own investigation.

In *Irish Chain* (Berkley, 1995), Benni discovered more bodies while sponsoring a prom for senior citizens at the Oak Terrace Nursing Home. One victim, Miss Rose Ann Violet, had been Benni's grade school teacher. The other, Brady O'Hara, once perceived to be racially prejudiced, had befriended Japanese-Americans after Pearl Harbor. Benni probed the history of area Japanese-Americans during and after World War II. She weighed loyalty to handsome local minister Rev. MacKenzie Reid against her special feeling for Gabe Ortiz.

By *Kansas Troubles* (Berkley, 1996), Gabe and Benni were married so she had a new family to accommodate—Gabe's. The couple traveled to rural Kansas, where they became immersed in relationships among Gabe's boyhood friends, their spouses and lovers. The death of Tyler Brown, an ambitious young woman who abandoned her Amish husband to become a country singer, left unanswered questions. Who had been the father of her child? Who hated her enough to bash her head in? Old loyalties played out against new ones as Gabe and Benni worked together to find the killer.

Gabe had been unable to express his grief about personal losses in his life as *Goose in the Pond* (Berkley, 1997) began. This caused the distance between him and Benni to grow. Her concentration on the Storytelling Festival sponsored by the Art Museum was distracted when she found the corpse of storyteller Nora Cooper while jogging. Nora's estranged husband was having an affair with one of Benni's close friends so she could not resist involving herself.

Although Benni and Gabe married, she kept the name Harper. Big celebrations coming up as *Dove in the Window* (Berkley, 1998) began. The traditional post-Thanksgiving barbecue teamed with a display of the art of Western Women for Heritage Days in San Celina. The best part for Benni was the party at her dad's ranch. That was complicated by the presence of Wade Harper, her former brother-in-law. He (although married) and ranch hand Kip Waterman had competed for the attentions of art photographer Shelby Johnson. When Shelby was murdered, both men were suspects. There was another romance going on that didn't suit Benni. Grandma Dove was being courted by Pulitzer Prize winning photographer Isaac Lyons.

Benni had known little of her mother, Alice Louise, the orphaned child brought up by an older cousin. In *Mariner's Compass* (Berkley, 1999), an unexpected legacy turned her focus towards her parents. The old gimmick of an heiress required to spend two weeks alone in the decedent's house was given an interesting twist. Benni's inheritance earned her enemies and put stress on her recent marriage. She survived with the help of new and old friends. Throughout the story, Benni thought about her mom who had been present for such a small portion of her life. Grandma Dove had filled her space.

The importance of mothers and birth families was brought home to Benni again in *Seven Sisters* (Berkley, 2000) when Gabe's son Sam, a college student, announced his plan to marry his pregnant girlfriend. Bliss, a police officer on Gabe's staff, was a member of a distinguished but dysfunctional local family. During the engagement party at the Seven Sisters Ranch, a member of the family was murdered. Bliss and her twin sister Joy tried to balance their loyalties to family and to justice. The plotting was ingenious and the characters, strong. Ford Hudson, a persistent sheriff's detective, drew Benni into the investigation while Gabe was preoccupied with his son and visiting ex-wife Lydia. Benni's inability to conceive a child was not a problem for her. She was ambivalent about motherhood.

Elvia Aragon, Benni's best friend, and her fiancé Emory who was Benni's cousin, joined Gabe, Benni and her grandmother Dove on a trip to Sugartree, Arkansas in *Arkansas Traveler* (Berkley, 2001). Forty years after the civil rights movement, race still mattered in Sugartree. The struggling white Baptist church and the African-American Baptist church were considering a merger. African-American Amen Tolliver, a childhood friend of Benni's, was running to unseat Grady Hunter the current white mayor. When Grady's son Toby, a difficult young man, was murdered the police department focused on Tolliver's nephew, Quinton. Gabe and Elvia as Hispanics were surprised at the bigotry to which they were exposed. Elvia was unsure if she should marry Emory considering the treatment she received in his hometown. Benni not only had to solve a murder but to reunite two people she loved.

With two happy weddings in the offing, Benni was in despair during *Steps to the Altar* (Berkley, 2002). Her friend Elvia was to wed Emory, Benni's cousin. Even more of a surprise was the marriage of Grandma Dove to Isaac Lyons. Benni and Gabe's marriage was in deep trouble. She diverted herself by investigating the fifty-year-old murder of Garvey Sullivan

Sunshine and Shadow (Berkley, 2003) showed Bennie as a young housewife/college student in 1978. Her blissful marriage to Jack Harper, her contacts with author Emma Baldwin and Emma's sullen son, Cody. Author Fowler skillfully wove the past into the lives of Emma, Benni, and Gabe in 1995. Emma had returned to San Celina after almost two decades. Benni's joy in seeing her again was tempered by the recent murder of Luke Webster, an old pal of Gabe, and attempts on her life.

Benni's dad was unable to help Shawna Abbott, the daughter of his dead friend Joe Darnell in *Broken Dishes* (Berkley, 2004), but Benni agreed to take over the task. Shawna and Johnny were transforming their cattle ranch into a "guest" (not "dude") ranch. Benni and Dove helped get speakers, staff, and attendees for the first two-week session, which focused on quilting. Fowler created fascinating supportive characters, including the reappearance of "Hud" (Det. Ford Hudson) who came on scene when human bones were discovered on the ranch.

Two events: an imposed assignment (by Dove) to help direct a children's church play, and a visit from Gabe's cousin Luis, led to traumatic outcomes for Benni and Gabe in *Delectable Mountains (*Berkley, 2005). Benni and Dove were to replace the director, who was called away by a family emergency, in an original production of *Pilgrim's Progress-The Joyful Journey* at the San Celina First Baptist Church. After a rehearsal, Benni discovered the body of custodian Walt Adams in the church sacristy. The subsequent theft of a valuable violin from the nearby Catholic mission museum might be connected. The problems between Gabe and Luis were not shared with Benni but she was aware of their tensions. Benni's compassion for children made it impossible for her to stay on the sidelines. This was a sensitive, moving narrative.

Based on her prior experience when she met Kathryn, Gabe's mother, Benni worked hard to prepare for her Christmas visit in *Tumbling Blocks* (Berkley, 2007). It was a different Kathryn who arrived, a warm affectionate woman who surprised them by bringing along Ray Austin, her new husband. Gabe didn't handle this well. Benni had problems at work too, getting ready for the Art Museum's Outside Artist Exhibit, which was to feature a recently donated painting by reclusive Abe Adam Finch. With all that on her plate she didn't need an assignment from her boss, Constance Sinclair, to solve a murder.

An excellent series. In 2008 Fowler began a new series featuring Love Mercy Johnson, a photo-journalist/café owner. Good news, a new Benni Harper *State Fair* (2010).

Sally Harrington

Author: Laura Van Wormer

Talk (Mira, Ontario, 1998) contained several of the characters who appeared later in the Sally Harrington series, but she was not included.

Sally (Sarah) Harrington left a major position on a frothy Los Angeles magazine to return to her Castleford, Connecticut hometown. Not only had she become disillusioned at the quality of the work she was doing, but an ambitious lover had dumped her. On her return to Castleford where her mother still lived, she revived a romance with her high school boyfriend, Assistant District Attorney Doug Wrentham. Doug had married and divorced while Sally was attending UCLA and working in California. Sally's mother, Belle, had survived what was then considered to be the accidental death of Dodge, her architect husband. She had raised Sally and her brother Bob by teaching school.

Sally worked part-time at the local newspaper in *Exposé* (Mira, 1999) until dynamic magazine editor Verity Rhodes hired her to write a profile of Cassy Cochran, president of the Darenbrook Broadcasting System (DBS). This offered an opportunity to rejuvenate Sally's career and gain a foothold in New York City. Leaving Doug behind, she found a more exciting replacement in Spencer Hawes. The problem was finding the flaws in Cassy Cochran that would spice up an article to the level Verity expected. Back in Castleford, the death of an initially unidentified man stirred up suspicions that the accident that killed Sally's father had been murder.

Sally's new lover, book editor Spencer Hawes' acquiescence in a proposed sexual triad with movie starlet Lilliana Martin so repulsed Sally in *The Last Lover* (Mira, 2000) that she ended their affair. When first Lilliana and then Spencer disappeared, an assumption was made that they had left together. Anchorwoman Alexandra Waring's offer of a top-level job at DBS headquarters in New York City came at the right time. Union leader Cliff Yarlen, Lilliana's reputed lover, was murdered shortly after he spent time with Sally. She felt compelled to find his killer to save her job and protect herself. The suspect in Sally's father's death had not been prosecuted and was making Castleford uninhabitable for the Harrington family.

Sexually explicit pictures of Sally and Spencer were circulated in Castleford. Nevertheless, she had wearied of the big city pressures and returned home. During *Trouble Becomes Her* (Mira, 2001), she still had responsibilities as a witness in a West Coast trial based on an inter-family mob killing. The complexities of the Arlenetta-Presario gangster feud became more personal when, on a visit to the Presario estate, a corpse was deposited in Sally's rental car.

The Bad Witness (MIRA, 2002) was bloated with repetitions of events occurring in the prior book. Its 433 pages also included at least four subplots: (1) a surprise as to the motive for Sally's father's death; (2)the lesbian relationship between Alexandra Waring and actress Georgianna Hamilton Ayres; (3) the professional relationship between Sally and Alexandra as it affected her future at DBS; and (4) the end of one romance for Sally and the beginning of a new one. But the focus of the narrative was the trial of Jonathan Small, member of the Presario family, for the murder of gangster Nick Arlenetta and its roots in the feud between their families. Sally witnessed an attack on Lilliana Martin, Jonathan's sister, after which she covered the trial for DBS.

Just after Sally had been offered her own morning television show by DBE in *The Kill Fee* (MIRA, 2003), she and members of her family became the victims of a major conspiracy. Uncle Percy, now in a residential home, Gregory House, was offered $10,000 for a five acre piece of land he didn't know he owned. This offer was from an environmental trust, but the land was vital to a major real estate project whose backers would not tolerate opposition. Both Sally and her mother felt vulnerable. Alexandra Waring's attractive but married brother David tempted Sally from her current relationship with Paul Fitzwilliam.

The on-going saga continued in *Mr. Murder* (Mira, 2006) which included several changes in Sally's life. She was finishing her stint as special projects administrator for Alexandra Waring and would soon co-anchor the DBS Morning Show with former law professor Emmett Philps. The past continued to haunt her however. Several men who had reason to harm Sally were killed. After each incident, Sally received a bouquet of white roses. Sally accompanied Alexandra to a West Coast meeting of television affiliates. While there they marketed the Darenbrook Broadcasting System. Sally was reunited with the love of her life, but someone else wanted her for himself.

Kate Harrod

Author: Laura Coburn

Katharine "Kate" Harrod's parents died when she was in her teens, leaving her to the care of a young aunt who lacked the warmth of Kate's mother. An early unsuccessful marriage produced no children. Dissatisfied with her job as a librarian, Kate entered the San Madera, California Police Academy. There she found the focus her life had been lacking. Kate's second marriage to Jonathan had been marred by the death of Emily, their first child. When son Tommy was born, she felt secure. Jonathan's career as an architect allowed him to work at home, eliminating the need for child-care expenses. Kate's absorption in her work desensitized her to Jonathan's growing unhappiness with their lifestyle. Only when he suffered a breakdown, did she realize that he was no longer supportive of her work. By that time, Kate had become supervisor for the homicide unit, requiring long hours, weekend and night work, and heavy pressure. When Jonathan found this intolerable, he moved out threatening to seek custody of Tommy. Kate's devotion to her job had become more important to her than her fifteen-year marriage.

Kate's involvement in the death of young Billy Schuyler was personal in *A Desperate Call* (Onyx, 1995). The boy had been playing in the Harrod yard hours before he disappeared. Although the case precipitated the separation from Jonathan, it validated Kate's commitment to her work.

In *An Uncertain Death* (Onyx, 1996), Kate was diverted from her focus on the suspected killer of teenager Connie Hammond by her attachment to Mabel, an elderly woman who reminded her of her mother. Revelations that Kenneth Branscombe, Mabel's brother and Connie's coach, might have had romantic feelings for the girl made him the obvious suspect. The suspicions against Kenneth were diminished, then reinforced. Confusing.

The discovery of infant Lucy, smothered by duct tape, in San Madera was followed by that of a murdered nude woman in the Stockton jurisdiction during *A Lying Silence* (Onyx, 1997). The adult victim was found to be Meryl Masters, a social worker, who had cared for Lucy in her mother's absence. This connection brought detectives from both departments into the case. Complex relationships between the mother and father of the child and with the adult victim emerged. Kate, acting as lead detective, contended with insubordination from a member of her team, while falling in love with another. On a lighter note, Kate built a bond with her son Tommy (now nine-years-old) by purchasing a drum set and arranging for them both to take lessons.

Kate was concerned in *A Missing Suspect* (Onyx, 1998) that her failure to properly question Becky Symons may have contributed to the young woman's murder. Becky's unhappy marriage suggested several suspects, providing Kate with the problem of choosing among them in a comparatively simplistic narrative.

Beth Hartley

Author: Kathleen Anne Barrett

In her early forties, Beth Hartley was still working towards success in her personal and private lives. She had been married twice (one divorce, one death), with no children from either spouse. Her years as an attorney with a large firm had been wearisome. When she inherited a huge lakeside home from her Aunt Sarah, she turned it into a legal research office, working on referrals from other attorneys. Over a period of time she built up business, developing a loyal staff of employees, which included her best friend since grade school, attorney Emily Schaeffer, and secretary Janice Grezinski.

As *Milwaukee Winters Can Be Murder* (Avalon, 1996) began, Janice needed help. Her brother Dave, a college student, had been found dead with an empty pill bottle and a suicide note nearby. This seemed an open and shut case to the police department. Janice was adamant that Dave would never kill himself even though he had financial problems. Beth contacted Dave's friends, the doctor at the clinic where he did part-time computer work, and his girlfriend. She found an ally and a potential romance in Brian McHenry, a detective whom she hadn't seen since they attended school.

Milwaukee Summers Can Be Deadly (Avalon, 1997) tapped into Beth's inability to say no. This time it was sixteen-year-old Peter Barry, her neighbor who sought help. His father had been murdered. The motive might be personal because Phillip Barry was a philanderer, but something was awry at his office. His secretary, Anna Schulz who wanted to talk privately to Beth, was also killed.

Unlike many other sleuths who are uncomfortable prying into other peoples' lives, Beth considered investigating murders as a hobby. In *Milwaukee Autumns Can Be Lethal* (Avalon, 1998) someone disagreed, threatening Beth and those she loved. She had discovered the body of Don Balstrum, a Marquette University Law School classmate, when she delivered papers. Beth methodically questioned the victim's family and friends. Detective Brian McHenry was making no discernible progress on the case, but handled the competition well.

These were linear narratives for light reading.

Author Barrett has also written three mysteries for the Thumbprint series, designed for adult new readers But whatever happened to spring in Milwaukee?.

Matilda Haycastle

Author: Michele Bailey

Matilda Haycastle's mother Claire, was a Frenchwoman who, while working as an interpreter, met and married English academic Malcolm Haycastle. Matilda was born after the couple had settled in England. She went through the motions of British girlhood; the Girl Guides, the boarding school, and time at a University, but was restless. Her stint at secretarial school facilitated her travels through Europe, which was subsidized by short-term employment. After working in Switzerland and France, Matilda settled in Brussels, Belgium where her facility with languages was an asset.

Her indulgences were the opera, Arnold Schwarzenegger movies, and a car that she maintained herself. She had no compelling goals except, perhaps, a vague desire to be a movie producer. Her insistence on independence often came across as rudeness. She did not consider herself promiscuous, but had serial relationships with men that occasionally continued as friendships. Matilda was portrayed as extremely attractive to men, more for her spirit than her appearance.

In *Dreadful Lies* (Macmillan, 1994), Matilda checked on the household and cat of a friend of a friend. The cat, Hortense, was ungrateful. The friend of a friend, Connie Trevor, failed to return. With no compelling motive for involvement, Matilda searched Connie's past to understand her disappearance. Luc Vanderauwera, a married police officer, was hostile initially, but became Matilda's lover. Powerful forces wanted the investigation scotched, but Luc and Matilda were too stubborn to quit.

The romance with Luc did not survive *The Cuckoo Case* (Macmillan, 1995), partly because Luc was a suspect in the murder of his wife, Marie-Paule. Matilda had become attached to Daniel, the ten-year-old child of their marriage. Matilda searched the tangled relationships of Luc and Marie-Paule and their impact on the boy, recently injured in an accident. When Daniel learned that Luc was not his birthfather, he asked Matilda to find out who was. Dr. Marius Charpentier joined in Matilda's quest. When he realized that she did not share his feelings, he left the country on a mission, but rented his attractive home to her. Matilda, still trying to domesticate Hortense, her recently acquired cat, soon had houseguests.

In *Haycastle's Cricket* (Macmillan, 1996), Matilda's brilliant but eccentric Uncle Edward was in Brussels attending a scientific conference. He brought along bumbling American assistant Byron Kaplan, a vendetta with prominent environmentalist Phillipe Andrieu, and a propensity for trouble. The result was that he became a murder suspect when Andrieu was shot. Clearing Uncle Edward's name was a high priority for Matilda as their relationship entered a new phase.

Matilda may be an acquired taste, at least for American readers, but she was worth the experiment.

Lucinda (Cinda) Hayes

Author: Marianne Wesson

After age forty, Cinda still had no strong personal connections. She had married Michael, a graduate student, when she was in law school in Colorado, but subsequently they divorced. Her father, a former attorney, was in a nursing home; her mother, dead. Cinda grew up in Texas, but affected by the murder of John F. Kennedy, chose not to live there. Her closest family was a sister, Dana, married to Jerry, and their sons, Woody and Louis. She had neither children nor pets. Maybe there was no room in her life for them. Cinda began her professional career in the Boulder County District Attorney's office. When she left the agency after ten years, she was chief of the Sex Crimes Prevention Unit. She was a careful litigator who had built up an ensemble of resources. Her personal feelings included need for legal protection for women and children and opposition to the death penalty.

The offer of a job as director of the local Rape Crisis Center was just what Cinda needed in *Render Up the Body* (HarperCollins, 1998). She was burned out by her experiences at the Boulder County District Attorney's Office. So why did she allow herself to be appointed as appellate attorney for convicted/rapist murderer Jason Smiley? He had been condemned to death on the grounds that he had committed a murder in the course of a crime, but maintained that he had not committed the crime. He did not want to hear Cinda's explanation that she was not working on the question of guilt, but on raising technical issues that might lead to a retrial or a lesser sentence. The deeper Cinda got into the trial record, the more difficult it became for her to limit her involvement. Her work at the Rape Crisis Center suffered. Her concerns about her best friend, ADA Tory Meadows distracted her, and she just might be in love.

Business was slow at the private practice office that Cinda now shared with Tory Meadows, so in *A Suggestion of Death* (Pocket Books, 2000) she agreed to appear on the Bar Association's radio question and answer program. One questioner, a young woman, enquired as to when a suit must be filed by a child endangered by a parent. Cinda knew how complex the answer must be so she agreed to contact the woman personally. Before she could do so, Morgan, the daughter and campaign manager for Professor Harrison McKay, candidate for state Senator, came to her office. Sensitive to the potential conflict of interest if this connected with the young woman who called in, Cinda ended the conversation abruptly. That decision led to her involvement with Drew, Harrison's younger daughter, now calling herself Mariah, who had vague memories of a frightening experience with her dad and a group of local "militia" who rejected the current court system. An engrossing narrative with complex characters.

The impact of a snuff video with a young girl as a victim was devastating to Cinda in *Chilling Effect* (University Press of Colorado, 2004). She represented Peggy Grayling, the mother of nine-year-old Alison, who had been abused and killed by mentally disturbed Leonard Fitzgerald. There was evidence that Fitzgerald had played the snuff video repeatedly before he attacked the child in a manner patterned on the "fictional" death. Peggy was not satisfied that Fitzgerald had been imprisoned for life after a plea of not guilty by reason of insanity. A personal connection prompted Cinda to take the case, even though there were serious First Amendment issues. She and Tory changed their freedom of speech stance as applied to Alison's death. Her friends paid a heavy price. A compelling narrative but "chilling" indeed.

Wesson has a strong legal background, providing legitimacy and passion to her books.

Nanette Hayes

Author: Charlotte Carter

Nanette Hayes attended an Ivy League college. After graduation, she chose to live a helter-skelter life subsidized by the money she earned playing her saxophone on the streets and in the subways of New York and Paris. Her action may have been a reaction against her father, Edmund, the principal in a top prep school. He had left her African-American mother to marry a white woman. On occasion Nanette used her degree in French to earn money as a translator. She lived in an apartment near Gramercy Park so must have had adequate income. Nanette might be called unconventional. Had she been, it would have pleased her. Her role model had been her Aunt Viv who traveled the world, and lived dissolutely but had a great time doing it.

Nanette resented the treatment African-Americans received in the United States, but loved Paris where she had visited as a student. She distrusted authority, the police in particular. For recreation she played, sang or listened to music, drank quite a lot, and smoked pot. She was single, but sexually active.

Nan had problems with the men in her life. In *Rhode Island Red* (Serpent's Tail, 1997), Sig, the stranger whom she allowed to sleep on her couch, was a dishonest cop who was killed during the night. Walter, her regular boyfriend, and her new lover, Henry, could not be trusted. Go-go dancer Aubrey Davis, her friend since childhood, was the only one Nan could count on. Sig, Walter, and Henry all sought a legendary saxophone, once owned by Charlie "Bird" Parker. Nobody came out of the treasure hunt unscathed.

Nan returned to Paris in *Coq au Vin* (Mysterious Press, 1999) to find her missing Aunt Viv. Aunt Viv had distanced herself from her family for several years. Then a message came. She needed help. Within days Nan had made connections with Andre, a handsome violinist and researcher of African-American music. Other contacts were a pimp/thief who offered to help find Viv, and an elderly bistro owner who knew something of Viv's past life. What she couldn't be sure of was whether they wanted Viv found for their own needs or to help her. Nan returned home, sadder but wiser.

The end of her relationship with Andre sent Nan back to New York City. She was drinking heavily in *Drumsticks* (Mysterious Press, 2000). She had no regular work, just playing the sax on the streets until a friend gave her a rag doll for good luck. Good luck happened, but folk artist Ida Williams, who made the mojo dolls, was murdered. Nan pulled herself together to bring Ida's killer to justice. She had help from a hired gun, her father, and a disgruntled police officer. Andre returned. It was not clear whether that was good luck or bad.

Carter has a second more recent series featuring young Cassandra Perry, set in Cook County, Illinois in the Sixties.

Tamara Hayle

Author: Valerie Wilson Wesley

Growing up in a motherless home with an alcoholic father motivated Tamara to make it on her own. After five years as a police officer, she tired of the department's treatment of African-Americans, and opened her own detective agency in Newark, New Jersey. She had divorced De Wayne Curtis, father of her son

Jamal, and had moved on to a relationship with Basil Dupre. Still she was close to Jake Richards, who remained loyal to his mentally ill wife.

However, in *When Death Comes Stealing* (Putnam, 1994), Tamara could not ignore De Wayne's plea for help. Someone was killing his sons (by four separate mothers). Jamal might be next, so she researched De Wayne's past to find a vengeful killer, now close at hand.

Tamara's past underlay *Devil's Gonna Get Him* (Putnam, 1995). She was hired to investigate a man who had dumped her three years before. Her client, Lincoln Storey, a wealthy and ruthless African-American businessman, suspected his stepdaughter Alexa might be making a mistake in her affair with Brandon Pike. Tamara had mixed motives in taking the case: anger with Pike and the need for money as she was still driving a 1982 diesel Jetta. When Storey was murdered at a fundraiser, the focus changed. The number one suspect was the sister of Wyetta Green, a close friend of Tamara. The investigation reawakened in Tamara her mixed feelings for her own mother, and led to a belated forgiveness.

Where Evil Sleeps (Putnam, 1996) took place in Jamaica, on a vacation financed by Tamara's grateful friend, Wyetta. Feeling lonely, Tamara visited "the real Jamaica" with three strangers who had their own agenda for the evening. When she found herself on a murder scene without money or a passport, Basil Dupre returned. One of the three strangers, Sammy Lee, and a German tourist had been killed during a fracas that began when teenagers entered a sleazy bar firing handguns. The narrative was interrupted by frequent flashbacks to Tamara's marriage, her relationship with Basil, and the death of her brother, Johnny.

Tamara was drawn into the tangled lives of the Lennox and Raymond families by her sense of loyalty to Johnny in *No Hiding Place* (Putnam, 1997). Johnny, then a detective, had acted as Shawn Raymond's "Big Brother." His mother Bessie pleaded with Tamara to investigate Shawn's murder because the police were writing it off. Bessie was also concerned with the welfare of Shawn's two sons, born to different mothers. Tamara uncovered a tragic history of generational hatred and revenge set in inner city Newark. The narrative highlighted the pressures on young black males and the efforts of the women in their lives to protect them.

What looked like a terrific opportunity to earn a substantial fee from a celebrity client in *Easier To Kill* (Avon, 1998) turned into a series of tragedies. The investigation as to who threatened radio talk show hostess Mandy Magic by killing off her friends provided the paycheck, but left Tamara depressed. Her personal life was also at a low level. Jake Richards, unable to offer Tamara a lifetime commitment, had turned to another woman who would settle for less.

The search for runaway and pregnant teenager Gabriella Desmond took Tamara to Atlantic City in *The Devil Riding* (Putnam, 2000). She learned of the moral decay within the high-rise hotels and casinos. Basil's presence led to the death of a serial killer who targeted young prostitutes. Tamara's own agenda exposed evils from the past of a prominent African-American family that continued to affect their lives

Celia Jones and Tamara had been good time buddies in high school even though their paths had rarely crossed since then, but, in *Dying in the Dark* (Ballantine, 2004), Celia haunted Tamara's dreams. After she had heard of her murder, Celia's son Cecil, hired Tamara to find her killer. The answers she got were too late for Cecil, who was murdered a few days later. Many of the suspects had been high school classmates. The motive for Celia's death was one that a woman could understand. Wesley packed a lot of emotion and self-discovery into a crisp novel. When it ended, Tamara was ready to move ahead. She even had a new car.

As *Of Blood and Sorrow* (Ballantine /One World, 2008) began. Tamara thought life was going well for her. She had a steady prospect for marriage, used car salesman Larry Walton, and a meeting scheduled with Newark businessman Treyman Barnes II. All that changed when two individuals from Tamara's past made the scene. Peripatetic Basil Dupre wanted to resume their relationship. Lilah Love, with whom Tamara had a history, sought Tamara's help in recovering something that had been taken from her and in locating her daughter whom she had left in the care of her younger sister, Thelma Lee. Any chance that Tamara would take that assignment disappeared when Treyman Barnes II hired her to find his granddaughter whose mother Lilah was unfit to raise her.

The scatological dialogue, however relevant it may be to the setting, will not appeal to all readers.

Sharon Hays

Author: Sarah Gregory, pseudonym for Albert W. Gray

After a degree in drama from the University of Texas-Dallas, Sharon Hays set out to make her mark on Broadway. It was not the professional rejection that sent her back to Texas, but an unplanned pregnancy. Her lover Rob, another actor, had no interest in fatherhood. Sharon tackled both motherhood and law school with equal vigor and success. In her thirties, she had become a successful prosecutor with the Dallas County District Attorney's office. She resigned when sexually harassed by a co-worker. By then Melanie was eleven-years-old. Her father, Rob, had become a successful television actor, presenting Sharon with a problem. Did she have the right to deny Rob and Melanie some kind of relationship?

During *In Self Defense* (Signet, 1995), Sharon's professional problems were solved when criminal defense attorney Russell Black offered her a position. Black had an ulterior motive. He had agreed to defend Midge Rathermore, an obese mentally slow teenage girl, on a charge of hiring a hit man to kill her father. Assistant District Attorney Milt Breyer, who had harassed Sharon, was the prosecutor, confident of a guilty verdict.

As *Public Trust* (Signet, 1998) opened, convicted murderer Raymond Burnside, having exhausted his appeals, was scheduled for execution. Dycus Wilt, a client of Sharon, offered information that would prove Burnside's innocence. At first skeptical, Sharon reviewed the Burnside case and found justification for seeking a new trial. However the political and legal systems had a vested interest in protecting the original verdict.

In *The Best Defense* (Signet, 1999), Sharon agreed to help actress Darla Cowen, a long time friend now accused of murdering her lover David Spencer. Because Darla had returned to Los Angeles and Spencer had been killed in Dallas, the first legal hearing was for extradition. Darla had supported Sharon when she was a pregnant young actress. Now Sharon had to do more than keep Darla out of prison. She had to find a killer… or two.

Sharon's loyalty to her mentor Dallas attorney Russell Black was the only justification for getting involved with the Benedict family in *Capitol Scandal* (Signet, 1999). Texas Congressman Will John Benedict was the major suspect in the murder of Courtney Lee, an intern in his District of Columbia office. Sharon's prior contacts with Will John (whom she dated in college), his mother (U.S. Senator Mattie Ruth), and his lecherous father Paul (a former law professor) had been traumatic. Melanie, Sharon's teenage daughter, would have to be left behind in Dallas while her mother was in Washington. The narrative painted a depressing picture as to the behavior of our representatives in Congress.

These were interesting narratives with an engaging sleuth.

Amanda Hazard

Author: Connie Feddersen, a.k.a. Carol Finch

Amanda moved her home, and eventually her business, from Oklahoma City to rural Vamoose, Oklahoma. She divided work as an accountant between her farmhouse and the small office she maintained downtown. Amanda, unsure of herself and relationships since her divorce seven years earlier, did not possess the cool calculating characteristics attributed to accountants. She was a trim blonde who never forgot what it had been to be a fat child. Amanda balanced her right wing philosophy with an emotional and impulsive response to events in her personal life.

She had nothing but friendly feelings for client William Farley even though in *Dead in the Water* (Zebra, 1993) he was a demanding businessman. She discovered his body out on the range. The police discredited her description of the scene of the crime. The narrative was replete with double entendres and sexual fencing with "irresistible" police Detective Nick Thorn.

Amanda did not disclose her sexual relationship with Thorn in *Dead in the Cellar* (Zebra, 1994). This led him to believe that she was ashamed of his blue-collar orientation. Her close friendship with Elmer Jolly, reclusive scientific farmer, made her reluctant to accept his death as an accident.

Amanda's image softened in *Dead in the Melon Patch* (Zebra, 1995). She entered home-canned goods at the county fair, baby-sat for grungy children, and hired their mother to help the family survive. She recruited Jenny Long, her former rival for Nick's affections, to be her office manager. Amanda interfered in Nick's investigation of the murder of Sheila, the multi-married granddaughter of "Miz Lula" MacAdo. Amanda checked out the husbands (and their wives) with whom Sheila had dallied, until one emerged by her failure to comply with Miz Lula's sense of order.

In *Dead in the Dirt* (Kensington, 1996), Nick disengaged from Amanda only to save her life. He feared that the local murder of Will Bloom was connected with major drug dealing by a master criminal. There was no way to keep Amanda out of the investigation. She had found the body, so she had to find the killer.

A corrupt local official, Commissioner "Dusty" Brown incurred Amanda's wrath in *Dead in the Mud* (Kensington, 1997), when he ignored her complaints about poor roads. His subsequent death might have been an accident. Amanda believed otherwise based upon his poor reputation and a clue (the letter "S" scratched in the mud beside his body), which had been washed out by the time the police arrived. Humor was provided through the worn-out gag about her disasters at the beauty parlor and the efforts of two reluctant prospective mothers-in-law to manage her bridal shower.

Dead in the Driver's Seat (Kensington, 1998) played it for laughs as she and Nick prepared for their wedding. Car dealer Frank Lemon consistently drove his red 4X4 at excessive speeds, but there was a question as to whether or not it was Frank who drove the vehicle into the river. Frank's body was in the car, but the driver's seat was not set for his girth. Lots of shenanigans at the wedding ceremony, but the trip to the reception was even more harried.

What was new in *Dead in the Hay* (Kensington, 1999) now that Amanda and Thorn were married? Very little! Amanda continued to find bodies; this time, client Harvey Renshaw, a retired air force mechanic who now had an oil well. Thorn remained reluctant to recognize that murder might be involved. Amanda consequently made him look like a fool. The staff at the local beauty parlor made Amanda look like a fool. There's only one real surprise.

On to *Dead in the Pumpkin Patch* (Kensington, 2000) which had the same pattern even though Amanda was very very pregnant, due to deliver in two weeks. This time the body of her client Nettie Jarvis was in a pumpkin patch and Nick humored her because she was pregnant. She solved the case barely in time to deliver. Amanda was officious, ignorant of the law, and inconsiderate of her husband's standing in the community.

Dr. Bernadette "Bernie" Hebert

Author: Catherine Ennis

Dr. Bernadette "Bernie" Hebert utilized her Ph.D. in analytical chemistry in the Louisiana State Crime Lab, located in New Orleans. Her father, a police officer, and her mother were both deceased. She had been aware of her lesbian orientation since she was eighteen years old. Vi, a music director, had been her lover for eight years when the series began.

In *Clearwater* (Naiad, 1991), Bernie may not have mourned her Uncle Albert, but she investigated his murder at the request of her cousin, Albert, Jr. The suspect, a former teacher who had been involved with Bernie, may have been a victim of Albert's blackmail. A license plate near the scene of the crime was traced to a candidate for mayor.

Another cousin, Helen, head of the epidemiology section of the Health and Hospitals division in New Orleans, sounded an alarm in *Chautauqua* (Naiad, 1993). A potential crisis from cholera in Lake Charles caused Bernie to take a short-term transfer to the University. This created problems with Vi, an unstable and difficult woman. Bernie sought the pattern in the deaths that had occurred after eating seafood from Lake Charles.

Helen Hewitt

Author: Lynda La Plante

Helen Hewitt, a tall self-contained divorcée, had worked diligently to move to the rank of Governor III in the English penal system. At this level she had been the assistant director of a woman's prison, but that did not satisfy her. Even as Barfield Prison for males exploded in a riot, she was being interviewed for a promotion.

In *The Governor* (Pan, London 1995), Helen was appointed to head Barfield, an unusual achievement for a woman. The facility housed high-level security inmates including child molesters. The death of molester Michael Winchwood during the riot had been declared a suicide. Even though she was facing massive resistance from staff, Helen insisted upon a broader investigation.

Helen's successes did not ensure her continued employment at Barfield. In fact, as *Governor II* (Pan, 1996) began, she was working as a trainer in hostage situations. The poor showing of her successor in a hostage situation facilitated Helen's return as Governor of Barfield. By now she had won the loyalty of her staff, but she faced a myriad of problems, one of which endangered her unborn child.

Although Helen was the protagonist, much of the interest in the narratives came from the vignettes of individual prisoners. The series was the novelization of television programs by La Plante. She has at least a quartet of female sleuths; latest, Detective Anna Travis

Karen Hightower a.k.a. Bast

Author: Rosemary Edghill, pseudonym for Eluki Bes Shahar

As Karen Hightower, she was a designer, working semi-independently at Houston Graphics. As Bast, the life she really lived, she was a white witch in a coven. She indicated at one point that she had been married and divorced. Her home was a small low rent apartment on the fifth floor of an older building in New York City. Wiccan was described as a "neo-pagan earth-centered religion". Karen read Tarot cards for others, but because she was a third degree Wiccan she did not charge for her services.

Bast was comfortable in her own Wiccan group in *Speak Daggers to Her* (TOR, 1994) so had little contact with her friend, Miriam. Miriam could not seem to settle down in a group, moving from one to another in search of something that none provided. When a friend told Bast that Miriam was dead, she had a sense of guilt. She took upon herself (1) notification of kin, then (2), at her sister's request, disposing of Miriam's property, which included a sought-after Khazar book, and (3) seeking the evil man who had marked Miriam for death.

Bast's coven, Changing, was sponsoring an ecumenical gathering of pagan groups to occur on Mayday as *Book of Moons* (TOR, 1995) opened. Ned Shelton, who had sought entry into the Changing group, but been rejected, disrupted the festivities. He announced his possession of a grimoire of Mary Stuart, Queen of Scotland. The document purported to prove that Mary had been a witch. Poor Ned did not realize that his proclamation would bring him ridicule and death. Bast felt guilty that she had failed Ned, but barely escaped with her own life. She felt disconnected from Changing, and considered withdrawal.

Bast had dropped out of the coven headed by Lady Bellflower by *The Bowl of Night* (TOR, 1996). She accompanied Julian, a ceremonial magician who worked at the Snake, a bookstore/gathering place for witches, to a HallowFest in upper New York State. Pagan groups of all kinds were welcome to attend. The closeness she had hoped for with Julian seemed within reach. Instead, after a brief encounter, Julian absorbed himself in an archaic ritual, the Tesoraria. Local tensions against the pagan gatherings at Paradise Lake mounted when a fundamentalist preacher was found dead in the woods. Bast's values were in conflict. She solved them and the murder in the only way she knew how.

Marti Hirsch

Author: Miriam Ann Moore

Martha ("Marti") Hirsch was an unreconstructed rebel plagued by bouts of depression, an affinity for pot, and an allergy to alcohol. After a miserable high school existence, she had attended all female Quincy College in the Berkshires where she experimented with lesbian sex. She transferred to the University of California at Berkeley, which nurtured her negative feelings about authority and encouraged her enjoyment of literature and daytime serials. Enraged by U.S. action in Vietnam, Marti left the United States to travel, spending time in an Israeli kibbutz. She reveled in her role as the family rebel, embarrassing her extended family on multiple occasions by her attire and behavior. She disliked children, and while battling discrimination publicly, had many intolerances of her own.

Her father, Maury, a moderately successful theatrical agent, had shared his enthusiasms for old movies and the New York Giants football teams with Marti. He and her mother, a onetime chorus girl, now lived in Florida. They had initially had a close relationship, but Marti and her dad had been estranged for years. After her return to the United States, Marti, single and in her late twenties, decided to be a writer. She quit her job as reader at a publishing house, and took part-time employment as secretary to Dr. Karl Hammerschmidt, a blind psychiatrist. One of her perks was some non-authoritarian counseling. She needed it. She also did occasional entertainment reviews for an alternative newspaper, *New York Night*, during which she took cheap shots at people whom she disliked.

Marti had met Jana Crowley at the Jerusalem airport. They traveled through the British Isles, and shared an apartment in New York City. When Marti introduced Jana to pianist David Price and his music, there was instant chemistry, and Marti lost a roommate. *Last Dance* (Avon, 1997) was set in 1978. As the narrative began, Jana had just discovered David's dead body. She had run from the building, called Marti in a panic, asking her to pick up David's eight-year-old daughter Lorraine from school. Marti renewed her acquaintance with former classmate Jerry Barlow now a teacher at the school. Frustrated by poor police work and multiple suspects, Marti solved the case at some personal sacrifice in friendships. Sated with the slick urban types, she convinced Jerry, who had always loved her, to give up his job and roam the U.S. with her.

Stayin' Alive (Avon, 1998) picked up on Jerry and Marti three years later in 1981. They were living in a trailer he won in a Las Vegas poker game. Marti had sent her manuscript for the Price murder book to an agent, was taking classes at UNLV, and ghostwriting themes for overworked and undereducated college athletes. Jerry had a job at the Paradise Hotel and Casino where he accompanied singer Donny Brooks. Brooks, a compulsive drinker and womanizer, was arrested when Dorothea Jones, manager of the Paradise, was brutally murdered. Marti put together a motley crew to prove Donny's innocence.

For a short time after she found her old friend artist Jana Crowley dead in her laundry room, during *I Will Survive* (Avon, 1999), Marti thought she might have been the intended victim. She and Jana had common enemies, particularly since Marti had been working as Jana's gofer. Finding Jana's killer became an obsession for Marti. Her relationship with Jerry Barlow, now her husband, was threatened. This too was set in 1981 and contained considerable retrospective material.

Holly-Jean Ho

Author: Irene Lin-Chandler

As her name and appearance suggested, Holly-Jean Ho was the diminutive, dark-haired daughter of an English father and a Hakka Chinese mother. She had an English name, Deirdre H. Jones, which she rejected. Her father was a sweet Christian man who had won a Distinguished Service Cross and had been a prisoner of war. He had been a serviceman in Taipei when he met and married Holly-Jean's mother. Holly-Jean had never attended college. Instead she worked with a circus knife thrower, learning a skill she used in her business affairs. After the circus, she ran an herbal teashop and a kung fu dojan. Finally she studied computers and developed the expertise that enabled her to open her own investigative agency.

By her thirties, Holly-Jean had engaged in multiple partner sex and was a heavy drinker. She worked both sides of the criminal scene. Her agency, based in London where Mrs. Howell-Pryce ran the office, had extensive business in Europe and Asia. Holly-Jean had expertise in electronic and intellectual property, and in the mediation of commercial disputes among her clients, which included Chinese criminal triads. Her propensity for deception and mischief had earned her a Fei-Ying Bang lien from the triads that was later lifted.

For recreation she meditated, practiced Tae Kwan Do (where she earned a black belt), and enjoyed classical music, but was content with "pub grub" for food. Her personal habits included flossing her nostrils with a silver chain and scraping her tongue. Her pet was a three-legged neutered Siamese cat.

Holly-Jean's intention to limit her investigations to software piracy went down the drain in *The Healing of Holly-Jean* (Headline, 1995). Her current cases involved gang rape, disappearances, and drug smuggling. None of them went well. When she realized that she had been a pawn in a contest between major Chinese triads, Holly-Jean achieved a measure of success and survived a final betrayal.

In *Grievous Angel* (Headline, 1996), the spicy stew of child pornographers, international Internet crime, and negotiations among Asian triads may be too much for the average palate. Holly-Jean may be good to her mother and kind to animals, but she was as likely to add to the crises, as to solve them. The narratives resembled those featuring espionage heroines in the 1960s.

Holly-Jean had never dealt with probate matters, but in *Hour of the Tigress* (Headline, 1999), Hamish McIlvuddy made her an offer she could not refuse. Only after she agreed to seek other possible heirs to a Scottish lairddom, did Holly-Jean realize that the control of vast resources coveted by powerful Chinese triads was at stake. She traversed the slums of Manila and the outreaches of China to locate alternatives to Hamish's claim, leaving mayhem and murder in her trail. The existence of an older sister, Frangipangi Johns, whom her mother had been forced to release for adoption because she had been born on an ill-omened day, was revealed.

Dido Hoare

Author: Marianne Macdonald

Dido, whose name had been chosen by her academic parents from the legendary Queen of Carthage, lived in a small house behind her Islington antiquarian bookshop. A short unhappy marriage to Davey had ended. Their son Benjamin was born later, to become the center of her life. Also assuming a major role was her father, Barnabas, a retired Oxford professor, who was aging but determined to involve himself in Dido's affairs; professional, that is. Not that she had personal affairs, except for a low-level romance with Paul Grant, a married detective inspector. Part-time employee Ernie Weekes helped out in the shop.

Even with the assistance of her widowed father, Dido had difficulty making a financial success of the bookstore during *Death's Autograph* (Hodder & Stoughton, 1996). A stalking car pursued her through the night. A threatening note was left with Barnaby. A burglar, who stole only cash and stamps, ransacked her shop. The murder of Prof. Job Warren, a prominent U.S. librarian to whom she planned to sell the Ireland Collection, convinced Inspector Paul Grant that he needed to keep a close eye on Dido. She and Barnabas researched the history of the Ireland Collection while, fortunately for her, Paul Grant watched carefully.

As *Ghost Walk* (Hodder & Stoughton, 1997) opened, Dido had almost convinced herself that the problems of Tom Ashe, an elderly squatter, were not her concern. Her instinctive kindness to the old man led to an elegant gift and a role as executor of his will when he was murdered. She also attracted the attentions of greedy nationalistic and religious fanatics in a struggle for an historic document.

All her book knowledge did not protect Dido from the manipulations of elderly "Her Majesty" (Clare Templeton Forbes) or the sexual blandishments of American Prof. Jay Reslin in *Smoke Screen* (Hodder & Stoughton, 1999). Clare Forbes was the mother of poet Orrin Forbes' daughter, Georgina. Dido's thrill at the possible acquisition of valuable books and manuscripts by Forbes blinded her to danger. After Clare's murder, Barnabas' acuity and Ernie Weekes' insistence on adding a computer extricated Dido from personal and professional disasters.

Phyllis, Ben's nanny, seemed pleasant enough, working to support an invalid husband. Her call for help in *Road Kill* (St. Martin, 2000) thrust Dido into a struggle between crooked and ambitious cops, former robbers and the confederate who had hidden their loot. She and her erstwhile beau Detective Paul Grant balanced personal relationships against their responsibility to the law. At the conclusion Dido felt betrayed and guilty but ready to move on.

A plea from childhood friend Lizzie Waring brought Dido and three-year-old Ben to a rural Somerset area during *Blood Lies* (Hodder and Stoughton, 2001). Dido had anticipated that Lizzie and Mickey, her husband of three years, might be having marital problems. The situation was far worse. Mickey's father (on whose estate Lizzie and he resided) had senile dementia. His brother Teddy had returned from prison after serving a sentence for the death of a young woman. The Warings were not popular in the Castle Hinton area. There was an interesting bibliographic slant to Dido's investigation into not just one, but two murders in the past.

The suicide of regular customer Timothy Curwen, who paid for his last book on Dickens with a rubber check, drew Dido into a prolonged adventure in *Die Once* (Hodder & Stoughton, 2002). Even the revelations as to Curwen's source of income and the possibility that he was still alive did not deter Dido from involving herself. Once she had possession of the Dickens book, she was hooked. Everyone wanted to get his or her hands on it. In retrospect, Dido showed extraordinary solicitude for a man who participated in drug dealing.

Dido took a risk when she purchased a perceived medieval manuscript from old acquaintance, Gabriel Steen, in *Faking It* (Severn House, 2006). Gabriel, a book runner who searched through markets, house sales and street vendor stands for unrecognized treasures, was in a hurry to sell after he received a phone call. It was days later when Dido learned that he had been killed within hours after leaving her shop. Mysterious men, including Steen's partner, Ishmael Peters, drifted in and out of the narrative, but the real mystery was in the manuscript. Very interesting.

Three Monkeys (Severn House, 2006) was something of a disappointment. Dido played Good Samaritan by rescuing a monkey, visiting his elderly vagabond owner who discovered body parts in an alley, providing shelter for a teenage prostitute, and befriending an abused wife Some of her efforts aided Scotland Yard and local police in a major investigation but there were too many loose ends at the conclusion.

This was a highly literate British series, not available in all bookstores, but worth the search.

Vicky Holden

Author: Margaret Coel

Vicky Holden, a divorced Native American attorney, had returned to the Wind River, Wyoming Arapaho Reservation after working for a major Denver law firm. Her two adult children lived elsewhere. After her divorce from their abusive father Ben, Vicky had left Lucas and Susan with their grandmother while she completed college and law school. By the time she was ready to return to them, they were independent. For two years Vicky lived off-reservation in Lander, Wyoming. She was a direct descendant of Chief Black Night, a major figure in tribal history. Her detecting evolved through her association with Rev. John O'Malley, a Jesuit priest stationed on the reservation while he coped with alcoholism. He mixed well with the Native Americans, better than many of the priests who acted as his assistants.

The death of tribal chairman Harvey Castle in *The Eagle Catcher* (University Press of Colorado, 1995) uncovered deceit within personal relationships and in the past acquisition of Indian lands. Vicky and Father John foiled greedy oil companies, but also revealed the secret that caused Castle's death.

In *The Ghost Walker* (Berkley, 1996), the future of the Jesuit mission was put at risk by an ambitious scheme to build a recreational center on the property. Initially the return of Vicky's estranged daughter Susan to the reservation did not connect with the death of former convict Marcus Deppert. Later, Father John's investigation put him at odds with Vicky's need to protect her daughter.

Some members of the tribal council perceived the government plan to store nuclear waste on the reservation as economic assistance to the Arapahos in *The Dream Stalker* (Berkley, 1997). A dying man, Gabriel Many Horses, contacted Father John with a potential confession, which could destroy their optimism. By the time Father John arrived the man was dead. Unemployed men desperate to support their families were pitted against environmentalists, many of them from out of state. Vicky mobilized opposition to the plan with her letters to newspapers. As a result, she found herself an "outsider" from her own people just when she and Father John needed their help to solve a murder. Vicky and Father John became painfully aware that they must avoid intimacy because their feelings had gone beyond friendship. His younger assistant was urging the elimination of many programs that Father John believed were essential; i.e. AA, literacy.

Under the Federal Native American Grave Protection and Repatriation Act, public facilities were required to restore sacred artifacts to Native American tribes. In *The Story Teller* (Berkley, 1998), Vicky was hired to facilitate returns to the Arapaho Nation. On a peripheral issue, tribes vied to qualify for reparations for the Sand Creek Massacre. A ledger, which might substantiate the Arapaho claim, had been listed among the Arapaho artifacts, but had disappeared. The death of Todd Harris, a young ethno-history graduate student, brought Vicky and Father John into a working relationship, tenuous because they realized the hazards involved.

The strong ties within Arapaho families and their deep affection for their children made it unlikely that any girl would be adopted outside the tribe. In *The Lost Bird* (Berkley, 1999), actress Sharon David came to Vicky seeking her birth parents. This quest paralleled Fr. John's search for the killer of Fr. Joseph Keenan, an aging Jesuit philosophy professor who had returned to the reservation where he had once been a pastor. A gripping and emotional narrative with personal overtones for both Vicky and Father John.

The tension between Fr. John and Vicky seemed to have been resolved by her decision to give her former husband Ben a second chance. In *The Spirit Woman* (Berkley, 2000), Laura Simmons, a college friend of Vicky's, came to the area to finish a biography of Sacagawea, the Shoshone woman who guided the Lewis and Clark expedition. The discovery of the skeleton of Charlotte Allen, a prior biographer, was followed by Laura's death. Father John was reluctantly preparing for transfer to an academic post in Wisconsin. Vicky was struggling with burnout, ambivalent feelings about Ben, and her own possible relocation to Denver.

Father John remained at the reservation assisted by Father Don Ryan, who brought problems of his own, during *The Thunder Keeper* (Berkley, 2001). Vicky was sharing her Denver home with her son Lucas who was employed in the computer industry there. She needed distance from Ben and Father John and from the knowledge that she had killed, albeit in self-defense. Two separate incidents brought Father John and Vicky together. He could not forget the confession of a man who had participated in, but not committed a murder, and who believed other murders would follow. Vicky had witnessed the hit-and-run killing of a man who wanted to meet her on a matter of "life and death." Her persistent involvement in the "accident" prompted Lucas to challenge Vicky. She was as addicted to danger as Ben was to alcohol. He might be right, but she returned to the reservation.

Vicky's return to a solo practice in Landers and employment by the tribe to solve water pollution issues did not bring her the peace of mind she expected in *The Shadow Dancer* (Berkley, 2002). Ben, now the successful manager of the Arapahoe Ranch, had expectations of a reunited family. His murder after a quarrel with Vicky cast suspicion on her. Fr. John, fearful that St. Francis's Mission would be shut down, found time to look for Dean Little Horse, the grandson of parishioners. In their separate ways, both Vicky and Father John felt the answer to their problems lay in the shadow ranch where Orlando, messiah of the Ghost Dancer Cult, revived an historical belief in the restoration of Indian supremacy.

The relative merits of gambling casinos on Native American reservations was explored in *Killing Raven* (Berkley, 2003). Lodestar Enterprise loaned the tribe money to build and equip a casino. In exchange they were awarded the contract to manage the facility. Lakota attorney Adam Lone Eagle was hired as legal counsel for the Great Plains Casino. Later, he offered Vicky, then barely making a living, a job as his assistant. She agreed with a personal agenda, if she found evidence of corruption, her loyalty was to the tribe.

Christine Nelson, the new curator at the Arapaho Mission on the Wind River Reservation, brought in an exhibition of early 20th century still photos as *Wife of Moon* (Berkley, 2004) began. In 1907, photographer Edward Curtis had hired local men and women to pose as the attackers on a village and the residents, but he abandoned the project when Bashful Woman was killed during the re-enactment. Father Damien Henley, the new assistant pastor, arranged for presidential hopeful U. S. Senator Jaime Evans to visit the area. The concordance of these events had unexpected results; the murder of Denise, a descendant of Bashful Woman; suspicion that T. J. Painted Horse had killed her; and the disappearance of Christine Nelson. Fr. John was the primary in this book, but Vicky had her moments. She and Adam Lone Eagle had become personal and professional partners.

In 1874, enraged by raids on their own people, Shoshone warriors, escorted by U. S. troops commanded by Captain Bates, massacred a village of Arapahoes. Over 125 years later, as explained in *Eye of the Wolf* (Berkley, 2005) there remained bitterness between the two tribes that shared the Wind River Reservation. Vicky, against Adam's wishes, was defending Arapaho ex-convict Frankie Montana on a charge of assaulting three Shoshone college students. Their failure to appear at a preliminary hearing was explained when Fr. John found their bodies on the Bates battlefield. The potential for inter-tribal violence loomed, even after the police focused on Montana.

Vicky was aware when she agreed to seek a new trial for convicted killer Travis Birdsong in *The Drowning Man* (Berkley, 2006) that neither her law partner and lover, Adam Lone Eagle nor their primary client, the Arapahoe-Shoshone Joint Council, would approve. It had taken considerable work for Adam to get the council business. When Adam was called away on personal business, Vicky was left in charge. Travis had not been charged with the murder of his close friend Raymond or the theft of the petroglyph for which both men were believed to be guilty. He was convicted of manslaughter, but protested his innocence. Father John had been chosen by the thieves of a second petroglyph, *The Drowning Man,* as the go-between to deliver a quarter of a million dollars in exchange for the religious relic. It was a delicate operation. The earlier petroglyph had never been recovered. The council wanted Father John to be sure this one was, but Ted Gianelli of the FBI had his own ideas as to how to handle the matter. An impetuous gesture on Father John's part complicated Vicky's life.

Coel reached into the 1970's for *The Girl with Braided Hair* (Berkley, 2007) when AIM (the American Indian Movement) made violent protests against the discriminatory treatment under which Native Americans suffered. The discovery of the skeleton of a brutally murdered young woman sent both Father John and Vicky into a search for her identity and her killer. When Vicky was attacked, it became apparent that he (or they) were still alive and probably on the reservation. Information about possible suspects was withheld by those who feared becoming victims. A horrifying statistic was quoted: The primary cause of death of Native American women is murder.

Other books in this series: *The Woman Who Climbed to the Sky; Stolen Smoke* could only be located in one library in Arizona. They were identified as short, possibly novellas. Meantime Coel introduced a new sleuth, investigative reporter Catherine McLeod. Next in the Vicky Holden series: *The Silent Spirit* (2009)

Primrose "Rosie" Holland

Author: Jo Bannister

Like Clio Rees Marsh, one of two other Bannister English female sleuths, Primrose "Rosie" Holland had given up her career as a doctor for something totally different. She retired from her position as a pathologist at the West Country Hospital to become an "agony aunt" or advice columnist. Her crisp, no-nonsense approach in *Primrose Path* was a hit, swelling the circulation of the *Skipley Chronicle.* She was drawn into criminal investigations where she worked with Detective Superintendent Harry Marsh (see Clio Rees Marsh in Volume 2). Her contributions were not always welcomed. She was a plump, well-built woman in her forties who was outspoken and unsubtle. Her personal assistant on the column was Alex Fisher, a younger woman who became romantically involved with Matt Gosling, the publisher. Another conspirator was Arthur Prufrock an elderly retired teacher, with a passion for ornithology.

Rosie had brushed off Fiona Morris' concerns about her missing brother, Philip, in *The Primrose Convention* (Macmillan, 1997). She took a second look when the disappearance extended to seven weeks. Because Philip was an amateur ornithologist, Rosie sought help from Prufrock. Young Shad Lucas, the son of a gypsy woman, accompanied Rosie to Philip's apartment where he received emanations that indicated that Philip had been abducted. Prufrock, a World War II veteran, showed surprising skills when pitted against a big time smuggler.

Although Rosie had offers from larger newspapers, she chose to stay with the *Chronicle.* Her editor, Dan Sale, was skeptical that she might be too close to the story in *The Primrose Switchback* (Severn House, 1999). Shad Lucas, now employed as Rosie's gardener, had returned to consciousness in the Crewe railroad yard. His special gifts gave Rosie and Inspector Marsh no reason to doubt Shad's insistence that a young woman had died on the premises. Rosie and Marsh felt strongly that Shad had been a victim, but local opinion was less understanding. The deceased, young television researcher Jackie Pickering, had participated in a hoax that made Rosie look foolish. Prufrock came to the rescue again.

Bannister has a third series with a female sleuth, featuring Brodie Farrell.

Barbara Holloway

Author: Kate Wilhelm

Barbara Holloway had been raised by her parents who lived by ideals, which she carried into her law practice. Actual legal work in the firm, where her father Frank Holloway was a partner, disillusioned Barbara. When she felt that Frank had sold her out in a criminal case, she left to spend the next five years traveling. During that time, she worked at low-level jobs and would have probably continued to do so had Frank not contacted her for help. She was described as having dark brown hair and blue eyes with a muscular body. Even when Barbara returned she was unwilling to return to a large firm, preferring to conduct business out of her small home or a local restaurant.

Oregon criminal statutes require a "qualified" attorney to defend the accused in any trial that might result in a death sentence. As *Death Qualified* (St. Martin, 1991) began, realizing that he was being drugged, Tom Mann discontinued his medication. He then returned to his family after a five-year absence. When Tom was murdered, his wife Nell was charged with the crime. Barbara took Nell's case partly because the prosecutor was Tony De Angelo, her former lover. She, Frank, and dedicated mathematician Mike Dinesen found the killer.

Author Kate Wilhelm did an excellent job on the cross examinations in *The Best Defense* (St. Martin, 1994) a narrative hard to set aside. Barbara's defense of Paula Kennerman, a battered wife, pitted her against the judiciary and the local press. She used law students and her father to gather information about smuggled abortion drugs and illegal immigrants.

During *Malice Prepense* (St. Martin, 1996 apa *For the Defense*) Frank Holloway defended young brain-damaged Teddy Wendover, who had been accused of killing the man considered by some to be responsible for his disability. Barbara disapproved until she delved deeper into the case. She uncovered a conspiracy motivated by greed, not revenge. John Mureau, a mining consultant, fearful that he was unworthy to love Barbara, drew new hope from their shared investigation.

Frank Holloway had never seen Barbara as happy as she was when she and Mureau returned to Oregon in *Defense for the Devil* (St. Martin, 1999). Barbara's level of contentment was fragile, subject to her consuming professional responsibilities. When she opposed the District Attorney's office to free Ray Arno, a man she believed to be innocent, she could not let go, whatever the cost.

In *No Defense* (St. Martin, 2000), the action was driven by relationships between parents and their children, i.e. the need to protect a vulnerable child, the grief at the loss of a son, the willingness to sacrifice, the hunger for vengeance. Frank, then Barbara, took an interest in the affairs of young Lara Jessup, accused of murdering her husband. Vinny Jessup, Lara's second husband was wealthy, older, and had terminal cancer. What initially seemed to be a car accident was determined to be murder. The locals had always considered Lara a trophy wife. Powerful community leaders considered her fair game. Good legal maneuvering and use of non-courtroom tactics worked for Barbara but she accepted that she was a driven woman.

The framework of *Desperate Measures* (St. Martin, 2001) focused on the murders of Gus Marchand, an honest but narrow-minded man, and Hilde Franz, the principal at the high school attended by Gus' children. The conflict of interest between Barbara who represented Alex Feldman, a bright but physically deformed young man to whom Gus had taken a dislike, and her father Frank who represented Hilde enhanced the narrative. Hilde and Alex became suspects when Gus was murdered. The two attorneys had to protect their own clients first, and then find the real killer. Alex, a brilliant cartoonist whose facial deformities made him a target for prejudice and vigilantism, formed a poignant relationship with a beautiful woman who saw beyond his façade.

Surgeon David McIvey was a candidate for murder in *Clear and Convincing Proof* (MIRA, 2003). He was a controlling husband to Annie. As the son of one of the two doctors who had begun Kelso/McIvey Rehabilitation Clinic, he had no interest in carrying out his deceased father's plans. Dr. Thomas Kelso, the aging co-founder knew that David planned to replace the charitable facility with a moneymaking surgical clinic. This would affect Darren Halvord, director of the physical therapy department. When McIvey was murdered, the Clinic Board of Directors hired Barbara to defend both Annie McIvey and Darren Halvord, if, and when, they were charged. Barbara skirted the boundaries of unethical behavior, defending two clients whose interests might be in conflict.

A chance visit to a bistro to hear a new pianist in *The Unbidden Truth* (Mira, 2004) motivated Barbara to defend Carol Frederick on a charge of murder. Carol's unusual talent had drawn the attention of a group of charitable women who planned to subsidize her future musical education. Now they agreed to subsidize her defense against the charge of murdering Joe Wenzel, member of a powerful local family. Wenzel had been sexually harassing her. Barbara's defense was complicated by information revealing that Carol, a foster child, might have a hidden identity. It was not enough to find out who killed Wenzel, but why Carol had been chosen as the scapegoat. Terrific characterizations.

Wally Lederer turned a liability into an asset in *Sleight of Hand* (Mira, 2006). He had two convictions for theft before an elderly comic urged him to use his ambidextrous skills as a pickpocket into a legitimate business. When Wally was accused of stealing a valuable gold ship replica by former friend car dealer Jay Wilkins, he sought Frank Holloways's advice. He recommended Barbara. All of her skills were needed when Jay was murdered. Again the case was complicated. Jay's wife, restaurant cashier Meg, had died mysteriously the week before his murder.

Barbara was at a crossroads as *A Wrongful Death* (MIRA, 2007) began. Darren Halvord, the man in her life, wanted a more permanent relationship. Her work as an attorney was emotionally draining, causing her to consider a teaching position. In order to clarify just what was best for her, she rented an isolated cabin near the water. Within days she was embroiled in the life of Elizabeth Kurtz, who, together with her son Jason, occupied a nearby cabin. Elizabeth had acquired valuable information that made her a target. When Barbara provided initial support to Elizabeth and Jason, she was harassed by the police and stalked by an unidentified enemy. Gripping narrative with fine characterizations.

When controversial author David Etheridge came to Barbara for advice about a court order in *Cold Case* (MIRA, 2008) neither appreciated the extent of the charges against him. He had accepted an invitation from Chloe McCrutchen to rent the apartment adjacent to the home she shared with her husband, State Senator Robert McCrutchen. David only planned to be in Eugene for a short period of time, but it was long enough for him to be accused of two murders. Twenty-two years before, the McCrutchen family had held a college graduation party for Robert. There had been an unpleasant incident between Robert and his fellow student Jill Storey into which David intervened. Jill was strangled to death later that night. No charges were brought at that time. Now David and Barbara anticipated that he would not only be charged with Jill's death but with the more recent murder of Robert McCrutchen. Barbara, her dad, and Bailey Novell spent a lot of time investigating, but the courtroom scenes were kept to a minimum.

Wilhelm's plots were intricate and her courtroom scenes well researched.

Patricia Anne Tate Hollowell

Author: Anne George

See: The Tate Sisters, page 790.

Mary Russell Holmes

Author: Laurie R. King

See: Mary Russell, page 711.

Samantha Holt

Author: Karen Ann Wilson

Samantha Holt's father was a surgeon. She preferred working with animals. Her personal life had been disrupted when she was left waiting at the altar, leaving her afraid of a commitment. An attractive blonde from Connecticut, she moved to Paradise Cay, Florida. Her degree as a veterinary technician earned Samantha a job with Dr. Louis Augustin's clinic. She was comfortable with Augustin, lab assistant P. J. Thompson, and the older receptionist Cynthia Caswell.

In *Eight Dogs Flying* (Berkley, 1994), the staff agreed with Dr. Augustin that the incidents occurring to dogs currently or previously owned by his former wife Rachel were not accidents. They might be connected to her charges that a local importer, Stellar Enterprises, sold spoiled meat. When Rachel was accused of murdering two men, one with a knife from her kitchen, the staff proved she was being framed. Samantha took on the role of "Watson" not "Holmes," which was reserved for Augustin.

In *Copy Cat Crimes* (Berkley, 1995), Samantha was diverted by the attentions of Det. Sgt. Peter Robinson. A basket of infant kittens whose care was paid for by counterfeit bills connected with the murder of regular clinic client Arnie Silor. Augustin expected Samantha to join him in break-ins, burglary and the discovery of more corpses. Coincidence played a large part in the plotting.

Paradise Cay was disturbed by a planned expansion of high-tension lines in *Beware Sleeping Dogs* (Berkley, 1996). Because local citizens were concerned about the potential impact on human life and the environment, Dr. Augustin and Samantha checked the area personally, only to stumble across a naked corpse with a five-pointed star carved on his forehead. Local corruption, wild dogs with nerve damage, possible connections to Wicca, and Samantha's concern about her relationship with wealthy Michael Halsey kept the pages turning.

In *Circle of Wolves* (Berkley, 1997), Samantha was the driving force rather than Dr. Augustin. Through her volunteer activity as a pet therapist at a facility for the elderly, Samantha became concerned that frail residents were being shunted into the more expensive units, including the psychiatric wards. These moves were based less on their needs than on the greed of the management. Still humiliated by having been left at the altar, Samantha delayed telling her mother that she and Michael Halsey were engaged.

Good reading.

Alison Hope

Author: Susan B. Kelly

If it were correct that men prefer women who are shorter, less intelligent, less educated, and with a lower income, Alison could qualify for spinsterhood. She was a tall redhead with a Cambridge degree and a computer software business, who had no difficulty attracting suitors, including Inspector Nick Trevellyan. Nick, formerly of the London Criminal Investigation Division, had transferred to the rural Hop Valley. Alison, the late and only child of a rector and his wife, was cautious about making a lifetime commitment, but she and Nick forged a long-term relationship.

Alison and Nick met in *Hope Against Hope* (Scribners, 1990) when she was suspected of the murder of her cousin and business partner, Aidan. Her claim that the partnership had ended carried no weight against the written survivorship agreement by which she benefited from his death. Alison established a formidable presence, but Nick did the detecting.

By *Time of Hope* (Scribners, 1992), Alison and Nick were living together, although he kept his apartment. Their Venetian holiday was interrupted when Nick was recalled by the death of young pregnant "Frisco" Carstairs. Frisco's skill as a gardener had been matched by her indiscriminate sexual affairs. Alison intervened because Ben Lawson, virginal son of her cleaning woman, was a serious suspect. Good cleaning women were hard to find.

The couple took separate tracks in *Hope Will Answer* (Scribners, 1993). Alison went undercover in a computer company to determine who was siphoning money from client accounts. Nick's temporary sergeant, an aggressive young woman, was not only interested in professional advancement but in Nick as they probed juvenile rapes.

Nick was primary in *Kid's Stuff* (Scribners, 1994), although Alison added moral support and a significant clue to his investigation of murder and child sexual abuse. Nick doubted that pornographer Arturo Bottone committed suicide in the barn of his wealthy wife's stable, but he found it difficult to confront the probable killers.

Death Is Sweet (Constable, 1996) began as Nick and Alison visited friends in London. Their host, Peter North who was married but attracted to nubile tennis instructor Louise Baron, became the primary suspect when she was killed. The actual killer, once confronted, confessed without pressure, neatly finishing off Nick's investigation. Alison was reduced to dog walking and other domestic chores.

The series improved, and had good prospects for the future but instead Kelly switched over to a police procedural series featuring Superintendent Gregory Summers

Martine "Marty" Hopkins

Author: P. (Patricia) M. Carlson

Martine "Marty" Hopkins, whose career plans were interrupted by an early marriage and pregnancy, eventually became a deputy sheriff in Nichols County, Indiana. The fact that family friend Sheriff Wes Cochran facilitated her employment caused resentment from male officers. Marty needed work, and her one-year in college had not prepared her for professional employment. Brad, her charming but unreliable husband, drifted from place to place seeking a job in broadcasting. Marty, who was described as a tall brown-haired woman, stayed behind to provide a home for their nine-year-old daughter, Chrissie.

Sheriff Cochran sought to protect Marty from the violence of law enforcement in *Gravestone* (Pocket, 1993). He sent her to evaluate Judge Hal Denton's claims that attempts had been made on his life, rather than to the shallow grave of a dead child. Cases involving children were hard on Marty. She uncovered the racial hatred, family discord, and revenge that led to both Denton's death and the child's.

Bloodstream (Pocket, 1995) returned Brad to Nichols County, sober, employed and eager to re-establish their family in Memphis. Even though Chrissie was devoted to her father, Marty was no longer sure that their marriage was viable. She was preoccupied with the deaths of two teenage boys and the abduction of a girl, hampered by an election campaign and the manipulations of land speculators. The resolution was unexpected.

Marty's personal chaos had to take a back seat in *Death Wind* (Severn House, 2004, almost a decade later than the prior book). It was she who filed for a divorce from Brad, but he took the offensive, seeking joint custody of Chrissie (now 13). Chrissie was devastated by their bickering and resentful of Marty's professional responsibilities. Marty had two major cases to deal with: (a) The Nichols County investigation of Stephanie Stollnitz's death in the lobby of the bank where she worked and (b) the mysterious death of punk rock band singer, Hoyt Heller. All this with a hurricane adding to the chaos.

It was a traumatic experience for Marty to be assigned to the arson/murder of Zill Corson in *Crossfire* (Severn House, 2006). She had never recovered from the death of her father in a burning car when she was twelve. Although Sheriff Pierce tried to sideline Marty, she came up with the information that tied Zill's death to others. Brooklyn Assistant District Attorney Liv Mann, daughter of a prior victim, flew to Indiana with questions about her father's death. He had gone to high school in Indiana with another of the victims and with former sheriff Wes Cochran. This is an exceptionally taut narrative with good characterizations.

Carlson is also the author of the Maggie Ryan series. (See Volume I)

Stevie Houston

Author: Tracey Richardson

Stevie Houston discarded the name, Stephanie, but retained strong feelings about her family. She could not understand the disconnect between herself and her parents that began when her twin sister Sarah drowned in the swimming pool. They did not approve of Stevie's career as a policewoman, considering that she had a university degree. Her older brother and sister had not only married and had children but also followed their father's footsteps by becoming corporate attorneys. Stevie's lesbian sexual orientation placed another gap between her and her parents who still lived in Calgary, Alberta, Canada.

She entered the police force in Toronto. Even with the university degree, Stevie started as a traffic cop and worked on the fraud squad before achieving status as a homicide detective. During her probationary period in the unit she overstepped her authority on several occasions bringing down the wrath of her supervisor, Lt. Jack McLemore. Stevie was fortunate in having Detective Ted Jovanowski assigned as her partner and coach. Ted was only four years away from retirement, but he accepted Stevie, recognized her strengths and tried to help when her need for independence was overwhelming. She was physically impressive at 5' 9" and 170 pounds, and knew it, using her appearance to intimidate suspects. In her first appearance, Stevie met the woman, Dr. Jade Agawa-Garneau, who was to dominate her personal life throughout the series.

The death of Father Gregory McCleary, a beloved parish priest, in what seemed to be an auto-erotic accident in *Last Rites* (Naiad, 1997) came at a time when Stevie was still on probation and inexperienced. Ted's heart attack put her in a difficult position. She was incapable of taking the lead on the case, but unwilling to settle for the decisions of her supervisor. Two subsequent deaths reinforced Stevie's conviction that Father McCleary had been killed because of his sexual orientation and his message of tolerance and inclusion in the Catholic Church. Acting without official support and at risk to herself and Jade, she proved her point. There was a price to be paid.

Lesbianism featured in *Over the Line* (Naiad, 1998) in combination with corruption in a small town police force. Jade who had done the autopsies convinced Stevie that the deaths of police officer Gina Walters and Harding Scott, her friend and coworker in the Shelton police force, were murder. The matter was taken to McLemore, thence to higher provincial authorities. Ted had recovered from his heart attack, but was not well enough to go undercover in the Shelton force. Stevie took on the assignment. She found allies there and needed them. Jade and Stevie who were living together added a dog, Tonka to the household.

Stevie's relationship with Jade interfered with her investigation in *Double Take Out* (Naiad, 1999). When ruthless businessman James Hedley was murdered, his wife Vanessa's lack of an alibi placed her in a precarious position. Jade had no part in that alibi, but she and Vanessa had shared an affair while still at the University. Stevie's persistence and reassurances from Jade made it possible for her to look elsewhere for suspects. James Hedley was in deep financial trouble. That combined with his use of salacious photographs and videos for blackmail had earned him enemies.

Jerusha "Jeri" Howard

Author: Janet Dawson

Jerusha "Jeri" Howard, the divorced daughter of divorced parents, was drawn to domestic traumas that erupted into murder. Jeri's birth family had been divided by her parent's divorce. Her brother Mark remained close to their mother, a successful Monterey restaurateur. Jeri's sympathies lay with Tim, her professor father. She had ended her marriage to Det. Sgt. Sid Vernon. Her solo detective agency was located in downtown Oakland, California. She shared her home with two cats, fat Abigail and skittish Black Bart. Jeri was described as a tall redhead.

In *Kindred Crimes* (St. Martin, 1990), Philip Foster whose wife Renee had disappeared, first hired, and then fired Jeri. He could not eliminate her from the investigation. The search for Renee reached back into Jeri's high school days. Renee's brother Mark, who was a classmate, had killed his parents. Mark had served his sentence, and been paroled. Without Jeri's help he would have been convicted of a more recent murder.

In *Till the Old Men Die* (Fawcett Crest, 1993), her dad, Prof. Tim Howard, found his colleague, Dr. Lito Manibusan dead in a parking lot. Jeri was motivated by concern for her father, but the investigation extended into current and past Philippine-American politics. Lt. Commander Alex Tongco, USN, Manibusan's nephew, intruded into the investigation and into Jeri's life.

In *Take a Number* (Fawcett Columbine, 1993), Ruth, an abused wife, sought missing assets, possibly profits of drug smuggling by her husband, Chief Petty Officer Sam Raynor. Tongco entered the controversy when Raynor was murdered, as did Sid Vernon. Ruth's attorney wanted her to claim self defense. Jeri had an alternative: Ruth was being framed.

What was supposed to be a vacation combined with bonding for Jeri and her estranged mother Marie became a rash of investigations in *Don't Turn Your Back on the Ocean* (Ballantine, 1994). Cousin Bobby was a suspect in the murder of his girlfriend, Ariel Logan. Someone was maiming sea gulls, Jeri's mother's restaurant was plagued with disruptive accidents, and her suitor was unacceptable. It wasn't much of a vacation.

During *Nobody's Child* (Fawcett, 1995), Jeri was hired by Mrs. Naomi Smith, who suspected that a recently discovered corpse was that of her daughter, Maureen. The girl had left home before her high school graduation and had made no contact over the years. Jeri had help on this one: her Dad, her friend Cassie, and her ex-husband, Sid. Residents of the seedier part of town filled in the blanks as to what Maureen Smith had been doing for the past three years. Maureen's killer became less important than the future of a child who might be carrying a fatal disease.

Coincidences abounded in *A Credible Threat* (Fawcett, 1996). Five women, including Sid Vernon's daughter Vicki, occupied a home owned by Sasha, an African-American law student. Because of her affection for Vicki, Jeri investigated threats, obscene phone calls, and vandalism at the residence. When the incidents spread to Jeri, she sought the terrorist in her past.

Jeri developed an affection for Darcy Stefano, the rebellious teenager she tracked down in Paris during *Witness to Evil* (Fawcett, 1997). It was impossible to ignore the young woman's cry for help. Darcy had run away from the strictly disciplined boarding school to which her uncaring mother had sent her. She had left behind suspicion that she might have murdered a member of the staff.

The unexplained death of new client Rob Later sent Jeri undercover in a formerly respected corporation during *Where the Bodies Are Buried* (Fawcett, 1998). Bates, a food production company, had recently been taken over by industrial sharks. Posing as a temporary employee, Jeri followed the information gathered by Later to find his killer.

What little Jeri knew about horse racing came from occasional trips to the track with her beloved Grandma Jerusha. In *A Killing at the Track* (Fawcett 2000), she was hired by David Vanitsky, part owner of Edgewater Downs, to investigate threats against trainer Molly Torrance. When jockey Benita Pascal was killed, Molly faced a new danger, as a suspect in the murder. Enjoyable, credible and interesting.

Scam and Eggs (Five Star, 2002), a collection of short stories by Dawson included two in which Jeri appeared.

Mention has been made of another Jeri Howard book *The Missing Child.* This may be another form of *Nobody's Child* mentioned above.

Dawson created picturesque subordinate characters and employed themes of interest to women. Her skills notably improved over the series.

Sara Howard

Author: Caleb Carr

The series, set in the 1890's, featured Sara, then a secretary at the New York Police Department. She had grown up in the Gramercy Park area, daughter of a wealthy family. Although her mother was an invalid, Sara's father taught her to shoot a gun, gamble and ride a horse on their country estate. He was now deceased. After attending college, Sara worked first as an assistant to a visiting nurse who practiced in a tough area of town. Her goal was to be the first female police officer in New York City.

The Alienist (Random House, 1994) went beyond the usual confines of a mystery. Psychologist Laszlo Kreizler was recruited by Theodore Roosevelt, the current police commissioner to investigate the mutilation deaths of prostitutes. The search was to be carried out secretly because both Roosevelt and Kreizler were distrusted by the conservative municipal leadership. The narrative was related by crime reporter John Schuyler Moore who had attended Harvard with Roosevelt and Kreizler. They put together a team including brothers Lucius and Marcus Isaacson, both detective sergeants with special skills (law and medicine) and Sara Howard. The plan was to create a profile of a man who could commit such horrors, perhaps one who had been abused himself. They hoped to identify him before he could commit another murder, but were opposed by powerful interests: proprietors of whorehouses, religious leaders, conservatives and those who preferred to ignore the harm done. Sara played a significant role, spurring the others on when they were thwarted and threatened.

The Angel of Darkness (Random House, 1997) reinstated the team, this time the narration was done by Stevie Taggert whom Sara had helped in the prior book. Sara recruited the members of the group one at a time after Senora Isabella Linares, wife of a Spanish diplomat came to her for help. Sara had opened her own investigation agency by this time. Kreizler was the last recruited but he could not refuse when he learned that Senora Isabella's infant daughter had been kidnapped. The extended narrative detailed the identification of the kidnapper, her ties to the Hudson Dusters (a gang with both juvenile and adult members), and an incredible history of murder. Kreizler, as before, saw the kidnapper as the product of her childhood. Others were not so forgiving. A courtroom duel with Clarence Darrow illuminated the story.

These are terrific narratives.

Sharyn Howard

Author: Joyce and Jim Lavene

Sharyn was the third generation in her family to serve as sheriff in Montgomery County, North Carolina, even though she had never been a deputy. She had won her position in a special election after her father (T. Raymond) was killed in action. Sharyn had earned a law degree but never took the bar exam. Sharyn's mother, Faye, approved of her other daughter, college student Kristie, who conformed more closely to the image as to what a young Southern woman should be. Ernie Watkins, the chief deputy who had hoped to be promoted, was initially hostile to Sharyn. This was not an easy time to be sheriff. The community's population had expanded. There were more outsiders, some tourists. Marriage was definitely not on her mind, but Dr. Nick Thomopolis, the medical examiner, showed interest in Sharyn.

Last Dance (Avalon, 1999) was a simplistic narrative. An experienced mystery reader will be aware early on who was the killer of two young women. Sharyn had been a teenager when classmate Leila Bentley was murdered at the high school parking lot. Her father, then sheriff, had arrested a drunken youth, Ronnie Smith. Smith was due to be executed in the near future. Now Sharyn is investigating the death of Carrie Sommers, who had stayed after the prom to help with cleanup. She cannot ignore the similarities between the two killings.

What had been intended as a long overdue vacation for Sharyn ended abruptly in *One Last Good-bye* (Avalon, 2000). Tom Metzger, Pulitzer Prize winning author had come to Diamond Springs to investigate a fifty-year-old plane accident. Captain Billy Boots had over flown the lake to make contact with his girlfriend, Mary Sue, but crashed into the water. Sharyn had several major murder cases waiting for her: Boots' death, that of co-pilot Joseph Walsh, and Metzger's. Faye, Sharyn's mother was romantically interested in State Senator Carson Talbot.

Sharyn had a worthy pair of opponents in *Until Our Last Embrace* (Avalon, 2001): a wily killer and the manipulative district attorney, Jack

Winter. Winter, who showed a personal interest in Sharyn, wanted her to join his staff as an attorney. When the ravaged body of Darla Richmond was found in a wooded area, the first assumption was that a bear was responsible. The examination by Nick Thomopolis caused Sharyn and Ernie Watkins to suspect Darla's husband, Donald. Sharyn may be a smart woman, but she was totally dense about Nick's feelings for her. The narrative was more skilled than the prior two.

Ernie Watkins had become Sharyn's most trusted friend and deputy but as *The Last to Remember* (Avalon, 2001) opened, he was behaving strangely. His problems receded in her mind on a stormy night with multiple emergencies. Civic leader Beau Richmond burst into the sheriff's office to confess to a forty-year-old murder, only to be found later hanging from a beam. Sharyn and her staff were not only held responsible but possible murder suspects. On a personal level, Sharyn was unhappy as Faye and Carson Talbot moved towards an engagement.

Sharyn considered not running for another term as sheriff as *For the Last Time* (Avalon, 2001) began. The reopening of a twenty-five-year-old case, one which had baffled her grandfather Jacob, had been followed by the discovery that not one, but two killings had taken place at the time. She could not leave until these cases had been dealt with. The assumption was that the killer murdered a second time to cover up the first death. Sharyn risked the displeasure of her family and retribution from Jack Winter by opposing the redevelopment of the Bell's Creek campground.

An assailant injured Senator Carson Talbot, Faye's fiancé, during a Revolutionary War re-enactment in *Dreams Don't Last* (Avalon, 2002) but that was the least of his problems. Soon afterwards he was suspected of killing an elderly woman with whom he had shared a past and homeless Vietnam veteran Willy Newsome. Sharyn's family problems interfered with her professional responsibilities. Kristie, her sister, was acting erratically and claiming that Sharyn would take revenge on those who called her to task. This was another short book with many characters from prior narratives. The Lavenes were churning them out quickly.

The election for sheriff was held during *Last Fires Burning* (Avalon, 2003), but the community was more concerned about the drought and fires on Diamond Mountain. Sharyn's plan to divert wild animals from the town antagonized the county commissioners. A series of deaths and fires in town were variously attributed to a gambler's enforcer, and protestors, including Sharyn's Aunt Selma. There was history behind the incident. Sharyn and Nick were dating seriously.

Dinner with Nick was interrupted in *Last Rites* (Avalon, 2004) by the discovery of insurance salesman Clint Walker's corpse. He had been buried in his car in a deep hole at a neglected cemetery eight years before. Clint's lecherous behavior had earned him so many enemies that it took time to weed them out. A second murder complicated the process. The narrative ended with a hook for the next book, an annoying technique. Incredible that no fuss had been made when Clint disappeared.

Sharyn was safely elected to four more years as sheriff, but in *Glory's Last Victim* (Avalon, 2004), she over-reached on several occasions. While she had a series of burglaries to contend with, she devoted considerable personal time to prove that Sam Two Rivers had not killed coed Lynette Ashe. There was a personal reason for her interest. Sam was Aunt Selma's beau. Lynette's death connected with a series of crimes over more than a century.

Last One Down (Avalon, 2004) was short, crowded and implausible. Reluctantly Sharyn and two of he deputies had flown to an isolated law enforcement training center on a nearby mountain side, leaving behind a suspicious death. At the training site, they encountered multiple attacks and murders while the rains poured and the creeks rose. Ernie, Nick and the rest of the squad remained behind to deal with additional deaths and injuries. Eventually they joioned forces for a showdown with an incredible killer.

The Sharyn Howard mysteries are rarely self sustaining, depending upon the reader's knowledge of prior books. In *Before the Last Lap* (Avalon, 2005) Sharyn pulled her staff together after Deputy Ed Robinson and his wife Trudy (Sharyn's assistant) are both suspected of murder. Trudy had been privately investigating the death of her first husband, who was killed driving a car owned by Duke Beatty. She took risks to learn whether Duke was responsible for the crash or might have been the intended victim. When she disappeared, returning only after Duke and his chief mechanic were murdered, Ed confessed to both crimes to protect her. All of this took place against the on-going background of a rural county which was controlled by the "good old boys", some in public office; others more shadowy figures. Sharyn's fear that her father may have been a member of the group motivated her concern. The FBI wanted her to hold off on her investigation of the murders to protect an on-going project of their own.

Concerned that state senator and former district attorney Jack Winter was responsible for her father's death, Sharyn chose an unusual method of investigation in *The First Shall Be Last* (Avalon, 2007). She encouraged romantic advances from Winter, which necessitated rejecting county coroner Nick Thomopolis. Her behavior confused and angered many of her friends and co-workers. Her plan was initially shared only with FBI Agent Brewster who was investigating the possibility that Winters and other members of the "good old boy" club were connected to the drug trade. Several people died in the process.

The series had deteriorated. Meanwhile the Lavenes had two other series in process. One featuring Prof. Margaret "Peggy " Lee, who turned her back on her academic career to open a garden shop; the other, former cop, now a stock car racer, Glad Wyczhewski.

Emma Howe

Author: Gillian Roberts

See: Billie August, Page 26

Lil Hubbert

Author: Gallagher Gray, a pseudonym for Katy Munger

Lil Hubbert was an octogenarian, who assisted her fifty-five-year-old bachelor nephew in solving mysteries. Retired after sixty years in the fashion industry and limited slightly by hearing problems, she had retained her common sense, good appetite, and zest for life. Lil had always been special to Theodore (T. S.) Hubbert, providing the warmth and excitement denied him by a cold and unappreciative mother. Aunt Lil was described as "sturdy", white-haired, favoring pants suits, bright colors, and multiple accessories.

As *Hubbert & Lil; Partners in Crime* (Fine, 1991) began, T. S., a banker, was recalled by Sterling and Sterling when Robert Cheswick was stabbed in the partners' room. He shared dinner and his problems with Aunt Lil, and she never let go of the investigation. She encouraged T. S. to renew his acquaintance with wealthy widow Lilah Cheswick, and acquired an admirer of her own, messenger Herbert Wong.

In *A Cast of Killers* (Fine, 1992), Lil recruited T. S. to work at the St. Barnabas soup kitchen where Emily, a former actress but whose name was then unknown, had collapsed and died. Quite a few of the patrons of the soup kitchen were elderly women with theatrical backgrounds. Lilah Cheswick used her connections to gain access to the morgue, the autopsy, and the diagnosis of cyanide poisoning. When the police ended Lil's volunteer work at St. Barnabas, she attended as an eligible recipient. T. S. had always wondered why Lil, capable of so much love, had never married.

In *Death of a Dream Maker* (Ivy, 1995), T. S. learned about Max Rosenbloom, Lil's former employer and the man she had always loved. After decades apart, Max was en route to meet with Lil when he was killed by a car bomb. Lil had to know who did it and why. The police, the Rosenbloom family, and gang leader Jake the Snake were interested in Lil, because she was a major beneficiary in Max's will.

During *A Motive for Murder* (Ivy, 1996), Lil parlayed her position on the Board of Directors of the Metro Ballet Company into investigating a murder. Bobby Morgan, a former child star, whose son Mikey had a major role in *The Nutcracker* production, had been killed. Bobby was a ruthless promoter who had enough enemies to keep Lil busy. T. S. came along for the ride, preoccupied with learning how to dance so he could spend more time with Lilah Cheswick.

Lil was portrayed as vital, without that hint of patronizing that often taints the literary characterizations of the elderly. Author Katy Munger moved on to a new series. See: Casey Jones.

Harriet "Harry" Hubbley

Author: Jackie Manthorne

Harriet "Harry" Hubbley, a lesbian, had been a physical education teacher in the Montreal, Quebec school system for three decades. On a personal level, she and Judy Johnson had been lovers for eleven years, but not always in a monogamous relationship. Harry had grown up in Spruce Bay, a small fishing village in Nova Scotia. Her parents had retired and now lived in Vancouver.

During *Ghost Motel* (Gynergy, Canada 1994), Harry and Judy vacationed together on Cape Cod, but each found romance elsewhere. Harry's interlude with a female police officer came about during a murder investigation.

When, in *Deadly Reunion* (Gynergy, 1995), Harry attended a thirtieth high school class reunion, she did so alone. Judy would not attend unless she was publicly acknowledged as Harry's partner. The twenty-three graduates, or those who also attended, were rife with possibilities for murder. Wayne Williams, who boasted of his affairs, was an obvious prospect for the victim.

Last Resort (Gynergy, 1995) described Harriet's visit to her friend Barbara Fenton in Key West, Florida. When Barbara was killed, Harriet inherited a controlling interest in a guesthouse, which motivated her to find the murderer.

Harriet attended her last gym teacher's convention as *Sudden Death* (Gynergy, 1997) opened. With the inheritance of a Florida guesthouse plus $300,000 in investments, she no longer needed to work through the Canadian winters. Among the attendees were current lesbian couples and former lovers. When Julie, a flirtatious member of the group, was murdered, there were multiple suspects. Harriet met Raven, a much younger woman with whom she developed a relationship.

At fifty and still depressed by the end of her affair with Judy Jackson, Harriet was not in a party mood. However, in *Final Take* (Gynergy, 1998) a college friend convinced her to join Butch and Richie, male homosexuals, at the San Francisco Gay and Lesbian Film Festival. The death of Fran, Richie's sister and their hostess, created tensions within the group. Raven, Fran's former lover now intimate with Harriet, was a vulnerable witness.

Honey Huckleberry

Author: Margaret Moseley

Honey Huckleberry lived her life by schedule. Perhaps it would be unfair to diagnose her as obsessive-compulsive, but order ruled her life. A tiny redhead, who worked as a book representative in Texas, Honey moved about the state visiting independent booksellers on behalf of publishers. Her parents had been late in life to have children, and perhaps unprepared for her birth. There was a hint that the pregnancy had contributed to her mother's poor health and eventual death.

Honey had enjoyed a close and companionable relationship with her now deceased father, a researcher who assisted in the development and patenting of inventions. He, at times. purchased the rights to inventions that the originator had tired of trying to market. He had a secret name for his daughter, "Lydia" known only to a few intimates. Not that Honey never left home. She had attended Tarrant County Junior College and earned a degree in English from TCU. Honey's isolated and introverted upbringing may explain her rigidity and fears (including a terror of entering the pantry where foods were stored).

Her reclusiveness did not apply on the road where she made friends among the booksellers whom she served. She and Harry Armstead, a retired British Royal naval officer, had an ongoing affair that was restricted to her visits to him at South Padre. His dog Bailey, a Golden Lab, became her pet too.

There was a surfeit of Stevens in Honey's life. The first had been unorthodox accountant Steven Bondesky who had worked with her dad. Perhaps the most important had been Steven Hyatt, a friend since high school. Neither Honey nor Steven Hyatt had fit in with the cliques at their school, so they had bonded. He had driven her to her classes when her dad needed to remain home with her mother. They used "Lydia" and lines of poetry to communicate with one another after he became a Hollywood director. Frequently, the most useful Steven in her life was her mechanic, Steven Miller, who took care of Honey's car and checked on the house for her when she was on her route.

Honey's metamorphosis began in *The Fourth Steven* (Berkley 1998), triggered by a phone call from a man who identified himself only as Stephen, but was privy to intimate details in Honey's life. The death of Steven Miller in Honey's home introduced her to Silas Sampson, a Fort Worth police detective. Bookseller and friend Janie Bridge induced Honey to do some detecting on her own. All of a sudden the reclusive Honey had a life filled with excitement, a cupboard full of money, and several beaus.

Honey was surprised when she attended a local library dinner in *Grinning In His Mashed Potatoes* (Berkley, 1999). She was invited to sit at the head table with the guest of honor, author Twyman Towerie. Towerie was under the mistaken impression that Honey was a detective. When he dropped dead in his mashed potatoes, Honey did not accept the official designation of natural death. She suspected he had been killed by one of his four former wives. She and Janie went undercover to learn which one, or two, or more was involved.

Catastrophes piled up in Honey's life during *A Little Traveling Music, Please* (Berkley, 2000). Steven Bondesky who handled her considerable investments had disappeared, leaving her account empty. Hurricanes, floods, and tornadoes complicated the search for Bondesky. Then it got worse. Harry Armstead disappeared, leaving Bailey with Honey. She could make no plans in her personal life until she found Harry again. She and two friends set off for England where he had last been seen. Unfortunately they were not the only ones looking for Harry. There was a teasing end to *A Little Traveling Music*. Unfortunately there were no more in the series. Moseley has also written two well-received standalones.

Emma Hudson

Author: Sydney Hosier

Not only has Sherlock Holmes been credited with a wife (See: Mary Russell), and a daughter (See: *In the Dead of Winter* by Abby Penn Baker), but series have been created around other women in his life. (See: Irene Adler). Now his housekeeper, Mrs. Emma Hudson, traded upon their connection. Emma, a short plump woman in her sixties, utilized Holmes' name and implied that they worked together professionally when it suited her. She was the widow of William, who had run a ship chandler's business, but, after his death, depended for her income on renting rooms in her large house. Holmes was her most distinguished lodger.

After her first experience as an investigator, Mrs. Hudson came to rely upon old friend Violet Warner, widow of William's partner. Violet's forte was OBE (out-of-body experiences) during which she could project her "self" to other locations and view the actions of suspects. Sherlock Holmes (but not Arthur Conan Doyle) would have been appalled at such tactics. He had encouraged Mrs. Hudson in her reading, her use of libraries, and her efforts at self-education. She had other talents—she had considered becoming a painter, and still did landscapes.

As *Elementary, Mrs. Hudson* (Avon, 1996) opened, Violet, then working as a housekeeper at a Surrey estate, contacted Holmes for help. He was in Scotland, so Mrs. Hudson presented herself as a substitute. Violet believed that Lady Agatha, the doyenne of Haddley Hall, had been murdered. Her astral spirit had witnessed the death, but she was unable to identify the killer. Mrs. Hudson, who had been introduced to the household as a friend of Violet, stayed on to prove Will Tadlock, a young groom's helper, innocent of the murder of an initially unidentified young woman. After her stint at Haddley Hall, Violet moved in with Emma at the rooming house.

Sherlock referred a noble client (a young Sir Winston Churchill) with an unusual case to Mrs. Hudson in *Murder, Mrs. Hudson* (Avon, 1997). Churchill's concerns about an international saboteur were put aside when he was assigned to cover the Boer War in South Africa. Violet and Emma persevered in their investigation, assisted by well-lubricated Irishman Paddy O'Ryan, and saved the British House of Commons from a disaster.

Initially Emma opposed Violet's idea of running advertisements for their services in the newspaper. In *Most Baffling, Mrs. Hudson* (Avon, 1998), she eagerly followed up on Jane Bramwell's response to the ad. Bramwell's husband had been shot during a game of charades at their home, but none of those present could recall seeing a gun or a killer. For all of Mrs. Hudson's charm, the resolution may not satisfy astute readers.

Emma Hudson's adventure in *The Game's Afoot, Mrs. Hudson* (Avon, 1998) might like many of Sherlock Holmes' cases have been condensed into short story form. While vacationing in Brighton, Emma and Vi encountered ghosts and pseudo ghosts (one seeking love; the other, a stolen jewel).

Light entertainment.

Robin Hudson

Author: Sparkle Hayter

Thirty-five-year-old Robin Hudson was a tall redheaded New York City television news reporter for All News Network (ANN). After mishandling two high priority assignments, she was relegated to the network's Special Reports Unit. This was not the first setback in her life, so she coped. Robin's father died when she was ten. Her mother had been diagnosed as chronically mentally ill (she believed herself to be the "rightful queen of England"). Robin was concerned about her own mood swings, sufficiently so that she refused to have children. Her husband could not cope with the situation so the marriage ended. Her subsequent romances were casual. Robin kept an ill-humored alley cat named Louise Bryant, rarely ate meat and grew poison ivy to inhibit burglars. She collected singing and talking condoms activated by body heat. She had a morbid preoccupation with murders, keeping a scrapbook of clippings begun when she was a crime reporter. Louise Bryant became an asset as a star in commercials.

What's A Girl Gotta Do? (Soho, 1994) was overpopulated—too many co-workers, and too many suspects in the death of private investigator Larry Griff, who knew too much about Robin's past. Even when Robin learned that Griff had been investigating her and other sexually harassed females, she was vulnerable. Fortunately Louise Bryant came to the rescue.

Robin's memories of her Aunt Maureen were negative, based on her effort to get custody when Robin's mother was mentally ill. As *Nice Girls Finish Last* (Viking, 1996) opened, Aunt "Mo" came to visit, just as Robin became a murder suspect. She had made, but did not keep, Dr. Herman Kanengiser's last appointment before he was murdered. Already on shaky ground at ANN because of pranks attributed to her, Robin investigated the doctor's connections with other staff members, sado-masochism and double billing.

Robin was executive producer of *Special Report*, but that did not keep her from a Halloween revel with old friends in *Revenge of the Cootie Girls* (Viking, 1997). Their bar tour was interrupted by news that Robin's naive young intern Kathy was missing. Her rescue was based upon clues in a treasure hunt; the answers to which referred back to (a) a vacation in New York City which Robin had taken while a college girl, during which she and a friend picked up two

Italian strangers, and (b) the cruelties which school girls inflicted upon one another by their cliques and rejection of the "outsiders."

A casual encounter with a confused scientist in *The Last Manly Man* (Morrow, 1998) eventually connected with Sparkle's latest production, a series on the man of the future, and with the discovery of a corpse on the beach. During the assignment and the investigation, she worked with vegetarian environmentalists, protestors of the horny bonobo apes and most reluctantly with Rob "Rambo" Ryan, her competitor for airtime. Her store of information was enhanced when she learned that women could urinate standing up if they used a funnel. Who said mysteries were frivolous?

The Chelsea Hotel was a port in a storm for Robin when her apartment building burned at the beginning of *The Chelsea Girl Murders* (No Exit Press, 2000). Her occupancy of friend Tamayo's suite was marred by runaway lovers, disappearing incomes, and murder. The cast of characters was eclectic as befitted the historic hostelry.

Robin Hudson was not a run of the mill sleuth, nor was Sparkle Hayter a commonplace author. Both were flaky and occasionally crude, but fun. Hayter turned to writing standalones.

Jo Hughes

Author: Linda Mather

Jo Hughes was described as an Englishwoman in her mid-twenties with dark curly hair. When she could not live on her income from writing a weekly horoscope column for a Coventry newspaper, she accepted a part-time position with Macy and Wilson, a detective agency. Her personal life was fairly boring: a cat named Preston, regular swimming at an indoor pool, occasional fun times with her best friend Maurisha, and a couple of one-nighters with Bill Macy, her employer.

Her first assignment for the agency in *Blood of an Aries* (St. Martin, 1994) was to check out three individuals to see if they might be friends of young accountancy student Grahame Holte. The challenge expanded as Holte, lecherous college professor Edward Pinder, and Pinder's American lover all died mysteriously. When she met strangers, Jo used astrology as an introductory topic to check personality traits of suspects and victims. Her identification of the killer came as a result of hard work.

The disappearance of his brother Sean prompted Connor Fitzpatrick to visit the detective agency in *Beware Taurus* (Macmillan, 1994) when Jo was the only staff person available. She accepted the case, but needed the help of Alan, the other Macy and Wilson investigator, to discover why Sean had disappeared and why so many people had been looking for him.

Another family affair, the death of her sister Monique, sent Toni Carlyle to Jo for an astrological reading in *Gemini Doublecross* (Macmillan, 1997). Monique had been depressed because her affair with John, a mysterious stranger whom Toni had never met, had ended. When Toni felt herself to be in danger, Macy assigned Jo as her companion. Both sisters had sought companionship through lonely-hearts advertisements.

Although the series was referred to as "Zodiac Mysteries," the impact of astrology was minor.

Liu Hulan

Author: Lisa See

Liu Hulan was a member of the upper society in China, a "Red Princess." Her family had once been major landowners. The Jiang family (her mother's) had been royal entertainers—singers, dancers, and puppeteers to the Court. The revolution was anathema to them. Hulan's parents, Jinli Jiang and her husband, had rejected their families and allied themselves with the rebels. Initially that led to a happy situation in which her father held a post in the Ministry of Culture. However the period of cleansing brought about by Mao and the Red Guard placed them all at risk. Hulan, at age twelve, was placed in a rural community to learn peasant virtues. Patriotic fervor and/or the desire to save oneself led individuals, even children, to denounce others.

When her father was accused of malfeasance in office and Jinli severely injured in a fall, family friend Zai intervened to get Hulan out of China. She was sent to the United States, and placed in a Connecticut boarding school during a time when her father was in a Chinese labor camp. Even when the Mao regime ended, Hulan remained in the United States where she attended USC. She went on to law school, and finally took employment at Phillips, McKenzie law firm. There she met and fell in love with David Stark.

When Hulan returned to China, ending the relationship, she found her mother in a wheelchair, only competent to converse on special occasions. Her father, who never forgave what he perceived as his daughter's betrayal, had become Vice Minister at the powerful Ministry of Public Security. Hulan became employed there; first, as a tea girl, then as an investigator. Zai, her father's subordinate, played an important role in her advancement. Hulan did not live with her parents, although she visited her mother every day. Instead she lived in the Jiang home, which had been restored to the family. She was dedicated to her duty to China.

When the United States and Chinese governments agreed to cooperate in investigating the death of two young men in *Flower Net* (HarperCollins, 1997), Hulan and David Stark were reunited. Their prior connection was known, but it suited the needs of powerful people in both countries. Billy Watson, son of the U.S. Ambassador to China, and Guang Henglai, son of a powerful Chinese businessman, had been killed under similar circumstances. Linking their deaths was easy; finding why they had to die was more difficult. The resumption of her affair with David had potentially serious consequences.

As *The Interior* (HarperCollins, 1999) began, Hulan was pregnant. Even the risk to her unborn child did not turn her from her duty to China. She traveled to the rural areas to answer the plea of old friend Ling Suchee whose daughter Miaoshan had been murdered. When Hulan became aware that female workers in American-owned plants were being mistreated, she broadened her investigation. David Stark, who had previously worked for the U.S. Attorney's office, was now legal counsel for the Knight factory. He was the father of her child and wanted to be with her. The narrative tackled the moral issues involved when an American corporation establishes factories in foreign countries.

It will take a discerning reader to absorb all the background information about ancient China, current China, and its potential future provided in *Dragon Bones* (Random House, 2003), but it will be a rewarding experience. Liu Hulan and David were dispatched to Site 518 where archeologists hurried to retrieve artifacts that would be buried when the land was flooded by the Three Gorges Dam. Liu Hulan was ordered to abandon her current investigation of a cult, which threatened the government, and find the killer of young American archeologist, Brian McCarthy. David's task was to retrieve items that had been stolen from the site. Although they worked separately, they shared a common enemy and revitalized their relationship.

The books provided a fascinating background that explored China's recent past and the current status of the individual, the family, the neighborhood, and the government.

See wrote at least three other novels relating to China that were well received.

Leah Hunter

Author: Sarah Lacey, pseudonym for Kay Mitchell

At age twenty-five, Leah Hunter had not recovered from her affair with a married man. Her employment as a tax inspector in Bramfield, Yorkshire, where she had attended a female college, provided few opportunities to meet eligible men. She had a poor relationship with her parents, actually disliking her father. As a substitute, Leah depended upon Dora, an elderly friend from whom she rented a garage. After her car was seriously damaged, Leah drove a souped-up Morris Minor with a BMW engine. An attractive brown-haired woman, she kept physically fit with regular workouts at a health club and training in self-defense. She did not hesitate to use martial arts and weapons to protect herself.

Leah needed to be physically fit in *File Under: Deceased* (St. Martin, 1993) when a casual encounter in an art gallery placed John Thorne, a dying undercover agent, in her arms. She survived threats, battering, burglaries, arson, and a romantic interest in Sgt. David Nicholls, the investigating officer, before learning who her real adversaries were.

Grace Howe was not deterred by the police department's disinterest in the disappearance of her eighteen-year-old son Andy in *File Under: Missing* (St. Martin, 1994). She and Dora convinced Leah to search for him. He had disappeared from a party held by his employer, music producer Dean Wilde. Leah had assorted allies: Charlie, the used car dealer; Sid, a pimp with contacts; Neal Anderson, an attractive former classmate; and Darius Dixon, a local reporter. It was Sgt. Dave Nicholls of the Regional Crime Squad who was there when she needed him. She and Nicholls never moved in together or made a commitment but saw one another frequently.

During *File Under: Arson* (St. Martin, 1996), Leah, recuperating from a bullet wound, returned to action when fifteen-year-old Billy was found hanging in his jail cell. The boy had been arrested for arson based on his juvenile record. Leah and Nicholls believed he had been set up. Her work with tax abuse cases aided her investigation of a major arson scam until her suspects retaliated, claiming that Leah had solicited a bribe. She had the life of another teenager, as well as her professional reputation, at stake.

As *File Under: Jeopardy* (St. Martin, 1997) began, Leah saw college friend Jeannie Johnson being escorted out of jail. Jeannie, a customs inspector, would not discuss her predicament but she left a packet for Leah with her mother when she disappeared. Mrs. Johnson was hospitalized after a hit-and-run accident, the packet disappeared, and a badly injured Jeannie was rescued from a canal. Leah persisted, learning about the real Jeannie, the crime syndicate, and justice outside of the law.

Leah took considerable risks, but had national health insurance coverage and some unconventional friends.

Lexy Hyatt

Author: Carlene Miller

Lexy, now in her thirties, was a tall redheaded reporter in Orlando, Florida. She had been an English teacher, but left when a new rigid principal was appointed. She had become disillusioned by the cruelty to gay and lesbian students in the school, three of whom had committed suicide during her tenure. She was lesbian and hung out at the Cat, a gay bar. She was athletic, played softball during her school years, and liked to hike.

The Cat, owned by Marilyn Neff, was the site of a murder in *Killing at the Cat* (New Victoria, 1998). Independent insurance broker Darla Pollard's body was found in the storage room. Lexy was there at the time and acquainted with most of the others present. She had a divided loyalty. Now a reporter on *The Ledger*, she could provide first hand information on the incident, but she wanted to protect the Cat and her friends from homophobic publicity. During her investigation, Lexy met a new woman, Wren Carlyle.

Forced to cancel a trip with Wren, Lexy was talked into spending her vacation on Marilyn Neff's boat *Willow*, during *Mayhem at the Marina* (New

Victoria, 1999). She was not a water person but she came to care deeply for those who were: "Cap" Andrew MacKay, owner of the marina; his friend, widow Meg Gilstrap; and most particularly young Charlie, a delinquent who had been paroled to Detective Roberta Exline's care. Not everyone was welcoming. Steve, Cap's estranged son, schemed to shut down his dad's marina. When Steve was murdered, Lexy feared that the police would arrest one of her new friends. She wanted to be sure that it was the guilty one.

Wren and Lexy had settled into their new home by *Reporter on the Run* (New Victoria, 2001), but there were problems at the *Ledger.* When Rose and William Standish died together in a plane crash, the ownership of the newspaper went to their twin children: Andrew, a reckless playboy, and Andrea, who had spent the last decade working on the *Ledger.* But each owned only 40% of the stock. The remainder had been acquired by a right wing couple, Christopher and Nelda Cross. Andrea encouraged Lexy and two co-workers to take part in an orienteering event, part of Women's Health Week. The death of Andrew Standish cast suspicion on Andrea, but he had earned many enemies.

Reiko Ichiro

Author: Laura Joh Rowland

Readers of the first three books in the Sano Ichiro series set in late Seventeenth century Japan would be unlikely to anticipate the role that Sano's wife Reiko would come to play. He, a former teacher and tutor, had earned a position as a yoriki, a senior police officer in Edo (Tokyo), based upon a favor owed to his family by that of Katsuragama Shundai. He was ostracized within the police structure by other yorikis, who got their jobs through nepotism and their upper class status. Nothing in his previous training had prepared Sano for his new job, but he was bound as a samurai to follow Bushido (the Way of the Warrior, i.e. obedience to superiors). This obligation had been drilled into him by his father, a former ronin, and now the elderly owner of a martial arts academy, who had high hopes for his only son. Ronins were warriors who had lost their masters and operated on their own. Some became outlaws, but the Ichiro family code would not allow that. The shogun, Tokugawa Tsunayoshi, was the titular head of the country, but Chamberlain Yanagisawa who was also his lover, held real control. Sano's early success caused Yanagisawa to see him as a rival. He was a dangerous enemy. As the series progressed and Sano rose to more important roles, his list of rivals increased

In *Shinju* (Random House, 1994) Sano was assigned to investigate and quickly close the deaths of lower class artist Noiyoshi and upper class Niu Yukiko. Their bound together bodies had been discovered in the river, and their deaths assumed to be Shinju (double suicide). Sano's training as a teacher gave him a second code to follow; find the truth. He did so with serious consequences to himself.

By *Bundori* (Villard, 1996) Sano had a new job and title as Honorable Investigator of Events, Situations, and People on the staff of the shogun and lived in a mansion. After the death of a member of the shogun's inner circle, he was assigned to ferret out the killer, who collected trophies from his victims. In so doing Sano met Aoi, a ninja (person trained in martial arts) who totally captivated his heart. Again, by including Yanagisawa in his circle of suspects, he set himself up for repercussions. His father had made tentative approaches to Reiko's father as to a possible marriage for Sano, but his current status made that an unlikely prospect.

During *The Way of the Traitor* (HarperCollins, 1998) Yanagisawa took his revenge by sending Sano (now engaged to Reiko) to Nagasaki, the only port where foreign ships were allowed to dock. There were rumors of corruption and smuggling, which led to murders. Still deeply in love with Aoi, Sano postponed the wedding again because of his transfer. He took with him young Hirata, his assistant whom he came to trust. As before Sano got himself in trouble with the local authorities, some of whom had ties to Yanagisawa; some of whom were involved in the smuggling. At times Sano's struggles with his responsibilities and the conflicts that arose when he must protect his country and when he sought justice grew wearisome.

It was time for a change, and in *The Concubine's Tattoo* (St. Martin, 1998) that included the marriage ceremony between Sano and Reiko, whose father was wealthy Magistrate Ueda. Lady Harume, currently the shogun's favorite concubine was tattooing her body, unaware that the ink she was using had been poisoned. Sano who was assigned to investigate her death found unexpected help from his new bride. The conventional role of a wife would not have allowed such cooperation, but Reiko was the only child of her widowed father. She had been raised with opportunities, education, and expectations equivalent to that provided for a son. The narrative contained a substantial amount of explicit sex of a perverse nature. Homosexuality and pederasty seem to have been accepted in court circles, the shogun being a practitioner. The developing relationship between Sano and Reiko was loving and considerate of her needs.

Left Minister Konoe, a powerful figure in the less powerful world of the Edo Imperial family was murdered in *The Samurai's Wife* (St. Martin, 2000). Sano, reeling from Chamberlain Yanagisawa's coup to humiliate him, was relieved to be sent to Miyako to solve the crime. Although Reiko and two assistants, detectives Fukida and Marume, accompanied Sano, he had no local contacts on which he could rely. The Imperial Family had been relegated to a ceremonial role generations before. Yanagisawa, secretly came to Miyako, planning to further mislead and disgrace Sano. Reiko disregarded Sano's restrictions, spending time with Lady Jukyoden, mother to young emperor Tomohito, and Lady Asagao, his chief consort. Both she and Sano withheld information from one another. Tomohito, still a teenager, chafed at his diminished role, finding encouragement within his court for intrigue.

Reiko really pushed the envelope in *Black Lotus* (St. Martin, 2001). She was now the mother of a son, and for a considerable period of time had devoted herself to family affairs. Sano's request for her help was eagerly accepted. She was to question Haru, a teenage novice at the Black Lotus Temple. Haru had been found in a semi-conscious state near to a burned out house in which three corpses had been discovered. She was the prime suspect for everyone but Reiko, who became her champion. Reiko made every effort to divert Sano's attention to the evil aspects of the Black Lotus Temple. This was dangerous as many powerful people were adherents of the temple and its high priest, Anraku.

The shogun demanded an immediate solution to the death of young Lord Mitsuyoshi as *The Pillow Book of Lady Wisteria* (St. Martin, 2002) began. The young man, who was not only a cousin of the shogun and his potential heir, but also the son of powerful Lord Matsudaira, had been murdered at an upscale "place of assignment" in the red light district. Lady Wisteria (who previously appeared in *Shinju*, see above) had been his companion for the evening. She had a history with Sano. Her help in an earlier case had motivated him to secure her freedom from a brothel. Lady Wisteria had disappeared from the enclosed and guarded "pleasure quarter". Was she a witness, a victim, or an accomplice to murder?

The abduction of the Shogun's mother (Lady Keisho-in) and three companions in *Dragon King's Palace* (St. Martin, 2003) unleashed assorted agendas for Sano and Hirata. Their wives, Reiko and the pregnant Midori, were among the companions who had accompanied Lady Keisho-in, as was the unstable wife of Chamberlain Yanagisawa. Yanagisawa, at this time, was battling the forces of Lord Matsudaira whom he tried to identify as responsible for the abduction. The shogun was devastated by his mother's possible fate. Separate forces were sent to trace the kidnappers. Reiko was determined to devise her own rescue, but the only one of her companions who was even close to being functional was Lady Yanagisawa. They were imprisoned on the island of the Dragon King, who was determined to avenge a wrong done to members of his family. Coincidentally Reiko resembled the deceased woman whom he had loved.

Battles between the supporters of Chamberlain Yanagisawa and Lord Matsudaira formed the background for *The Perfumed Sleeve* (St. Martin, 2004). The shogun was blissfully unaware of their armed rivalry, as he was of most conditions in Edo. When Senior Elder Makino died, he left a message, requesting that in the case of his death, Sano should investigate. He was only allowed to proceed under the supervision of representatives of the two major suspects. Reiko, not yet recovered from her abduction, gathered her courage and went undercover as a servant in the Makino household, which included his wife, concubine, and a houseguest.

Success, in the form of his promotion to the role of Chamberlain to the shogun had not brought contentment to either Sano or Reiko by *The Assassin's Touch* (St. Martin's 2005). He was immersed in administrative details. She was bored by inactivity and loneliness. His assignment to investigate a series of unexplained deaths to other recently promoted court officials was a difficult, but initially welcomed, challenge. Reiko and her father, magistrate Uedo, exceeded their authority when he asked her to investigate murder charges against Yugao, whose family had been sentenced to hinin (a lower caste) status as a result of her father's misdeeds. While Sano struggled within the system, Reiko explored the sleazy segments of the community, exposing herself to danger and Sano to humiliation.

Initially Reiko was more victim than sleuth in *Red Chrysanthemum* (St. Martin, 2006). Hirata and his men had found her dazed and naked in the bed of Lord Mori. Reiko had gone to Mori's estate, and met with his wife in the hope of rescuing a missing four-year-old boy whose mother had rented him to Mori, a pederast, for a night from which he never returned. Sano had difficulty proving her innocence at a time when she was pregnant with their second child. He had problems of his own, having been falsely accused of treason to the shogun and given a limited period of time to prove both him and his wife Reiko innocent. Reiko investigated those who might have reason to hate her. Hirata's marriage suffered from his determination to further rehabilitate himself after a serious injury. Hoshima, former lover of Lord Yanagisawa (now exiled), used his position as commissioner of police to thwart Sano's investigation.

Both Sano and Reiko were devastated by the disappearance of their eight-year-old son, Masahiro, as *The Snow Empress* (St. Martin, 2007) began. When the shogun insisted that Sano go to the island of Ezogashima to investigate conditions, Sano might have refused had not his rival Lord Matsudaira revealed that his men had kidnapped the boy and taken him to the island. Wan and emaciated Reiko insisted on accompanying Sano, his detectives, and troops on the voyage. A shipwreck off the Ezo coast left only a small group who were taken prisoners, first by the Ezos (native tribe); then by the troops of Lord Matsumae. Sano struck a bargain with Matsumae, whereby he would identify the killer of Tekari (Matsumae's mistress) if allowed the freedom to also look for his son. Reiko through her contacts with the females on the island and Hirata, who had added Ainu spiritualism to his esoteric martial arts, worked separate paths. Reiko had made the decision to leave her newly born daughter, Akiko, in Midori's care.

As the Eighteenth century began, Sano and Reiko's personal and political lives were in chaos during *The Fire Kimono* (St. Martin's Minotaur, 2008). Acts of violence against the households of Sano and of Lord Matsudaira further inflamed the enmity between them. Sano was diverted to a more personal problem. After a heavy storm, the skeleton of Tadatoshi, a cousin of the shogun, was discovered. He had disappeared 43 years earlier during the Great Longsleeves Kimono Fire that killed 100,000 and destroyed most of Edo Castle. A highly respected official, Col. Doi Nao Katsu had accused Sano's mother, Etsuko, of kidnapping and murdering Tadatoshi. He demanded her execution and the executions of all members of her family. Reiko's role was restricted as Sano battled a long-time enemy. She tried to gather information from Etsuko, fought like a warrior to protect her children from an assassin, and sought to regain the love and trust of her daughter, Akiko.

The narratives provided an excellent, well-researched background of conditions in Seventeenth century Japan, then governed by a dictator, the shogun. Supporting characters, such as Hirata, his wife Midori, the exceedingly dangerous Lady Yanagisawa and her husband, the totally incompetent shogun, and those who sought to influence him, were well drawn.

The series continued in 2009 with *The Cloud Pavilion.*

Laura Ireland

Author: Linda Mariz

Among the tallest and most athletic of the modern sleuths was blonde blue-eyed Laura Ireland who, at 6' 1", capitalized on her height and proficiency in volleyball. In addition to working on a Ph.D. in archeology at UCLA she played for a professional team, the Gatoraders of Gainesville, Florida.

While attending the National Championships in *Body English* (Bantam, 1992) Laura learned that her former lover Larry Todd, a professor at Washington State University, had been murdered. Todd had kept letters that might jeopardize Laura's career. Her efforts to retrieve the documents attracted the attention of even taller detective Theo Talbot.

In *Snake Dance* (Bantam, 1992), the scene shifted to Redemption Parish, Louisiana where the Talbot family had been a major producer of sugar. Just about every cliché of the decadent extended Southern family was used to describe Laura and Theo's ill-omened visit to a family reunion. Theo's irresponsible use of Laura as a decoy to flush out a killer was an eye-opener. A disappointing second offering.

Hannah Ives

Author: Marcia Talley

Middle age seemed to Hannah Ives (a worrier by nature) to be a placid and fulfilling time in her life. Her rebellious daughter Emily had kept the household on edge for years by running away as a teenager. Now she was out West, living with her college dropout boyfriend Daniel Shemanski, (who preferred to be called Dante in his new career as a masseuse). Hannah had worked her way up from a clerk position to head of the Archives and Records at Whitworth & Sullivan Law Offices. Her husband Paul was a tenured professor at the U.S. Naval Academy in Annapolis. Then it fell apart, beginning with a diagnosis of breast cancer.

The physical aftermath of cancer treatments and the subsequent loss of her job due to downsizing sent Hannah off to visit her widowed sister-in-law Connie at the Ives family farm in *Sing It to Her Bones* (Dell, 1999). A charge of sexual harassment against Paul, and Hannah's discovery of a corpse kept her at the farm. The victim Katie Dunbar, a pregnant teenager, had been dead for years, stashed away in the cistern on a vacant farm. Thinking of her own daughter, Hannah set out to investigate, a decision that she shared with too many people. She was less than kind to Paul, denying him the support he had given her during her cancer treatments.

Their marriage restored to tranquility, Hannah's sense of security was threatened from another source in *Unbreathed Memories* (Dell, 2000). Now charges of sexual abuse were brought against her father, retired Captain George Alexander, USN by Hannah's sister Georgina who had been seeing psychologist/therapist Diane Sturgis. During therapy sessions, memories of sexual abuse had emerged. Sturgis' murder placed Captain Alexander in a vulnerable position. Struggling with the collapse of her mother, Hannah used the Internet library to learn more about false memories, incest, and the personal history of Dr. Sturgis.

The saga of Hannah and her family continued in *Occasion of Revenge* (Dell, 2001). Her father's drinking had been at a social level until the death of his wife. Then it became a concern. Even more so, when George came under the influence of Darlene Tinsley, a predatory female who had buried three prior husbands. Her death and George's disappearance focused attention on him as the probable killer. Fortunately George and Hannah benefited from the intervention of a kind but flaky neighbor.

Cancer survivors have a loyalty to one another akin to those who served in the military so, in *In Death's Shadow* (Avon, 2004) Hannah rejoiced when she reconnected with Valerie Stone. Valerie had been considered terminal, but her cancer had gone into remission. Yet within a short time after she and Hannah began jogging together, Valerie died. Had Hannah not been aware that Valerie had sold the beneficiary interest in her life insurance, she would never have suspected that she might have been murdered. Aided by her "honorary grandmother", novelist Naddie Browley, Hannah uncovered a scheme to prey on the dying and the elderly.

The old adage "No good deed goes unpunished" came true for Hannah in *This Enemy Town* (Avon, 2005). To help Dorothy Hart, currently undergoing chemotherapy for breast cancer, Hannah agreed to assist in creating the sets for the Naval Academy's production of *Sweeney Todd*. Dorothy, the wife of an admiral stationed in the Pentagon, had a son in the cast. On the set Hannah encountered Jane Goodall, who as a midshipman had accused Paul of sexual misconduct. Sometime after they had a violent quarrel, Jane was murdered. Hannah was arrested, questioned; and, placed in a cell until bail was arranged. She had to prove her own innocence.

Through the Darkness (Avon, 2006) had no room for humor. During the rush to get Dante's Spa Paradiso opened for business, someone abducted ten-month-old Timmy, Dante and Emily's son and Hannah's grandson. Talley did an excellent job of detailing the involvement of local police, the FBI, and volunteers. Neither Hannah nor Emily could let the experts take over. The pain, fears, and anger of the entire family made the narrative hard to read, but impossible to put down.

It was Hannah's sister Ruth's desire to have a great wedding reception with a band and dancing that set the tone for *Dead Man Dancing* (Severn House, 2008). Ruth's fiancé, Hutch, had competed in ballroom dancing while in college. It was something of a surprise to learn that his partner had been Kathleen O'Reilly, now the co-owner of J & K Dance Studios. Hannah and Paul, her father George and his steady girlfriend Neelie Gibbs, all signed up for lessons. Hannah, whose granddaughter, Chloe was a student at the studio, was appalled by the pressure placed on nine-year-old Tessa by her ambitious mother. Others were concerned about Tessa for different reasons; strong enough to justify murder?

Talley edited *I'd Kill for That,* and *Naked Came the Phoenix,* serial novels by assorted female mystery authors. Next announced: *Without a Grave* (2009); *All Things Undying* (2010)

Kate Ivory

Author: Veronica Stallwood

When Kate Ivory approached an investigation, she proceeded with thorough research, as she would for one of her historical novels. She was an attractive single resident of Oxford, although not a graduate of the University. Kate enjoyed her membership in the Fridesley Runners, a group that exercised regularly over the local terrain.

The narrative developed interesting group dynamics in *Death and the Oxford Box* (Scribners, 1993) when the Runners helped Rose Smith, a vulnerable young woman devastated by her husband's desertion and his theft of valuable enameled boxes. A harebrained scheme to secure the boxes was sabotaged by murder, blackmail, and chicanery among developers.

Vivi, an anonymous character in *Oxford Exit* (Scribners, 1995), released his anger through submissions in his writing course. Was he also the hacker who tinkered with the computer listings at the Bodleian Library to conceal the theft of out-of-print books? Kate went undercover at the Bodleian to find the murderous hacker, making the right connections when she took over her friend Emma Goldby's writing class.

Oxford Fall (Macmillan, 1996) approached the murder of Chris Townsend, an unfaithful and dishonest Oxford administrator, on two levels. His confederates and a woman whom he had betrayed hassled Kate, who had been assigned to his responsibilities for a summer program. At a higher level Chris, now deceased, found himself outside the Garden of Eden, sharing his past with the angel Zophiel, guardian of the Gate. Zophiel theorized that Chris had been killed because of his long time cruelty to others. The hell of it was that Chris could not accept who really had killed him. An unusual treatment.

Five itinerant squatters came into Oxford as *Oxford Mourning* (Scribners, 1996) began, one with murder on her mind. Kate, eager for a new approach to enliven her next historical novel about writer Maria Susanna Taylor and her actress sister, Ellen Ternan, contacted Olivia Blacket. Olivia, a tutor at Leicester College, had recently discovered Taylor's notebooks. Kate could not, however, be kept out of Olivia's office, her love life, or the investigation of her murder, the next to occur.

The agent for Kate's publisher would have her believe that being chosen to accompany gothic romance writer Devlin Hayle on a book signing tour was a stroke of good fortune. In *Oxford Knot* (Macmillan, 1998), Kate learned otherwise. Hayle was a disaster, and had attracted enough enemies (bookies, relatives of his mistress, and collaborators whose work he had appropriated) to keep them both in suspense as they moved through the countryside. When her dear friend Andrew Grove was found dead in Kate's entryway, she realized that she too had a nemesis following her.

Andrew's death left Kate feeling guilty and depressed as *Oxford Blue* (Headline, 1998) opened. Her recovery began with a change of location to a nearby rural community, but accelerated with a visit from Roz, the mother who had ignored her for years. Roz and Kate intervened when they felt the local police were treating the death of young Donna Paige too lightly. Donna had worked as a gardener, but had a dangerous lover. Roz was a sprightly character who played a major role in the investigation. Questions as to why she had separated herself from her child for ten years went unanswered. She came at a time when Kate considered herself a magnet for murder because so many people close to her had died.

When Kate returned to her Agatha Street home in Oxford, Roz accompanied her. In *Oxford Shift* (Headline, 1999), she had her latest historical romance ready for the publisher and no contract for a new book. Emma Dolby, a friend who had figured in an earlier narrative, ended Kate's sense of contentment. An injury to Sam, Emma's husband, had forced her to take on extra work. Joyce Fielding, Emma's mother who had agreed to provide childcare for the Dolby brood, had disappeared. Kate, with the help of Roz and George, Emma's affable brother-in-law, undertook to search for her. Excerpts explained Joyce's decision to leave and her problems in finding shelter. As Roz and Kate looked for Joyce by trying to understand what would cause her to leave, they also explored why Roz had abandoned Kate when she was only seventeen.

By *Oxford Shadows* (Headline, 2000), Kate had lost her sense of personal security. Roz remained in the Agatha Street house. Kate moved in with George Dolby who occupied a home that had been passed down in his family for several generations. Imprisoned in the house by her own fears, Kate learned of Chris and Susan Barnes, two London area children who had been evacuated to Oxford and lived in that house under the control of Miss Elinor Marlyn during World War II. As the insidious character of Miss Marlyn emerged, Kate went out into the community to learn more about the lives of evacuated children and the homes in which they were placed. An engrossing narrative, but it was time for Kate to get back to work.

During *Oxford Double* (Headline, 2001), Kate described herself as "not easily taken in." Yet, she agreed to courier a mysterious package from a slight acquaintance (a man she had seen earlier wearing a disguise). She was aware that he and the man to whom she delivered the packet died within a short time, as had an inquisitive couple living next door. Yet she withheld valuable information from the police until she was personally attacked. Unreal behavior from a woman of her experience and imagination.

Bits and pieces of horror stories based on credit card fraud came to Kate in *Oxford Proof* (Headline, 2002). Minor amounts such as that sustained by her friend Emma, and a total wipeout of the assets held by Kate's new editor Neil Orson were part of the story. Much of the narrative was the first person account of how young Viola Grant started her criminal career; then was absorbed into the network of a big time operator with chilling results.

The fact that Kate was familiar with Oxford and yet not a part of the academic community caused her friend, Dean of Women Faith Beeton, to seek her help in *Oxford Remains* (Headline, 2004). Faith was concerned about charges made by second-year student Daisy Tompkins against her tutor Joseph Fechan. Fechan for all of his intelligence was socially inept and had few friends among the staff, faculty or students. Faith trusted him and wanted Kate to read Daisy's file and appraise the likelihood of the charges. The narrative used alternating chapters of Fechan's first person character development with Kate's investigation.

Kate and Roz had never been close but in *Oxford Letters* (Headline, 2005), Kate was concerned. Not just because Roz seemed more tired and weaker but because her new friends, Marcus and Ayesha Freeman had so much influence over her mom. They were kind, but ever present, even had a key to Roz's home. At first, everything Kate learned about the Freemans was reassuring, almost too good to be true. Avril, Roz's business partner, was also worried about the Freemans and the threatening solicitations that she and Roz (and eventually Kate) were receiving.

By *Oxford Menace* (Headline, 2008) government agent Jon Kenrick had sold his place and moved in with Kate. He wanted them to buy a larger home, preferably in the suburbs or country, and consider a family. Kate was having enough trouble fitting Jon into her house, not ready for more change. Sam Dolby, Kate's young friend, had a short-term internship at an Oxford lab run by Blake Parker. Protestors against the use of animals in testing new drugs had the staff, including Sam's girlfriend, Kerri Ashton, on edge. Even more so after the office building was bombed and staff members were personally threatened. When Sam left to spend time teaching in a rural Chinese school, Kate promised to look after Kerri. That became impossible.

Author Veronica Stallwood created fascinating characters, both within the university community and on the fringes of society.

Jolene Jackson

Author: Paula Boyd

Jolene had made changes in her life by her mid-forties. Danny, the father of her two children, had dumped her for a "bimbo". Once the children were grown and in college, Jolene set up a small greeting card business, making limited use of her journalism degree from the University of Texas in Austin. She felt she had left Texas behind, now lived in Colorado. She enjoyed her car-truck, which she called Tahoe, and seemed content with her current life.

Jolene made her entrance in *Hot Enough to Kill* (DIOMO, 1999) with a bang, several bangs in fact. She returned from her home in Colorado to Kickapoo, Texas to rescue her 72-year-old mother, Lucille. Considering that Lucille whacks people on their heads with her purse in which she carries a Glock 9mm, you wouldn't think she needed much help. Lucille's married beau, Kickapoo mayor Big John Bennett, had been murdered. Sheriff Jerry-Don Parker, who had been the love of Jolene's life didn't know if Lucille was a target or a killer. No one was safe from this murderer, not even the cops.

Only three months had elapsed since Jolene's prior somewhat disastrous visit to Kickapoo, TX, but another trip couldn't be avoided in *Dead Man Falls* (Diomo, 2000). Jolene traditionally hosted her mother Lucille's Dairy Queen birthday party and it was time. It was also time for a big local celebration the inauguration of man-made Redwater Falls, designed to bring tourists into the area. There were compensations. The visit meant seeing Sheriff Jerry-Don Parker again. He had been her high school boyfriend until hated rival Rhonda Davenport told him lies about Jolene. When the corpse of Calvin Holt washed over the falls in its first burst of water, Jolene dashed down river to assist in retrieving the body. In Calvin's hand were sheets from their high school yearbook, indicating prospective targets, which included Jolene and Jerry-Don. He was the sheriff of Bowman county so the murder occurred out of his jurisdiction, but he helped out the authorities in Redwater Falls, notably detective Rich Rankin. Jolene's high school years had been traumatic, a rapacious principal, an incompetent English teacher, both of whom Jolene exposed, and the hatred of Rhonda. Before she was through, Jolene learned a lot more about Rhonda and about herself.

After a considerable delay, Paula Boyd's *Turkey Ranch Road Rage,* is slated for publication in 2010.

Cassidy James

Author: Kate Calloway

By age thirty-one, Cassidy James had settled into a comfortable life in a lakeside home near Cedar Hills, Oregon. She still mourned the loss of her lover Diane but was facing the reality of life alone. Diane had bequeathed a comfortable estate to Cassidy relieving her of financial concerns. No longer interested in teaching, she initially apprenticed herself to Jake Parcell, an elderly private investigator. Later she set herself up as an independent operator, working out of her home on cases that interested her. Her companions were a pair of mixed breed cats, Panic and Gammon. Cassidy enjoyed cooking, and enviably had no problem maintaining her weight. She worked out regularly, and became an expert at martial arts.

When *1st Impressions* (Naiad, 1996) began, the body of unpopular Walter Trinidad had been recovered from Lake Rainbow. His niece Erica hired Cassidy to investigate. This was not the only local concern. A young girl had disappeared. When Kate and Erica came upon the killers, they were in serious danger. Their rescue came at the hands of Jess Martin, a dishonorably discharged veteran, and his tiny daughter, Jessie. Erica, who had a relationship with Cassidy, returned to California to pursue a career opportunity and another woman.

2nd Fiddle (Naiad, 1997) made Cassidy aware that someone was intimidating and blackmailing local residents to obtain control of their property. Her concern for young Jessie, still recovering from her traumatic experience, brought psychologist Maggie Carradine into Cassidy's life. Maggie and Cassidy became suspicious of a religious right wing group that sponsored military retreats. Neither Maggie nor the primary villain was content to be "second fiddle."

In *3rd Degree* (Naiad, 1997), Multiple assaults had the entire town up in arms. They were affecting women and doing financial damage to the community. When real estate broker Susie Popps was murdered after an assault, probably because she recognized her attacker, Cassidy made a serious error.

Wealthy lesbian doctor Allison Crane hired Cassidy to pose as her "girlfriend" in *4th Down* (Naiad, 1998), hoping she could prevent another murder attempt. Several days at an isolated retreat camp gave Cassidy an opportunity to meet the suspects in a prior killing at the risk of her own safety.

In *5th Wheel* (Naiad, 1998), Cassidy's best friend, police office Martha Harper, sought her help in investigating the murders of young women. The victims had been mutilated and killed, their bodies left along highways. The young women were connected to a local college so Cassidy went undercover as a teaching assistant in the Theatre Department.

Cassidy was aware that Maggie had returned from Europe after nursing her former lover Cecily through cancer treatments. As *6th Sense* (Naiad, 1999) opened, she could not reject Maggie's plea for help. Maggie was dreaming about murders before they occurred. Cassidy joined Maggie's therapy group because several of the participants had been connected to the victims. Repairing the relationship between Cassidy and Maggie was a significant subplot.

Cassidy might be in *7th Heaven* (Naiad, 1999) now that Erica Trinidad, (see *First Impressions)* her former lover had returned. They worked together to confound a group of mean-spirited gamblers who risked other people's reputations.

Native American Grace Apodaca had been a friend, so in *8th Day* (Bella Books, 2001), Cassidy was disposed to help Grace's cousin, Connie. Connie had been convicted of murder and sentenced to prison after an automobile accident. Given the expectations of a long prison stay, she had relinquished her rights to daughter Maddie to her husband's parents. After an appeal based on inadequate representation, Connie was freed for time served. She wanted time with Maddie. Daniel and his second wife had found the girl ungovernable at age thirteen, and sent her to Camp Turnaround, a behavior modification program in an isolated area. A coded message from Maddie indicated that Annie Sisson, a friendly counselor, had been murdered. Cassidy took a position at Turnaround where she and Grace found an ally in Jo Bell a horse trainer, who became close to Cassidy.

Dewey James

Author: Kate Morgan

The weight of Jane Marple's impact on the mystery genre can be seen in the frequency with which her name is still used to characterize female sleuths over age fifty. Dewey James was announced as a "thoroughly modern Miss Marple." Dewey, a retired librarian, lived in a small town amidst Kentucky horse country. She was the widow of the local police chief, a tall, athletic, and silver-haired woman with blue eyes. Dewey presumed upon her husband's friends for inside information, although she considered Fielding Booker, his replacement, totally incompetent. She owned her own horse, which she rode regularly, had a Labrador Retriever for company, enjoyed reading, helping at the library, and literacy programs. She quoted the classics pretentiously, and considered herself the local "eccentric." Dewey had attorney George Farnham for her beau and ally.

A Slay at the Races (Berkley, 1990) began when bank executive Donald Irish was found dead in a racehorse's stall. The authorities wanted the animal destroyed, but Dewey and George proved that Irish had been murdered. That wasn't enough for Dewey though; she had to solve the case.

In *Murder Most Fowl* (Berkley, 1991), Dewey joined a bird watching group. While organizing the sanctuary's professional library, Dewey found clues to the murder of college professor Otis Marion. Marion had been sent to evaluate the Farrand State University grant that kept Evergreen solvent.

Dewey had new challenges in *Home Sweet Homicide* (Berkley, 1991). She and George were taking ballroom dance lessons for the Hamilton High Homecoming. Broadway star Jenny Riley, a younger alumna who had agreed to provide the entertainment, was killed. As a librarian, Dewey was sensitive to issues that would not have occurred to Police Chief Booker.

Mystery Loves Company (Berkley, 1992) concerned Harrison Powell, a handsome stranger who ingratiated himself into the community until he was murdered. The victim had presented himself as the son of a missionary couple who were friends of local rector Cedric Hastings. Only when he was dead did Dewey investigate the methods Powell had used to enter the community.

Days of Crime and Roses (Berkley, 1992) transported Dewey to New York City where she visited her college roommate, then preparing for a fifth wedding. Jane Duncan had become a powerful wealthy woman, serving on the board of the Pincus Foundation. When foundation director Lainie Guiles was killed, Dewey carried on an investigation parallel to that of the police department.

Wanted: Dude or Alive (Berkley, 1994) took Dewey and George to Los Lobos, a Southern California inn that was targeted by a local publisher. The inn had been plagued with "pranks," rumors of ghosts, and the death of two employees. Local corruption led to Dewey's arrest but George came to the rescue, deepening Dewey's appreciation of him.

Dewey's standing in the community and George's interim appointment to the board of the elite Jefferson school drew them into controversy when the headmaster disappeared in *The Old School Dies* (Berkley, 1996). The discovery of Victor Salgo's corpse in a rental car made those who wanted his job primary suspects, but Dewey, George, and an inquisitive young boy probed deeper.

The books were diverting but lacked realistic deduction.

Gemma James

Author: Deborah Crombie

The changing times have been reflected in the increased number of male sleuths with female subordinates who play an active, often independent, role in the investigations and eventually rise to higher status. Scotland Yard Superintendent Duncan Kincaid worked with chestnut-haired Gemma James, a divorced single mother living on a sergeant's salary. Kincaid, also divorced, showed an interest in women, even a mild recognition that the redheaded Gemma was one. She had a basic education but her potential for advancement was limited by the family income. Her parents lived above their bakery shop, where she had worked until she entered the Criminal Investigation Department. Her sister Cynthia had a more conventional and remunerative career as a beautician. Rob, Gemma's former husband, was frequently late with his child support, and paid little attention to their son, Toby.

Kincaid was the primary sleuth in the first two narratives, calling upon Gemma for assistance as needed.

In *A Share in Death* (Scribners, 1993), Kincaid vacationed in a time-share suite in Yorkshire, at the time when Sebastian Wade, an intrusive assistant project manager, was electrocuted. Kincaid investigated, contacting Gemma to lend a hand.

In *All Shall Be Well* (Scribners, 1994), reclusive Jasmine Dent, a neighbor for whom Kincaid had great affection, might have killed herself. Kincaid was sure she had been murdered. He had no compunction about including Gemma in his investigation on an unofficial basis until he could get permission from the department.

In *Leave the Grave Green* (Scribners, 1995), they investigated the drowning of Connor Swann, an upstart Irishman married to Julia, the artistic daughter of a well-known musical couple, Sir Gerald Asherton and his wife Dame Caroline. Duncan and Gemma moved beyond their alliances and biases to find the killer, but also beyond their professional relationship. Duncan was relieved, Gemma appalled by this change in their status. The intimacy they had reached could not easily be sustained if they were to work together; yet, their former camaraderie was gone.

As *Mourn Not Your Dead* (Scribners, 1996) began, both were uncomfortable at a time when they needed to work together. Alistair Gilbert, commander of a police division, had been found dead in the family kitchen. The government wanted the case handled delicately, particularly since there were hints of police corruption. Gilbert's treatment of subordinates and members of his family provided motives for murder.

During *Dreaming of the Bones* (Scribners, 1997), Gemma did not take kindly to Duncan's involvement in the death of literary figure Lydia Brooke. His interest came at the request of Victoria McClellan, Duncan's former wife who had walked out of their marriage with no explanation twelve years before. She was working on a literary biography of Lydia, and had noted differences between prior attempts at suicide and the method of her death. Victoria persisted in questioning those close to Lydia and reviewing her letters. The narrative followed three women: Victoria, Lydia, and Gemma on parallel tracks. Victoria's subsequent death was perceived as a heart attack. Gemma and Duncan now knew too much to stop. Their lives were changed by disclosures flowing out of the investigation.

Kissed a Sad Goodbye (Bantam, 1999) skillfully wove the experiences of English children sent to the country during World War II to escape the Blitz into the mysterious death of Annabelle Hammond, a young woman executive. Kincaid and Gemma had conflicts of their own to surmount. Unforgettable emotions from the past had doomed Annabelle to disaster. Author Deborah Crombie's suspects were, as always, engrossing.

Significant events occurred in the lives of Gemma and Kincaid during *A Finer End* (Bantam, 2001), but the focus of the narrative was on the city of Glastonbury, the ruins of an abbey in the center of town, and the impact of the dead on the living. Edmund, a young monk and Alys, a child from the past, powerfully affected the living, including Jack Montfort, Duncan Kincaid's cousin. Montfort had a special gift of communicating with Edmund and Alys. A subsequent hit-and-run accident and murder did not take place in Gemma and Kincaid's jurisdiction but they journeyed to Glastonbury on Jack's behalf. A complex investigation of the recent history of those involved and the Twelfth century struggles in the abbey and its environs were meshed in a fascinating narrative. Gemma was in training for promotion that would entail a transfer. Duncan and his newly discovered son Kit had become deeply attached to one another.

Gemma and Kincaid had reached a high point in their personal life as *And Justice There Is None* (Macmillan, 2002) began. They were moving into a large home that would accommodate Gemma's son Toby, Kincaid's son Kit, and a hoped for child of their own. Technically they worked in separate jurisdictions but the savage murders of a young wife, her vindictive husband and a seemingly unconnected jewelry dealer had the same modus operandi. What tied the victims together?

Two parallel incidents that led to murder occurred in *Now May You Weep* (Morrow, 2002). An unacceptable romance between a young widow and a former beau now married occurred at the end of the Nineteenth century. Although their descendants were unaware of the details of the murder that followed, a feud between their families persisted a century later, exacerbated by their connections to whiskey distilleries. Gemma knew none of this when she agreed to accompany her friend Hazel Cavendish to the Scottish Highlands where they would attend a cooking school taught by John Innes. There were multiple relationships that complicated matters, including Hazel's with a former lover, now married. When Innes was murdered, Gemma worked with the local police inspector. Kincaid was busy. Kit's abusive grandmother was seeking custody.

Although Gemma worked for Metropolitan Police and Kincaid for Scotland Yard during *In a Dark House* (Morrow, 2004), they managed to join forces on a variety of cases. Aided by female firefighter Rose Kearney and arson investigator Bill Farrell, they solved an abduction, a disappearance, a series of fires, and two murders. They were still unmarried although they shared a household.

There were suspicious deaths and murders in *Water Like a Stone* (Morrow, 2007) even when Kincaid and Gemma took the boys to spend Christmas holidays with his parents, Hugh and Rosemary. Juliet, Kincaid's sister, was there with her children but at odds with her investment counselor husband, Caspar Newcombe. While remodeling an old barn, Juliet had discovered the mummified body of a tiny girl. A few days later, former social worker Annie Constantine Lebow was found murdered. After leaving her husband, Annie had been living on a narrow boat on the English river system. The narrative was about more than murder, about the lives of the river people, the burnout of workers in children's services, and relationships. This was a remarkable book.

Although they shared their personal lives, Gemma and Kincaid usually made every effort to keep their professional lives apart now that they were working in different units, but in *Where Memories Lie* (Morrow, 2008), this was not possible. Gemma became involved in her friend Erika Rosenthal's concerns about a diamond brooch that had been designed by her father in Germany. It had been entrusted to Erika's care, taken from her, and now was listed for auction. The subsequent deaths of individuals connected to the brooch resulted in Duncan's taking responsibility for the investigation. Gemma used her aide Melody Talbot and the case files of decades old murders to direct Duncan to a solution.

An exceptional series, directed towards those who enjoy British procedurals with romantic aspects. The narratives were literate and compelling. Next: *Necessary as Blood* (2009)

Jessica "Jesse" James

Author: Meg O'Brien

Jessica "Jesse" James, a tough newspaper reporter, was 5' 4", slim with brown hair and green eyes. After working hard to get through college at Ithaca State and to get a job, she risked it all by her drinking. She entered detox several times. The drinking and her anti-authoritarian attitudes made it necessary for her to work freelance.

In *The Daphne Decisions* (Bantam, 1990), Jesse uncovered a scheme to bilk the elderly in the Rochester, New York area. Her self-destructive behavior and her relationship with crime boss Marcus Andrelli were relieved by the comic touches provided by three juvenile delinquents and an endearing child who attached herself to Jessica. Jessica, who frequently commented that she disliked children and dogs, could not avoid them.

In *Salmon in the Soup* (Bantam, 1990), Jessica exposed a child pornography racket, and was temporarily concerned that Marcus might be involved. His power and criminal activities seemed to be part of his attraction for Jessica.

Jessica was appealing in *Hare Today, Gone Tomorrow* (Bantam, 1991). She reunited with her mother Kate, who had been living in California. Jessica and Kate's feelings for one another were complex. There was nothing comic about Kate's relationship with con man Charlie Browne. Jessica was at least willing to check things out when Browne was accused of murder utilizing Tark, Andrellis' bodyguard. Now aware of the existence of Marcus' unacknowledged son, whom he avoided for fear it would put the boy at risk, Jessica visited the child regularly.

By *Eagles Die Too* (Doubleday, 1992), Jessica was still fighting alcoholism, fueled by concern that Marcus was spending time with another woman. She was aware of a scam, but unsure just how Marcus, and Charlie Browne, now married to Kate, might be involved.

The final Jessica James appeared four years later. It was published in London and received limited attention in the United States. In *A Bright Flamingo Shroud*, (The Women's Press, 1996), Jessica was free of her dependence on alcohol. She had left the newspaper to work freelance, currently on a screenplay. This project was delayed by the appearance of Johnny James, who claimed to be her paternal grandfather. Rescuing "Gramps" and his lady friend from mobsters sent Jessie to Florida and the protection of Marcus Andrelli.

The bang up ending exploited a boat made famous in an Esther Williams film but later purchased by Andrelli.

The series had excellent supporting characters, but the plots needed more attention, particularly in the closing chapters. O' Brien switched to standalones, well received by readers.

Liz James

Author: Karen Hanson Stuyck

Liz James, a divorcee in her thirties, was employed as the public relations director at a mental health clinic in Houston. Her unhappy marriage to Max, a type A attorney, had resulted in four miscarriages but no children.

Caroline, Liz's college roommate, had made few contacts over the last ten years, but in *Cry for Help* (Berkley, 1995) she sought out Liz, confused and upset. Liz, resenting the intrusion at that time, dismissed her abruptly; then was horrified when she learned that Caroline had supposedly killed herself. Suicide seemed unlikely to Liz, as it did to Caroline's eight-year-old son, Jonathan, but both knew that Caroline's mother had a similar death at about the same age. Concern for Jonathan, whose father resented her interference, and a sense of guilt made it impossible for Liz to stay out of the investigation.

Partly because she was dating Nick Finley, the investigative reporter who helped her solve Caroline's murder, *Held Accountable* (Berkley, 1996) found a slimmer happier Liz. She became involved in the death of a fellow-employee, therapist Gina Lawrence, who had been threatened by her former husband. However, when Liz received threats to her own life, she realized that the killer had a broader focus and was close to hand.

Liz made some major changes in her life prompted in part by a workshop on womanpower during *Lethal Lessons* (Berkley, 1997). Not all of the other participants in the workshop were so moderate. One ran down her husband in the parking lot. The provocative workshop leader Kate Quinlan became a suspect in her husband's murder. Liz's investigation was simplified when the killer panicked.

Elena Jarvis

Author: Nancy Herndon

Elena had been a student at New Mexico University, when she met police officer Frank Jarvis on a backpacking trip. She was one of five children of Sheriff Ruben Portillo and his ex-flower child wife, Harmony Waite. Elena's parents did not approve of her hasty marriage to a man who coveted danger by working undercover for the Narcotics Squad of the Los Santos, Texas police department. Frank and Elena's delicately balanced relationship did not survive her decision to join the police department and her rapid promotion to detective in the Crimes Against Persons Unit. Frank was vindictive and angry, and given to practical jokes to release his frustrations. Elena wanted no more to do with him although she lived in the house they had bought together. As the series opened she was in her late twenties, a dark-haired conscientious professional who frequently encountered sexual discrimination in her work, but persevered.

Elena was dispatched to evaluate an alleged assault by a bursting snail in *Acid Bath* (Berkley, 1995). She dismissed the matter, making a friend of Professor Sarah Tolland. When Sarah's former husband, poet Gus McGlenlevie, was killed, Elena was reproved for her failure to charge Sarah with the earlier incident. Friendship had to be ignored, but that did not stop Elena from learning more about the victim and his killer.

Herndon's tart touch continued in *Widows' Watch* (Berkley, 1995) when she introduced Elena's visiting mother Harmony, whose weaving avocation had become a business. Elderly residents primarily occupied Elena's neighborhood. Harmony, busy renovating Elena's trashed home, fit right in. She comforted the widow of mean-spirited Boris Potemkin who had been killed in mid-afternoon while his wife played bridge. She ingratiated herself at the Senior Center and at the Police Department, calling attention to a series of such murders. It was Elena, however, who restrained her fellow officers from a rash arrest, and found the pattern in the deaths.

During *Lethal Statues* (Berkley. 1996), Elena paired with Herbert Hobart University security officer Tey Vasquez to investigate the death of Annalee Ribbon, the only African-American student. While Vasquez focused on the members of Annalee's family and other minority students, Elena broadened her search to include members of a right-wing group. The killer was too close to be seen until Vasquez was ready to arrest the wrong person. Elena acquired a new romantic interest, Professor Michael Futrell of the criminology department.

Elena took on an elephantine task in *Hunting Game* (Berkley, 1996),. Someone had sneaked into the zoo and given food to Pansy, a gentle elephant, that caused Pansy to go berserk and kill her trainer. The incident connected with the bizarre death of the zoo administrator's brother, Arnold Mandel, a promiscuous sweatshop owner. Local powers urged the arrest of labor organizer Alope Randall, but Elena found a killer closer to home. Her relationship with Futrell foundered when his twin brother Mark was murdered in Elena's apartment.

Elena's recent cases had left her plagued by flashbacks and nightmares. She realized her condition affected her work, but was reluctant to seek professional help. In *Time Bombs* (Berkley, 1997), Elena worked a series of escalating explosions with members of the local police, FBI, and ATF bomb squads. She did her share in identifying the perpetrators, but succumbed to her need for help, and sought it.

The death of Hope, wife of mayoral candidate Wayne Quarles, while she accompanied police officer Monica Ibarra on a "walk around" caused political repercussions in *C. O. P. Out* (Berkley, 1998). Elena and Leo Santos were assigned the case until she was suspended for her aggressive investigation of the victim's family. Undeterred and with the support of her immediate superiors, she went undercover to seek the truth. Leo and his wife, Concepcion (great name for the mother of quintuplets) were having difficulty coping with the care of five infants. Herbert Hobart University had provided support in exchange for the right to research the children's development. Elena's friend, Professor Sarah Tolland, pushed hard to get additional room and childcare assistance for the family.

The wealthy students and staff at Herbert Hobart University were aware of their importance to the community, but in *Casanova Crimes* (Berkley, 1999) they learned they couldn't get away with murder. Nor could they cover up the death of young women through unprotected sex, or the impact of a male student who had thirty-one female partners although he was HIV positive. Elena's honorary degree at the university did not deter her when she uncovered multiple sexual irregularities among staff and students. She evaluated the affections of her current beau, divorced professor and musician Rafer Martin.

Irreverent narratives with a novel heroine and humorous side characters.

Jazz Jasper

Author: Karin McQuillan

Running a safari was an unusual job for a woman, but Jazz Jasper was an unusual woman. Devastated by her divorce, she abandoned her training as an art historian to work for a commercial tour company in Africa. Later, she went independent as "Jazz Jasper, Safaris."

Jazz was ripe for trouble in *Deadly Safari* (St. Martin, 1990) and she found it. Advertising executive Cliff Edwards and his client Boyce Darnell wanted to photograph professional models against the scenery of the Serengeti. Darnell's death from an apparent heart attack was followed by the murder of copywriter Lynn Alexander. Lynn and Jazz had been college roommates. Although they hadn't seen each other for a while, it was Lynn who had arranged for Jasper Safaris to handle the junket. During the investigation, Jazz had romantic interludes with both environmentalist Dan Striker and Inspector Omondi.

In *Elephants' Graveyard* (Ballantine, 1993), Emmet Laird was just what Africa needed, a rich American willing to put his money where his interest was. Unfortunately his family did not share his concerns. Someone murdered Laird at his campsite overlooking an elephant watering hole. Jazz needed a solution because the publicity was ruining her safari business. Jungle justice prevailed.

Jazz and Dan Striker had been lovers for sometime but in *The Cheetah Chase* (Ballantine, 1994), their relationship ended. His love for the Kenya that used to be made it impossible for him to remain there. Her love for Kenya caused her to stay. The death of investigative reporter Nick Hunter, who had boasted of a major coup, was important to Jazz. She shared the passion of Nick and his coworkers for preserving animals from human predators. This was a tense narrative in which Jazz settled for "a" compromise.

An excellent series. Wish there were more books coming, but I have not identified any new ones.

Kate Jasper

Author: Jaqueline Girdner

Kate Jasper was short, dark, plump, childless in her late thirties, initially sharing her home with a cat (C. C. for Cool Cat). A separated, then divorced young woman, Kate put her imagination to work designing and selling humorous gift items through the mail via "Jest Gifts."(for example, shark earrings for female attorneys. The administrative tasks were hers. The manufacturing was farmed out. The finished products were stocked and shipped from a Marin County warehouse.

With a job that averaged sixty hours a week, it's no wonder she visited a chiropractor in *Adjusted to Death* (Diamond, 1991). On entering a treatment room, she found fellow patient Scott Younger dead from a broken neck. Chiropractor Maggie Lambrecht, concerned about publicity, urged Kate to investigate, but she became attracted to the prime suspect, burly but homely Wayne Caruso. Wayne, who had been the bodyguard for the victim, inherited a substantial source of income.

The divorce from husband Craig was finalized in *The Last Resort* (Diamond, 1991) just when he needed Kate to prove he had not murdered his fiancée. Kate, for all her prowess as a detective, failed to identify the killer and had to be rescued. On another level, Wayne gave Kate an ultimatum: no more sex until they married.

She was too busy in *Murder Most Mellow* (Diamond, 1992) to be concerned. Kate's weekly support group was upset when software designer Sarah Quinn received threatening phone calls. They took it even harder when she was electrocuted in her bathtub. Kate felt guilty that she had taken Sarah's fears so lightly. The least she could do was to investigate.

In *Fat-Free and Fatal* (Diamond, 1993), Kate, a vegetarian, and her psychic electrician friend Barbara Chu took a low fat, low cholesterol cooking class. Sheila Snyder, the owner of the vegetarian restaurant where they met, was murdered. It became clear that the woman's abusive behavior towards her daughter Topaz motivated the killer; but which observer had resorted to murder?

Wayne was devastated in *Tea-Totally Dead* (Berkley, 1994) when Vesta, his mentally ill mother, was poisoned. He was convinced that a member of his family killed her. Kate, who had worked for a while in a mental hospital, felt competent to handle the matter. In the conclusion she surprised Wayne by proposing marriage. She didn't say when.

During *Stiff Critique* (Berkley, 1995), Kate joined a writer's group, which like other settings into which she was placed, contained a strange group of individuals. Kate's friend, African-American attorney Carrie Yates, was suspected of murdering fellow author Slade Skinner. The victim had been writing a book that may have included personal information about others in the group. The suspects therefore came from within the group. After multiple meetings, one member revealed her guilt. That's one way to get out of more meetings.

Past relationships continued to play a major role in the series during *Most Likely to Die* (Berkley, 1996). Kate (nee Koffenburger) Jasper reunited with fellow members of the Gravendale High class of 1968. The special group with whom Kate had associated gathered at the home of Sid Semling, whose school day pranks had elements of cruelty. Someone wired the pinball machine to shock the guests and kill the host. Since the machine had belonged to Kate, she had to get involved.

During *A Cry for Self-Help* (Berkley, 1997), Wayne and Kate researched weddings through a seminar group. Their leader, charismatic Sam Skyler, fell or was pushed, over a cliff. The group had been observing a scuba diving ceremony so closely than no one witnessed the incident. Several members of the group had motives to kill Sam. His fiancée and his son would inherit the Skyler Institute For Essential Manifestation. Other motives manifested themselves.

In *Death Hits The Fan* (Berkley, 1998), Shayla Greenfree, a best selling author who had capitalized on the popularity of crossover science fiction/mysteries, was poisoned in front of an audience that included Kate and Wayne. The owner of the bookstore where the event had been held was Ivan Nakagawa, a close friend. Just before she expired, Shayla had called out Kate's name. Kate investigated syringes and poisons without results. She had to use her karate moves to rescue a diminutive science fiction writer who was on the right trail.

While Wayne lay ill with pneumonia during *Murder on the Astral Plane* (Berkley, 1999), Kate worried about her propensity for murder scenes. Barbara Chu, who repeatedly led Kate into trouble, suggested that they attend a soiree at the home of Justine, an African-American lesbian psychic. As part of the process, the attendees sat in a circle with their eyes covered by masks. When the masks were removed, Silk Sokoloff, a vicious newspaper columnist, had been throttled. Another set of outlandish suspects, and poor Wayne being ignored or staggering along as Barbara and Kate question one suspect after another.

A zany setting, a nursery where plant lovers bemoaned the destruction of their flowers by deer, and quirky characters, including police officers, contributed to the complexities of *Murder, My Deer* (Berkley, 2000). The murders of two doctors who were members of "Deer Abused" were overwhelmed by the frantic activity, some of which was the result of Wayne and Kate's secret marriage.

It was a little difficult to accept that rugged Wayne Caruso needed a sensitive support group but that was the premise in *A Sensitive Kind of Murder* (Berkley, 2002). Other members had serious hang-ups and so did their spouses and significant others. When journalist Steve Summers was run down by Wayne's car, Wayne, Kate and her visiting Aunt Dorothy sought information on the suspects but also the victim.

Average plotting but lots of colorful background and zany characters.

Hepzibah Jeffries

Author: Emily Brightwell, a house name, but believed to be written by Cheryl Arguiles

The Mrs. Jeffries series explored the problems of Victorian domestics in London so well dramatized by the television series, *Upstairs, Downstairs.*

Mrs. Jeffries had little physical description beyond the paperback cover. She was the widow of a village constable, an intelligent woman with the administrative skills to organize a household. Housemaid Betsy, footman Wiggins, arthritic cook Mrs. Goodge, and burly coachman Smythe completed the domestic detective unit. Hepzibah coordinated their activities and conveyed significant information to her overwhelmed employer, Inspector Gerald Witherspoon. This allowed him to take credit for the solutions. Eventually he blossomed with some skills of his own.

The Inspector and Mrs. Jeffries (Berkley, 1993) set the pattern of a bumbling shy police inspector who solved the murder of the unpopular Dr. Bartholomew through the efforts of his domestic employees. Not illogical. The secrets of the rich or noble houses were well known below stairs, the servants forming a vast intelligence network.

In *Mrs. Jeffries Dusts for Clues* (Berkley, 1993), pretty housemaid Mary Sparks had been misused by lecherous gentry. Luty Belle Crookshank, Witherspoon's unconventional American neighbor, made friends with the servants, asking their help to find the young woman.

In *The Ghost and Mrs. Jeffries* (Berkley, 1993), the servants in another household headed by Abigail Hodges, a domineering penny pinching older wife, were released to enjoy a night on the town, leaving their mistress to a killer.

A slump in the stock market during *Mrs. Jeffries Takes Stock* (Berkley, 1994) prompted Inspector Witherspoon to demand household economies at an unrealistic level. Mrs. Jeffries manipulated the menus to bring his parsimony under control while uncovering stock market fraud.

Inspector Witherspoon turned out to be more intelligent than his staff gave him credit for in *Mrs. Jeffries on the Ball* (Berkley, 1994). He allowed Mrs. Jeffries to play Cupid, placing him on site of a murder at a society ball, but he handled the situation adequately.

Mrs. Jeffries on the Trail (Berkley, 1995) found the staff "out of sorts" because they had no mysteries to solve. To add to their relish for action, they pitted the males against the females in solving their next case. Fortunately both genders worked together when wealthy Harlan Bladestone sought the killer of flower seller Annie Shields, a woman he had abandoned before her birth.

In *Mrs. Jeffries Plays the Cook* (Berkley, 1995), much was made of the absence of Mrs. Goodge, causing other member of the staff to cook the meals. They managed this while helping kleptomaniac Minerva Kenny and retrieving stolen goods. That was not enough. William Barrett, the judgmental neighbor who was going to expose Minerva, was murdered. The series had become highly patterned.

Something new was added in *Mrs. Jeffries and the Missing Alibi* (Berkley, 1996). Inspector Witherspoon was suspected of murder. An unknown person, who resembled Witherspoon and claimed to be him, was noted at the scene of the crime. Not only did this put rival detective Inspector Nigel Nivens, in charge of the case, but it cut off the staff's access to information. Still, with the help of Constable Barnes, Witherspoon's loyal assistant, and a friendly medical examiner Dr. Bosworth, they managed.

Mrs. Jeffries Stands Corrected (Berkley, 1996) was even more frustrating for Hepzibah. Her encouragement of Inspector Witherspoon had surprising results. He considered himself competent to solve the murder of prosperous tavern keeper Haydon Dapeers using his "inner instincts." While the staff busily gathered information about all suspects, the Inspector surprised them.

Miffed that the Inspector had developed skills on his own, the staff was determined to prove their value in *Mrs. Jeffries Takes the Stage* (Berkley, 1997). Homosexual theatre critic Ogden Hinchley, who had a reputation for ruthless reviews, was murdered. The actors and production staff at the theatre who had financial and professional stakes in the success of a new play were the primary suspects, but the motive was more obscure.

Assigning Niven to burglary cases and leaving murders to Witherspoon had temporarily resolved the relationship between Inspector Witherspoon and his professional rival. In *Mrs. Jeffries Questions the Answer* (Berkley, 1997), they were supposed to work together on a case in which Hannah Cameron may have been murdered because she interrupted a burglary. The downstairs staff plus Luty and her butler Hatchet were determined to prove that this was Witherspoon's case, and did so.

As *Mrs. Jeffries Reveals Her Art* (Berkley, 1998) began, Nanette Lanier, a small shopkeeper, asked the downstairs staff to help her locate Irene, a missing model. They were initially unaware that this search was connected to the murder of wealthy art dealer James Underhill. Underhill, a guest, had been poisoned as Inspector Witherspoon called upon the prominent Grant family to inquire about Irene. With the help of coachman Smythe's underworld connections and maid Betsy's contacts in the art world, Irene was found and the Inspector and his household scored another coup.

In *Mrs. Jeffries Takes the Cake* (Berkley, 1998), she rallied her troops once again when news came that the household of M. P Andrew Frommer had been disrupted by murder. Mrs. Goodge, whose prior participation had been limited to conferring with tradesmen and servants, took the initiative in isolating a killer.

Inspector Witherspoon's decision to make an arrest for the murder of Mirabelle Daws, an Australian woman visiting England, in *Mrs. Jeffries Rocks the Boat* (Berkley, 1999) was based on solid evidence. Still, he was prevented from a serious error by the work of Hatchet (Luty Belle's butler), Wiggins (the footman) and Mrs. Jeffries. Smythe and Betsy settled for a long engagement to avoid leaving their friends in the Witherspoon household, even though he had shared with her the knowledge of his wealth.

Annabeth Gentry's maid Martha had met Betsy during a prior case. In *Mrs. Jeffries Weeds the Plot* (Berkley, 2000), she shared with Betsy the "accidents" that had plagued her mistress. All had occurred since Miss Gentry's bloodhound Miranda had unearthed the corpse of pickpocket Tim Porter. Under Mrs. Jeffries' leadership the household gang fanned out to investigate the victim and a second corpse found by Wiggins and Smythe.

In *Mrs. Jeffries Pinches the Post* (Berkley, 2001), the household took on a murder case without anyone requesting their help. They had become addicted to crime solving. The death of ruthless businessman Harrison Nye in the yard of an empty house was assigned to Inspector Witherspoon. Mrs. Jeffries and her gang probed the past connections between the victim and the owner of the house. They intercepted a mysterious letter to determine the motive for the crime, and then set a trap for the killer.

Mrs. Jeffries and her confederates included the recently returned Lady Ruth Cannonbery and formed an alliance with Constable Barnes in *Mrs. Jeffries Pleads Her Case* (Berkley, 2003). Inspector Witherspoon was assigned to re-evaluate the death of inventor Harlan Westover, which had been designated a suicide by the resentful Inspector Nigel Niven. Constable Barnes played an increasingly large role in managing the Inspector when he was on duty.

The Witherspoon household was still concerned because murderess Edith Durant was at large in *Mrs. Jeffries Stalks the Hunter* (Berkley, 2004). They put that aside and went into action when lecherous Sir Edmund Leggett was shot to death shortly after the announcement of his engagement to American heiress Beatrice Parkington. The servants gathered information about the obvious suspects: Beatrice who did not wish to marry Edmund; her sweetheart who detested him; Edmund's abandoned mistress, and cousin Roland who would now inherit the title. It was character that provided Mrs. Jeffries with the clues to the killer.

Not one but two deaths, a decade apart, kept Inspector Witherspoon perplexed in *Mrs. Jeffries Sweeps the Chimney* (Berkley, 2004). He had trouble making the connection between the recent murder of elderly cleric Jasper Claypool who had just returned from India and the discovery of a skeleton in an abandoned cottage. The connections were there: Claypool was the majority stockholder in Claypool Paint Factory which owned the cottages. His heirs included twin nieces and nephews Eric and Horace (who were in the family business currently undergoing reorganization).

Whoever killed Sir George Braxton in *Mrs. Jeffries and the Silent Knight* (Berkley, 2005) must really have hated him. Sir George had been lured to his garden during the night, struck down, and had his head pushed under the icy water of his pond. The murder took place out of Inspector Witherspoon's jurisdiction, but his involvement was requested by the Home Secretary. Sir George was not only an hereditary baronet, but also a distant cousin of the Queen. All three of Sir George's daughters, an in-house "cousin", houseguests and the servants were questioned by Witherspoon and Barnes. Mrs. Jeffries and the household ensemble hoped not to involve Luty Belle because she had been ill, but with Wiggins' help she contributed her bit. All the others carried out their usual roles, contacting sources. Each contributed a piece to the puzzle, which was completed when Mrs. Jeffries' solution was triggered by a carol.

The kitchen crew at Witherspoon's house was investigating another murder in *Mrs. Jeffries Appeals the Verdict* (Berkley, 2006) with one major difference. Pickpocket Tommy Odell had been arrested, tried and convicted of killing Caroline Muran and injuring her husband, Keith. He was scheduled for execution. Blimpey Groggins, one of Smythe's snitches, convinced the crew that Tommy was incapable of murder. It was a delicate matter because Inspector Niven had handled the case.

Mrs. Jeffries and members of Inspector Witherspoons' household were ready for a new adventure when *Mrs. Jeffries and the Best Laid Plans* (Berkley, 2007) began, Betsy most of all. She and Smyth were to be married and she was overwhelmed by the details. Inspector Witherspoon and Barnes were called to an adjacent studio at banker Lawrence Boyd's home. Boyd's corpse had been discovered when the fire department dealt with arson. Guests and staff present at the home when the police arrived were questioned over a period of time. Mrs. Jeffries and ensemble found out additional information. She synchronized the evidence into a solution and spurred the Inspector to make an arrest. It was Betsy's plans that went awry.

Mrs. Jeffries outdid herself in *Mrs. Jeffries and the Feast of St. Stephen* (Berkley, 2007). Stephen Whitfield died at his own table surrounded by guests who seemed to have no motive for poisoning him. Not that he was well liked though. Because of the coming holiday season and pressure by nasty Inspector Niven, Inspector Witherspoon was ordered to come up with a quick solution. His usual accomplices gathered up information re the guests, while Mrs. Jeffries encouraged her employer and made subtle suggestions. Barnes, as always, played a significant role. A surprisingly good conclusion raised this narrative to a level above the usual.

Even before Inspector Witherspoon was assigned to the case in *Mrs. Jeffries Holds the Trump* (Berkley, 2008), medical examiner Dr. Bosworth came to the kitchen for help. He had participated in the autopsy of an acquaintance, Michael Provost, during which he detected evidence of murder. However the police were treating the death as suicide or accident. Solicitor Anthony Tipton, alerted by Provost's housekeeper, convinced the Chief Inspector to assign Witherspoon to review the case. As usual, all members of the kitchen crew, including Luty, Hatchet, and Ruth Cannonberry, participated in the investigation which led to members of an exclusive London club. Again, this was a well-constructed narrative.

Due in 2009: *Mrs. Jeffries in the Nick of Time* and *Mrs. Jeffries and the Yuletide Weddings; Mrs. Jeffries Speaks her Mind* (2011)

Mrs. Jeffries Learns the Trade is a three for one, containing *The Inspector and Mrs. Jeffries; Mrs. Jeffries Dusts for Clues; The Ghost and Mrs. Jeffries. Mrs Jeffries Serves Two* contains *Mrs. Jeffries and the Best Laid Plans; Mrs. Jeffries and the Feast of St. Stephen.*

A reader might ask: while the servants followed lovesick young nieces, frequented seedy taverns, or set séance traps, who was feeding the horses, polishing the silver and tending to the clothes? These employees would not last a week at the Bellamys of Eaton Place.

Claire Jenner (Claiborne)

Author: Sophie Dunbar

Tiny blonde Claire Jenner was a survivor. Baptized Evangeline Claire, the only child of a Danish au pair and a Cajun fisherman, she had been raised by older relatives when her parents died an untimely death. A graduate of Marcel's Institute de Beauté in New Orleans, she worked until she met and married wealthy Dan Louis Claiborne after knowing one another just a few weeks. The marriage ended when she discovered that she was not the only recipient of his passion. Even though Dan was a top rated attorney, Claire won a substantial divorce settlement, a home and a location for her own beauty shop. Dan and Claire remained emotionally attached, rebuilding their relationship after the divorce.

During *Behind Eclaire's Doors* (St. Martin, 1993), the death of Angie Labiche, who worked for Claire but pursued Dan, made him vulnerable to suspicion. In clearing the way for their reunion, Claire solved the murder and the theft of a perfume formula.

A Bad Hair Day (St. Martin, 1996) focused on a special event during which local beauticians provided emergency services to women whose hair had been badly cared for. One beneficiary was to have been Duchess Crowe, who claimed marriage to a deceased member of the British nobility, but was running a nightclub in New Orleans. The inter-relationships among the suspects were confusing, and Claire had become a sycophantic wife.

With time on their hands, Claire and Dan accepted "Tinker" Bell's invitation for a holiday at her Mississippi Gulf Resort in *Redneck Riviera* (Intrigue, 1998). Hurricane Babe hovered along the coast. Beauty pageant contestants had historic prejudices and current rivalries to spice their competition.

Gambling interests had a stake in creating havoc. Tinker hoped that Dan and Claire would solve her problems.

Claire was to play an important role in her friend Charlotte's wedding in *Shiveree* (Intrigue, 1999) as matron of honor, hairdresser, and eventually detective. The groom's former wife was murdered in the bridal chamber. Multiple suspects emerged from among the guests. The narrative lagged under the weight of detailed descriptions of bridal attire.

Author Sophie Dunbar has a new series featuring Ava and Frank Bernstein.

Sister Joan

Author: Veronica Black, pseudonym for Maureen Peters

Sister Joan had been an art teacher, whose relationship with a Jewish lover did not survive their religious differences. At thirty, she experienced a calling to the contemplative life, not because she felt unsuited for the secular world, but as a higher choice. She left behind her Yorkshire home and her parents, covered her blue-black hair with a veil, and became a nun. Hers was a semi-cloistered order, dedicated to chastity, poverty, and obedience. As might be expected of a mature professional woman, obedience came the hardest.

Mother Frances, the dying superior of Cornwell House, had made the Order aware that there were problems among the sisters in *A Vow of Silence* (St. Martin, 1990). Joan was sent to Cornwall with orders "to keep her eyes open and report back" to the Mother House. No one expected she would encounter two mysterious deaths and evidence of a cult.

In *A Vow of Chastity* (St. Martin, 1992), Joan was disturbed by the uncharacteristically subdued behavior of her students in the elementary school. She sensed evil, which she connected to the disappearance of sacred objects from the public chapel. Her visits to the students' homes, including a gypsy encampment, and her close cooperation with Detective Sergeant Alan Mill created controversy but uncovered a killer.

A three month retreat, a period reserved for solitary contemplation, was recommended by Joan's superiors in *A Vow of Sanctity* (St. Martin, 1993), dispatching her to a remote, Calvinistic area of Scotland. Her prayers and concentration were distracted by local reaction to the disappearance of storekeeper Dolly McKensie's husband Alisdair. Joan kindled the consciences of those who concealed the truth.

Joan's return to the convent of the Daughters of Compassion in *A Vow of Obedience* (St. Martin, 1994) was marked by change. Her small school had been closed and the students transferred to a larger facility. Joan's superior assigned her temporarily to the kitchen and the novitiate (residence of those not yet accepted into the Order). On Joan's farewell visit to the little school, she discovered the corpse of young Valerie Pendon dressed as a bride. A short time later twenty-year-old Tina Davies was found dead near a gypsy encampment, similarly dressed

During *A Vow of Penance* (St. Martin, 1994), Joan worked to organize the convent scrapbook. The project made her aware of mutilations of trees and shrubbery that had taken place twenty years before. The recollection became important when similar mutilations occurred, simultaneous with the death of housekeeper Mrs. Fairly at the priest's house. Mrs. Fairly had called Joan, asking to meet with her but never appeared. Sgt. Mills declared her death to be suicide. Joan had access to possible suspects when Mother Dorothy appointed her to serve as housekeeper to the two priests until an acceptable replacement could be found.

The membership of the religious community was aging, so a visit by Sr. Marie and Sr. Elizabeth, two prospective postulants, in *A Vow of Devotion* (St. Martin, 1995) was welcomed. Sr. Elizabeth seemed paranoid. She may have reason to be fearful. Not so welcome were mysterious red roses, intruders on the convent grounds, and murder.

Joan left the convent temporarily in *A Vow of Fidelity* (St. Martin, 1996) for a reunion with fellow art students in London. Three out of ten graduates had died recently in suspicious accidents. On her return, Joan shared the information about the deaths with Sgt. Mills. When the group visited the convent on a retreat, they brought jealousy, guilt, and revenge to the religious setting.

The convent abandoned the idea of raising money by hosting retreats, but found itself in need of other income sources in *A Vow of Poverty* (St. Martin, 1996). Joan was set to work cleaning storerooms in the hope of finding valuables. The storerooms contained material left on the premises by the Tarquin family, prior owners of the property. There was treasure to be found, but death too. Joan's research of the Tarquin family and the life of her name saint, Joan of Arc, brought knowledge that placed her own life in danger.

A sense of restlessness caused Joan to ride her horse Lilith beyond her usual route in *A Vow of Adoration* (St. Martin, 1998). At an abandoned stone building, she discovered the corpse of an unknown man. She went to the nearest dwelling, that of antiquarian Michael Peters, to call the police. The postmortem determined that the victim had died a natural death. The long-term disappearance of Peter's younger wife Crystal made it impossible for Joan to detach herself from the case. With Sgt. Mills initially on vacation, and Constable Petrie down with measles, Joan relied on a confusing ally. One of the weaker plots in the series.

Concern for a close friend of Mother Dorothy and the need to take Sister Marie into town for dental surgery provided Joan with reasons to visit St. Keynes Hospital during *A Vow of Compassion* (St. Martin, 1998). However, too many incidents of mismanagement, too many errors, and several too many deaths convinced Joan that there was a pattern of murder.

When no new postulants presented themselves to join the Daughters of Compassion in *Vow of Evil* (Hale, 2004) the new superior, Mother David, decided to rent out the house the postulants had formerly occupied. The new tenants were unusual: a mother, two daughters, a son-in-law and an Italian friend, but their characters had been vouched for by Father John Fitzgerald. There seemed to be no reason to connect them to the small acts of cruelty and destruction that began even before their arrival. Evil was present, but as Joan's friend reclusive Brother Cuthbert predicted, only prayer can overcome it. Sister Joan's efforts were an answer to the prayers.

Hilda Johansson

Jeanne M. Dams

In this series, set in the early 1900s, Hilda Johansson was the head housemaid for Mr. and Mrs. Clement Studebaker of South Bend, Indiana to whom she was fiercely loyal. Hilda, whose parents still lived on their Swedish farm, had a limited education. Like many immigrants, the Johansson children had come to the United States individually, and then helped their siblings to do the same. Hilda's serious older sister Gudrun, younger more mischievous sister Freya, and brother Sven were already nearby and employed. All saved to bring others over in the future.

Hilda was a single woman, as marriage would probably have meant the end of her wage earning, but found herself reluctantly attracted to fireman Patrick Cavanaugh. Patrick's ethnic and religious background was anathema to a devout Swedish Lutheran. This was a time when not only did Americans scorn immigrants, but the individual immigrant groups sought to maintain their solidarity. Immigrants had been lynched in Indiana.

The setting and period were refreshing, and Hilda engaging in *Death in Lacquer Red* (Walker, 1999). The death of wealthy female missionary Mary Harper shortly after her return to her brother's South Bend home was blamed upon Chinese refugee Kee Long. This bigotry motivated Hilda to investigate, recruiting Patrick, Freya, and other domestics in the cause.

The assassination of President McKinley by Leon Czolgosz, a middle European immigrant in *Red, White, and Blue Murder* (Walker, 2000) stirred up nativist feelings in South Bend. Both John Bolton, coachman in the Studebaker household, and Flynn Murphy, brother of Hilda's friend Nora, may have been in the group that met with Czolgosz when he visited the area. While McKinley lay near death, two men were found murdered at a construction site. Wealthy but brutish building executive Roger Warren, had been wrapped in an American flag. The connection made between the presidential attack and the use of a flag in the murders led the community to believe that the killings were politically motivated. Hilda and James Oliver, a more reasonable businessman, barely prevented a lynching.

Patrick Cavanaugh's Irish Catholic family objected to his association with Hilda in *Green Grow the Victims* (Walker, 2001). Nevertheless, they recruited her when his uncle, Daniel Malloy disappeared after the murder of Republican

John Bishop, his political opponent in the election for the county council. Hilda, with many misgivings, believed in Daniel. She risked her reputation to find him, and risked her life to prove his innocence. Even though united in their appreciation for Hilda's accomplishments, Patrick's family could not accept their relationship. Her own Protestant family, grateful for the assistance of Malloy in obtaining passage to the United States for Hilda's mother and siblings, remained equally unaccepting. Still they were in love.

Hilda's mother and younger siblings had moved to South Bend by *Silence Is Golden* (Walker, 2002). Younger brother Erik had problems settling in and keeping a job. Hilda feared he would run away. Her concern was intensified when Erik's friend Fritz disappeared while attending a circus performance. Young boys in the South Bend area were being molested and murdered. Hilda took it upon herself to see that Erik was safe.

Erik's plea that Hilda investigate the murder of his favorite teacher, Miss Jacobs, came at a difficult time in *Crimson Snow* (Perseverance, 2005). Clem Studebaker had died, leaving his home and business to Col. George, his son. Hilda's best friend at work, Norah, had married, moved out and was working elsewhere as a daily. As head housemaid, Hilda found it difficult to keep the younger maids attentive to their work. However, elderly attorney Robert Barrett, who had known Miss Jacobs and was a possible suspect in her death, prevailed upon Col George to allow Hilda to get involved. Patrick Cavanaugh also had changes in his life. His uncle Dan Malloy had offered Patrick a partnership in his dry goods business. He wanted Hilda to marry him and share his good fortune. There were two hurdles: Hilda's Swedish Protestant family and Patrick's Irish Catholic relatives.

The transition from maid at the Studebaker residence to a life as Mrs. Patrick Cavanaugh with a home and servants of her own was not always easy for Hilda in *Indigo Christmas* (Perseverance, 2008). She did not feel accepted by her new upper class acquaintances; yet, her old friends and her family were uncomfortable with her elevated status. Plus which she was bored, but that didn't last. Dear friend Norah, now Mrs. Sean O'Neill, was in the last stages of her first pregnancy when Sean was accused of theft and jailed. For Norah's sake and that of her child, Hilda had to discover who was responsible for the arson, murder, and possible theft of a wallet at Walter Miller's farm. Dams did an excellent job of awakening Hilda to the fact that she too might be judgmental.

Dams has a second series, featuring American widow Dorothy Martin who made a new life for herself in England. (coverage in this volume)

Caroline "Fremont" Jones

Author: Dianne Day

Caroline "Fremont" Jones was a free spirit, casting off her New England roots to set up a secretarial business in San Francisco in 1905. She had a Wellesley education, but her father and stepmother were determined that she make an advantageous marriage. There was no rapport between Fremont and her father's second wife. Safety and security were not high on Fremont's wish list. An inheritance from her mother provided the financial security needed to underwrite her independence. She opened a small office above a bookstore on Russian Hill, advertising her services to the public. "Typewriter" was a novel occupation at the time. Dropping her given name, Caroline, she used Fremont to honor the General, a distant relative. She was lucky to find a friendly landlady, Maureen O'Leary.

The Strange Files of Fremont Jones (Doubleday, 1995) introduced troublesome clients. Edgar Allan Partridge had prepaid for the typing of his eerie short stories, but never returned to pick up the finished product. Concerned because she had been paid in advance, Fremont used clues from Partridge's stories in her investigation. Li Wong had hired Fremont to type a statement to be used in case of his death, which occurred a week later. When Fremont discovered his killer, she shared the information with his goddaughter, Meiling, who became a close friend.

Fremont's first thought when the San Francisco earthquake struck in *Fire and Fog* (Doubleday, 1996) was the safety of her typewriter. Artifacts found by Fremont when she checked her office building for damages made her a target of smugglers. Her next concern was a place to live, taking her from the frying pan to the fire. She did meet and become close to a mysterious lodger, Michael Archer. Fremont never had a dull moment, and that was the way she wanted it.

When Fremont moved to the Carmel area in *The Bohemian Murders* (Doubleday, 1997), her expectation was that she would enjoy an expanded relationship with Michael Archer. That was his name when he had roomed at the O'Leary boarding house. In Carmel he was known as Misha Kossoff, a return to his roots. Michael (as he shall be referred to herein) was twenty years older than Fremont. He had also become suspiciously intimate with Artemesia Vaughn, a seductive artist. Vulnerable and intimidated, Fremont secured a temporary position as a lighthouse keeper on the nearby coast. She alerted the authorities when she saw the body of a woman floating on the waves. Fremont's determination to discover the identity of "Jane Doe" made someone uncomfortable. She continued her typewriting. The passages that she typed for Artemesia may distort the flow of the narrative for some.

Fremont was happy to receive a visit from her aging father in *Emperor Norton's Ghost* (Doubleday, 1998). However, she was unwilling to grant his dying wish, that she legalize her relationship with Michael. While Michael concerned himself with the impact that Gregor Rasputin was having on Imperial Russia, Fremont allowed herself to be drawn into the world of spiritualism by battered wife Frances McFadden.

Death Train to Boston (Doubleday, 1999) was more of an adventure than a mystery. En route by train to Chicago, Michael and Fremont were separated. An explosion on the railroad car in which she was riding tossed Fremont into the wilderness. Her rescuer, unorthodox Mormon Melancthon Pratt, planned that when she recovered from her injuries, she would provide him with the children, denied him (to his way of thinking) by his five current wives. Old enemies from both Michael's and Fremont's pasts made their reunion more difficult but with Meiling's help, they managed.

Although still handicapped by injuries, Fremont continued her trip to Boston to visit her ailing father in *Beacon Street Mourning* (Doubleday, 2000). His subsequent death left her a wealthy woman, but she wanted more. She wanted proof that Augusta, her stepmother, had killed her father. Michael and Fremont had announced their engagement to please her father, but they did not follow through on their wedding plans. She was willing to settle for a household with her new cat, Hiram.

These books were entertaining cozies.

Casey Jones

Author: Katy Munger

Casey Jones asked for no sympathy and provided little. Her parents had been murdered in Florida when Casey was seven. The grandfather who had raised her taught her self-reliance and self-acceptance. An unfortunate early marriage contributed to her problems. She was arrested while transporting drugs at the request of her husband. It was unclear whether or not Casey was aware of her cargo, but it was she who was sentenced to two years at the Florida Women's Correctional, of which she served 14 months. Her conviction was a heavy blow to her grandfather. Casey left Florida with unfinished business: the murders of her parents, clearing her own name, and dealing with her former husband. She headed north, but stopped in Raleigh, North Carolina. That was far enough. Raleigh was a comfortable setting for a woman who preferred the country.

She was described as a "big girl," taken to mean solidly built, weighing about 160 pounds. Her size did not bother her. Casey could put away a dozen donuts without guilt. She was at various times, blond, redheaded, and a mixture of black and blond.

Her personal relationships with men after the divorce were initially casual. One police detective estimated that she had slept with half the men on his force. She developed an ongoing relationship with Burly Nash, who had been rendered paraplegic by a motorcycle accident. His physical limitations in bed meant she looked elsewhere for sex on occasion.

By the time the series opened, more than a dozen years had passed since she was released from prison. She put to use the computer skills, some unorthodox, that she had learned while institutionalized. Because she had a felony record, Casey could not apply for a private investigator's license, but she did the "legwork" for Bobby D (Dodd) who fancied himself a Nero Wolfe clone. Technically she was his receptionist. Bobby was a compulsive eater, indolent to the point of inertness, but had contacts throughout the community that provided inside information. Eventually he developed a sincere relationship with wealthy widow Fanny Whitehurst. Bobby was given to acquiring electronic gadgets for the agency (cigarette pack cameras, targeted hearing devices to eavesdrop through walls) that came in handy.

Until *Legwork* (Avon, 1997) Casey's assignments had been run of the mill. The chance to serve as bodyguard for senatorial candidate Mary Lee Masters was a step up. The discovery of a corpse in Mary Lee's car parked in her driveway changed the focus. The victim was identified as Thornton Mitchell, a contributor to the campaign of Mary Lee's opponent. First, she was ordered to find Mary Lee's wandering husband Bradley; then to find the killer. Casey was one tough cookie, but then so were Mary Lee and the killer.

Talk about a hopeless case! Time was out for Gail Honeycutt in *Out of Time* (Avon, 1998). Her appeals exhausted, she would be executed by the end of a month for the murder of her husband, Durham police officer Roy Taylor. The boys in blue, including Bill Butler, stonewalled when Casey sought files to review the case. She looked elsewhere for allies and found them, including dogs. By the time Butler rallied around, Casey had the matter well in hand.

Casey had ample opportunity to mix with the rich and powerful in *Money to Burn* (Avon, 1999). Her fifteen-hour shift as bodyguard for tobacco researcher Tom Nash failed. He died in his basement laboratory when the building was set on fire after Casey had left. Tom's fiancée Lydia Talbot, the daughter of tobacco magnate Randolph Talbot, hired Casey to discover whether or not her father was responsible for the death. Lydia may have lost her true love, but both Bobby and Casey seemed to have found theirs.

It looked for a while like Casey had met her match in *Bad to the Bone* (Avon, 2000). Tawny Bledsoe passed herself off as a battered wife with a small daughter. She hired Casey to find the child whom her African-American husband Robert Price had kidnapped. When Tawny's check bounced, Casey realized she'd been set up to finger Price as a killer. This was a complex narrative during which many of the supporting characters developed identities. Burley had been in a depressed period, unable to help, but Bobby Dodd, bartender Jack O'Neill, and Fanny Whitehurst expanded their roles.

Duke University in Durham was in real trouble during *Better Off Dead* (Avon, 2001). Women were being assaulted, raped, and finally murdered on or near the campus. Casey was drawn into the case of victim Helen Pugh, who had identified prominent professor David Brookhouse as her attacker. When a jury found Brookhouse innocent, he sued Helen. She became so traumatized that she was unable to leave her home. Casey solved part of the isolation problem by installing herself, Bobby, Fanny Whitehurst, and Burly Nash in Helen's home. Burly's work on the Internet helped Casey find the pattern even though he was moving away from his dependence on her.

Next: *Bad Moon on the Rise* (2009)

Sam (Samantha) Jones

Author: Lauren Henderson

Sam (Samantha) Jones, a sculptor who lived in a small former warehouse, found her friends among the artistic community in London. Unable to live on the proceeds of her art, she worked as a weight lifting teacher in a gym, and as an assistant in an art gallery—anything to continue to sculpt. Her formal education had been at an art school, but she apprenticed herself to a blacksmith after graduation. She was single, but had serial affairs, and may have been bisexual. She avoided meat although she was not a strict vegetarian. Her preferred clothing included leather jeans, Doc Marten boots, and whatever else was handy. She used "speed," and was obsessive about finishing anything she started. Her opinions were clear and difficult to change; e.g. she detested both tourists and hippies.

In *Dead White Female* (Hodder & Stoughton, 1995), Sam felt a special bond with Lee Jackson, her tutor in art school. Alone, among the partygoers, she did not accept that Lee had fallen while drunk and died accidentally. The search for truth brought more deaths, ending in an unsatisfactory compromise that had nothing to do with justice.

There were too many females in *Too Many Blondes* (Hodder & Stoughton, 1996), all of them enamored of Derek Brewster, the black weights instructor at the gym where Sam exercised. Derek's main interest was Linda Fillman, the gym manager. When she was murdered, the others lined up as suspects. Sam, who taught part-time at the gym made the necessary connections: identified the killer, found a buyer for a sculpture, and seduced a detective sergeant.

Sam could not bring herself to cooperate with the police department during *Black Rubber Dress* (Hutchinson, 1997). She ran a solo investigation of the murder of Bill, the doorman at the Mowbray Steiner Investment Bank Building where Sam's sculpture was located. Bill may have been a blackmailer. She justified her independent probe on the grounds that the corpse was found under her mobile, *Thing III*. Out of her social milieu, Sam was never out of her depth as she moved among the high (on drugs) and mighty suspects.

Burned out by preparation of an exhibition of her mobiles, Sam took a busman's holiday in *Freeze My Margarita* (Crown, 1998). She created a forest of mobiles for a stage production of *A Midsummer Night's Dream*. The petty jealousies and gnawing ambitions of cast members caused interruptions and nasty incidents during the rehearsals. The discovery of a woman's corpse on the premises could hardly be ignored. Sam had a new well-matched lover in Hugo Fielding, the male star of the production, but her former beau, Detective Inspector Hawkins came in very handy.

Sam's efforts to remain monogamously linked to Hugo Fielding while she visited New York City in *Strawberry Tattoo* (Hutchinson, 1999) left her adequate time to enjoy the city and its inhabitants. She became acquainted with the staff and artists in the Bergmann La Touche Gallery where she and three other young Brits were exhibiting. Two murders, one in Strawberry Fields, Central Park, marred the visit. A chance to renew a teenage friendship with Kim Tallboy added to her enjoyment. There were interesting insights as to how a boozing, drug enhanced artist saw New York City's East Village.

Hugo, Sam's lover, carried a major role in a teleplay during *Chained!* (Random House, 2000). Because Sarah, the film's heroine, was to be a sculptor, Sam was hired to serve as advisor and double. Double, she was when kidnappers abducted her instead of Sarah. The kidnapping was followed by two savage murders. In the belief that her abductors were connected with animal rights advocates whom Sarah had offended, Sam sent Lurch, her youthful assistant, undercover. Then she had to rescue him.

Loyalty to her friend Tom Connelly motivated Sam (and Hugo, somewhat more reluctantly) to visit him during *Pretty Boy* (Hutchinson, 2001). Realizing that he could not support himself as a poet, Tom had taken a job as a primary school teacher in Lesser Swinford. During the initial visit on New Year's Eve, Sam met Janine Burrows, a single mother whom Tom was romancing. She returned alone to extricate Tom when he was accused of killing Janine who had rejected his attentions. Sam, an outsider in Lesser Swinford, managed to upset a significant number of local residents during her investigation of other suspects, and to alienate Hugo, perhaps forever.

The narratives were witty, astringent, erotic, and common, like the heroine. You either like her or you don't. She might be fun to know but you wouldn't want her to marry your brother.

Henderson's new series protagonist is sixteen-year-old Scarlett Wakefield.

Texana Jones

Author: Allana Martin

Growing up in El Polvo, Presidio county, along the Texas/Mexican border, Texana Jones spoke Spanish and English and had friends in both countries. She managed a trading post, while her husband Clay worked as a veterinarian. Texana had ended an earlier short-term marriage, but there were no children in either case. A bobcat, Phobe, served both as a pet and a watchdog for the store. Texana was friendly, but not to be trifled with. On occasion, she enjoyed smoking a good cigar.

Texana's interest in the spiritual brought her into contact with Rhea Fair in *Death of a Healing Woman* (St. Martin, 1996). Texana was still mourning the deaths of her friends, Maria Elena Ortega-Deed and her husband Bill. Their killer had not yet been found. When Rhea failed to pick up her week's supply of groceries at the trading post, Texana went to check on her. She found the place in disarray and Rhea, dead. A young woman who had been visiting Rhea had disappeared. Although Rhea had two living sons, her past was obscure until

Texana delved into it to discover the cause of her death. She sought justice, but it took a white dog to provide the final verdict.

Mid-July was no time for tourists along the border, so, in *Death of a Saint Maker* (St. Martin, 1998), Texana was not sure just why Professor Boyce Aply and his inquisitive wife Pat had chosen to park their RV near her store. However, to be sociable, Texana invited Pat to accompany her to a chapel dedication across the Mexican border. The Saint Maker, an elderly carver, was found dead on the premises. Texana's resistance to the idea that the man had been killed by a pit bull put her into conflict with smugglers, corrupt Mexican police, and a powerful rancher.

Dental work across the border was more economical, but Texana paid a heavy price for her trip in *Death of an Evangelista* (St. Martin, 1999). En route home, she entered a cab which contained a corpse. The Mexican police were quick to take her into custody. Her release came only when she dropped the name of Gordon Suarez (see prior). This infuriated Texana's neighbor Claudia Reyes because the cabdriver, her cousin, remained in jail. The victim was a German who had connections to a U.S. prisoner-of-war facility. Texana found herself caught in religious controversy between powerful members of the Catholic faith who feared the growing power of a charismatic Protestant minister, Evangelista. She was harassed. Old friends turned on her, whether because of the history of the camp or the religious fury was not immediately clear.

A dominating father (now deceased) had tied the seven Spivey daughters to the land until all were over age sixty. As *Death of a Mythmaker* (St. Martin, 2000) began, Ellie Spivey rebelled out of love for charming con man Julian Row. Julian's murder opened his past and cast suspicion on a man whose life he had destroyed. The new sheriff not only ignored Texana's insistence that he had arrested the wrong person, but also accused her and Clay of drug smuggling.

Texana, her family, and friends had been associated with the 1961 production of a movie based on a raid by Mexican Pancho Villa. Forty years later in *Death of the Last Villista* (St. Martin, 2001) a television company containing members of the original cast returned to the area for a production based on the movie. What many remembered about the financially unsuccessful film was the murder of a technical advisor, Jacinto Trejo, who, as a boy, had followed Villa on his raids. What Texana learned was the impact of the earlier production on members of the cast and her own family.

Clay's arrest for the murder of Zanjiu Mehendru seemed like an error that would quickly be rectified as *Death of the River Master* (St. Martin, 2003) began. Six weeks had passed since the River Master was killed. Perhaps Clay had been randomly chosen as a scapegoat. He had a solid alibi for that night. What Texana and Clay had not accounted for was the level of corruptibility in the Mexican police and judiciary. Only when Texana realized that Clay was a target, could she rally a defense.

A solid series.

Tyler Jones

Author: Joan M. Drury

Tyler Jones was a lesbian newsprint reporter in San Francisco. She had attended the University of Minnesota earning a degree in journalism. She maintained a close relationship with her activist mother who lived in San Francisco but was a native of Northern Minnesota. Tyler initially drove a Volkswagen and named her dog after Agatha Christie but called her "Aggie." She had attained recognition, not only for her regular column *Womenswords* on feminist issues, but also for her book, *The Undeclared War: Violence Against Women.* Tyler described herself as a large woman with dark hair in her late thirties, currently without anyone special in her life, but having a large circle of friends. When she recognized that she had a drinking problem, she became active in Alcoholics Anonymous and no longer used alcohol.

In *The Other Side of Silence* (Spinsters, 1993), Tyler discovered a corpse in a park near her home. The victim, Dr. Jason Judd, had expressed his anger towards Tyler. Fortunately there were other suspects within the Judd family. Tyler pursued her own investigation until silenced by organized activists against men who mistreated women.

The death of her mother was not only a personal tragedy for Tyler, but, in *Silent Words* (Spinsters, 1996), it sent her on a quest for the truth. Her mother's dying words told her to unearth the skeletons back home in Northern Minnesota, and she did, but at the cost of life. Tyler found new friends, gained knowledge about her own family, and challenged the cover up of an old murder.

Closed in Silence (Spinsters, 1998) found Tyler, now forty-two, preparing to attend a reunion with five classmates from the 1970s, one of whom (Julie) had been her lover for almost five years, but was now in a heterosexual marriage. The group met on an island off the Washington State coast, providing an isolated setting for sexual intrigue and murder. The discovery of a murdered male on the island led to disclosures by members of the group as to their lives over the past seventeen years, but not to the identification of the killer. Tyler had her suspicions but she chose not to reveal them.

Carol Jordan

Author: Val McDermid

Detective Inspector Carol Jordan had reached her rank by age thirty. Her advancement was facilitated by her degree in sociology from Manchester University. Her initial placement had been in London where she had an extended affair with a doctor. It did not survive when she was assigned to Bradfield. There she, her brother Michael (a software designer) and her cat Nelson shared a flat. Nelson accompanied her on a later move to Seaford. A blonde of average height, Carol enjoyed well-designed clothes, but made her purchases at second hand shops. She exercised regularly at a local gym but had few personal interests. The series featured Carol and Dr. Tony Hill

While in Bradfield in *The Mermaids Singing* (HarperCollins (U.K.), 1995), she was selected by Assistant Chief Constable John Brandon to serve as liaison with Home Office psychologist, Dr. Tony Hill. Brandon had decided that savage murders that had been previously treated as three separate cases were the work of a serial killer. Hill's expertise as a profiler was to be used to advise the Bradfield Police Department. Not all staff welcomed this assistance. Carol not only respected Tony's skills but was also physically attracted to him. Unfortunately so was the killer. Tony's personal problems made him vulnerable to the blandishments of a seriously warped character. The narrative followed the patterns of a police procedural interspersed with excerpts reflecting the killer's progress from one murder to the next.

What had begun as a test exercise for Tony Hill's fledgling profiler class in *The Wire in the Blood* (HarperCollins, London, 1997) became an official case when bright rookie detective Shaz Bowman tied a series of teenage disappearances to popular celebrity Jacko Vance. Carol, still working to gain acceptance in her East Yorkshire community, was not a member of Hill's National Offender Profiling Task Force (NOPTF), but she consulted with them. Shaz's murder created a breach between the profile group and police departments. Without local support, Carol and Tony gathered unofficial allies to make their case, putting the sadistic killer in a vise.

Carol was thrilled at the opportunity to work with NCIS (National Criminal Intelligence Service) as *The Last Temptation* (St. Martin 2002) began. The assignment was for her to go undercover, thereby attracting Tadeusz Radecki, an international criminal and major drug dealer. Her allure for Radecki would begin with her close physical resemblance to Katerina Basler, his deceased lover. Carol, who hadn't seen Tony Hill for two years, reached out to him for help in assuming this new persona. She also involved him in the search for a serial killer. Both paid a heavy price for their successes, but found strength from one another.

It wasn't easy for Carol to go back to the office in *The Torment of Others* (St. Martin, 2004). She was not sure she could ever return to police work after she had been assaulted. It took her former supervisor, John Brandon and the promise of a new unit handling special crimes to lure her. The disappearances of two young boys and the emergence of a serial killer of prostitutes were her first challenges. Carol knew she could depend on some loyal members of her prior group and on Tony Hill. These were difficult cases: the bodies of the missing boys had not been located. Derek Tyler had been found guilty of killing four streetwalkers and was now in prison. Yet new killings with a similar M.O. cast doubt on his guilt. Were these copycat killings? Carol had to fight a weakness of her own. She was drinking heavily.

Tony Hill, hospitalized after a murderous attack by an axe-wielding patient, in *Beneath the Bleeding* (HarperCollins, 2007), was in no condition to solve crimes. The ricin poisoning of local football player Robbie Bishop had Bradford in mourning. Chief Constable John Brandon demanded quick results. Carol's unit split along several different lines of enquiry: gamblers, stalkers, even terrorists. Meanwhile Tony, with help from Paula McIntyre, stuck to his theory that the motive for Bishop's death lay in his past and was part of a pattern. Even the possibility that terrorists were responsible made it necessary for Carol to contend with the arrogant interference of the new Counter Terrorism Command.

A BBC television series was based on Tony and Carol, using material from the books, but was not always faithful to the original character roles.

McDermid has two other series (Kate Brannigan, covered in this volume, and Lindsay Gordon, covered in volume 1.) She has also written standalones. Next: *Fever of the Bone* (2010).

Charlotte Justice

Author: Paula L. Woods

Charlotte Justice had been in the Los Angeles Police Department for thirteen years during which major riots took place in African-American neighborhoods. Her husband, Keith, who had been her professor in college, had been dead for twelve of those years. He and their daughter, Erica had been murdered. Her family home, referred to as "the Nut House," was shared with her parents and a boxer named "Beast." Her mother Joymarie was a social worker. Her father Matt was a chemist who had worked for Max Factor in Hollywood. In the process he had developed a line of cosmetics designed for African-Americans. Charlotte was described as "light-skinned." Her brother and sisters were all high achievers. Her work on a Ph.D. dissertation ended when Keith and Erica were killed. After a period of severe depression, she dropped out of school and entered the police department.

At work, Charlotte's partner in the elite Homicide-Robbery Special Unit was Gena Cortez, a Hispanic. The two women had not bonded initially, but developed a good working relationship based partly on having to deal with discrimination against females, African-Americans, and Hispanics in the LAPD. Charlotte's work was characterized as methodical. Her outside interests included watching African-American movies, collecting artworks by promising artists, enjoying sports and single malt Scotch.

Inner City Blues (Norton, 1999) took place during major rioting in Los Angeles minority neighborhoods. Charlotte chanced upon Dr. Lance Mitchell, an African-American doctor, being hassled by fellow police officers. Her intervention may have saved Mitchell from abuse, but led to his being a suspect in the murder of Cinque Lewis. Lewis, a former leader of the Black Freedom Militia, was believed to have been the man who killed Keith and Erica. Inner-city

Los Angeles may be new territory for some readers: violent, drug-ridden, economically depressed, but populated by many courageous, ambitious, and mutually supportive African-Americans.

As *Stormy Weather* (Norton, 2001) began, Angelo Clemenza had been tried and convicted for the serial murders of nursing home residents. When similar cases arose, detective Billie Truesdale wondered if a mistake might have been made, if Clemenza had an accomplice who continued to kill, or if there were a copycat murderer at large. When former film director Maynard Duncan died, Charlotte and Billie considered all three of these alternatives. They uncovered a motive for Duncan's death that had nothing to do with mercy killing. Charlotte began to see her persistence as obsession; her delay in responding to the overtures of emergency room physician Aubrey Scott as a failure to put her past behind her. It was time to move on.

Just back on the job after a suspension was lifted, Charlotte was determined to prove herself in *Dirty Laundry* (Ballantine, 2003). The discovery of the body of Vicki Parks, ex-reporter, now working in Mike Santos campaign to become mayor, thrust her into several lines of investigation. Who was the person who called in the discovery? Why did he disappear after making the call? After a second death, the murder of a fellow police officer, Charlotte's problems increased. Politics involving "dirty laundry" (revelations of past activities in candidates' lives) led to the possibility of police corruption and racial discrimination.

Burned out or not, Charlotte could not pass up the chance to rework an unsolved case in *Strange Bedfellows* (Ballantine, 2006). Eve, her therapist agreed. A drive-by shooting had resulted in the deaths of Malek Shareef and the long-term hospitalization of Chuck Zaccari, CEO of CZ Toys. Chuck's young third wife, Alma, was relegated to a wheelchair and her premature daughter was potentially handicapped. This resonated with Charlotte whose husband and daughter had been murdered. Zaccari's toy company had been on the brink of a major agreement with Shareff's "Beautiful Dolls" corporation. Charlotte was at odds with her supervising detective over a sexual harassment case. The LAPD was under pressure from the FBI and SEC who were investigating financial irregularities at CZ Toys. What rankled the most was the realization that her own family had concealed information about the deaths of her husband and daughter.

Alison Kaine

Author: Kate Allen

Alison Kaine, a Denver Colorado police officer, was described as having a good relationship with her father and working well with her male police partner. That's the good news.

During *Tell Me What You Like* (New Victoria, 1993), Alison was drawn into the sadomasochistic underworld of hard-core lesbians. Her explorations led to an attraction to a dominatrix. The narrative revolved around a young boy who had been raised by a quartet of women and who, as an adult, murdered lesbians.

In *Give My Secrets Back* (New Victoria, 1995), Alison investigated the death of an author who wrote a lesbian book series, *Blaze Bad Girls*. She had been electrocuted by a vibrator while in her bathtub. The official decision was that the death was accidental. Alison disagreed because the files of a pending book were missing.

The stress of her investigations and her current relationship sent Alison to New Mexico in *Takes One To Know One* (New Victoria, 1996) to assist "land lesbians" in building an adobe house. Not only did a former lover join her on site, but Alison also discovered the corpse of a domineering Native American.

Just a Little Lie (New Victoria, 1998) crossed the line for me. I could not finish it. Alison had taken a leave of absence from the Denver Police Department to work for a friend who was putting on a "leather event". Really raunchy.

A high level of explicit sex and brutality with mystery coming in a weak third.

Jackie Kaminsky

Author: Margot Dalton

With her background, Jackie Kaminsky might well have ended up a criminal rather than a police detective in Spokane, Washington. Her mother, who had abandoned Jackie, died of a drug overdose. Her father had decamped even before she was born. Irene, her disgruntled grandmother raised Jackie and younger cousins Joey and Carmelo in Los Angeles. Lacking a sense of family in her home, Jackie found it on the streets, joined a gang and participated in crime up to and including armed robbery. That last caper put her in a juvenile detention facility for two years. She emerged determined not to return and to help others to avoid the experience.

She became a street cop in Los Angeles. After a decade on the streets in Los Angeles and Spokane, she was promoted to detective. Jackie burned out on the "mean streets" of Los Angeles, so moved to Spokane where she felt more comfortable. Her contacts with Gram became more and more acrimonious as the old woman became a serious alcoholic. Jackie had not yet developed a personal base in Spokane. Her lover and partner in Los Angeles, Officer Kirk Alveson, had been killed in action. As a consequence of her unhappy childhood, Jackie was plagued with uncertainties as to her own worth. Even when offered love, she mistrusted it, leaving her unable to make a commitment.

A blonde with short hair, Jackie wore slacks and blazers at work. She had never developed much of a personal wardrobe and spent little money on herself, but was skilled enough to make some of her own furniture. She had always wanted to play the flute, but settled for listening to flute music. Jackie was proud of her ethnic and racial heritage, which included Cherokee, West

Russian, and African-American. Her life experiences had made her suspicious, even prejudiced, against the rich and powerful who seemed able to manipulate the legal system.

Jackie was assigned primary responsibility in *First Impression* (Mira, Toronto, 1997), when three-year-old Michael Panesivic was abducted from a mall where he had been shopping with his mother. The custody and visitation battles between Michael's divorced parents caused the police to assume that a family member had taken Michael. That changed when itinerant carpenter Paul Arnussen appeared, claiming to have a "flash" which told him that Michael was underground, but alive. A skeptical Jackie was unsure whether Paul was the kidnapper, a psychotic or her only chance to locate the child. Along the way she achieved one of her objectives by rescuing abused teenager Angela Gerard who had taken to the streets.

Paul had become a standard in Jackie's life by *Second Thoughts* (Mira, 1998), but he had difficulty accepting the dangerous aspect of her work. Jackie's first homicide was dramatic to the point of incredibility. Six people, including Jackie, received letters that disclosed hidden secrets and promised death or degradation. Four of the potential victims were related by marriage or family relationships. Jackie had been granted primary responsibility in the deaths of Maribel Lewis and her son Stan and had no intention of giving up on the case.

Jackie's continued insecurities threatened her relationship with Paul in *Third Choice* (Mira, 1998), which related to his ultimatum that they marry, at least live together, or end it. She became involved in the disappearance of loving husband and father John Stevenson even before he was connected to a crime. Jason Burkett, John's employer, and his wife Norine were coping with the death of their daughter Angela in a hit and run accident. An undeniable murder joined the two cases, upgrading the need to find John Stevenson. A personal revelation made it equally important for Paul and Jackie to make the right choice for their lives.

If there had been any possibility that a pregnant Jackie Kaminsky would settle for a desk job in *Fourth Horseman* (Mira, 1999), it ended when she and Paul unearthed two skeletons. She had purchased a home for herself and her expected child, unwilling to move to Paul's farm. With official approval she questioned her new neighbors to learn the circumstances that caused the deaths of young Maggie Birk and the infant buried beside her thirty years before. Red herrings abounded. There was a happy ending for a change, which included son Danny, and a black cat Shadow.

The narratives tended to be long. Dalton wrote romances and gave space to introspection on the part of her characters. They could be classified as soft police procedurals—crisp on the outside; a little soggy in the middle.

Sarah Keane

Author: Michael Molloy

At introduction, Sarah Keane was an English widow in her late thirties, still numbed by the death of her husband. Jack, a television foreign news reporter, had died when the Land Rover in which he had been riding was struck by rocket fire. They had three children who had also lost a father— serious and unusually mature Emily, who wanted to be a doctor like her grandfather, and the boisterous twins, Martin and Paul. Sarah spent most of that first year compulsively cleaning house or feeling sorry for herself. Jack had often been overseas on assignments. She seemed to be treating his death as a temporary absence. Before her marriage, Sarah had worked on the local newspaper, the *Gazette*, but that was seventeen years ago. Her education had not included college. She had attended a boarding school run by the Sisters of Charity because her mother (now deceased) had serious health problems. Religion affected her attitudes but she no longer practiced the Catholic faith.

As *Sweet Sixteen* (Sinclair-Stevenson, 1992) began, Sarah experienced a short period of tear-filled exhaustion, then an awakening that life had to go on. For one thing, Jack's insurance money was running out. Feeling that reporting was her only skill, she contacted her friend George Conway, news editor at the *Gazette*. He offered her occasional work. An elite unit, headed by George's ambitious assistant, was handling the major news story, three murders by a mutilating serial killer. All victims had recently reached their sixteenth birthdays, as Emily would within a short time. Sarah's personal life improved through contacts with Superintendent Colin Greaves of the local police station but within her circle of new and old friends and enemies at the *Gazette* was a killer.

In *Cat's Paw* (Sinclair-Stevenson, 1993), there was a rather touching narrative of the redemption of unpopular news reporter Cat Abbott, thanks to professional psychic Doreen Clay. This was against a background of vicious struggle between two Northern Irish gangs in London. While Sarah and Colin moved closer to an accommodation in their personal lives, their professional roles were endangered by the gang war.

Having just finished an exhausting expose of the fate of homeless children, Sarah looked forward to pleasant Christmas holidays with Colin and the children in *Home Before Dark* (Heinemann, 1994).In one fell swoop, the atmosphere at the Gazette changed. Instead of Brian Meadows as editor they had former television personality Simon Marr, inexperienced but charismatic. News editor George Conway was shunted aside for Alan Stiles. Fanny Hunter, Sarah's archenemy, was exultant. The order from Board Chairman Sir Robert Hall was to soft pedal sex stories, but that couldn't apply to a serial killer who had murdered three women, only to have the fourth, actress Vickie Howard, survive to tell her story…or could it. Marr's current priority was the disclosure of a threat of a national disaster and how to use the possibility for his own advancement.

It all started when reinstated news editor George Conway came up with a great idea for Sarah's next assignment in *Dogsbody* (Heinemann, 1995). She was to go out and earn a living, starting without any money, to dramatize the plight of street people. This led to a job for solicitor John Latimer, who handled the legal affairs of the Nightingale family. First, she was to go undercover at the Corinthian Club, which included Sir Silas Nightingale and his entourage. They, and other men about town, used the Corinthian for Regency level pranks, gambling, and orgies. It got worse. Colin learned of the assignment, made it his business to be on hand, even if he had to risk his life. Bizarre, even grotesque at times.

Irene Kelly

Author: Jan Burke

Irene Kelly, a former newspaper reporter, was working in public relations in Las Piernas, California when her friend and mentor Conn O'Connor, was killed by a packaged bomb during *Goodnight, Irene* (Simon & Schuster, 1993). Irene returned to the *News Express* to investigate a long forgotten case, which probably motivated O'Connor's murder. She had driven him home the night before. The next morning he went out to pick up the paper, lifted a package and was blown up. She was in no mood for romance, but did not reject the help of detective Frank Harriman.

Frank wanted Irene to spend Thanksgiving with his family in *Sweet Dreams, Irene* (Simon & Schuster, 1994). Although Irene did not intend to share the rest of her life with her 20-pound tomcat, "Wild Bill Cody," she was not ready to join the Harriman family. Instead she involved herself with a political campaign that erupted into murder. She had been contacted by young Jacob who had become involved with a Satanic cult, hoping to convince his friend Sammy to leave the group. Unfortunately for his father's campaign for District Attorney, Jacob's picture was taken. Jacob convinced Sammy to go to the Casa de Esperanze, a shelter started twenty-four years ago by Mrs. Althea Fremont. Irene worked there as a volunteer. The identification of Althea's killer became Irene's priority.

Suffering from anxiety and physical handicaps, Irene moved in with Frank and marriage was definitely in their future as *Dear Irene* (Simon & Schuster, 1995) opened. Her injuries did not keep her from returning to work part-time. She became the recipient of messages from a killer, who couched his announcements of murder in Greek mythological terms. Irene's investigation reached back to the working women of World War II.

In *Remember Me, Irene* (Simon & Schuster, 1996), a chance meeting with Lucas, an unrecognized acquaintance, left Irene with a sense of guilt. Lucas' involvement with prominent Las Piernas businessmen led to a suicide, a retirement, a heart attack, and his own death. Frank, now Irene's husband, was concerned about her excursions into the tougher parts of town and the higher echelons of Las Piernas power.

Frank's marriage to Irene made him suspect at the police department when there were "leaks" to the press in *Hocus* (Simon & Schuster, 1997). Frank disappeared, leaving his gun at a murder scene. Hocus, a group of "pranksters," who had turned to kidnapping and murder, may have abducted Frank. He had rescued two traumatized boys who witnessed a killing. Under pressure by her editor to get an exclusive story, but assisted by the mother-in-law who had hitherto been critical, Irene had only one goal: to rescue her husband.

Liar (Simon & Schuster, 1998) mixed family discord and murder. Irene's sister Barbara had decided just where she was going to be buried in the family plot, only to learn that someone else had co-opted the lot. Aunt Brianna's burial had been authorized by Irene's Aunt Mary, even though Brianna and her "husband" Arthur had been estranged from the rest of the family for years. It might have ended there except that Irene was the beneficiary in Brianna's will. Much of the information she gathered about Brianna's death and that of Arthur's prior wife could not be relied upon. Not an easy read.

Teenager Gillian Sayre, dissatisfied with the police department response to her mother's disappearance in *Bones* (Simon & Schuster, 1999), contacted Irene every time an unidentified female body turned up. When Nicholas Parrish was tied to the death of another woman four years after Julia Sayre's death, he plea-bargained. He would lead the authorities to Julia's grave if no death sentence were imposed. Irene was included in the group that flew, and then backpacked, to the isolated site. Parrish escaped and continued his depredations, taunting Irene that she would be added to the list of his victims. Who had killed Julia was no longer the question. What was left for Irene to discover was the connection between the Sayres family and Parrish.

During *Flight* (Simon & Schuster, 2001), Frank was the primary, assigned to review decisions made earlier by members of his department. The death of young Seth Randolph, who was the lone survivor of "pirates" who boarded his father's yacht, had been blamed on detective Philip Lefebvre. He had subsequently disappeared. His plane crashed, the result of tampering. Frank was treated with hostility when he disputed the earlier findings in the case. Lefebvre had left a son behind who deserved to have his father's name cleared.

Bloodlines (Simon & Schuster, 2005) continued the saga of the interconnected relationships between Jack Corrigan and rival reporter Helen Swan in the Thirties. Corrigan and his youthful protégée, Conn O'Connor, who rose from paperboy to crime reporter on the Las Piernas newspaper, were tied to Irene because O'Connor had been her mentor. The 465 page narrative covered their personal and professional lives from 1936 to the current time, detailing those who loved or hated them. O'Connor had never stopped searching for the killer of his sister, Maureen in 1936. Irene took up that challenge. Very moving but could have used genealogy charts to limit confusion.

Irene's article about children abducted by the non-custodial parents triggered unrest among members of the Fletcher clan in *Kidnapped* (Simon &Schuster, 2006). It had all seemed so innocent when Graydon and Emma Fletcher, unable to have children of their own, adopted and fostered close to two dozen, now adults. But there was no safety in numbers. As the original children married, had children of their own, the group expanded. The first tragedy had been the death of Graydon's "son" Richard and the disappearance of Richard and Elise's daughter, Jenny. The trail to find Jenny absorbed Irene, Frank, and members of Jenny's family. The children, Jenny and others in her new household carried much of the action and drama.

This is a fine series that combined good characterizations with above average plotting. Burke's short stories have been published in major mystery magazines and collected in *Eighteen.* Her most recent book, *The Messenger* (2008) fits into the supernatural genre. Next: *Disturbance* (2011)

Virginia Kelly

Author: Nikki Baker

Virginia Kelly combined three minority factors in her persona. She was an African-American female lesbian sleuth. Virginia, motivated to succeed by her father and mother, earned a degree in electrical engineering and a Masters in Business Administration. Her parents accepted that she was a lesbian, who, after leaving their home, shared an apartment with white accountant Emily Karnowski in a white Chicago neighborhood. She was a small woman in her late twenties with short wiry dark hair. She worked as a securities analyst developing investment opinions on mutual funds. She existed on fast food when not sharing her home, was chronically late for work, and drove a convertible in Chicago's cold winters. Her only companion was an untrained cat named Sweet Potato.

In the Game (Naiad, 1991) concerned itself with the homosexual community, other lesbian couples, their meeting places and methods of communication (newspaper ads). Bev, an African-American lesbian friend, contacted Virginia for help when she suspected her lover Kelsey of infidelity. She needed her more when Kelsey was murdered. Virginia's interest in the case led to an affair with lesbian attorney Susan Coogan which complicated matters with Emily Karnowski.

The Lavender House Murder (Naiad, 1992) took place in Provincetown, where Virginia vacationed at a residence frequented by lesbians. She came to the attention of the police when she discovered the corpse of Joan di Maio. Virginia was suspected by the local police. The mystery aspect of the narrative was overlaid with details of lesbian life.

Long Goodbyes (Naiad, 1993) took Virginia to her hometown for a high school reunion at the request of Rosalee Paschen, the woman who had dominated her early lesbian life. There was little time for nostalgia. While working her way through tangled relationships, Kelly exposed a dangerous pedophile.

By *The Ultimate Exit Strategy* (Bella Books, 2001) Virginia was in her early thirties and working for Whytebread, Greese, Winslow, & Shoat as a stock analyst. WGWS was in the early stages of a merger with a larger firm when CEO Wes Winslow collapsed and died of poison. The chief detective on the case was a former lover of Virginia. Two staff members who had agreed to talk to Virginia about some of the shenanigans at the firm were murdered.

Zoe Kergulin

Author: Trudy Labovitz

Zoe, a non-observant Jew, was a licensed private investigator who specialized in corporate work in rural West Virginia. She had previously been an investigator for the U. S. Department of Justice in D.C. The reason why she left her job in D. C. was eventually explained. Her educational background included Cornell and Stanford, both of which she had attended on scholarships. Her graduate degree had been earned at Georgetown. She had joint majors in criminal justice and anthropology. Zoe, who had multiple siblings, had never married and, although she enjoyed her nieces and nephews, did not intend to have children of her own. Cats were more her style, including "Hot Fudge", a three-legged specimen whom she rescued from a trap.

Zoe's retreat to rural West Virginia in *Ordinary Justice* (Spinsters Ink, 1999) followed the incident in which she killed Paul Martin. Martin had attacked Karen O'Malley, Zoe's best friend. The death was ruled to be justifiable homicide, but she cashed in her pension and moved out of town. Zoe purchased a large rundown house in Bickle County where her beloved cousin Ethan McKenna was the sheriff. As the narrative began, Zoe met Susan Rourke, an abused wife who was hiding from her husband, Patrick. When Susan disappeared, the search found not her body, but Patrick's. Motivated by her own loss, Zoe sought to protect Susan from being framed for his death. No loving couples appeared in the narrative. Except for cousin Ethan and Dorsey (a hippie) all the men were depicted as brutal. Tolerance should be a two-way street

Ethan and his deputy, Rosalyn Fitzgerald, were shot in her driveway in *Deadly Embrace* (Spinster's Ink, 2000). Rosalyn did not survive. Zoe's first, rather paranoid, theory was that the attack was meant to avenge her killing of Paul Martin. While Ethan languished in the hospital, FBI agent Libby Gordon took over his office and made it clear that Zoe's help was not welcome. The FBI slant on the case was that the attacker was either a member of Ethan's staff or Rosalyn's husband Kirk. Zoe evaluated testimony from unstable teenager Ren Bertram, which conflicted with information from state agent Andrew Prescott and dyslexic Sheriff Shep Tuttle of adjoining Feller County

Joanne "Jo" Kilbourn

Author: Gail Bowen

Deadly Appearances (Douglas, Canada 1990) introduced Joanne "Jo" Kilbourn as a speechwriter and college teacher with a passion for politics. Her husband Ian had served as Attorney General and as a member of the Provincial legislature before his murder by hitchhikers. Joanne was so terrified of flying that on one occasion she drank gin for breakfast to prepare for the flight. Joanne and her three children (daughter Mieka and son Peter, who entered college, and younger son, Angus) initially lived in Regina, Saskatchewan. The children matured over the series. Joanne, who rounded out her life with enthusiastic cooking and appreciation of the arts, was still working on her Ph.D. dissertation when party leader Andy Boychuk, for whom she wrote speeches, was murdered. The supporting characters were richly developed. The dialogue was literate without being pretentious and the tension, gripping.

Joanne and the children moved to Saskatoon in *Love and Murder* a.k.a. *Murder at the Mendel* (St. Martin, 1993), because Mieka and Peter were attending college there. Her personal life was complicated by Mieka's decision to leave college and begin a catering business with her lover, Greg Harris. Chaos came with the death of artist Sally Love, who had been Joanne's friend since childhood. Joanne knew that Sally had been deeply affected by the death of her father in a tragic incident that almost cost her life and the life of her mother. Joanne dealt with the loss of a friend and of her own illusions, but she added Sally's daughter Taylor, a loving and talented child, to her household.

By *The Wandering Soul Murders* (St. Martin, 1994), the Kilbourn family had returned to Regina, absorbed in preparations for Mieka's marriage. Peter had a disturbing relationship with Christy Sinclair who was attracted to the warmth and security of the Kilbourn family. Her death and that of a teenager working for Mieka sent Joanne into the past, into the wilds of Saskatchewan, and into a temporary relationship with politician Keith Harris.

Kevin Tarpley, the slow-witted youth convicted of Ian's murder, was killed in a prison yard as *A Colder Kind of Death* (St. Martin, 1995) opened. Joanne reassessed the circle of political friends who had surrounded her married life to evaluate their possible involvement in his death. Inspector Alex Kequahtooway, who managed to be on scene whenever needed, treated Joanne's connection with the subsequent death of Maureen Gault, Kevin's girlfriend, seriously.

Julie Evanson-Gallagher had been a long time acquaintance, but something less than a friend. In *A Killing Spring* (McClelland & Stewart, 1996), Joanne was reluctant to get involved when Julie's new husband died in what seemed to be an autoerotic accident. Based on her own impression of Reed and a visit at the scene with Alex, Joanne agreed with Julie that this could not be suicide. She had no idea at that time that Reed's death would be connected to the sexual harassment of Kellee Savage, a handicapped student who was later found dead. The affair between Joanne and Alex, a Canadian Indian, was threatened when she over-reacted to bigotry.

Judge Justine Blackwell was approaching the end of her career when, in *Verdict in Blood* (McClelland & Stewart, 1998) she reached the conclusion that some of her decisions had been unnecessarily harsh. Her concern became obsessive, but was tempered by a fear that she might have degenerated into senility. Justine and Joanne's mutual friend, Hilda McCourt, was recruited to help Justine assess her stability and to act as executor in a new will which disinherited her three daughters, leaving her assets to a controversial facility for former convicts. The death of Justine, followed by a serious attack on Hilda, drew Joanne into the controversy. She was focused on a breach between her and Alex over treatment of his son Eli's reaction to the death of his mother. The parallels to *King Lear* and the connections between Eli's bouts of amnesia and Justine's death were subtly woven into the narrative.

Burying Ariel (McClelland & Stewart, 2000) was more than a dirge for the loss of a bright and caring young woman. Ariel Warren, a fellow lecturer of Joanne's at the University, had also been a childhood friend. She was taken aback when ardent feminists seized upon Ariel's death as a "cause" which could be exploited for the movement. If Ariel had been murdered, surely a man must be responsible, they argued. Charlie Dowhanuik, their suspect, also a childhood friend, had been too dependent on Ariel to let her go. It had to be someone else. Willie, a slow learning Bouvier des Flanders, was added to the Kilbourn household.

Long time friend, television producer Jill Osiowy, asked Joanne to be the matron of honor at her wedding in *The Glass Coffin* (McClelland & Stewart, 2002). The bridegroom-to-be, documentary producer Evan MacLeish, had two previous marriages, each of which had ended in suicide. What horrified Joanne was the fact that Evan had videotaped his spouses and their tragic endings. Before the wedding took place, best man Gabe Leventhal was murdered. Alex was in charge of the investigation in which Jill was a suspect.

Gail Bowen packed more mystery, romance, and tragedy into the 234 pages of *The Last Good Day* (McClelland & Stewart, 2004) than most authors provide in their 400+ narratives. Joanne, Taylor, Angus and his girlfriend Leah Drache were spending the summer at Lawyers' Bay, a gated community of members of the Falconer Shreve law firm. Joanne rented a cottage from former partner Kevin Hynd. At the annual Canada Day celebration, attorney Chris Altieri confided his guilt and need to make amends to Joanne, but by morning he had killed himself. The reasons for his suicide were poignant and affected all members of the Falconer Shreve Inner Circle.

Joanne was confident about her feelings for wheelchair bound attorney Zack Shreve in *The Endless Knot* (McClelland & Stewart, 2006) although she had several warnings that he was a shark in the courtroom and a philanderer in his personal life. Their bonds were tested when Zack served as defense attorney for right wing businessman Sam Parker, accused of attempting to murder journalist Kathryn Morrissey. She had written a book, based on confidential information which exposed tragedies in the lives of young people. In covering the trial for Nation TV, Joanne saw a different side of Zack. Aspects of the case involved both of Joanne's daughters.

As usual, author Gail Bowen skillfully wove the elements of friends and family into a stark tale of prostitution and abuse in *The Brutal Heart* (McClelland & Stewart, 2008). Joanne's new husband, Zach Shreve, revealed secrets of his own past when call girl Cristal Avila was murdered. With some difficulty, they kept their marriage afloat. Joanne was observing the parliamentary campaign of Ginny Monaghan, potential candidate for prime minister. That too became problematic when revelations about Ginny's life and that of her former husband Jason Brodnitz surfaced as a result of a custody battle. The treatment was unusually brutal for this excellent series.

A most enjoyable series, featuring a vibrant and caring woman. The Canadian series featuring Jo became available in the United States when St. Martin's Press published several of the books. The series is best read in chronological sequence to get the full flavor of the characters. *Joanne Kilbourn: Her Investigations* and the *Further Investigations of Joanne Kilbourn* each contain several of the books mentioned above.

Another alternative, the first four in the series have been made into television shows in Canada.

Next: *The Nesting Dolls* (2010)

Sal Kilkenny

Author: Cath Staincliffe

Sal Kilkenny, a University graduate and single mom to Maddie (age four initially), was an unorthodox English private investigator. She had survived a personal attack in a previous murder investigation. Even though wounded she refused to find less dangerous work. Her drab basement office was located in Manchester. She and Maddie shared nearby lodgings with Ray Costello and his son, Tom. She and Ray were friends, not lovers, sharing childcare responsibilities and expenses. She was a vegetarian, loved to garden, and swam at a public pool. A dog, Digger, was part of the household. Later, the attic apartment was rented out to Sheila, a carpenter who could cook, bake, and baby-sit with Maddie on occasion.

She was desperate for work when Mrs. Hobbs hired Sal to find her sixteen-year-old son, Martin in *Looking for Trouble* (Crocus, Manchester, 1994). A £1,000 retainer convinced her to take the case. She felt differently when she learned that her client was not Martin's mother and that he was terrified of returning to his parents. The murder of J.B., an artist who had befriended Martin, started Sal on the trail of a major child pornography ring.

Elderly Agnes Donlan, who was concerned about the welfare of her friend Lily Palmer, consulted Sal in *Go Not Gently* (Headline, 1997). Lily's health had deteriorated since she entered the Homelea Nursing Home. The case expanded into a wholesale investigation of the process of medicating, diagnosing, and treating elderly men and women. In an unrelated case Sal was concerned that she might have directed attention to a client whose unfaithful spouse had been murdered.

Although Sal seemed undaunted by the physical abuse and danger connected to her job, her housemate Ray Costello voiced his concerns in *Dead Wrong* (Headline, 1998). An assignment to prove young Luke Wallace had not killed his close friend, Ahktar Khan, pitted Sal against a cold killer and his employer. There were casualties along the way, and a threat was made to Sal's daughter Maddie.

Roger Pickering came to Sal with what appeared to be a hopeless quest in *Stone Cold Red Hot* (Allison & Busby, 2001). He wanted her to find his older sister Jennifer who had disappeared 23 years before. Initially Roger and Jennifer's friends had been told that she had gone on to the University; then, dropped out of school; and finally, that she was a disgrace whose name was never to be mentioned. Now their mother Barbara was dying. Roger hoped to effect a reconciliation between mother and daughter. Sal also undertook an investigation of harassment by neighborhood youths against a refugee family from Somalia. Bigotry she learned was not confined to lower class neighborhoods.

The death of Miriam Johnstone was determined to be suicide, yet in *Towers of Silence* (Allison & Busby, 2002), her family needed to know how their mother had slipped into depression so quickly. Sal made them aware that the police seemed to have a basis for their judgment. Still it was true that black victims in Manchester did not always get equal treatment, so she took a look. In a separate case, also involving a family, Sal tailed a teenage boy to see why he was disappearing for short periods of time

In *Bitter Blue* (Allison & Busby, 2003) Sal suffered blows to her self-esteem. Her daughter Maddie was in trouble at school, unwilling to share her problems with her mother. Her platonic relationship with Ray Costello had changed. Moreover a client weakened her sense of competence at her job. Lucy Barker needed help. Lucy, a hotel receptionist, had a miserable childhood, and had not recovered from an unhappy engagement. So why was someone breaking and entering her home and sending threatening letters. No one was giving Sal the information she needed.

Sometimes you win; sometimes you lose. That's the way it was for Sal in *Missing* (Alison & Busby, 2007). She dealt with three cases: (1) a well-to-do rock band singer hired her to find his birth mother; (2) Trisha Marlowe's best friend, Janet Florin, had been missing for a week when Trisha hired Sal. Her currently unemployed husband Mark was left with their two children. Trisha was certain that Janet would never abandon her kids; (3) Ramin Yalik, still awaiting the news on his application for refugee status, was concerned by the disappearance of his younger brother, Berfan, whose application had been denied. Berfan had been tortured by the authorities in his homeland and was determined not to return there. Staincliffe added personal touches as Sal dealt with the continued change in her relationship with Ray and bad health news for her best friend, Diane.

Sal had a scatological vocabulary. The narratives were gritty and gruesome, but will hold the persistent reader's attention. Cath Staincliffe has recently published at least two mysteries featuring DCI Janine Lewis.

Katy Kincaid

Author: Celestine Sibley

See: Kate Mulcay, page 597.

Libby Kincaid

Author: Kerry Tucker

Libby Kincaid, who was abandoned by her father, then orphaned by her mother's early death, had been raised by relatives in Rochester, New York. Uncle Garth triggered her interest in photography. The Rochester Institute of Technology trained the tiny chestnut-haired Libby for a career as a photojournalist. Although based in New York City, she frequently traveled about the world for a newsmagazine, *American.*

Libby put aside her professional interests in *Still Waters* (HarperCollins, 1991), when, after years of occasional contacts with her brother Avery, she returned to Darby, Ohio for his funeral. Avery had been found, a presumed suicide with his badly wounded dog at his side. Whatever Libby knew about Avery, she was certain that he would never have let an injured animal suffer, so his death could not have been suicide.

Libby's grief motivated her to take leave from her job during *Cold Feet* (HarperCollins, 1992). She worked on a photo-book featuring an African-American tap dance group, the Nonpareils, most of whom were now elderly men. In the midst of this project, Libby was diverted by the appearance of her father Max who had recently won (and was quickly spending) the proceeds of the New Jersey Lottery. When one of the Nonpareils was murdered, suspicion fell on a fellow dancer, but also on Libby. Her experience in a New York City jail, although harrowing, did not discourage her from finding the killer.

Death Echo (HarperCollins, 1993) returned Libby to Ohio where she located Mavis Skye Rihiser, the reclusive writer whom she had been seeking. There were complications When Libby and Dan Sikora (a friend of her brother Avery, and now Libby's lover) returned from a camping trip, Dan's former girlfriend Pam Bates needed help. Pam had also been close to Libby's brother Avery. Her former foster mother, Lydia Butcher had been acting mysteriously; i.e. writing a will, not showing up at her job. Lydia was Mavis Skye Rihiser's sister. After an interval during which Libby returned to New York City, Pam contacted her again with concerns about both sisters. They were justified. Lydia was killed when an arrow was shot into her back. There was history for these two women that Libby researched.

Drift Away ((HarperCollins, 1994) located Libby temporarily in Boston where she taught photography at Harvard. Attorney Andrea Hale, a college friend, had disappeared along with client Mark Le Clair, whose escape she might have assisted. With the approval of Jack, Andrea's husband and Libby's former lover, Libby moved into their new but empty apartment, taking a job at the law firm where Andrea was employed. She not only reentered Andrea's recent past, but her college days to find a killer and a relationship.

Above average, but a lot of the characters seemed to be somebody's former lover which got confusing.

Lisa King

Author: Gail E. Farrelly

Lisa King, who grew up in the Bronx, was a respected member of the financial world by age forty. She boasted a Ph.D., and had worked her way up to an associate professorship of finance at Yonkers University. She was described as tiny, and temperate in her appetites.

Lisa represented her university at a Boston conference in *Beaned in Boston* (Chicago Spectrum, 1995). Among the other conferees were lecherous professor Richard Duncan and a half-dozen men and women who had reason to hate him. Garrulous chambermaid Katie Maguire found Duncan dead in his hotel room. Det. Celeste Barclay and Sgt. Roy Clarkson welcomed Lisa's input as to the members of the group. A fourth member of their strategy group was Celeste's widowed father Martin, now Chief of Security at the Sheraton Hotel where the group met. They divided up the possible suspects, met to confer, and began several romances.

Duped by Derivatives (Chicago Spectrum, 2000) followed five years later. Lisa refreshed her real world knowledge of finance by spending a sabbatical as a "visiting scholar" at Reilly Investment Company on Wall Street. Several of those who had featured in the prior narrative were now in New York City. Former police sergeant Roy Clarkson had opened a detective agency. Katie Maguire was his assistant. Roy's agency had been hired to identify the prankster who plagued the Reilly Investment Company at a time of low morale among staff and clients. Clients had suffered losses when the derivative market sagged. Staff members feared losing their jobs, a serious possibility. Chief Executive Officer George Reilly made a deadly error by his insensitivity to vulnerable associates.

The series ended after just two books.

Willow King

Author: Natasha Cooper, pseudonym for Daphne Wright

Willow King, a staid, self-controlled civil servant in the Department of Old Age Pensions in London, had a second life as romance novelist Cressida Woodruffe. Her part-time position, ostensibly limited so that she could "care for Aunt Agatha," made possible a lavish lifestyle from Friday through Monday.

Willow's secret was threatened in *A Common Death* (Crown, 1991 apa *Festering Lilies*) when Algernon Endelsham, her department head, was murdered. Should she reveal her second identity, using Richard Crescent, her banker lover, for an alibi? She decided to solve the killing before disclosure was necessary, but shared her identity, her bed, and her life with Tom Worth, the inspector in charge of the case.

In *Poison Flowers* (Crown, 1991), Willow, the repressed child of elderly parents, was reluctant to make a total commitment to the luxurious life of Cressida. As Cressida, currently between books, she consulted Tom, now promoted to Chief Inspector, about a recent series of poisonings. Tom had confided that the department could not agree as to whether or not the murders were committed by a serial killer. Willow sought the pattern in the poison deaths as she and Tom developed a profile of the potential serial killer.

Tom and Willow were on an Italian vacation in *Bloody Roses* (Crown, 1993) when Richard Crescent, Willow's former lover, made his "one call." He had been charged with killing Sarah Allfarthing, a fellow bank employee whom he claimed to love. Willow went undercover at the bank, blending aspects of her two personas.

There was considerable uncertainty in Willow's life in *Bitter Herbs* (Crown, 1993). The genre of romance novels that had fueled her career as Cressida was in a slump, so she embarked on a monograph on former novelist, Gloria Grainger. Willow's investigation of Grainger's death coincided with her participation in a government committee investigating prison inmates. Clever medical detection exposed Grainger's killer. Self-examination made Willow aware that her fear of commitment was destroying her relationship with Tom Worth.

Marriage with Tom solved that problem and, during *Rotten Apples* (St. Martin, 1995), Willow settled midpoint between the demure repressed civil servant, Willow, and the flamboyant wealthy romance novelist, Cressida. She was recruited to investigate abuses of citizen rights by the Inland Revenue (comparable to the U.S. Internal Revenue Service). The staff at IR was hostile to any inference that their treatment of art historian Fiona Fydgett led to her suicide. Someone was determined to stall the investigation. The narrative ended with red herrings unresolved.

The Drowning Pool (St. Martin, 1997) a.k.a. *Fruiting Bodies*, opened with Willow in the hospital. Difficult as it was to give birth to her first child, she endured a dour midwife, agitating protestors outside the facility, medical complications, and the murder of Alexander Ringstead, her obstetrician. The arrival of Lucinda was greeted with delight by her parents, but Willow was required to remain in the hospital because of potential hemorrhaging. She intended to put that time to good use by interfering in the police investigation, but overdid it as usual.

Editor Jane Cleverholme had lingering doubts that *The Daily Mercury*, on which she worked, may have influenced the jury to convict an innocent man in *Sour Grapes* (St. Martin, 1998). She dealt with this concern by suggesting that graduate student in criminology Emma Gnatche, investigate the case as part of her thesis. Accountant Andrew Lutterworth had been sentenced to four years in prison for the hit-and-run death of a young mother and child. Although initially he insisted that his car had been stolen, he confessed to the incident; then recanted and said the confession was a response to police bullying. Emma wrote to her old friend Willow, seeking her insights and was invited for the weekend. They followed two lines of enquiry. Emma used technology, including a lie detector test. Willow researched the death of Philip, Andrew's fourteen-year-old son, and its impact on his wife, Jemima.

Cooper tapped an interesting vein of fantasy. Women leading everyday lives may well covet a second exciting existence. In reading Willow they can have one without risk. Her current series features English barrister Trish Maguire. (see this volume)

Lucy Kingsley

Author: Kate Charles a.k.a. Kate Chase

Lucy Kingsley, a divorced artist, closely connected to the Church of England, played an increasingly significant role in the series that featured attorney David Middleton-Brown. She lived in London, near to her beloved Victoria and Albert Museum. A strawberry blonde, her brief marriage as an art student to a faculty member had ceased to be important in her life. She had several short-term but unhappy relationships before she met David. She was very attracted to him, even when she learned that he had once had a homosexual affair.

David was an expert in religious antiquities. During *A Drink of Deadly Wine* (Mysterious Press, 1992), he was consulted by his former lover, Father Gabriel Neville, now happily married and under consideration for archdeacon. Neville was being blackmailed for a past affair, told to resign his position or be exposed. When the woman, believed to be the blackmailer, was killed, Lucy worked with David on the investigation.

By *The Snares of Death* (Mysterious, 1993) David was working with a London church. Rev. Robert Dexter, the new pastor of St. Mary, the Virgin, was determined to eradicate all papist elements in his new parish, in part by selling or destroying art works. He not only found serious opposition in the congregation but in his household and was murdered in the church. Lucy's involvement led her into danger, but moved their relationship further. David rescued her, and then wondered if he could have a successful long-term heterosexual relationship.

He and Lucy not only could but did, in *Appointed to Die* (Mysterious, 1994) when he temporarily moved into her London apartment. David was in the process of selling his prior home and establishing himself with a London firm. Lucy's father, Canon John Kingsley, had served at Malbury Cathedral so she could not reject a request to design the program cover for their Music Festival. However her visits to Malbury became entwined with the politics engendered by the controversial new Dean. When the death of distinguished cleric Canon Arthur Brydges-ffrench cast suspicion on all residents of the Close, Lucy called David.

Lucy and David were living together in *A Dead Man Out of Mind* (Mysterious, 1995), but found it too close for comfort when Lucy took in her disapproving niece. At the same time, both Lucy and David were involved in the problems of two city parishes both headed by the same pastor, but having difficulty retaining curates. Several murders and thefts of church silver brought Lucy and David on board in an official capacity. It took Lucy, David, Ruth (the fourteen-year-old niece), and old friends Gabriel and Emily Neville to work this out.

When it was time for David to move into the home he inherited, Lucy wanted separation to clarify their relationship as *Evil Angels Among Them* (Mysterious, 1996) began. Young Rev. Stephen Thorncroft and his new bride Becca had idealized the life they would lead in his new parish. She was soon disillusioned by obscene phone calls that she concealed from Stephen. Parish politics erupted when vacancies occurred among the lay leadership, causing Stephen to seek advice from David and Lucy. The death of social worker Flora Newall, who visited a lesbian mother about her daughter's welfare, was murder. The mother became the obvious suspect. Lucy and David unearthed several others whose secrets the social worker held, and a killer who wanted power.

Intriguing settings. Using a similar background, author Charles began a new series featuring curate Callie Anson

Sara Kingsley

Author: Anne Wilson

Sara Kingsley was the grandchild of Polish Jews on her father's side. Her maternal grandparents had died in Germany during World War II. She did not practice Judaism, but was proud of her heritage. She had been under great pressure by her father (now deceased) to achieve success. Her mother, still alive, was more concerned that Sara, divorced from her unfaithful husband David, was raising their children alone. Daughter Hannah attended elementary school. Son Jacob was enrolled in nursery school. Sara's degree was from the London

School of Economics, but she worked as a community counselor for the Acton Counseling Centre (partly funded by grants).

In *Truth or Dare* (Women's Press, London, 1995), Sara was portrayed as an unconventional heroine. She was a risk taker, exposing both herself and her children to harm. She had been unable to help either her friend Caroline Blythe or a later client who turned out to be James Blythe's mistress when they came to her for counseling. When Caroline died, presumably a suicide who injected herself with cocaine, Sara refused to believe her friend capable of killing herself or leaving her body to be found by her daughter. Sara threw caution to the wind, telling all suspects that she was probing into the matter. Predictably she became the next target.

Sara had both professional and personal problems in *Governing Bodies* (Women's Press, 1997). Mona Pearson, the black female principal of a school had been found standing over the corpse of Tony Thornley, a hostile member of the governing body, with a knife. At the very least, Sara and others wanted Mona to get a fair trial. Even Mona was unsure of her own innocence. On a personal level, Sara was betrayed by her own body, which evidenced a powerful desire for Pete Corelli, a twenty-three-year-old man who sought a personal relationship.

Kate Kinsella

Author: Christine Green

After Kate's father's death, her mother had moved to Australia for what Kate considered a "second childhood." Left alone, she upgraded her nursing skills, specializing in medical and nursing investigations. A single woman, whose police officer lover had been killed, she wanted a new career. Kate's top booster was funeral director Hubert Humberstone, above whose facility she had located her office. Hubert was a very inquisitive man, eager to share in the details of her investigations; a rather strange man, with a shoe fetish and attachments to unusual women. Kate was slightly shorter than the average Englishwoman, and had greenish blue eyes.

As *Deadly Errand* (Walker, 1992) began, Kate was contacted by Nina Marburg who rejected the police conclusion that the murder of her niece Jacky on the hospital grounds was a random killing. Kate had chosen to work only in medically related private investigations, but this was close enough, as she needed work. She went on staff at Riverview Medical Center because she decided that only undercover work at the facility could substantiate her judgment that an employee had killed Jacky.

In *Deadly Admirer* (Walker, 1992), Kate worked in the emergency room at Longborough General Hospital where district nurse Vanessa Wootten was treated for a drug overdose. Wootten not only wanted Kate's nursing skills, but her services as a detective. Someone had been following her and she feared for her life. Kate with the assistance of Humberstone and vicar's son Christopher Collicot saved Vanessa from the police and a killer.

Kate's arm's length relationship with Hubert became somewhat closer in *Deadly Practice* (Walker, 1995), although not romantic. When she was broke he helped her find work as a nurse and as an investigator. After her assignment turned dangerous, he abetted her in a burglary, and bailed her out when she was caught. In order to investigate the death of nurse Jenny Martin, Kate accepted a job at Riverview Medical Facility where she became embroiled in the politics and family dynamics of the staff. The police had been willing to blame Jenny's murder on a local delinquent, but Kate found a alternate suspect.

Kate journeyed to the Isle of Wight during *Deadly Partners* (Walker, 1996), at the request of elderly Elizabeth Forrester, seeking to find Nigel, a nephew who co-owned a hotel there. En route Kate met Caroline Uxton, who was eager to join in the search. When Caroline was discovered dead in the missing man's cabin, Kate concentrated on the connections between Caroline and Nigel. She had to because unfriendly DCI Formbridge considered her a major suspect.

Kate had returned from a yearlong sojourn in New Zealand by *Deadly Bond* (Severn House, 2001). Hubert Humberstone had gone to great lengths to update her office décor and equipment. He believed that she had to expand her practice beyond the medical to general investigations. Within days she had been hired to protect Lorraine Farnforth, a potential murder witness. Unfortunately for her reputation Lorraine was killed while Kate slept in the adjacent room. Kate's return was followed by a visit from her mother Marilyn, a coquette even in her fifties. She matched well with Hubert.

All of Kate's nursing skills, limited as they now were, came in handy during *Deadly Echo* (Severn House, 2002). She rescued Megan Thomas, a new mother who had been impregnated after drinking a drug-laced beverage. The conspiracy to merchandise infants born to naïve young women was too valuable for the criminals to allow Kate to reveal their crimes.

Kate hadn't had any cases more challenging than "maritals" recently but, in *Deadly Choice* (Severn House, 2004), she was not sure that she wanted to get involved with Helen Woods' problems, Helen, whom Kate barely remembered from their school days, was living at Tamberlake, a "haunted " house. Her fiancé, Paul Warrinder whose family owned the home, traveled a lot, leaving Helen there alone. Eventually Kate agreed to visit. Within days she discovered good reasons for Helen's concerns.

By *Deadly Night* (Severn House, 2005) Kate had tired of being a private investigator. No wonder. Her discovery when helping Hubert that the corpse of 92-year-old Ivy Waites showed signs of rape was just the beginning. The inside information that Alvira Trees had also been raped could not be followed up on, because Alvira refused to talk to Kate and Hubert or the police. Young Zoe Burrows was murdered in her family's garden shed. Additional murders, rapes, and a disappearance continued, as the list of suspects burgeoned until a bizarre ending.

Victoria Decker-White hired Kate to go undercover in Fair Acres Private Hospital during *Deadly Web* (Severn House, 2005) Her husband Rupert died after eating a peanut concealed in a canapé at the hospital's New Year's Eve party. Staff had been warned to avoid peanuts as ingredients. Victoria, an administrator on leave from Fair Acres, arranged for Kate's employment as an aide.

Hubert meant nothing but the best for Kate in *Deadly Retreat* (Severn House, 2007) when he arranged for a three-week stay at Peace Haven in Wales. He may have been unaware that it was the preparation house for persons in the Witness Protection Program. Although Kate's stay was short, it was long enough to involve her in Fran Rowley's life. Fran, formerly a successful solicitor, had pleaded guilty to the charge of smothering her two-year-old son, Ben. Her only friend Malcolm Talgarth was a former co-worker. There seemed to be no one else who could have killed the child. First Kate convinced herself that Fran was innocent; then, she had to convince Fran.

Author Christine Green has two other series: one featuring Fran Wilson (elsewhere in this volume) and a new series featuring D.I. Thomas Rydell and Denise Caldicote

Fran Tremaine Kirk

Author: Ruthe Furie

Fran Tremaine Kirk, a tall redhead, escaped from her marriage to private investigator Dick Kirk, with her life and a badly maimed dog. Kirk had been physically abusive, and divorce did not end his harassment. During *If Looks Could Kill* (Avon, 1995), Fran abandoned her car when Dick attacked her. Returning with police support, she found him dead. Dick's mother blamed Fran for the death. Although she received Dick's life insurance, Fran needed work to survive emotionally and financially. Her new employer William Lighfoot combined a Buffalo private detective agency with a dating service (call girls) and suspect catalog sales. Fran needed her survival skills and her experience working in Dick's agency to investigate arson, robbery, and murder.

A trip to Europe with Dick's mother, Marsha, was the setting for *A Deadly Pâté* (Avon, 1996). Their relationship had been brittle, but they worked together when Marsha's sister, Annee was accused of the murder of her philandering French husband. There were inventive touches and an incredible solution.

A Natural Death (Avon, 1996) brought stability to Fran's life through a romance with Detective Ted Zwiatek. However, she put her love life on hold to investigate contrived murders at an organic farm, the motives for which were hidden under a patina of family togetherness.

The narratives became more compelling over the series.

Kirsten

Author: David J. Walker

Kirsten and her husband attorney Dugan, worked together in Wild Onion, Limited. Her skills as a private investigator were based upon her relentless and sometimes reckless style. Kirsten's deceased father had been a police officer. She had followed in his footsteps, but was unable to deal with the structure. A stint in a large security firm was also too restrictive for her. She professed a dislike for violence, but occasionally resorted to it. Her decision to retain her maiden name was symptomatic of her need to be independent—financially and personally—from anyone. That left it unclear as to how she paid her office rent as she spent much of her time on cases that never paid off. Dugan had attended law school while a member of the police force.

In *A Ticket To Die For* (St. Martin, 1998), Kirsten set out to find and get a statement from Lynn Bulasik, a missing witness for sleazy attorney Larry Candle, only to find Lynn dead in the adult bookstore where she worked. Kirsten recruited Dugan in an effort to track down a second possible witness, but outpaced him, as she stole keys, burglarized offices, and risked assault, battery and rape. The narrative was split into segments relating to Kirsten, Dugan, and Rita (one of Larry Candle's clients) but at the cost of losing tension.

Eudora Ragsdale, the African-American mother of twin daughters, devoted considerable time and effort to fighting entrepreneur John Michael Hurley's plan to replace Emerald Woods with a shopping mall. In *The End of Emerald Woods* (St. Martin, 2000), she became the victim of a campaign to damage her reputation. Larry Candle referred Eudora to Kirsten and Dugan when she was arrested for embezzlement. Four subsequent murders made it clear that the vendetta against Eudora was of a personal nature. Kirsten manipulated a conclusion that protected both Eudora and Emerald Woods. Coral, a ten-year-old neighbor girl, became part of the solution.

In *A Beer at a Bawdy House* (St. Martin, 2000), Bishop Peter Keegan sought help from Kirsten. Only in bits and pieces did Keegan reveal the incident that made him a target for blackmail. Only gradually did the role of his brother, Police Chief Walter Keegan, emerge. Kirsten and Dugan enlisted ex-cop Cuffs Radovich in the investigation, which dealt with a quartet of murders.

Kirsten's uncle Mike had been very special for her in the old days, the one she went to for help, but in *All the Dead Fathers* (St. Martin, 2005), it was Mike, now a defrocked priest, who needed help. He had a sexual relationship decades ago with a seventeen-year-old girl who came to him for counseling. The girl died; the family was paid off, but neither Dugan (who had defended Mike on the civil case) or Kirsten ever felt the same about Michael. After the Sun-Times published a list of 18 former priests charged with sexual abuse, the murders and mutilation began. Many of the priests were housed in a residence on a Catholic college campus. Kristen hired Cuffs Radovich to assist in security at the priests' house. This got even more serious when Dugan was abducted.

Walker also has a series featuring ex-attorney, private investigator Malachy Foley.

Next: *Too Many Clients* (2010)

Amanda Knight

Author: Margot J. Fromer

Amanda Knight, the director of nursing at JFK Hospital in Georgetown and the wife of businessman Ken James should have been a happy woman. Instead, she came across as self-centered and judgmental; a tyrant, intolerant of the slightest error in her subordinates.

In *Scalpel's Edge* (Diamond, 1991), libidinous Dr. Leo McBride was found with a scalpel in his trachea. Amanda, and eventually Lt. Paul Bandman, realized that his death had not occurred as a result of the incision but from some obscure source. The investigation took on international aspects before it ended.

Amanda was loyal to her friends. She shared a supportive friendship with gay Dr. Eddie Silverman, who assisted her in her investigations. In *Night Shift* (Diamond, 1993), diagnostician Aaron Zurman was murdered at JFK Hospital. His was only the first death in the highly regarded transplant unit. The reader was made aware that a trio of killers were involved in the death. Ken, Amanda's husband, rescued her when her efforts to protect the reputation of the hospital became dangerous.

Michelle "Micky" Knight

Author: J. M. Redmann

Micky Knight was a New Orleans private investigator, not overburdened by scruples. Life had dealt her a series of tragic blows. Her mother, when a pregnant teenager, had married Lee Robedeaux, an older man who was not the father. When Micky was five, her mother left, but wrote regularly. Lee had been a good father to Micky, but he died when she was ten, leaving her to the cruel ministrations of Aunt Greta. Uncle Claude, her husband, had never taken part in his wife's mental and physical abuse of Micky, but he ignored it. Bayard, their older son, had sexually abused Micky almost from the time she arrived until she ran away at eighteen. The letters and cards from her mother had ended when Micky moved in with Uncle Claude and Aunt Greta. Micky's letters were returned. Emma Auerbach, a rich older woman who had asked nothing in return, subsidized Micky's education as she had those of other young women.

Micky went to college in New York City where her mother had lived but found no trace of her. The third Robedeaux brother, Charlie and his wife Lottie had been supportive, offering a refuge to Micky. Their son, Torbin, had understood. He, too, was homosexual, even more blatantly so, becoming a drag queen in his adult life. Although Micky was aware that her mother was of Greek heritage, she had no idea who her father was, not even whether her dark skin and hair indicated an African-American lineage. When she reached adulthood, she changed her name from Robedeaux to Knight. The possibility that her mother was still alive had not been a priority. For a period of time during her twenties, Micky had been promiscuous. Frequently characters in the narratives were former lovers. She had problems with alcohol.

Realizing that client Karen Holloway had manipulated her, Micky seduced her and ruined her reputation with her grandfather, causing her to be disinherited. During *Death by the Riverside* (New Victoria, 1990), she had continued contacts with the Holloways of One Hundred Oaks. She went underground for the local police who suspected that the property was being used as a dispersal site for drugs. After serious revelations as to her complicity in murder, Micky fell in love with Dr. Cordelia James.

In *Deaths of Jocasta* (New Victoria, 1992), Micky provided security for Emma Auerbach's annual party for gays and lesbians. Among the guests was Micky's former lover Cordelia, the woman she considered the love of her life, but with whom she had had little recent contact. During the evening the body of Vicky Williams, who had bled to death after a botched abortion, was discovered in the nearby woods. Cordelia contacted Micky professionally because she was receiving abusive phone calls and faxes. She needed her even more when a second corpse was found in the clinic at a time when only Cordelia was working. Pro-life protestors were picketing the clinic. That's where Micky looked first for her suspects.

In *The Intersection of Law and Desire* (Norton, 1995), Karen, Cordelia's manipulative cousin, convinced Micky to help her cope with a blackmailer. The investigation intersected with Micky's concern about the daughter of a friend who had become depressed. Motivated by the abuse that she had suffered as a young girl, Micky cooperated with the police. This was an emotionally charged narrative.

Attempts by a mother to find her lesbian daughter whom she had rejected because of her lifestyle, and a young man's search for his birthmother in *Lost Daughters* (Norton, 1999) motivated Micky to seek her own parents. Although she was preoccupied by a series of deaths and disappearances of young women, several of whom were clients of Cordelia, Micky followed her personal quest to a surprising outcome.

The series contained considerable explicit sexual material.

Next: *Death of a Dying Man* (2009); *Watermark* (2010)

Deborah Knott

Author: Margaret Maron

Deborah Knott's family was from the old South. The Knotts had been in North Carolina since the 1700s, if not always in a distinguished capacity. Her father Kezzie was best known for the quality of his bootleg liquor. After being sent to prison on income tax evasion, he returned to his tobacco farm. A room at the farm was reserved for Deborah, a sandy-haired blonde with blue eyes. She had left home when her mother died, to live with her Aunt Zell and Uncle Ash. Deborah's mother had been Kezzie Knott's second wife, but she raised his sons, had more of her own, and a daughter, Deborah, then she died of cancer. After Deborah graduated from West Colleton High School, she attended college and law school before returning to Cotton Grove, Colleton County to practice law. Her first appearance was in a short story that won an Agatha award.

In *Bootlegger's Daughter* (Mysterious Press, 1992), young Gayle Whitehead for whom Deborah had babysat needed help. She and her mother had disappeared from the family home eighteen years before. Later Gayle had been found alive, her mother dead. Deborah uncovered the scandal behind the death. Unfortunately she lost her campaign for county judge.

With considerable support from her father, Deborah was appointed judge in *Southern Discomfort* (Mysterious, 1993). She and her niece, Annie Sue, helped WomenAid to construct low cost homes for single mothers. Coming late in the evening to the site, Deborah found Annie Sue naked and semi-conscious, claiming that the building inspector had tried to rape her. Later the inspector's body was discovered with his head knocked in, making Annie Sue a murder suspect.

Deborah moved into a summer home on Harker's Island while she worked as a substitute judge in *Shooting at Loons* (Mysterious, 1994). On a leisurely boat excursion, Deborah discovered the body of Andy Bynum, a leader in the Independent Fisherman's Alliance. Her investigation forced her to examine her responsibilities as a judge. At a lonely time in Deborah's life, she met attractive conservation warden Kidd Chapin.

In *Up Jumps the Devil* (Mysterious, 1996), Chapin visited Deborah in Colleton County, as did Allen Stancil, with whom she had shared a short-term marriage. Allen's cousin and uncle were murdered under circumstances that made him a suspect. As much as Deborah wanted to forget she had ever loved Allen, she did not believe him a killer. Deborah, her dad, and her brothers, wrestled with the encroachment of developers on the land they loved.

While acting as a substitute judge in High Point, North Carolina during *Killer Market* (Mysterious, 1997), Deborah visited the massive furniture market. The event had attracted so many visitors that Deborah could find no place to stay. Matilda Jernigan, a mysterious older woman, befriended Deborah and drew her into the complex professional and personal relationships among furniture designers, manufacturers, and merchandisers. The death of Chan Nolan, an attractive executive, had personal implications for Deborah. She had not been as intimate as he claimed, but he was part of her early past. Even her lofty position did not protect Deborah from suspicion of murder.

Seventeen-year-old A.K., son of Deb's half-brother Andrew, was already in trouble as *Home Fires* (Mysterious Press, 1998) began. A.K. hung around with two high school dropouts. Deb was horrified to learn that they were responsible for bigoted graffiti and vandalism in a local cemetery. All three had been charged with vandalism and convicted. Assistant District Attorney Cylvia De Graffenried, an African-American, thought the sentence of weekends in jail was too lenient. The anti-African-American venom went far beyond the graffiti. Two African-American churches were torched, in one of which a body was discovered. Fortunately A. K. had solid alibis for several of the events. Out of town activists became involved. The conflicts between Cylvia and Deborah personalized local feelings.

The pace of *Storm Track* (Mysterious Press, 2000) mimicked that of oncoming Hurricane Fran, building slowly: Deborah's warm encompassing family (readers may need the chart to keep track); the tension between African-American pastor Ralph Freeman and Clara, his rigid wife; the chronic infidelity of attorney Jason Bullock's wife, Lynn. As the storm menaced Colleton County, the human pressures increased in intensity: theft, blackmail, murder. Some of the personal damages were irreparable.

Out of the red clay of North Carolina's pottery industry, Maron fashioned another narrative that explored family dynamics in *Uncommon Clay* (Mysterious, 2001). Although Deborah was unceremoniously (and with great humiliation) dumped by game warden Kidd Chapin, she had a supportive family. Amos Nordan, patriarch of an intergenerational family and pottery business, saw his heritage dwindle as his sons died mysteriously. Deborah, who had been assigned temporarily to the local court, saw red as Amos' grandsons became targets.

The carnival came to town in *Slow Dollar* (Mysterious Press, 2002) bringing back memories from Deb's childhood. She had already met Tally Ames of Ames Amusement, when she appeared as plaintiff in Deb's court. They bonded quickly so when Tally's older son Braz was murdered, Deb took a special interest. This was a fascinating rendition of carney life (note the glossary) and of the strong ties that bound the Knott family together. A terrific narrative

The excitement generated by the news that Deborah and Deputy Dwight Bryant were engaged in *High Country Fall* (Mysterious Press, 2004) was so disturbing to Deborah that she accepted a week-long assignment as a relief judge in the North Carolina hill country. She and Dwight had settled for a marriage based on friendship and good sex, but she wondered if that would be enough. Deborah bound over young Danny Freeman for trial in the murder of gerontologist Dr. Carlyle Ledwig. Deb's cousins, twins May and June, stoutly defended Danny and looked for an alternative suspect. A second allied murder convinced Deborah that the twins might be right. She learned a lot about herself and Dwight during the week.

Keeping their potential professional conflicts of interest at bay posed problems for Dwight and Deb in *Rituals of the Season* (Mysterious Press, 2005). When bright ambitious Asst. District Attorney Tracy Johnson was assassinated while driving her daughter to a medical appointment, several possible motives emerged. Deb was at the edges of Dwight's investigation, but played a strong role in determining whether or not Martha Hurst, now on Death Row for murder, was really the killer of her stepson.

Winter's Child (Mysterious Press, 2006) was more Dwight's book than Deb's. They'd been married only a month when he visited his eight-year-old son Cal in Sharpsville where Cal lived with his mother, Jonna. Dwight had married Jonna on the rebound when he felt that Deborah could never love him. Within hours of Dwight's arrival in Sharpsville, Jonna and Cal disappeared. Jonna's corpse was discovered later in her car. Deborah joined Dwight in his search for his son. Deborah used her computer skills to discover the motivation for Jonna's death. Together they reopened an earlier case of murder which, had connections to Colleton County.

The narrative's warm depiction of Deb and Dwight working with love to include his eight-year-old son Cal into their new marriage in *Hard Row* (Warner, 2007) was balanced against a chilling murder investigation. The discovery of body parts along a highway initially provided no clues as to the victim's identity. Gradually information provided an answer but the killer's motive did not emerge until later. Meanwhile owners of acreage formerly planted with tobacco were turning to other crops. Mexican laborers were doing much of the fieldwork. Not everyone welcomed their presence. Engrossing.

Candace Bradshaw came from a dirt-poor dysfunctional family, determined to make something of herself as *Death's Half Acre* (Grand Central Publishing, 2008) began. Hard work and marriage to her older employer Cameron, head of Bradshaw Management, led to a position as chairman of the County Board of Commissioners. Her murder, initially assumed to be suicide, opened a kettle of worms because Candace had misused her position to her own profit. Her estranged husband, Cameron, and their spoiled daughter, Dee, struggled to get the family business and their personal lives under control. It was Dwight's case but Deb needed to locate Candace's secret cache of information before anyone else did. Kezzie was busy with an interesting scam of his own.

The motivations were credible, the plots were complex, and the characters were delightful. Author Margaret Maron raised her skill level and her popularity even higher than in the Sigrid Harald series. Both Deborah (four short stories) and Sigrid (two) were featured in *Shoveling Smoke* (Crippen & Landru, 1997). Deborah appeared in other short story anthologies. Next: *Sand Sharks* (2009); *Christmas Morning* (2010)

Sgt. Kathy Kolla

Author: Barry Maitland

Kathy Kolla's life changed when her father, a government official, ran his car into a bridge, ending his life before his improprieties could be revealed. At fourteen, she and her mother moved in with her left-wing Uncle Tom until they could get welfare help. Within two years, Kathy's mom, a victim of depression, had also died. She set her sights on a career in the London police force and had risen to the rank of sergeant when the series began.

Kathy was awed by the opportunity to work with Detective Chief Inspector David Brock on the death of Meredith Winterbottom, an elderly woman who lived in an ethnic London neighborhood as *The Marx Sisters* (Hamish Hamilton, London 1994) began. Meredith was one of three sisters who occupied a residence in Jerusalem Lane, an area coveted by developers. One after another, small shopkeepers had sold out to the real estate interests, but Meredith, who owned the house, had resisted. The case languished and was closed. When another of the sisters was clearly murdered, Brock requested Kathy as his assistant again. For personal reasons, she was unsure she wanted to rejoin his team. Together they explored the character of the neighborhood, its connections with Karl Marx, who had lived there, and the risk to the surviving sister.

Sgt. Kolla's transfer for training in a provincial force during *The Malcontenta* (Penguin, 1995) had disastrous results. Initially she had been assigned only juvenile and domestic cases by hostile supervisor, Detective Inspector Ric Tanner. When put in charge of a high profile case, the death of Alex Petrou, a staff member at the pricey Stanhope Clinic, the lack of support from Stanhope director Stephen Beamish-Newell and Tanner caused Kathy to go beyond her authority. When DCI Brock, came to her rescue, both were severely disciplined. Their efforts to uncover the powerful individuals involved in a cover-up were met with violence.

The murder of Angela Hannaford in *All My Enemies* (Penguin, 1996) was tied to similar crimes involving an amateur dramatic society (SADOS). Brock was preoccupied with setting up a new unit at headquarters. Kathy found substitute allies in initially hostile Indian Det. Sgt. Leon Desai, who coordinated the gathering of physical evidence, and in her troubled Aunt Mary, who went undercover at the theatre as a seamstress. There were some bizarre connections in the narrative, tying murder to drama. Leon Desai and Kathy later became lovers.

Kathy's belief in Brock's integrity sustained her during *The Chalon Heads* (Allen & Unwin, London, 1999) when he was suspended for theft of a valuable stamp. Even when reassigned to the Fraud unit where she aided an investigation into kidnapping, murder, and forged postage stamps, Kathy was determined to prove Brock innocent. A complex narrative that demanded the full attention of the reader.

The fact that his long time nemesis, Greg "Upper" North, had been seen at the new mammoth mall was enough to send Chief Inspector Brock there in *Silvermeadow* (Orion, 2000). However, he and Sgt. Kolla were diverted into the disappearance and then discovery of the body of young Kerri Vlasich, a part-time worker at the mall. Brock and Kolla's work was hampered by the local police and the reluctance of the mall management to have unfavorable publicity. The possibilities of other such disappearances, of drug dealing in which mall staff was involved, and a daring robbery kept the tension high. Kathy's relationship with Scene of the Crime investigator Leon Desai was woven into the narrative.

In *Babel* (Orion, 2002), Kathy and Brock dealt in changes in their community. It was not only the cultural differences that accompanied an influx of immigrants, but also the disparity between those promoting scientific advances and the reaction against the disciplines imposed by changes in society. Against this background a weary unsettled Kathy, considering retirement, rallied to help Brock and his unit in the investigation as to who murdered philosophy professor Max Springer.

Brock and Sgt Kolla were assigned to take over an investigation that had been on-going for months in *The Verge Practice* (Allen & Unwin, 2003). Charles Verge had disappeared shortly after his second wife Miki was murdered. There was some evidence that he had died. His imperious mother Madelaine insisted that Charles had been murdered and framed. He was a prominent architect, but according to his first wife Gail, Charles had seemed different lately. The death of rival architect Sandy Clarke complicated matters, but a confession provided a simple solution to the case, one approved by the authorities. It did not suit either Brock or Kolla however.

Whatever private life Kathy or Brock had before the disappearance of six-year-old Tracey Rudd was put aside as *No Trace* (Allen & Unwin, 2004) progressed. Tracey was the third young girl to disappear from the Northcote Square area. She was the child of nouveau artist Gabe Rudd, who transformed the crises in his life into art, lucratively in the case of his deceased wife, Jane. Kathy and Brock after distinguishing Tracey from the two prior victims were obsessed with finding her still alive. The suspects included not only erratic artists and dealers, but also Sir Jack Beaufort, head of a commission currently investigating "police efficiency". At this point, both Kathy and Brock had no life beyond their work.

Kathy and Brock were assigned to investigate the murders of two teenage delinquents in *Spider Trap* (St. Martin, 2007) but, in the process, the skeletons of three black men were discovered nearby. One skull was missing. MP Michael Grant blamed crime in the South London district he represented, not on fellow Jamaicans, but on the family of Spider Roach. Roach had moved out of the Cockpit Lane area and become gentrified. It became clear the he might be responsible for all five murders, but legal maneuvering, turf protection by criminal justice organizations, and CYA attitude by Brock's supervisor stifled the investigation. Two men who had been important in Kathy's life; Attorney Martin Connell, who represented the Roach family, and Tom Reeves, Special Branch investigator, played major roles in the narrative.

A compelling series. Coming : *Dark Mirror* (2009) *All My Enemies*(2009)

Leigh Koslow

Author: Edie Claire

Even though Leigh Koslow was temporarily unemployed in the first narrative, she refused to return to her parents' home. Leigh's mother, Frances Morton Koslow, was far more overbearing than her twin sister, Lydie. Each of the sisters had a single daughter. Leigh and Cara, Lydie's daughter, had a close relationship. Leigh's father, Randall Koslow, was a veterinarian in Avalon, a suburban area of Pittsburgh, Pennsylvania where the family lived. In her youth, Leigh had helped out at his animal clinic, but chose to study journalism at the University of Pittsburgh. She owned a black Persian cat, Mao Tse, and a pair of caged finches. Leigh's career had been as a copywriter for an advertising agency but these were tough times in the business. She had been let go as a result of mergers, bankruptcy, and cutbacks on three separate occasions. Edging up to thirty she did not want to become dependent on her parents' hospitality. Leigh's two closest friends during college, detective Maura (Mo) Polanski, and budding politician Warren Harmon, continued to play roles in her life.

In *Never Buried* (Signet, 1999), Leigh had an opportunity to meet her own needs and help Cara at the same time. Cara's husband Gil was in Japan on business while she was in the final months of her first pregnancy. They had purchased a home in Avalon, but only recently occupied it. Leigh moved in to offer Cara companionship while she polished up her resume. The house had a tragic history. The discovery of an embalmed corpse in the back yard, threats, and an arson attempt made it clear that someone wanted the women to abandon the house. Mo Polanski lent a hand until she too had family problems.

The new advertising agency partnership among Leigh and former associates at her prior job was working well, but not making enough money for Leigh to live on during *Never Sorry* (Signet, 1999). Utilizing the skills she had learned helping her dad in his veterinary office, she took a part-time job at the zoo. She was delighted to assist Dr. Mike Tanner, the zoo veterinarian on whom she'd had a teenage crush when he apprenticed with her dad. Her attachment to Mike added motive to the charges of murder against Leigh when cat keeper, Carmen Kaslow, was killed. Carmen, one of the women connected to Mike since his divorce, had been a problem for Leigh since high school days. The help of attractive female attorney Katherine Bowser was a blessing and a curse. Warren Harmon found her very attractive.

The third Morton sister, Bess Cogley, had always been a special favorite of Leigh's. Aunt Bess faced a quandary in *Never Preach Past Noon* (Signet, 2000). She was deeply devoted to her new church, The First Church of the New

Millennium, but believed the pastor, Rev. Reginald Humphrey might be a con man. Humphrey's disappearance, the discovery of his corpse by Leigh and the arrival of Noel, Humphrey's glib missionary wife, raised new problems. There were secrets within the church that needed to be exposed, but others that were best left hidden. Warren, whose uncle was arrested for the murder, reassessed his feelings for Leigh just in time.

Warren and Leigh had married by *Never Kissed Goodnight* (Signet, 2001), but he was too busy running for the Pittsburgh City Council to monitor her activities. Cara March, Leigh's cousin, had never met her father, Mason Dublin who had left her mother before Cara was born. The appearance of Cara and her wealthy husband Gil on a national television program *Movers and Shakers* brought Mason back into Cara's life in a terrifying manner. Mason may not have been a perfect husband and father, but he wanted to protect Cara and her son even if it cost his life.

Only the flimsy excuse that she was protecting her father, veterinarian Randall Koslow, allowed Leigh to get involved in the affairs of wealthy Lilah Murchison in *Never Tease a Siamese* (Signet, 2002). True Lilah's cat held the key to the identity of the child she had given away. Also true, threats were being made against persons at the veterinary clinic. Lilah had purportedly died in a plane crash and her new will left the bulk of her estate to an unidentified "real" child. This news was hard on her adopted and greedy son, Dean, but created a variety of suspects for the murders.

The series featured complex plots usually centering on members of the heroine's family.

Loretta Kovacs

Author: Anthony Bruno

Loretta Kovacs was another female sleuth who was constantly trying to live up to her father's expectations. She was not svelte and trim, and constantly fought her attraction for sweets. Her dad was an attorney, as was her only sister, but Loretta had chosen social work. Although she earned a Master's Degree in Social Work at Columbia, her career had been one crisis after another. She bungled a job as assistant warden at a prison, failed as a staff counselor, and as a parole officer. Loretta had lost her nerve when terrorized by female prison inmates and could not pull her life together. Hanging on to tenure in the New Jersey Department of Corrections, she was relegated to the "jump squad" to retrieve parole violators. Julius Monroe, her new supervisor, reading her record, had little hope that Loretta would succeed, but reluctantly agreed to give her a one-week tryout. The good news was the assignment to work with tough Frank Marvelli; the bad news was that they had to locate and return an adept con woman.

Loretta had been terrified when she entered the "jump squad" office in *Devil's Food* (Forge, 1997). The tryout week sent her and Marvelli on the trail of devious Martha Lee Spooner, an employee of Weight Away, a "fat farm."

Marvelli was preoccupied with his seriously ill wife, so Loretta improvised. She was pitted against a biker hired to kill Martha Lee, with whom she had established rapport. Both had weight problems.

Marvelli's wife had died by *Double Espresso* (Forge, 1998). Loretta felt free to improve their relationship when they were assigned to bring in Sammy Teitlebaum, a hired gun who just happened to be Marvelli's brother-in-law. Sammy had an assignment of his own, to locate and kill Gus Rispoli, who snitched on gangster Taffy DeMaggio. The race was on. Loretta and Marvelli needed to locate My Blue Heaven, the special prison where Rispoli was confined, before Sammy did. They were kept busy, unable to separate their allies from their enemies, but muddled through. After seeing the buxom Loretta dressed up to divert Taffy, Frank became aware of her charms.

If "kinky" is a reader's favorite flavor, *Hot Fudge* (Forge, 2000) will satisfy the appetite. The search for Ira Krupnuk, parole jumper and master criminal, teamed Marvelli with Vissa Mylowe, a voluptuous female parole officer. Loretta reacted by following the pair to San Francisco where Ira, under a new identity, was ensconced as a partner in a prosperous ice cream company. From there on the diversions took over, dominating the humor and warmth that had enhanced the two prior narratives.

Interesting premise and pairing with Marvelli. Bruno had another series with two male protagonists, Bert Gibbons and Mike Tozzi.

Thea Kozak

Author: Kate Flora

Thea Kozak, a tall dark-haired woman in her late twenties, had tried social work and journalism before she became a Boston-based educational consultant to private schools. She and her employer (later business partner) Suzanne Begner, advised schools on how to attract more and better students. The death of David, Thea's husband, in a car accident had devastated her personal life, but she remained close to her family.

Thea's sister Carrie, blonde and petite, had been adopted by her parents, but never felt completely at home. She bore no physical resemblance to her adopted family, and wanted to find her birth parents. As *Chosen for Death* (Forge, 1994) opened, Carrie, then working as a waitress in Camden, Maine, was killed during a sexual assault. State police investigator Andre Lemieux was unable to break into the defensive silence of Carrie's family, until Thea helped. When she visited Camden to clear up Carrie's affairs, she discovered a second family who wanted their secrets kept. Still unable to handle David's death, she avoided a commitment to Andre.

In *Death in a Funhouse Mirror* (Forge, 1995), Thea offered her sympathies to Eve, her college roommate, whose mother had been viciously murdered while walking a dog. A complex narrative explored the distortions and differences between Thea's view of Eve, her multi-faceted mother, and her father, who might be a killer. A subplot concerned Thea's role as partner in the firm, when a disgruntled female employee accused her of sexual harassment.

There were problems at work during *Death at the Wheel* (Forge, 1996). Pressure from Linda, Thea's mother, caused her to focus her attention elsewhere. Julie Bass, a vulnerable young woman who reminded both Linda and Thea of Carrie, was accused of murdering her husband. Thea exposed herself to multiple injuries to find the real killer; then was jolted by a crisis that caused her to reassess her priorities. The plan of Andre Lemieux and Thea to live together faltered.

As *An Educated Death* (Forge, 1997) began, Thea believed she had broken through Andre's depression. The healing was put on hold when Thea was called to address an emergency situation at Bucksport School. Laney Taggert, a pregnant student, had ventured out during the night onto thin ice and drowned. What headmistress Dorrie Chapin wanted was advice on how to handle the situation with students and parents. Others on staff believed Thea was hired to solve a murder. Her investigation was invasive enough to provoke an attempt to kill Thea. Andre wanted her to back off and let the police handle the matter. She expected him to understand that she took her responsibilities as seriously as he did.

NAGS was the unpleasant acronym for the National Association of Girl's Schools, meeting in Hawaii during *Death in Paradise* (Forge, 1998), but there was a considerable amount of dissension. Thea, not feeling well at all, was on the Board of Directors and was a speaker at the conference. She was not the only one who found director Martina Pullman overbearing, but she was a primary suspect when Martina was murdered. Rory Altschuler, Martina's assistant who had alerted Thea that Martina was missing, became a major part of the puzzle. Without her usual support from Andre, Thea received help from "kid spy" Laura Mitchell, and good advice from Ed and Marie Pryzinski as to her personal life.

Andre was thrilled at the prospect of fatherhood, eager to marry Thea, but in *Liberty or Death* (Forge, 2003) he was prevented from doing so. A right-wing militia group took him hostage as he was en route to the wedding ceremony. They demanded the release from prison of Jed Harding, a former Vietnam veteran. Pregnant or not, Thea could not stay out of the action. She went undercover in Harding's hometown of Merchantville, Maine, as an abused wife. Merchantville served as the headquarters for the Katahdin Constitutional Militia. Her efforts to locate where Andre might be held, eventually drew the attention of the KCM. A taut poignant narrative.

Thea and Andre were enjoying marital bliss in *Stalking Death* (Crum Creek Press, 2008) when Suzanne, her partner in EDGE, called. St.Matthew's, an elite New Hampshire prep school, was in crisis mode and needed advice. Shondra Jones, a sixteen-year-old scholarship student, claimed that she was being stalked. Headmaster Todd Chambers insisted that her allegations were unfounded, particularly since they targeted Alisdair MacGregor, grandson of a major donor to a new building on campus. Only Jamison, Shondra's older brother (also a student there) and a few teammates believed Shondra....until Thea arrived. A compelling story although it was hard to believe that so many corrupt or evil persons were to be found in a small isolated community.

Flora has begun a new series featuring Joe Burgess.

Merry Kramer

Author: Gale G. Roper

After four years, living with her family in Pittsburgh and vainly hoping that her current boyfriend Jack Hamilton would propose, Merry (formerly Merrileigh) moved to Amhearst where she found work as a reporter on *The News.* She moved into one of four units in a carriage house and became affiliated with the local church and their bell choir. Merry was very devout, read a chapter of the Bible every night. She had one brother, Sam who was a student at Penn State. The apartment was shared with a cat, Whiskers, which she acquired from the local animal shelter.

Merry had only been in Amhearst three months, when, in *Caught in the Middle* (Zondervan, 1997), she found Patrick Marten's body in the trunk of her car. It had been a tough day. She had to leave her car at the garage where Patrick worked so it could be inspected. By the time she picked it up to attend a night meeting, a storm was brewing. Driving home, she swerved to avoid a car and almost hit a pedestrian. The subsequent death of attorney Trudy McGilpin, the local mayor, was followed by shots at Merry and her new friend artist Curt Carlyle in the church parking lot. Trudy's death did not seem to be connected so there could be two killers out there.

Jolene, the secretary at *The News*, was an enigma to Merry in *Caught in the Act* (Zondervan, 1998 She had separated from her husband, Arnie, because of "irreconcilable difference" aka infidelity. Yet, she seemed stunned when she found Arnie dead. Merry was busy with a story on "His House", a refuge for girls in trouble, during which she brought together a youthful mother and a childless couple. Still Merry found time to seek out Arnie's killer. It was a good thing she was busy because Jack Hamilton had temporarily moved to Amhearst and was complicating Merry's romance with Curt Carlyle.

Staff at *The News* continued to get personally involved in criminal activities during *Caught in a Bind* (Zondervan, 2000). Family page editor Edie Whatley was devastated when her husband Tom disappeared under suspicious circumstances. Her fifteen-year-old son Randy was more disturbed when a bloody corpse was discovered in the classic car destined to be his birthday present. Warmth and compassion about the plight of women who had been abused by spouses enriched the narrative. Merry continued to take risks without backup, but artist Curt Carlyle loved her anyway.

Merry did it again, found a corpse, this time while jogging with Jolene during *Caught Red Handed* (Steeple Hill, 2007). They responded appropriately by calling the police, but Merry went a step further. She went to victim Martha Colby's home, entering when she found the door open, and appropriated Martha's journal before a neighbor chased her off. Plans for her marriage to artist Curt Carlyle were disrupted, not only by attempts on Merry's life, but on a conflict between Merry and Curt's further professional aspirations.

Each book featured a Christian service, i.e. aid to pregnant young women, supports for abused women. Plotting was occasionally flawed. Roper has other series with a strong emphasis on Christian lifestyles.

Kimberley "Kimmey" Kruse

Author: Susan Rogers Cooper

Currently a redhead, Kimmey Kruse was a tiny woman, who spent most of her time on the road, traveling from one gig to another as a standup comedienne. She maintained a residence in an apartment at the residence of her best friend, prosperous Texas attorney Phoebe Love. Kimmey considered herself discriminating. She had only a half dozen lovers over the years.

One of those ex-lovers, handsome and successful Cab Neusberg, was the headliner on Kimmey's bill in *Funny as a Dead Comic* (St. Martin, 1993). The circumstances of Cab's death during a one-night stand with Kimmey at Kaiser's Komedy Klub narrowed the suspects to other performers and their entourages. Sal Pucci, the assigned detective, interspersed his investigation with offers to sleep with Kimmey, one of which she finally accepted. The narrative was larded with jokes calculated to offend religious, racial, and gender groups.

Funny as a Dead Relative (St. Martin, 1994) provided a total change in scenery, out of the nightclub circuit and back to West Texas. Because Paw-Paw, Kimmey's grandfather, needed in-home care after a broken leg, Kimmey canceled a television appearance. Her arrival coincided with a major family picnic, to which Cousin Leticia returned after many years estrangement, only to die of anaphylactic shock from a wasp sting. Kimmey's insistence that Leticia had been murdered did not sit well with the police, or with handsome cousin Will for whom Kimmey lusted. Detective Pucci took his vacation in Texas, a gesture that was received with scorn by Kimmey, but she needed his help.

Interesting. Cooper has two more extensive series, one, featuring Sheriff Milt Kovak; the other, cozy E. J. Pugh.

Magdalene la Bâtarde

Author: Roberta Gellis

Occasional references to the background of brothel keeper la Bâtarde gave her earlier name as Arabel de St. Foi, and that of her husband as Brogan. He was described as a knight, but one who behaved with jealousy and brutality. His need to possess her utterly included suggesting that she wear the unsanitary and uncomfortable chastity belt. References were also made to her great beauty that attracted the attention of other men, driving Brogan to distraction. His murder at her hands, possibly in self-defense, was only hinted at, but she disappeared after his death. Lovers were mentioned but it was unclear whether they were taken before or after Brogan's death. Her financial problems forced her to work in a whorehouse. She was rescued by Lord William of Ypres. He sent her up in her own establishment, convinced the local bishop to rent her a former convent (referred to as the Old Priory Guesthouse), and provided her with protection. Magdalene's continued physical response to his generosity was based on gratitude rather than romantic love.

Lord William served as commander of the mercenaries of King Stephen in 1130, a period of considerable turmoil in England and Normandy. Matilde a.k.a. Maud, the only daughter of Henry I of England, had been assured the throne by promises the barons made to her father. However they reneged on this commitment and installed Stephen of Blois, a grandson of William the Conqueror. Stephen's reign was beset by rebellions. His brother Henry of Blois was the bishop who presided over the diocese in which Magdalene's business was located.

She was well spoken in both English and French and still a great beauty. By the time the series had begun Magdalene had adequate staff so that she no longer had to service customers. Her life experiences were such that she was fiercely independent, and unwilling to sacrifice her financial freedom. A marriage or any formal liaison would have placed her resources under the control of a man, something she would never again tolerate. Her household initially consisted of three whores and a cook/housekeeper. The clientele was select, paying high prices for the quality of service and the assurance of confidentiality. This was assured because the lovely Sabina, although an accomplished musician, was blind; the sensuous Ella was slow-witted; and dark skinned Letice was mute. All, including Magdalene, were excommunicated for their activities. The church considered Dulcie, the cook/ housekeeper, acceptable. The establishment was technically registered as a place where embroidery was done, not totally incorrect. The inhabitants did beautiful embroidery sold at the markets and on orders from churches.

Magdalene had achieved a measure of security by *A Mortal Bane* (Forge, 1999). Baldessare de Firenze, a papal messenger who had been misdirected to the Old Priory, chose to avail himself of its services, but was murdered on the nearby church steps. Brother Paulinus, the sacristan of the adjacent monastic house, made accusations immediately that Magdalene or one of her women was responsible. Magdalene learned quickly that the packet carried by the victim contained a papal bull and letters to King Stephen that were of great political and religious import. The investigator appointed by Bishop Henry, Sir Bellamy of Itchen, sought more than Magdalene's cooperation. She was tempted to succumb to his romantic overtures, but not yet.

Sabina's departure to become the leman (mistress) of Mainard, a successful but physically deformed saddle maker, left Magdalene short of staff in *A Personal Devil* (Forge, 2001). She did not make Sir Bellamy (familiarly called Bell) aware that she serviced only men seeking emotional rather than physical comfort. He went out of his way to recruit a replacement, Diot, who had been badly treated by prior whoremasters. Magdalene had held Bell at bay on a personal level, but she did not hesitate to call upon his services when Mainard was suspected of murdering his vindictive wife Bertrild. Bertrild had vilified, threatened, and blackmailed so many that the problem was in singling out her killer. An accommodation was reached between Bell and Magdalene.

The year 1136, as presented in *Bone of Contention* (Forge, 2002) was a tempestuous time. Stephen's claim to the throne was disputed by his cousin, Robert of Gloucester, and he had come to fear the growing power of the Bishop of Salisbury. Magdalene's loyalties were to William of Ypres, head of Stephen's mercenaries, and to Sir Bellamy, knight of the Bishop of Winchester. Those created potential conflicts of interest. Anticipating problems William asked Magdalene to visit Oxford where Stephen was holding a conclave of his supporters. One of Williams' men, Niall Arvagh, was the primary suspect in the death of obnoxious Aimery St. Clair. If the stabbing was done by Niall, was it because he and Aimery desired the same woman? Enemies of William preferred to believe he had ordered the killing for political reasons. Magdalene and Sir Bellamy cooperated on the investigation.

The relationship between Magdalene and Sir Bellamy had fascinating aspects in *Chains of Folly* (Five Star, 2006) but it and the murder mystery were submerged in a complex and difficult to understand civil war. Stephen's half-sister Matilda and her forces sought to topple him from his throne. Ambitious politicians and landowners made cautious decisions as to whom to support. Sir Bellamy, who was on the staff of Bishop Winchester, sought Magdalene's help when the corpse of a prostitute was found in Winchester's bedroom. Magdalene's whores helped Sir Bellamy to identify the victim and seek out her killer. In the process he and Magdalene grew closer, partly because she shared the story of her husband's death and her own complicity.

Author Roberta Gellis had an established reputation for historical novels before she entered the mystery field. The series portrayed the limited options available to females of lower rank and income in the medieval period.

Devonie Lace-Matthews

Author: Gina Cresse

Devonie had a life plan: a career as a database administrator. She spent thirteen years in that capacity for a communications company. When that ended, not necessarily the way she had anticipated, thirty-six-year old Devonie moved on to Plan B: life on a 36' sailboat docked at a San Diego marina with dreams of becoming a treasure hunter. Her Aunt Arlene and Uncle Doug were in the yacht business. Her romantic life had also fallen apart. She had been dumped after a long time affair.

Devonie purchased the contents of a storage unit at an auction in *A Deadly Change of Course-Plan B* (Avalon, 1998), starting her off on an improbable adventure. The contents in storage included $500,000 and information about a conspiracy. American banks and politicians were underwriting Mexican drug traffic. She survived unscathed but her friends paid a terrible price for her "lone ranger" methods. She wasn't meticulous about the money either.

A reader might conclude that Devonie was more of a nuisance than a help in *A Deadly Bargain-Plan C* (Avalon, 2000). True she located billionaire Gerald Bates's sunken yacht. However her subsequent investigation may or may not have assisted Bates personally. Her confidence shaken, she made Dr. Craig Matthews happy.

Diane Perkins was the character first introduced in *A Deadly Change of Heart* (Avalon, 2001). Slimmer and trimmer, she found a job on the *San Diego Union Tribune*. Her husband, Brad, had lost interest in her and she knew it. Even the revelation that he was in serious business trouble, did not deter her from handing him the divorce papers. There was no Plan B for Diane. When she interrupted two men standing over a suitcase full of money, they dropped her over a cliff. A year later, Devonie went to another auction, this time, cars seized by the police department. Inside the orange Ford Explorer she purchased, there was an envelope from Diane to Brad. That was enough to convince her that Brad was may have been responsible for what happened to Diane. The police, who had determined that her death was an accident, weren't interested so Devonie went solo again.

Ronnie Oakhurst followed in her inventor father's footsteps during *A Deadly Change of Power* (Avalon, 2002) developing alternative power sources for engines and generators. She encountered resistance, ranging from disbelief to violence. Devonie interrupted an attempt to kill Ronnie, becoming her dedicated supporter. The results, a "free-to-run" engine that liberated the individual. Lots of luck

Lou Winnomore, regularly played the same numbers in the lottery, but in *A Deadly Change of Luck* (Avalon, 2003) he died before he could collect on a big win. Devonie purchased the vacant Winnomore home from his estate as an investment. For a short time she had possession of the winning ticket, just long enough to learn the motive for Lou's murder

There was some improvement over the series, but it still abounded in coincidences and confessions.

Dee Laguerre

Author: Kirk Mitchell

Dee Laguerre was a female sleuth who operated in a male atmosphere, as a ranger for the Bureau of Land Management (BLM). The series dialogue was often at the locker room level, realistic for the settings. There was an emphasis on action, as opposed to the deductive process.

Dee, more formally Dominique, was the daughter of a Basque sheep herding family whose acceptance in cattle country was insecure from the beginning. Her parents had died as a result of exposure to the cold after an accident. Dee always felt different, even rejected; an attitude that was reinforced when her lover, Cinch Holland, married the young woman he had impregnated while Dee was away at college. Although she had earned a master's degree in resource management, Dee never felt adequate.

BLM employees in general received hostile treatment because government land and laws affected the economic success of ranchers and farmers. On a personal level, Dee was active in a government employee organization that was concerned about the environment and about the connections between officials and special interest groups. That made her a renegade at work, where an atmosphere of resentment already existed for those who benefited from minority advancement programs. Dee had to be tougher, work harder, and fend for herself.

Her marriage to Tyler Ravenshaw, an environmental attorney from a socially prominent family, had failed. Tyler saw problems from the security of an air-conditioned office, a controlled courtroom, or a conference of dedicated supporters. Dee knew too much about the hardships of ranching, the fight for grazing and water rights, and the burden of paperwork that led to the sale of centennial ranches. She left Tyler, took specialized training, and was stationed in her home territory in Nevada.

The economic needs of the ranchers and environmental concerns were at odds in *High Desert Malice* (Avon, 1995). The struggle was complicated for Dee when Cinch, for whom she had never ceased to care, killed deer to protect his pasture. Did he also kill two federal officials, or was Dee his alibi for the time of the murder?

The struggle between historic land rights and the demands of an urbanized society provided motives for murder in *Deep Valley Malice* (Avon, 1996). Dee, then stationed in California, clashed with local sheriff Tyrus Foley in the investigation of explosions that endangered the water supply to Los Angeles. Her emotions were at stake as a result of the death of Sid Abramowitz, a disabled friend from the Bureau of Alcohol, Tobacco, and Firearms, and her attachment to an ambitious official. Duty and loyalty overcame romance again.

The series would be particularly interesting to environmentalists. In addition to his series featuring FBI agent Anna Turnipseed and BIA agent Emmett Parker, Mitchell has written several historical standalones.

Barrett Lake

Author: Shelley Singer

Barrett Lake, a transplanted Midwesterner who had been raised by Jewish adoptive parents, was teaching at the Berkeley, California Technical High School as *Following Jane* (Signet, 1993) began. Barrett had been contacted by private investigator "Tito" Broz in his search for Jane, a missing student. Jane, who worked at a local grocery, had disappeared shortly after the murder of teacher William Anderson. Barrett's dissatisfaction with her current life and her concern for Jane caused her to join the Broz Agency as a part-time investigator. Her successful solution in the case posed a dilemma that she solved by teaching on a reduced schedule to maintain her pension and benefits, but continuing to work for Broz.

A fourteen-year-old boy, David Minsky, disappeared in *Picture of David* (Signet, 1993), kidnapped by those who wanted revenge on his father Lev. Clearly David was alive, but in torment and fear. Barrett took considerable physical risks, but prevailed with the help of a spunky senior citizen who shared her duplex.

Sara Henry, a fifteen-year-old lesbian rejected by her parents, was the focus in *Searching for Sara* (Signet, 1994). Robert Nygard, her gay uncle, hired the Broz agency to find Sara somewhere in the streets of San Francisco. Young runaways, those who would protect them, and those who would abuse them were suspects when muralist Steve O'Connell, a volunteer at the Loughlin Street Youth Center, was murdered.

Interview with Mattie (Signet, 1995) kept Barrett on the streets. Mattie, an abused youth, was murdered shortly after being quoted in a news story. Editor Oz Overstreet was deluged with letters accusing the publication of setting the boy up for death. Barrett believed that the culprit was on the newspaper staff.

Although the themes were repetitious, these were well-written and sensitive to the problems of teenagers. Singer also wrote the Jake Samson/ Rosie Vicente series (see Volume 2).

Julia Lambros

Authors: Takis and Judy Iakovou

This series featured a delightful pairing of a Greek husband and American wife, with occasional touches of Nick and Nora Charles. This Nick was a soccer coach turned restaurateur who would have disdained Nick Charles' dilettante ways. Julia, who had qualified as a speech therapist, met Nick while attending Parnassus College. When soccer succumbed to football in the college budget and love evolved into marriage, the Lambros turned to a typical Greek venture, a restaurant. This was not a simple matter for a Yankee female and a male immigrant still on green card status because Delphi, Georgia was "good ole boy" territory. However, years of hard work had brought success, including the constant morning presence of the Buffaloes, local businessmen who mooched free coffee in the restaurant kitchen. At home the Lambros had a Scotch terrier named Jack.

Julia had just returned to work after a miscarriage that left her depressed in *So Dear to Wicked Men* (St. Martin, 1996). The death of Glenn Bohannon while eating a restaurant breakfast brought unpleasant notoriety. The tensions escalated when it was determined that Glenn had been poisoned. The local sheriff decided it might be the Lambros' way to eliminate possible competition. Glenn had been considering opening a Mexican restaurant and had negotiated with local businessmen for services and equipment. The Lambros knew they had been set up, probably by one of the Buffaloes, but they had to find the killer themselves.

Julia was aware that discrimination still lingered in the South. She had a strong reminder of its impact on individuals in *Go Close Against the Enemy* (St. Martin, 1998). Nick was totally pre-occupied dealing with IRS agent Richard Fortunata; so, it was Julia who stepped in when young April Folsom was accused of murdering Walter Fry, deacon of the Mount Sinai Tabernacle Church where her father was pastor. Fry had opposed the burial of April's deceased infant in the church cemetery, because the child was of mixed parentage. With help from elderly Alma Rayburn, Julia sought other suspects. At the end, she became aware that she had prejudices of her own. She needed to understand and appreciate that white Southerners had virtues that she had been unwilling to recognize.

There Lies a Hidden Scorpion (St. Martin, 1999) combined an ingenious series of plots set within the Greek-American culture in Florida when Nick, Julia and cousin Spiros journeyed there to attend a family wedding. The bride-to-be Kate was Nick's god-daughter. A nasty car accident and some gruesome packages caused the family of the groom to consider canceling the wedding. The couple worked with Spiros and Miss Alma to implicate those who would stop the marriage even if it took murder to do so.

Julia and Nick appeared in a novella, *Another Curse* in the anthology, *Deadly Morsels* (Worldwide, 2003) during which food inspector Marcia Lowery shut their business down because an unlabeled bottle found in their supplies contained moonshine. Marcia had a history of making trouble, had already been dismissed from one federal job, and was being divorced from her husband. She had contacted the federal Bureau of Alcohol, Tobacco, and Firearms Agency to investigate the Lambros possible involvement in an interstate moonshine operation. Her mysterious death just made things worse.

Gloria Lamerino

Author: Camille Minichino

Growing up had been difficult for Gloria Lamerino. Her domineering mother was endlessly critical, never satisfied with her hardworking intelligent daughter. Gloria's fiancé, Al Gravese, had been killed three months before they planned to marry. Gloria earned a Ph.D. and spent her working years in California. At fifty-five, she was a good-humored, stocky woman whose dark hair was graying. There had been no man in her life since Al. Upon retirement, Gloria moved from the West Coast back to Revere, Massachusetts. Her parents were both dead, but she had a sense of unfinished business. Gloria relied upon her long time friendship with Frank and Rose Galigani who ran a local funeral parlor. Her special talents made her valuable to the Revere police department where she first met Detective Matt Gennaro, whom she found attractive.

Science had been a passion for Gloria since high school and framed her thinking processes. During *The Hydrogen Murder* (Avalon, 1997), that was just what Gennaro needed. Eric Benson, a scientist whose team was on the brink of a major discovery, was dead. The clue to his killer lay in Greek scientific symbols. Gennaro sought help from Gloria, but then more...he wanted to be a part of her new life in Revere.

Matt and Gloria had been dating decorously since the hydrogen case ended, but in *The Helium Murder* (Avalon, 1998), she moved on to the second chemical element and a chaste exchange of kisses. Gloria's knowledge of "mole," an expanded number, explained the murder of Congresswoman Margaret Hurley. To overcome the killer, Gloria had to pass the "acid" test. Gloria's pragmatic view of life (she had renounced or ignored her Catholic faith) abandoned her when there was a hint of murder.

In *The Lithium Murder* (Morrow, 1999), just the fact that deceased custodian Michael Deramo worked in confidential university laboratories kindled Gloria's suspicions. A search of his home added to her belief that he had been murdered, and that his death was connected to a research project. Gennaro's insistence that she stay out of trouble did not carry weight when Carlo Massino, Deramo's supervisor, was murdered. Gloria's knowledge of Italy and the Italian language, not her scientific background, provided significant clues.

In prior books, Gloria had operated under the auspices of a police department. In *The Beryllium Murder* (Morrow, 2000), she not only lacked this support, but was also met with hostility by Inspector Dennis Russell of the Berkeley Police Department. Gloria had returned to California for two reasons—to visit her dear friend Eldine Cody and to inquire into the death of scientist Gary Larkin. She found it difficult to believe that so conscientious a researcher would be careless with dangerous material. She used her professional methodology (charts, chronology, narratives) to locate a blackmailer, an embezzler, and a killer. However, she was singularly guileless in her search for proof.

The news that Matt had prostate cancer left Gloria reeling in *The Carbon Murder* (St. Martin, 2004) but she made time for an elementary investigation. Mary Catherine Galigani, her beloved god-daughter had returned to Revere from Houston, "M.C" like Gloria was a chemist involved in carbon research. There were other recent visitors in Revere from Texas, and two of them had been murdered. Gloria's special skills made it possible for her to tie motive to murder.

Gloria's methodology of crime solving (attention to details; careful research; interviewing all suspects) ran into obstacles in *The Boric Acid Murders* (World Wide, 2004). Yolanda Fiore, former public relations employee at Charger Street laboratory, had been murdered at the local public library. Gloria, just off the plane from California, was having a welcome back dinner at the Galigani home when detectives arrived to take John, the younger son, to the police department for questioning in Yolanda's death. Rose, his mother, was Gloria's oldest and dearest friend so Gloria had to be careful. Matt Gennaro, who might otherwise have been assigned to the case, was unable to take part officially because of his friendship with the family. He and Gloria managed however, trading information with Matt's partner George Berger. In the process Gloria and Matt made plans for their own future.

The week before Elaine Cody's wedding in *The Nitrogen Murder* (St. Martin, 2005), Gloria was supposed to be relaxing. She and Matt, still recovering from prostate cancer surgery, had flown to San Francisco for the event. Gloria was to be maid of honor at the event. Instead, she investigated connections between prospective bridegroom Phil Chambers and a recent murder victim, Lokesh Patel, both of whom had worked on developing an innovative nitrogen-based explosive. Furthermore, Phil's daughter Dana, an EMT for a private ambulance service, had transported Patel to a trauma center, only to see her partner, Tanisha Hall, shot down. Matt and Gloria set a wedding date.

Married only four months, the last thing Gloria wanted was in-law problems, when in *The Oxygen Murder* (St. Martin, 2006), she, Matt and the Galiganis went to New York City. Matt arranged to spend their first night in town with documentary filmmaker Lori Pissano, the niece of his deceased first wife. He had been like a father to young Lori. When Gloria stopped off at Lori's apt/studio the next morning, she discovered Amber Keenan, Lori's camerawoman, dying. By the time help arrived it was too late. Matt and Gloria needed to know how close Lori was to Amber and about possible misuse of her assignments. Gloria's new documentary was a study of oxygen and its impact; when was it too much; when, not enough. Gloria and Lori eventually worked together while Matt coordinated with his NYPD pal, Buzz Arnold.

Years after the death of her mother, Gloria was still subject to measuring her achievements by what Josephine would have said (usually criticism). Matt Gennaro had made a difference. The voices were quieter, less frequent, and more often ignored.

An enjoyable series. Next: *Fluorine Murder* (2010)

Skip (Margaret) Langdon

Author: Julie Smith

Skip Langdon, an "ungainly" upper class renegade, chose police work as a career, scandalizing her New Orleans family. She lived apart from her socially prominent parents in a small apartment. Her father had rejected her. Her mother and brother Conrad were obsessed with the impact of her occupation on their social standing. Skip had always been a rebel even though she attended exclusive schools and made her debut. During college, she smoked pot, sold drugs, and had an abortion arranged by her mother. She walked a precarious line; too upper class and educated to be fully accepted by her fellow police officers; and too unconventional to be trusted by the staid New Orleans social world.

Skip was on street duty in *New Orleans Mourning* (St. Martin, 1990) when Chauncey St. Amant was shot while riding in the Mardi Gras parade. The problems within the St. Amant family were common knowledge in Skip's social circles. Aided by the films of friend Steve Steinman, Skip solved the murder but was unable to follow it through. Depressed, she questioned her commitment to police work.

By *The Axeman's Jazz* (St. Martin, 1991), Skip had been promoted to detective. She hunted a serial killer, who claimed ties to a 1919 murderer, the Axeman. The task force methodically sifted through records, psychological profiles, and witnesses during a narrative interspersed with chapters on the tormented killer.

In *Jazz Funeral* (Fawcett Columbine, 1993), Steve Steinman returned to report on the New Orleans Jazz and Heritage Festival. The death of festival producer Ham Brocato focused Skip's attention on the wealthy and contentious Brocato family.

During *New Orleans Beat* (Fawcett, 1994), Skip questioned the quality of her relationship with Steve, who was deeply involved in the Hollywood scene. Professionally, she was skeptical of the "accidental" death of computer geek Geoffrey Kavanagh who had investigated his father's death through the fantasy world of a billboard network. Geoffrey, who had been trying to rescue a cat while climbing a ladder, was found by his mother, Marguerite. Both Geoff's girlfriend, Lenore Marques, and his gay friend, Layne Bilderback, believed he had been murdered.

In *House of Blues* (Fawcett, 1995), the death of domineering restaurateur Arthur Hebert, and the kidnapping of his daughter Reed, and granddaughter Sally sent Skip into the dregs of the New Orleans underworld. Arthur was in the process of turning his new venture, a restaurant at a casino, over to Reed who had been responsible for much of the planning. Nina Phillips, Reed's African-American assistant, tried to carry on, hassled by Sally, Reed's mother. There was a suspect with connections.

The mood deepened in *The Kindness of Strangers* (Fawcett, 1996); no blues, no Mardi Gras; instead, an emphasis on graft, guilt, and perversion. Skip had placed herself on six-month leave because she experienced flashbacks of the incident in which she had killed a man. Looking for something to occupy her mind, she made a dangerous choice by opposing the election of Errol Jacomine, a popular religious leader whom she instinctively mistrusted. She suffered retribution from Jacomine and his followers. Skip researched his background, placing herself and someone she loved in danger. The tension started early and was sustained.

As *Crescent City Kill* (Fawcett, 1997) opened, Skip was still dealing with remorse. Jacomine was bent upon revenge, and his latest crusade was through an anonymous "jury" which executed persons who did not meet their right wing criteria. He had already involved one of his sons in the group, but was determined to include his granddaughter, even if she had to be kidnapped. The girl, Lovelace, fled from her Midwest campus, seeking security with a sympathetic uncle who lived in New Orleans. Jacomine's maniacal schemes ended in a hostage setting during which Skip risked her life. Hopefully Jacomine will not be a continuing nemesis in the series.

Skip and Adam Absolve (once her partner, now her supervisor) interviewed Councilwoman Bebe Fortier whose husband had left her stranded in the airport during *82 Desire* (Fawcett, 1998). Russell Fortier had been the Property Manager for United Oil Corporation, whose "mature" oilfields may have been more valuable than the company realized. Russ' decision to jettison an unhappy marriage and expose corruption in the oil industry set off responses that led to murder. Four narrative strands; Skip, Russ, Talba Wallis (African-American part-time private investigator and budding poetess), and Jane Storey, volatile local reporter, figured in the solutions.

Skip Langdon had a cameo role in *Louisiana Hotshots* (Forge/ Doherty, 2001), which focused on Talba Wallis as an aspiring private investigator. Talba's poetry, written under the name, Baroness de Pontalba, was a minor asset, but she was also a computer whiz. A new series in which Talba will be the primary seemed to be the future with Skip playing minor roles. However *Mean Woman Blues* (Forge, 2003) also published as *Boneyard Blues* brought Earl Jacomine and Skip back into action. He had never given up his desire for revenge. With the help of his first wife Rosemarie Owens, Jacomine had re-invented himself as a Dallas talk show host, Mr. Right. Even with his current success, Jacomine struck out at Skip. First a sniper shot; then, she and Steve Steinman were framed for robbery and corruption. Again subsequent narratives focused on Talba Wallis.

The narratives were long, complex but featured good characterizations and atmosphere.

Meg Langslow

Author: Donna Andrews

Meg Langslow had defied convention and the wishes of her large and ditzy family, by moving to Washington, D.C. to pursue a career as a blacksmith. She had not disregarded her college education and her ties to Yorktown, Virginia, but needed space. A tall woman in her thirties, she was developing terrific upper body strength and a reputation for original and intricate ironwork. She, her married sister Pam and her younger brother Rob were horrified when their parents divorced. Her father James, a retired doctor, was a great mystery fan. Her mother Margaret, a cool and collected woman, had admitted to a Parisian fling in her youth. They were eventually reunited.

Three summer weddings drew Meg back to Yorktown in *Murder with Peacocks* (St. Martin, 1999). She was to be maid of honor in all three: the wedding of Margaret, her mother, to innocuous appearing neighbor Jake Wendell; the wedding of her brother Rob to Samantha Brewer; and the wedding of her best friend and business partner Eileen to her longtime beau Barry. The last was the only one of which she approved. Meg's father had seemed complacent about Margaret's nuptials until the death of Jake's visiting sister-in-law was followed by several "accidents." An easy read lightened by Meg's zany relatives and her new boyfriend Michael Waterston's efforts to explain that he was not gay, even though he filled in at his mom's bridal boutique.

What Meg and Michael had in mind was an intimate vacation at Aunt Phoebe's primitive cottage on Monhegan Island, off Maine. What occurred was close to a family reunion in *Murder with Puffins* (St. Martin, 2000). Her parents, brother, aunt and a family friend were already occupying the place when they arrived. Hurricane force winds trapped them on the island. The murder of justly unpopular artist Victor Nesnick created a crisis because both of her parents and Aunt Phoebe were logical suspects.

Yorktown was hosting a battle reenactment and colonial craft fair in *Revenge of the Wrought-Iron Flamingos* (St. Martin, 2001). Michael, the attractive drama professor of whose gender preferences Meg was now confident, served in a French unit during the battle which was stage managed by his domineering mother, Dahlia. Meg's efforts to maintain her professional standing as an ironworker were sabotaged by a special order of pink flamingos for personal friend, Mrs. Fenniman. Having a corpse found in her sales tent didn't help either. The narrative featured interesting information about colonial times, but there were more caricatures than characters.

Unable to continue her work as a blacksmith because of a hand injury, Meg worked as office manager at Rob's software company during *Crouching Buzzard, Leaping Loon* (St. Martin, 2003) The Mutant Wizard's staff included a practical joker/ blackmailer, a porno king, and a killer. Not surprisingly, their mascot was a one-winged buzzard. Could this conglomerate feature in a readable mystery? Andrews made it work. Ted Corrigan, the prankster/blackmailer, was murdered. Meg had to work the case, because Rob was the primary suspect.

Michael Waterston's contract with the TV series, *Porfinia, Queen of the Jungle* created problems for his full time job as a college professor in *We'll Always Have Parrots* (St. Martin, 2004). His required appearance at a series fan conference gave Meg grief too, as she watched the female Amblyopians fawn on Michael. Her original plan to sell her home-made swords at the conference took second place when the star of the show, domineering actress Tamerlaine Wynncliffe-Jones was murdered.

It had seemed relatively simple in *Owls Well That Ends Well* (St. Martin, 2005). Michael and Meg could purchase the huge but neglected Sprocket manor house at a low price IF they assumed the responsibility for selling the contents, and paying 7% of the net profits to Sprocket heirs. Not only did at least one Sprocket heir, Barrymore, appear to monitor the auction, dozens of Meg's extended family joined in the festivities, hoping to earn some money in the process. The discovery of slippery antique dealer Gordon McCoy's corpse in a trunk sent Meg on an extended track as she looked for a killer to whom she was not related or was not an associate of Michael.

With a background of remodeling the historic Sprocket home she and Michael had purchased, Meg still had time to share in Caerphilly activities during *No Nest for the Wicket* (St. Martin's Minotaur, 2006). Edwina Sprocket had left behind a leaky roof, 23 boxes of mementoes, and a prank that created controversy after fifty years. Extreme Croquet (played on rough terrain, using animals' legs as alternative wickets) was the rage. While playing on Mrs. Fenniman's team, Meg discovered the corpse of Lindsay Tyler. Lindsay had ties not only to members of the other three contending teams, but also to Michael.

Michael and Meg were keeping a secret as *The Penguin Who Knew Too Much* (Thomas Dunne, St. M, 2007) began, but they weren't the only ones. They planned to elope during a Memorial Day party to avoid a huge family wedding. However Meg's father signed them up to temporarily provide housing for displaced zoo animals. While Dr. Langslow was creating a habitat for penguins in the home Meg and Mike had purchased, he discovered a corpse. What followed was the usual credible chaos that Andrews handles so well.

Andrews' wickedly funny sense of humor was augmented by a well-developed mystery plot in *Cockatiels at Seven* (Thomas Dunne, St. Martin's Minotaur, 2008). Karen Walker, a friend whom Meg had not seen in years, stopped by long enough to leave her toddler, Timmy in Meg's care, "just for a while". Karen did not return to Meg's home or to her job at the college financial office where she worked. Searching for Karen, Meg came upon the corpse of Jasper Walker, Karen's estranged husband. Then it got complicated. Meg's dad and her recently discovered grandfather, Dr. Montgomery Blake, had a mysterious project going on. Timmy, an endearing child, caused Meg to re-evaluate her feelings about having a family.

Meg would have taken more enjoyment in the annual Caerphilly Holiday parade during *Six Geese A-Slaying* (St. Martin's Minotaur, 2008), if she had not reluctantly agreed to serve as "Mistress of the Revels", a fancy name for organizing the parade. This year's motif was the Twelve Days of Christmas. There were potential problems; i.e. the young woman portraying the Virgin Mary was ready to deliver her baby; heavy snow was predicted, there were hordes of animals which necessitated clean-up crews. The locals were delighted that the Washington Star-Tribune had sent Ainsley Werzel to report on the festival. Not so delighted when the big story was that someone had murdered Santa Claus (the detested Ralph Doleson, selected only because the costume fitted him).

Author Donna Andrews also has a series featuring artificial intelligence personality (female) Hopper Turing. Next: *Swan for the Money* (2009); *Stork Raving Mad* (2010)

Renee LaRoche

Author: Carole laFavor

When Renee ("Renie") LaRoche left the reservation in the Sixties, she sought an education, and then, the justice that she felt had been denied her Native American people. She spent years as part of a radical movement designed to force the government to respect the economic and social rights of Native Americans. After twenty years, she returned to the Ojibwa reservation in Minnesota where her grandmother, Granny Flandreau, and Great Aunt Lydia still lived. She then spent four years being reabsorbed into her native culture, teaching part-time at the reservation school, earning extra money by beading and basket weaving. During those years, Renie was involved with Samantha Salisbury, a Caucasian college professor. She shared her home with her daughter Jenny, and cocker spaniel Mukwa. Renee worked well with the reservation authorities, serving on a police-community task force for youth.

Theft of Native American relics from a local high school display was a concern in *Along the Journey River* (Firebrand Books, 1996). Renie and tribal police chief Hobey Bulieau suspected that it was connected to other such incidents. Private collectors were willing to purchase these artifacts without questioning their provenance. Two suspicious deaths, one that of tribal chieftain Jed Morriseau; the other, the car accident of stranger Peter Thompson, in the area, were connected to the robberies. Renie had concern for the sanctity of historic caves on property owned by her family, but also for helping young Billy Walking Bear make peace with his heritage.

Cal, a former lover and fellow radical, contacted Renie in *Evil Dead Center* (Firebrand, 1997) asking that she investigate the death of an unidentified Native American female. The local coroner had written off her demise as the result of alcohol and hypothermia but no toxicology report had been filed. The woman had been buried as a Jane Doe, although the authorities had information identifying her as Rosa Mae Two Thunder. When a suspect was identified, Cal and Renie utilized Native American skills (woodsmanship and tracking through the Boundary Waters) and a modern cell phone to keep in contact with Hobie Bulieau.

Hester Latterly

Author: Anne Perry

Hester played a significant but supporting role in the Inspector William Monk series. She had been living in reduced circumstances (on the charity of her surviving brother) since she returned from nursing in the Crimean War. Another brother had died in the Crimea. Her father committed suicide after financial reverses. The Crimean experience, although it carried little weight in England, had given Hester confidence in her abilities and a desire for independence. A spinster in her late twenties had few employment options in Victorian England. Callandra Daviot, an influential friend, tried to place Hester advantageously, but her assertive behavior made it difficult. She worked in hospitals until her insubordination forced her to confine her practice to private homes.

Inspector Monk had never been the same since his head injury. Partial amnesia caused a new found humility and compassion, but left important blanks in his memory. He struggled with hopeless cases requiring diplomatic handling, assigned by unfriendly supervisor Runcorn. In *The Face of a Stranger* (Fawcett Columbine, 1990), Monk met Hester while investigating the death of Hon. Joscelin Gray, a veteran whom Hester had nursed during the war. Monk and Latterly clashed initially, but they developed a working arrangement based upon mutual respect.

Monk was assigned to discover the killer of young widow "Tavie" Haslett in *A Dangerous Mourning* (FawcettColumbine, 1991). His conclusion that her killer was a member of a prominent household was reluctantly accepted. Callandra Daviot arranged that Hester, recently fired for insubordination, be hired to care for Tavie's bereaved mother. Callandra also subsidized a private enquiry business when Monk was fired for his refusal to arrest a young footman for the murder.

Hester had a stronger part in *Defend and Betray* (FawcettColumbine, 1992) when she convinced barrister Oliver Rathbone to defend Alexandra Carlyon, charged with murdering her husband, General Thaddeus Carlyon. This was no simple task as Alexandra had confessed to causing the fall that ended in his death. The General's sister Damaris was convinced that Alexandra was innocent. Rathbone hired Monk to investigate. Together Monk and Hester challenged public perceptions about the roles of husband and wife, revealing a scandal likely to have remained hidden.

Hester's role was less important in *A Sudden Fearful Death* (Fawcett-Columbine, 1993). Monk investigated the death of Prudence Barrymore, a young nurse who had served in the Crimea. The probe led to unwelcome disclosures about the practice of medicine on female patients and the abuse of family intimacy in Victorian households. In order to assist Monk, Hester obtained the position formerly held by Prudence as nurse to Sir Hubert Stanhope, a surgeon who was a major suspect.

Although Hester's problems were the primary plot in *The Sins of the Wolf* (FawcettColumbine, 1994), she was victim and suspect, not sleuth. While on a temporary assignment, Hester became the primary suspect in the death of wealthy Scottish widow Mary Farraline. Her friends, Lady Callendra, Rathbone, and Monk, rallied to obtain her release from prison. Although her Scottish advocate, James Argyll, obtained a "not proven" verdict, neither Hester nor Monk would settle for anything less than the identification of the real killer. Their joint investigation pushed them into a new, but tenuous, level of intimacy.

They withdrew from one another in *Cain His Brother* (Fawcett-Columbine, 1995), seemingly frightened by a single encounter. Monk investigated the disappearance of Angus Stonefield, and the possibility that Caleb, his evil brother, had murdered him. The psychological underpinnings for the narrative were obvious, but author Anne Perry writes so well that the narrative would be hard to put down. Hester had only minor impact, saving Monk from a vengeful woman.

Monk's investigations and Oliver Rathbone's trial expertise dominated *Weighed in the Balance* (FawcettColumbine, 1996). Hester's incisive interview with a murder suspect was responsible for winning a civil suit for slander against Countess Zorah Rostova. When former Crown Prince Friedrich, who abandoned his claim to the throne of a small German principality for the love of Gisela (a commoner) died, Rostova had accused Gisela of murder.

The presence of traumatized and beaten Rhys Duff and his murdered father in the odious St. Giles section of London could not be explained to Scotland Yard as *The Silent Cry* (Fawcett Columbine, 1997) began. Rhys had been rendered mute by the experience. Hester was hired to provide home care for him after his release from the hospital. Monk, meantime, had been hired by sweatshop owner Vida Hopgood to find the brutes who were abusing her employees, women who supplemented their income on the streets. Their paths met when Monk suspected that Rhys might have been more criminal than victim. They eventually worked together to find the killers, restoring some of the rapport they had built earlier.

Sir Oliver Rathbone made an impulsive decision to represent young architect Killian Melville as the defendant in a breach of promise suit in *A Breach of Promise* (Ballantine, 1998). Melville, who had been attentive to Zillah, the daughter of his business sponsor Barton Lambert, denied that he had sought her hand in marriage. In a parallel plotline, Hester, currently employed as nurse for seriously damaged British veteran Gabriel Sheldon, was approached by Martha Jackson. Martha, maid to Perdita (Gabriel's wife), was desperate to find her two handicapped nieces. Leda and Phemie had been institutionalized after becoming orphans, then placed with one tavern keeper after another.

By *The Twisted Root* (Ballantine, 1999) Monk and Hester had married. Their great joy in the intimacy overcame their individual needs for independence and control, but not without effort. Monk's happiness made him sympathetic to the plight of young Lucius Stourbridge whose fiancée, Miriam, had disappeared before the wedding. James Treadwell, nephew of the family cook, who had driven Miriam away from the ceremony, was found dead. Oliver Rathbone defended Miriam and Cleo Anderson, her foster mother, when they were accused of murder. Hester stayed involved through her volunteer work at North London Hospital and in the home of disabled veteran John Robb. They had become a team. The ending was extremely well done.

The morality of slavery and selling munitions concerned not only the representatives of the Confederacy and the Union, but the family of Daniel Alberton, who had guns to sell. However, in *Slaves of Obsession* (Ballantine, 2000) Alberton's murder was initially blamed upon his sixteen-year-old daughter Merrit, and Union sympathizer Lyman Breeland. Daniel's beautiful widow Judith who had lost a husband, did not intend to lose her daughter, so hired Monk. Unpleasant revelations of Monk's past surfaced, but Hester was living in the present and their shared future. She and Monk traveled to the United States, following the troops to Bull Run to find young Merrit Alberton and assist in proving her innocence.

Hester had seen little of her brother Charles since her marriage, so in *Funeral in Blue* (Ballantine, 2001) she knew his visit was a serious matter. He shared his concern that his wife Imogen was in trouble and asked Hester to talk to her. This problem was engulfed by a broader crisis—the trial of Hester's friend (and the man whom Lady Callandra loved) Dr. Kristian Beck for the murder of his wife, Elissa. Elissa carried a burden of guilt that led to excesses of which her husband and father were unaware. Monk was hired privately by Lady Callandra, but found an unexpected ally, Inspector Runcorn. Charles' concerns eventually meshed with Monk's investigation. In the process of probing Kristian and Elissa's years in Vienna, Monk's need to resurrect his own past grew.

Hester and William Monk suffered from a failure to communicate in *Death of a Stranger* (Ballantine, 2002). Her efforts to end a usury system that forced young gentlewomen into prostitution uncovered information that was only belatedly available to Monk. Katrina Harcus, a mysterious woman with a secret agenda, had hired Monk to investigate financing of a new line for the Baltimore & Sons railroad. Monk had only hazy recollections of the role he had played as a young banker in a prior investigator of fraud which ended in the imprisonment and death of his former mentor Arrol Dundas, sixteen years before. Complications arose when Nolan Baltimore, president of the railroad, was murdered in the red light district and Katrina died of a fall. The past was becoming clearer, causing Monk to fear what he might learn about himself. Oliver Rathbone was a tremendous help.

The need for money motivated Monk's decision to investigate the theft of ivory tusks from the ship *Maude Idris* in *The Shifting Tide* (Ballantine, 2004). None of his experience or training had familiarized him with the London dockside. He wondered why ship owner Clement Louvain did not want the River Police involved, even though a watchman had been murdered. A connection emerged when Louvain brought a seriously ill woman to the clinic for street women run by Hester. The horror of Ruth Clark's death forced both Monk and Hester to expose themselves to danger.

As *Dark Assassin* (Ballantine, 2005) began, a new sewage system had been designed for London to avoid the repetition of the Great Stink of '58. Monk, under financial pressure, accepted a job with the River Police, the one formerly held by heroic Inspector Durban (killed in prior book). Fearing for Hester's safety he had insisted that she no longer work at the Clinic, but he did not want her to return to private practice where she would have to live in her patient's home. The drowning after a fall from the Waterloo Bridge of a young couple, Mary Havilland and Toby Argyll, became the focus of Hester and Monk's lives. Hester, whose father had killed himself, shared Monk's belief that Mary had killed herself, as had her father James, months before. James, an engineer for the Argyll Company digging an underground sewage tunnel, had protested that adequate safety measures were not being taken.

Hester's roles varied in individual books. Her need for independence and Monk's arrogance initially impeded a romantic relationship. Next book: *Execution Dock* (2009)

Author Anne Perry is a compelling writer, combining historical expertise with absorbing narratives. *The Christmas Visitor* (Ballantine, 2004) was a holiday offering which was connected to the Monk/Latterly series only through Oliver Rathbone's family. Perry is even better known for her Thomas and Charlotte Pitt series. She currently has a third series set in the first World War.

Lauren Laurano

Author: Sandra Scoppetone a.k.a. Jack Early

Lauren Laurano had been attacked and raped while on a heterosexual date by hoodlums who killed her companion. She graduated from Smith College, and then worked for the FBI, where she met Lois, another agent with whom she had a lesbian relationship. Their affair, discovered by the agency when Lauren accidentally killed Lois, caused her dismissal. She was petite and trim with brown hair going gray in her forties. Her father, a self-centered attorney, and her mother, a long time alcoholic, had by this time accepted their only child's relationship with psychotherapist, Christine "Kip" Adams. As the series began, Lauren had become a private investigator in New York. Her relationship with Kip was initially monogamous, and portrayed more on an emotional than a physical level.

Everything You Have Is Mine (Little Brown, 1991) began when lesbian friends asked Lauren to counsel Lake Huron, who had been date raped by a man she met through an ad. Lake's apartment had been searched and the man's letters stolen; then she was discovered, hanged. Lauren, convinced that Lake had been murdered, not only wanted her rapist but her killer because she was not at all certain they were the same person.

During *I'll Be Leaving You Always* (Little Brown, 1993), Lauren examined several of her relationships while solving the murder of her closest friend, Megan Harbaugh. Megan was more and less than the woman Lauren had known, but she did not deserve to be shot down by someone she had trusted.

My Sweet Untraceable You (Little Brown, 1995) defied credulity. Lauren, whose caseload was bare, needed a new client. Did she want to work for "Boston Blackie" who believed his mother had been killed by his father 38 years before and that his real grandfather was a rich and powerful man? She did, and set out on a confusing chase involving multiple births, cross-dressing, and greedy killers. Kip, Lauren's lover, was stressed by the approaching death of her brother Tom from AIDS and their commitment to assist his suicide. Lauren's relationship with Kip suffered from Tom's death and Lauren's absorption in her computer.

As *Let's Face the Music and Die* (Little Brown, 1996) began, Kip had accepted a temporary position out of town. Although upset by this decision, Lauren became involved with an e-mail pen pal who was looking for a short-term romance. Professionally, she helped her friend Elissa who had inherited a fortune. Unfortunately Elissa was suspected of murdering her Aunt Ruth from whom she had received the bequest. Lauren sought a killer while she was threatened by a man who had reason to hate her. Insightful, with a high level of tension.

In an effort to save their relationship, Lauren and Kip took a vacation on Long Island in *Gonna Take a Homicidal Journey* (Little, Brown, 1998). The plan was to help their friends Jenny and Jill renovate their recently purchased home. The death, called suicide, of Bill Moffat, came to Lauren's attention when she stopped in at the local bagel/breakfast shop. Jean Ashton, Bill's cousin, asked Lauren to investigate. Bill had been active in a local struggle between established food providers and fast food outlets seeking to move into town. Bill was president of AFF (Anti-Fast Food), and had some serious enemies in this struggle. Even Bill's mistress agreed that he would never consider suicide, leaving his wife Toby to care for their handicapped daughter. His death connected with other murders, including those of children. Lauren's involvement caused added stress between Lauren and Kip, already weakened by infidelity and the gap between their income levels.

Lauren Laurano was one of the first lesbian sleuths to appear in mainstream hardcover mysteries. Scoppetone's new series, set in the 1940's, features Faye Quick who took over for her private investigator boss when he went into the service in World War II.

Rosie (Rosalynd) Lavine

Author: Melisa Michaels

Rosie Lavine was a petite private investigator in Berkeley, California at an unstated future time. She wanted to be a police officer, but lacked the necessary height to qualify. Hers was a two-person firm, shared with Shannon Arthur. They had a humdrum business, mostly repossessing cars for the banks that had subsidized their purchases. Rosie enjoyed her gin and classical music but suffered from depression during the Christmas season. Although the cause was not clear to her, she connected it to a childhood experience. There was no one to ask, because Rosie had run away from home at age eleven; then, hung out in the seedy Haight-Ashbury area of San Francisco. She had married unsuccessfully.

Teenage Candy Cayne, a roadie with an Elf Rock group, drew Rosie into a different world in *Cold Iron* (ROC, 1997). Elfs were a subspecies of being, small in stature with Spock-like ears. They were capable of mating with humans and their progeny were known as Haflings. Cold Iron was composed of two elfs and two halflings. Candy feared that elfling Jorie, the lead singer of Cold Iron, might be murdered. Rosie agreed to accompany the band on its tour, presenting herself as Candy's cousin. Jorie became intensely involved with Rosie, ferreting out the cause for her nightmares and fears, but left her with a new worry. Had she fallen in love with a killer?

It was Kyriander Stone (the halfling whom Rosie loved) who recommended her agency to investigate "troubles" in Fey Valley during *Sister to the Rain* (ROC, 1998). The Valley was a communal enterprise by a mixture of artistic humans, halflings and trueblood elves. Discovering the nature of the troubles (sightings, strange music) was only the first step in Rosie and Shannon's case. By then, a reckless youth had been murdered and Shannon, ruthlessly attacked. When the killer revealed herself, justice was provided not by human standards, but by the laws of Faeria, a land that Rosie was privileged to visit.

Sierra Lavotini

Author: Nancy Bartholomew

Sierra Lavotini, a tall blond exotic dancer currently working at the Tiffany Club in Panama City, Florida, had ventured far from her Philadelphia roots; even farther, from her parochial school upbringing. Of her four brothers, three were firefighters like her dad; the fourth was a police officer. It was not that they had become estranged, but that they worried about her far too much for Sierra's taste. Growing up with four brothers had its advantages. She was assertive, a risk taker, and handled a car like a professional racetrack driver. A major crime figure, Moose Lavotini, from the New Jersey Lavotinis, was not a relative, although Sierra often claimed a connection. Before she moved to Florida and after the death of her lover in a gang war, Sierra lost the child she had been carrying. Now she shared her trailer home with a Chihuahua named Fluffy.

Not since Gypsy Rose Lee has such a voluptuous, free-spirited stripper made the mystery scene. *The Miracle Strip* (St. Martin, 1998) put a strain on Sierra's loyalties. Her pal Denise Curtis, bartender at the Tiffany Club, was in deep trouble. Denise's dog Arlo was being held for $100,000 ransom. The size of the ransom should have warned Sierra that Denise had a sideline, even more so when the corpse of Joey V., a drug courier, was discovered in Denise's motel room. Sierra risked her job, health, and a possible relationship with handsome cop Detective John Nailor to help a friend.

Sierra felt she and Nailor were moving towards something special until, in *Drag Strip* (St. Martin, 1999), he kissed an unknown woman in her presence. When Ruby Diamond, a naïve young stripper who had been Sierra's protégée, was murdered at a dirt racetrack, Sierra took it as a personal affront. With Nailor coming and going mysteriously, she had to rely on other allies: Raydean, her mentally ill neighbor, her visiting brother Al, and their mother.

Sierra may have dropped the name of her "uncle" Moose Lavotini once too often in *Film Strip* (St. Martin, 2000) but "what's a girl gonna do" when her fellow strippers are being murdered. John Nailor may be back in her personal life, but Sierra shared her detecting with Raydean, Pat (the landlady at the trailer court), and her visiting brother Francis. A trio of rival mobsters also pitched in to help.

Sierra was devastated to learn in *Strip Poker* (St. Martin, 2001) that her inept employer Vincent Gambuzzo had lost ownership of the Tiffany Gentlemen's Club in a poker game. Four hijackers had interrupted the game. In the subsequent melee, one of the players, Denny Watley, was shot. Based on the fact that his prints were on the gun, the police arrested Vincent for the murder. The subsequent owner Big Mike Riggs brought a low class tone to the strippers' performances, exposing more flesh and encouraging more contact with the customers. Sierra led a revolt. The others depended on her to prove Vincent innocent and restore dignity to their exotic dancing. She did better than that, although there were conflicts of interest with Detective John Nailor.

Using fairly sordid backgrounds, Bartholomew created a cast of wannabees, mentally ill females, and raunchy males, revealing the loyalties, the humor, and the survival skills that kept them going. The narratives had pace, imagination, and warmth.

Aimee Leduc

Author: Cara Black

The death of Aimee Leduc's father, Jean-Claude, in a car explosion five years before, had ended their close relationship and partnership in Leduc Investigations. They had been working in cooperation with the Commissariat on a case when his van exploded. Aimee's hand still bore scars from when she had tried to open the vehicle door. Her father had been a detective in the Paris Commissariat who had quit to work with his father. Aimee was the third generation in the business.

After his death, she limited her work to computer forensics, working primarily in providing security to large corporations. She and her partner, dwarf Rene Friant, had depended to a great extent on a contract with Eurocom. The contract had recently been broken, leaving the agency in serious debt. Not only had Eurocom turned their business over to an American agency, but they were withholding payment for work already done. This put Leduc in serious trouble with the tax authorities.

Aimee's mother, an American who had worked for the Paris *Herald Tribune*, left when Aimee was eight. Her father refused to discuss his wife's whereabouts or the reason for her departure. While an exchange student in New York, Aimee had searched unsuccessfully for a trace of her mother. Later in the series, Aimee came to believe that her mother, a political activist, might not only be alive, but living in Paris. At thirty-four, Aimee lived in a rundown apartment on Isle St. Louis, which she had inherited from her grandfather. She could neither afford repairs nor could she sell because of the tax consequences. She had recently purchased a Bishon Frise puppy, which she named Miles Davis.

For those who were alive during World War II, it is painful to remember the plight of the French Jews during the German Occupation. For the young it is good to learn so that such atrocities will not reoccur. During *Murder in the Marais* (Soho Press, 1999), Aimee went beyond her original commitment to encode material for Soli Hecht, a representative of Temple E'manuel. The finished product was to be delivered to Lili Stein. After Aimee found Lily mutilated and dead, Hecht offered even more money for the identification of her murderer. Aimee came to realize that Lili's death and Soli's subsequent "accident" were efforts to conceal the identity of a man who had betrayed his friends and neighbors to the Nazis. A tour de force.

Once again Aimee allowed personal considerations to influence her choice of cases. In *Murder in Belleville* (Soho, 2000), she agreed to help Anais de Froissart, wife of an influential government official, but also the sister of Aimee's friend, Martine. What had seemed a domestic dispute expanded into a murder investigation; then became a government scandal and international intrigue. Those who sought peaceful methods and who provided humanitarian aid for illegal foreign residents were sabotaged by rivals for power. Aimee used her computer skills and Le Figaro to foil a political coup. Some understanding of the French political system and the French/Algerian war would simplify the narrative for readers.

Even with the agency's finances in dire straits, Aimee was diverted into a private investigation in *Murder in the Sentier* (Soho, 2002). She needed to know whether or not her mother (Sydney) was alive; the degree to which she had been involved in terrorist activities, and whether or not she had any responsibility for the car bomb that killed Jean-Claude, her father. Operating without police support, even from her godfather, Morbier, Aimee probed the history of the Baader-Meinhof group, the remnants of which were seeking loot that Sydney might have hidden.

At lunch with agency client Vincent Csarda, Aimee noted an attractive older woman wearing a silk Chinese jacket identical to her own as *Murder in the Bastille* (SOSO, 2003) opened. After the woman left, Aimee noted that she'd left her cell phone behind. Instinctively responding to a call, Aimee went to return the phone. Then her world collapsed, an attack left her blind. The woman, reporter Josiane Dolet, was murdered nearby. Rene who had previously limited himself to office work, was pressed into service. Attractive ophthalmologist Dr. Guy Lambert provided more than professional attention. With the help of friends and software programs to enable the blind to use a computer, she persisted.

While still recovering from the injury to her eyes in *Murder in Clichy* (Soho, 2005), Aimee was drawn into an international controversy when she agreed to help Linh, a new acquaintance at the Cao Dae temple. Linh, a nun, asked Aimee to deliver an envelope in exchange for a package. The transfer went awry when a passing motorcyclist murdered the other party to the exchange, art gallery owner Thadee Baret. Aimee fled the scene with a substantial certified check and a knapsack filled with Asian antiquities (subsequently stolen). She also acquired a pair of stalkers, some doubtful allies, and a quick course in the history of the French defeat in Vietnam. This adventure put her relationship with Dr. Lambert at risk.

Depressed by the end of their relationship, Aimee joined her childhood friend Laure Rousseau at a retirement party in *Murder in Montmartre* (SOHO, 2006). Laure and her partner Jacques Gagnard left the group without explanation. When Laure did not return, Aimee went looking for her. She found critically injured Laure and dying Jacques on a scaffold attached to a building under construction. The worst came when the police charged Laure with having murdered Jacques. With little help from the inexperienced defense attorney assigned to Laure, Aimee and Rene conducted their own investigation. It led into Corsican politics, arms smuggling, and "Big Ears". More fortuitously it answered Aimee's questions about her father's record.

It was strange from the beginning of *Murder on the Ile Saint-Louis* (SOHO, 2007). An unknown woman left a newborn baby at Aimee's door. Meanwhile what had been planned as a peaceful protest against Amstrom Oil Company by MondeFocus turned into a riot. Armed security forces claimed that the permit for the protest had been revoked. Bottle bombs were discovered on the premises. Both the government and MondeFocus blamed young Polish born activist Krzyszof Linski for the melee. Even though Aimee and Rene had Amstrom's public relation firm, Regnault as a client, they took personal and professional risks to protect the baby whom Aimee grew to love, to find her mother, and to identify the "bad man" who had killed and would kill again. A hint at the conclusion increased the possibility that Sydney, Aimee's mother, was alive and nearby.

Murder in the Rue de Paradis (SOHO, 2008), for all of its brilliance is a difficult book for those without a basic knowledge of the conflicts between Sunni and Shia'a; bond between Turks and Kurds. On a personal level, Aimee was forced to learn these distinctions when Yves Robert, the foreign correspondent whom she had never been able to forget, returned to Paris. To her surprise, he announced his intention to settle down and proposed marriage. Her joy was short lived. Her next sight of Yves was as a corpse in the morgue. The authorities wrote off his death as the result of a homosexual encounter, a decision Aimee could not accept.

This was a fascinating series. Expected in 2009, *Murder in the Latin Quarter; Murder in the Palais Royale* (2010)

Heaven Lee

Author: Lou Jane Temple

Katherine O'Malley went through a variety of names over the years. Her parents had been killed in a car accident. Through marriage she added, and dropped a series of married names: Martin, McGuinne, Wolff, Steinberg, and Kelley. To add luster to her profession as a chef and restaurateur, she finally became Heaven Lee. All her marriages except one had ended in divorce. None had left her wealthy. Her Kansas City restaurant staff was eclectic, to say the least; gay waiters, a former ace reporter as the maitre d', a green-carded immigrant; and a burned-out artist who dressed in khaki although he had never been in the service.

This was not Heaven's first career. She earned a law degree between husbands McGuinne and Wolff; then, practiced in the field of entertainment law. Her association with a drug deal led to her disbarment and three years probation.

As *Death by Rhubarb* (St. Martin's Dead Letter Paperbacks, 1996) began, the restaurant was crowded. This was Monday night when the gay waiters planned to do their female impersonations. Jason Kelley (husband #5) needed to borrow Heaven's car. The business was being picketed by the 39th Street League of Decency, members of which entered and accosted the diners individually. Two of the diners happened to be Sandy Martin (husband #1) and female guest Tasha Arnold, his new assistant. When Tasha collapsed and died of poison, it was not surprising that Heaven made the top ten list of suspects. So did Jason who had been dating Tasha.

During *Revenge of the Barbecue Queens* (St. Martin, 1997), Heaven served as a judge at the Barbecue World Series. She was also a member of the Queens team competing in a parallel contest against the Male Chauvinist Pigs. Pigpen Hopkins, captain of the all-male team, was discovered drowned in barbecue sauce, after he had been knocked unconscious with a meat tenderizer. Kitchens can be dangerous places. Varied suspects had motives for the elimination of Pigpen. The most practical was based upon Pigpen's special sauce recipe, which was to be offered to the highest bidder.

During *A Stiff Risotto* (St. Martin, 1997), Heaven and two staff members attended a festival for chefs held in Aspen, Colorado under the auspices of the *Real Deal* magazine. The first 500 to register were to select the top chef from among four nominees. Lida Lunch, the *Real Deal* editor had an agenda of her own. Others had a plan to embarrass candidates for the best chef award with some nasty accidents and insinuations. The contenders had multiple connections in their pasts. Away from her twenty-six-year-old Kansas City lover Hank, Heaven flirted with Australian winegrower Rowland Alexander and Texas barbecue expert Bo Morales. Among her other questionable behaviors were her concealment of evidence and of Lila's corpse.

All the average reader needs to know about bread making was provided in *Bread on Arrival* (St. Martin's Paperbacks, 1998). Heaven and Pauline, the chief baker at Café Heaven, took part in a convention held by Artos, an organization of individual bakers (as compared to large commercial bakeries). Within Artos and among others attending the meetings, there were divergent theories as to how the world's needs for bread should be met. The intensity of the disputes led to strange deaths, which Hank (Heaven's young lover, a doctor) helped her to solve. The affair between Hank and Heaven made it difficult for her to criticize her daughter Iris, who had a much older lover.

Kansas City had a celebration planned to open a museum honoring the Negro Baseball League and to renovate the Ruby Theater where local jazz had been spawned. In *The Cornbread Killer* (St. Martin, 1999), Heaven signed on to coordinate the food preparation for the gala events in her neighborhood of 18th and Vine. Honored visitors, including a new restaurateur, jazz greats, a documentary film producer and former baseball players, gathered to work out their problems with the past. Heaven survived a concussion to restore a jazz relic and solve a mystery.

A law school friend, Mary Whitten, invited Heaven to New Orleans in *Red Beans and Vice* (St. Martin, 2001) to serve as one of several chefs for a benefit dinner to raise money for an order of nuns. Upon her acceptance, she received a scurrilous letter libeling her business, making her reluctant to leave at that time. Putting her fears aside, she joined in the planning of the menu. An antique cross belonging to the nuns was stolen as the group met. Vicious remarks were painted on the convent walls. Herbs from the nun's garden were poisoned. Someone was determined to sabotage the benefit. When Truely Witten, Mary's husband, was murdered, Heaven remained in New Orleans to offer comfort...and to investigate. Was the murder a progression from the earlier incidents or were there two agendas of destruction?

Death Is Semisweet (St. Martin, 2002) was light and frothy for all of the death and destruction it included. Heaven's friend, Stephanie Simpson, owner of the new Chocolate Queen Candy Shoppe, had revealed her connection with the Foster chocolates family. The downing of the Foster blimp; the murder of Oliver Bodden, representative of WACC (West African Cocoa Company, and vandalism of both chocolate shops and Heaven's restaurant brought Sgt. Bonnie Weber into the case. Realistic motives existed for several members of the Foster family to feel they had been cheated of their inheritance.

This combination of food, forensics, and fluff may not appeal to everyone's taste, but the characters add flavor and the reading goes down easy. Although cuisine remained important in her narratives, Temple changed sites and times and characters in later books. Temple's new historical series features immigrant Irish cook, Bridget Heaney.

Lt. Tory Lennox

Author: Tony Gibbs, pseudonym for Wolcott Gibbs, Jr

Tory Lennox was the daughter of a well-to-do family that had hoped that she would get a traditional education and marry a traditional husband. Instead she attended the U.S. Coast Guard Academy, determined to get posted at sea. Her appointment to a desk job in Washington, D.C. was not what she had in mind for a career. When California congresswoman Linda Goodell recruited Tory to go undercover on the West Coast to ferret out graft within the Drug Enforcement Agency, she took the assignment eagerly. This meant going outside the chain of command and set Tory up for disciplinary action, but in D.C. there was no action at all.

Chief of Harbor Security for Santa Barbara, Neal Donahoe, prided himself on his independence from the system, but he found U.S. Coast Guard Lt. Lennox a necessary ally in *Shot in the Dark* (Mysterious Press, 1996). A boat manned by DEA "cowboys" had been scuttled and the agents killed by occupants of a vessel that they had intercepted. The first step was to find the sunken vessel, but this had to be done carefully so as to prevent a DEA cover-up.

Neal Donahoe had a new supervisor, Maria Acevedo, as *Fade to Black* (Mysterious, 1997) opened. Maria was not going to tolerate a slapdash household living on a barely seaworthy boat tethered at the docks. Tory's sympathy for Erling Halvorsen and his five children aroused Halvorsen's erotic interest in her. Meanwhile, Tory's attention to recent changes in artwork by a blinded painter alerted her and Neal to a major scam. They balanced their ambitions against their need to be together.

For another series by author Tony Gibbs with a seaside flavor see Gillian Verdean in Volume 2.

Catherine LeVendeur

Author: Sharan Newman

Catherine LeVendeur was a novice at the convent headed by Heloise in this series set in Twelfth century France. Heloise, whose love affair with the famous theologian Father Peter Abelard had scandalized Christendom, sent Catherine on a secret mission in *Death Comes As Epiphany* (TOR 1993). Catherine, only eighteen but learned, was to return home, as if in disgrace, to investigate unauthorized changes in a psalter. Her parents reacted to her return differently: her devout mother, with unbelieving horror; her father, a converted Jew who concealed his origins, with understanding. While accomplishing her mission, Catherine lost her heart and her vocation to Edgar, a handsome young Scotsman.

A comparatively tall brunette, Catherine returned to the convent in *The Devil's Door* (Forge, 1994) but only to make arrangements for release from her temporary vows. She and Edgar were caught up in theological disputes, anti-Semitism, and the death of the beautiful Countess Alys whose bequest of land aroused controversy.

Catherine and Edgar had married by *The Wandering Arm* (Forge, 1995). Rather than living in luxury, they went undercover as a penniless artisan and his wife. Their mission was to discover a missing relic and the powerful individuals behind its theft. Their failure to do so would have increased the suspicion that the Jewish community was seriously involved in wrongdoing. They had to succeed.

Catherine and Edgar joined a procession of pilgrims en route to the shrine of St. James in Campostella, Spain during *Strong as Death* (Forge, 1996). After a stillbirth and two miscarriages, they sought intercession for a healthy child. Among their company were Catherine's father Hubert, her Uncle Eliazar, and Cousin Solomon, but also a seeker of vengeance for crimes committed decades before.

The Twelfth century, disturbed by political and religious controversy, provided a contentious background for *Cursed in the Blood* (Forge, 1998). It was the cruelty of the powerful and the rage of the oppressed that caused Edgar, Catherine, the infant James, and Solomon to journey to Scotland. They survived but not intact, returning to Paris with a new member of the family, Edgar's half-sister, Margaret. Their return coincided with the recruitment of men for the Second Crusade and the re-emergence of anti-Semitism, which placed Catherine and her family at jeopardy.

In *The Difficult Saint* (Forge, 1999), Catherine and her father, Hubert, put aside their personal concerns to travel to Germany and rescue her sister. Agnes had been accused of murdering her new husband, Lord Gerhardt. Against a background of religious dissension, the LeVendeur family accomplished their mission at the cost of making decisions that would split the family again. Edgar played a significant role, coping as best he could with a vital loss.

Troops were gathering in Paris, including those of the elite Knights Templar, for the Second Crusade in *To Wear the White Cloak* (Forge, 2000). Edgar, Catherine and their family returned from Germany. The discovery of a dead man garbed in the white cloak of the Knights brought attention to the home previously occupied by Hubert and now by Catherine and Edgar. Fears that scrutiny might expose Hubert's return to his Jewish faith motivated them to find the killer. The vengeance of Jehan, a disappointed suitor of Catherine's sister, and the dynastic hopes of two fathers complicated their efforts.

Astrolabe, the son of Heloise and Abelard, came to Catherine and Edgar for help in *Heresy* (Forge/Tom Doherty, 2002). At the request of friends, he had sought out Eon, a confused man who thought he was the son of God. Realizing he could not convince the man to leave his followers, Astrolabe prepared to leave himself. He agreed to escort Cecily, a young nun seeking refuge from those who had turned her convent into a brothel. During an attack by those who wished to capture Eon and his followers, Cecily was murdered, the scene arranged to make Astrolabe suspect. At this time the Pope had called together a great meeting at Reims. Catherine in the mid-stage of a second pregnancy agreed to attend to help Astrolabe identify the real killer. Slow reading due to names, titles and relationships

Gargenaud, Catherine's maternal grandfather, called all his descendants to come at once to the family castle in Boisvert in *The Witch in the Well* (Forge, 2004). The spring that had nourished the inhabitants of the castle thanks to sprightly ancestress Ando Nenn was dwindling. Even more serious was the news that Lord Olivier was marching on the castle, claiming ownership. Strange happenings occured to Catherine, Edgar and their children, to her brother Guillaume and his family, and to her overbearing sister Agnes and her family. The dead walked. Spirits appeared and disappeared within the castle. Gargenaud and his heir, grandson Seguin, prepared for a siege with Edgar's help. Catherine, Margaret, and Agnes searched for the secrets of a family treasure.

The Outcast Dove (Forge, 2003) was Solomon's book. Catherine was busy having a baby, a son, named Peter after Abelard.

The narratives personalized the theological disputes and religious prejudices of the period within a credible framework.

Wynsome "Wyn" Lewis

Author: David Kaufelt

Wyn Lewis was a workaholic real estate broker and attorney who returned to her hometown on Long Island after her marriage ended. The Lewis family (she had reverted to her maiden name and earned her law degree after the divorce) belonged to the inner circle of Waggs Nook Harbor residents. Her deceased father, Hap, had been an easygoing but respected real estate dealer, often consulted by those in difficulty. Her mother, a former high school principal, had tired of Long Island life and moved to Manhattan to become Vice Chancellor of the City University of New York. Wyn was financially successful, enabling her to subsidize a group home for troubled teenagers. Her former husband, Nick Meyers, had remarried. Still he continued to involve himself in Wyn's life, disapproving of her relationship with Tommy Handwerk, local master carpenter. She was a blonde, very attractive at thirty-six, cool and determined.

The Lewis books were mysteries superimposed upon a *Peyton Place* like setting, in which Wyn's character development was subordinated to the fascinating and libidinous supporting characters. In *The Fat Boy Murders* (Pocket, 1993), the remaining members of an elitist high school group, the Fat Boys, were threatened with extinction. Wyn, who was involved with the victims and the suspects as a friend, an attorney, and a broker, was drawn in further when her uncle Fitz, a former NYC police commissioner, helped the chief of police.

Another local group, the women who remained year round on Long Island (widowed or divorced; well educated and upper middle class, but not genuine locals), was the focus of *The Winter Women Murders* (Pocket, 1994). With time on their hands, considerable energy and ambition, the widows sponsored a literary arts symposium which featured controversial feminist notables with local ties. When group leader Sophie Comfort Noble died, her potential successors squabbled over the right to dictate the course of the literary organization. Wyn busied herself with the murder of freethinking author Keny Blue. Feeling neglected, Tommy Handwerk found more agreeable companionship. He wanted a marriage and children; Wyn was slowly realizing that she might too.

The boom in construction in Waggs Neck Harbor, as *The Ruthless Realtor Murders* (Pocket, 1997) began, had its negative aspects. Someone was murdering real estate brokers. The victims had been connected with a series of suspicious land transfers. Wyn had been an innocent part of those negotiations. Ambitious police lieutenant Pasko had his own motivation for connecting the recent deaths to murders he had failed to solve in the past. He kept a salacious eye on Wyn, but so did Tommy, now her husband.

The narratives dealt with past events in Waggs Neck Harbor, which had its share of abuse, greed, illegitimacy, and struggles between those who wanted to update the community and those who fought change.

Gilda Liberty

Author: Della Borton, pseudonym for Lynette Carpenter aka D. B. Borton

Gilda Liberty and the members of her extended family had spent their working lives in show business. Having retired from professional life, her parents, aunts and uncles had returned to their Eden, Ohio roots. Her parents, Douglas and Florence, had been a song and dance team. Assorted aunts and uncles had worked in make-up, wardrobe, or as cameramen, actors and actresses. Gilda at fifty plus, contented herself with managing the Paradise, a rundown theatre bequeathed to her by her Aunt Mae. She had been married, produced a son John, now an adult Her subsequent lesbian relationship with Liz had ended, leaving her lonely. In her investigations she utilized the various skills of family members. A helpful genealogy chart was provided.

The Liberty clan members should wear numbers on their jerseys like a football team in *Fade to Black* (Fawcett, 1999). Then the reader could identify individuals during the introductory narrative and remember the role each one played: heavy drinker, practical joker, hairstylist, innkeeper, but also killer and arsonist. The Libertys gathered in Eden, Ohio for the funeral of Aunt Mae, an Oscar winning actress. Gilda had mixed feelings when she learned that she would inherit a substantial sum of money if she took over management of Mae's beloved Paradise Theater for five years. She had no technical expertise to run the projectors. Her seventeen-year-old nephew Duke handled that part of the process. After what she went through ferreting out the mystery of "Rosebud", managing a theater should be a breeze.

During *Freeze Frame* (Fawcett, 2000), Duke needed help with the projectors. Gilda's niece, Faye McCadden, needed help with the documentary she was producing dramatizing the gender differences in high school athletics. A deal was made. Faye would help Duke in exchange for space to work at the Paradise and some assistance from Gilda. The first assignment had Gilda roaming a mall taking background video footage while Faye interviewed and photographed the participants in a cheerleader contest for very young girls. Something in their footage may have endangered the athletic department at Buckeye State University.

Leo Mayer, a shirttail connection to the Liberty family, had deteriorated as a result of Alzheimer's in *Slow Dissolve* (Fawcett, 2001). His third wife Shirley had two goals: (1) to get control of Leo's money, now handled by his sons, for his own protection and (2) to find "Auggie," a figure from his past whom Leo desperately wanted to contact. Pulled into the case by family and by her association with private detective Sammy Styles, Gilda had a third goal: to keep Leo and Shirley alive. The narrative delved into a fascinating aspect of American films before World War II. As D. B. Borton, she wrote the Cat Caliban series, covered in this volume.

Readers interested in African-American films in that period are directed to Richard Lupoff's books featuring Bart Lindsey and Marvia Plum. (See Volume 2).

Robin Light

Author: Barbara Block

Robin Light, who identified herself as having been a drug using, card carrying liberal in the Sixties, seemed too young to qualify. Her tastes were more than liberal: She ignored parking tickets, drank Scotch, smoked pot, and shared sex with a wounded police officer in his hospital bed. A tall woman with carrot colored hair, her marriage had ended when her husband Murphy overdosed in his parked car. Robin was extremely depressed after his death, even resorting to self-mutilation to assuage her loss.

Robin took control of Noah's Ark, the Syracuse, New York pet shop she inherited from Murphy. She shared her home with two cats and a dog named Zsa Zsa, existed primarily on junk food, and drove a yellow Checker Cab. A college graduate, she had worked as a substitute teacher, photographer and journalist, but quit to write a book about the standoff on the St. Marie Indian Reservation. Gradually she took control of her alcohol abuse.

As if lizards and exotic birds weren't enough excitement, someone left a package at the shop for John Blount, Robin's assistant, in *Chutes and Adders* (Kensington, 1994). The contents were deadly. When Murphy's connection with endangered species was uncovered, Robin was at risk from the police and a killer. African-American police officer, George Samson, a pal of Murphy's, gave Robin the benefit of the doubt and much of his spare time.

Martha, a repulsive tarantula, saved Robin when she helped old friend Lynn Stanley, suspected of murder, and became entwined in a disturbed family relationship in *Twister* (Kensington, 1995). Robin had accompanied Lynn to a dismal house in a tough neighborhood where Lynn expected to retrieve something her husband Gordon had left there. When Lynn did not come out, Robin went in and found her standing over the corpse of Brandon Douglas. Unexplainably Lynn confessed to manslaughter one. Douglas had been an employee of the family business. After the subsequent death of Janet, Brandon's half-sister, Robin used expired credentials as a reporter to investigate.

In Plain Sight (Kensington, 1996) featured a cast of supporting characters, most of whom were related to one another. The narrative blended the disappearance of schoolgirl Estrella Torres with the murder of dog-loving housewife Marsha Pennington, who had been in the process of a divorce. Custody of the dogs had been a settlement issue. Robin's relationship with George Samson moved beyond friendship.

The memory of Murphy, Robin's deceased husband, came back with a vengeance in *The Scent of Murder* (Kensington, 1997) when a strange young girl pleaded for help in his name. Amy drifted in and out of Robin's life, usually with the police on her trail. Her stepfather had been killed, and she was a suspect. Robin followed her through discos and warehouses, exposing herself to arrest and physical injury to pay a debt that was Murphy's, not hers.

In *Vanishing Act* (Kensington, 1998), Bryan Hayes convinced Robin to investigate the disappearance of his sister Melissa, a college sophomore. Her interviews with Melissa's roommates, boyfriends, and professors brought forth a variety of possible reasons why Melissa might have chosen to leave school voluntarily. Robin had an "inspiration" as to what really happened to her. Inspirations make solutions too easy.

Robin was a pushover for a sad story in *Endangered Species* (Kensington, 1999). She agreed to help Eli Bishop recover a suitcase he had smuggled in from Cuba purportedly full of cigars. His roommate Nestor had disappeared at the same time as the suitcase. Too late, Robin learned that Nestor had been murdered, that the contents of the suitcase were far more valuable than cigars, and that Eli's employer was prone to violence.

Noah's Ark occupied very little of Robin's attention during *Blowing Smoke* (Kensington, 2001). Income from her work as an unlicensed private investigator was keeping the store afloat. That meant taking cases that had an emotional impact: (1) finding Bethany, a teenage runaway, and returning the girl to a father who had given up on her; (2) investigating Pat Humphrey, a pet psychic whom three siblings suspected was bilking their mother; then, (3) working for the siblings' powerful mother, Rose Taylor, when Pat Humphrey was found dead. Robin, who had not been in touch with her own mother in years, wondered about families. George Samson, who left the police force to work on an academic Ph.D., backed away from Robin and her affinity for violent crime.

Private investigator Paul Santini had been an occasional employer and a substitute lover for Robin, but in *Rubbed Out* (Kensington, 2002) he involved her in a disastrous case. Currently estranged from George Samson and tempted by an exorbitant fee, Robin set out to find Walter Wilcox's wife, Janet. Janet had emotional problems, had been seeing a therapist, and had a possible history of sexual abuse. Wilcox was desperate to find her; so was Santini. Before she was through, Robin was desperate too as she was pulled into the machinations of Russian gangsters.

Robin had enough failure in her life, as *Salt City Blues* (Severn House, 204 GB) began, to make her cautious about taking on new projects. George Samson was spending time with his mistress Natalie with whom he recently had a son. Robin hesitated to tell him to pack up and leave her home. Noah's Ark was in serious financial trouble. Her private investigation business wasn't bringing in any money, so Robin worked two nights a week bartending at Ian Yates "Shamus' Bar." A casual contact with Freddy Sanchez involved Robin in a series of murders. She couldn't back off not only because Ian asked her to help Freddy's mom, but because Manuel, her employee at the pet shop might be in trouble. He frequently was.

Nothing much had changed as *No Good Deed* (Severn House, 2007) began. George no longer shared her home, but he kept stopping by the store. Ian had become the man she depended upon when she was in trouble, although there was no romantic involvement. Manuel continued to get into trouble, this time with his Onondoga pals, Chad and Jellybean. John Gabriellos (who was referred to as Robin's partner without any explanation) asked Robin to check on his gay lover, Trent Goodwell. Was he "seeing" Benny Gibson? There was a lot going on, all of it bad. It took a lot for Robin to catch on. John was lying to her. Manuel was lying to her. George had been lying to her for years. Thank goodness for Ian.

The series showed promise, but was no cozy. At times Robin seemed just plain dumb.

Margaret Loftus

Author: C. J. Koehler

Margaret Loftus, a tall dark haired police officer, was teamed with Det. Sgt. Ray Koepps, a former priest. Both differed from the average police officer so took comfort in their association. Margaret had an on-going romance with a steady but unidentified stockbroker. Ray, whose affair with a married woman had triggered his withdrawal from the priesthood, was unattached.

During *Profile* (Carroll & Graf, 1994), the police department contacted mental health professionals in their search for a serial killer. Dr. Lisa Robbins responded, revealing her concerns about an unnamed patient. Lisa became a suspect when the next victim was her husband's lover. The characters of Margaret and Ray were subordinate to Lisa, but well developed.

Ray's religious training failed him in *Mind Games* (Carroll & Graf, 1996), when he and Margaret investigated a murder at Friar's Close, an experiment in communal living. His attraction to a suspect led him to lie under oath, carry out unauthorized surveillance and use excessive force. Margaret had only a minor role.

Whitney Logan

Author: Mercedes Lambert (pseudonym of Douglas Anne Munson)

Whitney Logan rejected her East Coast family, moving to California where she used an inheritance to attend law school, and enter criminal law practice. This was a risky move for the tall blonde who had excellent grades, but limited experience in the specialized field. She was single, but sexually active. Her emotional stability was shaky, deteriorating seriously by the final book in the series. It was very important for Whitney to succeed in her chosen career, spurred by her father's disapproval and his declaration that she would never make it as an attorney. Even when she barely kept her office running, Whitney chose not to ask her parents for financial help.

Harvey Kaplan, Whitney's landlord, had been a top notch criminal defense attorney, but crossed a line that made it necessary for him to retire from practice. He was insistent that he would never again appear in court but on occasion advised Whitney in her cases.

On her first major case in *Dogtown* (Viking, 1991), Whitney enlisted hooker Guadalupe "Lupe" Ramos, to find missing domestic Carmen Luzano, who may have been an illegal immigrant. Whitney soon discovered that her client Monica Fullbright was not to be trusted, but by that time she was too involved in Carmen's other identity to end her investigation. The trail led through the seamiest areas in Los Angeles, the drug trade, and the complexities of Central American politics. Lupe ended up in jail, but the two women had become friends. Lupe's street smarts were an asset to Whitney.

Whitney's fascination with Lupe continued in *Soultown* (Viking, 1996). When Lupe was released from prison, Whitney was waiting, offering apologies, a ride home, and eventually a job in her office. They pursued a killer who had robbed the savings of five elderly Korean women, but found themselves enmeshed in Lupe's domestic problems, feuds within the minority population of Koreatown, and the laundering of drug money. Lupe and her five-year-old son Joey lived with her mother and her no-good brother Hector, but at least she had somewhere to go at the end of the day. Whitney went home to Jack Daniels for consolation.

Ghosttown (Five Star, 2007) was more than a mystery narrative. A court appointment brought Whitney to the jail to meet Tony Red Wolf who had been charged with a drunk and disorderly misdemeanor. From then on she was totally focused on him. Although he had rejected her help initially, he called her during the night, asking her to meet him at the San Gabriel mission. He was waiting to show her the dismembered body of Shirley Yellowbird. This was murder and Whitney was unsure as to what role Tony had played in the death but she desperately wanted a big case, a breakthrough. Over the next weeks, she also developed feelings for Tony. He took her into a sleazy world, populated by Native Americans (Tony was a Choctaw "breed"), Hispanics, and other minorities. Whitney ignored her responsibilities as an officer of the court, becoming more and more unstable, delving into Native American spiritualism.

Even more interesting than the narrative itself was how it came to be published. Viking who had published the first two books rejected *Ghosttown* and the direction that Lambert was taking with her heroine. The terms of her contract denied Lambert the right to merchandise the book elsewhere. In an extensive "Afterword," Lucas Crown detailed author Lambert's deterioration; i.e.her inability to write, her burnout as an attorney in abusive custody situations, and times when she was a street person. She eventually found employment teaching English in the Czech Republic, but kept in regular contact with Crown. A move back to the United States was necessitated when her cancer returned. She left the unpublished narrative in Crown's hands. After her death in 2003 and the expiration of the Viking rights on the characters, Crown took it upon himself to get *Ghosttown* published. Although she had a niche readership, not everyone will enjoy the series. Even fans may be disappointed in the final book. These were complex murky narratives with an unconventional sleuth.

Lavinia London

Author: James R. McCahery

Elderly sleuths have never gone out of style, but Lavinia London had a slow start. She was a tall widow in her seventies who had left New York City for an upstate vacation home shortly before the death of her husband. Lavinia had worked as a radio/television actress. Her daughter Tracey lived with her husband and daughter Susanne in New York City.

When Lavinia accompanied a friend to make arrangements for a deceased family member, they found local undertaker Leo Frame dead in one of his coffins during *Grave Undertaking* (Knightsbridge, 1990). Lavinia's contact with the investigation came through her friendship with local sheriff Tod Arthur. Two more murders occurred before Lavinia and the sheriff baited the killer into an attack.

Friendship enticed Lavinia into a murder investigation again in *What Evil Lurks* (Kensington, 1995). Her research for an autobiography crossed paths with an investigation into the death of Henry Blaine. He was a former radio soap opera star, who had been financing his retirement through blackmail. Lavinia avoided the classic gimmick of serving as bait for the killer, but found an attractive beau, who might instead have been the killer.

Lavinia made one more appearance in *Deep and Crisp and Even*, a short story in the anthology *Murder Most Merry.*

Emma Lord

Author: Mary Daheim

Emma Lord gave birth to her son, Adam, after an affair with Tom Cavanaugh; then, built a life for herself and their child. Through her newspaper connections she continued to see Tom occasionally. He developed an interest in the boy as he grew older. An unfortunate aspect to the narratives was the ridicule of Sandra, Tom's wealthy but mentally ill wife. An attractive trim and tiny woman with brown hair untouched by gray, Emma never married, although she had male friends. She raised Adam, while parlaying her experience on a big city newspaper and an unexpected inheritance into ownership of a weekly newspaper in Alpine, Washington. Her parents had been killed in a car accident. Her only brother Ben was a Catholic priest. Emma's employees at the *Alpine Advocate* were her support system, led by house and home editor Vida Runkel who knew all there was to know about everyone in Alpine and her business manager, Leo Walsh. Eventually Adam also became a priest. Vida's romance and her obsession with her obnoxious grandson Roger were given considerable space.

In *The Alpine Advocate* (Ballantine, 1992), Chris Ramirez, grandson of Neeny Doukas who "owned" the town, returned after a fourteen-year absence. Emma, at Adam's request, provided Chris with transportation and lodging, and then, support and defense when his gold hunting cousin Mark was murdered.

The Alpine Betrayal (Ballantine, 1993) focused on actress Dani Marsh who had grown up in Alpine. Dani returned reluctantly to star in a movie to be filmed on location. Her former husband Matt and her estranged mother offered no welcome. When Matt was poisoned at a local gathering, Vida had the background information, which Emma needed to discover a killer.

During *The Alpine Christmas* (Ballantine, 1993), Father Ben substituted for the ailing pastor, and Adam returned for the holidays. The Nyquist family's problems with pranksters escalated when Oscar revealed to Emma that someone was trying to kill his daughter-in-law Bridget. His problems were overshadowed by the discovery of female corpses (or portions thereof) traced to hookers from the "big city." Yet there was a connection, Bridget had gone to school with one of the victims.

Emma at forty-two was still waiting for Tom Cavanaugh in *The Alpine Decoy* (Ballantine, 1994). Racial incidents were new to Alpine, but the deaths of two African-American men at a time when the Campbells, a local family, were hosting Marilynn Lewis, a young African-American nurse, awakened the town's xenophobia. Emma searched the origins of the victims, tracing their ties to Alpine, before heading for a rendezvous with Cavanaugh at a statewide conference.

Emma needed to leave town for a while after her romantic interlude, so in *The Alpine Escape* (Ballantine, 1995) she rambled along the Washington coast. Car problems stranded Emma at the home of Mavis Fullerston, a friend who had discovered old bones in her newly acquired house. With time on her hands, Emma researched the family who had occupied the home, but called on Vida and close friend Sheriff Milo Dodge for help.

During *The Alpine Fury* (Ballantine, 1995), the visit of "Bobby" Lambrecht, the local boy who became a major bank executive, aroused suspicions that the Bank of Alpine might be absorbed by a larger institution. The murder of bank official Linda Lindahl, whose family controlled the local facility, did not seem a coincidence to Emma. Ed Bronsky, her advertising manager, had resigned upon inheriting a fortune. He stayed around as a humorous character.

Ed's replacement, Leo Walsh, although still abusing alcohol to deal with the pain of his divorce, kept Emma off balance as *The Alpine Gamble* (Ballantine, 1996) began. The community needed industry, but was a mountainside spa the solution? When Stan Levine, one of the two developers, was murdered at the site, the project was jeopardized. Milo Dodge had difficulty coping with another murder on his turf, but he was there for Emma when she realized that Tom would never leave his wife. Feeling revitalized by this decision, Emma looked elsewhere for companionship. She and Sheriff Dodge had been spending time together, but he maintained a four-year relationship with disabled potter Hortensia Whitman.

During *The Alpine Hero* (Ballantine, 1997), both Milo and Emma delved into the relationships in the Whitman family. Emma had discovered the body of a woman who had been receiving a facial at the local beauty salon. The victim had taken an appointment initially meant for Hortensia, and was identified by Hortensia's brother Trevor as his wife, Kay. Trevor had a past. He had been sent to prison for killing Hortensia's abusive husband. Who had been the intended victim?

Ursula O'Toole Randall returned to her hometown in *The Alpine Icon* (Ballantine, 1997), prepared for a third marriage, but not to die. Emma and

Vida persisted in their belief that Ursula had been murdered. Her will provided motives for her death, but so did her involvement in parish politics. Adam announced his intention to study for the priesthood.

Emma needed to get away as *The Alpine Journey* (Ballantine, 1998) opened. An emergency call from Vida made it clear that she had not left murder behind. Audrey Imhoff, Vida's niece in Oregon, had been killed. Her husband Gordon was missing. Their teenaged children were unsupervised. Vida's family pride and Emma's loyalty necessitated a depressing search for a killer. Emma's personal life became more solitary.

Emma's decision to end her affair with Milo Dodge ended their friendship too. That was only one of her problems during *The Alpine Kindred* (Ballantine, 1999). *Advocate* reporter/photographer Carla Steinmetz was not only pregnant, but had accepted a job at the new community college. That made it Emma's responsibility to cover the latest local scandal and the death of Einar Rasmussen, Jr, a major donor to the college and head of a trucking business.

The Advent days before Christmas were usually happy ones for Emma. During *The Alpine Legacy* (Ballantine, 2000), she was consumed with anger. Crystal Bird, editor and publisher of an alternative newspaper, viciously attacked Emma for what she perceived as a failure to fight for women's rights in the Alpine community. The charges triggered animosity against Emma. The stakes went higher when Crystal was found dead under circumstances that pointed to Emma. A romantic interlude with Tom Cavanaugh lifted her spirits temporarily, but even discovering the killer brought only limited satisfaction. She realized that Tom was drawn to women who needed him. Father Ben and Vida both accused Emma of relishing her role as victim.

Emma and Vida took their act on the road again in *The Alpine Menace* (Ballantine, 2000) to rescue her shiftless cousin Ronnie. Much as Emma loved Seattle, she believed that the local police department looked no further than Ronnie when his live-in lover was throttled. The victim, Carol Stokes, had recently been reunited with the child whom she had given up for adoption eighteen years before. Maternal feelings ran amok.

Emma had a major decision to make in *The Alpine Nemesis* (Fawcett, 2001). After all these years of waiting, Tom Cavanaugh, now a widower, had asked her to marry him. Strangely enough she wanted time to think it over. Emma was preoccupied with growing competition from the new radio station. KSKY could provide up to the minute news while *The Advocate* was a weekly paper. It had been scooped on the disappearance of snowboarder Brian Conley. Determined not to let that happen again, Emma put out an extra when the Norwegian Hartquists shot and killed three of the Irish O'Neills. Her efforts to connect a disappearance (which turned out to be murder) with the assassination of the O'Neill brothers were successful but only after Emma suffered a tremendous loss.

A confusing mélange of family names and relationship began *The Alpine Obituary* (Ballantine, 2002) but they roused Emma out of the half-life she had been living since Tom Cavanaugh was murdered. Vida talked Emma into investigating a threatening note sent to Judge Marsha Foster-Klein who had handled the case of Tom's killer. Distraught widow June Froland insisted that her husband had been murdered. Spencer Fleetwood, owner of the radio station, suggested joint ventures. The narrative mixed three time frames, causing confusion for a reader. At the least Emma came to realize that others suffered a loss and survived.

There was no question about who shot Hans Berenger, dean of students at Skykomish Community College in *The Alpine Pursuit* (Ballantine, 2004). College president Nat Cardenas fired the shot from a gun supposed to hold blank cartridges during the premiere performance of a play put on by the local dramatic club. So who made the switch? Milo would like the killer to be cocaine dealer Darryl Eckstrom whom he eventually arrested. Emma gathered additional information. Her decision will come as a shock, even a disappointment

The Alpine Quilt (Ballantine, 2005) was a poignant narrative during which Emma was personally affected by what she learned and how she handled the truth. Vida was out of town when Genevieve Bayard, a former resident of Alpine, returned after many years. Her son Buddy and his wife Roseanna welcomed this rare visit, but it was Annie Jeanne Dupre, childhood friend of Genevieve, who was most excited. When Genevieve died after eating a meal at the rectory, where Jeanne was the housekeeper and Father Ben was the substitute pastor, Annie Jeanne was ill and devastated. Emma wanted the story for the Advocate, but she also wanted to protect Father Ben and Annie Jeanne. Vida, who had returned, wanted nothing to do with the investigation. She'd never liked Genevieve. Why?

The death of Tim Rafferty, who worked part-time for the radio station in *The Alpine Recluse* (Ballantine, 2006) was determined to be murder. Tim had been stabbed to death before his home was set on fire. He left behind: Tiffany, his pregnant wife; Delia, his mother who suffered from Alzheimer's, and Beth, the 911 operator who took care of Delia. Baffled by the case, Milo Dodge was intrigued by sightings of "Old Nick", a recluse. Emma with some help from Vida probed deeper, till she touched a nerve.

Emma and her author were contemplative in *The Alpine Scandal* (Ballantine, 2007). Prodded by Vida's advice and her own loneliness, Emma gave thought to a future in which The Advocate was the only significant factor in her life. The death of well-liked and exceedingly competent Elmer Nystrom was more than a news story to Emma and Vida. They had received a premature obituary on Elmer in the mail, which prompted a visit to his wife, Polly. Taking advantage of Polly's offer of some fresh eggs, they entered the chicken house where they discovered Elmer's body. Sheriff Milo Dodge was in and out of the hospital during the narrative. Emma and Vida used their regular sources and some possible suspects to acquire information about Polly and Elmer. What was there in his life that would lead to his death? Not up to usual standards for the series.

Tom Cavanaugh, the man in Emma's life, was dead but in *The Alpine Traitor* (Ballantine, 2008) she couldn't get him off her mind. His son Graham, daughter Kelsey and her husband Dylan Platte had arrived in Alpine. At least so it seemed at first. Dylan informed Emma that the Cavanaugh siblings who had inherited Tom's newspaper chain, intended to buy the Advocate. They were negotiating to buy Ed Bronsky's house and move to town. It became more complex when "Dylan" turned out not to be Dylan according to the fingerprints on his corpse. Emma had to reassure herself of Tom's love for her while dealing with staff problems and Tom's family. Some issues were left unresolved...six more letters in the alphabet. Next: *The Alpine Uproar* (2009); *The Alpine Vengeance* (2011)

These were pleasant narratives mixing hometown humor, sympathy for those who live and work in the Northwest, and mystery. Daheim has a second extended series, featuring Bed and Breakfast owner Judith McMonigle (Flynn), also in this volume

Dottie Loudermilk

Author: Gar Anthony Haywood

Dottie and Joe Loudermilk were middle class African-Americans who had retired in their early fifties to become "lifers" on the highway, traveling in style in Lucille, their beloved Airstream trailer. Joe, a former police officer, was less interested in murder than Dottie, but she cunningly cajoled him into helping when their children were involved.

In *Going Nowhere Fast* (Putnam, 1994), Dottie and Joe returned to the motor home, only to find a dead man on the toilet and their youngest son, "Bad Dog" a.k.a. Theodore, in trouble. Dottie doggedly pursued evidence that the victim, Geoffry Bettis, was a witness against the mob, protected by the FBI.

Their older daughter "Mo" a.k.a. Maureen was a tax attorney who handled the Loudermilk's finances and the most stable of the children. She threw up her hands in *Bad News Travels Fast* (Putnam, 1995) when her brother, Eddie, the family political activist, was accused of murdering Emmett Bell, an angry and aggressive protestor. Dottie was unwilling to let Eddie's fate be decided by the Washington, D.C. police department. She and Joe battled politicians, Capitol police, and blackmailers to free Eddie and influence the killer to confess.

These were engaging people in a well-written series.

Haywood also has a series featuring Los Angeles private investigator Aaron Gunner.

Philipa Lowe

Author: Roger Ormerod

Philipa Lowe's marriage to Graham Tonkin had ended badly. After an unexplained scandal he left his job to paint. From then on, Philipa maintained their home in Penley. She moved to America, but had never sought a divorce. Her father had been a police superintendent and the author of a definitive book about Raymond Chandler.

Her decision to stop off from a Swiss vacation to attend Graham's funeral in *Hung in the Balance* (Constable, 1990) had negative repercussions. Graham had purportedly driven his car over a cliff. She had no hope of an inheritance. Nor did she have any expectation that the corpse was not Graham's, although she knew that he did not drive. She certainly had no reason to believe that she would be accused of murder. Graham had obtained a divorce under the false pretense that she could not be located. Then he amended his will to name her, by personal name rather than the designation "wife," as his heir. This might have been ridiculous except that he had achieved considerable recognition as a painter. Although Anna Treadgold, Graham's current mistress, insisted that Philipa should be arrested, Inspector Oliver Simpson was both cautious and attracted to Philipa. This was a taut and complex narrative.

Philipa had developed a successful personnel management agency in New York City that assisted major corporations in locating, testing, and hiring employees. Given a lucrative offer for the business, she decided to return to England in *Bury Him Darkly* (Constable, 1991) by way of a leisurely trip on the Queen Elizabeth 2. What seemed to be a chance friendship with fellow passenger Bella Fields turned into a major murder investigation with roots in the past. Bella, a well-known television actress, had been taken into custody when she disembarked from the ocean liner. Her father had disappeared ten years before. Now his corpse had been found in her hometown of Horsely Green. Detective Inspector Oliver Simpson, Constables Jennie Lyons, and Terry Alwright joined with Philipa to prove Bella's innocence when the local inspector seemed determined to convict her.

It was bridegroom Martin Reade who was the three-time loser in *Third Time Fatal* (Constable, 1992). His first wife, Amanda, was killed the night before he was to wed Heather Payne, longtime friend of Philipa. Amanda's naked body had been discovered in Martin's bed. As he and Heather prepared to leave for their American honeymoon, Martin was arrested for bigamy and fraud based on charges filed by Jean McBride whom he had also "married." Philipa's knowledge of British cars and their motors helped her sift through competing theories as to who killed Amanda.

Given the prior narratives, *A Shot at Nothing* (Constable, 1993) was a disappointment. Philipa wanted to marry Oliver Simpson, but he balked at the difference in their financial status. He was unwilling to live in a house owned by his wife. Oliver reluctantly assisted Philipa when she negotiated to buy Collington House in the Penley area. Its owner Clare Steadman, imprisoned for the murder of her unpopular husband Harris, returned as they were inspecting the premises. This added another complexity. At one time there had been a relationship between Oliver and Clare. Furthermore as part of her protestation that she was innocent of Harris Steadman's death, Clare implied that Oliver might have killed him. Another death occurred because Philipa persisted in an investigation, leaving her to wonder if she might best have let the past bury its dead.

Ormerod is also the author of the Inspector Richard Patton/Amelia Trowbridge series, covered in Volume 2.

Victoria "Vicky" Lucci

Author: Suzanne Proulx

Victoria Lucci made it clear that her last name was pronounced to rhyme with lucky, and that she was not related to Susan Lucci, the soap opera actress. She was, in fact, a risk manager for Montmorency Hospital located in midtown Manhattan. Vicky had followed a long and rocky road to get to this point. Her original goal had been to earn a nursing degree, followed by employment at a Boston hospital. While there she had dabbled in illegal drugs. Presumably, she had never been charged for her offenses because she entered law school and earned a degree. A few years working in a legal aid program had led to her current position.

Some pressure (internal or external) forced Vicky into a drug rehabilitation group. She no longer indulged in drugs (maybe a little pot), but smoked even though doing so during work hours forced her out into the cold. Her alcohol intake was restricted to wine, which she occasionally overdid enough to earn a hangover. Her sexual interests were frequently men who were already married. Their assignations might be carried out in strange settings; e.g. a room off the hospital morgue. A rape while in law school had convinced Vicky to carry pepper spray in her purse, hide some under her pillow, and keep a baseball bat under her bed.

For such a tiny woman, she was ferocious. Vicky had an amicable relationship with her brother Bob and his wife, Happy. She baby-sat with their children. Not so, with her mother whom she identified as a nag and a cheapskate.

Bad Blood (Fawcett Gold Medal, 1999) provided a sense of constant stress, frequent interruptions in Vicky's workload, and general chaos. She focused on missing drugs from the hospital pharmacy, potential law suits for malpractice, and tampering with the blood supply. The primary question was who would risk the lives of patients to delay or stop a potential merger of Montmorency with a for-profit chain. The narrative was cluttered with characters, although patients were often referred to not by name but as "Downs Syndrome child", or "man from Texas".

The background and the on-going characters were established by *Bad Luck* (Ballantine, 2000), which made the narrative easier to read. The pressures on Vicky continued. A problematic day began when she struck a black cat with her car. This was followed by the disappearance of her supervisor Jette Wakefield; the mysterious descent into a coma after facial surgery of the wife of prominent staff doctor Dennis Devoss; and an awareness that the hospital computers had been compromised. At least Vicky had acquired a steady lover, Glenn Rossmore who was separated from his wife and living across the hall. She also acquired the black cat.

Peter Lookabough still blamed Dr. Cynthia Hawthorne and Montmorency Hospital for the stillbirth of his daughter and the hysterectomy performed on his wife, Barbara in *Bad Medicine* (Fawcett, 2001). Peter's resentment simmered even though Vicky had agreed to drop all financial charges for the procedures. His entrance into the hospital with a gun created a hostage situation not only for Vicky but also for a young couple whose child was being delivered. Once said, the narrative degenerated into endless negotiations and bickering.

Declared Dead (Fawcett, 2002) was the best plotted of the series. The narrative began when Jenna McLaren stopped by at Vicky's office with her own death certificate. The emergency room misunderstanding occurred when Jenna's young sister, Marnie arrive in no condition to clarify her identity. Her death raised far more problems than mistaken identity because she had participated in the test of an experimental drug produced by High Plains Research Institute. Vicky had recently been contacted with a lucrative offer of employment at HPRI. Some technical details were confusing, but with the help of former lovers and beaus, Vicky worked her way through to a solution. Her employment situation was even more confusing. She'd resigned at Montmorency. Could she return? What about the job she had begun at HPRI?

Marti MacAlister

Author: Eleanor Taylor Bland

African-American policewoman Marti MacAlister found life in Chicago unbearable after her husband Johnny's death was termed a suicide by the Police Department. She transferred to nearby Lincoln Prairie, hoping to leave behind gambling, prostitution, drug dealing, and murder, but they had preceded her. Marti was tall and imposing, with four commendations from her ten years on the Chicago Police Department. Her children, Theo, initially aged nine, and Joanna, almost fifteen, put down roots in Lincoln Prairie. The family shared a house with Sharon, a divorced teacher, and her daughter. Paramedic Ben Walker became Marti's friend through work and his role as Theo's scoutmaster. Marti and her partner Vik Jessenovik, who had grown up in Lincoln Prairie, shared an office with vice cops Slim and Cowboy, bypassing racial and gender tensions.

In *Dead Time* (St. Martin, 1992), two children, Georgie and Padgett, overheard a murder. The next morning schizophrenic Lauretta Dorsey, a former Navy therapist, was found dead. Vik and Marti, knowing that the children had been in the vicinity, had to locate them before the killer did.

Slow Burn (St. Martin, 1993) handed Vik and Marti a heavy caseload: arson at a clinic; the death of a young African-American man and the search for his sister; the killing of an impoverished elderly woman in a nearby apartment; and the reappearance of a pimp who preyed on teenage girls. The subplots were skillfully blended, and pragmatically addressed the racial problems that Marti and her family encountered.

Gone Quiet (St. Martin, 1994) began slowly with the death of Henry Hamilton, an elderly church deacon, but mounted in horror as Marti and Vik uncovered the chaos this old man had brought into the lives around him. A short-term substitute supervisor tested the partners, but Vik had the political connections needed to clear the case without interference.

The anniversary of her husband Johnny's death created tension for Marti and the children in *Done Wrong* (St. Martin, 1995). Her memories and anger intensified when the deaths of two of Johnny's fellow police officers confirmed her feeling that Johnny, a good cop, had been punished for his honesty.

Keep Still (St. Martin, 1996) found Marti awakening to the possibility that there might be another love in her life. Ben had become more than a family friend. Two major homicide cases (the death of elderly Sophia Admunds, who fell down her basement stairs, and the drowning of motel manager Liddy Fields in the facility's pool) came together.

Marti and Vik were preoccupied with the murder of Ladiya Norris, a young woman who had been under the influence of an older man, in *See No Evil* (St. Martin, 1998) and in helping the Vice Squad identify a Halloween flasher. Perhaps that was why she failed to notice signs of an intruder in her own home. Ghosts and a cat played roles in alerting Marti to death and danger.

The realization that discrimination had permeated the criminal justice system during the Sixties came home to Vik and Marti as they investigated the murder of former actor Barnabas Cheney, elderly member of a prominent family, in *Tell No Tales* (St. Martin, 1999). Both were on edge: Marti was making the transition to married life and an expanded family. Vik was dealing with his wife's illness and a reappraisal of the men who had shaped his youth.

In contrast to their own families where obstacles were overcome by love, Marti and Vik encountered dysfunctional relationships leading to arson, fraud, bombing and murder in *Scream in Silence* (St. Martin, 2000). A badly abused elderly woman had a son with an unreasoning hatred for anyone who offended him. A spoiled young man killed women for the pleasure he derived. A woman scarred by a teenage experience was unable to lead a normal life. These strands were woven into a blend of cozy and police procedural.

Relationships between mothers and their daughters dominated the narrative strains in *Whispers in the Dark* (St. Martin, 2001). Marti and Vik saw no way to solve the mystery surrounding the single arm found in a forested area until they connected the incident to body parts discovered as long as twenty years ago. They were drawn into the Lincoln Prairie artistic community, which may have included the killer as well as the victims. Sharon, Marti's closest friend since childhood, had been secretive about "Mr. Wonderful", the new man in her life. Neither Sharon's dying mother nor her neglected daughter Lisa were aware of the direction this relationship was taking.

As a police officer, Marti was sensitive to her own vulnerability and that of her family, but in *Windy City Dying* (St. Martin, 2002) she was unprepared for the viciousness of a recently released killer. Adrian Quinn had spent his prison time planning revenge on the police officers, attorneys, judge, and jurors who had put him behind bars. First, he would kill the loved ones of those against whom he sought revenge. The complexity of Quinn's strategy made it difficult for Marti, Vic and their allies to find the pattern.

The death of a student archeologist while excavating on the estate of the powerful Josiah Smith sent Marti and Vik on a journey into African-American and Native American history in *Fatal Remains* (St. Martin, 2003). In the 1850's, Idbash Smith had served as a receiver on the Underground Railroad. He had also made purchases of Potawatomi land as the tribal members were forced to relocate. A more primitive form of retribution had caused "accidents" over the generations to male members of the Smith family. Josiah's decision to sell the land triggered a series of murders investigated by Marti and Vik. As often happens, the cover-up of past misdeeds led to current violence

In *A Cold and Silent Dying* (St. Martin, 2004) the connections between Mart's personal and professional lives caused problems. She had been supportive to her long time friend Sharon in the past. In rescuing Sharon from De Vonte Lutrell, the most recent "Mr. Wonderful", she incurred his wrath. A devious and sadistic man, Lutrell wanted Sharon's money and Marti's life. This occurred at a time when the atmosphere at the department was tense because of

Lt. Gail Nicholson, the new unit supervisor, who was unwilling to take Lutrell as a serious threat. There were, as always, other cases that demanded attention

A Dark and Deadly Deception (St. Martin, 2005) went far beyond Lincoln Prairie for its plotlines. Vik and Marti had dual responsibilities: (1) to the regular homicide unit, still headed by Lt. Nicholson. She demanded results on the identification of a skeleton found when a downtown building was remodeled; (2) as members of the Northern Illinois Regional Task Force, they were assigned to the death of minor actress Savannah Payne-Jones. Savannah was part of a unit filming background scenes on the nearby highway. Her body had been discovered in the Des Plaines River. The background to the crimes involved characters from mid-Europe, an American serviceman, and an artist in jewelry.

Author Eleanor Taylor Bland did an excellent job of melding current social issues into tense narratives set in a midwestern community.

Devon MacDonald

Author: Nancy Baker Jacobs

Devon MacDonald, a thirty-three year old red-blonde, switched from schoolteacher to private investigator at a time of personal crisis. Her husband Noel disappeared shortly after their only child had been killed in a traffic accident. Devon, unable to return to a classroom filled with children near in age to her deceased son, searched for a new career. She settled into a partnership with ailing but avuncular private detective Sam Sherman. Devon, the child of older parents, always felt unwanted, confirming her stance on abortion in favor of "wanted" children.

Devon had a child-related case in *The Turquoise Tattoo* (Putnam, 1991). Dr. Ben Levy, whose child needed a bone-marrow transplant, hired her to find children whom he parented through a medical school sperm bank. Finding such a child was just a first step for Levy.

Noel, whom Devon had not divorced, sought a reconciliation in *A Slash of Scarlet* (Putnam, 1992), but she was hesitant. She was searching for Brentwood Peters, a charming con man who had bilked several local women out of their savings. Devon went undercover as a potential victim, setting up an isolated confrontation.

In *The Silver Scalpel* (Putnam, 1993), Devon searched for pregnant teenager Kerry Hammond at a time when St. Cloud, Minnesota was divided into Pro-Life and Pro-Choice supporters. Violence caused a fire at the Women's Medical Center, killing two occupants. Monica, Kerry's older sister, feared that one of the victims might have been Kerry. Devon investigated the activities of a fundamentalist religious group.

Devon's cases arose out of contemporary social problems, and tackled controversial issues. Besides a number of standalones, Jacobs has a series featuring Hollywood reporter Quinn Collins.

Maggie MacGowen

Author: Wendy Hornsby

Margot Eugenie Duchamps MacGowen, had settled for "Maggie." She was 5' 7" tall, and had her nose redone because it had a bump. The daughter of a college professor, she had worked as a news anchor, then as a Los Angeles documentary filmmaker. She met and married Scott, whom she came to know when he visited her parents to offer condolences for the death of her brother Marc in Vietnam. Maggie's sister Emily had responded to Marc's death by rebellion, conspiring to bomb a university building, thereby causing the death of a graduate student. In reparation, Emily became a doctor and dedicated her life to charitable work. After Maggie's divorce, she settled for shared custody of their daughter, Casey and received ownership of the family home in San Francisco. They shared it with an ugly dog, named Bowser.

As *Telling Lies* (Dutton, 1992) began, Maggie responded to Emily's call, but arrived too late to save her from a savage attack causing brain damage. The attack occurred at the time when Aleda Weston, a fellow participant in the bombing, had surrendered to the police after 22 years in hiding. The investigation, centering on the current lives of the ex-rebels, was compelling. Maggie developed a relationship with twice-divorced police detective Mike Flint.

In *Midnight Baby* (Dutton, 1993), Maggie worked with Guido Patrini on a film about children and their mothers, contrasting the neglected with the overindulged. She met fourteen-year-old Pisces who survived on the street by the "Badger Game", and worked with Sly, a nine-year-old thief and blackmailer. This exposed her to a world where children were sold for sex or inheritances, even by their own parents.

Mike Flint was anticipating retirement as *Bad Intent* (Dutton, 1994) opened. For all the intensity of their relationship, Maggie was a career woman unwilling to make a long-term commitment. In an atmosphere of racial politics, Mike had been accused of manufacturing evidence that sent African-American Charles "Pinkie" Conklin to prison. Maggie's interest in clearing Mike's name influenced the documentary film that she and Guido Patrini were producing, creating tensions between them.

Maggie tackled a major project under the auspices of a television network in *77th Street Requiem* (Dutton, 1995), reviewing the killing of police officer Roy Frady, who had been a close personal friend of Mike. Her conflict of interest and her resentment of network pressure added to her concern. Evidence indicated that Frady's killing was connected to the Symbionese Liberation Army (SLA), Patty Hearst, and possible police involvement.

Maggie's life was in personal disarray as *A Hard Light* (Dutton, 1997) began. Her daughter, Casey, still a teenager, was considering a transfer to a Boston dance school. Mike Flint, burned out as a detective and revolted by a current case where teenagers tortured a young man, wanted to retire. A substantial offer had been made for the home that Maggie and Scott had occupied in San Francisco. She could use the money. Scott, now married and practicing law in Denver, was desperate to purchase the house. Into this confusion came a mystery from the past. Vietnamese refugees, employees of a museum, had assisted in the transfer of valuable artifacts to prevent them from being confiscated by the Communist regime. Some of those items were turning up for sale; and there were rumors of smuggled gold. Maggie turned her attention to the refugees. She would juxtapose their story with Mike's case on the teenagers in her next documentary. A complex, well-plotted story.

Maggie could be fearless and ruthless, loving but ambitious and successful, if not always likeable. The series had an explicit sexual flavor. After a considerable hiatus, Maggie returns in *In the Guise of Mercy* (2009) and *The Paramour's Daughter* (2010).

Kathryn Mackay

Author: Christine McGuire

Kathryn Mackay, a petite young divorcee, held her own in a courtroom. After Kathryn's father died, she had been raised by her mother and a strict stepfather in Kansas City, Missouri. The strictness provoked rebellion and, but for a kindly public defender, Kathryn might have ended up as a lawbreaker instead of an attorney. In tribute to her mentor, Kathryn went from law school to the public defender's office. Embittered by the system, she transferred to the district attorney's office. Her marriage to fellow attorney Jack Hallam ended in divorce. His subsequent death was hard on their daughter Emma. She and Emma lived in Santa Rita, northern California.

As *Until Proven Guilty* (Pocket Books, 1993) began, the district attorney's office investigated sadistic killings by a man who courted attention, sending puzzles to the police. The media took advantage of leaks at headquarters to provide the notoriety the killer desired. Slowly the list of suspects was narrowed, although the killer fought back. The narrative contained considerable explicit brutality.

During *Until Justice Is Done* (Pocket, 1994), the police department and district attorney's office suffered from burnout. The extensive crimes, the legal loopholes, and the revolving door limited their capacity to deal with new cases. Witnesses feared to testify. Kathryn's former husband had been shot down in a courtroom. Emma panicked every time she was separated from her mother. Someone was taking the law in his or her hands, killing rapists who evaded conviction. Kathryn had more than her reputation on the line.

As *Until Death Do Us Part* (Pocket, 1997) began, the primary investigator for the prosecution lost his arm when a package intended for the defense table exploded. His replacement, Dave Granz, had become very close to Kathryn and to Emma since Jack's death. Emma's special need for Kathryn's attention at this time had to compete with her mother's heavy caseload. It included: the prosecution of an HIV carrier who continued to have sex with women, an investigation as to the source of the bomb, and a series of deaths of men found in bondage situations killed by incendiary devices placed on their bodies. The narrative was interspersed with vignettes about "Angel," the serial killer.

What was initially construed as a house fire in *Until the Bough Breaks* (Pocket, 1998) was declared murder/arson by Medical Examiner Morgan Nelson. Attorney Lawrence Lancaster was already dead when the fire broke out. Finding the culprit was only the first step. The accused based her defense on the battered wife syndrome. Kathryn's focus was distracted by rape charges against her lover, investigator Dave Granz.

The sudden death of Kathryn's boss, District Attorney Hal Benton, in *Until We Meet Again* (Pocket, 1999) led to her appointment as acting district attorney. Her efforts to solve the mysterious deaths of young Hispanic girls were sabotaged by Chief Deputy District Attorney Neal McCashill, a rival for that promotion. Her investigation of possible sexual abuses at a county medical facility brought her personal and professional lives into conflict again. The man who currently met her needs was Dr. Robert Simmons, director of the facility where the abuses occurred.

Although she had been elected as district attorney of Santa Rita County by *Until The Day They Die* (Pocket, 2001), Kathryn did not concentrate on the conventional administrative and public roles of the office. She assumed personal responsibility for the highly publicized cases of infant kidnappings, working the crime scenes with her former lover Dave Granz, now in the Sheriff's department. She was still obsessed with locating Dr. Robert Simmons.

Kathryn had made enemies in her career, and they were avid to take revenge in *Until the Final Verdict* (Pocket, 2002).When indicted murderer Dr. Robert Simmons (formerly Kathryn's lover) was extradited from Spain to the United States, he was accompanied on the plane by Kathryn and Sheriff Dave Granz, who married while they were in Spain. Simmons' death from digitalis was blamed on Kathryn, not as negligence, but as deliberate murder, punishable by execution. The prosecuting attorney who replaced her was vindictive, and allowed great leeway by the judge. Dave and Emma were terrified, but they and the friends that Kathryn had earned over the years rallied to her support. Very interesting courtroom maneuvering.

Dave and Kathryn were well established in their jobs and marriage by *Until Judgment Day* (Pocket, 2003). Not that there were no problems. Kathryn was in a high-risk pregnancy due to RH factors. Dave had recently received a second serious head injury in the line of duty that worried Kathryn and Dr. Morgan Nelson. Professionally, there were even more problems. One after another a total of six Catholic priests were assassinated. The Bishop went to jail initially rather than release the personnel records of the first two victims. Suspicions as to motives for the crimes ranged from embezzlement to pederasty. With both Kathryn and Dave somewhat incapacitated, Chief Inspector James "Jazzbo" Miller and Inspector Donna Escalante of the District Attorney's staff carried the load for the investigation during this gripping narrative.

These were raw, terse narratives. Kathryn came across as rather unstable to hold high office.

Joanna Mackenzie

Author: Margaret Duffy

Her work as an English police officer had given Joanna Mackenzie valuable experience. When terminated, she put her hard-earned skills to good use as a private investigator. Her cases occasionally brought her into contact with her former lover, Chief Inspector James Carrick. Joanna had been dismissed because of her affair with Carrick at a time when his wife was dying. There were problems in the new workplace. She was irked with her partner Lance Tyler. He co-opted the glamorous overseas assignments, relegating her to lost dogs and petty theft.

In *Dressed to Kill* (St. Martin, 1994), Joanna's probe of missing yard shrubs segued into the murder of their unpopular client Mrs. Amelia Pryce, and the theft of a valuable church reliquary. Both Carrick and Joanna were at risk of serious injury as they followed the intertwined trails of their cases. He wanted to resume their relationship, but she was deterred by the awareness of how much she physically resembled his now deceased wife.

Carrick's career was at risk in *Prospect of Death* (St. Martin, 1996) when he was discovered in a wrecked car with an elevated alcohol blood content. He had spent the earlier evening with fellow Scots, celebrating the birthday of Robert Burns. Joanna enlisted the help of Patrick Gilliard (see Volume 2, Ingrid Langley Gilliard), a character from another series by Duffy, to prove that Carrick was being framed to cover up a murder.

The relationship between Joanna and James Carrick was in a precarious state as *Music in the Blood* (Piatkus, 1997) began. His wife Kathleen was dead. Still, the affair he had with Joanna while she served as his sergeant had led to an official reprimand for him and a forced resignation by Joanna. Further estrangement arose when Carrick became involved with opera star Kimberley Devlin. Devlin had been buried alive after a hit-and-run accident. Carrick's interest in her attacker became part of a large-scale investigation by MI5. Patrick Gilliard and Joanna, who was now his employee, went undercover at a Scottish castle to end the smuggling of criminals into the United Kingdom.

Joanna and James Carrick were married as *A Fine Target* (Piatkus, 1998) began. She was out of town taking university courses when Carrick was notified that an abandoned car belonging to Patrick Gilliard had been found. It was not Patrick's body that lay nearby but that of his brother, Larry. Patrick and his wife Ingrid were the target of killers, remnants of a police unit that had gone beyond its authority. Neither Ingrid nor Joanna had any role in the action.

See, under Ingrid Langley Gilliard, (Volume 2) three narratives in which James Carrick played a supportive role. Joanna made a minor appearance in *So Horrible a Place* (Allison & Busby, 2004), but was in the early stages of a pregnancy during *Dead Trouble* (Allison & Busby, 2004); and had no significant role in *Tainted Ground* (Severn House, 2006), or *Blood Substitute* (2008) although Carrick continued to play a role in the Gilliard series.

Good character development, intriguing plots from an established author.

Kate MacLean

Author: Noreen Gilpatrick

Kate MacLean had left the San Francisco Police department under a cloud. Unsure whether or not she was meant to be a police officer, she worked as a waitress in a variety of locations, then applied at the Eastside Police Department outside Seattle. She was assigned to paperwork until Sam Morrison took her on as his partner. Part of Kate's problem was her tendency to get over-involved, particularly in cases where children were at risk. She lived on a houseboat for a while, but preferred a shore residence because of her love for gardening.

Because she was first on the scene during *Final Design* (Mysterious Press, 1993), Kate had primary responsibility for investigating the death of Catherine Fletcher, a partner in a struggling graphic arts business. Insurance coverage made the surviving partners suspect, but Kate probed Catherine's personal relationships: the husband whom she reamed in the divorce settlement, the daughter and grandson she ignored for years, the second husband who had been replaced by a lover. Kate persisted until she found the killer.

Although Kate and her partner, Sam Morrison, had become intimate, as *Shadow of Death* (Mysterious, 1995) opened, he gave his marriage another chance. For Sam that meant a transfer to the duty desk, and no ongoing contacts with Kate. This left her to deal alone with a major murder investigation. The corpse of pregnant student Sarah Taft from highly structured religious Woodhaven Academy was found in a nearby forest. The administrators of the school and church were indignant that any guilt might be attached to a member of their staff, but cooperated when a second murder occurred.

Kate bucked the system that, in turn, denied her adequate support, not an ideal situation for a female officer.

Annie MacPherson

Author: Janet L. Smith

After her parents' divorce, Annie MacPherson lived initially with her mother, who was married to a Hollywood producer. At fifteen, she joined her father in Seattle. A redheaded Phi Beta Kappa, Annie earned a magna cum laude degree in English before entering law school. After graduation she worked five years in the prosecutor's office, then turned to private practice.

Annie served as the power of attorney for Dorothy Lymon in *Sea of Troubles* (Ballantine, 1990). After her former husband died, Dorothy had inherited a plush resort in the nearby San Juan Islands. Annie was sent to arrange its sale. When guest Daisy Baker disappeared, Nicholas Forrester, the potential purchaser, threatened to sue. Annie solved the disappearance and subsequent murder, not only to protect her client, but because she was attracted to the prime suspect, adventurer David Courtney.

Back in Seattle, Annie protected her interests when, in *Practice to Deceive* (Fawcett Columbine, 1992), she and her partner were absorbed by Kemble, Laughton, Mercer & Duff, the firm in which her father had practiced. The death of confidential secretary Nancy Gulliver alerted Annie to the reason for her recruitment.

Loyalty to former college friend Taylor North motivated Annie to visit winemaking country in *A Vintage Murder* (Fawcett, 1994). Taylor's friendship had once been important to Annie, but after a misunderstanding, they parted without resolving their problems. When Taylor's abusive husband Stephen Vick was murdered at a winery gala, she was the obvious suspect. The second most likely suspect was Galen Rockwell, an attractive wine maker who had been Taylor's lover.

An underrated series, deserving of more notice.

Royce Madison

Author: Kieran York

Royce Madison had found acceptance in her hometown, Timber City, Colorado (population: 3,000). Her deceased father, Grady had been a popular Timber County sheriff. Her mother, Molly, ran the local bakery, Molly's Kitchen. The Madison family were among the early pioneers in the area. After three years in the Denver Police Department, Royce moved back home and was hired by her father's replacement to serve as a deputy. Because of strained feelings between Molly and Royce, she stayed at her grandmother Dora's rural home. Her closest friends in town were Gwen Ives and Nadine Atwell, honorary aunts who co-owned the local newspaper. They had a lesbian relationship, which made them supportive of Royce's sexual orientation.

During *Timber City Masks* (Third Side Press, 1993), Gwen and Nadine were not supportive of Royce's affair with supercilious teacher Valeria Driscoll. Valeria spent much of her leisure time with wealthy heiress Trish Chandler-Sumner, preferring to keep her relationship with Royce sub rosa. Trish's murder brought Royce into conflict with the current sheriff, Yancy Sumner. Sumner's indolent brother Luther was Trish's widower and poised to inherit a fortune. Yancy provided Luther with an alibi and diverted the investigation to a young Native American, Ray Tierra-Blanca. Once involved in her own probe of Trish's death, Royce found clues to the murder of her father.

By *Crystal Mountain Veils* (Third Side, 1995), Royce had turned her attention to new veterinarian Hertha White but that too posed a problem. Royce had been named acting sheriff, but was opposed in a forthcoming election. Her rival was backed by a right wing coalition that did not favor a woman sheriff, particularly one with a lesbian lover. Royce's big case was the murder of vitriolic reporter Sandra Holt. Holt had come to Crystal, where movie star Godiva was shooting a film. Costar Tyler McDermott was the son of a judge and of a leader of the right wing coalition. In solving these cases, Royce earned the respect of the men who served under her.

Matty Madrid

Author: P. J. Grady

Matty was very much a creature of the distinct Northern New Mexico culture and upbringing: close to her high school friends who became resources when she needed help, fiercely independent, and suspicious of government beyond her own community, Santa Fe. Her family was Hispanic and Catholic, although she did not let Catholicism rule her personal decisions. Matty (baptized Marta) dropped out of high school when she became pregnant, but managed to earn a GED. When the series began she was in her late twenties and taking courses at the Sante Fe Community College, working toward an associate degree. She managed all this in spite of being the sole parent for Esperanza, her twelve-year-old daughter, who was brain damaged as the result of a fall when she was a toddler. "Mingo" (Darryl) Minguez, Esperanza's father, had walked out when Esperanza was injured. He was a prisoner at the New Mexico Penitentiary, as the first book began, serving a ten-year sentence. Although she had been profoundly affected by his desertion, Matty visited him once every two weeks. Her parents were deceased, but her extended family pitched in to help care for Esperanza when Matty was at work. Her grandmother, a victim of Alzheimer's, lived with them, but could not be relied upon. Matty had been a sheriff's deputy, but had problems with working within the system. Now she operated as Marta Madrid, private investigator. Marty had an interested suitor, Zeke Fresquez, a curator at the local Museum of Indian Arts and Culture, but she was unable to make a commitment. That might have changed had there been a third book, but that didn't happen. Matty drove a 1983 Toyota, which she called "the Red Menace", lived on fast foods, and liked her beer.

As a deputy sheriff and a frequent visitor to Mingo, Matty had some acquaintance with what goes on within a prison, but in *Maximum Insecurity* (Avocet, 1999), she learned a lot more fast. The mother of deceased inmate Isaac "Gordo" Gonzalez hired Matty to investigate his death which occurred while he was bench pressing in the prison exercise room. No guard had been present at the time. The ruling, which was handled internally, was that he had died as a result of an accident. It was not devotion to her son that motivated Erlene Gonzalez to pursue this matter. She intended to made some major money through a lawsuit.

The prison, which housed medium and maximum security inmates, was rife with drugs, violence, and sexual relationships. Matty couldn't let go once she got started, but needed help from old high school pals, an honest attorney-general, and Zeke. Along the way, she acquired a dog (renamed Ruggles) who attached herself to Esmerelda. This was a short (189 pages) narrative, heavily overpopulated with characters.

During *Deadly Sin* (Avocet, 2001), Matty was contacted by her Uncle "Cipi" Cipriano Vigil, who asked her to call on Father Nick Jelenik, pastor of San Geronimo parish. A statue of San Miguel (St. Michael the Archangel), which was an important part of the church's Good Friday ritual, had been stolen from its place on a side altar. Father Nick, in turn, asked Matty to visit Dionne Quigley, who had been receiving threatening messages. Dionne and her husband Gerald (a major figure in the community and particularly among right wing Catholics affiliated with Dextera Dei) did not belong to San Geronimo parish; however she was a volunteer in the church's soup kitchen. Dionne did not want her husband to know the charges made against her in the letters, but after her murder in the church itself, they were exposed. As in the prior book, Matty had to contend with powerful figures who were determined to prevent her from learning the truth. This was a taut well-plotted narrative.

Lt. Gianna "Anna" Maglione

Author: Penny Mickelbury

Twenty years in the Washington D.C. police department had earned Gianna Maglione the leadership of the Hate Crimes Unit. She and her lesbian lover, African-American newspaper reporter Mimi Patterson, shared professional interests in the community, but from widely different perspectives. Gianna was tall with mahogany hair and hazel eyes. Her sexual orientation was not so much a problem in her job as was her tendency to ignore administrative tasks in favor of fieldwork.

The personal relationship between Gianna and Mimi was complicated by their professional responsibilities. In *Keeping Secrets* (Naiad, 1994), Gianna was determined to suppress information about a serial killer in order to protect her investigation. Mimi insisted on the right of the public to know and the need to inform potential victims. After the third victim, a pattern emerged. The killer targeted gay married men who continued to have homosexual affairs.

During *Night Songs* (Naiad, 1995), Gianna convinced her supervisors that the Hate Crimes Unit should handle crimes against prostitutes. The "Daniel Boone Killings" consisted of knives thrown from passing cars. Her task was more difficult because of the high profile suspects.

Although both Gianna and Mimi were sensitive to the need to keep their careers separate in *Love Notes* (migibooks, 2001), it was not always possible, and at time might be beneficial to share information. Both were under intense pressure at work. The Hate Crimes Unit was targeted by budget cutters.

Gianna was focused on the deaths of several middle-aged women (possibly lesbian) who had recently moved to the D. C. area. Nevertheless she had to accept another major assignment from her director. IRA supporters were smuggling guns to Ireland, but Jamaican gangs wanted to intercept them. Mimi who had successfully outed a corrupt official, was under fire because the man had killed himself. From a variety of sources, she became aware of (1) the serial killings; (2) the physical and emotional stresses many middle-aged women felt before and during menopause; and (3) her own limitations in dealing with the human aspects of her personal and professional lives. Some explicit sex may offend potential readers of the series.

Gianna and the members of her Hate Crime Unit in the DC police department had no idea of the gap in their coverage until in *Darkness Descending* (King's Cross, 2005) Prof. Natasha Hilliard was murdered. The hate angle was obvious. She had been attacked shortly after leaving The Snatch, a lesbian bar, and led a double life. Better known as a PhD history professor who was lesbian, she also presented herself as Tosh, a masculine aggressive persona, considered a subset of lesbianism. Only then did the Hate Crimes Unit learn that an entire precinct headed by Inspector Frank O'Connell had a policy not only of ignoring attacks on lesbians, but encouraging them. Mimi Patterson used her resources to expose the corruption and paid a price.

Mickelbury has two other series on which she has concentrated more recently: One featuring Carole Ann Gibson (covered in this volume); the other New York PI Phil Rodriguez

Magdalena "Maggie" Maguire

Author: Kate Bryan, pseudonym for Ellen Recknor

Maggie Maguire was a private investigator, a novel occupation for a female in the last quarter of the Nineteenth century. The job utilized the substantial list of skills that she had developed in her peripatetic young life. When Maggie was two her mother died and her care was left to her father, "General" Custis Maguire. He was a huckster who ran a traveling circus in the Western states. Maggie received a grounding in classical education from the General who had attended an unnamed university. Over the course of thirteen years she had also learned jujitsu, knife throwing, marksmanship, card tricks, animal training, roping and riding, wire walking, tumbling and juggling. Her most unusual skill, which came in handy, was mesmerism (hypnosis).

Her ability as a contortionist made her valuable to her father as a shill when he sold his patent medicines. This unconventional education came to an end when the "General" realized that Maggie's increased physical maturity had attracted the attention of male members of his troupe. At age fifteen she was sent to Miss Sophia Beckmyer's Academy for Young Ladies of Good Breeding and Refinement. Given her ethnic heritage of Irish, English, Scotch, Dutch, French, Spanish, Portuguese and Mandan Indian, her "good breeding" may have fallen short. Her propensity for wild and explosive pranks eliminated any claims of refinement.

When the "General" died leaving Maggie without financial security, both she and Miss Sophia were happy to end her schooling. Given the small amount of money she had available, Maggie went to Chicago where she applied for work at the Pinkerton Detective Agency. Her tenure there ended when she quit, disappointed at the low level assignments she was given and appalled at the excessive use of force when the Pinkertons raided Jesse James' family home. She moved to San Francisco, recruited her somewhat older cousin Grady Maguire (out of jail), and set up M. Maguire & Co, Discreet Inquiries. She achieved some success over eight years, including regular work from Quincy Applegate of Western Mutual Specialties.

Puritanical, but crooked, timber baron Horace Hogg had willed a fortune to his missing daughter Harriet. At his death, Quincy Applegate hired Maggie to find the young woman in *Murder at Bent Elbow* (Berkley, 1998). There were conditions for the inheritance: Harriet was to present herself as a virginal, sober and stable young woman. This might not come easy for a child who had been abducted by Indians at the age of six, and only returned to society as a young woman. Maggie hesitated to take the case until she met the secondary beneficiary, Ralph Scaggs. When she found Harriet (now known as Hattie), a dirty drunken whore in Bent Elbow, Maggie contended with those who sought to learn Hattie's secrets and then kill her.

A Record of Death (Berkley, 1998) was more than faintly reminiscent of Agatha Christie's *And Then There Was None.* Oh, the guests invited to a free vacation on Cutthroat Island were not all murderers. Each guest had been invited by a person or group he or she was unwilling to offend. Their host, Sam Warden, made known to the group via an Edison "talking machine" that he was intent on revenge. Maggie and Grady were among the invitees.

Maggie could refuse Quincy Applegate nothing, so, in *Murder on the Barbary Coast* (Berkley, 1999), she went undercover as Magdalena Obermyer to the Children of Golgotha. Brother Ascension, an ex-convict who induced his followers to bequeath him money, masterminded the cult. Grady, Otto Obermyer, and Quincy set up a scam to counter the con man before another person died suddenly.

These were romps into history with a dauntless heroine. Flaws may be found, but it is better to just enjoy.

Trish Maguire

Author: Natasha Cooper, pseudonym for Daphne Wright

Trish Maguire, an English barrister and Queen's Counsel, had a caseload focused on children.

She had a difficult childhood, an absentee father and a hypercritical stepfather, which factored into her approach. As an expert in this field, she spent spare time writing a treatise on the subject. Trish was programmed to burnout due to her need for success, and her emotional ties to the children whose cases she handled. She had no long-term relationship with a man, but has had serial short-term affairs. The question of how to prevent the abuse and neglect of children oppressed her because all of the solutions suggested (abortion, sterilization, and state intervention) had been ineffective or failed to meet the criteria of personal freedom that Trish espoused. Pondering these alternatives had slowed down her work on the book.

In *Creeping Ivy* (Simon & Schuster, 1998), Charlotte, the four-year-old daughter of Trish's cousin Antonia, disappeared. The police focused on the child's nanny (Nicky); on Antonia's lover (Robert Hithe), and on Antonia's former husband (Ben) who never believed Charlotte was his child. Trish had to move carefully because her innocent interest in the child had been manipulated by Antonia to add her to the suspect list.

Kara Huggate, a friend and a caring social worker, was brutally assaulted and murdered shortly before she was to testify in Trish's case as *Fault Line* (Simon & Schuster, 1999) began. Perhaps Trish's involvement might have stopped then had not another client, Blair Collons, insisted that his firing and Kara's murder were motivated by their investigation of corruption in local government. The narrative also introduced Chief Inspector William Femur, his lesbian assistant "Cally" Lyalt, and cocky young constable Steve Owler. George Henton, the solicitor who had been Trish's lover, quarreled with her because she refused to even meet with her long absent father. George returned when Trish needed him.

Trish was not acting as a barrister when she involved herself in the reinvestigation of Deb Gibbert's conviction for murder during *Prey to All* (Simon & Schuster, 2000) She was providing legal advice to her friend Anna Grayling's television documentary on the case. Deb had been convicted of killing her contentious invalid father. Her primary supporter, MP Malcolm Chaze, was subsequently murdered. Trish concentrated on Deb's troubled family and the possibility that the doctor who testified against her might have been prejudiced. To some degree, Trish's sympathy for Deb was based on similarities in their lives. Both had difficult relationships with their fathers. Trish's father, Paddy Maguire, had recently reinserted himself in her life. Trish's relationship with George had reached the point where they talked about having a child together.

With George in the United States as *Out of the Dark* (Simon & Schuster, 2002) opened, Trish learned of her pregnancy and then suffered a miscarriage. When eight-year-old David was struck by a car in front of Trish's loft apartment, her initial response was to summon help. Her involvement escalated when she learned that David had been sent to Trish by his terrified mother, Jeannie Nest. When Jeannie was found brutally murdered, both Trish and the authorities probed the connections between David, Jeanne, and the Maguire family. Paddy Maguire needed help. George returned to surprising news.

Trish's life had changed by *A Place of Safety* (Simon & Schuster, 2003) due to the addition of her young half-brother, David. George was not often in agreement with Trish as to how to raise the traumatized boy. Paddy was not involved. Her professional mentor, Antony Shelley, thought David's care interfered with Trish's focus at work. That did not inhibit him from saddling her with the job of pleasing merchant banker Henry Buxford. Buxford was uncomfortable with recent decisions made by his godson, art historian Toby Fullwell, as director of the Gregory Bequest Gallery. Interspersed in the narrative are episodes in the romance, pregnancy, marriage and postwar problems of Army nurse Helene Gregoire and Jean-Pierre Gregoire in 1916.

Trish's involvement in a civil trial made it impossible for her to accompany George and David on their trip to Australia in *Keep Me Alive* (St. Martin's Minotaur, 2004). Although she missed them, she rarely had time to focus on it. Will Applewood, the primary claimant in a suit against a major supermarket chain, needed not only her legal skills but personal support. Serious food poisoning which put Trish's friend Carol Lyatt in the hospital forced Trish into taking responsibilities in a possible child abuse case. She drafted Will to follow-up on the poisoning which led to the discovery of one murder and caused a second one. A mild flirtation ended when she realized how much she needed George and David. There were too many subplots for one book

The pasts of two well-established men were under serious scrutiny in *Gagged and Bound* (St. Martin's Minotaur, 2005). Trish had been recruited to advise biographer Beatrice Bowman on a potential libel suit, based on the journals of Jeremy Morton, the confessed bomber who spent twenty years in prison for the deaths and severe injuries to children on a school bus. Although he had taken full responsibility for the tragedy initially, the journals identified the bomb maker, "Baiborn" which was also the private nickname of a member of the House of Lords. Seeking help from her friend, Inspector Caro Lyatt, Trish took on another challenge. Caro had information that Inspector John Crayley, her rival for an important post, was "on the take" for the notorious Slabbs crime family. At the expense of her current caseload and at risk for herself and her half-brother David, Trish investigated both men. The Slabbs were notorious for punishing those who crossed them with gags, bindings, torture and murder.

Sam Foundling wasn't even Trish's client, although he had been seventeen years ago, but in *Evil Is Done* (St. Martin's, 2007, published in England as *A Greater Evil*), it was a good thing he had called upon her that morning. When he returned to his studio, he found his wife Cecelia dying. Had it not been that Trish provided him with the semblance of an alibi, he would have been sent to jail. He needed to be free because Cecelia had been over eight-months pregnant and the child had been saved. Trish was representing Leviathan Insurance in a construction case. The Arrow building was almost brand new, but major cracks were appearing in the structure. Unfortunately George's firm, Henton,

Maltraver, represented another party in the case. A possible conflict of interest there. This was not up to usual standards. Too talky.

Now a newly appointed Queen's Counsel (QC), Trish did not see defending Clean World Waste Management (CWWM) as an opportunity in *A Poisoned Mind* (St. Martin's Minotaur, 2008). In fact her personal sympathy went out to Angie Fortwell, the plaintiff in the case who was acting as her own attorney. Angie's husband John had died when tanks of dangerous waste belonging to CWWM blew up. The tanks were situated on land leased from the Fortwells and John had been hired to check on them regularly. The explosion also contaminated the Fortwell's farmland. The narrative followed Angie as she and her lawsuit were appropriated by Friends Against the Destruction of the Earth (FADE). Trish hoped to reach an equitable solution but needed more information to do so. Meanwhile, there were problems at home, where David had introduced Jay, an unstable teenager, into the equation with surprising support from George.

Sgt. Kathleen Mallory

Author: Carol O'Connell

Kathleen Mallory's origins were obscure, but they had been painful and surfaced in her dreams. She resisted delving into them, as had been recommended by the police psychologist. She had been rescued from the streets as a child of ten or eleven by New York City Detective Lou Markowitz, and cherished by his wife, Helen as if she were their own. Mallory joined the police force, reaching the rank of sergeant and earning distinction for her work with computers. Lou did not want Kathleen on the streets. He was unsure how much she had been marked by the experiences of her early life. Helen had sent Kathleen to parochial schools but she preferred Judaism. Neither faith made any deep impression on her, although she had a strong need for structure. She found it in computers and the Special Crimes Unit. She permitted almost no one to use her first name. She was "Mallory." She was interested in her appearance, but her apartment was sterile, organized to the point of obsession.

During *Mallory's Oracle* (Putnam, 1994), Lou Markowitz was killed in an "unfashionable" neighborhood, investigating serial crimes against wealthy older women. Lou's replacement, Lt. Jack Coffey, believed that Mallory was too emotionally involved to be effective, so he placed her on compassionate leave. This did not deter her from following the case, finding the killer, but escaping death only with the help of her eccentric friend Charles Butler.

While still recuperating, Mallory was sent to check on a death in a public park in which the victim had initially been identified as "Mallory" in *The Man Who Cast Two Shadows* (Putnam, 1995; apa as *The Man Who Lied to Women*). Following the trail of a jacket she had donated to charity, Mallory discovered the victim's identity, and moved into a posh residential hotel where the killer was one of several suspects. She maintained her partnership with Charles, investigating a young boy who might have paranormal powers, but who might also be a vicious killer. Her psychological limitations made Mallory unappreciative of Charles' fierce love.

Killing Critics (Putnam, 1996) placed Mallory in the Manhattan art world, following a trail first made by Markowitz. There had to be connections between the deaths of young dancer Aubry Gilette a decade before and that of artist Dean Starr. Starr had been stabbed in the presence of witnesses, who assumed his corpse was performance art. Hampered by bureaucratic and political interference, Mallory used religion, the Mafia, and those who loved her to determine whether the recent deaths were motivated by revenge or a fear of disclosure. The narrative left the reader uncertain as to Mallory's future.

When Mallory appeared in *Stone Angel* (Putnam, 1997) a.k.a. *Flight of the Stone Angel*, she was in Dayborn, Mississippi, the town where a mob had stoned her mother, Dr. Cassandra Shelley. Mallory did not need to know why, only who. She did not welcome the appearance of Charles Butler, who followed her there, or Sgt. Riker, who hoped to keep her from murder. Within hours after she arrived, Babe Laurie had been killed with a rock, and Sheriff Tom Jessop had placed Mallory under arrest. He and others of his clan had been part of the murderous mob from which Mallory had fled as a child. Charles persisted through lies, confusion, and violence that left the community in shambles, and Mallory still unhealed.

On her return to duty in *Shell Game* (Putnam, 1999) Mallory met a killer as cold, joyless, and intelligent as she. The death of second-rate magician Oliver Tree when a complex illusion misfired, introduced her to other more practiced illusionists. The group had a history, stretching back to their experiences in the Second World War, which had deeply affected their lives. The narrative was complex to the point of confusion, unsustained by emotional content. Readers who had hoped for some redemptive quality in Mallory after she resolved her childhood recollections, may be disappointed.

Fans of the Kathy Mallory series will find little fault in *Crime School* (Putnam's, 2002) an extended police investigation of a serial killer. Mallory and Riker were convinced that the hanging of aging hooker Sparrow, to whom both had ties, was connected to a similar crime two decades before. Had these and other similar attacks been done by one man, or were the most recent copycats? In answering these questions, the narrative gave considerable space to Mallory as a street child, her use of a third rate western book series, and the possibility she might have been guilty of arson and murder. Some of the diversions will annoy those not already involved in Mallory's history.

Riker, who has played an important role in Mallory's life since her childhood, was hurting in *Dead Famous* apa *The Jury Must Die* (Putnam's, 2003). Although his physical wounds had healed, he remained emotionally drained and subject to panic attacks. Mallory was determined to return him to active status. The opportunity presented itself when Riker, now working for his brother's crime scene cleaning service, came to care for Johanna Apollo, a disabled employee. He was unaware that the humpbacked but attractive woman had been a Chicago psychiatrist. Jo Apollo had evaded the Witness Protection Plan, instituted for jurors who had given a not guilty verdict in the trial of radio shock celebrity, Ian Zachary. A series killer, "The Reaper" was murdering the jurors with surprising assistance. As far from cozy as you may want to go

Mallory found herself at odds with her closest allies, Charles Butler and Riker, in *Winter House* (Putnam's, 2004). Nedda Winter had returned 58 years after her disappearance from the house in which nine members of her family and their household had been murdered. Her presence came to the attention of the Serious Crimes unit when Nedda admittedly killed an intruder known to be a professional hit man. She had murdered Willy Ray Boyd with an ice pick, the same weapon used in the Winter Massacre decades before. To Charles Butler and Riker, Nedda was a victim needing protection, sometimes from Mallory. She considered greed and money to be the primary motive for murder, which whatever her methods might be, led Mallory to a surprising killer. This case was personal.

Mallory's encounter with Savannah Sirus, the woman who had been her mother's roommate, sent her on a sentimental journey (as much as Mallory can be sentimental) in *Find Me* (Putnam's, 2006 apa as *Shark Music*). Savannah turned over letters from Mallory's birth father, Peyton Hale, written as he traversed old Route 66. Riker became involved because Savannah was found dead in Mallory's apartment after she had taken unauthorized leave. Tracing Peyton's route, stopping at the points of interest that he mentioned, Mallory became involved with a convoy of bereaved parents, individuals whose children had disappeared. They had come together through the efforts of elderly Paul Magritte who counseled via the Internet. FBI agent Dale Berman had an agenda of his own, which endangered members of the group. In their belief that the serial killer was traveling within this structure, Mallory (joined by Riker and Charles) frequently tangled with Berman over protection for the members of the convoy. Along the way, she made significant and life-changing discoveries. This is a memorable read even for those who have not read the entire series.

It may not be possible to like Mallory, but it is difficult to forget her, once encountered. A stunning series. It is important for readers to be aware that the Mallory books are regularly published in England with different titles. Mysterious Press released a limited edition of *Mysterious Profile* that is not part of the series. It consists of profiles of major sleuths including Mallory however.

Wanda Mallory

Author: Valerie Frankel

Wanda Mallory was a redheaded New York City private investigator who had been a researcher for a pornographic magazine. She was 5' 7", in her late twenties, usually dressed in Hanes T-shirts and jeans, but only occasionally wearing underwear of any brand. A Dartmouth graduate, she "fondled" her gun (named "Mame"). Her lover and assistant, photographer Alex Beaudine may have been attracted by her frequently mentioned mammary glands.

In *A Deadline for Murder* (Pocket, 1991), although hired by publisher Belle Beatrice to shadow her lover Johann Pesto, Wanda was quickly dismissed as the bearer of bad news. Belle was strangled a short time later, and the police believed that Wanda either committed the crime or knew the killer.

In *Murder on Wheels* (Pocket, 1992), Alex and Wanda split when head biker Storm Bismark hired her to recover money he owed loan shark "Saint" Nick Vespucci. Before Bismark could pay his debt, the money had been stolen from his safe. The investigation was punctuated by brutality, booze, and blither.

In *Prime Time for Murder* (Pocket, 1994), Wanda was hired to protect Sabrina Delorean, mistress of ceremonies for a television dating game. Sabrina survived the show, but Wanda's investigation of her past cast grave doubts on Sabrina's explanation of why she was a target.

During *A Body to Die For* (Pocket, 1995), Wanda, while trailing her current lover Max, met Jack Watson, a former pro tennis player who hired her to investigate Amaleth, his wealthy wife. When Amaleth's lover was murdered, Jack was arrested. Wanda frequented the athletic club run by Amaleth seeking another suspect. She ended up in the hospital, but with a wedding ring and a valuable formula to provide for her future. The pace was frenetic. The characters were eccentric, but not always appealing.

Hannah Malloy

Author: Annie Griffin, pseudonym for Sally Chapman

Although Hannah Malloy and her sister Kiki Goldstein were featured as partners in the series, Hannah emerged as the dominant character. Over the narratives, Kiki was more passive—a not too bright plump little woman who at sixty still thought of herself as a femme fatale. She rarely thought of anyone else, in fact. She was constantly in pursuit of a man, eligible or ineligible, interested or almost unaware of her. Part of Hannah's involvement in cases came through protecting Kiki. She was a co-dependent in her tolerance for Kiki's outlandish attire, her schemes to get male attention, and her self-centered reactions to tragedy. Both sisters had been married twice; both had lovers outside of marriage. Physically Hannah was tall, slim, and, when she chose to be, strikingly attractive. Like Kiki, a dyed blonde, she tinted her hair auburn.

Hannah was traditional only in comparison to Kiki. She was one year older, and had been employed as an executive secretary to the head of a major corporation. Still, she had been a hippie and protestor in the Sixties and had a wild side that emerged on occasion. In retirement she devoted time to her poetry, her garden (particularly roses) and to volunteer work (principally with cancer patients). She had been a cancer victim, undergone a double mastectomy, and for a considerable period of time avoided intimacy with males. Following the mastectomy, Hannah chose not to have reconstructive surgery, but found an alternative that satisfied her. There had been a third sister, who died leaving behind a daughter, Lauren. Lauren, an accountant, was as virginal and naïve as Kiki was sexually aggressive.

As the series began, Kiki was living with Hannah in her home in Hill Creek, California where both had grown up. The women shared the use of Kiki's elegant 1992 Cadillac convertible. Sylvia Plath (a pet Vietnamese pig), and Teresa E. Eliot (a dog) completed the household. The sisters had an agreement that whatever their sexual adventures might be, none would be carried out within the confines of the shared home. Both women were members of the Hill Creek Rose Club and frequented the Book Stop Coffee House and Ellie's Lady Nail's emporium. The best gossip came from the latter.

Hill Creek was near San Francisco but had developed its own character. Most of the residents were wealthy, educated, and absorbed in whatever was currently popular as to variants in style, food tastes, personal development, and political attitudes. Naomi, neighbor and local psychic who communicated messages from a long deceased Native American, Red Moon, was a good friend and frequent accomplice. John Perez, a retired chief of police from a nearby city, became Hannah's friend, then lover. He finally accepted her need for danger and was there when she got into trouble.

As *A Very Eligible Corpse* (Berkley, 1998) began, Hannah was bored by her everyday life. She had her garden, the pets, her twice-a-month poem in the local paper and the volunteer work but they did not add up to much in the way of excitement. Thanks to Kiki, she soon had more stimulation than she wanted. Dour Arnold Lempke vowed to expose the Church of Revelations where his daughter Lisa was a member. When both Arnold and Reverend Swanson, the director of the church, were murdered, Kiki was arrested. She proved to be resilient while incarcerated—losing weight, exercising, and making friends with her hooker cellmate. Hannah was determined to prove Kiki's innocence. For the first time in years, Hannah felt a sense of purpose.

Matters of the heart were significant in *Date with the Perfect Dead Man* (Berkley, 1999). Kiki pursued screen director Frederick Casey when he attended the Hill Creek Film Festival, only to find him dead in bed. Lauren, the niece who had been sedately dating Detective Larry Morgan, fell madly in love with Casey's actor son, Brad. Even Hannah was affected. In Perez's absence, she enjoyed the admiration of Casey's partner, Hinkley Bowden. Hannah was certain that the wrong person had been arrested for Casey's death and that of his assistant Angie. Some of what she learned was painful.

Geraldine Markham, retired botany teacher, had been a mentor to Hannah. In *Love and the Single Corpse* (Berkley, 2000), Geraldine and five members of her 1955 botany class met at the tree they had planted that year. Aware that Geraldine was ill, Hannah agreed to meet with her soon to discuss a problem. Not only was Geraldine murdered in her hospital bed, but Mendoza, her hired killer, lay stabbed to death in the room. Against all advice, Hannah sought the person who had hired Mendoza. She discovered a Geraldine whom she had never known in the process.

Hannah's determination to prevent Signatech, a software producer, from moving into Hill Creek motivated her to run for mayor in *Tall, Dead, and Handsome* (Berkley 2001). The subsequent demise of her two rivals for the position raised Hannah to the level of murder suspect, causing her to be ostracized within her social circle. One victim, as in prior narratives, had been the object of Kiki's love fantasies. Author Annie Griffin's seemingly deliberate failure to make clear the last name for a character was annoying.

An interesting series. Griffin, writing as Sally Chapman, is also the author of the Julie Blake series.

Munch Mancini

Author: Barbara Seranella

This series (set in California in the 1970s) presented Munch Mancini as a tiny auto mechanic with an incredible history. Munch's mother had been a hippie vagrant who died when Munch was nine. Most of their life together had been spent in communes. Her putative father, "Flower George" Mancini, was not only abusive but tried to pimp Munch. This proved to be more than she could handle so she shot him, but not mortally, and took off. Over the years, Munch had supported herself anyway she could, including prostitution. She discovered that working as an auto mechanic was safer in the long run. Her real name, Miranda, just didn't fit. She had begun her drug and alcohol abuse in her preteens. Munch loved machinery and was attracted to bikers, but was rejected by "Satan's Pride" because of her addictions. She supplemented her income later by setting up a limousine service with one vehicle, a carefully cared for Cadillac.

In *No Human Involved* (St. Martin, 1997), Munch set out to learn who had killed Flower George. Mace St. John, an experienced detective, believed Munch was innocent of the crime. He was able to prove that George had already been dead when Munch took a shot at him. This did not clear Munch's record by any means. She had been arrested no less than thirteen times for assorted crimes under different names. She had been made pregnant by Sleaze Garillo, but aborted the child, leaving her infertile.

Now living in Venice Beach, California, Munch was walking the straight line as *No Offense Intended* (HarperCollins, 1999) began. She was under a suspended sentence with three years probation hanging over her head. One of the conditions was that she stay away from felons, but it wasn't easy. Jon "Sleaze" Garillo sought Munch's help for his infant daughter before he was killed. Munch's risk taking sent her back into an unsavory atmosphere. Equal attention was paid to the painstaking police work of Det. "Jigsaw" Blackstone who competed with FBI agents in solving Garillo's murder. Now Munch had another reason to stay straight, a child who needed a mother.

Munch remembered those who helped her kick her drug addiction. In *Unwanted Company* (HarperCollins, 2000), she reached out to help teenage friend Ellen Summers. Recently released from prison, Ellen needed a job and a place to stay. Her potential employment as a driver for Munch's limousine service turned into a disaster. Not only was Ellen not to be relied upon, but Munch had allowed two dubious characters and their female companions to rent the service. When the two women were murdered, guess who was at risk?

Within a short period of time during *Unfinished Business* (HarperCollins, 2001) Munch learned of the death and mutilation of Diane Bergman and the rape of Robin Davies. Both women had their cars serviced at the garage where Munch had recently been promoted to department manager. Mace St. John, a detective who seriously tested Munch's current relationship with Garret Dimond, drew her into the investigation. However when she began to question a possible connection between the incidents and the garage, her adopted daughter Asia, was threatened. Never one to back away from a challenge, Munch persisted but it was twice as hard as she had anticipated.

Good deeds got Munch into a lot of trouble during *No Man Standing* (Scribner's, 2002). Asia's best friend, Lindsay Ramsey, aroused Munch's protective instinct. Unfortunately Noreen, Lindsay's mother, considered Munch a home wrecker and took revenge. Ellen Summers, see above, was hiding a hoard of counterfeit money, sought by both the Feds and the Mob. Too stubborn to abandon her old friend, even though these guys were playing for keeps. Munch had to balance her altruism against a need to protect Asia and the life they had built together.

Munch was celebrating her ninth year of sobriety, employment, motherhood, and ownership of a house when in *Unpaid Dues* (Scribner's, 2003), the other shoe dropped. It was not that she had forgotten the years when she, Sleaze John, Jane Ferrar, and "Thor" had shared drugs, sex, and a total disregard for the law. Mace St. John made the first connection between Munch and the recently discovered corpse of Jane Ferrar. With the addition of fourteen-year-old Nathan Franklin, son of a long time friend, Munch had even more to lose by getting involved.

When Munch didn't have problems of her own, she bought into someone else's as in *Unwilling Accomplice* (Scribner's, 2004). She had never had respect or affection for Lisa Slakum, Sleaze John's sister who had gone into a Witness Protection Program with Charlotte and Jill, her two daughters. Still she could hardly turn Lisa down when she wanted the cousins to meet. Within a week, Charlotte (now 13) was missing; Lisa was in jail, and Jill had been added to Munch's elastic household. In her minimal spare time, Munch searched for Charlotte who may have been involved in crimes masterminded by a "Fagin" like criminal.

Munch thought she had it made in *An Unacceptable Death* (St. Martin, 2006) began. All arrangements had been made for her wedding to police officer Rico Chacon. Admittedly Rico was currently undercover, but they managed occasional meetings. Then it hit. Rico was dead, shot not by criminals, but by fellow police officers in a gun battle. He had been considered a turncoat, fighting on the side of the drug dealers. Two major drug figures sought revenge for the deaths of those killed in the fray. Delaguerra, the Mexican jefe, wanted to recover a missing cocaine shipment. All Munch wanted was to clear Rico's name.

Great series. Serenella has just issued the first in a planned series featuring Charlotte Lyon, a crisis manager.

Dr. Calista "Cal" Marley

Author: Bill Pomidor

Cal Marley and her husband, Plato, left medical school with ambitions as high as their student loans. They purchased a huge rundown house and dilapidated furniture. Their household included an aging Australian shepherd dog (Foley) and a cat (Dante). Plato, who had attended Siegel, the Cleveland area medical school, had a large number of geriatric patients in his general practice office. Cal, a Chicago native with a degree from more prestigious Northwestern University Medical School, was a forensic pathologist and deputy coroner. Both held teaching positions at Siegel Medical College. She was a tiny blonde whose painstaking work made her intolerant of any less competent approach to medicine.

During *Murder by Prescription* (Signet, 1995), the couple spent their first wedding anniversary at a geriatric conference at which Plato was a presenter. The stay at Chippewa Creek Lodge was also an opportunity for Plato and other professionals to confer on a proposed textbook. When two members of the group died ostensibly from natural causes, Cal insisted on autopsies, researching combinations of drugs that might mask murder.

The Anatomy of Murder (Signet, 1996) found Cal and Plato tutoring failure-prone medical students in anatomy. All Cal had in mind was helping the students, but their cadaver was that of university researcher and former Vietnam Army nurse Marilyn Abel whose death may have been too convenient.

By *Skeletons in the Closet* (Signet, 1997), Cal had become assistant professor of anatomy at Siegel Medical College, deputy coroner, and was on staff at Riverside General, where Plato was the primary physician in geriatrics. The discovery of a skeleton in the excavations for an addition to the College harkened back to similar corpses attributed to the Kingsbury Killer, who had never been identified. Cal investigated discrepancies in the skeleton collection of the college. There were nine more skeletons than there should have been. The death of medical researcher Marvin Tucker at an award dinner connected to the most recent skeleton. Both Cal and Plato had a professional interest in tracing the skeletons to patients who had died prematurely.

Cal had been an important witness in the trial of mentally ill Jimmy Dubrowski, convicted as the Westside Strangler. Riverside Hospital's top managers were drafted into a survival bonding experience in *Ten Little Medicine*

Men (Signet, 1998). The isolated setting provided a splendid opportunity for a killer to begin a campaign of revenge. Long hours with little personal time had become weariness for both Cal and Plato. They needed to make changes in their lives.

In *Mind Over Murder* (Signet, 1998), Jimmy Dubrowski escaped, leaving Cal vulnerable. She and Plato thought they would never be safe until Jimmy was returned to prison. Fortunately for Jimmy, they found another solution. That problem solved, Cal had a special Christmas gift for Plato.

Catchy and interesting

Stephanie "Stevie"Marriner

Author: Robert S. Levinson

Stevie had been only sixteen when she was swept off her feet by Neal Gulliver, then a Los Angeles crime reporter. They married. The marriage lasted seven years, during which Stevie developed a sense of self, and respect for her own talents. Over the seven years since the divorce, Stevie won two daytime Emmy's for her performances in *Bedrooms and Boardrooms*, a daily soap opera, but she really wanted a career on the stage or at least in the movies Neil had lost the crime beat, but was kept on as a columnist. They stayed in touch because she valued his advice. He tolerated the fact that she had affairs, but was obsessed with Stevie, willing to take any time or interest she would grant him. Her dad had abandoned the family when she was five, leaving Stevie with a man-chasing neglectful mother. She had hired investigators to locate her father, but without success.

The Elvis and Marilyn Affair (Forge, 1999) was a disappointment. Sure, the tantalizing thought of a secret correspondence between two major celebrities was a draw. What followed was as excessive as anything to come out of Hollywood: too many characters, too many relationships, endless name-dropping, and too many crises. A tontine type series of deaths among aging movie retirees kept Neil busy. Stevie was both a suspect and a potential victim. Her self-centered personality may not endear her to a reader like it did poor Neil. The narrative introduced side characters who became part of the ensemble: Detective Lt. Ned De Santis and Augie Fowler, who had mentored Neil as a young reporter, but retired to a monastery of his own creation, the Spiritual Brothers of the Rhyming Heart.

Stevie played a more aggressive role in *The James Dean Affair* (Forge, 2000), because Nico Mercouri, the victim of a killer at the Hollywood Post Office, was dear to her. She, Nico, and Neil had been at the post office for the premiere of a commemorative James Dean stamp. The killer escaped but connections evolved tying Nico's death to those of others who had worked with Dean in *Rebel without a Cause* or *Giant.* ; i.e. Natalie Woods, Nick Adams, and Sal Mineo. More recent murders or attacks produced witnesses who identified the culprits as looking like James Dean. Was he really dead? Levinson has a fondness for hostage situations in his conclusions. Stevie showed considerable courage in such incidents.

The John Lennon Affair (Forge, 2001) was bad enough to make the prior two look good. Stevie and Neil continued their relationship on the same level. She had affairs with co-stars, producers, and directors, but was quite annoyed when Leigh Wilder to whom Neil had been engaged before he met Stevie appeared on the scene. The narrative explored just where Neil, Stevie, and Augie had been when John Lennon was murdered and how they reacted. Neil and Augie were instrumental in setting up the first *Imagine That* rock fest, which raised money to combat the gun lobby. Martin Halliwell, a U.S. Treasury official, approached Neil and Steve about becoming involved in a similar event to be held on the San Gorgonia Indian reservation. His pitch was that crime boss Aaron Lodger was using the event to launder money. Don't you believe it? Before they were through the narrative tied in not only Lennon's death, but also the attempt to kill Ronald Reagan, and plans for another high-level assassination. Real life history put no limits on Levinson's imagination. At any rate, Stevie and Neil ended up in Aaron Lodger's good graces. He was a man who got things done, took care of his friends and his enemies. Stevie, by now, had shed *Bedrooms and Boardrooms* for triumphs on the stage.

Not only Stevie and Neil, but Levinson had widened their horizons by *Hot Paint* (Forge, 2002), the best of the series. As the result of a gift from Aaron Lodger, Neil and Stevie entered the art world. He had presented them with a boxed set of eleven Andy Warhol lithographs. Each featured a famous painting and its owner. It was Augie Fowler who arranged for them to meet Zev Neumann and Ari Landau, Mossad agents who wanted to locate other sets of the lithograph, but particularly one containing the 12th segment. Several of the art collectors pictured on the lithographs had died mysteriously. Ari and Zev shared the history of art confiscated by Nazis from German and French Jewish collectors during the Holocaust. Some paintings had been restored to their owners' families; others seemed to have disappeared while in the possession of U.S. military forces in Europe. A new character, professional killer Clegg, stole the show. Another new character, sleepwalking Maryam Zokaie, almost stole Neil.

There certainly is a niche market for Levinson's work: movie and music buffs, conspiracy addicts, and those attracted to celebrities of all kinds. Neither Stevie nor Neil was a character to admire or connect with. She was ambitious, self-centered, and promiscuous. He was a long time wimp.

Cat Marsala

Author: Barbara D'Amato

The titles, *Hardball, Hard Tack, Hard Luck, Hard Women* sounded clipped, competent, and explosive. Chicago reporter, Cat Marsala, who was short and stocky with dark hair and eyes derived from her Italian heritage, met those expectations.

Still single in her early thirties, she worked freelance in a city with strong newspapers. She juggled on-going relationships with two "steady" beaus: John Banks, an establishment type stockbroker who was there when she needed him, and Mike Murphy, a stereotypical alcoholic reporter who needed her. Cat had a parrot named "Long John Silver." Her brother Teddy had been convicted and sent to prison because of his drug activities.

It was a chance to interview drug legalization activist Louise Sugarman that enticed Cat to a sherry party in *Hardball* (Scribner's, 1990). While she was sitting next to Louise, a bomb exploded killing the activist and leaving Cat partially amnesiac. Cat's strong feelings about drug trafficking wouldn't let her leave this one alone.

A cruise on a Lake Michigan sailboat hosted by the socially prominent Honeywell family, Cat's assignment in *Hard Tack* (Scribner's, 1991), sounded promising. It was a chance to see how the other half lived. She did not enjoy the internal tensions that surfaced in the close confines of the boat. Obnoxious fellow guest Chuck Kroop, a business rival and a lech, had his throat slit. This took some doing because after getting drunk and violent, Chuck had been given an injection to quiet him down and stashed in a locked room. Obviously not suicide. Cat sought the submerged motive for murder.

A trip downtown with her mom put Cat on a murder scene in *Hard Luck* (Scribner's, 1992). The victim, lottery executive Jack Sligh whom she had planned to interview, dropped on her unexpectedly from an upper story window. Sligh was to attend a meeting with representatives of other states to consider a multi-state lottery, but he had dissension within his own agency. Cat's employment prospects improved after media attention. She had the ground floor on this story.

She was commissioned to produce a television segment on hookers in *Hard Women* (Scribner's, 1993). Anxious to score on this one, Cat immersed herself in the milieu of prostitution. Her empathy so impressed Sandra Love, a high-class escort service employee, that when she was savagely beaten, she came to Cat for refuge. Sandra ended up dead, but she left a trail of infected men behind.

In *Hard Case* (Scribner's, 1994), Cat investigated a university hospital trauma center, spending five days in the midst of surgeons, nurses, and administrators who were trying to save lives, and one who was a killer. Dr. Sam Davidian, the trauma surgeon and a suspect in the death of unit administrator Dr. Hannah Grant, offered Cat a third choice in the romance field. Mike Murphy was still fighting alcohol. John Banks was still boring. She had to be certain that Sam wasn't a killer.

Cat appeared more vulnerable during *Hard Christmas* (Scribner's, 1995). Tired of murder and mayhem, she chose a "soft" assignment, tracing the growth, sale, and use of Christmas trees. The De Graafs of western Michigan wanted to keep the family tree farm, even though it was a marginal operation, or did they? Was there among the group someone who would kill to capitalize on the value of the land for development? Cat's special feeling for thirteen-year-old Nell made her reluctant to pry into the family's secrets, but she could not be silent once she learned the truth.

In *Hard Bargain* (Scribner's, 1997), Cat responded to an emergency call from old friend Chicago Chief of Detectives Harold McCoo. She investigated a questionable shooting by police officer Shelly Daniels. Daniels had taken a domestic violence call to the home of her sister Marie that resulted in the death of her abusive brother-in-law, also a police officer. McCoo's handling of the case and leaks about the investigation from within his squad damaged his reputation at a time when top officials were jockeying for appointment to replace the current police superintendent. Careful review of the evidence by Cat saved Daniel's job and McCoo's reputation.

Cat had barely presented a visiting Dalmatian with a meaty bone in *Hard Evidence* (Scribner's, 1999) when her dinner guest (and lover) Dr. Sam Davidian identified the bone as human. The most prestigious supermarket in Chicago asked Cat to identify the victim and the killer before their reputation went down the drain. The background of the setting was well researched but may be more than the readers want to know about meat departments.

Author Barbara D'Amato integrated the mystery in *Hard Road* (Scribner's, 2001) into the Oz series by author Frank Baum, who had been a friend of her father. Cat's brother Barry, the director of an Oz Festival at Chicago's Grant Park, was suspected of murder partly because of Cat's testimony. Tom Plumly, head of festival security, had died of a knife in his chest, shortly after colliding with Barry. Cat had been a witness to the collision. Loyalty was important to the Marsala family. Cat had to find the killer or be ostracized.

D'Amato did remarkable research on the background of her narratives. This was an excellent series set in the Midwest. Although I have not uncovered any further Cat Marsala books, she may have been mentioned in D'Amato's other two series featuring Police Chief Polly Kelly and Suze Figueroa.

Jennifer Marsh

Author: Judy Fitzwater

Jennifer Marsh's desire to be published verged on fanaticism. It was more than financial success that she needed. Her deceased parents had left her a trust fund that paid the rent. She had attended college but remained in her hometown. She and her partner Dee Dee Ivers ran a small but profitable catering business in Macon, Georgia. Dee Dee handled the meat dishes because Jennifer was a vegetarian. Her specialty was vegetable bouquets. The nine unpublished mystery novels on her closet shelf were a constant prod to her dissatisfaction. She was not alone in her ambition. She regularly attended a writer's critique group, most members of which were still waiting for publication. Others included: Teri, an African-American who wrote suspense novels; April, married and pregnant again who did children's books; Leigh Ann, who favored romance in her life and her fiction; and

Monique, an older woman who had published once and only once. All took part in her investigations.

What made Jennifer even wackier was the way that she expressed her desire to have a child. She had already named this unconceived being, Jaimie, and carried on conversations with her/him. For the time being she settled for Muffy, her adopted greyhound. Her long time romance with investigative reporter Sam Culpepper was chaste to the point where it must have been difficult for him.

It was unreal to believe that Jennifer was willing to die in *Dying to Get Published* (Fawcett Crest, 1998). On the other hand she gave consideration to killing literary agent Penney Richmond. Plan A was to do so while leaving a trail that would draw police attention, but having an alibi that would prove her innocence. Plan B was needed when she ended up in jail for a murder she had not committed. Her potential alibi, attractive reporter Sam Culpepper, was willing to help solve the murder.

Emma Walker had been a friend in need to Jennifer, but, in *Dying to Get Even* (Fawcett, 1999), Jennifer seemed unlikely to return the favor. She had come upon a dazed Emma at the site of her former husband Edgar's murder, holding the weapon in her hand. Raised Baptist, Jennifer could not lie on the witness stand when called by the prosecution. Gathering her critique group together, she hoped to make amends for her testimony by finding the real killer.

Obviously babies were important to Jennifer. In *Dying for a Clue* (Fawcett, 1999), she had two touches with reality. First, her experience in tagging along with sleazy private investigator Johnny Seeman could be dangerous. On their first outing he was shot and a nurse murdered. Second, she learned how deep was the bond between parent and child, for an adopted child as well as a birth child. The imaginary Jaimie was hard to stomach.

Jennifer knew that graduates attended class reunions primarily to gloat over their achievements—family, career, and financial success—so why would she attend one in *Dying to Remember* (Fawcett, 2000)? Leigh Ann, her pal from the critique group, did not want to go alone to the Riverside High School All Classes Reunion and had registered them both. A letter from Danny Buckner, her senior prom date, tipped the balance. Others had their own agendas for attending: to relieve guilt, to prove innocence, to resurrect the bones of a missing classmate. Jennifer had a strange ally in investigating Danny's death; his wife, Sheena, her worst enemy in high school.

In *Dying to Be Murdered* (Fawcett, 2001), Jennifer had to be talked into accepting $1,000 to spend a week at the home of Mary Bedford Ashton. Mary was convinced that she would be killed. Jennifer's job was to chronicle the events in the Ashton mansion so that the murderer would be identified and prosecuted. Mary was the second wife of wealthy Shelby Ashton. Her insistence on the potential murder had warranted a competency hearing. A bloody bedroom and a missing corpse, if there was one (Mary was not to be found) ended Jennifer's stay, but not her sense of duty.

The society pages had a lot to answer for in *Dying to Get Her Man* (Fawcett, 2002) The engagement announcement of 39-year-old Suzanne Gray to criminal defense attorney Richard Hovey appeared on the same day as the report of Hovey's death. After his funeral, Suzanne was found dead on his grave. A second spurious engagement announcement caused Jennifer to believe that Sam was unfaithful.

The last three in the series showed considerable improvement. They presented Jennifer more favorably, dropped her childish fantasy, and had better plotting.

Dorothy Martin

Author: Jeanne M. Dams

Dorothy Martin, a recent widow, had left southern Indiana to settle in England, a move that she and her husband Frank had planned before his death. They had been retired teachers. Dorothy purchased a rundown Seventeenth century gatehouse in Sherebury, an English cathedral town. She knew she would need time and money to bring the home up to her standards, but Dorothy enjoyed the challenge. Now she had time to read old friends— Agatha Christie, Ngaio Marsh, Dorothy L. Sayers, and new ones Ellis Peters and Charlotte MacLeod. Her friendly manner and distinctive hats drew attention among the locals, and encouraged friendships with neighbors.

One contact, that with Chief Constable Alan Nesbitt, came about during *The Body in the Transept* (Walker, 1995). Dorothy tripped over a corpse in the Cathedral. The death of unpopular Canon Billings was no accident. Dorothy methodically listed her suspects, followed a few red herrings, but eventually confronted a killer with a literary motive.

Alan saw Dorothy on a decorous level; although, in *Trouble in the Town Hall* (Walker, 1996), he made it clear that marriage was on his mind. Murder was on Dorothy's. She and cleaning woman Ada Finch had discovered the corpse of an unknown young man in the controversial Town Hall. The preservationists wanted the building repaired through local contributions. Major murder suspect Archibald Pettifer wanted to renovate it as a mall. Because Alan was preoccupied with a royal visit, Dorothy took the murder investigation on herself.

Holy Terror in the Hebrides (Walker, 1997) a.k.a. *Death in Fingal's Cave* was a disappointment. Dorothy's "vacation" on Iona (an island off the coast of Scotland) forced her into contact with a group of squabbling religious advocates. When Bob Williams, the least popular member of the lot, fell to his death from the rocks in Fingal's Cave, Dorothy looked at his companions for a killer. Without Alan in support and isolated by a severe storm, she allowed her imagination to run rampant. When he rejoined her, Alan set Dorothy's mind at ease and made her an acceptable proposal.

Her intervention in murder investigations had provided stimulation in Dorothy's life. During *Malice in Miniature* (Walker, 1998), she was unable to restrain herself when her friend Ada's son Bob was accused, first, of theft from a major collection of miniatures at Brocklesby Hall, which was determined to be a misunderstanding; then, of murdering housekeeper Emma Lathrop. Even after Bob was exonerated, Dorothy persisted, sifting among other possible suspects until there was only one remaining. Alan had been offered a prestigious appointment at Bramshill Police Staff College. Awed by the social demands that would be made upon her as his wife, Dorothy withheld her approval of the move.

During *The Victim in Victoria Station* (Walker, 1999), while Alan was in Zimbabwe for a conference, Dorothy totally ignored police procedure. Upset when there was no mention of a death she had observed while riding the train, she enlisted friends to determine who the victim had been and why he had been murdered.

Who would kill kindly biologist Kevin Cassidy, formerly a professor at Randolph University where Dorothy's deceased husband Frank had worked? Cassidy had suspected that he was in danger, so, in *Killing Cassidy* (Walker, 2000), he arranged a $5,000 bequest to Dorothy, conditioned on her return to Hillsburg in the United States to collect the money. The letter accompanying the check revealed Cassidy's suspicions. Without status and treated with hostility by local police and suspects alike, Dorothy and Alan came to believe that there were grounds for Cassidy's fears. When Dorothy had been despondent about a miscarriage, Cassidy had spurred her back into activities. She owed him justice.

Like many criminal investigators in retirement, Alan never forgot the case which he had failed to solve. In *To Perish in Penzance* (Walker, 2001), Dorothy convinced Alan to vacation on the Cornish coast where, thirty years before, a young blonde woman had died of a drug overdose. Within days, Dorothy and Alan were helping the local police with the death of another young woman. Not only was Alexis Adams found in the same cave as the prior victim, but she was also her daughter. Alan found the local police cooperative. Dorothy, as always, took a strong role in questioning suspects and possible witnesses, using her intuition to good advantage.

Only a casual contact with young Miriam Doyle and her mother Amanda was needed to get Dorothy to champion them in *Sins out of School* (Worldwide, 2003). John Doyle, Amanda's controlling husband had been murdered. Her behavior after she discovered the body made her a suspect. Dorothy looked elsewhere, investigating others who had reason to hate Doyle. Amanda kept her secrets, but Dorothy had Alan's expertise and influence on her side. A pleasant narrative with good characterizations.

Winter of Discontent (Forge, 2004) was permeated with Dorothy's concern about the future for her and Alan. In the course of investigating the disappearance and death of town historian Bill Fanshawe and the murderous attack on his young assistant Walter Tubbs, Dorothy and her elderly neighbor Jane Langland interviewed a quartet of men and women connected to a World

War II RCAF (Royal Canadian Air Force) base in England. Jane and Bill Fanshawe had been lovers before he was declared missing in action, only to be discovered later in a Nazi prison. They came together decades later when he was hired to run the Sherebury museum. Dorothy learned a great deal about the impact of WWII on the British during her interviews.

Cozy and low key. *A Dark and Stormy Night*, identified as a Dorothy Martin book, has been scheduled for 2010.

Saz (Sarah) Martin

Author: Stella Duffy

Saz Martin, who had been raised in Kent, now lived in South London where she shared a relationship with Dr. Molly Steele (of Asian and Scottish parentage). Her parents accepted her lesbian orientation. They retained some hope that it was a temporary phase or that Saz would "settle down." Her sister Cassie had a more conventional life, the wife of Tony and mother of four children. Professionally, Saz was a private investigator. It remained to be seen how professional she was.

Calendar Girl (Serpent's Tail, 1994) was a disjointed narrative, almost experimental in its presentation, particularly when Maggie Simpson, a comedian who was embroiled in a lesbian affair, carried the narration. Meanwhile, Saz was hired by John Clark, a heterosexual male who, although married, had an asexual relationship with a woman whom he had met regularly until she disappeared. John had loaned the mystery woman a sizeable amount of money. This was a case worth investigating. It took Saz to New York City where she worked undercover (very little) at the Calendar Girl Casino.

As *Wavewalker* (Serpent's Tail, 1996) opened, Saz received a recent picture of Dr. Max North and his heiress/sculptor wife Caron, an older picture of Max, plus twenty £50 notes. A subsequent phone call from an unidentified woman told Saz to investigate Max, who had merchandised a system of group therapy in England. Max, an American from a prosperous background, had a conventional medical and psychiatric education, but there was a substantial gap in his resume and personal history. Saz's client, for very personal reasons, wanted Saz to explore that time period. After her investigation, Saz wondered if her client might be as dangerous as Max.

Beneath the Blonde (Serpent's Tail, 1997) first explored an earlier time spent together by two young girls, one of whom obsessed about the relationship when the other moved away. The second focus was on the current stalking of singer Siobhan Forrester. Two members of the musical group, *Beneath the Blonde*, were murdered before Saz, who had been hired to guard Siobhan, uncovered the events that haunted the group. It had seemed a wonderful opportunity for Saz to recover from the trauma and burns incurred in a prior case, but instead the case tested her sexually, emotionally and physically. She returned to her lover Dr. Molly Steele with secrets she could never reveal.

The decision to have a child involved intricate planning. Saz's egg would be fertilized by sperm from Chris Marquand, a gay friend. Molly, who had better health insurance, would be inseminated and bear the child. In *Fresh Flesh* (Serpent's Tail, 1999), there were unforeseen results. Chris' interest in finding his own birth parents had been put on hold when his adopted father was alive. Now, a father-to-be, he asked Saz to research the matter. Her investigation unearthed a conspiracy to sell infants. The children, now adults, had differing reactions to the disclosures. For one, there was a rage that he vented on Saz.

Saz's slow recovery from burn injuries and the birth of their daughter, Matilda, led to a change in lifestyle for Saz and Molly in *Mouth of Babes* (Serpent's Tail, 2005). Her maternity leave ending, Molly returned to her medical practice while Sal accepted the role of stay-at-home mom. It seemed to be working until (1) Molly's dad died, requiring her to spend more time with her mother in Scotland; (2) suppressed memories of Saz's high school years came back to haunt her. She reconnected with other members of the gang that had been so important to her in those years. Saz's commitment to stay home and out of trouble went down the tubes. Duffy exposed the impact of schoolyard bullies on their victims and their own lives.

Duffy and Lauren Henderson co-edited *Tart Noir*, an anthology of 20 short stories about "Bad Girls".

Kate Martinelli a.k.a. K.C.

Author: Laurie R. King

Although Katerina Cecilia (K.C. or Casey), then Kate Martinelli, was raised in an Italian Catholic family no parents or siblings appeared in the narratives. Her sexual orientation was only hinted at in *A Grave Talent* (St. Martin's 1993) where her lover, Lee Cooper, was not initially described as a female. Lee, a therapist, had been a teaching assistant at the University of California-Berkeley when Kate was a student. Until they met, Kate had considered herself heterosexual. Lee took part in an investigation of child murders by Kate and her crusty supervisor, Al Hawkin. The climax left Lee handicapped and Kate traumatized by her "outing" as a lesbian San Francisco police officer. Lee eventually earned a PhD and had a practice as a psychotherapist. They shared a home, which accommodated Lee's handicap, made possible by her personal wealth.

Kate spent a year behind a desk after the incident but was ready to return to work in *To Play the Fool* (St. Martin, 1995). In this context, the "fool" was not an irresponsible individual, but one who had detached himself to play the role of the jester. Brother Erasmus, a suspect in the killing of a street person, was such a man: difficult to find, even more difficult to understand. Kate sought the reason for his Biblical quotations and three-track life before she could induce him to testify against a killer.

On medical leave, Kate provided childcare for Jules, Al Hawkin's twelve-year-old stepdaughter while he was on his honeymoon in *With Child* (St.

Martin, 1996). Part of Kate's plan was to visit Lee, who had ended her "smothering" relationship with Kate. En route, Kate was disabled by a headache. She awoke the next morning to find Jules missing in an area terrorized by a serial killer who wrote the police stating she was not one of his victims. Lee and Kate worked together to find Jules and erase suspicion that Kate had killed the girl.

The anger, not only by females who had been physically and/or sexually abused by men, but also by those who empathized with them, burst into violence during *Night Work* (Bantam, 2000). Kate, who was generally sympathetic but not to the level of vigilantism, investigated the murders of males who had abused women and girls. Her involvement went beyond the professional level when her friend, lesbian minister Roz Hall, fanned the women's rage to flames. Lee and Kate were considering parenthood, hopefully a girl baby.

Fans of the Sherlock Holmes and Kate Martinelli series, would naturally look forward to *The Art of Detection* (Bantam, 2006). Kate and Lt. Al Hawkin were assigned to investigate the death of Sherlock Holmes enthusiast and memorabilia collector, Philip Gilbert. His body had been found inside a coastal gun emplacement. The possibility that Gilbert might have uncovered an unpublished Doyle story offered a potential motive for his murder. Kate's access to the manuscript made her aware that there were parallels between Gilbert's death and that of a young army lieutenant in 1924 that Holmes, under one of his many aliases had investigated. However it also created the possibility, unpleasant and unlikely to some, that Arthur Conan Doyle would have written a novel about the relationship between a gay Army lieutenant and a street youth. The entire manuscript was included in the book, causing some dislocation in the flow of the contemporary plot. At least there was a happy ending for Kate and Lee. They were to be married under a current law, the first lesbian couple to marry in San Francisco. By this time their daughter Nora was three years old.

Her publication through mainstream St. Martin's and Bantam plus an Edgar Award, can be seen as recognition both of author Laurie R. King's writing and of more general acceptance of the sub-genre. What distinguished Kate from some lesbian sleuths was the discreet treatment of physical intimacy.

Genevieve Masefield

Author: Conrad Allen

The closed setting of a huge ocean liner proved to be ideal for this series. There was historic value as the series began in 1907 when instability in Europe was developing. The names of the ships evoked memories: e.g. the Lusitania, later sunk by the Germans, influencing the United States to enter World War I. There was room for multiple suspects as the large ships contained up to 2,000 passengers and appropriate size crews. Yet as in the Golden Age, the mysteries often centered around the well-to-do located in First Class accommodations.

Genevieve, an Englishwoman, had left her native country to get away from repercussions when her engagement to Nigel Wilmshurst, a member of the minor nobility, ended. Her fiancé's description of the break-up was generally accepted, rather than her own. Admittedly she, a small town girl, had been partly attracted by his wealth and social standing.

George Porter Dillman, a former ship designer/actor/Pinkerton man, was the primary sleuth in *Murder on the Lusitania* (St. Martin's Minotaur, 1999) but Genevieve made a strong showing. Both were passengers on the maiden voyage of the huge Cunard vessel, which was England's latest entry in the race with Germany for commercial control of the oceans. George was undercover as a passenger, but actually was employed by the Cunard Line as an investigator. His duties on this trip went beyond gambling and minor thefts. There were thefts, but they were certainly not minor: diagrams of the ship stolen from the cabin of the chief engineer and a priceless musical instrument. Annoying freelance reporter Henry Barcroft seemed an obvious suspect for the thefts; even after he was murdered in his cabin. But the thefts continued. Genevieve provided George with essential clues at the right time and proved she could handle herself in an emergency.

In *Murder on the Mauritania* (St. Martin's Minotaur, 2000) Genevieve and George were learning to work together and in the process, moving closer to a personal relationship. The Mauritania was a huge ship carrying over 2,000 passengers. Most in third class were immigrants. Genevieve traveled in first class where she quickly made friends and the usual male admirers; George in second class, kept in regular contact with her. November was a poor time to travel particularly with a shipment of gold bullion intended to rescue United States banks. A profusion of small thefts could be dealt with; in fact, George believed he had already identified the thief. When his suspect disappeared, he and Genevieve had to deal with two sets of criminals who had designs on the bullion. Only acute observations and good luck brought by a black cat saved the day.

Realizing that he and Genevieve might be becoming too obvious on the Cunard Atlantic line ships, in *Murder on the Minnesota* (St. Martin's Minotaur, 2002), George agreed to serve on the U. S. Minnesota, a combined cargo/passenger ship headed for Japan and China. Genevieve was annoyed that he had made these plans without consulting her, but agreed to accompany him. Only then did he reveal, that this was not a routine trip. There were suspicions that smuggled goods were included in the cargo, and he had already identified the possible criminal. The murder of proselytizing Catholic priest, Father Liam Slattery, was an unexpected complication. As usual, Genevieve worked primarily with the female passengers, but also elicited attention from men because of her beauty. There was a lot of table talk as both Genevieve and George mingled with different individuals during meals.

The growing relationship between Genevieve and George was sidelined during *Murder on the Caronia* (St. Martin's Minotaur, 2003), possibly by the pressure of their responsibilities. Purser Paul Taggart had made them aware that there might be smuggled drugs on board the Caronia. As the passengers arrived, George and Genevieve noted a couple being escorted on board, under arrest by Scotland Yard Inspector Ernest Redfern and his sergeant, Ronald Mulcaster. Genevieve had her usual admirers and a young friend Isadora who was kept sequestered by her parents Also on board was Theodore, a world-class cyclist going to Europe for a major race. The passengers presented an interesting group involved in drugs and romance.

The new assignment took some getting used to in *Murder on the Marmora* (St. Martin's Minotaur, 2004). It featured a smaller ship, but a much longer voyage, all the way to Australia via Egypt. There were fewer passengers; only first and second classes. A significant difference for George was that for the first time he had to work with a purser who was openly hostile. When the thefts mounted up, followed by the murder of agreeable Walter Dugdale, purser Brian Kilhendry made it clear that George and Genevieve had better solve these crimes because he ran a "clean ship". Things were even more difficult for Genevieve. Among the passengers were her former fiancé, Nigel Wilmshurst and his new bride Araminta.

The four-day voyage from Bombay to Aden in *Murder on the Salsette* (St. Martin's Minotaur, 2005) found the young couple still in honeymoon mood but required to pose as single passengers. The Salsette, an elegant vessel, was smaller and therefore more subject to motion on the water. This was to be a short voyage without expectations of serious problems. Genevieve mixed primarily with female passengers; e.g. Tabitha Simcoe and her wheelchair bound mother, Constance. George made contacts with male passengers such as: Dudley Nevin, a British expatriate who had left England "under a cloud"; rigid retired British Army Romford Kinnersley; MP Sylvester Greenwood, and psychic Guljar Singh. After a series of thefts and a murder both Genevieve and George learned more about these casual acquaintances. George felt it necessary to rebuke Genevieve for her impulsive actions.

Precarious cargo was being conveyed on board in *Murder on the Oceanic* (St. Martin's Minotaur, 2006). Not gold bullion this time but priceless art treasures purchased in France by J. P. Mellon, owner of the White Star Line. Mellon ignored advice, preferring to keep his purchases in his suite, relying on his bodyguard, Howard Reidel, a former NYPD captain. Reidel was savagely murdered and a portion of the artwork stolen. There were other thefts minor in comparison. As has become commonplace, Genevieve was the object of unwelcome male attentions; but this time George had a serious admirer too.

By *Murder on the Celtic* (St. Martin's, 2007), Genevieve had tired of their unsettled life. She disliked traveling under the pretense of being a single woman. George soothed her, nothing bad would happen on the *Celtic*, a smaller, older but very luxurious vessel. Within hours of embarking, George learned that murder suspect Edward Hammond was assumed to be on board. It was too late to return to New York harbor where police could arrest him. Problems mounted.

Genevieve had two suitors who made a contest of their pursuit. A new bridegroom disappeared and several thefts were reported. The first, by Arthur Conan Doyle, whose annotated first edition of *A Study in Scarlet* had disappeared while he and his wife attended a séance.

They were fun reads.

Caroline Masters

Author: Richard North Patterson

Caroline Masters, a tall dark American woman in her forties, who was estranged from her family, made minor appearances in two early books by author Richard North Patterson. During *Degree of Guilt* (Knopf, 1992), she presided over the murder trial of Mary Carelli, a prominent television reporter. Christopher Paget, father of her son, Carlos, had defended Carelli. Paget and Carelli had appeared earlier in *The Lasko Tangent* (Ballantine, 1979) but Caroline wasn't involved.

Paget, in love with his unhappily married assistant Terri Peralta, became the murder suspect in *Eyes of a Child* (Knopf, 1994) when Terri's husband was killed. He chose Caroline, then in private practice, to defend him. Politics had influenced district attorney McKinley Brooks' decision to prosecute. Paget had been considering a race for U. S. Senator. Caroline's expert cross-examinations of prosecution witnesses weakened its case, but it was really Paget's book.

The focus changed in *The Final Judgment* (Knopf, 1995) (republished in 2000 as *Caroline Masters)* when Caroline became the primary character. She had a traumatic childhood during which she saw her unfaithful mother's fatal crash and suffered from the domineering control of her father. Depressed by the loss of her lover, Caroline left everything connected to her family in New England. She went to law school in California, eventually becoming a candidate for the U.S. Supreme Court. At that moment, her professional life had to be put on hold. Her niece Brett, who had a special claim on Caroline, was on trial for murder.

The tension in *Protect and Defend* (Knopf, 2000) arose from Republican control of the Senate and the recent election of a young Democratic president. The stage for conflict was set by (1) new legislation requiring the consent of one parent for an abortion of a minor when the fetus was viable; (2) the litigation brought by Mary Ann Tierney, a fifteen-year-old daughter of pro-life parents, seeking to have that law declared unconstitutional; and (3) a vacancy on the Supreme Court that could affect the outcome of that case. President Kilcannon nominated Caroline, then an appellate court justice. He and Chad Palmer, chairman of the Senate Judiciary Committee, had to deal with a woman's right to an abortion within their own families or relationships. Caroline's past was up for scrutiny, exposing an action taken many years before that affected her life and the lives of others in her family. The narrative explored the personal and political impact of a question that divided the country. Like the prior appearances, this was a gripping narrative with well-developed characters and a dramatic conclusion.

Molly Masters

Author: Leslie O'Kane

Molly and Jim Masters were married when the series began, but separated temporarily due to his transfer to the Philippine Islands. By the time Jim applied for transfer back to the United States, Molly and their two children were occupying her parents' home in upper New York State. It had been seventeen years since Molly had been in the Albany suburb of Carlton, and she had mixed feelings. She was able to continue her work, designing personalized greetings to be sent via fax machine, while caring for Karen (age seven) and Nathan (only five). The Masters family had previously lived in Boulder, Colorado where Molly had established "Customers for Friendly Fax," and where she felt better integrated into the community. Molly had credibility as she had a college degree in journalism.

Molly's return to Carlton in *Death and Faxes* (St. Martin, 1996) brought reminiscences of her prickly relationship with teacher Phoebe Kravett, whom Molly had unfairly criticized in the school newspaper. Mrs. Kravett, seemingly holding no grudge, had designated Molly as the administrator of a trust to fund scholarships for local students. Burdened with guilt, Molly had to make certain that one of her classmates had not murdered Phoebe.

Jim, Molly and the children remained in Carlton during *Just the Fax, Ma'am* (St. Martin, 1996). Preston Saunders, the philandering husband of a high school classmate, entered Molly's cartoon in a contest sponsored by a pornographic magazine. When Preston died, Molly, feeling a need to strengthen her local reputation, risked life and limb to find his killer.

The Cold Hard Fax (Fawcett, 1998) placed Molly in the basement, as she witnessed the murder of the previous owner of her home through a small window. The victim, Helen Raleigh, had been digging in the Masters' yard. That was surprising. When Molly dug into Helen's past, she was even more surprised.

Molly's plans for a working vacation in the Denver area during *The Fax of Life* (Fawcett, 1999) went awry. The resort rented for her workshop was rundown. Unsure that she would even be paid and dismayed by the participants' dislike for one another, Molly was ready to take her children and go home. That became impossible when participant Allison Kenyon's body was found in Molly's unit. She was perceived as a suspect, although she had no motive. Molly continued to risk her life although her children were still young.

As a parent, Molly took an interest in the local schools during *The School Board Murders* (Fawcett, 2000). As a daughter, she was even more concerned about accusations that her father, Charlie Peterson, was unfit to serve on the local school board. When Sylvia Greene, his primary accuser, was murdered during a closed session of the board, the problem escalated. Her husband Jim and Sgt. Tommy Newton were bypassed again when Molly risked her life to clear her father's name.

Molly's life was heavily focused on the schools again in *When the Fax Lady Sings* (Fawcett, 2001). She took part in a PTA fundraiser, appearing as one of seven clowns in a skit. Someone wearing a clown suit murdered Corinne Bullock, the director of the production, during the dress rehearsal. Even with a closed pool of suspects, Molly couldn't leave this one for the police to solve. Her business, faxable greeting cards, was not doing well. She needed to find a job that would keep her busy. The locals were referring to her as "Typhoid Molly."

Patty Birch moved to Carlton in order to be near her divorced husband Randy and his new young wife, Amber in *Death of a PTA Goddess* (Fawcett, 2002). She quickly put her talents (and she had many of them) into community activities, becoming president of the PTA. Her popularity took a dive when it was disclosed that she had encouraged four high-school girls to surreptitiously tape PTA Board meetings and private conversations. Molly, having left her coat behind, returned to Patty's house after the video showing and found her dead. The video itself did not seem to justify murder so Molly and her elitist pal Stephanie Saunders sought a more credible motive. Molly and Jim were having a difficult time adjusting to daughter Karen's new activities: taking driving lessons and dating.

Witty, but warm; loaded with red herrings and technicalities, but with credible killers. Molly was less credible; making tremendous demands on her husband's patience, risking her children's welfare; a loose cannon.

O'Kane has a second series featuring Allie Babcock who provides therapy for dogs and their owners.

Angela Matelli

Author: Wendi Lee

Angela Matelli grew up in a large family that needed all the help it could get. Her dad had abandoned them. Thanks to a hard working mother, Angela entered college, and then left Boston to join the Marine Corps where she served in the military police. While in the Corps, Angie drove for Colonel Ev Morrow until their awareness of mutual attraction caused him to transfer her rather than incur the jealousy of his unstable wife, Earlene. After six years service, she returned to the Boston area, going into business as a solo private investigator. Angela invested her savings in an apartment building, partly occupied by family members.

She was *The Good Daughter* (St. Martin, 1994). An early client, Tom Grady, had been a partner of Angela's uncle, a police officer. He worried about his daughter's relationship with ex-convict Brian Scanlan, and well he might. Brian was connected to ILAP (International League for Advancement of Peace), an organization tied to IRA terrorism. Angela was in personal danger because she continued her investigation after Grady was killed. Angela utilized their common Marine Corps background to enlist the support of Detective Lee Randolph.

In *Missing Eden* (St. Martin, 1996), Ev Morrow, now stationed in California, needed Angie to find his daughter taken by Earlene to Boston. Angie found where fourteen-year-old Eden had been living but she had disappeared. The ravaged body of Rachel McCarthy, Eden's best friend had been found on the seashore. Angie resisted her feelings for Morrow, but she could not abandon his child.

Deadbeat (St. Martin, 1999) had an interesting plot: the theft of credit cards; then, their expansion to new accounts on which major expenditures were made. Thanks to her widespread contacts, Angie traced Lisa Browning, one member of the gang who was killed shortly thereafter. Angie worked with the police department, but she had to save her own life with aikido. A heavy dose of the Matelli clan.

There was never a choice when Al, Angela's brother with Mafia connections, disappeared in *He Who Dies* (St. Martin, 2000). Family came first with Angela, even without her mother urging her to find Al. Finding Al became a problem when (1) they found his friend Eddie dead in Al's condo; (2) the police considered Al the most likely killer; and (3) most seriously, the Mafia found him first. Al had decided to go "straight" to preserve his marriage. The Mafia reacted very negatively. Angela called upon her network of cops, reporters, computer experts, and family members for help.

The Haitian Department of Tourism will give no thanks to Lee for *Habeas Campus* (St. Martin, 2001). Angela was hired by Dr. Don Cannon of Hartmore College, Vermont to determine whether or not student Amy Garrett was alive. She had been found "dead", taken to the morgue, but had subsequently been seen on the street. Cannon was concerned that Amy might have been dosed with zombie dust. The fact that her body, not yet embalmed or autopsied, had disappeared from the mortuary convinced Angie but not the local police department.

Angela was an interesting character, independent for her own needs but overburdened with the problems of her sisters. She had potential for further development.

Nell (Mary) Matthews

Author: Eve K. Sandstrom

Nell Matthews' lack of trust in men traced back to her childhood. Her parents' divorce, her father's disappearance, and her mother's death had scarred her. She might have understood her dad's need to leave, but not his failure to return when her mother died. Fortunately she had kindly grandparents who provided for her needs. College romances, even with the academic whom she referred to only as "Professor Tenure," never reached the level of commitment. Nell became the daytime "violence beat" reporter (police, sheriff's office, and fire department) for the Grantham, Oklahoma *Gazette*. She shared a house with her gay landlord Rocky Rutledge, graduate student Martha Henry, and nursery school teacher Brenda.

Nell and police officer Mike Svenson met in *The Violence Beat* (Onyx, 1997). Mike, the son of Irish Svenson, the deceased Grantham police chief, had returned to his hometown after reaching the rank of senior detective in the Chicago Police Department. People were skeptical of this decision as he had to start all over as a police officer, but his experience and skills were put to good use as head of the negotiating team. Mike rescued Nell and a small child in a hostage situation. Their subsequent romance had to survive a serious conflict of interest. Bo Jenkins, the hostage taker had been murdered, but not before giving Nell a cryptic message referring to Mike's father who had died in an "accident". Nell balanced her responsibility to the *Gazette* against a need to help Mike clear his father's name.

By *The Homicide Report* (Onyx, 1998), Mike and Nell were nearing the end of a six-month period, after which they agreed to marry or end their relationship. That seemed less important when the death of unpopular *Gazette* copy editor Martina Gilroy had personal ramifications for Nell far beyond the crime itself. Martina had hinted that she was aware of information about Nell's family, particularly her father, Alan. The search for Martina's killer brought about a tender reunion, and the fear that it might not last.

In *The Smoking Gun* (Signet, 2000), Mike Svenson, now Nell's unofficial fiancé, killed Paul Howard, the man who attacked Patsy Raymond, the director of the Grantham Women's Shelter. Mike, a skilled hostage negotiator, had a profound sense of failure. Not only was Paul the son of the most powerful woman in the Grantham area, but within twenty-four hours Cherilyn Howard, Paul's wife was killed. This was not Nell's beat, but she could not leave the case alone because she had failed to respond to Cherilyn's call for help.

Nell is an interesting sleuth but the narratives have too many coincidences.

Eve K. Sandstrom has a second series featuring Sam and Nicky Titus.

Dr. Lauren Maxwell

Author: Elizabeth Quinn

After the death of her veterinarian husband Max in a plane crash, Lauren Maxwell lived with her son Jake, daughter Jessie, and Nina Alexeyev who had been Max's partner. Although Nina was a lesbian, there was nothing but friendship between the two women. Both missed Max. Lauren, a Ph.D. in biology from the State University of New York-Buffalo, had moved to Alaska because of Max. She remained there as an investigator for the Wild America Society. Her previous experience had been with the Alaska Fish and Game Commission.

Out in the wilderness in *Murder Most Grizzly* (Pocket, 1993), Lauren came upon the ravaged corpse of her friend Roland Taft, a solitary man who had devoted his life to the study of the grizzly bear. Dismayed with the official theory that Roland had been carrying a gun when attacked by a bear, Lauren solicited the help of Belle Doyon, a traditional Athabascan. Together they sought the ties between Taft's death and hunting parties, an angry father, and a vengeful government official.

Belle Doyon was shot but not killed in *A Wolf in Death's Clothing* (Pocket, 1995), possibly because of her opposition to expanded oil leases. Lauren, concerned with her son Jake's behavior, arranged for him to help the Indians gather fish and game for the winter. She remained nearby to monitor latent hostility by recent white settlers against the natives. Lauren's awareness of Athabascan mythology and tradition enabled her to distinguish between the need for scientific research and the right of the tribe to honor its dead.

Lauren met an attractive Russian botanist in *Lamb to the Slaughter* (Pocket, 1996) when she served as a guide for scientists meeting in Denali Park. Konstantin Zorich worked with Lauren to discover why the murder of renowned botanist Arkady Radischev was necessary.

Federal legislation authorizing the capture of orca whales for scientific research aroused environmentalists in *Killer Whale* (Pocket, 1997). The murder of Sam Larrabee, nephew of Lauren's best friend Vanessa, followed by the explosion of fisherman Charley Massett's boat, united Lauren, Vanessa, and biologist Owen Stuart against the whale hunters. French biologist Raoul D'Onofre had a government permit to capture 12 orcas. Lauren's two goals, to prevent the capture of the orcas and identify the killer, clashed in a thrilling conclusion.

Dr. Haley McAlister

Author: Janice Kiecolt-Glaser

Haley McAlister, at forty, had a comfortable professional life as a clinical psychologist and college professor in Houston, Texas. Her personal life was shattered when Ian, the man with whom she had shared the prior eight years, died in a car accident. She referred to herself as a "widow" so perhaps they had been married, although she did not share his name. Haley had a prior short marriage when she was twenty-two.

Personal tragedy was not new to Haley. Her mother had died after the birth of her younger brother. Within a year, Haley had been diagnosed with leukemia. Although she recovered, she spent the years from age thirteen to fifteen in virtual seclusion. Even when she returned to school, she sensed reluctance on the part of her schoolmates to become close. Her personal isolation had given her sensitivity to the unspoken messages that people conveyed by their posture, facial expressions, and what they said. She turned this and her Ph.D. in psychology into a specialty; i.e. lie detection.

Unfortunately her experiences had made her less, not more sympathetic with the people she treated. She avoided individual therapy, preferring to work with groups. She exercised regularly, running and swimming at a health club. She lived in suburban Piney Point Village. Like many female sleuths she had an antique car: a 1960 Corvette convertible, which she treasured. Considering the risks she took, Haley was wise to have Pavlov, an impressive Great Dane, as a regular companion.

The death of graduate student Alicia Erbe in *Detecting Lies* (Avon, 1997) reinforced Haley's reluctance to give individual therapy. Alicia had requested special attention while a member of a therapy group. The police and Haley's colleagues perceived her death as suicide—not a happy result for a treating professional. A lawsuit by Alicia's previously neglectful parents was a real possibility. It didn't help that Alicia's body had been found in a car parked outside Haley's office building. Haley became convinced that Alicia had been murdered. To protect herself, she investigated Alicia's associates at the college.

Haley had seen Kitty Evanston very briefly as a possible test subject for memory loss after surgery. As *Unconscious Truths* (Avon, 1998) began, Kitty withdrew from the test group, planning to go to a different hospital for a second surgery. She was convinced that she had been under anaesthetized during a prior operation, causing her great pain and subsequent nightmares. Kitty's death occurred just as Haley began work on the renewal of a National Institute of Health grant to the Anesthesiology Department. Her interview with staff revealed a hostile work environment, exacerbated by nasty pranks. When the suspected prankster was murdered, Haley connected his death to Kitty's. She had no trouble in identifying liars from among the suspects. There were several.

Cassidy McCabe

Author: Alex Matthews

Cassidy McCabe was willing to take on almost any task. That was not necessarily a virtue in a social work trained therapist. A tiny divorcee in her thirties, Cassidy had a solo practice conducted from her home in Oak Park, Illinois. She had a stray cat (Starshine) for a companion, but allowed her house and yard to deteriorate. Although Cassidy advised others as to their personal crises, she had never recovered from her father's abandonment when she was five or from the end of her marriage to an unfaithful man. On at least one occasion, her reach so exceeded her grasp as to endanger her client. Cassidy's solo practice denied her the professional support of peers.

Cassidy was comfortable in tolerant and diverse Oak Park, which bordered on a tough Chicago area. In *Secret's Shadow* (Intrigue Press, 1996), she was stunned to learn that a client, Ryan Hollister, whom she had been treating for two years, had killed himself. Not only was the family threatening to sue, but Cassidy became convinced that Ryan had been murdered. Although Cassidy became romantically involved with Ryan's half-brother, newspaper reporter Zach Moran, she still kept in touch with Kevin, her feckless former husband.

During *Satan's Silence* (Intrigue, 1997), Cassidy not only shared a client's problems with Zach who used the material as the starting point for an investigative report, but went beyond her professional skill level. Based on information gained during this session, Cassidy uncovered serious child abuse and sacrifice.

Vendetta's Victim (Intrigue, 1998) alerted Cassidy to a man who preyed upon vulnerable women, introducing himself at funerals, and then seducing them into medically risky relationships. Her mother (Helen), never a resource, became a problem when she planned to marry wealthy industrialist Roland Mertz, whose children warned Cassidy that he was abusive.

Her responsibility as a citizen did not weigh heavily on Cassidy in *Wanton's Web* (Intrigue, 1999). She abetted Zach in the concealment of a crime, the murder of Zandra, the woman who bore his son seventeen years before. Zandra, who had been a hooker, now ran her own establishment. Proving that Zach was innocent of the crime took longer. Her sense that Zach's social background was superior to her own often seemed unduly important.

There was something for everyone in *Cat's Claw* (Intrigue, 2000). Zach, by now married to Cassidy, was having problems separating himself from an undercover role. Cassidy's neighbors were murder victims and cat killers. Toss in Mary McCabe, Cassidy's eccentric but lovable grandmother, and an emotionally needy stepson, Bryce Palomar. Unfortunately the ingredients were not a comfortable mix.

Never before *Death's Domain* (Intrigue, 2001) had Cassidy's personal and professional lives been so conflicted. A series of events (publication of her obituary, references to a regrettable incident in her past, and threats) consumed her life. Certain that the taunter was both dangerous and vengeful, Zach and Cassidy examined her past to avert a second tragedy. Zach too had problems, coping with Bryce, his recently discovered son. This may be the best of the series so far.

By the time of the ceremony in *Wedding's Widow* (Intrigue, 2003), Cassidy had been Claire Linden's therapist for over two years. She had counseled Claire out of an abusive marriage, but feared that marrying Max O'Connell would be a mistake. That problem was solved when a sharpshooter killed Max during the ceremony. Relinquishing her role as therapist Cassidy joined Zach in an investigation of the murder, focusing on the kind of man Max was.

Blood's Burden (Intrigue, 2006) showed continued improvement. Although Cassidy had a history of involving herself in other people's business, this time is was her business, and Zach's. His son Bryce was the obvious suspect when Kit Hopewell, his live-in girlfriend, was brutally murdered. There was no sign of forced entry. Bryce was the only other person known to be in the locked house. The couple had been arguing publicly. Kit was known to be involved with other men, and had a history of discord in her parental family. When Zach got busy, Cassidy took over. They spent some time discussing the possibility of having their own child, but it would involve a major change in their lives.

Cassidy didn't have enough to worry about in *Murder's Madness* (Veiled Interest, 2007) so she allowed herself to become involved with the new tenant in Zach's condo, Delia Schiff. Zach had been reluctant to rent to Delia, but, even after Cassidy was made aware that Delia was schizophrenic, she convinced him to do so. Zach was having on the job problems with a new editor who had a grudge against him, causing him to drink too much and be depressed. Delia's frantic call that she had seen a "Dark Angel" and a man hanging from the rafters, meant that the police had to be called. At that point, Delia disappeared.

The narratives used italics at times to express Cassidy's inner thoughts; sometimes, this became wearisome. The plotting improved in the later books.

Christina McCall

Author: William Bernhardt

Ben Kincaid was the dominant character in the legal series in which Christina McCall made regular supporting appearances. Ben was a former government attorney who went into private practice in Oklahoma City. He was eagerly recruited by the large law firm in which Christina, a divorcee in her thirties, worked as a paralegal. She was as out of place in the money grasping, status conscious firm as was Ben. He was distinguished by his idealism; Christina by her strawberry colored hair, unconventional dress and inappropriate use of French phrases. She eagerly assisted Ben in burglary, and when his success forced him out of the firm, she quit her job. Eventually she attended law school, graduated, and assisted Ben in cases. Mike Morelli, Ben's former brother-in-law also featured in many of the cases.

In *Primary Justice* (Ballantine, 1992), Ben was handled a difficult task, arranging an adoption for Sanguine Enterprises vice-president Jonathan Adams and his wife Bertha. Jonathan had come upon Emily, an amnesiac child, and had taken her in. Before any serious plans for an adoption could be made, Jonathan was murdered. Richard Derek, Ben's supervising attorney, told him to stay away from the murder investigation. Ben was denied use of the firm's resources, but Christine, cut corners, helped in a burglary at Sanguine, and was personally at risk because of her activities. Ben was fired. Christina quit in protest.

In *Blind Justice* (Ballantine, 1992), Christina was employed by another large firm, while Ben opened his own struggling office. In the prologue, a man put drops in a carafe to drug someone, who turned out to be Christina. She had docilely drunk the beverage as requested by her date for the evening. When she came to, reputed drug dealer Tony Lombardi was dead and she was the primary suspect. With Christina in jail, Ben faced a hostile judge and prosecutors who were willing to bend the rules to convict her.

During *Deadly Justice* (Ballantine, 1993), Ben tried corporate law. Christina served as his legal aide. She and his private office staff saw him as betraying his ideals for advancement. Eventually Christina and Ben's former brother-in-law police Lt. Mike Morelli saved Ben from himself and his unscrupulous legal associates.

Christina was so appalled at Ben's defense of white supremacist Donald Vick in *Perfect Justice* (Ballantine, 1994) that she declined to work with him. He and other members of his staff successfully proved that Vick was the dupe of a sinister organization and the victim of a vengeful woman.

Except for benefiting from a fashion update by Ben's mother and a date with Ben, Christina played no significant role in *Cruel Justice* (Ballantine, 1996). Ben had accepted what seemed to be a hopeless case when he agreed to defend young developmentally disabled African-American Leeman Hayes in a murder case. Hayes had been kept in the justice system for ten years without a trial. Reminiscent of the better Perry Masons, Ben synthesized the information gained during interviews into a brilliant cross-examination that exposed the real killer. Other subplots included child abductions, molestation, and Ben's revision of some of his negative feelings about his father

In *Naked Justice* (Ballantine, 1997), a novel that included overtones of the O.J. Simpson trial, Ben defended Wallace Barrett, a former football star (now the first African-American mayor of Tulsa) who was accused of murdering his wife and two small children. Ben, currently caring for, and learning to care about, his eighteen-month-old nephew Joey (who had figured in the prior book), needed a productive case. Christina had informed him that they were not making expenses. Ben came to believe that Barrett, whom he knew slightly as a parent at day care, was incapable of killing his children, and successfully defended him. Christina made Ben aware of a tricky highway curve that saved his life when he was stalked by an enemy from the past, but otherwise only served as emotional support.

By *Extreme Justice* (Ballantine, 1998), Ben had given up the practice of law and work on his book, turning to music to make a precarious living. When a precariously balanced corpse "dropped in" on his combo's opening night, the police department targeted Earl Bonner, the proprietor of the jazz "Emporium" and a past friend of victim Lily Campbell. Ben put his lawyer hat back on and enlisted the support of his former associates, including Christine, to help Earl. It was more comfortable than he had expected.

Ben barely remembered George Zakin, the environmental activist whom he had successfully defended in a murder trial six years before. In *Dark Justice* (Ballantine, 1999), their paths crossed again. Ben, on a book signing tour in a small Washington state town, learned that Zakin was charged with murder. Although Ben sympathized with the environmental group involved, he deplored their violence. Christine and other staff members were summoned to help.

Ben was fatigued by a prior case, but not too tired to see Cecily Elkins in *Silent Justice* (Ballantine, 2000). Cecily's son had been one of eleven victims of leukemia caused by industrial pollution. Ben put his firm at financial risk to file a class action suit against Blaylock Corporation, the polluter that would be represented by the firm for which Ben had previously worked. Mike Morelli had a case that ran parallel to Ben's, the murders of Harvey Pendergast, an executive at Blaylock, and the subsequent deaths of his wife and child. The cases eventually fused. Christine, now going to law school, remained at Ben's side cheering him on when he was ready to quit and sharing his danger.

The characteristics that Christina treasured about Ben were his downfall in *Murder One* (Ballantine, 2001): his devotion to his client, his belief in confidentiality, and his vulnerability to a woman who manipulated him. She stood by helplessly as his legal assistant until the point when he was arrested for murder, jailed, and treated very badly. By that time, she had graduated from law school with a distinguished record. She not only represented Ben as his attorney but also cooperated with him as he identified the real killer without compromising his ethics.

Christina added color and realism to Kincaid, but took a long time to develop as a character. She began as a Della Street clone, but her decision to go to law school moved her up a notch. As an attorney, she may hit the big time. The narratives usually began with a mysterious prologue, and ended with an unexpected revelation.

Readers of *Criminal Intent* (Ballantine, 2002) will make their own judgments as to the guilt or innocence of controversial Episcopalian priest, Father Daniel Beale. Was he guilty of killing three women in his parish community? Although he was charged with the murders, Ben defended Beale with a personal commitment. Beale, then pastor of Ben's church, had served as a friend and mentor to Ben when he was a boy. Now Ben had an opportunity to return the favor. Others were not so well inclined to excuse Beale, not even his wife Andrea. One good thing, he told Ben to look at Christine. She had served as second chair in the trial, giving the opening statement. It was a token appearance.

When flavorist Frank Faulkner was murdered in *Death Row* (Ballantine, 2003), his wife and all but one of their children were slaughtered with him. Ben defended Ray Goldman, a co-worker of Frank at Prairie Dog Flavors. After repeated appeals failed over a seven-year period, Ray was about to be executed when Erin Faulkner, the surviving child, revealed that she had identified Ray under pressure from the prosecution. Erin and her best friend died in purported suicides. Goaded by his new partner, Sgt Kate Baxter, Mike Morelli carried out a parallel investigation to Ben's and Christina's. At the end Ben struggled to tell Christina how important she was to him.

There was no way that Ben would agree to defend accused killer Johnny Christensen in *Hate Crime* (Ballantine, 2004). Sure it was his kind of case, an unpopular defendant who admitted he had brutally attacked gay restaurant manager Tony Barovick, but denied that he had killed him. Ben had a history with Ellen, Johnny's stepmother, that made him unwilling to get involved. Christina took the case. Later, Ben joined in.

The series made another switch in focus, setting the crimes in Washington, D. C. or focusing on politics.

Oklahoma Senator Tod Glancy made an unpleasant television appearance in *Capitol Murder* (Ballantine, 2006) after a video of his sexual encounter with young intern Veronica Cooper was distributed to the media. Bypassing the slick Eastern attorneys, Glancy contacted law school classmate, Ben Kincaid to help control the situation. Ben, Christina, and members of their staff, arrived at the Capitol only a short time before Veronica's badly abused body was discovered in Glancy's hideaway office. The narrative was heavy on courtroom drama

Capitol Threat (Ballantine, 2007) was disappointing. It was not the sensational revelation that Thaddeus Raush, Circuit Court of Appeals judge nominated for a Supreme Court vacancy, was gay. Raush himself announced the fact and identified his partner, Ray Eastlick. It was not even the nasty manipulations within the Senate Judicial Committee, which had to move the nomination to the floor for determination. The real turnoff was the larding of the book with major segments following Al Loving, long time investigator for Ben Kincaid and now acting as his research assistant. He descended into the seamiest transvestite and gay hangouts in the D.C. area. There was gratuitous sex and violence. No indication that Loving was reporting to Ben until late in the narrative. In the end, it was clear. Everyone had a price, even Ben Kincaid. Although she took part in planning sessions, Christina was more focused on getting important environmental legislation passed and in getting Ben to set a date for their wedding.

You can take the boy out of the country but you can't take the country out of the boy; i.e. Ben Kincaid was not ready to be Oklahoma's senator in *Capitol Conspiracy* (Ballantine, 2008). Having been a witness to a terrorist attack in Oklahoma City that left the First Lady and seven others dead, plus Major Mike Morelli grievously injured, Ben was vulnerable. President Franklin Blake, his chief of staff Tracy Sobel, and the director of Homeland Security Carl Lehman pushed a constitutional amendment that in time of "clear and convincing danger" would allow the president and his Emergency Security Council to temporarily set aside the Bill of Rights. Ben supported the plan. Christina and Loving set out to investigate the April 19th tragedy in Oklahoma City against heavy odds. Next: *Capitol Offense* (2009)*; Capitol Betrayal* (2010)

Give Bernhardt credit for tackling controversial issues. He has moved on to a new series, featuring Susan Pulaski, a Los Vegas cop.

Emily "Blue" McCarron

Author: Abigail Padgett

Blue McCarron had been raised Episcopalian, as would be appropriate since her father was an Episcopalian priest. As an adult she was unaffiliated with a church and considered eccentric by many. She was vegetarian, but that did not mean being different in California. Her mother, Betsy had died in a car accident when Blue and her twin brother were thirteen. A close family friend,

Carter Upchurch, Blue's godmother, had assumed a maternal role in her life. Her brother David moved from juvenile delinquency to armed robbery and was sentenced to a Missouri prison. His redemption by a church visitor had led to a reconciliation between Blue and David.

Blue had become a computer whiz as a subjunct to her practice as a social psychologist at the Ph.D. level but rarely used the title, "Dr." Her doctoral dissertation *Ape* in which she made comparisons on the gender characteristics of apes and human had been published. As a social psychologist, her work was in predicting trends and advising businesses, rather than in clinical work so she did not need a client accessible office.

Blue's decision to purchase a vacant desert motel, where she lived and had her office, was based on the end of a relationship. The old motel went cheaply because there was no water on the premises. Misha, her lesbian lover, had left without explanation. As a result, Blue resigned her teaching position at San Gabriel University, although she continued to teach young girls at a juvenile detention center. Her subsequent African-American lover Roxie Bouchie, a forensic psychiatrist, maintained a home in nearby San Diego.

It was time for Blue to cut off the crippling depression after Misha's disappearance. In *Blue* (Mysterious Press, 1998), she agreed to assist in the defense of Muffin Crandall, a sixty-one-year-old widow who was held for trial in the murder of a drug dealer whom she said had invaded her home. What distinguished these revelations was that the corpse had been stored in a freezer for five years until a power failure made its presence obvious. Blue arranged to have Roxie Bouchie evaluate Muffin's mental stability, but before any defensive strategy could be developed, Muffin was poisoned in the jail infirmary. At that point Blue thought it was over and planned to concentrate on locating Misha, but it had just begun. The ensuing struggle involved two of the most important people in Blue's life.

As *The Last Blue Plate Special* (Mysterious Press, 2001) began, Blue was designing polls for political candidate Kate Van Der Elst. A fundraiser was disrupted by the news that California State Assemblywoman Dixie Ross had died of a stroke. Blue and Roxie thought it strange that another female California state senator had died in a similar incident only two weeks before. Evidence mounted that a serial killer was targeting women who had achieved success in occupations previously dominated by men. In Blue's personal life, she was forced to make a painful decision.

Author Abigail Padgett is also the author of the "Bo" Bradley series, covered in this volume.

Dr. Gail McCarthy

Author: Laura Crum

In spite of the fact that her parents died before she entered college, Gail McCarthy never gave up her dream of becoming a veterinarian. She worked at other jobs until she graduated from the University of California-Davis with her D.V.M. A job at the Santa Cruz Equine Practice returned Gail to hometown Santa Cruz. In addition to her elderly and ill-humored Australian Cattle Dog (Blue), she had rescued a gelded quarter horse (Gunner) from euthanasia, and adopted an injured tabby cat. Fiercely independent and living in a small cabin, Gail had never married although she had a relationship with an older man, Lonny Peterson. She was a tall, dark-haired woman in her thirties, who enjoyed winter sports.

In *Cutter* (St. Martin, 1994), the investigating officer considered the death of cutting horse trainer Casey Brooks on a well-schooled mount to be an accident, but Gail was unconvinced. Casey had been harsh in his criticism of other trainers and owners, and his death occurred shortly after horses in his care had been poisoned. Her method of detection was to ask questions until the threatened killer retaliated.

Gail stumbled on two corpses in *Hoofprints* (St. Martin, 1996). After she found the murdered bodies of Cindy and Ed Whitney, Gail barely missed death at the hands of a sniper and was threatened by a hired killer. Only a chance encounter put her in a position to end her fears.

A training session at Lake Tahoe gave Gail a chance to ski while earning education credits as *Roughstock* (St. Martin, 1997) began. Her former vet school roommate, Joanna Lund, was diverted by the attentions of thrice-divorced Jack Hollister. Jack's murder placed suspicion on Joanna and sent Gail on the trail of his three former wives and others who would benefit from his death.

In *Roped* (St. Martin, 1998), rancher Glen Bennett was plagued by accidents (some deadly), but he refused to bring in law enforcement. His daughter Lisa, a high school friend of Gail's, was frantic, aware that the incidents were escalating and that some member of her family was probably involved. On a personal level, Gail moved to a larger place, but not with Lonny who had finally filed for divorce.

Just before Gail took off on a long awaited solo trip into the mountains in *Slickrock* (St. Martin, 1999), she discovered the dying Bill Evans, a veterinarian who did not want to live. Something in that encounter made Gail sense danger. As she traversed the hills and meadows with her horses and dog, meeting other groups of campers, she was cautious. Which of the other riders could she trust? A redheaded stranger, Robert "Blue" Winter, seemed her best bet, and her future. Lovely descriptions of the terrain.

The relationship with Lonny had ended by *Breakaway* (St. Martin, 2001). Whatever had been there for either of them was not strong enough to keep Lonny from moving away or to cause Gail to go with him. She was aware that, even with a partnership in the veterinary practice and the home she had carefully constructed, she was depressed. Intellectually, she knew that the early death of her parents and the struggle for her career had developed a need for independence that limited her personal future. Nicole Devereaux, an expatriate artist, whose horse had been sexually abused by a human male, intrigued her. Nicole refused to involve the police, but Gail wondered if the crimes might escalate.

As *Hayburner* (St. Martin's Minotaur, 2003) began, Gail was making a fresh start. Therapy and a vacation had pulled her out of depression. She planned to break her own colt, Danny, and was ready for a new man in her life at age 37. There was a challenge: a series of barn fires at ranches that boarded and trained thoroughbred horses. In assisting in rescue operations and treating injured animals, Gail focused her attention on possible suspects. The sheriff's department had targeted a disaffected teenager. Painful though it proved to be, Gail looked for a arsonist with a more obvious motivation. Being a veterinarian is something that Gail was good at; she was less skilled as a psychologist.

Sometimes it's nice to read a taut straight-lined mystery like *Forged* (St. Martin, 2004). Within a short time Gail was involved with two deaths. First, farrier Dominic Castillo was shot while shoeing Gail's horse in her barn. His dying declaration that he killed himself carried no weight with the police. There were both men and women who had suffered from Castillo's lechery, many of whom were clients of Gail's practice. A second death provided a motive, which many readers will recognize. Gail acquired another injured horse (Twister) but was giving thought to having a child with her husband Robert "Blue" Winter.

Gail, now seven months pregnant and totally preoccupied with the imminent birth of her son in *Moonblind* (Perseverance Press, 2006), had taken leave from her job at Santa Cruise Equine Practice. It was not so easy to separate herself from the plea for help she received from her cousin, Jenny Parker. After establishing a successful thoroughbred breeding farm in Michigan, Jenny had divorced Charley, her husband of twenty years, and bought a ranch in California. There were matters that Jenny was unable to leave behind that prompted her fear that she was being stalked. Gail was the only one to whom she confided these secrets. Gail had to balance her desire to help Jenny against her reluctance to take any risks that might endanger her pregnancy. This was a delightful read, proof that good mysteries need not be blown up to 400 pages.

The birth of son Mac had a profound impact on Gail in *Chasing Cans* (Perseverance, 2008). She took leave from her work at Santa Cruz Equine Practice and became a stay-at-home mother. No bottle feedings, no day care, and only her husband Blue as backup. Circumstances forced Gail to make adjustments. She was the closest witness when barrel racehorse Dancy Doc reared up, causing the death of neighbor Lindee Stone. She was also present when a horse seriously injured another rider at Lindee's stables. Gail convinced Detective Jeri Ward that these were not accidents.

The primary plots were interspersed with warm, fuzzy James Herriott-like tales that animal lovers will enjoy. *Going, Gone* (2010)

Lara McClintoch

Author: Lyn Hamilton

Lara McClintoch had made a business out of her knowledge of antiques. She and husband Clive Swain had been partners in a shop located in the Yorkville area of Toronto. The collapse of their marriage ended cooperation between them at least initially. Clive opened up a nearby store. Lara continued with a series of business partners (most recently, Sarah Greenhalgh) and lovers (Lucas May who remained a friend after their affair ended). Clive's second wife Celeste had sufficient resources to indulge him in a business without immediate prospects for success. Lara's shop cat, Diesel, lasted through many of the changes. Lara had been raised in a middle class Presbyterian home. She now inclined toward an earth mother concept of life, like that which existed in Malta centuries before and still lingered. Late in the series, Clive returned as a partner in Lara's antique business, although they had no personal relationship.

A cryptic message from Lara's old friend, Dr. Hernan Castillo Rivas, sent her to Merida, Mexico in *The Xibalba Murders* (Berkley, 1997). Within days his corpse was found in the museum where he had formerly served as director. Fortunately Lara had good friends in Merida where she had spent part of her early years. With their aid she was able to overcome those who conspired to sell indigenous artifacts to foreign dealers. Among her newer friends was one whose loyalty she came to doubt. On Lara's return she repurchased an interest in the antique shop, which she had sold to settle her divorce from Clive.

Martin Galea, a prominent Toronto architect with whom Lara had briefly considered an affair, sought her out in *The Maltese Goddess* (Berkley, 1998). He wanted someone to prepare his Maltese home for an important meeting. Considering that he made many purchases at her shop and that the trip would be something of a vacation, she agreed. When the newly purchased furniture arrived in Malta, an unfamiliar chest contained Galea's body. Attractive Sgt. Robert Luczka of the RCMP, who was assigned to work with the Maltese police, assisted Lara in preventing an assassination.

The Moche Warrior (Berkley, 1999) was set in the coastal region of Peru where a pre-Incan treasure brought together smugglers, archeologists, and killers. Lara joined them incognito to save her business and her reputation. She had purchased at an auction a box of Peruvian antiquities that included the warrior, an ear ornament. Subsequently her shop had been robbed and a corpse, that of a man she knew as "Spider", was left behind. RCMP Sgt. Rob Luczka had a conflict of interest: his responsibility as a police officer and his growing affection for Lara.

Lara accompanied her friend Alex Stewart to Ireland to claim an inheritance in *The Celtic Riddle* (Berkley, 2000). The decedent, Eamon Byrne, had left behind a dwindling fortune, a squabbling family and a vengeful enemy. A hidden treasure meant to restore the family solidarity was to be located through clues left by the testator. Lara and her friends raced a killer and almost lost.

Clive had a great idea, an antiques and archeology tour to Tunisia with Lara in charge, as *The African Quest* (Berkley, 2001) began. Of the more than a dozen applicants who signed up, there were several with hidden agendas: revenge, blackmail, and destruction of an enterprise. Lara was without her usual resources as she sought the connections between a Fourth century treasure ship sunk off the Tunisian coastline and the murderous incidents that were plaguing her tour group. The historical sub-text described the treachery on board the treasure ship and a young boy who lived to denounce the traitor.

While in Rome during *The Etruscan Chimera* (Berkley, 2002), Lara agreed to purchase a bronze statuary for billionaire art collector Crawford Lake . Her contacts for the assignment were elusive and untrustworthy. Visiting the current owner, Robert Godard, she realized that the Bellerophon statuary was a fake. She was led down a false trail, risking arrest for smuggling. That was bad enough but someone murdered Godard.

The Thai Amulet (Berkley, 2003) took Lara to Bangkok where Rob's daughter, Jennifer was traveling with her Thai lover, Chat Chaiwong. Chat was the heir to a family dynasty, child of an elderly man and his second wife. Chat's marriage to Jennifer, a foreigner, would face opposition. Before Lara left Canada, she had agreed to locate antique dealer Will Beauchamp, who had abandoned his wife and disabled child. Lara explored decades old deceits and current murders. Unable to foresee any justice, she provided her own, but with misgivings.

A chance encounter in *The Magyar Venus* (Berkley, 2004) brought Lara back in contact with five women with whom she had shared apartments during her college days. She joined them at a gala at the Cottingham Museum where curator Karol Molnar displayed his latest acquisition, a 2500-year-old figurine, the Magyar Venus. The man called Molnar was in fact Charlie Miller, whom she had loved and lost twenty years before. Anna Belmont, one of the former housemates, died in a plunge from a bridge after quarreling with Molnar. Lara had been so intoxicated that she was not sure that she had no role in Anna's death. The surviving four believed the Venus was a fake so Lara flew to Budapest to examine the documentation of its authenticity.

Although the initial murder, that of antique dealer Trevor Wylie, took place in Toronto, most of the action took place in Orkney Islands off the coast of Scotland in *The Orkney Scroll* (Berkley, 2006) Lara's professional reputation had been tarnished in her evaluation of an art nouveau writing desk which had been a factor in Wylie's murder. Tracing the provenance of the desk took Lara, not only across the ocean, but back a thousand years in history to the Viking occupation. She worked with allies whom she did not trust, followed clues that had to be deciphered, and became a suspect of theft and a subsequent murder. The narrative included excerpts of the saga of "Bjarni the Wanderer". Far more enjoyable were Lara's lyric descriptions of Orkney, its convivial residents, and history.

The Chinese Alchemist (Berkley, 2007) is a worthwhile, but at times cumbersome read. It combined the tale of Imperial Concubine Lingfei and eunuch Wu Yuan during the T'ang Dynasty and a dangerous mission undertaken by Lara. Her elderly friend Dory Matthews had been born of an English mother and a Chinese Communist in 1944. Dory and her mother Vivien left China after a period of unrest, leaving behind her father and a young brother, Anthony. Dory asked Lara to attend a New York City auction and bid on a silver box, one that had personal meaning for her. It seemed a simple task, but the withdrawal of the box and Dory's subsequent death sent Lara on a much farther journey to Beijing again to purchase the silver box.

Lara could not remember have taken a vacation. Her travel had always been connected with her business; however, in *The Moai Murders* (Berkley, 2008) she agreed to accompany her ailing friend Moira Meller on a trip to isolated East Island. They arrived at their hotel to learn that most guests were there to take part in the First Annual Rapa Nui Moai Conference. The participants included a few acknowledged professionals but the conference was dominated by ambitious amateurs who were interested in the thousands of carved images (moai) on the island and the seemingly indigenous rongorongo language of the inhabitants. There was a considerable amount of hostility among the delegates, much directed at primary speaker Jasper Robinson who promised to reveal a surprising discovery. Although there was a considerable amount of material describing the island and its descent into poverty, even slavery, related to the invasion of foreign elements, the motive for several deaths came not from ancient history, but more recent events. Lara's investigation was aided by RCMP Rob Luczka, the man in her life and probably in her future. Although he was not on scene, they communicated via the Internet and telephone, but also in her dreams.

This is an excellent series.

Shirley McClintock

Author: B. J. Oliphant, pseudonym for Sherri Tepper a.k.a. A. J. Orde

Even though she was officially retired and twice widowed, Shirley McClintock would scoff at senior citizen discounts. Ms. McClintock (she used her family name, not that of either husband) had left a responsible position in the federal government to return to her family's Colorado ranch. With the help of foreman J.Q. (John Quentin), Shirley ran a herd of pedigreed Belted Galloways.

Life had not always been that simple. A drunken driver had killed her son, Sal. Son Marty disappeared in the Amazon jungle; after which Martin, her first husband, died of grief and heart problems. A second shorter marriage to Bill was ended by cancer. She and J.Q. shared a physical relationship, but marriage was not in their plans. Shirley was physically robust at 6' 2"; the only sign of aging, her graying hair. Her politics were diverse. She was adamantly pro-choice and intolerant of fundamentalist religions, but contemptuous of "knee jerk" liberals, particularly ACLU members. She promoted the responsibilities of minorities, including the primacy of the English language. However vehement Shirley could be on ideology, on a personal level, she championed the underdog and the vulnerable.

During *Dead in the Scrub* (Fawcett, 1990), while hunting deer with realtor Charles Maxwell, they discovered a skeleton. Later Charles was murdered, and his wife Gloria arrested. Shirley agreed to take responsibility for their daughter, Allison, (eleven, going on eighteen thanks to her parents). The skeleton was eventually identified as that of William Dietz, deacon of a fundamentalist church. It did not seem coincidental to Shirley that Charles Maxwell's last big sale was to Rev. Orrin Patterson, pastor of that church. Gloria, out on bail, was also murdered. Shirley would fight to keep Allison who might be the next victim.

By *The Unexpected Corpse* (Fawcett, 1990), Shirley and J.Q. had added twelve-year-old Allison to the household as a foster child. Shirley was an only child, but she had an extended family of cousins, aunts, and uncles. She was present at the intended burial of the ashes of her uncle January Storey, his most recent wife Billie-B, and cousin Willard. Willard's box contained priceless Revere silver. Shirley agreed to act as executor, but also as sleuth as the bodies piled up.

Martin, Shirley's first husband, had bequeathed her property in the District of Columbia, necessitating a trip to make financial arrangements. On her return in *Deservedly Dead* (Fawcett, 1992) she was aghast at the changes. Land speculator Eleazar Azoli had not only damaged the environment but also created ill feeling among other residents. Shirley solved Azoli's murder and Allison's personal problem, but could not restore her sense of belonging.

Death and the Delinquent (Fawcett, 1993) took Allison, Shirley, and J.Q. to a guest ranch in New Mexico where seriously disturbed April (age 13) became friendly with Allison. While they were trail riding, a sharpshooter shot Shirley's mule, causing her to fall and damage her knee. A second shot killed April. There was more to come, an abducted infant, another murder. Seeking a solution for the deaths while on crutches, Shirley realized her need for a fresh start. The change was not that simple. Colorado had been the McClintock home for four generations.

Even after six months as the proprietor of a New Mexico guest ranch in *Death Served Up Cold* (Fawcett, 1994) Shirley was unsettled. She was having a problem with memory lapses. On the advice of Xanthippe Minging, a teacher who had joined the ménage to tutor Allison, she discontinued a medication for insomnia to which she had become addicted. Shirley needed all her faculties. Not only had guest Alicia Tremple been murdered and her cabin burglarized, but Allison's relatives schemed to get custody of the child for mercenary reasons. Shirley's solution to the murder was intriguing, but distasteful.

A Ceremonial Death (Fawcett, 1996) was overloaded with Shirley's opinions on schools, the legal system, and families. Allison was having difficulty integrating into the local school, hassled by a clique headed by Dawn French, a jealous classmate who resented her achievements. When Allison discovered Dawn's corpse, she was not a serious suspect, but Shirley connected the death with another recent murder. Shadow Dancer aka Bridget McCree, a cosmic healer, had been left naked, her body marked with symbols. The locals toyed with the idea of extraterrestrials because there had been some animal mutilations in the area. Shirley deemed the local sheriff to be totally incompetent so set to work to find the killer. Instead, the killer found her.

Renting cottages to guests was not without its dangers. Shirley suffered from destructive children, demanding mothers of the bride, and free-spending honeymooners in *Here's to the Newly Dead* (Fawcett, 1997). The honeymooners, having borrowed a shovel from Shirley, went off to plant a tree. When they did not return she followed their trail and found them both dead. She needed all of her self control when there was a possibility that her son Marty might still be alive after sixteen years.

This was one tough lady who ran roughshod over opposition. Under the name A. J. Orde, Oliphant/ Tepper had another series featuring interior decorator Jason Lynx and detective Grace Willis (see Volume 2)

Dr. Anna McColl

Author: Penny Kline

Anna McColl was a clinical psychologist who worked in a group practice in Bristol, England. She had never married but had serial affairs. She could have used a little help herself for her obsessive-compulsive behaviors.

As *Dying to Help* (Macmillan, 1993) began, Anna's lover David, had returned to his former wife Iris. Her evenings and weekends were lonely but there were challenging cases at the office. She was planning a research project on "frequent attendees" (hypochondriacs or those perceived as such). Young Jenny Weir had been referred by her general practitioner because of her continued visits. Diane Easby asked Anna to exonerate her brother, Keith Merchant, from a charge of murdering social worker Karen Plant. The two cases merged in a credible narrative with a rambling introspective style.

Readers may need access to a diagnostic codebook to enjoy *Feeling Bad* (Macmillan, 1994). Anna dealt with anxiety neurosis, incest, sibling rivalry, homosexuality, and sexless marriages. It all began when Luke Jesty, still burdened with guilt because of sister's death six years before, fell apart. He had been present when Paula Redfern was catapulted into traffic and killed. Anna needed more information about both Luke and Paula to verify that she had not misdiagnosed his condition. She was diverted by an emotional response to a suspect.

Anna's plans for a two-week vacation had to be cancelled in *A Crushing Blow* (Macmillan, 1995). She used the time to help Geraldine Haran with her agoraphobia. During her visits to the Haran home, Anna became aware of Geraldine's interactions with her husband, her son and those relatives who occupied the other portion of the duplex. As her concern for Geraldine progressed, Anna probed into the death of lonely widower Walter Bury who was murdered in a nearby forest. The narrative was marred by excessive red herrings and tag ends.

Social scientist Maggie Hazeldean had scheduled an appointment to meet with Anna. In *Turning Nasty* (Macmillan, 1995), she died before the consult could take place. Bill, Maggie's estranged husband, and their son Ian could not put closure to her death until they knew who had killed her. Among the suspects were not only associates of Maggie but also clients of Anna, so she shared the family's need to know. By now Anna had her Ph.D. and was Dr. Anna McColl. Again, there were many diversions into subplots.

Sally Luckham, aged twelve, had narrowly escaped abduction at the hands of a woman as she walked home from school. She was referred to Anna to get a coherent description of the incident and the person involved. During *Ending in Tears* (Macmillan, 1997), persons who were suspects in the death of Tom Luckham, Sally's recently deceased father, contacted Anna. She realized that she might know more than the killer wanted her to. On the more positive side, Anna found that Professor Owen Hughes' absence for an exchange program in Australia was a relief. Inspector Howard Fry was her new admirer. The narrative began well, but was overpopulated.

Living in Dread (Severn House, 1998) was just plain cluttered. Anna, whose house had been damaged by fire, rented the annex to a home owned by Eric Newsome, unaware at the time that his wife Nikki had been murdered months before. Eric was perceived by many, including the police, as the primary suspect, although no charges had been brought against him. Anna took a personal interest in Eric and Nikki's son, Charlie (6 years old). Unfortunately so did someone else. Using this frail connection, Anna made it her business to seek other possible suspects in the murder, including men with whom Nikki might have been involved. Too frequently characters from prior books were presented without adequate background information.

Kline also has a juvenile series featuring Karen Cady.

Karen McDade

Author: Emer Gillespie

With no intent to minimize the trauma of rape, it can be said that Karen McDade might have taken steps on her own behalf to recover from the tragic event. Jack, her lover at the time, had become increasingly possessive and jealous. His interpretation of her innocent encounter with a male friend drove him into a frenzy that culminated in rape. She received no encouragement from the London police who said that, given the couples' past sexual history, it would be her word against his. Nevertheless she declined to follow up on suggestions of counseling. She drew back from all but the closest friends and declined to join a group where she could share her sense of betrayal. Instead she moved to a different home address where she slept during the day. She worked as a film editor during the night hours, sequestered in a third floor room at her office at Finest Cut.

Karen's mother had been killed in a car accident when she was eleven. Her father never recovered from the loss, and they both feared intimacy. She had no brothers or sisters. Her constant companion was Job, a huge Bouvier des Flandres, who accompanied her everywhere that the law and her boss allowed. Lacking family resources, she overwhelmed her good friends John and Sarah. Sarah and Karen had been friends since they met as students at the North London Polytechnic. Sarah had chosen marriage and a family. Karen had decided that she would never have children, fearing that she would harm them by dying. Sarah's husband John had helped Karen when her career was at a standstill by suggesting that she take a course in film editing. Even with her handicaps Karen was successful in her work for Finest Cut, an independent production company. Her most recent project had been a series on women from a variety of different backgrounds and nationalities done for Nordic Communications. Her work was well appreciated by her boss, Bob Wilkes.

Given that chaotic a life, Karen's discovery of a young woman's body in the alley near the offices in *Virtual Stranger* (Headline, 1998) accentuated her fears. Had Jack located her? Was he the man who had plagued her with sexually taunting on the phone? Three years and four months had passed since the rape, but it was always fresh in her mind. She finally recognized that the victim, young Katie Sewell, had appeared in an independent film made by Rob Benson that she had edited. Was the killer someone she knew or worked with?

Karen took a leave of absence from Finest Cut during *Five Dead Men* (Headline, 1999) to work with Rob Benson on a documentary. Their film focused on a civic renovation project and its impact on the environment. The confluence of death on the construction site and Karen's reconnection with estranged members of her family had a devastating impact on her. Rob, waiting patiently for her to recognize his feelings, and faithful dog Job shared in the repercussions from betrayal and death.

Tally McGinnis

Author: Nancy Sanra

Tally had earned a degree in criminology and attended the police academy, but after some time as a San Francisco police officer, she moved and changed her career plans. Now sharing a bayside condo with her lesbian lover, Katie O'Neill, she opened her own detective agency with Katie, as office manager. Tally's father Patrick had been a workaholic district attorney, and Tally modeled herself on him. Harry Sinclair, San Francisco chief medical examiner, had been a friend to Patrick and a surrogate father to Tally. After Patrick's death, her mother began dating Sinclair. Eventually Cid Cameron, also a former police officer, became the third partner in the detective agency.

Relationships dominated *No Witness* (Rising Tide, 1995) Lt. Cid Cameron, San Francisco Homicide, made Tally aware that wealthy computer consultant Cathy Dorset had been murdered and her lover, Pamela Tresdale, arrested. Cid, a long time friend, knew that Pamela had dumped Tally for Cathy Dorset. Tally's first instinct was to defend and protect the woman with whom she had shared five years. She resisted that impulse when she realized that the police would then focus on her as a suspect. Katie O'Neill helped locate the "other woman".

Although attorney Rita Cruz contacted Tally to investigate the murder of nurse Melinda Morgan in *No Escape* (Rising Tide, 1998), she was particularly concerned with the defense of her client, Dr. Rebecca Tolliver, who had been charged with the crime. One unusual clue: a red rose left by the victim's bedside made Tally and Cid (now her partner in the agency) decide to take the case. The red rose connected the murder to their nemesis, Marsha Cox, a suspect in a prior case.

Tally, Katie and Cid were among 200 plus passengers on a Panamanian registered cruise ship tour for lesbians in *No Corpse* (Rising Tide, 2000). They had hoped for a restful vacation but were assigned to a table with five quarrelsome women. The women, formerly roommates while attending the University of Washington, shared a terrible secret. One, then another, was murdered. Tally and Cid wondered who might hate them all. Vincenzo Pallino, a friend of Cid's who was director of security on the vessel, accepted their help. Explicit lesbian intimacies were woven into the narrative, which may deter some readers.

Donna Haskell pleaded with Tally and Cid to investigate the murder of her talented daughter, Johanna, in *No Evidence* (Bella Books, 2005). Months after her disappearance, Johanna's body had been found on a semi-deserted beach, a victim of sadistic abuse. There was considerable explicit sadistic torture in the narrative. The local police had not charged anyone with the crime although one suspect had been arrested and released. Tally and Cid reactivated the investigation, enlisting the help of the San Jose College security office because Johanna had been a student there. Identifying the probable killer was not the problem. Suddenly, on page 161, with multiple questions unresolved, the book ended with *to be continued.* No subsequent book has been located.

Nuala Anne McGrail

Author: Andrew M. Greeley

Nuala McGrail could not possibly be as lovely, as bright, and as engaging as narrator Dermot Coyne described her. She was the child of low-income parents in the Gaelic speaking section of western Ireland. After she won a scholarship to Trinity College, she moved to Dublin. At nineteen she was close to graduation but lacked the funds to continue.

In *Irish Gold* (Forge, 1994), Coyne visited Ireland to research his grandparents' involvement in the battle for Irish independence from 1917 to 1924. Dermot had been devoted to Nell Pat, his grandmother, and believed that her journals would explain why his grandparents left Ireland in 1920 and never returned. A chance encounter with Nuala in a student pub provided Dermot with a translator and an object for adoration. The translations were a potential danger to English authorities and their Irish allies. Nuala's youth and innocence kept Dermot from taking advantage of her, although she was deeply in love with him.

The terrain changed in *Irish Lace* (Forge, 1996) and the blend of a past conspiracy with the present was more labored. Nuala's degree entitled her to a Morrison visa and a job as an accountant at a prominent Chicago firm. Chicago and its environs were the home of the Coyne family, which took Nuala to its heart. She became preoccupied with emanations from an area formerly used as a Civil War prison camp for Confederate soldiers. Nuala's stay in Chicago was jeopardized by her contacts with Irish revolutionaries who frequented the pub where she sang. She and Dermot set the date for their wedding.

The McGrail and Coyne clans gathered for the event in *Irish Whiskey* (Forge, 1998). When Nuala and Dermot visited a local cemetery, she had another of her intuitive flashes; the grave of James "Sweet Rolls" Sullivan, a bootlegger who rivaled Al Capone, was empty. This information came in handy when Nuala needed leverage. A former friend charged Dermot with stock manipulations. It took Cindy Hurley, his attorney/sister, and Nuala, to prove his innocence. Interference with wedding plans by Nuala's pompous older brother didn't help, but it padded out the narrative.

Greeley continued his mix of Irish mysticism and history in *Irish Mist* (Forge, 1999), exploring the assassination of Kevin O'Higgins who had brought stability to Ireland after Michael Collins' death. En route to a Dublin charity concert, Nuala had a "spell" concerning the assassination of a politician whom they assumed to be O'Higgins. Their investigation into his murder must have upset someone (perhaps information about a possible affair between British hero, Hugh Tudor, and the widow of a distinguished general). There was an attempt to abduct Nuala and one to kill her (foiled by an Irish Wolfhound, which they adopted).

Poor Dermot. In *Irish Eyes* (Forge, 2000), he realized that baby daughter, Nelliecoyne, had inherited her mother's "fey" (the ability to see into the past or future). Screams from the child as they visited the family cottage on Lake Michigan sent Nuala and Dermot into a voyage of discovery. Although distracted by the antics and death of ambitious music critic Nick Farmer, they connected a one hundred-year-old shipwreck to a lost treasure. An engrossing view of Chicago Irish in the 1890s.

Nuala and Dermot visited western Ireland in the present, and in the past during *Irish Love* (Forge, 2001). They now owned an ample bungalow near the Connemara coast. Within weeks of their occupancy there were bombings, and shots were fired. Nuala and Dermot immersed themselves in the journal left behind by Chicago reporter Ned Fitzpatrick describing the vicious destruction of a local family during the 1880s. They learned about the local feuds that scapegoated one man and the incompetent and unjust English police, court system, and politics that allowed innocent men to go to the gallows. Nuala and Dermot uncovered a greedy plot to destroy the local community. When she came to Ireland, Nuala had been suffering from post-partum depression that forced her to put her career on hold. Her experiences, although stressful, and the time spent with her parents restored her balance. She sang again.

Irish Stew! (Forge, 2002) blended the Coyne's investigation of an attack upon attorney Seamus Costelloe with reporter Ned Fitzpatrick's century old account of the Haymarket bombing. Costelloe had earned his enemies and was sure that he had warned them off, but family members asked Dermot and Nuala to probe deeper. In 1886 German and American Socialists had been targeted by prominent Chicago businessmen who feared them and the unions that might follow. They had easily corrupted the police who turned a peaceful protest and a single bomber into a campaign to rid Chicago of foreign terrorists. Nuala's involvement was slightly diminished so that she could care for their premature daughter.

Irish Cream (Forge, 2005) introduced the John P. O'Sullivan family to whom those words meant the "cream of society". By this they meant the Irish Catholics, preferably graduates of Notre Dame, who had risen to the top (including themselves, of course). The lone holdout was Damien, who was derided, detested and harassed by his family. He was hired by Dermot and Nuala as tender for their children and Irish wolfhounds. On another track, Dermot was reading the journal of Irish priest Fr. Richard Lonigan, who had been rusticated to an isolate west coast parish at the period between the famine and the Land League. Lonigan's struggle with the British constabulary over the murder of an estate manager, the wounding of Lord Robert Skeffington and his affection for his widowed housekeeper were detailed. Dermot now had the plot for his next novel.

Nuala's sense of danger was at high in *Irish Crystal* (Forge, 2006). She had reason to be concerned. Federal agents had taken her green card and her citizenship papers were on hold. She was harassed by agents from Homeland Security who were operating on false information. There were hassles with the church too. Dermot was at odds with their current pastor and both were concerned about the nun who taught Nelliecoyne's first Communion class. Nuala's sense of danger extended to their friends John and Estelle Curran and their extended family. The bombing of the Curran home occurred while they were traveling in Europe.

Dermot and Nuala were off on one of their personal crusades in *Irish Linen* (Forge, 2007) to locate Desmond Dooley, peripatetic son of a prominent Irish Catholic family in Chicago. His parents initially sought their help. Simultaneously, they were reading another of the narratives stored in Father George's church. The author was Timothy Clarke, Lord Ridgewood, a Catholic in Ireland whose family lived on the border between Ireland and Northern Ireland in the 30's and 40's. While studying in Germany awaiting assignment within the Irish diplomatic service, Timmy met Annalise, the love of his life, then only sixteen. He became a close friend of Claus von Stauffenberg, whose love for the real Germany and adherence to his Catholic ideals made him a natural enemy of the Nazi movement. Von Stauffenberg became a distinguished Army officer, but risked his life to end the war. This narrative far out shadowed the search for Des Doolin partly because of its historical accuracy.

Nuala's psychic gifts combined with her skill in wielding a camogie stick in *Irish Tiger* (Forge, 2008). When the wedding plans of John Patrick (Jack) Donlan and Maria Angelica Connors were sabotaged, they were referred to Nuala and Dermot for help. It was needed because scandalous but false gossip escalated into physical violence after the couple (both widowed with adult children) were married. Nuala, with the help of family attorneys, was also coping with professional difficulties. The original contract for her annual Christmas show had been cancelled and an effort was made to prevent Nuala from seeking another sponsor.

Next: *Irish Tweed (2009)*

You don't have to be Irish to enjoy the series, but it helps. Greeley has a second mystery series featuring Bishop Blackie Ryan of the Chicago Diocese.

Annie McGrogan

Author: Gillian B. Farrell

Annie McGrogan, a New York City actress, spent her "at leisure" hours as a part-time private investigator. She was a slender redhead with serious aspirations, having studied under such legitimate drama teachers as Geraldine Page and Jeff Corey. Her ability to disguise herself on stage or at work was an asset. As she detected, she absorbed impressions to use in her stage and screen portrayals. Annie had ended her ten-year marriage to Patrick for a handsome lover, who then dumped her.

In *Alibi for an Actress* (Pocket, 1992), Annie maintained a platonic relationship with her partner, Sonny Gandolpho. They were assigned to guard television soap actress Lucinda Merrill, but became her alibi when her unfaithful husband was murdered. Annie's personal life merged with her professional responsibilities in a taut narrative.

During *Murder and a Muse* (Pocket, 1994), she explored the nature of relationships, while researching her part in a new movie by unconventional director Alan De Lucca. Until he was murdered, Annie had been drawn to De Lucca. She had invested her professional skills in the movie, and needed the pragmatic Sonny to help her return to reality.

Imaginative premise.

Madison McGuire

Author: Amanda Kyle Williams

Lesbian sleuths are frequently portrayed as police officers or private investigators. Madison McGuire offered an interesting alternative, espionage agent. The reluctance of government security forces to employ homosexuals was acknowledged in the series. Madison, whose mother died when she was five years old, spent her adolescence in England where her father, who worked for the CIA, had been stationed. Professionally, she preferred to work alone, but had allies within the espionage trade who came to her assistance on occasion, including Max Rudger, an ex-IRA agent.

Madison had been forced to resign from the CIA during *Club Twelve* (Naiad, 1990). Her lover, Elicia planned to use Madison's car to get groceries. As she entered the vehicle, another car drove by. She was fatally shot. From that point on, Madison had a goal, the destruction of an international conspiracy for world domination. She demanded the support of the CIA or threatened to carry on alone. She was unprepared for betrayal.

Although Madison initially lost her security clearance, she was recalled in *The Providence File* (Naiad, 1991) to infiltrate the Palestinian Liberation Army, presenting herself as a renegade CIA agent. Her current partner, tax attorney Terry Woodall, resented her return to duty.

In *A Singular Spy* (Naiad, 1992), Madison was employed as a trainer at the Clandestine Entry Program Center until Lyle Dresser, a disloyal CIA employee, was murdered in Geneva. The agency sent McGuire with a handpicked team to uncover other moles, considering the task force expendable.

The Spy in Question (Naiad, 1993) provided Madison with a new interest, singer Dani Stone, and a new assignment for the CIA. A small American unit was sent into Peru to destroy drug production sites. Madison was to contact Enrique Navarro, a populist leader willing to fight the Senderos, betrayers of the peasants they had promised to liberate. Surprisingly naive after two decades of government employment, Madison was shocked at the duplicity of the political system. She and others, who were concerned about the integrity of the CIA, disregarded their orders.

The books provided interesting plots and did not limit themselves to lesbian or feminist issues.

Judith Grover McMonigle (Flynn)

Author: Mary Daheim

Judith was a tall gray-haired, ex-librarian widow. She had married Dan McMonigle on the rebound. He might not have realized that he was second choice, but something was bothering Dan because he ate himself to death. With son Mike off to college, Judith remodeled the spacious Seattle family home into a bed and breakfast, adding her querulous mother, Gertrude, to the household. Gertrude became an overworked gag that detracted from Daheim's otherwise light touch. Her husband, Donald, who had suffered from rheumatic fever as a child, had died an early death.

In *Just Desserts* (Avon, 1991), former opera star Oriana Bustamanti commandeered the entire establishment while her home was being fumigated. Her husband Otto had been expected to make a major announcement as to his estate plans at a family dinner. The hired entertainer, fortuneteller Madame Gushinka aka Wanda Rakesh, was poisoned during tea and cream puffs. Anxious to protect her reputation, Judith solved the murder, which meant spending time with Lt. Joe Flynn, who had jilted her twenty years before.

Judith and her cousin, Renie (Serena) Jones vacationed in Canada during *Fowl Prey* (Avon, 1991). They connected with the reunion of producer Max Rothsides' original theatrical team. The death of street peddler Bob-o, and his parakeet stimulated Judith and Renie to play detective with long distance help from Joe Flynn.

Judith's active Catholicism was evident in *Holy Terrors* (Avon, 1992) when she catered the parish post-egg roll repast. The death of volunteer Sandy Frizzell cancelled the meal, but the revelation of Sandy's gender was even more of a shock. Flynn, freed of his marriage, was ready to try again with Judith.

Their long delayed honeymoon occurred as *Dune to Death* (Avon, 1993) began but Joe suffered a disabling injury. Unwilling to postpone her honeymoon again, Judith invited Renie to join her at the cottage while Joe languished in the local hospital. Judith and Renie had a dead landlady to test their skills.

In *Bantam of the Opera* (Avon, 1993), while Joe was in New Orleans for a conference, Judith provided "bed and breakfast" for egotistical opera star Mario Pacetti and his retinue. A dose of poison finished Pacetti, but did not alter Judith's propensity for high-risk investigations.

When Judith and Renie visited the family cottage to bury Dan's ashes in *A Fit of Tempera* (Avon, 1994), they became acquainted with artist Riley Tobias. Before Tobias was murdered, he gave Judith a landscape, touching off a search for a parent, a painting, and an obvious killer.

Judith and Renie agreed to cater the family birthday party for "Uncle Boo" in *Major Vices* (Avon, 1995), knowing that they would earn little appreciation. Boo's death in the locked room of an isolated family home put Judith in a quandary. Joe was out of town, and his rival, Det. Buck Doerflinger was handling the case. Judith proceeded as usual. She hid clues, tampered with evidence, and found the killer.

In *Murder, My Suite* (Avon, 1995), Judith (now Judith Grover McMonigle Flynn) recovered from the disastrous visit of gossip columnist Dagmar Chatsworth and her entourage at the bed and breakfast. She and Renie headed for a free week at a Canadian ski resort. Her neighbors were the Chatsworth entourage who had brought their problems with them. Murder followed, but the narrative diverted to scenic descriptions, Judith's unwarranted jealousy of her husband's contacts in an investigation, and mother jokes.

The foursome, Judith, Renie and their spouses, journeyed to England in *Auntie Mayhem* (Avon, 1996). While the men fished in Scotland, the wives visited a magnificent but undercapitalized manor home. The potential heirs to the estate were considering making it into a "bed and breakfast" facility, but ninety-four year old Aunt "Pet" had to die first. Her death set Judith and Renie to detecting. Fortunately, their husbands arrived in time to rescue them.

Nutty As a Fruitcake (Avon, 1996) was set during the Christmas holidays, when Judith's exuberant, even excessive, celebration clashed with Joe's negative memories of Christmases past. The death of neighbor Enid Goodrich did not spoil Judith's enthusiasm, but the arrest of Enid's long-suffering husband George did. Many people had a motive for disposing of Enid. Judith intended to exonerate George. There was a handy network of Bed and Breakfast facility owners who assisted one another in crisis times.

In *September Mourn* (Avon, 1997), Judith and Renie traveled to isolated Chavez island to substitute for ex-high school classmate Jeanne Barber in running her three cabin hostelry. Obnoxious guest H. Burrell Hodge died shortly after Renie had cracked a plate over his head. Judith looked among the permanent residents of the island for others with motives to kill, and found more than she needed. Her intrusive questions were tolerated by the suspects to an unrealistic degree.

Her son Michael's wedding created a crisis for Judith. Was this the time to tell him about his father? The time to talk never came during *Wed and Buried* (Avon, 1998). Judith witnessed a "bride's" murder on an adjacent hotel rooftop during the reception. Patient Joe agreed to check. A corpse did show up the next day, but it was the groom's. Judith's insistence on carrying on a parallel investigation in a case with no friend or relative involved got no support from Renie and created problems for Joe.

Judith decided to end her catering services. In *Snow Place to Die* (Avon, 1998), she accepted a final assignment to accommodate Cousin Renie. She would provide an evening meal for the management staff of a telephone company holding their annual retreat at an isolated lodge. The winter weather made it impossible for Judith and Renie to leave as the corpses increased and the suspects dwindled. Agatha Christie would be pleased.

It may take special skills to keep track of the cops and criminals (with assorted aliases) who filled Judith's bed and breakfast in *Legs Benedict* (Avon, 1999). The narrative was heavily seasoned with coincidences and sweetened by personal pathos. Those who were regular fans of the series knew what to expect and would enjoy.

Daheim pulled out all the stops in *Creeps Suzette* (Avon, 2000). Judith and Renie were persuaded to investigate murderous attempts on the life of rich, reclusive dowager Leota Burgess. Creepers (the family home) and the family lineage were well populated by ghosts and evidence of miscegenation, murder and suicide, mental instability, infidelity and racial prejudice. Murders spanning sixty years were solved but only with the help of Detective Edwina Jefferson and newly licensed private investigator Joe Flynn.

A mystery tour in their area took Judith and Renie to the Alhambra in *A Streetcar Named Expire* (Avon, 2001) where a woman's corpse had been discovered behind a wall during a remodeling of the building from apartments to condominiums. Within minutes of her entry into the Alhambra, Judith discovered the corpse of Aimee Carrabas, an exorcist who had been hired by George Guthrie to cleanse the building. Joe was hired to investigate Aimee's murder, but Judith and Renie went one step backward. Convinced that the deaths were connected, they focused on former resident Dorothy Meacham. She had disappeared decades before, after which her husband Harry moved to California. The couple had a daughter, Anne-Marie, whose whereabouts were unknown. Gertrude in a lucid moment helped by recalling Dorothy, Harry, their child, and a mysterious foreign woman.

Renie and Judith were booked for orthopedic surgery at Good News Hospital during *Suture Self* (Morrow, 2001). They occupied their recovery time by investigating the deaths of three other patients. All three had recovered well from surgery, only to die unexpectedly. Renie's complaints against the food and medication became tiresome. Judith not only solved the crimes but also assisted in a parallel case on which Joe was working.

During *Silver Scream* (Morrow, 2002), Daheim threw everything in, including the kitchen sink. She had reluctantly agreed to accommodate superstitious movie producer Bruno Zepf and his ensemble, who were in town for the premiere of his latest masterpiece, *The Gasman*. What a bunch of prima donnas! Whatever loyalty they had to Bruno or to fellow workers washed away when Bruno was discovered with his head under water in the Hillside Manor kitchen sink. Since the plugged up sink and a faulty cupboard door were Judith's responsibility, she feared a crippling lawsuit. Murder seemed a preferable alternative.

The prospect of a relaxed vacation lured Judith and Joe from Hillside Manor in *Hocus Crocus* (Morrow, 2003). The Bed and Breakfast was closed for repairs anyway. Renie and Bill Jones were going to the Lake Stillasnowamish Resort Casino on a Native American reservation, so that she could attend a conference and gamble in her spare time. Both couples ended up bringing extra baggage: Gertrude and Aunt Deb. While in the neighborhood, Renie and Judith wanted to check on work being done on inherited family property. A friend of Joe's provided the quartet with tickets to the dinner show of the Great Mandolini. When Judith discovered the corpse of Salome, the illusionist's assistant, the narrative got frenetic, even incredible.

This Old Souse (Morrow, 2004) went over the top, but that's the hallmark of the series. Neither Renie, the instigator, nor Judith, the confirmed busy body, had a good reason for spying on the home of Dick and Jane Bland. The reclusive family had occupied a once lovely home for 50 years allowing it to deteriorate. Every year they received a mysterious package from Austria. What became Judith's business was that while she was snooping around, someone put a corpse in her car trunk. The police found her story difficult to believe; readers may, too.

Fatigued by her work at the Bed and Breakfast and the constant arguments between Joe and Gertrude, Judith was ready for a vacation in *Dead Man Docking* (Morrow, 2005). She and Joe had already made plans when Renie invited Judith to accompany her at no cost on a cruise to the South Pacific. Renie, a graphic artist, had a contract to promote designs for Cruz Cruises that might be jeopardized by a recent move. The cruise would provide her with an opportunity to solidify her position with Cruz. The ship, *San Rafael,* never left the harbor. First CEO Magglio Cruz was found dead in a grand piano; then, two important staff members were murdered. The addition of engaging characters from the 1930's; i.e. clones of Jean Harlow, Nick and Nora Charles added nostalgia.

Saks and Violins (Morrow, 2006) had too much of foul-mouthed Gertrude; too much of Renie's obsession with Oscar (a small ape) and Clarence (a bunny), stuffed animals whom she personalized. Across the cul de sac lived Rudi Wittner and his younger companion, pianist Taryn Moss. Wittner chose to house some of his frequent guests, including his mentor Dolph Andreas at Judith's bed and breakfast. Rudi had antagonized many of the neighbors by his nude violin practice in his yard. Still it was Andreas who was poisoned, by rhubarb! Rudi did suffer a loss. His $350,000 violin bow was stolen. Even with her artificial hip, Judith managed to straighten things out.

Judith and Renie had been hoping for a warm California vacation as *Scots on the Rocks* (Morrow, 2007) began. Instead they ended up in a cold drafty castle on Scotland's North Sea. The castle was owned by whiskey entrepreneur Philip Fordyce and occupied by his gnome-like son, Chuckie. Mr. and Mrs. Gibbs served as chauffeur, butler, cook, and housekeeper during the off-season. While Joe and Bill took off with Inspector Hugh MacGowan on a fishing trip, Judith and Renie embroiled themselves in the murder of Harry Gibbs, the grandson of the two servants. Harry was also the husband of young heiress Moira who owned the controlling interest in an offshore oil company. Renie's rude, violent, and ridiculous behavior, sometimes prompted by her latent jealousy of Judith, went beyond humorous to annoying. She was suffering from a serious eye problem while Judith's artificial hip limited her movements. Due to a misunderstanding, the local police were tolerant of their activities.

Vi Agra Falls (Morrow, 2008) had a great title but a confusing case of characters. Another member of the Buss family turned up every time you thought you had them straight. Vivian, (Joe's ex-wife), returned to the neighborhood with Billy Buss, her latest husband. She horrified nearby homeowners with the announcement that she planned to tear down her home and the recently purchased adjoining property in order to erect a condominium. Where did Vivian get that kind of money? An overcrowded narrative included five of Vivian's husbands and four of her children. One husband had already died; another did not survive Vivian's big celebration.

Characters in the *Bed and Breakfast* books were reminiscent of past television series; e.g. Judith's mother resembled Sophie, the wisecracking, ill-humored senior citizen on *The Golden Girls.* Judith played Lucy Ricardo to cousin Renie as Ethel Mertz. By #17, the series moved up to hardcover. *Loco Motive* is scheduled for early in 2010. Some may prefer the Emma Lord series also by Daheim.

Kathy McNeely

Author: Louis Charbonneau

A less common category for female sleuths has been scientists, except for the recently popular pathologists and longtime favorite archaeologists. Kathy was a Ph.D. level zoologist studying the impact of oil spills on Antarctic birds.

She kept warm with handsome archeologist/adventurer Brian Hurley during *The Ice* (Fine, 1991). Kathy had rescued birds earlier when the *SS Kowloon* oil spill contaminated the area. Her more recent assignment, funded by the National Science Foundation, was to predict the spill's long-term impact by tabulating the survivors. The U.S. team headed by marine biologist Dr. Carl Jeffers accommodated a Russian expedition, a film company, and American business interests seeking precious minerals. The prize was valuable enough to incite murder.

Kathy's reputation preceded her so that, although her technical skills were unassailable, scientist Jason Cobb wondered whether she was a prima donna in *White Harvest* (Fine, 1994). She rescued him from death, and worked with an Eskimo hunter and an undercover agent to fight the human predators who ravaged the walrus herds.

An interesting diversion from the private investigators, housewives, and policewomen.

Camilla McPhee

Author: Mary Jane Maffini

Camilla McPhee, who had not recovered from the death of her lover Paul, had two resources: her extended family and Justice for Victims, the non-profit agency she founded to represent the victims of crimes. At age thirty-two she considered herself the ugly duckling, short, dark and stocky, as compared with her three sophisticated, tall, slim blonde sisters. Camilla had been the "caboose" in the family, a birth, which her mother did not survive. Her father Donald, principal at St. Jim's high school, was well known in the community. Her sisters had married well, although Alexa was widowed. They worked at finding an appropriate spouse for Camilla. The McPhee family had its roots in Nova Scotia, but had settled happily in Ottawa, the national capitol of Canada.

Initially Camilla had practiced criminal law. Her dismay at the limited attention paid to the victims of crime led her to establish Justice for Victims, which she ran from a cluttered office. Her father, who had a proclivity for rescuing the children and grandchildren of friends, induced her to hire young Alvin Ferguson. Once Camilla got beyond the annoyance of Alvin's presence (he played rock music on his radio) and his appearance, she found him to be capable and loyal. There was some relief in sending him off on research projects so she could complete the necessary paperwork on her desk. She had achieved some success with Justice for Victims, partly because she had a highly developed network of friends in the police department, the Royal Canadian Mounted Police, the legal profession, and social services groups. Neighbor Violet Parnell joined the ensemble.

Camilla had known Robin Findlay since kindergarten, too well to believe that she would kill vitriolic columnist Mitzi Brochu in *Speak Ill of the Dead* (RendezVous Press, Toronto, 1999). The police, notably Sgt. Conn McCracken, considered the fact that Robin was discovered at the scene of the crime with bloody hands to be significant evidence. Mitzi had targeted dozens of prominent persons in her columns, usually female, and generally those who carried more weight than Mitzi considered acceptable. Camilla rallied her resources, including an attractive man who reawakened feelings dormant since Paul's death.

Everyone wanted serial abuser Ralph Benning put away for a long time during *The Icing on the Corpse* (RendezVous, 2001). Someone did something about it and murdered him. The police turned their attention to his former wife until she too was found dead; then, to Camilla's client, Lindsay Grace who had testified against him. They finally arrested social activist Elaine Ekstein who enjoyed the attention. With help from Alvin Ferguson and her elderly neighbor Violet Parnell, Camilla targeted the killer in time to attend her sister Alexa's marriage to Det. Sgt. Conn McCracken.

Camilla thought she would be glad to have Alvin out of her office as *Little Boy Blues* (RondezVous, 2002) began. He had found a job at an art gallery, but she had relaxed too soon. Collect calls from the Ferguson family in Sydney made Camilla aware that Alvin's handicapped younger brother Jimmy was missing. Alvin was in a state of shock, so Camilla and Violet Parnell drove him to Sydney, Nova Scotia only to return to Ottawa for a dramatic finish.

Remembrance Day (November 11th, celebrated as Veterans' Day in the U. S.) drew great crowds in *The Dead Don't Get Out Much* (RendezVous, 2005) and Camilla's dear friend, former WAC veteran Violet Parnell always marched in the parade. This year she was upset, collapsed. She "had seen a dead man". When Violet disappeared from the hospital, Alvin and Camilla learned that she had flown to Italy. Leaving disappointed beau Ray Devereau behind, Camilla followed. The narrative provided clues to Violet's strange behavior through letters sent to her by her friends, Betty and Hazel, by Harry whom she had loved, and by Walter whom she had married.

There was never a dull moment for Camilla in *The Devil's in the Details* (Rondezvous, 2004). She barely remembered Laura Brown, a casual acquaintance from her days at Carleton University. So why had Laura, mysteriously dead, selected Camilla for both her next of kin and heir? Certain that there were other family members, Camilla began investigating. The search led her into personal danger both from the killer and from the police who now suspected her of not only Laura's death but several others. This was a very engrossing book with a historical background that is still relevant.

Add author Jane Maffini to the list of female mystery novelists from Canada. I don't know how she got in here. Her second McPhee book didn't come out until 2001, but I was too engaged in the series by that time to cut her out. Author's privilege, I guess. She has also written mysteries featuring romance writer Fiona Silk and, more recently a series on Charlotte Adams, a professional organizer. Next: *Law and Disorder* (2009).

Sutton McPhee

Author: Brenda English

Sutton McPhee was deeply attached to her younger sister, Cara. Sutton had been twenty-five, living away from the family home in Hilton, Georgia and Cara, nineteen and in college, when their parents had been killed in a traffic accident. The sisters were very different. After her parents died, Cara quit college to return to Hilton where she immersed herself in church work. Sutton used her journalism degree to work her way up from a small Georgia newspaper to a larger one in Tallahassee. It was there that she met, married, and divorced Jack Brooks, a city planner whose rigidity she found intolerable. After Sutton moved on to a better job as the education reporter with the *Washington News*, Cara was lonely. She moved to the D.C. area to be closer to Sutton, but they did not share a home. Sutton had a condo in Alexandria, drove an ancient Volkswagen Beetle, and studied yoga. Cara lived near her job as secretary for the Bread of Life Church in West Springfield, Virginia until her death. Sutton had few close relationships after Cara's death until she met Noah Lansing and his young son, David. Before Noah, she had enjoyed sex without requiring any commitment.

In her professional life, Sutton had developed a network of personal resources in the police department, which proved valuable when she could not obtain information through regular channels. The best of these was police public information officer Bill Russell.

Cara's murder in a parking lot adjacent to an ATM was initially assumed to be a random killing in *Corruption of Faith* (Berkley, 1997). Although the police continued to think so, Sutton unearthed evidence that Cara had been unhappy and disappointed with people whom she had trusted. Sutton took advantage of her position on the newspaper, motivated by a need for revenge against those who had found Cara too dangerous to live. She feared she might be fired, but was promoted to police reporter.

Two cases—the rape and murder of senatorial aide Ann Kane and the murder of the well-respected wife of county supervisor Hub Taylor— merged in *Corruption of Power* (Berkley, 1998). Sutton's "hard headed" pursuit of information led to a conflict with attractive detective Noah Lansing. Lansing had painful memories of personal damage caused by a young reporter, setting up a hostile impression of Sutton. When Sutton and Lansing cooperated, they became so attracted to one another that she had to worry about a conflict of interest.

Sutton was more than a reporter in *Corruption of Justice* (Berkley, 1999). She had investigated the deaths of police officer Dan Magruder and foundation director Robert Coleman. Now she was the witness who could tie the cases together. She jousted with Noah Lansing (whom she loved) and with rival *News* reporter, Sy Berkowitz (whom she detested). Sutton's need for independence made it difficult for her to accept protection from others. Perhaps she feared she might come to relish it; at least, she realized it was a facet of Lansing's love for her.

Portia McTeague

Authors: Faye Sultan and Teresa Kennedy

As the series began, Portia McTeague was in her forties, working in Charlotte, North Carolina as a forensic psychologist, but available for court appointed roles in adjacent states. She usually acted for the defense, but in the second narrative voluntarily sought to be on the investigative team as a profiler. Her origins were in small town Mississippi where she received little attention from her alcoholic father or her social climbing mother. There had been no siblings. A cousin had raped her when she was eleven. He pimped her to his friends, getting her cooperation through drugs. A second rape took place while she was in college. When she became pregnant, her parents gave her $10,000 and sent her off on her own. The child presumably was given up for adoption.

Portia later adopted Alice (at age six) at the request of the girl's mother. Alice became the center of Portia's personal life. She had parlayed the $10,000 from her parents into a Ph.D. in psychology, but she still needed help. Therapist Dr. Sophie Stransky continued to see Portia after retirement. Portia was claustrophobic, had no sense of direction, read while driving on superhighways, and hated cats. Her other support was attorney Declan Dylan, bound to a wheelchair by a car accident. He was a rich widower who cared very deeply for Portia. On the positive side, Portia volunteered time to work at Charlotte's Help Line.

Portia was already feeling burnout when she let Dylan convince her to serve as an expert witness for defendant Jimmy Wier in *Over the Line* (Doubleday, 1998). The question was not whether Jimmy had killed two elderly women while delivering groceries. Dylan wanted a verdict of not guilty by reason of insanity or at least a life sentence, rather than legal execution. Portia felt personal pain as she delved into the childhood abuse suffered by Jimmy. The pressure broke down some of her own defenses, allowing her to face her past.

Portia's decision to phase out her forensic work for criminal defendants and concentrate on a clinical practice in *Help Line* (Doubleday, 1999) did not provide the expected peace of mind. She was, in fact, bored with the more humdrum aspects of her work. Her affair with private investigator Alan Simpson and her personal and therapeutic relationship with Dr. Stransky were disrupted by Portia's venture into profiling. She allied herself with law enforcement on a serial murders case, unaware that she had been led into danger and, even worse, had endangered a friend.

She was a troubled woman, seeking to solve other people's problems, while personally addicted to danger and darkness.

Jayne Meadows

Author: Steve Allen

Steve Allen and Jayne Meadows may have had a more egalitarian marriage than most Hollywood couples during the 1980's, but Jayne was a supporting player in Steve's mystery series. She is a real person, born to American missionaries in China, who developed a comfortable reputation as an actress and television comedienne. Her sister, Audrey, was best remembered for her work as Jackie Gleason's wisecracking wife in *The Honeymooner* skits. A brother, Edward, became a corporate attorney. Jayne married Steve, who was then divorced with children, and they had a son. She was tall, redheaded, and witty, confrontive with those who annoyed her, but sympathetic and maternal with the vulnerable.

In *The Talk Show Murders* (Delacorte, 1982), in which a crude rock star was killed during the Toni Tonielle show and *Murder on the Glitter Box* (Zebra, 1989) wherein Steve substituted as host of a major television show, only to have a guest poisoned on stage, references were made to Jayne, but she never appeared.

Murder in Manhattan (Zebra, 1990) brought the Allens to New York City, where Steve had a small part in a film, the cast of which was embroiled in arguments and affairs. While Jayne shopped till she dropped, Steve survived a ship explosion, a cold swim, and a helicopter rescue.

As *Murder in Vegas* (Zebra, 1992) began, the Allens interrupted a vacation so Steve could assist old friend Bobby Hamilton in presenting a Vegas show. Jayne befriended Bobby's promiscuous daughter, while Steve defended him on a murder charge.

The Murder Game (Zebra, 1993) brought the Allens back for a reprise of a game show on which Jayne had appeared during the Seventies. Several suspicious deaths occurred to members of the original cast making Jayne very uncomfortable, and sending them out to sea with a corpse.

The Allens were invited on the maiden voyage of *Atlantica*, a fabulous ocean liner, in *Murder on the Atlantic* (Zebra, 1995). Steve's only responsibility was to perform one evening, but he involved himself in the family troubles of ship owner Marius Wilmington and the deaths of his heirs. Jayne had a larger role in the detection in this one.

Wake Up to Murder (Kensington, 1996) reunited the Allens with Cat Lawrence, whom they had befriended as a young girl. Needing a replacement for her co-anchor on a morning talk show, Cat recruited Steve. Jayne traced suspects when a series of accidents ended with murder, but her talents were underutilized.

In *Die Laughing* (Kensington, 1998), the Allens discovered a corpse while attending a funeral, but not the one expected to be in the coffin. Allen repeated plotting that he had used in an earlier book to explain whether or not comic Benny Hartman was really dead.

Considering Allen's verbal wit and breadth of knowledge, his mysteries were a disappointment. There could have been more of Jayne's acerbic touches; less of Steve's personal philosophy and name-dropping.

Possible other: *Murder in Hollywood* (1988) could not be located.

Elizabeth "Tenny" Mendoza

Author: Melanie McAllester

Few people called Tenny Mendoza "Elizabeth." The nickname "Tenny" was a backhanded tribute to her tenaciousness. She held a graduate degree, but chose employment as a police officer in Bayview, California. Her family, four siblings and her parents, was supportive of her career choice and her sexual orientation. Tenny described herself as one-half African-American and one-half Mexican. She had been successful as a homicide investigator in Bayview but was chosen by her captain to work on a three-person team investigating the serial rapes of lesbians that took place in two different California jurisdictions.

In *The Lessons* (Spinsters, 1994), Tenny worked with lesbian patrol officer Ashley Johnson and prejudiced sexual assault officer Steve Carson. The police procedural aspects of the narrative were matched by the gradual development of a good working relationship among the three detectives. Each learned a lesson, but not the ones the rapist was trying to teach.

The local police force was ready to write off young Kelsey Sabatos' abduction as a domestic dispute in *The Search* (Naiad, 1996) on the premise that her father had taken the child from his former wife and her lesbian lover. Carter, Kelsey's mother, and Tenny, her former lover disagreed. The ties between Tenny and Carter, and between Tenny and Kelsey were so powerful that she quit her job, traveled to Chicago, then Brazil to bring Kelsey home. In so doing, she uncovered a child-selling ring.

Dr. Anne Menlo

Author: Maxine O'Callaghan

Petite child psychologist Anne Menlo practiced in the Phoenix/Scottsdale area where she shared a suite with two other Ph.D. professionals, Andrew Braemer and Cynthia Lynde. She chose to live in a more isolated area near Cave Creek. Detective Bern Pagett had shared her home for a while, moving toward marriage, but it never happened. He continued to visit, staying over several nights a week, but they were no longer on the wedding track.

Commitment was difficult for Anne, a matter she frequently discussed with Rosemary Biederman, who had been her advisor in the Ph.D. program at Arizona State University. Multiple sclerosis had diminished Rosemary's professional career but she always made time for Anne. Anne had relied upon Rosemary during her college years when she failed to recognize that a child under her care was being sexually abused. After Nicki Craig killed herself at age ten, Anne's sense of guilt never totally left her. She volunteered regularly at a child abuse center.

Unlike Bern, Anne relished the outdoors. Her one and a half-acre property included a natural basin where wildlife came to drink the water. She rode her mountain bike up and down the hills for exercise. Anne's parents lived in San Diego but they did not figure in the narrative; nor did her brother Kevin. Bern had convinced Anne to be on call for the Phoenix police department in cases where children needed immediate care. Given her tendency to become personally involved, this may have been a mistake.

During *Shadow of the Child* (Jove, 1996), Anne not only found it difficult to work on a case managed by Bern, but she found herself drawn to three-year-old Danny Lewis. The boy had been kidnapped and then discovered by the police in a home where a woman had been murdered. Initially mute, Danny responded to Anne. She was determined to protect him, even from Bern's questions. Bern suffered both physical and emotional damage from their experience. They also acquired a badly mistreated half Doberman, half Black Labrador dog named Duke who only gradually allowed himself to be cared for.

In *Only in the Ashes* (Jove, 1997), the only way that Kathleen Graley could cope with the death of her young daughter was to know how and why Rachel had died. With some misgivings, Anne agreed to investigate. The fire that consumed the house in which the child's body had been found was determined to be arson. Bern was assigned the case. In a parallel situation, Anne sought the mother of an "abandoned" girl, Chrissie. Both struck an emotional chord in her: the mother grieving for Rachel, the child, seeking her mother. An engrossing read. Readers who enjoy her might try O'Callaghan's earlier series featuring Delilah West (Volume 2).

Calliope "Cal" Meredith

Author: Marsha Mildon

Mildon did not provide a lot of background on Cal. She was a tall, heavyset Canadian private investigator living in and around Victoria, Vancouver Island. She had very negative feelings about religion.

Cal was still depressed by the death of her lover, Liz as *Fighting for Air* (New Victoria, 1995) began. The death of Ethiopian doctoral student Tekla Takale while diving brought back the horror of the accident that took Liz's life. Soon Cal was too busy to dwell on the past. Her friend, diving instructor Jay Campbell was accused of causing Tekla's death by criminal negligence. Cal had originally been a member of the group learning to snorkel, but had to drop out due to an ear infection. Jay had been drinking heavily when she filled the oxygen tanks for the divers. Cal had become personally interested in Jay and was determined to prove that one of the other divers had deliberately substituted a tank filled with carbon monoxide. There were a half-dozen suspects whose motives surfaced.

Although the model of a Minoan goddess ship figured as a significant symbol in *Stalking the Goddess Ship* (New Victoria, 1999) the narrative focused on the current relationships of faculty wife Lily Barton. The primary suspects in Lily's death were archeologist Marguerite Delaney (studying the Minoan ships) and her lover, Stephanie Rogers, owner of a diving resort. Cal and her lover Jay had difficulties of their own. As friends and guests at the resort, they both had vested interests in finding an alternative suspect, focusing on the men in Lily's life. They came to realize that the pursuit of justice outside of the legal system may lead to excesses, even with the best of intentions. The involvement of child pornography lent a sinister cast to the narrative.

Ophelia O. Meredith

Author: Tanya Jones

At age thirty-two, Ophelia O. Meredith had a number of significant achievements. She was a solicitor in the firm of Snodsworth, Parrish, Ranger located in Rambleton, Yorkshire, England. She had a happy marriage to Malachi, owner of a computer consulting business called Wet Nose Solutions, a reference to their three Labrador Retrievers. She was expecting her sixth child, all of whom had been named after Popes due to the Catholic faith she and Malachi practiced. Even daughter, Joan, could claim a papal designation, although with a cloud over it. The boys had such cumbersome names as: Pius, Innocent, Urban, Hygenus, and Adeodata (called Dodie), sure to make them the subject of ridicule on the school playground. The dogs were also gifted with unusual names: Digabyte (Gigi), Megabyte (Meg), and Reredorter (Rea). To house this motley group, Ophelia and

Malachi had recently purchased a rundown property, Moorwind Farm. He had difficulty in planning and carrying out income producing employment.

Faced with the loss of her job in *Ophelia O. and the Mortgage Bandits* (Headline, 1995), she did not hesitate to hide the corpse of her new employer. She needed money to redeem the family's abducted Black Labrador, more money than she could obtain as an attorney, so she reluctantly pursued a circular Ponzi scheme. Fortunately for her peace of mind, extraneous events, an enterprising secretary and the brighter than expected Meredith children saved her from further felonies (and sins).

As *Ophelia O. and the Antenatal Mysteries* (Headline, 1995) began, Ophelia had limited time for other activities; just surviving was an effort. However, she and her friend Polly thwarted a legal scam designed to bilk the medical profession. At the conclusion, she produced and Malachi delivered a second daughter. Fortunately, Malachi's business had become successful.

The religious orientation was treated with humor, rather than ridicule, for a change.

Laura Michaels

Author: John Miles, pseudonym for John Bickham

Aspiring social worker Laura Michaels was a dark-haired divorcee with a nine-year-old daughter. While completing her graduate degree, she worked part-time at Timberdale Retirement Center.

Her personal life improved in *A Permanent Retirement* (Walker, 1992) when she met Deputy Sheriff Aaron Lassiter during his investigation of an apparent suicide by Timberdale resident Cora Chandler. Laura's suspicion that the death might be a homicide was incited by obsessive mystery fan/resident Maude Thuringer. Maude was one of several minor characters whose peculiarities became routine: Judge Emil Young, whose ponderous speech slowed down the dialogue; Still Bill Mills, whose "malapropisms" suggested he should have a brain scan; and Ken Keen, who suffered from memory loss and an overabundance of male hormones.

The notably inefficient administrator at Timberdale hired a professional acting group to entertain the residents with a mystery weekend in *Murder in Retirement* (Walker, 1994). The death of obnoxious impresario J. Turner Redwine provided Laura and Aaron with too many suspects, but she persevered even with amnesia brought on by a blow on her head.

The regulars reappeared in *A Most Deadly Retirement* (Walker, 1995) during which mysterious lights, attacks on residents, and the apparent suicide of a possible suspect kept them busy. Administrator Judith Epperman avoided responsibility; Maude Thuringer played Jane Marple; and social director Francie Blake vamped investigator Aaron Lassiter while Laura probed the record of a man who had killed before and was willing to kill again.

Limited character development over the series.

Maris Middleton

Author: Kaye Davis

The name was a clue. Her father had wanted a son, to be named for his two favorite baseball players, Roger Maris and Mickey Mantle. She was stuck with Maris Mantle Middleton. Her sister was tabbed Landry Middleton, but settled for Lana and a conventional marriage. Maris' sexual orientation had been accepted by her family, but posed problems when Mary Ann, her lover of ten years, was diagnosed with terminal cancer. Her employer, the Texas Department of Public Safety, did not have a policy that allowed compassionate leave for non-marital partners. Maris chose to leave the agency where she had worked as a forensic chemist. After Mary Ann's death, she cashed in her pension benefits and an insurance policy to fund her own business as an "independent crime scene specialist." Although she had excellent contacts with law enforcement agencies and enough referrals to keep busy, Maris was depressed and drinking heavily as the series began. Her only comfort was Earnhardt, her border collie, named after Dale Earnhardt, the NASCAR racer.

Maris was still mourning Mary Ann when she met FBI agent Lauren O'Conner in *Devil's Leg Crossing* (Naiad, 1997). Lauren had taken a leave of absence from her Chicago office to investigate the disappearance of her niece, Karin. Karin, who lived in a small Texas town, had been spending time with dubious characters. There was also suspicion that she might have been the victim of sexual abuse by a family member. Dissatisfied with the local police investigation, Lauren sought out Maris whom she had met briefly in the past. The two women developed a personal relationship, but the results of their probe had unexpected consequences.

By *Possessions* (Naiad, 1998), Lauren had transferred to the Dallas FBI office. Maris, who had working relationships with both the Texas Rangers and local sheriff's departments, was hired to do the lab work on a grisly murder in Pierce County. A package sent to her home contained a single black dress shoe and a menacing message that tied the recent death to a series of killings. Gradually Maris and Lauren, together with local law enforcement, developed a profile: a male, connected to police work, who hated lesbians. As they came closer to his identity, the killer targeted Maris.

When retired sheriff Nelda "Sherf" Archer was brutally beaten to death in *Until the End* (Naiad, 1998), Maris and her friend Gayle Blessing were determined to find the killer. Current sheriff Odell Wilbarger had good intentions, but both women brought special skills to the investigation. They believed that the motive for Sherf's death originated in a bank robbery during the 1940s, the loot from which had never been found. Besides capturing the killer and recovering the missing treasure, Maris proved the innocence of a young driver accused of vehicular homicide.

As an independent professional, Maris had to be very cautious about her area of authority in *Shattered Illusions* (Naiad, 1999). She had support from her lover Lauren O'Connor and from Chief Deputy Sally Trent who were aware of Maris's expertise. The problem was Police Chief Kenedy who had jurisdiction over the rapes/murders of three young women in a veterinary clinic. Kenedy, seeking a quick solution, focused first on the boyfriend of one of the victims; then, on a mentally disabled man. Maris went beyond the obvious, to a third suspect with whom she had a history. The narrative included explicit sex and violence, more than could be skimmed over. Maris and Lauren became involved in the problems of Lauren's sister Irene, and in the unstable lesbian relationship between pregnant Shannon Stockwell (formerly Maris's lover) and her new partner attorney Robin Fisher.

Author Kaye Davis had the technical background to provide credibility to the narratives. She offered more than some readers would want to know about mutilations, sexual activity, and serial killers.

Brenda Midnight

Author: Barbara Jaye Wilson

A small town girl from Belup Creek, Brenda Midnight moved to New York, settling finally in a Greenwich Village neighborhood. She married and divorced four times. A job with Needleson Brothers (hatmaking materials) led her to launch her own business. She put her artistic skills to work as a milliner, not a seller of headwear, but a designer and creator of original hats. Her shop was called Midnight Millinery, and was distinguished because she was unwilling to make exact copies of any hat. Her customers could be assured that they would not encounter another woman wearing the same hat. She advertised her product by wearing hats on almost every occasion. Her other constant fashion accessory was a five-pound Yorkshire terrier, named Jackhammer.

Whatever Brenda's last name had been in Belup Creek, she chose not to use it in New York. Noting a sign on the premises, which included the word "Midnight," she appropriated it for her last name. She struggled to make a living in her shop on West Fourth Street. Brenda was active in a neighborhood association that met at Pete's Café. She was a vegetarian who controlled her "risks" by neither flying nor eating meat. Initially she was so straitened by finances that she slept under her cutting table. This persisted until she was bequeathed a studio apartment. Brenda was a tiny woman but in good physical condition and fearless. She had loyal friends who created an ensemble approach to the series.

Carla Haley inveigled Brenda into doing the headpieces for the high society wedding of attorney Ashley Millard in *Death Brims Over* (Avon, 1997). Carla, who had designed the gowns, was found dead shortly after Brenda was robbed of the headgear by a mysterious "Lady in Pink." Brenda rallied her friends: television actor Johnny Verlane, computer expert Chuck Riley, and self-retired artist Elizabeth Franklin Perry. Plan A was to infiltrate the law office where Ashley worked. They had to improvise. There was no Plan B.

The first step to enjoying *Accessory to Murder* (Avon, 1998) was accepting that there was a good reason for moving Buddy Needleson's corpse from his business premises to the exterior of the morgue. Once done, the reader can enjoy the machinations of Brenda and her friends after they realized that (1) Buddy had been murdered, (2) they had interfered with a potential police investigation, and (3) that Johnny Verlane's agent Lemmy Crenshaw was the first choice of the police for killer.

Death Flips Its Lid (Avon, 1998) was a convoluted narrative during which ex-husband Nado P. Sharpe visited Brenda because he had quarreled with his new wife. Against her better judgment, Brenda allowed him to escort her to Johnny Verlane's going away party. Brenda left early. Nado stayed behind only to become witness, or maybe a suspect, in the murder of apartment building owner Royce Montmyer. Typically, he panicked, fled from the scene, and stole a police car. Coincidentally Montmyer was a romantic rival of another of Brenda's good friends. More coincidentally there was an influx of former friends from Belup Creek. Brenda had to get involved. As usual she rallied her more dependable friends to find the real killer.

Chuck Riley, the reclusive computer genius who facilitated many of Brenda's investigations saved her life in *Capped Off* (Avon, 1999). It all began when she waited in an outer room at Castleberry's Department Store to show her line of hats to well-respected buyer Doreen Sands. Why would she get involved when Sands' corpse was discovered in her office? Probably because someone planted a gun in Brenda's purse where her detective friends, Turner and McKinley, found it.

The pain of having mistaken a real kidnapping of her friend Dweena (formerly Edward) for a ruse to entice her to a surprise birthday party in *A Hatful of Homicide* (Avon, 2000) was mingled with guilt. Once Dweena was freed, she wheedled Brenda into trying to retrieve the $50,000 ransom she had paid. Not that it was Dweena's money or Brenda's. That was part of the problem. Another problem was Dweena's sidelines; i.e. what she referred to as her "diplomatic vehicle relocation project" (she boosted cars of diplomats) and SOB (Save Our Brothels), an effort to halt the demolition of older buildings in the neighborhood. When murder was done, everybody lied, even the corpse.

Credibility took a vacation in *Murder and the Mad Hatter* (Avon, 2001) when Brenda agreed to marry sleazy talent agent Lemmy Crenshaw. Never mind that she loved television actor Johnny Verlane or that Lemmy tricked her into the arrangement. Somewhere under the froth of a stolen bra collection, a fictional plan to resuscitate New York City, time travel romances, and the loss of a lucky fountain pen, there was a murder.

Interesting side characters, but plotting weakened by the multiplicity of issues.

Francesca Miles

Author: Melissa Chan, pseudonym for Jocelynne Scott

Francesca Miles was both a private investigator and film critic in Melbourne, Australia. She lived with Luana Joyschild Adams, her lesbian lover. An earlier marriage to Tony Sanford had failed. Francesca was a strong feminist; still, she worked well with Inspector Joe Barnaby in New South Wales Police Department. They had met when Francesca marched against Australia's involvement in the Vietnam War and he policed the crowd. She was allowed to take part in interviews he conducted when they shared an interest in the case. She preferred to serve clients who were involved with feminist causes, even though they didn't always pay well. Her second job and her great interest was the movies. Although she had attended law school and earned a master's degree that included courses in criminology, Francesca was an outsider who relied on her instincts.

Based upon their friendship, Inspector Joe Barnaby made Francesca an integral part of his investigation in *Too Rich* (Spinifex Press, Australia, 1991). She was allowed to accompany him to the penthouse where unfaithful businessman Daniel Gleixner had lived with his mistress. He had died under suspicious circumstances, which pitted his wife Rose against the mistress, Elizabeth. Francesca was included in the interviews with family members, two of whom subsequently died. She did not share her version of the case with Joe Barnaby, only with the killer.

The murders of affluent Sydney widows had never been solved, but, in *One Too Many* (Artemis, 1993), the focus shifted to Melbourne where wealthy widows again became targets of a killer. The modus operandi was similar in nature. Was this the same killer or a copycat? Inspector Barnaby, who had arrived to represent the New South Wales Police, called on Francesca for her insights. Her efforts were augmented by friends and family members of the victims. Officially Barnaby was advised by the local FBI profiler who focused on a type: young, repressed male. Even a confession from a man who fit that profile to a degree did not satisfy either Francesca or Barnaby. There was considerable discourse as to women's rights and images in the narrative.

One after another, Melbourne community leaders were being murdered during *Guilt* (Artemis Press, Melbourne, 1993). Luana, Francesca's lover, was the estranged daughter of Gordon Burton Adams, the first victim. When Barnaby came from South Wales to see if a murder in his jurisdiction was connected, he included Francesca in his investigation. Patterns emerged but Francesca and Joe interpreted them differently. For different reasons both opted for a simple solution.

Lydia Miller

Author: Eleanor Hyde

Although her roots and her family were still in Ohio, Lydia Miller had become a New Yorker. She turned her clothes sense and experience as a model into a well paying job on *Gazelle*, a fashion magazine. A tall blonde, she reflected elegance and control.

However, as *In Murder We Trust* (Fawcett, 1995) began, her equanimity had been overwhelmed by Manhattan's heat. She had declined an invitation from Adam Auerbach, a wealthy twice-divorced man, to visit his place in the Hamptons; then, changed her mind when the electricity failed. She was surprised to find Adam dead when she arrived; even more surprised to learn that she had inherited a substantial bequest. It was no surprise that she became the prime suspect for cantankerous Detective Barolini. Fortunately Kramer, his assistant, not only trusted Lydia but also shared her love for John Steinbeck. Lydia was active in the investigation, but put herself into serious danger by concealing information.

Disillusioned by the backbiting in the design field, Lydia tendered her resignation at *Gazelle*; then, agreed to take a sabbatical as *Animal Instincts* (Fawcett, 1996) began. Her experience, coupled with volunteer work at an animal shelter, alerted her to extravagant claims for a "youth" product and a thriving trade in stolen pets. A confusing narrative.

Robin Miller

Author: Jaye Maiman

Robin Miller, first a romance writer, then a private investigator in New York, was still searching for her place in life. She was distrustful of firearms because they had caused the death of her sister. Yet, she had killed in self-defense. Her father never spoke to Robin after her sister's death, and died before they could be reconciled. Her sexual relationships had been difficult. Two of her lovers were killed. She desired women, but was uncomfortable with that realization. Robin studied the disciplines of Tae Kwon Do, but existed primarily on junk food.

In *I Left My Heart* (Naiad, 1991), the death of Robin's lover, investigative reporter Mary Oswald, might have been caused by anaphylactic shock, suicide, or murder. Knowing Mary's care with medications, Robin believed it had been murder. Mary had been Robin's lover when they both worked in New York. They had parted when Robin was experiencing a difficult time with her father's death after their long estrangement. Before she finished her investigation, Robin realized that she had never known the real Mary. Robin's career as romance writer Laurel Carter went into eclipse when she was "outed" as a lesbian during the investigation of Mary's death.

By *Crazy for Loving* (Naiad, 1992), Robin worked in Tony Serra's detective agency. When David Ross, the errant husband whom Robin was trailing, was murdered, Tony pulled Robin off the case. Pooley, a twelve-year-old African-American boy, was arrested for the killing, a solution unacceptable to Robin.

In *Under My Skin* (Naiad, 1993), a vacation provided little relief. While visiting friends in the Poconos, Robin's flashbacks to an unhappy childhood were interrupted when potential client Noreen Finnegan was murdered. Noreen, a recovered alcoholic, had been searching for her siblings.

Robin's relationship with television chef K. T. Belleflower faltered during *Someone to Watch* (Naiad, 1995). A primary murder suspect, Lurlene, had been K. T.'s childhood friend. There were others with a motive to kill, necessitating serious risk taking behavior by Robin. Robin was also searching for Julie Reed aka Judith Ryan who had stolen from her 52-year old client Abigail Whitman.

Baby, It's Cold (Naiad, 1996) placed Robin in a difficult situation. She had been seeing Phyllis Roth for several weeks when Michael, the son of Phyllis and Matthew, her gay former husband, was kidnapped. Robin agreed to investigate without contacting the police. The narrative explored the hunger of some gays and lesbians to have children. K. T. Belleflower returned.

San Francisco police detective Tom Ryan, who had worked with Robin at the time of Mary Oswell's death, had been a good friend, even a surrogate father. In *Old Black Magic* (Naiad, 1997), when she and K. T. Belleflower visited New Orleans, Robin became aware of a murder closely resembling the death of Tom's estranged wife years before. At first, Tom discouraged Robin's involvement, but agreed to have his former police partner Theobald Sweeney, now a private investigator, contact her. Sweeney was a crude and bitter man, but he wanted justice for Tom Ryan. K. T.'s pregnancy was terminated by a miscarriage. She and Robin planned another artificial impregnation.

What should have been a joyous time for Robin and K. T. deteriorated during *Every Time We Say Goodbye* (Naiad, 1999). They were delighted that K.T.'s most recent pregnancy was going well. Her desire to move to the suburbs had only half-hearted support from Robin. They agreed that Sydney (K. T.'s fourteen-year-old niece) needed help but they had to combat Sydney's parents to provide it. Robin's mom, from whom she had been estranged, was seriously ill. Cathy Chapman, Robin's rapacious former lover, had come to New York to convince Robin to work with her to bring down Charles Ballard, one of Serra Investigative Agency's major clients and therefore one of Robin's.

Sex was explicit to a degree that not all readers will find acceptable. The titles of the books are derived from songs of earlier decades.

Kate Millholland

Author: Gini Hartzmark

Katharine Anne Prescott Millholland had a pedigree longer than her name. Her wealthy Chicago area family had sent her to North Shore Country Day,

Bryn Mawr, and the University of Chicago Law School. Yet life had not been kind. Her brief marriage to Russell Dubrinski, disapproved of by her family, had ended when he died of brain cancer. Kate was not close to her parents—a father addicted to alcohol, and a mother who valued her social position and reputation above her children. Her brother, Teddy had committed suicide. Kate's decision to practice law was acceptable because she practiced Mergers and Acquisitions in Callahan Ross, a corporate firm. With little personal life, Kate became so obsessed by her work that her clothes were selected by her secretary or through a personal shopper. She gobbled M & Ms in times of stress.

In *Principal Defense* (Ivy, 1992), corporate raider Edgar Eichel threatened Azor, a major client of Callahan Ross. The matter became personal when Gretchen, the teenage ward of Azor CEO Stephen Azorini, was found dead. Gretchen was the daughter of Stephen's brother, Joey. The Azorini family was connected with the Mafia, so Kate had to tread carefully as she uncovered evidence of sexual and financial misconduct. Even when injured and amnesiac, Kate fought to save Azor and its attractive CEO with the help of investigator Elliott Abelman.

Kate had become a partner in Callahan, Ross by *Final Option* (Ivy, 1994). That did not protect her from suspicion of murder when she found Bart Hexter, a major client, dead in his wrecked vehicle. Kate searched for missing files to defend Hexter Commodities from federal charges, going to great lengths to save herself from a too humble killer.

In *Bitter Business* (Fawcett Columbine, 1995), Kate dealt with the business affairs of the contentious Cavanaugh family, in which she found parallels to her own. Not only was there a possibility that Jack Cavanaugh's irresponsible younger daughter Lydia would sell her shares in the closely held family corporation, but someone killed both his secretary Cecelia Dobson, and Dagny, his reasonable older daughter. Lover Steve Azorini wanted a live-in relationship, but found competition from Elliott Abelman.

Fatal Reaction (Ivy, 1998) was set in a background of international finance and biochemical experimentation, but Millholland mastered these complex fields. When Danny Wohl, a key player in the negotiations, was murdered, Steve Azorini called on Kate to find the killer and thereby save his corporation from financial ruin. She did so with help from Elliott Abelman and her mother, Astrid. Kate's relationship with Azorini was seriously weakened.

In a somewhat lighter vein during *Rough Trade* (Ivy, 1999), Kate was diverted from representation of sleazy twin restaurateurs who wanted an IPO (initial public offering) by the plight of her best friend, Chrissy Rendell. Jeff, Chrissy's husband, was suspected of murdering his father Beau Rendell, the owner of a Milwaukee, Wisconsin football franchise. Her secretary Cheryl, Elliott, and a beefy football player helped Kate survive. Meantime, she moved beyond her affair with Azorini.

The Prescott-Milholland families had been major supporters of the Prescott Memorial Hospital where Kate's roommate Claudia held a fellowship during *Dead Certain* (Fawcett, 2000). When the Board of Trustees voted to sell the hospital to a profit-making corporation (HCC), Kate and her mother Astrid were horrified. Prescott Memorial had a significant patient population from the underprivileged, who would no longer be served by the change. A series of post-operative deaths at the hospital complicated the struggle to keep the facility independent and endangered first Claudia's job, then her life.

An interesting combination of love and business.

Tori Miracle

Author: Valerie S. Malmont

Her early years as the daughter of an American diplomat had provided Tori Miracle with extensive travel and an elegant lifestyle. Her world crashed when her younger brother Billy, whom she was supposed to be watching, wandered off and died from snakebite while they were in Thailand. After Billy's death, Tori's mother became an alcoholic. Her institutional costs were not covered by health insurance. Tori's father consoled himself with a younger woman and his work. Tori, a college graduate, had some success with a book. However when she lost her job as a crime reporter, she barely had enough money to subsidize her mother's care, pay her rent, and feed two cats (Fred and Noel). A tiny woman in her mid-thirties, her personal life was equally dismal; e.g. a fiancé who dumped her because she had spent too much time working on her book.

As *Death Pays the Rose Rent* (Simon & Schuster, 1994) began, Tori visited Alice-Ann, her college roommate, now married to Richard, a wealthy publisher living in Lickin Creek, Pennsylvania. Richard, as a descendant of the town founder, annually received a single rose as a tribute from the community in a well-attended festival. Tori's arrival with the cats did not help the deteriorating relationship between Alice Ann and the unfaithful Richard. He had recently embarked on a money-raising scheme, the details of which he had not shared. Richard was found dead and Alice-Ann was among the suspects. Lickin Creek had a history, which included real estate fraud, an invention by Thomas Edison, Civil War history, and underground tunnels. Lots of action but the tunnels were better connected than the plot. Tori had not been totally accepted in Lickin Creek: too well traveled, an accomplished linguist, and a published author.

Lickin Creek might be a small town, but in *Death, Lies, and Apple Pies* (Simon & Schuster, 1997) it was heavily populated with characters. Tori returned to the area to continue her relationship with chief of police Garnet Gochenauer. Garnet's widowed sister Greta, who had moved in with him, was a leader in the opposition to a local nuclear waste depot. Underemployed and unemployed men and women wanted jobs. Landowners who would benefit supported the project. Motives for two unexplained deaths multiplied. Tori's life was threatened on several occasions before the killer disclosed himself.

Tori adjusted to the changes in her life during *Death, Guns, and Sticky Buns* (Dell, 2000). Police Chief Garnet Gochenauer must have misunderstood her intentions because he took leave to advise the Costa Rican police. Her full-time position at the *Chronicle* drew her into a reenactment of a Civil War execution sponsored by Lickin Creek College for Women. The firing squad's ammunition had been tampered with causing the death of former congressman Mack Macmillan. Tori's reputation as a harbinger of disaster motivated her to discover who had substituted real bullets for the blank wads. Her courage and sense of humor made it possible to survive her own depression at the need for a breast biopsy.

Health did not seem to be a problem for Tori in *Death, Snow, and Mistletoe* (Dell, 2000). She had mixed feelings about the news that her father was to marry the much younger woman who was bearing his child. She was affected, as were all the citizens of Lickin Creek, by the disappearance of five-year-old Kevin Poffenberger while roaming the woods with older cousins. The discovery of a skeleton revived memories of another five-year-old boy who had disappeared thirty-seven years before. The news left one woman heavy with guilt; another, burning for revenge.

Death, Bones, and Stately Homes (Perseverance Press, 2003). Was a fun read, even considering the salacious aspects of the murders. Tori's reputation in Lickin Creek was still focused on her involvement in murder and arson. Nevertheless, when she and her pal Alice-Ann discovered the skeleton of former high school music teacher Rodney Mellott in the springhouse of Morgan Manor, Tori agreed to keep it a secret until Alice-Ann's fund raising tour of homes ended. Rodney and his fiancée, Emily Rakestraw, had been believed to have eloped four decades before. Tori needed to share her concerns with Garnet Gochenauer, still in Costa Rica, but he had never responded to her letters. When Mellott's skeleton disappeared, it only added to the problems.

Intricate plots and interesting, but eccentric, characterizations.

Meredith "Merry" Mitchell

Author: Ann Granger, pseudonym for Ann Hulme

Merry Mitchell was a convent educated British career diplomat who, by age thirty-five, had been stationed in a variety of foreign countries. Tall, slim, and hazel-eyed with brown hair, she had served with dedication and competence, earning the respect of her colleagues.

In *Say It with Poison* (St. Martin, 1991), Merry returned to England to attend the wedding of Sara, the child of cousin Eve and Mike, the man whom Merry had loved. Mike's death had never been satisfactorily explained until Merry, with the assistance of Chief Inspector Alan Markby, solved two murders.

Merry accepted a post in London, commuting from Bamford, Markby's location, in *A Season for Murder* (St. Martin, 1992). She approached the affair with Alan cautiously, unwilling to limit her independence. He sought her help in the investigation of a tragic hunting death that might have been murder.

During *Cold in the Earth* (St. Martin, 1993), Merry rented a London apartment but house-sat in Bamford during her vacation. Markby was unhappy with the continued development of his hometown by real estate brokers. The tensions in the community increased when a bulldozer uncovered a corpse. As an outsider, Merry offered Markby a different perspective of the suspects, many of whom he had known from childhood.

In *Murder Among Us* (St. Martin, 1993), Alan and Merry were invited to the grand opening of a posh restaurant and inn. Their evening out was interrupted by a chase after a nude protestor who led pursuers to a corpse.

Merry, who would not live with Alan, but would be desolate if he were out of her life, had a change of heart in *Where Old Bones Lie* (St. Martin, 1994). She purchased a small cottage in Bamford. She spent her vacation helping her archeologist friend Ursula Gratton, who suspected her former lover of killing his wife. Old and new disappearances vied with hippies and skeletons for attention.

Fixing up her new home preoccupied Merry for the first half of *A Fine Place for Death* (St. Martin, 1995), while Alan and his temporary assistant, Sgt. Helen Turner, investigated the death of a young hooker. However, Merry became heavily involved when a second teenager, who had sought her help, was brutally murdered. Operating independently and against Alan's advice, she worked with an elderly retiree to find more than one killer.

Even during their spare time, Merry and Alan could not escape murder. In *Flowers for His Funeral* (St. Martin, 1995), wealthy Alex Constantine died in their presence from a "thorn" prick at a flower show. Merry was shocked to learn that the grieving widow was Alan's former wife, Rachel, and irritated to find that he was expected to provide support and counsel. The Secret Service became very interested in the case because Constantine had a prior identity in Lebanon. That did not keep Alan and Merry out of the investigation. Markby accepted a promotion that would require a transfer. Excellent read.

Actually, as *Candle for a Corpse* (St. Martin, 1996) began, Markby worked at the regional office, but continued to make his home in Bamford. When gravediggers found bones that should not be there, and proof of an undetected murder surfaced, Alan took responsibility for the case. Merry was in the neighborhood when the bones were discovered, knew many of the suspects, and made it her business to know them better, even peering through their windows.

A Touch of Mortality (Headline, 1996) concentrated on Alan's role because police procedure was the key to the killer in what seemed to be a neighborhood feud. Merry's friendship with a victim aided in the solution.

Merry and Alan were determined to avoid controversy on their vacation in Parsloe St. John, but, as *A Word After Dying* (St. Martin, 1998) evolved, they found it impossible. Initially Alan agreed to take part in the investigation of the death of elderly recluse Olivia Smeaton. Merry was appalled that Alan coveted the Smeaton house as a retirement home. The community, rife with rumors of Satanism, made it clear that Alan and Merry were not welcome.

Alan made the deductions to solve the murders in *Call the Dead Again* (St. Martin, 1999), but the characterizations that will remain in the reader's mind were the females: (1) Merry, unable to commit to Alan; (2) Kate, the hidden daughter of a prominent attorney who became a catalyst for disaster; and (3) Carla, the attorney's wife, overwhelmed by a sense of betrayal.

Hugh Franklin remarried too soon after the death of his wife in *Beneath These Stones* (Headline, 1999). Too soon, because neither he nor Sonia realized how miserable she would be in an isolated farmhouse. After a bitter quarrel, Sonia left one evening. The next day, her corpse was found. Hugh's daughter Tammy had vital information that could solve the case and absolve her father of suspicion.

Death in its many forms, including murder and wartime service had diminished the Oakley family. By 1999, as *Shades of Murder* (Headline, 2000) began, two elderly sisters were believed to be the end of the line. As they considered selling the rundown manse, another possible heir threatened their precarious position. Friends, including Merry and Alan, rallied to protect the spinsters from Jan Oakley, who claimed to be a cousin. His death by arsenic poisoning threatened the sale of the property and the status of the sisters.

Alan and Merry went to Lower Stovey to consider purchasing the old vicarage in *A Restless Evil* (Headline, 2002). The vicarage, and the village, had deteriorated since the time, 22 years before, when the newly promoted D.I. Alan Markby investigated a series of three rapes by the "Potato Man". His failure to solve the case had always rankled him. Within weeks the bones of an unidentified person were discovered in the woods, and Ruth Aston, a retired teacher who cleaned the church, was murdered. While Alan used his police skills, Merry mixed with the locals, getting impressions of individuals and the tensions among them.

Merry drew Alan into the affair of the poisoned pen letters sent to Alison Jenner in *That Way Murder Lies* (Headline, 2004). When Fiona, Alison's stepdaughter, was murdered, the investigation carried out by D. I. Jessica Campbell under Alan's supervision followed two tracks: Fiona's death; and the 25-year-old case in which Alison had been tried and found not guilty of the death of her wealth great-aunt. Merry and her friend Toby Smythe visited Cornwall where the earlier murder had taken place, drawing the killer's attention.

The series contained above average writing. Merry was an independent heroine who had a significant role. Granger has a second series featuring footloose actress Fran Varaday.; and a more recent series with Lizzie Martin.

Michelle "Mitch" Mitchell

Author: Doug Allyn

Michelle "Mitch" Mitchell placed a high value on her independence. As a motherless teenager, she had refused to consider an abortion when she became pregnant and ran away from her father's home. She bore a son, Corey, and supported him without the help of the man she believed to be his father. While working as a diver for Exxon Oil on the Texas Gulf, Mitch (as she preferred to be called) earned a degree in marine biology. Her commitment to a career ended her engagement to a man who wanted her to lead a more conventional life. When her father died, after years of estrangement with only minor exchanges through the mail, Mitch was surprised to inherit his bar/grill/diving facility on Lake Huron. Corey, then in the middle grades, did not return to Michigan with his mother, but continued his education in Texas.

When she returned to Huron Harbor, Mitch's intention was to sell out as soon as it could be arranged. However, as *Icewater Mansions* (St. Martin, 1995) opened, entranced by the lake and out of sheer stubbornness, she turned down an offer to purchase and began to renovate the "Crow's Nest." New complexities entered her life when doubts arose as to whether her father had died a natural death. Then the man whom she believed to be Corey's grandfather sought custody of the boy.

By *Black Water* (St. Martin, 1996), Mitch had placed Corey in boarding school and made a commitment to Huron Harbor. Her skill as a deep-water diver drew her into the disappearance of Jimmy Calderon who came to town searching for a father he had never known. His brother, Ray, believed that Jimmy had been murdered and would not leave Huron Harbor until he found the killer. Always an outsider herself, Mitch and her friend Sheriff Charlie Bauer became Ray's allies.

Mitch wanted her son Corey to live with her, but, during *A Dance in Deep Water* (St. Martin, 1997), the parent-child relationship was tense. As Mitch learned about her own mother's family, she grappled with her hatred for the father who wronged his wife and child. She and Corey grew closer. Along the way, she dove deep into a flooded mine to determine whether or not her father was a killer.

Allyn's narratives were concerned with family relationships, particularly the emotional ties between children and parents. He has another series featuring Dr. David Westbrook.

Tess Monaghan

Author: Laura Lippman

Theresa Esther Weinstein Monaghan, better known as Tess, worked as a reporter on the *Baltimore Star* until it collapsed. There being an overabundance of unemployed reporters in Baltimore, she chose another profession, private investigator. Tess had lots of connections in the city. The Monaghans and Weinsteins were well represented in government circles. Her dad was a city liquor inspector; her mother, a secretary for the National Security Agency. Uncle Donald was in state government. Aunt Kitty Monaghan, who owned a Fells Point bookstore, offered the upstairs for an office/apartment. Tess, who had attended nearby Washington College where she was on the crew, still rowed for exercise. She was a tall brown-haired woman, fiercely independent, trying to survive without a steady source of income. Her lover at the time the series began was Jonathan Ross, a reporter on the *Baltimore Beacon & Light*.

In *Baltimore Blues* (Avon, 1997), a simple assignment trailing attorney Ava Hill for her fiancé Daryl Paxton, produced evidence that Ava had been spending time with senior attorney Michael Abramowitz at O'Neal, O'Connor, and O'Neill. Abramowitz's murder after a fracas with Paxton focused suspicion on him. Tess and her rowing coach, paraplegic attorney Tyner Grey, had more than one mystery to solve. Who had killed Abramowitz? Who had paid him to cover up another murder? Tess' sense that she had achieved some form of justice was tempered by the fact that not everyone came out unscathed.

Tyner offered Tess a full-time position as investigator for his law office with the understanding that she would earn enough hours to qualify for a license. In *Charm City* (Avon, 1997), she investigated staff at the local newspaper to determine who had authorized the reinsertion of an investigative report. Management had ordered the material withdrawn until there was further verification of fraud involving the purchase of a National League basketball franchise. The intended purchaser, "Wink" Wynkowski, committed suicide after the story was printed. Bar-owner "Uncle" Spike Orrick, a shirttail relative of Tess who was brutally beaten in what might have been a robbery, had left his greyhound Esskay in Tess' keeping. The blending of these two incidents resulted in an engaging narrative in which management rivalries, spousal abuse, cruelty to animals, and fraudulent reporting played parts. The romance that had developed between Tess and "Crow," a guitar player who made it big in the music business, faltered, but Tess kept the dog.

By *Butchers Hill* (Avon, 1998), Tyner had forced Tess to go it alone, so she was operating out of Aunt Kitty's upstairs. Two new cases came in the same day. Luther Beale had been sent to prison after killing one of a group of foster children who had terrorized his neighborhood. Released after serving his sentence, he wanted to make amends to the surviving children. Unfortunately, as Tess located the children they were murdered. In the second case, "Mary Brown" hired Tess to find her half-sister, missing for thirteen years. Gradually Tess discovered the identity of her client and her reason for employing Tess.

Texas was foreign to Tess, but in *In Big Trouble* (Avon, 1999, rereleased in 2009), that was where her concern for Crow took her. Inklings that he was in big trouble forged an alliance between Tess and Crow's parents. They hired her to find their missing son. The search led Tess to two recently deceased ex-convicts, and then connected with a twenty-one-year-old tragedy that still motivated murder. The plotting and characterizations were excellent.

In *The Sugar House* (Morrow, 2000), tracing a "Jane Doe" victim had begun as a favor for Tess' dad, Patrick. It did not end there. Ruthie Dembrow wanted one thing: the name of the young victim for whose death her brother had been sent to prison. He had been knifed shortly after his arrival. The trail of "Jane Doe" was still there to be followed from an unhappy home to an institution for young rich and vulnerable bulimics. The facility was still functioning, although its financial procedures were suspect. The search ended with favors: one, by Patrick, could cost his job; another, that Tess could accept graciously. She had continued to live above Aunt Kitty's bookstore but Kitty and Tyner Gray were very much in love, and three was a crowd.

A client for whom she refused to provide services during *In a Strange City* (Morrow, 2001) enticed Tess and Crow to be present on January 19th when an anonymous figure annually visited the grave of Edgar Allan Poe. Two visitors appeared that night; one was murdered, but not necessarily by the other. Clues and messages deposited at Tess' home drew her deeper into Poe's life and its relevance to Baltimore history. The destructive nature of those for whom "collecting" became an obsession was a significant factor in the narrative. At this time, Tess lived in her new home. Crow was a frequent visitor. She was still working for Al Keyes agency in order to earn the necessary training for an independent investigator's license.

Although Tess maintained good relationships with her mother's family, she was unfamiliar with the traditions of Orthodox Judaism, as *By a Spider's Thread* (Morrow, 2004) began. Her new clients, wealthy furrier Mark Rubin's search for his missing wife Natalie and their three children engaged her sympathy although he was difficult to deal with personally. He withheld information about his and Natalie's private lives too long. Fortunately, Tess' Uncle Donald Weinstein had connections within the Maryland prison and criminal justice systems that provided leads. The search, which went beyond state borders, elicited help from members of Tess' female private investigator's group, Snoop Sisters. A compelling narrative.

Both Crow and Tess bought into good deeds in *No Good Deeds* (Morrow, 2006) with inevitable results. Crow had taken in Lloyd Jupiter, an African-American teenage delinquent who worked a flat tire scam. He provided a meal, a place to stay and protected Lloyd even when he realized the potential danger. Tess, more pragmatic, had been leery of Lloyd and noticed his reaction to the name, of recently murdered Assistant District Attorney Gregory Youssef. Still she promised not to turn Lloyd in. Before they were through, Tess was barely surviving heavy pressures by a DEA agent, an FBI agent, and an Assistant U. S. attorney to disclose who had provided her with information.

Tess gave more and more signs of arrogance and repressed violence in *The Last Place* (Morrow, 2002). Her connections with Aunt Kitty, her occasional employer Tyner Gray, even with Crow had weakened. Her pal Whitney Talbot had conned Tess into trapping sexual predator Mickey Pechter. The physical abuse they took on Pechter sent Tess to court on a charge of felony assault. Even though she was ordered to meet with a therapist for anger control, Whitney convinced Tess to follow up on what were labeled "domestic violence cases" by a consortium of voluntary organizations. There was much more than domestic violence involved. Tess had a new ally, toll road cop Carl Devett, but an old enemy.

Lippman combined two worlds with which she was familiar in *Another Thing to Fall* (Morrow, 2008). Flip Tumulty, young television writer/producer trying to escape his father's shadow, brought his cast and crew to Baltimore to film *Mann of Steel.* He paired twenty-year-old Selene Waites, a much sought after starlet, with Johnny Tampa, who was making a comeback. A series of incidents that cost time and money prompted Flip to hire Tess to be Selene's "bodyguard", just as the vandalism turned murderous. The thoughts of the killer were interposed into the narrative. Lippman, the wife of a television producer, skillfully contrasted the manipulations of Hollywood against the Baltimore background.

That same year Morrow released a collection of short stories and a novella by Lippman, *Hardly Knew Her.* Tess appeared in two of the stories and an interesting interview. She had a real surprise for her readers. According to Mystery Scene Magazine (Number 107, 2008) she and Crow were going to have a baby! The story, *The Girl in the Green Raincoat* was to be published in serial form in the New York Times Magazine. I have yet to locate it. What did emerge was two standalones by Lippman that were well received.

The Baltimore background was authentic and colorful. A worthwhile series to be read from beginning to end.

Hester Latterly Monk

Author: Anne Perry

See: Hester Latterly, page 462.

Adele Monsarrat

Author: Echo Heron

Adele Monsarrat was dedicated to nursing. She had become a fixture at Ward 8 of Ellis Hospital in Marin County near San Francisco. The ward in general, and Adele in particular, had a reputation for wackiness that was well earned. She was a tall, slim, dark-haired woman in her thirties who insinuated herself into murder investigations. Like the hospital administration, the police tolerated her because she had valuable skills.

From childhood Adele had been fascinated by police work. She had discovered the bodies of a neighbor woman and her child as a youngster and was instrumental in the arrest of the killer husband. During high school she worked for a security business, learning to pick locks and disarm alarm systems. She graduated from high school at sixteen. During her nurses' training at the University of California, Adele also studied drama. Over the years, she collected a closet full of costumes, which she used undercover with wigs and make-up.

She was a vegetarian, but addicted to peanut butter, potato chips, and popcorn. She avoided alcohol and had no interest in drugs. Frequent mention was made of her "crazy woman" laugh. Given the descriptions of her days at Ward 8, maybe she needed to be a little crazy to survive. Although she had been raised Catholic by her widowed librarian mother, Adele considered herself one-half agnostic and one-half atheist. If she worshipped anything, it was nature. She saw a lot of it because she religiously ran eight to twelve miles each morning.

Adele's early marriage to Vietnam veteran Gavin Wozniac ended in divorce. He had taken off for a period of years justifying her petition to terminate the marriage. On his return, they eventually established a civilized friendship. He married again, this time to someone more tolerant of his idiosyncrasies. She did not. During their marriage, Gavin had taught Adele some martial arts skills and how to handle a gun. For support, she relied on her close friendship with fellow nurse Cynthia O'Neil, on the non-human companionship of Nelson, her vegetarian Black Labrador, and eventually on her feelings for Detective Tim Rittman. When none of these were available, she relied on help from imaginary friends, including some well-known fictional detectives. Adele drove a 1978 Pontiac station wagon named the Beast, tolerating its frequent bad moods. She was less tolerant of HMOs and the pressure they placed on hospital administration to replace nursing staff with cheaper, untrained workers.

Readers should be warned not to read *Pulse* (Ivy, 1998) just before surgery. The patients on Adele's ward were very sick. Many of her fellow workers were in bad shape—mentally ill and/or promiscuous to an alarming degree. They were dying off more quickly than the patients, and these were not natural deaths. The narrative, which contained many vignettes concerning hospital care, could have used editing.

Ward 8 had barely recovered from a serial killer scare when, in *Panic* (Ivy, 1998), it was overwhelmed by mysterious deaths seemingly from a viral disease. The initial patient was Iris Hersh, the daughter of a doctor, but she may have infected her nurse, Cynthia O'Neil. Adele put the rest of her life on hold as she fought to save Cynthia while investigating the Hersh family during her rare off work hours.

Adele bonded with the amnesiac patient she dubbed "Mathilde" in *Paradox* (Ivy, 1998). The young woman had been discovered badly burned at the scene of a car accident. Inside the vehicle was the corpse of a young child. Detective Tim Rittman, who had achieved status close to that of a co-protagonist although he had not become Adele's lover, believed that Mathilde was complicit in a series of murders. Adele disagreed, risking both their lives to prove him wrong.

During *Fatal Diagnosis* (Ballantine, 2000), Adele's work environment was unpleasant because the nursing staff was overburdened and administration sought budget cuts by replacing senior staff with new hires. Adele's devotion to her patients might have assisted in their recovery but it made her a prime target for dismissal. She and fellow nurses Cynthia O'Neill and Wanda Percy were alerted to the possibility that patients who had prior surgeries in Europe were potential murder victims. Adele needed the combat expertise that she had learned from her Green Beret ex-husband and help from Cynthia and Tim Rittmann to survive the enemies she acquired while investigating a scheme, which threatened not only individuals but also communities.

The narratives included intricate plotting and focused on serial killers, and the frenzied atmosphere of Ward 8. They provided flashes of wacky humor.

Lane Montana

Author: Kay Hooper

Lane Montana, a licensed private investigator in Atlanta, advertised her skills as a "finder of lost objects." She claimed an "instinct," although when tested at Duke University for Extra Sensory Perception, she flunked. Lane survived financially through inherited investments. She was a small, green-eyed dark haired woman in her early thirties, who shared her Atlanta loft with a Siamese cat, "Choo". Lane was very close to her artist brother, Jason. Her widowed mother's multiple marriages may account for Lane's single state.

In *Crime of Passion* (Avon, 1991), Jeffrey Townsend failed to identify the object he wanted found during the message he left on Lane's answering machine. When she arrived at his home, he was dead. Police considered her presence in the electronically secure Townsend home, her delay in contacting them, and the erasure of Townsend's message to be suspicious. That seemed reasonable, but Lt. Trey Fortier not only believed Lane but tainted evidence, and then shared access to department records and facilities with her. Their affair created a definite conflict of interest.

House of Cards (Avon, 1991) focused on the new relatives acquired when Lane's mother married Englishman Adam Rowland. During a stay at the ancestral home, Larry, the innocuous appearing insurance executive married to Aunt Emily Buford, was murdered. Lane knew there was a killer in her family tree, but had to identify the right person.

The series did not continue but Hooper has an extended series featuring Noah Bishop and psychic Cassie Neal.

Britt Montero

Author: Edna Buchanan, a well-known Miami reporter

Britt Montero mirrored the reporter that author Buchanan was in reality: tireless, ambitious, intolerant of police brutality, and stimulated by her work. Britt was a blond, green-eyed Cuban/American whose father had been executed by the Castro government. Her mother worked as manager of an "upscale fashion house." Their relationship was strained, because after Britt's father died, her mother farmed her out to assorted relatives in Florida. Britt survived two years at Northwestern University in Evanston, Illinois, but transferred to a warmer climate to graduate. Aged forty, as the series began, she was a crime reporter for the *Miami Daily News*. Britt, who considered television reporters unnecessarily intrusive, prided herself on being a print journalist. She not only carried a gun, but supported handgun ownership. She had never married, sharing her home with a cat, Billy Boots.

In *Contents Under Pressure* (Hyperion, 1992), Britt's sources at the police department dried up when she asked questions about the death of D. Wayne Hudson, a former football player who had fled when pursued by night shift police. Hudson's wife asked Britt to search beyond the obvious reason for the pursuit. Attractive Sgt. Ken McDonald was willing to help so long as it did not jeopardize his job.

Miami, It's Murder (Hyperion, 1994) began with Britt depressed by the end of her relationship with McDonald. The narrative blended two story lines: (a) the suspicion of retired detective Dan Flood that gubernatorial candidate Eric Fielding had committed a murder 22 years before; and (b) a series of murders, seemingly executions of criminals who had escaped justice through technicalities.

By *Suitable for Framing* (Hyperion, 1995), Britt, comfortable with her status at the *Daily News*, had no qualms about helping novice reporter Trish Tierney. She realized that she was being undermined in time to save her reputation. She was less fortunate in helping Howie, a young African-American drawn into crime by his friends; then, betrayed by the juvenile justice and social services systems.

Britt had resolved to stay out of Cuban politics, but in *Act of Betrayal* (Hyperion, 1996), she had no choice. She was focused on a pattern of missing boys. The *Daily News* wanted her insider status, as the daughter of hero Tony Montero, for a series on Cubans in Miami. Juan Carlos Reyes, a powerful candidate for leadership in Cuba after the anticipated demise of Castro, and Jorge Bravo, a struggling patriot who no longer accommodated American goals, both sought Tony's journal, which identified a traitor. Britt's daytime activities were still exciting, but her nights were haunted by dreams of a man she had killed.

In *Margin of Error* (Hyperion, 1997), Britt's editor offered her a "plush assignment," sharing her workdays with charismatic movie actor, Lance Westfell as he prepared for a role as a reporter in a film set in Miami. The world of make-believe left Britt confused as to who were the victims, who, the villains in an over blown narrative. Not up to Buchanan's standards.

Britt, although exposed to crime and criminals, believed that environment, not genetics could cause individuals to be evil. This conviction did not survive in *Garden of Evil* (Avon, 1999). She ignored the needs of elderly Althea Moran, and misjudged her own ability to cope with a killer. She became aware of a destructive family trait that could well be carried on by a child yet unborn. This was a character building experience for Britt.

Deception by a son, cruelty by one husband, and a lack of trust by another all entered into the tragic resolution of Kaitlin Jordan's death in *You Only Die Twice* (Morrow, 2001). Although no corpse had been discovered, R. J. Jordan had been convicted of his wife Kaitlin's death in 1991. After multiple appeals had failed, he was due to be executed. When Kaitlin's body washed upon on a Miami Beach shore, Jordan won his freedom, but the casualties had only begun. Britt wanted to know where Kaitlin had been during the years after she disappeared and why she returned to Florida just before R. J. was to die. Terrific plotting.

Britt's encounters with a badly scarred corpse and with Sgt. Craig Burch of the Miami Cold Case Squad Unit began *The Ice Maiden* (Morrow, 2002). The body in the morgue was probably a member of the gang that had abducted young Sunny Hartley and her boyfriend Ricky Chance fourteen years ago. Sunny, who survived, had been raped and wounded. Ricky was murdered. Although Burch was denied authorization to reopen the case, the CCU squad cooperated with Britt in reviewing the matter. Sunny, now a sculptress, was "the ice maiden" unwilling to relive her horrible experience. There were dramatic and horrifying surprises as Britt proceeded, but, on the positive side, she was planning a wedding.

Britt took a leave of absence after a shocking death, going off by herself to an isolated island, as *Love Kills* (Pocket, 2008) began. When Miami's Cold Case Squad (headed by Britt's romantic rival Lt. K.C. Riley) identified the remains of an excavated body as child abductor Spencer York, they needed to talk to Britt. Her pal, photographer Lottie Dane, lured Britt back to work at the *Miami News*. While together in the Bahamas, Britt and Lottie had found a camera which was a major clue in a more recent death. She was pregnant with Ken's child, hard up for cash, but determined to reclaim the police beat and follow up on what she believed to be a serial killer. This was a poignant story, combining the Montero series with Buchanan's new series featuring the Cold Case Squad, as did the prior book. Next: *Legally Dead* (2009)

Britt would be unbelievable, if it were not that Edna Buchanan is too. New series, featuring U. S. Marshal Michael Venturi

Kellie Montgomery

Author: Valerie Wilcox

Sailing Puget Sound off Seattle was more than a hobby for Kellie Montgomery. It filled her life after her husband Wendell died. Harbormaster Bert Foster, who had formerly been married to Kellie's sister, found her a job at Sound Sailing, maintained at the exclusive Larstad's Marina. Against her daughter Cassie's wishes, Kellie sold the family home and used the proceeds to purchase the forty-foot-sloop *Second Wind* on which she made her home. She had taught in the Seattle school system for fifteen years, but at age forty wanted something different. Cassie, who had been adopted by Kellie and Wendell, was attending school out East so the sloop offered all the space Kellie needed. She may have been insensitive as to how vulnerable Cassie felt losing her beloved father and the home she grew up in. A peripatetic cat named Pan-Pan joined Kellie's crew.

Kellie was part of an extended family, dominated by her older sister Donna. Donna's power arose not only from her formidable personality but from her role as trustee of a fund created when their parents were killed in a car accident. Besides Donna, Kellie had another sister and three brothers. Their parents had enjoyed a close marriage. Mom, a Mormon, had descended from Brigham Young. She and Kellie's dad, an Irish Catholic, had raised their family in Maine. Kellie and Wendell were the first of the family to move to Seattle; followed by Donna and Bert.

Even with her job as manager of the sailing school, there must have been a void in Kellie's life. To the dismay of Detective Allen Kingston she was drawn to murder investigations. On one occasion that occurred before the events in the first narrative, she had "assisted the police." That only increased her passion for detecting.

While sailing, Kellie had noted a drifting yacht and called the Marina for a rescue as *Sins of Silence* (Berkley, 1998) began. She recognized the victims when she prematurely boarded the ship: Donald Moyer, the attorney who processed Cassie's adoption, and his wife Miranda. Kellie's motive for aggressively seeking their killer was based on concern that the potential purchasers of Larstad's Marina might blame Bert Foster for poor security measures. That convinced her, but not Kingston. When Cassie returned on vacation, determined to find her birth parents, Kellie had another reason to want to know more about Donald and Miranda Moyer.

Things held dear by Kellie were endangered in *Sins of Betrayal* (Berkley, 1999). Detective Allen Kingston had not been in touch. Was it because his new partner Melody Connor was a tall blonde? Her favorite sister, Kate, was drinking heavily. Was she ill? The management of Larstad's Marina was considering punitive measures against owners who lived on board their boats. This could mean Kellie would have to move the *Second Wind* elsewhere. Juggling all this, Kellie tracked down a pair of aging lovers whose marriage might make them targets for murder.

Former neighbors Paul and Sharon Crenshaw were Kellie's first customers for her new charter service in *Sins of Deception* (Berkley, 2000). Martin Petrowksi, long time pal of the Crenshaws, and employee of Pierpont Engineering and Construction, and his son Jason came along. The voyage through the San Juan Islands was interrupted when Paul, Pierpont C.E. O., was arrested for the murder of Jewell Jessup, a high priced prostitute. Although Sharon and Kellie believed Paul, there was considerable physical evidence connecting him to the crime. While he was out on bail, Sharon was similarly murdered and Paul disappeared. Ignoring Det. Allen Kingston's orders, Kellie took on responsibility not only for Tiffany, the Crenshaw daughter, but for solving the crime. At the same time, Kellie was dealing with daughter Cassie's search for her birth mother.

The narratives read well, and expressed a deep love for sailing and for the Seattle area.

Claire Montrose

Author: April Henry

A sparse childhood and lonely teenage years had contributed to Claire Montrose's personality. Her unwed mother spent a large amount of time watching television after she was awarded disability payments for a fall incurred while shopping at a Portland grocery store. Her sister Jean did not finish high school, but went to beauty school and was working at a mortuary at the time of the series. Claire's high school years had been grim. Her after school hours were spent working at a pizza parlor, using her wages not for personal needs but to pay family bills. This experience caused her to live sparsely and avoid debt. Her first full time job was with the Oregon Department of Transportation Special Plate Department. As a hobby she collected names of cute license plates. She was a single woman in her early thirties, tall with red gold hair.

As *Circles of Confusion* (Harper Paperbacks, 1999) began, Claire's bland existence was electrified by an inheritance from Aunt Cady, a spinster who had served in the Women's Army Corps in Germany during World War II. Among Aunt Cady's meager possessions were a diary and a small but intriguing painting. Spurred on by dissatisfaction with her current life, Claire flew to New York City for an appraisal. Naïve but not stupid, she shared her story with two attractive men who differed as to the authenticity of the painting: a Vermeer (very rare), a Van Meegeren (excellent fake), or a more amateur effort. It was worth killing for. A well-done art story. Dante Bonner, one of the experts whom Claire had consulted in New York City, wanted to remain a part of her life.

In *Square in the Face* (Avon, 2000), Claire and Dante shared a long distance romance. Each was emotionally attached to their home locale. Claire had no confidence in marriage based on her family's experience. Her mother and sister both had children outside of marriage. One of her grandmothers had married five times. Claire's heart melted when she learned that her friend Lori's three-year-old son had been stricken with leukemia and needed a bone marrow transplant. The best potential donor was a daughter that Lori had given up for adoption. Lori thought the best person to find that child was Claire.

Claire vacillated about attending her twentieth high school reunions but, in *Heart Shaped Box* (HarperCollins, 2001), she decided to go. She lived in Portland, so could easily drive to nearby Minor, Oregon. Some of her classmates seemed unchanged. Cindy Weaver, former prom queen and head cheerleader, was still vivacious and hungry for attention. Others had exceeded early expectations: Richard Crane, the shy but intelligent yearbook photographer, had become a software multi-millionaire. Sawyer Fairchild, then a student teacher, was a rising politician. When Cindy was murdered during the first night party, Claire defended the innocence of Logan West who had spent most of the intervening years fighting schizophrenia. Museum curator Dante Bonner escorted Claire to the event and served as her Watson.

Claire's roommate, "Charlie" was stunned when in *Buried Diamonds* (St. Martin, 2003), Claire showed her a valuable diamond ring, she had discovered. The ring had been found in a stone wall on the property of local philanthropists, Allen and Mary Lisac. Allen had given it to his fiancée, Elizabeth, but they never married. Shortly after Allen's return from Korea, Elizabeth had hung herself. Charlie, already scarred by her memories of a German concentration camp, discovered the body. The discovery of the ring led to other questions. Had Elizabeth killed herself or had she been murdered? She'd been pregnant. By whom? Major portions of the narrative were retrospective, Charlie's life in 1952 and her experiences in a concentration camp. This was as much her story as Claire's.

An excellent series. Too bad it ended.

Dr. Jean Montrose

Author: C. F. (Francis) Roe

Jean Montrose was the doctor that rural Scottish (and American) communities long for—a compassionate general practitioner dedicated to her patients. Her marriage to Steven, owner of the local glass works, occasionally suffered from her lack of attention. Their daughters, Lisbie and Fiona, reluctantly accepted additional home responsibilities and the absence of their mother at critical moments, but paid a price. Jean's work at autopsies established a working partnership with Chief Inspector Douglas Niven.

In *A Nasty Bit of Murder* (Signet, 1992) a.k.a. *The Lumsden Baby* (Headline, 1990), she was uncomfortable with the crib death of an epileptic infant and the subsequent death of his aristocratic but alcoholic father. Her probe into their deaths was interspersed with glimpses of a rural practice, reminiscent of James Herriott's veterinary series.

During *A Fiery Hint of Murder* (Signet, 1993) a.k.a. *Death by Fire* (Headline, 1990)), local superstition and modern lasers vied for the responsibility for arson and death by incineration. Jean's absorption led to a brush with infidelity and a failure to notice Lisbie's alcoholism.

In *A Classy Touch of Murder* (Signet, 1993) a.k.a. *Bad Blood* (Headline, 1991), the Montrose family drove through the placid countryside, only to discover a wrecked car whose driver had been shot. Victim Graeme Ferguson had been engaged to marry Ilona, the beautiful daughter of the Earl of Strathalmond. Both Graeme and his politically ambitious brother Roderick were less than admirable. Jean made Doug Niven aware than the real killer would never pay for the crime.

A Bonny Case of Murder (Signet, 1994) a.k.a. *Deadly Partnership* (Headline, 1991) focused on the tangled lives of two couples: entrepreneur Donald Tarland and his psychologist wife, Teresa, and local restaurateurs Bob and Louise Fraser. The murders of Frasers' flirtatious daughter Caroline and Tarland's partner, Mac MacFayden, led Doug Niven and Jean to uncover the cold calculating plot to use Caroline's death for financial advantage.

A Torrid Piece of Murder (Signet, 1994) a.k.a. *Fatal Fever* (Headline, 1992) centered on Dr. Derek Sutherland, who failed both as an anesthesiologist and as a father; on Ann McIvor, whose ambitions for her son, Jeremy led to callous disregard for others; and on haunted cleric Duncan Sinclair, who tried to protect a boy from a vengeful killer.

In *A Relative Act of Murder* (Signet, 1995) a.k.a. *A Death in the Family* (Headline, 1993), seductive Moira Dagleish used men for gratification. Her politically powerful uncle, Alistair Dagleish, used his office to enhance his career. Moira's death targeted other men in her life, leaving the one man who dominated it for Jean to discover.

Doug Niven could not ignore Jean as a suspect in *Hidden Cause of Murder* (Signet, 1996). The growing antipathy between her and Diane Taggart, her new partner, was known to the community, and was exacerbated by Taggart's charges against Jean to the Medical Board.

The death of abusive bully Robertson Kelso after surgery in *A Tangled Knot of Murder* (Signet, 1996) produced several suspects. The primary was surgeon Hugh Kirkwell who had reason to hate his patient. As in many prior narratives, Jean kept Inspector Douglas Niven from making a serious error.

Readers are cautioned that, except for the last two narratives, the American and English editions have different titles. These were cozy, reader friendly books.

Abigail Moon

Author: Marjorie Eccles

The British based series was an ensemble, with Sgt. Abigail Moon as a contributing member. Widowed Inspector Gil Mayo was the series protagonist. Over a period of time Abigail became his preferred professional partner, but his personal relationship was with Sgt. Alex Jones. Abigail had a life of her own, a small place with a garden for puttering, and an on-going affair with Ben Appleyard, editor of the local newspaper. The series based on Mayo included several books during the 1980s and early 1990's before Abigail was introduced.

Abigail joined Mayo's team in *The Company She Kept* (St. Martin, 1996). She acted as his assistant when he connected the recent murder of Angie Robinson to a death fourteen years before. The earlier victim was a woman whom no one missed but no one forgot. Abigail had a short-term affair with a man in her unit who returned to his wife and a seriously ill son.

Mayo was available for significant interviews, but Abigail, now an inspector, was in charge of the murder investigation in *An Accidental Shroud* (St. Martin, 1997). The violent death of antique jewelry dealer Nigel Fontenoy involved a fascinating array of suspects connected by birth, complicity, and greed. Fontenoy's cousin, Jake Wilding, seemed an obvious choice. He needed money, but, when questioned, he diverted them to other possibilities.

Two seemingly unrelated crimes, the death of out-of-town businessman Philip Ensor and that of young Patti Ryman, who had been delivering newspapers, divided the resources of Gil Mayo's unit in *A Species of Revenge* (St. Martin, 1998). Only as the evidence was gathered did they collectively realize how closely the crimes were entwined. Had Patti seen Philip's killer? Was the killer among the residents of new development Ellington Close? Abigail's personal life played no part in the narrative. Her interviewing skills contributed to the success of the investigation.

In *A Death of Distinction* (St. Martin, 1998), Alex Jones, burned out and physically damaged, resigned from the police force. She joined her sister in an interior decorating business. Abigail could not consider such an alternative. Her career was too important. Gil and Abigail investigated the murder of recently retired prison administrator Jack Lilburne. He had been governor of a prison for juvenile offenders. In that capacity he had considerable impact on the lives of prisoners, some of whom were now in the vicinity. Flora, Jack's daughter, had been injured in the explosion that killed her father. She might be in danger of another kind in the hospital.

Ben Appleyard's decision to leave Lavenstock left Abigail emotionally adrift in *Killing Me Softly* (St. Martin, 1999). Soon she was too busy to focus on her own needs. Drugs were pouring into the area. Initially there were no connections to the death of unfaithful husband Tim Wishart. Three lines of enquiry met as the narrative developed. Women were disappearing from the community, one of whom was desperately in need of help. Early portions of the books described the potential victims, the killers, and suspects.

The Superintendent's Daughter (St. Martin, 1999) gave Abigail her opportunity to head the investigation into Kat Conolly's death. Gil had been taken off the case because of Kat's close friendship with his missing daughter Julie. Still the emphasis of the story was on Kat: her devotion to her womanizing father, the mystery of her parentage, the men she loved and left, and the man she wanted but could not have. Structurally the narrative moved back and forth among characters at a mildly confusing rate.

A Sunset Touch (Constable, 2000) had an intricate plot revolving around the descendants of Jerzy, a Free Polish airman during World War II, and his English lover. Abigail was assigned to the death of Stefan Kaminski. He had encouraged Jerzy's son Tadeusz to come to Lavenstock. The fire in which Kaminski perished was at first believed to have caused the death of Tadeusz's children. When Jerzy escaped Poland, he had brought along a valuable painting. Inspector Martin Kite, was simultaneously investigating an attack on Cecily Haldane, wife of the local vicar. Ben Appleyard, the roving reporter, had returned from the East and sought to re-establish his relationship with Abigail. This was a complex narrative which required careful reading.

Abigail's request for promotion to Detective Chief Inspector would entail a transfer. In *Untimely Graves* (Constable, 2001), the Lavenstock police department was under pressure from higher authorities to solve three murders: those of a young athlete, an unidentified woman, and the bursar of prestigious Lavenstock College, Charles Wetherby. Breakthroughs came when the "mystery woman" was identified and a relationship established between her and the bursar.

Author Marjorie Eccles' supporting characters—the victims, their families, the suspects, and the criminals—were well drawn. Eccles packaged more plotting, character building, and nuances into a 200 plus page book than some others do in twice the space. The Abigail Moon books have been mentioned as a possible BBC television series. Eccles continues to write police procedurals, historical mysteries, but no more recent Mayo/Moon narratives were located.

Eccles has introduced what may become a new series featuring D.I. Dave Crouch and Sgt. Kate Colville in *Killing a Unicorn*.

Phyllida Moon

Author: Eileen Dewhurst

At age thirty-eight, Phyllida Moon had resigned herself to a midlevel career as an actress in English repertory theatre. It had not met the goals she set when she trained at RADA (Royal Academy of Dramatic Arts). Then, neither had her marriage to Gerald, who was incapable of fidelity. Gerald, the stage manager for the company, went too far when he dallied with a cast member. Phyllida's loyalty to the Independent Theatre Company had been based partly on her affection for the prior producer. When ill health forced him to resign, he was replaced by Wayne Cryer who had no appreciation for Phyllida's work. At the point of quitting before she was fired, Phyllida had a generous offer to work in a forthcoming television serial.

As *Now You See Her* (Severn House, 1995) began, she decided to stay on in Seaminster, the town in which the company was currently playing. She let Gerald know that he was no longer a part of her life. The television series in which she would be cast as a female detective would not begin production for several months. Phyllida decided to seek employment as a private investigator with Peter Piper's agency to gather background. She accomplished this by role playing, setting herself up in various guises to gain information about possible incest, the mysterious death of a young student, and a teacher who took advantage of his students.

Phyllida took on two distinct personas in *The Verdict on Winter* (Severn House, 1996)—one as a daily domestic, the other as a receptionist in an art gallery. In both cases she was observing the behavior of art expert David Lester. Lester's widowed sister, who shared his home, attributed the changes in David to anonymous letters implying that he was selling a forged painting. When David was murdered, he was blamed for possible art fraud at his gallery. Phyllida's powers of observation enabled her to discover a different motive for David's death.

The police department's lack of interest in the simultaneous disappearance of Carol Hargreaves and Maggie Trenchard sent their husbands to Peter Piper's agency in *Roundabout* (Severn House, 1998). When the women's bodies were discovered, Chief Superintendent Kendricks accepted help from the ubiquitous, "Mary Bowden" (the name by which Phyllida was known to the Seaminster Police). She had some concern about her need to submerge herself in these false identities and she reexamined who Phyllida Moon was.

After a successful two months in London performing in *A Policeman's Lot*, Phyllida found herself eager to return to Seaminster and her multifaceted job with Peter's agency. As *Double Act* (Severn House, 2000) began, he had a major assignment ready for her. She was to audition for a local dramatic society in order to observe young Paul Harper who might have fallen in with drug dealers. Phyllida watched the interactions among members of the theatre group. The death of the major contributor, writer/producer Henry Hutton, provided more than enough drama. During the case, Phyllida took on two separate roles: one previously used, Mary Bowden; and a more dramatic stint as Mrs. Sonia Sheridan, a visitor from American.

Phyllida's unexpected gallbladder surgery disrupted her plans to seek out attractive Dr. Jack Pusey who had relocated to Edinburgh as *Closing Stages* (Severn House, 2001) began. However it suited the needs of Detective Chief Inspector Kendrick who wanted an undercover agent in Stansfield Manor to look for evidence that dementia patients were being euthanized. During her recuperation, Phyllida became familiar (in one case very familiar) with members of the staff and other patients. She returned later as Miss Henderson, a health care worker. The narrative was interspersed with the dilemma of a medically oriented family watching a loved one succumb to Alzheimer's.

No Love Lost (Severn House, 2001) exposed the dangers of unrequited love and jealous love. Peter Piper's Detective Agency had been hired by Hugh and Sandra Jordan, parties in a marriage, each suspicious that the other had been unfaithful. When Sandra was savagely murdered, Phyllida's input was made available to the police. She had her own love, Dr. Jack Pusey, to be considered. They had reunited, shared wonderful time together, and married. His son, James, became close to Phyllida.

Chief Superintendent Maurice Kendrick approached the Peter Piper Agency in *Easeful Death* (Severn House, 2003), not in his official capacity however, but as a concerned uncle. His niece Samantha, whose father had recently died, had joined a non-religious cult headed by "The Enabler", Charles Henderson. Phyllida, still recovering from a loss of her own, went undercover. Librarian Sally Hargreaves played the role of her niece as they mixed with the "Bridgers" who focused on death; then, on murder. Dr. Jack Pusey had made Phyllida aware that under all her disguises, she was a really lovable person.

With some justification, Phyllida was appalled by her behavior when she witnessed the murder of Basil Wright in his jewelry store as *Naked Witness* (Severn House, 2003) began. She had fled from the scene to protect the private persona of Phyllida Moon Pusey. Contacts with her boss Peter Piper and DCS Kendrick did nothing to comfort her for that decision. The killer had taken a note on which her name and address were written. Ronald, Basil Wright's assistant, had disappeared. Phyllida could not resume her personal life until the killers were identified so she reappeared as Amy Pearson, an American visitor. Her plan was to acquaint herself with Basil's family, where she might find a killer.

Much was made of Phyllida's mousy unprepossessing appearance as compared to the roles she played. She coveted the self-possession and allure that she portrayed when being someone else.

Dewhurst has several other series, including those featuring Helen Johnson, and Neil/Cathy McVeigh Carter, both covered in Volume 2.

Teodora "Teddy" Morelli

Author: Linda French

It could have been worse, Teddy Morelli had sisters named Delizia; Tomasina, and Elizabetta and brothers, Raffaele, Carlo, and just plain Joseph, Jr. Joseph senior had met his wife, referred to in the series as "Marmee", in Italy where she performed Shakespeare for tourists on street corners. He had been an engineer, a designer of cockpits for Boeing Aeronautics. Joseph, Sr. had died; Marmee still played an important role in her children's lives.

Teddy was tiny, a former gymnast, now a history professor at Rainwater University in Bellingham, Washington. She had a Ph.D. with a specialty in Western American History. Her sister Tomasina a.k.a. Tabor was a female professional wrestler. Dr. Aurie Scholl, a fellow professor at the University, had discarded Teddy for what seemed to be a better marriage. When it ended in divorce, he wanted a second chance. Since he had used some of her original material in a professional publication without giving her credit, Teddy was hesitant. Teddy's current project was researching Chinook (the jargon, as distinguished from the language) used by the white traders and Native American hunters and fishers along the Pacific Coast.

Talking Rain (Avon, 1998) opened in Vancouver, British Columbia. Teddy had traveled there to watch Tabor fight. She was the villainess in her competitions. Tabor was gay, a fact she unsuccessfully tried to hide from Marmee. Tabor had a devoted male suitor, a wrestler named "Steamboat" Stevens who was also aware of Tabor's sexual preferences, but loved her anyway. Tabor had been sharing a home in the Bellingham area with Margaret Zimmerman, an author of children's books. When they returned from Vancouver, Margaret was dead. The sisters were whirled into a succession of wild events: treasure hunting, embezzlement and burglary. Another suspicious death was blamed on Teddy. A little knowledge of Chinook helped.

Teddy had never been a big fan of her sister Daisy's husband, botanist Leo Faber. In *Coffee To Die For* (Avon, 1998), she was however impressed by his genetically altered mocha coffee. When Leo was murdered, there was a mad rush to find the greenhouse where he had been growing his R-19 beans. Some of the seekers didn't care "beans" about coffee. Leo had a sideline in marijuana. Teddy, pulling a reluctant Aurie Scholl along, was determined to get there first, even if it killed her.

Alert always to her need for tenure at Rainwater State University, Teddy paid her dues in *Steeped in Murder* (Avon, 1999). She escorted potential donor, Sally Pickett-Patchett, around the area, but drew the line at embellishing the reputation of Sally's ancestor, General George Pickett. When Ira Dedmarsh, chairman of the history department, was murdered, Teddy cooperated with the police and provided living quarters for Dedmarsh's attractive replacement. Fortunately the Pickett-Patchetts were not only Civil War buffs, but also rock and rollers.

Cordelia Morgan

Author: Bett Reece Johnson

Cordelia Morgan was a hired gun, trained by The Company to kill. For a dozen years this had been her life. As the series began she was burned out. She had been angry since childhood. Her mother had finally left her abusive husband, going to what seemed to be a refuge, a female village in New Harmony, North Dakota. The place was destroyed in a massacre, which the FBI either sanctioned or covered up. Cordelia's mother, Rachael, had died in the flames.

She returned to her father, a man involved in horses and gambling. Through him she met Psichari Pasonombre, who mentored her into working for The Company. He became her surrogate father, although she later feared his wrath when she walked off the job. Cordelia had not explained her reasons. She was fleeing from Simon Cruz, the man with whom she had lived for two years. He was also involved with The Company. She had stolen information to protect reclusive feminist author Anna Lee Stone. She did this aware that Stone's controversial book might have triggered the New Harmony massacre in which Rachael died, but that it had also given Rachael the courage to flee from a brutal husband.

Psichari knew that Cordelia had already exceeded the usual length of service with The Company. He had given her one more assignment in *The Woman Who Knew Too Much* (Cleis Press, 1998). He sent her to investigate the suspicious death of raunchy old reclusive Jasper Blankenship in New Mexico. Under an assumed persona, Cordelia joined the environmental protest group to which Blankenship belonged. They were resisting efforts to transfer water rights, a transfer that might increase pollution. Cordelia's sympathy for this group and her growing affection for Anna Lee Stone put her at odds with The Company.

Cordelia was in flight when, in *The Woman Who Rode to the Moon* (Cleis, 1999) she agreed to help Claire James, a friend of her mother. Claire's alienated daughter Camilla had been found hanging in a barn at El Gato, an enclosed Colorado community that Claire had begun. Under a false identity, Cordelia moved into El Gato where she crossed paths with J. S. Symkin ("Sym"). Both Cordelia and Sym were aware that there was evil at El Gato. It appeared in the greed of a land developer, but more seriously in the brutality and sexual excesses of two men. Sym was vulnerable. Cordelia was vengeful. At the end, Cordelia was on the run again.

Two women, each with a notorious past, met in a parking lot in Los Tierras as *The Woman Who Found Grace* (Cleis, 2003) began. Cordelia, now using her mother's first name, was still evading Simon Cruz, traveling in a motor home, pulling her horse in a trailer. When an earthquake damaged the motor home and injured the horse, Grace Frost offered Cordelia a place to stay while repairs were made. Grace's past was as lurid as Cordelia's. She had been convicted of murdering two women friends, sentenced to death; then put in a mental hospital. Her thirty-two years of institutionalization ended thanks to investigative reporter Julia Simmons. Julia cast doubt on the original verdict; then provided Grace with a place to stay. Cordelia needed a temporary place to stay; Grace needed to be rescued from the memories that haunted her and to be reawakened to what she had forgotten. Johnson explained in the preface that she had based Grace on Winnie Ruth Judd, a famous killer in the 1930's. The narrative was weakened by too many transitions from Cordelia to Grace as narrator and from the past to the present.

Johnson's prose, particularly as it related to settings, was exceptional, but the plotlines were convoluted.

Taylor Morgan

Author: Megan Mallory Rust

Taylor Morgan's life had been focused on airplanes since her father taught her to fly his Cessna 185. Flying is a way of life in Alaska because of the scarcity of highways. She worked as a pilot for Tundra Air Charter in Bethel, but eventually found that boring. A new job as pilot for LifeLine Air Ambulance offered more challenges. She settled into a remote cabin on the outskirts of Anchorage, which required a four-wheel drive vehicle in the winter—her choice, a Suzuki Sidekick. Her lover, pilot Steve Derossett who also worked with LifeLine, spent much of his time at the cabin, but Taylor was often alone. She had decided against having a pet because her schedule was so uncertain. She was obsessed with planes and thought best just sitting in a cockpit. On occasion, she ignored regulations to transport passengers in need of immediate help.

There was a loneliness to being the only female pilot at LifeLine, so in *Dead Stick* (Berkley, 1998), Taylor welcomed new employee Erica Wolverton. When Taylor conducted Erica's check flight, she was impressed with her cool demeanor and technical skills. She grieved when Erica was among five persons killed in a plane crash. The NTSB (National Transportation Safety Board) representative made a preliminary decision that Erica, the copilot, had panicked and caused the crash when the pilot had a heart attack. Taylor had noted several anomalies at the scene of the crash that convinced her that someone had tampered with the aircraft.

Out of gratitude to her former employer, Tundra Air Charter, Taylor used vacation time to help them out during *Red Line* (Berkley, 1999). This entailed leaving Anchorage and Steve behind, going to Bethel on the edge of the tundra. The Yukon-Kuskokwin Delta contained small, isolated, and impoverished villages, most of which prohibited alcohol. A few flights involving serious injuries convinced Taylor that someone was smuggling liquor via planes. What profit would there be in such a venture? At least enough to kill for.

The murder of experienced Lear jet pilot Carter Masterson left LifeLine short of trained staff in *Coffin Corner* (Berkley, 2000). Taylor and Steve ignored the Anchorage police in the investigation of Masterson's death. Instead, they focused on reasons why fellow pilots might have killed him. Lear jet pilots were the cream of the crop, and they knew it. Taylor wondered if murder could be motivated by the desire for professional advancement. She was dying to fly a Lear herself.

Little of Taylor's background, appearance, or interests (beyond the need to fly) emerged in the narratives, but the technical details and descriptive material were excellent.

Ruthie Kantor Morris

Author: Renee B. Horowitz

When the series began, Ruthie Kantor Morris was a widow in her fifties. There had been no children in her marriage to Bob, although she had endured three miscarriages. Her work as a pharmacist sustained her. She had helped out at her dad's drug store as a teenager and earned a degree in pharmacy. By that time family owned drug stores had become passé. She was employed by a pharmacy in a Food Go supermarket in Scottsdale, supervising a younger professional and a technician. While at the university, Ruthie had been deeply in love with fellow student Michael Loring. Her parents placed heavy pressure on Ruthie to end the romance because Michael was not Jewish. In deference to their wishes, she did so. Her marriage to Bob had been a happy one, but she never forgot Michael. She had an excellent job, and owned a home with a swimming pool large enough to swim laps, but she was lonely.

Ruthie was meticulous in her pharmacy work so was concerned during *Rx for Murder* (Avon, 1997) when Harry Slater, a favorite customer, died from a drug reaction. Betsy, Harry's much younger wife, and waitress Denise Seaford, who had an eye on Harry, were both suspects. This caused a conflict of interest for Ruthie when she learned that Betsy was Michael Loring's daughter. His presence reawakened her feelings, but even he might be a suspect.

Exacting and cautious as Ruthie might be, she was accused of substituting the wrong medication in *Deadly Rx* (Avon, 1997). Young Amy Brookman needed pain medication, antibiotics, and Methergine to control bleeding after a miscarriage. When she died, the medication in her blood stream was Coumadin (a blood thinner). Amy's parents planned to sue both Ruthie and Food Go for negligence. Ruthie could lose her license, taking away the primary focus in her life. Her friends Denise Seaford and Michael Loring rallied to help her. Unfortunately Michael seemed interested in another woman.

Although the page count of *Rx Alibi* (ClockTower, 2002) was relatively short, that was partly due to the smaller print. Ruthie's latest brush with murder came about because her dear friend waitress Denise Seaford was one of a half-dozen suspects in the murder of female attorney Andrea Felder. Denise was seeing Andrea's husband, Sterling Harraday, and providing part-time day care for Andrea's handicapped father, Amos. Amos, Sterling, and Denise all wanted Ruthie to do her own investigation.

Interesting series, which ended too soon.

May Morrison

Author: Nancy Star

The entertainment scene has always been popular in mysteries e.g. the theater-based novels of Ngaio Marsh during the Golden Age. The focus currently has been on movies and television. May Morrison, a divorcee with two daughters, was employed as a New York City television talk show producer. Part of her job was to keep the volatile Paula Wind (of *Paula Live*) under control. Todd, May's former husband, was now comfortably married to a tissue paper heiress. May had a tough schedule, with childcare being an ever-present problem. Her own mother Shirley lived in Florida, and had no desire to lend a hand.

During *Up Next* (Pocket, 1998), there was a touch of the *Murphy Brown* ensemble. May had Pete Jackson repairing her house to provide comic relief. While a killer watched from above, James Barnett, producer of a rival talk show, fell 39 floors down to the sidewalk from his apartment. The possibility of suicide seemed even less likely when two more television personalities died shortly thereafter. Even though Detective Paul O'Donnell was personally attracted to May, he could not eliminate her as a suspect. Eventually she seemed more likely to be the next victim.

May planned an episode on alternative medications for *Paula Live*. In *Now This* (Pocket, 1999), her perspective was changed by a series of mysterious deaths. The victims had been unrelated except by attendance at a luxurious spa or through friendship with May's friend and neighbor, Stacey Blum. Although May had ignored Paul O'Donnell's advice and offer of a gun, she did accept a more appropriate gift, an engagement ring.

Star's more recent books have been written for children and adolescents.

Zen Moses

Author: Elizabeth M. Cosin

Childhood had been erratic for Zen (actually Zenaria). She was the child of Russian Jewish and Gypsy emigrants. Her father, who was a partner in the family cigar shop, died. His brother Sam kept the business going. Her mother, part Gypsy, took off in the family station wagon and joined a commune in Idaho. She had no siblings, but was close to her cousin Danny. While a sports writer, she had carried out a successful expose of a crooked agent/attorney. As the series began, she had become a private investigator, having been tutored by her friend Bobo La Couceur, who was available to help when needed. Zen enjoyed gardening, blues singers, and mountain bikes but was a little too fond of alcohol. She lived in a small earthquake damaged house in Santa Monica with FEMA funding. Like many female sleuths, she favored cats.

Cousin Danny Moses was believed to have died twelve years before, but in *Zen and the Art of Murder* (St. Martin, 1998), his fresh corpse turned up in the freezer room of Zen's favorite pub. All those years, Zen and Uncle Sam thought Danny had been one of the dozen members of Guru Tama Tai's cult who joined hands and jumped off a cliff into the sea. While determined to find Danny's killer, Zen had to keep working. Television personality Latisha Maxwell hired Zen to locate her father, Harry Winchester. Unfortunately she was not the only one seeking Winchester.

Zen's relationships in *Zen and the City of Angels* (St. Martin, 1999) tended to the extremes, from solid loyalty to deep enmity. Two men she had humiliated in the past: disbarred attorney Eddie Cooke and detective Vince Lennon, were on the negative side. Bobo, her mentor, and attorney Jim Gray on the other extreme. Zen couldn't turn down Jim's request that she locate a missing dog. Her success led Jim and Zen into a maze of pain, guilt, and the possibility that one or the other would be charged with murder. With limited time, Zen tried to help unstable Sherrie Sanger and her foul-mouthed ten-year-old daughter Emily. Biggest mystery: who pays Zen's frequent hospital bills. Didn't sound like she had health insurance.

Kate Mulcay

Author: Celestine Sibley

Katy Kincaid, later to become Kate Mulcay, appeared in a single mystery in the Fifties, *The Malignant Heart* (Doubleday 1958), as a "damsel in distress" newspaper reporter at the Atlanta Searchlight. She lived then with her handicapped father, a cop disabled on duty. She was a dauntless redheaded heroine who risked danger to learn which of her fellow reporters had killed the women's editor Paula Reynolds and Garrity, an elderly reporter. Police Lieutenant Benjamin Mulcay, who was to become Katy's husband, came to her rescue.

By the current series, Kate was widowed. During the marriage, Ben had discussed his cases with Kate. After his death, Kate left Atlanta for a rural log cabin, bringing along her pet cat (Sugar) and dog (Dalmatian, Pepper). She remained active as a stringer for big city newspapers. Although independent, she did not see herself as a militant feminist, preferring to judge people by other standards than gender.

In *Ah, Sweet Mystery* (HarperCollins, 1991), Kate would not believe that her elderly neighbor Miss Willie Wilcox killed her stepson Garney, even after she confessed. She proved otherwise. There were interesting touches, such as when Georgia grande dame Miss Marlowa Walton showed them "how it's done" at a Nelson Eddy-Jeanette MacDonald festival.

In *Straight As an Arrow* (HarperCollins, 1992), Kate vacationed on Ila Island off the West Florida coast. Her host and hostess, permanent residents Phil and Nora Noble, suspected that the increased murders and dangerous attacks on the island were connected to the struggle between environmentalists and developers.

Kate wanted full-time work in *Dire Happenings at Scratch Ankle* (HarperCollins, 1993) and was assigned to the Georgia political beat. She was interested in the transition from "good old boy" representatives to blow-dry legislators. What seemed at first to be a generous effort to restore Native American lands to Georgia ended in the disappearance and deaths of state representative Return Pickett and his lover, Edie Putnam. The ending was downbeat, unusual for the series.

Kate appeared to be too wise and worldly to be duped by a young reporter (à la *All About Eve*), as depicted in *A Plague of Kinfolks* (HarperCollins, 1995). It was also difficult to believe that even Southern hospitality would allow her to become the victim of such sleazy relatives as Edge and Bambi Green, the Texan cousins who appropriated her home. These situations formed the background for Kate's investigation into the death of neighbor Bets Dunn.

Spider in the Sink (HarperCollins, 1997) was episodic, showing Kate as a soft touch who reached out to everyone who sought her help. She would have plucked a spider out of the sink rather than kill it. Yet when charming new Episcopalian priest, Rev. Jonathon Craven, paid court to Kate, she was unable to give him the benefit of the doubt. This narrative portrayed Kate as in her late forties, younger than before. An older Lady Bountiful, Iris Moon, was killed shortly after installing two street persons in her guesthouse. The police assumed the "guests" had killed her, but Kate went beyond the easy answer.

Author Celestine Sibley was an excellent writer with skills honed as a reporter. Her narratives moved with style and grace. She had written extensively about the city she loved, Atlanta.

Lorelei Muldoon

Author: Wenda Wardell Morrone

It was a wonder that Lorelei Muldoon had developed any social skills at all. She was the daughter of Professor Hank Muldoon, a theoretical scientist in the field of mathematics and computers. He was an undemonstrative father with tunnel vision. Lorelei inherited a somewhat lower level of mathematical and theoretical expertise. It was sufficient for her to establish her own fledgling New York City company, which aided corporations in protecting their computer systems from hackers. On her staff (in fact half of her staff) she had young computer whiz Rudy Persich. Lorelei had identified Rudy as the hacker who diverted $50,000 from his father's business accounts to subsidize his purchases of sports memorabilia. That was one way to get parental attention. Rudy's court requirement of public service was carried out as a teacher at the COBOL school, where unemployed adults received training to make them competent for jobs.

Lorelei realized very quickly that her trip to Senator Fred "Bandit" Coleman's isolated cabin in *No Time for an Everyday Woman* (St. Martin, 1997) was a mistake. A mistake that Bandit paid for with his life and put Lorelei at risk. There were hidden agendas, and personal relationships that pushed the narrative from intricate into confusing. Lorelei was on the run most of the time, but when she settled down to the spreadsheets, she saw the pattern that led to murder.

In *The Year 2000 Killers* (St. Martin, 1999), Rudy had developed a device that would minimize the problems of Y2K systems that interacted with those that were damaged. He was unaware that, when he shared his Y2K bridge disk with the COBOL students, he was triggering a disaster. Terrorists killed Rudy, kidnapped Lorelei, and manipulated Natalie Cordoniu, a ten-year-old computer whiz, to carry out a massive transfer of foreign assets. Hank, Lorelei's father joined her and a hard-edged Y2K government team to foil this scheme. Although blinded by personal considerations, Hank succeeded in doing so. This was a tense narrative, hard to put down

Phoebe Mullins

Author: Karen Sturges

Phoebe, a widow in her late forties, had come to realize that she had spent almost all of her life as an adjunct; first, to her father (acclaimed musician Yannis Angelopoulos) and later, to her husband, conductor Mischa Mullins). Although she had hoped for a personal career as a ballet dancer and had been accepted at School of American Ballet, her widowed father insisted that she travel with him throughout Europe as he played his concerts. Her subsequent marriage to Mischa (whom she called Mike) included a similar arrangement. She became fluent in three foreign languages, learned to handle the travel and business arrangement for the two men, and generally smooth their paths in the classical music world. Phoebe wanted children, but a miscarriage left her infertile.

She was unsure that this was as devastating to Mischa as it was to her. The one joy she did not divest herself was dance, as she continued to work out at studios wherever they were located. Almost all of her life had been spent in urban areas. Although they traveled almost constantly, she and Mischa leased a Manhattan rent controlled apartment, a bargain considering its size. She needed that break, because the investment broker who handled the couples' finances, had depleted them as a result of his gambling addiction.

Finances forced Phoebe to look for a job, and in *Death of a Baritone* (Bantam, 1999) that was something of a blessing. Her position as secretary to former opera star Anna Varovna brought her back into the world of music. Varovna operated a school for serious music students, the Varovna Opera Colony, at her Long Island estate. Each summer she produced three operas, the first of which included former graduates of her school and successful professional musicians or teachers in the cast. Students performed in the two later productions. Handsome baritone Frank Palermo played a leading role in *Cosi fan tutte.* It was well known among his fellow performers that Frank had was seriously allergic to penicillin, and that.his latest enthusiasm was his membership in a religious cult, Children of Truth. A fundamental precept of the cult was that nothing should be concealed or lied about; members did not lie and counseled others to tell the truth even when it was harmful. Whoever substituted penicillin for Frank's vitamin pills obviously was uncomfortable with this doctrine. Phoebe was encouraged by Anna to find the killer because "she was someone people talked to". They did.

Another opportunity opened up for Phoebe when the summer ended. An invitation from Aunt Portia, her mother's estranged sister, came as a pleasant surprise in *Death of a Pooh-Bah* (Pocket, 2000). Portia Carpenter Singh had left home as soon as she was eighteen, traveled the world, married three times, but after the death of her third husband, returned to Northampton, Massachusetts, where she had grown up. Interested in becoming reacquainted, she agreed to subsidize the first production of Derek Bowles' Northampton Repertory

Company, Gilbert & Sullivan's *Mikado.* The performance and rehearsals were held in the Old Church Theater which had terrific acoustics. When director Harry Johns and Bowles learned of Phoebe's background, they recruited her as choreographer, then as stage manager for the production. There were problems. Local businessman and retired pediatrician, E. Foster Ballard, was as arrogant and demanding as the role he played, "Pooh-Bah". After a series of "incidents", Ballard was murdered. On a more personal level, Phoebe found herself attracted to Harry Johns; but less so to "Bear" Ben Solliday, Aunt Portia's friendly neighbor. She met musical director Nadine Gardner, who seemed so familiar, and she was.

These stories brought music at a classical level to life, much as Iain Pears did with art, that I was looking forward to another in the series. The best information I could find indicated that Karen Sturges died.

Clare Cliveley Murdoch

Author: Ann Crowleigh, pseudonym for Barbara Cummings and JoAnn Power

See: Clare and Miranda Cliveley, page 165.

Kate Murray

Author: Peg Tyre

Kate Murray was a crime reporter, who had worked her way up from copy girl to researcher, and finally reporter on the *New York Daily Herald.* A tiny woman with dark hair and brown eyes, she was single and on the rebound from an affair as *Strangers in the Night* (Crown, 1994) began. Work was not going well. After mishandling a big story because of her naïve trust in a mother's description of her son, she had been placed on six months probation. The murder of African-American nurse Margaret Severing on her doorstep offered Kate a chance to redeem herself. Dominick, a young drug addict who had witnessed the crime, contacted Kate, but she considered him a crank caller. John Finn, the detective assigned to the case, was fighting his own depression, and his unresolved attraction to Kate.

Kate left the *Daily Herald* when an unacceptable new owner took over during *In the Midnight Hour* (Crown, 1995), finding work on a local television station. Finn, who had succumbed to alcohol, was reassigned to a narcotics squad, which he realized was "on the take." He and Kate reconnected conveniently when she prevented his "buddies" from learning that he was taping their conversations. She risked her job on Channel 7 to direct police squads to a major drug delivery. Finn, once aware that he was to be a father, cleared his name and gave up alcohol.

Jordan Myles

Author: Martina Navratilova and Liz Nickles

An injury incurred while mountain climbing forced Jordan Myles to abandon a promising career as a professional tennis player. Encouraged by sports doctor Gus Laidlaw to find related work as a physical therapist, Jordan entered college and earned a degree. She became associated with the Desert Springs Sports Science Clinic near Palm Springs California in partnership with Gus Laidlaw and Bill Stokes, a former Olympic marathon runner. Her relationship with Gus, a divorced man, had become more personal. Her own short marriage to sportscaster Tim Tulley ended when she was injured. Jordan had many friends on the circuit, and was welcomed and respected in her new role, but missed the excitement of being a performer. Her constant companion, except when she went to England, was a Jack Russell terrier, "A. M." named after Alice Marble, the U.S. tennis champion of a past generation.

Her lifestyle kept Jordan on the road, dressed for comfort not for style, eating vegetarian whenever possible, and occasionally behind on her paperwork. In the old days, there had been a manager to pay bills, make reservations, and remind her of appointments. The physical therapy work was supplemented by television opportunities as a color commentator at major tennis tournaments and on an interview series.

The Total Zone (Villard, 1994) found Jordan at Madison Square Garden to attend an award ceremony for Marissa Storrs, a lesbian tennis legend who had been a friend to her. She was summoned back to Desert Springs to care for Audrey Armat, a promising newcomer whose parents controlled her personal and professional lives. Jordan realized that Audrey's problems were more than physical, but played no part in her disappearance. Fearing bad publicity for the Sports Clinic, Jordan worked with disheveled but competent Noel Fisher ("The Fish") to find Audrey and learn what had caused her disappearance.

In *Breaking Point* (Villard, 1996), Jordan was welcomed by the professional staff and invited to a soiree at the Global Sports greenhouse across from Roland Garros where the French Open was held. When Catherine Richie, a computer expert who may have used her skills illegally, crashed through the building's glass ceiling to her death, Jordan was too late to resuscitate her. It was not too late to trace a killer. Jordan and one-time competitor Kelly Kendall played doubles as investigators, and won.

The rapport between Gus Laidlaw and Jordan had been intermittent at best but, in *Killer Instinct* (Villard, 1997), there was a serious rupture. Although he assured her that they had a great future together, that future was not to be with the Sports Clinic. Under the influence of commercial magnate Trent Byers, Gus envisioned a line of herbal products to enhance performances of both professional and amateur athletes. He wanted Jordan to tout "Duration" on her television show. Her reluctance infuriated him, but she was concerned about a series of unfortunate mishaps to tennis players. Fortunately the "Fish" was available to lend a hand.

Alice Nestleton

Author: Lydia Adamson, pseudonym for Frank King

It wasn't necessary for a reader to like cats and theatre to enjoy Alice Nestleton, but it helped. She had been raised in rural Minnesota by her grandmother, and then trained at the prestigious Guthrie Theatre in Minneapolis. Alice was very selective about her theatre roles. As she explained, perhaps too frequently, she was only interested in the avant-garde. This contributed to her limited finances but provided her with ample time to solve mysteries. She now lived in New York City, but Alice traveled if the part was right. Physically she was tall, very thin, with blonde hair going gray. Since her divorce, there had been temporary liaisons, but the man who most consistently figured in her life was Anthony Basilio, a struggling theatrical designer. Tony had always loved Alice, even though he married someone else. Her feeling for him was based on loneliness.

In *A Cat in the Manger* (Signet, 1990), cat-sitting brought about Alice's discovery of Harry Starobin's body. Alice was living in a cottage on the run-down Starobin Long Island estate. When his wife Jo learned that seventy-nine-year-old Harry had led a secret life, she hired Alice to find his killer. The place to start was the $381,000 in cash stashed away in a bank lockbox.

A Cat of a Different Color (Signet, 1991) found Alice teaching an acting course at the New School for Social Research. An unusual breed of cat, presented to her by student Bruce Chessler, led Alice into a murder investigation. Unable to handle a third cat at this time, Alice farmed "Clara" out to her neighbor Mrs. Oshrin. When she learned that Bruce had been murdered and "Clara" had been abducted, Alice needed Basilio's help and his recollections of road shows.

During *A Cat in Wolf's Clothing* (Signet, 1991), a New York Police Department special unit hired Alice at $300 a day to help them solve seventeen murders tied together by an abandoned mouse and a disappearing cat at each scene of the crime.

Barbara Roman was the nicest friend Alice ever had. In *A Cat By Any Other Name* (Signet, 1992), Alice refused to believe that Barbara had jumped out of a window during a meeting of her garden club. Initially no one agreed. When Tim, Barbara's roaming husband, was killed, the police took a second look. This was the pick of the litter in an otherwise routine series.

During a performance of the *Nutcracker Ballet* at Lincoln Center in *A Cat in the Wings* (Signet, 1992), former ballerina Lucia Maury was arrested for the murder of principal dancer Peter Dobrynin, missing for three years. Alice and Lucia had been roommates. Her family hired Alice to investigate.

Devastating reviews of her latest theatrical role inclined Alice to take time off in *A Cat With a Fiddle* (Signet, 1993). She delivered a cat to violinist Beth Stimson in rural Massachusetts. Beth was convening with other members of the Riverside String Quartet at the Covington Center for the Arts. The death of concert pianist Will Gryder was considered the act of a juvenile burglar, but not by Alice.

Alice took advantage of Tony's absence during *A Cat in a Glass House* (Signet, 1993) for a torrid affair with Sonny Hoving, an ambitious young Eurasian detective. While enjoying a Chinese dinner, Alice witnessed the murder of waitress Nancy Han that made no sense until she traced a kitchen cat and foreign medications for male impotency.

She needed a vacation by *A Cat With No Regrets* (Signet, 1994), so a role in a film to be made in rural France seemed promising. The death of the primary backer, Dorothy Dodd, within minutes of their landing put a crimp in the production. Alice's harebrained scheme to smoke out a killer was unprincipled.

Who better than Alice to investigate the death of Martha Lorenz, volunteer for Village Cat People, in *A Cat on the Cutting Edge* (Signet, 1994)? The murderer's trail led through the cat shelter foundation to the secrets of a Bohemian group that included poetess Edna St. Vincent Millay.

What do actresses do when they are "at leisure"? Anything they can, so in *A Cat on a Winning Streak* (Signet, 1995) Alice performed in an Atlantic City Casino. She did not anticipate the murder of Adele Houghton, a woman whose cat brought her such luck that she was banned from the casinos. Adele had come to Atlantic City with three college friends. The quartet met every year at a different site. Marketing manager of the casino Art Agee asked Alice to investigate. Then he was murdered.

Her niece, Alison Chevigny, convinced Alice to pose for negligee ads in *A Cat in Fine Style* (Signet, 1995) exposing her to the world of advertising and the murder of their host Niles Wiegel. Cats played a part, but more important was the breach between Tony and Alice. His attraction to a young make-up artist made him a suspect in her death.

In *A Cat Under the Mistletoe* (Dutton, 1996), "Roberta," a neurotic cat in Alice's care, needed psychological treatment, but when Alice visited therapist Wilma Tedescu's office, she found her dead. Aaron Stoner, a detective whom Alice was seeing regularly, recalled a similar murder ten years before. There had to be a connection. Somewhere among Wilma's clients was a killer.

Aaron Stoner became more important in Alice's life when her affair with Tony ended during *A Cat in a Chorus Line* (Signet, 1996). The blow-up came after she and Tony witnessed the murder of old friend John Cerise. The killer confessed, but Alice could not end it there. She had to know why elderly composer Peter Krispus left his money to his cats, and how Cerise had earned two million dollars. Tony's accusation that Alice had abandoned the theatre to dwell upon cats and detection could not be easily dismissed.

Alice was depressed by her breakup with Tony and the lack of opportunities in the theatre as *A Cat on a Beach Blanket* (Dutton, 1997) began. A chance to housesit in the Hamptons offered her solitude, which she enjoyed for a very short period of time. Her need for companionship drew her into the community of the wealthy New Yorkers who had purchased oceanfront property, and were tearing down the shacks of fishermen. While attending a poetry reading, Alice became acquainted with members of an artistic group, one of whom was blown up before the afternoon ended. Alice's insistence on investigating the murder and then, in an admission of failure, entertaining the suspects, may have led to a second death.

In *A Cat on Jingle Bell Rock* (Dutton, 1997), Alice was very much at leisure, when old friend Jack Rugow invited her out for a drink. Jack, the producer and director of a repertory company, was concerned about funds for Sustenance House, which provided services for the poor. Jack had come to depend on an anonymous annual donation, but this year none had been received. Alice discovered donor Frank Loeb too late. He was dead and so was Will Holland, another member of the Sustenance House Board of Directors. Were there cats in the narrative? Of course, a pair of Siamese who led Alice to information about comfort pets, theft, and the cause of Loeb's defection and death.

A Cat on Stage Left (Dutton, 1998) was the sixteenth in a series that was showing signs of wear. Mary Singer would pay $2,500 if Alice would care for her cat, but as Singer exited the car, her chauffeur shot her and left. Who was the heavily disguised chauffeur and who had occupied the backseat of the car? The cat carrier contained a stuffed feline, not a real animal, but Alice waited a long time to check the stuffing. With the help of Sam Tully, writer of a television private investigator series, Alice researched the play that tied the suspects together, and the suicide that led to murder.

In *A Cat of One's Own* (Dutton, 1999), Jake, a cat with the skills of Willie Sutton, escaped. Later its owner, Amanda Avery, a friend of Alice, was murdered. Alice had succeeded in finding the distinctive cat. Now she had to find a killer. The plot had major holes, but then reality was not a high priority in this series.

A Cat With the Blues (Signet, 2000) found Alice becoming quirkier. Her search for the killer of fellow actor Elias Almodovar and for a cat kidnapper lacked authenticity. Her flashes of intuitive thinking were erratic. The quick trip love affair was contrived.

The axiom that "no good deed goes unpunished" held true in *A Cat With No Clue* (Signet, 2001). An anniversary gift from Alice to a married couple led to a triple homicide. Her pals initially helped in the possible connection to a prior child abduction, but grew tired of Alice's theorizing.

Alice got more than she was asking for in *A Cat Named Brat* (Signet, 2002) when her job to cat sit for travel guide writer Louis Montag ended in his death and the cat's disappearance. Alice was considered suspect by the assigned detective. Two more related deaths kept her on the trail of Brat, the six-toed feline. After pursuing other areas of investigation, Alice and Sam Tully focused on finding Brat.

Alice couldn't even take a bus to a sale without getting involved in murder during *A Cat on the Bus* (Signet, 2002). A fellow passenger drew a gun and shot four people before exiting the bus, leaving a caged cat behind. This factor brought Alice a job offer from the NYPD Retro Squad. Director Louis Nessem believed this incident was connected to a case three years before, although no one had been killed then. Alice, who had been enjoying a long-term role on a television show, was juggling it and a personal life, which included two ardent lovers.

Under the name Adamson, King has two other series: Dr. Deirdre Nightingale and Lucy Wayles. Under his own name he had a short series featuring Sally Tepper.

Jane Nichols

Author: Maureen Tan

Jane Nichols was a survivor, but it wasn't getting any easier. As a child, she had been present when her parents were assassinated in Greece. Jane's dad had been in the diplomatic service. Her mother seemingly was a charming hostess and helpmate. Jane had been in the car with her parents when they were ambushed and murdered. Her grandfather raised her, then passed her along to his friend "Mac," Douglas MacDonald, who recruited her into England's MI5 (Internal Security). While posing as an Irish stewardess, Jane survived an attempt to kill her only because her lover Brian intervened, causing his death. Five years later, a bloody incident in Belfast where she was undercover with the I.R.A., left her so burned out that she could no longer function professionally. She had worked with partner John Wiggins, steely, dispassionate, and deadly.

Fortunately she had inherited money and the income from her second occupation, as the author of a mystery series, featuring P.I. Andrew Jax. Jane used the name "Max Murdoch" as her literary pseudonym, and her literary agent Dora Hollingsworth handled her business affairs.

When Dora arranged for Jane to attend a writer's conference in Atlanta, Georgia in *AKA Jane* (Mysterious Press, 1998), Jane saw a picture in the newspaper that forced her to return to espionage, the face of Jim O'Neill, the man who had ordered her death and caused Brian's. MI-5 made it impossible for her to carry out her own vengeance, but offered her support and supplies to bring O'Neill to justice. Jane, struggling to maintain an identity of her own, juggled her feelings for the new man in her life, and her need to erase guilt from the past.

The losses in Jane's life had made her leery of commitments. In *Run Jane Run* (Mysterious Press, 1999), she left her comfortable existence and her lover, police chief Alex Callaghan, behind in Savannah, Georgia, to take a new assignment. MacDonald sent Jane and John Wiggins to rescue Hugh, the dissolute nephew of a prominent Member of Parliament, Sir William Winthrup.

Hugh was being held hostage at a family estate in Scotland. Jane had flashbacks after meeting members of the Winthrup family, a sense that Sir William may have played an important role in her life.

Terrific books. Never let up on the tension.

Alix Nicholson

Author: Sharon Gilligan

The gift of a camera had made photography an important part of Alix Nicholson's life and a second source of income. A native of Southern Missouri, her home life had been unhappy. Her mother died of cancer when Alix was twelve. The tension between her and her stepmother Ellen led to truancy and rebellion. Her career as a Missouri high school teacher was disrupted when two female students misused cameras and photographic equipment to take nude photos. The fact that she was a lesbian made that incident more serious. Although she did not lose her teaching certificate, she was fired. After the termination, she expanded her photography career and worked as a substitute teacher in the Dubuque, Iowa school system.

At age forty, Alix was a tall blonde woman who dressed casually. The longest relationship in her experience ended because her lover did not approve of Ann's selection for an assistant. Brian, a former student, eventually died of AIDS.

It was for Brian as much as the potential for a documentary that Alix went to Washington, D.C. in *Danger in High Places* (Rising Tide Press, 1993) for a ceremony celebrating the AIDS quilt. Contention as to how government money should be divided between AIDS research and research focusing on cancer in women caused nurse Sandra Hastings to disrupt the rally. When Sandra was murdered, Alix's pictures of the rally uncovered the killer, proving the innocence of lesbian Congresswoman Hallie Shepherd.

Danger! Cross Currents (Rising Tide, 1994) harkened back to Alix's years as a high school teacher. An opportunity to teach a course in photography at a California college reunited her with Leah Claire. Leah had been accused of murdering Meredith Coates, her lesbian lover, a woman whose greed and indiscretions had earned her multiple enemies.

Dr. Deirdre "Didi" Nightingale

Author: Lydia Adamson, pseudonym for Frank King

Deirdre "Didi" Nightingale must be taken with a grain of salt. She was a licensed veterinarian who returned from a year's service in India to a local practice in Duchess County, New York. Didi lived on an inherited estate with four resident servants who were paid no wages. Two of the servants, Charlie, who served as her veterinary assistant while promoting his own remedies, and the cook, Mrs. Tunney, were elderly. The situation with the other two, Abigail in her early twenties and Trent Tucker at nineteen was less credible.

A diminutive brunette with pale green eyes, Didi was single, and scarred by a bitter ending to her relationship with a professor at the University of Pennsylvania Veterinary College. Both of her parents were dead, her mother more recently. Didi accepted a role as head of the household.

She had always looked upon Dick Obey as her best booster, so his death in *Dr. Nightingale Comes Home* (Signet, 1994) was not only a surprise, but also a personal loss. She could not believe that Obey, drunk or sober, could have died from an attack by stray dogs. Didi's probe uncovered a Dick Obey that she had never known, and startling information about her household and her recently deceased mother.

Perhaps because of her experience with elephants in India, or because she had always loved the circus, in *Dr. Nightingale Rides the Elephant* (Signet, 1994) Didi served as veterinarian for Dalton's Big Top during their stay in Duchess County. Didi could not prevent the tragic death of chorus girl Ti Nolan whose head had been crushed by elephant Dolly, but she successfully treated mysterious illnesses in the menagerie. Almost too late, Didi brought a fatal connection to the attention of the authorities.

Through the death of her friend Mary Hyndman, Didi learned about the old style German Shepherds raised by the monks of Alsatian House in *Dr. Nightingale Goes to the Dogs* (Signet, 1995). An elderly recluse, Mary had a Shepherd pup that disappeared when she died. She purportedly had left money to the monks. Taking Abigail with her, Didi checked out the monastery, its specialized training, and the method by which dogs were allotted to prospective owners. Her presence triggered a death for which Abigail was a suspect.

In *Dr. Nightingale Goes the Distance* (Signet, 1995), the suicide of distinguished veterinarian Dr. Samuel Hull and an injury to a horse he was tending forced Didi to deal with her unresolved feelings for Dr. Drew Pelletier, the college professor with whom she had a short affair. Was he an unscrupulous scientist, a killer, or merely a philanderer?

Didi took advantage of an opportunity to commune with nature in *Dr. Nightingale Enters the Bear Cave* (Signet, 1996). She joined a scientific expedition into the Catskill Mountain Forest Preserve. The area was presumed to be isolated but the group met with murder, treachery, and a monster bear.

She considered pigs to be highly intelligent animals, but they brought nothing but trouble to Didi in *Dr. Nightingale Chases Three Pigs* (Signet, 1996). She was suspected of killing Clifford Stuckie, a wealthy pig farmer whom she barely knew, because love letters addressed to her were found in his possession. A second death, that of retired professor Hiram Bechtold, was connected. Police Officer Allie Voegler balanced his unrequited love for Didi against the evidence, but he joined her probe into illicit activities on the pig farm.

Didi's presence at the Blessing of the Animals in *Dr. Nightingale Rides to the Hounds* (Signet, 1997) made her a witness to the assassination of reclusive

John Brietland. He had made enemies when the family factory closed, putting locals out of work. It was not clear that Brietland was the intended victim nor whether or not the killer had been a "hired gun." Another suspicious death had taken place at the same site seven years earlier. Didi and Allie Voegler worked out their personal relationship while muddling through to an unsatisfactory conclusion.

Dr. Nightingale Meets Puss in Boots (Signet, 1997) took Didi's household to New York City where Abigail was hired to sing at a nightclub. Her employer Carl Schirra was shot when he took the stage to make the introduction. Although Abigail, Trent, Charlie and Mrs. Tunney returned home, Didi stayed on, visiting Ilona Baer, a former veterinary school classmate whose clientele included killers by proxy.

In *Dr. Nightingale Races the Outlaw Colt* (Signet, 1998), Allie was unable to handle the death of his friend and fellow police office, Wynton Chung. After he was suspended from his job, Allie depended on Didi to investigate a series of murders dramatized by a mysterious colt. Their relationship survived but Allie's professional record was damaged.

1999 was not a good year for Didi. Business was slow. She was concerned about paying her bills and maintaining her staff. *Dr. Nightingale Traps the Missing Lynx* (Signet, 1999) had an incredible plot. The death of television weatherman Buster Purchase was tenuously connected to the uncovering of a pre-Civil War Underground Railroad station. Flimsy plotting.

Didi faced a dilemma in *Dr. Nightingale Seeks Greener Pastures* (Signet, 2000). The farm animal business in her area was diminishing. It became necessary for her to develop skills in other veterinary specialties. With that in mind, she attended a conference in Atlantic City. The murder of conference speaker Eleazar Wynn was tied to the deaths of persons involved in horse racing and gambling. Friend Rose Vigdor and former beau Allie Voegler made unwise choices that damaged their ties to Didi. The ongoing saga of Charlie's money-making schemes did nothing to help.

The murder of best friend Rose Vigdor six months after she left Hillbrook was incomprehensible to Didi during *Dr. Nightingale Follows a Canine Clue* (Signet, 2001). There were so many questions. Why had Rose disappeared, and then returned to the area without making any contact with Didi? Why had Rose been living at a Zen Buddhist retreat under a false name? Had she set the fire that burned down the retreat house? Most important: who had killed her and why? Didi seemed out of control. Her behavior was so bizarre as to be inconsistent with her character. Charlie was bizarre, but that was a way of life for him.

The Nightingale narratives included unrelated veterinary cases, and numerous episodes involving Charlie and the other servants. They did not always advance the plots and occasionally interrupted them, but added humor and warmth.

Chicago Nordejoong

Author: Victoria McKernan

She might not rank with the top female investigators, but Chicago Nordejoong was no carbon copy. Her deceased mother was Trinidadian; her sea-going father, a Norwegian ship captain. Chicago, named after the city, was a tall, lithe, dark-haired woman, who shared her father's love of adventure. Her mother had died when Chicago was five, but she kept in touch with relatives in Trinidad. Years of travel with her father had provided her with little formal education, but a smattering of foreign languages and the ability to curse in all of them. Chicago made her home on her boat, which was harbored in U.S. and Caribbean ports as the whim and job opportunities took her. She taught scuba diving and captured rare fish for sea museums and aquariums. Her short but happy marriage to Stephen had ended when drug smugglers killed him. She had little interest in most domestic skills, but enjoyed weaving. Unconventional to the limit, her pet was an eight-foot boa constrictor named "Lassie."

As *Osprey Reef* (Carroll & Graf, 1990)) began, Alex Sinclair, a government investigator, rescued Chicago and Umbi, her Hawaiian assistant, from attacking sharks. Sinclair was researching the use of fish as receptacles for smuggled drugs. Chicago became a prickly and somewhat unreliable ally when Sinclair learned that local law enforcement officials were involved in the criminal activity. Before she was finished, Chicago suffered from the "bends" and a romantic attachment to Sinclair.

When Sinclair moved on to the Caribbean and a new career as a pilot for a small airline, Chicago felt rejected. However, in *Point Deception* (Carroll & Graf, 1992), he returned to find Chicago preparing for a two-year cruise. He had ferried a mutilated corpse identified by U.S. Senator Robert Wattles as that of his daughter Angelica. Chicago's trip was postponed while she and Sinclair tangled with munitions makers, industrial polluters, and crooked politicians. In the course of their struggle, Chicago learned more about the roots of Sinclair's inability to make a commitment.

Chicago and Sinclair were together as *Crooked Island* (Carroll & Graf, 1994) began, but she sensed his restlessness as they cruised the Caribbean. Conspiracies to locate and to conceal evidence that a living descendant of the Stuarts might threaten the legitimacy of the current British monarchy came just in time. The discovery of a medallion in fish guts by ten-year-old Annabel Lee fed into the ambitions of a Scottish Jacobite group. Personal danger did not dissuade Chicago and Sinclair from playing a significant role in the outcome.

These were mystery adventures with a novel heroine and complex plotting.

Pat North

Author: Lynda La Plante; *(Robin Blake was listed as having adapted the material from the television program,)*

This was another of author Lynda La Plante's novelized television series. Although it covered territory similar to *Prime Suspect,* it neither attained the recognition, nor developed the female character of that series to the same extent. It was perhaps more similar to the American television series, *Law and Order,* in that it followed a case through both the investigation and the prosecution.

Trial and Retribution (Pan, 1997) was an ensemble presentation that covered a case involving the family of five-year-old Julie Harris who was sexually abused and murdered near a low-income housing development. Attention was given to the police officers involved in that case including Detective Inspector Pat North and over-zealous Constable Colin Burridge and to the prosecutors and defense attorneys, particularly Belinda Sinclair, the novice defense counsel. At this point, Pat was thirty-five, lived with her boyfriend Graham and was stationed at the Southampton Street Station House in the Criminal Investigation Division.

In *Trial and Retribution II* (Pan 1998), the emphasis remained on the victims, suspects, and process. Inspector North and her supervisor, Detective Superintendent Michael Walker carried their roles as investigators with limited personal development. Walker was shown to have an unhappy marriage and some personal interest in Pat. Justice did not prevail in the courtroom, but another solution emerged.

Walker and Pat moved into an apartment in *Trial and Retribution III* (Pan, 1999). There seemed to be no potential conflict of interest because she had been transferred to the vice squad while Mike was stationed in the Metropolitan Area Major Investigating Pool. Then, fifteen-year-old Cassie Booth disappeared while delivering newspapers. Obsessive wine merchant Steve Warrington, who had demanded action from Pat on a possible brothel in his neighborhood, became a suspect. Walker and Pat dealt with different approaches to the case. Their relationship survived although Pat suffered considerable trauma.

Mike and Pat continued to live together although he had not divorced his wife by *Trial and Retribution IV* (Macmillan, 2000). The Home Office selected her for advanced placement. She was assigned to a team reassessing the conviction of James McCready. Mike, who had been the arresting officer, was accused on appeal of homophobia, suppressing evidence and having a personal grudge against McCready. There were consequences for both of them in the outcome.

As *Trial and Retribution V* (Macmillan, 2001) began, reclamation workers in a North London neighborhood uncovered the skeleton of a teenage woman in the backyard of 54 Hallerton Road. Mike Walker was assigned to the case at a time when Pat was relegated to administrative tasks. The initial investigation expanded, and received considerable publicity, as more skeletons were found. Enquiries and forensic results focused on the occupants of the house from 1981 to 1983. Difficulty arose in discovering the identity of the victims and their ties to the suspects. Pat showed an interest and made valuable suggestions. The personal relationship between Pat and Mike was in serious trouble: the divorce in abeyance, Pat's attraction to a more understanding man, and their inability to communicate with one another.

Trial and Retribution VI (Macmillan, 2002) was an engrossing read. Just when Michael Walker's divorce was finalized, Pat, now a detective inspector, had her first big assignment. Michael was up for promotion to Commander. Their relationship had problems, partly because Lynn, his former wife, had made an imprudent choice for a new boyfriend. While Pat was absorbed in the disappearance of music teacher Jane Mellor, Mike's focus shifted from preparation for the promotion interview to the protection of Lynn and their two children. LaPlante has at least four series based on female sleuths; latest, Detective Anna Travis

Tru North

Author: Janet McClellan

Tru North, a lesbian police detective in Kansas City, Missouri, had to work at it. She earned a bachelor's degree at the University of Missouri-Kansas City before entering the police department. Unfortunately, she tested out in the bottom half of her police training class. Some real blunders on the job; e.g. shooting at her reflection in a department store mirror, didn't help. However, she was dedicated to her work and meticulous at a crime scene where she used a tape recorder to capture her impressions. Major O'Donoghue, a female professor of criminal justice at UM-KC, had encouraged her career. Fellow officers perceived Tru as obsessive-compulsive and overly assertive, but she worked companionably with partner Tom Garvan.

Possibly because she had attended a three-week FBI training course on serial killers, Tru was assigned to a case involving a series of bombings as *K.C. Bomber* (Naiad, 1997) began. Tru suspected that her supervisor Captain Rhonn wanted her to fail so she could be fired. Her personal life was in disarray. A three-year relationship had just ended, leaving her with a sense of rejection. Tru used her computer skills to identify a suspect, outlasted her supervisor, and found a new love.

A sense of unease kept Tru on the case, even after she had arrested Karen Bayborn for the murder of her lesbian lover Sandra Vondameier in *Penn Valley Phoenix* (Naiad, 1998). The lack of information about Sandra puzzled Tru. Her computer and a set of fingerprints illuminated the victim's past and her probable killer.

As was shown in *River Quay* (Naiad, 1998), Tru had a problem with relationships. She had moved from a nine-month relationship with Eleanor to six-months with Marki, and then found herself involved with C. B. Belpre, an assertive arson investigator. They were initially hostile with one another while turf protecting on the death of a man in a burned-out building. Beyond their personal problems, they failed to properly identify the victim. The most stable element in her life was a cat, Poupon.

Fortunately, Tru's new supervisor ignored the negative personnel reports left by Captain Rhonn and gave her a fresh start in *Chimney Rock Blues* (Naiad, 1999). He offered her a choice assignment as the homicide representative on a Metro committee investigating serial murders. While checking out a scene of the crime, Tru saw a suspicious car, but was knocked unconscious and suffered amnesia, causing her to be restricted to desk duty for a while. Later, she was assigned to transport Valerie, a young alcoholic who had been housed in a rural jail because of crowding. The attacker who intercepted Tru and Valerie was probably the serial killer, but the conclusion left unanswered questions.

McClellan provided excellent background as to police procedures. There were detours into sexually explicit interludes.

Kali O'Brien

Author: Jonnie Jacobs

Kali O'Brien, a single attorney practicing in a large San Francisco law firm, had rarely returned to Silver Creek, California since her high school graduation. After her mother committed suicide, her father took the slower route, killing himself with alcohol. Nevertheless, when her brother John and sister Sabrina thought themselves too busy, it was left to Kali to clear up the estate and take on her dad's springer spaniel, Loretta. Her relationship with her siblings was always tense.

As *Shadow of Doubt* (Kensington, 1996) began, she took an evening off to attend a party held by old friends, Jannine and Eddie Marrero. When Eddie, a popular high school coach, was murdered, the local police focused on Jannine as the killer. At the request of Jannine's mother, and with the help of local publisher Tom Lawrence, Kali searched Eddie's life for other motives. Darryl Benson, the chief of police who had loved Kali's mother, was dubious, but the killer realized Kali was on his trail. Kali's big city job and her romance with a top litigator ended. She stayed on in Silver Creek, establishing a solo practice with the help of senior attorney Sam Morrison.

When, in *Evidence of Guilt* (Kensington, 1997), Sam needed her help on a major murder case, Kali agreed. Defendant Wes Harding was the local "bad boy," the stepson of a prominent doctor. Kali remembered having a crush on him in high school. The crime, a vicious killing of a young mother and her daughter, was slowly tied to Wes by physical evidence. With little help from her client and Sam in the hospital, Kali persisted until again the murderer took action against her.

The trial attorney's worst nightmare is a client who lies to his lawyer. In *Motion To Dismiss* (Kensington, 1999), Kali had no choice but to take the case.

Grady Bennett, the husband of Kali's best friend Nina, was accused first of rape, then of murder. Based on diligent research, she managed a Perry Mason breakthrough in the courtroom to win the case. During the investigation, she lost a friend and reconnected with a former lover.

Kali had a history with psychologist Steven Cross. During *Witness for the Defense* (Kensington, 2001), she agreed to represent his sister Terri Harper and her husband Ted in an adoption proceeding. Right wing radio commentator Bram Weaver, who derailed the adoption by claiming to be young Hannah's father, was murdered. When Terri was accused of the killing, Kali took on her defense, even though that required her to work with Steven Cross. She had two strategies: (1) to weaken the prosecution case, and (2) to identify an alternative suspect in order to create reasonable doubt. In the end, she was left with no doubt at all. Being around Hannah reawakened Kali's desire to have a child.

There's a good narrative in *Cold Justice* (Kensington, 2002), but it's burdened with coincidences and red herrings that diminish its impact. Kali and Anne Bailey had worked at the district attorney's office at the time of the Bayside Strangler cases. Owen Nelson, now running for governor, had been the head prosecutor. Dwayne Davis, the convicted killer, had recently been executed. Then, a series of murders with strong resemblances to the Bayside Strangler deaths occurred. Anne was the first victim. Kali agreed to short-term employment at the DA's office, focusing on Anne's death and working with attractive detective Bryan Keating.

Intent to Harm (Pinnacle, 2003) was a taut narrative that will grip the reader's attention and, even over 368 pages, never let go. Kali agreed to meet a client known only as Betty in a secluded setting. They were ambushed. Betty was killed; Kali injured. Although her initial role was that of victim and witness, Kali became involved in two additional tasks. Manuel Escobar, the police department's suspect as Betty's killer, was a friend of the family. Moreover, even though her recollection of the event was hazy, she did not believe him to be the attacker. A second phone call alerted Kali to what Betty might have wanted to discuss with her: a murder, which had never been solved.

Kali's relationship with her older brother John and her sister Sabrina had never been close, but in *The Next Victim* (Pinnacle, 2007) that changed. Kali had been casual about responding to John's call for help until Sabrina made her aware that he was dead. Both learned that John had been the primary suspect in the murder of two women, wealthy Sloane Logan Winslow and her housekeeper, student Olivia Perez. Although Sloane and John had enjoyed a youthful affair, they were currently at odds about the future of Logan Foods where John was employed. His connection to Olivia came as a surprise. The narrative explored Kali's personal growth and made her aware of her fear of intimacy.

A very competent series set within a small town legal system. Jacobs is also the author of the Kate Austen series covered elsewhere in this volume.

Rachel O'Connor

Author: Mary Freeman, pseudonym for Mary Rosenblum

Rachel O'Connor, the daughter of a Jewish mother (Deborah) and an Irish father (Will) was raised in Oregon. The O'Connor family owned a prosperous orchard adjacent to the city of Blossom. After college and the death of her father, Rachel's Uncle Jack had assumed she would return to work in the orchard. Instead Rachel, aware that she would chafe under Jack's authority, chose to set up a business, Rain Country Landscaping, which proved to be quite successful.

Within hours in *Devil's Trumpet* (Berkley, 1999), Rachel lost client Henry Bassinger to violent death and signed new client Dr. Joshua Meier who would profoundly affect her life. Jeff Price, Rachel's high school beau, had returned to Blossom where he joined the local police force. Jeff, who had moved to California after graduation, had been with the Los Angeles Police Department. When Julio, Rachel's youthful assistant, became a suspect in Henry's death, she probed into the old man's past. A reclusive dreamer at his death, Henry had spent a short interlude of his life away from his domineering father. During that time he had enjoyed a career as a musician, fathered a son, and laid the seeds for his own murder and the death of a teenage boy. Jeff and Rachel found they still enjoyed one another's company.

Plans to annex 200 acres of undeveloped land to the city of Blossom in order to regulate its growth raised a storm in *Deadly Nightshade* (Berkley, 1999). Uncle Jack O'Connor who felt the prospects of the family orchard would be damaged led opposition to the proposal. When Bob Dougan, the swing vote on the city council, was murdered, Jack was indignant because Jeff, now chief of police, had questioned him. Jack laid it on the line with Rachel: side with the family or with him. A vicious attack on Jeff made it clear to Rachel where her loyalties lay. A missing jacket, a Ponzi scam and a faked appointment led Rachel and Jeff to a crazed killer in time to prevent a second death. Rachel had introduced Dr. Meier to her mother early in the series but did not realize that their interest in one another would lead to an elopement.

Botanists Eloise and Carl Johnston had enjoyed a loving marriage, marred only by the death of their seventeen-year-old daughter Linda. The widowed Eloise hired Rachel in *Bleeding Heart* (Berkley, 2000) to renovate the garden she and Carl had created. Her intention was to bequeath the property to a conservancy group. Eloise's sudden death by an overdose of digoxin focused suspicion on her caretaker, young April Gerard. Rachel was certain that the girl was innocent and that Eloise's biography in process had motivated the killer. She was half-right. Rachel was distracted by concerns that her mother might have tired of her marriage; the truth was equally disturbing but Deborah and Dr. Meier faced it together. Rachel's own romance moved forward when she accepted an engagement ring from Jeff.

Jeff and Rachel's wedding was just a few months away as *Garden View* (Berkley, 2002) began. They rarely had time to talk about it. The city of Blossom was suffering from vandalism. Jeff's new deputy Bert Stanfield, a former big city cop, campaigned for his version of "tough love" policing. Rachel had been delighted to win the contract to landscape the grounds at Garden View Retirement Village. She overcame the technical problems on the job more easily than the awareness that there was a killer, probably on staff. Interesting secondary characters.

In all cases, suspicions cast on individuals about whom Rachel had come to care motivated her investigations.

Kendall O'Dell

Author: Sylvia Nobel

Kendall O' Dell was a tall redhead, living in Castle Valley, Arizona where she worked for the local newspaper, the *Castle Valley Sun*. She had originally come from the Philadelphia area, where her parents, and her brother Patrick and his wife still lived. Her father was a retired newspaper reporter, who had served as a foreign correspondent during the Vietnam War. She had inherited his love for the job. Her intense focus on her work doomed her early marriage to a pharmacist. Both the end of a subsequent romance and her asthma had been factors in the decision to move to a drier climate. Morton Tuggs, then editor of the *Castle Valley Sun*, owed her dad, Bill O'Dell, a favor. He hired Kendall as a reporter for the paper, which was owned by his wife's family.

Kendall found relief from her asthma in Arizona, but in *Deadly Sanctuary* (Nite Owl Books, 1998), there were other hazards. Her predecessor at the *Sun* had disappeared in the midst of an investigation. Kendall walked a tight line. What had happened to unpopular reporter John Dexter? What might happen to Kendall if she continued to probe the deaths of two runaway girls? She was torn between the blandishments of attorney Eric Heisler and the challenges of reporter/rancher Brad "Tally" Talverson.

On slight acquaintance, Kendall offered to drive young Angela Martin to an inherited mining claim in *The Devil's Cradle* (Nite Owl, 2000). They were not made welcome in nearby Morgan's Folly. Angela had presented herself as Audrey Martin, a child who had purportedly died along with her mother Rita fifteen years before. At stake was control of a decommissioned mine, that if reopened could provide jobs for the area. As Angela/Audrey struggled to make sense of who she was, Kendall investigated the death of the young woman's father.

Kendall jeopardized her planned vacation with Tally in *Dark Moon Crossing* (Nite Owl, 2002) by diverting her attention to strife along the U.S./Mexican border. Mexican nationals who entered illegally faced resentment and hostility from local ranchers. Some perished in the desert. Some were captured and relocated to their own country by the Border Patrol. Others, including family members of Lupe Alvarez, who worked in the advertising department of the paper, disappeared mysteriously. Best if the earlier books were read first.

There was something for everyone in *Seeds of Vengeance* (Nite Owl, 2006). Kendall and Tally's plan to tell her mother, Ruth, that they were engaged to be married had to be postponed. Judge Riley Gibbons, Ruth's former brother-in-law, had been savagely murdered. His headless corpse had been found on his own estate, now housing his wife (La Donna) in a guest cottage and his mistress (Marissa) in the main hotel building. Once informed of the death, Ruth offered Kendall a deal. She would accept the marriage if Kendall investigated Riley's murder. Then, reporter Grant Jameson, Kendall's former fiancé, came to town to cover the case. Toss in a small ghost, a trophy-hunting killer, and gold-covered chocolates.

Some of the romantic dialogue was fulsome, but the plotting was above average, clues well planted in the narratives. A good offering from a small press.

Maureen O'Donnell

Author: Denise Mina

A sexually abusive father made Maureen O'Donnell's childhood a living hell. Her alcoholic mother, Winnie, was into denial and self-pity, leaving none for her daughter. As a child, Maureen had been discovered in a cupboard under the stairs with blood between her legs. Michael O'Donnell was never charged. She was not the only one of the children to suffer from his attentions, but it was never discussed among them. Maureen was labeled "crazy" when she had her breakdown, but received little professional treatment.

Given that background it was remarkable that she managed several years studying art history at Glasgow University before another breakdown caused her to drop out. She eventually finished her degree. She was the youngest of the O'Donnell children. Marie, the eldest had become a bank executive who married well and lived in London. Una, a civil engineer, dominated her kindly husband Alistair. Brother Liam, who was closest to Maureen, fared the worst. He dropped out of law school to become a drug dealer.

What treatment Maureen received after her college breakdown amounted to a four month period in Northern Hospital during 1996, followed by a referral to Rainbow Clinic where she was unsuccessfully treated as "Helen" by Angus Farrell. He referred her to Dr. Louise Wishart of Albert Hospital who provided help. At the time the series began, Maureen was working as a ticket seller at a movie theatre.

Maureen's liaison with therapist Douglas Brady in *Garnethill* (Bantam, 1998) ended when he was found dead in her apartment. Although his dalliance with Maureen was totally unprofessional, she was envisioned by the police, not as a victim, but as a suspect in his murder. Bolstered by her close friend Leslie

Findlay and her brother Liam, Maureen chose not to be a victim, but to bring the culprit to justice on her own terms.

Maureen's helpful involvement in the Brady case did not win her any support from the Glasgow Police Department in *Exile* (Carroll & Graf, 2001). In a gesture of support to Leslie Findlay, Maureen looked for abused housewife Ann Harris, who disappeared from a Glasgow women's refuge, only to be found murdered in London. Maureen's reformed brother Liam warned her to stay out of it because "hard men" were involved. She traveled to London to learn more about Ann, her disappearance and her death. She was financially self-sufficient at this point, but deeply troubled. Her father Michael had returned to Glasgow and reconnected with her mother and her two sisters. Not everyone realized that Michael was still a dangerous man where children were concerned.

None of Maureen's problems had been resolved as *Resolution* (Bantam, 2001) began. Angus Farrell had been charged with two counts of murder, but there was a serious possibility that he would not be convicted. His release would put both Maureen and her vulnerable friend Siobhan McCloud at great risk. The birth of her sister Una's daughter intensified Maureen's fears about her father. She had almost exhausted the windfall from Douglas Brady, only to learn that the Internal Revenue expected her to pay £6,000 in inheritance tax. Fighting her alcoholism, Maureen sought solutions that would not result in her arrest and imprisonment. The trilogy ended as she did so.

A powerful trilogy. Mina continued her mystery writing with a series featuring Paddy Meehan.

Jake O'Hara

Author: Noreen Wald

Jake O'Hara (baptized Jacqueline Grace after two of her mother's heroines of the times, Jackie Kennedy and Grace Kelly) preferred to be known as Jake. She had attended the finest schools her mother could afford: Convent of the Sacred Heart for high school and Manhattanville for college. Jake earned a bachelor's degree that she put to work as a ghostwriter, writing fiction and non-fiction to be published under the name of her client.

There was a support group in New York called Ghostwriters Anonymous where such writers gathered to share their contempt for their employers, bemoan the lack of credit they received for their work, and talk about plans to write their own books. Like AAA, the individuals referred to themselves at meetings only by first names and the initials of their last names. Over the series, the individual Ghostwriters who assisted Jake in her investigations included morbid Modesty Meade, gay Too Tall Tom, and quiet but successful Jane Dowling.

Maura, Jake's mom, was a constant presence in her life. Her marriage to Jack O'Hara, an ex-Marine who became a salesman, had not lasted. Jake loved her dad and mourned his eventual death. Maura and Jake managed quite well in an inherited co-op apartment in the exclusive Carnegie Hill area of New York City.

Jake's life was thrown into confusion in *Ghostwriter* (Berkley, 1999). She had become the center of attention for several handsome men, including a hypno-therapist, an attorney, and a NYPD detective. However, membership in Ghostwriters Anonymous was decimated by murder. The worst news was that the recent victims were all associated with Edgar-winning crime novelist Kate Lloyd Conners. Jake had just hired on to ghostwrite Kate's latest book. Although the modus operandi for the killings was quirky, the narrative read smoothly with witty dialogue.

The murder of caustic book critic Richard Peter in *Death Comes for the Critic* (Berkley, 2000) had enough suspects to fill a jury box. Jake benefited from Peter's death. Under the *qui bono* theory, she could have been included. The Ghostwriters pitched in, eliminating suspects. Unfortunately the killer eliminated several more. Jake juggled her feelings for high-powered attorney Dennis Kim and NYPD detective Ben Rubin. Her mother Maura would have settled for either one to get Jake married.

Two of the three celebrity panelists at a Greater New York Crime Writer's Conference died of poisoning in *Death Never Takes a Holiday* (Berkley, 2000). The holiday was St. Patrick's Day. The poison was administered in green beer served by a leprechaun. Motives abounded for the deaths of a dying U.S. Senator and a former actress who promoted creative cruises. Jake went overboard in investigating the disparate motivations, which included theft of the Faith diamond, euthanasia services, and a thirty-four-year-old rape case. The Ghostwriters pitched in to help as always.

As *Remembrance of Murders Past* (Berkley, 2001) began, Maura O'Hara witnessed the murder of Father Billy Blake while waiting in the confessional. No way could Jake stay out of this case. Her mother, now engaged to former district attorney and prospective U.S. Senator Aaron Rubin, was in danger. The Ghostwriters had questions to ask. Jake's involvement was more personal. The murder of Karen Scanlon had coincided with Jake's birth thirty-four years ago, and she felt her presence in her dreams and responses to people and settings. A spookier slant on murder.

There were flaws. Not everyone likes astral clues. The multiple suspects, helpers, and motivations cluttered the narratives. That should not keep a reader from having fun with Jake.

Enter Dying (Berkley, 2002) brought Jake to the realization that she would have to make some personal decisions. Maura, who would soon be Mrs. Aaron Rubin, would be spending much of her time in Washington, D. C. Would Jake stay on in the co-op her mother had inherited or would she find a place of her own? How much longer, at age thirty-four could she keep attorney Dennis Kim dangling, while she was still attracted to NYPD homicide chief Ben Rubin? Her involvement in the murder of aging actress Elaine Eden pushed Jake toward crises. Through Dennis, she had been hired to ghost/edit the script for Elaine's starring role in the production of *Susie Q*, a musical based on a novel Jake had ghost written. Elaine's death on stage during a rehearsal had her replacement, her co-star, the composer, director and producer all pointing fingers at one another. An indecisive ending as to romance.

Freddie O'Neal

Author: Catherine Dain

Freddie O'Neal, who grew up in Reno, graduated from the University of Nevada-Reno. Fortunately, she did not gamble, except for an occasional Keno card, because she had no luck at all. After Danny, her unfaithful father, deserted his family, her mother married a man for whom Freddie had no affection. The man she loved, Rob McIntire, married someone else. A tall rawboned blonde, Freddie ran a small-time detective agency out of her home. Her support system consisted of political reporter Sandra Herrick, African-American veteran Deke Adams now a guard at a local casino, and two cats, Butch and Sundance.

As a teenager, Freddie had a major crush on Mick Halliday, now a Los Vegas gambler. In *Lay It on the Line* (Jove, 1992), Joan, Mick's wife, hired Freddie to find the absconding caretaker for her ailing father. Freddie and Deke found the stolen car, but with a trunk full of cocaine. When Joan's prominent sister was murdered, Joan was the primary suspect.

Freddie's flying lessons came in handy in *Sing a Song of Death* (Jove, 1993). She flew the jet carrying singer Vince Marina when the pilot collapsed. Before she could determine the cause of the pilot's illness, Vince was murdered. He had refused a bodyguard initially although there had been a prior attempt on his life. Freddie's subsequent investigation involved both personal friends and hardened casino owners.

In *Walk a Crooked Mile* (Jove, 1994), it became vital for Freddie to locate her father. She began her search with Sam Courter, a Marine Corps buddy of Danny O'Neal. There were powerful forces that wanted Danny kept quiet, even if they had to kill him. An extensive search led Freddie to believe that Danny, dead or alive, had been a witness to murder.

By *Lament for a Dead Cowboy* (Berkley, 1994), Sam Courter had become the man in Freddie's life, but he had never forgotten the woman he married. On a shared trip to Elko, Nevada for a cowboy poet gathering, their relationship was tested. Sam was accused of murdering cowboy poet Carl Baxter, who had "stolen" his wife and he refused to discuss his case with Freddie.

In *Bet Against the House* (Berkley, 1995), Ted Scope's business flourished under his direction, but his death created consternation. His will left widow Gloria in control, and she reveled in it. Their three children disagreed on everything except to fight the will. Freddie was hired to get "dirt" on Gloria. By the time Gloria was murdered, Freddie had become her ally, and was determined to find the killer. Before her death, Gloria did Freddie a favor. She introduced her to an attractive university professor who made up for Sam's absence.

Professor Curtis Breckinridge helped Freddie face two crises during *The Luck of the Draw* (Berkley, 1996). When Al, her stepfather, had a heart attack, Ramona, Freddie's mom, moved in with her temporarily. That was a domestic crisis. Freddie's search for a student debtor involved her in university politics and murder at a more serious level.

Freddie felt contentment in her life with Breckinridge, but it all went up in gun smoke as *Dead Man's Hand* (Berkley, 1997) began. Hispanic teenager Jamie Morales held up Freddie and Curtis in a mall parking lot. Within minutes Curtis had been wounded and Freddie had killed his attacker. Within days, Curtis was in the local hospital under the watchful eye of his aristocratic mother and Freddie was the darling of the right wing gun lobby. Her life was unalterably changed. She had to make major decisions, as did Curtis, but not today.

Author Catherine Dain has a new series featuring Faith Cassidy, a former actress, now a therapist. She has also published a collection of short stories, *Dreams of Jeannie and Other Stories* and participated in at least two anthologies.

Allison O'Neil

Author: Lauren Wright Douglas

Blending in was not one of Allison O'Neil's goals. A redhead by nature, she dyed her hair assorted colors, had a pierced eyebrow and a black cat tattoo. Her clothes were shabby and funky. Her father, William Martin, had decamped when Allison was four. Mother Maureen returned to her maiden name. She died when Allison was a college senior. At that point Allison lost interest in graduation and dropped out. For a while she worked in a bookstore. As the series began, she was running a mail order mystery and science fiction book search business out of her home. The business was called Lorien, after the home of the elves in *Lord of the Rings.*

An unexpected bequest sent Allison to Lavner Bay, Oregon in *Death at Lavender Bay* (Naiad, 1996). The community was a gathering place for lesbians. Aunt Grace, with whom she had no contact since her mother's death, had left Allison $10,000 and an attractive bed and breakfast hostelry. Permanent residents who paid no rent inhabited the B&B. Allison's original intention was to sell the place and return to her California home. Her conviction that Aunt Grace had been murdered kept her there long enough to learn the truth and to delay plans to sell. Allison added a new boarder and a potential lover when she involved Kerry Owyhee, a Native American private investigator in her probe.

Aunt Grace was known for her generous hospitality to those in need. In *Swimming Cat Cove* (Naiad, 1997) Allison, plagued by empty rooms at the bed and breakfast, wondered if she could survive. Osie, the eleven-year-old daughter of the inn's caretaker, and private investigator Kerry persuaded a reluctant Alison to give sanctuary to a nine-year-old girl threatened by a neglectful father and his pornographic acquaintances.

Author Douglas has a longer series featuring Caitlin Reece (see Volume 2)

Kathleen O'Shaughnessy

Author: Ruth Raby Moen

Kathleen O'Shaughnessy provided limited personal background. Her father, a Vietnam War veteran, had abandoned the family. She had been deflowered at her senior prom, had attended Kitsap Lutheran College where she took courses in journalism, and then worked for a law office. She was described as having blonde curly hair and being very proud of her red 1973 Porsche.

Only One Way Out (Flying Swan, 1994) had the later copyright date but the events narrated preceded those in *Deadly Deceptions*. Kathleen accompanied her fiancé Casey on a Labor Day weekend trip into the Cascade Mountain range. By the end of the first day, they had become lost, found a corpse, and had their car disabled. Then it got worse. At the conclusion Kathleen changed boyfriends and careers, taking a job on the *Seattle Gazette*.

Kathleen was dissatisfied with her assignments at the *Seattle Gazette*. At thirty-one, she was ready for change. A phone call from Camille Cloud, a young mystic on the Suquamish Indian Reservation, during *Deadly Deceptions* (Flying Swan Publications, 1994) was a potential solution. Camille indicated that her father, tribal leader Joe Cloud who opposed leasing land to a gambling combine, had been abducted. En route via a car ferry, Kathleen noticed a family group in which two children were treated very badly. Kathleen's intervention brought her into contact with a handsome conniver who hoped to involve her in his schemes. She bumbled through kidnapping, child abuse, smuggling and twins split at birth, but she earned her scoop.

What had begun as routine coverage of the Skagit County Fair in *Return to the Kill* (Flying Swan, 1996) ballooned into sex scandals, murder, and the discovery of municipal corruption. Kathleen's sister Patti, whom she hoped to visit, had remarried. Her new husband Dwayne was involved in a potentially violent militia movement. Kathleen's efforts to protect Patti's son Jeffrey and his young friend Billy put them all in danger. Billy's dad, Deputy Sheriff Benjamin Jack, was an attractive ally.

These were earnest narratives but the small print made them difficult to read. Moen used a different spelling for Kathleen's last name in her later books. Another potential book in the series, *In Harm's Way*, was not located on the Internet or in libraries.

Victory "Torie" O'Shea

Author: Rett MacPherson, pseudonym for Laurette Allen a.k.a. Lauretta Dickhenber

Torie O'Shea's obsessive-compulsive strain, which can be a handicap, worked well for her as a genealogist, where attention to detail was important. It had helped in her prior job in a bank. If genealogy was her passion, her income came primarily from work at Gaheimer House, a historical society that also prized methodical precision. Torie was married to Rudy, had two daughters, and was pregnant with their third child as the series began. They lived on a two-acre piece of land near New Kassel, Missouri where they raised chickens. She sang privately with her Dad's band, although he had been divorced from her mother due to his chronic infidelity. In her early thirties, weight was another problem for Torie at 5' 2".

Torie's mother had contracted polio as a teenager, forcing her to spend her life in a wheelchair. She had been unable to finish high school as a result of the inadequate programs for the handicapped in West Virginia at that time, but was an accomplished artist. Torie's real name, Victory, was a celebration of her birth, because her mother thought she would never be able to bear a child. Torie had a tense relationship with her mother-in-law who blamed her because Rudy no longer practiced his Catholic religion. Torie did not have a close personal relationship with her boss, elderly Sylvia Pershing, president of the New Kassel Historical Society, but they had mutual respect. Enough so that Sylvia entrusted Torie with personal documentation of her youthful relationship with wealthy Hermann Gaheimer, which enabled Torie to release Sylvia from a sense of guilt.

Local businesswoman Norah Zumwalt made it clear in *Family Skeletons* (St. Martin's Paperbacks, 1997) that her purpose in seeking a five-generation genealogy was to find her father. Eugene Counts had served in World War II, leaving before he could marry her mother, and never returning. Before Torie could make her aware that Eugene was not only alive, but also lived nearby, Norah was murdered. Her current relationships, two estranged children and an unfaithful beau, provided as many suspects as did Torie's extended investigation of Eugene Counts. Torie was reminded that she had a husband and two vulnerable children to consider. The motivation of the killer seemed weaker than that attributed to other suspects.

Rudy was a very patient man in *A Veiled Antiquity* (St. Martin, 1998). He did not remonstrate with Torie when she searched a house in which a murder had been committed while their two children were present. Fortunately he was unaware that she had stolen (no other word for it) a packet hidden in victim Marie Dijon's home. Torie marshaled her genealogical materials, her history books, and her allies to trap a killer. They added a lost dachshund named Fritz to the household.

Torie was looking to her own family's past in *A Comedy of Heirs* (St. Martin, 1999). She had learned that her great-grandfather, Nate Ulysses Keith, had been murdered fifty years before. His wife, Della Ruth had kept the family in the home at gunpoint as Nate died slowly outside. A clipping describing the murder sent Torie back into her family history. Her generation had no knowledge of the circumstances of the death. She wondered if it was too late to find Nate's killer. Torie's quest reunited her with her father and led her to accept the man who was to become her stepfather.

Torie had no idea why one-hundred-and-one-year-old Clarissa Holt had insisted that she be present at the reading of her will in *A Misty Mourning* (St. Martin, 2000). Clarissa was not even dead when the invitation was issued. She was murdered soon after Torie and Grandma Gert arrived. The will bequeathed a three-story boarding house plus ten acres of West Virginia land to Torie because of a kindness shown to Clarissa three generations earlier. Along with the bequest came the obligation to clear herself as a suspect in Clarissa's death. It did not help that Torie was seven months pregnant with her third child.

Killing Cousins (St. Martin, 2002) may be the best of the series so far. Readers who remember their own childhoods or had contacts with children of an impressionable age will not dismiss it lightly. Torie swallowed hard when Jalena, her mother, married Sheriff Colin Brooke, then set off with him on a three- week honeymoon in Alaska. Torie experienced some post-partum depression after Matthew's birth. She had two major projects to keep her mind occupied. (1) Colin had purchased the contents of reclusive jazz singer Catherine Finch's estate. Torie was to select the saleable items and catalog them for Colin's antique shop; (2) Sylvia Pershing assigned Torie to a biography of Catherine Finch who had ended her career after the disappearance of her infant son, Byron. The projects intermeshed.

For a genealogist locating an unknown relative can be an achievement, but in *Blood Relations*(St. Martin, 2003) Torie was furious. She did not want to believe that Stephanie Connelly was her half-sister. Oh, the potential infidelity was no surprise. That's why Jalena had divorced Dwight. What hurt was that he had not told her. It was a relief to be diverted by the news that the low level in the Mississippi had put the Phantom steamboat partly above the waterline. The ship had sunk over eighty years ago, but myths about it still abounded. Why hadn't the captain survived? What happened to the Huntleigh heiress whose body was never found. Was there really a fortune in Arkansas diamonds left on board?

Aunt Sissie, to whom Torie was devoted had seemed highly stressed when she urged Torie to visit her Olin, Minnesota home in *In Sheep's Clothing* (St. Martin, 2004). Sissie seemed tired and frail but was primarily concerned with a novel/diary written 150 years before by a young Swedish immigrant. Sissie wanted Torie to use her genealogical talents to identify the author and learn what had become of her. Sheriff Brooke lent a hand, but took it hard when he was arrested for murder. Sylvia Pershing died, leaving Gaheimer House and considerable investments to Torie.

Although it was understandable that Torie was depressed by Sylvia's death in *Thicker Than Water* (St. Martin, 2005), her obsession with a photo postcard sent to Sylvia in 1950 was strange. The photo showed a young girl at a Dubuque railroad station. The message referred to a "forgotten promise". The natural tensions rising from Torie's new wealth were exacerbated by a visit from Rudy's mother and some dissension in the Historical Society. Someone was sneaking into Gaheimer House, even attacked Torie in a crowd.

There were changes in the O'Shea family during *Dead Man Running* (St. Martin, 2006). They were moving to the country, building a home that Torie and Rudy had planned together. At least that would take them away from current mayor and neighbor Bill Castlereagh. Colin Brooke was opposing Bill in the mayoralty election. Torie checked out Bill's life and family history. In this investigation, Torie came to realize that her aggressive behavior has made Rudy a frequent object of ridicule. Is she capable of change?

The news that the Kendall house and its contents were for sale excited Torie in *Died in the Wool* (St. Martin, 2007). Glory Anne Kendall, a gifted quilter, had died decades before. Torie's excitement grew when she and quilt expert Geena Campbell visited the house and inspected some of Glory's work. Yet, there was a dark side to purchasing the building. It had been the site of three horrible deaths, each victim a child of Sandy Kendall. His shell-shocked veteran son Rupert had hung himself. Soon afterwards Sandy's beloved daughter Glory died from drugs; finally, elder son Whalen shot himself. There was worse to come. Torie couldn't let go until she learned what it was.

MacPherson is one of the current authors who can write a reasonably concise mystery that is a fascinating read, as in *The Blood Ballad* (St. Martin's Minotaur, 2008). New information caused Torie to question facts in the family genealogy she had spent years to construct. Was her grandfather the bastard of famous fiddler Scott Morgan? Had Scott Morgan appropriated and copyrighted songs written by grandfather Keith? How did this connect to the decades old mystery of what happened to Beth Morgan, Scott's daughter-in-law, and to the recent murder of a descendant? Sylvia Pershing had left behind some of the answers in her meticulous records.

A solid series that improved over the years.

Laura Owen

Author: Louisa Dixon

At age thirty-eight, attorney Laura Owen had been appointed Commissioner of Public Safety in the state of Mississippi with the responsibility to enforce drug laws. She had attended "Ole Miss" for her undergraduate degree, earned a law degree at Virginia, and spent several years defending indigent clients in the criminal courts. Laura married architect Semmes Owen and they had a young son, Willis.

Semmes died in a car accident during *Next to Last Chance* (Genesis Press, 1998). Laura's decision to leave a comfortable job as an attorney in the state auditor's office for a more politicized position in government brought chaos into her life. Her son Will's life was threatened and she was framed for the murder of suspected drug smuggler Tom Hillman. Fortunately during her brief tenure in office, she had gained the confidence of her appointee for head of the State Patrol. Her achievements made her a target of rivals within the Mississippi political community.

Time had passed by *Outside Chance* (Genesis Press, 1999). Laura had been appointed Commissioner of Public Safety and head of the State Highway Patrol. She still mourned Semmes death, but was showing an interest in Vic Regis, Chief of Staff to Governor Gibbs Carver. Although Laura was aware of political corruption in the state government, she did not play a central role in the purported death of Brent Wexler, Carver's chief fundraiser. Her primary contribution was in the investigation of financial irregularities. She had previously worked in the State Auditor's office and put that expertise to work. I am indebted to my daughter-in-law, Vonne Meussling Barnett for this review. The book was not available to me at the time the initial Volume 3 was published, and it was too good to replace.

A third book in this very interesting series, *No Chance at All* had been announced, but Louisa Dixon withdrew it from Genesis Press. No information was available at this time as to whether or not it was published elsewhere.

Veronica Pace

Author: Philip Luber

The death of Veronica Pace's mother by a burglar had influenced her decision to become a prosecuting attorney after graduation from Harvard Law School. After serving as assistant district attorney for Bristol County, Rhode Island, she joined the FBI. Only a child when her mother died, she had been traumatized because she had seen the killer and felt guilty that she had survived. Her father had remarried a younger woman whom Veronica had difficulty accepting. She was a determined young woman, jogged regularly, set goals and attainted them ruthlessly. Not all of her desires could be met. She was unable to bear children.

Veronica was not the primary character in the series in which she appeared. Harry Kline, a widowed semi-retired psychiatrist, who had achieved notoriety for his book on Vietnam veterans and had independent means, had that role. When, during *Forgive Us Our Sins* (Fawcett, 1994), Harry researched family members of victims for a forthcoming book, he met Veronica. He contacted her on receiving pictures and notes sent by "Artie" who had killed a seemingly unrelated series of individuals. Together Veronica and Harry traced the deaths tied together by a penny left with the victims, but encountered the killer at personal risk. Kline decided not to write the book on victim's families, and began seeing patients again.

In *Deliver Us From Evil* (Fawcett, 1997), Veronica played an ancillary role, competing with a younger woman for Kline's attentions, but working out of the area on another case. Kline solved the mystery of a hit-and-run death, although concealing information from the police department, and forced a shoddy therapist to surrender his license. Veronica and her family had become very fond of Melissa, Harry's daughter. Melissa's initial resistance to Veronica as her father's romantic interest helped Veronica accept her own stepmother as a friend.

By *Pray For Us Sinners* (Fawcett, 1998) Veronica had moved into the housekeeper's vacant apartment on Kline's estate, although he was still mourning his deceased wife. The prologue returned to the night when Veronica entered her mother's room, and saw her killer who said, "Until we meet again" as he exited. She had never been able to erase this memory. Veronica took a leave of absence, reviewed the case file, revisited her family home now occupied by a Mafia don, and offered a substantial reward for information leading to the identification of the killer. It was Kline who made the decision as to the outcome of the case.

Harry Kline was not happy when Veronica's former lover Steven Farr stopped in during *Have Mercy on Us* (Fawcett, 1999). Harry needed personal time to talk to Veronica, but he was also irritated by Steven's over-familiarity. Purportedly Steven had come to the area to meet with his fiancée Sandi O'Neill; after which they were to go on a camping trip. Harry had already been made aware by Chief of Police Alfred Korvich and Detective Kay Wheaton of the savage murder of an unidentified woman near Walden Pond. He contacted them when he became aware that Steven had been unable to reach Sandi for several days. As an FBI agent, Veronica made Steven aware that he would need to be cooperative with the police; as a friend, she offered him a place to stay, an apartment over their barn. Subsequent murders and local resentments over a real estate development near Walden kept both Harry and Veronica busy.

Exciting concepts and good characterizations.

Lorraine Page

Author: Lynda La Plante

Lorraine Page was a former police officer who subsequently ran her own investigation agency in Los Angeles. Upset by the death of her police partner, she had begun drinking. Under the influence of alcohol, Lorraine had caused the death of a young boy. Her guilt precipitated even heavier drinking which wrecked her marriage and ended her future in the police department. As the series began, Lorraine had been divorced from Mike Page for over five years, during which he had custody of their two daughters, Sally and Julie. She had no contact with the girls. Lorraine planned to deal with her scarred face by surgery sometime in the future. Her regular companion was a dog, "Tiger," part wolfhound and part Malamute.

As *Cold Shoulder* (Macmillan, 1994) began, Lorraine had been helped to recovery by Rosie Hurst, a fellow alcoholic. The need for money to buy liquor had led Lorraine into the clutches of a serial killer. After she escaped from him, she could not deny her responsibility to identify him. Her return to sobriety correlated with her role in his capture. The change in her life did not include a reunion with her children at this time.

In *Cold Blood* (Macmillan, 1996), Anne Louise Caley, indulged daughter of faded actress Elizabeth Seals, and her husband, real estate developer Robert Caley, disappeared. The police and initial investigators had no luck in finding the girl. A chance encounter sent the case to newly founded Page Investigations, which consisted of Rosie Hurst and Lorraine. Their investigation was saturated with betrayal, voodoo, and death. They were the only happy survivors, emerging wealthy, but not necessarily healthier or wiser.

Cold Heart (Macmillan, 1998) was the final narrative in the trilogy. As it began, Lorraine seemed to have a new life. The one million-dollar bonus she had earned on the prior case subsidized a new office, a new truck and car, the down payment on a new home, and the financing for her plastic surgery. Her new client was Cindy Nathan, young wife of a major studio executive who had been found dead of gunshot wounds in his swimming pool. When Cindy was found dead, the easy answer would have been suicide from guilt. Instead Lorraine uncovered fraud and made plans for her own future. It would include a reunion with her daughters, and more time with a man who loved her as she was then, but she paid a price.

La Plante has had a stable of winners over the years, mostly BBC series that were novelized; the latest is detective Anna Travis

Julian Palmer

Author: Jonathan Stone

Julian was a strange woman, who changed from one book to another. Some of her actions were unbelievably naïve, even foolish. The murder of her father, which took place in the family home when she was a child, had a profound effect on Julian's development. She was reluctant to share her past with others. Frequent mention was made of her beauty, her coal-black hair, startling features and the impact they had on men. Although she originally came from a small Southern town, she had attended and excelled at the Police Academy, leading to a position on the New York City Police Department.

Julian had two reasons for applying for an internship position at Cannanville, New York in *The Cold Truth* (St. Martin, 1999). Born and raised in the South, she relished the concept of deep snow, something she had never experienced. More seriously, she was impressed by the reputation of the Cannanville chief of police, Winston "Bear" Edwards. He boasted that he solved murders within two weeks. How many had there been in his thirty years in a small town? However he hadn't been smart enough to realize that "Julian", his new intern, was female until she walked into his office ready for duty. Edwards was struggling with a recent murder, the savage stabbing of waitress Sarah Langley. He had been unable to pinpoint her killer in what he referred to as "a perfect crime". The appearance of "psychic" Wayne Hill provided new clues and new directions. Julian was impressed by Edward's thorough research, but had ideas of her own as to who killed Sarah.

The Heat of Lies (St. Martin, 2001) brought "Bear" Edwards back into Julian's life. She had risen to the rank of lieutenant in the Troy, NY police department. Their parting had been acrimonious to say the least. His decision to visit her was unclear; her desperate attempt to use him to solve a troubling murder brought her into conflict with her superior officer. The death of Francis Ryan, father of two young daughters, bore a considerable resemblance to that of Julian's father's murder. She and her sister Stephanie had been about the same ages as Alyshia and Annabelle Ryan. The connection also resonated with Edwards. The engrossing narrative was built upon too many unlikely plot devices.

Tom Hartley was the primary viewpoint character in *Breakthrough* (St. Martin, 2003), an underachieving forty-year-old man still living with his mother. A chance encounter with beautiful business executive Laura Hodges changed all that. He speculated on the stock market based on that meeting; then was shocked to learn that Laura, who had so fascinated him, was dead. He needed to know more about her, about the silver cylinder she carried in her brief-case, the acquisition of inventor Nathan Cartmann's company. Like the fictional character in the movie, *Laura* she re-entered his life. Julian Palmer, temporarily working as an insurance investigator, provided a counter balance. She was taking maternity leave without pay to care for the child of a teenager, but working part-time for an insurance agency that had a financial interest in the turmoil at Peale Investments, Laura's employer. Tom and Julian were lonely people who bonded, as he grew to know Julian, he also learned more about Laura.

Charlotte "Charlie" Parker

Author: Connie Shelton

Charlie Parker and her brother, Ron, had been close since childhood, but the death of their parents in an air crash when she was sixteen deepened that relationship. Their father, a scientist, worked for Sandia Labs doing top-secret work during the Cold War. Their mother, a member of a wealthy and prominent family, spent her time in Junior League and country club activities. During the first years after the accident, Charlie lived with her grandmother. When old enough she moved next door into the home her parents had occupied before their death, sharing it with a mixed breed dog, named Rusty. She had become a tiny auburn-haired woman in her thirties without a husband or children. Another brother, Paul, occasionally visited with his wife and two rambunctious children. Charlie did not initially have a private investigators license. Her experience came when she uncovered theft in the trust fund left to her by her parents, and again when she assisted a neighbor who was being defrauded by an insurance agent. Bolstered by her accounting degree, CPA certification, and experience with a major corporation, Charlie opened an investigation agency with recently divorced brother Ron.

Loyalty was important to Charlie, so why in *Deadly Gamble* (Intrigue, 1995) did she agree to find a valuable watch for Stacy North, the woman who "stole" her fiancé years before? When gambler Gary Detweiler who had stolen the watch was murdered, Stacy needed help. Connie, realizing that Stacy was tied to a controlling husband, lent a hand. Stacy deserved it. She'd saved Connie from an unhappy marriage.

That investigation left Charlie tired and depressed so she headed to Kauai, Hawaii in *Vacations Can Be Murder* (Intrigue. 1995). She spotted the corpse of Gilbert Page during a helicopter tour of the island. Charlie's personal interest in pilot Drake Langston drew her into the murder investigation. She must have failed to take the ethics course in business school. She entered private offices, read personal and business mail, and lied about her identity.

At the time of her parents' death, Charlie had asked few questions. Fifteen years later, in *Memories Can Be Murder* (Intrigue, 1995), she couldn't stop asking them. Why had reports of the Sandia plane crash been removed from the FAA office? Why had the fact that the crash had been caused by a bomb brought on board in the pilot's carry-on been concealed? Why were people even now willing to burn buildings and kill informants when the need for secrecy about the Sandia project was long past? People were getting hurt!

With heartache at her separation from Drake Langston and a headache from fourteen stitches in her head, Charlie returned to New Mexico in *Partnerships Can Kill* (Intrigue, 1997). High school friend Sharon Ortega had financial and personal problems in her restaurant business—some of which stemmed from her partner David Ruiz. Charlie's expertise was needed not only in auditing the books, but also in determining whether or not David committed suicide. The business insurance would be ineffective unless Charlie could find a killer, someone other than Sharon. In her spare time, Charlie protected Ron from a predatory female.

A casual visit to a small New Mexican town in *Small Towns Can Be Murder* (Intrigue, Press 1998) spurred Charlie's interest in the miscarriage and death of Cynthia Martinez, a young Hispanic woman whose husband might be an abuser. Combating the silence of the isolated community, Charlie uncovered a vicious conspiracy.

Drake had moved from Hawaii to New Mexico where he was building up a charter flight business. His plan to fly ski charters to Taos in the New Mexico Mountains during *Honeymoons Can Be Murder* (Intrigue, 2001) had a dual purpose. Besides the income, it would provide him and Charlie a delightful place to spend the early days of their marriage. Included in the deal Drake had worked out was the rental of a secluded cabin in the woods. Because their own home was being remodeled, this fit into Charlie's plans too. Two new cases for RJP Investigations came with the site: the need (1) to prove their new friend Eloy Romero had not murdered his priest brother; and (2) to check a possible case of false identity. Charlie, as usual, had no compunction about stealing and reading privileged material; then concealing the information.

Dorothy Schwartzman was not an ideal client for RJP Investigations during *Reunions Can Be Murder* (Intrigue, 2002). Charlie actually disliked Dorothy and mistrusted her motives. What she hired them for was to search for her father, long time prospector Willie McBride. Too much pressure from Dorothy and her brother Felix sent Willie and his pal Bud Tucker up in the hills. One was found dead; the other became a suspect until an explosion changed the picture.

Competition Can Be Murder (Intrigue, 2004) took Charlie and Drake to the coast of Scotland when they went to help old friend Brian Swinney. Brian, operator of the Air-Sea Helicopter Company, needed to spend time with his dying mother. Charlie and Drake would fulfill his contract to ferry men and materials to and from coastal oil rigs. Only after they arrived were they aware of the hostility of the unionized oil workers who aligned themselves with fellow unionists operating a water transport system

Balloons Can Be Murder (Intrigue, 2005) was a disappointing entry in the series. Attorney and balloonist Rachael Fairfield came to RJP Investigations because she was receiving threatening letters. These arrived as she was preparing to set a new class record during the annual Albuquerque International Balloon Fiesta. Because Rachael had testified against her own father in a child molestation case, she believed he was the letter writer. While Ron watched William Fairfield, now released from prison, Charlie acted as Rachael's bodyguard, but looked elsewhere for suspects. Incredible plotline.

Charlie and Drake planned a low-key vacation at Watson's Lake, but in *Obsessions Can Be Murder* (Intrigue, 2006), it just didn't happen. They arrived in town on the fourth anniversary of a gas explosion that destroyed the home of David and Earleen Simmons, killing housekeeper Bettina Davis. David, who had been seen leaving town the prior afternoon, had never returned. Earleen was more interested in the insurance than her missing husband. Only Amanda Zellinger, David's daughter by a prior marriage, was concerned. When she heard that an investigator was in town, she hired Charlie. Drake had been called back to work so that fit into Charlie's plans. Ron, back in Albuquerque, provided significant information about the Simmons and Zellinger families.

A light series from an enterprising publisher. Next: *Holidays Can Be Murder* (2009); *Gossip Can Be Murder* (2010)

Lily Pascale

Author: Scarlett Thomas

Lily Pascale, who made frequent references to the fact that she had one green eye and one blue eye, was, at age twenty-five, a lecturer in English Literature at a Devon University. Her area of specialty was mystery fiction. For a period of time due to a temporary vacancy she served as acting head of the department. While in London, Lily had hoped for a career as an actress. Her parents were divorced. "Mum", who coordinated the Women's Studies program at the university, was writing a novel. Henri, Lily's French-born father, practiced psychiatry in London where he entertained his many female friends. Her younger brother Nat, who had a different father, was attending the local university. For all of the cosmopolitan elements in her life, Lily remained rather innocent, and unaware of her impact on others. She disliked flying, but smoked. When younger she and her dearest friend Eugenie, now deceased, had learned magic and card tricks. She enjoyed puzzles and riddles. Lily shared her Devon home with a half-Siamese cat, Maude.

A sudden decision to flee London in *Dead Clever* (Hodder and Stoughton, 1998) sent Lily back to her maternal home and a part-time position at the university. She was to replace an instructor in Contemporary Literature who had quit suddenly. New to the faculty, she was appalled to learn that one member of her class had been savagely murdered and a second student had died of a drug overdose. The attractive man with whom she had a date might be connected to these tragedies. Something sinister was happening on the campus.

Lily's fifteen minutes of fame as a crime investigator caused former college friend Jess Mallone, now a freelance journalist, to ask for help during *In Your Face* (Hodder & Stoughton, 1999). Jess had written a magazine article about three women who had been stalked. The day it was published, all three were murdered. With time on her hands, Lily went to London to escape the end of a romance and meet with Jess. Not only had Jess disappeared, but Lily also wondered if she had ever known her at all. The narrative was interspersed with the killer's responses to self-questioning.

Seaside (Hodder & Stoughton, 1999) was like the little girl with the curl in the middle of her forehead. When it was good, it was very very good. It wasn't always good however. Emma Winter offered Lily 10,000 pounds to find to discover which of the two Carter twins was dead (Laura or Alex); who had killed her and why. Lily could use the money but there was more than that involved. The victim had left a suicide note signed "Laura", but the survivor said that it was Alex who had been murdered. The character study of the interaction between the twins was interesting. The narrative was well plotted, but the third person inserts were distracting.

Martha Patterson

Author: Gretchen Sprague

After a successful career in the Trusts and Estates Division of Reilly Whitman, a prestigious law firm, attorney Martha Patterson had too many skills to waste her time. The death of her husband Edwin, former owner of an airfreight business, had left her lonely but financially secure. Her son Robert was married and lived with his wife and two children in California. Martha had been born and raised in Nebraska, the daughter of a state Supreme Court Justice, but she intended to stay in New York City. A chance encounter with Howard Wallace, who had interned at Reilly Whitman but turned to public service work, led to her volunteer job at West Brooklyn Legal Services (WBLS). She had been warned to avoid the "Mother Teresa Syndrome." Still Martha took a personal interest in the people she served. She could not help contrasting their lives with those of her former wealthy clients. In her late sixties, she remained a physically active woman. Tennis was no longer an option but she chose to walk, rather than ride, whenever possible. She was interested in modern art and had a social life.

Meeting Wilma Oberfell at WBLS on her first day at the office in *Death in Good Company* (St. Martin, 1997) made an impact on Martha. Not only did Wilma seem distrustful of other staff members, but Martha was impressed by her excellent grammar. She was surprised that Wilma followed her home; then, left without speaking. When Martha went to Wilma's home to check on her, she was dead. Although she had other legal work to deal with, the murder of Howard Wallace, who had introduced her to the agency, convinced Martha that something was terribly wrong with WBLS.

Martha had moved on from WBLS by *Maquette for Murder* (St. Martin, 2000). She still volunteered for Sunny Searles' social services projects, but was also busy doing legal research for small firms. Because he had shown an interest in modern sculpture, she invited her accountant, Joe Gianni to accompany her to a showing by her friend, Hannah Gold. In the mid-hours of the night, Martha was awakened by a frantic phone call from Hannah. She had been struck on the head, her maquette (a scale model of a larger piece) had been destroyed and her handsome young assistant Kent Reed was dead. Fortunately, Phil Sharpman, who had worked with Hannah in the prior case, was involved. Unfortunately, Martha waited to share what she had learned with him.

Being a retired attorney posed a problem for Martha in *Murder in a Heat Wave* (St. Martin, 2003). Friends and acquaintances were too eager to fill her time with their problems. Would she be a candidate for the co-op board? The current board chairman Arnold Stern had been murdered, leaving a half-dozen potential suspects. Had there been kickbacks after a recent remodeling of the lobby? Could she keep confidential a revelation by an eight-year-old witness? Would she review the will of her dying friend, Irene Xendopoulis? Some matters could be delegated; some ignored, but not murder.

A solid series. Sprague had just begun a new series, but died shortly after the first book was published.

Dr. Andi Pauling

Author: Lillian M. Roberts

Andi Pauling, a tiny blonde, grew up in southern Illinois, near St. Louis. Her mother had a painful death from cancer while Andi was in college. She did not have a close relationship with her father, who had not been supportive of her career plans. Andi had never forgotten fellow veterinary student Ross McRoberts. He had been there to help her with her studies. The possibility of a romance between them ended when she rebuffed an overture, a decision she later regretted. Ross married Eastern socialite Kelsey Vallice shortly after graduation and moved to Kentucky. Andi joined Dr. Doolittle's Pet Care in Palm Springs California run by Dr. Philip Harris. Eventually she became a part owner of the business. Harris' death revealed serious financial problems. Andi ran the clinic alone for a while; then Dr. Trinka Romanescu, who had worked for the Animal Emergency Center, joined her. Trinka would be the managing partner in charge of finances. They occasionally disagreed as to the need for new equipment, hiring of additional staff, and Andi's overly generous nature. She had a problem saying "no," dressed very casually, and over the years had adopted numerous dogs and cats in need of homes. She did not, however, want children because they might bring heartbreak. Marriage was only a remote possibility in her plans.

Andi was still playing catch-up with her bills when Dr. Ross McRoberts reappeared in *Riding for a Fall* (Fawcett Gold Medal, 1996). His marriage had ended. He was planning to relocate, but was temporarily caught up in polo playing. He was also temporarily short of funds, so Andi offered him lodging. Andi's experience with animals had been directed toward small pets, rather than horses. Ross drew her into the wealthy world of competitive polo. She was unprepared for the vicious attacks on Ross' horses, the murder of devious Berto Gutierrez with whom Ross had quarreled, and Ross' strange behavior.

When Andi saw the injured dog in *The Hand That Feeds You* (Fawcett, 1997), she realized that its condition was the result of a commercial dogfight. Within days Willard Hanes, the dog's owner, had been viciously murdered and Nikki, his mute eight-year-old daughter, had disappeared. Andi, who had found the corpse, was unable to leave the matter to the authorities. Her instincts told her that dog fighting was minor compared to other aligned activities. Clay Tanner, the attractive owner of a neighboring horse farm, showed a personal interest. Until her health concerns were settled, Andi could not respond.

Andi had euthanized a seriously ill Sheltie belonging to philanthropist Gilda Hopkins several years before *Almost Human* (Fawcett, 1998) began. She was shocked to receive a videotaped plea from Gilda, asking for help in her own death. Andi had never forgotten her mother's painful cancer death. Her visits to Gilda made her vulnerable to charges that she had murdered the woman. The narrative gave close to equal attention to the treatment of Sally, a chimpanzee and her endangered infant.

Author Lillian M. Roberts did not hesitate to take on serious issues, i.e. animal and child abuse, drugs, and euthanasia.

Karen Pelletier

Author: Joanne Dobson

Karen Pelletier's parents were low-income emigrants from French Canada. She initially seemed destined to live a life much like her mother's. Married and pregnant by eighteen, she left her brutish husband when his anger spilled over on their daughter. Determined to make a life for herself and young Amanda, she went back to school part-time while working at a variety of menial jobs, eventually earning a Ph.D.

Karen's first professional work was at a New York City College where she began a significant affair with police captain Tony Gorman. Their relationship had real importance to Karen, but not enough to reconsider her decision to take a more prestigious offer from Enfield College in Massachusetts. Tony, who wanted a wife and children, accepted her decision and married someone else. As the series began, Amanda was a Georgetown University student; Karen, an untenured professor at the private school.

Karen's expertise in the works of Emily Dickinson was a significant factor in *Quieter Than Sleep* (Doubleday, 1997). It may have been the reason why Professor Randy Astin-Berger sought an opportunity to talk to her just before he was murdered. The exposé of a killer led also to new information about Dickinson's involvement with a libidinous historical figure. Karen's romantic interest in college president Avery Mitchell might have seemed mutual. However, Mitchell was careful to avoid a conflict of interest and hoped to reconcile with his wife. Karen's awe of the sophisticated Mitchell blinded her to the more humble talents of a local police lieutenant.

Karen was popular with most of her students, but she experienced considerable problems with the college administration in *The Northbury Papers* (Doubleday, 1998). The head of her department was disdainful of Karen's interest in the works of Serena Northbury, whose Nineteenth century novels they considered unworthy of academic attention. Karen's discovery of members of the Northbury family in Enfield, coupled with the death of wealthy descendant Edith Hart, made her a murder suspect. She was a collateral beneficiary of a trust that established a department at Enfield to explore the works of American women writers. While seeking an unpublished Northbury novel, Karen frightened a killer who thought she knew too much already. Fortunately the officer on the case was the same Lt. Piotrowski whom she had met in the earlier book.

The ultimate betrayal to academics, plagiarism, played a role in two separate mysteries in *The Raven and the Nightingale* (Doubleday, 1999). First, was the recent death of Elliot Corbin, an arrogant and ambitious professor in Karen's department; second, the purported suicide of a young poetess involved with Edgar Allan Poe a century before. Karen's contacts with Lt. Charlie Piotrowski made a slight move toward friendship, but daughter Amanda strengthened her ties to her own past. The conclusion left untidy endings in the lives of supporting characters.

A flip remark by Karen, nominating *Oblivion Falls* as the outstanding book of the Twentieth century during *Cold and Pure and Very Dead* (Doubleday, 2000) brought reclusive author Mildred Deakins to public attention after fifty years of anonymity. The attention was unwelcome and became worse when Martin Katz, the reporter who publicized Karen's recommendation, was murdered. *Oblivion Falls* had been a roman à clef. Karen believed that the motive for Katz's murder and a subsequent killing lay in events described in the book and reflected in Mildred's personal life. The killer was close enough to touch. The narrations were interspersed with excerpts from *Oblivion Falls.* Well done, but there were too many coincidences. The experience made Karen more understanding of her own mother.

A major conference on the mystery was to take place on the Endfield campus when *The Maltese Manuscript* (Poisoned Pen Press, 2003) began. Crimes were occurring as they prepared. Valuable books were stolen from the college library. Famous author Sunnye Hardcastle was to be a featured speaker. Over the narrative, she became a nuisance to Karen who was to escort her; then a confederate when they and Amanda investigated the thefts and a murder. By this time Sunnye had become a friend. Karen needed a friend because she and Charlie were not getting along. She was tempted by her high school friend, Dennis O'Hanlon, now a private investigator and very knowledgeable about thefts of books from college libraries.

These were literary mysteries, but Karen was free of the intellectual arrogance of some academic sleuths. She showed genuine interest in her students, particularly those who shared her background.

Daisy Perika

Author: James Doss

Daisy Perika, an elderly Native American who had outlived two husbands, gradually tempered her Christian religion with a return to the shamanism of her Ute tribe. Her visions and signs alerted her when trouble was on the horizon. Tribal policeman Charlie Moon was the real focus of the series which was subtitled in his name, although Daisy was an on-going resource character in the narratives.

The Shaman Sings (St. Martin, 1994) concerned the death of Priscilla Song, university researcher who had recently made a significant breakthrough.

Scott Parris, the local police chief, and Anne Foster, an attractive young reporter, were unwilling to settle for the obvious suspect, Priscilla's lover, but it was Daisy who snared the killer.

Daisy had a larger role in *The Shaman Laughs* (St. Martin, 1995) when her friend and confidante, Nahum Yaciiti, disappeared. Her "favorite nephew," police officer Charlie Moon, searched for the old shepherd. Daisy, in peril of losing her homestead to a government proposal to store nuclear waste, also disappeared. Cattle mutilators and killers were no match for Daisy's dreams and her consultations with Pitukupf, a dwarf spirit who lived in the canyon.

Daisy was having visions as *The Shaman's Bones* (Avon, 1997) began, and she wanted Chief of Police Scott Parris to be aware of trouble to come. His decision to postpone his vacation based on her prophecy was fortunate. Ambitious Ute tribal member Provo Frank abandoned his wife Mary's corpse and fled with his daughter, Sarah, to the reservation and Daisy's protection. The bone of contention was a whistle, a sacred emblem of power. The manner of Mary's death and the prospective danger to Sarah caused Daisy to call upon her spiritual powers and Pitukupf.

The Sun Dancers of the Ute Mountain Tribe were tested for endurance. They fasted from food and liquids in a continuous dance, seeking a dream vision and the power it provided. During *The Shaman's Game* (Avon, 1998), two dancers died, seemingly of natural causes, but there were rumors of a witch. Charlie and Daisy attended the summer dances on the mountain: he, in his professional capacity; she, because she was determined to deal with the witch. Another watcher sought revenge for the death of a young Shoshone dancer. At the end, Charlie did not know, or did not want to know, who had intervened to silence the witch, but he grieved.

Father-daughter relationships played important roles in *The Night Visitor* (Avon, 1999). Daisy provided foster care for Sarah Frank, an orphaned half-Ute child. The daughter of a greedy landowner had her eye on Charlie Moon. Paleontologist Moses Silver and his archeologist daughter Delia dug up ancient bones on the Nathan McFain land adjacent to Daisy's. Nathan was not about to let all the credit go to strangers. Con man Horace Flye, who had been working on the dig, disappeared, leaving his daughter Butter uncared for. Charlie took her to Daisy. Daisy played a diminished role. Buffoonery, archeology and Native American mysteries created an uneven mix and a tricky ending.

North American mysticism was diluted in *Grandmother Spider* (Morrow, 2001) by an infusion of Maggody-like humor. A series of unlikely events occurred on April Fool's Day in the territory next to the Southern Ute jurisdiction. Scott Parris and Charlie Moon cooperated in the investigation of the murder of attorney Miles Armstrong and the disappearances of Tommy Tonompicket and Dr. William Pizinskil. This tied in to sightings of a mysterious object that resembled a giant spider and to the Ute mythology of Grandmother Spider. Charlie had problems on the job but inherited a substantial ranch. He had begun to take over the series.

Strange things were happening on the Ghost Wolf Mesa during *White Shell Woman* (Morrow, 2002). The discovery of an ancient pictograph that might lead to buried treasure aroused considerable interest among the archeologists. The murder of April Tavishutz, a bright young student who was working on the site, set Charlie and Daisy on parallel tracks. He had been hired by the Tribal Council to carry out Special Investigations. Daisy's help was sought by a possible suspect in April's murder. Fortunately the case went to the dogs.

Dead Soul (St. Martin, 2003) was almost completely Charlie's book. Daisy shared her meetings with a dead young woman and her vision of an explosion but that was it. Charles helped his neighbor, U. S. Senator Patch Davidson, the victim of an attack that left him confined to a wheelchair. Charlie, using Daisy's input, wove together disparate incidents into an incredible narrative of revenge.

There was one level of deception after another in *Witch's Tongue* (St. Martin's Minotaur, 2004). One night a white woman, Kicks Dogs, camping on the mesa overnight, awakened to find her husband, Jacob Gourd Rattle, had disappeared. Elsewhere robbers stole coins and cameos from Jane Cassidy's personal museum. Chaos followed. The total of corpses mounted. Other victims were injured. Charlie played a role in unraveling all the cases; thereby, impressing FBI Special Agent Lila Mae McTeague, acquiring a new cowhand and additional acreage for his ranch. Daisy's role was relatively insignificant.

Shadow Man (St. Martin, 2005) had it all. The interplay between Charlie and police chief Scott Parris, and scurrilous villains who had double-crossed Colombian drug runners. One such villain, orthodontist Manfred Blinkoe, had been the target of attempts on his life. Daisy's encounters with the spirit world provided clues, but also made her a target. Father Raes Delfino tried to help Daisy reconcile her native religion with Catholicism.

Doss' use of vernacular and cozy dialogue among the characters in *Stone Butterfly* (St. Martin's Minotaur, 2006) should not be allowed to lull the reader into complacency. The book is a taut, well-plotted narrative, in which Daisy played a vital but subsidiary role. Young Sarah Frank, who had appeared in earlier books, was caught up in the deadly rivalry between wealthy Raymond Oates and his half-brother Ben Silver, who had something that Raymond wanted. When Ben, who employed Sarah at his home, was murdered, she fled creating suspicion that she was the killer. Sarah had been living with her Papago cousin Marilee in Utah. She sought refuge with Charlie Moon (on whom she had a major crush) and Daisy in Colorado. Charlie, who was still entranced by FBI agent Lila Mae McTeague, had been a friend of Sarah's father. There were others besides the police who were looking for Sarah; someone paid the price.

Doss' narrative style changed in *Three Sisters* (St. Martin's Minotaur) and not necessarily for the better. This narrative featured a one-way conversation between author and reader that many will find annoying. The term "three sisters" did not in this case refer to the granite appendages on the mesa, but to

Cassandra, Beatrice, and Astrid Spencer. They were daughters of Joe Spencer who had left his property in a survivorship trust. After Astrid was mauled to death by a bear, her husband Andrew Turner married Beatrice. Cassandra's fame as a television psychic was enhanced by her predictions of serious crimes. Charlie was in charge, but it was Daisy's recollections of the three girls in their youth that provided a significant clue.

Using his folksy narrator style, Doss described a series of semi-humorous, semi-tragic events in *Snake Dreams* (St. Martin's Minotaur, 2008). Daisy had been forewarned by the *pitukupf* that Chiquita Yazzi (deceased) would be contacting her. Chiquita was concerned about her seventeen-year-old daughter Nancy, left at the mercy of her predatory stepfather, Herman Wetzel. Daisy and Sarah Frank (who lived with her) reached out to help Nancy when Herman was murdered and Nancy's 34-year-old beau became a suspect. Millicent Muntz, the retired schoolteacher who was Herman's landlady, teamed up with Daisy to protect Nancy, who was more resourceful than they realized.

Author James Doss writes lovely mystic prose, enhanced by his descriptions of the Western landscape, but his narratives lack the reality of Margaret Coel and Tony Hillerman.

Next: *The Widow's Revenge (2009).*

Jane Perry

Author: Frances Ferguson, pseudonym for Barbara-Serene Perkins

Jane Perry had an eclectic background. Her father was a British Army general whose postings had taken them to Saudi Arabia, Sweden, Italy and Germany. She spoke several European languages, had a college degree and certification as an attorney. She had been deeply disappointed by her lack of opportunities to get into the Criminal Investigation Division in London.

Jane's move to a rural English police department seemed a good idea as *Missing Person* (Headline, 1993) began. Unfortunately, chauvinistic DCI Morland had just replaced the progressive female detective inspector. Nevertheless Jane with the help of charming sergeant Steve Ryan solved serial murders, prevented the assassination of a Spanish prince, and identified an arrogant killer. She would bear scars from her efforts, but probably earned a promotion.

Jane's personal and personnel problems received considerable attention in *No Fixed Abode* (Headline, 1994). Her tempestuous relationship with veterinarian Adrian Reston was endangered when his partner Quentin Hurst was suspected in one of her cases. When her current superior officer, DI Dan Crowe, resigned, Jane applied for the post, but did not receive serious consideration. Jane's persistence and independence worked against her. She investigated the death of Old Mary, a mentally ill vagrant, after Crowe's replacement told her to drop the case. It seemed likely that Old Mary had seen something and had to be silenced

In *Identity Unknown* (Headline, 1995), Jane's opportunity for promotion to detective inspector came...but at a cost. She had to leave the Criminal Investigation Division (CID) and move into Community Relations. In that role she attended the funeral of local dignitary Richard Musthill and witnessed the discovery of a headless corpse in the grave. Superintendent Annerley, who remembered her successes, insisted that she use her current post to gather information in the case. Jane found herself attracted to a mysterious cult leader at a time when she and Adrian were at odds.

The best part of Jane's new position was the opportunity to liaise with European police forces and use her language skills in *With Intent to Kill* (Headline, 1996). The abandonment of a truckload of immigrants on the highway took place as Jane drove by after such a meeting. The next morning while searching for the escaped immigrants, the police found the body of journalist Lionel Hughes. Hughes' current wife insisted that his prior spouse, now living in France, was the most likely suspect. Jane went beyond this supposition. She used a handsome Sûreté officer to develop another possibility. At least this time she arranged for backup when she ventured into danger. She would still prefer to work in CID, but not if it meant a transfer and leaving Adrian.

Karen Perry-Mondori

Author: Catherine Arnold

Karen Perry-Mondori's colleagues and adversaries perceived her as an adept criminal lawyer who used trickery when necessary to give her clients the full benefit of the law. She did not do her own research nor factual investigations, but was skilled in courtroom tactics. A tiny brown-haired woman practicing in Clearwater, Florida with an established firm (Hewitt, Sinclair, and Smith), she had earned her position. Karen had been estranged from her mother for years and never knew who had been her father. A good marriage to neurosurgeon Carl Mondori had made that less important in her life. They had a daughter, Andrea, initially six-years-old who was cared for by au pairs while her parents worked.

Motivated by the courage of witnesses in a prior case who risked their jobs for the truth, Karen agreed to defend Jack Palmer in *Due Process* (Signet, 1996). There were many reasons not to do so. There seemed to be an open and shut case against Jack for killing Dan De Fauldo, the husband of a woman he had purportedly raped. The De Fauldos were neighbors of Carl and Karen. Carl and the managing partner of her firm cautioned her to avoid the case. Jack Palmer probably could not pay her fees. The well-developed narrative provided credible courtroom scenes and an absorbing conclusion.

Karen could not explain, even to herself, why she agreed to defend aging Mafioso Angelo Uccello. He was admittedly a drug dealer, but in *Imperfect Justice* (Signet, 1997) she believed he had been framed on the current charges. State and federal investigators and judicial officials aligned themselves against her defense. Her mother Martha visited to insist that she withdraw. Karen and her family paid a price for her persistence. Even what seemed to be a final victory had a bittersweet twist.

There was no way for Karen to separate her personal and professional feelings in *Wrongful Death* (Signet, 1999). After receiving a videotape that portrayed him in pederast activity, her brother Robert was discovered shot in the head. Numbed with grief and trying to help Robert's widow and twin sons, Karen could not put aside her need for justice. She believed the tape had been faked, and intended to find out how and by whom.

The stakes for Karen escalated with each narrative. In the beginning she was protecting her client from being framed by an individual. By *Class Action* (Signet, 1999) she pitted herself against the federal government (CIA and FBI) in her defense of Herman Gaylord, a vagrant accused of murdering Gerald Brock, his best friend. At times, Karen's zeal for justice outweighed her responsibility to her husband and her daughter. In the conclusion she realized that she had been manipulated, but had enough faith in the American public to release frightening information.

An excellent series that should attract female attorneys who read mysteries, but be enjoyed by many others.

Maddy Phillips

Author: R. D. Zimmerman

Blind and paraplegic, Maddy Phillips had isolated herself on a Lake Michigan island far from her former professional life in Chicago. Her vision problems arose from retinitis pigmentosa. Her physical injuries came as the result of a collision caused by a drunken bus driver. That ended her career as a forensic psychologist, but the insurance settlement made her financially independent. Maddy remained on the island year round with Alfred and Solange, husband and wife servants, and two mastiff dogs, Fran and Ollie. Maddy's father had been killed in a plane crash; her mother suffered from Alzheimer's. Maddy retained her interest in the world, her sense of humor, and her strong influence on her brother Alex. He allowed her to hypnotize him as to past activities and was guided by her questions. The relationship was close to unhealthy.

In *Death Trance* (Morrow, 1992), Alex's former lover Dr. "Toni" Domingo was killed, shortly after the death of Liz, her younger sister. Through hypnosis Maddy retrieved information that had defied Alex's conscious memory. When Maddy identified the killer, the knowledge was painful.

During *Blood Trance* (Morrow, 1993), former patient Loretta Long contacted Maddy in a panic. Alex, sent to bring Loretta to the island, found her standing over her stepmother's corpse with a knife. Attempts to injure Alex suggested that he had suppressed knowledge that would identify the killer.

After the solution, Alex quit his job as a technical writer to work full time for Maddy.

The action moved from the Midwest to Russia in *Red Trance* (Morrow, 1994), and required an even greater suspension of belief. Maddy had corresponded for years with wealthy Russian hypnotist Dr. Pavel Kamikor from whom she concealed her accident and her confinement to a wheelchair. Alex returned to Russia,where he had lived as a student, to find oppression replaced by commercialism at a level conducive to murder.

Quirky. Zimmerman moved on to a series, featuring recently outed news reporter Todd Mills.

Joanna Piercy

Author: Priscilla Masters

Joanna Piercy's promotion from detective sergeant to detective inspector in a rural English police department was not universally popular with staff. On the positive side, she had the advantage of a college education with a degree in psychology and had recently scored a major success. Her ambition and coldness did not endear her to those whom she supervised. Nor did the fact that she was involved with married pathologist Matthew Levin. Joanna's parents had divorced. Her mother never recovered from her father's remarriage to a much young woman.

As *Winding Up the Serpent* (Macmillan, 1995) began, Joanna needed the respect and approval of her co-workers. Proving that the mysterious death of unpopular nurse Marilyn Smith was murder could earn that respect. Joanna and Sgt. Mike Korpanski were under pressure to break through the silence of those who were glad Marilyn was dead. Over the series, Korpanski came to respect Joanna, which helped with other personnel. Unhappy with her private life, Joanna concentrated on her work, trying to end the affair with Matthew Levin.

Joanna and Mike's investigation into the death of an initially unidentified abused ten-year-old boy in *Catch the Fallen Sparrow* (Macmillan, 1996) produced many suspects, all guilty of something. Dogged persistence kept the police team working until significant clues appeared. It took a mother's devotion to get a confession. The intensity of the search kept Joanna's mind off the fact that Matthew was giving his marriage a second chance. At times, Joanna wondered if part of Matthew's allure was his limited availability. Did she really want him in her life full-time?

The rape and death by garroting of single mother Sharon Priest in *A Wreath for My Sister* (Macmillan, 1997) produced a quartet of possible suspects with whom she had been sexually involved. By the process of elimination, Joanna and Mike focused on a man who had killed before and might kill again. For a while it looked as though there might be a future with Matthew but she finally realized that it was not his wife Jane who was her rival for his affection. It was his daughter, Eloise.

Joanna, who resented Matthew's attachment to Eloise, learned more about parental love in *And None Shall Sleep* (Macmillan, 1997). After an accident while riding her bicycle, Joanna left her hospital bed to take over the investigation of the disappearance of solicitor Jonathan Selkirk, a patient on the floor below. The discovery of Selkirk's "executed" body necessitated the involvement of the Regional Crime Squad because his killer was presumed to be a paid assassin. The task of finding who had hired the killer remained the responsibility of Joanna and her staff. Two associated deaths emphasized for Joanna the devotion of parents to their children, particularly for an only child. The idea of a pregnancy distorting her body and limiting her activities was abhorrent to Joanna.

Even Joanna's cat ran away in *Scaring Crows* (Macmillan, 1999). An isolated rural family came to the attention of the police department. Elderly Aaron Summers, who was dying of cancer, and his mentally disabled son Jack had been shot to death. Aaron's daughter Rosie had disappeared, but Joanna was reluctant to treat her as a killer. Joanna was on the brink of purchasing a house with Matthew when she pulled back. His expectations that Eloise would spend considerable time with them and that they might have children of their own were unrealistic. She was honest about the fact that she did not like children and had no intention of getting pregnant.

Neither Joanna nor her assistant, Sgt. Mike Korpanski were in good humor as *Embroidering Shrouds* (Macmillan, 2001) began. At the office they were plagued by a series of burglaries that had escalated into vicious assaults. Mike had a visiting mother-in-law who upset his household. Joanna was dreading a visit from Eloise. She and Matthew had a shared residence and a loving relationship, but she knew he felt guilt at having divorced Eloise's mother. Eloise detested Joanna. When the most recent burglary included murder, it would have been easy to attribute it to the same source as prior incidents had it not been for the character of the victim. Nan Lawrence, a bitter woman, had tormented the lives of her siblings and a former lover and had twisted the character of her great nephew. Good police procedural although Joanna's treatment of Eloise seemed harsh.

Joanna's lack of interest in children was apparent early on in *Endangering Innocents* (Allison & Busby, 2003); or perhaps she felt that possible abuse and neglect were the responsibilities of other agencies. She and Mike took action when Horton Elementary School personnel reported that a van owned by Joshua Baldwin often appeared nearby when the children were being released from school. Baldwin seemed innocuous so they settled for warning him off. When five-year-old Maddy Wiltshaw disappeared, Baldwin was the obvious suspect. Chief Superintendent Colclough advised Joanna not to narrow her investigation so quickly. A search for Maddy in the adjacent rural area was complicated by an outbreak of foot-and-mouth disease. Farmers did not welcome searchers. Joanna had her own problem, which threatened her personal life.

Locating an errant wife seemed more of a domestic matter than one for Joanna's unit in *Wings Over the Watcher* (Allison & Busby, 2005). She felt some empathy for Beatrice Pennington, whom she had met through her cycling club. If "Beattie" had rejuvenated herself and found romance elsewhere, more power to her. Prodded by her husband Arthur, Joanna and Mike had gone through the motions; contacted their disinterested children, her associates at the library, and her long time pals, Jewel and Marilyn. Everything changed when Beattie's corpse was located along a rural road. Joanna's focus was diverted by the changes in her own life. Dr. Matthew Levin and she had parted with some friction. He was still interested in having a family and she had not been able to meet that need and wasn't sure she wanted to.

Author Priscilla Masters has new series, featuring Dr. Megan Banesto; the coroner Martha Gunn, and antique dealer Susanna Paris and multiple excellent standalones.

Anna Pigeon

Author: Nevada Barr

Widowed Anna Pigeon, mourning her handsome actor/husband, left their New York City apartment to rebuild her life. After training as a law enforcement officer in the National Park Service, she was assigned to the Guadeloupe Mountains Park in West Texas. The expansive park and the solo assignments provided solitude, perhaps more than was wise. The only link to her past was her sister Molly, a psychiatrist with whom she maintained regular telephone contact. Anna tried to fill the void in her life with alcohol and a lover, but was unsuccessful. At thirty-nine, she was a physically strong woman wearing her copper hair tinged with gray in a long braid, sharing her successive homes with her cat, Piedmont. Anna had attended a Catholic school system for academic reasons, but had no tie with organized religion.

In *Track of the Cat* (Putnam, 1993), Anna was jolted out of her isolation. While patrolling in search of wild lion spoor, she found the corpse of fellow ranger Sheila Drury. The official diagnosis was that the death resulted from an animal attack. Anna was convinced that a staff member had murdered the woman.

By *A Superior Death* (Putnam, 1994), Anna had left her beloved desert behind for the rigors of Isle Royale in Upper Michigan. Now her mode of transportation was by boat, a new experience. The ranger post was rife with rumors about hard drinking ranger Scotty Butkus, whose wife was missing. Two Canadian divers found a sunken ship that had one more corpse than expected. It was at this point that Anna met FBI agent Frederick Stanton. He was the first man to whom she had been seriously attracted since her husband's death.

Anna returned to the Southwest in *Ill Wind* (Putnam, 1995), but the position at Mesa Verde, Colorado lacked the solitude she craved. She assisted in the rescue operations of injured or ill park visitors, policed domestic abuse and industrial theft by staff and contract workers. The local environmentalists and Native Americans resented park improvements that might damage Anasazi relics. When a series of tragedies occurred, some claimed that the ancient gods were angry. Anna saw human hands at work in the death of park employee Stacy Meyers, and human greed in the illnesses that threatened the young and vulnerable. She faced her own vulnerability by finally admitting to herself and sister Molly, "My name is Anna, and I am an alcoholic."

Anna needed all of her wits during *Firestorm* (Putnam, 1996) when rangers from the Southwest responded to a major California fire. Not only did she and emergency medical workers have to abandon a seriously injured man as they fled from a firestorm, but Leonard Nims, a survivor from their group, was murdered.

Anna's next assignment was on the Cumberland Island beaches off Georgia's coast in *Endangered Species* (Putnam, 1997). She and other National Park Services personnel helped volunteers who assisted rare turtles to spawn their eggs on the shore. When a drug interdiction plane carrying NPS personnel crashed, there was no doubt about sabotage, only about who had been the intended victim. While Anna investigated, the two most important persons in her life, her sister Molly and FBI agent Frederick Stanton faced a crisis of their own with implications for Anna.

Claustrophobia had always been a problem for Anna. It became unavoidable in *Blind Descent* (Putnam, 1998) when she entered a recently discovered extension of Carlsbad Caverns to rescue a survey team. One member of the team was Anna's dear friend Frieda who had been seriously injured in a suspicious fall. Curt Schatz, a member of the survey team, filled the void in her personal life since neither Molly nor Frederick had been close to her recently.

Molly's devastating illness brought Anna to her bedside in *Liberty Falling* (Putnam, 1999) where Frederick Stanton joined her. He had stayed away because Molly's love for Anna made her unwilling to return his love. Rather than spend her nights at Molly's apartment, Anna stayed with her friend Patsy Silva on Liberty Island in New York harbor. Investigating the mysterious deaths of teenage tourist Agnes Tucker, who had been abducted from her mother's home by her father, and James "Hatch" Hatchett, a friendly park policeman, provided Anna with the diversion she needed as her sister lay deep in a coma. Anna's prodigious visual memory aided her as she roamed the island at night, uncovering a vicious plot but ending a valuable friendship.

In *Deep South* (Putnam, 2000), seeking career advancement, Anna moved up in the National Park system by accepting a district ranger position at the Natchez Trace Parkway. She anticipated hostility toward a Yankee female in a supervisory position. In investigating the murder of teenage Danni Posey, Anna saw both the bigotry and tolerance of Mississippi, the cruelty and kindness, the weight of past history and glimmerings of hope for the future. Her awakening to potential love for Paul Davidson, the reverent sheriff, was accompanied by mistrust of his motives. The conclusion left her physically battered but at peace with herself.

What she had hoped would be an easy assignment to allow her to recuperate from her injuries turned out otherwise in *Blood Lure* (Putnam, 2001). She was detached to a DNA research project at Glacier National Park. Her experience and increased knowledge were to be useful on her return to Natchez Trace. Her superiors had a hidden agenda. Anna, who had always loved solitude and exposure to nature, was shaken by inexplicable behavior on the part of both humans and animals. The death of young Rory Van Slyke's abusive stepmother Carolyn, changed Anna's status from researcher to investigator. Solid police work tied together disparate clues: the value of "Boone & Crockett" trophies, the need for young boys to bond with pets and role models, and unusual bear activity. She returned to Mississippi and Paul, having done her best.

At times during *Hunting Season* (Putnam's, 2002) Anna was more prey than hunter. The death of good old boy Doyce Barnette occurred on federal park land. His killer had not only moved the body but had planted evidence of an auto-erotic episode. Anna was diverted by concerns about where her affair with Episcopalian priest/sheriff Paul Davidson was going and by staff problems.

Barr, who has moved her physical settings around the United States, took on a new dimension in *Flashback* (Putnam's, 2003) i.e. time. Molly, Anna's sister, had sent her a packet of letters which had been written to their great-great-grandmother. Molly thought she might find them diverting in her temporary assignment as Acting Supervisory Ranger at isolated Fort Jefferson in the Dry Tortugas. The author of the letters, great-great Aunt Raffia, had lived at the Fort shortly after the Civil War because her husband, a Captain in the Union army, had been in charge of a rebel prison. Dr. Samuel Mudd, of the Lincoln conspiracy, had been one of the prisoners. Boredom was not a problem for either Raffia or Anna. The current chaos on Dry Tortuga helped Anna to make a personal decision. Engrossing but the change in time and multiple characters require attentive reading.

Whatever beauty existed in Yosemite National Park, as depicted in *High Country* (Putnam's, 2004), was overwhelmed by the sense of evil, the cruelty and violence of the narrative. Months before, Anna (preparing to marry Paul Davidson) was sent to the park to work undercover as a waitress. Four young part-time employees had disappeared on the same day, too many to be a coincidence. Although there were a few dependable characters in the narrative, too many were deeply flawed from "pot' hunters to hit man. Even Anna showed a violent streak that surprised her.

Long time Anna Pigeon fans may find *Hard Truth* (Putnam's, 2005) weighted heavily with explicit violence. Anna had an inauspicious welcome to her new job at Rocky Mountain National Park. She and Paul had agreed to put their jobs first in the next year and then re-evaluate. Her subsequent adventures might impact on her decision. Paraplegic former climber Heath Jarrod and her 71-year-old aunt, Dr. Gwen Littleton, had discovered Beth Dwayne and Alexis Sheppard, two of the missing teenagers from a church youth group. The fate of the third girl (Candace Watson age 13) was unknown. Beth Dwayne's immediate attachment to Heath drew Anna, Gwen, and Heath into her family, a polygamous community. Anna had personnel problems to death with: Rita Perry, an experienced ranger who had unexplained absences, and Ray Bleeker, backcountry warden who did not live up to his resume.

During *Winter Study* (Putnam, 2008) Anna returned to Isle Royale (see *A Superior Death* above), this time in the winter. She witnessed the struggles between wolves and moose, but more critically the antagonism between employees of Homeland Security and those of the Wolf Study. The fifty-year-old Wolf Study needed the isolation of winter for their continued work, but it was endangered by Homeland Security's insistence that the park be open to the public year round for defense purposes. Something was amiss in the three wolf packs. There was erratic behavior by wolves and evidence of a super wolf, which may have been the offspring of a wolf/dog mating. The weather was freezing; the accommodations, primitive; and the atmosphere, beset with tensions not always clear to Anna, a newcomer to the group. The antagonisms between and within the two groups erupted in murder and a disappearance. The narrative had a factual background because the Wolf Study exists and is near to completion.

Next: *Borderline* (2009); *Burn* (2010)

This has been a great series. Barr writes lyrically about settings, animal life, and characters, but the more recent tendency to gratuitous violence is offsetting.

Josie Pigeon

Author: Valerie Wolzien

Josie Pigeon had perceived herself as rejected by her parents and the father of her child when she became pregnant as a college freshman. She cut herself off from them completely. While employed as a waitress, she worked on a Habitat for Humanity house, where she met Noel Roberts. Noel changed her life. He rescued her at a time when she wondered how she would provide for Tyler Clay, her infant son. Noel offered Josie a job on his construction crew, Island Contracting, on one condition. She would commit herself to two years work. The work became a career. Tyler was thirteen when Noel died. He left the business to Josie and provided a trust fund for Tyler's education, which meant boarding at an off-island prep school. Josie had not been the only recipient of Noel's generosity. Each member of his all-female construction crew had been recruited at a time of crisis, offered a job, and a chance to change her life. Josie continued

Noel's practice of purchasing from local independent suppliers that earned their loyalty.

When Josie took over in *Shore to Die* (Fawcett Gold Medal, 1996), Island Contracting was remodeling a decrepit mansion that had recently been purchased by Mr. and Mrs. Cornell Firbank III. The Firbanks wanted cheap quality. Josie tried to meet their needs because, if this project were successful, it would bring in more business. She lost credibility for common sense when she hid a corpse found on her construction site. Sam Richardson, a former prosecuting attorney who recently purchased an island liquor store, collaborated with Josie. They decided the only way to avoid arrest by local police was to find the killer. It didn't help that someone removed the corpse. Interesting but there were loose ends.

When finishing carpenter Amy Llewellyn, who worked for a competing construction firm, was murdered in *Permit for Murder* (Fawcett, 1997) the circle of suspects was small. It included members of Josie's work crew and her estranged lover Sam Richardson, because the corpse had been discovered on Josie's work site. Considering the resemblance to an earlier case, Chief of Police Michael Rodney focused his suspicions on the all-female crew.

Murder connected to Josie's crew occurred again in *Deck the Halls with Murder* (Fawcett, 1998). The victim was Caroline Albrecht, a new employee. Even the incompetent local police knew where to look for the killer, i.e. among her coworkers. That didn't mean that they arrested the right one, of course. On a personal level, Josie was preoccupied with the coming holiday, her resumed romance with Sam, and Tyler's vacation. Her deadline for the remodeling of a home to suit quadriplegic Hugh Sylvester did not allow for workers to be murdered or arrested. Josie might know how Caroline died, but could she convince the authorities that her theory was sound.

Remodeling an A-frame house to suit an unknown client presented problems for Josie and her new crew in *This Old Murder* (Fawcett, 2000). She added to the complexities by agreeing to have their work taped for a Public Broadcasting series on home repair and renovation. Courtney Castle, the temperamental star of the show, had a history with Josie. This created problems when her corpse was located on site. Nothing new there. Along the way Josie reassessed her relationship with her parents. Chad Henshaw, son of Wolzien's other female sleuth, made a minor appearance.

Hurricane Agatha wiped out Point House, the site of Island Contracting's premiere project in *Murder in the Forecast* (Fawcett, 2001). Only Josie and one other person knew that the owner's corpse disappeared along with the building, i.e. the killer. As always a new member of her crew aroused suspicion. Something different occurred. Chief Rodney, now enamored of Sam's mother Carol, offered to help Josie find the killer.

Although there were interesting aspects to Josie's visit to New York City in *A Fashionable Murder* (Fawcett, 2003) the narrative bogged down with interminable interviews with minor characters who had known interior decorator

Pamela Peel. Josie had come to New York to help Sam Richardson prepare his apartment for sale. The sale became less important when Pamela's corpse was discovered by Josie in a window seat in the apartment. Pamela and Sam had been a couple for years before he retired and moved to the Island. Josie's effort to prove Sam was no killer was aided by her former employee Betty Patrick, now married and living in Manhattan and by Sam's mother Carol. A lot of time was spent shopping.

Although the wedding date had been set for Labor Day weekend, gowns and catering were not high on Josie's list in *Death at a Premium* (Fawcett, 2005). She had a major reconstruction of a former bed and breakfast, "Bride's Secret", to be completed by the end of the summer. The new owners, wealthy Seymour Huggins and his wife, wanted the estate returned to a single-family dwelling. No surprise to the police or readers of the series that two dummies and then a real corpse were discovered on site. Unfortunately Josie was functioning with a new crew, one of whom could not be covered by her insurance. Ending was a stretch.

There were admirable elements to the series; however, on occasion, Josie's identification of the killer was not always substantiated by evidence that would justify an arrest, trial, and/or conviction. Several narratives had a subplot concerning Tyler's teenage adjustments.

Susan Henshaw, another of Wolzien's sleuths, was covered in Volume 2 of Mystery Women

Molly Piper

Author: Patricia Brooks

Molly Piper, a tiny woman at 4' 9" working as a Chicago police officer, was shot while acting inappropriately on duty; then allowed to resign. She went to the village of Grace on Prince Island, Washington where she became a private investigator. Molly had skills beyond her experience, was highly organized, and a former gymnast. She built up a coterie of friends, including Attorney Eugene Mulholland in Grace and Simon Emmershaw, a semi-retired private investigator in Olympia. Timothy Gray, also a former Chicago police officer, had been there for Molly when she was raped at age twenty-one, and now lived nearby on the mainland. Molly's current home was an old camper, parked on land owned by Free, an African-American who owned a bookshop.

Mary Alice Abbott had only vague recollections of an older sister Alice, even when she received her letters in *Falling from Grace* (Dell, 1998). When Alice failed to appear for a planned meeting, Mary Alice hired Molly to find her. A serial killer known as the Crucifixer because of his methods resurfaced on Prince Island at this time. Mary Alice's dysfunctional family kept Molly preoccupied even as she almost became a victim herself.

In *But for the Grace* (Dell, 2000), unpopular businessman Edmond Anderson Bercain hired Molly to investigate the unknown members of the

Liberation Brigade who had placed WANTED posters around town, alleging cruel and criminal behavior in his past. She began by contacting a group of squatters, many of whom had been evicted or felt cheated by Bercain. By the next morning, Bercain had been found dead after a citywide celebration of New Year's Eve. Her new client was Bercain's widow. Molly's personal life was in disarray because her current lover Jake had become disinterested. Feeling rejected, she concentrated on following up on anonymous letters slipped under her door relating to the murder, and on the problems of two suspects, a teenage squatter and a Native American youth, both of whom had reasons to dislike Bercain.

Rose Piper

Author: Hilary Bonner

At age 33, Rose had risen to the level of DCI under Superintendent Titmuss in the Avon and Somerset constabulary based at the Southmead Police Station. By the second book, she had become deputy chief of Children's Protective Services. Rose was married to Simon, but things weren't working out. An effort to revive the marriage failed. Rose's father had died young of cancer. She was not close to her mother, who reminded her of Hyacinth Bucket of the *Keeping Up Appearances* BBC program because of her pretensions. Rose had problems with delegating, and occasional impulsive decisions.

Although it might be classified as a police procedural, *A Passion So Deadly* (Heinemann, 1998) was much more. The narrative explored Rose's consuming interest in serial killings of male prostitutes and its impact on her marriage. Her search for a mysterious Mrs. Pattison, who had patronized the victims, succeeded, but did not satisfy her.

After the prior narrative which caused the breakup of her marriage, Rose was vulnerable as *For Death Comes Softly* (Heinemann, 1999) began. She had this high tension job in Children's Protective Services. It was difficult to believe that a woman who had risen from constable to this position, would fall deeply in love with Robin Davey, heir to the island of Abri, where she vacationed. They had met when she almost drowned. He was a widower, engaged to a lovely young woman. She returned to work focusing on a difficult child abuse case. Serious problems with the abuse case and the death of Robin's fiancé not only discredited Rose professionally, but sapped her self-esteem.

Bonner has a second series featuring Karen Meadows, also a police professional, but most of her later work was in standalones.

Jimi Plain

Author: Victoria Pade

Finances forced Jimi Plain into selling the home that she and her children had shared since the divorce eight years ago. Her former husband was referred to as "Uncle Dad' because, even though his biological connection to their two daughters was established, he withheld both emotional and financial support. By moving out of Colorado he managed to avoid paying the court-ordered child support. Whenever the law caught up with him, he moved again. The neglect affected each child differently: Chloe at nineteen eagerly sought contacts with her father; Shannon, then seventeen, had written him off. The solution that presented itself was to move into the large family home owned by Jimi's grandmother (Gramma), a fierce Italian woman. She had already subdivided the place to provide a basement level apartment for Jimi's cousin, detective Danny Delvecchio. Jimi purchased the home from Gramma; then, shared the upper floors with her. The third floor provided Jimi with the office out of which she worked as a free-lance technical writer on catalogues, training material, etc. A miniature schnauzer, Lucy, completed the household. Jimi had been raised a Catholic but no longer practiced her religion to the dismay of both Danny and Gramma. She was approaching forty as the series began.

A divorce support group had provided Jimi with comfort. By *Divorce Can Be Murder* (Dell, 1999), she was beyond active participation, but assisted as a volunteer when called on by therapist Audrey Martin. The group involved in this narrative was disrupted by the connections among its members. After Bruce Mann was murdered, Jimi tried to balance her loyalty to the group (which included her best friend) and to the law (as represented by Danny). Subsequent deaths made the choice easier. The plot could be considered a wake-up call for wives to be knowledgeable about their husband's finances. However, some readers may be offended by the concept that while divorce is intolerable to some, murder may not be.

The membership in the New You Center for Dating in *Dating Can Be Deadly* (Signet, 1999) had been a gift to Jimi from Gramma, Chloe, and Shannon. She went reluctantly to avoid hurting their feelings. After her personal counselor Steffi Hargitay was murdered in her office, Jimi returned to check out the suspects for cousin Danny. She must have asked too many questions. The frequent reviewing of the potential suspects added length to the narrative.

Charlie Plato

Author: Margaret Chittenden

Charlie Plato had grown up in Sacramento. She was a tall redhead who had been on her own since her parents were killed flying their Cessna in a thunderstorm. She spent twelve years in Seattle where she married young plastic surgeon Rob

Whittaker. She had met Rob when she applied to work in his office, but their lifestyles never meshed. At thirty, after they divorced, Charlie went in a totally different direction with her life. She invested her inheritance in a business. Along with TV western star Zack Hunter and two other friends, she purchased and managed a country and western tavern, "Chaps," located on the San Francisco peninsula. Zack was a silent partner with a half share. Charlie was an active manager helped by her best pal, Savanna Seabrook. Prudent for her age and state in life, Charlie did not engage in sex with Zack who was a womanizer. Allergic to cats and afraid of dogs, she shared the loft over the tavern with "Benny" her Netherland dwarf rabbit.

With time on his hands, Zack ran for the local city council in *Dead Men Don't Dance* (Kensington, 1997) and convinced Charlie to be his campaign manager. The discovery of deceased Gerald Senerac (Zack's opponent in the race) in Zack's car trunk created political and legal problems. His alibi was Senerac's wife!

While attending her self-defense class in *Dead Beat and Deadly* (Kensington, 1998), Charlie noticed bruises on Estrella Stockton, a mail order Philippino bride. Suspecting an abusive husband, Charlie offered her help. Estrella's murder prompted her husband Thane to enlist Zack and Charlie in proving his innocence; that he had been physically abused and threatened with murder by Estrella. Research into Estrella's checkered past revealed that she was capable of violence, but who killed her?

The aftershock from an earthquake in *Dying to Sing* (Kensington, 1996) uncovered the skeleton of an older man in the Chaps flower garden. He had been dead for several months, the death occurring just about the time that Zack purchased the property. Damages to police department computers made it difficult to identify the victim, but someone knew. A mysterious phone caller demanded $5,000 owed him by John Doe (later identified as Walt Cochran, once a popular singer, more recently a vagrant who read the Wall Street Journal at the public library). Zack and Charlie sought information. Someone else destroyed it, killing an elderly librarian. Along the way, Savannah got a new beau and Zack got a new series. Nothing for Charlie except satisfaction. Zack made moves on her but was too unreliable to consider after marriage to an unfaithful husband.

Charlie had been aware that bartender and partner Angel Cervantes had a deep secret in his past. In *Don't Forget To Die* (Kensington, 1999), she learned that his mother had been murdered. His father Vincenzo, the primary suspect, had fled with a younger woman. When Vincenzo's corpse was discovered in the area, the police questioned Angel and his brother Miguel. All mysteries were solved except whether or not Charlie finally succumbed to Zack's seductive powers.

Savanna Seabrook graduated from an alternative high school where teacher Reina Diaz had motivated many of the students. Reina's murder in *Dying To See You* (Kensington, 2000) took place at Chaps during a twenty-year class reunion. Which of her devoted students had killed this highly regarded woman? Charlie and Zack found the answer deep in the past but not before serious damage to their business.

A light, bouncy series. Don't expect significant character studies or intricate plotting.

Stephanie Plum

Author: Janet Evanovich

Being unconventional had become a way of life for Stephanie Plum. To her mother's dismay, she had shown no interest in marriage since her divorce from Dickie Orr. Her Italian-Hungarian heritage was not responsible for her quirks: beer for breakfast, disinterest in physical possessions, and devotion to a pet hamster. She was tall, brown-haired and initially out of work. Behind on car payments, Stephanie blackmailed her cousin Vinnie into a job as a skip tracer for his New Jersey bail bond business.

As *One for the Money* (Scribners, 1994) opened, Vinnie set her on the trail of police detective Joe Morelli, accused of murdering an unarmed suspect. Stephanie preferred to believe that Joe was merely seeking a witness to prove his innocence. She had always let Joe sweet-talk her, even when they were high hormonal teenagers. Armed with pepper spray, handcuffs, and a gun, Stephanie set out in the car she stole from Morelli.

Morelli continued to play a major role in Stephanie's investigations. In *Two for the Dough* (Scribners, 1996), her search for absconding defendant Kenny Mancuso turned into a murder probe. Grandma Mazur's absorption in local wakes provided Stephanie with an opportunity to observe the suspects. Gran's 1953 Buick became transportation when Stephanie's Jeep was stolen. Morelli's special assignment to trace stolen army equipment dovetailed with Stephanie's search for Kenny.

Cousin Vinnie was not interested in the fact that candy store owner "Uncle Mo" was popular with all the neighbors in *Three to Get Deadly* (Scribners, 1997). All that concerned him was that Mo had disappeared, failing to appear in court in a case in which Vinnie had posted his bail bond. With the help of "Ranger" (Carlos Manoso) her co-investigator, Stephanie reluctantly sought Mo, earning the disapproval of her extended family, until she found a corpse on the store premises. While evading the police, including Morelli, Stephanie had a hair-raising experience, had to deal with her ex-husband, and fought off attackers while defending her hamster, Rex. Lula, African-American ex-hooker, now a clerk at Vinnie's, carried a lot of weight in future narratives.

The first three books were combined in *Three Plums in One* (Scribners, 2001)

Stephanie was led on a merry chase in *Four to Score* (St. Martin, 1998) by bail jumper Maxine Nowicki who had vicious killers on her trail. Stephanie acquired a new assistant (Lula) and a new enemy (who torched her car and apartment) driving her into the willing arms of Joe Morelli. Business as a bail enforcer was depressed and so was Stephanie.

Stephanie and Morelli ended their affair because of divergent plans for their future. He had no intentions of marrying. In *High Five* (St. Martin, 1999), she took on odd jobs: (1) at her family's request to look for missing Uncle Fred who may have blackmailed a killer, and (2) to assist Ranger in a series of funny escapades which may be illegal, but to Ranger were "morally right." Author Evanovich teased her readers with "the lady or the tiger" ending. Whom did Stephanie invite to share the evening? Morelli or Ranger?

Ranger had been a friend and mentor to Stephanie. In *Hot Six* (St. Martin, 2000), she refused to execute Vinnie's order to find him. Ranger had jumped bail when questioned about the death of gangster Homer Ramos in a burned building. Homer was the son and heir apparent of Alexander Ramos, a major black market gun dealer. The action was non-stop from that point on. The narrative mixed a voracious Golden Retriever, semi-suicidal friend Carol Zabo, and at least two sets of rival gangsters. Cars blew up. Joe and Stephanie suffered from repeated coitus interruptus. Lula and Grandma Mazur added to the distractions.

Eddie DeChooch was an old man with limited hearing and vision. He should have been an easy pick-up for bounty hunter Stephanie in *Seven Up* (St. Martin, 2001). However, Eddie was a retired gangster used to solving problems with a handgun, and well able to elude both Stephanie and Ranger throughout the narrative. Stephanie freed three hostages, replaced a human heart, and overpowered a deranged widow, but she couldn't bring Eddie in without making a deal with Ranger.

Readers who like Christmas and like Stephanie Plum may not necessarily enjoy *Visions of Sugar Plums* (St, Martin, 2002). Christmas related mysteries have become very common, and do not always reach the level of quality expected of a series. The mixture of fantasy, whimsy, and terror in this one didn't come off. Diesel, ex-biker male with supernormal powers, showed up in Stephanie's kitchen just before the holidays. They have missions, which may not mesh. He is to return high-powered John Ring to his retirement home. She has to produce toy maker Sandy Claus in court. It's harder to swallow than bad fruitcake.

No good deed goes unpunished, Stephanie realized in *Hard Eight* (St. Martin, 2002). Her search for Evelyn Soder and her daughter Annie was not a job assignment from Vinnie's bond agency. Mabel Markowitz, friend and neighbor of Stephanie's parents, had put her home up as a custody bond for Evelyn. It was designed to provide access to Annie for her father, Steven. Mabel wasn't the only one at risk. Stephanie, after rejection by Morelli, was vulnerable to Ranger who felt she owed him big time. Stephanie was further harassed by snakes, bunnies and bears plus a corpse on her couch. Albert Klahn, Evelyn's ineffectual attorney, and Valerie (Stephanie's sister) became regulars in the series. Valerie and her two children had moved in with mom and dad.

The cast of characters is getting longer and so are the books.

To the Nines (St., Martin, 2003) is likely to have the reader laughing out loud. Not that murder, especially in multiples, can be even remotely funny, but the efforts by Stephanie and her ensemble had their hilarious moments. Stephanie was assigned to locate Samuel Singh, who was working on a temporary visa at Tri-Boro Tech. If Samuel was not known to have left the U.S. by the end of his visa period, Vinnie was out big money. Instead Samuel disappeared.

Even in the bloody *Ten Big Ones* (St. Martin, 2004), author Evanovich kept the laughs coming. Stephanie and Lula managed to arouse the hatred of the Comstock Street Slayers, a local gang. Morelli's efforts to rein Stephanie in backfired. She moved out. "Junkman", an out-of-town hitman, was hired to deal with Stephanie. While working to find an apartment for Valerie and her ménage, rehabbing cross-dressing Sally Sweet, and hiding out in luxury, Stephanie was scared and she ought to be.

Stephanie went from the frying pan into the fire in *Eleven on Top* (St. Martin, 2005). Burned out by her experience chasing bail jumpers, she quit. She couldn't leave her past behind. Someone hated her and wanted her to suffer. Stephanie's hunt for a replacement job was hampered when Lula, now doing Stephanie's job, sought her help. Finally, Ranger hired her to work in his corporate security agency. They focused on the disappearance of four different men. There had to be a connection and Stephanie was determined to find it. Her efforts to give up sweets had emotional side effects.

Evanovich may be spreading herself and Stephanie too thin, as she inserts extra narratives between the numbered books. *Plum Lucky* (St. Martin's 2007) was more of the usual. Stephanie's contrary Grandma Mazur stole a bag of currency, making her the target of the gangster to whom it belonged. Lula added her regular flair for disaster as she became involved with former jockey, Snuggy O'Connor, who talks to horses and was convinced he could make himself invisible. The gimmicks overwhelmed the plot.

This was also true of *Plum Lovin'* (St. Martin, 2007). Diesel, (see prior) returned with a proposition he figured Stephanie couldn't refuse. He had access to Annie Hart who was on Stephanie's wanted list. If she would carry out Annie's promise to five individuals to solve their problems by Valentine's Day, he would turn Annie over to her. One complication was that Annie had accepted Deisel's protection because an angry Bernie Beaner was out to get her. Another was that among the five was Albert, Stephanie's prospective brother-in-law. There were some nice moments, but too much sleaze mixed in with an abduction, hives, and Deisel's efforts for a one-nighter with Stephanie while Joe Morelli was working overtime.

Stephanie and Lula had a stack of FTA's (Failed to Appear cases) to clear up as *Twelve Sharp* (St. Martin, 2006) began. They worked their way through them with the usual comic aspects, but office manager Connie advertised for additional help. Lots of the 310 pages went into that struggle. Underlying the funny stuff (Lula and Grandma Mazur's ventures into show business) was a tragedy. Carmen Manoso, who claimed to be Ranger's wife, stalked Stephanie.

A Ranger wannabee abducted Julie, who definitely was Ranger's daughter. Overwhelmed Ranger needed Stephanie's help and he got it.

Lean Mean Thirteen (St. Martin, 2007) had little new to offer: (1) Stephanie trying to deal with her romance with Morelli (kinder than ever expected) and her attraction to Ranger; (2) wild chases after FTA (Failure to Appear) guys who are notably eccentric; (3) Lula's aberrant behavior and Grandma Mazur's eccentricities. The major narrative line featured Stephanie's short-term ex-husband, attorney Dickie Orr. Because Stephanie became violent toward Dickie in his office, she was a prime suspect when he disappeared. She not only had the police watching her, but also Joyce Barnhardt, her rival for Dickie's affections in the past. Dickie had not done well as an attorney, failing to make partner in his original firm. He connected with three less reputable and less qualified practitioners who led him astray. The new firm was making money but Ranger and Morelli wanted to know how. Redeeming episode: a Costco lunch.

Fearless Fourteen (St. Martin, 2008) was more of the same. The series had become repetitious. Sure, it was a concern that FTA Loretta Rizzi couldn't put up money for her rebonding; that Loretta's brother Dom, recently released from prison, couldn't get his hands on the nine million dollars that he and three friends had stolen from a bank; and that Morelli was accused of having fathered Loretta's child, now a teenage junkie. Even the addition of Brenda, a sixty-one-year old singer trying to rejuvenate her career with help from Lula and Grandma Mazur, didn't alleviate the boredom. Time for Stephanie to pick a man to whom she can make a real commitment.

Murder is not funny but Evanovich has added a lot of quaint touches to the series. She sets her scenes well, combining realistic ethnic dialogue with action and humor.

Next: *Plum Spooky, Finger Lickin Fifteen* (2009)

Rachel Porter

Author: Jessica Speart

The educational background for her entry into a career in the U.S. Fish and Wildlife Service seemed skimpy, but Rachel Porter received basic training at the Academy in Glynco, Georgia before her assignment to the New Orleans area. She had sought a placement in the Slidell office where Charlie Hickok was in charge after being inspired by a television program on his achievements. Not only was Charlie a misogynistic curmudgeon, but Rachel underestimated the cultural differences between New York City and Louisiana. Her prior experience had been as an actress, struggling for small roles on Broadway, television and in commercials. Now, Rachel, already in her thirties, raised by a Jewish mother and stepfather, had to learn a new way of life. Her stepfather, Dr. Sandy Berman, had adopted Rachel, but graciously insisted that she retain her birth father's last name. Rachel actually got along better with Sandy than with her formidable mother.

Charlie Hickok routinely sent Rachel out on cold and unsuccessful attempts to catch poachers. Even when caught, the local authorities rarely prosecuted small time offenders. Nepotism, graft, and political manipulation were taken for granted. Although the official Fish and Wildlife station was in Slidell, Rachel lived in the French Quarter of New Orleans. She and Terri Tune, her gay landlord who was a professional female impersonator, became close friends. The area had experienced an increase in right wing politics. Neo-Nazi groups demonstrated against gays and minority groups who received little protection from the police department. Over the series, her supervisors perceived Rachel as a wild cannon. They were right.

Once the reader accepts the improbabilities inherent in Rachel's career change, *Gator Aide* (Avon, 1997) moved swiftly. The presence of a dead alligator at a murder site necessitated the attention of an agent from the Fish and Wildlife Service. Charlie Hickok must not have realized that once Rachel got on an exciting case, it would be impossible to get her off...particularly when she was working with attractive homicide detective Jake Santou. The victim of the murder was Valerie Vaughn, a topless dancer who had suspicious connections to local politicians and businessmen.

Anyone who thought all they could lose in Las Vegas was their money had better read *Tortoise Soup* (Avon, 1998). Rachel wanted to leave the bayous, but was lonely for Jake Santou. Federal agents were unwelcome in the Nevada deserts, hated by ranchers because of the emphasis on endangered species, by mine owners for regulations, and by real estate developers because the government owned most of the land. When elderly recluse Annie McCarthy was murdered, Rachel challenged the local, state, and federal governments to find the killer. Annie had staked a gold claim on eighty parcels of land. Efforts to deal with 350 stolen tortoise eggs were somewhat less dangerous. Santou came to visit and to propose.

Rachel picked up new allies wherever she relocated; next, the Miami area in *Bird Brained* (Avon, 1999). They were rarely co-workers or police. Her crusades led her far beyond the bounds of her job description, when she investigated the murder of smuggler Alberto Dominguez. Dominguez had been involved in the exotic bird trade, but Rachel smoked out additional culprits. Terri Tune, her former landlord in New Orleans, joined her, and partied with her current lesbian landladies, Sophie and Lucinda. Add in a retired military man and a smart mouthed cockatoo for help in solving the murder. Colorful characters, yes. Careful plotting, not necessarily.

Rachel's next transfer was to the El Paso, Texas area in *Border Prey* (Avon, 2000). Her immediate concern was the death of her only snitch, Timmy Tom Tyler, an entrepreneur who smuggled animals across the Mexican border. Timmy Tom was small-time, but Rachel moved on to bigger game, i.e. erratic scientist Dr. Martin Pierpont and powerful rancher Frederick Ulysses Krabb (better known by his initials). Unfortunately, Krabb was currently married to Rachel's long time friend Lizzie Burke.

During *Black Delta Night* (Avon, 2001), Rachel was reunited with her former supervisor Charlie Hickok and Jake Santou, the man she couldn't forget. Having Charlie available made it easier to get unofficial permission for a dangerous undercover mission. Fishermen on the Mississippi River were hired to catch the endangered paddlefish, whose roe was similar to caviar. Santou made an undercover appearance as a shady character. Pooling their resources they ended up without egg on their faces.

The U.S. Fish and Wild Life agency must have thought Rachel could come to no trouble on the Blackfoot Reservation area of Montana, but they underestimated her again in *A Killing Season* (Avon, 2002). Sure, there was a problem with the grizzly bears. Actually two problems: someone was trapping them, but also the Native Americans blamed the grizzlies for the disappearances of reservation dwellers. There were resentful members of the "Indignant Blackfeet Arise" group, counterpoised against "The United Christian Patriots" (who were neither Christian nor patriotic). Accompanied by attractive tribal game officer Matthew Running, Rachel stirred up enough trouble to bring the FBI, in the person of Santou, to the rescue.

Now in Georgia, Rachel formed an alliance in *Coastal Disturbance* (Avon, 2003). Not the romantic kind she has with Santou, but a crusade against pollution with fellow Fish and Wildlife employee Gary Fletcher. They were stymied in their efforts to prove that a chemical plant near the Georgia coast was discharging excess amounts of deadly mercury. Both were warned, then threatened if they did not back off. Santou, working undercover, was equally vulnerable. He may have been betrayed.

When Dr. Mark Davis, professor at Stanford's Endangered Biology Department contacted Rachel in *Blue Twilight* (Avon, 2004) it didn't seem like anything to get too excited about. Endangered butterflies! Nevertheless she followed up on a connection to a larvae collector in the San Bruno Mountain area, learned of the monetary values attached to rare species, and the benefits in pollination from the lowly butterfly. There was some concern about the disappearance of butterfly expert John Harmon, but the police were not reacting to it. Eric Holt, a friend of visiting Terri Tune, distracted Rachel's attention. His 14-year–old daughter Lily had run away in the midst of a custody dispute. This brought back Rachel's guilt. She had known that her older sister, Rebecca's intent to run away, but had not alerted her mother. Rebecca had disappeared. Jake, badly injured in a prior narrative, was fighting pain and depression with alcohol and pills, but pitched in when needed.

Fodor would not approve of *Restless Waters* (Avon, 2005) wherein Rachel, now assigned to Hawaii, was exposed to sights never seen by tourists. Jake, on leave from the FBI because of back injuries, and Rachel moved in with Jake's old pal, Kevin O'Rourke. While Jake and Kevin lolled in the sun or surfed the waves, Rachel chafed under the supervision of Norm Pryor. He believed in "see no evil, hear no evil" and wanted Rachel to follow that precept. She heard about the propagation of exotic animals from other countries that threatened the native Hawaiian species. She saw the corpse of potential informer Sammy Kalahiki floating in the water off a coral rock. By ignoring Pryor's orders, Rachel invited retaliation from the killers and those who protected them.

New York City was home to Rachel, so in *Unsafe Harbor* (Severn House, 2006), she accepted reassignment to the adjacent New Jersey Port Authority. This enabled her to live in the lower East side neighborhood she remembered from childhood, and to share a home with Jake Santou. He had been reassigned to the New York office. Jack Hogan, Rachel's supervisor, kept her on a tight rein, clearing up unfiled citations left behind by her predecessor. That couldn't last. Not after the corpse of socialite Bitsy von Falken was discovered. Not when Magda, a friendly vendor who discovered the body and stole a clue, was killed. A telephone informant set Rachel on a trail of bloody diamonds, smuggled ivory, and personal revenge.

Author Jessica Speart took on worthwhile causes in her narratives; i.e. the protection of endangered species including female émigrés. She implicated the business and government interests, which not only tolerated abuses, but also benefited from them. The historical backgrounds and physical descriptions were credible and well researched.

Kathleen "Kit" Powell

Author: Julie Robitaille

Kit Powell had eclectic tastes: boxing and Jane Austen. A redhead whose father ran a sports bar, and whose ex-husband had been a jock, she reported sports for a San Diego television station. She had previously worked as a television writer, but moved on screen when the regular sportscaster was too drunk to appear.

Kit's assignment put her on scene in *Jinx* (Council Oak Books, 1991) when Barry Bludhoff, the stepson of team owner Daphne Collier and the general manager of the Sharks football team, was killed in a fall out of a skybox. Daphne had inherited the team when her third husband was killed also in an accident. She moved the team from Galveston to San Diego. Barry's widow owned stock in the team, but did not live to dispose of it. Someone was taking sports too seriously.

Iced (St. Martin, 1994) involved Kit in the serial murders of homeless persons in San Diego. It was in her role as sportscaster covering the skating championships that Kit met trainer Therese Steiner. Her death was somehow tied to the killings of the homeless and the bigotry of the "White Nation". Kit's underground work put her in danger, but not out of action.

Kate Power

Author: Judith Cutler

The British police system allowed accelerated advancement for recruits with college degrees. In her late twenties, Kate Power, who had a master's degree from Manchester University, was a sergeant in the Birmingham CID (Criminal Investigation Division). She attended the local Baptist church at the urging of her Aunt Cassie, but had been involved with a married man, now deceased. When Aunt Cassie entered the nursing home, Kate had the use of her house and was busy fixing it up. In her spare time, she coached a youth football team. There was some evidence that Kate had a drinking problem but was working on it. As the series developed, there was even more evidence that she fell too easily into romantic and/or sexual affairs with co-workers and superior officers, not recommended in any line of work.

The move to Birmingham was a flight from Kate's memories of Robin, her lover who had been killed. She could not mourn him properly, that was for his wife and children. In *Power On Her Own* (Hodder & Stoughton, 1998), Kate encountered a new set of problems: the hostility of fellow workers at the West Midlands CID, the adjustment of Great-Aunt Cassie to the nursing home; and the renovation of the old woman's house for her use. Most chilling was the probability that among her new friends at work and in the community were members of a pederast ring and a killer.

By *Staying Power* (Hodder & Stoughton, 1999), Kate had moved from London and made friends on the Birmingham force. She contended with Detective Constable Selby's insubordination and misogyny. She was not his only victim. DC Colin Roper, who kept his homosexuality in the closet, was Kate's partner. They tied together several major cases involving pharmacy thefts, drug dealing, family violence and fraud. Selby's behavior eventually accelerated to the point where charges could be brought.

Kate's transfer to the specialized Major Incident Team during *Power Games* (Hodder and Stoughton, 2000) might have offered professional opportunities. Instead it placed Kate under hostile supervision from Inspector Nigel Crowther, whose spectacular advancement on the force had been fostered by his politically prominent mother. Kate had her own admirers in Inspector Graham Harvey and Superintendent Rod Neville to protect her reputation. When she discovered an unidentified body at her tennis club, she sought the woman's identity and her killer with a persistence that created problems for Crowther.

Another transfer, this time to the Birmingham Fraud Squad, brought more misery to Kate in *Will Power* (Hodder & Stoughton, 2001). Her immediate supervisor Inspector Lizzie King was volatile to the point of hostility, a problem recognized but not understood by others in the squad. Kate's assignment to a forgery case expanded to a murder investigation, allowing her to liaise with the CID unit to which she had previously been attached. Again working with her secretive and guilt-ridden lover Graham Harvey and under the direction of Rod Neville, who had no qualms about office romances, she needed to get her personal priorities in order.

The good news in *Hidden Power* (Hodder & Stoughton, 2002) was that Kate had passed the exam for detective inspector and was waiting for an opening in her new status. The bad news was that in the interim she was seconded as a detective sergeant to the Devon and Cornwall Constabulary under the direction of DCI Earnshaw, a woman who had worked her way up in the system and didn't intend to risk her position. Kate was to go undercover as a cleaner at a Sophisticasun time share complex. It wasn't the hard work that troubled Kate. It was being teamed with Det. Sgt. Craig Knowles, her pseudo common law husband. He was abusive and uncooperative beyond the role set out for him. Still he was the local representative; she was the out-of-towner. The only friendly faces were those of building manager Gary Vernon and his family. Vernon might be involved in criminal activity, but Kate came to care deeply for his children.

Kate took over as an Inspector at the Scala House police station as part of her mid-management training in *Power Shift* (Hodder & Stoughton, 2003). This shift put her back in uniform presiding over an understaffed unit with personnel problems. Three investigations meshed bringing Kate into professional contacts with her current lover Rod Neville, her former lover Graham Harvey, and the women in their past and present lives. The cases involved (1) the smuggling of Eastern European juveniles into the United Kingdom for prostitution, (2) the death of Joe Gardner, the trucker who had helped Natasha, one of the young women being transported, to escape, and the disappearance of Phil Bates, a member of Kate's unit. On a personal level, Kate had to make arrangements to supplement Aunt Cassie's income so she could remain in the nursing home. She took a lot of punishment in this one, but she dumped a man who betrayed her.

Cutler has tremendous versatility. In addition to the Sophie Rivers series, covered in this volume, she has at least three others. (1) Parson Tobias Campion, an historical sleuth; (2) Chief Supt Frances Harman, a police procedural; and (3) Josie Welford, a pub owner in a culinary series. Tremendous breadth and depth to all of her work.

Narcissa Powers and Judah Daniel

Author: Ann McMillan

Narcissa Powers' mother died when she was fifteen; her father, when she was nineteen. Her husband Rives Powers had tutored her brother Charley. Rives died of tuberculosis, leaving her a widow at age twenty-one. Their baby died shortly after birth. At twenty-three, Narcissa became one of an ensemble which included Judah Daniel, a former slave who had expertise as an herbalist; Dr. Cameron Archer, the supervisor of the Medical College of Virginia Hospital; and Brit Wallace, an English reporter.

The terminal illness of her beloved brother Charley, a medical student, had sent Narcissa to Richmond in *Dead March* (Viking, 1998) in time to realize that he might have been murdered. After a brief visit in the home of Dr. Edgar Hughes, Charley's professor, Narcissa moved in with her sister-in-law Mirrie, an outspoken opponent of secession. The State of Virginia made its choice and prepared for war while Narcissa focused on the activities of the "resurrection men" who stole corpses from their graves for medical research. Her sensitivity to the plight of African-Americans was heightened by attendance at a slave auction and her alliance with free African-American Judah Daniel. Narcissa and Judah worked together as practical nurses at the overflowing army hospital, while investigating Charley's death.

In *Angel Trumpet* (Viking, 1999), Narcissa and Judah worked in the Medical College of Virginia Hospital under Dr. Archer. They were expected to watch over Archer's headstrong young female cousin Jordan who had returned from a Maryland boarding school for young ladies. They also had the task of interrogating slave servants who were suspected of killing members of their plantation families. Although Judah's herbal skills and Narcissa's probing affected the plot, Cameron and Brit identified the killer.

Civil Blood (Viking, 2001) was an ambitious narrative, fueled by the fear, greed and passion of a dozen characters. Narcissa and Judah, with a common goal—preventing the spread of smallpox in Richmond—set out to locate a jacket and a considerable amount of money that carried the smallpox virus. Rival youth gangs, a philandering entrepreneur, and the women he betrayed complicated their search.

Richmond, the capitol of the Confederacy was under siege by Union troops as *Chickahominy Fever* (Viking, 2003) began. Susy Reynolds, a free African-American servant in Jefferson Davies' household, had been placed there as a spy. When she retrieved a letter from General Wise detailing the weaknesses in the Confederate defenses, her intent was to get it to McClellan. Narcissa and her sister-in-law Mirrie were guests of abolitionist Louisa Ferncliff, who had placed Susy in the Davis household. Narcissa and Judah connected only at the conclusion. There were other narrative lines: a mother determined to keep her wounded son from returning to his regiment; the fate of an infant who might be returned to slavery.

A fascinating series.

Patricia "Pat" Pratt

Author: Bernie Lee

Ignoring the unfortunate choice of surname, this was another "couples" series. Patricia Pratt, the mother of two college age children, was a successful financial consultant, who lived in Oregon with husband Tony, a freelance mystery writer.

In *Murder at Musket Beach* (Fine, 1990), the couple rented a cottage in a small Pacific coast town. Although Tony wanted a vacation from mysteries, they tripped over a corpse on the beach shortly after they arrived. Fortunately local power broker/grocer Martin Ross vouched for them when the police came. Tony and Pat followed separate paths to investigate, but finally combined what they had learned, including plans to make money off a real estate deal.

A Japanese film company hired Tony to make location arrangements near an Indian reservation as *Murder Without Reservation* (Fine, 1991) began. When Pat joined him, her role was more that of victim than investigator. Even with such action standbys as stampedes, kidnapping, robberies, and the murder of handsome Japanese actor Dennis Shimada, the narrative failed to hold together.

Murder Takes Two (Fine, 1993) took the Pratts to London where advertising executive Gary Bonham was murdered during the filming of commercials. Only on their return to Oregon did they identify the killer. Pat took an active role in protecting Tony when he confronted a suspect, but the killer was obvious, and the motive was weak.

Nick and Nora needn't worry about the competition.

Dr. Amy Prescott

Author: Louise Hendricksen

Dr. Amy Prescott was a slim divorcee who had been raised by her father and followed in his footsteps as a forensic pathologist. She initially worked in the Western Washington State Crime Lab; later, she formed a consulting firm with her father. Amy maintained an apartment in Seattle, but spent much of her time on an offshore island where the family owned property. Her mother had left the family when she was eleven. Amy was fiercely independent of all men, even her father, which may have contributed to her failed marriage. She shared her island cottage with Cleo, a black Cocker Spaniel, and Marcus, a Manx cat. Amy was described as tall and brown-haired. One of her closest relationships was with her Aunt Helen, who had become a substitute mother.

Cousin Oren, Helen's son, was a murder suspect in *With Deadly Intent* (Zebra, 1993) when his provocative fiancée Elise disappeared. The sheriff of Lomitas Island resented the Prescott family, and was uninterested in any other explanation for the missing woman. Amy teamed with Simon Kittredge, formerly Elise's lover, to disclose the truth about the disappearance.

Simon remained important to Amy in *Grave Secrets* (Zebra, 1994). He was kidnapped in Idaho where he investigated unfortunate investments made by his father. He had left a message on Amy's answering machine. She went to look for him, even though he was interested in another woman. Rock Springs, Idaho was controlled by elements unlikely to share their secrets with Amy.

Amy was four-months pregnant by her Native American lover, Nathan Blackthorn, as *Lethal Legacy* (Zebra, 1995) began but had no intentions of telling him he was the father. Nathan had returned to the reservation and married within the tribe. Yet she needed his help when her friend and fellow doctor, Cam Nguyen, was accused of murdering his wife. The police solution was too simplistic for Amy; so she followed a trail of Asiatic intrigue through back alleys and topiary gardens.

Gin Prettifield

Author: Cecil Dawkins

Although Gin (Ginevra) was part-Sioux Indian, she rarely mentioned the fact because it had become so politically correct to be Native American. That was not her style, although she frequently wore an expensive silver conch belt. She was a tall, dark woman who had been raised in the Mora Valley of New Mexico, and now worked as assistant director of the Waldheimer Museum in Santa Fe, which had an unusual collection of Old Masters. Gin rented a small unit in a compound where the inhabitants shared a semi-communal existence and an interest in the arts. Before settling down, she had attended Barnard College, earning a degree in art history, and traveled extensively throughout the British Isles.

In *The Santa Fe Rembrandt* (Ivy, 1993), even though she was competent, Gin wondered why she had been hired by the Museum for such a responsible position. Her confidence was shaken when she discovered that forgeries had been substituted for priceless artwork. When a member of a tour group was attacked with a Remington sculpture, Gin was uncertain whether or not the crimes were connected.

In *Rare Earth* (Ivy, 1995), Gin vacationed at her family home in the Sangre de Cristo Mountains where she discovered a bear hovering over a mutilated body. The ranger to whom she reported the incident returned with her, but the body had disappeared. The victim was probably a member of a well-known rock band expected to perform at an area festival, but which one? Complex motives and unexplained relationships early in the narrative diminished the impact of the action.

Tina Martinez and Reuben Rubens, members of the communal group to which Gin belonged, were featured in author Cecil Dawkin's *Clay Dancers* (Ivy, 1994). She did not appear.

Laura Principal

Author: Michelle Spring a.k.a. Michelle Stanworth

The daughter of a truck driver dad and hairdresser mom, Laura Principal managed an advanced degree from Cambridge, which qualified her as an academic historian and teacher. Her father Paul died after a long illness. Laura ended her marriage when it no longer met her needs. Then, she became a private investigator working for her divorced lover Sonny Mendlowitz. Laura owned a Cambridge home, and a shared-interest in a renovated Norfolk barn cottage (Wildfell) with university librarian Helen Cochrane. While in London, she lived in Sonny's apartment. Although she loved Sonny, she had a need for

Wildfell and friendships with other women. During her investigations, Laura frequently compared herself to fictional detectives.

As *Every Breath You Take* (Orion, London, 1994) opened, Laura and Helen lowered the Wildfell expenses by taking in a third party, Monica Harcourt. However the new arrangement created tensions, and Monica's murder was no solution. Because Laura had involved herself in the affairs of several other friends, when she was attacked at her office, it was unclear whether or not the attack was connected to Monica's death. Laura and Helen risked further danger before the culprit was found. Too many ambitious plots tripped over one another.

A similar problem existed in *Running for Shelter* (Orion, 1995). Laura was managing the office and caring for Sonny's sons while he was in Europe. She accepted an assignment to find the thief plaguing the theatre where producer Thomas Butler was preparing a new play. She agreed to trace the missing paintings from Marcia Shields' home without involving the police. She involved herself in the plight of immigrants whose services were abused by their employers. Laura risked personal injury and police charges to rescue a victim when the police were reluctant to act on her information. She resolved the conflict between her relationship with Sonny and her need for privacy.

During *Standing in the Shadows* (Ballantine, 1998), Laura was hired not to prove the innocence of foster child Daryll Flatt who had allegedly murdered Geraldine King, his widowed caretaker, but to learn his motive. Detective Inspector Nicole Pelletier, a former student of Laura's who had worked the case, had no sympathy for the boy even though he came from a deeply disturbed background. Laura probed the social services management of Daryll's case and cases of lonely women, which placed the "facts" in a different light.

While Sonny was obsessed with expanding the agency to Europe, Laura immersed herself in the disappearance of a young college student in *Nights in White Satin* (Ballantine, 1999). The cruel treatment experienced by Katie Arkwright at the hands of sadistic Cambridge men was enough to drive her away, but had she committed murder before she left? An examination of Katie's past showed a troubled childhood and some unsavory employment

Laura had given little thought to having a child until *In the Midnight Hour* (Orion, 2001). Olivia Cable had seen a teenage boy who resembled the young man her missing son might have become. She and her husband Jack had spent twelve years searching for their child. Jack did not want Olivia crushed by another disappointment so he hired Laura to check the young man's background. Laura' s awareness of Olivia' s deep sense of loss caused her to confront her own feelings about having Sonny's child.

The narratives were distinguished for their excellent physical descriptions.

E. J. (Eloise Janine) Pugh

Author: Susan Rogers Cooper

E.J. Pugh, a tall redhead, had no taste for violence. She was a happily married young woman in her thirties with children, living in small town Texas. Her parents, an over-involved mother and a passive father, lived in Houston. She had three sisters. The older two, Liz who managed a small theatre, and Nadine, a nurse, had never been close to E.J. Cheryl, a few years older, had been too close for comfort. Over the years, E.J. had contributed to the family income by writing two dozen romance novels. Her husband, Willis, an engineer, was a stabilizing influence in her life.

But in *One, Two, What Did Daddy Do?* (St. Martin, 1992), E. J. had no choice. Drawn to the neighboring house, she found a family slaughtered with only Bessie, a four-year-old girl, as a survivor. The local police were content to file the case as murder-suicide but E.J. knew the family well. She would not take the chance that Bessie was in danger, and eventually persuaded Detective Elena Luna, a former Army MP, to help trace the clues found in a teenager's journal.

By *Hickory, Dickory, Stalk* (Avon, 1996), Bessie had become a part of the Pugh family in the process of adoption. The house formerly occupied by Bessie's parents had been purchased by a strange family, whose elder son, Brad, was found stark naked and definitely dead in E. J.'s car. He was no favorite of E. J.'s who suspected him of vicious pranks. Whoever had been harassing E.J. set about framing her for Brad's death.

Home Again, Home Again (Avon, 1997) was Willis' book, not E. J.'s. At a time when he was dealing with his fortieth birthday, he had developed a compulsion to climb Enchanted Rock. His disappearance after he and a friend set out to make the climb set E.J. on his trail with the help of their friends. She had to do some soul searching about her role in the deterioration of their relationship. Equally interesting was Willis' adventure among rural Texans who could not afford to let him go, but were reluctant to kill him. He weighed the quality of his marriage and his need for some validation for his forty years of life.

E.J. had stopped Brenna McGraw from killing herself. Now she had to bring security into the teenager's life. But, in *There Was a Little Girl* (Avon, 1998), that became more difficult when Brenna was accused of killing her mother, recently released from prison. E. J.'s mother-in-law Vera, formerly hostile, became an ally. Police officer Elena Luna, E. J.'s friend and neighbor, had no sympathy for E. J.'s amateur antics and neither did Willis.

During *A Crooked Little House* (Avon, 1999), figures from the past threw Willis and E. J.'s lives into turmoil. Willis and Vera had always blamed the death of her younger son, Dusty, on his immature wife, Juney. Vera had cared for Juney during her pregnancy, then took sole care of baby Garth when Juney left. Vera had been devastated when Juney reappeared and took little Garth away after a year. When Juney dropped Garth off a second time, Vera was determined to seek custody of the boy. After Juney was accused of murder, Vera put aside her feelings and helped E.J. prove her innocence.

E. J.'s involvement in murder investigations was very hard on Willis. Aware of this, she discussed with her therapist, Anne Comstock, why she allowed herself to be drawn into these matters when it so obviously created a problem for her husband. *Not In My Back Yard* (Avon, 1999) confronted two of the most terrifying fears of a mother: (1) the possibility of terminal illness and (2) proximity to a child molester. E.J. was torn between her repugnance for a convicted pederast and compassion for his wife and nine-year-old son. Her tactics when Michael Whitby was murdered went over the line. She lied, made unfounded accusations, and bullied suspects.

Only E. J.'s mother, Louise, thought a vacation shared by her daughters would lead to bonding in *Don't Drink the Water* (Avon, 2000). The enmities among the siblings had begun in their childhood and were too serious to be erased in a week, even in the lovely Virgin Islands. The discovery of a woman's corpse in a cistern exacerbated the problem. The victim, whom E.J. remembere having seen on the ferry dock and walking the beach, was identified as Tracy Bishop. E. J.'s history of involvement in crime put her on the suspect list of the local police. While investigating Tracy's background, E.J. reviewed her childhood, seeking clues to the rivalry between her and her sister Cheryl.

It had been years since E.J. got involved in a murder investigation, but in *Romanced to Death* (Severn House, 2008) she was ready for one. The American Romance Writers Association had nominated E. J.'s latest book for a "Lady", an award to be presented at the convention in Austin. Although E. J. had never met Jane Dawson aka Maybellle La Rue, her prospective roommate, they had been in contact for some time, and already bonded. Jane's murder took place against a background of jealousy, charges of plagiarism, and insights into the negative aspects of fame as a romance writer. Things weren't much better for E. J. on the home front. Elizabeth (formerly Bessie), now thirteen and raised as part of E.J. and Willis' family, had become involved via the Internet with "Tommy", who shared frightening information about the tragedy that happened to her birth family.

A good series dealing with sensitive issues. Author Susan Rogers Cooper has another major series featuring Deputy Sheriff Milton Kovak and a shorter one featuring comedienne Kimmey Kruse.

Recently announced: *Full Circle* (2011)

Sarah "Quill" Quilliam

Author: Claudia Bishop, pseudonym for Mary Stanton

Sarah "Quill" Quilliam had established herself as an artist in New York City, but her personal life was in disorder. She turned her back on urban life, and joined her recently widowed sister Meg in operating the Hemlock Falls Inn. Quill served as the business manager for the inn located in rural New York State, while

Meg, a petite trained chef, ran the kitchen. They relied on a dedicated staff initially including part-Native American manager John Raintree and "born again" head housekeeper Doreen Muxworthy.

When, during *A Taste for Murder* (Berkley, 1994), Mavis Collinwood, companion to Amelia Halllenbeck, was injured after a fall from a balcony, she threatened a lawsuit. Local car dealer Gil Gilmeister was killed in an accident, but initially there seemed to be no connection between the incidents. Mavis' subsequent death was obviously murder. John Raintree may have been one of the targets of a blackmailer. Quill found a killer who tried to put her out of business.

The inn needed a public relations coup, so when television hostess Helena Houndswood came to stay in *A Dash of Death* (Berkley, 1995), the staff catered to her every mood. She came to the inn, because she was considering the purchase of land in the area and was to interview the winner of a design contest sponsored by her program. Unfortunately the winner was a group (employees of a local paint manufacturer), which gradually decreased in size as members were murdered. Quill solved the mystery before her beau Sheriff Myles McHale could. He was surprisingly constant, given that she frequently withheld information needed to solve the murders.

Their relationship was threatened in *A Pinch of Poison* (Berkley, 1995) when Myles indicated that he wanted marriage and a family. Marriage was acceptable to Quill, but she did not believe she could continue her career if she became a mother. The continued existence of the inn was threatened when the members of the Rudyard Kipling Condensation Society revived a long buried hatred. Myles and Quill worked together well enough to declare a truce.

The varied plot lines of *Murder Well-Done* (Berkley, 1996) were hard to swallow. A gender issue had divided the local Chamber of Commerce into feuding sections. The inn was to host the wedding dinner of deposed Senator Alphonse Santini to the heiress of a Scottish-Italian Mafia clan. Myles had been defeated for re-election and his successor was less tolerant of Quill. The new town justice sentenced her to jail for passing a school bus. When Nora Cahill, provocative television anchor, was murdered with a knife from the inn, she was returned to jail. Even a murder committed while she was incarcerated was blamed on her! Too many ingredients of dubious quality to go down easy. Not up to the standard of prior books.

During *Death Dines Out* (Berkley, 1997), a pseudo-vacation in West Palm Beach turned into a disaster for Quill and Meg when they were caught between vengeful socialite Tiffany Taylor and Verger, her powerful ex-husband. What was anticipated to be Meg's chance to earn back her third star as a chef ended up in a murder/kidnapping. On their return home, good times were back in upstate New York and particularly for tourism.

Among the few guests at the inn during *A Touch of the Grape* (Berkley, 1998) were a quintet of elderly ladies who merchandized craft kits. A series of arson/murders thrust suspicion on Quill and Meg as owners of heavily mortgaged property, but money was not the motive for the crimes. Revenge was.

Quill was betwixt and between during *A Steak in Murder* (Berkley, 1999). Her lover Sheriff Myles McHale was doing industrial espionage for General Electric. Her suitor John Raintree was available to help with business decisions and crime solving. The restaurant (the Palate Gourmet) that she had received in trade from Marge Schmidt was operating at a profit. In turn, Marge was doing well with the inn at Hemlock Falls, which she had purchased, mortgage and all. So why was Quill miserable? The consensus from sister Meg and friends was that Quill used these distractions and the murder investigations to avoid the real problems in her life. An acknowledged artist, she no longer painted. Unimpressed by these insights, Quill involved herself in a triple murder that featured Texas cattlemen and Russian venture capitalists. Then she turned back the clock.

Quill was not at her best during *Marinade for Murder* (Berkley, 2000). It was understandable. The negotiations for the Finnish acquisition of a minority interest in the inn, enabling the sisters to repurchase, were not going well. Meg, whose participation in the inn's future was essential, had been offered a lucrative position at a New York City restaurant. Horvath Kierkegaard, the Finnish representative who loved American fast food, was insisting upon changes in the inn's menus. Quill's relationship with Myles had ended with John Raintree as a probable successor. She had too much on her plate. To make it worse, her dog was accused of murder!

Quill was suffering from a variety of health problems as *Just Desserts* (Berkley, 2002) began. She diligently searched out possible diagnoses in Merck's Manual. It could be stress because she'd fallen in love with Ben Harker, a New York City artist, and was spending less time at the inn. That meant she hadn't kept up on events: the meteorologist's conference arranged by television weatherman Boomer Dougherty; the cityoflove.com dating service promoted by Doreen Muxsworthy-Stoker; and the inn's web page designed by Joss Roberts. Even the release of George Nash from prison didn't register right away. As teenagers, Meg and Quill had been present when Nash and two accomplices took off in a stolen car. When the car crashed, infant Evan Ross, who had remained in the vehicle while his father went into a store, died. One of the best of the series.

Andy Bishop was a competent caring doctor so, in *A Puree of Poison* (Berkley, 2002) when three of his elderly patients in the local hospital died in one week, most assigned no blame to him. That was not enough for Andy. He had looked for a pattern; the only one he found was that all had recently eaten at the inn. As Meg's suitor, he wasn't about to challenge her cooking, but he talked to Quill about his concerns. She had a lot on her plate, but knew that she had to protect the inn's reputation.

As Quill's psychiatrist explained to her in *Fried by Jury* (Berkley, 2003), all she had on her mind was (1) a potential and disastrous confrontation between two fast food magnates who would be staying at the inn, and (2) an equally hostile exchange between Meg and famous chef Banion O'Haggerty, both candidates to judge a deep fry cooking contest. When O'Haggerty was murdered, Quill needed to focus to protect Meg. The psychiatrist helped.

March was supposed to be a quiet time at the inn, but in *Buried by Breakfast* (Berkley, 2004) Quinn was overwhelmed. The jury in a civil lawsuit against ROCOR, the real estate developer of property near the inn, was sequestered there. Friends of the Dead were protesting against ROCOR's plans to relocate an historic cemetery to accommodate a golf course. The ROCOR development was rumored to include an inn that would compete with the inn at Hickory Falls. A hitherto distant cousin, Clarisande was coming to visit so Meg could teach her to cook. Venomous Carol Ann Spinoza had won local support for a "Peoples Police Force". Then wrestler Bouncer Muldoon, a missing juror, was found dead. He had been Marge Schmidt's husband, an added complication. Too many issues were left hanging at the conclusion.

The dynamics between Quill and Meg were an important part of *A Dinner to Die For* (Berkley, 2006). As the older sister, Quill had a powerful influence on Meg when they were young. She was relieved that Meg, a widow, seemed to have found happiness with fiancé Dr. Andy Bishop. Yet Meg seemed tense, fighting with replacement chef Jerry Grimsby. Leo "Boom-Boom" Maltby, brought an entourage with him as guests at the inn. He was reputed to be planning a "nudie" nightclub for the community, which aroused "Women Against Crimes Against Women". When Quill did not support their protest, they encouraged others to take their business somewhere else. Staff realignment had caused a mutiny. How did the corpse of small time hood, Antonia Caprese fit in?

The International Association of Pet Food Producers (IAPFP), guests at the inn during *Ground to a Halt* (Berkley, 2007), was one of the smallest and most contentious gatherings ever to meet there. Arrangements had been made by newcomer to the Chamber of Commerce, Pamela Durbin. Pamela, who owned a pet shop, was also a major investor in Vegan Vittles, a vegetarian pet food distributor. Pamela and Marge Schmidt were vying for the attentions of farmer Harland Peterson. Quill, now married to Myles and no longer living at the inn, was having a problem with her isolated new home. While acting as a volunteer for a first grade school trip to a pig farm, Quill discovered a corpse identified as Lila Longstreet, bookkeeper for Max Kittleburger, president of Pet-Pro Protein. Based on the assumption that her killer was connected to IAFPF, members were required to stay at the inn until the investigation was completed.

Quill believed that she had come up with an acceptable solution to the inn's financial problems in *A Carol for a Corpse* (Berkley, 2007). It wasn't easy for her to contact *L'Apertif* magazine editor Lydia Kingsfield, who had been her high school nemesis. They made a deal whereby Kingsfield Publishing would lease the inn for four weekends to showcase Lydia's television show *Good Taste* and set up a joint merchandizing project to introduce Meg's jams, jellies, and chutneys to the public. It became more complex when Lydia's husband, egocentric and powerful Zeke Kingsfield, became involved. Lots of side issues, some very productive.

A Plateful of Murder, scheduled to be published in 2009 includes the first two books in the series plus recipes from the inn at Hemlock Falls.

Bishop, who had a real winner in the anthology *A Merry Band of Murderers*, also has a new series featuring Dr. Austin McKenzie, a retired veterinarian, and has more recently introduced The Beaufort and Company, a paranormal series located in the South.

Death in Two Courses (2010) includes the third and fourth books in the series plus recipes. Due in 2010, *Toast Mortem*.

Garner Quinn

Author: Jane Waterhouse

Author Garner Quinn's preoccupation with true crime may have resulted from watching her father, a criminal defense attorney. Dudley Quinn had rejected Garner's alcoholic mother He had provided for his child's financial needs, but showed little personal interest in the girl. He was a hedonistic egotist who filled his home and his life with beautiful people. Garner's upbringing was watched over by Cilda Fields, the African-American housekeeper. As a child Garner had fantasized that attractive sculptor Dane Blackmoor, who frequented the Quinn home, might be her real father, and that she might be the product of her mother Gabrielle's affair. Blackmoor's interest was far from paternal, even with Garner in her preteen years. None of this prepared her for marriage. Her short-term union with attorney Andrew Matera produced little happiness, except for her daughter Temple who shared her New Jersey home. Her focus was on her career. As one project ended, she became desperate to begin another book. When she covered a trial, she became a part of the defense, even contributing to their plans.

As Garner left behind the legal team that had won the acquittal of Jefferson Turner, putative serial killer, in *Graven Images* (Putnam, 1995), she was contacted by Dane Blackmoor, who offered himself as the subject of her next case. He was suspected of killing Victoria Lynn Wood, a young woman whom he had used as a model for his work. The narrative explored Garner's need to know more of her mother, now deceased, to connect with her dying father, and to cope with her continued fascination with Blackmoor.

Garner was thirty-seven as *Shadow Walk* (Putnam, 1997) began, burned out by her short but highly successful career and determined to move her life in another direction. She could not, however, turn her back on what had been one of the most intensive relationships in her life, a high school friendship with Lara Spangler. Lara, her mother, grandmother, and two brothers were killed by her father, who then disappeared. Shortly before his "suicide," T.J. Sterling, a rival author, had hinted that he had located Gordon Spangler. Convinced that Spangler had killed Sterling, Garner set out to hunt him down.

The letter from Dane, eagerly awaited by Garner, never arrived in *Dead Letter* (Putnam, 1998). Instead there were threatening, erotic messages from CHAZ, a stalker. Garner was referred to the Corbin Security Agency for protection and found a loving friend in owner Reed Corbin. When the agency was unable to provide the safety it had promised, Garner made her own plans.

Garner was a flawed but fascinating character.

Imogen Quy

Author: Jill Paton Walsh

In her thirties, Imogen Quy settled contentedly into her deceased parents' home in Cambridge, England. She had abandoned her plans to become a doctor, and entered nursing school instead. After graduation she secured a position with the University. She dated, but remained single. Her first love, a fellow medical student, had rejected her, and the right person had never come along. Boarders, primarily students and staff at Cambridge, supplemented her income.

As *The Wyndham Case* (St. Martin, 1993) opened, Imogen was called to the library in her capacity as university nurse. Crispin Mountnessing, the librarian in charge of the exclusive Wyndham collection, had discovered the body of first-year student Philip Skellow. Imogen's continued involvement came at the request of Sgt. Mike Parsons. She discovered how a practical joke and an unfortunate scuffle ended in tragedy; then found the plunderers of the Wyndham case.

In *A Piece of Justice* (St. Martin, 1995), Fran, one of Imogen's roomers, was hired to ghost the biography of Gideon Summerfield, an otherwise undistinguished mathematician whose single great discovery made him a candidate for the Waymark Prize. Imogen learned that three prior ghostwriters had either disappeared or died mysteriously. The origins of Summerfield's discovery became apparent to Imogen, as did the reasons why murder was necessary to hide the truth. These were intricate narratives. The characterization of Imogen was not broadly developed, but the plotting was excellent.

The "Takeover King" Sir Julius Farran received a mixed welcome when he visited St. Agatha's in *Debts of Dishonor* (Hodder & Stoughton, 2006). Imogen had been assigned to entertain him, but instead had to warn off hecklers. When Sir Julius died in a fall off a cliffside, Imogen remembered his comments about dangerous enemies. The involvement of Andrew Duncombe, once Imogen's lover, now a director of the Farran Group, drew her into a complex puzzle. The second death of an Farran executive was clearly murder. On her own, Imogen put the pieces together and forced a solution that she could live with.

Walsh did it again in *The Bad Quarto* (Hodder & Stoughton, 2006), a thought provoking narrative, which dealt with gray areas and the responsibility of those who have to make decisions. Imogen came upon the scene of John

Talentine's death. A Cambridge Climber (group who individually made dangerous ascents on campus structures) he had attempted the jump from Harding's Folly, only to be killed. Two years later John's death was questioned in a dramatic expose. Had he been murdered or was he the victim of carelessness? Imogen was involved on several levels: nurse for the Kyd Players who were presenting an abbreviated version of *Hamlet*; witness to an intrusion of the Tower Room from which Talentine had fallen, and confidante of the Master, Sir William Buckmote. Excellent narrative.

In another series, author Jill Paton Walsh took on a formidable task, continuing the Lord Peter Wimsey/Harriet Vane series and did very well.

Caro Radcliffe

Author: Carole Hayman

Caro (Caroline) Radcliffe experienced more than a physical change in life during her forties. She had been a researcher for a television production company when she married Sebastian. Twenty years of his infidelity had produced daughter Jade, now off to Oxford, and considerable dissatisfaction. Sebastian was a prominent television producer, who had returned from one liaison during the Christmas holidays, only to disappear. Caro resided in the coastal town of Warfleet.

Missing (HarperCollins, 1996) concentrated on Caro's evolution into a novelist and a lesbian. The only corpse was an individual not closely connected to the primary characters. Sebastian, who had left Caro and found happiness with Delia Henderson, was now missing. Delia was the guardian of Sebastian's son by a deceased lover. A sub-plot involving young Warren Peabody, son of the Radcliffe housekeeper and interested in Jade, was convoluted.

By *Greed, Crime, Sudden Death* (Vista, 1998), Warfleet and Caro had their hidden depths revealed. She had used the events of her recent past as the background for her first successful novel. Jade was now working for the television production company where Sebastian had held a prominent position. Jade had discarded Warren, but was shocked to learn that he was having an affair with Caro. Warfleet reeled under the news that the estate of the Marquis of Tolleymarch might be turned into a theme park. This time there clearly was a murder. Victim Charlie Fong had made a dramatic entry into the media business and was behind the plans for the theme park. There were also rumors of drug and gun smuggling in the taverns and hotels, now filled with reporters, police and FBI agents. Cluttered.

Agatha Raisin

Author: M. C. Beaton, pseudonym for Marion Chesney

Agatha Raisin had always pushed herself, leaving school at fifteen to work in a local biscuit factory; then, attending business college. Beginning as a secretary, she achieved management status in a public relations agency. The child of alcoholic parents, she married Jimmy Raisin who had a drinking problem. They had separated, but neither had taken the ultimate step of divorce. Agatha was in her early fifties when she sold her lucrative public relations business.

The self-centered, competitive Agatha Raisin responded to life in the Cotswold village of Carsely with a series of learning experiences and disasters. She learned that the qualities that made for success in the business world were not held in high esteem among the locals. She disliked housework, was totally inept in a kitchen, and knew little or nothing about gardens. Yet she wanted to be included in the life of the village. She possessed none of the small talk or courtesies that might have attracted acquaintances, but in the way of small towns, she gathered a circle of friends. She added cats to her household, and enjoyed swimming. A stocky woman with brown hair and eyes, Agatha was no beauty, but was definitely interested in men, and particularly in neighbor James Lacey.

When, in *Agatha Raisin and the Quiche of Death* (St. Martin, 1992), she learned of the quiche competition, it seemed an opportunity to make her presence felt. And so it did. The purchased spinach quiche, which she entered as her own, poisoned the contest judge later in the day.

In *Agatha Raisin and the Vicious Vet* (St. Martin, 1993), her overtures to Lacey were counterproductive. Veterinarian Paul Bloden took her to dinner, but made an appeal for his new animal hospital. However, when Bloden was killed by equine medication, Agatha found an interest she could share with Lacey—murder.

The two early themes, Agatha's competitiveness in local contests and her interest in Lacey, combined in *Agatha Raisin and the Potted Gardener* (St. Martin, 1994). She had returned from a European vacation to find Lacey had diverted himself with Mary Fortune, a newcomer who excelled in cooking and gardening. Agatha sold herself into six months servitude with a London public relations firm in an effort to win prowess as a gardener and regain her rapport with Lacey. After her rival was brutally murdered, Agatha and Lacey teamed to find the killer.

Six months in London was about all Agatha could handle. During *Agatha Raisin and the Walkers of Dembley* (St. Martin, 1994), she was relieved to return to the countryside. Her tour de force with Lacey, finding the killer of Jessica Tartinck, the aggressive leader of the local hiking group, brought him to a proposal.

It would be too much to expect a wedding to go smoothly for Agatha. In *Agatha Raisin and the Murderous Marriage* (St. Martin, 1996), Jimmy, her first and current husband, was the uninvited guest. When he was murdered near Agatha's home, she and the now-estranged James combined to learn who else had a motive to kill him.

James left Carsely, taking the planned Greek honeymoon alone. In *Agatha Raisin and the Terrible Tourist* (St. Martin, 1997), she set out in pursuit. Her companions in the Turkish sector of Cyprus included two couples and two singles attached to the couples. They formed an ill-sorted group, but within it were a victim and a killer. Agatha encountered James during the murder investigation; however, it was tightfisted but attentive Sir Charles Fraith who offered his support.

A commercial plan to purchase a share of the water from a century-old spring that flowed onto public property aroused considerable controversy in the community during *Agatha Raisin and the Wellspring of Death* (St. Martin, 1998). Agatha's discovery of the body of Robert Struthers, a member of the Anscombe Parish Council, just before a deciding vote brought her into the fray. She accepted a position as public relations manager of Anscombe Water, the group seeking a franchise, and a personal relationship with a co-owner of the company. James and Agatha conducted individual probes but coordinated their efforts in the end. This cooperation did not extend to a romantic future. Maybe it was time for Agatha to move on.

Agatha had a hair-raising experience in *Agatha Raisin and the Wizard of Evesham* (St. Martin, 1999) when she and Charles interfered in a police investigation. They believed that hairdresser Mr. John was seducing and blackmailing female clients. His murder whetted their appetites for detecting until they discovered the naked truth.

Depilated to her roots, Agatha headed for a seaside resort in *Agatha Raisin and the Witch of Wyckhadden* (St. Martin, 1999). It was a dismal place during off-season. Elderly singles who spent the evenings playing Scrabble populated the Grand Hotel. Agatha's presence and her visit to a local psychic provoked excitement, followed by two murders. She regained her looks but not her spirits. Romance with kind local inspector Jimmy Jessop did not survive. Her only acquisition was another cat, named Scrabble.

Agatha never did discover the source of the strange lights at the end of her garden during *Agatha Raisin and the Fairies of Fryfam* (St. Martin, 2000). She had rented a cottage in the small village in Norfolk in the hope that her absence would kindle James Lacey's interest. Although she succeeded in that respect, her friends predicted a marriage would not last. She did stumble upon the killer of upstart businessman Terence "Tolly" Trumpington-James and helped solve the theft of a valuable painting.

Regular readers aware of Agatha's strong personality and the entrenched habits of James Lacey would not be surprised at the travails of their marriage in *Agatha Raisin and the Love from Hell* (St. Martin, 2001). Less predictable would be the shared suspicions of infidelity, the public quarrels, and James' departure leaving behind evidence of a bloody struggle. James, at first thought of as a victim, became a suspect when Melissa Sheppard, with whom he had an affair, was found dead. Agatha was aroused from her depression by Sir Charles and dear Mrs. Bloxby, the vicar's wife, who assisted in locating James and flushing out the killer.

Agatha, desolate because James was currently in a Benedictine monastery and Sir Charles had married, sought solace on an island off the coast of Chile as *Agatha Raisin and the Day the Floods Came* (St. Martin, 2002) began. What did that have to do with the rest of the narrative? Very little except that it made Agatha suspicious of the death of bride-to-be Kylie Stokes. Enlisting help from new neighbor John Armitage and ex-employee Roy Silver, Agatha checked out Kylie's so called friends and the man who loved her.

There was a lesson there somewhere for Agatha in *Agatha Raisin and the Haunted House* (St. Martin, 2003). Perhaps that she should avoid charming gentlemen who move in next door. Or that, if she was going to solve mysteries, she should get an investigator's license and charge for her services. She stretched the patience of Sgt. Bill Wong and Margaret Bloxby as she and her gentlemen friends took a lesson in Seventeenth century British history to dispel a modern ghost.

James, having disappeared from the monastery and John Armitage, only interested in a "quickie", might have made Agatha vulnerable, but in *Agatha Raisin and the Case of the Curious Curate* (St. Martin, 2003) she backed off when handsome curate Tristan Delon suggested investment opportunities. Delon had so increased church attendance that when he was murdered in the vicar's office, poor Rev. Bloxby was suspected. This could not be allowed to happen to dear Margaret Bloxby, his wife, so John Armitage and Agatha worked together, most of the time.

When Agatha did decide to open a private investigation agency, she did it with a flair in *The Deadly Dance* (St. Martin, 2004). She rented an office, hired a secretary, and two part-time assistants. Secretary Emma Comfrey developed strong feelings for Sir Charles Fraith. After some small time cases, the agency was hired by Catherine Laggat-Brown to guard her daughter Cassandra at an engagement party. Cassandra had received a threatening note. Agatha's quick thinking thwarted a sniper, but her investigation had just begun.

Agatha was in the doldrums as *The Perfect Paragon* (St. Martin's, 2005) began. No one had replaced James Lacey in her life. Her staff at the detective agency had been decimated by resignations. Business was so lousy that Agatha agreed to represent businessman Robert Smedley who suspected that his dowdy wife Mabel was being unfaithful. That necessitated recruiting new staff: competent secretary Helen Freedman; her shaved-headed nephew Harry Beam who was taking a year off from school; and seventy-six year old Phil Witherspoon. All turned out to be assets. The team not only discovered the body of missing teenager Jessica Bradley, but was hired by Mabel Smedley when Robert was murdered.

At some point, the reader of the series will tire of the off-again, on-again relationship between Agatha and her former husband, James Lacey, but not probably not in *Love, Lies and Liquor* (St. Martin, 2006) James' plan to take Agatha on a nostalgic visit to remote (and now rundown) Snoth-on-Sea, Sussex was a disaster. A nasty exchange between Agatha and a fellow guest at the hotel, Geraldine Jankers, brought her to the attention of the police. The discovery of Geraldine's body on the beach where she had been strangled with Agatha's missing scarf led to serious problems. Agatha and her agency staff searched Geraldine's past for other suspects. What a past! Her current husband was #4. #2 had recently been released from prison. Agatha soldiered on even when she became a target.

Initially Agatha put aside a letter from Phyllis Tamworthy in *Kissing Christmas Goodbye* (St. Martin's Minotaur, 2007). Phyllis' contention that a member of her family intended to kill her seemed outlandish. Agatha had more immediate problems to deal with: hiring and training new intern Toni Gilmore and preparing a traditional Christmas holiday in the hope that James Lacey would share it. After meeting Phyllis, Agatha and her current guest Roy Silver agreed to attend a family gathering, meet the Tamworthy offspring in the light of Phyllis' plan to change her will. No surprises. Phyllis barely survived dinner so Agatha rallied her support system: Sir Charles, members of her staff (Phil Marshall, Patrick Mulligan, and the surprising Toni) to consider which of the siblings did the crime. Phyllis had made so many enemies that they had to check outside the family.

Agatha was as smart and tough as ever when it came to murder in *A Spoonful of Poison* (St. Martin's Minotaur, 2008) but as vulnerable as ever when it came to romance. She agreed to manage public relations for a church fete partly because attractive George Selby was the fete chairman. All Agatha's hard work in making the event a success was undermined when someone spiked the jam in the jam tasting contest with LSD, causing two deaths. Agatha and her young assistant Toni Gilmour worked together on the case, but there too difficulties arose.

Agatha was pugnacious, unrepentant, and crude; and those were her positive characteristics. Next: *There Goes the Bride* (2009); *Busy Body* (2010). The publisher has also reissued early Agatha Raisin books in couplets (two books in one cover).

Beaton has a second extended series featuring Constable Hamish Macbeth.

Gwenn Ramadge

Author: Lillian O'Donnell

Gwenn Ramadge, a tiny blonde who had been a model, became a private detective. The only child of a wealthy New York family, she had graduated from Barnard College. During an unfortunate love affair, she became pregnant, ending her work as a model and initiating her career with Hart Security and Investigations. When her lover showed no interest in marriage and her child miscarried, Gwenn stayed on at the agency, eventually becoming the owner.

She preferred corporate work, but Gwenn could not turn down an important client. In *A Wreath for the Bride* (Putnam, 1990), Anne Soffey asked her to investigate a murder that had occurred at the wedding of her daughter Mary. When the wedding car blew up, a bridesmaid then checking the luggage was killed. Daughter Mary disappeared at sea on the honeymoon. A second new bride was found dead while her drunken husband slept. Gwenn was piqued by the similarities among the cases.

This experience convinced Gwenn that she wanted no more to do with murder. In *Used to Kill* (Putnam, 1993), she had no choice. Businessman client Douglas Trent had informed his office that he would be returning early from a business trip. No one had told his wife Emma, a dance teacher. When she returned from her studio and found him dead and the safe robbed, she was stunned. She was also suspected because of a report by Hart Security. Later Gwenn needed a vacation and a chance to assess her relationship with Sgt. Ray Dixon, so she spent time in Cuernavaca at her parent's home.

By *The Raggedy Man* (Putnam, 1995), Gwenn was bored and ready to take on new challenges. Her first case, suggested by Dixon, was to prove the innocence of Jayne Harrow, a young policewoman who had been suspended for drug possession. Jayne had broken the code, turning in fellow police officers for dealing drugs obtained in raids. Gwenn hired her. On her first assignment, Jayne was found dead. The police preferred to label her death a suicide. Gwenn and Ray proved that Jayne died because she knew too much. Disturbed by the police corruption, Sgt. Ray Dixon retired and considered a career as a private investigator.

Gwenn was hired to probe thefts on board the cruise ship *Dante Alighieri*, in *The Goddess Affair* (Putnam, 1997), but was diverted into the investigation of the drowning in the ship's pool of Minerva Aldrich. Minerva, whose cancer was in remission, was in the center of a family squabble over control of Goddess Designs, the firm founded by her deceased mother. Theft, smuggling, drugs, and financial mismanagement were entangled in a murky plot.

Readers may remember that Lillian O'Donnell was also the author of the Norah Mulcahaney and Mici Anhalt series covered in Volume 1.

Carmen Ramirez

Author: Lisa Haddock

Carmen Ramirez, the daughter of an Irish-American mother and a Puerto Rican father, had been raised by a loving but strait-laced Baptist grandmother in Frontier City, Oklahoma. Her father was still alive, but her mother had died when Carmen was young. After graduation from journalism school, she remained in her hometown, working at the local newspaper, sharing her apartment with two cats. Carmen had accepted her lesbian orientation, but had no expectation that her grandmother or the community would do so.

During *Edited Out* (Naiad, 1994, but set in 1985), Carmen and her lover Julia Nichols investigated the death of Diane Barrett, a lesbian teacher who had died when suspected of killing a twelve-year-old girl two years before. They questioned whether Diane's death was correctly labeled suicide, or if there had been a cover-up. It was too serious a matter to cover up if the murderer of the child was still at large.

During *Final Cut* (Naiad, 1995, but set in 1987) Julia, a student at Frontier City University, was one of a group starting a lesbian/gay organization. A visit from Toni Stewart, a bisexual friend from Carmen's college days, ended in her death. Toni's family wanted the matter settled quietly. Carmen uncovered an anti-homosexual group that enforced their views with murder.

The narratives had excellent plotting, but evidenced a strong anti-male bias.

Lucia Ramos

Author: Mary Morell

Lucia Ramos, one of the early Chicana series sleuths was a lesbian police officer working in San Antonio, Texas. After a stint in juvenile, she had been assigned as a rookie detective in homicide.

In *Final Session* (Spinsters, 1990), her investigation of the death of psychotherapist Elizabeth Freeman showed that Freeman was a destructive personality who had seriously damaged patients by sexual abuse. Lucia looked for the killer among current and former patients and members of their families until she discovered a tie-in to Freeman's personal life. Lucia became sexually involved with Dr. Amy Traeger, an older woman psychologist who worked with her on the case.

In *Final Rest* (Spinsters, 1993), Lucia went to Alabama to assist Amys Aunt Meg who had been arrested for murder. Amy and her aunt were both lesbians and victims of incest. Lucia's credentials as a police officer gained cooperation from local officials while Amy rallied the gay community for further support. The plot had merit, but the explicit sex will deter some readers.

Precious Ramotswe

Author: Alexander McCall Smith

Precious Ramotswe had been the only child of a prosperous father, a man who had worked the mines and suffered lung damage as a result. He had built up a substantial cattle ranch over the years. Her mother died when she was only four. Precious had an excellent education for a female in Gaborone, Botswana (formerly Bechuanaland Protectorate). A cousin had home schooled her initially. She continued through regular classes and Sunday school until age sixteen. By then she excelled in art and mathematics, assisted by a remarkable memory. Her interest in detection asserted itself in her first full-time job. While doing office work for a bus company owned by a family member, she caught an employee stealing.

Precious had no intention of continuing her father's cattle business after his death. She sold the extensive herd, which included white Brahmin bulls. With the proceeds she purchased a small building at the outskirts of Gaborone and established the No. 1 Ladies' Detective Agency, the first of its kind in Botswana. Adding to her fame was the fact that she did not charge clients for whom she failed to get satisfactory results. Her methods of detection were based on a book by Clovis Anderson: observation, deduction, and then analysis. Her personal beliefs centered on the god Modimo who rewarded and punished appropriately in the hereafter.

Precious was a dark, heavyset woman in her thirties when the series began. She loved her country, loved Africa, and wanted to be nowhere else. Precious had not been fortunate in her marriage to musician Note Mokoti. They had been immediately attracted to one another, but she could not abide his life style. After the loss of a premature infant, she made a life on her own. She had no problem finding suitors. A wealthy factory owner proposed but was rejected. Mr. J.L.B. Matekoni, owner and chief mechanic at the Tlokweng Road Speedy Motors, was successful on his second offer of marriage.

All of this information was gradually introduced in *The No. 1 Ladies' Detective Agency* (Polygon, 1998), which included a series of cases, both humorous and serious.

The path of true love did not always run smoothly in *The Tears of the Giraffe* (Polygon, 2000). J.L.B. and Precious had to choose a house in which to live. Hers was in better condition. Florence, J. L. B.'s lazy maid, was unacceptable to Precious so became a formidable enemy. As a gift to his bride, J.L.B. surprised her with two children in need of a home: Motholali, an eleven-year-old handicapped girl and her brother, Puso, age five. He was a very kind man and she appreciated that quality in him. At work, Precious had added an assistant Mma Grace Makutsi. There were moral questions in the cases they handled: how much to tell of what she learned in an investigation and the appropriateness of blackmail to learn the truth.

The couple's happiness was shattered in *Morality for Beautiful Girls* (Polygon, 2001) when J.L.B succumbed to depression. His business was going well and could be turned over to an assistant. Precious cut her caseload, adjusted her expenses by moving into a smaller office in J. L. B.'s garage and renting out her building. She continued to take a few cases, (possible domestic poisoning, investigating potential candidates in a local beauty contest) but her real concern was her husband's recovery.

The Kalahari Typing School for Men (Anchor U.S, 2003) is an antidote for much of what is available today in the media. Precious and Grace Makutsi solved problems (less than murder) with intelligence and charm. Precious and Mr. Matekoni provided a home for the two orphans and gave aid to the orphans home. Botswana's charm was based not on oil or scenery but by the warmth and integrity of the characters portrayed.

The Full Cupboard of Life (Pantheon, GB, 2003) retained the charm of the earlier books. Precious' investigation of the suitors for a wealthy woman was the only plot in which she had a strong role. The fearful parachute jump and the exposure of fraud by a rival garage were primarily concerns of J.L.B. Matekoni. Mma Potokwane, matron of the orphan farm, played a decisive role in the fraud problem.

The cases coming into the lives of the primary characters in *In the Company of Cheerful Ladies* (Pantheon, 2004) were all solvable. Charlie, the older apprentice at the car repair shop, left for the charms of a rich older woman, but Precious found an acceptable substitute. Romance came into the life of Mme Grace Makutsi when she least expected it. A threat to Precious' marriage was dealt with satisfactorily.

Precious and her ensemble continued to handle small matters that made a big difference in people's lives in *Blue Shoes and Happiness* (Pantheon, 2006). Mr. Polopetsi, former convict who had been unjustly convicted, had become part of the staff at the #1 Ladies Detective Agency and also worked at the garage. The problems dealt with ranged from blackmail to giving romantic advice to Grace Makutsi. Grace had shocked her fiancé by revealing that she was a feminist. All services were provided without recourse to the police although she did bring a dishonest doctor to the attention of his profession.

The episodic pattern of life at the #1 Ladies' Detective Agency and the Tle Kweng Road Speedy Motors was disrupted during *The Good Husband of Zebra Drive* (Pantheon 2007). Charlie, Mr. J.L. B.'s mildly competent apprentice, has decided to start his own business. After obtaining an ancient Mercedes-Benz, he intended to start a taxi service, the #1 Ladies' Taxi Service. More seriously, Grace Makutsi, now engaged to furniture storeowner Phuti Radiphuti, had become resentful of the minor chores (making bush tea), and the gentle reprimands from Precious when she interfered in conversations with clients. She had money to spend on clothes and her general appearance. Impulsively, she quit her job at the agency and resolved to find a position of greater importance. J.L. B. decided he would like to do some investigating, and filled in on one of the cases that Grace Makutsi would probably have handled. Precious took on the most serious case: three deaths in the Intensive Care Unit of the Mochudi Hospital, each occurring at about the same time on Fridays to occupants of the same bed. Grace returned to her job.

The Miracle at Speedy Motors (Pantheon, 2008) contains a message for readers of all ages and races. It is not the big miracles, but all the little ones that make life worth living for those who can settle for less than perfection. There were problems: (1) threatening letters to Precious, (2) Mme. Manka Sebina, who had no family, hired Precious to trace her roots, (3) Grace Makutsi and her fiancé Phuti were preparing for a joint household. Most important to J. L. B. was the possibility that doctors in Johannesburg might be able to enable their foster daughter Motholeli to walk again. Next: *Tea Time for the Traditionally Built* (2009); *The Double Comfort Safari Club* (2010). Earlier Precious Ramotswe books are also being reissued in sets.

These were charming stories in a new setting. Seven of the books were included in a television series shown over HBO in 2008-9. They were terrific. All parts were well cast. Hopefully there will be more of them. Unlike so many television series based on mysteries, this one did not distort the characters or change the plots in discernable ways.

Smith has several other mystery series (1) featuring Isabel Dalhousie and her Sunday Philosophy Club, set in Scotland; (2) Dr. Moritz-Maria von Igelfeld, re The Portugese Irregular Verbs; (3) the 44 Scotland Street Series based on the residents of a boardinghouse; and (4) a new series called Corduroy Mansions set in London scheduled for the summer of 2010.

Sonja Joan "Sunny" Randall

Author: Robert B. Parker

As a feminist Sunny Randall's mother had talked the talk, but never walked the walk. She was horrified by her daughter's decisions. She had not approved of Sunny's marriage to Richie Burke, whom she had known and loved since grade school. The Burke family was notorious then, and still held sway over criminal operations in part of the Boston area. Nor had she approved of their divorce or understood their continued close relationship.

Sunny earned a degree in social work, but never used it. She had joined the police force following in her father's footsteps, but that did not last either. Becoming a private investigator allowed her more independence. That seemed to be the byword for Sunny. She could not handle being controlled. Richie had come to realize this, although not necessarily to understand it. He could be forgiven his confusion, because when push came to shove, Sunny often turned to him for help in her investigations. Their divorce had been unusually congenial. She refused alimony. He insisted that she have full ownership of their home, although she could not afford the upkeep. The only possible controversy was placement of their bull terrier, Rosie. Sunny was granted custody with visitation rights for Richie. As the series began she was working on a master's degree in fine arts and selling some of her paintings.

Sunny had close friends, although her perfectionist sister Elizabeth was not among them. Julie, a psychiatric social worker, and Spike, the gay part-owner of bar-restaurant Beans & Rice, were always there when she needed them.

As *Family Honor* (Putnam, 1999) began, Sunny still needed to be with Richie. They met for dinner once a week (which eventually included more intimate weekends). Her assignment to locate Millie Patton, a runaway fifteen-year-old girl, pitted Sunny against professional criminals. To save Millie, vulnerable because she had overheard a conversation that led to murder, Sunny not only took personal risks but she invoked the power of the Burke family. Her role as mentor to Millie paralleled a similar relationship that Spenser had with Paul Giacomin in another Parker series.

Millie had disappeared from the scene by *Perish Twice* (Putnam, 2000), during which most of Sunny's time was occupied by pro bono work. It was unclear how she survived without alimony, personal wealth, or paid employment. She proved to no one's satisfaction that her sister Elizabeth's husband was unfaithful. She comforted her dear friend Julie whose therapeutic skills were ineffective to deal with her own drinking and infidelity. Finally, although she was initially paid for this one, she located the man who was stalking feminist Mary Lou Goddard. Sunny continued on the case after Mary Lou fired her. A woman resembling Mary Lou had been found dead in her office. The presence of pimps and hookers in the case brought Sunny into conflict with African-American criminal elements. Again Richie (who was not personally involved in crime), and his father and uncle (who were) came to her rescue. Independence went just so far for Sunny.

When Sunny agreed to escort romance author Melanie Joan Hall on a bookselling tour in *Shrink Rap* (Putnam's, 2002) she had no idea that her relationship with men, and Richie in particular, would become an issue. Melanie Joan's husband, psychotherapist Dr. John Melvin, was stalking her. His need to control women contrasted with Sunny's need to be independent of the men in her life. She became a patient of Dr. Melvin to gain evidence that would lead to an arrest and conviction.

The revelation that Richie planned to marry threw Sunny for a loop in *Melancholy Baby* (Putnam's 2004). She wasn't sure she could manage without him. Taking college student Sarah Markham's case didn't help Sunny's stability. Sarah felt certain that she had been adopted by the couple who raised her as their own child. They insisted she was wrong, but refused to provide DNA. This had to be more than Sarah's fantasy. Otherwise why would someone kill Sarah's father, George Markham? Dr. Susan Silverman (see Volume 1) did her best to help Sunny understand why she couldn't handle marriage. Susan hadn't been able to do so either.

Actress Erin Flint was close to physical perfection and she knew it in *Blue Screen* (Putnam's, 2006) . Her professional and personal lives were controlled by wealthy entertainment czar Buddy Bollen, on whose estate she lived. Erin's career had been built on the "Warrior Woman" series, but Buddy had big plans. He wanted Erin, a fine athlete, to play in a movie about Babe Didricksen, and to play center field for his floundering major league baseball team. Misty Tyler, Erin's sister, had also served as her trainer. When Misty was murdered, Buddy worried that Erin had been the intended target. Sunny had already been hired to be Erin's bodyguard, now she was to identify the killer. Parker not only brought Susan Silverman into the act, but Jesse Stone played a significant role in the investigation.

There was almost as much about Sunny's personal life (a potential reconnect with Richie, the dynamics of her parents' lives, and a test to the limits of friendship) in *Spare Change* (Putnam's, 2007) as there was mystery. The re-emergence of a serial killer, nicknamed the "Spare Change Killer" after twenty years had caused local authorities to hire Sunny's dad, Phil, as a consultant. He had handled the prior unsolved cases. Phil hired Sunny as his assistant. There seemed to be no motive for the crimes but a strictly followed modus operandi. When Sunny's intuition focused on one suspect, she ignored legal niceties. Her therapist, Dr. Susan Silverman, played a role as did Quirk and Belson from the Spenser series.

High Profile (Putnam's, 2008) was a Jesse Stone novel. Sunny who began an affair with Stone in a prior book, served only as a patsy for him. She agreed to bodyguard Jenn, his promiscuous former wife, who claimed she had been raped and was being stalked. Stone had the high profile murder to deal with and couldn't baby-sit Jenn himself.

Author Robert B. Parker's dialogue and warm relationships enriched the series. He continues his Spenser series in which Susan Silverman plays a continually weaker role, writes occasional Westerns and has a third series featuring former big city cop Jesse Stone, now chief of police in a Massachusetts small town. On occasion protagonists visit in one another's series.

Sunny Randall books are being reissued in sets or collections.

Tammi Randall

Author: E. L. Wyrick

Tammi Randall was not born in Patsboro, where she practiced law. However, she had been raised in a Southern Georgia town about the same size. Her rigidly religious mother and alcoholic father had left her with a spiritual belief that was unconnected to church membership. Her undergraduate degree had been in psychology and her law degree was from local Catledge University.

Her strong feeling for the underdog led Tammi to the practice of public law in the Teal County Legal Aid Society. Frequently this meant the dirty and scurrilous, the poor and undereducated, the petty crimes and repeated complaints. Occasionally, she and her friends: African-American businessman Mitch Griffith, school administrator Dan Bushnell, and Dan's wife Meg, became involved in criminal investigations. Tammi was mentored and supported by Bernard Fuchs, a seasoned attorney who worked part-time for Legal Aid. Her salary was average to low. She drove a Yugo which barely made it through the Georgia hills, and lived rent-free in an older home, acting as house sitter. At twenty-seven, she remained single, cautious about her relationships with men after a badly handled sexual interaction in the back seat of a car at age seventeen.

During *A Strange and Bitter Crop* (St. Martin, 1994), Tammi represented young African-American James Cleveland against charges of double murder. When one of his accomplices tried to end Tammi's investigation by vehicular assault and rape, she defended herself. Her distrust of men was exacerbated by the betrayal of a man she had come to love. (Because this book was not available to me in 2000, it was reviewed by my daughter-in-law, Vonne Meussling Barnett. I considered re-doing it myself, but Vonne had done such a fine job of it that I saw no reason to replace her version.)

By *Power in the Blood* (St. Martin, 1996), Tammi was working out at a self-defense class, swimming several days a week, and practicing with a pistol, determined never again to be defenseless. Her therapist, Dr. Josie Beam, was concerned that Tammi might overreact to a threat. A request to handle a lucrative real estate matter was tempting; however, her client, movie actor Lawton Fletcher, was dead on arrival. Tammi had to understand Fletcher and why he wanted to buy the nearby town of Warrendale, Georgia before she could identify his killer. She did meet an attractive man along the way, and found friends to share her home.

Claire Rawlings

Author: Carole Bugge

Claire Rawlings was well established in New York City as the editor for mystery books at Ardor House. She had a comfortable life: drove an old brown Mercedes, exercised with hand weights, and enjoyed classical music and national public radio. Initially she shared her apartment with Ralph, an all white cat. That changed when she teamed up with thirteen-year-old Meredith a fellow redhead who like Claire had never come to terms with her mother's death. Meredith Lawrence more or less adopted Claire who had known her mother in college. Detective Wally Jackson eventually became part of their "family," adding a much needed balance.

Claire's social circle in New York City during *Who Killed Blanche DuBois?* (Berkley, 1999) included old friends from her college days in North Carolina. Blanche DuBois was more than a friend; she was a best selling author on Claire's list. When first Blanche, then another member of the alumnae group, were murdered, Claire felt vulnerable. Meredith and Detective Wallace Jackson were there when Claire realized that not every friend could be trusted.

Rejected by her stepmother and ignored by her passive father, Meredith became Claire's ward as *Who Killed Dorian Gray?* (Berkley, 2000) began. Claire was still suffering nightmares from her near escape from death. An invitation to spend a pleasant week at Ravenscroft art colony near Woodstock seemed likely to provide the relaxation she needed. Her only task would be to lecture to the artists and writers attending the camp. The campers included some who had previous ties to one another. During a late night ramble to the bathhouse, Claire found the body of Maya Sorenson a.k.a. Dorian Gray. She had help in solving this and a subsequent murder from Meredith, who ran away from summer camp to join Claire.

Claire and Wally Jackson might have benefited from a travel guide in *Who Killed Mona Lisa?* (Berkley, 2001). Instead they relied upon a recommendation from Claire's boss, Peter Schwartz, in selecting a vacation hideaway. Hide away from whom? Not only did Meredith join them, but they were also stuck with a sorry group of staff and residents at the Wayside Inn in South Sudbury, Massachusetts. As in a Golden Age mystery, when beautiful young waitress Mona Lisa Callahan was murdered, the group was isolated by a snowstorm. Claire and Meredith found clues through an historic Secret Drawer Society.

These were well written books. Claire was portrayed as an intelligent, well-educated woman who had a strong sense of history and literature. Meredith, who was looking for a mother substitute, grew throughout the series. Author Carole Bugge has a second series based on Sherlock Holmes.

Savannah Reid

Author: G.A. McKevett, pseudonym for Sonja Massie

Food was a major focus of Savannah Reid's life. About thirty pounds overweight at age forty, she compensated by scrupulous attention to her appearance. While a police officer, she had earned a black belt in karate. The oldest of nine children of an alcoholic, irresponsible mother and assorted fathers, Savannah remained single, sharing her San Carmelita, California apartment with two black cats (Cleopatra and Diamante). Her mother remained in Georgia, but the travails of her siblings were frequently brought to Savannah's attention.

In *Just Desserts* (Kensington, 1995), Savannah, then a police officer, felt sandbagged in her efforts to find the killer of Jonathan Winston, husband of an activist city council member. When her investigation threatened local public figures, Savannah was fired on the excuse that she had failed physical standards by not losing weight. Beverly Winston, Jonathan's wife and chief suspect, hired Savannah to continue. Her efforts were hampered by the arrival of Atlanta, her youngest sister who had become uncontrollable in her mother's home. In her new roles as substitute mother and private investigator, Savannah showed promise, founding her own Moonlight Magnolia Agency.

During *Bitter Sweets* (Kensington, 1996), Savannah's morale was severely tested when her search for Lisa Mallock, the "sister" of a client, ended in the woman's murder. Not only had she been duped by real estate broker Brian O'Donnell, the man who pretended to be a brother, but Lisa's daughter Christy was missing. With the help of her two gay assistants, Ryan Stone and ex- Brit John Gibson and her former police partner detective Dirk Coulter, Savannah made the best of a bad case.

In *Killer Calories* (Kensington, 1997), Dirk was in charge of the investigation wherein middle-aged actress Kat Valentina died in a sleazy health spa. Valentina, who was a part-owner of the facility, had a high alcohol content, so an accidental death was assumed, but an anonymous client hired Savannah to review the case. Savannah went undercover at the Royal Palms Spa where the staff included several with serious motives for wanting Kat dead.

A series of vicious rapes escalated into the murders, not of the victims, but of police officers who worked the cases. During *Cooked Goose* (Kensington,

1998), Captain Harvey Bloss of the San Carmelita police did not want Savannah participating in his department's investigation of the local rapist. He could not maintain his opposition when his estranged daughter Margie turned to Savannah for help after escaping the rapist. The deaths and disappearances of several police officers and the rapes were tied together by the presence of ornamental rings on victims. On a personal level, she delivered her sister Vidalia's second set of twins. The exposure of the rapist was unusual because the man had none of the obvious characteristics of a serial rapist.

Regular business had to be put aside in *Sugar and Spite* (Kensington, 2000) when Dirk Coulter, Savannah's best friend and former partner, was arrested for the murder of his ex-wife Polly. Dirk might be foul mouthed, sloppy, and inconsiderate, but he did not kill Polly. Savannah's loyal band (John Gibson, Ryan Stone, and office manager Tammy Hart) rallied around when the top brass at the police department showed little interest in other suspects.

Savannah, noted for her healthy appetite and generous girth did not usually spend time at Beauty pageants. In *Sour Grapes* (Kensington, 2001), she had two good reasons for attending the Miss Gold Coast Beauty Queen Contests. She was working security there with Ryan Stone. Her sister Atlanta Reid, thinner than ever, was a contestant. Savannah might be faulted for focusing on the wrong suspect, but Atlanta came through with a bang.

You can take a girl out of the country but, as *Peaches and Screams* (Kensington, 2002) showed, you can't take the country out of the girl. It was sister Marietta's third wedding that drew Savannah back to McGill, Georgia. Within minutes of her arrival, she learned that her younger brother, Mason, had been arrested for the murder of Judge Patterson. Savannah used her wiles and her nagging on her former beau Deputy Tom Stafford to gain access to Mason and to the scene of the crime. Dirk and Tammy flew to the rescue. John and Ryan provided support, helping to identify an alternative killer. This was the best so far of the series, displaying poignancy in Savannah's efforts to rescue her beloved Gran, helping her to realize that love can be crippling.

The job of discovering who was sending threatening letters to television chef, "Lady Eleanor Maxwell" came at the right time for Savannah in *Death by Chocolate* (Kensington, 2003). She needed the money. She did not need the grief of dealing with the dysfunctional Maxwell family. She also did not need a visit from her unhappy sister Cordele, who shared her angst about her unhappy childhood endlessly. When Eleanor was killed, Savannah still had a job to do because the letter-writer might be the murderer.

Savannah explored new territory in *Cereal Killer* (Kensington, 2004) when she was hired to go undercover, but not much of it, as the 'before" model in a Slenda Flakes commercial. Two attractive "after" models had died under suspicious circumstances and a third disappeared, cases on which Dirk Coulter was working. The models' agent Leah Freed wanted Savannah to do a parallel investigation, uncover even more. Dirk seemed comfortable allowing Savannah to push the envelope on ethical conduct and benefit from what she learned. The San Carmelita police department, aware that no one else would work as Dirk's partner, lent a blind eye to Savannah's close involvement.

Given that Savannah had developed an extraordinary crush on Lance Roman, cover boy for romantic novels, what could please her more than to be a contestant in a reality show, *Man of My Dreams*, as *Murder a la Mode* (Kensington, 2005) opened. The prize was two weeks vacation with Lance. The contest was to be filmed at Blackmoor Castle, a shoddy replica of an English redoubt built by Texas businessman R. K. Breadstone. Someone was eliminating the contestants, the hard way. Fortunately Ryan and Gibson were available. Murder was bad enough but Savannah had to wear a corset and ride a horse.

Good hearted Tammy Hart, Savannah's assistant, thought she was doing her overweight cousin Abigail Simpson a favor in *Corpse Suzette* (Kensington, 2006) when she entered her name in a contest for a free makeover at Emerge. Abigail won, came to Georgia where Savannah offered her a place to stay. Surly, thin-skinned Abigail had to be convinced to take part in the services offered by Emerge. Her scheduled appointment with plastic surgeon Dr. Suzette DuBois was cancelled when DuBois disappeared. Dirk, in his official capacity, worked with Savannah who had been hired by Suzette's former husband and business partner, Sergio D. Allessandro to find Suzette.

Savannah was awed at the opportunity to serve as actress Dona Papalardo's bodyguard in *Fat, Free and Fatal* (Kensington, 2007). Dirk Coulter, who was investigating the murder of Kim Dylan, Dona's personal assistant, had recommended Savannah. It was a good time to be moving over to Dona's mansion. Jesup, Savannah's sister, had turned up with a weird husband that she'd known only two days before they married in Las Vegas. Kim had died wearing Dona's clothes so it was assumed that Dona had been the target. A well plotted mystery.

During their early years on the San Clemente police force, Savannah and Dirk had found Maggie, a missing girl, too late, so in *Poisoned Tarts* (Kensington, 2008) they were determined to find 18-year-old Daisy O'Neil. Daisy had made the mistake of attaching herself to the Skeleton Key Three, a trio of attention seeking, self-centered semi-celebrities at her school. Daisy was smarter, but the trio were thinner and richer. Their leader, Tiffany Dante, the only child of wealthy and powerful Andrew Dante, had a personal grudge against Daisy. Although Savannah had no official status, she called on her regulars: Tammy, John and Ray, plus Gran, to help find Daisy.

A competently plotted series with good characterizations. Next: *A Body to Die For* (2009); *Wicked Craving* (2010) and *A Decadent Way to Die* (2011)

Cassandra Reilly

Author: Barbara Wilson

Cassandra Reilly was a free spirited translator of Romance languages. She was described as a tall, middle-aged woman, with hazel-green eyes who had received most of her education through her travels, having left her Michigan home at sixteen. Her widowed mother had seven children, but Cassandra never liked her siblings, and had few contacts with them. Essentially rootless, she maintained a rented room in Hampstead, England, another in Oakland, California, but roamed Europe on an Irish passport.

During *Gaudi Afternoon* (Seal, 1990), Cassandra found work translating a book, but was diverted into the search for Frankie Steven's husband. Somewhat later Cassandra realized that Frankie was a transsexual, fighting his/her former spouse for custody of their child. Neither one came across as a responsible parent, although they finally reached an accommodation.

Cassandra returned in *Trouble in Transylvania* (Seal, 1993) en route to China via Vienna. She encountered a strange group of acquaintances traveling to a Romanian health spa, and decided to join them. Dr. Pustulescu, the inventor of a youth serum, was electrocuted at the spa while demonstrating a treatment. One of Cassandra's traveling companions, Bree, asked for help. Her grandmother, Gladys Bentwhistle, was suspected of murder.

The Death of a Much-Travelled Woman (Third Side Press, 1998) was a set of short stories during which Cassandra unmasked killers, but could not always bring them to justice. She wrote her own book as she traveled in Hawaii, rural England, Central Europe, Scandinavia, and Russia. She stayed with friends, lived on a shoestring, and found lovers and former lovers along the way.

As *The Case of the Orphaned Bassoonist* (Seal, 2000) began, Cassandra had just returned from an unrewarding journey to a tropical island, only to be urged to come at once to Venice. Her friend and landlady Nicola Gibbons, currently attending a symposium on Vivaldi, was in danger of arrest. Someone had stolen a valuable bassoon left in Nicola's care. Cassandra had no contact with the local police; nevertheless, she investigated the personal, sexual, and professional lives of the musician-suspects. Background included art history insights into the Pieta, the female orphans trained by choirmaster Antonio Vivaldi and the possibility that among them had been unrecognized composers of musical scores for bassoonists. The best of the series.

Barbara Wilson is also the author of the Pam Nilsen series.

Nina Reilly

Author: Perri O'Shaughnessy, pseudonym
for Pamela and Mary O'Shaughnessy

When she lost her job as an appellate attorney and her marriage became unbearable, Nina Reilly moved to Lake Tahoe, temporarily living with her younger brother Matt and his family. She brought along her eleven-year-old son Bobby, who knew that Nina's husband was not his father. Nina had withheld information about the man who was. She realized a day would come when Bobby would demand the information. Over the series, Nina had a short but happy marriage that ended when her husband died. Her longest relationship was with Paul van Wagoner, a private investigator. Paul, himself twice divorced, had an abiding love for Nina, but played "Herbie" to her "Momma Rose" (a la *Gypsy)* as she focused on her career and Bobby. Sandy Whitefeather, Nina's Native American secretary, played significant roles in several of the narratives.

During *Motion to Suppress* (Delacorte, 1995), Nina reassessed her original intention of practicing only civil law when Sandy Whitefeather, brought in Misty Patterson as a client. Misty knew she had struck her husband, believed he had left the house on his own; but denied that she had killed him and deposited his body in Lake Tahoe. Misty's pregnancy reminded Nina of her own vulnerability before Bobby was born, so she took the case. With the help of Paul van Wagoner, a San Francisco investigator, she not only handled the courtroom battles, but also probed Misty's past to relieve her of guilt. Although van Wagoner had no affinity for either marriage or fatherhood, he fell in love with Nina and wanted more than a casual affair.

In *Invasion of Privacy* (Delacorte, 1996), Bobby's need to know became unbearable when Terry London, a treacherous client in an invasion of privacy case, forced the issue. Terry's murder brought Kurt Scott back into Nina's life. Scott, a former forest ranger who had left her pregnant and alone a decade earlier, was identified as Bob's father. When he was arrested for Terry's murder, Nina fought a rival attorney for the right to prove him innocent.

Having discouraged Paul van Wagoner's romantic interest, Nina reached out to Collier Hallowell, a widowed prosecuting attorney in *Obstruction of Justice* (Delacorte, 1997). Hallowell had never recovered from the hit-and-run death of his probation officer wife Anna, three years before. When he and Nina climbed Mount Tallac, they encountered the contentious de Beers family whose expedition ended in the death of the father, Ray. Van Wagoner's investigation of Anna's death intersected with the possibility that Ray's death had not been an accident. Hollowell and Nina faced one another in the courtroom and at the edge of death. Van Wagoner, who had responded to Nina's rejection by a relationship with a seductive artist, was there when Nina needed him.

The potential of a multi-million dollar contingency fee was not Nina's only motive for taking a complex palimony case in *Breach of Promise* (Delacorte, 1998). She felt compassion for Lindy Markov whose business and personal relationship with her partner/lover Mike had never been legalized. Lindy's stake in their successful business disappeared when Mike left her for a younger woman. The palimony trial was disrupted when juror Cliff Wright died of an allergic reaction to delivered food. It wasn't enough that they won the case. Van Wagoner and Nina had to discover who arranged for Wright's lunch. He helped out but his relationship with Nina was troubled.

Nina's chance at happiness in *Acts of Malice* (Delacorte, 1999) was endangered by her representation of ski instructor James Strong, a man accused of killing his brother Alex. Philip Strong, their father, was the owner of the up-scale Paradise Ski Resort. His reactions and those of Alex's wife mystified Nina. Collier Hallowell, who had returned from a period of mourning for his deceased wife ready to renew his relationship with Nina, warned her off the case. She waited too long to scrutinize her obligations to Jim Strong when they conflicted with her sense of justice. Van Wagoner, who had left the area to work in Washington, D.C., remained in waiting for Nina, protective of her interests even from a distance.

Nina's son Bob was probably the only friend that sixteen-year-old Nikki Zach had. In *Move to Strike* (Delacorte, 2000), Bob talked Nina into representing the girl when she was accused of murdering her uncle, Dr. William Sykes. Nina needed something to jolt her out of her inactivity, but she couldn't manage alone. Paul van Wagoner, when contacted, was reluctant to be with Nina again, a mixture of pain and guilt. His investigation into a plane crash and mining claim combined with Nina's courtroom skills to unearth a triple killer.

On reflection, Nina should have realized in *Writ of Execution* (Delacorte, 2001) that Jessie Potter was not the ideal client. Only reluctantly did she even reveal her identity. As the recent winner of a seven-million-dollar jackpot at Prize's casino, she had obligations to the Internal Revenue Service which could not be ignored. Her solution, marriage to mere acquaintance Kenny Leung, would provide her with another name. However, this brought a new set of problems. Jessie feared vengeance from the father of her deceased husband. She had another equally insidious enemy, the men who had arranged to win the jackpot themselves. Paul van Wagoner was on scene to help, but the on-again, off-again connection was becoming tedious.

Nina found herself in serious trouble during *Unfit to Practice* (Delacorte, 2002), but she earned a lot of it. Driving home after a tough day in a court custody hearing and office time preparing for the next day, she used a back-up car key when she couldn't find her regular one. When she awakened the next morning, the car in which she had left three client files had disappeared. There were serious repercussions for the clients concerned in those cases. When she was charged with negligence and called before the California Bar Association tribunal, she became more of a victim than a protagonist. Paul enlisted the services of attorney Jack McIntyre, Nina's former husband, to represent her. They needed to determine who had stolen the car and misused the information contained in the files.

Moving to Paul's home in Carmel in *Presumption of Death* (Delacorte, 2003) did not solve Nina's problems In fact, she acquired new ones. When Wish Whitefeather, Sandy's son who had moved to Carmel to work for Paul, was charged with arson and murder, Nina had no status in the local legal community, no formal office to work from, and until Sandy returned from her new job in DC, had no secretary. The victim, Danny Cervantes, had been a childhood friend of Wish, and they had resumed their relationship when Wish moved to Carmel. Wish and Danny had hiked up into the hills, according to Wish, to see if they could photograph the arsonist who was terrorizing the area. When a burned corpse was located, Wish, who had been injured and sought medical help elsewhere, was arrested and jailed. Paul and Nina sought proof that there were others on the hill; later, they uncovered the identity of a third man but what was his role? Given the publicity the fire and murder elicited, the solution to the problem was hard to believe.

Although initially Nina had shared Paul's small home, even when Bob joined them, by *Unlucky in Law* (Delacorte, 2004) she had moved into a small home in Carmel, which she had inherited from an aunt. This did not meet Bob's needs. He was unhappy in the Carmel school system, missed friends and family in Tahoe; just didn't "belong". Paul gifted Nina with a beautiful engagement ring, hoping to solidify their plans, but her acceptance was lukewarm. These problems were shunted aside when Nina's mentor, octogenarian attorney Klaus Pohlmann, recruited her for second chair in the murder trial of Stefan Wyatt. When Stefan was stopped for a minor driving violation, a bag of bones was noted in the back seat of his car. Stefan, already a two-time loser, couldn't afford even a grave desecration conviction, much less a murder connected to Konstantin Zhukovsky. The tangled relationships between the Wyatt and Zhukovsky families: their possible connections with the Romanovs, and the intervention of a murderous Russian were fascinating, if not always plausible.

Case of Lies (Bantam Dell, 2005) is not the book you read before you go to sleep. On her return to Tahoe, Nina agreed to represent Dave Hanna in a civil suit against a motel, claiming that staff negligence contributed to the death of his wife Sarah. She had been shot during a melee when a masked man robbed three young visitors to Lake Tahoe. The trio left town before they could be questioned about their attacker. Aware that a man similar in description had been seen in the area, Nina and members of Sarah Hanna's family insisted on pursuing the case. Excellent characterizations of the three young witnesses.

Show No Fear (Pocket, 2008) was billed as a Nina Reilly prequel. Long time readers of the series may find it difficult to connect the Nina in this narrative to the Nina they have admired and enjoyed. The story of her mother Ginny's illness and death, of brother Matt's problems and the return of Richard Filsen to seek custody of Nina's son Bob, certainly filled in gaps in Nina's history. At that time she was going to law school and working at Klaus Pohlmann's law firm. The interaction of the partners, which then included Paul Van Wagoner, added interest, but the narrative seemed jerky, disconnected. Nina, Paul, and Matt were less attractive characters. This was not anywhere near the standard of the series. Question: when was it written? If Kurt Scott was Bob's father in *Invasion of Privacy*, how does Richard Filsen fit in?

The narratives varied in their quality, combining some incisive courtroom scenes with other less interesting legal maneuvers. For all of Nina's technical skills, she seemed obsessive about her cases, envisioning herself a "savior" for those in need when actually Paul's investigations made many of her successes possible. Her angst about his presence in her life became boring.

Regan Reilly

Author: Carol Higgins Clark

Regan Reilly was the daughter of Luke, a funeral director, and Nora, a suspense novelist whose maiden name had been Regan. A trim brunette, Regan had spent her junior year abroad at Oxford. She became a private investigator located on the West Coast, but her life changed when she met Detective Jack Reilly. They married and her adventures continued through their honeymoon and travels. Luke and Nora frequently appeared in the series.

As *Decked* (Warner, 1992) opened, Regan was attending the tenth reunion of her classmates in St. Polycarp's hallowed halls, remembering the disappearance of her roommate, Greek heiress Athena Popolous. After Athena's skeleton was discovered, Regan's disclosure that she had a journal and pictures of that period brought the entire Reilly family into the case.

During *Snagged* (Warner, 1993), Regan attended a Florida wedding, only to become enmeshed in the problems of another guest, the bride's uncle. Richie Blossom, a long time inventor, should have known that the hosiery industry would not welcome runless pantyhose. Luke and Nora, Regan's parents, were along to justify the "mortuary jokes," but could not resuscitate the weak plot.

Iced (Warner, 1995) found Regan and her parents in Colorado where rival art thieves plundered the rich, including their host and hostess Sam and Kendra Wood. Eben Bean, an ex-convict, had been employed by the Woods as a caretaker. He, was assumed to have committed the crime because he had disappeared, but Regan believed him innocent. She did not throw in the towels but used them to rescue Eben and restore him to his family.

Twanged (Warner, 1998) was as overcrowded as a New York City cocktail party. Regan had been hired to bodyguard Brigid O'Neill. Her story and that of the historic Irish fiddle that brought her fame, were overwhelmed by the ensemble of guests at Chappy and Bettina Tinka's place on the ocean. Yes, there were murders, at least attempts, and the theft of another violin in Ireland...

Regan had a dozen interesting suspects to consider in *Fleeced* (Scribner's, 2001). Her friend Thomas Pilsner, manager of the formerly prestigious Settler's Club, needed help to locate missing diamonds that were to have been donated to the Club. Donors Ben and Nat Carney, two retired jewelers who were club members, both died the night the jewels disappeared. Jack Reilly (no relative), the New York police detective with whom Regan had planned to spend time, had been sent to London. She had other resources in sorting out what began as theft but included arson and murder.

Author Carol Higgins Clark combined her talents with those of her mother, Mary Higgins Clark in *Deck the Halls* (Scribner's, 2000) during which Alvirah Meehan (Mary's sleuth) and Regan Reilly shared a Christmas story. A pair of disgruntled bumblers kidnapped Luke Reilly and Rosita, his driver from the funeral home. Hints dropped by Luke in a phone message and clues from friends brought about a rescue in time to save Luke and Rosita from a frigid death.

Lucretia Standish, wealthy widow in her nineties, was preparing to marry Edward Fields, a much younger man, in *Jinxed* (Scribner's, 2002). In her exuberance, she decided to share eight millions dollars with her deceased husband (Haskell)'s relatives. Regan was hired to find actress Whitney Weldon who was Haskell's great-niece. In a game of lost and found and lost again, Regan was opposed by a hit man.

Greed and ambition were powerful motivators in *Popped* (Scribner, 2003) wherein wealthy entrepreneur and balloon enthusiast Roscoe Parker pitted a pilot production of a reality show by Danny Madley against a pilot sitcom produced by Bubbles Ferndale. On Danny's reality show three married couples competed for a one million dollar prize. Lots of dirty tricks. Danny, who had gone to school with Regan, hired her to discover who was sabotaging his show.

Mary Higgins Clark and Carol Higgins Clark collaborated on *The Christmas Thief* (Scribner, 2004). Regan, her parents, and detective Jack Reilly joined Alvirah and Willy Meehan at a Vermont ski lodge. Alvirah, feeling sorry for Opal Fogarty who had lost her lottery ticket to con man Packy Noonan, invited her to come along. Packy, recently paroled from prison, had hidden loot in a nearby tree. The lightweight narrative had the Reillys cavorting around seeking a ninety-foot-tree destined for Rockefeller Center and a small flask full of diamonds.

When winter weather hit the East Coast in *Burned* (Scribner, 2005)Regan abandoned her plans to visit Jack and accepted her friend Kit Callan's invitation for an Hawaiian weekend. She arrived shortly after the body of hotel employee Dorinda Dawes washed up on the beach. Hotel manager Will Brown, for reasons of his own, suspected she had been murdered and hired Regan to investigate. There had been a series of incidents that plagued hotel guests. Dorinda had been wearing a seashell lei when her body was discovered, one that had been stolen from a local museum thirty years before.

Hitched (Scribner, 2006) may be the best of the series. Regan and Jack were to be married in a short time,. When she went to pick up her wedding gown, she discovered Clarissa and Alfred, the designer duo, tied up and her gown missing. Regan was only one of five April brides whose gowns would not be available The narrative followed the five brides-to-be, their intended spouses, and the two bungling robbers. Jack helped Regan in the search and, as a bonus, recognized a disguised bank robber.

Credibility was in short supply in *Santa Cruise (*Scribner, 2006), another collaboration with Mary Higgins Clark) when Alvirah and Willy invited the senior and junior Reilly couples to join them on the maiden voyage of the rehabbed Royal Mermaid. "Commodore" Randolph Weed had purchased and renovated the ship. At the suggestion of his public relations man, Dudley Loomis, the passengers (all of whom had distinguished themselves for charitable acts or had won the trip at a charity auction) rode free. Two stowaways had sneaked on board with the connivance of a staff member. Santa garbed guests, obnoxious but charitable children, and a pseudo-invalid were among the passengers. Lots of coincidences were needed to make it work.

Coincidences abounded again in *Laced* (Pocket Star, 2008) when Jack and Regan honeymooned at Hennessy Castle in Ireland. This was planned as a vacation and a chance to meet with Regan's relatives, but they were set up for trouble. Slick jewelry thieves John and Jane Doe, who had a grudge against Jack, had learned of the Reilly trip. They stole an antique lace tablecloth from the Castle just to embarrass him. Sheila and Brian O'Shea, also fellow guests, were working a scam on wealthy Irish-American Dermot Finnegan. Lots of atmosphere with the ghost of lace maker May Reilly, a superstitious housekeeper/artist, and a visit from Luke and Nora.

Regan and Jack shared an eerie night in New York City during *Zapped* (Scribner's, 2008) along with a variety of confused characters joined together by connivance and coincidences. Lorraine, just off the plane from London, learned that the loft apartment owned by her estranged husband Conrad, had been sold to the Reillys who acquired it to expand their own adjacent apartment. She needed to retrieve letters that, if exposed, could ruin her theatrical career. Unstable Georgina who had abandoned her fellow attendees at a conference, including Kit, Regan's best friend, took off with a young man. Kit involved Regan in the pursuit of the couple because Georgina was dangerous. Over the narrative they acquired a posse, which included Conrad, Lorraine's husband. Carol Higgins Clark suffers from unnecessary comparisons with her mother. She is a good mystery writer.

Dashing Through the Snow (Scribner's, 2008) was a joint effort between Mary Higgins Clark and Carol. They reduced the traditional twelve days of Christmas to: "six eager sleuths, five lottery winners, four nasty crooks, three sub-plots, two anguished lovers, and one bang up ending. The six sleuths were the double set of Reillys, plus Alvira and Willy Meehan who met up with them at the first Festival of Joy in Branscombe, New Hampshire. Five employees of venerable Conklin's Market regularly purchased a joint lottery ticket. This time Duncan, head of produce dropped out just before the ticket won $160 million. There was a second ticket, owner not identified that would share in the prize, an engagement ring of dubious provenance, and a missing heiress to provide action.

Next: *Cursed* (2009), *Wrecked* (2010)

Maggy Renard

Author: Barbara Sohmers

Maggy's career as an actress languished after her marriage to Fred Renard. He continued to be successful as a television and stage actor, a playwright, and author of thrillers. They preferred spending time together to working separately but at times it could not be avoided. Maggy was deeply in love with her husband who was twenty years older than she. Yet, at times she regretted the missed opportunities to advance her own career. They had met when Fred, then divorced, directed Maggy in her first appearance on stage. References to "The Fox" in the titles were to Renard, the French word for "fox."

Ile de Marees (Island of Tides) off the French coast had always been a special place for Fred. He and Maggy had vacationed there in their own cottage, but in *The Fox and the Puma* (Sodef Press, 1997), Fred purchased a bar-restaurant. His residuals were such that he could afford to take time off. The planned "vacation" deteriorated into a lot of work, complicated by (1) the murder of promiscuous summer visitor Regine Rothmann; (2) the disappearance of her daughter Dominique. (3) the escape of Carrere, a convicted rapist from the local prison; and (4) a second escape, a puma from a visiting circus. Fred and Maggy found real life drama to be more nerve wracking than writing fiction.

While Fred was shooting a film in Provence during *The Fox and the Pussycat* (Sodef, 1998), Maggy made an unusual career decision. Disappointed at her lack of opportunity for dramatic roles, she signed on as singer and mistress of ceremonies at The Pussycat, a strip tease joint in Paris. It was a learning experience, not the least of which was increased awareness of ritual female mutilation in some African countries. Maggy wanted to be the heroine, not a victim, but when performers at the Pussycat were murdered, Fred stepped in to save the day.

Although the narratives and dialogue were witty, both dwelt upon serious sub-themes: anti-Semitism and female circumcision.

Efforts to locate a possible third book, *The Fox and the Serpent's Tooth,* were unsuccessful

Susan "Sukey" Reynolds

Author: Betty Rowlands

Sukey Reynolds had been an English police department photographer working at crime scenes until her divorce from Paul. She found it impossible to care properly for their son Fergus while on the force. Instead she became a civilian employee of the local police department. Paul, who had remarried, was no longer part of her life. During the series, she dated divorced Inspector Jim Castle.

As *An Inconsiderate Death* (Severn House, 1997) began, the prologue revealed that of three men who had robbed a bank, two had been arrested and convicted. Neither the identity of the third man nor the location of the stolen money had ever been discovered. Sukey's position as civilian photographer for the scene of the crime unit did not have official status. Nevertheless, she played a prominent role in sorting out two murders, aided by pictures she had taken. Inspector Jim Castle, who had known Sukey when she was on the force, did much of the investigating and volunteered to fill the vacant space in her life.

It was unfortunate that Sukey discovered the corpse of her former husband's current wife, Myrna, in *Death at Dearley Manor* (Severn House, 1998). Naturally, she had to be removed from the case asserted Inspector Jim Castle. Naturally, according to Castle's supervisor, he too had to be removed. That created problems because her former husband Paul Reynolds was the primary suspect and their son Fergus insisted that Sukey prove his innocence.

By *Copycat* (Severn, 1999), Inspector Jim Castle was accepted as Sukey's lover although they maintained some discretion in the presence of fifteen-year-old Fergus. Her role as a civilian scene of the crime officer differed from Castle's but they frequently worked the same cases. Castle was certain that Manuel Rodriguez masterminded a series of art thefts, a theory confirmed by Pepita, an undercover female agent. Sukey's close resemblance to Pepita made her a target of a vicious international gangster. She rebelled against Jim Castle's personal authority.

The deaths of two participants in the RYCE (Restore Your Cosmic Energy) program seemed more than a coincidence to Sukey in *Touch Me Not* (Severn, 2001). Using her own time, encouraged by Fergus and family members of the deceased, she signed up for the therapeutic sessions. Sukey was experiencing real benefits until day four when "Xavier," the cult leader was murdered. Whatever positive influence the program may have had until then, it did not deter Sukey from taking independent action without a backup. She had a tight line to walk on a personal level. She remained bitter against her former husband Paul, who had abandoned her and Fergus years before, but recognized that Fergus loved his father.

It became increasingly difficult to be sympathetic to Sukey in *Dirty Work* (Severn House, 2003). She had insight, or a hunch, that the death of Eve Stanton was connected to the disappearance of Matt Braine, a street magazine seller. These events became tangled with two subsequent murders and a series of break-ins and robberies. Sukey, who wanted to return to the regular police work, went far beyond her role as a Scene of Crime adjunct, motivated by her concern for Matt Braine.

Sukey did it again in *Deadly Obsession* (Severn House, 2004) when she exceeded her authority to investigate what she believed to be murder. Arthur Soames had fallen, or been pushed, down a flight of outside stairs. His fiancée Elspeth Maddox and his daughter Sabrina each thought the other had been responsible. Sukey was able to achieve an armistice between the two women, who looked to the past for an alternative killer with Sukey's help. The police had ruled the death to be an accident and were unwilling to get involved even when Sabrina disappeared.

During *Party to Murder* (Severn House, 2005) Sukey and Jim Castle still spent personal time together, but he wanted their relationship kept secret. He worked with a new bright and attractive partner, Sgt Dalia Chen who accompanied him on investigations. When Sir Digby Kirtlings' young estate manager Una May was strangled at his country manor, Sukey and her partner Mandy, had roles as crime scene officers, necessitating that they work with Jim Castle. Sukey's son, who was attending a nearby university, had become a friend of Anne-Marie Gordon, niece of the Kirtling housekeeper Miranda Keene. When Anne-Marie disappeared, Sukey increased her involvement in the case.

Sukey was cautiously integrating herself into a new role, no longer a Scene of the Crime operator, but a regular detective constable in the Criminal Investigation Division as *Alpha, Beta, Gamma....Dead* (Severn House, 2007) began. It had meant moving and only rarely seeing Inspector Jim Castle who had been important in her life. The move made sense because she had been placed on the fast track for promotion. A skeptical Sgt. Rathbone took Sukey along to the Mariner's Hotel where archeologist Dr. Edwin Whistler had been discovered dying by Prof. Stephen Lamont. Lamont, who was scheduled to meet Whistler to receive valuable artifacts (including a letter purported to have been written by St. Paul), became a serious suspect because he needed money to subsidize medical costs for his chronically mentally ill sister Hester. Sukey thought of a different line of enquiry and did her Lone Ranger act to Rathbone's dismay.

Sukey and her best pal Constable Vicky Armstrong happened to be at the library in *Smokescreen* (Severn House, 2008) when irate spectator Wendy Downie accused romance writer Jennifer Cottreall of murder. The drowning of Jennifer in her bathtub at her Woodlands estate, cast suspicion on Wendy who was mentally ill, and had objected to the death of a fictional character. That was too easy. Sukey and Rathbone checked out other members of the Woodlands household and Jennifer's professional associates. Next: *A Fool There Was (2009)*

Readers may also be interested in the Melissa Craig series by author Betty Rowlands.

Caroline Rhodes

Author: Mary Welk aka Mary V. Welk

Caroline (later referred to as Cari by some people) attributed her good fortune in solving mysteries to her nurses' training and attention to detail. Her happy marriage to Ed was cut short when he was struck down by a hit-and-run driver while jogging. The accident occurred close to home at a time when Caroline was watching. She suffered from profound depression, causing her three children to have her committed to a mental hospital. Caroline was smart enough and well educated enough to get her act together sufficiently to be released but depression remained a problem. She had been primarily an emergency room nurse, but chose not to return to her position at Ascension Hospital in Niles, Illinois. Under some pressure from her son Martin and his wife Nikki, she sold the family home and moved to rural Rhineburg. Martin, who was studying for his PhD, was a graduate assistant to rotund Professor Carl Atwater. Carl, in his seventies, was thirty years older than Caroline, but became important in her recovery. There was no indication of a romantic interest on the part of either of them. Caroline's two daughters remained in the Chicago area. Krista was an art teacher at a high school and an artist in her own right. Kerry, the youngest of the children, was still in college, studying theater. Caroline's finances did not allow her to be idle. In exchange for a suite of rooms in the student nurses' dormitory at Bruck University, she acted as housemother. Her skills in the emergency room earned her a place at St. Anne's Hospital as a float staff nurse. St. Anne's was connected to Bruck University, where Martin was continuing his education. There was considerable friction on the campus. Ambitious university president Garrison Hurst was decimating the liberal arts programs to raise money for a football stadium.

Caroline was on duty in the psychiatric unit of St. Anne's as *A Deadly Little Christmas* (Kleworks, 1998, republished in 2007 as *A Merry Little Murder*) began. She had left the recreation room where patients were decorating a donated tree to gather up the refreshments. Before she could return, the tree lights were plugged in, causing the tree to explode, shooting branches into the room leading to the deaths of seven people including student nurse Gail Garvy. Martin had confided most of Caroline's background to Professor Atwater, and he became her partner in investigating who was the intended victim of the exploding tree, and who, the killer. In the course of her probing, Caroline became acquainted with wealthy and prominent ninety-year-old Alexsa Stromberg Morgan, who began as an adversary, but became a co-conspirator.

Something Wicked in the Air (Kleworks, 1999, republished in 2009 as *The Rune Stone Murders*) added to Caroline's ensemble. Postmistress Emma Reiser, for whom Nikki had been working part-time, had died in what seemed to be an accidental fall. Not only was her death not what they thought at first, but Emma had secrets known only to a small part of the community. In the back room of the post office, which was also her home, she ran an efficient bookie joint. The night before her body was discovered, erratic professor Andrew Littlewort had posted a package containing what he believed to be a Nordic rune. If so, it would be an amazing discovery challenging concepts as to how far inland the Vikings had traveled. The rune had not only disappeared, but was believed to have been the murder weapon. All this took place during the annual Festival of Knights, a pageant that included jousting, parades, and a fortune telling booth.

Molly O'Neal, nurse manager of the Ascension Hospital's emergency room, had been a friend and mentor to Caroline, so in *To Kill a King* (Kelworks, 2000), she could not ignore Molly's plea for help. A weak summertime schedule made it possible for Caroline to move back to Niles for several months, taking a position at the hospital. Dr. Roger MacDuffy, emergency room director, was a martinet who used circumstances and a badly worded employee contract to dismiss any staff who opposed his decisions. Molly, a dedicated nurse, balked when he cut back on staff and facilities for the emergency room during renovations. Roger had alliances, professional and sexual, with staff members. When his slavish mistress, Director of Nursing Angela Horowitz, was murdered, Roger pointed a finger at Molly. Not only did Caroline rally her Rhineburg ensemble (which now included Police Chief Jake Moeller, his antique dealer wife, and the three Bruck brothers who were in charge of security at Bruck University) but she was offered entrée to the hospital through Adam Horowitz, Angela's father, a man with dubious connections.

There were plotting problems in *The Scarecrow Murders* (Hilliard Harris, 2004) but it provided an interesting exploration of the tensions on the Bruck campus. Garrison Hurst was determined to have a college football team, which necessitated a stadium. To get the necessary money, he had to accept conditions from banker Trace Golden, Sr. who was determined that his son, also Trace, would star on the team. Unfortunately Hurst had contracted to allow the Moore Sisters' Rodeo to use the new field on the Friday night before the Homecoming Game. This would leave the turf in unacceptable condition. The game was an important fund raising tool as rich alums were expected to attend. Coach Wade Wilkins was a cruel bully who enjoyed inciting disagreement among his players. Martin, Caroline's son who had been a track star as an undergraduate, had been recruited as a pass receiver. So when the town and campus divided between feminists favoring the rodeo and their male relatives and students protesting for the football, Caroline had a foot in both camps. She needed them because when Trace, Jr. was murdered, Martin was the primary suspect. The ensemble, now expanded by a sextet from the Rhineburg Boarding House and Home for Gentle Women, pitched in.

Entertaining.

Emma Rhodes

Author: Cynthia Smith

Emmy Lou Rhodes dropped her birth name early on, choosing Emma in honor of Emma Peel, a character in *The Avengers* television series. Her early life had been exemplary—wonderful parents, educational achievements, the potential of her 165 IQ, an almost photographic memory, and a law degree that led to a coveted position in a Wall Street law firm. Yet Emma wanted something different. A life of excitement, freedom from financial concerns, the ability to pick and choose her assignments, and work that could be accomplished within two-week spans because she was easily bored. Emma's impatience showed in her serial monogamous relationships with men, but she retained many of her former lovers as friends. She parlayed a degree in art history from Sarah Lawrence, her law degree, ease with languages, musical skills, and a sympathetic persona into a unique vocation, private resolver. Her standard plan included no retainer but a $20,000 fee payable only on success within two weeks. She always succeeded. Among her possessions were apartments in New York City and London, plus a villa in Portugal. The homes were embellished by valuable art works and furniture given her by grateful clients. Her own tastes were expensive. She purchased Porthault bed sheets at $1,000 apiece, bought designer clothes and indulged her taste for jewelry. She attended the theatre, but preferred ballet and opera.

Emma developed a network of powerful friends who assisted in her investigations. Abba Levitar, a Mossad official, was a resource but never a lover. Black Scotland Yard Inspector Caleb Franklin was both. Interestingly, she maintained an excellent relationship with her parents who lived in Rye, New York. They had always encouraged her, supported her decisions, and relished hearing of her important clients and friends.

As *Noblesse Oblige* (Berkley, 1996) began, Emma earned the gratitude of the Belgian royal family by rescuing a small boy from an attempted kidnapping. The introduction led to a two-pronged case: to end attempts to kill Spanish diplomat Count Bernardo de Rojas Sandoval and to discover where he had fled. Moving seamlessly throughout Europe and England, Emma solved two murders and a series of abductions.

She sought relaxation in her Portuguese casita where she mingled with an assortment of expatriates in *Impolite Society* (Berkley, 1997); then, acquired a new case almost immediately. An American couple, Martin and Anne Belling refused to believe their son, Rev. Peter Belling, had committed suicide or that he was involved with drugs. Peter had become involved with Leida Van Dolder, a maladjusted single mother. Emma's probe expanded to drug traffic in the area. With Abba and Caleb's help, she solved multiple problems. They could not help the fact that she had fallen deeply in love with a man whom she could not marry.

An encounter on an English train started Emma's next case in *Misleading Ladies* (Berkley, 1997). She earned a double fee by saving a marriage, identifying a misguided killer, and securing an inheritance for a young woman. Although Emma varied from her serial monogamy in this episode, her heart still belonged to Lord Mark Croft, heir to a dukedom. She postponed decisions as to marriage because she had little respect for titles or the lifestyle of the nobility. She retained family values, e.g. believed that parents, not servants, should raise children.

A casual visit to Sotheby's auction house in *Silver and Guilt* (Berkley, 1998) set Emma on an extended adventure. First, to reclaim an heirloom candelabra for Lady Margaret, a member of the English nobility; second, to solve the murder of its most recent owner Bootsie Corrigan, a personal friend. Bootsie had been poor, became rich, and still drove a hard bargain, perhaps too hard. Along the way, Emma stabilized a marriage, arranged a political career, and restored dignity to an impoverished family. Not bad for a two week job.

Emma's assignment in *Royals and Rogues* (Berkley, 1998) took her to Russia to evaluate conditions in a factory subsidized by an American foundation. She was startled by the pervasiveness of the Russian mafias, the corruption of the criminal justice system, and the tolerance of these conditions by the community. When her young friends, Stosh Tambovskaya and the Countess Irina, were murdered, Emma was advised to return home. This was a crucial decision for her. Was she a dilettante to abandon a case when it became hazardous? No, she was a professional, and remained.

As awed as the reader may be with Emma's skills, equal credit should be given to the broad knowledge of the author in art, music, European history, architecture, and literature. Author Cynthia Smith's plotting was above average. Her clues tracked and were valid for the arrest, trial and conviction of criminals unlike many other light mysteries.

Schuyler Ridgway

Author: Tierney McClellan, pseudonym for Barbara Taylor McCafferty

Schuyler Ridgway had survived her divorce and the need to support a family with limited job experience and two years of college. She found work as a real estate agent. Her two adult children became college dropouts without any real purpose in life. Schuyler's life in Louisville, Kentucky was dull, but at least she no longer had to put up with her ex-husband's upper class pretensions.

Schuyler's life took an unexpected turn in *Heir Condition* (Signet, 1995). She was notified of a bequest from wealthy developer Ephraim Cross. The members of the Cross family were equally surprised and assumed that Schuyler had an affair with the deceased. No one believed she had never met the man, particularly since she had no alibi for his murder. In fact someone tried to frame her for the crime. Matthias Cross, son of the victim, was determined to learn the truth about his father and Schuyler.

Matthias, a college professor, remained an important part of Schuyler's life in *Closing Statement* (Signet, 1995). So did detectives Reed and Costello who once again were called upon to investigate a crime in which Schuyler was involved. She had discovered the corpse of Edward Bartlett, a former client who was suing her. Bartlett's last words should have identified the killer, but a misunderstanding and the passage of time delayed the solution.

Schuyler's difficulty in expressing her feelings for Matthias finally resolved itself in *A Killing in Real Estate* (Signet, 1996) during which she discovered another corpse when taking clients to view a house for sale. The victim was fellow real estate agent Trudi Vittitoe, who had been "stealing clients" from Schuyler. That left her as either a suspect or the next target.

By the time Schuyler met murder again in *Two-Story Frame* (Signet, 1997), the gimmick of having the same police detectives handle the case and consider her a suspect had worn thin. The more interesting angle was that the victim was Kim, the fiancée of Schuyler's former husband Ed, to whom Schuyler was showing a house for sale. Schuyler spent a considerable portion of the narrative complaining about Ed and their children, before she came up with a conclusion that competent detectives could have reached earlier.

McClellan, under her real name Barbara Taylor McCafferty co-authored a series with her twin sister, Beverly Taylor Herold. Their twin protagonists, Bert and Nan, were presumably named after the Bobbsey twins.

Lil Ritchie

Author: Phyllis Knight

Lil Ritchie, a Virginian by birth, had worked for years in Texas; then, settled in Maine. A tall rawboned lesbian with graying dark hair, she had been a country musician before she became a private investigator. Her musical career was ruined by a false accusation that she had murdered member of her band. She still enjoyed music (especially early jazz, blues, and rock), cooked Southern style, and swam for recreation.

In *Switching the Odds* (St. Martin, 1992), Lil was hired to find young Jesse Cooper who ran away from prep school to find his alcoholic birth father. Jesse could run, but he could not hide, because he and his pal Greg had witnessed a murder which may have involved a family friend.

During *Shattered Rhythms* (St. Martin, 1994), Lil helped Andre Ledoux, a guitarist whose work she had always admired. Ledoux's erratic behavior and eventual disappearance worried the other members of his combo, who thought he might have relapsed into drug addiction. Lil followed his trail to Northern Maine and into Canada. She was unable to prevent his death, but she resolved to turn his killers over to the police. Knight's physical descriptions of New England and Canada and their history were well integrated into the narrative.

Sophie Rivers

Author: Judith Cutler

By her thirties, Sophie Rivers had become a lecturer at William Murdoch College in Birmingham, England. She led a simple life: enjoyed cooking (excellent curries); did the Canadian Air Force exercises, sang with the Midlands Choral Society, was an excellent pianist, as well as a cricket fan (her father had played professionally). Scared off by the thefts of automobiles in Birmingham, she had no car. She used public transportation, walked, or rode her bicycle to the college campus. There were a few problems. Sophie liked her gin a little too much and her taste in men had been unwise. William Murdoch bore no resemblance to the famed British universities. The students were primarily from immigrant homes, eager to rise above their parents' status. A kind woman, Sophie was frequently drawn into their personal problems. A problem of her own, a decision made when she was young, was dealt with during the series.

When, during *Dying Fall* (Piatkus, 1995), ambitious student Wajid Akhtar was murdered on campus, Sophie discovered the corpse. A short time later, she was devastated by the death of her close personal friend George Carpenter, the bassoonist in the local symphony orchestra. With help from a college porter, Sophie avoided becoming another victim. Sophie had enjoyed the company of DCI Chris Groom, but he was too bland for her taste.

By *Dying To Write* (Piatkus, 1996), Sophie was focused on a writer's workshop where unfortunately the male attendees offered little interest. Moreover the week at the isolated institute was very hard on the females involved. Nyree Compton had died, Kate Freeman disappeared, and there had been several attacks on females. Chris Groom was called in, but was unable to save Sophie from a sense of guilt and disappointment. She might be scholarly, but she learned slowly out of the classroom.

In *Dying On Principle* (Piatkus, 1996), a temporary assignment to George Muntz College for a computer project provided Sophie with a more convenient commute, but put her on someone's hit list. The college's top management staff was anti-union, rarely available, and on the take. Sophie removed musician Simon Webster from her list of admirers, but added a randy fraud squad inspector and a ruthless entrepreneur. Inspector Chris Groom remained at the top of the list but Sophie was not ready to make any commitments.

Sophie's attachment to her slightly younger cousin, rock star Andy Rivers, was a pivotal factor in *Dying For Millions* (Piatkus, 1997). Chris Groom was away for training. After a series of malicious acts, Pete Hughes, a worker on Andy's final performance was murdered Pete had fallen from a gantry after drinking from Andy's flask. A parallel assignment, finding technical internships for students, placed Sophie in a dangerous conflict of interest. This forced her to balance her feelings for Andy against her loyalty to Chris.

As *Dying For Power* (Piatkus, 1998) began, Sophie had returned to William Murdock College tanned and refreshed from a vacation. What she found there was chaos. Ethnic groups clashed as to proper attire and the appropriate behavior of female students and staff. Some minority groups were harassed by others. This was no minor problem for Sophie whose own attire was criticized. There were fires, attacks on staff, and murder. The new administration could not, or would not, take proper action; in fact, it supported charges against Sophie.

Chris had been promoted to Chief Superintendent in a nearby jurisdiction as *Dying To Score* (Headline, 1999) began. His relationship with Sophie had diminished to friendship. Good thing because at this point Sophie met the man she had been waiting for, cricket player Mike Lowden. Not even the accusation that Mike had killed fellow player Guy Timpson could change Sophie's feelings. Timpson was a dirty player who had made many enemies, including Mike. At the conclusion, she was a happy woman, facing the future, secure with the two most important men in her life, one a minor surprise.

It had seemed like a well-coordinated decision in *Dying by Degrees* (Headline, 2000). Mike would be in Australia for cricket matches; Sophie would take a sabbatical from William Murdoch College to earn a masters degree at the University of West Midlands. She would join Mike for the Christmas holidays. They would have a small wedding on his return to England. Sophie had always enjoyed her teaching, and felt confident that she had done a good job. She was assigned to part-time work, teaching English to Asian women, and failed miserably. Could it be because the membership in the group changed regularly? Were her students qualified for the course? She had to rely on Chris Groom when her problems connected with the murder of fellow teacher Carla Pentowski.

Sophie's participation in the Big Brum Bookfest was intended to be casual volunteer activity during *Dying By The Book* (Piatkus, 2001). Her commitment quickly expanded when project director Brian Fairweather became seriously ill at a time of crisis. Authors who were to headline the event had been threatened. Novelist Marietta Coe was murdered. Someone was stalking attractive blondes and Sophie fit the description. Her personal problems were resolved along the way.

With Mike overseas with the English cricket team and Sophie finishing her Masters degree in education at the University of West Midlands in *Dying in Discord* (Headline, 2002), they decided to keep their wedding plans secret. Unfortunately Sophie found herself the recipient of unwelcome sexual attentions by male and female staff and students. Nasty rumors circulated as to her sexuality. When murders connected to gay and lesbians occurred, Sophie was considered a suspect by local police. In the alternative they were willing to use her as a "tethered goat"

Mike and Sophie had moved into a new home and were planning a blessing ceremony to announce their marriage, as *Dying to Deceive* (Headline, 2003) began. Sophie agreed to archive major donations of cricket memorabilia for the Warwickshire Cricket Club. Then it all fell apart. Both curator Greg Bigg and many of the valuable antiquities disappeared. Mike and Sophie split up over his resentment of her contacts with Chris Groom. Scandalous rumors of fixed cricket games cast doubt on players, including Mike. Although she asked a lot of questions, Sophie was more victim than sleuth.

Cutler has two police procedurals, featuring female protagonists: Kate Power (this volume) and more recently Chief Superintendent Frances Harman; a culinary series featuring Josie Welford, and an historical male sleuth, Parson Tobias Campion. She is an extremely versatile writer.

Nan Robinson

Author: Taffy Cannon

Nan Robinson, who had been divorced for three years, lived in a condo in Playa del Ray near Los Angeles. A graduate of the UCLA Law School, she worked as an attorney/investigator for the California State Bar. Leon, her former husband, had remarried and there was no contact. Her father, who died in a car wreck, had been an alcoholic. She still attended meetings of the Adult Children of Alcoholics. In her mid-thirties, Nan remained unsure of what she wanted to do with the rest of her life.

Before *A Pocketful of Karma* (Carroll & Graf, 1993) began, Nan had befriended computer expert Debbie Fontaine, a young woman from her hometown. When Debbie's mother contacted the Bar office in search of her daughter, Nan was surprised. Debbie no longer worked there. For old time's sake, Nan tried to find Debbie, who had become involved with an obscure cult, "Karma, The Past Lives Institute." First Debbie's corpse, then that of her abusive former husband were found. The police would settle for murder/suicide, but Nan believed that Debbie had been a danger to someone at PLI. She hoped it was not the man with whom she had fallen in love.

In *Tangled Roots* (Carroll & Graf, 1995), Nan left her work behind to visit her sister Julie, who ran a small flower and orchard business with her husband Adam. When Shane Pettigrew, the heir to his primary competitor, was murdered, Adam was charged even though he and Shane had been friends since childhood. There were other suspects, but no one seemed interested in pursuing the investigation, even when Shane's domineering father died mysteriously. Nan took on the challenge, prodding defense attorney Ramon Garza until she discovered the killer.

When Nan's high school class in Spring Hill, Illinois announced their twentieth reunion, she attended during *Class Reunions Are Murder* (Fawcett Crest, 1996). She was not the biggest surprise at the gathering. That was Brenda, the "class tramp," who had left town pregnant. The father of her child was the obvious suspect when she was murdered, but Brenda had more than one secret that gave her power over fellow classmates.

Author Taffy Cannon created memorable characterizations and interesting plots. She completed Rebecca Rothenberg's manuscript for *The Tumbleweed Murders* and, writing as Emily Toll, has a new series featuring travel director Lynne Montgomery.

Benedetta "Bennie" Rosato

Author: Lisa Scottoline

Bennie Rosato made her living as a defense attorney in criminal actions or as a plaintiff attorney in civil cases, specializing in matters, which involved civil rights and police brutality. She had an adversarial relationship with the Philadelphia police. Benny had never had it easy. She was the child of Carmella Rosato, a single mother who had never identified her daughter's father. Although Benny had a good income, her mother was chronically mentally ill and required twenty four-hour care. Carmella lived in Benny's home, where a nurse cared her for during the daytime. This did not leave much time for a personal life.

For a time after Bennie and her law partner Mark Biscardi ended their affair, they continued to practice together. But, as *Legal Tender* (HarperCollins, 1996) opened, Benny learned that Mark, now seriously involved with Eve Eberlein, an associate in their firm, was preparing to leave. Angered by the secrecy of his betrayal, Bennie blew her top. When Mark was murdered during a period of time when Bennie had no alibi, she found herself dealing with the Philadelphia police department.

By *Rough Justice* (HarperCollins, 1997), Bennie headed a small all-female law firm. Rosato and Associates. The firm served as local counsel for hotshot attorney Marta Richter in her defense of slumlord Elliot Steere when he was accused of murder. The case had already gone to the jury and Marta was confident of an acquittal, when Steere bragged of his guilt. Marta returned to the Rosato firm, determined to undermine her own case with the assistance of two young attorneys. They were unaware of why she wanted further investigations, but risked their reputations and safety. Bennie, who kept in touch with the case at crucial moments, did not play a major role in the narrative. She did save Marta from making a serious mistake.

Bennie could not separate her private life from her profession during *Mistaken Identity* (HarperCollins, 1999). She defended Alice Connolly, a woman who was probably her twin sister, on the charge of murdering her lover, Detective Anthony Della Porta. Bennie had been raised by her chronically ill mother in the belief that she was an only child abandoned by her father. Neither was the truth. That still left the question: did sister Alice kill Della Porta? If not, who did?

The Vendetta Defense (HarperCollins, 2001) was only a peripheral part of the Rosato series. Attorney Judy Carrier was a member of the firm headed by Bennie. Judy took on the defense of Tony Lucia an Italian septuagenarian who considered murder to be a necessity given the wrong that had been done to his family. Judy carried the narrative, but it was Bennie who showed her how to win.

Was there anything more that could go wrong as *Dead Ringer* (HarperCollins,2003) opened. Bennie won her big civil suit, but her client went bankrupt and couldn't pay his fees. Bennie was fighting to become lead attorney on a class action suit against the top litigator in that specialty, Bill Linette. Her landlord has threatened to evict her for non-payment of rent. Someone stole her wallet and made charges on her credit card. So who returns to town? Vindictive Alice, her identical twin, whose behavior is casting doubts on Bennie's sobriety.

Attorney readers may swallow hard at the histrionics and questionable legal practices. (See also Mary DiNunzio, another member of Bennie's staff, covered in this volume because Bennie makes supporting appearances in some of the books). Bennie also appeared in a supporting role in *Courting Trouble* (2003) which featured Anne Murphy, new attorney in the Rosato and Associates firm.

Danielle "Dani" Ross

Author: Gilbert Morris

Dani Ross' life had taken several different directions. She had studied to be an accountant at Tulane University and worked for the Attorney General's Office in Massachusetts. Then she fell in love with Jerry, a divinity student. When he died in a tragic accident shortly after they had quarreled, her guilt led her to believe that she should take his place in the missionary field. Her graduate work at Hayworth Divinity School was interrupted by news that her father was ill. Dan Ross ran a detective agency in New Orleans, but could not continue after a serious heart attack. His wife Ellen, and two younger children, Rob and Allison, were incapable of keeping the business afloat. Dani saw a different responsibility, one that she could not ignore. She was a devout Christian who did not take these matters lightly. Dani was tremendously proud of her great-great-grandfather, a colonel in the Confederate Army, and drew inspiration from his courage at Pickett's unsuccessful charge at Gettysburg.

In *Guilt by Association* (Revell, 1991), she knew that she would have to hire additional staff at the agency but Dani was hesitant about hiring rebellious Ben Savage. He had been recommended by a police chief but with the comment that he had lost his job as a Denver detective for insubordination. It turned out to be a wise choice. Within a month Dani had been abducted and imprisoned in a silo along with ten others. They were to be punished for an unknown transgression. Ben, who followed up on her disappearance, was added to the group. She imparted her religious beliefs to members of the group suffering from their captivity and danger. Ben's physical skills, gained when he worked as an aerialist in a circus, led to their escape. Together they figured out which of their fellow prisoners was the killer.

Well-known actor and playwright Jonathan Ainsley convinced Dani to come to New York City in *The Final Curtain* (Revell, 1991). There had been threats, followed by attempts on his life, as he began production of his comeback play. Dani was to go undercover as a wardrobe mistress, prompter and understudy. When leading lady Amber LeRoi was murdered, Dani assumed her role. Ben joined the crew in time to save more than one life. Dani's religious beliefs transformed several characters. Her deductive skills uncovered five members of the group who had committed crimes.

During *Deadly Deception* (Revell, 1992), Dani took her Christian beliefs (and her .38 revolver) into the home of crime syndicate boss Dominic Lanza. He hired Dani and Ben to guard his four grandchildren against attacks by a rival gang. The closeness between Dani and Ben made it possible for them to communicate when she and a four-year-old boy were kidnapped.

Someone was extorting money from men and women on the rodeo circuit. Ben's sister came to him for help just as he and Dani had another of their quarrels in *Revenge at the Rodeo* (Revell, 1993). She heard next of Ben when he turned up in a Dallas hospital. Luke Sixkiller, currently on suspension for alleged abuse of a prisoner, accompanied her. Both took undercover jobs on the rodeo circuit until they identified the "creeps" who had gone beyond threats to mayhem and murder. Luke had a conversion experience which brought him closer to Dani in Ben's absence.

Dani faced her biggest challenge in *The Quality of Mercy* (Revell, 1993). Tommy Cain was out of prison, determined to kill those who had caught and convicted him, including Dani's father. When he succeeded, Dani's pain was so great that she lost touch with her faith. She wanted revenge, not consolation, ignoring the advice of those who loved her.

Eddie Prejean, an innocent man facing execution in a Mississippi prison, reached out to Dani in *Race with Death* (Revell, 1994), the conclusion of the six book series. Only a gubernatorial pardon could save Eddie Prejean and Governor Layne Russell wanted Eddie dead. Ben and Dani found the trail that led to Russell's personal connection to the victim. Dani, helpless in a swamp, had found her way to safety. Ben, desperate with fear that she might be dead, found his way to faith in God.

It was Dani's reputation as a devout Christian that sent Rev. Alvin Flatt to her in *Four of a Kind* (Crossway, 2001). He was at first glance an elderly, shabbily dressed man, but his message was powerful. He had been sent by God, after a life of sin, to build a church (Greater Fire Baptized Church of Jesus Christ) in a disreputable part of New Orleans. His success in attracting members to his congregation was threatened by hoodlums. Lenny Valentine, a merciless crime lord, needed the land on which Flatt's church stood in order to build a mall. Dani sought help from two men who were important in her life: her investigator Ben Savage and police lieutenant Lucas Sixkiller. Even though her support of Flatt's church placed Dani and members of her family in danger, she came to believe in Flatt's sense of mission. Ben had a reason of his own to challenge Valentine.

The narrative placed considerable emphasis on religious values. They were well plotted with interesting characterizations. Continuing characters were used to illustrate the power of Dani's intercession even if not immediately effective; e.g. two criminals who did not seek repentance in their first appearance, died after a change of heart in subsequent books.

Ruby Rothman

Author: Sharon Kahn

Although she could never escape her role as the widow of a rabbi, Ruby Rothman was a skilled computer consultant and had become part-owner of The Hot Bagel in Eternal, Texas. Her only child Joshua was initially a college student. The Rothman household had shrunk to Ruby and a three-legged golden retriever named Oy Vey. Members of her former husband Stuart's congregation, particularly Essie Sue Margolis, kept their eyes open for an acceptable beau for Ruby. She was a warm and witty woman, who was less comfortable in larger groups. The Rothmans had lived in Eternal for twenty-one years, but Ruby loved New York City and enjoyed her visits there. She had a support system: members of the Temple; her Lebanese partner in the bagel shop Milt Aboud; and Nan, a legal secretary and law student with whom she corresponded on the Internet. Ruby's e-mail letters were utilized as parts of the narrative.

Ruby had almost accepted her widowhood when, in *Fax Me a Bagel* (Scribner's, 1998), a tragic event made her aware that Stu Rothman might have been murdered. A prominent temple member (Essie Sue's sister) died of cyanide poisoning after eating a bagel at Milt's shop. The possibility that the bagel might have been intended for Ruby and subsequent "accidents" confirmed her suspicions. Two trips to New York City, during which she learned the traditions of the bagel business and probed the relationships among members of a prominent bagel-making family, enlightened her as to possible motives.

Essie Sue's relentless campaign to sell matzo balls to raise money for a statue to honor her sister provided an opening for more unscrupulous dealings in *Never Nosh a Matzo Ball* (Scribner's, 2000). While Essie Sue spent her time sponsoring a marriage for Rabbi Kevin Kapstein, Ruby sought the connection between a recent murder and the residents of the Fit and Rural Ranch. Ruby, peddling her computer skills, infiltrated the Ranch, which provided a weight reduction plan, but received a cool reception.

The hot pastrami in *Don't Cry for Me, Hot Pastrami* (Scribner's, 2001) was only the second prize. The first prize in Essie Sue's moneymaking lottery, a cruise in the Caribbean, was won by Ruby. She would go as part of a tour group from her Temple headed by Rabbi Kevin Kapstein. Willie Bob Gonzalez, the professor who was to deliver the lecture series on "Jews of the Inquisition" died, while boarding. Rabbi Kapstein retained possession of his materials and, thanks to Essie Sue, was named as his replacement. Kapstein, a less than fluent speaker, needed help so Essie Sue volunteered Ruby. This gave her an opportunity to learn more about the Diaspora of the Spanish Jews, but again made her a target for a killer. Ruby proved to be a survivor. She also met an attractive Jewish travel writer who promised to keep in touch.

Essie Sue was unstoppable when she decided upon a plan of action in *Hold the Cream Cheese, Kill the Lox (Scribner, 2002).* She was determined to have Rabbi Kevin Kapstein prepare her twelve-year-old cousins for their Bar Mitzvah, to be followed by the best repast ever offered. The lox had to be perfect, but the master lox preparer in Eternal, Texas was murdered before he could audition. Lox was also a problem for Ruby's business partner, Milt Aboud. Rising prices and lower quality might force a change in supplier. A trip to Alaska with her friend Nan gave Ruby an opportunity to checkout the Acme Jobbers, who supplied the lox in question. That riled Acme up but did not solve Herman Guenther's murder.

Just the fact that Essie Sue and Freddie Fenstermeier were co-chairmen of the Temple Rita Reunion in *What Big Giver Stole the Chopped Liver?* (Scribner, 2004) was enough to doom the event. Essie Sue, permanent chairman of the Temple Board, and Freddie, grandnephew of the donor who originally subsidized the temple, detested one another. Their rivalry infected the event, climaxing when an uninvited guest was found dead, face down in the ice bucket where the liver mold (made by Essie Sue) had rested. The Austin police wanted to know why Max Cole had been murdered by Essie Sue's brass pestle, the prints on which were those of Hal Margolis (Essie Sue's husband). Essie Sue wanted to know where her platter was.

Group travel had always been hazardous for Ruby, especially when shared with members of Temple Rita and organized by compulsively bossy Essie Sue Margolis, but in *Out of the Frying Pan, into the Choir* (Scribner, 2006), the violence started before the Temple Choir left Eternal, Texas. They had been invited to compete in an interdenominational Choir Fest in Lake Louise, Canada. During a fund raiser, organized by Essie Sue, soprano Serena Salit collapsed and died. By the time Ruby departed with the choir and supporters, she was suspicious that she might be traveling with a killer. Her cell phone not only kept her in contact with Lt. Paul Lundy, it contributed to the solution to the murders.

Trudy Roundtree

Author: Linda Berry

Trudy was the only female in the police department in the southern Georgia town of Ogeechee. Her original goal had been to teach so she had earned a degree in English from a local teacher's college. Her husband Zach was killed while hunting. However her prior employment had been with an Atlanta advertising agency. That ended after an unhappy affair with a staff member. She and her cats now lived in a house bequeathed to her by her grandmother. Not all family members were happy with this arrangement. Her grandmother also had been successful in convincing Trudy's cousin, chief of police Henry Huckabee to hire her as a police officer.

Trudy was inexperienced, but managed adequately in *Death and the Easter Bunny* (Write Way, 1998). With Henry hampered by a severe allergic reaction, she investigated the arson/murder of Reed Titter. Reed had bragged about his expectation of big money so they suspected he was blackmailing someone. Trudy was slow to put that motive together with squealing brakes, an Easter Bunny, and an automatic oven.

Hubcaps were significant and confusing in *Death and the Hubcap* (Write Way, 2000). Local eccentric Tanner Whitcomb fantasized that the hubcap he held in his hands was the steering wheel of a vehicle so no one got excited when he said he'd run over someone. Trudy checked it out, only to find the victim of a hit and run with tire tracks on his body. The driver's license in his wallet identified him as Lester De Loach, but he was vaguely familiar to Trudy. She recognized him from a visit to an Atlanta art gallery. A missing hubcap involved four teenagers whose punishment yielded the clue that identified the killer.

Henry Huckabee, Trudy's boss and cousin, thought he was providing her with light duty in *Death and the Icebox* (Thomson Gale, 2004) when he assigned her to research a thirty-year-old homicide. Trudy had been at the Riggs' farm when an old icebox containing a young woman's body was unearthed. Even with her left hand immobilized by an accident, she used newspaper files, the long memories of her friends and high school scrapbooks to not only identify the victim but those who were complicit in young Karen Willard's death and burial.

Elderly Althea Boatright went beyond eccentric. She was just plain mean in *Death and the Walking Stick* (Five Star, 2005). Shortly after she had killed Charlie Sykes by pinning him to a wall with her "runaway car", Althea was found dead. She lived in a separate set of rooms at the home owned by her son Leland Grinstead and his wife Clarice. The house had been inherited by Althea when her second husband Rowland Boatright died. His children from a first marriage deeply resented the loss of the family home to the upstart Grinsteads. Althea's bridge playing pals (including Trudy's Aunt Lulu) were certain she had been murdered because not only was the walking stick found in a room not hers but it was nowhere near her body. Very homespun solutions solved the crimes.

The Stubbs family held their reunion to coincide with the closing weekend of Ogeechee's Bicentennial in *Death and the Family Tree* (Five Star/ Thomason/Gale, 2007). Four generations of Stubbs gathered, some from out of town. They were a contentious group, but no one expected that their disagreements would end in murder. Yes, there was an upset when young Kevin Purvis made it known that he had secretly married Gretchen Holland, a fellow college student. Mildly senile Great Uncle Julian plummeted down the stairs clutching a framed family tree at a time when Trudy was at the Bed and Breakfast investigating a possible theft. The B and B was owned by Della and Willie, two members of the Stubbs family. Chief of Police Hen Huckabee needed Trudy on the case because his wife Trina was a Stubbs.

Death and the Crossed Wires (2009)

Mary Russell

Author: Laurie R. King

The Beekeeper's Apprentice (St. Martin, 1994) was a compilation of notes left behind by an elderly woman, relating to incidents in her youth. Mary Russell had been a fifteen-year-old orphan, living near the Suffolk Downs with a disgruntled aunt, when she met Sherlock Holmes. She was tall, blond, athletic, and lonely, tortured by guilt because her ill humor might have contributed to the death of her parents and brother. During a stroll on the Downs, she met Holmes, now retired and began a relationship that shaped her life. Mrs. Watson became a second mother; Sherlock a mentor and friend. Gradually she joined in his investigations, traveling disguised as a gypsy to rescue a missing American child.

Once freed from her aunt, she moved from being Holmes' pupil to acting as his associate. They incurred the wrath of a criminal who targeted Watson, Holmes, and Mary for death. With Holmes' powers fading, Mary, by then an Oxford student, persisted until they faced their adversary. By her twenty-first birthday, Mary was almost six feet tall, a student of the martial arts, and increasingly devoted to Holmes.

In *A Monstrous Regiment of Women* (St. Martin, 1995), their personal relationship changed, frightening both with its sexual implications. Mary involved herself in the charismatic religious movement of Margery Childe, which explored the female component of God. The deaths of devotees to the New Temple of God provided funds for Margery's movement, causing Mary to wonder whether she was victim or killer? A vicious and greedy murderer dragged Mary to the depths of drug addiction before Holmes rescued her. The ending may shock Holmes' fans.

Mary did not consider herself a Christian. Her mother had been Jewish. Still, she shared Holmes interest in *A Letter of Mary* (St. Martin, 1997). An amateur archeologist, Dorothy Ruskin, contacted them regarding a papyrus message from Miriam (Mary) from the town of Magdala re Joshua (Jesus). Dorothy, because her sight was failing, turned custody of the letter and the carved wooden box in which it had been contained over to Holmes. The provenance of the letter seemed authentic. Its impact on the Christian world would be to indicate that women played a strong role in the early life of the Church. A short time later, Mary and Sherlock learned that Dorothy had been killed in a traffic accident. Convinced that she had been murdered, each went undercover to investigate major suspects. There was an interesting appearance by "Peter" (Wimsey?) who recognized Mary, but did not betray her.

Although Sherlock and Mary had been married for over two years in *The Moor* (St. Martin, 1998), she was still learning about him. His peremptory telegram summoning her to the home of aging scholar Rev. Sabine Baring-Gould distracted Mary from her work, but she acquiesced. The moor (Dartmoor) had no attraction for her at first. As she and Sherlock investigated first rumors, then murder, reminiscent of his prior case, *The Hound of the Baskervilles*, its bleakness and the people who inhabited the moor enthralled her. A phantom coach carrying Lady Howard accompanied by her black dog vied with a more recent death on the moor. The narrative moved slowly. Perhaps like the moor, it required time and attention to develop a real interest.

Nursing their physical and emotional wounds, Mary and Sherlock left England as *O Jerusalem* (Bantam, 1999) began. The narrative was out of sequence, covering a period before Mary and Sherlock had married. Mycroft, Sherlock's brother, had offered several alternative locations in which they could serve England. Mary chose Jerusalem, the homeland of her people, then occupied by British troops. She and Sherlock traveled together with Mary dressed as a young man under the auspices of suspicious British allies. They noted the contemptuous treatment English soldiers gave to occupants of Jerusalem. Tensions among different racial groups ran high. There had been a series of murders causing Mycroft to fear for the safety of General Edmund Allenby. Their relationship moved to a different level during their travails.

Mary and Sherlock had barely resettled themselves in their country home, when, in *Justice Hall* (Bantam, 2002) they received a visit from their former comrade Ali Harz, now revealed to be a member of the illustrious Hughenfort family. Ali convinced them to accompany him to Justice Hall, home of the Duke of Beauville. Ali's older cousin, Marsh had left England to serve his country under the auspices of Mycroft Holmes. He had returned only when two deaths made him heir to the Dukedom. Ali and Marsh both desired to return to the desert they loved, but could do so only when the family heritage was preserved by a legitimate heir to the title. The narrative went beyond the deaths of potential heirs to the horrors of war on young men, the responsibilities of those who made battlefield decisions as compared to the plans of the military hierarchy, and the summary execution of those who opposed the decisions.

There must have been times when Holmes looked back with longing to the days at Baker street, even his beekeeping retirement; i.e. when as in *The Game* (Bantam, 2004) brother Mycroft sent him and the intrepid Mary Russell off to India. Their mission was to locate Kimball O'Hara, the prototype for Kipling's *Kim* . Working sometimes together, then separately, they journeyed to the principality of Khampur, which bordered Russia. While Mary used her friendship with two young Americans to meet the irascible maharajah, Holmes traveled as a native magician.

The decision, in *Locked Rooms* (Bantam, 2005) to return to London via San Francisco so that Mary could deal with matters pertaining to her father's estate, seemed sensible. What confused Mary was the experience of three dreams which upset her and worried Holmes. On arrival in San Francisco, Mary consulted Henry Norbert, the family attorney, and visited the empty family home, unoccupied since 1914. This came about because Charles Russell's will insisted that no one except family and someone accompanied by family could enter the premises. The first two dreams made sense when Mary realized she had been present during the 1906 earthquake. The final dream, the locked room, metaphorical in nature, became clear only after an investigation shared with a Chinese bookseller and former Pinkerton agent Dashiell Hammett.

King is one of the most literate and compelling authors in the current mystery field. Although *The Art of Detection* (Bantam, 2006) refers to Sherlock Holmes at a time when he and Mary Russell might have been in the U. S., it is a Kate Martinelli book. (covered elsewhere in this volume)

Next: *The Language of Bees* (2009), *The God of the Hive* (2010)

Carol Sabala

Author: Vinnie Hansen

Carol, a baker at *Archibalds* family restaurant, aspired to be a detective. She nurtured this dream with her library of real crime, mysteries, and reference books about detection. She was a tall redhead, married to Chad, a roofer, but had no interest in having children. She was physically active, played on a volleyball team.

Her car was a 1966 Kharman Ghia. Carol's mother at 73 was still active and independent. Her father Geraldo, possibly Mexican, had died. There was a brother Donald, who had died of AIDS. Chad's mother had given Carol a menorah, causing her to believe that she was of Jewish descent. Chad had been raised by his grandparents, but recently Mary, his mother, had moved back into his life, calling him everyday, seeking rides and attention. Carol did achieve a start on her dream, working part-time for alcoholic investigator J. J. Sloan. David Shapiro, who became her lover in later narratives, worked part-time for Community Care Licensing, but also was a "nudie" photographer. This didn't seem to bother Carol.

Chef Jean Alcee Fortier was the star of the Archibald kitchen in *Murder, Honey* (Xlibris, 1999) at least until someone murdered him. Carol's shift began at 3:30 AM so that fresh breads and rolls would be available for breakfast. Fortier had been poisoned, collapsing into the dough. His reputation as a chef was equaled by his reputation as a womanizer, including fellow workers. Carol wanted to solve this case, even though Chad was concerned about the risks. She didn't pay much attention to his ideas.

Author Hansen's seventeen years as a teacher provided authentic background in *One Tough Cookie* (Xlibris, 2000) for problems in an understaffed, badly equipped high school. The students had varied levels of motivation and assorted ethnic backgrounds. Carol became involved when she agreed to provide a demonstration for home economics teacher Alvina Jameson's cooking class. Eldon, restaurant manager at Archibald's, gave her time off with pay because his friend Alvina had a hidden agenda. Carol was to investigate a case of cookie poisoning which had affected several faculty members. The cookies had been baked as a class project to raise money. Within days the incidents escalated to murder. Jennifer Padilla, a pregnant student, refused to name the father of her child, although there had been rumors of sexual harassment by at least two male teachers. When she was found dead of a fall, there was no stopping Carol from getting involved, no matter how Chad felt about it.

Rotten Dates (Mainly Murder, 2003c) related many changes in Carol's life. She initiated a divorce; then was aggrieved at how quickly Chad found a replacement. Her mother (Bea) moved into a rooming house in Santa Cruz. She and Carol had bonded in a surprising manner. Suzanne Anderson, Carol's friend and co-worker at Archibald's, urged her to initiate or respond to an ad in a newspaper dating service. At this point the narrative became sexually explicit, even kinky, to a point that will make some readers uncomfortable. Carol had two "clients": Bea who was concerned about a "strange" neighbor, and Suzanne whose unconventional cousin Beverly may have been killed by someone she met through a dating ad. A real disappointment.

It was concern for her mother, Bea, that led Carol to Harbor View Estates in *Tang Is Not Juice* (Mainly Murder, 2005). She was aware that Bea, feeling her age, was considering a move there. While on a visit, they met (and Bea bonded with) resident Gladys Mills. Gladys' subsequent death had a hint of murder. Bored by baking and entranced by becoming a private investigator, Carol finagled her way into a job. Gladys' son Rusty had been disappointed when Glady's personal assistant at Harbor View, Chrissie Locatelli, inherited the family home. He wanted proof of undue influence, but Carol went beyond her assignment.

Next: *Death with Dessert* (2009)

Amelia Sachs

Author: Jeffrey Wilds Deaver

Lincoln Rhyme, former head of the forensics unit at the New York Police Department, was a quadriplegic confined to a wheelchair. He wanted to die and his doctor had agreed to help. Three factors intervened: (1) a difficult case which he may be the only person able to solve; (2) a fearsome enemy, "The Bone Collector," who dangled clues to taunt Rhyme, his ultimate target; and (3) Amelia Sachs, who made his life worth living.

A tall attractive redhead, she had been an advertising model; then, became a patrol officer like her father. The onset of arthritis limited her choices to retirement or transfer to the information unit. Her personal life had been on hold since her lover Nick, a bent detective, ended their relationship. When his criminal affiliations were discovered, Nick cared enough about her to put distance between them. Her father had been dead for three years. Mother Rose lived near Amelia's apartment in Brooklyn. Amelia was an excellent pistol shot, cast her own bullets and reloaded her own ammunition. She also carried a switchblade that she learned to use as a kid in Brooklyn.

It had been Amelia who discovered the first victim as *The Bone Collector* (Viking, 1997) began. By the time Rhyme's former comrades on the police force went to him for help, Amelia had been accepted as a member of the scene of crime team. Rhyme was impressed enough to insist that she become his contact with the police. She would be his eyes at the scene of the crime, wearing an earphone connection to keep in touch. Their relationship grew, a fact noted by the Bone Collector, whose modus operandi was based on that of a killer described in a book *Crime in Old New York*.

The federal government's efforts to prosecute arms dealer Phillip Hansen were hampered when he dropped evidence into the ocean from a plane. Of the three witnesses against Hansen, a contract killer known as the "Coffin Dancer", had eliminated one, Edward Carney of Hudson Air Charters. Rhyme's cooperation was assured in *The Coffin Dancer* (Simon & Schuster, 1998) because the Coffin Dancer had killed his laboratory assistant Claire Trilling, the woman he loved. The first responsibility for Rhyme's special squad was to protect the remaining witnesses: Carney's widow Percey Clay, and top Hudson pilot Brit Hale. The second was to capture and convict Coffin Dancer. Rhyme wanted more than justice. He wanted vengeance. Amelia was very much a part of the action, angry with herself because during one contact she had an opportunity to kill Dancer and failed to do so, angry at Rhyme because he resisted her sexual overtures.

Rhyme had a walk-on in *The Devil's Teardrop* (Simon & Schuster, 1999) which pitted document expert Parker Kincaid against a threadening "Digger" shortly before the end of the millennium.

When Rhyme went to the University of North Carolina's Medical Center in *The Empty Chair* (Simon & Schuster, 2000), he was aware of the risks involved in the experimental treatment he would receive. It would be worth it if the end result would be increased mobility. He did not expect to be drawn into the hunt for Garrett Ganlon, a teenage boy accused of murder and kidnapping. Nor did he anticipate that Amelia would dispute his findings and those of the local authorities. Her independent actions caused her to be indicted for murder. She was saved before sentencing when Rhyme uncovered a sinister plot. She repaid his efforts by saving his life.

An inter-agency force requested help from Rhyme and Amelia in *The Stone Monkey* (Simon & Schuster, 2002). A notorious smuggler, nicknamed the "Ghost," was about to land Chinese immigrants off the Long Island coast. When the Chinese vessel noted the presence of the Coast Guard, chaos followed. The ship was blown up. Swimmers dispersed. Somewhere in New York City there were two families seeking a life in America. The "Ghost" was determined to prevent them from achieving that goal. As his victim count mounted, he added Amelia to the list. Lincoln and Amelia were talking about having a child but she had a history of endometriosis. Dr. John Sung, one of the immigrants, was treating her with acupressure and herbal meds or was that his agenda?

As a technical exercise in legerdemain, *The Vanished Man* (Simon & Schuster, 2003) will probably receive considerable praise. A professional magician who no longer worked at the trade had nourished resentment against the Cirque Fantastique, now playing in New York City. As a prelude to a final act of violence, he killed a series of innocent victims using methods based on famous illusions. Rhyme and Amelia were assigned to the case and with the help of Kara, a student magician, matched wits with the conjurer.

Sixteen-year-old African-American Geneva Settle was the target of a paid assassin in *The Twelfth Card* (Simon & Schuster, 2005). She was clever enough to evade Thompson Boyd when he came upon her in the library of the Museum of African-American Culture and History. Considering Boyd's expertise, she was fortunate that Rhyme and his crew were called in to investigate and protect Geneva. Geneva had been at the museum to research her ancestor, Charles Singleton, a former slave. He had served in the Union Army and become a property owner in New York State, only to be rejected by his people when he was accused of embezzlement. Not only a good mystery but a learning experience.

Talk about the dance of the seven veils, the "Watchmaker," criminal mastermind in *Cold Moon* (Simon & Schuster, 2006) had at least that many. The complex narrative that entwined two cases: (1) brutal even sadistic murders at each of which a clock had been left behind were referred to Rhyme by City

Hall; and (2) a murder case on which Amelia, at her own request, was the lead detective. She became a threat to powerful forces in the NYPD, learned things that made her wonder if she wanted to be a cop. Kathryn Dance added her skills in kinesthetics. Kathryn went on to appear in a book of her own, possibly the beginning of a series.

Rhyme and Sachs were nearly outwitted in *The Broken Window* (Simon & Schuster, 2008) by a computer mastermind. Rhyme's estranged cousin Arthur was arrested and jailed for the murder of Alice Sanderson. Having declared his innocence, Arthur relied upon the legal system to prove that this was a case of mistaken identity. Aware of the circumstantial evidence, his wife Judy was less optimistic so contacted Rhyme for help. He was sufficiently impressed to check further, researching similar cases, which featured murder, rape, and theft. Someone with access to vast amounts of personal information might be a serial killer. Rhyme and Sachs' involvement did not go unnoticed.

Next: *The Burning Wire* (2010)

These were spellbinding narratives; different in tone from Deaver's other series featuring Rune. New series featuring Kathryn Dance, California investigator and Deputy Brynn McKenzie.

Dr. Maxene St. Clair

Author: Janet McGiffin

Maxene St. Clair was a M.D./Ph.D., meaning that she had earned both a medical degree and a doctorate in science. Her marriage to another doctor failed. After six years of teaching and research, she left the academic setting, taking an equally high-pressure job as an emergency room doctor at St. Agnes' Hospital in Milwaukee, Wisconsin. A redhead in her late thirties, Maxene used photography as a relaxation, and her cat, "Ruby" for company.

During *Emergency Murder* (Fawcett, 1992), Maxene worked the late shift when Nanette, the wife of prominent surgeon Hank Myer, arrived close to death dressed as a hooker. The immediate diagnosis was heart failure. An autopsy indicated that she been poisoned by an obscure substance, last known to have been used in Maxene's college lab. Investigator Joe Grabowski, who had dated Maxene before her marriage, was inclined to give her the benefit of the doubt.

In *Prescription for Death* (Fawcett, 1993), Joe played a larger role. Among the regular admissions to the emergency room were prostitutes brought in by their pimps after hard sex and abuse. Maxene made a personal visit to the rooming house where Latoya was close to death. Before the ambulance could arrive, a drive-by killer had wounded another hooker and artist Wyoming Syzinski, Joe's boyhood chum. Joe and Maxene were present later when a heavy wooden sculpture fell and injured artist Soren Berendorf who subsequently died. They connected the incidents.

Maxene joined the ranks of politicians in *Elective Murder* (Fawcett, 1995) when there seemed to be a bounty on female legislators in Wisconsin.

Democratic state senator Irene Wisnewski from Milwaukee had asked Maxene to come to Madison and testify on a pending bill. Irene was less interested in emergency room services than in preventive care. Maxene's primary goal was to protect state funding for emergency room treatment, but she had to solve a murder to do so.

McGiffin has also contributed to a series of mystery books designed for those who are learning English as a second language.

Laney Samms

Author: Carol Schmidt

Laney Samms co-owned a bar in California that attracted a lesbian clientele. Her constant companion was a German Shepherd called "Radar." Her business partner was Anne Nickolai, a female veterinarian with whom she had lived for twenty years. Laney was described as a woman in her forties whose hair had turned from dark to silver.

In *Silverlake Heat* (Naiad, 1993), Laney found her long time affair with Anne stultifying and ended it. She became involved in a destructive relationship with the wife of an Episcopalian priest, and a murder investigation in which the killer manipulated her.

Laney bought full control of the bar, but left it to be managed by a friend in *Sweet Cherry Wine* (Naiad, 1994). She moved to a guesthouse on the Los Angeles estate of Kitt Meyers, a music entrepreneur. Kitt provided Laney with free rent and a small salary for house-sitting and minor clerical work. Laney and Kitt intervened in an attack on a young woman whom they recognized as a former rock star. The recovery of Hayley Malone needed more than financial and medical assistance. A malevolent ghost had pursued her from childhood.

By *Cabin Fever* (Naiad, 1995), Laney's relationship with Hayley was floundering. Her stay at Kitt's estate ended when she was almost killed by a bomb placed in Kitt's car. Laney moved again, this time to Upper Michigan where she worked to establish a lesbian summer camp, threatened by the hostility of the local residents.

Charlotte Sams

Author: Alison Glen, pseudonym for Cheryl Meredith Lowry and Louise Vetter

Although she had a financially successful husband, Charlotte Sams wanted more. Their son Tyler was twelve, and she had time on her hands. Her best pal Lou Toreson had retired from her position at Ohio State University to carry on a private psychology practice. Charlotte, who lived in Clintonville, a suburb of Columbus, Ohio, decided on her own career as a freelance journalist concentrating on feature stories about the area. Once on scene, murders occurred, and Charlotte and Lou solved them.

In *Showcase* (Simon & Schuster, 1992), the setting was a local art show, which might be displaying copies, not original art-works. Prof. Phil Stevenson, who was married to Charlotte's cousin Melanie, gave his expert opinion that a white jade necklace was a fake. No one paid too much attention because Phil had been drinking. But maybe someone did pay attention because he died the next day. His death was accepted as a heart attack by the authorities, but Charlotte and Lou knew better.

The Columbus zoo was highlighted in *Trunk Show* (Simon & Schuster, 1995) when elephant handler Jerry Brobst, whom Charlotte was to interview, was found dead in the elephant yard. Neither vandalism to her car, nor the efforts of African-American homicide detective Jefferson Barnes, kept Charlotte and Lou from interviewing suspects, rifling files, and interfering in the investigation. There were some interesting suspects.

The narratives were well-handled.

Dr. Meredyth "Mere" Sanger

Author: Robert W. Walker

Meredyth Sanger a.k.a. Mere was a silver-blonde psychiatrist, born and raised in Seattle, Washington, but practicing in Houston, Texas. Her parents had been educators. She had attended Duke University. The primary protagonist in the series was Lucas Stonecoat, a Native American who had been relegated to the "Cold Room" of the Houston Police Department. His job was to check unsolved murders to see if they had been mishandled or if new information made it wise to reopen the case.

Lucas had been disabled since a drunken driving accident while working for the Dallas Police Department. After that, there was no future for him in Dallas. He moved to Houston where he started as a rookie, but had not conquered his drinking problem. He had contempt for laws and regulations that enhanced the rights of the accused. On occasion Mere, in her job as psychiatrist for the 31st Precinct, pushed to have Lucas involved in her cases. They became his cases, not hers. His viewpoint, personal life, and actions dominated the series.

Lucas hoped that Mere would be part of his future. Her assistant was Randy Oglesby, a computer nerd who helped Lucas on the sly. Although she had an interest in Lucas, Mere had other lovers, but no marriages. She carried a weapon and was proficient with it, unusual for a police psychiatrist. Mere's police salary was only a portion of her income as she also had a lucrative private practice.

Randy, Lucas and Mere became interested in a series of mutilations and deaths by crossbows during *Cutting Edge* (Jove, 1997). Randy knew something about bows because he had constructed a computer game based on crossbows. Mere met Lucas in the records unit when she went there to research murders stretching back ten years and taking place in a variety of locations. A recent victim had been local judge Charles Mootry. Not only were their efforts unappreciated by Lucas' superior officers, but they were decoyed first out of the area; then, into danger. The narrative was extremely violent with villains and protagonists both quick to kill.

FBI agent Dr. Kim Desinor (who also appeared in author Robert W. Walker's Jessica Coran series) added her visions to Mere's psychological insights and Lucas' Native American mysticism in *Double Edge* (Jove, 1998). Another serial killer terrified a segment of Houston's community, the families of young African-American males. Lucas could not resist keeping tabs on the latest victim, Lamar Coleson, who had disappeared but might still be alive. Guided by Kim's dreams and visions, Lucas and Mere raced against the clock. Lucas made time to reinvestigate the death of Minerva Roundpoint, a young Native American woman, whose son could not rest until her killer was identified.

Cold Edge (Jove, 2001) was not for the faint of heart, or for those who believe that police officers should abide by the civil rights of those who have been suspected of or arrested for crimes. Lucas and Mere joined in the hunt for a depraved serial killer, or perhaps two separate killers, the Scalper and the Beheader. Lucas, under heavy pressure at work, juggled his romantic and family connections. He was angry that the authorities assumed the Scalper was a Native American, but he behaved brutally to get information from a suspect.

Any reader who can make it through the early chapters of *Final Edge* (Jove, 2004) may well enjoy the well-written police procedural that follows. Lauralie Blodgett and her adoring lover, veterinarian Arthur Belkvin, are on a murderous rampage motivated by incidents in Lauralie's early life for which she blamed Mere. The unsavory murder of young Mira Lourdes was the start of a long trail left by Lauralie to entice Mere and Lucas into her intrigue. Too much detailed savagery.

A reader who enjoyed Mere should try Walker's other series featuring Jessica Coran.

Lacey (Sherlock) Savich

Author: Catherine Coulter

It was certainly not the financial rewards that caused Lacey to seek a career in the F.B.I. She had planned to be a musician, and had considerable talent as a pianist. She had a dramatic change of heart, sold her piano, dropped out of college for a year; came back with a new major in Forensic Science. She added a master's degree in Criminal Psychology from Berkeley. Her father's example certainly had an impact. He had been a district attorney; then a judge. Her mother, who was chronically mentally ill, had little influence on Lacey. The family housekeeper, African American Isabelle Tanner, was closer to Lacey than her mother was. A family trust fund supplemented Lacey's income. It was the brutal death of her half-sister Belinda that caused Lacey's turnabout. From that time she was focused on becoming an investigator and finding Belinda's killer.

Coulter's books were essentially an ensemble series based on the FBI. Characters like Lacey and Dillon Savich (whom she married) came and went in individual books. In some they played major roles; in others, made minor appearances. Dillon, for example, appeared in *The Cove* (Jove (1996) before Lacey joined up.

There are hurdles to enjoying *The Maze* (Putnam's, 1997). It is necessary to believe that the FBI would recruit and train Lacey Sherlock without uncovering the traumatic events in her past. Then the reader must swallow hard and accept a serial killer who employs a dramatic modus operandi, leading the victims into a maze with string Finally when Lacey has achieved success in identifying the String Killer, she wondered if she might have failed to achieve her goal. She already had her eye on her boss Dillon Savich. He was good for her; stable and dependable.

The Target (Putnam's 1998), absorbing though it is, has little to do with the FBI or with Lacey and Dillon. Judge Ramsey Hunt, burned out by media attention, retreated to an isolated Colorado cottage. He was there when six-year-old Emma Santera ran away from a vicious child molester. Hunt had bonded with Emma and with her mother, Molly. Dillon and Molly's mobster dad helped them avoid the villain. Lacey? Now married to Dillon, she was busy bearing their son.

Barely recovered from an attack while in Tunisia, FBI agent Ford "Mac" MacDougal left DC in *The Edge* (Putnam's, 1999) to be at his sister Jilly's bedside. She had driven her Porsche at high speed over a cliff. Fortunately she was rescued by a passing trooper. Fragmentary remarks by Jilly while still in a coma sent Mac to confront librarian Laura Scott. This became complicated when both he and Laura fell instantly in love. Mac had a lot to learn about Laura, but also about Jilly, her husband Paul, and the pharmaceutical product they were producing. What had brought them to Edgerton, an obscure town in Oregon? About half way through, Dillon and Sherlock joined their friend Mac in seeking a solution. They had no idea of what they would be up against. The narrative was a mixture of hot romance, eerie dreams, police procedural, and thriller.

Riptide (Putnam's, 2000) focused on Rebecca Matlock who was employed as a speechwriter for the New York governor. When the police ignored her concerns about a stalker, Rebecca changed her name and moved to Riptide, Maine. They and she were unaware that she had been chosen as a victim because of her father. Dillon and Lacey were recruited to help guard Rebecca.

During *Hemlock Bay* (Putnam's, 2001) an FBI case involving Lacey and Dillon was woven into the troubles of Lily, Dillon's sister. Lily and Dillon had each inherited eight of grandmother Sarah Elliott's paintings. Lily's life had been tragic: two bad marriages and the death of her daughter. Now she was a potential victim. Lacey had a minor role.

Lacey and Dillon were the continuing characters in this narrative and she played a decisive role in the outcome, but *Eleventh Hour* (Putnam's, 2002) centered on "Nick", a homeless young woman who had witnessed the murder of

Fr. Michael Joseph Carver. She had seen the killer leave the confessional holding a gun. Father Carver was the twin brother of FBI Special Agent Dane Carver, who went immediately to San Francisco to assist in the investigation. "Nick", who gave a false last name and withheld any information about her past, was obviously fleeing from a perceived danger. The rationale for Fr. Carver's death and other s associated with it was pitifully weak. Once that had been dealt with, the focus shifted to "Nick" and her problems. By that time, Lacey and Dillon were very involved.

Six-year-old Sam Kettering had been kidnapped from his Virginia home and transported to Jessborough, Tennessee as *Blind Side* (Putnam's, 2003) began. He escaped and was rescued by Sheriff Katie Benedict and her five-year-old daughter Keely. Sam remained endangered. His father, Miles Kettering, a former FBI agent, contacted Lacey and Dillon to protect the boy and discover the motive behind the attacks. Lacey had a chance to shine in this one, protecting Dillon from an aggressive female.

Callie Markham, investigative reporter for the Washington Post in *Blow Out* (Putnam, 2004) met Lacey and Dillon when her stepfather, a U. S. Supreme Court judge, was murdered in the court library. She convinced them to let her take part in the investigation while on leave from her job. As so often happens in a Coulter novel, Cassie met Ben Rowen, a Metro police detective who totally disapproved of her, and they fell in love. Succeeding murders and amorous activities in the court chambers filled out the narrative. It was finally decided that a professional assassin was involved, but motivation and the gathering of substantial evidence was glossed over. Lacey did well, but paid a price.

Elderly Moses Grace and his attractive young companion Claudia had a vendetta against Dillon in *Point Blank* (Putnam's, 2006), cause unexplained. Agent Ruth Warnecki had problems of her own. While spelunking in a Virgina cave, she was overcome by fumes, struck on the head and abandoned in the woods. When found by Sheriff Dixon Noble, she did not even know her name. Someone did because two men tried to kill her. Fingerprints led Lacey and Dillon to Dixon's house, triggering Ruth's memory. On a return to the cave, they found the body of young music student Erin Bushnell. The narrative moved back and forth from Lacey and Dillon's efforts to arrest Moses and Claudia to Ruth and Dixon's search for at least one killer.

Let's face it. Coulter writes romances. It's not an easy transition. She fails on the details. Her focus is primarily on the victims and the suspects. Lacey and Dillon are on the cleanup squad. Dillon and Lacey had significant roles in *Double Take* (Putnams, 2007) but two other lawmen got the action and the love affairs. FBI agent Cheney Stone rescued widow Julia Ransom from an assassin. Julia was suspected of the murder of her husband, psychic August Ransom, The San Francisco police decided that the attack was by a disgruntled accomplice. Cheney knew better. Virginia sheriff Dixon Noble had almost accepted that his missing wife Christie was dead, and had come to care for FBI agent Ruth Warnecki. Then he learned that Christie might be alive in San

Francisco. The two stories meshed, but credibility depends upon ignoring coincidences.

Tailspin (Putnam's, 2008) contained many of the narrative elements of *Eleventh Hour* but they were more skillfully integrated into the narrative. Rachael Abbott, having escaped from an attempt to drown her, was en route to her Uncle Gillette's isolated cabin near Parlow, Kentucky when the plane carrying FBI Special Agent Jackson Crowe and his passenger, Dr. Timothy MacLean, crash-landed, only to explode. She aided Jackson in transporting Dr. MacLean to safety, then guiding Jackson to medical attention in Parlow. Meanwhile Jackson's Mayday signal had alerted the FBI. Lacey and Dillon were sent to the site by helicopter. Three attempts had previously been made on MacLean's life. He was a psychiatrist who because of frontal lobe dementia was revealing confidential information on important patients. Rachel's story was equally compelling. Next: *Knockout* (2009); *Whiplash* (2010)

Readers are advised that recently published *Double Jeopardy* (Berkeley, 2008) contains *The Target* and *The Edge* and *The Beginning* (Berkeley, 2008) covers *The Cove* and *The Maze.*

Hillary Scarborough

Author: Paula Carter (A possible pseudonym)

See: Jane Ferguson, page 260.

Dr. Kay Scarpetta

Author: Patricia Daniels Cornwell

Kay Scarpetta had been raised in a poor Italian-Catholic home, marred by her father's illness, then death, from leukemia. She grew to be a petite blonde, extremely bright, and having almost total recall of written material. Her resume included: an undergraduate degree at Cornell, a medical degree from Johns Hopkins, plus a law degree. As the series began she was employed as the chief medical examiner in Richmond, Virginia, which was stated to have the second highest per capita rate of homicide in the United States.

Her childless marriage to Tony Benedetto ended in divorce, but Kay had an endearing relationship with her niece Lucy Farinelli, who became an integral part of the series. Lucy, from the time she was ten years old, was tied more closely to Kay than to her own mother. Kay added other supports to her life as the series progressed, the most important of which was her affair with FBI profiler Benton Wesley. The job consumed Kay's life despite her efforts to keep an emotional distance from the murder victims, yet retain compassion for their survivors. Her idea of a good time was a small dinner, usually Italian-American food, that she cooked for friends. Privacy, a sense of separation, was important to Kay so she lived on a one-acre suburban lot. For many years investigator Pete

Marino had a significant role in Kay's life. Later their relationship became stormy. Her more lasting connection was to Wesley whom she eventually married.

In *Postmortem* (Scribner's, 1990), Kay searched for a pattern in the serial murders of women. The investigation after the fourth death focused on Lori Petersen's husband Matt as the logical suspect but Kay was unconvinced. At risk from office politics, she received help from Lucy, who was already precocious at the computer, profiler Benton Wesley, and ambitious reporter Abby Turnbull.

Body of Evidence (Scribner's, 1991) introduced Kay's former lover, attorney Mark James, who represented deceased author Beryl Madison and Beryl's mentor Cary Harper. Madison's work in progress mirrored her relationship with Harper, leading Kay to puzzle over the human aspects of Beryl's life and death.

By *All That Remains* (Scribner's, 1992), Kay had developed an additional ally, police officer Pete Marino whose initial resentment of Kay became wholehearted acceptance. All worked with Kay when she was investigating a series of "couple" killings. The recent disappearance of Deborah, the daughter of Patricia Harvey, a high-ranking federal government spokeswoman, put heavy pressure on agencies for quick results. Scarpetta's persistence and knowledge of blood types pinpointed the killer.

During *Cruel and Unusual* (Scribner's, 1993), bureaucrats tried to stifle Kay's investigation of the death of a savagely mutilated child. The incident was similar to a crime for which Ronnie Joe Waddell had been sentenced and executed. Fingerprints could not lie, or could they? Lucy visited in time to help Kay pursue an enemy through agency computers that had been manipulated to conceal data.

Lucy was a college student by *The Body Farm* (Scribner's, 1994) working as an intern in a highly secret FBI unit at Quantico. Kay, Benton Wesley, and Pete Marino were simultaneously assigned to a child's murder that resembled earlier atrocities by the elusive Temple Gault. Kay fought Marino to find the real killer, and the FBI to prove that Lucy was not a security risk because of her sexual orientation.

In *From Potter's Field* (Scribner's, 1995), Gault returned with a personal vendetta, using for his own purposes a computer system designed by Lucy, which connected the FBI to municipal police departments. He was suspected of killing an unidentified young woman in Central Park. Benton (by now Kay's lover), Marino and Kay were consultants. Kay discovered the motive behind "Jane's" death, delving into the Gault family history to trap the man who taunted her with his killings.

Serial killers were not a primary concern in *Cause of Death* (Putnam, 1996), during which Kay investigated the murder of Ted Eddings, a reporter poisoned while diving in a restricted area. She battled local authorities to tie the death to the activities of a religious cult, only to learn that her probe was secondary to a federal effort to thwart illegal munition sales. Kay's relationship with Benton was on hold as his marriage ended. Her ties to Lucy weakened as the younger woman developed her own personal and professional lives.

Another serial killer occupied Kay's attention during *Unnatural Exposure* (Putnam, 1997). Ambitious FBI agent Percy Ring was eager to connect a recent corpse to prior cases, but Kay found significant differences in the modus operandi, including the possibility of a serious virus. Her probe was complicated because Deadoc, the series killer, had singled Kay out. He familiarized himself with her life and tantalized her with picture clues on his murders. Kay found Deadoc, who did not fit the usual profile of a series killer. She also freed herself from the memory of her deceased lover Mark James, making room for Benton in her life.

Scarpetta's Winter Table (Wyrick, 1998) was a diversion, appealing primarily to Cornwell devotees or cooks. A modest holiday tale served as the vehicle for recipes purportedly used by Kay, Lucy, and Pete Marino.

It was back to the hard stuff in *Point of Origin* (Putnam, 1998). Carrie Grethen had spent almost five years in a psychiatric hospital, planning revenge on Kay, Benton, and Lucy, her former lover. Carrie's escape coincided with a difficult arson case, which bore the marks of a serial killer. They followed a trail with Carrie always a step ahead of them, reaching a shocking end, which changed Kay's life forever.

As *Black Notice* (Putnam, 1999) began, Kay was given a letter that Benton had written before his death, forcing her to evaluate where grief had taken her. Protected by her friends, she became the target of an ambitious rival, deputy police chief Diane Bray. Kay and Marino focused on a murder, which pitted them against an international smuggling ring run by the powerful Chandonne family. The struggle awakened Kay's professional interest, but her personal life did not benefit from a short-term love affair. Lucy had also suffered from Benton's death, but her problems were magnified as she struggled to balance her duties with the Alcohol, Tobacco and Firearms Bureau and her responsibility to her current lover.

The Last Precinct (Putnam, 2000) could be compared to an old-fashioned icebox soup in which the cook utilized a meat bone, and then added all the left-over vegetables in the refrigerator. Kay's relationship with her dying father, with her husband Tony Benedetto, lovers Mark James, and Benton Wesley were all explored. Her conflicts with the criminal Chandonne family, with Carrie Grethen and Newton Joyce were woven into the plot. She faced new antagonists within the criminal justice system, notably Jaime Berger, a New York City prosecutor. There were connections to Kay's feud with Diane Bray. The accumulation of stresses had left Kay vulnerable when she was accused of killing Bray. Lucy, Marino, and Dr. Anna Zenner remained staunch allies but their ill-timed interventions were not always beneficial.

A second Scarpetta cookbook *Food to Die For* (Putnam, 2001), coauthored with Marlene Brown, tied individual recipes to dishes that appeared in particular narratives, and recipes from favorite restaurants. The pictures were terrific.

There were some fresh ingredients in *Blow Fly* (Putnam's, 2003) but its lengthy narrative relied heavily on prior books. Kay had left her job as Chief Medical Examiner for Virginia to work as an independent consultant. She relocated in Florida, but her next assignment took her to Louisiana where Jay Talley was murdering women who resembled Kay in appearance. His twin brother Jean Baptiste Chandonne was scheduled to be executed in a Texas prison. He would disclose information about his family's international criminal organization if Kay visited him and performed the lethal injection. Kay's friends reacted by manipulation and destruction. Distasteful. By now, Benton had done a J. R. (Dallas) and returned.

Kay agreed to return to Virginia in a consultant's role during *Trace* (Putnam's, 2004). Dr. Joel Marcus, current replacement for the position Kay had held, requested help in the mysterious death of Gilly Paulsson. Perhaps she returned because Benton had cancelled her planned visit to him in Aspen, the rationale for which he could not explain because it involved others. Kay and Benton suffered from a failure to communicate. Fortunately Pete Marino had no such problems.

All four of the primary characters in the Scarpetta series had difficult times during *Predator* (Putnam, 2005). Kay had moved to Florida to work for the National Forensic Society, far from Benton, the man in her life. More than distance separated them as they sought connections between vicious murders in Virginia and Florida. Benton was committed to the Predator project which used MRI's to study the responses of normal individuals as compared to habitual killers. Lucy, unhappy although her software patents had made her fabulously wealthy, guarded a secret even from Kay. Pete Marino felt totally cut off from Kay. There were those who sought to undermine these relationships. The ending left too many unanswered questions

The Book of the Dead (Putnam's 2007) would be an easy book to set aside. The first 100 pages (there are 405) contained enough crude sex, gory details of torture, and murder to turn off many readers. A serial killer (commonplace in the series) murdered a young female tennis star, an elderly Asian woman, and a young child. Kay became engrossed in tying these deaths together, identifying the killer and those who covered up for him. Her personally life was hectic. Kay's engagement to Benton Wesley caused an already unstable Pete Marino to deteriorate. A vicious enemy sought to destroy Kay's personal and professional lives. At this time Kay and Lucy were both living and working in Charleston, South Carolina.

Scarpetta (Putnam's, 2008) was bloated. The death of Terri Bridges would normally have no impact on Kay, who had married Benton and moved with him to Massachusetts. However they both had connections in New York City (Bellevue Hospital, John Joy School of Criminal Law). Diminutive Oscar

Bones, the prime suspect in Terri's murder, refused to talk to anyone except Kay, even though she had no recollection of having met him or Terri. Marino, now rehabilitated was working in Manhatttan Assistant District Attorney Jaime Berger's office. His assignment to the Bridges case forced both Kay and Benton to work with him. Lucy, now living in Greenwich Village, had a role in retrieving Terri's Internet files, exposing an improbable scenario that created a conflict of interest for all of the main characters. There were endless complications, extraneous characters, wearisome periods of soul searching, and boring technical details. Where was the Kay Scarpetta of the earlier books?

Kay had frequent struggles within the criminal justice system. Although Cornwell became an international favorite, her narratives grew longer and longer, each more dependent on prior books for understanding.

Next: *The Scarpetta Factor* (2009); *Port Mortuary* (2010)

Cornwell had a second less popular series featuring Judy Hammer and Andy Brazil; and a more recent series featuring District Attorney Monique Lamont.

Goldy Bear Schulz

Author: Diane Mott Davidson

See: Goldy Bear, page 63.

Cynthia Chenery "C.C." Scott

Author: Pele Plante, pseudonym for Patricia Planette

C.C. Scott, in her fifties, had a stable lesbian relationship with teacher Barbara Bettencourt. Her family life had been unremarkable, although her father suffered from depression. As an adult C.C. had wrestled with her own alcoholism, but had been dry for seventeen years thanks to her involvement with Alcoholics Anonymous. She worked as a therapist in California on a part-time basis. Barbara had difficulty in the work place due to parental concerns about her sexual orientation.

C.C.'s interest in the elderly motivated her in *Getting Away with Murder* (Clothespin, 1991). She suspected that a pseudo-supportive agency was duping older people through "living trusts."

While on vacation, C.C. was wary of local reactions to her lesbianism. In *Dirty Money* (Clothespin, 1993), she met other lesbians and male homosexuals at Abalone Beach. Unfortunately she also encountered her share of drug dealers, and a blackmailing killer from whom she had to be rescued. When she came too close to the killer, intervention by her friends made a difference.

Nicolette "Nick" Scott

Author: Val Davis, pseudonym for Robert and Angela Irvine

Scientific achievement was taken for granted in Nicolette "Nick" Scott's family. Her father was a distinguished professor of anthropology at the University of New Mexico, focusing on the Anasazi Indians. She had a Ph.D. in archeology, had earned kudos for her discovery of World War II airplanes in the Pacific, and was seeking tenure as a professor at the University of California-Berkeley. This concentration of energy on the past had its destructive aspect. Nick's mother Elaine suffered from chronic mental illness, a fact ignored by her father. Nick's childhood had been devoted to managing the household and concealing her mother's aberrations so as to avoid angering her father. Despite lingering resentment of her father's cavalier attitude, Nick spent summers working with him in the New Mexico desert or on Pacific islands.

During *Track of the Scorpion* (St. Martin, 1996), Nick was skeptical of elderly prospector Gus Beckstead's claim that he had located a World War II plane in the desert. Her expertise told her that such an event was unlikely. Nevertheless, she accompanied him to the site where the B-17 and its occupants were buried. The mission of the plane had been a secret one. Its exposure even now would be threatening to military and government officials. Nick needed her father and the survival skills he had taught her to combat the pressures placed on her investigation.

For all her complaints about her father's obsessions, Nick exhibited her own in *Flight of the Serpent* (Bantam, 1998). The narrative was about "Annie," a World War II B-24 bomber and the men who had flown in her. The plane had brought her crew back from 25 missions over Germany and the Ploesti oil fields of Romania. When Annie was decommissioned, former pilot John Gault purchased the plane. Before Gault's grandson Matt was blown to bits in his Cessna, Nick had heard a helicopter, seen its shadow, and noted Matt's physical appearance. She became a part of Gault's reconstructed crew bent upon learning why Matt died and taking revenge.

Nick's suspension by the her hostile department head Ben Gilbert, made her available to accompany her father and his college classmate Prof. Curt Buettner on an expedition in *Wake of the Hornet* (Bantam, 2000). The lure included a search for World War II airplanes located on Balesin, a neglected Pacific island. Villagers on the island adhered to the "cargo cult," a belief that if they built runways and decoy airplanes, others would come bringing valuable goods. The jungles on Balesin had secrets that Buettner intended to uncover, but that others would kill to conceal. Ingenious plotting.

Nick's father had always warned that airplanes would be the death of her. In *The Return of the Spanish Lady* (St. Martin, 2001), they nearly were. Her first assignment at the Smithsonian Institute was an expedition to northern Alaska to reclaim a World War II Japanese Aichi bomber. She and the Institute's administration were unaware that the sponsors of this quest, a pharmaceutical group, had a hidden agenda, one that put not only members of the expedition but society at risk. Fortunately in her misspent youth, Nick had learned some very handy lessons, including how to hotwire a vehicle.

Temporarily unemployed in *Thread of the Spider* (St. Martin, 2002) Nick signed on to accompany her father on a dig in Utah. They searched caves in gulleys created by flash floods. While Elliott focused on evidence of Anasazi and Fremont petrolyphs, Nick was diverted by the discovery of a 1937 Pontiac connected to folk heroes Knute and Nora Deacons. The discovery of presidential papers in the vehicle triggered a response in government and political circles. Unaware that her every move was being monitored, Nick and Prof. Reed Austin continued to research decades of murder.

Fascinating settings and plots.

Claudia Seferius

Author: Marilyn Todd

Claudia Seferius had considerable business ability, but in 13 B.C., she had limited opportunities to use it. A lesser woman would have devoted herself to the management of the household servants. Claudia was ambitious. She was an outrageous heroine; a former harlot/dancer who assumed the identity of a widow, Claudia Posedonius whose family had died during the plague. Actually her father had been an army orderly and her mother had committed suicide. Under this cover, she married Gaius Seferius, a wealthy wine merchant who had secrets of his own. When she met Security Agent Marcus Cornelius Orbilio she had neither the life experience nor the temperament to recognize a good man when she saw one. She didn't want Orbilio, but she discouraged any woman who did. The only true affection she seemed able to give was to an Egyptian cat, Drusilla, which she took everywhere.

In *I, Claudia* (Macmillan, 1995), she pitted her wits against Orbilio. He was a member of a noble Roman family who intended to pursue a political career when he had established his reputation. He had access to powerful members of the Augustinian government. Both Orbilio and Claudia sought the serial killer of six prominent Roman citizens. For him, it was part of his job. For Claudia, it was an effort to conceal the fact that the victims had purchased her services. She was addicted to gambling, and this time she won.

The death of her elderly husband Gaius provided Claudia with what should have been a comfortable inheritance in *Virgin Territory* (Macmillan, 1996), but she was unable to leave well enough alone. Within a short time she had gone into debt with her gambling and her right to Gaius' real estate was contested. In search of a solution she visited Sicily, escorting former vestal virgin Sabina Collatinus to her family home. The Collatinus estate was unsafe for virgins; not that Claudia had any such pretensions. Nevertheless, she benefited from having Orbilio on her trail.

Claudia should have learned that she was safer in Rome, but, in *Man Eater* (Macmillan, 1997), her bailiff Rollo insisted that she visit her vineyards. Set upon by hoodlums, she sought refuge at the nearby home of Surges Pictor. What a zoo that place was! Not just the animals either. Orbilio came to the rescue but had a difficult time convincing Claudia that the murders on the premises were designed to destroy her. In the larger world, the death of Agrippa, the premier general of the army and close friend to Augustus, created uncertainty.

A serial killer terrorized the Roman streets during *Wolf Whistle* (Macmillan, 1998). Rich merchants sought to take advantage of the civil unrest following the death of Agrippa to undermine Augustus. Orbilio was needed everywhere. He concentrated on saving two women whom he treasured: his youthful cousin Annia who was a potential victim of the serial killer and Claudia, who had acquired an obsessive admirer. She had little appreciation for Orbilio's efforts, but Claudia showed a warmer side to her personality in her treatment of an abandoned child.

Plague created panic in Rome during *Jail Bait* (Macmillan, 1999), but Claudia had more to fear. She had been stealing money from the repository of Sabbio Tullus. Orbilio, always mindful of her activities, secretly arranged a vacation for Claudia at Atlantis, an opulent resort. Once there, Claudia was enmeshed in murder investigations and the attentions of an attractive Spaniard. With Orbilio's help, she survived both.

To keep her wine business afloat in *Black Salamander* (Macmillan, 2000), Claudia joined a caravan of artisans and merchants visiting Gaul. She couriered a segment of a treasure map to rebellious tribal leaders as part of a deal to enhance wine sales. The expedition was a disaster. Orbilio, who joined the group belatedly, warned Claudia that her behavior could be considered traitorous. She was going to lose her head if she wasn't careful. Gaul was divided into more than three parts in this one.

Nowhere on her adventures throughout the Roman Empire had Claudia met a stranger group than the commune known as the Brothers of Horus in *Dream Boat* (Severn 2002). She went to their compound, seeking her willful step-daughter Flavia, who had faked her own abduction. Claudia's plans went awry, leaving her slave Junius in prison. Marcus who normally had powerful contacts was under house arrest because a female skeleton had been found in the wall of his family home. Eventually they all wound up in the fortified commune, ruled by a pair of brothers who flimflammed the members into a pseudo 'Egyptian community'. Feeling some guilt, Claudia realized that she may have been unfair to Orbilio.

Any port in a storm didn't work for Claudia in *Dark Horse* (Severn, 2002) She escaped her creditors and an angry racehorse owner in Rome to spend time on the island of Cressia. There Leo, a rival winemaker, was constructing a glorious villa for a new bride who would provide him with sons, unlike his first wife, Lydia. Saunio, the expert at illusionary art, was decorating the atrium with his magical touch. What Claudia failed to recognize was the allusions to real life in his work: Leo's purpose in discarding Lydia; the pirate Jason's needs; the connection between the "Ice Queen" Silvia and Orbilio, and an older man's desire to protect his son. A demonic killer was at work on the island so Orbilio appeared in his official capacity.

Perhaps the language is not always suited to the period and the characters are overdrawn in *Second Act* (Severn, 2003) but the plotting was exceptional. The identities of the "Digger" and the Saturnalia Rapist were well concealed. The banter between Claudia and Orbilio and among members of Caspar's traveling drama troupe was sparkling.

Desperate to save her failing business, Claudia journeyed to Hestria in *Widow's Pique* (Severn, 2004) in the belief that the King was interested in purchasing wine. Soon enough, she learned that the King had other expectations. He wanted Claudia to marry him. The King, whose older brother, wife, son, and daughter had died in "accidents", needed an heir, new blood in the royal lines. Although she was still waiting to meet the King, Claudia theorized that he was in danger from (1) his envoy Mazares or (2) Pavan, commander of the royal guard, or perhaps (3) Salome, the independent widow who provided refuge for abused women. Murders continued while Claudia dallied with Kazan, Mazares' unhappily married brother. The appearance of Orbilio provided some information but not enough to spare Claudia considerable pain.

Throwing caution and money to the wind in *Stone Cold* (Severn House, 2005) Claudia visited Santonum, the capitol city of Aquitania. She was determined to learn what had happened to her father, who (when she was ten) had failed to return from his annual stint as an orderly in the Roman Army of occupation. Once there she became the guest of Marcia, the richest woman in the area, but, Claudia discovered that Marcia was unable to purchase the loyalty and affection she desired. Orbilio, concerned about Claudia, had also come to Santorum but was diverted by an investigation into the abduction of street children. Marcia and the local druids scoured the countryside for the Scarecrow suspected in the disappearance of young attractive women. This was not a safe place for women, children, or Romans, Marcus discovered.

Sour Grapes (Severn House, 2005) saw Claudia off to a family vineyard in Tuscany. She was concerned about rumors that her mother-in-law Larentia (whom she supported) was being courted by wealthy horse trader Darius. Such a marriage might have financial implications for Claudia, still a widow. An eager Marcus Cornelius Orbilio suggested a marriage of convenience, but with negative results. There were strange things happening in Tuscany, signs of a vendetta that Claudia could not ignore because she might be a target.

Claudia felt she had no choice in *Scorpion Rising* (Severn House, 2006). Gabato, the assassin sent to kill her by rebel leader Scorpion, would let her live if she went to Santonum, Aquitania and investigated the death of his daughter Clytie. The child was a novice in the order of the Hundred Hands, an all female group dedicated to nature and opposed by the local druids. The leadership of the Hundred Hands had ignored Clytie's murder, focusing instead on false accusations by the druids that they were witches. Of course, Orbilio appeared. He was in charge of security police in this area, but allowed Claudia to inveigle him into her cause with dire results.

Whatever credibility the background material on early Rome might establish was dissipated by Claudia's vocabulary. In the First century, females were unlikely to ask, "What part of the word 'no' don't you understand?" The books are fun reads nevertheless. Todd's two most recent books have a different female series protagonist, (High Priestess Iliona), leaving poor Marcus adrift.

Beth Seibelli (Cole)

Author: Ed Stewart

Beth Seibelli was an investigative reporter who eventually married Reagan Cole, a San Francisco police sergeant. Beth's parents had always been seriously religious, but only experience led her to that state in her life. Activity had been more important than reflection for Beth. She played college level basketball and rode a motorcycle. Beth and Reagan each made serious religious commitments, but could not always mesh their professional assignments.

At times overwhelmed by its sheer length, *Millenium's Eve* (Victor, 1993) contained an interesting character study of television evangelists who, with some reservations, agreed to meet on Millennium Eve, December 31, 2000 in a show of Christian unity. Their exposure to a rescue mission, which practiced what it preached, and to bomb threats by a religious fanatic were powerful influences on the evangelists. Changes also occurred in the lives of Beth, a doubter, and Reagan Cole who learned to pray when there was no other alternative.

Shelby Hornecker Rider, one of the evangelists whose lives had been changed by their millennium experiences, gave up her television work to serve at Dr. No's King's House Rescue Mission during *Millennium's Dawn* (Victor, 1994). She and her new husband, Dr. Evan Rider, faced unexpected problems from a secret in Rider's past. Beth had drifted away from Reagan, partly due to his spiritual transformation. Tracking down a professional killer with Reagan provided her with a conversion experience that brought them together in spirit. The lives intersected in a dramatic conclusion. Some pruning could have made the book more interesting.

A near death experience gave pilot Cooper Sams a sense of destiny in *Doomsday Flight* (Victor, 1995). Under the influence of religious guru Lila Ruth Atkinson, he came to believe that the Second Coming of Jesus would occur on February 20, 2002 and that an airplane populated by believers could be spared the destruction of the earth. Beth was given an opportunity to interview the prospective passengers, even to accompany them on their journey. Her decision took into consideration Reagan's feelings and her pregnancy. The extended narrative covered the motivations of the passengers on the Doomsday Flight.

Dr. Susan Shader

Author: Joseph Glass, pseudonym of Joseph Libertson

Susan was a divorced psychiatrist, working as a profiler for the Chicago Police Department as the series began. Her husband Nick seemed to have primary custody of their son Michael. She and Nick, a civil liberties attorney, had lived in the Oakland, California area. Susan's skills expanded to include "second sight" at age ten after her parents were killed in a fire. She and her brother Quentin were raised by an aunt. Nick remarried Elaine. When in Chicago, Michael became very close to Detective David Gold, treating him as a second father. Even as a youngster, Michael had shown signs of sharing Susan's "gift". Susan shared her home with a roommate for a while, but was currently living alone. She did acquire a cat, Margie, from her roommate though. Over the series Susan developed a relationship with former NFL player Ron Giordano, now a professor of anthropology.

The dust jacket for *Eyes* (Villard, 1997) may appeal to fans of Patricia Cornwell . Although there are some interesting aspects to the psychic psychiatrist gimmick, this violent and sexually permeated narrative will not satisfy many serious mystery readers. David Gold involved Susan in a series of killings of females in which the eyes were gouged out. Her initial failure, then success, at identifying the serial killer led to danger for Michael and a raw sexually explicit conclusion.

Gore prevailed in *Blood* (Simon & Schuster, 2000). Susan's profession and her psychic paranormal skills were essential in identifying not just one, but several killers of young women. Calvin Wesley Train, a mentally ill serial killer, blamed her for his conviction and sought revenge. "The Undertaker" was responsible for several deaths, which had religious, sadistic, and sexual overtones. As a profiler, Susan sought the pattern among his victims, all young women. A third story line concerned Wendy Breckinridge, a seriously disturbed private client of Susan. Were there one, two, or three killers at work?

Desiree "Dez" Shapiro

Author: Selma Eichler

Desiree Shapiro continued as a New York City private investigator even after the death of Ed, her husband-partner, but she initially limited her practice to routine cases. She was a short plump woman who had accepted her weight and dealt with it by carefully choosing her clothes and accessories, but touched up her auburn hair. Desiree had been raised as a Catholic. Ed was Jewish. Religion didn't usually enter into the series. Ed and Desiree had no children, but she was close to his niece Ellen Kravitz. Stuart Mason, a divorced friend, had become a regular date and casual lover, but with no plans for a more structured relationship.

Desiree was unsure that she was capable of working a murder case until *Murder Can Kill Your Social Life* (Signet, 1994), when two deaths occurred in Ellen's apartment house. Neither Ellen nor Desiree knew the victims; but Desiree was concerned about Ellen's safety. Early on Desiree selected the brutish building custodian as her candidate for killer, but the final solutions were more complex and more painful for her.

She could not resist a handsome young man, particularly the younger brother of a childhood friend, so in *Murder Can Ruin Your Looks* (Signet, 1995), Desiree promised Peter Winters that she would discover which one of a pair of twins had survived a vicious attack. Peter was engaged to Mary Ann Foster, but no one knew whether she was the patient in the hospital, or the corpse in the morgue. Desiree learned the motive for the murder before she could understand why the bodies had to be defaced.

Doomed by her inability to say "no" even after she had been seriously endangered in earlier murder investigations, Desiree assumed risks again in *Murder Can Stunt Your Growth* (Signet, 1996). Elderly Evelyn Corwin insisted that her granddaughter, nine-year-old Catherine, did not die a natural death. Catherine, who had a congenital lung problem, had told her family that someone tried to run her down with a car. That had not convinced them at that time and it did not convince the police later. The Corwin family was so dysfunctional that there was no dearth of suspects.

Ellen Kravitz, Desiree's niece, was one of a group invited to the gracious home of newly divorced Sybil Miller in *Murder Can Wreck Your Reunion* (Signet, 1998). An unexpected guest was Raven Eber who not only had not been sent an invitation, but was heartily disliked by other members of the group. Her death by a plunge into the pool from an upstairs window could have been an accident, but the police were not taking it for granted. When the detectives questioned Ellen, Desiree took a hand.

Murder Can Spook Your Cat (Signet, 1998) focused on the death of Luella Pressman, a popular author of children's books, formerly married to Desiree's friend Kevin Garvey. Kevin suspected his ex-wife had been killed by one of her three step-daughters, but, prompted by a cat's water dish, Desiree took another look around.

Bruce Simon had been nothing but trouble for Desiree when they shared an affair. In *Murder Can Singe Your Old Flame* (Signet, 1999), suspected of murdering his wife, he was even worse as a client. Desiree made the same mistake the victim had, trying to have her cake and eat it too.

Desiree's comfortable relationship with dentist Al Bonaventure took a blow in *Murder Can Spoil Your Appetite* (Signet, 2000). She investigated the murder of Frankie Vincent, a politically inclined chiropractor. Her client, mobster Vito da Silva, had mentored Frankie's career and would not take "no" for an answer. He arranged the full cooperation of the Riverton, New Jersey police department, including a working relationship with attractive Lt. Lou Hoffman. Desiree was out of her territory and blindsided by the killer.

Desiree's brief encounter with philanthropist Miriam Weiden had left her with admiration. The news of her death in *Murder Can Upset Your Mother* (Signet, 2001) caused guilt. Miriam had sought Desiree's help when she felt threatened, but too late. Too soon, she learned that Miriam's charity was a façade; her friendships, in tatters; her lover, disenchanted. She was a woman whom only a mother could love. Personal plotting included Ellen's wedding plans.

Desiree didn't have an affair to cool off in *Murder Can Cool Off Your Affair* (Signet, 2002), but her life was cluttered. Ellen's wedding was coming soon. Desiree's secretary Jackie was having problems with her boyfriend Derwin. Her neighbor Harriet's randy father-in-law wanted to date Desiree, and a hit-and-run case on which she was helping Elliot wasn't working out. Perhaps that was why it took her so long to identify the killer of Edward Sharp, heir to his Uncle Victor's estate. John Lander, Desiree's client, was next in line for the bequest. Would he be the next victim?

Desiree's investigation into the death of Bobby-Jean, Mike's aunt who was a co-sponsor of a bridal shower for Desiree's niece Ellen, had unexpected ramifications in *Murder Can Rain on Your Shower* (Penguin, 2003). Mike, concerned that Bobby-Jean's death might have been poison, prompted him to ask Desiree to investigate. There were four female guests at the shower who had reasons to hate Bobby-Jean. Unfortunately the police focused on Allison Lynton, Mike's mother. Not up to Eichler's usual standards.

Young Vicky Pirrelli was so desperate to believe that her convicted father Victor was not a murderer in *Murder Can Botch Up Your Birthday* (Signet, 2004), that Desiree hadn't the heart to turn her down as a client. Victor had been found standing over the corpse of his mistress Christina Trent with the weapon in his hand. Although he plea-bargained, he died before he could be released. Ten years after the crime was committed, Desiree had to overcome pressure from other members of the Pirrelli family and play the numbers game to learn the truth.

Brusque attorney Blossom Goody was no particular friend of Desiree, so in *Murder Can Mess up Your Mascara* (Signet, 2005), she only reluctantly agreed to meet Blossom's cousin, Gordon Curry. Curry was concerned that someone was trying to kill him and was certain that he knew his potential murder's identity. He wanted Desiree to find evidence. She had barely started her search for suspect Roger Clyne, when she learned that Curry had been killed and a suspect arrested. The killer wasn't Roger Clyne; moreover, Clyne had been dead for months. Desiree agreed to stay on the case until it was solved. She expected Sgt Tim Fielding of the police department to cooperate with her even though she lied and withheld information.

It's not clear about the stockings, but Desiree did run on a lot in *Murder Can Run Your Stockings* (Signet, 2006) She had been hired by attorney Ben Berlin, whom she met on an airplane trip, to investigate the death of his favorite Aunt Bessie. Bessie had been found dead at the bottom of the basement steps by her son Joel. What made Ben suspicious was that the fall had been blamed on Bessie's high heels. He knew that she had had a prior accident and would not make the same mistake twice. There were two problems: was it a murder and by whom? Some good plot material but submerged under Desiree's personal relationships and her resentments.

Desiree was based in New York City so she was mildly resistant when attorney Blossom Goody sent her a client from small town Cloverton in *Murder Can Depress Your Dachshund* (Signet, 2007) Byron Mills had lost two adult sons recently and needed to know how this could happen. The night before well-liked Jordy was to donate a kidney to his older lecherous brother Cornell, Jordy was murdered in the hospital parking lot but his body moved to Cloverton. Cornell, depressed at what probably his last chance to survive, killed himself. Byron arranged for Desiree to meet with Naomi, Jordy's wife, who identified other contacts of the two brothers. In the end it was Des' copious interview notes and her extended enquiries that pulled the plug on the killer. Tootsie, the depressed dachshund, then made a complete recovery. In the narrative, Des showed increased understanding of the difficulties that Derek, nine-year-old son of her lover Nick, was dealing with and showed more tolerance for his misbehavior.

Eichler showed real skill tying a fictional murder mystery to a real one in *Murder Can Crush Your Party* (Obsidian, 2008). Romance author Belle Simone and her secretary Gary Donleavy sought out Desiree to make an offer she couldn't refuse. Belle had written a mystery narrative, which she wanted Desiree to read carefully. If Desiree, aided by three external clues supplied by Belle, could deduce who was the killer by a set date, she would be paid $24,940.00. A friendly waiter also hired her to tail his wife. Was she unfaithful? Niece Ellen and secretary Jackie also shared their problems.

A frequently used pattern in the series was a set number of suspects provided by the client and an ending when an attempt on Desiree's life revealed the killer. Yet in others, she developed her material and let the police take over.

Claire Sharples

Authors: Rebecca Rothenberg and Taffy Cannon

Claire Sharples, one of the new breed of highly educated sleuths, had a Ph.D. in microbiology but had burned out during her postdoctoral experience at MIT. On a more personal level, the end to an affair had left her depressed. An opening at the University of California Citrus Experimentation Field Station in Central California came at the right time.

During *The Bulrush Murders* (Carroll & Graf, 1992), arson and murder marred Claire's arrival at the station. The valley was torn between the major landowners and the small orchards. The California fieldwork was a totally different experience than Claire's laboratory experiments. Sam Cooper, the abrupt extension agent, helped Claire acclimate and solve the murder of Arturo

Rodriguez. Claire had arrived on the scene about the time that Arturo was struck down and a shed was set afire. The police wouldn't even consider arson, but Claire had heard a motorcycle leave the scene about that time.

The relationship with Sam was stressed by his strong commitment to the sons of his first marriage during *The Dandelion Murders* (Mysterious Press, 1994). Claire had befriended lonely Emil Yankovich, an organic farmer, but found his ambitious brother Bert's heavy use of pesticides unacceptable. The Yankovich brothers became suspects during a half-hearted investigation of the deaths of two immigrant farm workers and Los Angeles reporter Jonathan Levine. On one corpse, Claire spotted a "dandelion, but closer evaluation indicated that the flower was probably "Hulsea", an alpine flower. Dissatisfied with the police department's commitment, Claire moved into Levine's apartment in a marginal neighborhood and allied herself with the field workers who were exposed to potent pesticides and sexual harassment.

Sam and Claire were estranged in *The Shy Tulip Murders* (Mysterious, 1996). He had someone else in his life, a woman who wanted to share his two children. Claire had made it clear from the start that mothering was not part of her life. She opened new directions for herself: fixing up an isolated cabin, taking on extension duties in the California Central Valley, and her attraction to a young activist. She could not isolate herself from the ill feeling between the environmentalists and loggers, or from the violence that erupted. Sam, visiting the Valley as an expert during the murder investigation, convinced Claire to buy a weapon, but did not invite her back into his life.

Taffy Cannon's *The Tumbleweed Murders* (Perseverance Press, 2001) was a seamless rendition of the book begun by Rebecca Rothenberg. The descriptive material was as lovely as before. The pain and growth of Claire as she moved toward a new relationship with Ramon Corarrubias, the county small farm advisor, was handled with delicacy. The discovery of a long buried skeleton that might be the lost love of aging country music singer Jewell Scoggins captured Claire's sympathy and curiosity. Jewell's subsequent death only amplified Claire's need to know. She found a new ally, Ramon's cousin Yolie, who had been harassed for years for her attempt to focus public attention on an unscrupulous businessman. Claire never really got over Sam Cooper, but she and Ramon were headed for a commitment.

Lori Shepherd

Author: Nancy Atherton

See: Dimity Westwood, page 856.

Rei Shimura

Author: Sujata Massey

Rei Shimura's parents (her Japanese father, a psychiatry professor and American mother, an interior decorator) were permanently located in California. They might not understand Rei's need to move to Japan indefinitely, but they respected it. Their offer of a one-way airline ticket "home" was ongoing. Rei's father had a sister, Aunt Norie, living in Japan who, along with her son Dr. Tom, was a resource at times of trouble. As the series began, Rei was twenty-seven, a small dark-haired woman who subsisted on a vegetarian diet and shared her apartment with a fellow employee. Her Phi Beta Kappa key and master's degree in Asian art history had been of no immediate value. She supported herself by teaching English at Nichiyu (a kitchenware corporation that wanted bilingual employees). Eventually, Rei developed her own business as an "antique shopper" for wealthy Japanese collectors and foreign tourists.

Her insistence on making her own way in Japan still allowed Rei to splurge on a vacation trip to Shiroyama in *The Salaryman's Wife* (HarperCollins Paperbacks, 1997). The discovery of the nude body of Setsuko, wife of middle management businessman Seiji Nakamura, in the snow outside the local inn thrust Rei into controversy. She did not believe Setusko's death to be accidental or suicide. Whom could she trust among her fellow vacationers: the elusive Scottish solicitor Hugh Glendinning; the effusive American widow Marcele Chapman; certainly not Setsuko's offensive husband? She found answers in Setsuko's personal heritage and a career in an antique wooden box.

Rei's new profession as an antique shopper was at risk in *Zen Attitude* (HarperCollins, 1998). Her expertise fell short when she purchased an expensive *tansu* (dresser) for Nana Mihori, only to learn that she had seriously overestimated its value. She returned to the seller Nao Saki, only to learn that he had vacated the premises. When he was discovered dead, Rei followed up on Nomu Ideta, consignee of the *tansu,* who died shortly after her visit. Hugh Glendinning, by now Rei's lover, was preoccupied with the escapades of his younger brother Angus. Her investigation of the two deaths led to an even more valuable discovery.

Since Rei's affair with Hugh Glendinning had ended, Aunt Norie felt it was time for her to seek an appropriate Japanese husband in *The Flower Master* (HarperCollins, 1999). To that end, she enrolled Rei and herself in the flower arranging class at the Kayama School. Norie was well acquainted with the art of Ikebana and the staff. Too well, perhaps, because teacher Sakura Sato was found dead with a pair of Norie's pruning shears in her body.

The Floating Girl (HarperCollins, 2000) was a more complex narrative. To earn extra income, Rei took a part-time job as a columnist for the *Gaijin Times*, a publication directed to foreign readers. The owner intended a switch in focus, transforming the paper into manga (comic strips). Rei's assignment, a history of manga, led her into doujinski Showa, parodies of the commercial

Mars Girl comic. Three former college students produced the Showa. Nicky Larsen was murdered after talking to Rei. The case eventually involved the Yakuza (Japanese crime syndicate). Rei was aided in her search by her Japanese boyfriend, Takeo Kajama.

Rei displayed courage but a lack of wisdom in *The Bride's Kimono* (HarperCollins, 2001). A unique kimono, one of those she couriered from a Tokyo museum to the Museum of Asian Art in Washington, D.C., was stolen from her hotel room. Hana Matsura, a young Japanese woman who may have been connected with the theft, was subsequently murdered. The D.C. police department and the Japanese Embassy were suspicious of Rei who had delayed notifying either the authorities or the museum. She measured a new romance against her feelings for Glendinning.

During *The Samurai's Daughter* (HarperCollins, 2003) Rei's reconciliation with Hugh Glendinning encountered serious conflicts. The Japanese had been humiliated by the outcome of World War II and stressed with their potential future. Rei was researching the Shimura family history, focusing on her great-great-grandfather, a professor who had privately tutored the Emperor Hirohito. Hugh represented his law firm in a class action suit against a major Japanese corporation which had used slave labor in Phillipine mines. The death of Rosa Munoz, a potential plaintiff, an attack on another survivor, and evidence of resentment against Hugh and Rei made Japan seem less friendly.

Rei was restless for something to do in *The Pearl Diver* (HarperCollins, 2004). The opportunity to decorate the interior of Marshall Zanger's new restaurant, Bento, came just at the right moment. That is, until Kendall Johnson, Rei's American cousin, was abducted on the premises and business went sour. Andrea, the hard-faced club hostess, sought Rei's help in finding her missing Japanese mother. When Sadako disappeared, her husband Robert, had farmed Andrea out to a foster home. Rei's commitment to helping Andrea placed her in personal danger with serious repercussions, and changed her relationship with Hugh.

A surprise 30th birthday party thrown by Hugh for Rei did not produce the desired result in *The Typhoon Lover* (HarperCollins, 2005) They had been living in his apartment, now crowded by a visit from his brother, Angus and three friends. Hugh spent a lot of time carousing with them. So a job offer from the Sachler Museum, even though it consisted of undercover work, had some allure. The primary reward would be restoration of her visa to Japan. Her assignment focused on getting reacquainted with Takeo Kayama, visiting his summer home, checking on the presence of what might be a stolen antiquity, the ibex ewer. Japan had changed since Rei's last visit. Takeo had changed. He was to be married to Emi Harada, the daughter of the Minister of the Environment. Emi's death in a car crash, complicated both Rei's assignment and her relationships.

Rei tried something very different from antique shopping in *Girl in a Box* (HarperCollins, 2006) when she joined a highly secret agency working under the auspices of the CIA. Michael Hendricks, chief of OCI's Japan bureau, pulled Rei out of training prematurely for a special assignment. Keeping her own name, but changing her appearance and background information, she was to apply for a job at the main Mitsutan Department Store located in the Ginza. There had been hints that their profit statements were inflated. Operating solo with occasional phone calls from Michael, she took on serious risks, not knowing whom she could trust at the office. Michael became personally involved.

A cerebral hemorrhage struck Rei's father, Dr. Toshiro Shimura as *Shimura Trouble* (Severn House, 2008) began. She put everything aside to assist in his recovery. A trip to Hawaii to visit new-found cousins did not fit into that plan, but Toshiro insisted on going. They were to meet his brother, Hiroshi and his nephew Tom in Hawaii. Mike Hendricks fit himself into the plan. He and three pals from the Naval Academy were to take part in a sailboat race to Hawaii, where he could connect up with Rei. Her suspicions of the trip were well founded. Cousin Edwin wanted Rei there because of her connection (no longer important to her) with attorney Hugh Glendinning. He wanted Hugh to represent him and his family in a claim for valuable land. That became less important when Edwin's teenage son Braden was accused of arson and murder. For all of that Rei found a happiness beyond her expectations.

The narratives provided excellent background and a sense of the perplexities faced by someone trying to be loyal to two cultures.

Massey was one of several established authors who contributed short stories on their protagonists to *Tart Noir* (Berkley, 2002). She provided excellent background for her series.

Marla Shore

Author: Nancy J. Cohen aka Nancy Cane

Marla Shore had been haunted by an incident that occurred in her late teens. While babysitting a small child, she had answered an important telephone call, unaware that Tammy had left the house and fallen into the pool. The parents never forgave Marla for their child's death and she never forgave herself. They sued, but the price she paid went higher than that. She spent years educating people about the dangers of unenclosed pools, sought legislation to force owners to fence in pools, and encouraged swimming lessons. It had been very important to Marla's family that she marry well and that she marry a Jewish man. Attorney Stan Kaufman of the firm hired to defend Marla had seemed a perfect choice. Too late, Marla realized that Stan's was attracted to her because of her docility and youth.

After her divorce, she used the settlement money to finance her education and the establishment of a beauty salon in Palm Haven, Florida. By this time, Marla's father had died, but her mother Anita lived nearby. Her only brother was married with children. Her special companion was Spooks, a white male poodle. Marla's best friend was Tally Riggs, owner of a dress shop. She needed friends, particularly one who owned a dress shop because she was extremely conservative in her attire. The divorce had left her leery of entanglements. She spent considerable time working on environmental causes. Her former interest in gourmet cooking had to be abandoned when she became over-involved in causes. Stan, who had remarried, pressured Marla to sell jointly owned rental property. She wanted the continued income. His new wife wanted a more expensive home so he wanted the cash.

The events surrounding Tammy's death continued to shadow Marla's life in *Permed to Death* (Kensington, 1999). She and Bertha Kravitz, owner of Sunshine Publications, had been alone in the beauty parlor when Bertha ingested poison. Detective Dalton Vail said only lack of motive kept him from charging Marla with placing the poison in the powdered coffee creamer that was kept at the shop for Bertha's personal use. The motive existed so Marla needed to find the killer before Vail discovered an envelope that disclosed why Marla might want Bertha dead. The killer was aware that Marla was vulnerable.

Marla learned very little from her prior experience with murder. In *Hair Raiser* (Kensington, 2000), she used her recovery time from an injury to help her cousin Cynthia recruit chefs for a benefit. Someone was determined to sabotage the project—possibly someone on the board of directors of the environmental group holding the benefit. Heedless of Dalton Vail's warnings (they were dating) and undaunted by two murders, she made herself an easy target for very determined criminals.

Marla's connection to murder victim Jolene Myers was merely that of beautician to client, but, as she admitted to her mother in *Murder by Manicure* (Kensington, 2001), she was bored. Moreover she had been at the Perfect Fit Sports Club when Jolene drowned in the whirlpool. So had a half- dozen others who had reason to want Jolene dead. Some good came of her involvement. She bonded with Brianna, Dalton Vail's twelve-year-old daughter.

Marla was juggling too many balls in *Body Wave* (Kensington, 2002). She needed time to hire new staff for her beauty salon. Stan, her former husband. was accused of murdering Kimberly, his wealthy third wife, and made her an offer she couldn't refuse. He would sell her his half of their jointly owned rental property if she proved his innocence. What little time she had left was supposed to be her personal life. Dalton Vail, who suspected Stan, preferred to talk about their future. Marla went undercover as a nurses' aide to care for Kimberly's elderly grandmother, and to learn who else might want Kimberly dead.

Marla was present, in *Highlights to Heaven* (Kensington, 2003), when Dalton checked Goat's house for the presence of a dead body. The corpse was not that of Marla's quirky neighbor Goat, but he had fled the premises so was either a witness or a suspect. Marla could not let this alone, any more than she could stop intervening between Dalton and his teenage daughter, Brianna. She has a personal motive to stay involved. Four members of her clique at beauty school had died in suspicious accidents.

Died Blonde (Kensington, 2004) was another hair-raising tale, but this time some of the hair was antique. The murder of Marla's rival Carolyn Sutton, and that of a young girl were tied together by hanks of hair cut off their corpses. Dalton Vail asked for Marla's help on this one, but wished he hadn't when a third murder indicated she might be a target. Vail proposed, raising questions about their religious backgrounds, the possibility of children, and Marla's reluctance to move into the home formerly occupied by Vail and his deceased wife.

Vail was hesitant about meeting Marla's Jewish family at a Thanksgiving get-together arranged by her Aunt Polly in *Dead Roots* (Kensington, 2005). As a non-Jew, he was unsure of his welcome. That was the least of Marla's concerns. The gathering took place at Sugar Crest, a Florida resort that was facing problems. Should it be torn down to make way for a theme park or be remodeled? In the past Marla's mysterious grandfather Andrew and his wife Ruth had owned the property. The buildings were believed to be haunted so the current manager had hired "ghost busters" to investigate. After Aunt Polly died mysteriously, Dalton's plans for a romantic vacation had to be put on hold.

Marla had a problem saying "no" in *Perish by Pedicure* (Kensington, 2006), even to herself. She and her Dalton Vail had made a down payment on a new house. That contributed to the tension when she was overwhelmed by house guests including Georgia Rogers, her college roommate. Marla also had big plans for expanding her salon services, including a new location. In her spare time, Georgia had arranged for her to take part in the Luxor Products displays at a major beauty show. That sounded like fun until Chris Parks, Luxor director, was murdered and Georgia was suspected. Author Cohen did her readers a favor by pointing out the dangers of overdosing in the sunshine.

A Caribbean cruise underwritten by Dalton's parents in *Killer Knots* (Kensington, 2007) gave Marla a chance to know her prospective in-laws better. There were problems between Kate and Jordan Vail, and with Brianna's teenage rebellion, but they were minor compared to a series of attacks. Dalton and Marla were mistakenly seated with staff and volunteers from Camden Palms Museum of Art in Tampa, a group that had also been provided with free tickets. In this closed setting and on trips ashore, Marla came to realize that some of her fellow passengers (including one named Martha Shore) had concealed mistakes, misdemeanors, and murder in their past. Her investigation made her a target.

Cohen also writes science fiction. Next book in this series: *Crew Cut (2007)* had been announced but was nowhere available.

Kate Shugak

Author: Dana Stabenow

Kate Shugak was an Aleut Indian in her late twenties when the series began, only five feet tall, 110 pounds, but well able to take care of herself on land and at sea. Her skin was bronze, her hair black, and her eyes light brown. Her father

Stephan, who had died when she was a child, had raised Kate to be independent and courageous. Her grandmother Ekaterina Shugak, who raised Kate, no longer had an official position, but remained the most significant person in the community. Ekaterina, then eighty, and family friend Abel Int-Hout had shared her guardianship after her parents died. Kate left the tundra behind long enough to graduate from the University of Alaska in Fairbanks, but was drawn back to her people and the land they occupied. When arresting a child molester whom she was forced to kill, Kate's throat had been slashed not only leaving her with an ugly scar, but also impairing her vocal chords. She resigned from the Anchorage District Attorney's office, ended an affair with fellow investigator Jack Morgan and returned to her family village, living on land homesteaded by her father. Kate could handle isolation. She enjoyed chocolate, read extensively, liked The Nashville Network, and had "Mutt," her Malamute, for company.

As *A Cold Day for Murder* (Berkley, 1992) began, Ken Dahl, who had been assigned to find Mark Miller, the environmentalist son of a prominent Congressman, had been missing for two weeks. Jack Morgan convinced Kate to search for him because of her superior knowledge of the area. Her special assignment again cost her dearly.

An unidentified killer appeared early in *A Fatal Thaw* (Berkley, 1993) leaving a trail of seemingly unrelated murders, which almost included Kate. Ballistics indicated that the death of Lisa Getty, a seductive young woman, did not fit into the pattern. The intimacy of the community meant her quarry was someone whom Kate knew.

Kate took a different tack in *Dead in the Water* (Berkley, 1993). Tempted by the chance to earn money on a crab fishing boat, she boarded the *Avilda* as a deck hand. Two men had disappeared on the last voyage and the District Attorney's office had to know why, so they contacted Kate. Skipper Harvey Gault had claimed that the two men went ashore and never returned. The trip gave Kate an opportunity to visit the traditional Aleut Islands, where she received help from two women.

John King, the CEO of a major oil company in Alaska, was disturbed by evidence that his employees had easy access to drugs during *A Cold-Blooded Business* (Berkley, 1994). Once she was hired as a roustabout, Kate quickly became well acquainted with coworkers and staff. Her next assignment, as a driver for the public relations officer who gave tours of the site, made her aware that Native American artifacts were being dug up. That had to wait till she identified the drug dealers.

Play with Fire (Berkley, 1995) sent Kate, paraplegic Bobby Clark, and photojournalist Dinah Cookman into the re-growth area of a great forest after a fire. While hunting for morels, she found murder and religious mania, but could not bring herself to identify the killer. Like many of those who cherish their isolation, Shugak was critical of vacationers who wanted to share the wilderness for a short time but left it damaged. Romance blossomed between Bobby and Dinah, even though he was confined to a wheelchair.

Kate's sense of responsibility emerged in *Blood Will Tell* (Putnam, 1996). Her grandmother, a major figure in tribal politics, had been the dominant person in Kate's life. Nevertheless Kate had rejected any suggestion that she might take an active role in the affairs of the native people of Alaska. Ekaterina's age, the efforts to bribe her fellow council members, and the suspicious deaths of two supporters of native rights forced Kate to investigate forces that would open the wilderness to uncontrolled development.

Breakup (Putnam, 1997) described the coming of spring to Alaska; the emergence of the bears from hibernation, often with cubs; the relief of the residents from days of limited sunshine; and the resumption of outdoor life for Kate. Her sense of optimism was dampened when parts of an airplane dropped causing serious damage to her home, garage, snowmobile, and truck. Even more frightening was the discovery of the corpse of Carol Stewart by representatives of the National Transportation Safety Board while searching the forest near Kate's home. Although there was evidence of a bear attack, Kate wondered if Carol had been murdered before the bear arrived. Mark, Carol's husband, was determined to kill the bear. The apprehensive parents of Kate's friend Mandy Barnes could not understand why their daughter had abandoned her social position and wealthy lifestyle for Alaska. Kate had the intuitive, deductive skills and the persistence to tie these incidents together while doing some domestic counseling on the side.

A greedy brutal man (properly named Cal Meany) was murdered in *Killing Grounds* (Putnam, 1998). Still what readers may remember best after reading the narrative is the rush of excitement when the salmon returned, the stubbornness of commercial fishermen who plied their trade although hampered by government regulations, and the plight of the elderly natives who needed the fish to survive. State trooper Jim Chopin came to realize that, even though Kate had no official status, many tribal members perceived her as the successor to her grandmother's authority.

Nine men and a woman, top executives of a German software corporation, comprised the hunting group that Kate and Jack Morgan guided into the wilderness in *Hunter's Moon* (Putnam, 1999). While Jack and Kate resolved their differences to plan a life together, the hunters exploded into violence, motivated by ambition and greed. Jack's violent death led Kate to the brink of suicide, thwarted only by Mutt's intervention.

As *Midnight Come Again* (St. Martin, 2000) began, Sgt. Jim Chopin of the Alaska State Troopers had failed to locate Kate who had left her homestead, providing no information as to her destination. An undercover assignment with the FBI sent Jim north to Bering. Kate was working there under an assumed name. It took them both to outwit an alliance between Russian terrorists and greedy Americans. It took a near death experience to teach Kate that she wanted to live and to make Chopin aware that he wanted to share her life.

Gradually Kate re-embraced life, remembering Jack's plea that she care for his son Johnny. As *The Singing of the Dead* (St. Martin, 2001) began, the boy had hitchhiked from Arizona to Alaska, determined to remain. Kate provided a haven. The next step would be to fight for his custody, as his mother had relinquished his care to an unsympathetic grandmother. For that she would need money. Anne Gondaeff, a candidate for the Alaska State Senate, needed a bodyguard. As murder followed murder within the campaign entourage, author Dana Stabenow skillfully wove in the story of a hardworking hooker during the Gold Rush days. Ethan Int-Houk, a figure from Kate's own past, became a part of her future. A terrific read.

Stabenow is gifted. *A Fine and Bitter Snow* (St. Martin, 2002) is a taut narrative with character development, sex, violence, environmental concerns and murder all in 211 pages. The death of elderly environmentalist Dina Willner and the injury to her female companion Ruthe Bauman were puzzlers. Ranger Dan O'Brien, who had been urged to take early retirement, was found standing over the bodies. Disturbed Vietnam veteran Riley Higgins was found with the bloody weapon. Kate and State Trooper Jim Chopin asked a lot of questions. Too many for the killer. Mutt saved Kate's life when she was attacked. Kate suffered another loss, the death of her grandmother.

Stabenow brought her ability to create a setting and characters in Alaska, making them both unusual and credible, in *A Grave Denied* (St. Martin, 2003). When handyman Len Dreyer's body was discovered in a cave of the Grant Glacier, State Trooper Jim Chopin needed Kate's help. She was important to him in more ways than one. She paid a price for her involvement, but survived with the help of the community. Her efforts to make Johnny Morgan a part of her family added a touch of human interest. She is a remarkable heroine.

Charlotte Muravieff asked Kate to get her mother released from prison in *A Taint in the Blood* (St. Martin, 2004). No mean task considering that Victoria Muravieff, in prison for killing her older son thirty plus years ago, refused to cooperate. Victoria was a Bannister by birth, a member of a rich and powerful family. She had married Eugene, a Native Alaskan, and borne him three children. Kate was not sure that Victoria was innocent until she noted the fear and anger in the Bannister family at the possibility that she might be released.

Louis Deems and Kate had history so her interest in the results of his trial for murdering his third wife in *A Deeper Sleep* (St. Martin, 2007) was personal. Yet both she and Trooper Jim Chopin were prepared for a not guilty verdict. Two of Deems' prior wives had died of "accidents". He seemed impervious to the legal system. Several months later Deems was in trouble again. Johnny Morgan (14), who lived with Kate, had been at the Koslowski home when an intruder killed Mrs. Koslowski and her son Fitz. Johnny identified Deems in a line-up, but it didn't end there. It ended with secrets that Kate and Jim could not share with one another. The balance in their relationship had shifted over the past months.

The material about Alaska and its native inhabitants provided an interesting background to well plotted stories. Kate was a credible tough investigator. Next: *Whisper to the Blood* (2009); *A Night Too Dark* (2010); *Though Not Dead* (2011)

Jo Beth Sidden

Author: Virginia Lanier

Jo Beth Sidden was a wild, wild woman. Her childhood had been impoverished and her parentage uncertain. Her early marriage to Bubba, a battering psychotic, ended in divorce and his imprisonment. At age twenty-nine she was described as a tall, well-muscled woman. Jo Beth had built a life for herself as the breeder and trainer of bloodhounds in the southern Georgia area where she was raised. She not only bred the dogs, but also schooled police officers to use them. She assisted law enforcement officers in finding victims, killers, and persons lost in the nearby Okefenokee Swamp.

She would not take police referrals to locate bootlegger's stills or marijuana grower's fields. On occasion, she protected friends by destroying such evidence before the federal agents could gather it. Jo Beth did not have an alcohol problem, but she lit one cigarette after another, subsisted on a high caffeine intake when working, and, when under pressure, used "speed" tablets. She never cooked, survived on fast food, and paid a price with indigestion.

With self-assurance and insensitivity, Jo Beth interfered with the marriages and relationships of friends and guests, possibly in one instance, causing a suicide. Her reluctance to share information with the police may have led to a triple murder. She did not hesitate to involve others in her deceptions, including police chiefs and sheriffs with whom she had personal relationships, and a computer hacker "Little Bemis" who provided illegal access to information. Jo Beth had earned many of her enemies, but was innocent of the hatred from Bubba's father, a prominent local citizen. She made efforts to trace her own parentage.

Death in Bloodhound Red (Pineapple Press, 1995) was episodic, detailing Jo Beth's experiences with Tom, a developmentally disabled boy who died while lost in the swamp; the abuse of an elderly couple, and a returned Southerner whom she helped reclaim his inheritance. The profits enabled Jo Beth to add to her staff at the kennel. She disproved charges that she had attacked Bubba and forced corrupt sheriff Samuel Carlson out of office.

The House on Bloodhound Lane (HarperCollins, 1996) had a half-dozen subplots, but focused on the search for wealthy Frank Cannon whose disaffected sons plotted his kidnapping and potential death. By this time Jo Beth had 86 dogs, taught handling classes to police officers, and expanded her staff. The bad news was that Bubba had been released from prison and the system failed Jo Beth who should have been informed.

Jo Beth's disdain for the law extended to Judge Sanford Albee in *A Brace of Bloodhounds* (HarperCollins, 1997). The judge had taken advantage of his housekeeper Clara Ainsley, for years. Her daughter Gilly suspected he had also caused Clara's death. Jo Beth was sympathetic to Gilly and provided her with needed refuge. Her more immediate concern was finding the kidnapper of Peter, a small boy who had been camping with his family. Locating the child was only the first step; the "good old boys" were reluctant to believe that one of their own could be the culprit.

During *Blind Bloodhound Justice* (HarperCollins, 1998), Jo Beth kept a lot of secrets. Sheriff Hank Cribbs did not believe in coincidences, but he did not want to stir up a controversy. The medical parole of Samuel Debbs, convicted thirty years before of a double murder, was followed by the return of a now adult victim of kidnapping connected to the murders. Debbs sought Jo Beth's help. Once convinced of Debb's innocence, Jo Beth found a way to pinpoint a killer, yet spare an innocent victim from disclosure. Bubba returned with his leaded baseball bat, but Jo Beth dealt with him.

Perhaps Jo Beth's need to be alpha dog in the kennel and on the trail had affected her to the point where she had to dominate in her personal relationships. In *Ten Little Bloodhounds* (HarperCollins, 1999), she paid a price for her disregard for the feelings of those who loved her. She was hired first to find a cat, then to identify the killer of the cat's owner, officious Mrs. Alyce Cancannon. Jo Beth solved her personal problems in a manner that may leave some readers uncomfortable.

Jo Beth had barely taken down the electric fence and other precautions necessitated by Bubba, when, in *A Bloodhound to Die For* (HarperCollins, 2003) she acquired another unwelcome admirer Jimmy Joe Lane who had initially been sentenced to ninety days, but had ballooned the time to forty years by his multiple escapes. While in prison he developed a crush on Jo Beth, collecting newspaper article about her and the bloodhounds. She would be his "perfect mate". Fortunately Jo Beth devised a solution for Jimmy Joe, for her, and her patient beau Sheriff Hank Cribbs.

Lanier has great imaginative and descriptive powers. Unfortunately the series died when she did.

Phoebe Siegel

Author: Sandra West Prowell

Billings, Montana may seem a strange location for an Irish/Jewish private investigator, but Phoebe was no stereotype. She was a member of a large family which included a dead Vietnam veteran, a Catholic priest, a police officer whose death had been ruled a suicide, and a former drug addict. March was always a difficult time for Phoebe because her brother Ben's "suicide" had been attributed to an accusation that he took advantage of a juvenile. Her siblings with whom she maintained a prickly relationship called her "Fee." She had loved her father, a deceased police officer, deeply and still drove his 1949 Chevy truck. Phoebe was in regular contact with her mother, but shared her home only with a truculent cat, "Stud."

During *By Evil Means* (Walker, 1993), Mary Kuntz, mother of Jennifer who had made the accusation against Phoebe's brother Ben, sought help. Jennifer, then receiving treatment at a nearby sanitarium, had undergone a personality change. Phoebe's investigation gave her a chance to clear Ben's reputation.

The conflicts within the Native American community in Montana surfaced in *The Killing of Monday Brown* (Walker, 1994). Matthew Wolf, leader of a traditional faction, was accused when suspected grave robber Monday Brown was murdered. The Wolf family hired Phoebe to prove Matthew's innocence, giving her custody of artifacts discovered in Matthew's truck. Relying on her dreams and information from hookers, Phoebe believed that a German collector was the killer, but learned otherwise.

When Wallflowers Die (Walker, 1996) was exceptional. Phoebe investigated the decades old death of vulnerable young Ellen Maitland. She connected it to the death of ex-convict Frank Chillman, whose sister Rita, a prostitute, had been killed that same day. Sustained by her family, then in the throes of a religious crisis, and by Deputy Kyle Old Wolf she found a killer and exposed a conspiracy to delay justice. Kyle's platonic friendship had become very important to Phoebe.

Phoebe was competitive with most current private investigators.

Emily Silver

Author: Carol Brennan

Emily Silver had never adjusted to the structured life forced upon her at age nine by a rigid grandmother. Until then she had shared her parents' erratic lifestyle. Tuck, the father whom she adored, had been an unsuccessful playwright subsidized by his wealthy mother. Celia, her mother, an actress, kept the family afloat by working as a waitress. Their deaths had been officially designated as murder/suicide. As soon as she could, Emily ran off to seek a career as an actress. After limited success in Hollywood, she moved in with trucker Mike Florio, who provided safety within freedom, something she needed. He was seventeen years older and divorced, tolerant and patient, warm and accepting.

During *In the Dark* (Putnam, 1994), Emily's vague recollection that a third person with an unusual raspy voice had been in the apartment the night her parents were killed was reawakened. She heard that same voice in a darkened movie theatre. Mike calmed her hysteria by promising to investigate, but his visit to New York ended in his death. With only the name of "Dev," Mike's best friend, as a lead, Emily went to New York City to solve Mike's murder and the deaths of her parents. She reconnected with her dying grandmother, and located Dev, a.k.a. Paul Hannagan, now an investigator for a legal firm. After interviewing friends of Tuck and Celia, Emily came to know her parents as individuals, flawed in ways she had not expected. Emily and Dev's investigation and their sexual relationship forced her to rethink who she was.

In *Chill of Summer* (Putnam, 1995), murder again struck close to home. Emily and Dev lived in the house her grandmother had bequeathed her. Zach Terman, a womanizing author married to Emily's high school roommate, was left dead in the basement food locker. Emily investigated the tangled relationships of her friends until she found the guilty parties. On a personal level she coped with the presence of Liam, Dev's abusive father who now reeked of repentance and alcohol; and Dev's writer's block, which had plagued him since his first successful book.

Brennan had another equally short series, featuring Liz Wareham (covered later in this volume)

Margo Simon

Author: Janice Steinberg

Margo Simon had stress at home and at work. As the series began, she was a part-time reporter for San Diego's public radio station, KSDR, hoping for full time work. Her husband Barry Dawes, a professor at the Torrey Institute of Oceanography, expected their life to include regular visitation by the children of his first marriage: Jenny, a volatile teenager, and David, more amenable at age eleven. The household also included a golden retriever (Frodo) and a cat (Grimalkin).

She had been a rebellious student at the University of Wisconsin in Madison, where protests were commonplace; then, dropped out of college to follow her lover Rick to New Mexico where they subsisted on her pottery and his painting. When that relationship ended, Margo moved to San Diego. Work in a bookstore led to appearances on public radio. Enthusiastic about radio journalism, Margo returned to college and graduated from San Diego State. Her great personal enjoyments were dance and pottery, both of which relaxed her high-strung personality.

Margo covered a major art exhibition at the Capelli Foundation in *Death of a Postmodernist* (Berkley, 1995). Her prior research on the displaying artists provided insights into their personal lives. When installation artist Susana Contreras was killed on site, KSDR kept Margo on the story. The suspects were an eclectic group of artists, promoters, administrators, and critics. The most crucial observer might be a homeless woman whom Susana had befriended. Margo's success in the Capelli murder led to a full-time position on the staff, extended to include general news.

Her assignment in *Death Crosses the Border* (Berkley, 1995) was to evaluate the impact of maquiladoras, American-owned factories located across the Mexican border. The death of young pastor Ezekiel Holyrod of the Revelation of God Church, who had disclosed the miserable living conditions of the workers, was the beginning of Margo's journey into corporate deceit, religious duplicity, and political guile.

Margo's friend Paula Chopin glimpsed, but did not recognize, a killer/arsonist as *Death-Fires Dance* (Berkley, 1996) opened. Margo was drawn into the deaths of several "healers," not only through her reporting, but also as stepmother to Jenny, whose troubled boyfriend Nick Costas was a suspect.

Margo's interactions with Barry and the safety of her stepson David were at risk in *The Dead Man and the Sea* (Berkley, 1997). Oceanographer Hob Schreiber, a cruel and seductive faculty member at the Torrey Institution, had been murdered. The problem was the large number of persons who had feared and hated the victim. Margo had finally realized that her nightmares and flashbacks were symptoms of Post-Traumatic Stress Syndrome.

Leaving her marital problems unsolved at home, Margo journeyed to Israel in *Death in a City of Mystics* (Berkley, 1998). She and her sister Audrey were concerned because their mother Alice had been poisoned while visiting there. The sisters were aware that Alice had partial amnesia when she became conscious. They were not totally satisfied with the explanations of Batsheva Halevi, Alice's mentor in Israel. When he was murdered, Audrey was suspected until a letter sent by Alice before her illness was discovered. Margo's newfound connection with her religion released her from feelings of panic, fear and resentment. She left determined to make her marriage work. There was interesting background material as to the conflicts within the Israeli community.

Margo was an interesting, if not always endearing, sleuth who accepted challenges and persisted in her investigations, wondering at times if she had become too preoccupied with professional success. Author Janice Steinberg is an excellent writer.

Barbara Simons

Author: Carole Epstein

Barbara Simons had been terminated as vice president in charge of public relations at Pan Canadian Air when it was absorbed by an American corporation. She was looking for something to do. Her parents had reached a happy level in their marriage. Her father was a retired women's sportswear designer, and his wife waited on him hand and foot. Her mother was a terrible cook, but her husband never seemed to notice. Barbara was addicted to Coca-Cola and cigarettes, but did not drink alcohol. She was a tall auburn haired English-Canadian, as distinguished from the French Canadians among whom she lived and had worked in Montreal, Quebec. She was fluent in both English and French. Barbara had no tolerance for provincial nationalism, but had to be careful whom she offended.

In her forties, Barbara was unmarried, but had maintained a long-term peripatetic relationship with Sam Levine, who lived with his significant other in Connecticut. That part of her life was also close to crisis. Sam wanted to meet with her in Chicago to discuss their future...marriage...the end of the relationship...or something in between with more structure than they currently shared. Barbara was used to living well after many years of profitable employment. Her severance package allowed her to continue the good life for two years, and she had no incentive to make decisions as to her career future. She was sensitive to speech patterns as indicating the social class and educational background of others, and had disdain for those who did not meet her standards. She had one weakness, her great affection for her godchild, eight-year-old Robert, the son of a friend.

In *Perilous Friends* (Walker, 1996), Barbara showed herself capable of loyalty to her friends. Susan Porter's estranged husband Frank shared an apartment with a "blonde bimbo." Another pal Joanne Cowan, an investigative television reporter, was probing rumors of a gay tobacco smuggling ring. Her assistance was not without risk. After she and Susan searched Frank's apartment, someone murdered him. Barbara's undercover role as a lesbian gangster infiltrating the cigarette smuggling put her at odds with major Mafia figures. She surmounted considerable odds to survive this turmoil; then awaited Sam's visit with a Scarlet O'Hara like attitude of "I'll deal with that tomorrow."

Sam's visit never came off as *Perilous Relations* (Walker, 1997) began. Instead, she renewed her acquaintance with handsome Sgt. Greg Allard. While "riding along" in a police car, she became embroiled in the death of Walter Whitestone, who had been her boss at Pan Canada Airlines. His wife, sister, past and current mistresses, all of whom were suspects, sought Barbara's help in proving someone else guilty. The police considered Barbara as just another suspect so she had personal motivation for finding the killer.

Cecily Sinclair

Author: Kate Kingsbury, pseudonym for Doreen Roberts

Cecily Sinclair was the primary protagonist of the Pennyfoot Hotel series. She and her husband had transformed a deteriorating country estate house into a charming hotel frequented by the rich and idle of the English Nineteenth century. Unfortunately, her husband, Major James Sinclair, died of malaria soon after the project was completed. He left his friend and manager Baxter to assist Cecily. Baxter came to care for Cecily, but he was almost as frigid as the coastal weather, and had difficulty thinking of her in such personal terms. Cecily, a tall warm-blooded woman in her early forties whose light brown hair was beginning to gray, was lonely. She was initially unsuccessful in her efforts to induce Baxter to be more informal in their contacts. She did pressure him into sharing his light cigars with her, although he thoroughly disapproved.

Cecily, who had five brothers, was an active daring woman with little formal education but extensive experience gained while traveling with her husband during his military service. She and James had two sons, both of whom were serving overseas as the series began. The series regulars from the village included Phoebe Carter-Holmes, mother of the vicar who assisted in social events at the hotel; Madeline Pengrath, whose special powers aroused fear in the villagers; and several on-going or frequent guests. Each narrative had at least one semi-humorous subplot connected with guests and one involving relationships among the servants. The hotel, which catered to those seeking discretion, offered gambling and secluded accommodations for men who were accompanied by women to whom they were not married.

In *Room with a Clue* (Jove, 1993), loose bricks from a hotel parapet were believed to have caused the death of Lady Eleanor Danbury, a member of the nobility recently married to Robert, a younger, poorer man. He was arrested for the murder, but Cecily and Baxter proved his innocence.

In *Do Not Disturb* (Jove, 1994), Madeline Pengrath was suspected when two men died amidst quarrels relating to a new lighthouse intended to inhibit smuggling. The corpses were distinguished by a blue tint to their skins. A loyal friend, Cecily burglarized a corpse to get a list of victims, and picked up enough medical knowledge to explain the mysterious deaths.

Service for Two (Berkley, 1994) had an aura of evil, beginning with the substitution of a corpse in Dr. McDuff's casket. It wasn't that McDuff wasn't dead. His body had been dumped in Deep Willow Pond. The body was that of a London criminal. Using Baxter to gather information from the villagers, Cecily noted that a series of robberies had taken place at the homes of hotel guests. By now the series had become something of an ensemble with the servants' characters being explored (a la *Upstairs Downstairs* or the *Mrs. Jeffries* series)

The family of Lord and Lady Radley Sherbourne had gathered at Pennyfoot during the off-season in *Eat, Drink, and Be Buried* (Berkley, 1994). The corpse of Lady Sherbourne was found tied to a maypole on the Grange. The Maypole Dance was a vital spring festival in the area. Cecily questioned other family members even though they resented her interference. A drunken passerby, lost on his way home from the pub, had seen a caped headless horsemen near the body but the local police would prefer to blame gypsies.

During *Check-out Time* (Berkley, 1995), Michael, Cecily's son, returned to the village with Simoni, an African bride who became a suspect in the murder of obnoxious hotel guest, Sir Richard Malton. His equally obnoxious eight-year-old son Stanley annoyed staff and other guests. Someone on the premises was a hypnotist!

In *Grounds for Murder* (Berkley, 1995), housemaid Gertie awaited the delivery of her child (turned out to be twins); Baxter inched closer to a personal relationship with Cecily; and a multi-personality maid created confusion among the staff. Nevertheless, Cecily involved herself and Baxter in the murders of gypsy women in the area, using her friend Madeline Pengrath as bait.

Kilted Scotsmen invaded the community during *Pay the Piper* (Berkley, 1996). They stayed at the Pennyfoot en route to a London competition. After hotel footman Samuel Rawlins found the corpse of lecherous Peter Stewart in the butcher shop cellar, proprietor Tom Abbittson, was charged with murder. His wife begged Cecily to prove otherwise, and she did. She was less successful in working out her relationship with Michael and his pregnant wife.

An even greater blow to her pride awaited Cecily in *Chivalry Is Dead* (Berkley, 1996). She discovered the unwitting killer of footman Freddie Thompson and solved the kidnapping of eight-year-old Cynthia Chalmsford, but her hopes for the future were dashed by Baxter's announcement that he was seeking employment elsewhere.

Baxter returned in *Ring for Tomb Service* (Berkley, 1997). He had changed. He was self-sufficient and ready to approach Cecily as an equal. She had come to realize how important he was in her life, but was far too busy hosting a bicycle club, securing the return of a sacred vessel, and finding a killer, to listen to his plans.

Cecily introduced Baxter to staff as her business partner in *Death with Reservations* (Berkley, 1998). She had a more serious problem to consider. Among her guests were Bella DelRay, a pregnant music hall singer, her titled ex-lover Lord Sittingdon, and his wife Lady Katherine. Murder must be avoided, if possible.

Turnover at the Pennyfoot accelerated as illness and ambition struck in *Dying Room Only* (Berkley, 1998). Ivy Glumm assistant to magician Great Denmarric, disappeared and was discovered dead, Cecily could not leave the solution of the case to the incompetent police. Times had changed in England and the clientele at the Pennyfoot had deteriorated in numbers and in quality.

In *Maid to Murder* (Berkley, 1999), the servants looked elsewhere for their futures as one final killer wreaked havoc with the downstairs staff. Multiple murders were not good publicity for an establishment.

Four years later the series returned subtitled, "The Pennyfoot Holiday Series."

Initially the Baxters returned to Pennyfoot only as a temporary solution and favor for James' cousin Edward Sandringham. He had purchased the facility and turned it into a country club as *No Clue at the Inn* (Berkley, 2003) began. Hugh (Baxter now has a first name) was disinclined to take on the responsibility to manage the place since the former manager had died mysteriously, but Cecily was thrilled. She disliked the London fogs, missed her good friends, and was not deterred by a possible murder. She invited the former Pennyfoot employees to share Christmas at Pennyfoot County Club as their guests. Cecily's need to manage her own life and Hugh's desire to protect her clashed as the killings continued.

The Pennyfoot was open again, thanks to popular demand, in *Slay Bells* (Berkley, 2006). The arrival of Santa down the Pennyfoot Hotel chimney was to start the Christmas celebration. Instead it initiated a series of murders. Both Sid Porter, the "Santa," and Roland, a Pennyfoot footman, died mysteriously. Which one had killed the other and then died accidentally? Or was there a third party involved? Against Hugh's objections, Cecily intended to find out. Mysterious sightings, annoying pranks and marital misunderstandings delayed her progress.

Shrouds of Holly (Berkley, 2007) is light enjoyable reading. It's Christmas season again at Pennyfoot and a series of traditional events are planned. What wasn't planned was that (1) when Hugh and stable manager Samuel went hunting holly branches, their vehicle would return without either one of them, but containing a corpse. (2) Samuel was finally located, but had partial amnesia;

(3) victim Gavin Hargrove had recently inherited considerable property but earned enemies by his behavior. Cecily had two investigations going now: (1) find Baxter; (2) find the killer.

A busy holiday season at Pennyfoot Country Club was pending as *Ringing in Murder* (Berkley, 2008) began. Added to the regular Christmas festivities was the wedding of Dr. Kevin Prestwick to Cecily's long time but unorthodox friend Madeline Pengrath. The Club had a full house of guests including Sir Walter Hetherton, speaker of the House of Lords and his wife Lady Clara. A surprise party gift turned out to be a double disaster. Hugh wanted Cecily to hold off on an investigation until the two local police officials returned from vacations, but she was impatient. Other tensions between Madeline and Kevin, Gertie McBride and the father of her twins embellished the narrative.

Next: *Decked with Folly (2009); Mistletoe and Mayhem* (2010). Earlier books are being re-released in collections (two or more per book).

Kingsbury, a.k.a. Roberts, has a new series featuring Elizabeth Hartley Compton, referred to as the Manor House series.

Sydney Sloane

Author: Randye Lordon

Sydney Sloane was a tall strawberry-blonde private investigator in her late thirties, who lived in New York City. She had been a police officer before opening an agency with partner Max Cabe. Max, a chronic philanderer, deluded himself that he could woo Sydney from her lesbian orientation. Sydney's lover, a sculptor, had left her to study in Europe. Her mother had died of cancer. Her father, an attorney, was murdered in a courtroom by a pedophile. Sydney had never believed that her older brother David, who had a criminal record, had been killed in Israel.

In *Brotherly Love* (St. Martin, 1993), Sydney recognized David as an escaped murder suspect pictured in the newspapers. He had been cruel and sadistic, but she did not believe he was a killer. She set out to prove his innocence with the help of Gilbert Jackson, a family friend in the Police Department, and her Aunt Minnie, an unconventional senior citizen. In the course of her investigation, Sydney became involved with the victim's daughter, and discovered that she had a nephew.

Sister's Keeper (St. Martin, 1994) continued the focus on personal relationships. Caterer Zoe Freeman had grown up within the Sloane family, so her death in a traffic accident captured Sydney's attention. Even more so, because Zoe had built up a second identity, which indicated that she might be planning to disappear. The extended narrative also involved Sydney's sister Nora, who formed an attachment to a possible killer.

Father Forgive Me (Avon, 1997) found Sydney depressed. Debi, the fifteen-year-old girl whom she had traced for her parents, Tom and Joyce Cullerson, had jumped off a rooftop to her death. This might not have been the right time for Sydney to take on an investigation of the death of young Peter Long, found with drug paraphernalia on the scene. The police were willing to accept a suicide determination. Peter's sister Vanessa said he had been murdered. Either way, his death was an inconvenience to Wallace, his wealthy father, preparing to run for governor of his state, and about to introduce an improved computer chip that would enhance his business. Sydney took considerable personal risks to explore the relationships within the Long family and Wallace's business associates.

During *Mother May I* (Avon, 1998), Sydney reached out to a friend of her beloved Aunt Minnie. She proved that young Dr. Michael Callahan was innocent of the death of his wife. If so, of what was Callahan guilty? He had preferred prison to disclosing where he had been (and with whom) at the time his wife died. Sydney's affection for a ninety-two-year-old client was tinged with an awareness of her own vulnerability to the aging process. On a happier note, she and her current lover Leslie added a stray mixed-breed pup, Auggie, to their household.

Uncle Mitch had been dear to Sydney in her childhood, but totally rejected her when she revealed her homosexuality. Nevertheless, when Mitch was charged with arson and homicide in *Say Uncle* (Avon, 1999), his children came to Sydney for help. The family tie prevailed but led her into mayhem, more murder and an escape from a harrowing new career. Uncle Mitch had secrets of his own.

Sydney had to be coerced by Leslie to travel abroad in *East of Niece* (St. Martin, 2001). She took consolation in the fact that she could visit her niece Vickie and Vickie's fiancé Gavin Mason. As she and Leslie traveled the treacherous roads along the Mediterranean, they passed an accident. Even before Sydney learned that the victims were Gavin's parents, she suspected foul play. Gavin's disappearance after a secret marriage brought him to the attention of the police. They had discovered that the brakes on his parents' car had been damaged. Sydney received attention herself when her companion at a bistro died after eating a poisoned croissant. The investigation answered two questions for Sydney. "Yes," she wanted to continue as a private investigator, but "no," never again outside the United States.

Sydney had been stunned by the news that Police Captain John Cannady, husband of her college roommate Peggy, had been shot down in *Son of a Gun* (St. Martin's Minotaur, 2005). It got worse and more personal. The attacker was someone from Peggy's past, seeking revenge. Both Sydney and Peggy knew that the next target could be five-year-old Lucy, John and Peggy's daughter. Sydney, as godmother to Lucy, was determined that no harm would come to the little girl.

These were above average narratives. The lesbian relationships were treated with delicacy and dignity.

Grace Smith

Author: Liz Evans

By age twenty-eight, Grace Smith had undergone a considerable amount of rejection. Raised by a dedicated police officer father, she had joined the force. When she was set up in order to free a guilty defendant, her father and the police department both believed that she had accepted a bribe. She became a private investigator but the police officers she encountered in her cases remembered why she had been forced out. Her father, now confined to a wheelchair by an injury incurred in the line of duty, was even less forgiving. He had not spoken to her since her dismissal. Grace had one sister (married with children) and one brother.

The life she had put together since then was haphazard. Her professional status was as part of Vetch International Associates, a commune of six self-employed detectives all paying Mr. Vetch for the space and services provided. Vetch tossed his least rewarding cases to Grace. Her home in Seatown on the English coast was equally unstable, a basement apartment in a four story Edwardian house. Rent free, but hardly secure. Over a period of time she developed friendships, but it wasn't easy. She was well known for scrounging the use of phones, food, and equipment from other members of the commune.

Without money to pay her share of the office expenses as *Who Killed Marilyn Monroe?* (Oriel, 1997) began, Grace had no choice but to take on the investigation of Marilyn Monroe's death, even after she learned that Marilyn was a donkey. December Drysdale ran the family business, donkey rides for children on the beachfront. He was devoted to his beasts, naming them after his favorite American film actresses and actors. The fact that Marilyn had her throat slashed on the same night as a young prostitute convinced Grace to concentrate on the human murder. She remained one step ahead of everyone but the unsuspected killer. She did meet December's son Kevin who ran the Electric Daffodil, a popular pub, and found him very stimulating.

Even though she ended up with some doubts about her abilities as a private investigator in *JFK Is Missing!* (Orion, 1998), Grace had every reason to be proud of herself. She had tied together two complex cases: Henry Summerstone's search for a woman he hardly knew (or so he said) and a spoiled teenager's search for a married workman for whom she had a fancy. Although her mistakes in deduction made her vulnerable, Grace persisted. Finally, she had her personal life in sufficient order that she could reject a role as "the other woman."

Barbra Delaney, Grace's new client, in *Don't Mess with Mrs. In-Between* (Orion, 2000), could be charitably referred to as eccentric. Married first to a philanderer who left her with two children, one of whom died of leukemia, Barbra struck it rich with her second husband from whom she inherited a fortune. An accident caused her to consider a will. She intended to disinherit her only living child and divide her fortune among three strangers, identified only by pictures she had taken of them. Grace's assignment was to identify the prospects and evaluate their worthiness for the bequests. There were subjective decisions to make since cross-dressing, Native American enthusiasts, and murder were included in the mix.

Plotting was as devious as ever in *Barking!* (Orion, 2001) when Grace agreed to help accountant Stuart Roberts investigate the connection between a decades old murder and his own repressed memories as taped by his therapist. Aided by a flatulent part-bulldog, Grace worked her way through four separate murders, stretching back into the past. Amazing Grace.

Hannah Conti came to Grace in *Sick as a Parrot* (Orion, 2004), not because she wanted to locate her birth mother (she had already done that and been rejected), but because she wanted proof that Alison Wynne-Ellis had not committed murder. Alison, who had given birth to Hannah at age sixteen and put her out for adoption, was convicted of killing science teacher Trudy Hepburn. After twelve years in prison, she had been released and wanted a new start to her life. In her investigation, Grace managed to rile Alison, her high school classmates and family members. She found an attractive witty partner, Dane O'Hara who was considerable help. Parrot Tallulah whom Grace was temporarily fostering, was a total disaster.

Only because she needed the money did Grace agree to pass out informational material for the local tourist board in *Cue the Easter Bunny* (Orion, 2005). The bad news was that she had to wear face paint and an Easter Bunny suit to do so. While peddling her wares, she encountered Della Black who offered her a real job. Della's son Jonathan, who was a scriptwriter married to soap opera star Clemency Courtney, had been receiving threatening letters. Clemency, Jonathan, and Bianca Mendez who had become a "family" member had recently purchased a home in Seatown. Grace went undercover as a gardener, but insinuated herself into the household. Dane O'Hara returned on another of his crusades to remedy the failures that his police officer brother Declan had regretted as he lay dying. Dane needed Grace's help in investigating the disappearance of fourteen-year-old Heidi Walkinshaw fourteen years ago.

Grace is endearing, but stubbornly independent. She has few close connections, fearing to risk disappointment. These are fun reads, nevertheless.

Jane Smith

Author: Christine T. Jorgensen

See: Stella the Stargazer, page 765.

Marguerite Smith

Author: Marie Lee

Marguerite Smith began life as a Southie, the daughter of an Irish-American father and a French-Canadian mother. She moved out of South Boston when she was granted a scholarship to Radcliffe College. During college she met Joseph Smith, scion of a wealthy and prominent New England family, and with misgivings from both sets of parents, they married. After a seemingly happy marriage, which produced son Cornelius (Neil) and Alexandra (Alex), Joe sued for divorce to marry a younger woman. Marguerite could earn her own living as a teacher and was granted the house in the divorce proceedings, but her way of life was irreparably altered. Joe provided for the children, even subsidizing college, but Marguerite was deeply hurt by his rejection.

Marguerite had taken early retirement in her fifties as *The Curious Cape Cod Skull* (Avalon, 1995) began. She had been preparing for a visit from her niece Portia's husband Jeb, and their children, when she discovered a corpse in her shed. Jeb's insistence that he had not been on the premises put him high on the list of suspects when his alibi was broken. With an assist from her dog Rusty, Marguerite also found an ancient skull that tied into a list of library books found on the victim, archeologist Dr. Peter Dafoe. For Portia's sake, Marguerite delved into the books re Viking travels in America, until she discovered a motive that matched the crime.

Although she no longer taught, Marguerite kept an interest in her former students. She and her family were present at the internment of an elderly Native-American when a fresh corpse was discovered in the gravesite as *The Fatal Cape Cod Funeral* (Avalon, 1996) began. Victim Ethan Quade was the father of Rose, whom Marguerite had taught years before. Rose became a bone of contention as her maternal grandfather sought custody, as did Ethan's sister. Was Ethan guilty of embezzling funds from his employer? Red herrings abounded as Marguerite set herself to help Rose and clear Ethan's name.

Longing for the past and the temptation for a new romance brought Marguerite trouble in *The Mysterious Cape Cod Manuscript* (Avalon, 1997). Joe, her former husband, sought her help in finding an obscure book that would restore him to wealth. A handsome stranger made Marguerite look ridiculous in the eyes of the police when Joe was murdered. It took their daughter Alexandra, her husband Preston, and niece Portia to defend Marguerite from charges of double murder. Even the unpleasant police sergeant who suspected her was more effective than Marguerite in this case. She never suspected the killer even though she was on the trail of the mysterious journal.

A pleasant series with plotting difficulties that can be overlooked.

Guadalupe "Lupe" Solano

Author: Carolina Garcia-Aguilera

Lupe Solano was a tiny dark-haired Cuban-American, the U.S.-born daughter of refugees from Castro. Although her mother died of cancer, Lupe's father became a prosperous contractor, eager to gather his family together on his lavish Florida estate. Lupe had two sisters: Fatima, who moved back into the family home with her two children after a divorce, and Lourdes, who became a nun. After two years in college and a six-year apprenticeship, Lupe opened her own investigative agency. Ostensibly a Catholic, she shared her sexual favors with a select and seemingly non-competitive group of lovers.

In *Bloody Waters* (Putnam, 1996), Jose Moreno, an adoptive father, came to Lupe for help. His cancer-stricken daughter Michelle needed a bone marrow transplant. Lupe had met a child suffering from a similar illness while at her dying mother's bedside, and could not refuse. However, she had no idea then what a task she had undertaken: sleazy adoption attorneys, corrupt doctors, but happily, a mother superior who would deal with them.

When Lupe met with her best friend, Margarita Vidal, as *Bloody Shame* (Putnam, 1997) began, she seemed distraught but would not share her concerns. Preoccupied with assisting her sometime lover/attorney Tommy McDonald on a murder case, Lupe did not insist. When the pregnant Margarita died in a car accident, Lupe focused first on charges against Tommy's client, jeweler Alonso Arango, Sr. who claimed self-defense in the death of a purported burglar.

Luis Delgado, the Cuban refugee who repaired Lupe's Mercedes in *Bloody Secrets* (Putnam, 1998), did not share all of his past with her. His father had been defrauded of his share of diamonds smuggled into the United States by Miguel de la Torre, now a wealthy and prominent Cuban-American. Someone hired a professional killer to assassinate Luis after he came to the United States. Luis persuaded the man to take a diamond instead. The de la Torre's were friends of Lupe's family, sharing her father's obsession of returning to a capitalist Cuba. Lupe became so enamored of Luis that she was willing to embezzle funds for him. Good friends, including a call girl who would like to become a private investigator, helped Lupe, in spite of herself.

Two major conflicts in Lupe's life surfaced in *A Miracle in Paradise* (Avon, 1999). Although she did not practice her faith, she remained emotionally attached to the Catholic Church. Her Cuban heritage was extremely important to her, but, as with others of her generation, she realized that the past could not be regained. News that a miracle would occur at the Shrine of the Cuban Virgin on October 10th, a significant date in Cuban history, put these loyalties to the test. The rationale for the murders that followed the announcement tested credulity.

Lupe had never been to Havana. In *Havana Heat* (Morrow, 2000), it took two murders and the chance to recover a priceless tapestry to motivate her to make the trip. She risked her life and her current relationship with left-wing Cuban attorney Alvaro Mendoza to get there. Then she had to fight her way out.

The loyalty of many Cuban exiles to their homeland and to one another was very powerful. In *Bitter Sugar* (Morrow, 2001), Lupe agreed to help her father's childhood friend Tio Roman Suarez. Suarez had been contacted by a nephew with regard to an offer to purchase family interests in Cuban sugar mills appropriated by the Castro government. When the nephew was murdered after a quarrel, Tio Roman was charged with murder. As Lupe learned, loyalty could go only so far. There were problems in the Suarez family that had nothing to do with land or money.

Lots of local color; good, but not great. New release on Kindle, *Bloody Twist* (2010)

Bretta Solomon

Author: Janis Harrison

Her mother Lillie now deceased, had raised Bretta Solomon. Her father, who had tired of farming, deserted his family when she was eight. He did not totally forget them when his invention of a branding "gizmo" made him rich. Until Lillie died he sent an annual check. After that, Bretta merely received a birthday card and grapefruit for Christmas. She was unaware of whether he had remarried and/or had other children. Her husband Carl, a deputy sheriff, had shared his cases with Bretta, valuing her insights. He gave her credit when she assisted in an investigation, which did not sit well with his boss, Sheriff Sid Hancock. Carl died of a heart attack, leaving Bretta a childless widow in River City, Missouri.

Bretta opened a flower shop and made other changes in her lifestyle. By nature she was a highly organized person, self-described as a "planner." Formerly addicted to sweets, she cut back and lost weight. In an effort to keep her slimmer figure, she became an innovative cook.

In *Roots of Murder* (St. Martin, 1999), the death of Amish farmer Isaac Miller who had grown many of Bretta's flowers, reawakened her interest in criminal investigations. Neither the ire of the Amish bishop nor a python in her car could stop Bretta once she made up her mind. Two little girls, one whose life she altered, and one whose life she saved, had reasons to be grateful.

Using Carl's insurance money, Bretta purchased the Beauchamp mansion in *Murder Sets Seed* (St. Martin, 2000). Her plan was to turn it into a boarding house. The seller, Cameo Beauchamp-Sinclair, had an agenda of her own, bypassing her daughter Topaz, and adding Bretta to the sinister line of Beauchamp women. At a holiday dinner, Cameo announced that she was being blackmailed. Within hours, she had been strangled with Christmas lights. Cameo cancelled Bretta's house debt, but the murders had not ended. Bretta had ignored an invitation to visit her father in his Texas home. He came to hers.

During *Lilies That Fester* (St. Martin, 2001), Bretta expected hard work and challenges to her authority as head of the design contest at the Southern Missouri Flower Arrangers convention in Branson. She did not anticipate becoming involved in the desperate pleas of an elderly couple who wanted justice for the death of their daughter Stephanie, nor more pleasantly meeting DEA agent Bailey Monroe, a man who turned her thoughts to a romantic future. She realized that Carl would want her to go on living. The plight of overweight women was handled with insight and compassion.

The chance to provide the decorations for an elaborate wedding in *A Deadly Bouquet* (St. Martin's Minotaur, 2002) presented Bretta with a challenge. Evelyn Montgomery wanted everything to be perfect for her daughter's wedding, but frequently changed her mind. Other providers included four local women: a photographer, a caterer, wedding planner, and beautician. The death of beautician Claire Alexander seemed a mere annoyance to Evelyn, but caused consternation among the remaining providers. Bretta had to deal with her absentee father and a reunion with DEA agent Bailey Monroe.

Having her long lost father Albert McGinniss around in *Reap a Wicked Harvest* (St. Martin, 2004) was not always a blessing. He stumbled over the body of young lab assistant Marnie Frazier at the Parker Greenhouses' Customer Appreciation Day. He had pressured Bretta to join him in a detective agency, an offer she declined. This did not deter Bretta from investigating Marnie's murder. For whom was she a danger? Other Parker employees were also at risk. Bailey returned to brighten Bretta's life.

Knowing that she would not survive her latest struggle against cancer, Agnes Sutton had made what provision she could for her developmentally delayed adult son Toby, as *Bindweed* (2005) began. She left him advice, planned the menus for his meals, and introduced him to the merchants on Hawthorn street, who might employ him as a handyman. Bretta did so. Toby became part of the routine as he went from one job to another up and down the street. Bretta had agreed to visit Toby to investigate why someone had cut the tall hibiscus plant in his garden. He had been instructed by Agnes in the care of the hibiscus. Before they could meet, Toby was killed in a particularly vicious manner. There was no choice for Bretta. She had to investigate.

Helen Sorby

Author: Karen Rose Cercone

Helen Sorby went beyond unconventional for Pittsburgh in 1905. She was a feminist, pro-temperance, pro-union, and a socialist in a city controlled by industrialists. Since the death of their parents, she and her twin brother Tom, mapmaker for a fire insurance company, shared a residence, but not political views. Tom, deeply devoted to his sister, was far more accepting of the conditions. Both siblings were closely connected to their aunt, Patricia McGregor a.k.a. Aunt Pat, a comfortably situated widow. She was a strong supporter of the South Side Temperance League and had enlisted Helen to serve as her secretary.

Although she had only perfunctory allegiance to her Catholic upbringing, Helen had an elderly cousin, Father Regis Gillan, who counseled her at times. Helen's socialist views did not keep her from accepting help from Aunt Pat who had many valuable ties in the financial and industrial community, or from recruiting Tom to help her in her independent investigations.

Helen had a "marriage" that she initially sought to have annulled. The annulment became unnecessary when she learned that James Foster Barton was a bigamist. He had, in fact, made a habit of marrying well-to-do young women. Helen was not wealthy; however, she and Tom had expectations from Aunt Pat. They managed on Thomas' salary and the income Helen received from her freelance writing for New York City magazines. This connection provided her with access when she investigated. The local media were controlled by the oligarchy. She was writing *The Benefits of Socialized Pension Systems for Laboring Men*, a topic not likely to be a best seller. Helen lacked Thomas' training, but she was an excellent artist and draftsman. Her sketches were valuable to the police department in several cases. In her spare time she volunteered at Carey Settlement House.

Over the narratives, Helen developed a personal and professional alliance with Milo Kachigan, a detective with the Pittsburgh police department and later with the Allegheny County detective bureau. Milo had his own secret, his Armenian background. To be hired and promoted in his profession, it was obligatory to be Irish. The name Kachigan, Americanized at immigration, sounded Irish enough to get him hired. His presence at the Ancient Order of Hibernian hangouts didn't hurt. By the time he was "outed," he and Helen had been successful in their joint cases.

In *Steel Ashes* (Berkley, 1997), Milo and Helen met at the site of an arson/double murder. Based on his position and Irish sounding name, Helen expected him to be a mendacious bigot, oppressing more recent immigrants. Still they made a truce to learn who killed steelworker Josef Janczek and his socialist wife Lide. Attempts to kill or injure Milo and Helen failed but not for want of trying. They were less surprised to find betrayal from coworkers than they were by support from unlikely allies.

Helen's disdain for authority, including Milo, made it difficult for her to cooperative with him in *Blood Tracks* (Berkley, 1998). Milo contended with police corruption in a more personal way. He was framed on charges of bribery, but was never prosecuted so that his boss, Big Roge McGara could hold that possibility over his head. Both Helen and Milo were determined to find the killer of Lyell Osborne, a brilliant inventor on the payroll of Westinghouse Electric. The clashes between Westinghouse and the Penn railroad, a primary consumer of Westinghouse products, formed the background for the case. In this troubled atmosphere, Helen and Milo worked together. They got close enough to count.

Coal Bones (Berkley, 1999) had as many twists and turns as the coal mines. Milo investigated the murder of a coal company employee, initially without knowing the identity of the victim, or of the young Italian man apprehended near the body. It was a revelation to him that Helen's Italian relatives had a hand in much of the local villainy. She was balancing two projects: locating Emily, the missing daughter of coal baron Charles Murchison, and covering a coal strike by desperate miners. One impediment to a marriage between Milo and Helen was removed, but she clung to her belief in free love.

An excellent series. One of a large number of excellent series that ended after 2-3-4 books without explanation.

Anna Southwood

Author: Jean Bedford

Anna Southwood, the daughter of an Australian solicitor and his wife, had graduated from a Sydney University without any strong career goals. She married Clyde, a businessman whom she had met while in college, without much scrutiny as to what business he was in. Their life together floundered and they were separated when he died. The death left Anna a wealthy widow with an expensive home in Balmain. A tiny redhead who had been a "tomboy" as a child, Anna decided to spend Clyde's ill-gotten money to help others. She underwrote a monthly investigative newspaper for her friend, Lorna Temples, dabbled in Cordon Bleu cooking, radical politics, and detecting. The latter she accomplished by subdividing her home into residence and office, and employing Graham, an out-of-work actor, to front as the primary detective.

When, in *Worse Than Death* (HarperCollins, 1991, co-written with Tom Kelly), Anna investigated the disappearance of fourteen-year-old Beth, it was to defend her mother, Leonie Channing, from a charge of murder. Her efforts to connect the missing child with a similar incident in the past brought her into danger, but uncovered a nasty scandal. Undeterred by the risks, Anna continued both her altruism and her struggling agency.

A police officer sent Hilda Trelawney to Anna in *To Make a Killing* (HarperCollins, 1994). Hilda had never accepted the police decision that the death of her environmentalist husband Mark was an accident. Among the potential suspects were right-wing fanatics, real estate developers and tame politicians. They fought environmental legislation and the location of group homes for the developmentally disabled. Anna traced the family relationships that were the real cause of the murder, and met attractive police sergeant Ian McNeath, who became her lover.

By *Signs of Murder* (Angus & Robertson, Australia 1994), Anna realized that she needed her own qualifications as a private investigator. Hearing-impaired social worker Fiona Galloway hired Anna because she had been receiving threatening letters. Fiona connected the threats to Jackie Sims, a developmentally disabled adult who had been convicted of rape and murder. When Fiona was badly beaten, Anna reopened the Sims case to find the real killer.

Anna matured into a hard-edged investigator. The Australian series showed promise.

Diana Speed

Author: Tony Gibbs, pseudonym for Wolcott Gibbs, Jr.

Diana Speed, who had investigative experience from ten years in U. S. State Department Intelligence, was currently occupied as a troubleshooter for reclusive billionaire Roger "Rajah" Channing. She was a tall ash-blonde, educated at Wellesley, and a member of a socially prominent family. Her mother was a French Vicomtesse. Diana's former husband had been a Congressman. Disliking the artificiality of the Washington scene, she relocated in New York City as an executive in Channing's publishing company, Wild-Freeman.

Patrick Sarsfield, writer of historical romances, came to Wild-Freeman with an unusual offer as *Shadow Queen* (Mysterious Press, 1992) opened. An elderly woman and her daughter Marie, who were purported to be direct descendants of Mary, Queen of Scots, had possession of documents in which startling revelations were made. Sarsfield was murdered before he could deliver. The documents attracted both those who wished to save the British monarchy from embarrassment, and those who realized their commercial value. Diana sacrificed her relationship with Englishman Alan Trowbridge to uncover a plot to steal the material and dispose of Marie, the young "pretender."

During *Capitol Offense* (Mysterious Press, 1995), Diana developed a special rapport with recovering alcoholic Eric Szabo, another of Channing's investigators. They had not been expected to cooperate. Szabo was placed in Wild-Freeman as an editor, from which position he and Diana probed the death of power-hungry Congressman Philemon Fielding. His killer presumably was porn producer Magdalen Tyrell, who had been harassed publicly by Fielding. That was not the problem. What was Magdalen's next move?

Author Tony Gibbs was also the author of series featuring Lt. Tory Lennox in this volume and Gillian Verdean in Volume 2.

Lee Squires

Author: Christine Andreae

A mid-life crisis posed by the death of her four-year-old daughter Rachel from leukemia, and the dissolution of her marriage caused Lee Squires to abandon her career as an English professor and poetess and her opulent lifestyle in Washington D.C. She managed without a permanent residence, house-sat on a short-term basis, and took jobs whether they were academic or culinary as they came along. When under pressure, Lee contacted her mother, a practicing psychotherapist who lived in a communal setting back East.

In *Trail of Murder* (St. Martin, 1992), Lee signed on as cook for a Montana wilderness expedition. She knew little about Pete Bonsecours, the tour operator, or the wealthy participants. A series of accidents occurred, one fatal, within the close-knit group, exposing their fears and disloyalties. The victim of the fatal attack, wealthy Cyrus Strand, infuriated by a prior "accident", had publicly announced his intention to disinherit his family, leaving a lifetime trust for his third wife Luisa, but the final beneficiary would be a Wildlife Foundation. The adventure produced a romance with police officer Luke Donner, who was separated from his wife.

In *Grizzly* (St. Martin, 1994), tired of reading student papers, Lee took a break to serve as the cook at the J-E cattle ranch, where she and her family had often spent vacations. Lee had never forgotten the Fife brothers, whose parents had owned the J-E. Dave and his wife were now running the dude and cattle ranch, while "Mac," who had inherited the land, was obsessed by his study of grizzly bears. Lee entertained Japanese guests who were interested in purchasing the property. She located a grizzly killer, and solved a murder. Lee's affair with Donner ended when he returned to his wife and family. She resumed teaching on a part-time basis and returned to her poetry, but the lure of the wilderness was still a potent influence in her life.

As *A Small Target* (St. Martin, 1996) began, old friend Pete Bonsecours convinced Lee to cook for a small group journeying up to Lost Pipe Lake near the Flathead Indian lands. The party included Charlie Herron, a Los Angeles developer who wanted to locate a ski resort in the area, and Roland Redhawk, an environmental activist. Both were murdered at the site. Luke Donner reappeared to conduct the investigation with the help of Lee's insights and negotiating skills. She had misgivings about her role in capturing a wounded suspect.

Lee was not a happy heroine, but was a memorable character. Andreae has another series featuring fire fighter Mattie McCulloch.

Stella the Stargazer a.k.a Jane Smith

Author: Christine T. Jorgensen

Jane Smith, bored and burned out by her work as an accountant, made a radical change in her appearance, outlook, and employment. She became Stella the Stargazer, an astrologer and advice columnist for a second-rate weekly Denver newspaper. The pinstripe suits were exchanged for wildly colored voluminous outfits; the regular salary, for an irregular income with no benefits. Jane provided little information about her past: parents still alive, one brother and one sister; the education needed to be an accountant. Attention was given to her idiosyncrasies: an extra sense which affected her not only when she met people, but even in touching their correspondence, a fascination with lingerie, and a pet chameleon to whom she confided her problems. She had done volunteer work with a literacy program. The atmospheric conditions of mile high Denver cannot explain all this, but a reader who can accommodate the eccentricities will enjoy the Stargazer series.

In the opening narrative, *A Love to Die For* (Walker, 1994), Jane made the move to the *Daily Orion.* She fabricated some of the early letters. Others came from people she already knew. When Jane "saw" the corpse of Grace, the woman who produced her lovely lingerie, she was unsure whether she saw a real body or only an aura. Either way, the police saw her as their number one suspect.

Two disturbing letters began the mystery in *You Bet Your Life* (Walker, 1995). The first was a letter from Yvonne Talmadge, a woman seeking to avenge the death of her mother. The second was from Eddie Lorton, a husband whose wife left him on Stella's advice. Then, a rush to marriage by long time friend Amy Wilson sent Stella off to visit an old West gambling hall in Silverado.

Jane felt threatened in *Curl Up and Die* (Walker, 1997), but not enough to stay out of the love affair between her best friend, Meredith Spencer and Tony DeAngelo, a creative hair stylist at an exclusive salon. She had every right to be afraid: more threatening letters, "spells," and an astrological prediction in which she sensed doom for Meredith. When DeAngelo was murdered while both Meredith and Jane were on the premises, their problems had just begun.

Jane did not discount the story of abduction of his nanny Elena, told by young Steven Holman in *Death of a Dustbunny* (Walker, 1998). Unlike the police and Dustbunnies (the agency which had placed Elena in the household), she knew that the farewell note left by Elena was a fake. Based on her volunteer work, she was aware that Elena was illiterate. Steven's father was a reclusive man, isolating his motherless son. Jane took a special interest in the child, working as Elena's replacement until she figured out what was happening.

Even though she had an initial warning of tragedy, it was not Stella's extra-sensory power that led her to uncover a murderer in *Dead on Her Feet* (Walker, 1999). Instead she was motivated by her sympathy for lonely teenager Phillip Steadman, whose parents Barbara and Laurence managed the Magic Circle Theater. She invaded the privacy of suspects while working as an assistant director at the theater where Barbara had been killed. A second job was necessary because her publisher would not raise her salary. Stella had other concerns, Lips, the chameleon, had laid an egg.

These were simplistic narratives conducive to light reading.

Delta Stevens

Author: Linda Kay Silva

Delta Stevens was a lesbian police officer in California. After taking a bachelor's degree in social science, she initially intended to go to law school. She entered the police force with the plan that she would earn the money for tuition and then resign. However, she found police work so interesting that she stayed on. She loved to dance, collected baseball cards, but her job was her primary focus.

Delta was not a team player. She risked dismissal from the force on more than one occasion for her failure to share information with detectives on the case.

During *Taken by Storm* (Paradigm, 1991), when Delta's patrol partner and close friend Miles Brookman was shot in the line of duty, Delta did not accept the official line of "cop-killer" as an explanation. Miles had been checking drug thefts from the police department's evidence room. During his investigation, he had worked with Megan Osbourne, a childhood friend who had become a prostitute. Police computer expert Connie Rivera joined Delta in ferreting out which of their fellow cops were involved in drug dealing. They were aware that their investigation could lead to ostracism and retribution. In the course of the narrative, Delta began an affair with Megan.

Connie Rivera had graduated first in her class at Massachusetts Institute of Technology. Her involvement in humiliating practical jokes against a rival brought tragic results in *Storm Shelter* (Paradigm, 1993). Delta sensed a pattern in the escalating crimes in her patrol area. Only after several incidents did Connie tie the bizarre events to a video game left for her at the station. The obstacles that had to be overcome to win the game at each level were mirrored in the savage murders taking place. Knowing the identity of the perpetrator was not enough. They had to convince the homicide investigators of their theory. Meanwhile the crimes escalated to endanger those whom Delta and Connie loved.

Weathering the Storm (Paradigm, 1994) explored Delta's promise to Miles Brookman that she would protect children during the course of her work. Rogue behavior by Delta led her new captain to assign her as a patrol-training officer to Tony Carducci, a rookie with a directional handicap. Remembering how Miles had borne her early inadequacies, Delta tolerated a lot as they investigated a child pornography ring. Delta's personal heroism in the face of danger was weighed against her disregard for official orders. She won the approval of her new supervisor. Megan Osbourne, needing space from their relationship, left for a time-out in Costa Rica. Delta had urged her to take part in a "marriage" ceremony.

In *Storm Front* (Paradigm, 1995), Delta had two concerns: an assassin determined to kill Alexandria Pendelton, the female district attorney who wanted to be more than a friend to Delta, and Taylor, a female jewel thief who left a trail of clues for Delta to follow.

Delta had not approved of Megan's decision to accept an internship in the Costa Rican forests. In *Tropical Storm* (Rising Tide, 1997), her fears were realized when Megan became a prisoner of Colombian smugglers, headed by General Zahn. The gangs kidnapped women to work in gold mines. Delta recruited Connie Rivera, Sal (an electronics expert) and Josh (a former Vietnam veteran) to enter the tropical forest. All were aware that besides the smugglers, the forest held poachers and remnants of the Bribri, an indigenous tribe.

Storm Rising (Rising Tide, 2000) continued Delta and Megan's adventures in Costa Rica. As they were exiting in a helicopter, Delta was shot and fell into the water. The helicopter continued on without her, but Megan and Delta's oldest friend Connie Rivera believed she had survived. They rallied others: Sal and Josh, Gina Tarabini (Connie's pregnant lover), Tony Carducci from the police department, and Taylor, the jewel thief who loved Delta. In addition to rescuing Delta, Megan whose character had hardened as a result of her experiences, intended to rescue other kidnapped women whom she had left behind. Her need for revenge against General Zahn was overwhelming. These last three books are more adventure novels, than mysteries.

Thunderstorm, the last in the Delta Stevens series was self published by Linda Kay Silva in 2006. Although the plan to rescue Megan had been successful, it was at a great personal cost. Both Josh and the pregnant Gina had been killed. Dakota, the child of Gina and Connie Rivera, had survived thanks to an emergency caesarian performed by Delta. All were changed by their experiences. Delta had been deeply impressed by what she had learned from the Bribri. She looked at the world differently; the earth and its creatures, her relationships, even her job. Connie's reaction was even stronger. She separated herself from the others, softening only in Dakota's presence. They were sharing accommodations but in a more distant manner. Delta's workload was crushed by a series of murders, initially believed to be a war between two drug dealing gangs. Eventually she convinced herself and her former enemy, Detective Russell Leonard, that a third party was stirring up warfare between the two gangs. Was it the Mafia? Could a single person have committed the various forms of slaughter: bombs, throat slashing, sharpshooting rifles? Delta hoped that she was wrong about who that person could be. If that wasn't enough, the killer was leaving evidence pointing to Delta and her partner, Carducci, as the guilty parties. People are choosing sides, even Delta and the Mafia.

There were episodes of explicit lesbian sex during the narratives. Baseball fans will be annoyed to note that Mickey Mantle's name was misspelled and old time radio listeners will be irked to read that *Fibber McGee and Molly* was a children's program. A little research would eliminate such generational errors.

Blaine Stewart

Author: Sharon Zukowksi

Recovering alcoholic Blaine Stewart chose a difficult profession for a woman who needed to limit the stress in her life. She was a tall, redheaded private investigator, working in New York with her attorney/sister Eileen. Drug dealers had killed Blaine's husband Jeff, a government agent. Her subsequent miscarriage triggered her descent into alcoholism. Work, hard work, had been a blessing and made both sisters financially secure. The agency had an elite clientele; banks, insurance companies, and large corporations.

But, in *The Hour of the Knife* (St. Martin, 1991), Blaine was close to the edge. Eileen insisted that she take a vacation. Instead Blaine investigated the disappearance of college friend Amanda Johnson who enjoyed hacking into computer networks. Blaine held nothing back. She challenged the local authorities and broke into an office, while fighting off her recurrent nightmares with cigarette, coffee, and a compassionate doctor.

In *Dancing in the Dark* (St. Martin, 1992), Blaine divided her attention between a pro bono investigation into police harassment of African-American bodega owner Hurley Blake, and a far more lucrative case for Faradeux Industries. Faradeux sought a listing on the New York Stock Exchange, but W.A.R.M. (Worldwide Animal Rights Movement) was prepared to picket the announcement celebration. Blaine went undercover as a convert to the animal rights movement, where respect for life did not always extend to humans. Violence erupted in both cases. Eileen was seriously disabled when the agency office was bombed. Blaine did not seek relief in a bottle, although she cruised the toughest bars in the area for information.

Leap of Faith (Dutton, 1994) was a letdown from the earlier crisp narratives in its reliance on coincidences. Casual acquaintance Judith Marsden hired Blaine and Eileen to trace the surrogate mother who was bearing her child. Their investigation explored the potential abuses in the surrogate system as it developed into a business operation.

Blaine's marriage to FBI agent Dennis Halstead was in its fourth month when she received a call from her brother Dick in *Prelude to Death* (Dutton, 1996). Dick, who had been out of touch for two years, was charged with raping and killing Corrye Edwards, the poetess with whom he lived in Key West, Florida. Blaine rallied to Dick's defense instinctively, but risked Dennis' career and her own life when she challenged Cuban expatriates and powerful conservative forces within her own government.

The presence of a corpse on Blaine's doorstep drew her into the cutthroat world of international finance in *Jungleland* (Signet, 1997). Victim George Walden had managed funds at investment bank Kemble Reid. Blaine set out to learn what kind of man George had been. Was he involved in the theft of $500,000,000 in government securities or had he been about to expose the perpetrators? These questions consumed Blaine's work time until a more personal crisis occurred, the kidnapping of her niece Sandy. Now the question was: had Eileen's estranged husband taken his daughter, or was Blaine too close to finding George's killer.

A dauntless woman, fighting her alcoholism in situations often beyond her control.

Dr. Kellen Stewart

Author: Manda Scott

Dr. Kellen Stewart had begun her professional career as a medical student. By the time she had completed the requirements to practice, she discovered that she did not want to do so. Diverted for a short time into medical research, she left it all behind to become a psychiatrist. Her private life was nearly as chaotic.

After the death of her widowed mother, Kellen inherited a three-story building in Helensburgh, Scotland. She sold the building and used the proceeds to purchase a country place where she and her lover Bridget Donnelly could raise ponies and keep a stable. Somewhere along the way, Bridget and Kellen's relationship got off track. Kellen walked out, promising to come back.

As *Hen's Teeth* (The Women's Press, 1996) began, Kellen shared a Glasgow apartment with Canadian computer journalist Janine Caradice. Caroline Leader, a childhood friend and Bridget Donnelly's current lover, called Kellen to tell her that Bridget was dead. She believed that Bridget's death and the recent death of Bridget's brother Malcolm were connected. Kellen could not walk away this time.

The ties between Kellen and veterinary surgeon Nina Crawford had been two-way. After a suicide attempt, Nina had been referred to Kellen for therapy. Kellen, who now ran the stables with the help of elderly Sandy Logan, went to Nina when her livestock needed attention. In *Night Mares* (Headline, 1998), problems multiplied on both sides of the equation. Nina was coping with a series of unexplained equine deaths at her surgery. While Kellen monitored Nina's mental health, her mare that had just given birth to a prize foal was struck with the same symptoms as the dead horses. Someone wanted Nina either terrified or dead. Kellen, who had come to care for her more than she should for a patient, could not allow this to happen.

The discovery of friend Dr. Eric Dalziel's body while rock climbing was only the beginning in *Stronger Than Death* (Headline, 1999). Over short intervals, other medical associates of Kellen Stewart died under strange circumstances. Det. Stewart MacDonald focused on Eric's housemate Dr. Lee Adams. Lee and Kellen were long time friends, but Kellen could not prove Lee's innocence unless she would cooperate. The lesbian aspects of the relationships were not sexually explicit.

Scott is an excellent writer. Her sense of place, and descriptive powers were exceptional.

Teal Stewart

Author: J. Dayne Lamb

Teal Stewart, whose birth family had been poor and disorganized, was upwardly mobile at all costs. Her mother had trained as a concert pianist, but little was said about her father. By her thirties, Teal had parlayed her MBA from Stanford into work as a Certified Public Accountant at Clyborne Whittier. A tall, chestnut haired woman, she owned a three-unit town house on posh Beacon Hill in Boston. She had shared one unit with unconventional architect Huntington Huston a.k.a. "Hunt" for several years. Their affair cooled down to friendship with occasional bursts of loneliness, which brought them back together. They could not live with one another, regardless of their need. Argyle, the Scottish deerhound, who remained in Hunt's custody, suffered from the separation.

As *Questionable Behavior* (Zebra, 1993) opened, a dying man, editor Mark Konstat, collapsed in Teal's arms as she waited for the elevator in her office building. Her connection with the murder investigation hinged upon her developing relationship with Averill Cunningham, Konstat's best friend, her status as a witness, and her professional services in auditing the financial accounts of suspects. Her casual contact with a literate hit man and some assistance from a savvy secretary and a fledgling police detective enabled Teal to identify the killer and save herself.

In *A Question of Preference* (Kensington, 1994), Teal was preoccupied with her need to testify in an embezzlement case. Her dearest friend, artist Nancy Vandenburg, had asked for her help with threatening letters. Nancy's death left Teal feeling guilty, even when she learned that Nancy had a life she had never shared. Lt. Dan Malley, now engaged to Teal's secretary, saved the day in an action filled ending. There were strong female characters explored during the narrative. Partnership at Clyborne Whittier had been Teal's goal, but, once achieved, it presented a new set of problems.

During *Unquestioned Loyalty* (Kensington, 1995), office politics formed the background for a series of tragic deaths. Hunt disapproved of changes he saw in Teal as she accommodated herself to the system. Teal was torn between personal loyalties to coworkers and the firm's welfare. Working with Dan Malley, now married to her secretary, Teal went far afield to discover an unsuspected motive and killer.

These were not easy books to read because of the technical jargon and multiple suspects.

Emily Stone

Author: Kathryn Buckstaff

Emily Stone wanted to forget Blue Eye, Missouri, where she lived until she was six. Her dad, a quiet man who enjoyed his fishing and his booze, had left his failing hardware store behind, and moved his family to a Jacksonville, Florida trailer court. Her mother, an uneducated woman, was perceived by Emily as an embarrassment because of her limited interests and country philosophy. Emily was lonely in Florida, rejected because of her accent and appearance, but she persisted until she received a college education and a job as travel writer for the *Tampa Tribune*. She maintained a long-term relationship with an architect, but at thirty-eight felt unprepared for marriage and a family.

No One Dies in Branson (St. Martin, 1994) presented Emily with an unwelcome assignment covering the *Hot Country Awards* show in the tourist inflated town of Branson, Missouri, a short distance from Blue Eye. While investigating the death of Stella Love, a budding country singer, Emily uncovered hidden relationships among the suspects, but also came to appreciate the positive aspects of country and country music. The narrative was flawed by gushing comments about the "stars" that Emily met while in Branson (Johnny Cash, Louise Mandrell, and Glen Campbell).

By *Evil Harmony* (St. Martin, 1996), Emily had not only moved to Branson, but had become the acknowledged sweetheart (but not lover) of country star Marty Rose. Awed by the glitter of his life and his personal charisma, Emily was slow to realize that Marty was haunted by events in his past. The murders of two friends caused Marty to hire security guards, but his solution to the problem was unacceptable to Emily.

Lucy Stone

Author: Leslie Meier

Lucy Stone, a native New Yorker, moved to Tinker's Cove, Maine because of her interest in the environment and her marriage to carpenter Bill Stone. Although busy with three pre-teenaged children, she worked at Country Cousins, a Land's End clone, processing mail orders.

While on a break in *Mail-Order Murder* (Viking, 1991, also published as *Mistletoe Murder*), Lucy noticed an occupied car in the parking lot with the motor running and an exhaust pipe in the window. The managing director of the company Sam Miller III, who had been knocked unconscious and placed in the vehicle, subsequently died. Lucy was a potential witness who might be in danger.

Another pregnancy ended Lucy's employment, but left the family in financial straits, as *Tippy-Toe Murder* (Viking, 1994) began. This did not keep Lucy from investigating when "Caro" Hutton, a retired ballet teacher, disappeared. Lucy juggled her concerns about Caro with the murder of hardware storeowner Morrill Slack who had suffered from theft and the problems of a battered wife. No wonder she had limited time for preparing meals, attending Little League games, and sewing ballet costumes.

Lucy was still nursing her new daughter Zoe, when she embarked on a third murder investigation in *Trick or Treat Murder* (Kensington, 1996). A series of fires, the last of which had caused the death of summer visitor Monica Mayes, seemed targeted at historic properties. Buildings within the historical zone of the community could not be renovated without approval by a local commission. Lucy focused on Monica's marital difficulties until forced to deal with a killer who had money, not romance, on his mind.

With three of the children back in school and handy daycare available for Zoe, Lucy was restless as *Back to School Murder* (Kensington, 1997) began. A temporary job at the local newspaper and a night course in Victorian literature offered her chances for self-development. Instead she focused on a mysterious bombing at the elementary school, which fit a pattern of past crises. Local police arrested Josh Cunningham, a popular teacher who had roused the ire of right-wing parents, for the death of Carol Crane, the heroine of the bombing.

Lucy disagreed. A handsome college professor was a distraction to Lucy, but she returned to home and hearth without compromising herself.

Libraries ought to be safe places and library board members ought to be pillars of the community, but in *Valentine Murder* (Kensington, 1999) neither was true. At her first meeting as a board member, Lucy discovered the corpse of librarian Bitsy Howell. Since access to the building was limited, board members, including Lucy, were suspects. Her investigation placed the Stone children in danger amidst the snowstorm of the century.

The annual cookie exchange had been a tradition for Lucy and her friends. In *Christmas Cookie Murder* (Kensington, 1999), the event was a washout. Personal jealousies, rivalries and insecurities among the participants destroyed the holiday spirit. The murder of young childcare worker Tucker Whitney was attributed to her affair with an unfaithful husband. Lucy's personal knowledge of the suspect caused her to look further, perhaps too far for her own safety. More than the usual amount of action with smugglers, SWAT teams and corrupt officials.

When Native American activist Curt Nolan was killed after protesting against a gambling casino in *Turkey Day Murder* (Kensington, 2000), Bill, Lucy's husband, took a firm stance. She was not to investigate. On the other hand, long-time friend Miss Julia Talley urged Lucy to get involved. That, and her own curiosity tipped the balance. Curt had made so many enemies. Lucy looked in all the wrong places. When she identified the killer, it was a turkey that saved her neck. Toby was off to college; but Lucy added Nolan's Carolina dog to her household.

As *Wedding Day Murder* (Kensington, 2001) began, Sidra Finch, daughter of Lucy's best friend Sue, was engaged to marry Ron Davitz, an Internet entrepreneur whom she had met in New York City. Ron's overbearing mother substituted elaborate and expensive touches to the simple wedding that Sidra's family had envisioned. When Ron was found dead in the water before the ceremony, there were startling revelations about his financial empire. The ending was contrived.

Miss Julia Ward Howe Tilley was approaching her 90th birthday as *Birthday Party Murder* (Kensington, 2002) began. Lucy and her breakfast club decided on a major celebration for the spinster/former librarian. Lucy had a busy schedule: her job at the newspaper, a coeducational sleepover for daughter Sara's fourteenth birthday, and the need to do something about graying hair, facial wrinkles and an expanded waistline. She had never learned to say "no", not even to herself. When pal Rachel Goodman and her attorney husband Bob, asked Lucy to investigate the death of his partner Sherman Cobb, or when suspicious relatives took over Miss Tilley's household, who said "yes"? Lucy!

With some concern that her family would not survive without her, Lucy attended a Boston newspaper conference in *Father's Day Murder* (Kensington, 2003).It should come as no surprise to her readers that Luther Read, designated newspaperman of the year, was poisoned at the awards banquet. A minor connection to the Read family induced Lucy to investigate. The solution came only when she was pushed into it.

The Fourth of July, usually a community bonding experience in Tinker's Cover, was out of kilter in *Star Spangled Murder* (Kensington, 2004) Nudists, who preferred to be known as "naturalists", had taken over Blueberry Pond, the local fresh water swimming hole. Lucy could have handled that if her daughter Elizabeth hadn't joined them. Prudence Pratt, her holier-than-thou neighbor, brought charges against Kudo, the Stone's dog, for killing her prize chicken. Public demonstrations pitted members of Prudence's church against the naturalists. Toby (21) Lucy's son, was charged with assault after a fight with Wesley Pratt, Prudence's son. When Kudo was run over and Prudence was killed in a hit and run, the Stones became major suspects.

Lucy, wearing a green plaid coat, duck boots, and an oyster watch, accompanied by her college age daughter Elizabeth, invaded New York City in *New Year's Eve Murder* (Kensington, 2005). They had been chosen as one of six mother/daughter teams to take part in a "makeover" contest sponsored by *Jolie* magazine. The ten thousand dollar prize would come in handy for tuition. Shortly after *Jolie's* editor Nadine Nelson died of anthrax poisoning, Elizabeth came down with similar symptoms and had to be hospitalized. Lucy's friends from Tinker's Cover helped her with this one.

Anonymous messages sent to Pennysavers office in *Bake Sale Murder* (Kensington, 2006) detailed sexual harassment by senior football players against cheerleaders and junior varsity players. Ted, the newspaper editor, insisted that the messages could not be published or have a story written on them because the letters were unsigned. However, Lucy whose daughter Sara was a cheerleader did some investigating. It wasn't that she didn't have enough to do. She and her best friend Sue drew the new neighbors on Prudence Path into the bake sale to raise money for school costs of low-income families. The new and the old did not always mix well. Mimi, wife of the developer who had built the homes on Prudence Path, had already annoyed people by her suggestions. Chris took over the project like she'd been elected chairman, clashing with Sue. When Mimi didn't show up with her cookies, Chris sent Lucy to check on her. She was dead!

It seemed too much of a coincidence in *St. Patrick's Day Murder* (Kensington, 2008) that the headless body of Old Dan Malone was discovered in the harbor and that his younger brother, Dylan, a native of Ireland, appeared in Tinker's Cove. Stunned by the news of Dan's death, Dylan revealed that the two of them planned to remodel Bilge, the disreputable harbor side bar owned by Dan into a fine Irish pub and restaurant. Dylan, who had been hired to direct *Finians' Rainbow*, the centennial production of Our Lady of Hope parish, brought with him his actress wife Moira and his nine-year-old daughter Deirdre. Lucy and two friends agreed to take part in the musical chorus. Her kindnesses to the Malone family rebounded in chaos. That plus her reportorial curiosity led Lucy into danger. The solution was nothing to crow about.

The narratives were expanded with domestic details, and will be enjoyed best by those who like their mysteries seasoned with warmth and humor. One of the better cozy series. Next: *Mothers' Day Murder* (2009); *Wicked Witch Murder* (2010)

Dr. Michael Stone

Author: Anna Salter

Despite the name, Michael Stone was a female, named by her father while he was too drunk to realize his error. She became a forensic psychologist who specialized in child abuse, battered spouses, and custody cases. She devoted 80 percent of her time to a staff position at the Jefferson University Mental Health Clinic, and the rest to private practice in Vermont. Michael was the daughter of a gentle alcoholic father who practiced law in Wilson's Pond, North Carolina and his strong-minded wife. Michael's marriage to Doug ended after their daughter, Jordan, died of SIDS (Sudden Infant Death Syndrome).

Michael's life changed with Jordan's death. She maintained an interest in professional football, played in pickup coed basketball games, and rode horseback, but she separated herself from ownership. She occupied an isolated home that she stocked with 250 items, no more. Michael had serial relationships with married men after her divorce, but avoided any commitments. Under considerable pressure in her work, she returned on vacations to the inner coastal waters of North Carolina to refresh her spirit.

Shiny Water (Pocket Books, 1997) was an absorbing narrative, describing Michael's involvement in a child custody case in which allegations of child abuse had been made against Dr. Nathan Southworth, the father. After he was awarded primary physical placement, the children were murdered, and Sharon, their mother charged with their deaths. To protect her professional reputation and personal stability, Michael intervened in the investigation. She willingly accepted help from a convicted child molester, but feared dependence upon Adam Bowman, an attractive chief of police who shared her conviction that Sharon was innocent.

In *Fault Lines* (Pocket, 1998), Attorney Carlotta Young, Michael's best friend, warned her that the release from prison of Alex B. Willy, a former minister convicted of abusing children, could place her in danger. Michael had testified against Willy in court. Willy had won the right to a new trial on technical grounds, but the state would probably not retry the case. Willy's vendetta endangered not only Michael, but also the confidentiality and stability of her patients.

Personal relationships played a large role in the dilemma that faced Michael in *White Lies* (Pocket, 2000). Her respect for former mentor, deceased Dr. Reginald Larsen, influenced her to evaluate the competence of his son "Reggie", an anesthetist who was accused of sexual improprieties with his patients. Then, a long-term friendship with psychiatrist Marv Gliesen drew her into a case involving recovered memories of incest. Her never forgotten loss of a daughter to SIDS made it impossible for Michael to ignore the vulnerability of another woman's child. Finally her near death opened her up to a closer relationship with Adam Bowman, the Jefferson police chief.

What could induce Michael to agree to fill in as the psychologist in charge of a sex offender class at Nelson's Point Correctional Institution in *Prison Blues* (Pocket, 2002)? She was in the final trimester of a pregnancy, which had added seventy pounds to her small frame. Adam Bowman, father of the child, now sharing her home, would have preferred that she take it easy. Michael was motivated by her friendships for NPCI warden Gary Raines, and for Dr. Eileen Steelwater, the psychologist who had been fired from the position. Eileen had been discovered having sex with a prisoner. Raines had asked that Michael fill in for a short time until a permanent replacement could be hired. Complications came in bunches: the murder of a young sex offender; the efforts by a manipulative former attorney to control the sex offender classes; the possibility that drugs were being smuggled into the prison. Michael also became involved with eleven-year-old Aspasia, Gary's daughter, who had recently been diagnosed with diabetes. Aspasia refused to take her medications or control her diet, even though her parents rigorously insisted on her compliance. In her current position at the hospital where Aspasia was a patient, Michael intervened in the girl's care. This can be tough reading, although Salter managed to get human touches and a modicum of humor into her narrative.

Salter, a forensic psychologist, created an intriguing heroine and credible plots. Not for the squeamish.

Sergeant Stone

Author: Sarah J. Mason

Ponderous rural police Superintendent Trewley, and his brighter, younger, and better educated assistant Sergeant Stone were the protagonists in this series. Stone received chances to display her skills—a black belt in judo and medical training. She shared her private life with a traffic cop referred to as "What's his name" by Trewley. The couple were close enough to share a mortgage. "What's his name" had a degree in civil engineering. Stone was described as dark-haired with hazel eyes, capable of eating endless snacks without gaining weight to the dismay of her corpulent, always hungry superior officer.

Murder in the Maze (Berkley, 1993) offered rural English stereotypes and little action. The locals were gathered on the estate of newcomer Montague Rowles to celebrate their annual church bazaar when Isabel, the domineering wife of the local doctor, was murdered in the maze. After extensive questioning by Trewley, Stone's awareness of an obscure medical syndrome assisted in the solution.

In *Frozen Stiff* (Berkley, 1993), the incompetence, union stonewalling, and resistance to change in Tesbury's grocery chain headquarters hampered the efforts of management consultant Ken Oldham. When someone dispensed with him entirely, Trewley and Stone followed regular procedures.

Friday always seemed to bring weird cases, as in *Corpse in the Kitchen* (Berkley, 1993). Local aristocrat Miss Melicent Jervaux demanded police support in her efforts to evict a communal cult occupying adjacent land. A feud erupted between a bootier and a major manufacturer. These stresses might or might not account for the discovery of the corpse of Star, a member of the cult, in the kitchen of a nearby lodge. The methods of murder were ingenious, but the motive was weak.

During *Dying Breath* (Berkley, 1994), Stone's understanding of mercury poisoning helped Trewley in the determination of death of prominent scientist Dr. Basil Holbrook. Neither officer used much common sense in handling suspects.

Two murders in quick succession at a prominent girls' school confounded Stone and Trewley in *Sew Easy to Kill* (Berkley, 1996). A third occurred before they sewed the case up.

As *Seeing Is Deceiving* (Berkley, 1997) began, young "What's his Name" was busy directing traffic when three bank robbers drove past him. The cruel, well-organized thieves avoided detection for a considerable period of time even though a documentary film producer had videotaped their escapade. Their emphasis on crimes against oculists eventually solved the cases.

Stone (last name only provided) was an underdeveloped character with glib dialogue in a series in which other characters were better developed.

Writing as Hamilton Crane, author Sarah J. Mason was also the final author in the Miss Emily Seeton series. Another series, listed only as "Linford Mysteries" was noted on Amazon and Barnes and Noble.com.

Dr. Sylvia Strange

Author: Sarah Lovett

Sylvia Strange, a divorced woman, was described as a tall attractive brunette in her thirties who had earned a Ph.D. in psychology. Relationships had been difficult for Sylvia. Her father, besieged by alcoholism and depression, left when she was thirteen. Her next few years were notable for problems with drugs and the legal system. As an adult, she had infrequent contacts with her mother. An early marriage had ended in divorce, and an affair with an older man ended with his death. She was more successful professionally. Her practice, which included the evaluation of convicts under consideration for parole, led to a book on pathologies in prison inmates.

In *Dangerous Attachments* (Villard, 1995), Sylvia worked closely with her married friend Rosie Sanchez, an investigator at a New Mexico penitentiary. Sylvia had been hired by Attorney Herb Burnett to examine Lucas Watson, a seriously disturbed convict. Rather than parole, Sylvia recommended transfer to a psychiatric unit, earning not only his enmity but also that of his equally unstable brother and his father, a state senator. A parallel plot revolved around Rosie's search for the demented collector of body parts from prison inmates.

As *Acquired Motives* (Villard, 1996) began, Sylvia had ended her affiliation with the state prison, entering practice with Forensics Evaluation Unit, a private enterprise. Her employment as a defense witness in the trial of confessed rapist Anthony Randall was distasteful. Randall's release on a legal technicality fueled vengeance by a serial killer, whose identity was uncovered only after Sylvia delved into the childhood abuse of two lonely children. Her current affair with Police Officer Matt England was endangered by his desire for a long-term commitment, including a child.

It was a fluke that Sylvia was called to the hospital to work with Serena, a mute child, in *A Desperate Silence* (Villard, 1998). Serena was bright, but terrified. She had eluded a killer, driven her protector's car into a train, and survived. Sylvia and Serena developed a bond, which made Sylvia's involvement necessary to Serena's recovery. Sylvia fought off the authorities, possible relatives of Serena and the killer until she was sure that the child was safe. Matt surprised Sylvia with an engagement ring; she surprised him by accepting it.

Perhaps Sylvia should have refused to take part in John Dantes' psychological evaluation during *Dantes' Inferno* (Simon & Schuster, 2001). She had not come to grips with a personal crisis, the suicide of a patient whose release from the hospital she had authorized. John Dantes had been convicted as a bomber, but authorities suspected he had valuable information about other possible terrorist activities. Sylvia served with a group of experts (FBI, Los Angeles Police Department, and independent forensic guru Edmond Sweetheart) who suspected that Dantes had engineered the bombing of the Getty Museum and planned further depredations. How was he contacting his accomplices on the outside? Sylvia found Dantes attractive, worth saving, and her feelings were returned. Very complex characterizations and a narrative requiring close attention.

Dark Alchemy (Simon & Schuster, 2003) will be hard going for readers who find terminology like "dinoflagellates" indigestible. Edmund Sweetheart drew Sylvia into a psychological investigation of Dr. Christine Palmer who currently worked at Los Alamos National Laboratory. A suspicious number of Palmer's associates, either on site or as far away as England, had died mysteriously. Sylvia initially considered the case a witch hunt but changed her mind. Palmer was a brilliant biochemist who enjoyed the conflict with FBI agents with whom Sweetheart and Sylvia worked. Matt was understandably upset when Sylvia became a target as their wedding day approached.

Jane Stuart

Author: Evan Marshall

Jane Stuart came from the Midwest and attended the University of Detroit, but had few ties there. Both of her parents were dead. She was an only child. She met her husband Kenneth at her first job after college. He was her supervisor at Silver & Payne, a major literary agency in New York City. Because of stresses at Silver & Payne, partly due to the predatory nature of major executive Beryl Patrice, Kenneth quit his job and formed his own agency. He and Jane, by now his wife, moved their offices and home to a small New Jersey town, Shady Hills, about 25 miles west of New York City. Kenneth was able to take most of his writers along with him. His death in a traffic accident not only left Jane personally bereaved, but also decreased their client base. By that time she was in her late thirties and their son Nicky was nine. His favorite companion was Winky, a tortoiseshell cat who figured in several of the mysteries. Jane was comfortable in Shady Hills. She belonged to a knitting group, which provided her with emotional support and the best gossip in town.

Things had not been working out for Jane as *Missing Marlene* (Kensington, 1999) began. Her top author and romantic interest, Roger Haines was experiencing burnout. His latest book sold badly. His publisher dropped his option. Jane felt that his current manuscript needed a major overhaul, causing him not only to fire her, but also to undermine her reputation. Marlene, the nanny whom Jane hired out of affection for the young woman's mother, disappeared. Jane realized that Marlene had engaged in reckless behavior since joining her household in Shady Hills. She felt guilty that she had made so little effort to help Marlene get acquainted. The guilt and calls from Marlene's mother prompted Jane to delve into what might have happened.

Jane could not deny the loneliness in her life since Kenneth's death, but she became too involved to be obsessed by it during *Hanging Hannah* (Kensington, 2000). A *People* magazine profile of Jane as "Agent of Justice" tied her and other Shady Hills residents to the death of Hannah, a young developmentally disabled woman. Hannah's killing was followed by the murder of editor Holly Griffin who had arranged for Jane to represent superstar Goddess. Jane allowed attentive detective Stan Greenberg to chauffeur her as she questioned and researched but she did not share her findings with him. Winky earned her keep in this one. The premise that an indigent woman would have been allowed to stay on at a private facility without payment was difficult to accept. Reality check, please.

The memory of Kenneth whom she had loved dearly motivated Jane to accept his cousin Stephanie Townsend into her home in *Stabbing Stephanie* (Kensington, 2001). According to Stephanie she needed a place to stay until she could find an apartment. Carson & Hart, a publisher newly relocated in Shady Hills, would employ her. Stephanie convinced Jane to go undercover at the publishers. She was sure that something was wrong there. Stephanie was a big part of what was wrong, but it took Jane a while to figure that out. Winky, who visited the publisher to pose for a picture, opened the door to the solution. Light humor came from Jane's efforts to stay on the difficult Dr. Stillkin Diet. She was dating Detective Stan Greenberg regularly, and had improved her business status.

Ivy Benson, trying to rebuild her friendship with Jane in *Icing Ivy* (Kensington, 2002) tried too hard. She manipulated Jane into allowing her and her crude boyfriend Johnny Bagliere to attend an isolated retreat for aspiring writers. The group of students and instructors contained rivals, a blackmailer, and a killer. Ivy was the victim. Stan Greenberg's pleas that Jane leave the investigation to the police were ignored. As a single mother she had no compunction about placing herself in danger.

Tina Vale, new publisher of Corsair Books, had reason to dislike Jane. In *Toasting Tina* (Kensington, 2003) she planned to ruin the career of Jane's protégée Nat Barre, a pharmacist turned author. Tina's timely death solved that problem but spawned several others. For one thing Jane was a suspect. She had no faith that Stan could solve the case so she set out to do it herself.

"No good deed goes unpunished" Jane learned in *Crushing Crystal* (Kensington, 2004) when she agreed to investigate the death of Crystal Ryerson, sister of her housekeeper Florence. Jane and Florence knew that Crystal was self righteous. Her interference had caused a custody investigation, and threatened the job of a young media specialist. Fortunately, Jane's second good deed, allowing madcap singing star Goddess to gain experience for a movie role by working in her office, was more humorous than deadly.

The behaviors that provided motivation in the narratives were not closely linked to the way characters were presented. Marshall has a current series, subtitled "Hidden Manhattan mysteries"

Liz Sullivan

Author: Lora Roberts

Initially, Liz Sullivan's decision to live out of her 1969 Volkswagen van, avoiding relationships and subsisting well below the poverty level, seemed quixotic, even paranoid. She was hiding from Tony, her brutal former husband. She had divorced him while she was in prison for shooting him in self-defense. Hiding was not paranoid. It was prudent, because he continued to stalk her. A regular job or a permanent address would have limited her ability to move regularly, so she lived in the van, writing freelance articles, using the public library as a resource, She managed on thrift shop clothes and cheap food, supplemented by her section of a Palo Alto community garden plot.

Liz was a short, stubby woman with nondescript hair who found it easy to lose herself in the crowd. Her ties with her extended Irish family in the Denver area had been damaged when she dropped out of college to marry Tony. They had offered no support during the difficult period of her trial and imprisonment. Her husband's brutality had left her cautious in her relationships with men, but she taught writing at a senior center, enjoyed the companionship of other writers, and swam daily at a community pool.

The discovery of the corpse of Pigpen Murphy. a local street person, under her vehicle during *Murder in a Nice Neighborhood* (Fawcett Gold Medal,

1994) brought Liz to the attention of the police, and eventually led Tony to her van, but she survived.

However tenuous Liz's ties were with her family, she could not ignore the news that her mother was ill. In *Murder Mile High* (Fawcett, 1996), she returned to Denver. When someone deposited Tony's corpse on her parents' front porch, Liz protected herself and her family from hasty conclusions by the police department and the machinations of the killer.

An unexpected visit by a runaway teenage niece in *Murder in the Marketplace* (Fawcett, 1995) continued her prickly family relationships. Young Amy Sullivan's visit was tolerable because Liz had inherited a small home and income from the sale of adjacent property. Liz's entry into temporary work as a clerical exposed her to murder and caused her to be suspected by her coworkers. Not so with Police Officer Paul Drake, who became a friend and neighbor. Eventually Liz relaxed enough to have a nondescript black and white dog named Barker, probably for good reasons.

In a moment of weakness during *Murder Bone by Bone* (Fawcett, 1997), Liz agreed to care for a friend 's four children. Her strained domesticity was fragmented by their discovery of old bones and her discovery of a new corpse, that of archeologist Dr. Richard Grolen. The continued intimacy with Drake who provided overnight, but chaste, protection for Liz and the children aroused both positive and negative feelings in Liz.

She enjoyed growing, and sometimes selling, the vegetables she grew in a community garden. For Liz, gardens were a serene place, but when shared, they could become a source of wrangling and territorial disputes, as in *Murder Crops Up* (Fawcett, 1998). When murder did occur in the communal garden, Carlotta Houseman, an old enemy, suspected that Liz was the killer. Her close observation provided Liz with an alibi when a second death occurred. Niece Amy survived a personal crisis, but her life was changed. Paul's absence because his father was ill made Liz realize how important he had become in her life.

In *Murder Follows Money* (Fawcett, 2000), Liz's temporary employer warned her that her new assignment would be difficult. Escorting culinary expert Hannah Couch on her San Francisco tour went beyond difficult. Hannah's entourage included a killer, a kidnapper, and a potential suicide. Paul Drake was there for Liz and they moved closer to a commitment.

Dr. Evelyn Sutcliffe

Author: Leah Ruth Robinson

Dr. Evelyn Sutcliffe was a third-year resident working the emergency room at Manhattan's University Hospital on the upper west side of New York City. Prior to taking up medicine, Evelyn had been ABD (all but dissertation) toward a Ph.D. in English. As part of her studies, she had spent a semester at Oxford University. Her father, Evan Sutcliffe, had died in a car accident. Her mother Joan, a formidable personality who had served as a MASH nurse in

Korea, had remarried. Joan's second husband, pediatric neurologist Dr. Sandy Berman had adopted Evelyn although he insisted that she keep her birth father's last name in his memory. He was the man whom Evelyn thought of and referred to as "Dad." Sandy Berman had suffered a severe heart attack recently. Joan, who had been serially unfaithful, pulled herself together and paid more attention to him. Evelyn had two half-brothers: Alan, who was gay, studied at the Culinary Institute, and Craig, an assistant district attorney, had marital problems.

The man in Evelyn's life was staff psychiatrist Dr. Phil Carchiollo. Initially they both had apartments at the Doctor's Residence, a building that housed staff and provided office space for attending physicians' private practice. Phil moved out, wanting a more permanent home, and a more committed relationship. Evelyn felt pressured, unsure of her willingness to either move in with Phil or marry him. He had not always been that eager for commitment. He had dual relationships with Evelyn and another woman for some time. Beth, the "other woman" resided in London but returned to New York City on a regular basis. When she did, Phil was there for her. Beth's marriage changed the arrangements.

Evelyn was attracted to risk-taking charismatic men. She described herself as tall—six feet in shoes, with light brown hair. She was only minimally observant but shared the Jewish rituals of her mother and stepfather. Evelyn prided herself on her ability to focus on her work tasks, clearing herself of any emotional involvement in the patient. She described herself and other emergency room staff as "adrenaline junkies."

First Cut (Avon, 1997 *apa Intensive Care*) could be compared to a six-hour miniseries with an ensemble cast, members of which were described in detail. Evelyn had management responsibilities over other staff members, several of whom had professional or personal problems. Treatment of the third victim of a serial killer brought Evelyn and her staff into a murder investigation. The death of Theresa Kahr, whom Evelyn had mentored, could be attributed to the "Babydoll Killer" or might be a copycat. Evelyn was unsure of whom she could trust among her associates. The clues to the identity of the killers were artfully inserted in extensive details.

As *Unnatural Causes* (Avon, 1999) began, the relationship between Evelyn and Dr. Phil Carchiollo was disrupted by Elise Vanderlaende, a neurotic young woman who had inflated a minor contact into a belief that she and Phil were lovers. Not surprisingly Evelyn cast Elise as the prime suspect when poisoned mushrooms were delivered to her apartment, causing the death of dear friend Gary Seligman. Gary, a registered nurse, and others had been at Evelyn's apartment to celebrate an anniversary. The final outcome took place in the emergency room. Maybe a trifle too many trauma notes.

Doctors are not supposed to provide services to family members or close friends, but in *Blood Run* (Avon, 1999, but previously published in a different form in 1988), Evelyn had no choice. She was on duty in the emergency room when her friend Dr. Shelley Reinish arrived as a patient and left as a corpse. Evelyn, with her background in writing, was polishing up Shelley's book on emergency room physicians. Overcome by grief that she might have failed to note serious changes in Shelley's behavior, Evelyn probed until the connections came together.

The narrative over-focused on Evelyn's perceptions and feelings, and Phil's professional analysis of her feelings.

Cassandra "Cassie" Swann

Author: Susan Moody

Author Susan Moody, who had a long running series about globe-trotting, English-African photographer Penny Wanawake, switched to Cassandra Swann, a former biology teacher who taught bridge. Cassandra had been raised first by her pub-keeper father and grandmother, and then by an uncle in a rural vicarage. She had family: cousins Hyacinth and Primula, twins who were unbearably thin. Cassandra, who finished university in three years, had a strong visual memory that helped in playing bridge but also assisted her in solving mysteries. She was described as a divorcee in her thirties, who accepted her "womanly figure."

When, during *Death Takes a Hand* a.k.a. *Take-out Double* (Penzler, 1994), Cassandra arrived late for a bridge session, she found her fellow players dead at the table. They were members of a larger group, vacationing in a country mansion as part of a bridge tournament. Others in the group had connections based on their personal or professional lives, but it was the placement of the cards that directed Cassandra to the killer.

Grand Slam (Penzler, 1995) connected Cassandra's volunteer work teaching bridge to inmates at the local prison with her job as a paid partner for professional bridge player Roy Chilcott. When discharged by Chilcott, she tripped over the corpse of Lady Portia Wickham, an environmentalist. Someone wanted Portia dead and she had to know why.

The death of Cassie's father haunted her throughout *King of Hearts* (Scribner's, 1995), which had little or nothing to do with bridge. The mention of a horse named "Handsome Harry" set her to work questioning witnesses of Harry Swann's demise. Cassie became convinced that a quarrel outside his bar had been staged; the motive, murder. Her parallel investigation of the death of immigrant doctor Sammi Ray was transparent to a careful reader.

By *Doubled in Spades* (Scribner's, 1997), Cassie and her friend Natasha had started a bridge sundries business. She met amateur bridge player Naomi Harris who believed her husband wanted to kill her; and Lucy Benson, the child Naomi had given up for adoption. Male family members had preyed upon both women. Cassie involved faithful friend Charlie Quartermain in her investigation of Naomi's death. Charlie got no respect or affection from Cassie so it was not surprising that someone else recognized his worth.

In *Sacrifice Bid* (Headline, 1997), Cassie noted that a bridge acquaintance was more than willing to assist Charlie in his fund raising for the local nursing home. She was too busy worrying about Lolly Haden-White to care. Lolly, who also played bridge with Cassie, seemed distracted, making errors inconsistent with her skill level. When Lolly died mysteriously, Cassie believed her death was motivated by an incident decades before in Africa.

As *Dummy Hand* (Headline, 1998) began, a passerby had found Cassie badly injured by a hit-and -run driver. Charlie Quartermain, determined to find the offender, did not accept a voluntary confession by Bernard Price, a local schoolteacher. His investigation continued as Cassie slowly recovered her health and her memory. Then, the man who had blackmailed him into confessing one offense rather than face exposure for another, murdered Price.

Bridge had become peripheral in the later Swann books, but the cool mind and intense focus that made Cassie an exceptional player worked to her advantage in solving mysteries.

Kathryn Swinbrooke

Author: C. L. Grace, pseudonym for Paul Harding a.k.a. P. C. Doherty

This historical series centered on the relationship between a young female physician and a rough Irish mercenary during the Fifteenth century. Kathryn Swinbrooke, who had been trained to follow in her widowed father's footsteps, had married Alexander Wyville, an attractive but faithless man, who was missing in the War of the Roses. In her late twenties, she was dark-haired with blue-gray eyes and lived in Canterbury.

Kathryn met Colum Murtagh during *A Shrine of Murders* (St. Martin, 1993) when current pilgrims to Canterbury were poisoned in methods reminiscent of Chaucer's work. Kathryn, whose husband had allied himself with the losers in the War, became interested in Colum, even though she was aware that her husband might still be alive.

Colum worried about his countrymen in *The Eye of God* (St. Martin, 1994) because, as an Irishman allied with an English King, he was perceived as a traitor. The Eye of God, a valuable sapphire stolen by Richard of York from Ireland contained a secret that men would kill to protect or to learn. True to her own integrity and the spirit of the times, Kathryn remained chaste as she sought an annulment from her marriage.

In *The Merchant of Death* (St. Martin, 1995), Kathryn and Colum deduced that the suspects in a murder at the local inn were not brought there by chance but under pressure from a blackmailer. Kathryn took the lead in solving this murder, absolving Colum from blame in a purported death, and concealing the truth in another family tragedy.

Colum lived in Kathryn's home as a lodger, as *The Book of Shadows* (St. Martin, 1996) began. Two years and a day would have to elapse from Alexander's disappearance before she could seek permission to remarry within the church. Shortly after Kathryn attended Matthias, a dying former sorcerer, and learned of the *Book of Shadows*, Tenebrae, its current possessor, was murdered. He was an admitted necromancer who used the book not only for its spells, but also to blackmail. In addition to his death, the disappearance of the book was of concern to local officials, including Colum.

Although the War of the Roses had ended by 1472, with Edward IV on the throne, the potential for disruption still existed within the York faction as *Saintly Murders* (St. Martin, 2001) began. Neither of Edward's surviving brothers could be trusted, a source of great concern to their mother, Duchess Cecily. When Roger Atworth, a former soldier who had entered a monastery to repent for his sins, died, Cecily had two worries: had Roger destroyed the letters she had sent him, and had he died a natural death. Kathryn was selected by the archbishop of Canterbury to serve as Devil's Advocate in the process of proposing Atworth for sainthood. Implicit in that assignment was a close look at the circumstances of his death. The reward dangled before Kathryn was a search for Alexander Wyville, dead or alive.

Two puzzles emerged in *A Maze of Murders* (St. Martin, 2003) the theft of a ruby relic from a guarded locked chapel and the death of Sir Walter Maltravers who had loaned the jewel to the Greyfriar 's church. Sir Walter's beheaded body was found in the center of the guarded maze where he practiced penance for the breach of a sacred oath. The incidents were variously attributed to a pickpocket, to the remnants of a Byzantine Guard and to heavenly intervention. Kathryn used her wits and Colum, his powers of office and physical presence, to identify an earthly solution to the crimes. Kathryn and Colum will marry.

Colum and Kathryn's brief honeymoon ended when in *A Feast of Poisons* (St. Martin, 2004) Lord Henry Beauchamp invited them to his Kent manor. Beauchamp was to entertain three emissaries from King Louis XI of France. There were major foreign issues to be settled. Kathryn's assignment was to determine whether or not Beauchamp had killed his wife Lady Mary. She went far beyond that goal, solving a series of poisonings in the village of Walmer.

This continued to be an interesting series, with documentary material to illuminate the period.

Dodee Swisher

Author: Peter Abresch

Attendance at Elderhostels, short-term educational programs for persons age fifty-five or older, constitute one of the enjoyable perquisites of growing old. Individuals or couples share college dormitory or hotel accommodations, attend classes without the pressure to achieve, and make new friends. Jim Dandy, a recent widower, had only promised to attend the Elderhostel in

Bolder Harbor, New Jersey, to accompany an uncle. When the uncle died, his children convinced him to go anyway, although he had limited interest in bonsai. There he met Dodee Swisher, a tiny gallery owner and artist. After their first unplanned contact, they arranged to attend the same programs. Their intimacy grew accordingly. Her habit of sketching during classes provided them with clues when they encountered a mystery. He was the viewpoint character, but Dodee was the aggressor both in their physical relationship and their investigations. Gradually Dodee's background emerged. She had suffered from an alcoholic and abusive husband, whom she divorced when she feared for her children's safety.

Among the skills that Jim learned in *Bloody Bonsai* (Worldwide/ Writeway, 1998) were how to steal trees, burgle hotel rooms, and rescue damsels in distress. The damsel was Dodee who taught Jim that he had not lost his interest in, and aptitude for, lovemaking.

Dodee and Jim were reunited in Baltimore when they attended a culinary Elderhostel during *Killing Thyme* (Write Way, 1999). They were on the same wavelength as to resuming their physical relationship, but only Dodee's pressure kept Jim on the trail of a chef-killer. A senior citizen version of Ivan and Nan Lyons' *Someone Is Killing the Great Chefs of Europe*, but with a flavor of its own.

By the time Dodee and Jim met in *Tip a Canoe* (Write Way, 2001), he was evaluating their relationship. This was a very active Elderhostel in South Carolina's Santee Lakes Region. They added canoeing to their usual tasks of discovering corpses and identifying killers. By the conclusion, Jim was ready to make a declaration of love, to which Dodee responded wholeheartedly. A foul-mouthed attendee whose off-color sexual comments were inappropriate marred the cast of characters.

Dodee and Jim 's Elderhostel rendezvous in *Painted Lady* (Intrigue Press, 2003) blended religious faith, spiritualism, and human greed with a large dose of Western history. Before they began their trip down the old Sante Fe trail, a mysterious figure in Dodee's painting replicated the woman who had fallen or been pushed from a rooftop. Jim, who had hurried to assist the victim, was believed by some to have taken her notebook. If so, he might have clues to the whereabouts of a gold Mayan Falcon.

Jim and Dodee were attending a weekend culinary Elderhostel on the North Carolina coast in *Sheep in Wolf's Clothing*, a novella included in *Deadly Morsels* (Worldwide, 2003). They encountered the body of a local priest while walking on the shore. Dodee insisted on cutting classes to investigate.

Perhaps *Name Games* (Elderhostel, 2008) should also have been a novella. The narrative was slowed down by information about the flora and fauna to be encountered in the area of Mountain Retreat and Learning Center in Georgia. Dodie was enthusiastic about the wild river adventures offered by this Elderhostel. Jim spent much of his time at various levels of terror, not so much at the murder of government employee Howard Lesle or the fake FBI agents who appeared, or even the certainty that the "bad guys" had a mole in their group, as of his fear of traversing the swift rapids, falling down the "hidden cliffs" or making a fool of himself in front of Dodie. The "name game" was a clever plot device.

Zoë Szabo

Author: Lisa Kleinholz

Although she has only appeared in two books as of the time this was written, Zoë made a memorable entrance. She was the only child of a Broadway song and dance man and his artist wife. Her mother's death of cancer occurred after she had run away from home at age 16. Although her father prevailed upon her to return and visit her mother in the hospital, there was no real reconciliation. Zoë had been sexually active in her teens, and became part of the rock and roll music community. She did free lance writing on the music scene, including articles and reviews in Rolling Stones. When she met base guitarist and song writer Billy Harp, she fell totally in love with him, ignoring his reputation for wildness, the fact that his career was suffering, and that they came from totally different backgrounds. Billy's large family was Irish Catholic, although it never showed in his behavior. Zoë's father was a Jew who had emigrated from Hungary; her mother had been a lapsed Catholic. She held more closely to the Jewish traditions, but did not practice any religion. Their marriage produced two much-loved children; serious sensitive Keith age five as the first book began) and Smokie whose outlook on life was more reflective of Zoë's. Though she never stopped loving Billy, she found it difficult to stay behind with two small children and earn enough as a writer to support them, while Billy toured the world in furthering his musical career. When he was hospitalized in Kyoto, Japan after a serious overdose, that did it for Zoë. She returned to her father's Manhattan apartment.

Their reconciliation was based upon his commitment to avoid drugs, and her agreement to move to Graymont, Massachusetts, a town of 2500 population. By this time, Zoë's dad had died, leaving her enough money to purchase a home there, but they had huge personal debts run up by Billy. Zoë found a job as a reporter on the Graymont Eagle, but Billy became something of a househusband. He played with local bands, worked at writing new songs, and received some royalties from prior records. Semi-rural life was something of a shock to Zoë, although she believed Graymont was a good place to raise her children. She did not conform to local standards of dress and behavior. Her hair was punk. She had jewelry in four holes on her left ear and three on her right. Her skirts were short and her Mountbatten high heels had a tough time in Massachusetts' winter snows. Zoë's role model was Lois Lane (a la Superman) and she reported what she learned and deduced without regard to community mores. That led to conflict with Whit Smythe, the third generation publisher of the Eagle. He cut her stories and sometimes refused to print them. Fellow reporter Mark Polanski had an edgy professional relationship with Zoë. He had "stolen" her material more than once, but he also saved her life. Zoë did make friends: Eagle photographer Kate Braithwaite; Quaker Cletha Fair, and retired professor Morgan Swan who lived next door and frequently took care of the children when both Billy and Zoë had to be gone. There were conflicts of interest when her aggressive investigations clashed with personal loyalties.

Zoë wasn't the only one suffering from cultural shock in *Exiles on Main Street* (Harper, 1999). Cletha Fair and Prof. Peter Albright, who worked in Asian Studies at the local university, had been instrumental in bringing Cambodian refuges to Greymont. Both had spent considerable time in the Vietnam/Cambodian area. Cletha had adopted Prith, a young Cambodian. Zoë had written an article featuring the family of Song Touch, a bright young teenager. That gave her a head start when the corpse found in a car parked at the local mall turned out to be Chram Touch, Song's older sister. The extended narrative touched on the clash between Zoë's aggressive investigation and her local relationships. Her recklessness and interference caused irritation in the local police force.

It wasn't a foreign presence that created local hostility in *Dancing with Mr. D* (Avon, 2000), but the more common tensions between real estate developers and environmentalists. Cassandra Dunne's record as an activist determined to protect nature at all costs was well known. When she died after a mysterious fall from a 200-year-old maple tree on land destined to be developed, there were few mourners. Cassandra's righteousness had alienated other environmentalists who saw a role for compromise in their small community. When the local police determined Cassandra had been murdered, there was no stopping Zoë's determination, not only to identify her killer but to expose corruption. Her own life was in shambles. Billy had been lured away by charismatic singer Vivi Cairo, who needed him for a new album she was working on at a music studio in Vermont. Author Kleinholz did an excellent job of portraying Zoë's battles with her own needs, with Billy, and with Whit Smythe. Lois Lane lived and worked in Manhattan. She would have had a tough time in Greymont.

Alex Tanner

Author: Anabel Donald

Alex Tanner's work as a freelance researcher for television programs provided her with investigative experience. Her family background, an unknown father and an institutionalized mother, gave her empathy, but not pity, for the disadvantaged. She had spent her childhood in foster homes, buoyed up by her plan to become a private investigator like those she knew from reading mysteries. Her education, both college and secretarial training, prepared her for a career. By age twenty-eight, she owned a co-op apartment in London and had an independent pension plan. Unfortunately she had acquired no social graces and limited ability to bond with others. Alex was not over-scrupulous. On occasion, she stole books from libraries and read the papers on desks when she was left in an office. She was a shrewd judge of people, and capable of changing her mind.

In *An Uncommon Murder* (St. Martin, 1993), Sarah Potter's plight aroused Alex's sympathy. Sarah, after a lifetime of service as a governess to the Sherwin family, had been dismissed. Alex researched the death of Lord Rollo Sherwin in Africa during the Fifties and the disappearance of Lord Rollo's granddaughter whom Sarah had taught.

During *In at the Deep End* (St. Martin, 1994), Alex was hired by a posh London firm of solicitors to investigate the "state of mind" of seventeen-year-old Olivier de Savigny Desmoulins before he drowned in the pool at his boarding school. Using her television research connections as a cover, Alex became embroiled in the "evil" that pervaded Rissington Abbey, where a paramilitary curriculum was used to control unruly students. She and her assistant uncovered deceptions at several levels, and risked Alex's life in the endeavor. Television producer Barty O'Neill was the man in Alex's life, but without commitment.

In *The Glass Ceiling* (Macmillan, 1994), Barty and Alex hit some rough spots when he misunderstood her relationship with old friend Peter Barstow. A social worker friend convinced Alex to house and mentor Nick, a withdrawn teenage girl who would rather be homeless than fostered. These diversions did not deter Alex from following up on letters from a killer who wanted to be stopped. Alex explored the current lives of four young women who had been "pranksters" during their university days, and who were still playing games.

Alex planned to use her time in the United States during *The Loop* (Macmillan, 1996) visiting the sites where her favorite fictional sleuths had lived. Instead she fended off Barty's proposal of marriage and involved herself in model Jams Treliving's search for the love of her life...and the father of her unborn child. Both pursuits followed Alex back to England where she added a third concern. She needed to identify her biological father. That done, maybe she could move on in her life.

In *Destroy Unopened* (Pan, 1999), just when Alex most needed her underaged assistant, she (Nick) disappeared. That left Alex with the intriguing case of the unsigned love letters found by recent widow Hilary Lucas. The love letters made reference to a serial killer. Nick had left behind an unfinished case, the disappearance of Samantha, a young developmentally disabled woman. Barty was off in Africa, possibly in danger. She needed him to help her make an important decision about her future. The result was an intriguing narrative that left a reader with an appetite for more.

Alex was a no-nonsense investigator, who could go far. There were excellent reviews in England, but the series was not well known in the United States. "Smile, Honey" (1988) is a standalone.

Mary Alice Tate (Sullivan, Nachman, Crane)

Author: Anne George

See: The Tate Sisters, page 790.

Patricia Anne Tate (Hollowell)

Author: Anne George

See: The Tate Sisters, page 790.

The Tate Sisters

Author: Anne George

The Tate sisters were a study in contrast. Narrator Patricia Anne Tate Hollowell (nicknamed Mouse) was a petite, reflective, and well-organized mother of three, happily married to Fred Hollowell for forty years. She had taught high school English until she was sixty in a suburb of Birmingham, Alabama. After retirement she tutored children. Patricia Anne was careful about what she ate, promoted a vegetarian life style, and was allergic to alcohol. She continued to vote the Democratic ticket even after the Republican resurgence in the South, and had a soft spot for the hippies of the Sixties. Her dog, a mongrel named "Woofer," completed the household.

Mary Alice Tate Sullivan Nachman Crane, five years older, enjoyed life to the fullest with little concern for the future. Her lifestyle was subsidized by the considerable wealth she had inherited from her three deceased husbands, each of whom had been considerably older and to each of whom she had provided great joy and a child. She voted the straight Republican ticket, ate whenever and whatever she pleased, enjoyed a cocktail, and entertained lavishly. She shared her luxurious home with an overweight cat, "Bubba," and—for a time at least—with a "boyfriend." Physically, Mary Alice (called "Sister" by Patricia Anne) was a tall woman weighing at least 250 pounds. Her originally brunette hair had undergone subsequent variations. Mary Alice had two daughters and a son from her marriages. Son Ray had left the United States after being caught raising marijuana in a national forest. He ran a dive boat in Bora Bora. The sisters were one another's best friends, and their dialogue will resonate with anyone who has a loved sister as I do.

Author Anne George has subtitled each book in the series "A Southern Sisters Mystery."

As *Murder on a Girls' Night Out* (Avon, 1996) began, Mary Alice had purchased a country western bar. Shortly after she showed her new venture off to Patricia Anne, Ed Meadows, the seller, was murdered. Combining their skills and resources under protest from Fred, the sisters proved the innocence of Henry Lamont, a young man whom Patricia had taught in high school. On the side, they scouted for prospective husbands for their daughters among the suspects and investigators.

Although less hilarious, *Murder on a Bad Hair Day* (Avon, 1996) was enjoyable. The sisters' interest in primitive art involved them in the murder of gallery owner Mercy Armistead and art critic Ross Perry. Again Patricia Anne's sense of loyalty to a former student, this time Claire Moon who was Mercy's assistant, motivated her to take considerable personal risks to identify a tormented killer.

Mary Alice's daughter Debbie married Chef Henry Lamont as *Murder Runs in the Family* (Avon, 1997) began. The guests included Dr. Philip Nachman who matched up with Haley, Patricia Anne's widowed daughter. Another guest was Meg Bryan, Henry's cousin and a professional genealogist. Meg died precipitously after Patricia Anne requested information about Henry's family. The negative side of genealogy emerged as the sisters investigated judicial high jinks and family skeletons.

As *Murder Makes Waves* (Avon, 1997) began, Patricia Ann was bored by the routine of her life. She, her daughter Haley, and family friend Frances Zata accepted Mary Alice's invitation to visit her Florida condo. Mary Alice, who would be attending a Writer's Conference, had many friends in the area, more than one of whom were killers. The first victim had been Patricia Ann's new friend, the condo manager Millicent Weatherby, whose body washed up on shore. Fred prepared to merge his business with a major corporation, providing a future life of leisure and comfort for Patricia Ann. However, given the past, she might get bored again.

Weddings took the spotlight in *Murder Gets a Life* (Avon, 1998). Haley, Patricia Anne's daughter, announced her plans to marry Dr. Philip Nachman (his father had been one of Mary Alice's husbands). Ray, Mary Alice's son in Bora Bora, had married Sunshine Dabbs, who had won a trip to the island on *Wheel of Fortune*. Sunshine, a member of an extended family housed in a five-trailer compound back home, disappeared. A corpse was found, but it was not Sunshine's. Her family matched the sisters' in its complexity so keeping them all straight may be a problem for the reader.

Murder Shoots the Bull (Avon, 1999) when judged on its interesting characters and dialogue came off a winner. The narrative focused on the woes of Patricia Ann's happily married neighbor Arthur Phizer. He was accused of murdering Sophie Sawyer, the woman he had briefly married as a teenager. The couple had remained friends even after the annulment. Dying, Sophie had appointed Arthur to serve as executor and trustee of her extensive estate. There were too many coincidences for credibility, but then that's not what the series is all about.

A power struggle within a church and unrequited love were the motivations for murder in *Murder Carries a Torch* (Morrow, 2000). The narration was enlivened by contrivances such as artificial testicles as aids to childbirth, snake handling preachers, and Cousin Luke's wife Virginia who danced her way out of his life after forty years of marriage. On a more serious level, the sisters tripped over a corpse in their efforts to help their unlovable cousin "Pukey" Luke.

Mary Alice had opted for a fourth marriage to Sheriff Virgil Stuckey as *Murder Boogies with Elvis* (Morrow, 2001) began. The planning drew her and Patricia Ann into the problems of the groom's family. Stuckey's son and son-in-law were members of the Elvis kick line at a benefit performance when a fellow dancer was murdered. The victim was later identified as Russian Griffin Mooncloth, a former ballet dancer. Not only had Patricia Ann been watching from a front seat, but someone put the murder weapon in her purse. Had it not been for Mary Alice's trained karate kick, things could have been worse. The narrative glowed with the affection between the sisters and the love between Patricia Ann and Fred.

Bert and Nan Tatum

Author: Barbara Taylor McCafferty and Beverly Taylor Herald, themselves twins

As twins, Bert (Bertrice) and Nan Tatum may have been physically identical, but their attitudes were different. Nan, still single, worked as a disk jockey on a country music station in Louisville, Kentucky and enjoyed a casual lifestyle. Bert's husband had left her after twenty years of marriage. She had been highly domesticated, but was now alone. Her son Brian and daughter Emily were in college. She found employment through a temp office service, and lived in the other half of a duplex occupied by Nan. This provided her with an oversight into Nan's personal life of which she did not approve.

Nan hated to shop; Bert loved it. Nan remembered the unhappy parts of childhood. Bert saw it all positively. Nan went to work dressed in ragged jeans and a T-Shirt and had a foul mouth. Bert wore professional clothing and had a professional attitude.

When *Double Murder* (Kensington, 1996) began, the existence of the Sandersen family, killed twenty years before, had faded in the twins' minds. They vaguely remembered that the couple for whom they had baby-sat had been murdered while on vacation. So why were Bert and Nan being threatened, followed, and their homes ransacked by a person connected to that past incident? The alternating narrations distracted from the flow in an otherwise interesting plot.

As *Double Exposure* (Kensington, 1997) began, Nan had a problem with a persistent caller to her program, whom she had come to call "Looney Tunes." The woman, having heard of her prior success as an investigator, wanted Nan to solve a mystery. Nan was preoccupied with the new man in her life Crane Morgan, also a twin. He aroused her sympathy describing his grief at the suicide of his brother Lane. Lane may have committed the murder that Looney Tunes wanted solved. Bert came to rely on Hank Goetzmann, the stolid police officer who had dated Nan for a while.

The twins had promised never again to switch places because it got them in trouble. In *Double Cross* (Kensington, 1998), they did it again. They switched places and they got in trouble. Their shenanigans made it more difficult for the police to solve the murder of beautiful, but aggressive divorce attorney Stephanie Whitman. The only solution was to find the killer themselves. Bert's romance floundered over whether or not she was willing to "do it."

Although the explanation as to how Emily, Bert's daughter, confessed to murder was contrived, the dialogue or double monologue, in *Double Dealer* (Kensington, 2000) was witty. The twins harassed enough people while trying to learn who killed dishonest antique dealer Franklin Haggerty to force the murderer to attack them.

Nan pushed the envelope in *Double Date* (Kensington, 2001). She used Bert's name to enter an Internet dating service. Then she approached Derek Stanhope, whom she believed to be a respondent, as Bert. His wedding ring and obvious lack of recognition should have clued Nan into the fact that someone else might also have appropriated his name. When Stanhope was murdered, detective Hank Goetzman with whom Bert was considering marriage, suspected Bert of betraying their relationship and of murder. E-mail caused the problem but it also drew out the killer.

Light reading. Barbara McCafferty also wrote the Schuyler Ridgeway series as Tierney McClellan.

Aurora "Roe" Teagarden

Author: Charlaine Harris

Unlike many other librarian/sleuths, Aurora "Roe" Teagarden did not fade into the background as the series progressed. She became financially independent, had several meaningful relationships that went nowhere, and played a major role in each book. She was described as a tiny woman (4' 11") with brown hair and eyes. As the series began, Roe lived in and managed a Lawrencetown, Georgia town-house complex owned by her mother, Aida. Her father, a newspaperman, had moved after her parent's divorce and remarried. Like many librarians, Roe was addicted to books, most particularly to those based on actual crimes.

In *Real Murders* (Walker, 1990), Roe joined a club that met monthly to discuss true crime. Each member was responsible for preparing one program per year, researching a specific crime. Roe's assignment was the Wallace case, the factors of which were replicated when Roe found club-member Mamie Wright's corpse in the VFW kitchen. It seemed logical that a member of the Real Murder Club was involved. Roe, police officer Arthur Smith, and crime writer Robin Crusoe reviewed the Wallace case. When Phillip, Roe's six-year-old half-brother, visited, she feared a repeat of a child-killing case, and followed through until the boy was safe.

In *A Bone to Pick* (Walker, 1992), retired school librarian Jane Engle bequeathed Roe a home plus over one half million dollars. Convinced that Jane had some special reason for her bequest, Roe searched the house, finding a human skull. With the help of police officer Arthur Smith's pregnant wife Lynn Liggett, Roe drew out a killer who was ready to strike again. Roe had met an attractive man with only one perceived flaw. Rev Aubrey Scott was an Episcopalian priest.

Encouraged by her successful mother, Roe was working on a real estate broker's license as *Three Bedrooms, One Corpse* (Scribner's, 1994) began. When showing an expensive home to new plant manager Martin Bartell, Roe discovered the corpse of rival realtor Tonia Lee Greenhouse. Bantam-sized Roe used her eye for detail and a rock to clear Martin from suspicion. She had developed a passion for him.

Roe's marriage to Martin, a man of mystery, in *The Julius House* (Scribner's, 1995) included a surprise gift from her new husband. Martin purchased "The Julius House," from which a family had disappeared six years before. He was a sophisticated man, who was determined to protect Roe from the potential violence of his own business, the details of which he did not always share with her. Martin should have realized that Roe could not resist pursuing the mystery of the Julius family. Aware of potential danger, he arranged to have special security for his home, a married couple (Shelby and Angel Youngblood who lived on the premises).

Angel Youngblood was almost a bodyguard for Roe, but in *Dead Over Heels* (Scribner's, 1996) she could not protect her from a corpse dropped from a low flying plane. Victim, Det. Sgt. Jack Burns was a police officer who had been hostile to Roe. Subsequent incidents made it likely that the killer was someone who had an obsessive love for Roe.

In *A Fool and His Honey* (St. Martin, 1999), Martin was having health problems. Someone was slipping drugs into medication bottles. Martin's niece Regina descended upon the Bartell household without her husband but with a six-week-old baby. That should have been enough but at that point things went seriously wrong in Roe's life. When Regina's husband showed up he was dead on arrival. Not much room for humor in this narrative.

Roe's grief at Martin's death ended in *Last Scene Alive* (St. Martin, 2002). The return of former beau Robin Crusoe hastened the process but the cast and crew of *Whimsical Death* also came to town. The plot was based on the crime that Roe and Robin had helped to solve. Celia Shaw, the actress who would play Roe, was murdered in her trailer. Celia had a secret that explained why someone might kill her.

Roe had always liked Poppy Queensland, so she was distressed in *Poppy Done to Death* (St. Martin, 2003) when she failed to appear for the Uppity Women luncheon. She was even more distressed when she found Poppy dead. This was a family matter. Alida, Roe's mom, was married to John Queensland, Poppy's father-in-law. It got even more complex when Roe learned more and more about Poppy. There's another surprise, one that formalized Roe's relationship with Robin.

Author Charlaine Harris made Roe an engaging heroine, furnishing her with clever plots, but too often solutions depended upon mentally unstable killers. Harris has several series: (1) Lily Bard, covered in this volume: and (2) psychic Sookie Stackhouse who has a vampire boyfriend and (3) Harper Connelly, who after a lightning strike, gained extrasensory powers. The last two series began after 1999 and are therefore not included in this volume.

Sydney Teague

Author: Anne Underwood Grant

After her divorce, Sydney Teague made a life for herself and two children as owner of a small advertising agency "Allen Teague" in Charlotte, North Carolina. She denied herself alcohol, which had been a problem, but relieved tension with an occasional cigarette. Her former husband George paid little attention to the children, so Sydney made every effort to attend Joan's volleyball games and George, Jr.'s soccer matches.

Sydney's father had been a defense attorney. His moral courage in representing a young man accused of the rape and murder of a high school student was resented by Sydney. Her understanding came too late. They had been very close, but he died without resolution of the estrangement. Her widowed mother had moved to Asheville. Family support came from her brother, Bill, a corporate attorney who had failed at three marriages himself. She had good friends: her secretary Sally Ball, agency art director Hart Johnson, and real estate dealer Barbara Cates. Detective Tom Thurgood, who had been a lover, became a friend and a frequent tennis partner. She pushed her body's tolerance for stress. Frequent abdominal pains hinted at an ulcer.

The death of her good friend Crystal Ball and the arrest of Crystal's husband Fred were a shock to Sydney as *Multiple Listing* (Dell, 1998) began. Crystal was in the process of divorcing Fred, whose sister Sally Ball, was Sydney's secretary. Sydney did not believe that Fred had raped and killed his wife. With some professional and more personal help from widowed detective Tom

Thurgood, Sydney connected the fact that Crystal's house had been on a multiple listing with local real estate dealers, and that several other women whose homes were also on the list had been attacked and raped. This discovery did not end Sydney's conflict of interest as she had friends in the business.

Seth Bolick's obsession with the SNAKE project, developing a non-carcinogenic cigarette, touched Sydney in *Smoke Screen* (Dell, 1998). His desire to continue his father's crusade appealed to Roe's need to absolve herself from guilt as to her own father. Seth's death by nicotine poisoning, so closely patterned on his father's suicide, did not end the professional relationship. The Allen Teague Agency was still responsible for promoting the project. The local sheriff's decision to treat Seth's death as another suicide was well accepted by his family. Sydney believed he had been murdered. The narrative explored the plight of rural communities heavily dependent on tobacco as a cash crop, reminiscent of the Southern dependence on slavery in another century. A lost cause with dedicated adherents.

Cuttings (Dell, 1999) presented an interesting background, a gathering of floral designers in the Charlotte Convention Center, but the ending came across as contrived. Sydney had an interest in having FloraGlobal go well. Allen Teague had made the preliminary arrangements for the events and had ongoing clients who took part. One, two, and finally three significant participants were murdered. She and Tom Thurgood had different reactions to the possibility that Sydney might be next.

Grant's final book in the series, *Voices in the Sand* (2000), may have been self-published. It was remarkably different in its narrative style, more introspective and more descriptive of the setting. Sydney had no idea what she was getting herself into when she agreed to represent her Aunt Nan at the annual meeting of Dune's End Condominium Homeowners. The seaside and water had always been special to Sydney and her Uncle John but he was dead. With few allies on whom she could rely, she thwarted the plans of a powerful corporation.

Jane Tennison

Author: Lynda LaPlante

Little physical description was provided as to Jane Tennison in the novelizations of the popular *Prime Suspect* series. She could be nothing but what actress Helen Mirren portrayed her to be: a slim woman of medium height who wore her sandy colored hair in a short casual style.

Jane, initially assigned to white-collar crime, demanded the chance to head a major investigation. In *Prime Suspect* (Dell, 1993), she had her opportunity only because popular DCI Sheffield died of a heart attack while a case was in progress. The unit, which had strong loyalties to Sheffield, resented Jane from the start. She fought their passive/aggressive behavior, heightened when she ordered the release of their suspect. Only after she directed the team to credible evidence, did she win acceptance.

In *Prime Suspect 2* (Dell, 1993), Jane had just ended an affair when she met black detective sergeant Robert Oswalde at a training session and shared a one-night stand. Her ambitious supervisor Mike Kernan used the incident by assigning Oswalde to Jane's team currently investigating a murder with racial overtones. She and Oswalde managed the case successfully, but credit went elsewhere.

In *Prime Suspect 3* (Dell, 1994), the men in her new supervisory assignment resented Jane. She terminated a pregnancy, which at times she had seemed to welcome. Her professional skills were tested by official interference in an investigation of child pornography and prostitution. Jane used inside information to wrangle a favorable new assignment. She might not be one of the boys, but she had learned to play hardball.

It was not unusual for popular series to be novelized, but less frequently has the author of the television script done it. Actress Helen Mirren won an Emmy in 1993 for her role as Tennison, while the production won the award for best dramatic miniseries or special production in 1994. The television series was resurrected recently, but no book based upon the continued series has emerged. LaPlante probably just doesn't have time to write one. She has several other series, some from television shows: Jane Hewitt appeared in two books as the governor of a prison. Lorraine Page, a former police officer who became a private investigator appeared in three books. Detective Pat North was featured in at least five books. All of these three are covered in this volume. Dolly Rawlins, widow of a criminal who carried on for him, appeared in three books covered in Volume 2 of this series. New sleuth : Detective Anna Travis.

Iris Thorne

Author: Dianne G. Pugh

Iris Thorne was an overachiever, who arrived at work by 6 a.m. to get an early start at her West Coast stock brokerage. After a dirt-poor childhood and her father's abandonment when she was fourteen, Iris earned an MBA from the University of California at Los Angeles. She took a vacation in Paris before starting a job. There she met and fell in love with charming American photographer Todd Fillinger. On her return to the United States, she poured herself into her career. Iris drove a Triumph sports car, and was referred to as the "ice princess" by her fellow workers. She drank too much. There was a lighter, softer side to Iris, who had at one time been a special education teacher working with deaf children. She wondered about having a child of her own.

In *Cold Call* (Pocket, 1993), she was devastated when a street gang stabbed to death Alley, a handicapped "gofer" at the office. Iris had been unaware of ties between her agency and a major Mafia family. When she learned of financial misbehavior, she concealed money and information from the police. Iris was not overburdened with scruples, but someone paid for her transgressions.

Slow Squeeze (Pocket, 1994) failed to show Iris in a more favorable light. She was angry and vindictive when the wife of her lover John Somers sought reconciliation. At work, she competed with young Mexican broker Arturo Silva for the business of Barbie Stringfellow, a widow with money to invest. When Barbie was murdered, Iris solved the case to protect herself.

In *Fast Friends* (Pocket, 1997), Iris renewed acquaintances with Dolores Gaytan De Lacey ("Dolly"), the mother of childhood friend Paula. Dolly was having memory problems, not the least of which was that she couldn't remember executing a will in which she left valuable family land to her husband Bill. Dolly was sure she would never have bequeathed the property to Bill against her deceased father's wishes. When Dolly died, presumably a suicide, Iris had mixed loyalties. Bill, who had employed Iris' father, had helped to underwrite her college expenses. He wanted Iris to locate Paula, ostensibly so she could attend her mother's funeral, but did he have a more sinister motive? Complex, but interesting if read carefully.

Bridget Cross, the practical partner in the marital and professional relationship with her husband Kip, a computer genius, had serious problems in *Foolproof* (Pocket, 1998). Bridget, having caught Kip being intimate with their daughter's nanny, intended to divorce him. Their financial ties were not so easy to end. Bridget owned the majority stock share of Pandora, the software corporation built on Kip's creativity. She came to Iris to launch an IPO (switch from private ownership to a public stock corporation) with T. Duke Sawyer, a major dealmaker having a substantial interest. Kip opposed both the IPO and the involvement of Sawyer. When Bridget's murder was discovered, Kip was the obvious suspect. Iris had been named administrator of the Pandora stock fund; making her a target for a killer.

When Iris and Todd Fillinger met again as *Pushover* (Headline, 1999) began, it was at his invitation. He was now an entrepreneur in Moscow, seeking investors. She made the trip not only to check out the financial opportunity, but also because she still had a sense of guilt as to how their affair ended. She had a rewarding career and a solid relationship with her former boss Garland Hughes, but Iris needed closure. Within hours after he met her at the Moscow airport, Todd had been murdered. When Iris returned to Los Angeles, she could not let go. She learned more than she wanted to about Todd and about herself.

Judith Thornton

Author: Patricia D. Benke

After graduation from Stanford Law School in the Seventies, Judith Thornton worked her way up to Assistant (eventually Chief Assistant) in the San Diego District Attorney's Office. Her personal life did not fare as well. Marriage to a fellow attorney did not survive her workaholic behaviors. She and Steven developed a mildly congenial relationship for the sake of their daughter Elizabeth, but Judith never reconciled to his second marriage. Whatever marital problems she may have had, Judith was a fond mother and a devoted daughter. When her widowed mother declined into dementia, Judith designed an apartment for her in the home she and Steven had shared. She used her money to pay for nursing care, and spent leisure time at her mother's bedside. At times, Judith felt exhausted by her professional and personal responsibilities. She had her mind set on becoming a judge, using that goal to justify her concentration on work. There was no room for a relationship with a man after Steven left.

Judith's highly political supervisors in the District Attorney's office handed her a sensitive case in *Guilty By Choice* (Avon, 1995). Robert Dean Engle was clearly the brutal killer of young Kelly Solomon, but inexperienced police officers had gathered vital evidence without a warrant. The community would have had little tolerance for a failed prosecution, so it fell to Judith to develop admissible evidence.

In *False Witness* (Avon, 1996), Judith's ambitions for a vacancy on the California appellate court system were stymied by her devotion to duty. An elderly "tagger," who would identify the killer only if allowed to complete a mural on the hillside retaining wall, had witnessed the death of William Franklin Threadgill, a prosperous resident of Silverado Estates. The face of the killer was recognizable to Judith and to other Silverado residents, but could she prove her case?

In *Above the Law* (Avon, 1997), Judith's role was subordinate to that of two male Hispanics. Serafino Morales, a migratory worker, crossed the border each year to work the fields in order to provide for his family. When Rogelio Carrasco, a brutal co-worker, was murdered, the authorities were unsure whether Serafino was the killer or a witness. Young attorney Peter Delgado had been assigned to Judith's major crimes unit as a trainee. Peter had avoided dealing with the problems of migratory workers. He no longer had that option. It changed him.

The death of her mother caused Judith to be out of town in *Cruel Justice* (Avon, 1999) when the decision was made to prosecute Tom Russell for the sexual assault on his daughter. Judith did not consider it a viable case, but rather a political decision because the district attorney was up for election. Another factor was the animosity between Judith and prosecutor Aaron Mercer. She balanced her sense of personal ethics against loyalty to the district attorney's office.

Benke's experience as an appellate judge added to the credibility of the details in her narratives.

Alix Thorssen

Author: Lise McClendon

Alix Thorssen, although American, made frequent references to her Norwegian background to which she attributed her stoicism. She had grown up and gone to high school in Montana, but attended St. Olaf's College in Minnesota. That was a fine place to steep herself in her Norwegian heritage. She collected the comic book adventures of "Mighty Thor," a Nordic hero. Although Alix's original goal had been to support herself by painting, she accepted her limitations and opened an art gallery in Jackson Hole, Wyoming together with handsome Paolo Segundo. There she could continue her affiliation with art, but enjoy riding her horse, Valkyrie, and kayaking the white waters of the Snake River. Alix's income was supplemented by her work as an art fraud investigator.

In *The Bluejay Shaman* (Walker, 1994), an art fraud investigation made Alix available to her sister Melanie, when her husband, Wade, was arrested for murder. Wade, a college professor with a special interest in Native American traditions, had quarreled with Shiloh (Doris) Merkin, a former graduate student. She was deeply involved in Manitou Matrix, which combined feminism with Native American mythology. Whoever set Wade up for murder, also framed Alix for charges of vandalism. Fortunately, Alix found detective Carl Mendez who believed in her. Alix set a trap for the person she suspected as a killer, but was surprised at her catch.

In *Painted Truth* (Walker, 1995), Alix, her friend and kayak instructor Pete Rotondi, and art gallery owner Eden Chaffee were returning from the river when they realized that the Chaffee gallery was on fire. Only later did they learn that the corpse found inside might have been that of artist Ray Tantro, whose work was being displayed. He had hoped for a comeback with his showing sponsored by Eden. Alix overcame her panic when Paolo announced that he wanted to sell his share of the gallery. McClendon's conclusion was downbeat and unconvincing.

The Scandinavians have claimed with great pride that Vikings, not Christopher Columbus, first reached and traveled in North America. In *Nordic Nights* (Walker, 1999), the possible discovery of an historic rune stone put Alix's stepfather in jail for murder, her mother in the hospital, and Alix under ice. With Carl Mendez away for training, she was tempted by an attractive Nordic skier, but resisted.

The image of a wolf seen after her father's death had haunted Alix's memories. In *Blue Wolf* (Walker, 2001), the death of a wolf occurred about the same time as a request from painter Queen Johns. Queen Johns' son Derek had been killed in what had hastily been declared an accident. Years later, still distrustful of the police department and perceived by the locals as an eccentric, Queen Johns asked Alix to reopen the case. The pressures created by her probe brought unexpected results, one of which Alix deeply regretted.

McClendon is also the author of the Dorrie Lennox series.

Jordan Tidewater

Author: Naomi M. Stokes

Jordan, a graduate of the University of Washington and of the Police Academy, chose to return to the Quinalt Reservation. Like her father before her, she became sheriff of the Quinalt Indian Nation. Jordan's mother died when she and her twin brother Paul were born. Mika, her father, had suffered from problems with alcohol. Jordan's eight-year marriage to Roc ended, but he had been serially unfaithful for years. Jordan had custody of their son Tleyuk who was eight when the series began. They lived with Jordan's great-grandfather, an elder of the tribe, called "Old Man" Ahcleet.

In *The Tree People* (Forge, 1995) horrendous events occurred after a tree sacred to the Salish tribe was cut down by loggers. The evil spirit of Xulk, a shaman in centuries past, was released according to their mythology. Hannah McTavish, the CEO of Quinalt Timber, had threatened to run over protestors if they didn't move away to allow the tree to be cut down. She later regretted the act, considering the consequences; i.e. murder, accidents, and a flu like epidemic. Old Man Ahcleet was one of those affected by the "flu". He advised Jordan to purify herself to be able to deal with the evil forces. She needed all the help she could get. This was a beautifully written narrative.

During *The Listening Ones* (Forge, 1997) Stokes again blended Native American mysticism into her mystery. Jordan was deeply affected by the ceremonial treatment that led to the death of young Antonio Salinas. After his parents had died in South America, Antonio (who was the same age as Jordan's son) had been sent to the United States to be cared for by his uncle and grandfather. Jordan also had to deal with poachers on the reservation who killed bears, removed the saleable parts and left the bodies to rot or be eaten by wild animals. Again, on the advice of her grandfather, Jordan prepared herself to deal with the spirits, one of which was her deceased husband Roc, who sought to take her back with him to the Land of the Dead. Another tour de force by Stokes.

Abigail "Abby" Timberlake

Author: Tamar Myers

Fifty years before, a divorced woman in her forties might have been considered too old for a new life, but Abby Timberlake lived in the 1990s. She had always been a rebel; e.g. an anti-war protestor in the Sixties. Disaster seemed to dog her family. Her father, a traveling salesman for a clothing mill, had been killed when a seagull struck him while he was skiing.

Her husband Buford had exchanged her for a "blond bimbo" named Tweetie. Abby, a tiny woman who had the gray streaks in her brown hair tinted, lived in a rent-free home near Charlotte, North Carolina. She had turned her knowledge of antiques into a business enterprise, the Den of Antiquity. Buford, an attorney, had gained primary physical placement of their two children: Susan, now nineteen and at college, and Charlie, a seventeen-year-old high school student. Abby had close relationships with both children. She also spent time with her widowed mother who lived in nearby Rock Hill, South Carolina. Mama could be a comfort but she was excessively rude, made inappropriate choices in her male friends, and demanded a lot of attention from Abby. Her dear friend, C.J. (Jane) Cox figured in many of the narratives. C.J.'s whimsical (and probably incorrect) stories about her family became tiresome. They were a mistake to omit however because occasionally one contained a significant clue. Rob Goldburg and Bob Steuben, fellow antique dealers who shared a relationship, often assisted Abby in her investigations.

Abby's Aunt Eulonia had organized the Selwyn Avenue antique dealers, but they no longer considered her an asset in *Larceny and Old Lace* (Avon, 1996). She had let her store, Feathers 'N Treasures, deteriorate, but why would anyone strangle the old woman? Circumstantial evidence pointed to Rob, a gay member of the Association, but Abby did not believe him capable of murder. Six-foot-tall detective Greg Washburn came to agree with Abby and to value her personally. Their joint solution left Abby richer, although she lost the rent-free house.

Prompted by his diversion with a big-busted blonde, the romance with Greg had cooled by *Gilt By Association* (Avon, 1996). When Abby found the corpse of Arnold Ramsey in an armoire she had purchased from a dealer, she renewed her contacts with Greg in his official capacity. Abby had bought the armoire at Purvis' Auction Barn from the estate of Lula Mae Barras . Because she was convinced that the murder related to a secret contained within the four-piece-set of which the armoire was a part, Abby interviewed the members of the Barras family. A second murder and burglaries at the "Den" confirmed her suspicions but did not limit her investigation. Rob and his lover Bob shared their expertise and were lifesavers when needed. When Greg proposed, Abby was skeptical of his fidelity.

Abby had been too busy to talk to June Troyan when she stopped into the shop carrying a gray vase in *The Ming and I* (Avon, 1997). Only after the exiting June had been struck and killed by a car, did Abby find the vase had been left behind. It was a Ming, valued at well over $10,000. She was eager to keep the vase. There were others who were interested enough to vandalize her store, steal the vase, threaten her on the phone, and commit murder.

Greg took off on a vacation, to "clear his head" as *So Faux, So Good* (Avon, 1998) began. Abby was too busy to mind. First, their wedding announcement was found in the wallet of a dead man. Then her vaunted purchase of an antique tea service turned out to be questionable, sending her and three of her fellow antique hunters up North. There she became acquainted with Magdalena Yoder (a sleuth in author Tamar Myers' other series). Abby needed all the help she could get, because the killer was at hand.

Suspension of belief was required in *Baroque and Desperate* (Avon, 1999). Was it likely that a casual contact on an airplane would lead to an invitation to take part in a treasure hunt? Or that the maid at the wealthy Latham estate had been murdered at least once, and that C.J., Abby's dear friend, confessed to the killing? Someone stole everything in the Den of Antiquity in Abby's absence, and her insurance had lapsed. The credibility was missing too. Something good had occurred, her restless brother Toy was now top of his class at the Episcopalian seminary.

In *Estate of Mind* (Avon, 1999), an impetuous bid at the white elephant sale at the local Episcopalian church left Abby as the proud possessor of a missing Van Gogh. While she focused on how much the painting could sell for, others concentrated on taking it away from her.

In *A Penny Urned* (Avon, 2000), a surprise inheritance sent Abby, Mama, C.J., and her older friend Wynnell Crawford to historic Savannah, Georgia. There were more surprises: a cousin who became an aunt; hidden family secrets, and coin tricks. Greg's offer of an engagement ring forced Abby to make a decision.

Abby must have forgotten to take her medications when she held her Halloween party during *Nightmare in Shining Armor* (Avon, 2001). She invited guests whom she did not like or whom she hardly knew. Eccentric costumes and overindulgence in alcohol proved hazardous to the guests and setting alike. Finally in a huff, Abby sent them all home. Among the items left behind was an antique set of armor enclosing the corpse of Tweetie Timberlake, Buford's second wife. The new police detective, an attractive blonde, was not as impressed by Abby's explanations as her fiancé, detective Greg Washburn, might have been.

Abby's failure to recognize Lalique glassware might have led to murder in *Splendor in the Glass* (Avon, 2002). She was thrilled by the chance to broker the sale of Charleston doyenne Amelia Shadbark's collection. Within twenty-four hours, Amelia was dead and her glassware smashed.

Tamar Myers fans will know what to expect from *Tiles and Tribulations* (Avon, 2003): zany characters drawn together by some common interest. Here it was the "Heavenly Hustlers", a social group to which Abby's mom Mozella, belonged. Madame Woo-Woo was poisoned while presiding over a ghost busting séance at Abby's friend C.J.'s eighteenth century home. Abby did her usual "Had I But Known" bit but was rescued by her cat and C. J.

Abby had a problem saying "no" in *Statue of Limitations* (Avon, 2004) which precipitated unlikely results. Her pal Wynnell talked Abby into hiring her as an assistant in decorating the carriage house and servant quarters of the Webbfingers' estate. The property was being revamped into a Bed and Breakfast facility. Wynnell was assigned to renovate the adjacent garden. Marina Webbfinger, uppity even for a Charlestonian, quarreled with Wynnell. When Marina was found dead, Wynnell was accused of the murder. So again, Abby couldn't turn down a friend in need. She was certain that the killer was one of the current guests at the Bed and Breakfast. They were all hiding something bigger than a breadbox, smaller than a statue.

Abby and her two best friends, C. J. and Wynell, had another of their hectic adventures in *The Cane Mutiny* (Avon, 2006). It all began when Abby bid on and won the contents of a rental unit at Safe Keepers Storage. The contents included an extensive array of canes (aka walking sticks) and a skull. Unfortunately Abby had already notified the police of the skull by the time C.J. identified it as non-human. The discovery landed them both in jail for several hours. The frantic chase never ended as Abby hunted down the other high bidders for the unit, and researched the original renter, all of which kept the trio busy for 355 pages, larded with C. J.'s anecdotes about her extended family. C. J. 's knowledge of seventeen languages did come in handy however.

Abby forked over $10,000 for a wire and metal replica of the Taj Mahal at an auction in *Monet Talks* (Avon, 2005). One after another, the rival bidders had backed off. Inside the cage was a provocative mynah bird, which entertained Abby's customers at the Den of Antiquity. Not for long however, as the bird (Monet) was abducted. The ransom demand was for a real Monet, a painting! Abby investigated the other bidders with tension escalating. Her mother Mozella was in danger.

Abby, her family, and her associates seem to become wackier as the series progresses. By *Death of a Rug Lord* (Avon, 2008) C. C. had convinced herself that she was of Chinese descent and no longer wished to copulate with her husband (Toy, Abby's brother) because he was Caucasian. Abby's expertise with oriental rugs and her linguistic skills came in handy when she attended a party at newcomer Kitty Bohring's mansion. Passing herself off as a Germanic princess, she overwhelmed the fake Duke and Duchess who were guests of honor. Abby's efforts to clean a spill of Kitty's savonnerie carpet disclosed that it too was a fake. This set her off on an investigation as to how authentic oriental rugs might be exchanged for imitations.

Zany characters. Enjoyment requires a suspension of belief. Terrific titles. *Poison Ivory* (2009)

Elena Timofeyeva

Author: Stuart Kaminsky

Undoubtedly Inspector Porfiry Rostnikov was the dominating figure in the police procedural series in which Elena Timofeyeva appeared. He was a principled police official who had been shunted aside by political influence, but whose skills and intelligence made him valuable when difficult cases arose. Rostnikov built an ensemble within his unit (much like the Ed McBain stories he so admired). Like McBain, the group created by author Stuart Kaminsky was exclusively male, primarily featuring the dour Emil Karpo and the libidinous Sasha Tkach, until a single woman broke the barrier. For McBain, it had been Eileen Burke; for Kaminsky, it was Elena.

Elena had ties with the police bureaucracy. Her father had worked in military intelligence. Her Aunt Anna, a staunch Communist, had served as procurator, a post that made her Rostnikov's supervisor. When Elena moved to Moscow, Anna, though retired because of ill health, had sufficient influence to find her a position in the Special Investigations Office under Rostnikov. This was during the transitional period in Russia from the U.S.S.R. to Russia, a nation in which commercial and criminal forces challenged the power of the government. Elena was described as a brown-haired, rather plump woman, very intent upon her career. At one time she had attended college in Boston. She and Aunt Anna shared a tiny apartment.

In *Death of a Russian Priest* (Ballantine, 1992), Elena was assigned to work with Tkach whose former partner had been injured. Rostnikov and Karpo were assigned to the murder of Father Vasili, a rural priest who challenged the government, leaving Sasha Tkach and Elena to deal with the disappearance of a young woman, the daughter of Syrian diplomat Hassan Durahaman. The pattern of two or more plots, in one of which Elena played a role, continued.

During *Hard Currency* (Ballantine, 1995), Elena's skill in Spanish made her the logical choice to accompany Rostnikov to Cuba where they assessed the guilt of Russian engineer Igor Shemenkov in a murder case. Elena fended off an ardent Cuban police official while Rostnikov dealt with the political implications of the investigation. She questioned witnesses, visited a model Cuban prison, surveyed the scene of the crime, and shared with Rostnikov a private interview with Castro.

During *Blood and Rubles* (Fawcett Columbine, 1996), the unit was busy. Three cases were assigned to the officers. Elena and Karpo had been present when a tax squad invaded the home of elderly Natalya Dokorova whose brother Ivan had collected Czarist treasures. When Karpo was reassigned, Elena remained on the case because the treasures disappeared overnight. The other two subplots were more dramatic.

In *Tarnished Icons* (Ballantine, 1997), the murder of Russian Jews preoccupied Rostnikov. Karpo and Iosef (Rostnikov's son) sought a letter bomber. Elena worked with Sasha Tkach to find a serial rapist whose violence was escalating. Elena and Iosef became lovers.

The Dog Who Bit a Policeman (Mysterious Press, 1998) sent Elena and Tkach undercover to investigate dogfights and other criminal activities carried out by the Russian Mafia. Elena was considered dangerous and had to be rescued by Rostnikov. Iosef wanted to marry Elena. She cared for him, and felt no prejudice against his Jewish mother, a factor that had hampered Rostnikov's career.

The most significant strand of *Fall of a Cosmonaut* (Mysterious, 2000) was Rostnikov's assignment to find missing cosmonaut Tsimion Vladovka who had served on Mir, the Russian space station. Rostnikov soon learned that his quarry would be killed to protect a state secret. Elena, still engaged to Iosef, worked with Sasha Tkach on a theft meant to disguise a murder.

The dominating story line in *Murder on the Trans-Siberian Express* (Mysterious, 2001) was the recovery of valuable information from courier Pavel Cherkasov by Rostnikov and Sasha Tkach while traveling across the nation. Each member of the Office of Special Investigation squad had a role in the narrative. Iosef set himself up to entice a serial subway killer, but it was Elena who was attacked and injured, leading to plans for an immediate wedding.

A considerable period of time elapsed before the next in the series. The Office of Special Investigations, headed by Igor Yaklovev, was facing a takeover by a rival agency in *People Who Walk in Darkness* (Forge, 2008). The "Yak's" plan to avoid this crisis of bureaucracy was to assign Rostnikov three cases, each of which involved murder and smuggled diamonds. As usual, his unit was split into couples, each of which had the responsibility for one of the cases. Rostnikov chose Emil Karpo (still mourning the death of Mathilde, the prostitute who had been the only one he ever loved) to accompany him to Devochka, Siberia to investigate the death of Canadian geologist Luc O'Neil, who had been killed in a local diamond mine. Rostikov's son Iosef was paired with Zelach (a forty-three year-old man still living with his mother) to investigate the murders of two Botswanians, whose corpses had been deposited in a cemetery. Finally, Elena (who was engaged to marry Iosef) and Sasha Tkach took on the murder of Christiana Verovona, a prostitute, who had been killed on a train while acting as courier for money derived from the sale of smuggled diamonds. There were villains galore: brutal members of a Russian mafia who tortured the Botswanians for information; Christiana's drug addicted pimp; the hired gun of a London based corporate leader who had ordered one death and wanted more. It was CONFUSING.

Rostnikov appeared in at least four other Kaminsky narratives in which Elena had no role or a minor appearance. Kaminsky, a prolific writer had three other series: Toby Peters; Abe Lieberman; and Lew Fonesco.

Final in the series, *A Whisper to the Living* (2010)

Jacobia Tiptree aka Jake

Author: Sarah Graves

Jacobia Tiptree's parents disappeared from her life when she was three. Her father, an anarchist, allegedly mishandled the bomb with which he planned to blow up a Brink's truck. The blast killed his wife. Jacobia returned to her mother's family in the Tennessee hill country until she was grown. When she was sixteen, she took off for New York City where she fended for herself for several years. At some point, she had been sexually abused or raped. Not a great deal was revealed as to how she managed or where she obtained the funds and grants that enabled her to go to CCNY and into the investment field. However, she always had sympathy for young girls and women unhappy in their setting. It was impossible for Jacobia to change her activity level completely, but she made a mid-life correction in her setting. She quit her job as a well-paid money manager to move to tiny Eastport, Maine where she purchased a large, run-down mansion to serve as a bed and breakfast inn. Whenever possible she managed her own repairs and renovations, providing much of the humor in the series. Her husband Victor, a brain surgeon who had made a habit of infidelity, chose to follow her to Eastport. Both were deeply involved in the life of their son Sam whose dyslexia had led him into drug abuse. Sam's needs had been a primary reason why Jacobia had moved. She entered into a domestic partnership and eventually marriage with harbor pilot Wade Sorenson. The household also included Monday, a black Labrador.

Ellie White had become more than household help by *The Dead Cat Bounce* (Bantam, 1998). She was a friend, too good a friend to allow her to confess to a murder that Jacobia was certain Ellie had not committed. The victim had been Threnody McIlwaine, a former resident of Eastport who had ruined Ellie's father financially. Knowing Ellie's dedication to her dad, who cared faithfully for Hedda, his irascible invalid wife, Jacobia wondered whom Ellie was protecting. She challenged an ambitious investigator from the state district attorney's office and prodded local police chief Bob Arnold, but could not get Ellie to cooperate.

Jacobia, determined to renovate the sagging wreck of her home into a livable house, was changing herself by *Triple Witch* (Bantam, 1999). Part of the change came from her satisfying relationship with Wade Sorenson. She also had accepted that Victor had the right to be involved in Sam's life. She had adapted to Eastport where guns served a real purpose, friends could be counted on, and everyone knew more than they should about everyone else. This became important when Ellie and Jacobia found the body of Kenny Mumford, local ne'er-do-well, but a friend of Ellie's. Within a short time, Kenny's father and his girlfriend had been murdered. Jacobia learned that, even in Eastport, greed and infidelity existed and could lead to murder.

Victor's reasons for moving to Eastport were unclear to Jacobia as *Wicked Fix* (Bantam, 2000) began. She accepted his concern for Sam, but there was more to it. Putting aside their unhappy marriage, she helped to finance Victor's plan for a trauma clinic. Eastport needed the clinic. Jacobia needed Victor busy and out of her life. What she had not anticipated was the return of local bully Reuben Tate, who even as a boy had terrified his schoolmates. Tate's death did not end the problem. Instead it spawned a series of murders with Victor as the primary suspect in at least two.

Jacobia had been suspicious of Jonathan Raines from the moment they met in *Repair to Her Grave* (Bantam, 2001). He presented himself as a penurious graduate student seeking information on Jared Hayes, the Nineteenth century musician who had owned Jacobia's house. When Jonathan disappeared, his girlfriend Charmian Cartwright turned up. She claimed that he had been murdered while seeking a Stradivarius purportedly owned by Hayes. Jacobia was not sure she believed Charmian either. Amidst confusing clues, Jacobia coped with Sam's infatuation with a seductive teenager.

Faye Anne Carmody's abuse at the hands of her husband was well known in Eastport. In *Wreck the Halls* (Bantam, 2001), he was murdered and she was discovered in a bloody and confused state. Faye Anne received considerable public sympathy when she was arrested. Jacobia and her friend Ellie had a problem. Faye Anne did not claim self-defense. She insisted that she had not killed Merle. There were layers of intrigue among newcomers to the community, false names and appearances, stalking and blackmail. Other attacks took place before the killer went too far and had to be stopped. A side effect of the investigation was a restored memory of a fleeing car. Jacobia had a recollection of a car leaving her parents' home after the explosion. Could her father have survived? If so, was he still alive?

It took a nasty fall in *Unhinged* (Bantam, 2003) for Jacobia to come to the conclusion that busybody Harriet Hollingsworth had not left town, she'd been murdered. The purchaser of Harriet's house, Harry Markle, revealed that he had been the young cop who carried little Jacobia from the bombed building where her parents had purportedly died. The serial killer whom Harry claimed had followed him to Eastport targeted Jacobia and those she loved.

Jacobia needed all of her skills (CPR, carpentry and detecting) in *Mallets Aforethought* (Bantam, 2004) to rescue her pregnant friend Ellie's husband George from disaster. Good steady George was an obvious suspect when Jacobia and Ellie found the first two corpses. He wasn't responsible for the skeleton, but he'd threatened ruthless developer Hector Gosling. Jacobia wouldn't stop. She found two more corpses while George moved from suspect to victim.

Diamonds may be a girl's best friend, but it didn't turn out that way for Ellie and Jacobia in *Tool and Die* (Bantam, 2005). Kris Diamond totally bewitched Sam, causing him to dump Maggie, his ever faithful girlfriend. Kris' mom, Bella, had become Jacobia's frenetic housekeeper, driving them all to distraction. Her excuse for the obsession in cleanliness was that she was receiving death threats, presumably from her former husband. Jim Diamond had recently been released from prison after serving a sentence for embezzlement.

The chance for a short-term rental of the fixer-upper cottage that Ellie and Jacobia bought as an investment in *Nail Biter* (Bantam, 2006) had mixed results. They didn't know what they were getting themselves into. The tenants included a conman and his half-sister, a former cop, a wealthy woman and her mute teenage daughter, all attending a seminar on witchcraft. Dropping by to do some repair work, Jacobia came upon the corpse of Gene Dibble, a local street preacher. Further investigation provided evidence that Dibble was there on a drug deal. What mattered to Jacobia was that Wanda, the mute teenager, had disappeared. While Jacobia was mending fences with her father, Victor was dying. There's ghost stuff in here that doesn't bear mentioning.

Jemmy Wechsler had been there for Jacobia when she arrived in New York City in her early teens, so, in *Trap Door* (Bantam, 2007) she owed him big time. He'd made a lot of enemies. Most were dead or in prison. One was still actively seeking him so Jacobia and Wade agreed to let him stay at their lakeside cottage. She was aware that Walter Henderson, the retired hit man who still had Jemmy on his list, lived in Eastport. In fact he might have settled there just in case Jemmy sought refuge from Jacobia. Local bad boy Cory Trow didn't realize what he was up against when he had romantic trysts with Jennifer, Henderson's daughter. It was Jacobia and Ellie who found Cory hanging through a trap door in the Henderson barn. Murder or suicide? If murder, it would be convenient for Jemmy if Henderson were the killer. Sam has been off the wagon intermittently ever since Victor died. Maybe that's why Victor's ghost keeps hanging around.

The charming touches: Jacobia's happy marriage to Wade, the fellowship between Ellie and Jake, and all the tips on household repair continued to delight readers in *Book of Old Houses* (Bantam, 2008). The convoluted plot however was a disappointment. The saga of the book, which Jacobia's dad had found after a pipe burst in the cellar also continued. Horace Robotham, the book historian to whom Jacobia had sent the find for verification, was murdered. The book disappeared. Was it magical, a listing in blood of the owners of the house over the years, or a fake! Lots of characters wanted access to the book. Two more deaths followed. The conclusion was a let down, requiring pages and pages of explanations as to motivation and modus operandi.

In *A Face at the Window* (Bantam, 2008) the incompetence of the local and state police was unbelievable. Jacobia had been in touch with authorities in Manhattan who had reopened her mother's murder case. The original assumption that Jacob, Jacobia's father, had been responsible for her death had been disproved. The current investigation focused on New Jersey bar owner Ozzie Campbell, who had been at the Tiptree home that night. Jacobia, only three at the time, was a potential witness. Under these conditions it was incredible, that her husband, her father and his wife, her son, and the family dogs had made arrangements to be elsewhere. Not only did this leave Jacobia vulnerable, but also three-year-old Lee Valentine-White who had been left in Jacobia's care while her parents were on vacation.

Several of the book titles were Wall Street slang phrases, but explained in the text. Graves imbued her series with a great love of place (here in a northern locale), similar to that of Margaret Maron and Sharyn McCrumb in southern settings.

Next: *Crawlspace* (2009)

Nicky Titus

Author: Eve K. Sandstrom

Nicky Titus depicted the Oklahoma landscape and its sparse beauty, as seen through the eyes of a stranger in the land. She was a small woman with curly dark hair and brown eyes. The daughter of a widowed Army general, she had spent most of her adult life in urban areas, often in foreign countries. Nicky suffered agoraphobia when confronted with the flat, sparsely populated plains of the Southwest, and felt threatened by the closeness of the rural community. Her husband, Sam, an intelligence officer stationed in Germany, had taken inactive status when needed on the family ranch. Nicky, an artistic photographer, accompanied him, expecting their sojourn to be a short one.

In *Death Down Home* (Scribner's, 1990), Sam bypassed the local sheriff to discover why his father had been attacked and his brother killed. Sam's preoccupation with the investigation left Nicky feeling abandoned, but her pictures of the accident scene provided a significant clue. By the time Sam decided to remain in Oklahoma, Nicky felt accepted.

Sam became county sheriff in *The Devil Down Home* (Scribner's, 1991). Nicky, irritated by his taciturnity, made herself useful by taking photographs for his department, recording interviews, even studying law enforcement at a nearby college. A corpse in a benefit "Haunted House" unearthed local scandals ranging from closet Gothic authors to satanic pranks.

Meanwhile, back at the ranch...in *The Down Home Heifer Heist* (Scribner's, 1993), ranch hand Johnny Garcia became the number one suspect in cattle theft and murder. Even without a black hat, the villain was evident to readers, but the narrative was warm and enjoyable.

Note: author Eve K. Sandstrom's other series featuring Nell Matthews.

Rev. Ziza Todd

Author: David W. McCullough

Redheaded Ziza Todd, initially a student pastor, wore the clerical collar but no specific denomination was mentioned. Ziza (long "i") had attended Oberlin College, then a Rochester, New York seminary.

In *Think on Death* (Viking, 1991), the Olde Smyrna utopian community held its annual meeting just as ninety-three-year-old Nan Quick, last of the founding family, died. Aunt Nan could not have been a killer, but there were bones and a corpse in her home. Ziza came to officiate at the funeral but remained to solve the mystery.

Ziza relocated in Quarryville-on-the-Hudson during *Point No-Point* (Viking, 1992). Single at twenty-nine, she was assigned to provide youth services for a consortium of Protestant churches. She found herself caught between redevelopers and proponents of deceased sculptor Aladdin Barraclough as to the use of property. Readers were made aware that Dennis Morland who was scouting out the abandoned Barraclough iron foundry, had been murdered. His body was discovered elsewhere by elderly Miss Gatewood. Two more murders followed. The third, that of Adele Barraclough Bloodhorn, was treated as a suicide after murders. That didn't suit Ziza. The local pastors approved Ziza's plan to take her youth group to New York to assist vagrants, but drew the line when the street people returned the visit.

Nikki Trakos

Author: Ruby Horansky

Nikki Trakos was the darling of a large Greek family. Her father had retired to Florida but there were dozens of aunts, uncles and cousins in New York. Six-foot tall with big bones, long brown hair and blue eyes, Nikki could take care of herself. Bored by business school, she entered the Police Academy, where she distinguished herself by her intelligence and her interviewing skills. After working as a street cop, she became a detective investigator in Brooklyn. Still unmarried, she had adopted her nine-year-old niece Lara.

In *Dead Ahead* (Scribner's, 1990), Nikki and her partner middle-aged widower Dave Lawton, were expected to solve the murder of gambler Frank Sunmann in three days or "turn it over," so they cooperated. Nikki worked out the solution, but had to be rescued by her new partner.

In *Dead Center* (Scribner's, 1994), startled by Dave's proposal, Nikki insisted that they work separately to give her time and space. She needed his professional skills when the death of local politician Dean Zaporelli revealed an identity he had hidden from the voters and his family.

Ginny Trask

Author: Lee Wallingford

Recently widowed Ginny Trask coped with grief, loneliness and the need to support her nine-year-old daughter Rebecca. Finding it impractical to continue her art studies, she became a fire dispatcher for the Forest Service, while training for investigatory work. She met and became involved with fellow employee Frank Carver, a divorced former police detective, who served as a law enforcement officer for the Forest Service in Oregon.

In *Cold Tracks* (Walker, 1991), Ginny called on Frank officially when co-worker Nino Alvarez failed to appear. Ginny found Alvarez's body, but the murder investigation moved slowly. They discovered that Alvarez's death had important ties to the Whittaker and Meissner families. Len Whittaker was Ginny's boss in the Forest Service. Ginny's participation as Frank's assistant brought her daughter Rebecca into danger.

By *Clear Cut Murder* (Walker, 1993), Ginny had applied for transfer into the law enforcement division. Carver assigned her to the Coffee Creek district. A logging company was preparing to cut a prime section of old timber, the sale of which had been vigorously opposed by environmental groups. When environmentalist Ward Tomasovic was killed, Frank and Ginny coped with bumbling local officials and a killer's long repressed need for vengeance. In contrast to many couples in mysteries, Ginny and Frank were cautious about their personal relationship. Perhaps because he was older and her supervisor, but also because his marriage had ended in divorce, Frank postponed intimacy.

Tory Travers

Author: Aileen Schumacher

After the death of her husband, Tory Travers was fortunate to have her training as a structural engineer to provide for her and their teenage son, Cody. She had been raised in a wealthy family in central Florida, but became estranged. At nineteen, she had married one of her college professors, a man twice her age. During the series, her father, State Senator Tom Wheatley, contacted her. He arranged to have Cody spend a summer with him in Florida. Nine years of marriage to Carl and several years of widowhood had transformed Tory into a competent businesswoman.

In *Engineered for Murder* (Write Way, 1997), aware of the potential consequences to her company, she reported flaws in the construction of the new university football field. What she had not anticipated was that technician Bill Hartman would be murdered on the site. El Paso detective David Alvarez was assigned to the case. In working out her problems, Tory revealed the background of her estrangement from her father.

As *Framework for Death* (Write Way, 1998) began, Tory hadn't heard from David in months. When he needed a structural engineer, she responded immediately. Leonora Keaton Hinson, a wealthy but domineering woman, and her unidentified companion were found dead in a secret basement room. The floor above them had collapsed by accident or design. When an explosion seriously injured David, Tory took him home to nurse him. Good characterizations and plot.

In *Affirmative Reaction* (Write Way, 1999), the quality of Tory's engineering skills was called into question when her report on an abandoned development sharply disagreed with earlier tests. While inspecting storm sewers, she came upon the body of city employee Pamela Case, hanging upside down. Det. David Alvarez, currently on disability leave, was more than willing to share Tory's investigation. He was responsible for most of the evidence uncovered. The narrative took on the controversial issues of affirmative action to remedy past injustices to minorities and reverse discrimination.

In *Rosewood's Ashes* (Intrigue, 2001), when a heart attack struck Tom Wheatley, retired Florida state senator and Tory's father, she and David Alvarez flew to his bedside, unsure of their welcome. There were complications beyond Tom's health. Amy Cooper, an historian whom they had met on the plane, was struck down by a hit-and-run vehicle as she exited the airport. Cooper was connected to historical research and the legislative efforts to redress the harm done to the African-American residents of Rosewood by a vigilante attack twenty-three years before. Tory needed to know why her father, well known for his right wing viewpoint, supported the review of Rosewood's destruction. This was a mature, well-written book, the best of the series.

Melanie Travis

Author: Laurien Berenson

Melanie Travis was divorced from Bob, the father of her four-year-old son, Davey. Both of her parents had been killed in a car accident. She had supported herself and Davey as a teacher and camp counselor in Connecticut.

In *A Pedigree to Die For* (Kensington, 1995), Melanie responded when she was contacted by her Uncle Max's widow. Max had helped her father repeatedly over the years. Aunt Peg had two problems: Max's death of a heart attack which she believed had been provoked; and the disappearance of their kennel's top dog, Beau. Melanie posed as a potential purchaser of a stud poodle, bringing her into contact with those most likely to steal Beau or to antagonize Max. There were surprises ahead for Melanie (fewer for the reader) in disturbing news about Beau and Max, but a "beau" of her own in suspect Sam Driver.

The show class puppy given Davey by Aunt Peg interested Melanie in purebred poodles during *Underdog* (Kensington, 1996). The death of professional dog handler Jenny Maguire shortly after her best dog Ziggy had been killed aroused Melanie's suspicions. They were intensified when she realized that Ziggy was still alive. She concealed this information from Jenny's family. They were her primary suspects.

As *Dog Eat Dog* (Kensington, 1996) began Sam and Melanie were compatible. Then, a telephone call from her ex-husband created problems. Bob's oil well had come in. He was ready to play a major role in son Davey's life. Aunt Peg wanted Melanie to solve a murder and theft among the elite members of the Belle Haven Kennel Club. Barry Turk, a disreputable dog handler, had earned no kudos for his treatment of dogs or women. Melanie's sympathy for his pregnant lover caused her to investigate his death. There were lots of motives, but it is fair to say the killer, was not only least likely, but improbable.

When unpopular dog handler Barry Turk was murdered in *Hair of the Dog* (Kensington, 1997), there were more than enough suspects. Barry's pregnant assistant Alicia Devane came to Melanie for help. Not only was she top on the detective's list but she had been plagued with "accidents'. Some of the dog breeders and handlers were more promiscuous than their animals. Out of the myriad affairs, Melanie came up with the killer. She did one thing right. Dog groomer Bertie Kennedy's romance with Frank, Melanie's brother, had been a success.

Melanie's limited knowledge of dog breeding was sufficient to trap a killer in *Watchdog* (Kensington, 1998). She had promised Sam Driver that she would stay out of dangerous situations, but could not reject her brother Frank's plea for help. Frank had blithely gone into business with notorious land developer Marcus Rattigan. When Rattigan was murdered on the premises of Frank's new coffee house, he had no alibi and lied to the police.

Melanie's new position as a special tutor at exclusive Howard Academy did not seem likely to lead to murder and arson. However, in *Hush Puppy*

(Kensington, 1999), that was what followed her research into the history of Joshua Howard, founder of the school. When she entered a storage room, Melanie saw a young girl, Jane, who was being menaced by the caretaker Eugene Krebbs. When Krebbs was murdered, Jane, who was not a student at Howard Academy, was nowhere to be found. Melanie was devastated to learn that Sam Driver's former wife was in town, seeking a reconciliation. She busied herself rescuing Jane and finding hidden treasure.

Melanie, Sam, Sam's former wife Sheila, and her current partner Brian made for tense dinner companions in *Unleashed* (Kensington, 2000). Within weeks Sheila and Brian, who were developing a dog show magazine, were dead. Sam and Melanie's plans to marry were jeopardized. Melanie looked for Sheila's killer at Sam's request, but with concern that the solution to their personal problems would be more difficult.

Melanie had good reason to feel sorry for herself during *Once Bitten* (Kensington, 2001). Sam had taken time off to come to grips with Sheila's death. Not only was Melanie's brother Frank about to marry dog groomer Bertie Kennedy, but Melanie was expected to play an active role in the planning. Initially her assignment was to keep Aunt Peg from meddling. It expanded when wedding planner and dog handler Sara Bentley disappeared. Melanie had to find her, or do the planning herself. Bob, her former husband, returned for the wedding with an agenda of his own.

Hot Dog (Kensington, 2002) will not be to everyone's taste. Sam, Melanie's former fiancé, had returned but he would have to earn his way back into Melanie's trust. Bob surprised young Davey with a pony to be stabled at his new girlfriend Pam's pony farm. Aunt Rose, a former nun, needed a temporary home for Dox, a dachshund puppy which she intended to auction off. That infuriated Aunt Peg. Dox was dognapped in the midst of a custody battle between his breeder and her husband.

During the Poodle Club of America's annual specialty show in Maryland in *Best in Show* (Kensington, 2003) Aunt Peg, Melanie and Sam Driver performed well, but other owners and handlers cheated, bribed and murdered. When Betty Jean Boone, co-chairman of the raffle committee and owner of an outstanding entry was found dead, her sister Edith Jean carried on. Melanie had the upper hand in this one.

Stuffing is traditional for Christmas and *Jingle Bell Bark* (Kensington, 2004) had lots of it. The narrative had the basic mystery plot (death of friendly but inquisitive school bus driver Henry Pruitt), but the narrative was stuffed with advice on how to purchase a healthy puppy, decorations for the holidays, and the delivery of Bertie and Frank's infant daughter.

Taking Faith (her dog) to the South Avenue Obedience Club in *Raining Cats and Dogs* (Kensington, 2005) wasn't as easy as Melanie had expected. Obedience training is very different from dog show behavior. As a new member of the group, Melanie felt inadequate initially, but agreed to go along with the idea of visiting the Winston Pumpernill Senior Residence with their dogs. Paul Lennox, member of the Obedience group, initiated the visits because his Aunt Mary was a resident. Her death during the visit unsettled staff, residents, and the dog owners. She had been murdered which may have been a result of her plan to reunite with her estranged son Michael.

Davey had a surprise for Melanie in *Chow Down* (Kensington, 2006). He'd entered Faith via the Internet in Champions Dog Foods contest for a dog to represent their new product, Chow Down. Melanie had been unaware of the entry until she was informed that Faith was one of the finalists. She was surprised at the intensity of the other owners. Faith would compete against several different breeds. Melanie undertook a more formidable task, uncovering family and romantic ties among the dog owners and the company representatives who were to select the winner. Add on identifying the killer of Larry Kim, owner of the Yorkie. Big news for Sam at the end.

Bertie and Melanie joined Aunt Peg at the Symposium for Dog Judges, held in the Poconos, not because they had any interest in accreditation in *Hounded to Death* (Kensington, 2007), but just to relax. Bertie needed a rest from motherhood; Melanie was four months pregnant. Within hours of his controversial keynote speech, the naked corpse of Charles Evans was discovered in the Inn's hot tub. Melanie's reputation as a crime solver had preceded her so she was encouraged to get involved. Aunt Peg had additional concerns. She had arranged to meet her Internet pen pal Richard Donner for the first time, and there was a new dog in her life.

Melanie had taken a leave of absence from her teaching job in *Doggie Day Care Murder* (Kensington, 2008) to spend time with her infant son Kevin. Nine-year-old Davey welcomed his baby brother and was kept busy by Aunt Peg who was training him to show dogs in junior championship events. Melanie felt exhausted but not too tired to check out Pine Ridge Canine Care Center for her friend Alice Brickman. Alice, who was re-entering the workforce, needed a place for her Golden Retriever. That seemed simple enough until kennel co-owner Steve Pine was murdered. Steve's sister Candy who had heard of Melanie's investigations asked her to check into his death. Lots of doggie information, and friendly touches, but few surprises.

Technically well versed as to the competition among dog owners, trainers, and handlers, but no blue ribbons. Occasionally the bits of interesting dog information sat like undissolved lumps in the narrative.

Elizabeth Anne "Betty" Trenka

Author: Joyce Christmas

A tall, graying unmarried woman in her early sixties, Betty Trenka had been dismissed as out-of- date when her lifetime employer retired. He had been more than an employer to her. With an adequate pension and savings, she moved from Hartford, Connecticut to a rural setting in East Moulton. Needing to fill her time and reassert her usefulness, she sought employment. As much as she wanted to be known as Elizabeth, she always became "Betty" to new employers. Betty was feeling the aches and pains of growing old, but stayed active doing volunteer work at the library and taking part-time jobs.

In *This Business Is Murder* (Fawcett Gold Medal, 1993), Betty posted a notice card in the local grocery store, indicating her availability for clerical work. Jerry Preston, president of a local computer software firm, hired her to fill in for a few days during Denise LeGrand's vacation. When Denise was killed by a hit and run driver, Betty accepted a longer assignment, but not the official version that Denise's death was an accident.

As *Death at Face Value* (Fawcett, 1995) began, Betty was tutoring Carole, a young grocery store checker, in how to improve her employment opportunities when she disappeared. This connected with Betty's job—typing the autobiography of eccentric literary critic Crispin Abbott—who turned out to be a real pain. Then came an unexpected visit by hometown friend Viola Roman, who was fleeing from suspicion of murder. Lots of threads, but very tangled.

Sid Edwards was the only man Betty had ever loved. She wondered when she didn't hear from him after his retirement to Arizona. She learned in *Downsized to Death* (Fawcett, 1997) that he had been rendered helpless by a stroke. Eager to have access to Sid, Betty agreed to help his son Sid Jr. check his father's files. While Betty was in Hartford, Sid's wife, Mary was murdered. Betty possessed special knowledge that enabled her to tie motive to opportunity.

Back in East Moulton, Betty was restless. As *Mood to Murder* (Fawcett, 1999) began, she hired young Tommy Rockwell to work on her yard while she took a short-term position at the local schools. Robbery and assaults in the community aroused suspicion against Brad Melville who had been treated badly by East Mouton residents. He and his black-clad consort Raven were believed to have a Fagin-like control over disaffected teenagers, including Tommy Rockwell. Betty found herself in an insular village, cruel to strangers and outcasts.

Joyce Christmas is also the author of the Lady Margaret Priam mysteries. In *A Better Class of Murder* (Fawcett/Ballantine, 2000), the two women met. Betty was asked by neighbor Ted Kelso to size up software billionaire Gerald Toth. Toth wanted Ted, an accomplished computer programmer, to test a valuable new software system, ERP. While in New York City, Betty met Margaret who escorted her to glittering social events. The two became friends while solving a mystery that began with the death of Jane Xaviera Corso, a beautiful woman caught in a power struggle between software companies.

Lady Margaret and Betty took their show on the road again in *Forged in Blood* (Fawcett, 2002). Margaret invited Betty to accompany her on a trip to England for the wedding of her brother, the Earl of Brayfield, to a commoner, and then on to Rome where they would visit the home of Prince Aldo Castrocani (father of Paul, a character in the Priam series, See Volume 2). The narrative frequently degenerated into a travelogue although there were elements of theft and murder. En route, Margaret and Betty had become acquainted with noveau riche American couple Lester and Phyllis Flood, art forger Benedict Howe, and remittance man Max Grey.

Rose Trevelyan

Author: Janie Bolitho

Rose Trevelyan had been widowed after twenty years of marriage to David, a mining engineer. Her marriage had been a happy one. Left alone in her fifties, Rose took comfort, even joy, in her work as a painter and photographer. She had attended Art College as a young woman, but started again slowly with photography and watercolors; then, progressed to oil painting. The photography was her living; the painting, her passion. She lived by the sea in Newlyn, Cornwall, a wonderful place for an artist and a cook. Her parents were still alive. There had been no brothers or sisters. She and David had no children.

As *Snapped in Cornwall* (Constable, 1997) began, Rose's new friend, Gabrielle Minton, invited her to a dinner party. They never reached the main course. Rose found Gabrielle dead in her garden, seemingly the victim of a fall from her balcony. Barry Rowe, who used Rose's photographs on cards he sold in his shop, wanted to be a more important person in her life, but her feelings for him had not risen above affection. She received the attentions of Gabrielle's widower and the investigating officer, Detective Inspector Jack Pearce.

Her husband David's death had narrowed Rose's vision of her future. Ironically it was the death of dear friend Dorothy Pengelly in *Framed in Cornwall* (Constable, 1998) that awakened Rose to the need to reset her priorities. Dorothy, a reclusive woman who died suddenly, had two sons: Peter, dominated by an avaricious wife, and Martin, a developmentally disabled adult. The narrative explored how Dorothy's death changed her sons' lives. Rose, determined to prove that Dorothy had not taken her own life, persisted against the admonitions of Barry Rowe and Jack Pearce and the threats of the killer. She returned to painting with oils, opening a new chapter to her life.

In *Buried in Cornwall* (Constable, 1999), Jenny Manders, an artist's model whom Rose had met at a private showing, was murdered. Initially Rose did not connect her death to a prior psychic experience when she heard screaming from a mineshaft that contained an old skeleton. Rose added Nick Pascoe, formerly Jenny's lover, to her list of admirers. She continued to meet with Inspector Jack Pearce in the investigation of Jenny's murder.

Regardless of her beaus—faithful Barry Rowe, exciting Jack Pearce, and flirtatious art dealer Geoff Carter—Rose placed a high value on her independence in *Betrayed in Cornwall* (Constable, 2000). She was enjoying the first showing of her oil paintings but found time to help her friend Etta Chynoweth. Etta coped with a rebellious daughter, a married lover, and the death of a beloved son. Rose was determined to locate Etta's daughter Sarah, but it was Jack Pearce who paid the price for her efforts.

Hiring Rose to paint their joint portrait may have been an error for Louisa Jordan and Wendy Penhalligon in *Plotted in Cornwall* (Constable, 2001). They were unaware of Rose's connection to their nephew Joel, a student in her art class. More importantly they were unaware of her penchant for involving herself in the lives of others; i.e. a police investigation into the disappearance of Frank Jordan, Louisa's husband. Jack Pearce learned he couldn't forget Rose. Wendy's role in the narrative was confusing.

Life moved slowly for Rose as *Killed in Cornwall* (Allen & Busby, 2003) began. She was painting well and had an exhibit coming up. Her peace was shattered by a series of local burglaries and rapes, the last of which was murder. Further tension followed her mother's heart attack. There were two new men in the area who were questioned by Inspector Jack Pearce. He had hoped that Rose would not get involved. However, even when concerned about her mother's health, Rose was a person in whom people confided so she picked up significant pieces of information. Not that she couldn't make a mistake; actually, she made two.

Rose, while on the beach in *Caught Out in Cornwall* (Allison & Busby, 2003), was part of a crowd watching a lifeboat go out to rescue a yacht that had sent up a distress signal. She observed a small girl willingly accompanying a tall man off the premises. Only later did she learn that four-year-old Bethany, daughter of Sally Jones, had disappeared. This drew Rose into the affairs of Sally, her sister Carol, and Michael Poole, Bethany's father. The discovery of the child's body, the description of her clothing and Rose's growing awareness of the hostility between the sisters deepened her concern. She felt guilty for not having reacted more quickly.

Bolitho also has an artist's eye. Her descriptions are breath taking.

I am indebted to my daughter-in-law, Vonne Muessling Barnett, who reviewed *Buried in Cornwall* for me at a time when it was not available to me. It may be now but Vonne did such a fine review that I am leaving it intact.

Hannah Trevor

Author: Margaret Lawrence, pseudonym for M.K Lorens

Hannah Trevor would never have survived physically or emotionally without her Aunt Julia and Uncle Henry. Three children had been born to the marriage of Hannah and her husband James Trevor, a loyalist during the American Revolution. He was a domineering man, who thwarted her efforts to remove the children from a disease-ridden area. All three children died. James was willing to move to Maine when the Revolutionary War ended in defeat for his cause, but only as a stop on his way to Canada. Determined to have another child, Hannah seduced a married man. Their child Jennet was afflicted with deafness. Aunt Julia and Uncle Henry provided a home for Hannah and her child, but they were growing old. Johnnie Markham, their son and heir, might not be so generous. Hannah, who learned midwifery from Julia so she could support herself in the future, despised the inept Dr. Clinch who also served as coroner.

As *Heart and Bones* (Avon, 1996) began, Hannah and the local constable and blacksmith Will Quaid discovered the raped and murdered Anthea Emory. She was a reclusive young woman whose husband was on an extended surveying trip. A note describing three nights of abuse by local men (including Daniel Josselyn, father of Hannah's child) focused local attention on Josselyn as the probable killer. He was of distinguished English descent, but had given his loyalty to the revolutionary forces, serving with many of the local men under his command. Their war experiences had left him deeply disturbed. Hannah did not believe him capable of rape and murder; nor did his invalid wife Charlotte. Hannah had survived loving Daniel by staying away from him, although allowing him access to Jennet.

In *Blood Red Roses* (Avon, 1997), the body of her husband, who had been living in the area under an assumed name, was discovered. A killer had also slaughtered James Trevor's bigamous second wife and their three children. The authorities, already intent upon placing Jennet in indenture, focused on Hannah as the probable killer, forcing her and Daniel to work together to save themselves and their child.

The prelude to *The Burning Bride* (Avon, 1998) explored the tensions in the community that eventually led to rebellion by local farmers. They were forced to pay their taxes in non-existent silver, rather than the scrip with which they had been paid for their war services. Hannah was pregnant and preparing to marry Daniel, when the community exploded into violence. Daniel's recollections of the war and Hannah's bargain to save his life made it necessary for them to leave their homes behind and strike out for Canada. This was intended to be a trilogy, ending with this narrative.

Very well written, with absorbing historical details and characters. A subsequent book, *The Iceweaver* (Morrow, 2000) followed Jennet into adulthood. During that narrative Hannah, by then a widow, died.

Rita Trible

Author: C. N. (Carl) Bean

Rita appeared in only two books, but those who read them will not be surprised. Her character was flawed, not by her own fault, but by the background with which she was provided. Rita was a victim of childhood incest by her father. Her first marriage (to Steve) produced a son, Greg, to whom she was devoted, but the marriage did not survive her husband's brutality. Rita had successfully fought for sole custody of Greg. Rita's widowed mother Eva suffered from Alzheimer's, was a resident of a nursing home. Sean, her brother, and his wife Julie had acquired the family home. His leukemia was in remission, and he and Julie were regular backups in caring for Greg when Rita was hard pressed at work.

Her early experience in police work was as an investigator where her dogged pursuit of wrongdoers was an asset. As the series began she had been promoted to an administrative post as captain of the Wisconsin Criminal Investigation Division (WCD) located in Milwaukee. Unfortunately she lacked the skill set for this level of leadership and the officers under her command reacted. She had serious problems with Lt. Adam McCabe, the second ranking officer whom she had beaten out for the promotion. Her most reliable ally was African-American Charlie Dalton. Charlie was new to the unit, but had six years of experience in the Army Military Police and the Wisconsin State Patrol.

Appalled by the brutal murder of eleven-year-old Matthew Hammond (who was the same age as Greg) in *A Soul to Take* (Onyx, 1996), Rita insisted upon taking personal charge of the case and devoting major resources of the unit to it, thereby alienating McCabe and others in her unit. Further murders tinged with child abuse absorbed her energies and emotions at a time when Greg needed her. The basis for the conclusion had not been laid during the narrative. The news wasn't all bad. Rita did meet Mike Squires, an English teacher and coach at the local high school who came to play an important role not only in her life but in Greg's.

As she had in the prior book, Rita dealt with serious conflicts of interest in *With Evil Intent* (Onyx, 1999). Rita, given her personal history, was the wrong person to put in charge of multiple disappearances of youth and children in the Milwaukee area . Furthermore, the death of her friend, Madison CID official Jim Swearingen, had initially been labeled suicide brought on by charges of corruption, but the investigation grew much wider. It had broadened because of the strong-arm tactics of NCA (a national hospital corporation) seeking to acquire property in Milwaukee for a major healthcare center. The planned site would erase businesses and dwellings in a lower class African-American part of town. The suspicions that Jim was corrupt were based upon the fact that Al Hoeveler, now married to Jim's former wife Diane had ties both to NCA and to a gambling syndicate. Mike Squires, now married to Rita, might also be involved. This became even more confusing when it was learned that Scott Renneker, who purportedly had discovered Jim's corpse, was a major suspect in abuse and murder cases in other states.

Lucy Trimble (Brenner)

Author: Eric Wright

Lucy Trimble disposed of Geoffrey Brenner, her controlling husband of twenty-three years, the conventional way. She divorced him and left Kingston. She had prepared for the separation by carefully concealing an inheritance from her mother, buying a house in Longborough, Ontario, and finding working as a part-time library assistant. The house was ample for a bed and breakfast business. Her adult daughter Jill, who lived in British Columbia, was a dental hygienist. Lucy enjoyed a mutually satisfying relationship with the "Trog," Ben

Nolan an occasional guest at her bed and breakfast. Lucy was proud of her long-time Canadian heritage. Her father's family had been Loyalists during the American Revolution who, after the peace treaty, moved to Canada. Her mother's Welsh family moved from the British Isles before Confederation.

When a therapist encouraged her to get a life, she did just that. A bequest from David Trimble, her gambling addicted cousin, gave Lucy a second opportunity. At age forty-seven, she inherited his detective agency after years of reading mystery stories. Her first major case in *Death of a Sunday Writer* (Foul Play Press, 1996) was the exploration of David's death. He had been writing a mystery novel centered on horse racing. How much of it was based on fact? How much was fiction? Her other cases involved an agoraphobic wife, and a legacy left to a young boy who was transported to Canada in 1940, one of many who were removed from England during the bombings. Leaving the prosaic affair with the Trog behind, Lucy moved on to the more exciting and dangerous Johnny Comstock, a horse trainer of dubious morals.

In *Death on the Rocks* (St. Martin, 1999), Lucy's client Greta Golden, learned that the man she had considered a stalker was Michael Curnow, a British private investigator. He had been checking her for a possible inheritance. Financially independent, Greta was less concerned about a legacy than in the question of her parentage. To her knowledge her father had died as a result of a fall on a cliff in Cornwall at a time when her mother was in a nearby maternity hospital. Rival legatees questioned whether Aubrey Golden had been her father. Lucy was sent to Cornwall to find out. It was a convenient time to get away. The romance with Johnny had soured. Michael Curnow, a widower, was a pleasant and helpful companion during her investigation.

Author Eric Wright is an accomplished author, better known for his Charlie Salter series.

Baroness Ida "Jack" Troutbeck

Author: Ruth Dudley Edwards

The series featuring Robert Amiss, a rather aimless graduate of the better English schools, began in the Eighties, but was given new life when Baroness Ida Troutbeck, who preferred to be called "Jack", was added to the cast of characters. Robert, a former government employee, drifted about, knowing the right people, having a lovely and intelligent fiancée Rachel, but never finding his niche. His languid nature and his fiancée's frequent overseas postings left Robert vulnerable to the over-powering Jack.

She was a woman of considerable talent who had served as deputy secretary in the Department of Central Planning in Her Majesty's government. At early retirement she became first the bursar, then the Mistress of St. Martha's College, Cambridge. Based upon her achievements she was eventually created a Baroness and served in the House of Lords. These assorted placements gave her the opportunity to ridicule and lampoon government, politics, education, and the British nobility. On a personal level, Jack was rude, domineering, and arrogant. Her politics were conservative, even libertarian. Rules did not apply to her. She drove faster than allowed; smoked cigars where cigarettes were unacceptable, and had sexual liaisons with both genders. Robert became her emissary, her assistant, and perhaps, her stooge. When her participation in the series began, she was in her late fifties/early sixties Among the books which featured Robert before Jack entered the series are: *Corridors of Death*; *St. Valentine's Day Murders*; and *Clubbed to Death*.(all have been re-published by Poisoned Pen Press)

Jack enlisted Robert's support during *Matricide at St. Martha's* (HarperCollins, London, 1994 apa by Poisoned Pen Press, 2002) in a battle to determine the future of the College. The use of a major donation was at issue, with militant feminists and traditional scholars fighting to the death. Robert had some difficulty remembering where his loyalties lay. Spurred on by Jack he assisted in identifying a killer and in burying his own guilt.

Jack's admission to the House of Lords in *Ten Lords A-Leaping* (St. Martin, 1996, apa by Poisoned Pen Press, 2008) came at a propitious moment in English history. Animal activist groups had successfully navigated a bill protecting wildlife through the Commons. In the Lords, there was opposition from the proponents of fox hunting. A series of murders claiming the lives of nineteen members of the House of Lords raised suspicions against agitators. The killers were identified only when a survivor emerged as the intended victim.

After venting her spleen on government and academia, Edwards turned her attention to the clergy, specifically those of the Church of England, in *Murder in a Cathedral* (HarperCollins, 1996, apa Poisoned Pen Press, 2004). Baroness Jack, who had limited respect for any institution, convinced Robert to assist the new Bishop, David Elsworthy, now assigned to Westonbury. His clerics were divided between high-church homosexuals and right wing fundamentalists. Add in lesbian witches and aggressive shamans. Jack stirred the mixture, but three deaths had occurred before the killers' pattern and motives appeared.

In *Publish and Be Murdered* (Collins, 1998; Poisoned Pen Press, 1999), Robert, a Liberal in his political views, was recruited to manage a right wing journal, *The Wrangler*. Robert's appointment was opposed by the current editor who had the support of the trustees. Baroness Jack stepped in to ensure his employment. Robert, in his first full-time position in two years, made a dent in the financial problems of the journal, which were draining the assets of the Papworth Family Trust. When the editor and a trustee died in succession, not only Jack but also Robert's longtime friend, Chief Superintendent James Milton, used Robert to develop their case. The Baroness was less active in this one.

There were lots of mysteries in *The Anglo-Irish Murders* (Collins, 2000; apa Poisoned Pen Press, 2008)). Why would the British government sponsor a conference of English, Scots, Welsh, Northern and Southern Irish in Dublin? What could be accomplished in this effort to exchange and understand the culture and traditions of ancient enemies? Why was Baroness Troutbeck, well-known for her abrupt, even rude, behavior, appointed as co-chairman? Why did she accept? That was the easy one. Jack had family in Ireland whose home she had often visited and the conference was held in Dublin. Most of the original appointees had declined the honor. A series of murders further diminished the attendance. Edwards focused on the inconsistencies and the over-emphasis on the past, giving equal disdain to all nationalities.

Given the task of replacing the deceased chairman of the Knapper-Warburton Prize Committee in *Carnage on the Committee* (HarperCollins, 2004, Poisoned Pen Press, 2006), where else could Robert Amiss go but to Baroness Jack? Except for Amiss and a young Irish pop star, the committee was composed of bigots and self-seekers who traded literary favors like baseball cards. When three more committee members were murdered, the survivors sequestered themselves, and the media went wild. An explanation came from a source that only Baroness Jack had taken seriously. Robert solved his professional problems and reunited with Rachel.

Amiss even turned off his cell phone in *Murdering Americans* (Poisoned Pen Press, 2007 U. S.) to be sure that he and his recent bride Rachel were not harassed by Jack during their honeymoon. She had accepted a post as a Distinguished Visiting Professor at obscure Freeman University, Indiana. Jack didn't like the food, the hotel accommodations, and the difficulties she had bringing her pet parrot Horace along. She was disturbed when denied a permit to carry a firearm. Jack was shocked at the ultra liberal agenda at Freeman, which placed diversity and high graduation rates above academic achievements. She blamed President Henry Dickinson, Provost Helen Fortier-Pritchardson, and her bullying assistant, Ethan Gonzales and did not hesitate to challenge them. Jack went so far as to hire two young private detectives to investigate the trio. Two murders later, she flew to Europe to enlist Robert's support. Jack's casual dismissal of progress in the United States might not be well received at a time when the first African-American president was elected.

These are witty, knowledgeable mysteries with a scandalous touch.

Glynis Tryon

Author: Miriam Grace Monfredo

Glynis Tryon was an unconventional female for the pre-Civil War period. She had attended Oberlin College; then, worked as a librarian in Seneca Falls, New York. An attractive woman, she had rejected or at least postponed several marriage proposals by widowed police constable Cullen Stuart.

In *Seneca Falls Inheritance* (St. Martin, 1992), suffragettes converged upon Seneca Falls for a conference where women could issue their own declaration of independence. Glynis' work was interrupted by the death of Rose Walker, a woman searching for her birth parents. The legal rights of a woman to control her own property figured into a motive for murder. Glynis worked with Stuart and his enigmatic Indian deputy, Jacques Sundown.

Glynis' focus turned to the Underground Railway in *The North Star Conspiracy* (St. Martin, 1993). The death of slave catcher Lyle Brogan and his actress friend Luella, occurred when Cullen had left town for a new job. Glynis helped Niles Peartree, a young friend in love with a mulatto, when he was imprisoned and tried for offenses against the Fugitive Slave Act.

Glynis' feelings for Cullen and Jacques were highlighted in *Blackwater Spirits* (St. Martin, 1995). Murders, tied to the lynching of a young Seneca, were attributed to Jacques Sundown. The lynching victim had been his half-brother. Cullen was dismayed. Glynis set out to prove that Jacques was innocent. The relationship between Glynis and Cullen did not survive his suspicion that she was in love with Jacques.

Before *Through a Gold Eagle* (Berkley, 1996), Glynis had spent a year in Springfield, Illinois caring for a dying sister-in-law. When she returned to Seneca Falls, she was accompanied by her fashion conscious niece, Emma, and the corpse of a young man killed on the train. Before the victim died, he passed a gold coin and a bank note to Glynis. These later tied in to counterfeiting. Although Cullen had paid marked attention to another woman in her absence, he and Glynis worked together to uncover a counterfeiting ring which subsidized John Brown at Harpers Ferry. The romantic tension between Glynis and Jacques was alleviated when he left Seneca Falls, keeping in touch with her occasionally.

Both Cullen and Jacques taught self-defense to Bronwyn Llyr, Glynis' more adventurous niece and the daughter of her sister Gwen. During *The Stalking Horse* (Berkley, 1998), the self-defense skills came in handy as Bronwyn, then employed by Pinkerton, went undercover in the Confederacy to investigate sabotage to railroads. The plots gradually revealed to Bronwyn were insidious, calling upon her resources and those of new and old friends. Glynis was relegated to the role of chief worrier in this narrative.

The initial involvement of Glynis in the affairs of the Brent family was unrealistic in *Must the Maiden Die* (Berkley, 1999). She befriended Tamar, a mute indentured servant girl accused of murdering her employer, and correctly identified the killer. Niece Bronwyn, still in the Secret Service, worked with Jacques Sundown to cut off arms smuggled to the Confederacy, and with Glynis to locate hidden supplies.

Bronwyn and her sister Kathryn were the primary figures in *Sisters of Cain* (Berkley, 2000) while Glynis appeared only in a ten-page segment and by reference. Bronwyn served as a spy for the Union forces under the supervision of the U.S. Treasury. Kathryn, despite the opposition of Dorothea Dix to her youth, served as a hospital ship nurse under the auspices of the Sanitary Commission. Both the villainous Col. Dorian de Warde and the elusive Jacques Sundown made brief appearances.

Although Glynis had a cameo appearance in *Brothers of Cain* (Berkley, 2001), the emphasis was on her two nieces: Bronwyn Llyr, still a Union spy, and Kathryn, a dedicated nurse. They reappeared in *Children of Cain* (2002), which is the last of the Civil War trilogy.

The narratives were a reminder of the burdens that women and African-Americans suffered, and their struggle to obtain civil rights. The contributions of white males to both causes were not ignored. Glynis made a minor appearance coming to the Union hospital where Cullen Stuart lay ill with malaria.

Torrey Tunet

Author: Dicey Deere

Torrey Tunet came from a remarkable background. Her father Vladhad been a Romanian explorer, who died as a tourist boat captain off the shores of New Zealand. Her mother remarried, this time to a pharmacist. She grew up in a small town thirty miles from Boston, but had traveled extensively through her work. Torrey turned her remarkable linguistic skills into a career as a freelance translator through Interpreters International. She was working a Belgian/Hungarian conference in Dublin in the initial narrative, staying at a second rate hotel.

In *The Irish Cottage Murder* (St. Martin, 1999), wealthy Irish-American Desmond Moore offered Torrey a better accommodation in his refurbished Irish castle. He had two objectives in Ireland: (1) to earn a place among the local gentry, and (2) to wreak revenge on the English family who had owned the castle for their ill treatment of his ancestors. His most recent guests included several who had good reason to wish him dead. Unfortunately, when he was murdered, the local police considered Torrey a member of that group. Finding a Finnish corpse in the woods and appropriating a valuable piece of jewelry did nothing to help her cause.

Torrey returned to the Irish countryside in *The Irish Manor House Murder* (St. Martin, 2000) to write a series of multi-lingual books for children. With her own eyes, she saw her friend Rowena Keegan ride her horse roughshod over her grandfather, Dr. Gerald Ashenden. With her own lips Torrey lied to protect Rowena from prosecution. When Ashenden was killed in a subsequent accident, Inspector Egan O'Hare had no doubts as to who was responsible. Torrey and her lover Jasper O'Mara combined their talents to prove him wrong, sifting through decades of deceit that haunted the Ashenden family.

Dakin Cameron rescued Torrey from a pair of ruffians as *The Irish Cairn Murder* (St. Martin, 2002) began. A lucky break for him because when he needed a friend, Torrey came through for him. Dakin's mother Natalie, a widow soon to remarry, was blackmailed for an incident in her past. Two Canadians had come from Montreal: one, the blackmailer; the other, ready to stop him. Someone did, and Natalie was charged with murder. Torrey used her linguistic skills to solve this one

It was chance that had Torrey find eight-year-old Sharon waiting at the bus depot to be picked up by her Aunt Megan in *The Irish Village Murder* (St. Martin, 2004). Megan, the housekeeper at Gwathney Hall, had been en route to the town, but returned to the Hall for a sweater. There she found her employer, historian John Gwathney, dead of a gunshot wound. By the time Torrey and Sharon arrived, Megan had already called the Garda. As the village would have it, Megan who had been John's mistress, had been seeing potter Liam Caffrey. This made Megan and Liam suspects in the murder. Torrey was determined to prove otherwise with help from Jasper O'Mara. This time she not only used her language skills, but those as a thief and burglar.

Jane Turner

Author: Walter Satterthwait

Pinkerton agent Phil Beaumont narrated the series, set in the 1920s in England and Europe, but Jane Turner played a significant role. She was a tall young Englishwoman, relegated to work as a companion to a difficult older woman until Beaumont recruited her for the Pinkerton Detective Agency. The narration was interspersed with letters from Jane to her intimate friend Evangeline. She and Evangeline had been fellow students of a Mrs. Applewhite where Jane became proficient in French and German.

In *Escapade* (St. Martin, 1995), Jane had accompanied her employer Marjorie Allardyce to a country estate for a weekend shared by many distinguished guests, including Sir Arthur Conan Doyle and Harry Houdini. Beaumont was present to guard Houdini who had been threatened by Chin Soo, a rival escape artist and magician. In a broadly comic treatment, Beaumont and Jane cooperated to roust a ghost, solve the murder of the elderly but licentious Earl of Axminster, and protect Houdini. Beaumont was so impressed by Jane's help that he suggested to the Pinkerton Detective Agency that she be hired.

Masquerade (St. Martin, 1998) initially concentrated on Beaumont's Parisian assignment to probe the deaths of American Richard Forsythe and his German mistress Sabine again in a locked room. The French police had determined the case to be murder/suicide. Richard's mother did not accept that designation, even though his wife and other women of his acquaintance revealed his propensity for self-destructive behavior. Jane was present in France, assigned by the Pinkerton Detective Agency to act as nanny for the children of George, Richard's brother. Among the names dropped here were those of Ernest Hemingway, Gertrude Stein, and again Harry Houdini who helped in "locked door" situations. Working together and becoming personally interested in one another, Jane and Beaumont solved the initial case, but had to leave France hurriedly because Beaumont was wanted for murder. Next stop, Berlin to learn who may have tried to kill Adolf Hitler.

Cavalcade (St. Martin, 2005) provided a haunting reminder of the post World War I period when Germany, hobbled by reparation payments, suffered from brutal inflation. The economic conditions and the Russian Revolution influenced both Germans and foreign leaders to see merit in Adolph Hitler's new Nazi party. Pinkerton sent Jane and Phil to Germany to investigate an attempt to assassinate Hitler. They were appalled at the anti-semiticism and brutality they saw while checking who might have known that Hitler would be in the Tiergarten at that time. Both found it difficult to identify whom they could believe or trust. There was a bonus in the assignment for Jane.

Light and entertaining. Satterthwait is better known for his Joshua Croft series.

Dr. Samantha "Sam" Turner

Author: Marsha Landreth

Sam Turner was the second wife of a doctor, who had an adult son, Derek from his first marriage. A doctor herself, she had worked in a San Francisco hospital before her marriage. After her husband's death, she stayed on in Sheridan, Wyoming, fulfilling his dream of running a buffalo/cattle ranch. She was a slight blonde, who shared her home with a 200 pound yellow Labrador Retriever (Boomer), and a cat. Her father was still alive, but suffered from Alzheimer's.

As coroner in *The Holiday Murders* (Walker, 1992) Sam noticed the correlation between major holidays and violent deaths in the community. The murder on July 4th confirmed her theory of serial murders, but with an additional complication, this victim was under the Witness Protection Program. Was it a coincidence that Derek arrived in Sheridan to write an article on the buffalo ranch, and returned later for a Christmas visit? After Derek and Sam became intimate, he left town without explanation.

In *A Clinic for Murder* (Walker, 1993), Derek and Sam met again at a medical convention in San Diego. Their reunion was prompted by the disclosure of a mutual friend that Sam was pregnant. When she provided first aid to dying physician Dr. Doyle Smith, his last words "Murder, letter in safe" convinced her to search his hotel room, only to be arrested by the local police. Derek joined his investigative skills with hers as a pathologist, but both became targets for murder. The plot relied heavily on coincidence sending the couple on a honeymoon cruise with most of the suspects.

In *Vial Murders* (Walker, 1994), the series edged closer to science fiction when local deaths by smallpox were connected to a conspiracy to keep the virus alive for scientific research. Sam and Derek (currently a house-husband and father) did not work together, nor trust one another. They balanced personal and professional loyalties against the lives of local students. The narratives played upon the gender/culture clash as Sam moved from an urban medical system into a rural macho culture.

Anna Turnipseed

Author: Kirk Mitchell

Anna Turnipseed was an amalgam of races. Her mother had both Modoc Indian and Japanese blood. Her father was full-blooded Modoc. The Modoc line was distinguished in Native American history as descendants of Captain Jack, a great warrior. However, her more recent family relationships were less distinguished. She had been the victim of childhood incest.

After Anna's college degree in sociology with a minor in accounting from the University of California-Berkeley, she entered the FBI Academy, graduating first in her class. Anna settled in Las Vegas where she owned a small condo, but was frequently assigned to cases on Native American reservations.

There was horrifying violence in *Cry Dance* (Bantam, 1999). The narrative wove the needs and aspirations of Native Americans into the investigation of the death of Stephanie Roper, officer for the Bureau of Land Management. Her brutalized body had been identified by her car and DNA. Anna and Emmett Parker, a criminal investigator from the Bureau of Indian Affairs, were expected to work together investigating the connections among tribal insurrection, gambling on the reservation, and Jamaican gangsters. A man with every reason to hate Parker used Anna as bait in a trap.

The traumas of Anna's first year as an FBI agent were so serious that in *Spirit Sickness* (Bantam, 2000) she considered resigning. BIA investigator Parker who loved her, requested her participation in a major investigation, hoping it would restore her sense of competence. Navajo police officer Bert Knoki and his wife Amelia had been cruelly murdered. Working together and independently, with Anna taking on major authority, they followed a blood trail to a programmed killer. The complex narrative dealt with youth gangs on the reservation, a renegade Mormon cult, and Navajo traditions as to incest. Anna's own experience of incest personalized her involvement in the case.

Anna and Emmett were dispatched to Oregon to "keep order" and protect bones discovered by Basque shepherd Gorka Bilbau in *Ancient Ones* (Bantam, 2001). Bilbau had turned to fossil hunting to subsidize his alcohol problems. Early estimates touted by eminent archeologist Thaddeus Rankin identified the relicts as 14,500 years old and of Caucasian origin. The Native American tribes who occupied the area where the discovery was made sought possession of the bones under federal law and challenged Rankin's characterization of co-existing tribes as cannibals. Science was pitted against tradition. The narrative was chillingly explicit. Emmett's efforts to be patient as Anna overcame her trauma as an incest survivor were indicative of his strong feeling for her.

Emmett was beyond despair; his relationship with Anna survived only on the professional level when, in *Sky Woman Falling* (Berkley, 2003), they were both sent to a small Oneida reservation in New York State. The federal court decision, still not implemented, that the government had illegally taken substantial lands from the Oneidas, had caused a backlash from local whites. The whites feared that they would lose the homes and businesses they had built up over generations. This feeling even affected the judicial system. Brenda Two Kettles' shattered body had been found in a farmer's field, assuredly but inexplicably thrown from the sky, mimicking the Oneida myth of Sky Woman. Brenda had been en route to New York City, her purpose undisclosed, when she disappeared. She had reasons to fear not only white hatred but local Native Americans leaders because she opposed gambling and relocation. Anna and Emmett were caught in a tangle of local, reservation and federal bureaucracies.

Dance of the Thunder Dogs (Berkley, 2004) was Emmett's story in which Anna appeared only by reference.

Mitchell has another, shorter series featuring Dee Laguerre, a ranger for the Bureau of Land Management covered in this volume.

Mary "Ike" Tygart

Author: Polly Whitney

Ike Tygart's ex-husband, "Abby" Abagnarro, narrated the series. Ike existed only as Abby saw her, but he was madly in love and portrayed her with understanding, except for her decision to divorce him after a single infidelity. She was called "Ike" by Abby because of the denim overalls she wore, merchandised by a midwestern manufacturer, Ike Mason. She had grown up in Missouri, where she earned a graduate degree in journalism from the state university. Over the years Ike had a career as an investigative reporter roaming the globe. She had unmasked a lascivious Minnesota senator who harassed his female staff; had uncovered a terrorist training camp run by Israelis in the desert; and then turned to production of a news program for the All News Network (ANN), winning three Emmys for her skill. Abby, who served as director for Ike's show *Morning Watch*, was a native New Yorker from a large Italian-American family. His widowed mother Carole owned and managed Gypsy's, a restaurant patronized by nearby theatre personnel and patrons. In Abby's repentant eyes, Ike was naive and unforgiving, rooted in midwestern ideals of marriage. She considered the marriage had ended because the trust on which it had been based was no longer available. This did not mean they never made love. In fact, as Abby knew to his advantage, Ike was "turned on" by danger. She was described as a tiny highly organized blonde who had one blue and one green eye. In happier days they had entered dance contests together, and they continued to do most of their inner city travel on roller skates. Both Ike and Abby were creative and professional, and the background for the narratives was well researched.

The divorce was recent as *Until Death* (St. Martin, 1994) began. Abby was still begging for forgiveness. Connie Candela, the new co-anchor on *Morning Watch*, was discovered dead minutes before the show was to begin. Ike and Abby still had to produce a program, but they did so under the eyes of Captain Dennis Fillingeri, who found Ike attractive and Abby suspicious. Ike's expertise in the Mideast and Abby's careful eye for detail led to a spectacular conclusion, but no reconciliation.

By *Until the End of Time* (St. Martin, 1995), Ike had ended a romance with Fillingeri, but she and Abby had to work with him again. A chance attack on Abby tied into a serial killer who murdered homeless men found with their faces painted yellow. The subsequent murder of Dr. Hektor Stefanopolis, a researcher who had appeared on *Morning Watch*, made the connection between Abby's assailant and the serial deaths. Ike and Abby had a wild ride figuring it out.

A shotgun blast during a New York Knicks/Chicago Bulls basketball game at Madison Square Garden began *Until It Hurts* (St. Martin, 1997). Fans and players dropped to avoid injury. "The Big Chill," Archie Thorpe, a major star for the Knicks, did not rise. Abby and Ike, who attended the game with her sound technician Church Finnegan, were shocked to learn that Thorpe did not die from the gunshot, but had been stabbed by a sharp object. Abby, who had chased after the shooter, was reluctant to share his insights with unfriendly police detective Dennis Fillingeri. Thorpe's purchase of huge tracks of forest in Brazil, which he intended to clear to raise cattle, had made him no friends among environmentalists. That seemed a weak motive to murder compared with Thorpe's irresponsible romantic life or the impact of his retirement. The method of murder and its delivery were innovative.

These were well-plotted narratives, with clues planted to maintain the reader's interest; however, Ike and Abby never moved beyond their original characterizations.

Amanda Valentine

Author: Rose Beecham, pseudonym for Jennifer Fulton

Amanda Valentine had dual citizenship—American through her mother, and New Zealander through her father. She was eleven when her parents separated, leaving her in her father's custody. Although she had a Ph.D., she became a police officer, first in New York City, then in Wellington, New Zealand. An attractive blonde, Amanda had not totally recovered from the tragic shooting of her female lover on the steps of a police station.

During *Introducing Amanda Valentine* (Naiad, 1992), Amanda juggled an attack on a transvestite informer, financial transgressions in the municipal offices, and a serial murderer, known as the Garbage Dump Killer. She dealt with seductive television reporter Debby Daley on the personal level. She was successful in her investigations, but became disillusioned, and resigned her position to return to the United States.

The one-year hiatus in the United States ended, Amanda returned to New Zealand in *Second Guess* (Naiad, 1994). Political pressure was applied when Sybil Knight, daughter of a prominent Wellington family, was found dead in the "dungeon" of a lesbian nightclub. The owner of *Lynx* Casey Randall described Sybil as her best friend, but Kim Curtis was Sybil's housemate and partner. The medical examiner said the body had been moved there and that

Sybil had recently had an abortion. The Knight family all produced alibis. In a second case, truant children of welfare parents had disappeared. Detective Janine Harrison had indicated that she was in love with Amanda, but Amanda was still attracted to reporter Debby Daley.

By *Fair Play* (Naiad, 1995), Amanda was struggling to keep her understaffed unit functioning while many officers were diverted to deal with political demonstrations. As a result, she took personal charge of the murder of Bruce Petty, a gay Australian who had jumped bail on charges of financial mismanagement. She also involved herself in a case of lesbian rape with no sympathy for the perpetrator. The dialogue in this narrative was cruder and more sexist than in the earlier books.

Beecham had a second series after 2000 featuring Jude Devine, a detective for the Montezuma County Sheriff's office.

Tessa Vance

Author: Jennifer Rowe

Tessa's father, Senior Sgt. Doug Vance, was a legend in the police department. His utter devotion to his work unfortunately left little time for family. He was killed in action. Her mother was deeply disappointed when, after Tessa finished her university degree, she entered the Police Academy. She eventually rose to be a senior detective in the homicide squad. In order to please her lover Brett, Tessa asked for a transfer to the district in Sydney closest to the apartment they shared. This was Doug Vance's old stomping ground. His reputation was both a burden and a blessing for her. She was allowed to make the transfer, but was perceived as receiving special treatment. Her reputation was that she was "undisciplined" but intuitive. While in the prior unit, Tessa had testified against Brady Mumm a cold killer.

Tessa made an inauspicious start at her new precinct in *Suspect* (Ballantine, 1999) published as *Deadline* in Australia. Within days her life was in chaos. Brett, tired of competition from her work, decamped. Brady Mumm was paroled, and Tessa attributed anonymous phone calls and mischief to him. The homicide unit focused on a series of deaths with distinctive touches. Tessa played a substantial role in deducing the pattern of the killer, earning the respect of her new partner Steve Hayden. It was incomprehensible that neither Tessa nor her superior officers at the prior precinct notified her current inspector of the possible danger to Tessa from Brady Mumm.

The Haven, an estate owned by reclusive Rachel Bryde in *Something Wicked* (Allen & Unwin, 1998; Ballantine, 1999) was the setting for the bizarre death of aging pop star Adam Quinn. Quinn had joined the Bryde household, consisting of Rachel and her three socially isolated daughters, more than four years before. Steve and Tessa were sent from the Sydney police force because there was suspicion of homicide. Their technical skills were supplemented by a canny local constable, but matched against layers of deceit and horror and evil. Rowe added the haunting quality of Daphne du Maurier to a police procedural.

Rowe has a longer series featuring Verity "Birdie" Birdwood, covered in Part 1 of this volume.

Fran Varaday

Author: Ann Granger

Fran Varaday was a startling contrast to author Ann Granger's other female sleuth, Meredith Mitchell. Where Merry had been a diplomatic official, Fran, a frequently unemployed actress, was an outsider. Where Merry tended to be highly organized, Fran was a free spirit. She had been deeply affected by her mother's abandonment. She had attended a good private school at great sacrifice to her father and grandmother Varaday, but was asked to leave because of her behavior and appearance. Fran wanted to be an actress, but her drama course at the local technical school ended with her father's death and the increasing health problems of her grandmother.

When Gran died, there was no one to care for Fran. She took to the London streets at age sixteen. Over the ensuing years she had a variety of living situations: a commune of squatters, an dangerous apartment arranged by local government officials, and best of all a basement flat provided by a grateful client. When this ended, she slept in a friend's garage. She acquired Bonnie, (possibly a Jack Russell terrier) by default. Employment was no easier. Low-level jobs came along, but didn't last. Her friend, Ganesh Patel often supplied weekend or part-time work for her through his family's grocery businesses. Friendship was a possibility; a real emotional connection, less likely.

In *Asking for Trouble* (Headline, 1997), the young woman they knew as "Terry" joined the squatters' commune on Jubilee Street but she never bonded. After a summons to evict them all from the building, the group prepared to leave. At that point, they found Terry hanging from the light fixture in her room. Inspector Janice Morgan agreed that this was unlikely to be a suicide. Terry's grandfather, Alistair Monkton, paid Fran to research the years that Terry had been a runaway, and why anyone would want her dead. Ganesh reluctantly aided and abetted.

Even with a basement apartment and friendly landlady Daphne Knowles in *Keeping Bad Company* (Headline, 1997), Fran could not stay out of trouble. A chance encounter with boozy old Alkie Albie Smith involved her in the abduction of a wealthy young woman. The narrative provided lively twists and turns of plot. Former nemesis Sgt. Wayne Parry, almost became an ally. More alarmingly he became fond of Fran. She saw close relationships as a trap, and was wary of them.

In *Running Scared* (Headline, 1998), problems piled up for Fran at home and at work. Twin nephews wanted Daphne Knowles to deed over her home to them in order to avoid eventual death taxes. Fran was well aware of their distaste for her. Tig, a frightened juvenile, needed help to return to her country family. She had been "on the street" and was uncertain of her welcome. By now Fran thought of herself as being a part-time enquiry agent. Worst of all, an injured reporter had left damaging evidence in the store managed by Ganesh. When the reporter was murdered, Ganesh and Fran were targeted. They had every right to be scared.

The news that her mother Eva, who had abandoned Fran as a small child, was dying came to her via a private investigator in *Risking It All* (Headline, 2001). After years of feeling rejection, Fran had mixed feelings about Eva. Even more so when she visited her at the hospice, only to learn that her mother's dying wish was to know the welfare of a younger daughter, Fran's half-sister, whom Eva had given up for adoption. Rennie Duke, the investigator who had located Fran, was found dead by Fran and Ganesh Patel. Inspector Janice Morgan had dealt with Fran before and wanted more information than Fran was willing to give. Her prospects were looking up as the narrative ended.

No way was Fran going to work for P.I. Susie Duke during *Watching Out* (Headline, 2003). She was too busy with a part in *The Hound of the Baskervilles* to be produced in an upstairs room at the Rose pub. That wasn't enough to live on but Fran also waited on tables at the Pizzeria San Gennaro. She was not however too busy to help Ion Popescu, a sixteen-year-old Romanian refugee, find his brother Alexander. When Ion was murdered, she made time to identify his killer.

Mickey Allerton, owner of adult entertainment clubs in London, was no favorite of Fran's, but in *Mixing with Murder* (Headline, 2005), he made her an offer she couldn't refuse. She was to take a message to Allerton's runaway employee Lisa Stallard and convince Lisa to at least call him or Bonnie, Fran's dog, would die. Fran had no idea what a mess she was getting into when she set out for Oxford where Lisa's parents lived. Mickey had his minions watching her every move, but Lisa was a far more elusive target than either Fran or Mickey realized. Then, of course, there was murder.

It took only one quick look and Fran recognized "Mad Edna", an older woman she had known when she too was on the streets, but in *Rattling the Bones* (Headline, 2007) Fran couldn't let it go at that. It became clear to her that Edna was being followed by private detective Duane Gardiner. Who had hired him and his partner Lottie Forester? When Duane was murdered, Inspector Janice Morgan was in charge. She and Fran had a history. Fran was certain that Duane's murder was connected to Edna, but she couldn't convince Janice, so she'd have to do it herself. With help from a mysterious stranger, she "rattled the bones".

Note also: Granger's Mitchell and Markby series, covered in this volume. A new historical mystery series featuring Lizzie Martin has emerged.

Robin Vaughan

Author: Carolyn Banks

Robin Vaughan was a plump, brown-haired young woman. Her husband Jeet earned a comfortable living as food critic for the Austin *Daily Progress*, allowing her to indulge in her favorite, but expensive, sport of dressage. Her training exercises and competition brought her into the world of the wealthy and socially prominent.

Nika Ballinger, whose enthusiasm for dressage was not matched by her skill, was killed in what seemed to be an accident as *Death by Dressage* (Fawcett, 1993) began. Robin's awareness that Nika had been photographed with a horse not her own and in a habit designed for the highest level of skill dressage prompted her to investigate. A reward in the form of a second horse encouraged Robin to continue her detection.

In *Groomed for Death* (Fawcett, 1995), Robin accompanied Jeet to New York, where he negotiated a book contract. Surprisingly she managed to find horses, dressage, and murder through a casual acquaintance picked up on the city streets. She lied to her husband and to Flora Benavides, the new friend who was killed in what was perceived as an accident. Accidents did not happen to Robin's acquaintances, so she tied up New York traffic with a frantic gallop down the avenues, and complicated a formal investigation of a sweatshop operation.

Robin visited Mexico in *Murder Well-Bred* (Fawcett, 1995). She parlayed Jeet's assignment to describe Mexican food into a commission to write an article about Mexican horse ranches. Her recollection of a birthmark on a foreign dressage horse led her into danger, and may have contributed to several murders.

The Vaughan's return to Austin was short-lived because during *Death on the Diagonal* (Fawcett, 1996) Jeet managed a small town weekly whose deceased editor Townsend Loving had been a personal friend. This was expected to be a short-term assignment while a replacement could be found; nevertheless, Robin and her horses moved to Bead, Texas. Her first concern was to find a stable and exercise yard. In doing so, she discovered who had killed Loving.

A Horse to Die For (Fawcett, 1996) found Robin perplexed. The gift horse owned by her dear friend Lola Albright could be a killer or the reincarnation of a dead horse. Either way, someone took Robin's investigation seriously enough to want her out of the way.

Light fare for horse lovers.

Ronnie Ventana

Author: Gloria White

Ronnie Ventana, a former parole agent, became a licensed private detective hoping her Japanese language skills would provide her with work in industrial espionage. Her Mexican father had been a jewel thief; her mother, an American socialite who joined him in his escapades. Ronnie's three-year marriage to Mitch had ended eight years before the narrative began.

During *Murder on the Run* (Dell, 1991), Ronnie witnessed a murder while jogging along San Francisco Bay. While attending a professional meeting, she recognized the killer. Knowing her father's record, Lt. Philly Post of the SFPD had a problem with Ronnie's credibility. The man she had identified was Pete August, a former investigator for the District Attorney's office. With the help of "Blackie" Coogan, her sixty-five year old retired mentor, she avoided being caught in a dangerous vendetta.

Bink Hanover, a certified public accountant who had once saved Mitch's life, thought Ronnie could save him from vengeful Mary Solis, whom he referred to as the "Black Widow," in *Money to Burn* (Dell, 1993). Ronnie knew that Bink was undependable but quickly became so involved in his problems that she needed Mitch, "Blackie" and Lt. Post to put the matter to rights.

Ronnie allowed herself to be set up as a murder suspect in *Charged with Guilt* (Dell, 1995). Her assignment, to test the security of State Senator Payton Murphy's home, was bogus, and the senator was dead on her arrival. Ronnie not only had to prove her innocence, but protect herself and Buddy, a developmentally disabled youth, from vengeful killers.

The anniversary of the deaths of Ronnie's parents had special meaning for her. As *Sunset and Santiago* (Dell, 1997) began, she returned in the early hours of the morning to the street corner where their accident had occurred. In so doing, she was a witness to the dumping of an unidentified corpse. Young Marina Murieta, who had followed Ronnie, could identify one of those who dropped the body. The police placed no value on Marina's identification, even though the man was found dead later. Ronnie knew that the hostility which city prosecutor Harland P. Harper felt for the Ventana family was part of the problem. She could not understand why her friend Lt. Philly Post would cooperate with a cover-up.

Ronnie returned in *Death Notes* (Severn House, 2005) in a narrative steeped in the atmosphere of night clubs, alcohol, drugs, and pure jazz. Along with her pal Blackie Coogan, Ronnie attended the comeback performance of composer and tenor sax great Match Margolis. After a performance featuring several new compositions, Match was knifed to death. The rumor that he had told Ronnie the name of his killer put her in jeopardy not only with Lt. Post but with Match's family, friends, and band members. Note that this was published in England.

Child care was not among Ronnie's basic skills so in *Cry Baby* (Severn House, 2006) she was horrified to realize that her high school pal Analisa Bugatti had left her sitting in a restaurant with two infants of unknown origins. Suspense built when she realized there were others who desperately wanted possession of the children, enough to kill. Ronnie was unsure whether Analisa and her boyfriend Zach were victims or villains...maybe both. Excellent narrative.

White had clever plot twists and an engaging character. Her later narratives continued to show improvement.

Victoire Vernet

Authors: Quinn Fawcett, pseudonym for Chelsea Quinn Yarbro, and Bill Fawcett .

Madame Victoire Vernet was a petite young Frenchwoman married to Lucien Jeannot Vernet, a gendarme official attached to the Egyptian-based army of Napoleon Bonaparte. Victoire's family was middle class, but the nobility and monarchy had been displaced. She had a private education, encouraged by a mother who had managed the family business in her husband's absence. Victoire had no hesitation about accompanying her husband to Egypt although few reputable women were on the scene of Napoleon's military conquests.

In *Napoleon Must Die* (Avon, 1993), Lucien was held responsible when a golden scepter of symbolic importance to the Egyptians was stolen from booty confiscated by French soldiers. Napoleon decoyed Lucien with a mission, leaving Victoire as a possible accomplice under the care of Marmeluke Roustam Raza. Victoire's determination to discover who stole the scepter and killed the guard convinced Raza of her innocence. Together they provided information that saved Napoleon's life.

Napoleon's safety was at risk again in *Death Wears a Crown* (Avon, 1993). While Lucien traveled to Belgium on business, Victoire carried secret dispatches from the French coast to Paris. Even after her arrival in the capital city, she had to confound French exiles, British patriots, and members of the Imperial staff determined to depose Napoleon. As the narrative ended, Victoire, who was despondent about an earlier miscarriage, was happy to learn that she was pregnant.

Lightweight, but not everyone wants to challenge their intellect in his or her spare time.

Under the name Quinn Fawcett, there were two succeeding series; one based on Mycroft Holmes, the other on Ian Fleming. As Chelsea Quinn Yarbro she had a series beginning in the 1970's featuring Charles Spotted Moon and Morgan Studevant (see volume 1 of this series.)

Dr. Anne Vernon

Author: Alan Scholefield

Anne Vernon had been raised by her father Henry Vernon, a prosecutor and jurist in the British colonial service in Africa and later an advisor to independent African governments. Her mother, unable to cope with life in Africa, left the family home and returned to England when Anne was a small child. Subsequent contacts between mother and daughter had been rare. Anne returned to England for her medical training, finishing up at the distinguished St. Thomas' facility. She had tentatively accepted a position with a London medical practice, when she learned of her father's illness. During the interval when she was making arrangements for Henry's recuperation and move back to England, the firm rescinded its offer.

There had been alternatives for Anne. By that time, she had met and become pregnant by Paul, a young architect responsible for an addition to the medical facility where she was training. Paul's death in a tragic accident before they could be married left Anne with the joys and difficulties of raising her daughter Hilary ("Hilly"). The decisions to move to Kingstown, to accept a position in the medical service of the Kingstown Prison, and to purchase a large home jointly with her father, all came together at once. Her other option had been to accept the offer made by her lover, business tycoon Clive Parker, for marriage and a subsidized career in private practice. Clive had been an emotional resource for Anne after Paul's death. He loaned her the money to pay her share of the cost of the Kingstown house. Even with these connections, or perhaps because of them, Anne was unsure that she could make a future with Clive.

Burn Out (Headline, 1994) began with Anne's first days at the prison: her kind welcome by Dr. Tom Melville, head of the Medical Service; the hostility of Jeffrey Jenks, chief of the Nursing Services, and her empathy for former professional tennis player, Jason Newman. An avid tennis player, Anne had played a doubles match against Newman in her early teens, one that convinced her that she had no future in the game. He was in Kingstown on remand, awaiting trial. Anne's professional role was to evaluate his condition for the court, but she needed to know more about him. Henry Vernon became the investigator, meeting with the emotionally disabled members of Jason's family and probing into the background of the alleged victim.

Haunted by the suicide of a convicted prisoner, later shown to be innocent, Anne and Tom Melville made every effort to safeguard remand prisoner Mason Chitty in *Buried Treasure* (Headline, 1995). He had pleaded his innocence in the alleged death of Sharon Benson, a young woman with whom he had an affair. The failure to find Sharon's body was not only a flaw in the prosecution's case, but a source of anguish to her mother Lily. While Anne and Henry investigated the Chitty family background, Lily and newfound allies searched for the body. Watchman Malopo, Henry's law clerk and major domo in Africa, joined the Vernon household and added his skills to the search. Another interesting exploration of family dynamics, upper class attitudes to unwed pregnancy, sibling rivalries, and mother-daughter relationships.

Francesca Vierling

Author: Elaine Viets

The marriage of Francesca's parents, thought to be pillars of the church and the suburb of Crestwood, had been a fraud. Both were closet alcoholics who quarreled violently, leaving little time for their daughter. When Francesca was nine, her mother, enraged by her father's infidelity, killed him and shot herself. Her maternal grandparents were older and less wealthy, but they provided her with a stable environment and a sense of being loved.

Little was said of her education but she had been a columnist for the St. Louis *City Gazette* for 15 years when the series began. Francesca enjoyed her job, but was contemptuous of her immediate supervisor Charlie; of Hadley Harris III, the prudish managing editor; and of the sycophants who prospered under this regime. The *Gazette* was heavily beholden to its advertisers, and prided itself on being a clean wholesome publication. Charlie, a notorious letch, failed to live up to these standards. Georgia T. George, the assistant managing editor, was not only the most competent person on staff, but served as a mentor to Francesca. Both realized that the non-resident publisher was unlikely to support the female staff members.

Because of the popularity of her columns, Francesca was allowed considerable leeway. She was the free wheeling columnist on a hidebound newspaper. The *Gazette* had been a vital influence in the community, but the quality of staff had declined over the past decades. She spent more time at places like Uncle Bob's Pancake House than she did at the office. It was there that individuals sought her out with interesting tips for feature stories.

Francesca described herself as "Scrubby Dutch," one of the hardworking Germans who had built St. Louis into a thriving community. The downtown of St. Louis had deteriorated with the relocation of its more prosperous citizens to the suburbs, but Francesca preferred it. The personal rejection she had felt from neighbors and classmates after the tragedy of her parent's deaths left her prejudiced against their conventional lifestyle. She mixed with homosexuals, prostitutes, and minorities without patronizing them, still living in the building that had been her grandparents' home. Francesca was most at home in bars and libraries. Like many other female sleuths, she was attached to her ancient car, a 1986-88 blue Jaguar which she named Ralph. She described herself as a tall blonde in her late thirties. Among her resources were Marlene, the outspoken waitress at Uncle Bob's; Cutup Katie, an assistant medical examiner; and on occasion Detective Matt Mayhew.

Lyle Donnegan, Francesca's long time lover, was an English professor at a local university. He was there for her whenever needed, but she refused to move into his home. When depressed she insisted upon being alone. He offered marriage and security but she was not ready. She had been raised a Catholic but when she considered marriage, spoke of going before a minister, and dodged that question whenever possible.

Backstab (Dell, 1997) mixed a fond description of downtown St. Louis, Missouri and its residents with a mildly tawdry story of murdered transvestites and gay men. Author Elaine Viets provided great character studies, and interesting vignettes that illuminated the eccentricities of the Germanic culture of old St. Louis. Francesca challenged the administration at the *Gazette* to report honestly about conditions that Charlie and Hadley would prefer to ignore.

Viets delivered an engrossing mystery wrapped in an expose of the rich and righteous in *Rubout* (Dell, 1998). Sydney Vander Venter had an extreme reaction to her pending divorce from her powerful and wealthy husband. She took up with the Harley bikers, attending their ball, dressed fit to kill. Someone did. Francesca, also present at the gala, went beyond the easy suspects—the motorcyclists. A born and bred Southsider, she focused on residents of Ladue, where the Vander Venters resided. Fortunately she avoided a trip that the killer had planned for her.

Property values had risen due to the rehabilitation of homes on North Dakota Place in *The Pink Flamingo Murders* (Dell, 1999). The ramrod tactics of Caroline, a real estate dealer and the force behind the changes, aroused admiration in some, resentment in others; and finally murder in one. Francesca checked out Caroline's neighbors, treading carefully so as not to rile Charlie at the *Gazette*. Her concentration on the North Dakota murders blinded her to what was happening in her personal life.

Georgia T. George was the only management level employee at the *Gazette* that Francesca could tolerate, or even feel affection toward. So in *Doc in the Box* (Dell, 2000), she made herself available to transport Georgia to her radiology and chemotherapy appointments. Both women were appalled at the callous treatment the radiation therapy staff provided. Someone was even more ticked off. Doctors in the box-like Wellhaven Medical Arts Building, in the hospital clinic, and in their private offices were being shot. There was a great story there, a potential winner. Although nominated, Francesca did not win the McNamara award but came away with a prize.

The series provided good local color: what matters in St. Louis; the traditional foods and drinks; the variance in neighborhoods. If you want the inside story of St. Louis as seen by Viets, these are worth reading. Francesca took on all of the local powers: the Catholic Church, the police department, the *Gazette*, and city administration. She pointed out their flaws and worked with the "good guys and gals" in the system. She could be compared to Warshawski, except Francesca had a sense of humor. Actually Francesca rarely figured out the killer until she was face to face with him or her wielding a weapon. What's more she admitted this limitation.

Viets has two new series: *The Dead End Job Mysteries* featuring Helen Hawthorne and one showcasing shopper/investigator Josie Marcus. She has left St. Louis behind, but she took her quirky sense of humor and caustic wit with her.

Jackie Walsh

Author: Melissa Cleary

Jackie Walsh, a single mother, found all of the excitement she wanted when she added Jake, an Alsatian retired from the police department K-9 corps, to her household. Not only did Jake become a companion for Peter, her ten-year-old son, but he also protected their home in Palmer, Ohio. After her divorce, Jackie had returned to a larger city, where she was employed as a cinematographer in the Communications Department of Rodgers University. During the first three books, a continuing sub-plot was the search for the killer of Jake's owner, retired police officer Matt Dugan.

In *A Tail of Two Murders* (Diamond, 1992), Jackie discovered the corpse of Philip Barger, head of the Communications Department. Jackie's knowledge of intellectual theft helped Lt. Mike MacGowan solve the mystery. He became an important part of her life. MacGowan and Medical Examiner Cosmos Gordon were friends of Dugan and actively seeking his killer.

The internecine war among dog breeders in *Dog Collar Crime* (Diamond, 1993) flared when Basset fancier Mel Sweeten was murdered. MacGowan used Jackie and Jake for access into dogdom, and the case to ingratiate himself with the Walsh family.

Reporter Marcella Jacobs returned to Palmer from a high-powered job in Philadelphia in *Hounded to Death* (Jove, 1993). Her exposé of local politician Morton Slake became dangerous when Bambi, his mistress, was murdered. Jackie not only identified Bambi's killer, but also solved the murder of Matt Dugan. She and MacGowan carried on a circumspect courtship.

In *Skull and Dog Bones* (Jove, 1994), Ralph Perrin, the potential biographer of a pioneer female director, contacted Jackie shortly before he was found dead. With Jake seriously injured by a burglar, Jackie and Mike visited the West coast where the murder occurred, but a murky ending brought the solution back to Ohio.

The wealthy and stingy Goodwillie family was the source of problems in *First Pedigree Murder* (Berkley, 1994). Jackie pressured the family to donate money for a campus building. Mannheim, the kinder, gentler brother, was murdered on stage during the dedication. The clue to the killer might be a videotape of the ceremony. The narrative, interspersed with extraneous material, used a killer who had made only a minor appearance.

In *Dead and Buried* (Berkley, 1994), who would believe that Merida Green, a murderer Jackie helped to convict, would be paroled after 18 months? Or that she would join up with Jackie in solving the deaths of Palmer campus security chief Walter Hopfelt and Jake's former trainer Con Mitchell. An added pet, Maury, son of Jake, was an untrained undisciplined animal that author Melissa Cleary used for comic relief.

Maury played a larger role in *The Maltese Puppy* (Berkley, 1995) during which Dr. Linus Munch, a former Nobel Prize winner, came to the Palmer campus, only to be stabbed in the back.

Marcella Jacobs, Jackie's friend and an investigative reporter, went undercover at the local zoo during *Murder Most Beastly* (Berkley, 1996). She planned to expose shoddy conditions, but a nine-foot tall ostrich savagely attacked Marcella and her escort. Jackie investigated the death of the keeper who had escorted Marcella and probed a series of illnesses incurred by children who visited the zoo. A friendly gorilla lent a hand.

Frances Costello, Jackie's mother, was filling her hours with good deeds as *Old Dogs* (Berkley, 1997) began, which was fine until she involved her daughter. Winnie Swann, the elderly nursing home resident whom Frances visited, had exhausted her funds. She was certain that somewhere in the Swann home money had been secreted to sustain her. Mr. Swann, she declared, had been a bank thief. Incredible, but worth investigating. The "old dogs" were elderly men who had been undisciplined in their youth, one of whom would kill to keep their secret.

And Your Little Dog, Too (Berkley, 1998), the best book of the series, opened as Jackie, after hearing a dog whimpering, was led to the corpse of a homeless woman. Jackie did not accept the police decision to write the death off as exposure and alcohol, and investigated the problems of a powerful, but dysfunctional local family.

Mid-level television stars Lorraine Voss and Kurt Manowski came to Palmer during *In the Dog House* (Berkley, 2000) to perform in a film directed by a young Rodgers College graduate, John McBride. Jackie recommended another media expert, former producer Cameron Clark, to John when the original producer was sidelined. Clark proved to be a disruptive presence on the sets. When he was murdered, McBride, a former student of Jackie's, was suspected. Jackie, who felt responsibility for involving Clark in the film, used her California contacts to learn more about other suspects. Even then, she did not recognize the killer until she was in danger.

The books were at the low end of the sex/violence scale, attractive to those who prefer it that way, but had weak plotting. Some may be annoyed by the unrealistic skills and instincts Cleary ascribed to Jake and Jackie's acceptance by authorities as a reliable investigator.

Liz Wareham

Author: Carol Brennan

Liz Wareham was finding it difficult to live alone. She had been divorced twice. Her children were off to college. Her psychiatrist lover had just abandoned her.

Tense and lonely, she slept with the lights on, snuggling her two cats. Liz was a shopaholic, mildly dyslexic, and a terrible driver. Enough distinguishing characteristics for a new sleuth.

In *Headhunt* (Carroll & Graf, 1991), Liz had every right to be scared. In her work for The Gentle Group, a public relations firm, she arrived for an early meeting with client King Carter, only to find him stabbed to death. The investigating officer turned out to be former beau Lt. Ike O'Hanlon. Having a good cleaning woman around can be a great help!

In *Full Commission* (Carroll & Graf, 1993), Liz was more subdued, realizing that her interference in the prior case had tragic results. Riding home in a cab early in the morning, she witnessed an encounter between landlord Alfred Stover and Ada Fauer, a rent control protected tenant. Real estate broker Margaret Rooney feared that a member of her staff was responsible for vicious tricks sabotaging her sales, including the murder of Aristide Leonaides.

Liz frequently withheld important information from the authorities.

Brennan is also the author of at least two mysteries featuring Emily Silver.

Leigh Ann Warren

Author: Chassie West

Leigh Ann was a District of Columbia police officer when the series began in 1994. She took leave to return to small-town Sunrise, North Carolina. The second book did not appear until 2000; the third a year later; and the last in 2004 and might be considered a saga. Leigh operated both within the police system and on occasion on her own. Eventually due to an off-duty injury, she accepted disability retirement rather than work at a desk. She was African-American and a female, which in some police departments constituted two strikes, but shouldn't have in D.C.

Later books revealed more and more about Leigh's childhood. She vaguely remembered a fire in the family home when she was five that had left her an orphan. Cousins, who had four children of their own took her in, but for reasons not quite clear to her at the time, decided it wasn't working out.

"Miss Nunna" (Nunally Layton), a retired teacher in Sunrise, North Carolina, was a life-saver. She had taken in a prior foster child and was a pushover for lost dogs and cats, but Leigh was very special to her and she knew it. Although she graduated both from Howard University and its law school, her recollection of being saved from the burning house by a police officer motivated her to join the District of Columbia Police Force. It was on the job that she met "Duck" (Dillon Upshur Kennedy). At that time Leigh was engaged to Josh Mitchell, an undercover police officer, who was later killed on duty. Duck, a close friend of Josh, became her comforter, her resource, and her best friend. That lasted quite a while.

Leigh's return to Sunrise, the town where she had been raised and attended school, in *Sunrise* (HarperPaperbacks, 1994) was neither to visit Miss

Nunna, nor to attend the all-student reunion of Sunrise Township School. She was running away, horrified by an on duty incident in which Duck had been seriously injured, and in self-defense she had wounded his attacker. Initially she avoided becoming involved in the investigation of bones uncovered by Nunna's dog, even though it was she who alerted the local police. It became more difficult when popular Doc Webster, the medical examiner who was sure he could identify the victim, was murdered. Fortunately Duck arrived in time to help. Taking help was difficult for Leigh; taking orders from Duck was unacceptable. This was an excellent narrative with intricate plotting and good characterizations.

Her damaged knee had made it impossible for Leigh to continue active police work by *Killing Kin* (Avon, 2000) Her engagement to Duck had ended when he issued an ultimatum that she get a less dangerous job. Now she had neither Duck nor her career. The disappearance of Duck gave her something to keep her busy and in danger. She was shocked to learn that he had turned in his gun and badge, that he had transferred ownership of his condo to her, and changed his will. The scuttlebutt around the police department was that he had left under a cloud of suspicion; i.e. that he was using and selling drugs. There had been a plague of marijuana laced with PCB in the District. Knowing Duck, Leigh found it difficult to believe that he would disgrace his badge. She learned a lot more about him, before she understood what had sent him off on a personal crusade.

Leigh had known very little about her parents, who died in a fire when she was five-years-old, but in *Killer Riches* (Avon, 2001), she learned fast. Nunna and Walter (her new husband), traveling in the Airstream mobile home, had been abducted just as they returned to Sunrise. Their captor demanded that Leigh turn over the Silver Star awarded to her father for his Vietnam Service. The medal he insisted should have been given to him. The FBI was understandably skeptical so Leigh developed her own leads to her father's birth family; to a divided African-American community; to families divided by the spelling of their last name; to relatives, some of whom welcomed her while others rejected her and reviled her father.

By *Killer Chameleon* (HarperCollins, 2004), Leigh Ann had wedding plans. She couldn't believe all the bad things that happened to her at that point. At first they seemed to be coincidences (car spray-painted, food poisoning, false arrest), then it became obvious to her and Duck that someone was deliberately posing as Leigh Ann. That person picked up her wedding dress, cancelled honeymoon tickets, finally set her up as a murder suspect in the death of Claudia Hitchcock. Claudia was the twin sister to Miss Clarissa, Duck's cleaning woman. Leigh Ann looked for a connection. Things had been going so well. Her grandmother had offered her a lovely home that could be made into apartments. None of these things would work out unless she could identify her persecutor. The ending was endearing and humorous.

Penelope Warren

Author: Garrison Allen

"Big Mike," Penelope Warren's cat had top billing in the series, but Penelope deserved credit for the investigations. Penelope, who paid her dues in the Marine Corps and the Peace Corps, chose Empty Creek, Arizona as her home and the location of her mystery bookstore, "Mycroft & Company." Big Mike (actually Mycroft) was an Abyssinian alley cat Penelope adopted during her travels. He was totally spoiled, even having his own American Express card.

Penelope did not waste her three college degrees, including a Ph.D. in English Literature. She used them as an assistant professor at the local college. In her spare time, she rode her Arabian filly Chardonnay and enjoyed the company of Harris Anderson III a.k.a. Andy, the editor of the local newspaper. Mild mannered Andy had been slow to succumb to Penelope's seductive behavior, but learned fast once he realized what she had in mind; i.e. romantic and fantastic improvisations on love making. Penelope's life was frequently enlivened by visits from her sister Cassandra (an actress known professionally as Stormy Williams), who enchanted "Dutch" Fowler, the Empty Creek chief of police. Penelope's best female friend was Laney Henders, an author of erotic Westerns.

As *Desert Cat* (Zebra/Kensington 1994) began, Empty Creek was startled by the murder of Louise Fletcher, its most influential citizen. Louise had never been a close friend, but she chose Penelope to identify her attacker, leaving nebulous clues, which finally led to an obvious killer with a weak alibi.

In *Royal Cat* (Kensington, 1995), Penelope was persuaded to serve as "Queen" of the annual Elizabethan Spring Faire, which preoccupied the community every weekend during February and March. Not only did professional vendors and theatrical groups join in the Faire, but the Empty Creek businessmen prospered from the tourists. Penelope's predecessor as Queen, high school teacher Carolyn Lewis, had been murdered, so her first order of business was to find the killer.

The disappearance of a valuable Arabian stallion and the death of trainer Jack Loomis shortly before the Empty Creek Horse Show galvanized Penelope (and the local police) into action during *Stable Cat* (Kensington, 1996). She had been depressed and conscious of her age. A murder came at just the right time. Penelope's semi-legitimate status allowed her to question the suspects. She researched the lives of the trainer and the owners of the stallion, Horace and Maryanne Melrose. There were villains galore, and Penelope found them all.

Penelope had never abandoned her loyalty to the Detroit Tigers and Lions sports teams. In *Baseball Cat* (Kensington, 1997), she transferred her interest to the winless Empty Creek farm team. The discovery of the corpse of Peter Adcock, general manager of the Coyotes, in a dugout set Penelope on the trail of his killer. She considered herself an unofficial member of the local police department, interviewed and researched the players, club management and staff, and the denizens of the "Dynamite Lounge."

Dinosaur Cat (Kensington, 1998) had a cluttered cast of characters. The identification of dinosaur bones in the desert could be a threat to a major development or a boon to the local economy. Bone hunters from Japan, Israel, and Russia had been attracted to the site, but a subsequent explosion buried the bones under debris. The death of geology professor Millicent De Forest made it clear that rival factions were playing for keeps. Another explosion at the scene of the crime unearthed more recent human bones, which were traced back to the disappearance of Cornelius Hacker. This discovery resuscitated a feud between the Hacker and Mahoney families. Suspicions that a visiting expert had stolen elements of the Dead Sea Scrolls from a Russian museum complicated the investigation. This might be too complex a problem for humans, but the cat, "Big Mike" saved the day.

Penelope learned more about sister Stormy's work life when both had parts in a western movie shot in Empty Creek during *Movie Cat* (Kensington, 1999). Stormy had the more significant role but Penelope and her new alter ego, Elfrida Fallowfield, evened the score by identifying the killer of the movie's director, sleazy C. J. Masterly, and rescuing five potential victims. The cluttered manuscript added highly sexed screwballs from Los Angeles to the already overcrowded Empty Creek complement.

Penelope's level of involvement in detection was implausible, but the suspects and faithful readers ignored that fact.

Claire Watkins

Author: Mary Logue

Claire Watkins and her daughter Meg moved to Fort Antoine in northwestern Wisconsin from the Twin Cities in nearby Minnesota after her husband Steve died. He had been killed in a hit and run accident that Claire thought might have been retribution for her investigation into a drug gang, but she had never been able to prove it. She could no longer stay in the Twin Cities without Steve. Claire's younger sister Bridget was married and lived within thirty miles of Fort St. Antoine. Her prior experience as a trained police investigator helped Claire find employment in the sheriff's office in Fort St. Antoine, along the east side of the Mississippi River. Other deputies in the department initially resented her having a top-level position.

Meg, Claire's daughter, had a secret that almost cost her life in *Blood Country* (Walker, 1999). She had seen the redheaded man in a pickup who deliberately ran down her father. "Red" was aware that she was a danger to him. When he appeared in Fort St. Antoine, he tried unsuccessfully to kidnap Meg; then, did abduct Bridget. Claire traced the strands that led back to Steve's death. She discovered something she did not want to believe. The death of a friendly neighbor gave Claire her first chance to use the skills she had developed as a homicide investigator at the Minneapolis police department. As a bonus, she met pheasant farmer Rich Haggard who filled an empty place in her life and Meg's.

Wracked by nightmares and panic attacks in *Dark Coulee* (Walker, 2000), Claire held back from her growing attachment to Rich Haggard. Much as she needed his stability and warmth, her first priority at that time was solving the murder of isolated farmer Jed Spitzler. The most likely suspects for Jed's death were well-liked individuals in the community: a local mayor, the sturdy owner of a construction company, and Jed's teenage children. While working her way through her emotional problems with the help of a therapist, Claire reached out to Jed's daughter.

Claire's original motivation in moving out of the Twin Cities had been to get away from violence. In *Glare Ice* (Walker, 2001), she encountered brutality at several levels: the cruelty of a teacher to her daughter Meg, the avariciousness of a caretaker for an elderly woman, and an obsessive relationship that led to the deaths of two kind gentle men. Claire's experience in the Twin Cities made her alert to signs of abuse, but not necessarily in time to avoid murder.

The macabre story of a rural family gunned down on their farm had faded into obscurity until in *Bone Harvest* (Ballantine, 2004) a demand for the truth put the residents of Pepin County on edge. A man, who referred to himself as "Wrath of God", stole poisons from the Farm Cooperative and used them in escalating destruction. Claire sent Meg to visit her grandparents and put her relationship with Rich Haggard on hold till the truth emerged.

The narrative of *Poison Heart* (Ballantine, 2005) was not so much a "who done it" as a duel. The reader knows from the beginning that Patty Jo Tilde was an unscrupulous woman unwilling to wait until her elderly husband Walter died a natural death. Walter's daughter by a prior marriage sought Claire's help in preventing the sale of the family farm. It was no use. Patty Jo had a Durable Power of Attorney. When balked, she took action but not just against Walter.

Maiden Rock (Bleak House, 2007) explored the impact of methamphetamine on a rural Wisconsin community. Claire was intimately involved; as a deputy sheriff, but also as a parent when sixteen-year-old Krista Jorgenson leapt from historic Maiden Rock to her death on Halloween Eve. Meg, Claire's daughter, had left home in Krista's car en route to a party and was expected to stay overnight at the Jorgenson home. When Krista's mother called to let Claire know the girls had never returned, personal searches began. The Jorgenson car was located; then Krista's body; finally, Meg returned unaware of what had happened. She felt guilty, but she was not the only one; nor was Krista the only victim. This was a very moving narrative. Parents, teenagers, and teachers would benefit from reading it.

There was murder, all right, in *Point No Point* (Bleak House, 2008) but so much more. The discovery of a bloated male corpse in Lake Pepin delayed Claire's return for Meg's 16th birthday celebration. During the night, Rich received a call from his old pal, farmer Chet Baldwin who needed help. Chet had a problem: his wife Annie was dead, shot in the face. Claire had a problem. Although Chet and Annie had been friends, she had to deal with the matter professionally and Chet was a murder suspects. Rich had a problem. He saw Claire as overbearing, even cruel, in her treatment of Chet, who made it clear that he blamed himself for what had happened to Annie

A very well written series with an appealing heroine.

Logue is sensitive to rural and small town life and those who choose to or must live there.

Logue and her husband Pete Hautman co-author a juvenile series called Bloodwater Mysteries. Next: *Frozen Stiff* (2010)

Rev. Merrily Watkins

Author: Phil Rickman

As the series began, Merrily accepted a post as vicar of a Church of England parish in Hereford, England. She and her husband, Sean, had met when both were law students. A pregnancy ended her studies. Sean became quite wealthy, but relied on contacts within the criminal community. He died in a car accident while accompanied by his secretary/mistress. Merrily had been helping out in her church, counseling parishioners. A religious experience motivated her to study for the clergy. Thanks to help from her maternal uncle Ted Clowes she was assigned to Ledwardine, a village on the border of Wales. In addition to her traditional tasks, Merrily was also appointed Deliverance Consultant for the Diocese. That amorphous title was the equivalent of exorcist, and her assignment was the basis for most of the investigations in the narratives. She and her teenage daughter Jane had a tempestuous relationship, which mellowed over the series. Jane was embarrassed by her mother's choice of occupation and had no interest in organized religion, even dallied with paganism. Although Merrily's mother was alive, they were not close. Elderly neighbor Lucy Devenish became not only a friend to Merrily, but a mentor to Jane. After Lucy's death, her home was occupied by Lol (Lawrence) Robinson, a musician and songwriter who was emerging from a difficult past. Lol also occupied a significant role in Merrily's life; as her lover, a fact that seemed to be tolerated by the community and the clergy. Other characters such as Bishop Bernie Dunmore, his friendly but formidable secretary Sophie Hill, kindly trench digger Gomer Parry, Rev. Hugh Owen (former exorcist), Det. Sgt Andy Mumford and Inspector "Frannie" Bliss, Canon Sian Callaghan-Clarke, Detective Inspector (later promoted) Annie Howe, and Eirion, Jane's boyfriend, were among the regulars. Real life characters included Arthur Conan Doyle, author of the Sherlock Holmes mysteries; British composer Edward Elgar; and Nick Drake, a musician who committed suicide when young, and deeply affected Lol Robinson by this choice. Lucy Devenish, a fictional character, played a role even after her death.

Many of these characters appeared in the first of the series, *The Wine of Angels* (Macmillan, 1998). Merrily, newly arrived in Ledwardine, was insecure in her role as rector-to-be for the local church. Jane, almost sixteen, was rebellious. Seeking independence, she was drawn to Colette Cassidy, whose parents owned the local restaurant. Lol Robinson moved to town with beautiful Alison Kinnersley, only to lose her to local squire James Bull-Davies. All their plans were set awry when television playwright Richard Coffey and his lover, actor Stefan Alder, sought to produce a drama based on the life and death of 17th century priest Wil Williams.

The new young Bishop Mick Hunter appointed Merrily as the Diocesan Deliverance Counselor in *Midwinter of the Spirit* (Macmillan, 1999). His intent was that she would replace the current exorcist, Rev. T. E. B. Dobbs, who obstructed Hunter's plans for the future of the diocese. A casual contact with dying licentious Denzil Joy had left Merrily strongly affected by his post death presence. Jane was no help. She had been diverted into psychic experiences of her own by Roenna, an older, more sophisticated classmate. Lol, still trying to get his life in order, had been assigned by his therapist to assist with another patient, Katherine Moon. Katherine lived in a barn on the top of Denidor Hill, a place of historic significance. This 537 page epic traces Merrily's, Jane's and Lol's joint and individual efforts to combat a powerful center of Satanism. Awesome!

Practicing pagans, Robin and Betty Thorogood, purchased property in Old Hindwell which included St. Michael's (decommissioned by the Church of England) in *A Crown of Lights* (Macmillan, 2001). Their entry into the local community caused a reaction led by charismatic Rev. Nick Ellis, who was no longer affiliated with the Church of England diocese. Merrily's involvement began with her appearance on the television program *Livenight*, during which she was expected to represent a conservative viewpoint on the resurgence of paganism. She was disconcerted when mention was made of the presence of a pagan takeover of St. Michael's. The viewpoint characters in the narrative included not only Merrily and her teenage daughter Jane, but also Robin and Betty who were manipulated by other adherents of paganism, including Ned Bain. The backgrounds of Bain and Rev. Ellis, the sinister manipulations of local leaders, and Merrily's efforts to confront a self-centered killer were all explored in the 563 page narrative.

Jane was admitted into a shed on the school grounds where several classmates worked with an ouija board as *The Cure of Souls* (Macmillan, 2001) began. That was just the beginning of Merrily's involvement with young Amy Shelborne, the adopted daughter of a devout couple. Amy underwent a startling change in attitude and behavior causing her parents to seek help from the church. On a parallel track, former public relations executive Gerard Stock, now living in an unused hops kiln inherited by his wife Stephanie believed that an evil spirit resided in their home. It didn't get any less complicated as both Jane and her boyfriend Eirion; Merrily and Lol tried to restore some kind of order. Romanies (gypsies) who had helped to harvest the hops before the blight occurred still returned to the area of Knight's Frome, but were no longer welcome. Murder was involved as always. This was a lengthy but interesting read that would have benefited from a glossary (rural and/or Welsh terminology) and a cast of characters. These narratives did not belong in the horror category, but dealt heavily with the supernatural and religion. Commonplace motives such as greed and the struggle for power drove the action.

The Lamp of the Wicked (Macmillan, 2002) thrust Merrily into a cauldron of concerns in which all her personal and professional skills were needed. This began when trench digger Gomer Parry challenged the work of his professional rival wealthy Roddy Lodge as to the merits of Efflapure tanks. Arson and death at Gomer's place were ignored when Lodge was charged with murdering his paramour Lynsey Davies, a possibility that escalated into panic that Lodge might be a series killer. Merrily went beyond simple answers, challenging the local Development Committee.Was she dealing with mass hysteria, possible Satanism, hypersensitivity to electric impulses or just plain greed?

Jane had a strong role in *The Prayer of the Night Shepherd* (Macmillan, 2004) due to her employment at Stanner Hall Hotel. Ben Foley, former television producer, was convinced that his purchase of the hotel would pay off if he could make the connection between the building, the area, and the myths of Kingston to Arthur Conan Doyle's story, *The Hound of the Baskerville's.* He sought the attention of the Baker Street League; that failing, he recruited his old pal Antony Largo and a psychic group, The White Companions. Natalie Craven and her teenage daughter Clancy, had returned to the area; then moved in with unsophisticated farmer Jeremy Barrows. Jeremy farmed the Newt, a small acreage coveted by powerful but unstable neighbor Sebbie Dacre. Natalie's presence in the area stirred up feuds and myths of the Vaughn family in which female members had a murderous streak. Jane became very involved without telling Merrily who had problems of her own. The "miraculous "recovery of a young woman prayed for at Merrily's Sunday evening gatherings had created expectations of healing powers. More credibility was given to both the existence of an after-life and to the efficacy of the sacraments dispensed by Merrily.

Although *The Smile of a Ghost* (Macmillan, 2005) continues some themes of prior books (Jane's increased maturity, community acceptance of Lol as Merrily's lover) there's a fresh quality to the narrative. The forced resignation of Det. Sgt Andy Mumford had left him depressed, but the subsequent death of his nephew Robbie (a fall from the historic tower of Ludlow) turned him loose as a non-official detective. He enlisted Merrily's help to prove that Robbie had been murdered. She had already been assigned to investigate any possible connection with the eleventh-century death of Marion de la Bruyere in a similar fall, who supposedly still haunted the tower. Merrily was hampered by a new layer of supervision while Lol, now experiencing success in his music, had earned new enemies. Fascinating character Belle Pepper, once a Goth singer, now a resident of Ludlow, walked the streets at night with a lantern.

It doesn't take a degree in English musicology and/or archeology to appreciate *Remains of an Altar* (Quercus, 2006) but it would help. A series of car accidents on a stretch of road connected to appearances of a ghostly figure on a bicycle provided Merrily with an exhaustive assignment. Was a ghost, perhaps that of composer Edward Elgar, causing these incidents? Local pastor Syd Spicer, who had prior experience in the military, wanted an outsider to investigate. Upper Wychehill was less than a village but powerful commercial interests wanted to expand its horizons. To Jane's dismay their plans included building expensive homes on Coleman's Meadow, land that she and Gomer Parry believed to be an historical and mythical treasure. Acting independently (although Lol worked with both) Jane and Merrily incited protests, risked their reputations, and solved the mystery.

Rickman tied the significant facts of the murder of restorer Felix Barlow and the death (termed suicide) of his associate Fuschia together at the conclusion of *The Fabric of Sin* (Quercus, 2007). Getting to the conclusion was a difficult journey. Felix and Fuschia had been hired by the Duchy of Cornwall (Prince Charles' realm) to restore the Master House in Garway, located on the Welsh border. The building and its accompanying 92 acres had history connected to the feuding Newton and Gwilym families, but also to the Knights Templar, a secret organization suppressed in the Thirteenth century, but cherished by elements of the current order of Freemasons. Bishop Bernie had assigned Merrily to discover why Felix had refused to continue the restoration, but there was strong pressure to shut Merrily's investigation down after the deaths occurred. Elements of the story included information on Gnostics, St. Bernard of Clairvoux, the Cistercians, Druids, the Green Man aka Baphomet, and Jacques de Molay plus influences on the religious interests of Prince Charles...an overdose.

The ensemble aspect of the series pre-dominated in *To Dream of the Dead* (Quercus, 2008) when not only Ledwardine but the entire county was torn apart by plans to build a major by-pass that would damage ancient remains. The county council and its supporters advocated "progress" and stigmatized the opposition as pagans and terrorists. Jane was a major protestor, particularly of the Coleman Meadows area where historic stones were threatened by a real estate development. The beheading of councilman Clem Ayling was investigated by Inspector Frannie Bliss' nemesis, Detective Chief Inspector Annie Howe, who focused on opponents of "progress". Merrily, while delighted with Lol's resurgence as a composer and musician, faced criticism as too tolerant of paganism. Frannie Bliss, Jane, and Merrily had to work through personal problems at a time when the adjacent river flooded Ledwardine. Rickman's background for this conflict came from the real world. The Internet has considerable information as to the battle in Herfordshire over a new highway that would cross a winding series of stones that might rival those of Stonehenge.

Rickman is a terrific writer with an immense background of knowledge of religious, musical, archeological, and historical material. His books require serious attention from the reader, and yet in most case carry the action along successfully. Next, *Merrily's Border* (2009)

Lucy Wayles

Author: Lydia Adamson, pseudonym for Frank King

Lucy Wayles, a retired archivist who had been employed as director of the Urban Natural History Library of the City of New York, was entranced by feathered vertebrates a.k.a. the birds. In fact, she believed that in some previous incarnation, she had been an owl. She had many of the characteristics: wise, curious, and ready to pounce on prey. When she incurred publicity for her imprudent climb on an icy bridge to save a tufted duck, she was unceremoniously deprived of her position as president of the Central Park Bird Watchers. Unfazed, she began her own society, Olmstead's Irregulars. Recruits were few, although her long time suitor Markus Bloch, a researcher in viral genetics, remained loyal.

As *Beware the Tufted Duck* (Signet, 1996) began, Lucy was again at odds with the establishment. The police department had decided that her friend Abraham Lescalles had been murdered by one of the homeless who frequent Central Park. Lucy insisted that the killer was a "birder." Once she selected a primary suspect, Markus had to restrain Lucy from making a citizen's arrest. Just as well, as she had not yet properly researched the victim. When Lucy, a humorless woman, put her mind to a subject she was obsessive.

In *Beware the Butcher Bird* (Signet, 1997), Lucy followed up on the apparent suicide of Jack Wesley, a distinguished ornithological artist. Convinced that Wesley had been murdered, she rallied Olmstead's Irregulars to find his killer. Heedless of the danger to others, particularly Markus, she led them through the urban jungle of New York City. When finally disclosed, the motivation for murder was as obscure as a prehistoric ancestor to birdlife.

There was little improvement in the third narrative, *Beware the Laughing Gull* (Signet, 1998). As members of Lucy's bird group were murdered, jailed, or left town, new birders replaced them, not always copasetic with the original members. When Peter Marin became engaged, no one was too excited. He had never fulfilled any of his prior engagements. This time the ceremony would have been completed had not someone on roller blades shot the bride. Lucy insisted that the Olmstead Irregulars find the killer to clear Peter as a suspect. Aided by birdsong phonograph records the group succeeded in exposing a smuggling racket and identifying a killer.

Lucy was a domineering insensitive heroine whose antics and adventures were narrated by a devoted suitor.

Lydia Adamson is the pseudonym for Frank King. This is his third entry in the Mystery Women series as Adamson. The other two featured veterinarian Deirdre Nightingale and actress Alice Nestleton. As King, he also wrote a shorter series featuring Sally Tepper (covered in *Mystery Women*: Volume 2).

Fiona Wooten "Biggie" Weatherford

Author: Nancy Bell

Biggie Weatherford's husband Cuthbert had disappeared from her life after the Korean War. Her only son, an alcoholic, died; his wife, considered their child, young J.R., a burden so she left him behind in Biggie's care. J.R. (age eleven as the series began) was the focus of her life. She was eccentric, as only the extremely wealthy can be. Her behavior, keeping a catfish in the toilet bowl, washing greens in the bathtub, using an open refrigerator as an air conditioner might have labeled her otherwise. Owning about half of Kemp County, Texas protected her from the authorities and public retribution. She drove her car without a license and without concern for the traffic laws. People merely stayed out of her way.

Biggie and her supporting cast of characters were introduced in *Biggie and the Poisoned Politician* (St. Martin, 1996). They included Coye and Ernestine Sontag, the loyal tenants who farmed her land, and Monica, their partly-bald daughter who was J.R.'s best pal; the itinerant wannabe author Wade Hampton Crabtree whom she allowed to live above her garage; and her housekeeper/cook African-American Willie Mae who was into voodoo and whose recipes were an extra treat. Biggie, who had a deep interest in family history, would not tolerate the location of a sanitary landfill near her ancestral graveyard. The death of chief proponent Mayor Osbert Gribbons merely deflected her attention temporarily while she found his killer.

During *Biggie and the Mangled Mortician* (St. Martin, 1997), she had several projects in hand: to direct and appear in the local presentation of Gilbert & Sullivan's *H.M.S. Pinafore*, the renovation of the local depot, J.R.'s concern about the appearance of the Wooten Creek Monster, and finally, the murder of Monk Carter, the newly resident mortician. Unsure that the Texas Rangers could handle this matter, Biggie deployed her ex-convict houseman Rosebud to do the field investigations while she set to right other problems besetting the citizens of Job's Crossing.

Biggie and the Fricasseed Fat Man (St. Martin, 1998) divided her attention between the murder of local businessman Firman Birdsong and the threat that Jane Culpepper, J.R.'s maternal grandmother, would take him back to Montana with her. J.R.'s mother had shown little interest in the boy, but readily transferred her rights to her mother Janie whose second husband had recently lost a grandson in an accident. J.R. was on the brink of running away when Biggie solved both problems.

The gift of a swampy land parcel to the James Royce Wooten chapter of the Daughters of the Republic of Texas (Biggie Weatherford, president) brought unexpected consequences in *Biggie and the Meddlesome Mailman* (St. Martin, 1999). The local unit of the right wing Empire of Texas was holding training sessions on the property for anti-government activities. In a parallel plot line, Biggie and J.R. discovered the corpses of two officials, dangerously inquisitive postal employee Luther Abernathy and corrupt state politician Lefty Lovelace. She had to rely on the good will of teenager Buddy Duncan to save her life, but Biggie was right on target in solving the murders.

Biggie decided that Job's Crossing deserved an historical society equal to that of nearby Quincy, as *Biggie and the Quincy Ghost* (St. Martin, 2001) began. This necessitated overnight stays at the local inn, which prided itself upon having a ghost. It was J.R. who thought he heard a ghost and who discovered the corpse of Annabeth Baugh, a pretty young girl who worked at the inn. Biggie and J.R. combined to unearth historical secrets that the local inhabitants would just as soon have left in the past.

Although the basic plot line in *Biggie and the Devil Diet* (St. Martin, 2002) was poignant, there were problems in the execution. Rex Barnwell, the man in Biggie's young life, had returned to Job's Crossing. Although he was very ill, his wife was energetically turning the Barnwell Ranch into a "fat farm" for teenage girls. J. R. had problems of his own, two dates for the Homecoming Dance.

Stops just short of being too cute. Nancy Bell has begun a new series featuring Judge Jackson Crain and his thirteen-year-old daughter with a similar ambience.

Molly West

Author: Patricia Tichenor Westfall

Molly West had not been born in Appalachia but moved there fifteen years ago with her husband Ken. He had an opportunity for a faculty job in sociology at Sycamore State College in southern Ohio. Molly left an excellent position as benefits manager at a bank for a life in the country. The Wests had two children: Amanda, a graphic designer and Todd, who, after a rocky start, had finished college. Their rural life was not what Ken and Molly had planned. He had hoped for a more prestigious university. She had aimed for a bank presidency, but soon Molly was happy in Appalachia, even knowing that she would always be an outlander. Eventually Ken (nicknamed Dr. K) came to enjoy the area. More recently she had become associate director of the Tri-County Meal Van Service, delivering to shut-ins plus providing on-site meals at one location. In her fifties, Molly was otherwise undescribed. With an empty nest, Ken and Molly had taken an active role in the Puppy Rescue Association, acting as short-term foster caregivers for abandoned puppies.

One of those to welcome the Wests to the area was Dave Breyers, manager of a local mill, so in *Fowl Play* (St. Martin, 1996), Molly found it difficult to believe that he had killed his former wife. Cathy Breyers had been a shy young woman, less open to making new friends, but Molly discovered that Cathy had a secret life. Molly made good use of her connection with the local sheriff and of the wisdom and courage of Louella Chalmers Benton, an elderly woman to whom she brought food.

During *Mother of the Bride* (St. Martin, 1998), Molly was diverted into investigating the escape of convict Luke Sievers and the presence of bones too new to be of merely historical interest. Amanda, Molly's daughter, and her long time fiancé Bentley Cottingham of the Cleveland Cottinghams, decided to make it legal. The wedding was to be in her hometown with multiple bridesmaids from Amanda's high school years. There was one problem: the maid of honor, Bonnie Wheeler Sievers, was the potential target of her escaped husband Luke. Because of connections with Civil War re-enactments, the wedding decor would be strictly historical. The complications: gun smuggling, poisoning, and the discovery of bones were more recent.

Virginia West

Author: Patricia Cornwell

See: Judy Hammer, page 322.

Connor Westphal

Author: Penny Warner

At age thirty-seven, Connor Westphal preferred to be called C.W. as befitted her position as the editor of the Flat Skunk weekly newspaper, *Eureka,* published in the Mother Lode country of California. Before moving there Connor had worked for six years on the *San Francisco Chronicle.* Her parents who remained in San Francisco had turned over their rights to her grandparents' small diner and printing press to Connor. She hoped some day to renovate the diner, perhaps providing coffee equal to that she had enjoyed in San Francisco. In the meantime, she lived in the back rooms. She owned a 1957 Chevrolet, which she used for longer trips, but most of her transportation was by mountain bike. One of Connor's special features was the construction of mystery puzzles that she included in the paper. She was unable to compete with the rival *Mother Lode Monitor* in breaking news, but she did her best.

Connor dealt with her deafness by reading lips plus using both ASL (American Sign Language) and SEE (Seeing Exact English). Her parents had made a conscious effort to maintain Connor within the world of speech. Because she had lost her hearing at age four as a result of meningitis, she had a background as to speech sounds. Her telephone was equipped with TTY, which enabled her to send messages, but her reception had to be translated. Young Jeremiah (Miah) Mercer, son of the local police chief, ran a resale comic/CD/video game business in the former Hotel Penzance where Connor had her office. He worked part-time as Connor's assistant and translator. They exchanged favors as Connor collected "girlie" comics— "Archie and Veronica" and "Lulu.". Connor enjoyed Sierra Nevada beer and ate Dove bars for a pickup. She missed the great San Francisco coffee so mixed a cup of cocoa into regular coffee to create her own mocha. Unable to hear an alarm clock, she purchased a shake-awake bed to get her up in the morning.

Connor's personal life was shared with Dan Smith, initially a police officer, then self-employed as an investigator, and with her dog Casper. Casper, a Siberian husky, had been trained as a signal dog for the deaf. Her closest female friend was local mortician Del Ray Montez.

Lacy Penzance, of the illustrious local family, contacted Connor to place an ad seeking her missing sister Risa Longo during *Dead Body Language* (Bantam, 1997). Lacy's murder and the disappearance of hard drinking private investigator Boone Joslin caused Connor to investigate a pair of scams. Her companion, although sometimes he was a suspect, was Dan Smith, Boone's half-brother. Connor used her skills, a sense of smell and knowledge of comics, to identify a killer.

Trite but true, the earth moved for Dan and Connor (and everyone else in town) during *Sign of Foul Play* (Bantam, 1998). Two earthquakes and a series of aftershocks hit Flat Skunk. Initially the quake was blamed for the death of soils engineer Cullen Delancey. His body had been found at the site of a building constructed for the *Monitor*, the rival newspaper owned by the Truax family. Connor dug deeper. The corpses piled up. Clues from faulty lip reading and unclear signs led Connor to a crashing finish.

Flat Skunk had old buildings and old secrets to be dealt with in *Right To Remain Silent* (Bantam, 1998). Sparkle Bodie, a wealthy older woman, sought to preserve the town as it had been for her ancestors. Her son Esken and his wife Sonora preferred to change the town into a tourist attraction. Sparkle was so close to death that she had been taken to the funeral parlor, revived, only to be smothered to death in the hospital. Connor was appalled when Caleb, Sparkle's other son, was arrested. Caleb, who had been born deaf, had been treated as developmentally disabled, kept isolated, and never trained to communicate. He needed an advocate and Connor took the job.

Perhaps some new blood in Flat Skunk wouldn't be all bad. The locals seemed addicted to complex marital encounters, confused parentage, and lethal weapons in *A Quiet Undertaking* (Bantam, 2000). Dan Smith involved Connor in paint ball games, but some of their adversaries escalated to more dangerous weapons. Del Ray's mortuary was in serious trouble. Cremains (the residue after cremation), which had been destined for disposal in the ocean, were discovered in a common storage facility. The man responsible had been murdered. Careful readers may note an editing error: a major disclosure was prematurely revealed.

The Mark Twain short story about frog-jumping contests had been seized upon as a draw for tourists by the string of small California towns known as the Mother Lode communities. They had an annual frog-jumping contest as the centerpiece; plus art exhibits, food booths, bake sales, and other money making projects. In *Blind Side* (Perseverance Press, 2001), the Jubilee was marred by the death of the prospective winning frog and its owner Dakota Webster. The obvious suspect was Miah Mercer, Connor's assistant at Eureka, who always came in second. Miah and Dakota had been rivals for years. Connor followed clues to the local hospital, uncovering a more mercenary motive for multiple murders.

The last gold rush in Fat Skunk had taken place more than a century ago, but in *Silence Is Golden* (Perseverance, 2003), another one occurred when elderly prospector Sluice Jackson showed up with a gold nugget appraised at $2,000. Word spread quickly and people came in droves, including Josh Littlefield, who had been "close to" Connor at Gallaudet College, his former wife Gail, and their hearing impaired daughter Susie. There was friction between Gail (who wanted Susie to have a cochlear implant) and Josh (who opposed it). The discovery of an ancient skeleton, two murders and arson kept Connor busy and vulnerable.

The Hanging Dummy, an historical reminder of the Gold Rush Days, was replaced by a live corpse in *Dead Man's Hand* (Hilliard Harris, 2007). Zander Nicolas, a former hippie who shared a home and business with his common law wife India, was the victim. Sheriff Mercer was currently out of action, so Connor pursued the investigation with occasional help from Dan. Usual list of suspects who were actually quite unusual: a pair of religious leaders, a para-military redneck; a tree-sitting college student, and the CEO at the local Native American casino. Adding to the complexity was a visit from Connor's former college beau Josh Littlefield, who had purchased a nearby host town to set up a deaf community.

Connor took her interest in Nancy Drew to the heights. An adult, she still collected the books, played an active role when a crime was committed in her area, and took considerable risks. No mention made of her health insurance.

Aunt Dimity Westwood

Author: Nancy Atherton

Those who enjoy fantasy intermixed with romance and enlivened by mystery will relish this series in which a deceased benefactress, Aunt Dimity Westwood, reappeared (through entries in a journal) to advise those whom she loved on earth. Bobby MacLaren, Dimity's fiancé who had been killed during World War II, had left her money, which she used to help the needy through the Westwood Trust. On Dimity's death, Lori Shepherd, the daughter of Dimity's best friend, inherited Dimity's English cottage. Lori's father had also died during World War II, when she was three. She was a librarian, who had worked in a rare book department. When fire seriously damaged the collection and her marriage fell apart, Lori was delighted to move to England.

Aunt Dimity had been a continuing character in the bedtime stories that Lori's mother had told her, but her presence became very real when she took occupancy of the cottage in *Aunt Dimity's Death* (Viking, 1992) and read the 44-year correspondence between Dimity and her mother. Lori had two tasks as a condition of her bequest: to write an introduction to the Aunt Dimity stories as told by the letters, and to uncover and rectify a wrong done by Dimity during the war. The latter quest was accomplished with the help of young Bill Willis, whose Boston law firm handled Dimity's will. They married later.

Lori and Bill played no role in *Aunt Dimity and the Duke* (Viking, 1994) wherein Derek and Emma Harris, caretakers of Dimity's cottage, met and fell in love while solving the problems of a ducal family whose line of descent was in danger.

Lori was in sore straits again as *Aunt Dimity's Good Deed* (Viking, 1996) began. Her husband Bill Willis had been devoted during their courtship. On his return to the Boston law practice, he had little time for nurturing their marriage. Her planned second honeymoon faltered when Bill stayed behind. She went anyway, accompanied by her supportive father-in-law, Willis, Sr. Aunt Dimity's journal led Lori on a merry chase through family history and the English countryside to heal a centuries-old rift.

The tempest brewing in Finch as to who would have occupancy of the schoolhouse in the fall (the Harvest Festival committee headed by Peggy Kitch or the archeology students under the tutelage of Dr. Adrian Culver) came to a happy conclusion in *Aunt Dimity Digs In* (Viking, 1998). Misunderstanding, hidden agendas, and old time resentments gave way to explanations and apologies. Aunt Dimity helped Lori to understand the dynamics of local adults who had not outlived their childhood traumas during World War II.

Lori's poverty in her childhood had meant bleak Christmas holidays, so in *Aunt Dimity's Christmas* (Viking, 1999) she was going all out to make this year's a memorable event. The presence of an unknown tramp in her yard changed all that. With Bill back in the United States on an emergency, Lori and an attractive Catholic priest Fr. Julian Bright sought the identity of the ailing man and the circumstances that had brought him to Aunt Dimity's cottage.

Not so much a devil, but a long dead widowed father protecting his daughter to the point of denying her the right to love, was the background for *Aunt Dimity Beats the Devil* (Viking, 2000). Lori went to a border castle where the tragedy of Josiah Byrd, his rebellious daughter Claire, and her lover Edward had taken place. Her task was to appraise a library. Claire's ghost invaded Lori's spirit, threatening her marriage. With Aunt Dimity's guidance, Lori played cupid to lovers two generations apart.

Newcomer to Finch, Prunella Hooper had made few friends in the community. Her death as *Aunt Dimity: Detective* (Viking, 2001) opened, had occurred while Bill, Lori and their twins were in the United States visiting his family. On their return, Bill stopped off in London to finish some legal work while Lori and the children went on ahead. Within a short time after her arrival, Lori was scandalizing the locals as she and Nicholas Fox, a handsome male visitor, investigated Prunella's death. There were secrets in Finch. Each suspect pointed a finger at someone else. Lilian Bunting, wife of the vicar and Nicholas' aunt, wanted the truth to come out. Lori seemed to enjoy the attention she was receiving in Bill's absence. She explained to him that she gets carried away when she shares an adventure with someone. Bill took wise precautions to be more adventurous himself.

Aunt Dimity was delighted to revisit Hailesham Park, in *Aunt Dimity Takes a Holiday* (Viking, 2003). Lori would accompany her husband Bill, attorney to the current Earl Elstyn . Other family members on site included Derek and Emma Harris (a friend of Lori). To Lori's surprise Derek, the black sheep of the Elstyns, was also the heir apparent. Emma sought Lori's help. She was concerned that an attempt would be made on Derek's life, but he might not be the real target.

Lori's good friend Emma Harris prescribed a day hike to remedy her post-holiday exhaustion in *Aunt Dimity Snowbound* (Viking, 2004). A devastating storm isolated Lori and two fellow hikers at a partially restored country home. The caretaker made them aware of the enmity the now deceased householder had for Americans. By the time the weather abated, Lori and her friends had righted a decades old wrong.

There was more sugar than spice in *Aunt Dimity and the Next of Kin* (Viking, 2005) Dissatisfied with merely writing checks to charities, Lori did volunteer work at St. Benedict's homeless shelter and Radcliffe Infirmary. At Radcliffe she was directed by her friend nurse Lucinda Willoughby to Miss Elizabeth Beacham, a former legal secretary who was dying of cancer. The two women achieved instant rapport. Elizabeth's death was a shock to Lori. Even more shocking was a major bequest in Elizabeth's will and an assignment to find her younger brother Kenneth, the next of kin. In searching for Kenneth, Lori learned more about Elizabeth, an incredible woman. In her spare time she played cupid.

Threatening mail, including pictures of Lori and the twins convinced Bill in *Aunt Dimity and the Deep Blue Sea* (Viking, 2006) that he should find a safe place for his family. Sir Percy Pelham, a genial multimillionaire, had just the ticket: a helicopter ride to an isolated island off the coast of Scotland. Sir Percy had purchased the entire island to the initial dismay of the 200 residents. The castle had been modernized to accommodate guests. He provided bodyguards, Amien Hunter and Andrew Ross, for Lori and the boys. While Bill and Scotland Yard tried to identify Abaddon, the author of the threats, Lori and Aunt Dimity did their own investigating.

Bill, disturbed by Lori's failure to recover physically and emotionally from her experiences with Abaddon, devised a solution in *Aunt Dimity Goes West* (Viking, 2007). He arranged a vacation in the Colorado Mountains for Lori, the twins, and Annalise, their nanny. A family "cabin" (actually a luxurious home) near Bluebird had been made available by his client Danny Auerbach. Bill, who had fallen behind on his work, could not go with them. James Blackwell, the caretaker who was expected to assist Lori, disappeared, but young Toby Cooper would serve as driver, caretaker, and guide. It seemed to be working until the locals made Lori aware of the Lord Stuart curse. No wonder

Danny Auerbach's wife had refused to return to the cabin. With help from Toby and Rose Blanding, the local pastor's wife, Lori learned about the history of the area, the mine tragedy that had cost many lives, and the hostility that lived on.

Lori was in the throes of an anxiety attack as *Aunt Dimity: Vampire Hunter* (Viking, 2008) began. Her five-year-old twin sons were attending school part-time, causing her to worry constantly about what dreadful harm might come to them. A summons to the headmistress' office didn't help. The boys had terrified classmates with a story about seeing a vampire while they were horseback riding. Lori might not believe in vampires, but she wasn't taking any chances. Working with stable manager Kit Smith, who had problems of his own, she carried out an investigation while husband Bill was out of town.

Very light fare. *Aunt Dimity Slays the Dragon* (2009); *Aunt Dimity Down Under* (2010); *Aunt Dimity and the Family Tree* (2011) NB: *Introducing Aunt Dimity* contains the first two in the series

Charlotte Sue "Chas" Wheatley

Author: Phyllis Richman

Charlotte Sue Wheatley preferred to be called "Chas." Her personal history had made her mistrustful of men. During her marriage to Chef Ari Boucheron, she had traveled the world. After the divorce, they became friends, joined in their love for their daughter Lily

A Parisian romance with aspiring Chef Laurence Levain led to temporary joy, but ended too soon for Chas. A relationship with investigative reporter Dave Zeeger had been kept secret perhaps because she had lost hope that it would provide the commitment she wanted. During the time spent with chefs, Chas studied cooking. She ran a restaurant for a while, but needed a schedule more appropriate to a single mother. Friends encouraged her to try writing again, and to combine that skill with her knowledge of food and restaurants. She became the restaurant critic for the *Washington Examiner,* eventually achieving national syndication. She made her dinner reservations under false names to avoid recognition when possible, and noted not only the service, the quality and portion size of her own food, but also that of other diners. Under editor Bull Stannard, the *Examiner* was striving to establish itself in an area with tough competition from other news media.

Approaching mid-life she lived alone but was in regular contact with her daughter Lily Boucheron, a professional musician. She enjoyed food, reading mysteries, and walking. For her, walking was a way of life. She preferred it to driving around Washington, even through districts that others avoided. She donated her services as a cook to a woman's shelter and a food kitchen at various times. The narrative developed characters from among her co-workers, local chefs, and members of the police department. Two of the characters, both African-Americans, entertainment editor Sherele Travis and detective Homer

Jones struck up a romance. As an unofficial investigator, Chas often focused on wrong suspects for a considerable period of time, but persisted even at the risk of personal harm.

In *The Butter Did It* (HarperCollins, 1997), when Chas learned that Laurence Levain was dead, her horror had less to do with his reputation as a great chef than her recollections of their time together in Paris two decades before. That intimacy provided Chas with insights that were in conflict with the official determination that he had died of a heart attack. Dave Zeeger arranged for Chas to share her concerns with epicurean detective Homer Jones. Chas feared that she might learn that the killer was someone for whom she cared deeply.

Murder on the Gravy Train (HarperCollins, 1999) mixed sage advice about what can be learned from a menu with Chas' new assignment. She was to probe ways in which restaurants bilked their customers and tricks used by thieves to cheat restaurants. It became risky business. People were disappearing. Unknown corpses appeared on detective Homer Jones' case list. Chas simplified his task by identifying bodies, matching one bug against another, and finding a mole on the *Examiner* staff.

The new business reporter Ringo Laurenge was an untested ingredient in the *Examiner* newsroom mix during *Who's Afraid of Virginia Ham?* (HarperCollins, 2001). Management was impressed with his high level of production including his ventures into restaurant management, entertainment and the territories of other specialized reporters. His fellow workers considered him a poacher and plagiarist. Chas and her friend Sherele were among the first to recognize Ringo's destructive propensity. When he died after eating Sherele's ham rolls at an *Examiner* buffet, she was arrested. That created a problem for both Chas and detective Homer Jones, who was Sherele's lover.

Richman brought not only her knowledge of food and restaurants to her narrative, but a wicked sense of humor.

Blanche White

Author: Barbara Neely

Blanche White was a heavyset African-American who supported herself in her North Carolina hometown by domestic work. She had candid opinions of her white employers, and no reluctance to trick them. Not all of her opinions were well received; e.g. she believed prostitution should be legalized. Blanche was an excellent cook and a good friend, but never forgot a wrong. She was responsive but not subservient, and had no respect for the police department or the judicial system. Her closest ties were to Ardell, a friend from high school, to her own mother, and to Tafia and Malik, the niece and nephew she was raising

Her habit of writing checks with an insufficient balance in her account put her in court in *Blanche on the Lam* (St. Martin, 1992). She fled the scene after being sentenced to thirty days in jail. Her quick wits made it possible for her to find employment with a wealthy family whose prospective heir, developmentally disabled Mansfield needed a friend. Blanche learned enough to blackmail the family, but she also exposed a killer, and then headed for Boston, Massachusetts.

Blanche's move and some additional money enabled her to send her niece and nephew to excellent schools by *Blanche Among the Talented Tenth* (St. Martin, 1994), but with mixed results. While visiting a New England resort that catered to light-skinned African-Americans, Blanche became aware of prejudice within her own race and its impact on her niece. Not everyone at Amber Cove was unfriendly. Distinguished feminist Mattie Harris and handsome pharmacist Robert Stuart sought her company. When the "accidental" death of mean-mouthed Faith Brown was followed by the suicide of Mattie's godson Hank Garrett, Blanche probed the original death. She was enlightened and disillusioned, but with her strength and sense of humor she survived.

Malik's paper on the environment covered the impact of lead poisoning on children, including its potential for causing violent behavior in adolescents. In *Blanche Cleans Up* (Viking, 1998), Blanche took him to local meetings on the topic. She had been filling in as housemaid for prominent white politician Alister Brindle, so her friend Inez could go on vacation. Blanche had no trouble separating the "good guys" from the "bad guys" as she investigated the murder of Saxe Winton, the attractive young man who was Mrs. Brindle's trainer. She unmasked hypocritical politicians and counseled a pregnant teenager but accepted the help of ex-convicts who had their own kind of justice.

For eight years, Blanche had nurtured her hatred of Dave Palmer who had raped her when she was a servant in his sister's home. In *Blanche Passes Go* (Viking, 2000), she returned to Farleigh, North Carolina to work with her friend Ardell in her catering business. The memories were so strong as to blind Blanche to Palmer's possible involvement in a murder, to haunt her new relationship with a widower, and to cause an unfortunate death. The narrative brought insights into the individual and collective responses of African-American women to rape, abuse and a sisterhood of misery. Blanche's past had left her with powerful feelings against white people.

Jane Whitefield

Author: Thomas Perry

Jane Whitefield, a tall dark-skinned woman of partly Native American heritage, had not intended to spend her life breaking the law. It just happened that way, beginning with a young man who needed to leave the country during her sophomore year in college. What began as a single act of kindness developed into a personally rewarding and sometimes profitable business: creating new identities for people who deserved a second chance. She helped battered wives, children who were victims of incest, and those unjustly accused of crimes.

Jane knew little of her blond Irish-American mother who had appeared in New York City at age sixteen, and stayed there for a half-dozen years, but never talked about that time. When she met Henry Whitefield, she changed her life, becoming a model wife and mother in a small New York State town. Jane kept in regular touch with members of her father's Seneca tribe in the United States and Canada, and used them as resources.

Over the years Jane established a network of way stations and document replicators to create new personas for her fugitives. Despite her activities, Jane remained somewhat naïve. In *Vanishing Act* (Random House, 1995), she was vulnerable to John Felker, purportedly an ex-police officer framed for a crime. Felker had become an accountant after leaving the police force. He became a scapegoat with major money put in his bank accounts. Believing he had no chance to prove his innocence, he took $50,000 and ran. She gained a valuable ally in her cantankerous neighbor Jake Reinert.

Dr. Carey McKinnon had been a close friend, although one in whom she never confided her real occupation, but in *Dance for the Dead* (Random, 1996), their relationship became intimate to the point where marriage was a possibility. Before Jane could consider such a step, she had to overcome a devious enemy who threatened the life of Timmy Decker and to protect former embezzler Mary Perkins. Young Timmy had belatedly remembered coming home from shopping to find his parents dead . He was being raised as a son by Raymond and Emily Decker. Jane used up aliases, bank accounts, and separate identities that she had built over the years when she became the prey, rather than the rescuer.

Jane had an assignment to complete before she would be free to marry Carey as *Shadow Woman* (Random, 1997) began. Pete Hatcher's charm did not protect him from his employers at a Los Vegas casino when he knew too much about their plans for expansion. Jane's clever ruse to spirit him out of the state and into a new identity fell short, just as she was coming into her new identity as Mrs. Carey McKinnon. She reneged on her promise to Carey, but faced a formidable female adversary who was as dedicated as Jane herself.

Jane's resolve to forego future ventures in relocating threatened individuals lasted one year until Carey asked for her help in *The Face Changers* (Random, 1998). Only his sense of obligation to his mentor, surgeon Richard Dahlman, would justify Carey's placing Jane in danger. He did not realize then that Jane would be competing against a trio from her past. Help came from unlikely places, but Jane had to tread lightly every step of her way to protect Carey's career and their life together.

In *Blood Money* (Random, 2000), Jane found it impossible to reject Rita Shelford, a frightened young woman pursued by the Mafia. The reappearance of mob banker Bernie "the Elephant" Lupas with control over twelve million dollars in secret funds complicated the matter. The wall between Jane's past and present became more transparent.

Although credulity may be stretched, these were difficult to put down. After a ten year hiatus, Jane returns in *Runner* (2009).

Serena Wilcox

Author: Natalie Buske Thomas

Serena Wilcox was a tiny single woman, past thirty. She had survived the death of her fiancé and the loss of their child by a miscarriage. After a period of adjustment, Serena, who had attended college, entered on a career as a private detective. Unfortunately, her appearance was undistinguished. She lacked a professional wardrobe and training.

Serena made a late entry into *Gene Play* (Independent Spirit, 1998), characterized by short choppy chapters. The plot was ingenious, but the presentation weak. The machinations of an unlicensed doctor, a bigamist, and a cold-hearted con woman were explored. They preyed upon unmarried pregnant women and couples who desperately wanted children. Serena connected the dots along with Karyn, who became her partner, and attorney George Bowmann.

A venal businessman manipulated a commercial system, which allowed an individual to either visualize a prior period in his/her lifetime, or, at considerable expense, to take part in a self-designed "adventure" in *Virtual Memories* (Independent Spirit, 1999). Only the intervention of Serena and Karyn prevented customer Jack Miller from killing a man he had never met. Dan, an employee of Virtual Memories who had been duped by a conniving young woman, helped Serena track a greedy killer and save another life.

In *Camp Conviction* (Independent Spirit, 2000), Jack Miller came to Serena with concerns about a "family camp" with questionable practices. Karyn and Dan, now her fiancé, enlisted the help of Nolan, Dan's eight-year-old nephew, to pose as a family attending the camp. After they left, Serena took on a second case: a widowed computer devotee whose efforts to sell property adjacent to the family camp had been thwarted by picketers. They joined forces after Dan, Karyn and Nolan had narrow escapes from death. There was improvement in the series as it progressed.

Catherine "Cat" Wilde

Author: Jean Ruryk

Catherine "Cat" Wilde had dealt with multiple tragedies during her sixty-plus years. Her marriage to an unstable alcoholic had ended early. Their daughter and son-in-law were killed in a car crash. Her career as a producer of documentaries for radio and television had ended, and her work as a furniture restorer was all she had for income.

In *Chicken Little Was Right* (St. Martin, 1994), Catherine's most precious possession, the home she had worked so hard to own, was threatened. Her solution was unusual. She robbed a bank, taking a small child and his mother as a hostage. She then more or less adopted her hostages. However, a blackmailer, whose demands included assistance in murder, followed her home. Catherine had allies; a pair of gay antique dealers, a former advertising man who ran a gardening business, and a widowed ex-columnist with Mafia connections. She mixed her friends and her personal skills into a scheme to confound her oppressor.

Catherine's sense of loss after daughter Laurie's death never disappeared; in fact, it came back intimately in *Whatever Happened to Jennifer Steele?* (St. Martin, 1996). She recognized in a scabby dirty bag lady, the young girl who had been Laurie's best friend. Catherine fed Jennifer, cleansed her and saw to her medical needs, until the young woman regained her identity; not just as Laurie's friend, but also as a talented actress. With that knowledge came a realization that Jennifer was in danger, and would remain vulnerable until a killer could be identified.

Rena Kundera had a stall at a local flea market that she might lose because of major surgery. In *Next Week Will Be Better* (St. Martin, 1998), Catherine agreed to substitute for her. Her observations of how other vendors handled materials and customers made her suspicious that one might be dealing drugs or selling stolen items, and another might be a killer. Handicapped reporter Mike Melnyk and Catherine's antique hunting friends Rafe and Charlie helped her find a killer for whom beautiful things had become an obsession.

Catherine was an endearing sleuth who surrounded herself with new elements of family to replace her losses. Of course, one does have to overlook bank robbery and kidnapping. These were low key but emotionally well-grounded narratives.

Kate Wilkinson

Author: Lis Howell

The television business was chancy. Kate Wilkinson had been a full-time employee at LondonVision until her position was made part-time to accommodate a male co-worker. She had married Graham when he too worked for LondonVision, but it had not lasted. Graham took a new position in the Middle East. There had been no children. Kate had an abortion before the marriage, a miscarriage during it, and had no interest in a family. There were so many divergences of opinion between Kate and Rev. John Maple, an Episcopalian priest; yet, they became lovers. She was ardently atheistic, pro-choice, and pro-gay rights. His positions were more conservative and more religious. He did not try to influence her beliefs, and hoped she might give him the same tolerance. It had not been easy.

Kate was but one researcher among many for *Your Morning*, a television news show for women, as *After the Break* (Hodder & Stoughton, 1995) began. She had been ousted from her London job by Frank Rattle, and was not entirely happy to have him turn up in a supervisory role on *Your Morning*. Robert Pedlar, a researcher for the program, had committed suicide before Kate joined the staff. She and other workers suspected that Pedlar had been murdered. Kate's efforts to identify the killer were assisted by fellow researchers Jenny Sims and Dave Mitchell, and Jenny's sister, a social worker.

In between seasons in the television industry, Kate took on a special assignment in Cumbria, North England during *The Director's Cut* (Hodder & Stoughton, 1996). She accepted the job partly to accommodate her good friend Liz Jones, unaware that Liz was having an affair with erratic producer Andy de Salas. Anticipating a restful and productive interim in the country, Kate came to realize that small, inbred communities had their dark side. The locals were fiercely divided as to land use and new industries. The attitudes were reflected in the film they were working on, which was designed to showcase what could be accomplished in Northern England. The mysterious death of an elderly tyrant, the emergence of illegal dog fighting in the community, and a series of accidents added to the chaos. Rev. John Maple came to offer his assistance and support.

In *A Job to Die For* (Hodder & Stoughton, 1997), Kate was employed as general manager for a new food and health television channel expected to air in September. Unfortunately, she had some rather unstable associates on the payroll and among the stockholders. One was found dead in the canal near the office warehouse where the television station was located. Another intended to arrange that the new station would never become active. Explicit perverse material and unbelievable characters flawed the narrative. Because two of the above books were not available to me, I am indebted to my daughter-in-law, Vonne Muessling Barnett, for the reviews. Lis Howell has more recently authored a new series featuring three amateur detectives, called the *Norbridge Chronicle* mysteries.

Elizabeth "Liz" Will

Author: Dorian Yeager

Elizabeth "Liz" Will returned to her hometown Dovekey Beach in Maine, expecting little material success. A blond college graduate now in her thirties, all she wanted was supplies for her watercolors and space for a small art gallery. She was close to having a serious affair with uncommunicative Charles MacKay who headed a research project on a nearby island. Sal, her mother, had moved out of the family home when Liz and her sister Avis were grown to begin a career as a romance novelist. Frank, her dour and obstinate father, continued lobster fishing even as resources diminished.

One way for Liz to earn money was by crewing on Frank's lobster boat. In *Murder Will Out* (St. Martin, 1994), that idea ended in disaster when she recovered the body of town selectman Al Jenness from Frank's lobster pot. Al and Frank had frequently tangled in community affairs, most recently over the legalization of gambling and prostitution on the nearby islands. Liz not only agreed with Al, but also had shared an extra-marital affair with him. Still, she did not believe her father was a killer. With the aid of lesbian police chief Ginny Philbrick, the family Bible, and a tombstone, Liz made her point.

Summer Will End (St. Martin, 1996) found Liz chafing mentally and physically at the discipline she had set for herself. She rose early in the cold to harvest lobster; then, displayed her artwork to the tourists during the heat of the day. Both lobster and tourist seasons would end soon and she had to make the most of them. Accidents and incidents were felling tourists: heart attacks, shark and rattlesnake appearances, smoke and fire on the ferryboat, food poisonings. Liz was particularly concerned when Eamon, the husband of Elizabeth's high school friend Martha Robson, was at risk.

Yeager has a second series with a female sleuth, actress Victoria Bowering (see Part 1 of this volume)

Charlotte Willett

Author: Margaret Miles

Charlotte Willett was a young widow living in Bracebridge, Massachusetts in 1763. The period covered in the series came after the French-Indian war at a time when the first stirrings of resentment against England were surfacing. She had married Aaron Willett, a young Quaker who came to the area to visit, but stayed for love of Charlotte. They farmed together on family land for three years. Then, within a short period of time, both of her parents, her sister Eleanor, and Aaron died from contagious illnesses. Her remaining sibling Jeremy went to Edinburgh to further his education, leaving Charlotte in charge of the property which he, as the male child, had inherited. Working with hired hands (her friend Hannah Sloan and members of Hannah's family) and Lem Wainwright who needed a home, Charlotte spent her time lonely but busy. Her only companion at home was an elderly dog, Orpheus, but she was close to her neighbor Richard Longfellow.

Richard, a scientific farmer, was considered rather odd in Bracebridge. He had a glasshouse where he produced new species of plants and kept in touch with scientific discoveries, but he was respected enough to be elected a selectman. Richard had loved Charlotte's sister Eleanor, but she died before they could marry. Charlotte occasionally indulged in ice skating, reading, and spending time with her friends.

Charlotte was content with her good harvest and her friends as *A Wicked Way to Burn* (Bantam, 1998) began. Both she and Richard Longfellow were skeptical of drunken Jack Pennywort's tale of seeing wealthy Boston merchant

Duncan Middleton disappear in smoke and flames. Mercenary miller Peter Lynch was quick to plant suspicion on Gabriel Fortier, whose family had moved to the area from French Canada. Others hinted at witchcraft. Captain Edmund Montagu, representing the Crown, initially disdained the help of locals like Charlotte and Richard, but came to realize their value. Charlotte was responsible for many of the deductions that solved the mystery.

In *Too Soon for Flowers* (Bantam, 1999), visitors to Bracebridge brought tragedy with them. Dr. Benjamin Tucker came at Richard's request to inoculate volunteers against small pox, which was ravaging New England. Richard's younger half-sister Diana, Phoebe Morris who was engaged to Will Sloan, and Lem Wainwright were among the volunteers. Handsome David Pelham, a visitor from Boston, enlivened Diana's boredom with rural life. Two deaths linked to the inoculations created suspicion among the villagers. Richard, Captain Montagu, and Charlotte shared an investigation.

Singer Gian Carlo Lahte's physical condition was a matter of considerable concern in Bracebridge during *No Rest for the Dove* (Bantam, 2000). He had been castrated as a child to preserve the range of his voice. He visited Richard Longfellow because he was considering moving to the area. When fellow Italian Sesto Alba, also from Milan, was murdered nearby, suspicion lodged on Gian Carlo. Additional foreigners followed, creating a web of complicated relationships. The narrative covered the pre-Revolutionary war period with Captain Montagu justifying the Stamp Tax while Richard Longfellow supported the colonist's objections.

An island off the Bracebridge shore was home to elderly Catherine Knowles, her sister-in-law Magdalene, and a pack of marauding boars in *Mischief in the Snow* (Bantam, 2001). A cocky young man, Alexander Godwin, who boasted that he had expectations, met the women's everyday needs. His murder followed a quarrel with Lem Wainwright, Charlotte's protégée. She suspected that Lem might be involved in other local skullduggery, but she was certain he was not the killer. Diana (Richard's half-sister), by then married to Captain Montagu, had to re-establish their relationship after the death of their infant son. Richard and Charlotte's friendship gradually took on a more intimate tone.

Well-researched backgrounds.

Kay Williams

Author: William D. Blankenship

Kay Williams had been unfortunate with the men in her life. Her father, an architect whose skills had been diluted by alcohol, died young. She married, and then divorced, a man who was incapable of fidelity. By her thirties, she had parlayed her linguistic skills and her knowledge of antiques into a successful business. Not only did she maintain a shop in Ridgefield, Connecticut, but wealthy collectors hired her to represent them in auctions or to seek out valuable artifacts. This lifestyle kept her insulated from long term relationships and traveling extensively, but she relished it.

The Time of the Cricket (Fine, 1995) found Kay in Tokyo where she sought a sword once owned by the Emperor Meiji. Her negotiations with Turo Kajima, a local weapons dealer, had been successful, but, as she completed the transaction, a hired assassin murdered Kajima. The killer took the sword. Kay barely escaped with her life. However, at this point she had spent her client's money and had no sword in hand. Kay cooperated with Takeo Saji, a rebellious detective, in thwarting the Japanese Mafia. Their romantic affair was short-lived.

Kay returned to the United States from a successful buying trip in Singapore in *The Time of the Wolf* (Fine, 1998). She received a phone call from oil baron, "Billy Boy" Watkins. Watkins, another weapons collector, had learned that Jim Bowie's original knife left at the Alamo, was to be sold by the descendant of a Mexican who had been present at the battle. The weapon attracted the attention of bidders willing to spend millions to gain possession of the knife, including a hired killer. Kay's efforts to get the knife for Watkins, as the killer eliminated the competition, were hampered by the presence of her former husband Phil. Phil and his more vicious business partner intended to force Kay to subsidize their Caribbean resort venture. Treasury agent Roy Scanner, present to monitor possible counterfeit money, was seriously attracted to Kay, but her trickery in securing the knife, left him cold.

Ruth Willmarth

Author: Nancy Means Wright

Ruth Willmarth, in her forties, was at a crossroads. Her divorce from Peter, the man she dropped out of college to marry, was in process. Their older daughter Sharon was already in her second marriage and had two children. Still at home, she had Emily, a teenager, and Vic, in middle school. Also, she had more than thirty cows to care for on her Branbury, Vermont farm. The cows had literary or theatrical names: "Jane Eyre," "Zelda," and "Dolly Parton."

Ruth was well aware of the economic disparity in the Branbury area. Newcomers, known locally as "flatlanders," fled the cities rejoicing to find lower taxes and land prices, but demanding the level of services which higher taxes could provide. Locals could not afford the luxury of higher land prices or taxes.

There was a lot for Ruth to be angry about in *Mad Season* (St. Martin, 1996). There had been several barn fires in which arson was suspected. Bullies were making Vic miserable, taunting him as a smelly farm boy and physically abusing him. Worst of all, Pete, who had turned his back on Ruth and the farm, wanted to sell the property, which was in joint ownership. Ruth had centered her life on the land since Pete's desertion. Colm Hanna, who had loved and lost

Ruth to Pete in high school, became a source of strength. The murder of neighbor Belle Laroque and another unexplained death added to the stress.

What might be deemed instability elsewhere was perceived as merely eccentricity in *Harvest of Bones* (St. Martin, 1998). Ruth's friend Fay Hubbard was trying to run a bed and breakfast with limited experience. She took in elderly and confused Glenna Flint and her teenage grandniece Hartley without any idea of whether or not she would be repaid for their care. When a corpse was discovered on the property, Glenna insisted that it was not her husband Mac, who had disappeared. Another guest, Kevin Crowningshield who seemed familiar with the area, was seeking his missing wife Angie. When Angie was located, she was dying, possibly poisoned. Ruth, Colm and a pair of teenagers solved these multi-layered crimes. Ruth did work one thing out. She decided to give Peter the divorce he wanted.

Stan and Moira Earthrowl had purchased a Branbury area orchard, hoping to leave behind the tragic death of their only daughter Carol. In *Poison Apples* (St. Martin, 2000), Ruth and Moira became friends. Emily had summertime employment as a "picker" at the orchard, but most of the workers were Jamaicans. There were more than a few "bad apples" in the neighborhood, including Ruth's former husband Pete, now a greedy developer who would be satisfied to see the Earthrowls fail; Rufus Barron, the orchard manager who resented the foreign workers and coveted the property for himself; and religious cultists who harassed high school teacher Aaron Samuels for requiring students to read a controversial novel.

Family struggles intertwined in *Stolen Honey* (St. Martin's, 2002; republished in 2005). Ruth, put in long hours keeping her dairy farm afloat, burdened by her former husband's demands for payment of his share of the property. With daughter Emily going to college, Ruth survived party through the hard work of her handyman Tim and young Joey, the foster child Tim hoped to adopt. Donna Woodleaf, one of Emily's best friends, commuted to college from the farm owned by her beekeeper mother Gwen. The death of lecherous fraternity "boy" Shep Noble on the Woodleaf property placed Gwen, her Abenaki husband Russell and employee Leroy Ballinger under suspicion. Overshadowing Ruth and Gwen's concerns was a PhD research paper by Prof. Camille Wilmette, detailing eugenic practices allowed in Vermont during the 1930's, sterilization of women and children labeled "degenerate", primarily French-Americans and Native Americans. Very interesting material.

Ruth was overwhelmed as *Mad Cow Nightmare* (St. Martin, 2005) began. It was not the abnormal heat or the low milk prices. It was the invasion of the "travelers", Irish-American gypsies. When her hired man Tim left for a year's vacation in Alaska, Ruth had agreed to hire Darren O'Neill, a cousin of Colm's (her lover) as a farmhand. After Darren's arrival, the gypsies came in droves: Darren's lyrical wife Maggie; her teenage sister Liz, and their grandmother Boadie who brought along a pot-bellied pig all lived in a trailer on Ruth's property. More ominous, was the arrival of Nola Donahue, a possible carrier of the human form of Mad Cow disease. Enough said.

Wright is also the author of at least two juvenile mysteries.

Francesca "Fran" Wilson

Author: Christine Green

Francesca Wilson came to Fowchester shortly after she had been promoted to Detective Sergeant, but under a cloud. In her prior posting at Birmingham, she had turned in her lover, a fellow officer, for abusing a suspect. However necessary that had been for her own conscience, it cost her the support of her co-workers. She had few close ties. Her mother had died and her father had remarried. Her only sister lived in Canada. She was a small woman with dark hair, independent and clever. Superintendent Ringstead assigned Fran to Detective Inspector Connor O'Neill, whose descent into alcoholism after the suicide of his wife put him at risk. Theirs was a difficult pairing. He liked his shots and beer; she was a vegetarian. He was fighting his alcoholism, and needed someone close.

In *Death in the Country* (Bantam, 1995), the discovery of two sets of arms and hands in trash bags set Fran and Connor looking for not one body, but two: one male, one female. Suspects abounded, and most of them were guilty of something. The narrative was engrossing, but made more difficult by confusion as to the names of characters as it progressed.

In *Die in My Dreams* (Bantam, 1995), the improved relationship between Connor and Fran caused Ringstead to warn her not to get too close. When she requested a reassignment, he said no one else would have her. Two murders along the banks of the river close to a popular pub had alarmed the community. Ringstead considered the presence in the community of Carole Ann Forbes, a recently released woman who had been convicted of murder, an obvious solution, but Fran and Connor disagreed. They not only found the killer, but also investigated the original charges against Carole Ann.

The death of vicious Denise Parks while immobilized at a beauty parlor in *Fatal Cut* (Severn House, 1999) exposed the lives of her family; i.e. sister, daughter, and mother. The probe went beyond that to the heterosexual and homosexual liaisons of the staff at the beauty shop. Inspector Connor O'Neill's personal interest in Fran had to be shelved temporarily as they sifted through the list of suspects for the one who succumbed to murder.

Christine Green's other series featuring Kate Kinsella is covered in Part 1 of this volume

Lucie D'Arby Wilton (Archer)

Author: Candace Robb

Owen Archer, a former soldier incapacitated by the loss of an eye, found a new profession as "spy" or investigator for powerful English dignitaries beginning in the 1360s. Among his first suspects was the woman who would become his wife, Lucie D'Arby Wilton, apprentice apothecary to her husband Nicholas. Lucie began life as the daughter of Sir Robert D'Arby and his hostage French wife Amelie. The older soldier and his young bride had but the one child, disappointingly a daughter. Amelie died while pregnant with another man's child. Lucie was rejected by her father and placed in a convent. He returned to France to serve in the Hundred Years War. Nicholas, master apothecary in York and a friend of Amelie, offered Lucie an alternative to the restrictive life of the convent where she had been treated as the daughter of a promiscuous mother. The calm of their marriage had been broken only by the death of their child Martin of the plague.

In *The Apothecary Rose* (St. Martin, 1993), the deaths of an anonymous pilgrim and Sir Oswald Fitzwilliam, the ward of Archer's employer, the Archbishop, placed Nicholas and Lucie's marriage and their lives in jeopardy. Lucie, denied the rights and luxuries of her birth, was fiercely independent. After Nicholas died she became a master apothecary with Owen as her apprentice. Their love brought marriage, but Owen was frequently called away on missions for John Thoresby, Lord Chancellor and Archbishop. Lucie realized that Owen needed more than the routine life they led in York, but chafed when Owen rejected her involvement in his investigations, particularly where her expertise might be of value.

In *The Lady Chapel* (St. Martin, 1994), the murders of two prominent wool merchants occurred as a result of their political activities, but also through a deep seated need for vengeance for a past wrong. The complex narrative with major historical overtones was enlivened by on-going characters: Brother Wulfstan, in charge of the infirmary at the monastery; young Jasper de Melton, who became a part of the Archer household; Bess Merchet, an outspoken innkeeper who was Lucie's confidante; and Magda Digby, a midwife who operated without the approval of church or state. Lucie had been more suspect than sleuth in the first book, but achieved a supportive status in this book and others.

Lord Chancellor Thoresby and Brother Wulfstan sought Lucie's help in dealing with hysterical runaway nun Lady Joanna Calverley, in *The Nun's Tale* (St. Martin, 1995). Owen had the active role, roaming the countryside, and dealing with powerful English nobles while Lucie tended victims, and learned the background for their injuries.

Lucie's role in *The King's Bishop* (St. Martin, 1996) was reduced to hand wringing as Owen tried to save Ned Townley, a soldier/friend, from death. Ned was the primary suspect in several murders and there were those who would prefer that he not be taken alive. Once Lucie was a mother and had continued responsibilities in her work, it was logical that her participation would be reduced.

Lucie had only a background role in *The Riddle of St. Leonard's* (St. Martin, 1997), during which Bess Merchet assisted Owen. He investigated mysterious deaths among the corrodies (pensioners who had transferred assets to the hospital in exchange for lifetime care).

Lucie appeared only by reference in *A Gift of Sanctuary* (St. Martin, 1998) as her husband and father (with whom she had reconciled) journeyed to Wales in the service of the Duke of Lancaster to appraise the loyalty of the Welsh.

More than distance separated Lucy and Owen in *A Spy for the Redeemer* (Heinemann, 1999). His trip to Wales had been extended when the local Archdeacon pressured him into investigating the death of Cynog, a gifted stonemason. The separation was difficult for Lucie. The recent death of her father in Wales left a sizeable estate to be managed until her son Hugh reached his majority. Those who offered help to Lucie had agendas of their own: greed, a search for intimacy, or political power.

Considering the setting i.e., York, England in the Fourteenth century, it is no wonder that Owen Archer played the dominant role in *The Cross-Legged Knight* (Warner, 2003). Political and religious politics pitted William, Bishop of Winchester, against the Lancasters. He was blamed by Lady Pagnell for his failure to ransom her husband Sir Ranulf which led to his death. While in York negotiating a settlement, William was under the protection of Owen's forces representing Archbishop John Thorsby. Incidents that were perceived by William as a threat to his life must be investigated. The death of Cisotta, a midwife friend of Lucie, pulled her into the investigation. She had fallen, causing a miscarriage which plunged her into depression. Her determination to find Casita's murder involved her in Owen's responsibilities. By now Owen and Lucie had adopted young Jasper de Melton.

Lucie, pregnant with her fourth child, was in no condition to get involved in the death of Drogue, a river bargeman, during *The Guilt of Innocents* (Heinemann, 2007) Jasper, the teenage boy whom she and Owen Archer had adopted, was present when a group of boys from St. Peter's school came to the wharf to retrieve a small purse taken from young Hubert de Weston by Drogue. There was obviously much more at stake than a purse so Archbishop John Thorsby ordered Owen to investigate. This entailed some travel, leaving Lucie to take care of the younger children and herself.

There were heavy doses of history, essential to understand the motivations of the characters, which may deter some readers. Worth the trouble for a reader with the time and interest. Robb has a second more recent series, set in 13th century Scotland, featuring Dame Margaret Kerr.

Next: *A Vigil of Spies* (2009)

Holly Winter

Author: Susan Conant

The mystery heroine finally went to the dogs. It was about time after cats, cats, and more cats. Holly, a canine fanatic, informed her readers about dog care (no chocolate); responsibility (blame the owner, not the pet for misbehavior); and best breeds (the Malamute). Dogs were so pervasive in the series that even a dedicated dog lover might call "halt." Holly had no trouble recalling dog names and descriptions, but was hazy about the owners. She was a blonde, initially about thirty, with a veterinarian lover, and a widowed father who bred wolf/dogs. Having earned a journalism degree, Holly supported herself by writing a column for a dog magazine, and rented out an apartment building she owned.

During *A New Leash on Death* (Diamond, 1990), Holly and her Malamute Rowdy attended obedience training sessions where perfectionist Dr. Frank Stanton was murdered with a leash. With the help of friendly neighbor policeman Kevin Dennehy, Holly not only exposed murder, but also dog doping.

Dead and Doggone (Diamond, 1990) moved on to obedience trials. The problems of animals used in experiments, and the disappearance of Buck Winter's wolf/dog, vied for attention with the murder by grooming shears of cosmetologist Sissy Quigley.

By *A Bite of Death* (Diamond, 1991), Holly had added a second dog, Kimi, to her ménage. When PhD. psychologist Elaine Walsh, the previous owner, was poisoned, Holly was suspicious because the poison had been in cottage cheese which Elaine never ate. Holly used intimate dog behavior to uncover a deadly relationship.

In *Paws Before Dying* (Diamond, 1991), Holly's ego suffered when her untrained cousin Leah turned out to be a natural dog handler. Retired teacher and dog-owner Rose Engleman was found dead outside after a storm. The assumption was, that while walking her dog, she had accidentally touched a live wire. In her investigation Holly explored anti-Semitism and child abuse in a dysfunctional suburban family.

During *Gone to the Dogs* (Doubleday, 1992), Holly and her lover Steve Delaney followed the trail of missing veterinarian Oscar Patterson and a dog that need not have died. Holly and Rowdy saved Vietnam veteran John Buckley when he confronted the man who had killed a rare Chinook dog.

The series moved into hardcover with *Bloodlines* (Doubleday, 1992). Holly detested pet shops, which sold badly bred dogs. When "Puppy Luv" offered a Malamute pup for sale, she visited the store, only to learn that owner Diane Sweet had been murdered, and the puppy was gone. Holly's initial concerns were to rescue the pup and alert the SPCA; then leave Kevin Dennehy and the local police to solve the murder.

Ruffly Speaking (Doubleday, 1994) included several new characters and a good plot: Holly's neighbor Alice Savery, an isolated elderly woman who was unable to deal with dogs or children; deaf female minister Stephanie Benson; the death of Morris Lamb, a gay bookstore/restaurant owner; and Ivan, a precocious child looking for trouble. Holly became involved because she was doing an article on hearing-ear dogs for her magazine.

As columnist for *Dog's World*, Holly evaluated a summer training camp for dogs and owners in *Black Ribbon* (Doubleday, 1995). Maxene McGuire, the camp proprietor, was thwarted by disloyal staff, resentful guests, and "accidents" designed to ruin the camp's reputation. Eva Spitteler, a constant critic, was killed while using camp equipment without supervision.

Stud Rites (Doubleday, 1996) explored the rivalries and jealousies among competitors in Malamute dog shows. When the murder of Judge James Honeywell occurred, it was swathed in canine pedigrees, chilled by frozen semen, and solved by the process of elimination.

Animal Appetite (Doubleday, 1997) forced Holly into the "people" world when she accepted a challenge to write about something besides dogs. Holly researched the life of Hannah Duston, a colonial woman who had been captured by Indians; then, escaped after killing most of her captors. Holly conducted a parallel probe into the death of publisher Jack Andrews whose Golden Retriever was proof that he could not have committed suicide. A pleasing variation.

The Barker Street Regulars (Doubleday, 1998) tied a local murder investigation into Sherlock Holmes through several elderly devotees of the British sleuth, including nursing home resident Althea Battlefield. Holly and Rowdy had met them when they made their volunteer visits to nursing homes. When Jonathan Hubbell, Althea's visiting nephew, was murdered, the elderly sleuths wanted Holly and Rowdy to assist them in the investigation. Holly suspected that Ceci, Althea's wealthy sister, was being deceived by those who took advantage of her love for her deceased dog.

Holly contracted to write the text for a photographic study of famous dog shows hosted by heiress Geraldine Rockefeller Dodge in *Evil Breeding* (Doubleday, 1999). Her research introduced her to the malfunctioning Motherway family, which had for three generations hidden a nasty secret. The mix of Nazi spies, art thefts, and murder placed a heavy burden on Conant's narrative skills, resulting in a last chapter of extended explanations.

During *Creature Discomforts* (Doubleday, 2000), Holly returned to consciousness on a mountainside in Arcadia National Park, Maine. Amnesiac initially, through Rowdy, Kimi and the contents of her backpack, she returned to an awareness of her name. Only a re-enactment of her fall restored her memory and her connection to the death of chronic complainer Norman Abelard. There were two weddings to enliven the narrative but neither was Holly's.

With Steve Delaney married to disbarred attorney Anita Fairley, Holly devoted her attention to friends, human and canine, in *The Wicked Flea* (Berkley, 2002). Ceci Love introduced her to a group that allowed their dogs to run free in an area near her house. That would never do for show dogs. An undisciplined dog and a selfish breeder provoked a murder. The breeder (and victim) Sylvia Metzner had an avaricious family providing several suspects. The killer was exposed by a man who made a habit of it. Buck, Holly's widowed father, had married widow Gabriella.

Sometimes a favor is just a favor, but in *The Dogfather* (Berkley, 2003) favors got to be a problem. Holly had agreed to train mobster Enzio Guarini's elkhound puppy at no cost. Guarini, surrounded by his henchmen, worked hard at learning dog management skills. He was paranoid and had every right to be. "Blackie" Lanigan and Enzio were out to kill one another. Holly got caught in the middle, risking her life and almost ruining her reputation in the dog ring.

Vet Bruce "Mac" McCloud had been a mentor to Holly when she began merchandizing her book *100 Ways to Cook Liver* in *Bride and Groom* (Berkley, 2004). She and Steve Delaney (no longer married to Anita Fairley), now busy planning their wedding and honeymoon in Paris, got to know Mac, his author/wife Judith, and their two adult children. It was an exciting experience for Holly to be signing books at local bookstores. When there was a series of murders, Holly was surprised to realize how many of the victims she had met and how many were dog owners. Against advice from Steve, Holly checked things out. Too often, the killer's motives in the later books seem weak.

Psychologist Ted Green and his wife Eumie Brainerd-Green had bid high enough at a high school auction in *Gaits of Heaven* (Berkley, 2006) to win training lessons at Holly's group sessions. Their dog (or "person in fur' as they perceived him) was a mixed breed who was neither housebroken nor leash trained. His behavior was so destructive that Holly abandoned the possibility of group sessions, instead agreed to make housecalls. Ted and Eumie needed to be trained along with Dolfo. Their household was completed by Caprice, Eumie's daughter by a prior marriage, and Wyeth, Ted's son by his first wife. They detested one another. Although Ted was insistent that Eumie's subsequent death was a suicide, other therapists and friends disagreed. Busybody, Eumie might be, but she had been a generous soul.

Holly was alone (except for pets) in *All Shots* (Berkley, 2007), because Steve was doing the Minnesota Boundary Waters with his two dogs. While on a Malamute rescue mission, Holly discovered the body of a woman named Holly Winter. If that weren't enough, the victim had stolen financial documents from Holly's trash and entered the home of a third woman, also named Holly Winter, to obtain information. Lt. Kevin Dennehy helped to clear up the confusion but not before there were multiple complications including a search for a rare blue Malamute. More than a little confusing at times.

Susan Conant now has a cat series going, featuring Felicity Pride, and co-authors with her daughter, Jessica Conant–Park a series featuring Chloe Carter, subtitled "Gourmet Girl"

Hannah Wolfe

Author: Sarah Dunant

Hannah Wolfe, a Londoner whose politics, lifestyle, and approach to work were unconventional, was anti-establishment all the way. She was single in her mid-thirties. A three-year college education had prepared her for a job working for the European Economic Community, but she was too restless to work within the system. Her only sister Kate lived a more commonplace existence within marriage and parenthood, sometimes envying Hannah's adventures. Hannah had tried working as a solo private investigator, but, when the bills mounted up, returned to Frank Comfort's agency where she had learned the business.

In *Birth Marks* (Doubleday, 1992), elderly spinster Augusta Patrick hired Hannah to find the young ballet dancer whose education she had sponsored. When Carolyn Hamilton's pregnant corpse was found, Hannah's assignment was changed to finding a killer, who may have been connected to a job Carolyn had taken in Paris, a very intimate assignment.

Frank Comfort had a simple task for Hannah in *Fatlands* (Penzler, 1993), escorting Mattie Shepherd, a lonely fourteen-year-old boarding school student, to visit her scientist father in London. The assignment blew up, leaving Hannah with guilt, anger, and deep seated suspicions that Mattie's father was targeted for murder by animal rights extremists or by his own employer.

Hannah experienced doubts about her sexuality in *Under My Skin* (Scribner's, 1995). An undercover assignment at a beauty farm brought her into contact with a lesbian masseuse. She intervened in her sister Kate's marriage, almost with tragic results. These side issues did not prevent her from identifying the prankster who became a killer.

A provocative series with depressing undertones.

April Woo

Author: Leslie Glass

April was a second generation Chinese-American whose parents clung to the older traditions. Her mother Sai constantly encouraged April to make a good marriage, or at least to become educated in a field more prestigious than police work. However, for financial reasons, April had foregone full-time college. She took night classes that would lead to a degree. At the time she joined the New York Police Department, only a few detectives were Asians, much less Chinese. These were dark brooding narratives in which her co-protagonist was as likely to be psychiatrist Jason Frank as her police partner Sgt. Mike Sanchez.

April and Jason worked together in *Burning Time* (Doubleday, 1993), during which his actress/wife Emma was a pivotal character. Her appearance in a sexually oriented art film made Emma a target for mutilation and murder. When Emma disappeared, April was assigned to the case. April turned away from her domineering Chinese boyfriend. She had no physical relationship with Mike, although they were attracted to one another. He was married to an absentee wife dying of leukemia. Any potential romance between Mike and April moved glacially both because of their mothers' resistance to an interracial marriage and the demands of their work schedules.

During *Hanging Time* (Bantam, 1995), Jason's wife Emma sought professional advancement and recuperation in California, leaving him emotionally adrift. Milicia Honiger-Stanton came to him at that time very concerned about her sister. Camille Honiger-Stanton had been dominated by Milicia but had fallen under the influence of a strange man, Nathan Buck. According to Milicia, Camille or Nathan might be connected to the "boutique murders" to which April and Mike were assigned. The first victim of the boutique murders had been Maggie Wheeler, who worked at The Last Mango. She had been found hanging from a chandelier. Similar crimes followed. April prevented a serious injustice at the cost of missing her sergeant's exam.

In *Loving Time* (Bantam, 1996), Mike, now a widower, and April, now a sergeant, were assigned to two possible suicides: that of Ray Cowles, a mental patient who had been discharged from psychotherapy fourteen years before, and more recently that of Dr. Harold Dickey, a therapist who had treated him. If these were not suicides, there were multiple murder suspects: Dr. Clara Treadwell, head of the psychiatric center who had also treated Ray but was now a powerful and seductive psychiatrist, disenchanted spouses, and Bobbie Boudreau, a violence-prone former nurse.

Rick Liberty had moved beyond his fame as an African-American professional quarterback to becoming a successful businessman in *Judging Time* (Dutton, 1998). He was comfortable with his marriage to an attractive white actress. However when his wife Merritt and his best friend multimillionaire Tory Petersen died within minutes of one another, Liberty became the target of a murder investigation. April, now a sergeant at Midtown North, and Mike, a special homicide investigator, saw Liberty as only one of several suspects. Physical evidence, once it was properly evaluated, vindicated their uphill battle to prove Liberty innocent. They also reached a closer personal accommodation.

In *Stealing Time* (Dutton, 1999), it took a while for April to tie together three cases: the "suicide" of an alien worker in a sweatshop, the attack on young Chinese wife Heather Rose Popescu, and the disappearance of her child. Was it really Heather's child? The narrative explored the role of a woman in Chinese society and the workplace abuses of immigrants. April moved closer to Mike and a shared future as she freed herself at age thirty from her parent's domination.

April was still trying to cope with a hostile supervisor at work and a disapproving mother. She did not need additional problems. Yet, in *Tracking Time* (Dutton, 2000), she could not refuse to help Jason Frank. Mallow Atkins, whom Frank was training in psychoanalysis, had disappeared in Central Park. This was neither April's case nor her jurisdiction, but she intervened. Suspects included seriously disturbed teenagers whose needs had been ignored by their parents.

April and Mike's romantic plight and their investigations were subordinated to a mixture of explosive characters.

Successive murders of brides during, and before, their wedding ceremonies created not only professional but personal problems for April and Mike in *The Silent Bride* (Onyx, 2002). The same couturier who designed the dresses for Tovah Schoenfeld and Prudence Hay was providing the gown for the wedding of Ching Ma Dong, April's dearest friend. Talk of weddings also created a temporary rift between Mike (who wanted one) and April, who feared her parents' disapproval. With all that in the background, Mike and April were assigned to investigate the Bridal Killer.

Recent beneficiaries of substantial estates were at risk in *A Killing Gift* (Onyx, 2003). April who had come upon the body of her mentor Al Bernardino, chased his killer and almost became the next victim. Al's children and his former partner were obvious suspects until trophy wife Birdie Barrett died under similar circumstances. She had inherited a huge estate from her elderly husband. April's injury and her conflict of interest caused her to be shunted to the sidelines of the dual investigation. Undeterred, she sought the ties that connected Al, Birdie, and computer expert Jack Devereaux who had rescued her. April was definitely not a team player.

April's life had changed by *A Clean Kill* (Onyx, 2005). Not only had she and Mike married and purchased a home, but both had been promoted to command levels. She remained at the Midtown Detective Unit as commander while Mike was transferred to the 17th Precinct. However these designations became hazy when Mike talked April into assisting in the murder case of housewife Middy Wilson. A second death, that of Middy's friend and neighbor Alison Perkins, extended April's commitment. Sgt. Eloise Geol was working on a case involving strip clubs, handling unit meetings in April's absence, and researching information on the two victims and their nannies in the cases in Mike's unit. Burnout!

Glass populated her narratives with remarkable supporting characters, who were under heavy stress. Her primary characters developed over the series.

Susan Donovan Wren

Author: Charlene Weir

Susan Donovan had a tense relationship with her father, Attorney Patrick Donavan. Her mother, who had played violin in the San Francisco symphony orchestra, was more understanding of Susan's goals. In her mid-thirties, Susan was a dedicated San Francisco police officer who had earned a law degree and two commendations for valor. Then, she met Dan Wren, the police chief of Hampstead, Kansas. Their marriage was expected to end her professional career. She moved to Kansas, anticipating an uneventful adjustment.

Susan and Dan's honeymoon was short-lived. In *The Winter Widow* (St. Martin, 1992), he was shot in the back while investigating cattle rustlers. Susan intended to return to San Francisco, but not yet. She accepted an interim appointment to Dan's position because she did not intend to leave until his killer had been caught and punished. Susan made some false starts: chasing pigs, releasing a bull from his pen, and foiling her new sister-in-law's plan to sell the family farm. She survived with the help of initially hostile deputy Ben Parkhurst.

In *Consider the Crows* (St. Martin, 1993), Susan questioned "hippie" Lynnelle Hames in the isolated house she was renting. Lynnelle, who came to town to discover her parentage, was a danger to someone. When she was killed, Susan needed to know who was so vulnerable.

The current generation of the Barrington family had followed their mother into medicine in *Family Practice* (St. Martin, 1995), dominated by eldest daughter Dorothy. When Dorothy was murdered, her siblings were the logical suspects. Susan had another concern. The sole possible witness to Dorothy's death was young Jen Bryant, who had been left in Susan's care while her mother was out of town. Susan had to find the killer before another attempt was made on Jen's life.

Susan was the police chief in Hampstead during *Murder Take Two* (St. Martin, 1998); however, when the town was selected as a location by a movie production, her subordinates, Ben Parkhurst and Peter Yancy, were more personally involved. Established movie star Laura Edwards, who believed she was the target of a killer, looked to Ben, her former husband, for protection. Police officer Peter Yancy could not prevent two murders from occurring or separate his own family from involvement in the investigation. Susan came on strong in the resolution of the case, discarding a convenient suspect to identify the killer, and prevent a third murder.

Caley James was exhausted with flu and overwork as *A Cold Christmas* (St. Martin, 2000) began. Her furnace needed repair. She struggled to care for three children, eking out a living as an organist. Her irresponsible ex-husband Mat rated high on promises; low on performance. The last thing she needed was dead furnace repairman Tim Holiday in her cellar. Susan had only a passing acquaintance with Caley when she handled the investigation, but she reserved her decision as to moving back to San Francisco until the case was closed. She had questions. Why was Caley always tired? What was the connection between Mat James and the victim?

Grief, guilt and ambition motivated the characters in *Up in Smoke* (St. Martin, 2003) A widow herself, Susan was in good condition compared to Cass Storm whose husband and three-year-old daughter were killed by a drunken driver, or Mary "Em" Shoals whose daughter and unborn grandchild were killed by her sister-in-law. Presidential candidate Gov. Jack Garrett and his handicapped friend Wakely Fromm survived a forest fire in which six firefighters had died. The interactions which led to murder were intensified by political ambition. Garrett's were more than equaled by those of his wife Molly, and his campaign manager Todd Haviland. Susan had help from tough cop Demarco and her engaging reporter cousin Sean Donovan.

Edge of Midnight (Thomas Dunne, St. Martin's Miniature, 2006) was permeated with tragedy, explicit sex and violence. Two young women, accountant Cary Black and former juror Kelly Oliver, lived in fear. A third woman Lily Palmer had already died at the hands of a rapist killer. Attorney Arleta Coleridge, a friend of both women, encouraged Cary to leave her abusive husband and arranged shelter for her with Kelby who was hiding out in Hampstead, Kansas (Susan's jurisdiction). Although Susan endured a personal tragedy of her own, and participated in the investigation, novice cop Ida Rather stole the show.

These were well-plotted stories with interesting characters. Author Charlene Weir is an excellent writer, able to turn out a taut mystery free of the bloating now so pervasive in the genre.

Jolie Wyatt

Author: Barbara Burnett Smith

After her first husband Steve had deserted her and their infant child, Jolie worked hard to become a successful copywriter in Austin, Texas. A dozen years later, Matt had swept her and son, Jeremy, off to Purple Sage, Texas. Jeremy became deeply attached to Matt, but Jolie could not find a life for herself on the ranch or in the nearby small town, so the couple divorced. Her only close friends were fellow members of a writer's group; her only outlet, writing mystery stories, none of which had ever been published.

In *Writers of the Purple Sage* (St. Martin, 1994), Jolie became a prime suspect when local politician Volney Osler was murdered by a method carefully described in Jolie's manuscript. Who knew about the modus operandi? Only the fellow members of her writing group. Someone who knew Jolie well enough to plant evidence that tied her even closer to the crime. Many in the close-knit community knew she had quarreled with Osler. Matt and Jeremy helped her prove her innocence. Matt and Jolie resumed their relationship at a different level.

As *Dust Devils of the Purple Sage* (St. Martin, 1995) began, Jolie was a news reporter for local station WSGE. She aired the bulletin that young James Jorgenson had escaped from prison with the help of his sister Sharon, and was headed for Purple Sage, armed and dangerous. When Sharon's boyfriend Tim was murdered, James was assumed to be his killer. Jolie's investigation uncovered a bevy of female suspects.

Their non-marital status became a problem for Matt and Jolie during *Celebration in Purple Sage* (St. Martin, 1996). The town's centennial resulted in a host of visitors, including Matt's parents and his elegant former wife Cecily. Jolie needed her former mother-in-law's knowledge of the community to find the attacker of festival chairman Vera Meece and Sheriff Mac Donelly. With Mac seriously injured, his replacement Deputy Ed Presnell selected Matt as his number one suspect. Jolie was his second choice, so it was important for her to locate the man whom Vera had planned to meet at Camp John Seybold, formerly the location of a prison for captured German soldiers.

It might have been a mistake for Jolie and Matt to visit Austin in *Mistletoe from Purple Sage* (St. Martin, 1997). She planned to visit old friends, including former lover Michael Sherabian, at an office party. Jolie stopped at the restroom before leaving the group, only to find the corpse of copywriter Desi Baker, who also had history with Michael. Given a staff shortage, Jolie helped out at the agency where Desi had worked, making it possible for her to learn more about relationships. Because she was a suspect herself, Jolie had difficulty getting Sgt Ray Bohles to accept information from her. Still, she solved a crime and saved a child by Christmas morning.

Jolie had a lot of soul searching to do in *Skeletons in Purple Sage* (St. Martin, 2002) Dr. Bill Marchak, who had cared for her father in his last illness, was found dead in the water after a party in his honor. The party had been held at the home of Tom Green and his second wife, Leigh. Tom's first wife Bev had been a close friend of Jolie's so she made no effort to be kind to Leigh until it was too late. Jolie came to realize that her hasty judgments had put her into danger, Another complication arose when Irene, Jolie's mother, visited Purple Sage and began a relationship with Sheriff Mac Donnelly.

These were light but interesting. Barbara Burnett Smith began another series featuring Kitzi Camden.

Eva Wylie

Author: Liza Cody

Liza Cody, author of the series featuring engaging young private investigator, Anna Lee, introduced Eva Wylie, a dour self-centered female wrestler, who had obsessions rather than relationships.

In *Bucket Nut* (Chatto, 1992; Doubleday, 1993), Eva was determined to find her younger sister Simone lost to her during years in foster care. The girl's mother, a drunken prostitute, was unable to care for them both. Eva had few scruples. She lied, stole, bullied, and was a courier for drug dealers. However, on occasion, someone would appeal to Eva's weakness for the underdog; e.g. Eleanor Crombie, a drug ridden third-rate young singer who reminded Eva of her sister. Eva was a pawn of powerful drug interests. For her, survival was success.

What really mattered to Eva was her career as a wrestler, and it was endangered in *Monkey Wrench* (Chatto, 1994; Mysterious Press, 1995). She had worn out her welcome with fight promoters and the men at the gym where she trained. Nevertheless, she promised her friend Crystal that she would find out who killed her sister Dawn, a prostitute. This, plus her grudging involvement in teaching other prostitutes how to protect themselves on the streets, cost Eva her job and made her an accessory to murder.

In *Musclebound* (Mysterious, 1997), Eva reconnected with her sister. She would do anything to protect Simone. Eva tried to be fair with their irresponsible mother, but her overtures did not produce the affection and loyalty that she sought. Eva discounted Anna Lee's (See Volume 2) offers of employment and the friendship offered by a black wrestler, Keif. She focused on returning to the wrestling ring, but achieved it only by subterfuge.

These were gritty but depressing stories with a heroine to whom it was difficult to relate.

MacLaren Yarbrough

Author: Patricia Houck Sprinkle

MacLaren Yarbrough was a happily married woman, a rarity in mystery series in the Nineties. The Yarbrough family lived in small town Hopemore, Georgia where the couple had owned a hardware store. Unable to compete with the big chain stores, the Yarbroughs switched over to a feed and nursery business. She was described as petite, kept her hair honey brown with the aid of her beautician, and had become plump over the years. Joe Riddley, her husband, was devoted to MacLaren. Their two sons Ridd and Walker were grown and married.

Chapters in *When Did We Lose Harriet?* (Zondervan Publishing House, 1997) were alternately narrated by MacLaren and African-American librarian, Josheba Davidson. Young Harriet Lawson felt adrift after the death of the grandmother who had raised her. A placement in her aunt's home was unpleasant. At the end of the school year, she ran away. She had money enough to get to Alabama where she expected to meet the mother who had abandoned her at age two. Her brother's illness prompted MacLaren to visit Birmingham, Alabama, and to remain there while he recovered. She discovered an envelope containing $3,000 in a library book. Her plan to return the money involved her and Josheba in a search for Harriet; then, for her killer.

Thefts of antiques seemed minor compared to the murder and attempted murder that besieged Hopemore in *But Why Shoot the Magistrate?* (Zondervan, 1998). The magistrate in question was Joe Riddley who survived an attack. The target had been MacLaren who was close to discovering the killer of a young nurse who had been too attentive to her patients.

It was unlikely that MacLaren (or anyone else) would have invited the infamous Hiram Blaine to a party, but in *Who Invited the Dead Man* (Signet, 2002) he made an appearance at Joe Riddley's birthday celebration, as a corpse. Chief of Police Charlie Muggins was quick to focus suspicion on MacLaren, and then more seriously on Joe Riddley whose occasional rages concerned MacLaren. Hiram, who had fantasies about aliens, had been seeing someone in Hopemore. MacLaren's first concern was Joe Riddley but the best way to help him was to identify Hiram's killer.

The Yarbrough family was looking forward to the wedding of neighbor Maynard Spence and nurse Selena Jones as *Who Left That Body in the Rain* (Signet, 2002) began. Walker and his wife Cindy's children were to take part in the ceremony. Joe Riddley's gift was to be a partial payment for the used BMW that Maynard was purchasing from car dealer Skye MacDonald. The

MacDonalds (Skye, his wife Gwen Ellen, daughter Laura and son Skell) were very close to the Yarbroughs. Skell was upset that the BMW from the used car lot he managed had been sold by his dad to Maynard. He insisted that it must be returned because he had promised it to an important customer. The discovery of Skye's corpse, run over by his own abandoned car, and Skell's disappearance were too important to be left to incompetent police chief Charlie Muggins.

Sprinkle's *Who Let That Killer in the House?* (Signet 2002) was a dark tale. Hopemore, which had seemed a tolerant town, bristled with bigotry when African-American high school science teacher De Wayne Evans coached the all white girls baseball team. The celebration after a victory made things worse, resulting in graffiti at the school and De Wayne's home, then the discovery of his body. Woven into the narrative was another more subtle crime, involving the family of widow Sara Meg Stanton, her daughters and her younger brother, Buddy. Tensions built as the reader was given information yet unknown to MacLaren or the police. Mac and Joe Riddley turned their family home over to Ridd and Martha, purchasing a house in town.

MacLaren had a secret in her past, nothing evil, but something she would prefer not to share with her husband in *When Will the Dead Lady Sing?* (Signet, 2004). Former Congressman Burlin Bullock (the other party to her secret) came to Hopemore to promote his son Lance's candidacy for governor. There seemed to be no connection between this highly organized campaign and the fate of a homeless vagrant who trailed after the Bullock entourage, but one emerged.

Edie Burkett had survived her husband's death, his debts, and the stroke that left her father Josiah Whalen disabled, but, in *Who Killed the Queen of Clubs?* (Signet, 2005) she was viciously murdered. MacLaren, who had been concerned about Edie's forgetfulness, found her body. As a potential witness, she had no jurisdiction in the case, but members of her own family and those related to Edie drew her into the matter. Sprinkle's talent for depicting her Southern setting, the interplay among the suspects and the endearing relationship between Mac and her husband were well displayed in the narrative.

MacLaren's trip to Scotland with young friend Laura MacDonald was intended to ameliorate her disappointment in *Did You Declare the Corpse?* (Signet, 2006) because Joe Riddley planned a Gulf fishing trip with his younger son and two grandsons. The other members of the tour group, led by former stewardess Joyce Underwood, may have made beautiful music together, but individual members were contentious, violent, or greedy. The narrative portions detailing their progress to Auchnagar, included historical and descriptive material but also developed the characters. Within days of the arrival in Auchnagar, the body of wealthy tour member James Gordon from Georgia was discovered in a coffin in the small Catholic church. The members of the tour group were required to remain in Auchnagar, but that gave MacLaren time to uncover at least one killer.

Joe Riddley was pleased when MacLaren was invited to join the exclusive Magnolia Ladies' Investment Club in *Guess Who's Coming to Die* (Signet, 2007). MacLaren was appalled. The membership, except for her daughter-in-law Cindy, was composed of the richest women in town, some of whom she heartily disliked. At the first meeting she attended, Maclaren discovered the savagely abused body of wealthy Willena Kenan. Chief Muggins made it impossible for MacLaren to stay out of this one, because he focused on Cindy as his chief suspect. Her car keys had been discovered under Willena's body. Joe Riddley made life more difficult by refusing to tell even MacLaren where Cindy and her family had gone.

Joe Riddley had come to the end of his rope as *What Are You Wearing to Die?* (Obsidian, 2008) began, so he resorted to chains. When he heard that Robin Parker's truck had been found in a kudzu patch with Starr Knight's corpse inside, he cuffed MacLaren to the heavy office desk. It didn't work but, after all, this is a mystery series. Before long MacLaren sought out local taxidermist Trevor Knight, Starr's father and Robin's employer, just to bring food to the bereaved family, of course. As a result she met Robin and her two little girls. Bradley, Starr's four-year-old son, had been temporarily placed in foster care with Ridd and Martha so, it was only natural that she would take an interest. There were interesting cultural references to the decline of locally owned businesses in small towns, which personally affected Joe Riddley and MacLaren.

These were cozy, Christian-oriented narratives written by a skilled author.

Sprinkle had an earlier series featuring Sheila Travis, which was covered in Volume 2 of Mystery Women and a more recent one, *The Family Tree Mysteries,* featuring Katharine Murray.

Magdalena Yoder

Author: Tamar Myers

The Amish with their isolation from modern society formed the background for the Magdalena Yoder series set in Pennsylvania. The Yoder family had relaxed some of the practices of their antecedents, but Magdalena, a tall, well-built woman in her forties, was a faithful adherent of the Amish lifestyle. She had attended the local college earning an associate degree in English, but never graduated. Her younger, and more rebellious sister Susannah, had scandalized the family by marrying and divorcing a Presbyterian, and then earning a reputation as being promiscuous. Magdalena had remodeled the family home into the prosperous Penn Dutch Inn, which provided Susannah with a refuge between her expeditions into the outside world. Magdalena knew her sister's limitations and tolerated them, although she detested Susannah's current beau and eventual husband, local sheriff Melvin Stoltzfus. Initially, Magdalena's only romantic interest was an elderly veterinarian, Doc Shafor, who plied her with food and conversation.

Cousin Freni, whose cooking had earned the Inn an enviable reputation, found it difficult to cope with a vegetarian/animal rights convention in *Too Many Crooks Spoil the Broth* (Doubleday, 1994). The group arrived for the opening of deer season, planning to protest hunters. Isolated guest Heather Brown, who merely wanted to be left alone, and young Linda McMahon, a member of the vegetarian group, were killed by an obscure poison, hardly a recommendation for the Inn's cuisine.

In *Parsley, Sage, Rosemary, and Crime* (Doubleday, 1995), Magdalena leased the Inn to a film company for background scenes. She was unprepared for internal strife among the dramatic personnel and the unrestrained interest of the locals in becoming extras in the film. Magdalena, not only moved up to a major role after the death of the original scriptwriter, but attracted the interest of Aaron Miller, who had returned to the community to care for his father. The narrative was witty for such a restrained setting, although the plot was fragile.

The death of distant relatives took Magdalena, Susannah, and Freni to Ohio in *No Use Dying Over Spilled Milk* (Doubleday, 1996). Before Yost Yoder's body was in the ground, Magdalena learned that his death might be connected to a cooperative dairy that he and other Amish farmers had established when they became dissatisfied with the local milk purchaser. A stolid Amish farmer like Yost was unlikely to engage in bizarre behavior before his death. Aaron Miller joined Magdalena as soon as the weather and road conditions would allow. He did not arrive in time to rescue her (she had handled the killers herself), but he provided the happy ending with a proposal.

The big wedding day was at hand in *Just Plain Pickled to Death* (Signet, 1997), but one of the gifts included a corpse. Must have been the "something old" because the body had been pickled for twenty years. Sarah Weaver had disappeared long ago, but many of those who might have been responsible for her death would be guests at the wedding. With the Inn filled with non-paying relatives and soon to be in-laws, Magdalena made time to find another body, attend a funeral, and still get married.

Susannah's short-term employment with a paint company ended in disaster. She was back at the inn as a dependent in *Between a Wok and a Hard Place* (Signet, 1998). Also resident was Aaron's father. The only one missing was Aaron who flew to Minnesota to straighten some things out. After dropping him off at the airport, Magdalena seemed to have struck a body as she passed through town. Not only had the victim, a Japanese tourist, died previously, but Melvin Stoltzfus, asked Magdalena to help him solve the murder. One of the youths suspected of running over the body was later found dead. She knew the townspeople, including the teenagers who were downtown late at night, and had more information about guests at the inn. Some were behaving very suspiciously. Magdalena had never had it easy, but this narrative dealt her a cruel blow.

Freni's participation in a cooking contest was assured if she could secure the Penn Dutch Inn for several weeks. In *Eat, Drink and Be Wary* (Signet, 1998), Magdalena agreed to cancel all reservations and accommodate the contestants and judges. Little did she know that one man had been judged already and sentenced to death. There were so many motives for the murder of George Mitchell, the CEO of the sponsoring corporation, that Magdalena had to be close to death before she selected the appropriate killer.

As if the disaster of her pseudo-marriage to Aaron had not been enough, Magdalena's barn and inn were seriously damaged by a terrible wind in *Play It Again, Spam* (Signet, 1999). By the time the facility had been restored, the Washington, D.C., New York City and Los Angeles clientele had found a newer favorite. A request for rooms by World War II veterans had a hidden agenda, but so did a vicious Nazi criminal living under a false identity.

Magdalena's inn had a houseful of unusual guests in *The Hand that Rocks the Ladle* (Signet, 2000). It couldn't have happened at a more inauspicious time. Barbara Hostetler, Freni's daughter-in-law, delivered her babies, but triplets had been expected, not twins. Not only was Magdalena minus a cook, but she promised Freni to locate the missing infant. In the process they discovered the dead body of Dr. Ignatius Pierce, who had provided pre-natal care to Barbara. Retired cardiologist Dr. Gabe Rosen found Magdalena's whimsies attractive.

Magdalena may no longer number the rich and famous among her guests, but in *The Crepes of Wrath* (New American Library, 2001) she had a mixed bag: two African-American psychiatrists; two diminutive retired attorneys; one extremely tall physical education teacher, plus a television star whose wife was a medium. No problem. They all signed into the ALPO (Amish Lifestyle Plan Option), doing their own and some of Magdalena's cleaning to get the full experience. The drug-induced death of cook Lizzie Mast looked like murder. Even Melvin Stoltfus knew he couldn't solve the case so he turned it over to Magdalena.

Neither Freni nor Magdalena was considered a serious suspect in *Gruel and Unusual Punishment* (New American Library, 2002) when jail inmate Clarence Webber died after eating catered food provided by Penn-Dutch Inn. Her brother-in-law Melvin prevailed upon her to discover who had added arsenic to the gruel. Clarence had been a con-man with whom Magdalena had done business. However she had not succumbed to his blandishments as had the local women whom he had bigamously married.

Magdalena was surprised at the out-of-town guests who came to the Inn for Hernia Heritage Days in *Thou Shalt Not Grill* (New American Library, 2004). Only gradually did she learn: the legend of the Hostetler family treasure, and that her guests all had claims as heirs to a possible fortune. One guest, Buzzy Porter, annoyed others by playing practical jokes as they all searched for a buried time capsule. He, predictably, was murdered. Although Ida Rosen was not a guest, she made known her intention to move in with Gabriel and Magdalena when they married.

Colonel Custard's plans to create a five-star hotel in Hernia rain into serious problems in *Custard's Last Stand* (Signet, 2004). He had taken over all available rooms at the Penn Dutch, then surprised Magdalena with his project which was bound to have repercussions for her. She rallied the locals to have the building permit revoked, but, someone killed the Colonel. Another murder at the inn couldn't be left to the inadequate skills of Melvin Stoltzfus so Magdalena personally interrogated all suspects, but it was her deceased mother who put it all together. Gabe had two surprises for Magdalena: a gorgeous engagement ring and the chance to meet her future mother-in-law.

Rev. Arnold Schrock, pastor of Beechy Grove Mennonite Church during *Assault and Pepper* (New American Library, 2005), did not survive the chili served at a church supper. It had been laced with peanut butter, a substance to which he was known to be allergic. Melvin Stoltfus, now married to Susannah, had resigned his position as chief of police. Who then must solve the murder? The possibility that Schrock had a hidden life and may have been paying blackmail led to further discoveries.

In *Grape Expectations* (NAL, 2006) Magdalena became increasingly arrogant and bold. She was horrified to learn that fellow church member Ed Gingerich had sold his farm to Felicia and Vinny Bacchustelli, who planned to set up a vineyard. This was anathema to a teetotaler, but also might harm business at the Penn Dutch. When Felicia was found dead, the new chief of police Olivia Hornsby-Anderson made Magdalena aware that she might be a suspect, but also encouraged her help in the investigation. Magdalena had another search going. She needed a replacement pastor for her church who would preside over the wedding to her Jewish suitor, Dr. Gabriel Rosen.

Under her authority as mayor of Hernia, Magdalena undertook to investigate the murder of wealthy lech Cornelius Weaver in *Hell Hath No Curry* (NAL, 2007). It was not just that he seduced multiple females, but that he led them to believe, at least for a time, that marriage was in the offing. Emboldened by a new vision of herself as a beautiful woman, Magdalena still had to deal with her reputation as a mercenary, merciless, and rude person. There was some truth in these perceptions. The narrative, consisting primarily of interviews with the women in Weaver's life, was witty but repetitious. Not one of the better books in the series.

On the day of her wedding to Dr. Gabe Rosen in *As the World Churns* (Obsidian, 2008) Magdalena was notified that Melvin Stoltfus, in prison for murder, had escaped. This came in the midst of plans for the initial Hernia Holstein Competition. The Penn Dutch was totally booked for the event. As mayor of Hernia, Magdalena had major responsibilities. When her friend Doc Shafor was struck down by an attacker, young chief of police Chris Ackerman suggested that this might be an additional task for Magdalena. She was barely holding herself together: dueling with Gabe's mother for his attention and recovering from a shocking disclosure about her parents. The playful ridicule of Freni and Ida's colloquialisms and malapropisms grew tiresome.

Next: *Batter Off Dead* and *Batter Safe Than Sorry,* both announced for 2010

Fanny Zindel

Authors: Serita Stevens and Rayanne Moore

Fanny Zindel, a widowed sixty-five-year-old grandmother, had worked as an actress and modeled in Chicago department stores in her younger days. She still played tennis, attracted male suitors, and traveled about the world. She narrated, so could make all the wry philosophical statements associated with the role of Jewish mother/grandmother. Fanny was a friendly, warm personality, interested in everyone around her.

In *Red Sea, Dead Sea* (St. Martin, 1991), Fanny journeyed to Israel, not solely as a religious or emotional experience, but to search for her brother. Albert had disappeared, leaving a reputation as a traitor to the British. She and her friend Nathan Weiss were questioned at the Amsterdam airport for a murder in the men's room. Fanny's crochet scissors had been the weapon used. Her plans to meet her granddaughter were delayed. Fortunately Susan joined her, and they were allowed to proceed, carrying highly secret material given to her by an acquaintance.

Fanny would not tolerate an accusation of dishonesty against Susan, so, in *Bagels for Tea* (St. Martin, 1993), she challenged the authorities at her granddaughter's exclusive English boarding school. When both Mary Louise, the unpleasant young woman who accused Susan of cheating, and headmistress, Miss Kentworth, were murdered, Fanny called on her friend Nathan Weiss and his international contacts to find drug dealers, libidinous teachers, and two killers.

Wilhelmena "Helma" Zukas

Author: Jo Dereske

Helma Zukas fit into the stereotype of a small town (Bellehaven, Washington) librarian. She was described as tiny and trim, precise, and careful as to her appearance. She was attentive to her widowed mother, now resident in a retirement complex, and available for volunteer work such as the local crisis center. Helma, although solitary in her own habits, reached out to the troubled on the crisis line. Once curious, she was persistent in finding answers from her experience on the reference desk. She was a stubborn Lithuanian, born and raised in Michigan. Her best friend was unconventional six-foot tall artist, Ruth Winthrop, with whom she had little in common except affection.

During *Miss Zukas and the Library Murders* (Avon, 1994), a corpse was left in the library. Helma's resistance to computers and her reluctance to have anyone else cull her non-fiction section of the Bellehaven Library enabled her to find the killer of the man identified as Ernie Larsen. Unwed, but not impervious to the opposite sex, Helma assisted Chief of Police Wayne Gallant who found her attractive.

Compulsive about her responsibilities, Helma could not decline when she was reminded that she had promised to arrange the twentieth reunion of her high school class in *Miss Zukas and the Island Murders* (Avon, 1995). Having prudently invested the class funds, she could underwrite travel and lodging for the entire group at a nearby island resort. Once the group gathered, it was isolated by weather and a killer who had a secret to hide.

Helma was not at all certain that she wanted to be a member of the library team entered in Bellehaven's annual Snow to Surf Run in *Miss Zukas and the Stroke of Death* (Avon, 1995). She treasured memories of her youth, gliding along Michigan lakes in the canoe tailor-made for her by Uncle Tony. Friendship was important to Helma, and particularly her friendship for Ruth. So, against her better judgment, she involved herself in the murder of Joshman Lotz, an ex-convict who had brought misery to others all his life. Ruth had quarreled with Lotz hours before he was killed in the alley adjacent to her home. Burdened with two unsought responsibilities, Helma rose to the occasion.

The inability of Chief of Police Wayne Gallant to shed the trauma of his divorce and pursue a relationship with Helma in *Miss Zukas and the Raven's Dance* (Avon, 1996) made her vulnerable to the attentions of a new admirer. Her professional life was disturbed when her supervisor relocated her in a Native American Culture Center, where she was to complete the work of deceased cataloger Stanley Plummer. Plummer had been murdered because he had uncovered a secret in the archives. Neatness and organization were significant values for both Plummer and Helma so she was driven to complete his task, even at some risk to herself and a young Native American.

Unable to resist Ruth's blandishments about an adventure on her fortieth birthday in *Out of Circulation* (Avon, 1997), Helma set forth on a three-day hiking trip into the mountains. Helma prepared intensely for the trip and needed all her skills when a treacherous storm found her and Ruth sharing a cabin with a half-dozen wayfarers, including a murderer.

Helma's Aunt Em had been too important in her life to allow the eighty-seven-year-old widow to recuperate in a nursing home. In *Final Notice* (Avon, 1998), she took Em into her home. Em's treasured possessions included memoirs of her ill-spent youth during the prohibition era. What Em wanted to forget, someone else had every intention of finding out.

Because she believed that she had not committed the alleged traffic offense, Helma chose to serve 100 days of court ordered service at the Promise Mission for Homeless men during *Miss Zukas in Death's Shadow* (Avon 1999). The mission was located in a rundown area, but she had no idea that she would be involved in another murder case in which she was among the suspects. The victim, prominent businessman Quentin Vernon Boyd, was a member of the Library Board with whom Helma had disagreements. Tony, a slow-witted street person, confessed to the killing, but that was not enough to convince Helma that he was guilty. Ruth, who served along side Helma at the Mission, risked her own welfare when Helma came too close to the killer.

Helma did not take her ethical stance as a librarian lightly during *Miss Zukas Shelves the Evidence* (Avon, 2001). She was aware of the mysterious death of Professor Lewis Dixon, the son-in-law of her ex-boxer neighbor TNT Stone. Helma refused to divulge the name of the borrower of a book left at the scene of the crime and made it impossible for anyone else to do so. While Helma investigated, Ruth and Helma's mother took care of the ailing Wayne Gallant's children. Helma needed rescuing, and got it from a man she had always ridiculed. She and Wayne ended up in a promising romantic posture.

Helma awakened on her 42nd birthday with a sense of impending dread as *Bookmarked to Die* (Avon, 2006) began. Her inattentiveness and hesitation at work was apparent to her co-workers, causing director May Apple Moon to demand that she attend four group therapy sessions, each on a different topic. Helma needed her wits about her as she was launching a Local Authors Project. During the Authors' meeting and subsequent therapy sessions, Helma became acquainted with four women whose lives were enmeshed with one another. Two died under suspicious circumstances. Ruth, who had returned from Michigan because she couldn't paint there, helped Helma learn about the men involved.

Helma took some small satisfaction in the fact that she had been instrumental in Franklin Harrington's decision to donate the site for a new Bellehaven library and defray 51% of the total cost in *Catalogue of Death* (Avon, 2007). The city was totally unprepared for a rare and devastating snowstorm. Of course, ex-Michigander Helma uncovered her venerable skis and set out for work. Franklin was among the first patrons to brave the storm, spending some time with the microfiche and archives. Subsequently he left to make his regular visit to the excavation site. Within a short time, an explosion stunned the residents of Bellehaven. It was centered at the excavation site, killing Franklin, leading to a second death, and perhaps ending plans for a new library.

As an antidote to her grief when dumped by her long time beau, Ruth Winthrop created a series of paintings reflecting aspects of her past in *Index to Murder* (Avon, 2008). It was interesting in that two of them referred to men who had shared that past, but both of whom had been recently murdered. When the paintings were stolen, the police, Ruth and Helma sought a connection. What had Prof Vincent Jenson and chain saw artist Meriwether Scott had in common, besides Ruth? Ruth's sense of color and Helma's special skills led to an answer. On the side, Helma's supervisor May Apple Moon learned a lesson and Wayne Gallant waited for an answer.

Dereske has a second series, featuring Ruby Crane covered in this volume.

Author/Character Master List

Although some characters appear in all volumes of a shared series, only those in which a significant role is played will be listed. Books scheduled to appear in the future but not reviewed in this series are marked with the expected date of publication. Unfortunately publication dates can be postponed but every effort was made to get them correct. There are also differences in the date of publication depending on whether the book was published in the United States, Great Britain, Canada, Australia or other country. In the text, I used the date and name of publisher from the copy I reviewed.

Books identified in Hubin, Heising or some equally reliable authority but not available to me for review are listed as NA.

Occasionally titles are changed from one country to another. When possible I provided both titles.

In identifying new publications to be listed but not reviewed, I depended upon book review, magazines such as *Deadly Pleasures, Mystery Scene, Mystery News*, and newsletters from mystery bookstores. Information gleaned from the publications of Sisters in Crime and Malice Domestic helped me to stay reasonably well informed. Any errors are my own.

Andrews, Donna

Meg Langslow 459

Murder with Peacocks
Murder with Puffins
Revenge of the Wrought-Iron Flamingos
Crouching Buzzard, Leaping Loon
We'll Always Have Parrots
Owl's Well That Ends Well
No Rest for the Wicket
The Penguin Who Knew Too Much
Cockatiels at Seven
Six Geese A-Slaying
Swan for the Money (2009)
Stork Raving Mad (2010)

Andrews, Sarah

Emily "Em" Hansen 323

Tensleep
A Fall in Denver
Mother Nature
Bone Hunter
An Eye for Gold
Only Flesh and Bones
Fault Line
Killer Dust
Earth Colors
Dead Dry

Appel, William

Dr. Kate Berman. 74

Whisper...He Might Hear You
Widowmaker

Apostolou, Anna

Miriam Bartimaeus 52

A Murder in Macedon
A Murder in Thebes

Arnold, Catherine

Karen Perry-Mondori 639

Due Process
Imperfect Justice
Wrongful Death
Class Action

Atherton, Nancy

Dimity Westwood, Lori Shepherd 856, 737

Aunt Dimity's Death
Aunt Dimity and the Duke
Aunt Dimity's Good Deed
Aunt Dimity Digs In
Aunt Dimity's Christmas
Aunt Dimity Beats the Devil
Aunt Dimity: Detective
Aunt Dimity Takes a Holiday
Aunt Dimity Goes West
Aunt Dimity and the Deep Blue Sea
Aunt Dimity: Vampire Hunter
Aunt Dimity: Snowbound
Aunt Dimity and the Next of Kin
Aunt Dimity Slays the Dragon (2009)
Aunt Dimity Down Under (2010)

Ayres, Noreen

Smokey Brandon 105

A World the Color of Salt
Carcass Trade
The Juan Doe Murders

Bailey, Jo, pseudonym for Joseph Bailey

Jan Gallagher 284

Bagged
Recycled
Erased

Jane and the Man of the Cloth
Jane and the Wandering Eye
Jane and the Genius of the Place
Jane and the Stillroom Maid
Jane and the Prisoner of Wool House
Jane and the Ghosts of Netley
Jane and His Lordship's Legacy
Jane and the Barque of Frailty
Jane and the Madness of Lord Byron (2010)

Bartholomew, Nancy

Sierra Lavotini 467

The Miracle Strip
Drag Strip
Film Strip
Strip Poker

Bean, C. N.

Rita Trible 819

A Soul to Take
With Evil Intent

Beaton, M. C., pseudonym for Marion Chesney

Agatha Raisin. 673

Agatha Raisin and the Quiche of Death
Agatha Raisin and the Vicious Vet
Agatha Raisin and the Potted Gardener
Agatha Raisin and the Walkers of Dembley
Agatha Raisin and the Murderous Marriage
Agatha Raisin and the Terrible Tourist
Agatha Raisin and the Wellspring of Death
Agatha Raisin and the Wizard of Evesham
Agatha Raisin and the Witch of Wyckhadden
Agatha Raisin and the Fairies of Fryfam
Agatha Raisin and the Love from Hell
Agatha Raisin and the Day the Floods Came
Agatha Raisin and the Case of the Curious Curate
Agatha Raisin and the Haunted House
The Deadly Dance
Love, Lies and Liquor
Kissing Christmas Goodbye
A Spoonful of Poison
The Perfect Paragon
There Goes the Bride (2009)
Busy Body (2010)

Beck, K. K.

Jane da Silva 213

A Hopeless Case
Amateur Night
Electric City
Cold Smoked

Bedford, Jean

Anna Southwood. 763

Worse Than Death
To Make a Killing
Signs of Murder

Beecham, Rose, pseudonym for Jennifer Fulton

Amanda Valentine 830

Introducing Amanda Valentine
Fair Play
Second Guess

Bell, Nancy

Biggie Weatherford 852

Biggie and the Poisoned Politician
Biggie and the Fricasseed Fat Man
Biggie and the Quincy Ghost
Biggie and the Mangled Mortician
Biggie and the Meddlesome Mailman
Biggie and the Devil Diet

Benke, Patricia D.

Judith Thornton 798

Guilty By Choice
Above the Law
False Witness
Cruel Justice

Benjamin, Carol Lea

Rachel Kaminsky Alexander. 6

This Dog for Hire
A Hell of a Dog
The Wrong Dog
Fall Guy
The Hard Way
The Dog Who Knew Too Much
Lady Vanishes
The Long Good Boy
Without a Word

Benison, C. C., pseudonym for Douglas Whiteway

Jane Bee, Queen Elizabeth II 68

Death at Buckingham Palace
Death at Windsor Castle
Death at Sandringham House

Berenson, Laurien

Melanie Travis 813

A Pedigree to Die For
Dog Eat Dog
Hush Puppy
Once Bitten
Best in Show
Jingle Bell Bark
Chow Down
Doggie Day Care Murder
Underdog
Watchdog
Unleashed
Hot Dog
Hair of the Dog
Raining Cats and Dogs
Hounded to Death

Bernhardt, William

Christina McCall 533

Primary Justice
Deadly Justice
Cruel Justice
Extreme Justice
Silent Justice
Criminal Intent
Capitol Threat
Capitol Conspiracy
Capitol Offense (2009)
Blind Justice
Perfect Justice
Naked Justice
Dark Justice
Murder One
Death Row
Capitol Murder
Hate Crime
Capitol Betrayal (2010)

Berry, Linda

Trudy Roundtree

Death and the Easter Bunny
Death and the Hubcap

Death and the Icebox
Death and the Walking Stick
Death and the Family Tree
Death and the Crossed Wires (2009)

Birmingham, Ruth

Sunny Childs 156

Atlanta Graves
Fulton County Blues
Sweet Georgia
Blue Plate Special
Cold Trail
Feet of Clay

Bishop, Claudia, pseudonym for Mary Stanton

Sarah "Quill" Quilliam. 666

A Taste for Murder
A Dash of Death
A Pinch of Poison
Murder Well-Done
Death Dines Out
A Touch of the Grape
A Steak in Murder
Marinade for Murder
Fried by Jury
A Puree of Poison
Buried by Breakfast
A Dinner to Die For
Ground to a Halt
A Carol for a Corpse
Just Desserts
Death in Two Courses (2010)
Toast Mortem (2010)

Bishop, Paul

Fey Croaker 189

Kill Me Again
Twice Dead
Chalk Whispers
Tequila Mockingbird
Pattern of Behavior (novella in collection with the same name)

Black, Cara

Aimee Leduc 468

Murder in the Marais
Murder in Belleville
Murder in the Sentier
Murder in the Bastille
Murder in Clichy
Murder in Montmartre
Murder on the Ile Saint-Louis
Murder in the Rue de Paradis
Murder in the Latin Quarter (2009)
Murder in the Palais Royale (2010)

Black, Veronica, pseudonym for Maureen Peters

Sister Joan 402

A Vow of Silence
A Vow of Chastity
A Vow of Sanctity
A Vow of Obedience
A Vow of Penance
A Vow of Devotion
A Vow of Fidelity
A Vow of Poverty
A Vow of Adoration
A Vow of Compassion

Blake, Michelle

Lily Connor 171

The Tentmaker
Earth Has No Sorrow
Book of Light

Blanc, Nero, pseudonym for Cordelia Frances Biddle and Steve Zettler

Belle Graham

The Crossword Murder
Two Down
Crossword Connection
A Crossword to Die For
Corpus de Crossword
A Crossword Gift (ss collection)
Wrapped Up in Crosswords
Anatomy of a Crossword
A Crossworder's Delight
Another Word for Murder
Death on the Diagonal
A Crossword Holiday (ss and novella)

Brady, James

Lady Alix Dunraven 235

Further Lane | *Gin Lane*
The House That Ate the Hamptons | *A Hamptons Christmas*

Brennan, Carol

Liz Wareham 841

Headhunt | *Full Commission*

Emily Silver 748

In the Dark | *Chill of Summer*

Brightwell, Emily, a house name, but believed to be written by Cheryl Arguiles

Hepzipah Jeffries 397

The Inspector and Mrs. Jeffries | *Mrs. Jeffries Dusts for Clues*
The Ghost and Mrs. Jeffries | *Mrs. Jeffries Takes Stock*
Mrs. Jeffries on the Ball | *Mrs. Jeffries on the Trail*
Mrs. Jeffries Plays the Cook | *Mrs. Jeffries and the Missing Alibi*
Mrs. Jeffries Stands Corrected | *Mrs. Jeffries Takes the Stage*
Mrs. Jeffries Questions the Answer | *Mrs. Jeffries Reveals Her Art*
Mrs. Jeffries Takes the Cake | *Mrs. Jeffries Rocks the Boat*
Mrs. Jeffries Weeds the Plot | *Mrs. Jeffries Pinches the Post*
Mrs. Jeffries Pleads Her Case | *Mrs. Jeffries Sweeps the Chimney*
Mrs. Jeffries Stalks the Hunter | *Mrs. Jeffries Pleads the Case*
Mrs. Jeffries Appeals the Verdict | *Mrs. Jeffries and the Silent Knight*
Mrs. Jeffries and the Best Laid Plans | *Mrs. Jeffries and the Feast of St. Stephen*
Mrs. Jeffries Holds the Trump | *Mrs. Jeffries in the Nick of Time (2009)*
Mrs. Jeffries and the Yuletide Weddings (2009)

Brill, Toni, pseudonym for Anthony and Martha Olcott

Midge Cohen 166

Date with a Dead Doctor | *Date with a Plummeting Publisher*

Brooks, Patricia

Molly Piper 648

Falling from Grace | *But for the Grace*

Brown, Lizbie

Elizabeth Blair 82

Broken Star | *Turkey Tracks*
Shoo-Fly | *Double Wedding Ring*
Jacob's Ladder | *Cat's Cradle*

Brown, Rita Mae and her cat, Sneaky Pie

Mary "Harry" Haristeen 328

Wish You Were Here | *Rest in Pieces*
Murder at Monticello | *Pay Dirt*
Murder, She Meowed a.k.a. *Death at Montpelier*
Cat on the Scent | *Pawing Through the Past*
Claws and Effect | *Catch As Cat Can*
The Tail of the Tip-Off | *Murder on the Prowl*
Cat's Eyewitness | *Whisker of Evil*
Sour Puss | *Puss 'n Cahoots*
The Purrfest Murder | *Santa Clawed*

Riptide
Hemlock Bay
Blind Side
Blow Out
Point Blank
Double Take
Eleventh Hour
Tailspin
The Edge
Knockout (2009)
Whiplash (2010)

Crespi, Trella, pseudonym for Camilla Trinchieri

Simona Griffo 317

The Trouble with a Small Raise
The Trouble with Moonlighting
The Trouble with Too Much Sun
The Trouble with Thin Ice
The Trouble with Going Home
The Trouble with a Bad Fit
The Trouble with a Hot Summer

Cresse, Gina

Devonie Lace-Matthews 450

A Deadly Change of Course-Plan B
A Deadly Bargain-Plan C
A Deadly Change of Heart
A Deadly Change of Power
A Deadly Change of Luck

Crombie, Deborah

Gemma James 388

A Share in Death
All Shall Be Well
Leave the Grave Green
Mourn Not Your Dead
Dreaming of the Bones
Kissed a Sad Goodbye
A Finer End
And Justice There Is None
Now May You Weep
Water Like a Stone
In a Dark House
Where Memories Lie
Necessary as Blood (2009)

Crowleigh, Ann, pseudonym for Barbara Cummings and JoAnn Power

Mirinda and Clare Cliveley 165

Dead As Dead Can Be
Wait for the Dark

Crum, Laura

Dr. Gail McCarthy 537

Cutter
Hoofprints
Roughstock
Roped
Slickrock
Breakaway
Hayburner
Forged
Moonblind
Chasing Cans
Going, Gone (2010)

Cutler, Judith

Sophie Rivers 702

Dying Fall
Dying To Write
Dying On Principle
Dying For Millions
Dying For Power
Dying To Score
Dying By Degrees
Dying By the Book
Dying in Discord
Dying to Deceive

Kate Power 659

Power On Her Own
Staying Power
Power Games
Will Power
Hidden Power
Power Shift

Malice in Miniature
Killing Cassidy
Sins Out of School
The Victim in Victoria Station
To Perish in Penzance
Winter of Discontent

Hilda Johansson 404

Death in Lacquer Red
Green Grow the Victims
Crimson Snow
Red, White, and Blue Murder
Silence Is Golden
Indigo Christmas

Davidson, Diane Mott

Goldy Bear (Schulz) 63

Catering to Nobody
The Cereal Murders
Killer Pancake
The Grilling Season
Tough Cookie
Chopping Spree
Sweet Revenge
Fatally Flaky (2009)
Dying for Chocolate
The Last Suppers
The Main Corpse
Prime Cut
Sticks & Scones
Dark Tort
Double Shot

Davis, Kaye

Maris Middleton 565

Devil's Leg Crossing
Until the End
Possessions

Davis, Val, pseudonym for Robert and Angela Irvine

Nicolette "Nick" Scott 728

Track of the Scorpion
Wake of the Hornet
Thread of the Spider
Flight of the Serpent
The Return of the Spanish Lady

Dawber, Carol

Liz Gresham 313

Earthwork
Backtrack (NA)
Sounds Easy

Dawkins, Cecil

Ginevra Prettifield 663

The Santa Fe Rembrandt
Rare Earth

Dawson, Janet

"Jeri" Howard 361

Kindred Crimes
Take a Number
Nobody's Child
Witness to Evil
A Killing at the Track
Till the Old Men Die
Don't Turn Your Back on the Ocean
A Credible Threat
Where the Bodies Are Buried
Scam and Eggs (ss)

Day, Dianne

Caroline "Fremont" Jones 405

The Strange Files of Fremont Jones
The Bohemian Murders
Death Train to Boston
Fire and Fog
Emperor Norton's Ghost
Beacon Street Mourning

Deaver, Jeffrey Wilds

Amelia Sachs 715

The Bone Collector
The Coffin Dancer

Donald, Anabel

Alex Tanner 789

An Uncommon Murder
In at the Deep End
The Glass Ceiling
The Loop
Destroy Unopened

Doss, James

Daisy Perika 635

The Shaman Sings
The Shaman Laughs
The Shaman's Bones
The Shaman's Game
The Night Visitor
Grandmother Spider
White Shell Woman
Dead Soul
Stone Butterfly
Shadow Man
Three Sisters
Witch's Tongue
Snake Dreams
The Widow's Revenge (2009)

Douglas, Carole Nelson

Irene Adler 4

Good Night, Mr. Holmes
Good Morning, Irene apa *The Adventuress*
Irene at Large apa *A Soul of Steel*
Irene's Last Waltz a.k.a. Another Scandal in Bohemia
Chapel Noir
Castle Rouge
Femme Fatale
Spider Dance

Temple Barr & Midnight Louie 44

Catnap
Pussyfoot
Cat on a Blue Monday
Cat in a Crimson Haze
Cat in a Diamond Dazzle
Cat With an Emerald Eye
Cat in a Flamingo Fedora
Cat in a Golden Garland
Cat on a Hyacinth Hunt
Cat in an Indigo Mood
Cat in a Jeweled Jumpsuit
Cat in a Kiwi Con
Cat in a Leopard Spot
Cat in a Midnight Choir
Cat in a Neon Nightmare
Cat in an Orange Twist
Cat in a Hot Pink Pursuit
Cat in a Quicksilver Caper
Cat in a Red Hot Rage
Cat in a Sapphire Slipper
Cat in a Topaz Tango (2009)
Cat in an Ultramarine Scheme (2010)

Douglas, Lauren Wright

Allison O'Neil 620

Death at Lavender Bay
Swimming Cat Cove

Drury, Joan M.

Tyler Jones 412

The Other Side of Silence
Silent Words
Closed in Silence

Dudley, Karen

Robyn Devara 219

Hoot to Kill
The Red Heron
Macaws of Death
Ptarmageddon

Duffy, Margaret

Joanna Mackenzie 496

Dressed to Kill
Prospect of Death
Music in the Blood
A Fine Target
A Hanging Matter

Duffy, Stella

Saz Martin 520

Calendar Girl
Beneath the Blonde
Mouth of Babes
Wavewalker
Fresh Flesh

Dunant, Sarah

Hannah Wolfe 875

Birth Marks
Under My Skin
Fatlands

Dunbar, Sophie

Claire Claiborne Jenner. 164

Behind Eclaire's Doors
Redneck Riviera
A Bad Hair Day
Shivaree

Dunn, Carola

Daisy Dalrymple 203

Death at Wentwater Court
Requiem for a Mezzo
Damsel in Distress
Styx and Stones
To Davy Jones Below
The Case of the Murdered Muckraker
A Mourning Wedding
Gunpowder Plot
The Black Ship
The Winter Garden Mystery
Murder on the Flying Scotsman
Dead in the Water
Rattle His Bones
Mistletoe and Murder
Die Laughing
Fall of a Philanderer
The Bloody Tower
Sheer Folly (2009)

Eccles, Marjorie

Abigail Moon. 587

The Company She Kept
A Species of Revenge
Killing Me Softly
A Sunset Touch
An Accidental Shroud
A Death of Distinction
The Superintendent's Daughter
Untimely Graves

Edghill, Rosemary, pseudonym for Eluki Bes Shahar

Karen Hightower a.k.a. Bast 346

Speak Daggers to Her
The Bowl of Night
Book of Moons

Edwards, Grace F.

Mali Anderson. 11

If I Should Die
No Time to Die
A Toast Before Dying
Do Or Die

Edwards, Ruth Dudley

Baroness "Jack" Troutbeck 821

Matricide at St. Martha's
Murder in a Cathedral
Carnage on the Committee
Murdering Americans
Ten Lords A-Leaping
Publish and Be Murdered
The Anglo-Irish Murders

Eichler, Selma

Desiree Shapiro. 733

Murder Can Kill Your Social Life
Murder Can Stunt Your Growth
Murder Can Ruin Your Looks
Murder Can Wreck Your Reunion

Murder Can Spook Your Cat
Murder Can Singe Your Old Flame
Murder Can Spoil Your Appetite
Murder Can Upset Your Mother
Murder Can Cool Off Your Affair
Murder Can Rain on Your Shower
Murder Can Run Your Stockings
Murder Can Botch Up Your Birthday
Murder Can Mess Up Your Mascara
Murder Can Depress Your Dachshund
Murder Can Crash Your Party

Emerson, Kathy Lynn

Lady Susanna Appleton 15

Face Down in the Marrow-Bone Pie
Face Down on a Herbal
Face Down Among the Winchester Geese
Face Down Below the Eleanor Cross
Face Down Under the Wych Elm
Face Down Before Rebel Hooves
Face Down Across the Western Sea
Face Down Below the Banqueting House
Face Down Beside St. Anne's Well
Face Down O'er the Border

English, Brenda

Sutton McPhee 558

Corruption of Faith
Corruption of Power
Corruption of Justice

Ennis, Catherine

Bernadette "Bernie" Hebert 705

Clearwater
Chatauqua

Epstein, Carole

Barbara Simons 750

Perilous Friends
Perilous Relations

Evanovich, Janet

Stephanie Plum 652

One for the Money
Two for the Dough
Three to Get Deadly
Four to Score
High Five
Hot Six
Seven Up
Hard Eight
Visions of Sugarplums
To the Nines
Ten Big Ones
Eleven on Top
Plum Lovin'
Plum Lucky
Lean Mean Thirteen
Twelve Sharp
Fearless Fourteen
Finger Lickin' Fifteen (2009)
Plum Spooky (2009)

Evans, Liz

Grace Smith 756

Who Killed Marilyn Monroe?
J.F. K. Is Missing
Don't Mess with Mrs. In-Between
Barking
Cue the Easter Bunny
Sick as a Parrot

Evers, Crabbe

Petronella "Petey" Biggers 76

Murder in Wrigley Field
Murderer's Row
Bleeding Dodger Blue
Fear in Fenway
Tigers Burning

Fairstein, Linda

Alexandra Cooper 173

Final Jeopardy
Likely to Die

Fitzwater, Judy

Jennifer Marsh 516

Dying to Get Published
Dying for a Clue
Dying to Be Murdered
Dying to Get Even
Dying to Remember
Dying to Get Her Man

Flora, Kate

Thea Kozak. 445

Chosen for Death
Death at the Wheel
Liberty or Death
Stalking Death
Death in a Funhouse Mirror
An Educated Death
Death in Paradise

Fowler, Earlene

Albenia "Benni" Harper 331

Fool's Puzzle
Kansas Troubles
Mariner's Compass
Arkansas Traveler
Sunshine and Shadow
Delectable Mountain
Tumbling Blocks
Irish Chain
Goose in the Pond
Seven Sisters
Steps to the Altar
Dove in the Window
Broken Dishes
State Fair (2010)

Frankel, Valerie

Wanda Mallory. 507

A Deadline for Murder
Prime Time for Murder
Murder on Wheels
A Body to Die For

Frazer, Margaret, pseudonym for Mary Monica Pulver and Gail Bacon

Sister Frevisse. 278

The Novice's Tale
The Outlaw's Tale
The Boy's Tale
The Prioress' Tale
The Reeve's Tale
The Clerk's Tale
The Hunter's Tale
The Apostate's Tale
The Traitor's Tale
The Servant's Tale
The Bishop's Tale
The Murderer's Tale
The Maiden's Tale
The Squire's Tale
The Bastard's Tale
The Sempster's Tale
The Widow's Tale

Freeman, Mary, pseudonym for Mary Rosenblum

Rachel O'Connor. 614

Devil's Trumpet
Bleeding Heart
Deadly Nightshade
Garden View

Freider, Pat

Matty Donahue

Signature Murder
Privileged Communications

French, Linda

Teodora "Teddy" Morelli 591

Talking Rain
Steeped in Murder
Coffee To Die For

Green, Christine

Kate Kinsella 432

Deadly Errand
Deadly Practice
Deadly Bond
Deadly Night
Deadly Web
Deadly Admirer
Deadly Partners
Deadly Echo
Deadly Choice
Deadly Retreat

Francesca "Fran" Wilson . . . .

Death in the Country
Fatal Cut
Die in My Dreams

Greenwood, D. M.

Rev. Theodora Braithwaite 103

Clerical Errors
Idol Bones
Every Deadly Sin
Heavenly Vices
Foolish Ways
Unholy Ghosts
Holy Terrors
Mortal Spoils
A Grave Disturbance

Gregory, Sarah, pseudonym for Albert W. Gray

Sharon Hays 342

In Self Defense
The Best Defense
Public Trust
Capitol Scandal

Griffin, Annie, pseudonym for Sally Chapman

Hannah Malloy, Kiki Goldstein 508

A Very Eligible Corpse
Love and the Single Corpse
Date with the Perfect Dead Man
Tall, Dead, and Handsome

Grimes, Terris McMahon

Theresa Galloway. 285

Somebody Else's Child
Blood Will Tell

Guiver, Patricia

Delilah Doolittle 230

Delilah Doolittle and the Purloined Pooch
Delilah Doolittle and the Motley Mutts
Delilah Doolitte and the Careless Coyote
Delilah Doolittle and the Missing Macaw
Delilah Doolittle and the Canine Chorus
The Beastly Bloodline

Gunning, Sally, nee Carlson

Connie Bartholomew 50

Hot Water
Ice Water
Rough Water
Deep Water
Dirty Water
Under Water
Troubled Water
Still Water
Muddy Water
Fire Water

Haddad, C. A.

Becky Belski 69

Caught in the Shadows
Root Canal

Hansen, Vinnie

Carol Sabala 713

Murder, Honey
Rotten Dates
One Tough Cookie
Tang Is Not Juice

Harper, Karen

Elizabeth I 244

The Poyson Garden
The Tidal Poole
The Twylight Tower
The Queene's Cure
The Thorne Maze
The Queene's Christmas
The Fyre Mirror
The Fatal Fashione
The Hooded Hawke
The Queen's Governess (2010)

Harris, Charlaine

Aurora "Roe" Teagarden 793

Real Murders
A Bone to Pick
Three Bedrooms, One Corpse
The Julius House
Dead Over Heels
A Fool and His Honey
Last Scene Alive
Poppy Done to Death

Lily Bard. 35

Shakespeare's Landlord
Shakespeare's Champion
Shakespeare's Christmas
Shakespeare's Trollop
Shakespeare's Counselor

Harris, Lee, pseudonym for Syrell Rogovin Leahy

Christine Bennett 69

The Good Friday Murder
The Yom Kippur Murder
The Christening Day Murder
The St. Patrick's Day Murder
The Christmas Night Murder
The Thanksgiving Day Murder
The Passover Murder
The Valentine's Day Murder
The New Year's Eve Murder
The Labor Day Murder
The Father's Day Murder
The Mother's Day Murder
The April Fools' Day Murder
The Happy Birthday Murder
The Bar Mitzvah Murder
The Silver Anniversary Murder
The Cinco de Mayo Murder

Harrison, Janis

Bretta Solomon 760

Roots of Murder
Murder Sets Seed
Lilies That Fester
A Deadly Bouquet
Reap a Wicked Harvest
Bindweed

Harstad, Donald

Hester Gorse 296

Eleven Days
Known Dead
The Big Thaw
Code Sixty-One
The Heartland Experiment
A Long December

Hart, Carolyn

Henrietta O'Dwyer Collins. 168

Dead Man's Island
Scandal in Fair Haven
Death in Lovers' Lane
Death in Paradise
Death on the River Walk
Resort to Murder
Set Sail for Murder

Lewin, Jackie

Grace Beckmann 67

Death Flies on Final
Murder Flies Left Seat
Fear of Dying

Lin-Chandler, Irene

Holly-Jean Ho 348

The Healing of Holly-Jean
Grievous Angel
Hour of the Tigress

Linscott, Gillian

Nell Bray 111

Sister Beneath the Sheet
Hanging on the Wire
Dance on the Blood
Stage Fright
An Easy Day for a Lady a.k.a. *Widow's Peak*
Dead Man's Sweetheart a.k.a. *Dead Man's Music*
Blood on the Wood
Crown Witness
Absent Friends
The Perfect Daughter
Dead Man Riding

Lippman, Laura

Tess Monaghan 576

Baltimore Blues
Charm City
Butchers Hill
In Big Trouble
The Sugar House
In a Strange City
The Last Place
By a Spider's Thread
No Good Deeds
Another Thing to Fall

Livingston, Georgette

Dr. Jennifer Gray, DVM 305

The Dog Named Elvis Caper
The Deadly Dog-Bone
The Black Cat Caper
The Precocious Parrot Caper
The Telltale Turkey Caper
The Mischievous Monkey Caper
The Tenacious Terrier Caper
The White Elephant Caper
The Potbellied Pig Caper
The Pink Rabbit Caper
The Chattering Chimp Caper
The Unlucky Collie Caper (NA)

Logan, Margaret

Olivia Chapman 151

The End of an Altruist
Never Let a Stranger in Your House

Logue, Mary

Claire Watkins 845

Blood Country
Dark Coulee
Glare Ice
Bone Harvest
Poison Heart
Maiden Rock
Point No Point
Frozen Stiff (2010)

Lordon, Randye

Sydney Sloane 754

Brotherly Love
Sister's Keeper
Father Forgive Me
Mother May I
Say Uncle
East of Niece
Son of a Gun

Tippy-Toe Murder
Back to School Murder
Christmas Cookie Murder
Wedding Day Murder
Father's Day Murder
New Year's Eve Murder
St. Patrick's Day Murder
Wicked Witch Murder (2010)
Trick or Treat Murder
Valentine Murder
Turkey Day Murder
Birthday Party Murder
Star Spangled Murder
Bake Sale Murder
Mothers' Day Murder (2009)

Mercer, Judy

Ariel Gold 292

Fast Forward
Split Image
Double Take
Blind Spot

Meredith, Marilyn

Tempe Crabtree 180

Deadly Omen
Deadly Trail
Wingbeat
Judgment Fire
Unequally Yoked
Intervention
Calling the Dead
Kindred Spirits

Meyers, Annette

Olivia Brown 120

Free Love
Murder Me Now

Michaels, Melisa

Rosie Lavine 467

Cold Iron
Sister to the Rain

Mickelbury, Penny

Gianna "Anna" Maglione 500

Keeping Secrets
Darkness Descending
Night Songs

Carole Ann Gibson 289

One Must Wait
The Step Between
Where to Choose
Paradise Interrupted

Mikulski, Barbara and Oates, Marylouise

Sen. Eleanor Gorzack 297

Capitol Offense
Capitol Venture

Miles, John, pseudonym for John Bickham

Johnnie Baker 31

Missing at Tenoclock
Tenoclock Scholar

Laura Michaels 564

A Permanent Retirement
A Most Deadly Retirement
Murder in Retirement

Miles, Margaret

Charlotte Willett 866

A Wicked Way to Burn
No Rest for the Dove
Too Soon For Flowers
Mischief in the Snow

Mildon, Marsha

Cal Meredith 563

Fighting for Air
Stalking the Goddess Ship

The Body in the Basement
The Body in the Bog
The Body in the Fjord
The Body in the Big Apple
The Body in the Moonlight
The Body in the Bonfire
The Body in the Lighthouse
The Body in the Attic
The Body in the Ivy
The Body in the Snowdrift
The Body in the Gallery
The Body in the Sleigh(2009)

Paige, Robin, joint pseudonym for Susan Wittig Albert and William J. Albert

Kathryn "Kate" Ardleigh. 17

Death at Bishop's Keep
Death at Gallows Green
Death at Daisy's Folly
Death at Devil's Bridge
Death at Rottingdean
Death at Whitechapel
The Body at Epsom Downs
Death at Dartmoor
Death at Glamis Castle
Death at Hyde Park
Death at Blenheim Palace
Death on the Lizard

Parker, Barbara

Gail Connor 169

Suspicion of Innocence
Suspicion of Guilt
Suspicion of Deceit
Suspicion of Betrayal
Suspicion of Malice
Suspicion of Vengeance
Suspicion of Madness
Suspicion of Rage

Parker, Robert B.

Sunny Randall 681

Family Honor
Perish Twice
Shrink Rap
Melancholy Baby
Blue Screen
High Profile
Spare Change

Patterson, Richard North

Caroline Masters 525

Degree of Guilt
Eyes of a Child
The Final Judgment
Protect and Defend

Patti, Paul

Gabrielle "Gabe" Amato 11

Silhouettes
Death Mate

Pears, Iain

Flavia di Stefano 227

The Raphael Affair
The Titian Committee
The Bernini Bust
The Last Judgement
Giotto's Hand
Death and Restoration
The Immaculate Deception

Pence, Joanne

Angelina "Angie" Amalfi 8

Something's Cooking
Too Many Cooks
Cooking Up Trouble
Cooking Most Deadly
Cook's Night Out
Cooks Overboard
A Cook in Time
To Catch a Cook
Bell, Cook, and Candle
If Cooks Could Kill
Two Cooks A-Killing
Courting Disaster
Red Hot Murder
The Da Vinci Cook

Ripley, Ann

Louise Eldridge 241

Mulch
Death of a Garden Pest
The Garden Tour Affair
The Perennial Killer
Harvest of Murder
The Christmas Garden Affair
Death of a Political Plant
Death at the Spring Plant Sale
Death in the Orchid Garden
Summer Garden Murder

Robb, Candace M.

Lucie D'Arby Wilton 870

The Apothecary Rose
The Lady Chapel
The Nun's Tale
The King's Bishop
The Riddle of St. Leonard's
A Gift of Sanctuary
A Spy for the Redeemer
The Cross-Legged Knight
The Guilt of Innocents

Robb, J. D., pseudonym for romance novelist Nora Roberts

Lt. Eve Dallas 198

Naked in Death
Glory in Death
Immortal in Death
Rapture in Death
Ceremony in Death
Vengeance in Death
Holiday in Death
Conspiracy in Death
Loyalty in Death
Judgment in Death
Witness in Death
Betrayal in Death
Seduction in Death
Purity in Death
Reunion in Death
Portrait in Death
Imitation in Death
Visions in Death
Divided in Death
Origin in Death
Midnight in Death
Survivor in Death
Memory in Death
Interlude in Death
Innocent in Death
Creation in Death
Born in Death
Haunted in Death (novella)
Remember When
Strangers in Death
Salvation in Death
Promises in Death (2009)
Kindred in Death (2009)
Indulgence in Death (2010)

Roberts, Gillian

Billie August, Emma Howe. 24, 367

Time and Trouble
Whatever Doesn't Kill You

Roberts, Lillian M.

Dr. Andi Pauling, DVM 633

Riding for a Fall
The Hand That Feeds You
Almost Human

Roberts, Lora

Liz Sullivan 780

Murder in a Nice Neighborhood
Murder Mile High
Murder in the Marketplace
Murder Bone by Bone
Murder Crops Up
Murder Follows Money
Another Fine Mess (supporting role)

Robinson, Leah Ruth

Dr. Evelyn Sutcliffe 781

First Cut
Unnatural Causes
Blood Run

Robitaille, Julie

Kathleen "Kit" Powell 658

Jinx
Iced

Roddy, Lee

Laurel Bartlett 52

Days of Deception
Tomorrow's Promise
Yesterday's Shadows

Roe, C. F.

Dr. Jean Montrose 586

A Nasty Bit of Murder a.k.a. *The Lumsden Baby*
A Fiery Hint of Murder a.k.a. *Death by Fire*
A Classy Touch of Murder a.k.a. *Bad Blood*
A Bonny Case of Murder a.k.a. *Deadly Partnership*
A Torrid Piece of Murder a.k.a. *Fatal Fever*
A Relative Cause of Murder a.k.a. *Death in the Family*
A Hidden Cause of Murder
A Tangled Knot of Murder

Rogers, Chris

Dixie Flannigan 269

Bitch Factor
Chill Factor
Rage Factor

Roper, Gayle

Merry Kramer 447

Caught in the Middle
Caught in a Bind
Caught in the Act
Caught Red Handed

Rosen, Dorothy and Sidney

Belle Appleman 14

Death and Blintzes
Death and Strudel

Ross, Annie

Bel Carson 140

Moving Image
Double Vision
Shot in the Dark

Rothenberg, Rebecca

Claire Sharples 736

The Bulrush Murders
The Shy Tulip Murders
The Dandelion Murders
The Tumbleweed Murders *(completed by Taffy Cannon)*

Rowe, Jennifer

Verity "Birdie" Birdwood 78

Grim Pickings
Death in Store
Stranglehold
Murder by the Book
The Makeover Murders
Lamb to the Slaughter

Tessa Vance 831

Suspect a.k.a. *Deadline*
Something Wicked

Rowland, Laura Joh

Reiko Ichiro 376

Shinju
Way of the Traitor
Bundori
Concubine's Tattoo

Samurai's Wife
Pillow Book of Lady Wisteria
The Perfumed Sleeve
Red Chrysanthemun
Fire Kimono
Black Lotus
Dragon King's Palace
Assassin's Touch
Snow Empress
The Cloud Pavilion (2009)

Rowlands, Betty

Melissa Craig 182

A Little Gentle Sleuthing
Over the Edge
Malice Poetic
Smiling at Death
The Man in the Window
No Laughing Matter
Finishing Touch
Exhaustive Enquiries
Deadly Legacy
The Cherry Pickers
The Fourth Suspect
Sweet Venom

"Sukey" Reynolds. 695

An Inconsiderate Death
Copycat
Dirty Work
Party to Murder
Smokescreen
Death at Dearley Manor
Touch Me Not
Deadly Obsessions
Alpha, Beta, Gamma…Dead
A Fool There Was (2009)

Rozan, S. J.

Lydia Chin 158

China Trade
Mandarin Plaid
A Bitter Feast
Reflecting the Sky
The Shanghai Moon (2009)
Concourse
No Colder Place
Stone Quarry
Winter and Night

Rubino, Jane

Cat Austen 25

Death of a D.J.
Cheat the Devil
Raise the Dead
Fruitcake
Plot Twist
Cake Job (Novella in *A Deadly Morsel*)

Ruryk, Jean

Catherine "Cat" Wilde 863

Chicken Little Was Right
Next Week Will Be Better
Whatever Happened to Jennifer Steele?

Rushford, Patricia H.

Helen Bradley 99

Now I Lay Me Down to Sleep
A Haunting Refrain
Red Sky in Mourning
When Shadows Fall

Rust, Megan Mallory

Taylor Morgan 593

Dead Stick
Coffin Corner
Red Line

Salter, Anna

Dr. Michael Stone 775

Shiny Water
White Lies
Fault Lines
Prison Blues

Sandstrom, Eve K.

Nicky Titus 809

Death Down Home | *The Devil Down Home*
The Down Home Heifer Heist

Nell Matthews 528

The Violence Beat | *The Homicide Report*
The Smoking Gun

Sanra, Nancy

Tally McGinnis. 546

No Evidence | *No Corpse*
No Escape | *No Witness*

Satterthwait, Walter

Jane Turner 826

Escapade | *Masquerade*
Cavalcade

Saum, Karen

Brigid Donovan 230

Murder Is Relative | *Murder Is Germane*
Murder Is Material

Schmidt, Carol

Laney Samms. 718

Silverlake Heat | *Sweet Cherry Wine*
Cabin Fever

Scholefield, Alan

Dr. Anne Vernon 837

Burn Out | *Buried Treasure*

Schumacher, Aileen

Tory Travers 812

Engineered for Murder | *Framework for Death*
Affirmative Reaction | *Rosewood's Ashes*

Scoppetone, Sandra a.k.a. Jack Early

Lauren Laurano. 465

Everything You Have Is Mine | *I'll Be Leaving You Always*
My Sweet Untraceable You | *Let's Face the Music and Die*
Gonna Take a Sentimental Journey

Scott, Manda

Dr. Kellen Stewart 769

Hen's Teeth | *Night Mares*
Stronger Than Death

Scottoline, Lisa

"Bennie" Rosato, Mary DiNunzio, and Staff 705, 226

Everywhere That Mary Went (DiNunzio)
Moment of Truth (DiNunzio)
Legal Tender (Rosato)
Rough Justice (Rosato)
Mistaken Identity (Rosato)
Dead Ringer (Rosato)

The Vendetta Defense (Rosato & DiNunzio)
Courting Trouble (Rosato & DiNunzio)
Ladykiller (DiNunzio)
Killer Smile (DiNunzio)
Think Twice (DiNunzio 2010)

See, Lisa
Liu Hulan 373
Flower Net
Dragon Bones
The Interior

Seranella, Barbara
Munch Mancini 510
No Human Involved
Unwanted Company
No Man Standing
Unwilling Accomplice
No Offense Intended
Unfinished Business
Unpaid Dues
An Unacceptable Death

Shaffer, Louise
Angie DaVito. 214
All My Suspects
Talked to Death

Shah, Diane K.
Paris Chandler 150
As Crime Goes By
Dying Cheek to Cheek

Shelton, Connie
Charlotte "Charlie" Parker *628*
Deadly Gamble
Memories Can Be Murder
Small Towns Can Be Murder
Reunions Can Be Murder
Balloons Can Be Murder
Holidays Can Be Murder (2009)
Vacations Can Be Murder
Partnerships Can Kill
Honeymoons Can Be Murder
Competition Can Be Murder
Obsessions Can Be Murder
Gossip Can Be Murder (2010)

Sherman, Beth
Anne Hardaway 325
Dead Man's Float
Death's a Beach
Murder Down the Shore
Death at High Tide
The Devil and the Deep Blue Sea

Short, Sharon Gwyn
Patricia Delaney 216
Angel's Bidding
The Death We Share
Past Pretense

Sibley, Celestine
Kate Mulcay a.k.a. Katy Kincaid 597
The Malignant Heart (Katy Kincaid)
Straight As an Arrow
A Plague of Kinfolks
Ah, Sweet Mystery
Dire Happenings at Scratch Ankle
Spider in the Sink

Silva, Linda Kay
Delta Stevens 766
Taken by Storm
Weathering the Storm
Tropical Storm
Storm Shelter
Storm Front
Storm Rising

Simonson, Sheila

Lark Dailey (Dodge) 197

Larkspur
Mudlark
Malarkey
Skylark
Meadowlark

Singer, Shelley

Barrett Lake 453

Following Jane
Searching for Sara
Picture of David
Interview with Mattie

Smith, Alexander McCall

Precious Ramotswe 678

The No. l Ladies' Detective Agency
Morality for Beautiful Girls
The Full Cupboard of Life
Blue Shoes and Happiness
The Good Husband of Zebra Drive
The Double Comfort Safari Club (2010)
The Tears of the Giraffe
The Kalahari Typing School for Men
In the Company of Cheerful Ladies
The Miracle of Speedy Motors
Tea Time for the Traditionally Built (2009)

Smith, Barbara Burnett

Jolie Wyatt 880

Writers of the Purple Sage
Celebration in Purple Sage
Skeletons in Purple Sage
Dust Devils of the Purple Sage
Mistletoe from Purple Sage

Smith, Cynthia

Emma Rhodes 699

Noblesse Oblige
Misleading Ladies
Royals and Rogues
Impolite Society
Silver and Guilt

Smith, Janet L.

Annie MacPherson 497

Sea of Troubles
A Vintage Murder
Practice to Deceive

Smith, Julie

Skip Langdon 457

New Orleans Mourning
Jazz Funeral
House of Blues
Crescent City Kill
Louisiana Hotshots
The Axeman's Jazz
New Orleans Beat
The Kindness of Strangers
82 Desire
Mean Woman Blues

Smith, Sarah

Perdita Halley 320

The Vanished Child
A Citizen of the Country
The Knowledge of Water

Smith-Levin, Judith

Starletta Duvall 236

Do Not Go Gently
Green Money
The Hoodoo Man
Reckless Eyeballin'

Funeral Food
Mourning Shift
Cold Front
Foreign Body

Tell, Dorothy

Poppy Dillworth 225

Murder at Red Rock Ranch
The Hallelujah Murders

Temple, Lou Jane

Heaven Lee 471

Death by Rhubarb
Revenge of the Barbecue Queens
A Stiff Risotto
Bread on Arrival
The Cornbread Killer
Red Beans and Vice
Death Is Semisweet

Tesler, Nancy

Carrie Carlin 138

Pink Balloons and Other Deadly Things
Sharks, Jellyfish and Other Deadly Things
Shooting Stars and Other Deadly Things
Golden Eggs and Other Deadly Things
Slippery Slopes and Other Deadly Things

Thomas, Natalie Buske

Serena Wilcox 863

Gene Play
Virtual Memories
Camp Conviction

Thomas, Scarlett

Lily Pascale 631

Dead Clever
In Your Face
Seaside

Thomas-Graham, Pamela

Nikki Chase 154

A Darker Shade of Crimson
Blue Blood
Orange Crushed

Thompson, Victoria

Sarah Decker Brandt 105

Murder on Astor Place
Murder on St. Mark's Place
Murder on Gramercy Park
Murder on Washington Square
Murder on Mulberry Bend
Murder on Lenox Hill
Murder on Marble Row
Murder in Little Italy
Murder in Chinatown
Murder on Bank Street
Murder on Waverly Place (2009)
Murder on Lexington Avenue (2010)

Thurlo, Aimee and David

Ella Clah 161

Blackening Song
Death Walker
Bad Medicine
Enemy Way
Shooting Chant
Red Mesa
Changing Woman
Tracking Bear
Wind Spirit
White Thunder
Mourning Dove
Turquoise Girl
Coyote's Wife
Earthway (2009)
Never-ending-snake (2010)

(NB: Walsh has also continued the Dorothy L. Sayer series on Lord Peter Wimsey and Harriet Vane covered in Volume I)

Index of Characters – Volumes 1, 2, 3

1 refers to Volume I, 2 refers to Volume II, and 3 refers to Volume III of the series

C

1 refers to Volume I, 2 refers to Volume II, and 3 refers to Volume III of the series

G

M

1 refers to Volume I, 2 refers to Volume II, and 3 refers to Volume III of the series

1 refers to Volume I, 2 refers to Volume II, and 3 refers to Volume III of the series

Q

R

S

1 refers to Volume I, 2 refers to Volume II, and 3 refers to Volume III of the series

1 refers to Volume I, 2 refers to Volume II, and 3 refers to Volume III of the series

Book Titles Index

All titles were taken from my personal book reviews or from advance notices of future books and were rechecked for accuracy with recognized authorities such as Hubin, Heising, Twentieth Century Crime and Mystery Writers, and with newsletters by mystery book stores. Any errors are my own. Those titles marked with an asterisk (*) which are not reviewed are followed by a date. They are to be published soon but at a later date than this volume covers.

Title of Book	Author	Character
#		
12 Drummers Drumming	Diana Deverell	Casey Collins
1-900-DEAD	Tony Fennelly	Margo Fortier
1st Impressions	Kate Calloway	Cassidy James
23 Shades of Black	k.j.a. Wishnia	Filomena "Fil" Buscarsela
206 Bones	Kathy Reich	Dr. Temperance Brennan
2nd Fiddle	Kate Calloway	Cassidy James
3rd Degree	Kate Calloway	Cassidy James
4th Down	Kate Calloway	Cassidy James
5th Wheel	Kate Calloway	Cassidy James
6th Sense	Kate Calloway	Cassidy James
7th Heaven	Kate Calloway	Cassidy James
77th Street Requiem	Wendy Hornsby	Maggie MacGowen
82 Desire	Julie Smith	Skip Langdon
8th Day	Kate Calloway	Cassidy James
A		
Above the Law	Patricia D. Benke	Judith Thornton
Absent Friends	Gillian Linscott	Nell Bray
Absolute Instinct	Robert W. Walker	Dr. Jessica Coran
Absolution by Murder	Peter Tremayne	Sister Fidelma
Accessory to Murder	Barbara Jaye Wilson	Brenda Midnight
An Accidental Shroud	Marjorie Eccles	Abigail Moon
Acid Bath	Nancy Herndon	Elena Jarvis
Acquired Motives	Sarah Lovett	Dr. Sylvia Strange
Act of Betrayal	Edna Buchanan	Britt Montero
Act of Betrayal	Shirley Kennett	P. J. Gray
Act of Mercy	Peter Tremayne	Sister Fidelma
Acts of Malice	Perri O'Shaughnessy	Nina Reilly
Add One Dead Critic	Cathie John	Kate Cavanaugh
Adjusted to Death	Jaqueline Girdner	Kate Jasper
Affirmative Reaction	Aileen Schumacher	Tory Travers
The African Quest	Lyn Hamilton	Lara McClintoch
After the Break	Lis Howell	Kate Wilkinson
After-Image	Leona Gom	Vicky Bauer
Agatha Raisin and the Case of the Curious Curate	M. C. Beaton	Agatha Raisin
Agatha Raisin and the Day the Floods Came	M. C. Beaton	Agatha Raisin
Agatha Raisin and the Fairies of Fryfam	M. C. Beaton	Agatha Raisin
Agatha Raisin and the Haunted House	M. C. Beaton	Agatha Raisin
Agatha Raisin and the Love from Hell	M. C. Beaton	Agatha Raisin

Title of Book	Author	Character
Agatha Raisin and the Murderous Marriage	M. C. Beaton	Agatha Raisin
Agatha Raisin and the Potted Gardener	M. C. Beaton	Agatha Raisin
Agatha Raisin and the Quiche of Death	M. C. Beaton	Agatha Raisin
Agatha Raisin and the Terrible Tourist	M. C. Beaton	Agatha Raisin
Agatha Raisin and the Vicious Vet	M. C. Beaton	Agatha Raisin
Agatha Raisin and the Walkers of Dembley	M. C. Beaton	Agatha Raisin
Agatha Raisin and the Wellspring of Death	M. C. Beaton	Agatha Raisin
Agatha Raisin and the Witch of Wyckhadden	M. C. Beaton	Agatha Raisin
Agatha Raisin and the Wizard of Evesham	M. C. Beaton	Agatha Raisin
Ah, Sweet Mystery	Celestine Sibley	Kate Mulcay a.k.a. Katy Kincaid
An Air That Kills	Andrew Taylor	Jill Francis
Airtight Case	Beverly Connor	Lindsay Chamberlain
Akin to Death	Carroll Lachnit	Hannah Barlow
aka Jane	Maureen Tan	Jane Nichols
Alibi for an Actress	Gillian B. Farrell	Annie McGrogan
The Alienist	Caleb Carr	Sara Howard
All My Enemies	Barry Maitland	Sgt. Kathy Kolla
All My Suspects	Louise Shaffer	Angie DaVito
All Shall Be Well	Deborah Crombie	Gemma James
All Shots	Susan Conant	Holly Winter
All That Remains	Patricia D. Cornwell	Dr. Kay Scarpetta
All the Dead Fathers	David J. Walker	Kirsten
All the Dead Lie Down	Mary Willis Walker	Molly Cates
All the Old Lions	Carol Caverly	Thea Barlow
All Things Undying (2010)	Marcia Talley	Hannah Ives
The Alligator's Farewell	Hialeah Jackson	Annabelle Hardy-Maratos
Almost Human	Lillian M. Roberts	Dr. Andi Pauling
Along the Journey River	Carole LaFavor	Renee LaRoche
Alpha, Beta, Gamma...Dead	Betty Rowlands	Sukey Reynolds
The Alpine Advocate	Mary Daheim	Emma Lord
The Alpine Betrayal	Mary Daheim	Emma Lord
The Alpine Christmas	Mary Daheim	Emma Lord
The Alpine Decoy	Mary Daheim	Emma Lord
The Alpine Escape	Mary Daheim	Emma Lord
The Alpine Fury	Mary Daheim	Emma Lord
The Alpine Gamble	Mary Daheim	Emma Lord
The Alpine Hero	Mary Daheim	Emma Lord
The Alpine Icon	Mary Daheim	Emma Lord
The Alpine Journey	Mary Daheim	Emma Lord
The Alpine Kindred	Mary Daheim	Emma Lord
The Alpine Legacy	Mary Daheim	Emma Lord
The Alpine Menace	Mary Daheim	Emma Lord
The Alpine Nemesis	Mary Daheim	Emma Lord
The Alpine Obituary	Mary Daheim	Emma Lord
The Alpine Pursuit	Mary Daheim	Emma Lord
The Alpine Quilt	Mary Daheim	Emma Lord
The Alpine Recluse	Mary Daheim	Emma Lord
The Alpine Scandal	Mary Daheim	Emma Lord
The Alpine Traitor	Mary Daheim	Emma Lord

Title of Book	Author	Character
Aunt Dimity Takes a Holiday	Nancy Atherton	Dimity Westwood, Lori Shepherd
Aunt Dimity: Vampire Hunter	Nancy Atherton	Dimity Westwood, Lori Shepherd
Aunt Dimity's Christmas	Nancy Atherton	Dimity Westwood, Lori Shepherd
Aunt Dimity's Death	Nancy Atherton	Dimity Westwood, Lori Shepherd
Aunt Dimity's Good Deed	Nancy Atherton	Dimity Westwood, Lori Shepherd
Auntie Mayhem	Mary Daheim	Judith McMonigle (Flynn)
Authorized Personnel Only	Barbara D'Amato	Suze Figueroa
The Axeman's Jazz	Julie Smith	Skip Langdon
B		
Babel	Barry Maitland	Sgt. Kathy Kolla
Baby, It's Cold	Jaye Maiman	Robin Miller
Back to School Murder	Leslie Meier	Lucy Stone
Backstab	Elaine Viets	Francesca Vierling
Back Stage Murder	Shelley Freydont	Lindy Graham-Haggerty
Backtrack	Carol Dawber	Liz Gresham
Bad Blood	Linda Fairstein	Alexandra Cooper
Bad Blood	Suzanne Proulx	Victoria Lucci
Bad Blood a.k.a. A Classy Touch of Murder	C. F. Roe	Dr. Jean Montrose
A Bad Hair Day	Sophie Dunbar	Claire Claiborne Jenner
Bad Intent	Wendy Hornsby	Maggie MacGowen
Bad Luck	Suzanne Proulx	Victoria Lucci
Bad Manners	Marne Davis Kellogg	Lilly Bennett
Bad Medicine	Suzanne Proulx	Victoria Lucci
Bad Medicine	Aimee and David Thurlo	Ella Clah
Bad Moon Rising	Barbara Johnson	Colleen Fitzgerald
Bad News Travels Fast	Gar Anthony Haywood	Dottie Loudermilk
Bad to the Bone	Katy Munger	Casey Jones
Bad Vibes	Joyce Holms	Fizz Fitzpatrick
The Bad Witness	Laura Van Wormer	Sally Harrington
Badger's Moon	Peter Tremayne	Sister Fidelma
Bagels for Tea	Serita Stevens, Rayanne Moore	Fanny Zindel
Bagged	Jo Bailey	Jan Gallagher
Bait	C. J. Songer	"Meg" Gillis
Bake Sale Murder	Leslie Meier	Lucy Stone
The Ballad of Frankie Silver	Sharyn McCrumb	Nora Bonesteel
Balloons Can Be Murder	Connie Shelton	Charlotte "Charlie" Parker
Baltimore Blues	Laura Lippman	Tess Monaghan
Bantam of the Opera	Mary Daheim	Judith McMonigle (Flynn)
The Barker Street Regulars	Susan Conant	Holly Winter
Barking	Liz Evans	Grace Smith
The Bar Mitzvah Murder	Lee Harris	Christine Bennett
Bare Bones	Kathy Reich	Dr. Temperance Brennan
Baroque and Desperate	Tamar Myers	Abigail "Abby" Timberlake
Baseball Cat	Garrison Allen	Penelope Warren
The Bastard's Tale	Margaret Frazer	Sister Frevisse
Batter Safe Than Sorry (2010)	Tamar Myers	Magdalena Yoder
Bayou City Secrets	Deborah Powell	Hollis Carpenter
The Beach Affair	Barbara Johnson	Colleen Fitzgerald
Beacon Street Mourning	Dianne Day	Caroline "Fremont" Jones
Beaned in Boston	Gail E. Farrelly	Lisa King
The Beastly Bloodline	Patricia Guiver	Delilah Doolittle
Beat a Rotten Egg to the Punch	Cathie John	Kate Cavanaugh
Beat Up a Cookie	Denise Dietz	Ellie Bernstein
The Beekeeper's Apprentice	Laurie R. King	Mary Russell (Holmes)
A Beer at a Bawdy House	David J. Walker	Kirsten

Title of Book	Author	Character
Behind Eclaire's Doors	Sophie Dunbar	Claire Claiborne Jenner
Bell, Cook, and Candle	Joanne Pence	Angelina "Angie" Amalfi
Beneath the Ashes	Sue Henry	Jessie Arnold
Beneath the Bleeding	Val McDermid	Carol Jordan
Beneath the Blonde	Stella Duffy	Saz Martin
Beneath These Stones	Ann Granger	Merry Mitchell
The Bernini Bust	Iain Pears	Flavia di Stefano
The Beryllium Murder	Camille Minichino	Gloria Lamerino
The Best Defense	Sarah Gregory	Sharon Hays
The Best Defense	Kate Wilhelm	Barbara Holloway
Best in Show	Laurien Berenson	Melanie Travis
The Best Revenge	Stephen White	Lauren Crowder
Bet Against the House	Catherine Dain	Freddie O'Neal
Betrayal in Death	J. D. Robb	Lt. Eve Dallas
Betrayed in Cornwall	Jane Bolitho	Rose Trevelyan
A Better Class of Sleuth	Joyce Christmas	Elizabeth Anne "Betty" Trenka
Better Off Dead	Katy Munger	Casey Jones
Better Than Sex	Susan Holtzer	Anneke Haagen
Better to Rest	Dana Stabenow	Wyanet "Wy" Chouinard
Between a Wok and a Hard Place	Tamar Myers	Magdalena Yoder
Beware Sleeping Dogs	Karen Ann Wilson	Samantha Holt
Beware Taurus	Linda Mather	Jo Hughes
Beware the Butcher Bird	Lydia Adamson	Lucy Wayles
Beware the Laughing Gull	Lydia Adamson	Lucy Wayles
Beware the Tufted Duck	Lydia Adamson	Lucy Wayles
Beyond Ice, Beyond Death	Thomas McCall	Nora Callum
The Big Thaw	Donald Harstad	Hester Gorse
Biggie and the Devil Diet	Nancy Bell	Biggie Weatherford
Biggie and the Fricasseed Fat Man	Nancy Bell	Biggie Weatherford
Biggie and the Mangled Mortician	Nancy Bell	Biggie Weatherford
Biggie and the Meddlesome Mailman	Nancy Bell	Biggie Weatherford
Biggie and the Poisoned Politician	Nancy Bell	Biggie Weatherford
Biggie and the Quincy Ghost	Nancy Bell	Biggie Weatherford
Bindweed	Janis Harrison	Bretta Solomon
Bird Brained	Jessica Speart	Rachel Porter
Birth Marks	Sarah Dunant	Hannah Wolfe
Birthday Party	Marne Davis Kellogg	Lilly Bennett
Birthday Party Murder	Leslie Meier	Lucy Stone
The Bishop's Tale	Margaret Frazer	Sister Frevisse
Bitch Factor	Chris Rogers	Dixie Flannigan
A Bite of Death	Susan Conant	Holly Winter
Bitter Blue	Cath Staincliffe	Sal Kilkenny
Bitter Business	Gini Hartzmark	Kate Millholland
Bitter End	Joyce Holms	Fizz Fitzpatrick
A Bitter Feast	S. J. Rozan	Lydia Chin
Bitter Herbs	Natasha Cooper	Willow King
Bitter Instinct	Robert W. Walker	Dr. Jessica Coran
Bitter Sugar	Carolina Garcia-Aguilera	Guadalupe "Lupe" Solano
Bitter Sweets	G. A. McKevett	Savannah Reid
The Black Cat Caper	Georgette Livingston	Dr. Jennifer Gray
Black Delta Night	Jessica Speart	Rachel Porter
Black Diamond	Susan Holtzer	Anneke Haagen
Black Diamonds	Jon Land	Danielle Barnea
Black Lotus	Laura Joh Rowland	Reiko Ichiro
Black Notice	Patricia D. Cornwell	Dr. Kay Scarpetta

Title of Book	Author	Character
Black Ribbon	Susan Conant	Holly Winter
Black Rubber Dress	Lauren Henderson	Sam Jones
Black Salamander	Marilyn Todd	Claudia Seferius
The Black Ship	Carola Dunn	Daisy Dalrymple
Black Water	Doug Allyn	Michelle "Mitch" Mitchell
Blackening Song	Aimee and David Thurlo	Ella Clah
Blackout	John J. Nance	Kat Bronsky
Blackwater Spirits	Miriam Monfredo	Glynis Tryon
Blackwork	Monica Ferris	Betsy Devonshire
Blanche Among the Talented Tenth	Barbara Neely	Blanche White
Blanche Cleans Up	Barbara Neely	Blanche White
Blanche on the Lam	Barbara Neely	Blanche White
Blanche Passes Go	Barbara Neely	Blanche White
Bleeding Bones	Susan Wittig Albert	China Bayles
Bleeding Dodger Blue	Crabbe Evers	Petronella "Petey" Biggers
Bleeding Heart	Mary Freeman	Rachel O'Connor
Bleeding Maize and Blue	Susan Holtzer	Anneke Haagen
A Bleeding of Innocents	Jo Bannister	Liz Graham
A Blessed Death	Carroll Lachnit	Hannah Barlow
Blind Alley	Iris Johansen	Eve Duncan
Blind Bloodhound Justice	Virginia Lanier	Jo Beth Sidden
Blind Descent	Nevada Barr	Anna Pigeon
Blind Instinct	Robert W. Walker	Dr. Jessica Coran
Blind Justice	William Bernhardt	Christina McCall
Blind Side	Catherine Coulter	Lacey Savich
Blind Side	Penny Warner	Connor Westphal
Blind Spot	Judy Mercer	Ariel Gold
Blinded	Stephen White	Lauren Crowder
Blindsided	Clyde Phillips	Jane Candiotti
Blood	Joseph Glass	Dr. Susan Shader
Blood and Rubles	Stuart Kaminsky	Elena Timafeyeva
Ther Blood Ballad	Rett MacPherson	Victory "Torie" O'Shea
Blood Country	Mary Logue	Claire Watkins
Blood Dancing	Jonathan Gash	Dr. Clare Burtonall
Blood Diamonds	Jon Land	Danielle Barnea
Blood Game	Iris Johansen	Eve Duncan
Blood Lake	k.j.a. Wishnia	Filomena "Fil" Buscarsela
Blood Lies	Marianne Macdonald	Dido Hoare
Blood Lure	Nevada Barr	Anna Pigeon
Blood Money	Rochelle Majer Krich	Jessica Drake
Blood Money	Thomas Perry	Jane Whitefield
Blood of an Aries	Linda Mather	Jo Hughes
Blood on the Wood	Gillian Linscott	Nell Bray
Blood Orchid	Stuart Woods	Holly Barker
Blood Red Roses	Margaret Lawrence	Hannah Trevor
Blood Relations	Rett MacPherson	"Torie" O'Shea
Blood Run	Leah Ruth Robinson	Dr. Evelyn Sutcliffe
The Blood Tower	Carola Dunn	Daisy Dalrymple
Blood Tracks	Karen Rose Cercone	Helen Sorby
Blood Trance	R. D. Zimmerman	Maddy Phillips
Blood Will Tell	Terris McMahon Grimes	Theresa Galloway
Blood Will Tell	Dana Stabenow	Kate Shugak
Blood Work	Fay Zachary	Dr. Liz Broward
A Bloodhound to Die For	Virginia Lanier	Jo Beth Sidden
Bloodlines	Jan Burke	Irene Kelly
Bloodlines	Susan Conant	Holly Winter
Bloodroot	Susan Wittig Albert	China Bayles

Title of Book	Author	Character
Blood's Burden	Alex Matthews	Cassidy McCabe
Bloodstream	P. M. Carlson	Martine "Marty" Hopkins
Bloody Bonsai	Peter Abresch	Dodee Swisher
Bloody Roses	Natasha Cooper	Willow King
Bloody Secrets	Carolina Garcia-Aguilera	Guadalupe "Lupe" Solano
Bloody Shame	Carolina Garcia-Aguilera	Guadalupe "Lupe" Solano
Bloody Waters	Carolina Garcia-Aguilera	Guadalupe "Lupe" Solano
Blooming Murder	Jean Hager	Tess Darcy
Blow Fly	Patricia D. Cornwell	Dr. Kay Scarpetta
Blow Out	Catherine Coulter	Lacey Savich
Blowing Smoke	Barbara Block	Robin Light
Blown Away	David Wiltse	Karen Crist (Becker)
Blue	Abigail Padgett	Emily "Blue" McCarron
Blue Blood	Pamela Thomas-Graham	Nikki Chase
Blue Genes	Val McDermid	Kate Brannigan
Blue Plate Special	Ruth Birmingham	Sunny Childs
Blue Poppy	Skye Kathleen Moody	Venus Diamond
Blue Shoes and Happiness	Alexander McCall Smith	Precious Ramotswe
Blue Screen	Robert B. Parker	Sunny Randall
Blue Twilight	Jessica Speart	Rachel Porter
Blue Widows	Jon Land	Danielle Barnea
Blue Wolf	Lise McClendon	Alix Thorssen
The Bluejay Shaman	Lise McClendon	Alix Thorssen
The Body at Epsom Downs	Robin Paige	Kathryn "Kate" Ardleigh
Body English	Linda Mariz	Laura Ireland
The Body Farm	Patricia D. Cornwell	Dr. Kay Scarpetta
The Body in the Attic	Katherine Hall Page	Faith Fairchild
The Body in the Basement	Katherine Hall Page	Faith Fairchild
The Body in the Belfry	Katherine Hall Page	Faith Fairchild
The Body in the Big Apple	Katherine Hall Page	Faith Fairchild
The Body in the Bog	Katherine Hall Page	Faith Fairchild
The Body in the Bonfire	Katherine Hall Page	Faith Fairchild
The Body in the Bookcase	Katherine Hall Page	Faith Fairchild
The Body in the Boullion	Katherine Hall Page	Faith Fairchild
The Body in the Cast	Katherine Hall Page	Faith Fairchild
The Body in the Fjord	Katherine Hall Page	Faith Fairchild
The Body in the Gallery	Katherine Hall Page	Faith Fairchild
The Body in the Ivy	Katherine Hall Page	Faith Fairchild
The Body in the Kelp	Katherine Hall Page	Faith Fairchild
The Body in the Lighthouse	Katherine Hall Page	Faith Fairchild
The Body in the Moonlight	Katherine Hall Page	Faith Fairchild
The Body in the Sleigh	Katherine Hall Page	Faith Fairchild
The Body in the Snowdrift	Katherine Hall Page	Faith Fairchild
The Body in the Transept	Jeanne M. Dams	Dorothy Martin
The Body in the Vestibule	Katherine Hall Page	Faith Fairchild
Body of Evidence	Patricia D. Cornwell	Dr. Kay Scarpetta
Body of Lies	Iris Johansen	Eve Duncan
A Body to Die For	Valerie Frankel	Wanda Mallory
A Body to Die For	G. A. McKevett	Savannah Reid
Body Wave	Nancy J. Cohen	Marla Shore
The Bohemian Murders	Dianne Day	Caroline "Fremont" Jones
Bonded for Murder	Bruce Most	Ruby Dark
Bone Appetit	Carolyn Haines	Sarah Booth Delany
The Bone Collector	Jeffrey Wilds Deaver	Amelia Sachs
Bone Dancing	Jonathan Gash	Dr. Clare Burtonall
Bone Deep	David Wiltse	Karen Crist (Becker)

Title of Book	Author	Character
Bone Harvest	Mary Logue	Claire Watkins
Bone Hunter	Sarah Andrews	Emily "Em" Hansen
Bone of Contention	Roberta Gellis	Magdalene la Bâtarde
A Bone to Pick	Charlaine Harris	Aurora "Roe" Teagarden
The Bone Vault	Linda Fairstein	Alexandra Cooper
Bones	Jan Burke	Irene Kelly
Bones to Ashes	Kathy Reich	Dr. Temperance Brennan
Bones to Pick	Suzanne North	Phoebe Fairfax
A Bonny Case of Murder a.k.a. Deadly Partnership	C. F. Roe	Dr. Jean Montrose
Book of Light	Michelle Blake	Rev. Lily Connor
Book of Moons	Rosemary Edghill	Karen Hightower a.k.a. Bast
Book of Old Houses	Sarah Graves	Jacobia Tiptee
The Book of Shadows	C. L. Grace	Kathryn Swinbrooke
Book of the Dead	Patricia D. Cornwell	Dr. Kay Scarpetta
Bookmarked to Die	Jo Dereske	Wilhelmena "Helma" Zukas
Bootlegger's Daughter	Margaret Maron	Deborah Knott
Borderline	Nevada Barr	Anna Pigeon
Border Prey	Jessica Speart	Rachel Porter
The Boric Acid Murder	Camille Minichino	Gloria Lamerino
Born in Death	J. D. Robb	Lt. Eve Dallas
The Bowl of Night	Rosemary Edghill	Karen Hightower a.k.a. Bast
The Boy's Tale	Margaret Frazer	Sister Frevisse
A Brace of Bloodhounds	Virginia Lanier	Jo Beth Sidden
Brainwaves	Leonard Goldberg	Joanna Blalock
A Breach of Promise	Perri O'Shaughnessy	Nina Reilly
Bread on Arrival	Lou Jane Temple	Heaven Lee
Break No Bones	Kathy Reich	Dr. Temperance Brennan
Breakaway	Laura Crum	Dr. Gail McCarthy
Breaking Point	Martina Navratilova, Liz Nickles	Jordan Myles
Breakup	Dana Stabenow	Kate Shugak
Breakthrough	Jonathan Stone	Julian Palmer
Bride and Doom	Jean Hager	Tess Darcy
Bride and Groom	Susan Conant	Holly Winter
The Bride's Kimono	Sujata Massey	Rei Shimura
A Bright Flamingo Shroud	Meg O'Brien	Jessica "Jesse" James
Broken Dishes	Earlene Fowler	Albenia "Benni" Harper
Broken Lines	Jo Bannister	Liz Graham
Broken Star	Lizbie Brown	Elizabeth Blair
The Broken Window	Jeffrey Deaver	Amelia Sachs
Brotherly Love	Randye Lordon	Sydney Sloane
Brothers of Cain	Miriam Monfredo	Glynis Tryon
The Brutal Heart	Gail Bowen	Joanne "Jo" Kilbourn
Bucket Nut	Liza Cody	Eva Wylie
The Bulrush Murders	Rebecca Rothenberg	Claire Sharples
Bundori	Laura Joh Rowland	Reiko Ichiro
Buried Bones	Carolyn Haines	Sarah Booth Delaney
Buried by Breakfast	Claudia Bishop	Sarah "Quill" Quilliam
Buried Diamonds	April Henry	Claire Montrose
Buried in Cornwall	Jane Bolitho	Rose Trevelyan
Buried Treasure	Alan Scholefield	Dr. Anne Vernon
Burn (2010)	Nevada Barr	Anna Pigeon
Burned	Carol Higgins Clark	Regan Reilly
Burn Out	Alan Scholefield	Dr. Anne Vernon
The Burning Bride	Margaret Lawrence	Hannah Trevor

Title of Book	Author	Character
Castle Rouge	Carole Nelson Douglas	Irene Adler
The Catalyst a.k.a. The Strange Attractor	Desmond Cory	Dr. Kate Coyle
A Cat By Any Other Name	Lydia Adamson	Alice Nestleton
A Cat in a Chorus Line	Lydia Adamson	Alice Nestleton
Cat in a Crimson Haze	Carole Nelson Douglas	Temple Barr & Midnight Louie
Cat in a Diamond Dazzle	Carole Nelson Douglas	Temple Barr & Midnight Louie
Cat in a Flamingo Fedora	Carole Nelson Douglas	Temple Barr & Midnight Louie
A Cat in a Glass House	Lydia Adamson	Alice Nestleton
Cat in a Golden Garland	Carole Nelson Douglas	Temple Barr & Midnight Louie
Cat in a Hot Pink Pursuit	Carole Nelson Douglas	Temple Barr & Midnight Louie
Cat in a Jeweled Jumpsuit	Carole Nelson Douglas	Temple Barr & Midnight Louie
Cat in a Kiwi Con	Carole Nelson Douglas	Temple Barr & Midnight Louie
Cat in a Leopard Spot	Carole Nelson Douglas	Temple Barr & Midnight Louie
Cat in a Midnight Choir	Carole Nelson Douglas	Temple Barr & Midnight Louie
Cat in a Neon Nightmare	Carole Nelson Douglas	Temple Barr & Midnight Louie
Cat in an Orange Twist	Carole Nelson Douglas	Temple Barr & Midnight Louie
Cat in a Quicksilver Caper	Carole Nelson Douglas	Temple Barr & Midnight Louie
Cat in a Red Hot Rage	Carole Nelson Douglas	Temple Barr & Midnight Louie
Cat in a Sapphire Slipper	Carole Nelson Douglas	Temple Barr & Midnight Louie
Cat in a Topaz Tango	Carole Nelson Douglas	Temple Barr & Midnight Louie
Cat in an Ultramarine Scheme (2010)	Carole Nelson Douglas	Temple Barr & Midnight Louie
Cat in an Indigo Mood	Carole Nelson Douglas	Temple Barr & Midnight Louie
A Cat in Fine Style	Lydia Adamson	Alice Nestleton
A Cat in the Manger	Lydia Adamson	Alice Nestleton
A Cat in the Wings	Lydia Adamson	Alice Nestleton
A Cat in Wolf's Clothing	Lydia Adamson	Alice Nestleton
A Cat Named Brat	Lydia Adamson	Alice Nestleton
A Cat of a Different Color	Lydia Adamson	Alice Nestleton
A Cat of One's Own	Lydia Adamson	Alice Nestleton
A Cat on a Beach Blanket	Lydia Adamson	Alice Nestleton
Cat on a Blue Monday	Carole Nelson Douglas	Temple Barr & Midnight Louie
Cat on a Hyacinth Hunt	Carole Nelson Douglas	Temple Barr & Midnight Louie
A Cat on a Winning Streak	Lydia Adamson	Alice Nestleton
A Cat on Jingle Bell Rock	Lydia Adamson	Alice Nestleton
A Cat on Stage Left	Lydia Adamson	Alice Nestleton
A Cat on the Bus	Lydia Adamson	Alice Nestleton
A Cat on the Cutting Edge	Lydia Adamson	Alice Nestleton
Cat on the Scent	Rita Mae Brown	Mary "Harry" Haristeen & Mrs. Murphy
A Cat Under the Mistletoe	Lydia Adamson	Alice Nestleton
A Cat With a Fiddle	Lydia Adamson	Alice Nestleton
Cat With an Emerald Eye	Carole Nelson Douglas	Temple Barr & Midnight Louie
A Cat With No Clue	Lydia Adamson	Alice Nestleton
A Cat With No Regrets	Lydia Adamson	Alice Nestleton
A Cat With the Blues	Lydia Adamson	Alice Nestleton
Cat's Claw	Alex Matthews	Cassidy McCabe
Cat's Cradle	Lizbie Brown	Elizabeth Blair
The Cat's Eye	Marian J. A. Jackson	Abigail Danforth
Cat's Eyewitness	Rita Mae Brown	Mary "Harry" Haristeen
Cat's Paw	Michael Molloy	Sarah Keane
Catch As Cat Can	Rita Mae Brown	Mary "Harry" Haristeen & Mrs. Murphy
Catch the Fallen Sparrow	Priscilla Masters	Joanna Piercy
Catering to Nobody	Diane Mott Davidson	Goldy Bear (Schulz)

Title of Book	Author	Character
Catnap	Carole Nelson Douglas	Temple Barr & Midnight Louie
Caught Dead	Bridget McKenna	Caley Burke
Caught in a Bind	Gayle Roper	Merry Kramer
Caught in the Act	Gayle Roper	Merry Kramer
Caught in the Middle	Gayle Roper	Merry Kramer
Caught in the Shadows	C. A. Haddad	Becky Belski
Caught Out in Cornwall	Jane Bolitho	Rose Trevelyan
Caught Red Handed	Gayle Roper	Merry Kramer
Cause of Death	Patricia D. Cornwell	Dr. Kay Scarpetta
Cavalcade	Walter Satterthwait	Jane Turner
Celebration in Purple Sage	Barbara Burnett Smith	Jolie Wyatt
The Celtic Riddle	Lyn Hamilton	Lara McClintoch
Cemetery Murders	Jean Marcy	Meg Darcy
Cereal Killer	G. A. McKevett	Savannah Reid
The Cereal Murders	Diane Mott Davidson	Goldy Bear (Schulz)
A Ceremonial Death	B. J. Oliphant	Shirley McClintock
Ceremony in Death	J. D. Robb	Lt. Eve Dallas
Chain a Lamb Chop to the Bed	Denise Dietz	Ellie Bernstein
Chained!	Lauren Henderson	Sam Jones
Chains of Folly	Roberta Gellis	Magdalene la Bâtarde
Chalk Whispers	Paul Bishop	Fey Croaker
The Chalon Heads	Barry Maitland	Kathy Kolla
Chameleon	Shirley Kennett	P. J. Gray
Changelings	Jo Bannister	Liz Graham
Changing Woman	Aimee and David Thurlo	Ella Clah
Chapel Noir	Carole Nelson Douglas	Irene Adler
Charged with Guilt	Gloria White	Ronnie Ventana
Charisma	Jo Bannister	Liz Graham
Charm City	Laura Lippman	Tess Monaghan
Chasing Cans	Laura Crum	Dr. Gail McCarthy
Chatauqua	Catherine Ennis	Dr. Bernadette "Bernie" Hebert
The Chattering Chimp Caper	Georgette Livingston	Dr. Jennifer Gray
Cheat the Devil	Jane Rubino	Cat Austen
Check-out Time	Kate Kingsbury	Cecily Sinclair
The Cheetah Chase	Karin McQuillan	Jazz Jasper
The Chelsea Girl Murders	Sparkle Hayter	Robin Hudson
The Cherry Pickers	Betty Rowlands	Melissa Craig
Chestnut Mare, Beware	Jody Jaffe	Natalie Gold
Chickahominy Fever	Ann McMillan	Narcissa Powers, Judah Daniel
Chicken Feed	Alma Fritchley	Letty Campbell
Chicken Little Was Right	Jean Ruryk	Catherine "Cat" Wilde
Chicken Out	Alma Fritchley	Letty Campbell
Chicken Run	Alma Fritchley	Letty Campbell
Chicken Shack	Alma Fritchley	Letty Campbell
Child of Silence	Abigail Padgett	Barbara "Bo" Bradley
Children of Cain	Miriam Monfredo	Glynis Tryon
Chile Death	Susan Wittig Albert	China Bayles
Chill Factor	Chris Rogers	Dixie Flannigan
Chill of Summer	Carol Brennan	Emily Silver
Chilling Effect	Marianne Wesson	Cinda Hayes
Chimney Rock Blues	Janet McClellan	Tru North
China Trade	S. J. Rozan	Lydia Chin
The Chinese Alchemist	Lyn Hamilton	Lara McClintoch
Chinese Whispers	Peter May	Margaret Campbell
Chivalry Is Dead	Kate Kingsbury	Cecily Sinclair
Chopping Spree	Diane Mott Davidson	Goldy Bear (Schulz)
Chosen for Death	Kate Flora	Thea Kozak

Title of Book	Author	Character
Chow Down	Laurien Berenson	Melanie Travis
The Christening Day Murder	Lee Harris	Christine Bennett
Christmas Cookie Murder	Leslie Meier	Lucy Stone
The Christmas Garden Affair	Ann Ripley	Louise Eldridge
Christmas Morning (2010)	Margaret Maron	Deborah Knott
The Christmas Night Murder	Lee Harris	Christine Bennett
Chutes and Adders	Barbara Block	Robin Light
The Cinco de Mayo Murder	Lee Harris	Christine Bennett
Circle of Wolves	Karen Ann Wilson	Samantha Holt
Circles of Confusion	April Henry	Claire Montrose
A Citizen of the Country	Sarah Smith	Perdita Halley
Civil Blood	Ann McMillan	Narcissa Powers, Judah Daniel
Class Action	Catherine Arnold	Karen Perry-Mondori
Class Reunions Are Murder	Taffy Cannon	Nan Robinson
A Classy Touch of Murder a.k.a. Bad Blood	C. F. Roe	Dr. Jean Montrose
Claws and Effect	Rita Mae Brown	Mary "Harry" Haristeen & Mrs. Murphy
Clean Break	Val McDermid	Kate Brannigan
A Clean Kill	Leslie Glass	April Woo
Clear and Convincing Proof	Kate Wilhelm	Barbara Holloway
Clear Cut Murder	Lee Wallingford	Ginny Trask
Clearwater	Catherine Ennis	Dr. Bernadette "Bernie" Hebert
Clerical Errors	D. M. Greenwood	Rev. Theodora Braithwaite
The Clerk's Tale	Margaret Frazer	Sister Frevisse
A Clinic for Murder	Marsha Landreth	Dr. Samantha Turner
Close to the Bone	David Wiltse	Karen Crist (Becker)
Close to You	Mary Jane Clark	Eliza Blake
Closed in Silence	Joan M. Drury	Tyler Jones
Closing Stages	Eileen Dewhurst	Phyllida Moon
Closing Statement	Tierney McClellan	Schuyler Ridgway
The Cloud Pavilion	Laura Joh Rowland	Reiko Ichiro
Club Twelve	Amanda Kyle Williams	Madison McGuire
A Clue for the Puzzle Lady	Parnell Hall	Cora Felton & Sherry Carter
Coal Bones	Karen Rose Cercone	Helen Sorby
Coastal Disturbance	Jessica Speart	Rachel Porter
Cockatiels at Seven	Donna Andrews	Meg Langslow
Code Sixty-One	Donald Harstad	Hester Gorse
Coffee To Die For	Linda French	Teodora "Teddy" Morelli
Coffin Corner	Megan Mallory Rust	Taylor Morgan
The Coffin Dancer	Jeffrey Wilds Deaver	Amelia Sachs
Cold and Pure and Very Dead	Joanne Dobson	Karen Pelletier
A Cold and Silent Dying	Eleanor Taylor Bland	Marti MacAlister
Cold as Ice (2010)	Sue Henry	Jessie Arnold
Cold Blood	Lynda La Plante	Lorraine Page
Cold Call	Diane G. Pugh	Iris Thorne
Cold Case	Stephen White	Lauren Crowder
Cold Case	Kate Wilhelm	Barbara Holloway
A Cold Case of Murder	Jean Marcy	Meg Darcy
A Cold Christmas	Charlene Weir	Susan Donavan Wren

Title of Book	Author	Character
Cold Company	Sue Henry	Jessie Arnold
A Cold Day for Murder	Dana Stabenow	Kate Shugak
Cold Edge	Robert W. Walker	Meredyth "Mere" Sanger

Title of Book	Author	Character
Cold Feet	Kerry Tucker	Libby Kincaid
Cold Front	Kathleen Taylor	Tory Bauer
The Cold Hard Fax	Leslie O'Kane	Molly Masters
Cold Heart	Lynda La Plante	Lorraine Page
The Cold Heart of Capricorn	Martha C. Lawrence	Dr. Elizabeth Chase
Cold Hit	Linda Fairstein	Alexandra Cooper
Cold in the Earth	Ann Granger	Merry Mitchell
Cold Iron	Melisa Michaels	Rosie Lavine
Cold Justice	Jonnie Jacobs	Kali O'Brien
Cold Moon	Jeffrey Deavers	Amelia Sachs
Cold Shoulder	Lynda La Plante	Lorraine Page
Cold Smoked	K. K. Beck	Jane da Silva
Cold Tracks	Lee Wallingford	Ginny Trask
Cold Trail	Ruth Birmingham	Sunny Childs
The Cold Truth	Jonathan Stone	Julian Palmer
A Cold-Blooded Business	Dana Stabenow	Kate Shugak
A Colder Kind of Death	Gail Bowen	Joanne "Jo" Kilbourn
A Comedy of Heirs	Rett MacPherson	"Torie" O'Shea
Commitment to Die	Jennifer L. Jordan	Kristin Ashe
A Common Death a.k.a. *Festering Lilies*	Natasha Cooper	Willow King
The Company She Kept	Marjorie Eccles	Abigail Moon
Competition Can Be Murder	Connie Shelton	Charlotte "Charlie" Parker
Concourse	S. J. Rozan	Lydia Chin
Concubine's Tattoo	Laura Joh Rowland	Reiko Ichiro
Congregation	Virginia Stem Owens	Beth Marie Cartwright
Consider the Crows	Charlene Weir	Susan Donavan Wren
Conspiracy in Death	J. D. Robb	Lt. Eve Dallas
Contents Under Pressure	Edna Buchanan	Britt Montero
A Cook in Time	Joanne Pence	Angelina "Angie" Amalfi
Cook's Night Out	Joanne Pence	Angelina "Angie" Amalfi
Cooked Goose	G. A. McKevett	Savannah Reid
Cooking Most Deadly	Joanne Pence	Angelina "Angie" Amalfi
Cooking Up Trouble	Joanne Pence	Angelina "Angie" Amalfi
Cooks Overboard	Joanne Pence	Angelina "Angie" Amalfi
C.O.P. Out	Nancy Herndon	Elena Jarvis
Copy Cat Crimes	Karen Ann Wilson	Samantha Holt
Copycat	Betty Rowlands	Sukey Reynolds
Coq au Vin	Charlotte Carter	Nanette Hayes
The Cornbread Killer	Lou Jane Temple	Heaven Lee
The Cordelia Squad	Mary Anne Kelly	Claire Breslinsky (Benedetto)
Corona Blue	J. F. Trainor	Angela "Angie" Biwaban
Corpse in the Kitchen	Sarah J. Mason	Sergeant Stone
Corpse Suzette	G. A. McKevett	Savannah Reid
Corpus de Crossword	Nero Blanc	Belle Graham
Corruption of Faith	Brenda English	Sutton McPhee
Corruption of Justice	Brenda English	Sutton McPhee
Corruption of Power	Brenda English	Sutton McPhee
The Council of the Cursed	Peter Tremayne	Sister Fidelma
Countdown	Iris Johansen	Eve Duncan
Country Come to Town	Toni L. P. Kelner	Laura Fleming
Courting Disaster	Joanne Pence	Angelina "Angie" Amalfi
Courting Trouble	Lisa Scottoline	"Bennie" Rosato Law Firm
Coyote's Wife	Aimee and David Thurlo	Ella Clah
Crack Down	Val McDermid	Kate Brannigan
Crack Shot	Sinclair Browning	Trade Ellis

Title of Book	Author	Character
Crazy for Loving	Jaye Maiman	Robin Miller
Creation in Death	J. D. Robb	Lt. Eve Dallas
Creature Discomforts	Susan Conant	Holly Winter
A Credible Threat	Janet Dawson	Jeri Howard
Creeping Ivy	Natasha Cooper	Trish Maguire
Creeps Suzette	Mary Daheim	Judith McMonigle (Flynn)
The Crepes of Wrath	Tamar Myers	Magdalena Yoder
Crescent City Kill	Julie Smith	Skip Langdon
Crewel World	Monica Ferris	Betsy Devonshire
Crewel Yule	Monica Ferris	Betsy Devonshire
Crime of Passion	Kay Hooper	Lane Montana
Crime School	Carol O'Connell	Sgt. Kathleen Mallory
Criminal Intent	William Bernhardt	Christina McCall
Crimson Snow	Jeanne M. Dams	Hilda Johansson
Crooked Island	Victoria McKernan	Chicago Nordejoong
A Crooked Little House	Susan Rogers Cooper	E. J. Pugh
Cross Bones	Kathy Reich	Dr. Temperance Brennan
Crossed Bones	Carolyn Haines	Sarah Booth Delaney
Crossfire	P. M. Carlson	Martine "Marty" Hopkins
The Cross-Legged Knight	Candace M. Robb	Lucie D'Arby Wilton
Crossword Connection	Nero Blanc	Belle Graham
A Crossword Gift (ss collection)	Nero Blanc	Belle Graham
A Crossword Holiday (ss and novella)	Nero Blanc	Belle Graham
A Crossword to Die For	Nero Blanc	Belle Graham
The Crossword Murder	Nero Blanc	Belle Graham
A Crossworder's Delight	Nero Blanc	Belle Graham
Crosswords	Penny Sumner	Victoria Cross
Crouching Buzzard, Leaping Loon	Donna Andrews	Meg Langslow
The Crown of Lights	Phil Rickman	Rev. Merrily Watkins
Crown Witness	Gillian Linscott	Nell Bray
Cruel and Unusual	Patricia D. Cornwell	Dr. Kay Scarpetta
Cruel Justice	Patricia D. Benke	Judith Thornton
Cruel Justice	William Bernhardt	Christina McCall
A Crushing Blow	Penny Kline	Dr. Anna McColl
Crushing Crystal	Evan Marshall	Jane Stuart
Cry Baby	Gloria White	Ronnie Ventana
Cry Dance	Kirk Mitchell	Anna Turnipseed
Cry for Help	Karen Hanson Stuyck	Liz James
A Cry for Self Help	Jaqueline Girdner	Kate Jasper
Cryin' Time	Cecelia Tishy	Kate Banning
Crystal Mountain Veils	Kieran York	Royce Madison
Cuckoo	Alex Keegan	Caz Flood
The Cuckoo Clock	Michele Bailey	Matilda Haycastle
Cue the Easter Bunny	Liz Evans	Grace Smith
The Cure of Souls	Phil Rickman	Rev. Merrily Watkins
The Curious Cape Cod Skull	Marie Lee	Marguerite Smith
Curl Up and Die	Christine T. Jorgensen	Stella the Stargazer a.k.a. Jane Smith
Curly Smoke	Susan Holtzer	Anneke Haagen
Cursed	Carol Higgins Clark	Regan Reilly
Cursed in the Blood	Sharan Newman	Catherine Le Vendeur
Curtsey	Marne Davis Kellogg	Lilly Bennett
Custard's Last Stand	Tamar Myers	Magdalena Yoder
Cut and Dry	Jo Dereske	Ruby Crane
Cut to: Murder	Denise Osborne	Queenie Davilov
Cutter	Laura Crum	Dr. Gail McCarthy

Title of Book	Author	Character
Dead Beat	Val McDermid	Kate Brannigan
Dead Beat and Deadly	Margaret Chittenden	Charlie Plato
Dead Body Language	Penny Warner	Connor Westphal
The Dead Cat Bounce	Sarah Graves	Jacobia Tiptee
The Dead Celeb	Lindsay Maracotta	Lucy Freers
Dead Center	Ruby Horansky	Nikki Trakos
Dead Certain	Gini Hartzmark	Kate Millholland
Dead Clever	Scarlett Thomas	Lily Pascale
The Dead Don't Get Out Much	Mary Jane Maffini	Camilla McPhee
Dead Dry	Sarah Andrews	Emily "Em" Hansen
Dead Duck	Helen Chappell	Hollis Ball
Dead Famous apa *The Jury Must Die*	Carol O'Connell	Sgt. Kathleen Mallory
Dead Fit	Stephen Cook	Judy Best
The Dead Hollywood Mom's Society	Lindsay Maracotta	Lucy Freers
Dead in Hog Heaven	Carol Caverly	Thea Barlow
Dead in the Cellar	Connie Feddersen	Amanda Hazard
Dead in the Dirt	Connie Feddersen	Amanda Hazard
Dead in the Driver's Seat	Connie Feddersen	Amanda Hazard
Dead in the Hay	Connie Feddersen	Amanda Hazard
Dead in the Melon Patch	Connie Feddersen	Amanda Hazard
Dead in the Mud	Connie Feddersen	Amanda Hazard
Dead in the Pumpkin Patch	Connie Feddersen	Amanda Hazard
Dead in the Scrub	B. J. Oliphant	Shirley McClintock
Dead in the Water	Carola Dunn	Daisy Dalrymple
Dead in the Water	Connie Feddersen	Amanda Hazard
Dead in the Water	Dana Stabenow	Kate Shugak
Dead Letter	Jane Waterhouse	Garner Quinn
Deadline a.k.a. *Suspect*	Jennifer Rowe	Tessa Vance
The Dead Man and the Sea	Janice Steinberg	Margo Simon
Dead Man Dancing	Marcia Talley	Hannah Ives
Dead Man Docking	Mary Daheim	Judith McMonigle (Flynn)
Dead Man Falls	Paula Boyd	Jolene Jackson
A Dead Man Out of Mind	Kate Charles	Lucy Kingsley
Dead Man Riding	Gillian Linscott	Nell Bray
Dead Man Running	Rett MacPherson	Victory "Torie" O'Shea
Dead Man's Bones	Susan Wittig Albert	China Bayles
Dead Man's Fingers	Barbara Lee	Eve Elliott
Dead Man's Float	Beth Sherman	Anne Hardaway
Dead Man's Hand	Catherine Dain	Freddie O'Neal
Dead Man's Island	Carolyn Hart	Henrietta O'Dwyer Collins
Dead Man's Puzzle	Parnell Hall	Cora Felton and Sherry Carter
Dead Man's Sweetheart a.k.a. *Dead Man's Music*	Gillian Linscott	Nell Bray
Dead March	Ann McMillan	Narcissa Powers, Judah Daniel
Dead Men Don't Dance	Margaret Chittenden	Charlie Plato
Dead North	Sue Henry	Jessie Arnold
The Dead of Winter	Patricia Hall	Laura Ackroyd
Dead on Arrival	Patricia Hall	Laura Ackroyd
Dead on Her Feet	Christine T. Jorgensen	Stella the Stargazer a.k.a. Jane Smith
Dead Over Heels	Charlaine Harris	Aurora "Roe" Teagarden
Dead Reckoning	Patricia Hall	Laura Ackroyd
Dead Ringer	Toni L. P. Kelner	Laura Fleming
Dead Ringer	Lisa Scottoline	Benedetta "Bennie" Rosato
Dead Roots	Nancy J. Cohen	Marla Shore

Title of Book	Author	Character
Dead Soul	James Doss	Daisy Perika
Dead South	Winona Sullivan	Sr. Cecille Buddenbrooks
Dead Stick	Megan Mallory Rust	Taylor Morgan
Dead Time	Eleanor Taylor Bland	Marti MacAlister
Dead Time	Stephen White	Lauren Crowder
Dead to Rights	J. A. Jance	Joanna Brady
Dead White Female	Lauren Henderson	Sam Jones
Dead Wrong	J. A. Jance	Joanna Brady
Dead Wrong	Cath Staincliffe	Sal Kilkenny
Deadbeat	Wendi Lee	Angela Matelli
Deadfall	Sue Henry	Jessie Arnold
The Deadhouse	Linda Fairstein	Alexandra Cooper
A Deadline for Murder	Valerie Frankel	Wanda Mallory
Deadly Admirer	Christine Green	Kate Kinsella
Deadly Appearances	Gail Bowen	Joanne "Jo" Kilbourn
Deadly Bargain-Plan C	Gina Cresse	Devonie Lace-Matthews
Deadly Bond	Christine Green	Kate Kinsella
A Deadly Bouquet	Janis Harrison	Bretta Solomon
Deadly Care	Leonard Goldberg	Dr. Joanna Blalock
A Deadly Change of Course-Plan B	Gina Cresse	Devonie Lace-Matthews
A Deadly Change of Heart	Gina Cresse	Devonie Lace-Matthews
A Deadly Change of Luck	Gina Cresse	Devonie Lace-Matthews
A Deadly Change of Power	Gina Cresse	Devonie Lace-Matthews
Deadly Choice	Christine Green	Kate Kinsella
The Deadly Dance	M. C. Beaton	Agatha Raisin
Deadly Deception	Gilbert Morris	Danielle "Dani" Ross
Deadly Deceptions	Ruth Ruby Moen	Kathleen O'Shaughnessy
Deadly Decisions	Kathy Reichs	Dr. Temperance Brennan
The Deadly Dog-Bone	Georgette Livingston	Dr. Jennifer Gray
Deadly Echo	Christine Green	Kate Kinsella
Deadly Embrace	Trudy Labovitz	Zoe Kergulin
Deadly Errand	Christine Green	Kate Kinsella
Deadly Exposure	Leonard Goldberg	Dr. Joanna Blalock
Deadly Gamble	Connie Shelton	Charlie Parker
Deadly Harvest	Leonard Goldberg	Dr. Joanna Blalock
Deadly Harvest	Ellen Rawlings	Rachel Crowne
Deadly Justice	William Bernhardt	Christina McCall
Deadly Legacy	Betty Rowlands	Melissa Craig
Deadly Medicine	Leonard Goldberg	Dr. Joanna Blalock
Deadly Night	Christine Green	Kate Kinsella
Deadly Nightshade	Mary Freeman	Rachel O'Connor
Deadly Obsessions	Betty Rowlands	Sukey Reynolds
Deadly Omen	Marilyn Meredith	Tempe Crabtree
Deadly Partners	Christine Green	Kate Kinsella
Deadly Partnership a.k.a. *A Bonny Case of Murder*	C. F. Roe	Dr. Jean Montrose
A Deadly Pâté	Ruthe Furie	Fran Tremaine Kirk
A Deadly Practice	Leonard Goldberg	Dr. Joanna Blalock
Deadly Practice	Christine Green	Kate Kinsella
Deadly Retreat	Christine Green	Kate Kinsella
Deadly Reunion	Jackie Manthorne	Harriet Hubbley
Deadly Rx	Renee B. Horowitz	Ruthie Kantor Morris
Deadly Safari	Karin McQuillan	Jazz Jasper
Deadly Sanctuary	Sylvia Nobel	Kendall O'Dell
A Deadly Shaker Spring	Deborah Woodworth	Sister Rose Callahan
Deadly Sin	P. J. Grady	Matty Madrid

Title of Book	Author	Character
Deadly Trail	Marilyn Meredith	Tempe Crabtree
Deadly Web	Christine Green	Kate Kinsella
Deadroll	Greg Moody	Cheryl Crane
Dear Irene	Jan Burke	Irene Kelly
Death and Blintzes	Dorothy and Sidney Rosen	Belle Appleman
Death and Faxes	Leslie O'Kane	Molly Masters
Death and Restoration	Iain Pears	Flavia di Stefano
Death and Strudel	Dorothy and Sidney Rosen	Belle Appleman
Death and the Crossed Wires	Linda Berry	Trudy Roundtree
Death and the Delinquent	B. J. Oliphant	Shirley McClintock
Death and the Easter Bunny	Linda Berry	Trudy Roundtree
Death and the Family Tree	Linda Berry	Trudy Roundtree
Death and the Hubcap	Linda Berry	Trudy Roundtree
Death and the Icebox	Linda Berry	Trudy Roundtree
Death and the Oxford Box	Veronica Stallwood	Kate Ivory
Death and the Walking Stick	Linda Berry	Trudy Roundtree
Death at a Premium	Valerie Wolzien	Josie Pigeon
Death at Bishop's Keep	Robin Paige	Kathryn "Kate" Ardleigh
Death at Blenheim Palace	Robin Paige	Kathryn "Kate" Ardleigh
Death at Buckingham Palace	C. C. Benison	Jane Bee, Queen Elizabeth II
Death at Daisy's Folly	Robin Paige	Kathryn "Kate" Ardleigh
Death at Dartmoor	Robin Paige	Kathryn "Kate" Ardleigh
Death at Dearley Manor	Betty Rowlands	Sukey Reynolds
Death at Devil's Bridge	Robin Paige	Kathryn "Kate" Ardleigh
Death at Face Value	Joyce Christmas	Elizabeth Anne "Betty" Trenka
Death at Gallows Green	Robin Paige	Kathryn "Kate" Ardleigh
Death at Glamis Castle	Robin Paige	Kathryn "Kate" Ardleigh
Death at High Tide	Beth Sherman	Anne Hardaway
Death at Hyde Park	Robin Paige	Kathryn "Kate" Ardleigh
Death at Lavender Bay	Lauren Wright Douglas	Allison O'Neil
Death at Montpelier a.k.a. *Murder, She Meowed*	Rita Mae Brown	Mary "Harry" Haristeen & Mrs. Murphy
Death at Rottingdean	Robin Paige	Kathryn "Kate" Ardleigh
Death at Sandringham House	C. C. Benison	Jane Bee, Queen Elizabeth II
Death at the Spring Plant Sale	Ann Ripley	Louise Eldridge
Death at the Wheel	Kate Flora	Thea Kozak
Death at Wentwater Court	Carola Dunn	Daisy Dalrymple
Death at Whitechapel	Robin Paige	Kathryn "Kate" Ardleigh
Death at Windsor Castle	C. C. Benison	Jane Bee, Queen Elizabeth II
Death Brims Over	Barbara Jaye Wilson	Brenda Midnight
Death by Chocolate	G. A. McKevett	Savannah Reid
Death by Death	Claire McNab	Denise Cleever
Death by Dressage	Carolyn Banks	Robin Vaughan
Death by Election	Patricia Hall	Laura Ackroyd
Death by Fire a.k.a. *A Fiery Hint of Murder*	C. F. Roe	Dr. Jean Montrose
Death by Rhubarb	Lou Jane Temple	Heaven Lee
Death by the Riverside	J. M. Redmann	Michelle "Micky" Knight
Death Comes As Epiphany	Sharan Newman	Catherine Le Vendeur
Death Comes for the Critic	Noreen Wald	Jake O'Hara
Death Crosses the Border	Janice Steinberg	Margo Simon
Death Dance	Linda Fairstein	Alexandra Cooper
Death Dines Out	Claudia Bishop	Sarah "Quill" Quilliam
Death Down Home	Eve K. Sandstrom	Nicky Titus
Death du Jour	Kathy Reichs	Dr. Temperance Brennan
Death Echo	Kerry Tucker	Libby Kincaid

Title of Book	Author	Character
Death of the Office Witch	Marlys Millhiser	Charlie Greene
Death of the River Master	Allana Martin	Texana Jones
Death on a Silver Platter	Ellen Hart	Sophie Greenway
Death on the Cliff Walk	Mary Kruger	Brooke Cassidy (Devlin)
Death on the Diagonal	Carolyn Banks	Robin Vaughan
Death on the Diagonal	Nero Blanc	Belle Graham
Death on the Drunkard's Path	Jean Hager	Tess Darcy
Death of the Last Villista	Allana Martin	Texana Jones
Death of the River Master	Allana Martin	Texana Jones
Death on the Lizard	Robin Paige	Kathryn "Kate" Ardleigh
Death on the River Walk	Carolyn Hart	Henrietta O'Dwyer Collins
Death on the Rocks	Eric Wright	Lucy Trimble (Brenner)
Death Pays the Rose Rent	Valerie S. Malmont	Tori Miracle
Death Qualified	Kate Wilhelm	Barbara Holloway
Death Row	William Bernhardt	Christina McCall
Death Served Up Cold	B. J. Oliphant	Shirley McClintock
Death Takes a Hand a.k.a. *Take-Out Double*	Susan Moody	Cassandra "Cassie" Swann
Death Takes Passage	Sue Henry	Jessie Arnold
Death Too Soon	Audrey Peterson	Claire Camden
Death Train to Boston	Dianne Day	Caroline "Fremont" Jones
Death Trance	R. D. Zimmerman	Maddy Phillips
Death Trap	Sue Henry	Jessie Arnold
Death Walker	Aimee and David Thurlo	Ella Clah
The Death We Share	Sharon Gwyn Short	Patricia Delaney
Death Wears a Crown	Quinn Fawcett	Victoire Vernet
Death Wind	P. M. Carlson	Martine "Marty" Hopkins
Death With Honors	Ron Nessen, Johanna Neuman	Jane Day
Death with Reservations	Kate Kingsbury	Cecily Sinclair
Death, Bones, and Stately Homes	Valerie S. Malmont	Tori Miracle
Death, Guns, and Sticky Buns	Valerie S. Malmont	Tori Miracle
Death, Lies, and Apple Pies	Valerie S. Malmont	Tori Miracle
Death, Snow, and Mistletoe	Valerie S. Malmont	Tori Miracle
Death Understood	G. A. McKevett	Savannah Reid
Death's a Beach	Beth Sherman	Anne Hardaway
Death's a Beach	Winona Sullivan	Sr. Cecille Buddenbrooks
Death's Autograph	Marianne Macdonald	Dido Hoare
Death's Domain	Alex Matthews	Cassidy McCabe
Death's Half Acre	Margaret Maron	Deborah Knott
Death's Own Door	Andrew Taylor	Jill Francis
Deathday Party	Paula Carter	Jane Ferguson, Hillary Scarborough
Death-Fires Dance	Janice Steinberg	Margo Simon
Deaths of Jocasta	J. M. Redmann	Michelle "Micky" Knight
The Debt Collector	Lynn S. Hightower	Sonora Blair
Deck the Halls	Carol Higgins Clark, Mary Higgins Clark	Regan Reilly
Deck the Halls with Murder	Valerie Wolzien	Josie Pigeon
Decked	Carol Higgins Clark	Regan Reilly
Decked with Folly	Kate Kingsbury	Cecily Sinclair
Declared Dead	Suzanne Proulx	Victoria Lucci
Deep Freeze a.k.a. *Deep Waters*	Patricia Hall	Laura Ackroyd
Deep South	Nevada Barr	Anna Pigeon
Deep Valley Malice	Kirk Mitchell	Dee Laguerre
Deep Water	Sally Gunning	Connie Bartholomew
Deep Waters a.k.a. *Deep Freeze*	Patricia Hall	Laura Ackroyd
A Deeper Sleep	Dana Stabenow	Kate Shugak

Title of Book	Author	Character
Defend and Betray	Anne Perry	Hester Latterly (Monk)
Defense for the Devil	Kate Wilhelm	Barbara Holloway
Degree of Guilt	Richard North Patterson	Caroline Masters
Degrees of Separation	Sue Henry	Jessie Arnold
Déjà Dead	Kathy Reichs	Dr. Temperance Brennan
Delectable Mountain	Earlene Fowler	Albenia "Benni" Harper
Delilah Doolitte and the Careless Coyote	Patricia Guiver	Delilah Doolittle
Delilah Doolittle and the Canine Chorus	Patricia Guiver	Delilah Doolittle
Delilah Doolittle and the Missing Macaw	Patricia Guiver	Delilah Doolittle
Delilah Doolittle and the Motley Mutts	Patricia Guiver	Delilah Doolittle
Delilah Doolittle and the Purloined Pooch	Patricia Guiver	Delilah Doolittle
Deliver Us From Evil	Philip Luber	Veronica Pace
Dem Bones Revenge	Kris Neri	Tracy Eaton
Derailleur	Greg Moody	Cheryl Crane
Desert Cat	Garrison Allen	Penelope Warren
Desert Heat	J. A. Jance	Joanna Brady
Deservedly Dead	B. J. Oliphant	Shirley McClintock
A Desperate Call	Laura Coburn	Kate Harrod
Desperate Measures	Kate Wilhelm	Barbara Holloway
Desperate Remedy	Mary Kittredge	Edwina Crusoe
A Desperate Silence	Sarah Lovett	Dr. Sylvia Strange
Desperately Seeking Sushi	Jerrilyn Farmer	Madelyn Bean
Destroy Unopened	Anabel Donald	Alex Tanner
Detecting Lies	Janice Kiecolt-Glaser	Dr. Haley McAlister
The Devil and the Deep Blue Sea	Beth Sherman	Anne Hardaway
Devil Bones	Kathy Reich	Dr. Temperance Brennan
The Devil Down Home	Eve K. Sandstrom	Nicky Titus
The Devil Riding	Valerie Wilson Wesley	Tamara Hayle
Devil's Claw	J. A. Jance	Joanna Brady
The Devil's Cradle	Sylvia Nobel	Kendall O'Dell
The Devil's Door	Sharan Newman	Catherine Le Vendeur
Devil's Food	Anthony Bruno	Loretta Kovacs
Devil's Game	Patricia Hall	Laura Ackroyd
Devil's Gonna Get Him	Valerie Wilson Wesley	Tamara Hayle
The Devil's in the Details	Mary Jane Maffini	Camilla McPhee
Devil's Leg Crossing	Kaye Davis	Maris Middleton
Devil's Own Door	Andrew Taylor	Jill Francis
Devil's Trumpet	Mary Freeman	Rachel O'Connor
Devil's Workshop	Kate Gallison	Mother Lavinia Grey
Dial M for Meat Loaf	Ellen Hart	Sophie Greenway
Diamond Head	Marian J. A. Jackson	Abigail Danforth
Did You Declare the Corpse?	Patricia Houck Sprinkle	MacLaren Yarbrough
Die Dancing	Jonathan Gash	Dr. Clare Burtonall
Die in My Dreams	Christine Green	Francesca "Fran" Wilson
Die Laughing	Steve Allen	Jayne Meadows
Die Laughing	Carola Dunn	Daisy Dalrymple
Die Once	Marianne Macdonald	Dido Hoare
Died Blonde	Nancy J. Cohen	Marla Shore
Died in the Wool	Rett MacPherson	Victory "Torie" O'Shea
Different Women Dancing	Jonathan Gash	Dr. Clare Burtonall
The Difficult Saint	Sharan Newman	Catherine Le Vendeur

Title of Book	Author	Character
Digging Up Death	Triss Stein	Kay Engels
A Dilly of a Death	Susan Wittig Albert	China Bayles
Dim Sum Dead	Jerrilyn Farmer	Madelyn Bean
A Dinner to Die For	Claudia Bishop	Sarah "Quill" Quilliam
Dinosaur Cat	Garrison Allen	Penelope Warren
Dire Happenings at Scratch Ankle	Celestine Sibley	Kate Mulcay a.k.a. Katy Kincaid
The Director's Cut	Lis Howell	Kate Wilkinson
Dirty Laundry	Paula L. Woods	Charlotte Justice
Dirty Money	Pele Plante	Cynthia Cheney "C. C." Scott
Dirty Water	Sally Gunning	Connie Bartholomew
Dirty Work	Betty Rowlands	Sukey Reynolds
Disorderly Attachments	Jennifer L. Jordan	Kristin Ashe
Divided in Death	J. D. Robb	Lt. Eve Dallas
Divorce Can Be Murder	Victoria Pade	Jimi Plain
Do Not Disturb	Kate Kingsbury	Cecily Sinclair
Do Not Go Gently	Judith Smith-Levin	Starletta Duvall
Do Or Die	Grace F. Edwards	Mali Anderson
Do You Want to Know a Secret?	Mary Jane Clark	Eliza Blake
The Dobie Paradox	Desmond Cory	Dr. Kate Coyle
Doc in the Box	Elaine Viets	Francesca Vierling
Dog Collar Crime	Melissa Cleary	Jackie Walsh
Dog Eat Dog	Laurien Berenson	Melanie Travis
The Dog Named Elvis Caper	Georgette Livingston	Dr. Jennifer Gray
The Dog Who Bit a Policeman	Stuart Kaminsky	Elena Timafeyeva
The Dog Who Knew Too Much	Carol Lea Benjamin	Rachel Kaminsky Alexander
The Dogfather	Susan Conant	Holly Winter
Doggie Day Care Murder	Laurien Berenson	Melanie Travis
Dogsbody	Michael Molloy	Sarah Keane
Dogtown	Mercedes Lambert	Whitney Logan
The Dollmaker's Daughters	Abigail Padgett	Barbara "Bo" Bradley
Done Wrong	Eleanor Taylor Bland	Marti MacAlister
Don't Blame the Snake	Tony Fennelly	Margo Fortier
Don't Cry for Me, Hot Pastrami	Sharon Kahn	Ruby Rothman
Don't Drink the Water	Susan Rogers Cooper	E. J. Pugh
Don't Forget to Die	Margaret Chittenden	Charlie Plato
Don't Mess with Mrs. In-Between	Liz Evans	Grace Smith
Don't Turn Your Back on the Ocean	Janet Dawson	Jeri Howard
Doomsday Flight	Ed Stewart	Beth Seibelli
Double Act	Eileen Dewhurst	Phyllida Moon
The Double Comfort Safari Club	Alexander McCall Smith	Precious Ramotswe
Double Cross	Barbara Taylor McCafferty, Beverly Taylor Herald	Bert & Nan Tatum
Double Date	Barbara Taylor McCafferty, Beverly Taylor Herald	Bert & Nan Tatum
Double Dealer	Barbara Taylor McCafferty, Beverly Taylor Herald	Bert & Nan Tatum
Double Edge	Robert W. Walker	Meredyth "Mere" Sanger
Double Espresso	Anthony Bruno	Loretta Kovacs
Double Exposure	Barbara Taylor McCafferty, Beverly Taylor Herald	Bert & Nan Tatum
Double Murder	Barbara Taylor McCafferty, Beverly Taylor Herald	Bert & Nan Tatum
Double Negative	Leona Gom	Vicky Bauer
Double Shot	Diane Mott Davidson	Goldy Bear (Schulz)
Double Take	Catherine Coulter	Lacey Savich
Double Take	Judy Mercer	Ariel Gold

Title of Book	Author	Character
Dying for Chocolate	Diane Mott Davidson	Goldy Bear (Schulz)
Dying for Mercy	Mary Jane Clark	Eliza Blake
Dying For Millions	Judith Cutler	Sophie Rivers
Dying For Power	Judith Cutler	Sophie Rivers
Dying in Discord	Judith Cutler	Sophie Rivers
The Dying Light	Alison Joseph	Sister Agnes Bourdillon
Dying On Principle	Judith Cutler	Sophie Rivers
Dying Room Only	Kate Kingsbury	Cecily Sinclair
Dying to Be Murdered	Judy Fitzwater	Jennifer Marsh
Dying to Deceive	Judith Cutler	Sophie Rivers
Dying to Get Even	Judy Fitzwater	Jennifer Marsh
Dying to Get Her Man	Judy Fitzwater	Jennifer Marsh
Dying To Score	Judith Cutler	Sophie Rivers
Dying to See You	Margaret Chittenden	Charlie Plato
Dying to Sing	Margaret Chittenden	Charlie Plato
Dying To Write	Judith Cutler	Sophie Rivers
Dynamite Pass	J. F. Trainor	Angela "Angie" Biwaban
E		
The Eagle Catcher	Margaret Coel	Vicky Holden
Eagles Die Too	Meg O'Brien	Jessica "Jesse" James
Earth Colors	Sarah Andrews	Emily "Em" Hansen
Earth Has No Sorrow	Michelle Blake	Rev. Lily Connor
Earthway	Aimee and David Thurlo	Ella Clah
Earthwork	Carol Dawber	Liz Gresham
Easeful Death	Eileen Dewhurst	Phyllida Moon
Easier to Kill	Valerie Wilson Wesley	Tamara Hayle
East of Niece	Randye Lordon	Sydney Sloane
An Easy Day for a Lady a.k.a. Widow's Peak	Gillian Linscott	Nell Bray
Eat, Drink, and Be Buried	Kate Kingsbury	Cecily Sinclair
Eat, Drink, and Be Wary	Tamar Myers	Magdalena Yoder
Echoes from the Grave	S. D. Tooley	Samantha "Sam" Casey
Echoes of Death	Janet Harward	Josephine Blake
The Edge	Catherine Coulter	Lacey Savich
The Edge of Sleep	David Wiltse	Karen Crist (Becker)
Edited Out	Lisa Haddock	Carmen Ramirez
An Educated Death	Kate Flora	Thea Kozak
Eight Days to Live	Iris Johansen	Eve Duncan
Eight Dogs Flying	Karen Ann Wilson	Samantha Holt
Eight Miles High	D. B. Borton	Catherine "Cat" Caliban
Elective Murder	Janet McGiffin	Dr. Maxene St. Clair
Electric City	K. K. Beck	Jane da Silva
Elementary, Mrs. Hudson	Sydney Hosier	Emma Hudson
Elephants' Graveyard	Karin McQuillan	Jazz Jasper
Eleven Days	Donald Harstad	Hester Gorse
Eleven on Top	Janet Evanovich	Stephanie Plum
Eleventh Hour	Catherine Coulter	Lacey Savich
The Elvis and Marilyn Affair	Robert S. Levinson	Stevie Marriner
Embroidered Truths	Monica Ferris	Betsy Devonshire
Embroidering Shrouds	Priscilla Masters	Joanna Piercy
Emergency Murder	Janet McGiffin	Dr. Maxene St. Clair
Emperor Norton's Ghost	Dianne Day	Caroline "Fremont" Jones
The Empty Chair	Jeffrey Wilds Deaver	Amelia Sachs
The End of an Altruist	Margaret Logan	Olivia Chapman
The End of April	Penny Sumner	Victoria Cross
The End of Emerald Woods	David J. Walker	Kirsten

Title of Book	Author	Character
Face Down O'er the Border	Kathy Lynn Emerson	Lady Susanna Appleton
Face Down on a Herbal	Kathy Lynn Emerson	Lady Susanna Appleton
Face Down Under the Wych Elm	Kathy Lynn Emerson	Lady Susanna Appleton
The Face of a Stranger	Anne Perry	Hester Latterly (Monk)
The Face of Deception	Iris Johansen	Eve Duncan
Fade to Black	Della Borton	Gilda Liberty
Fade to Black	Tony Gibbs	Lt. Tory Lennox, USCG
Fair Game	Rochelle Majer Krich	Jessica Drake
Fair Play	Rose Beecham	Amanda Valentine
Faking It	Marianne Macdonald	Dido Hoare
Fall From Grace	Clyde Phillips	Jane Candiotti
A Fall in Denver	Sarah Andrews	Emily "Em" Hansen
Fall Guy	Carol Lea Benjamin	Rachel Kaminsky Alexander
Fall of a Cosmonaut	Stuart Kaminsky	Elena Timafeyeva
Fall of a Philanderer	Carola Dunn	Daisy Dalrymple
Fall to Pieces	Cecelia Tishy	Kate Banning
Fallen From Grace	Pat Welch	Helen Black
Falling from Grace	Patricia Brooks	Molly Piper
False Witness	Patricia D. Benke	Judith Thornton
False Witness	Patricia Hall	Laura Ackroyd
False Witness	Lelia Kelly	Laura Chastain
Family Honor	Robert B. Parker	Sunny Randall
Family Practice	Charlene Weir	Susan Donavan Wren
Family Skeletons	Rett MacPherson	"Torie" O'Shea
The Famous D.A.R. Murder Mystery	Graham Landrum	Harriet Bushrow, Helen Delaporte
A Far and Deadly Cry	Teri Holbrook	Gale Grayson
Farewell Performance	Donna Huston Murray	Ginger Barnes
Farewell, Conch Republic	Hialeah Jackson	Annabelle Hardy-Maratos
A Fashionable Murder	Valerie Wolzien	Josie Pigeon
Fast Forward	Judy Mercer	Ariel Gold
Fast Friends	Diane G. Pugh	Iris Thorne
The Fat Boy Murders	David Kaufelt	Wyn Lewis
The Fatal Cape Cod Funeral	Marie Lee	Marguerite Smith
Fatal Care	Leonard Goldberg	Dr. Joanna Blalock
Fatal Cut	Christine Green	Francesca "Fran" Wilson
Fatal Diagnosis	Echo Heron	Adele Monsarrat
Fatal Diagnosis	Mary Kittredge	Edwina Crusoe
Fatal Fashione	Karen Harper	Queen Elizabeth I
Fatal Fever a.k.a. A Torrid Piece of Murder	C. F. Roe	Dr. Jean Montrose
Fatal Instinct	Robert W. Walker	Dr. Jessica Coran
Fatal Reaction	Gini Hartzmark	Kate Millholland
Fatal Remains	Eleanor Taylor Bland	Marti MacAlister
A Fatal Thaw	Dana Stabenow	Kate Shugak
Fatal Voyage	Kathy Reichs	Dr. Temperance Brennan
Fatally Flaky	Diane Mott Davidson	Goldy Bear (Schulz)
Fate of Ravens	Tiina Nunnally	Margit Andersson
Fat Free and Fatal	G. A. McKevett	Savannah Reid
Fat-Free and Fatal	Jaqueline Girdner	Kate Jasper
Father Forgive Me	Randye Lordon	Sydney Sloane
The Father's Day Murder	Lee Harris	Christine Bennett
Father's Day Murder	Leslie Meier	Lucy Stone
Fatlands	Sarah Dunant	Hannah Wolfe
Fault Line	Natasha Cooper	Trish Maguire
Fault Line	Sarah Andrews	Emily "Em" Hansen

Title of Book	Author	Character
Flashback	Nevada Barr	Anna Pigeon
Flashpoint	Lynn S. Hightower	Sonora Blair
Fleeced	Carol Higgins Clark	Regan Reilly
Flight	Jan Burke	Irene Kelly
Flight of the Serpent	Val Davis	Nicolette "Nick" Scott
Flight of the Stone Angel a.k.a. Stone Angel	Carol O'Connell	Sgt. Kathleen Mallory
The Floating Girl	Sujata Massey	Rei Shimura
The Flourine Murder (2010)	Camille Minichino	Gloria Lamerino
The Flower Master	Sujata Massey	Rei Shimura
Flower Net	Lisa See	Liu Hulan
Flowers for His Funeral	Ann Granger	Merry Mitchell
Following Jane	Shelley Singer	Barrett Lake
Food to Die For	Patricia D. Cornwell	Dr. Kay Scarpetta
A Fool and His Honey	Charlaine Harris	Aurora "Roe" Teagarden
Fool's Puzzle	Earlene Fowler	Albenia "Benni" Harper
Foolish Ways	D. M. Greenwood	Rev. Theodora Braithwaite
Fool-Proof	Diane G. Pugh	Iris Thorne
A Fool There Was	Betty Rowlands	Sukey Reynolds
For Death Comes Softly	Hilary Bonner	Rose Piper
For Every Evil	Ellen Hart	Sophie Greenway
For the Last Time	Joyce and Jim Levene	Sharyn Howard
Foreign Body	Joyce Holms	Fizz Fitzpatrick
Foreign Body	Kathleen Taylor	Tory Bauer
Forged	Laura Crum	Dr. Gail McCarthy
Forged in Blood	Joyce Christmas	Elizabeth Anne "Betty" Trenka
Forget About Murder	Elizabeth Daniels Squire	Peaches Dann
Forgive Us Our Sins	Philip Luber	Veronica Pace
Found: A Body	Betsy Struthers	Rosalie Cairns
Four Elements of Murder	D. B. Borton	Catherine "Cat" Caliban
Four to Score	Janet Evanovich	Stephanie Plum
Fourth Horseman	Margot Dalton	Jackie Kaminsky
The Fourth Sacrifice	Peter May	Margaret Campbell
The Fourth Steven	Margaret Moseley	Honey Huckleberry
The Fourth Suspect	Betty Rowlands	Melissa Craig
Fowl Play	Patricia Tichenor Westphal	Molly West
Fowl Prey	Mary Daheim	Judith McMonigle (Flynn)
The Fox and the Puma	Barbara Sohmers	Maggy Renard
The Fox and the Pussycat	Barbara Sohmers	Maggy Renard
Foxglove	Mary Anne Kelly	Claire Breslinsky (Benedetto)
Framed in Cornwall	Jane Bolitho	Rose Trevelyan
Framed in Lace	Monica Ferris	Betsy Devonshire
Framework for Death	Aileen Schumacher	Tory Travers
Free Love	Annette Meyers	Olivia Brown
Freeze Frame	Della Borton	Gilda Liberty
Freeze Frame	Leona Gom	Vicky Bauer
Freeze My Margarita	Lauren Henderson	Sam Jones
Fresh Flesh	Stella Duffy	Saz Martin
Fried by Jury	Claudia Bishop	Sarah "Quill" Quilliam
A Fright of Ghosts	Helen Chappell	Hollis Ball
Frogskin and Muttonfat	Carol Caverly	Thea Barlow
From Potter's Field	Patricia D. Cornwell	Dr. Kay Scarpetta
Frost the Fiddler	Janice Weber	Leslie Frost
Frozen Stiff (2010)	Mary Logue	Claire Watkins
Frozen Stiff	Sarah J. Mason	Sergeant Stone
Fruitcake	Jane Rubino	Cat Austen

Title of Book	Author	Character
Go Not Gently	Cath Staincliffe	Sal Kilkenny
The God of the Hive (2010)	Laurie R. King	Mary Russell (Holmes)
The Goddess Affair	Lillian O'Donnell	Gwen Ramadge
Going, Gone (2010)	Laura Crum	Dr. Gail McCarthy
Going Nowhere Fast	Gar Anthony Haywood	Dottie Loudermilk
Golden Eggs and Other Deadly Things	Nancy Tesler	Carrie Carlin
Gone Quiet	Eleanor Taylor Bland	Marti MacAlister
Gone to the Dogs	Susan Conant	Holly Winter
Gone, Baby, Gone	Dennis Lehane	Angela Gennaro
Gonna Take a Sentimental Journey	Sandra Scoppertone	Lauren Laurano
Good Cop, Bad Cop	Barbara D'Amato	Suze Figueroa
The Good Daughter	Wendi Lee	Angela Matelli
The Good Diamond	Skye Kathleen Moody	Venus Diamond
The Good Friday Murder	Lee Harris	Christine Bennett
The Good Husband of Zebra Drive	Alexander McCall Smith	Precious Ramotswe
Good Morning, Irene apa *The Adventuress*	Carole Nelson Douglas	Irene Adler
Good Night, Mr. Holmes	Carole Nelson Douglas	Irene Adler
Goodbye, Charli	Diane Petit	Kathryn Bogert
Goodbye, Charli-Fourth Edition	Diane Petit	Kathryn Bogert
Goodbye, Charli-Take Two	Diane Petit	Kathryn Bogert
Goodbye, Charli-Third Time Lucky	Diane Petit	Kathryn Bogert
Goodnight, Irene	Jan Burke	Irene Kelly
Goose in the Pond	Earlene Fowler	Albenia "Benni" Harper
Gossip Can Be Murder (2010)	Connie Shelton	Charlotte "Charlie" Parker
Governing Bodies	Anne Wilson	Sara Kingsley
The Governor	Lynda La Plante	Helen Hewitt
Governor II	Lynda La Plante	Helen Hewitt
Grand Slam	Susan Moody	Cassandra "Cassie" Swann
Grandmother Spider	James Doss	Daisy Perika
Grape Expectations	Tamar Myers	Magdalena Yoder
Grass Widow	Teri Holbrook	Gale Grayson
Grave Deeds	Betsy Struthers	Rosalie Cairns
A Grave Denied	Dana Stabenow	Kate Shugak
A Grave Disturbance	D. M. Greenwood	Rev. Theodora Braithwaite
Grave Instinct	Robert W. Walker	Dr. Jessica Coran
Grave Misgivings	Kate Gallison	Mother Lavinia Grey
Grave Secrets	Louise Hendrickson	Dr. Amy Prescott
Grave Secrets	Kathy Reichs	Dr. Temperance Brennan
A Grave Talent	Laurie R. King	Kate Martinelli a.k.a K. C.
Grave Undertaking	James R. McCahery	Lavinia London
Graven Images	Jane Waterhouse	Garner Quinn
Gravestone	P. M. Carlson	Martine "Marty" Hopkins
Gray Matter	Shirley Kennett	P. J. Gray
Greed, Crime, Sudden Death	Carole Hayman	Caro Radcliffe
Greedy Bones	Carolyn Haines	Sarah Booth Delaney
Green Grow the Victims	Jeanne M. Dams	Hilda Johansson
Green Money	Judith Smith-Levin	Starletta Duvall
Grievous Angel	Irene Lin-Chandler	Holly-Jean Ho
The Grilling Season	Diane Mott Davidson	Goldy Bear (Schulz)
Grim Pickings	Jennifer Rowe	Verity "Birdie" Birdwood
Grinning in His Mashed Potatoes	Margaret Moseley	Honey Huckleberry
Grizzly	Christine Andreae	Lee Squires
Groomed for Death	Carolyn Banks	Robin Vaughan
Ground to a Halt	Claudia Bishop	Sarah "Quill" Quilliam

Title of Book	Author	Character
Haunted in Death (novella)	J. D. Robb	Lt. Eve Dallas
A Haunting Refrain	Patricia H. Rushford	Helen Bradley
Havana Heat	Carolina Garcia-Aguilera	Guadalupe "Lupe" Solano
Have Mercy on Us	Philip Luber	Veronica Pace
Hayburner	Laura Crum	Dr. Gail McCarthy
Haycastle's Cricket	Michele Bailey	Matilda Haycastle
He Who Dies	Wendi Lee	Angela Matelli
Headhunt	Carol Brennan	Liz Wareham
The Healing of Holly-Jean	Irene Lin-Chandler	Holly-Jean Ho
Healthy, Wealthy, and Dead	Suzanne North	Phoebe Fairfax
Heart and Bones	Margaret Lawrence	Hannah Trevor
The Heart Shaped Box	April Henry	Claire Montrose
Heart Trouble	Kathy Hogan Trocheck	Julia "Callahan" Garrity
The Heartland Experiment	Donald Harstad	Hester Gorse
The Heat of Lies	Jonathan Stone	Julian Palmer
Heavenly Vices	D. M. Greenwood	Rev. Theodora Braithwaite
Heir Condition	Tierney McClellan	Schuyler Ridgway
Held Accountable	Karen Hanson Stuyck	Liz James
The Helium Murder	Camille Minichino	Gloria Lamerino
Hell Gate (2010)	Linda Fairstein	Alexandra Cooper
Hell Hath No Curry	Tamar Myers	Magdalena Yoder
A Hell of a Dog	Carol Lea Benjamin	Rachel Kaminsky Alexander
Help Line	Faye Sultan, Teresa Kennedy	Portia McTeague
Hemlock Bay	Catherine Coulter	Lacey Savich
Hemlock at Vespers (ss)	Peter Tremayne	Sister Fidelma
Hen's Teeth	Manda Scott	Dr. Kellen Stewart
Here Lies a Hidden Scorpion	Tavis and Judy Iakovou	Julia Lambros
Here's to the Newly Dead	B. J. Oliphant	Shirley McClintock
Heresy	Sharan Newman	Catherine Le Vendeur
Hickory, Dickory, Stalk	Susan Rogers Cooper	E. J. Pugh
A Hidden Cause of Murder	C. F. Roe	Dr. Jean Montrose
Hidden Depths	Joyce Holmes	Fizz Fitzpatrick
Hidden Power	Judith Cutler	Kate Power
High Country	Nevada Barr	Anna Pigeon
High Country Fall	Margaret Maron	Deborah Knott
High Country Murder	J. F. Trainor	Angela "Angie" Biwaban
High Desert Malice	Kirk Mitchell	Dee Laguerre
High Five	Janet Evanovich	Stephanie Plum
High Profile	Robert B. Parker	Sunny Randall
High Seas Murder	Shelley Freydont	Lindy Graham-Haggerty
Higher Authority	Stephen White	Lauren Crowder
Highlights to Heaven	Nancy J. Cohen	Marla Shore
The Hippie in the Wall	Tony Fennelly	Margo Fortier
The Hireling's Tale	Jo Bannister	Liz Graham
The Historical Society Murder Mystery	Graham Landrum	Harriet Bushrow, Helen Delaporte
Hitched	Carol Higgins Clark	Regan Reilly
Hoakus Crocus	Mary Daheim	Judith McMonigle (Flynn)
Hocus	Jan Burke	Irene Kelly
Hold the Cream Cheese, Kill the Lox	Sharon Kahn	Ruby Rothman
Holiday in Death	J. D. Robb	Lt. Eve Dallas
The Holiday Murders	Marsha Landreth	Dr. Samantha Turner
Holidays Can Be Murder	Connie Shelton	Charlotte "Charlie" Parker
Holly Blues (2010)	Susan Wittig Albert	China Bayles

Title of Book	Author	Character
Hunting Season	Nevada Barr	Anna Pigeon
Hush Puppy	Laurien Berenson	Melanie Travis
The Hydrogen Murder	Camille Minichino	Gloria Lamerino
I		
I Left My Heart	Jaye Maiman	Robin Miller
I Will Survive	Miriam Ann Moore	Marti Hirsch
I, Claudia	Marilyn Todd	Claudia Seferius
I'll Be Leaving You Always	Sandra Scoppetone	Lauren Laurano
The Ice	Louis Charbonneau	Kathy McNeely
The Ice Maiden	Edna Buchanan	Britt Montero
Ice Water	Sally Gunning	Connie Bartholomew
Iced	Carol Higgins Clark	Regan Reilly
Iced	Julie Robitaille	Kathleen "Kit" Powell
Icewater Mansions	Doug Allyn	Michelle "Mitch" Mitchell
Icing Ivy	Evan Marshall	Jane Stuart
The Icing on the Corpse	Mary Jane Maffini	Camilla McPhee
Identity Unknown	Frances Ferguson	Jane Perry
Idol Bones	D. M. Greenwood	Theodora Braithwaite
If Cooks Could Kill	Joanne Pence	Angelina "Angie" Amalfi
If I Should Die	Grace F. Edwards	Mali Anderson
If Looks Could Kill	Ruthe Furie	Fran Tremaine Kirk
If No One is Looking	Jennifer L. Jordan	Kristin Ashe
If Two of Them Are Dead	Carol Cail	Maxey Burnell
Ill Wind	Nevada Barr	Anna Pigeon
Imitation in Death	J. D. Robb	Lt. Eve Dallas
The Immaculate Deception	Iain Pears	Flavia di Stefano
Immaculate Reception	Jerrilyn Farmer	Madelyn Bean
Immortal in Death	J. D. Robb	Lt. Eve Dallas
Imperfect Justice	Catherine Arnold	Karen Perry-Mondori
The Impertinent Miss Bancroft	Karla Hocker	Sophy Bancroft
Impolite Society	Cynthia Smith	Emma Rhodes
In a Dark House	Deborah Crombie	Gemma James
In a Strange City	Laura Lippman	Tess Monaghan
In at the Deep End	Anabel Donald	Alex Tanner
In Big Trouble	Laura Lippman	Tess Monaghan
In Colt Blood	Jody Jaffe	Natalie Gold
In Death's Shadow	Marcia Talley	Hannah Ives
In Memory of Murder	Janet Harward	Josephine Blake
In Murder We Trust	Eleanor Hyde	Lydia Miller
In Plain Sight	Barbara Block	Robin Light
In Self Defense	Sarah Gregory	Sharon Hays
In Sheep's Clothing	Rett MacPherson	Victory "Torie" O'Shea
Intent to Harm	Jonnie Jacobs	Kali O'Brien
In the Company of Cheerful Ladies	Alexander McCall Smith	Precious Ramotswe
In the Dark	Carol Brennan	Emily Silver
In the Dog House	Melissa Cleary	Jackie Walsh
In the Game	Nikki Baker	Virginia Kelly
In the Guise of Mercy	Wendy Hornsby	Maggie MacGowen
In the Midnight Hour	Michelle Spring	Laura Principal
In the Midnight Hour	Peg Tyre	Kate Murray
In the Still of the Night	Jill Churchill	Lily Brewster
In Your Face	Scarlett Thomas	Lily Pascale
An Inconsiderate Death	Betty Rowlands	Sukey Reynolds
The Incorrigible Sophia	Karla Hocker	Sophy Bancroft
Index to Murder	Jo Dereske	Wilhelmena "Helma" Zukas
Indigo Christmas	Jeanne M. Dams	Hilda Johansson

Title of Book	Author	Character
Jenny Rose	Mary Anne Kelly	Claire Breslinsky (Benedetto)
Jingle Bell Bark	Laurien Berenson	Melanie Travis
Jinx	Julie Robitaille	Kathleen "Kit" Powell
Jinxed	Carol Higgins Clark	Regan Reilly
A Job to Die For	Lis Howell	Kate Wilkinson
The John Lennon Affair	Robert S. Levinson	Stevie Marriner
The Juan Doe Murders	Noreen Ayres	Smokey Brandon
The Judas File	Rebecca Tinsley	Charlotte Carter
Judging Time	Leslie Glass	April Woo
Judgement Fire	Marilyn Meredith	Tempe Crabtree
Judgment in Death	J. D. Robb	Lt. Eve Dallas
The Julius House	Charlaine Harris	Aurora "Roe" Teagarden
Jungleland	Sharon Zukowski	Blaine Stewart
Just Desserts	Claudia Bishop	Sarah "Quill" Quilliam
Just Desserts	Mary Daheim	Judith McMonigle (Flynn)
Just Desserts	G. A. McKevett	Savannah Reid
Just Plain Pickled to Death	Tamar Myers	Magdalena Yoder
Just the Fax, Ma'am	Leslie O'Kane	Molly Masters
Justice Denied apa *Marital Privilege*	M. Diane Vogt	Judge Wilhelmina Carson
Justice Hall	Laurie R. King	Mary Russell (Holmes)
K		
K Falls	Skye Kathleen Moody	Venus Diamond
K. C. Bomber	Janet McClellan	Tru North
The Kalahari Typing School for Men	Alexander McCall Smith	Precious Ramotswe
The Kali Connection	Claudia McKay	Lynn Evans
Kansas Troubles	Earlene Fowler	Albenia "Benni" Harper
Keep Me Alive	Natasha Cooper	Trish Maguire
Keep Still	Eleanor Taylor Bland	Marti MacAlister
Keeper of the Mill	Mary Anne Kelly	Claire Breslinsky (Benedetto)
Keepers of the Gate	Jon Land	Danielle Barnea
Keeping Bad Company	Ann Granger	Fran Varaday
Keeping Secrets	Penny Mickelbury	Lt. Gianna Maglione
Kickback	Val McDermid	Kate Brannigan
Kidnapped	Jan Burke	Irene Kelly
Kid's Stuff	Susan B. Kelly	Alison Hope
The Kill Fee	Laura Van Wormer	Sally Harrington
Kill Me	Stephen White	Lauren Crowder
Kill Me Again	Paul Bishop	Fey Croaker
Kill or Cure	Mary Kittredge	Edwina Crusoe
Killed in Cornwall	Jane Bolitho	Rose Trevelyan
Killer Calories	G. A. McKevett	Savannah Reid
Killer Chameleon	Chassie West	Leigh Ann Warren
Killer Commute	Marlys Millhiser	Charlie Greene
Killer Dust	Sarah Andrews	Emily "Em" Hansen
Killer Heat	Linda Fairstein	Alexandra Cooper
Killer Instinct	Martina Navratilova, Liz Nickles	Jordan Myles
Killer Instinct	Robert W. Walker	Dr. Jessica Coran
Killer Knots	Nancy J. Cohen	Marla Shore
Killer Market	Margaret Maron	Deborah Knott
Killer Pancake	Diane Mott Davidson	Goldy Bear (Schulz)
Killer Riches	Chassie West	Leigh Ann Warren
Killer Smile	Lisa Scottoline	Mary DiNunzio

Title of Book	Author	Character
Killer Wedding	Jerrilyn Farmer	Madelyn Bean
Killer Whale	Elizabeth Quinn	Dr. Lauren Maxwell
Killer.app	Barbara D'Amato	Suze Figueroa
Killing at the Cat	Carlene Miller	Lexy Hyatt
A Killing at the Track	Janet Dawson	Jeri Howard
Killing Cassidy	Jeanne M. Dams	Dorothy Martin
Killing Cousins	Rett MacPherson	"Torie" O'Shea
Killing Critics	Carol O'Connell	Sgt. Kathleen Mallory
A Killing Frost	Margaret Haffner	Catherine Edison
The Killing Game	Iris Johansen	Eve Duncan
A Killing Gift	Leslie Glass	April Woo
Killing Gifts	Deborah Woodworth	Sister Rose Callahan
Killing Grounds	Dana Stabenow	Kate Shugak
A Killing in Real Estate	Tierney McClellan	Schuyler Ridgway
Killing Kin	Chassie West	Leigh Ann Warren
Killing Me Softly	Marjorie Eccles	Abigail Moon
The Killing of Monday Brown	Sandra West Prowell	Phoebe Seigel
Killing Raven	Margaret Coel	Vicky Holden
The Killing Room	Peter May	Margaret Campbell
A Killing Season	Jessica Speart	Rachel Porter
A Killing Spring	Gail Bowen	Joanne "Jo" Kilbourn
Killing Thyme	Peter Abresch	Dodee Swisher
The Kills	Linda Fairstein	Alexandra Cooper
The Kindness of Strangers	Julie Smith	Skip Langdon
Kindred Crimes	Janet Dawson	Jeri Howard
Kindred in Death	J. D. Robb	Lt. Eve Dallas
Kindred Spirits	Marilyn Meredith	Tempe Crabtree
King of Hearts	Susan Moody	Cassandra "Cassie" Swann
The King's Bishop	Candace M. Robb	Lucie D'Arby Wilton
Kingfisher	Alex Keegan	Caz Flood
Kissed a Sad Goodbye	Deborah Crombie	Gemma James
Kissing Christmas Goodbye	M. C. Beaton	Agatha Raisin
Knight and Day	Ron Nessen, Johanna Neuman	Jane Day
Knitting Bones	Monica Ferris	Betsy Devonshire
Knockout	Catherine Coulter	Lacey Savich
The Knowledge of Water	Sarah Smith	Perdita Halley
Known Dead	Donald Harstad	Hester Gorse
L		
The Labor Day Murder	Lee Harris	Christine Bennett
Laced	Carol Higgins Clark	Regan Reilly
The Ladies of the Vale	Andrew Puckett	Jo Farewell
The Lady Chapel	Candace M. Robb	Lucie D'Arby Wilton
Lady Vanishes	Carol Lea Benjamin	Rachel Kaminsky Alexander
Ladybug, Ladybug	Susanna Hofmann McShea	Mildred Bennett, Irene Purdy
Ladykiller	Lisa Scottoline	Mary DiNunzio
Lamb to the Slaughter	Elizabeth Quinn	Dr. Lauren Maxwell
Lamb to the Slaughter	Jennifer Rowe	Verity "Birdie" Birdwood
Lament for a Dead Cowboy	Catherine Dain	Freddie O'Neal
Lamp of the Wicked	Phil Rickman	Rev. Merrily Watkins
The Language of Bees	Laurie R. King	Mary Russell (Holmes)
Larceny and Old Lace	Tamar Myers	Abigail "Abby" Timberlake
Large Target	Lynne Murray	Josephine Fuller
Larger Than Death	Lynne Murray	Josephine Fuller
Larkspur	Sheila Simonson	Lark Dailey (Dodge)
The Last Blue Plate Special	Abigail Padgett	Emily "Blue" McCarron
Last Dance	Joyce and Jim Levene	Sharyn Howard

Title of Book	Author	Character
Last Dance	Miriam Ann Moore	Marti Hirsch
Last Fires Burning	Joyce and Jim Levene	Sharyn Howard
The Last Good Day	Gail Bowen	Joanne "Jo" Kilbourn
The Last Hostage	John J. Nance	Kat Bronsky
The Last Judgement	Iain Pears	Flavia di Stefano
The Last Lie (2010)	Stephen White	Lauren Crowder
The Last Lover	Laura Van Wormer	Sally Harrington
The Last Manly Man	Sparkle Hayter	Robin Hudson
The Last Noel	Jean Hager	Tess Darcy
The Last of Her Lies	Jean Taylor	Maggie Garrett
Last One Down	Joyce and Jim Levene	Sharyn Howard
The Last Place	Laura Lippman	Tess Monaghan
The Last Precinct	Patricia D. Cornwell	Dr. Kay Scarpetta
The Last Prophecy	Jon Land	Danielle Barnea
Last Puzzle and Testament	Parnell Hall	Cora Felton & Sherry Carter
Last Resort	Jackie Manthorne	Harriet Hubbley
The Last Resort	Jaqueline Girdner	Kate Jasper
Last Rites	Joyce and Jim Levene	Sharyn Howard
Last Rites	Tracey Richardson	Stevie Houston
Last Scene Alive	Charlaine Harris	Aurora "Roe" Teagarden
The Last Song Dogs	Sinclair Browning	Trade Ellis
The Last Suppers	Diane Mott Davidson	Goldy Bear (Schulz)
The Last Temptation	Val McDermid	Carol Jordan
The Last to Remember	Joyce and Jim Levene	Sharyn Howard
The Lavender House Murder	Nikki Baker	Virginia Kelly
Lavender Lies	Susan Wittig Albert	China Bayles
Law and Disorder	Mary Jane Maffini	Camilla McPhee
The Law of Betrayal	Tess Collins	Alma Bashears
The Law of Revenge	Tess Collins	Alma Bashears
The Law of the Dead	Tess Collins	Alma Bashears
Lay It on the Line	Catherine Dain	Freddie O'Neal
Leading an Elegant Death	Paula Carter	Jane Ferguson, Hillary Scarborough
Lean Mean Thirteen	Janet Evanovich	Stephanie Plum
Leap of Faith	Sharon Zukowski	Blaine Stewart
Leave the Grave Green	Deborah Crombie	Gemma James
Legal Tender	Lisa Scottoline	Benedetta "Bennie" Rosato
Legs Benedict	Mary Daheim	Judith McMonigle (Flynn)
Legwork	Katy Munger	Casey Jones
The Leper's Bell	Peter Tremayne	Sister Fidelma
The Lessons	Melanie McAllester	Elizabeth "Tenny" Mendoza
Let's Face the Music and Die	Sandra Scoppetone	Lauren Laurano
Lethal Legacy	Linda Fairstein	Alexandra Cooper
Lethal Legacy	Louise Hendrickson	Dr. Amy Prescott
Lethal Lessons	Karen Hanson Stuyck	Liz James
Lethal Measures	Leonard Goldberg	Joanna Blalock
Lethal Statues	Nancy Herndon	Elena Jarvis
A Letter of Mary	Laurie R. King	Mary Russell (Holmes)
Liar	Jan Burke	Irene Kelly
Libation by Death	Dorian Yeager	Victoria "Vic" Bowering
Liberty Falling	Nevada Barr	Anna Pigeon
Liberty or Death	Kate Flora	Thea Kozak
Lie Like a Rug	Donna Huston Murray	Ginger Barnes
Likely to Die	Linda Fairstein	Alexandra Cooper
Lilies That Fester	Janis Harrison	Bretta Solomon
The Listening Ones	Naomi Stokes	Jordan Tidewater
The Lithium Murder	Camille Minichino	Gloria Lamerino

Title of Book	Author	Character
Maltese Manuscript	Joanne Dobson	Karen Pelletier
The Maltese Puppy	Melissa Cleary	Jackie Walsh
Mama Cracks a Mask of Innocence	Nora DeLoach	Candi & Simone Covington
Mama Pursues Murderous Shadows	Nora DeLoach	Candi & Simone Covington
Mama Rocks the Empty Cradle	Nora DeLoach	Candi & Simone Covington
Mama Saves a Victim	Nora DeLoach	Candi & Simone Covington
Mama Solves a Murder	Nora DeLoach	Candi & Simone Covington
Mama Stalks the Past	Nora DeLoach	Candi & Simone Covington
Mama Stands Accused	Nora DeLoach	Candi & Simone Covington
Mama Traps a Killer	Nora DeLoach	Candi & Simone Covington
Man Eater	Marilyn Todd	Claudia Seferius
The Man in the Window	Betty Rowlands	Melissa Craig
The Man Who Cast Two Shadows apa *The Man Who Lied to Women*	Carol O'Connell	Sgt. Kathleen Mallory
Mandarin Plaid	S. J. Rozan	Lydia Chin
Manner of Death	Stephen White	Lauren Crowder
Maquette for Murder	Gretchen Sprague	Martha Patterson
Margin of Error	Edna Buchanan	Britt Montero
Marigolds for Mourning	Audrey Stallsmith	Regan Culver
Marinade for Murder	Claudia Bishop	Sarah "Quill" Quilliam
Mariner's Compass	Earlene Fowler	Albenia "Benni" Harper
The Marx Sisters	Barry Maitland	Sgt. Kathy Kolla
The Mask of Zeus	Desmond Cory	Dr. Kate Coyle
Masquerade	Walter Satterthwait	Jane Turner
Master of Souls	Peter Tremayne	Sister Fidelma
Masterpiece of Murder	Mary Kruger	Brooke Cassidy (Devlin)
Matricide at St. Martha's	Ruth Dudley Edwards	Baroness "Jack" Troutbeck
Maximum Security	P. J. Grace	Matty Madrid
Mayhem at the Marina	Carlene Miller	Lexy Hyatt
The Maze	Catherine Coulter	Lacey Savich
A Maze of Murders	C. L. Grace	Kathryn Swinbrooke
Meadowlark	Sheila Simonson	Lark Dailey (Dodge)
Mean Woman Blues	Julie Smith	Skip Langdon
Medusa	Skye Kathleen Moody	Venus Diamond
Melancholy Baby	Robert B. Parker	Sunny Randall
Memories Can Be Murder	Connie Shelton	Charlie Parker
Memory Can Be Murder	Elizabeth Daniels Squire	Peaches Dann
Memory in Death	J. D. Robb	Lt. Eve Dallas
The Merchant of Death	C. L. Grace	Kathryn Swinbrooke
A Merry Little Murder	Shelley Freydont	Lindy Graham-Haggerty
The Mermaids Singing	Val McDermid	Carol Jordan
Miami, It's Murder	Edna Buchanan	Britt Montero
Midlife Can be Murder	Jane Isenberg	Bel Barrett
Midnight Baby	Wendy Hornsby	Maggie MacGowen
Midnight Clear	Kathy Hogan Trocheck	Julia "Callahan" Garrity
Midnight Come Again	Dana Stabenow	Kate Shugak
Midnight in Death	J. D. Robb	Lt. Eve Dallas
Midsummer Murder	Shelley Freydont	Lindy Graham-Haggerty
Midwinter of the Spirit	Phil Rickman	Rev. Merrily Watkins
Millenium's Dawn	Ed Stewart	Beth Seibelli (Cole)
Millenium's Eve	Ed Stewart	Beth Seibelli (Cole)
Milwaukee Autumns Can Be Lethal	Kathleen Anne Barrett	Beth Hartley
Milwaukee Summers Can Be Deadly	Kathleen Anne Barrett	Beth Hartley
Milwaukee Winters Can Be Murder	Kathleen Anne Barrett	Beth Hartley

Title of Book	Author	Character
Mortal Spoils	D. M. Greenwood	Theodora Braithwaite
Most Baffling, Mrs. Hudson	Sydney Hosier	Emma Hudson
A Most Deadly Retirement	John Miles	Laura Michaels
Most Likely to Die	Jaqueline Girdner	Kate Jasper
Mother May I	Randye Lordon	Sydney Sloane
Mother Nature	Sarah Andrews	Emily "Em" Hansen
Mother of the Bride	Patricia Tichenor Westphal	Molly West
The Mother Tongue	Teri Holbrook	Gale Grayson
The Mother's Day Murder	Lee Harris	Christine Bennett
Mothers' Day Murder	Leslie Meier	Lucy Stone
Motion to Dismiss	Jonnie Jacobs	Kali O'Brien
Motion to Suppress	Perri O'Shaughnessy	Nina Reilly
A Motive for Murder	Gallagher Gray	Lil Hubbert
Mourn Not Your Dead	Deborah Crombie	Gemma James
Mourning Dove	Aimee and David Thurlo	Ella Clah
Mourning Shift	Kathleen Taylor	Tory Bauer
A Mourning Wedding	Carola Dunn	Daisy Dalrymple
Mouth of Babes	Stella Duffy	Saz Martin
Move to Strike	Perri O'Shaughnessy	Nina Reilly
Movie Cat	Garrison Allen	Penelope Warren
Moving Image	Annie Ross	Bel Carson
Moving Targets	Pat Welch	Helen Black
Mr. Big	Joyce Holms	Fizz Fitzpatrick
Mr. Murder	Laura Van Wormer	Sally Harrington
Mrs. Jeffries and the Best Laid Plans	Emily Brightwell	Hepzipah Jeffries
Mrs. Jeffries and the Feast of St. Stephen	Emily Brightwell	Hepzipah Jeffries
Mrs. Jeffries and the Missing Alibi	Emily Brightwell	Hepzipah Jeffries
Mrs. Jeffries and the Silent Night	Emily Brightwell	Hepzipah Jeffries
Mrs. Jeffries and the Yuletide Weddings	Emily Brightwell	Hepzipah Jeffries
Mrs. Jeffries Appeals the Verdict	Emily Brightwell	Hepzipah Jeffries
Mrs. Jeffries Dusts for Clues	Emily Brightwell	Hepzipah Jeffries
Mrs. Jeffreies Holds the Trump	Emily Brightwell	Hepzipah Jeffries
Mrs. Jeffries in the Nick of Time	Emily Brightwell	Hepzipah Jeffries
Mrs. Jeffries on the Ball	Emily Brightwell	Hepzipah Jeffries
Mrs. Jeffries on the Trail	Emily Brightwell	Hepzipah Jeffries
Mrs. Jeffries Pinches the Post	Emily Brightwell	Hepzipah Jeffries
Mrs. Jeffries Plays the Cook	Emily Brightwell	Hepzipah Jeffries
Mrs. Jeffries Pleads the Case	Emily Brightwell	Hepzipah Jeffries
Mrs. Jeffries Questions the Answer	Emily Brightwell	Hepzipah Jeffries
Mrs. Jeffries Reveals Her Art	Emily Brightwell	Hepzipah Jeffries
Mrs. Jeffries Rocks the Boat	Emily Brightwell	Hepzipah Jeffries
Mrs. Jeffries Stands Corrected	Emily Brightwell	Hepzipah Jeffries
Mrs. Jeffries Stalks the Hunter	Emily Brightwell	Hepzipah Jeffries
Mrs. Jeffries Sweeps the Chimney	Emily Brightwell	Hepzipah Jeffries
Mrs. Jeffries Takes Stock	Emily Brightwell	Hepzipah Jeffries
Mrs. Jeffries Takes the Cake	Emily Brightwell	Hepzipah Jeffries
Mrs. Jeffries Takes the Stage	Emily Brightwell	Hepzipah Jeffries
Mrs. Jeffries Weeds the Plot	Emily Brightwell	Hepzipah Jeffries
Muddy Water	Sally Gunning	Connie Bartholomew
Mudlark	Sheila Simonson	Lark Dailey (Dodge)
Mulch	Ann Ripley	Louise Eldridge
Multiple Listing	Anne Underwood Grant	Sydney Teague
A Multitude of Sins	Virginia Stem Owens	Beth Marie Cartwright
Mumbo Gumbo	Jerrilyn Farmer	Madelyn Bean

Title of Book	Author	Character
Murder Follows Money	Lora Roberts	Liz Sullivan
The Murder Game	Steve Allen	Jayne Meadows
Murder Gets a Life	Anne George	The Tate Sisters
Murder, Honey	Vinnie Hansen	Carol Sabala
Murder in a Cathedral	Ruth Dudley Edwards	Baroness "Jack" Troutbeck
Murder in a Heat Wave	Gretchen Sprague	Martha Patterson
Murder in a Hot Flash	Marlys Millhiser	Charlie Greene
Murder in a Nice Neighborhood	Lora Roberts	Liz Sullivan
Murder in Belleville	Cara Black	Aimee Leduc
Murder in Brief	Carroll Lachnit	Hannah Barlow
Murder in Chinatown	Victoria Thompson	Sarah Decker Brandt
Murder in Clichy	Cara Black	Aimee Leduc
Murder on Little Italy	Victoria Thompson	Sarah Decker Brandt
A Murder in Macedon	Anna Apostolou	Miriam Bartimaeus
Murder in Manhattan	Steve Allen	Jayne Meadows
Murder in Monmartre	Cara Black	Aimee Leduc
Murder in Retirement	John Miles	Laura Michaels
Murder in Scorpio	Martha C. Lawrence	Dr. Elizabeth Chase
Murder in the Air	Ellen Hart	Sophie Greenway
Murder in the Bastille	Cara Black	Aimee Leduc
Murder in the Forecast	Valerie Wolzien	Josie Pigeon
Murder in the Latin Quarter	Cara Black	Aimee Leduc
Murder in the Marais	Cara Black	Aimee Leduc
Murder in the Marketplace	Lora Roberts	Liz Sullivan
Murder in the Maze	Sarah J. Mason	Sergeant Stone
Murder in the New Age	D. J. H. Jones	Nancy Cook
Murder in the Palais Royale (2010)	Cara Black	Aimee Leduc
Murder in the Rue de Paradis	Cara Black	Aimee Leduc
Murder in the Sentier	Cara Black	Aimee Leduc
Murder in the Shadows	Ellen Godfrey	Janet Barkin
A Murder in Thebes	Anna Apostolou	Miriam Bartimaeus
Murder in Vegas	Steve Allen	Jayne Meadows
Murder in Wrigley Field	Crabbe Evers	Petronella "Petey" Biggers
Murder Is Germane	Karen Saum	Brigid Donovan
Murder Is Material	Karen Saum	Brigid Donovan
Murder Is Relative	Karen Saum	Brigid Donovan
The Murder Lover	Ellen Rawlings	Rachel Crowne
Murder Makes Waves	Anne George	The Tate Sisters
Murder Me Now	Annette Meyers	Olivia Brown
Murder Mile High	Lora Roberts	Liz Sullivan
Murder Most Beastly	Melissa Cleary	Jackie Walsh
Murder Most Fowl	Kate Morgan	Dewey James
Murder Most Grizzly	Elizabeth Quinn	Dr. Lauren Maxwell
Murder Most Mellow	Jaqueline Girdner	Kate Jasper
A Murder of Crows	Margaret Haffner	Catherine Edison
Murder Offscreen	Denise Osborne	Queenie Davilov
Murder on a Bad Hair Day	Anne George	The Tate Sisters
Murder on a Girl's Night Out	Anne George	The Tate Sisters
Murder on an Astral Plane	Jaqueline Girdner	Kate Jasper
Murder on Astor Place	Victoria Thompson	Sarah Decker Brandt
Murder on Bank Street	Victoria Thompson	Sarah Decker Brandt
Murder on Gramercy Park	Victoria Thompson	Sarah Decker Brandt
Murder on High	Stefanie Matteson	Charlotte Graham
Murder on Lenox Hill	Victoria Thompson	Sarah Decker Brandt
Murder on Lexington Avenue (2010)	Victoria Thompson	Sarah Decker Brandt

Title of Book	Author	Character
My Sweet Untraceable You	Sandra Scoppetone	Lauren Laurano
The Mysterious Cape Cod Manuscript	Marie Lee	Marguerite Smith
Mystery Loves Company	Kate Morgan	Dewey James
N		
Nail Biter	Sarah Graves	Jacobia Tiptee
Naked in Death	J. D. Robb	Lt. Eve Dallas
Naked Justice	William Bernhardt	Christina McCall
Naked Witness	Eileen Dewhurst	Phyllida Moon
Name Games	Peter Abresch	Dodee Swisher
Napoleon Must Die	Quinn Fawcett	Victoire Vernet
A Nasty Bit of Murder a.k.a. *The Lumsden Baby*	C. F. Roe	Dr. Jean Montrose
A Natural Death	Ruthe Furie	Fran Tremaine Kirk
Necessary as Blood	Deborah Crombie	Gemma James
The Nesting Dolls (2010)	Gail Bowen	Joanne "Jo" Kilbourn
Never Buried	Edie Claire	Leigh Koslow
Never-ending-snake (2010)	Aimee and David Thurlo	Ella Clah
Never Kissed Goodnight	Edie Claire	Leigh Koslow
Never Let a Stranger in Your House	Margaret Logan	Olivia Chapman
Never Nosh a Matzo Ball	Sharon Kahn	Ruby Rothman
Never Preach Past Noon	Edie Claire	Leigh Koslow
Never Sorry	Edie Claire	Leigh Koslow
Never Tease a Siamese	Edie Claire	Leigh Koslow
A New Leash on Death	Susan Conant	Holly Winter
New Orleans Beat	Julie Smith	Skip Langdon
New Orleans Mourning	Julie Smith	Skip Langdon
The New Year's Eve Murder	Lee Harris	Christine Bennett
New Year's Eve Murder	Leslie Meier	Lucy Stone
Next to Last Chance	Louisa Dixon	Laura Owen
The Next Victim	Jonnie Jacobs	Kali O'Brien
Next Week Will Be Better	Jean Ruryk	Catherine "Cat" Wilde
Nice Girls Finish Last	Sparkle Hayter	Robin Hudson
Night Mares	Manda Scott	Dr. Kellen Stewart
Night on Fire	Diana Deverell	Casey Collins
Nightshade	Susan Wittig Albert	China Bayles
Night Shift	Margot J. Fromer	Amanda Knight
Night Songs	Penny Mickelbury	Lt. Gianna Maglione
The Night Visitor	James Doss	Daisy Perika
The Night Watch	Alison Joseph	Sister Agnes Bourdillon
Night Work	Laurie R. King	Kate Martinelli a.k.a K. C.
Nightmare in Armor	Tamar Myers	Abigail "Abby" Timberlake
The Nitrogen Murder	Camille Minichino	Gloria Lamerino
Nights in White Satin	Michelle Spring	Laura Principal
No Birds Sing	Jo Bannister	Liz Graham
No Bones About It	Donna Huston Murray	Ginger Barnes
No Clue at the Inn	Kate Kingsbury	Cecily Sinclair
No Colder Place	S. J. Rozan	Lydia Chin
No Corpse	Nancy Sanra	Tally McGinnis
No Defense	Kate Wilhelm	Barbara Holloway
No Escape	Nancy Sanra	Tally McGinnis
No Evidence	Nancy Sanra	Taly McGinnis
No Fixed Abode	Frances Ferguson	Jane Perry
No Good Deed	Barbara Block	Robin Light
No Good Deed	Lynn S. Hightower	Sonora Blair
No Good Deeds	Laura Lippman	Tess Monaghan

Title of Book	Author	Character
No Hiding Place	Valerie Wilson Wesley	Tamara Hayle
No Honeymoon for Death	Mary Kruger	Brooke Cassidy (Devlin)
No Human Involved	Barbara Seranella	Munch Mancini
No Laughing Matter	Betty Rowlands	Melissa Craig
No Love Lost	Eileen Dewhurst	Phyllida Moon
No Man Standing	Barbara Seranella	Munch Mancini
No Offense Intended	Barbara Seranella	Munch Mancini
No One Dies in Branson	Kathryn Buckstaff	Emily Stone
No Reservation Required	Ellen Hart	Sophie Greenway
No Rest for the Dove	Margaret Miles	Charlotte Willett
No Rest for the Wicket	Donna Andrews	Meg Langslow
No Time for an Everyday Woman	Wanda Wardell Morrone	Lorelei Muldoon
No Time to Die	Grace F. Edwards	Mali Anderson
No Trace	Barry Maitland	Sgt. Kathy Kolla
No Witness	Nancy Sanra	Tally McGinnis
Nothing Else Matters	S. D. Tooley	Samantha "Sam" Casey
Nothing Gold Can Stay	Dana Stabenow	Wyanet "Wy" Chouinard
The Novice's Tale	Margaret Frazer	Sister Frevisse
Now I Lay Me Down to Sleep	Patricia H. Rushford	Helen Bradley
Now This	Nancy Star	May Morrison
Now May You Weep	Deborah Crombie	Gemma Jones
Now You See Her	Eileen Dewhurst	Phyllida Moon
The Nun's Tale	Candace M. Robb	Lucie D'Arby Wilton
Nutty As a Fruitcake	Mary Daheim	Judith McMonigle (Flynn)
O		
O Jerusalem	Laurie R. King	Mary Russell (Holmes)
Obsessions Can Be Murder	Connie Shelton	Charlotte "Charlie" Parker
Obstruction of Justice	Perri O'Shaughnessy	Nina Reilly
Occasion of Revenge	Marcia Talley	Hannah Ives
Of Death and Black Rivers	Ann Woodward	Lady Aoi
Officer of the Court	Lelia Kelly	Laura Chastain
Old Black Magic	Jaye Maiman	Robin Miller
Old Dogs	Melissa Cleary	Jackie Walsh
The Old School Dies	Kate Morgan	Dewey James
The Oldest Sin	Ellen Hart	Sophie Greenway
Once Bitten	Laurien Berenson	Melanie Travis
One Dead Tory	Stephen Cook	Judy Best
One for the Money	D. B. Borton	Catherine "Cat" Caliban
One for the Money	Janet Evanovich	Stephanie Plum
One Last Good-bye	Joyce and Jim Levene	Sharyn Howard
One Must Wait	Penny Mickelbury	Carole Ann Gibson
One Too Many (NA)	Melissa Chan	Francesca Miles
One Tough Cookie	Vinnie Hansen	Carol Sabala
One, Two, What did Daddy Do?	Susan Rogers Cooper	E. J. Pugh
Only Flesh and Bones	Sarah Andrews	Emily "Em" Hansen
Only in the Ashes	Maxine O'Callaghan	Dr. Anne Menlo
Only One Way Out	Ruth Ruby Moen	Kathleen O'Shaughnessy
Open House	Pat Welch	Helen Black
Ophelia O. and the Antenatal Mysteries	Tanya Jones	Ophelia O (Meredith)
Ophelia O. and the Mortgage Bandits	Tanya Jones	Ophelia O (Meredith)
Orange Crushed	Pamela Thomas-Graham	Nikki Chase
Orchid Beach	Stuart Woods	Holly Barker
Orchid Blues	Stuart Woods	Holly Barker
Ordinary Justice	Trudy Labovitz	Zoe Kergulin

Title of Book	Author	Character
Origin in Death	J. D. Robb	Lt. Eve Dallas
The Orkney Scroll	Lyn Hamilton	Lara McClintoch
Osprey Reef	Victoria McKernan	Chicago Nordejoong
The Other Side of Silence	Joan M. Drury	Tyler Jones
Our Lady of Darkness	Peter Tremayne	Sister Fidelma
Out of Circulation	Jo Dereske	Wilhelmena "Helma" Zukas
Out of Hormone's Way	Jane Isenberg	Bel Barrett
Out of the Dark	Natasha Cooper	Trish Maguire
Out of the Frying Pan Into the Choir	Sharon Kahn	Ruby Rothman
Out of Sight	Claire McNab	Denise Cleever
Out of Time	Katy Munger	Casey Jones
Outlaw Mountain	J. A. Jance	Joanna Brady
The Outlaw's Tale	Margaret Frazer	Sister Frevisse
Outside Chance	Louisa Dixon	Laura Owen
Ovation by Death	Dorian Yeager	Victoria "Vic" Bowering
Over the Edge	Betty Rowlands	Melissa Craig
Over the Line	Tracey Richardson	Stevie Houston
Over the Line	Faye Sultan, Teresa Kennedy	Portia McTeague
Owl's Well That Ends Well	Donna Andrews	Meg Langslow
Oxford Blue	Veronica Stallwood	Kate Ivory
Oxford Double	Veronica Stallwood	Kate Ivory
Oxford Exit	Veronica Stallwood	Kate Ivory
Oxford Fall	Veronica Stallwood	Kate Ivory
Oxford Knot	Veronica Stallwood	Kate Ivory
Oxford Letters	Veronica Stallwood	Kate Ivory
Oxford Menace	Veronica Stallwood	Kate Ivory
Oxford Mourning	Veronica Stallwood	Kate Ivory
Oxford Proof	Veronica Stallwood	Kate Ivory
Oxford Remains	Veronica Stallwood	Kate Ivory
Oxford Shadows	Veronica Stallwood	Kate Ivory
Oxford Shift	Veronica Stallwood	Kate Ivory
The Oxygen Murder	Camille Minichino	Gloria Lamerino
P		
Pack Up the Moon	Mary Anne Kelly	Claire Breslinsky (Benedetto)
Painted Lady	Peter Abresch	Dodee Swisher
Painted Truth	Lise McClendon	Alix Thorssen
Panic	Echo Heron	Adele Monsarrat
Paradise Interrupted	Penny Mickelbury	Carole Ann Gibson
Paradise Lost	J. A. Jance	Joanna Brady
Paradox	Echo Heron	Adele Monsarrat
The Paramour's Daughter (2010)	Wendy Hornsby	Maggie MacGowen
Park Lane South, Queens	Mary Anne Kelly	Claire Breslinsky (Benedetto)
Parsley, Sage, Rosemary and Crime	Tamar Myers	Magdalena Yoder
Partner in Crime	J. A. Jance	Joanna Brady
Partners in Crime	Gallagher Gray	Lil Hubbert
Partnerships Can Kill	Connie Shelton	Charlie Parker
Party to Murder	Betty Rowlands	Sukey Reynolds
A Passion So Deadly	Hilary Bonner	Rose Piper
The Passover Murder	Lee Harris	Christine Bennett
Past Pretense	Sharon Gwyn Short	Patricia Delaney
Pattern of Behavior (novella)	Paul Bishop	Fey Croaker
Pawing Through the Past	Rita Mae Brown	Mary "Harry" Haristeen & Mrs. Murphy
A Pawn for a Queen	Fiona Buckley	Ursula Blanchard
Paws Before Dying	Susan Conant	Holly Winter

Title of Book	Author	Character
Pay Dirt	Rita Mae Brown	Mary "Harry" Haristeen & Mrs. Murphy
Pay the Piper	Kate Kingsbury	Cecily Sinclair
Payment Deferred	Joyce Holms	Fizz Fitzpatrick
Peaches and Screams	G. A. McKevett	Savannah Reid
The Pearl Diver	Sujata Massey	Rei Shimura
A Pedigree to Die For	Laurien Berenson	Melanie Travis
The Penguin Who Knew Too Much	Donna Andrews	Meg Langslow
Penn Valley Phoenix	Janet McClellan	Tru North
A Penny Urned	Tamar Myers	Abigail "Abby" Timberlake
People Who Walk in Darkness	Stuart Kaminsky	Elena Timofeyeva
The Perennial Killer	Ann Ripley	Louise Eldridge
Perfect Circles	Greg Moody	Cheryl Crane
The Perfect Daughter	Gillian Linscott	Nell Bray
Perfect Justice	William Bernhardt	Christina McCall
The Perfect Paragon	M. C. Beaton	Agatha Raisin
Perfumed Sleeve	Laura Joh Rowland	Reiko Ichiro
Perilous Friends	Carole Epstein	Barbara Simons
Perilous Relations	Carole Epstein	Barbara Simons
Perils of the Night	Patricia Hall	Laura Ackroyd
Perish by Pedicure	Nancy J. Cohen	Marla Shore
Perish Twice	Robert B. Parker	Sunny Randall
A Permanent Retirement	John Miles	Laura Michaels
Permed to Death	Nancy J. Cohen	Marla Shore
Permit for Murder	Valerie Wolzien	Josie Pigeon
A Personal Devil	Roberta Gellis	Magdalene la Bâtarde
Picture of David	Shelley Singer	Barrett Lake
A Piece of Justice	Jill Paton Walsh	Imogen Quy
The Pillars of Solomon	Jon Land	Danielle Barnea
Pillow Book of Lady Wisteria	Laura Joh Rowland	Reiko Ichiro
A Pinch of Poison	Claudia Bishop	Sarah "Quill" Quilliam
Pink Balloons and Other Deadly Things	Nancy Tesler	Carrie Carlin
The Pink Flamingo Murders	Elaine Viets	Francesca Vierling
The Pink Rabbit Caper	Georgette Livingston	Dr. Jennifer Gray
Pisces Rising	Martha C. Lawrence	Dr. Elizabeth Chase
A Place of Safety	Natasha Cooper	Trish Maguire
A Plague of Kinfolks	Celestine Sibley	Kate Mulcay a.k.a. Katy Kincaid
Play Dead	Leslie O'Kane	Allie Babcock
Play It Again, Spam	Tamar Myers	Magdalena Yoder
Play with Fire	Dana Stabenow	Kate Shugak
Playing Dead	Lindsay Maracotta	Lucy Freers
Plot Twist	Jane Rubino	Cat Austen
Plotted in Cornwall	Jane Bolitho	Rose Trevelyan
Plum Lovin'	Janet Evanovich	Stephanie Plum
Plum Lucky	Janet Evanovich	Stephanie Plum
Plum Spooky	Janet Evanovich	Stephanie Plum
A Pocketful of Karma	Taffy Cannon	Nan Robinson
Point Blank	Catherine Coulter	Lacey Savich
Point Deception	Victoria McKernan	Chicago Nordejoong
Point No Point	Mary Logue	Claire Watkins
Point No-Point	David Willis McCullough	Rev. Ziza Todd
Point of Origin	Patricia D. Cornwell	Dr. Kay Scarpetta
Poison Apples	Nancy Means Wright	Ruth Willmarth
Poison Flowers	Natasha Cooper	Willow King
Poison Heart	Mary Logue	Claire Watkins

Title of Book	Author	Character
Poison Ivory	Tamar Myers	Abigail "Abby" Timberlake
A Poison in the Blood	Fay Zachary	Dr. Liz Broward
A Poisoned Mind	Natasha Cooper	Trish Maguire
Poisoned Tarts	G. A. McKevett	Savannah Reid
Popped	Carol Higgins Clark	Regan Reilly
Poppy Done to Death	Charlaine Harris	Aurora "Roe" Teagarden
Portrait in Death	J. D. Robb	Lt. Eve Dallas
Port Mortuary (2010)	Patricia D. Cornwell	Dr. Kay Scarpetta
Possessions	Kaye Davis	Maris Middleton
Postmortem	Patricia D. Cornwell	Dr. Kay Scarpetta
The Potbellied Pig Caper	Georgette Livingston	Dr. Jennifer Gray
Power Games	Judith Cutler	Kate Power
Power in the Blood	E. L. Wyrick	Tammi Randall
Power On Her Own	Judith Cutler	Kate Power
Power Shift	Judith Cutler	Kate Power
The Poyson Garden	Karen Harper	Queen Elizabeth I
Practice to Deceive	Janet L. Smith	Annie MacPherson
Pray For Us Sinners	Philip Luber	Veronica Pace
A Prayer for the Damned	Peter Tremayne	Sister Fidelma
The Prayer of the Night Shepherd	Phil Rickman	Rev. Merrily Watkins
Prayers for Rain	Dennis Lehane	Angela Gennaro
The Precocious Parrot Caper	Georgette Livingston	Dr. Jennifer Gray
Predator	Patricia D. Cornwell	Dr. Kay Scarpetta
Prelude to Death	Sharon Zukowski	Blaine Stewart
Prescription for Death	Janet McGiffin	Dr. Maxene St. Clair
Presence of Mind	Fred Hunter	Emily Charters
Press Corpse	Ron Nessen, Johanna Neuman	Jane Day
Pressed to Kill	Dolores Johnson	Mandy Dyer
Presumption of Death	Perri O'Shaughnessy	Nina Reilly
Presumption of Guilt	Lelia Kelly	Laura Chastain
Pretty Boy	Lauren Henderson	Sam Jones
Prey Dancing	Jonathan Gash	Dr. Clare Burtonall
Prey to All	Natasha Cooper	Trish Maguire
Primal Instinct	Robert W. Walker	Dr. Jessica Coran
Primary Justice	William Bernhardt	Christina McCall
Prime Cut	Diane Mott Davidson	Goldy Bear (Schulz)
Prime Suspect	Lynda La Plante	Jane Tennison
Prime Suspect 2	Lynda La Plante	Jane Tennison
Prime Suspect 3	Lynda La Plante	Jane Tennison
Prime Time for Murder	Valerie Frankel	Wanda Mallory
The Primrose Convention	Jo Bannister	Primrose "Rosie" Holland
The Primrose Switchback	Jo Bannister	Primrose "Rosie" Holland
Principal Defense	Gini Hartzmark	Kate Millholland
Principal Investigation	B. B. Jordan	Dr. Celeste Braun
The Prioress' Tale	Margaret Frazer	Sister Frevisse
Prison Blues	Anna Salter	Dr. Michael Stone
Private Lies	Carol Cail	Maxey Burnell
Private Practices	Stephen White	Lauren Crowder
Privileged Communication	Pat Freider	Matty Donahue
Privileged Information	Stephen White	Lauren Crowder
Profile	C. J. Koehler	Margaret Loftus
The Program	Stephen White	Lauren Crowder
Promises in Death	J. D. Robb	Lt. Eve Dallas
A Proper Burial	Pat Welch	Helen Black
Prospect of Death	Margaret Duffy	Joanna Mackenzie
Protect and Defend	Richard North Patterson	Caroline Masters

Title of Book	Author	Character
Rattling the Bones	Ann Granger	Fran Varaday
The Raven and the Nightingale	Joanne Dobson	Karen Pelletier
Ravenmocker	Jean Hager	Molly Bearpaw
Raw Data	Sally Chapman	Julie Blake
Razorbill	Alex Keegan	Caz Flood
Real Murders	Charlaine Harris	Aurora "Roe" Teagarden
Reap a Wicked Harvest	Janis Harrison	Bretta Solomon
Reckless Abandon	Stuart Woods	Holly Barker
Reckless Eyeballin'	Judith Smith-Levin	Starletta Duvall
Recognition Factor	Claire McNab	Denise Cleever
A Record of Death	Kate Bryan	Magdalena "Maggie" Maguire
Recycled	Jo Bailey	Jan Gallagher
Red Beans and Vice	Lou Jane Temple	Heaven Lee
Red Chrysanthemum	Laura Joh Rowland	Reiko Ichiro
The Red Heron	Karen Dudley	Robyn Devara
Red Hot Mama	Joanne Pence	Angelina "Angie" Amalfi
Red House	k.j.a. Wishnia	Filomena "Fil" Buscarsela
Red Line	Megan Mallory Rust	Taylor Morgan
Red Mesa	Aimee and David Thurlo	Ella Clah
The Red Scream	Mary Willis Walker	Molly Cates
Red Sea, Dead Sea	Serita Stevens, Rayanne Moore	Fanny Zindel
Red Sky in Mourning	Patricia H. Rushford	Helen Bradley
Red Trance	R. D. Zimmerman	Maddy Phillips
Red Wine Goes with Murder	Paula Carter	Jane Ferguson, Hillary Scarborough
Red, White, and Blue Murder	Jeanne M. Dams	Hilda Johansson
The Redbird's Cry	Jean Hager	Molly Bearpaw
Redneck Riviera	Sophie Dunbar	Claire Claiborne Jenner
The Reeve's Tale	Margaret Frazer	Sister Frevisse
Reflecting the Sky	S. J. Rozan	Lydia Chin
A Relative Cause of Murder a.k.a. Death in the Family	C. F. Roe	Dr. Jean Montrose
Remains of an Altar	Phil Rickman	Rev. Merrily Watkins
Remember in Death	J. D. Robb	Lt. Eve Dallas
Remember Me, Irene	Jan Burke	Irene Kelly
Remember the Alibi	Elizabeth Daniels Squire	Peaches Dann
Remembrance of Murders Past	Noreen Wald	Jake O'Hara
Remote Control	Stephen White	Lauren Crowder
Render Up the Body	Marianne Wesson	Cinda Hayes
Repair to Her Grave	Sarah Graves	Jacobia Tiptee
Reporter on the Run	Carlene Miller	Lexy Hyatt
Requiem for a Mezzo	Carola Dunn	Daisy Dalrymple
Resolution	Denise Mina	Maureen O'Donnell
Resort to Murder	Carolyn Hart	Henrietta O'Dwyer Collins
Rest in Pieces	Rita Mae Brown	Mary "Harry" Haristeen & Mrs. Murphy
A Restless Evil	Ann Granger	Merry Mitchell
Restless Spirit	S. D. Tooley	Samantha "Sam" Casey
Restless Waters	Jessica Speart	Rachel Porter
The Return of the Spanish Lady	Val Davis	Nicolette "Nick" Scott
Return to the Kill	Ruth Ruby Moen	Kathleen O'Shaughnessy
Reunion in Death	J. D. Robb	Lt. Eve Dallas
Reunions Can Be Murder	Connie Shelton	Charlie Parker
Revenge at the Rodeo	Gilbert Morris	Danielle "Dani" Ross
Revenge of the Barbecue Queens	Lou Jane Temple	Heaven Lee
Revenge of the Cootie Girls	Sparkle Hayter	Robin Hudson
Revenge of the Gypsy Queen	Kris Neri	Tracy Eaton

Title of Book	Author	Character
Revenge of the Wrought-Iron Flamingos	Donna Andrews	Meg Langslow
Rhode Island Red	Charlotte Carter	Nanette Hayes
The Riddle of St. Leonards	Candace M. Robb	Lucie D'Arby Wilton
A Ride on the Trojan Horse	Loretta Scott Miller	Elizabeth "Lisbee" Billings
Riding for a Fall	Lillian M. Roberts	Dr. Andi Pauling
Right to Remain Silent	Penny Warner	Connor Westphal
Rigor Mortis	Mary Kittredge	Edwina Crusoe
Ring for Tomb Service	Kate Kingsbury	Cecily Sinclair
Ringing in Murder	Kate Kingsbury	Cecily Sinclair
Rip Tide	Catherine Coulter	Lacey Savich
Risking It All	Ann Granger	Fran Varaday
River Quay	Janet McClellan	Tru North
Road Kill	Marianne Macdonald	Dido Hoare
Robin (NA)	Alex Keegan	Caz Flood
The Robsart Mystery a.k.a. To Shield the Queen	Fiona Buckley	Ursula Blanchard
Rode Hard, Put Away Dead	Sinclair Browning	Trade Ellis
Room with a Clue	Kate Kingsbury	Cecily Sinclair
Root Canal	C. A. Haddad	Becky Belski
Roots of Murder	Janis Harrison	Bretta Solomon
Roped	Laura Crum	Dr. Gail McCarthy
Rosemary for Remembrance	Audrey Stallsmith	Regan Culver
Rosemary Remembered	Susan Wittig Albert	China Bayles
Roses for Regret	Audrey Stallsmith	Regan Culver
The Rosewood Casket	Sharyn McCrumb	Nora Bonesteel
Rosewood's Ashes	Aileen Schumacher	Tory Travers
The Rotary Club Murder Mystery	Graham Landrum	Harriet Bushrow, Helen Delaporte
Rotten Apple	Stephen Cook	Judy Best
Rotten Apples	Natasha Cooper	Willow King
Rotten Dates	Vinnie Hansen	Carol Sabala
Rough Justice	Lisa Scottoline	Benedetta "Bennie" Rosato
Rough Track	Gini Hartzmark	Kate Millholland
Rough Trade	Gini Hartzmark	Kate Millholland
Rough Water	Sally Gunning	Connie Bartholomew
Roughstock	Laura Crum	Dr. Gail McCarthy
Roundabout	Eileen Dewhurst	Phyllida Moon
Royal Cat	Garrison Allen	Penelope Warren
Royals and Rogues	Cynthia Smith	Emma Rhodes
Rubbed Out	Barbara Block	Robin Light
Rubout	Elaine Viets	Francesca Vierling
Rueful Death	Susan Wittig Albert	China Bayles
Ruff Way to Go	Leslie O'Kane	Allie Babcock
Ruffly Speaking	Susan Conant	Holly Winter
A Rumor of Bones	Beverly Connor	Lindsay Chamberlain
Run Jane Run	Maureen Tan	Jane Nichols
Runemaker	Tiina Nunnally	Margit Andersson
Runner	Thomas Perry	Jane Whitefield
The Runner	Peter May	Margaret Campbell
Running for Shelter	Michelle Spring	Laura Principal
Running Scared	Ann Granger	Fran Varaday
The Ruthless Realtor Murders	David Kaufelt	Wyn Lewis
Rx Alibi	Renee B. Horowitz	Ruthie Kantor Morris
Rx for Murder	Renee B. Horowitz	Ruthie Kantor Morris
S		
Sacred	Dennis Lehane	Angela Gennaro

Title of Book	Author	Character
Sacred Hearts	Alison Joseph	Sister Agnes Bourdillon
Sacrifice	Clyde Phillips	Jane Candiotti
Sacrifice Bid	Susan Moody	Cassandra "Cassie" Swann
Sad Water	Teri Holbrook	Gale Grayson
A Safe Place to Sleep	Jennifer L. Jordan	Kristin Ashe
Saintly Murders	C. L. Grace	Kathryn Swinbrooke
Saks and Violins	Mary Daheim	Judith McMonigle (Flynn)
The Salaryman's Wife	Sujata Massey	Rei Shimura
Salmon in the Soup	Meg O'Brien	Jessica "Jesse" James
Salt City Blues	Barbara Block	Robin Light
Salvation in Death	J. D. Robb	Lt. Eve Dallas
The Samurai's Daughter	Sujata Massey	Rei Shimura
Samurai's Wife	Laura Joh Rowland	Reiko Ichiro
Sand Sharks	Margaret Maron	Deborah Knott
Santa Clawed	Rita Mae Brown	Mary "Harry" Haristeen
Santa Cruise	Carol Higgins Clark	Regan Reilly
The Santa Fe Rembrandt	Cecil Dawkins	Ginevra Prettifield
Satan's Silence	Alex Matthews	Cassidy McCabe
Savage Cut	Jo Dereske	Ruby Crane
Saving Death	Winona Sullivan	Sr. Cecille Buddenbrooks
Say It with Poison	Ann Granger	Merry Mitchell
Say Uncle	Randye Lordon	Sydney Sloane
Scalpel's Edge	Margot J. Fromer	Amanda Knight
Scam and Eggs (ss)	Janet Dawson	"Jeri" Howard
Scandal in Fair Haven	Carolyn Hart	Henrietta O'Dwyer Collins
Scaring Crows	Priscilla Masters	Joanna Piercy
Scarpetta	Patricia D. Cornwell	Dr. Kay Scarpetta
The Scarpetta Factor	Patricia D. Cornwell	Dr. Kay Scarpetta
Scarpetta's Winter Table	Patricia D. Cornwell	Dr. Kay Scarpetta
The Scent of Fear	Patricia and Clayton Matthews	Casey Farrel
The Scent of Murder	Barbara Block	Robin Light
The School Board Murders	Leslie O'Kane	Molly Masters
School of Hard Knocks	Donna Huston Murray	Ginger Barnes
A Score to Settle	Donna Huston Murray	Ginger Barnes
Scots on the Rocks	Mary Daheim	Judith McMonigle (Flynn)
Scorpion Rising	Marilyn Todd	Claudia Seferius
Scream in Silence	Eleanor Taylor Bland	Marti MacAlister
Sea of Troubles	Janet L. Smith	Annie MacPherson
The Search	Iris Johansen	Eve Duncan
The Search	Melanie McAllester	Elizabeth "Tenny" Mendoza
Searching for Sara	Shelley Singer	Barrett Lake
Seaside	Scarlett Thomas	Lily Pascale
A Season for Murder	Ann Granger	Merry Mitchell
Second Act	Marilyn Todd	Claudia Seferius
Second Guess	Rose Beecham	Amanda Valentine
Second Thoughts	Margot Dalton	Jackie Kaminsky
Secondary Immunization	B. B. Jordan	Dr. Celeste Braun
Secret's Shadow	Alex Matthews	Cassidy McCabe
Seduction in Death	J. D. Robb	Lt. Eve Dallas
See No Evil	Eleanor Taylor Bland	Marti MacAlister
Seeds of Vengeance	Sylvia Nobel	Kendall O'Dell
Seeing Is Deceiving	Sarah J. Mason	Sergeant Stone
Seeing Is Deceiving	Suzanne North	Phoebe Fairfax
Selective Memory	Jennifer L. Jordan	Kristin Ashe
The Sempster's Tale	Margaret Frazer	Sister Frevisse
Seneca Falls Inheritance	Miriam Monfredo	Glynis Tryon

Title of Book	Author	Character
The Sensational Music Club Mystery	Graham Landrum	Harriet Bushrow, Helen Delaporte
A Sensitive Kind of Murder	Jaqueline Girdner	Kate Jasper
September Mourn	Mary Daheim	Judith McMonigle (Flynn)
The Servant's Tale	Margaret Frazer	Sister Frevisse
Service for Two	Kate Kingsbury	Cecily Sinclair
Set Sail for Murder	Carolyn Hart	Hester Gorse
Settlement Day	Rebecca Tinsley	Charlotte Carter
Seven Black Stones	Jean Hager	Molly Bearpaw
Seven Sisters	Earlene Fowler	Albenia "Benni" Harper
Seven Up	Janet Evanovich	Stephanie Plum
Seventh Deadly Sin	D. B. Borton	Catherine "Cat" Caliban
Sew Deadly	Jean Hager	Tess Darcy
Sew Easy to Kill	Sarah J. Mason	Sergeant Stone
Sew For, Sew Good	Monica Ferris	Betsy Devonshire
Sex and Salmonella	Kathleen Taylor	Tory Bauer
Shades of Murder	Ann Granger	Merry Mitchell
The Shadow Dancer	Margaret Coel	Vicky Holden
Shadow Man	James Doss	Daisy Perika
Shadow of An Angel	Mignon F. Ballard	Augusta Goodnight
Shadow of Death	Noreen Gilpatrick	Kate MacLean
Shadow of Death	Alison Joseph	Sister Agnes Bourdillon
Shadow of Doubt	Jonnie Jacobs	Kali O'Brien
Shadow of the Child	Maxine O'Callaghan	Dr. Anne Menlo
Shadow Queen	Tony Gibbs	Diana Speed
Shadow Walk	Jane Waterhouse	Garner Quinn
Shadow Woman	Thomas Perry	Jane Whitefield
Shadows of Sin	Rochelle Majer Krich	Jessica Drake
Shakespeare's Champion	Charlaine Harris	Lily Bard
Shakespeare's Christmas	Charlaine Harris	Lily Bard
Shakespeare's Counselor	Charlaine Harris	Lily Bard
Shakespeare's Landlord	Charlaine Harris	Lily Bard
Shakespeare's Trollop	Charlaine Harris	Lily Bard
The Shaman Laughs	James Doss	Daisy Perika
The Shaman Sings	James Doss	Daisy Perika
The Shaman's Bones	James Doss	Daisy Perika
The Shaman's Game	James Doss	Daisy Perika
The Shanghai Moon	S. J. Rozan	Lydia Chin
A Share in Death	Deborah Crombie	Gemma James
Sharks, Jellyfish and Other Deadly Things	Nancy Tesler	Carrie Carlin
Shattered Rhythms	Phyllis Knight	Lil Ritchie
She Walks These Hills	Sharyn McCrumb	Nora Bonesteel
Sheep in Wolf's Clothing	Peter Abresch	Dodee Swisher
Sheer Folly	Carola Dunn	Daisy Dalrymple
Shell Game	Carol O'Connell	Sgt. Kathleen Mallory
The Shifting Tide	Anne Perry	Hester Latterly (Monk)
Shimura Trouble	Sujata Massey	Rei Shimura
Shinju	Laura Joh Rowland	Reiko Ichiro
Shiny Water	Anna Salter	Dr. Michael Stone
Shivaree	Sophie Dunbar	Claire Claiborne Jenner
Shoo-Fly	Lizbie Brown	Elizabeth Blair
Shoot, Don't Shoot	J. A. Jance	Joanna Brady
Shoot Him if He Runs	Stuart Woods	Holly Barker
Shooting at Loons	Margaret Maron	Deborah Knott
Shooting Chant	Aimee and David Thurlo	Ella Clah

Title of Book	Author	Character
Shooting Stars and Other Deadly Things	Nancy Tesler	Carrie Carlin
Shore to Die	Valerie Wolzien	Josie Pigeon
Short Cut	Jo Dereske	Ruby Crane
A Shot at Nothing	Roger Ormerod	Phillipa Lowe
Shot in the Dark	Tony Gibbs	Lt. Tory Lennox, USCG
Shot in the Dark	Annie Ross	Bel Carson
Shoveling Smoke (s.s)	Margaret Maron	Deborah Knott
Show No Fear	Perri O'Shaughnessy	Nina Reilly
Showcase	Alison Glen	Charlotte Sams
A Shrine of Murders	C. L. Grace	Kathryn Swinbrooke
Shrink Rap	Robert B. Parker	Sunny Randall
Shroud for a Scholar	Audrey Peterson	Claire Camden
Shroud for the Archbishop	Peter Tremayne	Sister Fidelma
Shrouds of Holly	Kate Kingsbury	Cecily Sinclair
The Shy Tulip Murders	Rebecca Rothenberg	Claire Sharples
Sick as a Parrot	Liz Evans	Grace Smith
Sign of Foul Play	Penny Warner	Connor Westphal
Signature Murder	Pat Freider	Matty Donahue
Signs of Murder	Jean Bedford	Anna Southwood
Silence Is Golden	Jeanne M. Dams	Hilda Johansson
Silence is Golden	Penny Warner	Connor Westphal
The Silent Bride	Leslie Glass	April Woo
The Silent Cry	Anne Perry	Hester Latterly (Monk)
Silent Justice	William Bernhardt	Christina McCall
The Silent Spirit	Margaret Coel	Vicky Holden
Silent Words	Joan M. Drury	Tyler Jones
Silhouettes	Paul Patti	Gabrielle "Gabe" Amato
Silicon Solution	M. Diane Vogt	Judge Wilhelmina Carson
The Silly Season	Susan Holtzer	Anneke Haagen
The Silver Anniversary Murder	Lee Harris	Christine Bennett
Silver and Guilt	Cynthia Smith	Emma Rhodes
The Silver Scalpel	Nancy Baker Jacobs	Devon MacDonald
Silver Scream	Mary Daheim	Judith McMonigle (Flynn)
Silverlake Heat	Carol Schmidt	Laney Samms
Silvermeadow	Barry Maitland	Kathy Kolla
A Simple Shaker Murder	Deborah Woodworth	Sister Rose Callahan
Sing a Song of Death	Catherine Dain	Freddie O'Neal
Sing It to Her Bones	Marcia Talley	Hannah Ives
The Singing of the Dead	Dana Stabenow	Kate Shugak
A Singular Spy	Amanda Kyle Williams	Madison McGuire
Sins and Needles	Monica Ferris	Betsy Devonshire
Sins of a Shaker Summer	Deborah Woodworth	Sister Rose Callahan
Sins of Betrayal	Valerie Wilcox	Kellie Montgomery
Sins of Deception	Valerie Wilcox	Kellie Mongomery
Sins of Silence	Valerie Wilcox	Kellie Montgomery
The Sins of the Wolf	Anne Perry	Hester Latterly (Monk)
Sins Out of School	Jeanne M. Dams	Dorothy Martin
The Siren Queen	Fiona Buckley	Ursula Blanchard
Sister Beneath the Sheet	Gillian Linscott	Nell Bray
Sister to the Rain	Melisa Michaels	Rosie Lavine
Sister's Keeper	Randye Lordon	Sydney Sloane
Sisters of Cain	Miriam Monfredo	Glynis Tryon
Six Bills	M. Diane Vogt	Judge Wilhelmina Carson
Six Feet Under	D. B. Borton	Catherine "Cat" Caliban
Six Geese A-Slaying	Donna Andrews	Meg Langslow

Title of Book	Author	Character
The Songcatcher	Sharyn McCrumb	Nora Bonesteel
A Soul to Take	C. N. Bean	Rita Trible
Soultown	Mercedes Lambert	Whitney Logan
Sound of Murder	Patricia and Clayton Matthews	Casey Farrel
Sounds Easy	Carol Dawber	Liz Gresham
Sour Grapes	G. A. McKevett	Savannah Reid
Sour Grapes	Marilyn Todd	Claudia Seferius
Sour Puss	Rita Mae Brown	Mary "Harry" Haristeen
Southern Cross	Patricia D. Cornwell	Judy Hammer
Southern Discomfort	Margaret Maron	Deborah Knott
Spanish Dagger	Susan Wittig Albert	China Bayles
Spare Change	Robert B. Parker	Sunny Randall
Speak Daggers to Her	Rosemary Edghill	Karen Hightower a.k.a. Bast
Speak Ill of the Dead	Mary Jane Maffini	Camilla McPhee
A Species of Revenge	Marjorie Eccles	Abigail Moon
Spider in the Sink	Celestine Sibley	Kate Mulcay a.k.a. Katy Kincaid
Spider Trap	Barry Maitland	Sgt. Kathy Kolla
The Spider's Web	Peter Tremayne	Sister Fidelma
The Spirit Caller	Jean Hager	Molly Bearpaw
Spirit Sickness	Kirk Mitchell	Anna Turnipseed
The Spirit Woman	Margaret Coel	Vicky Holden
Splendor in the Glass	Tamar Myers	Abigail "Abby" Timberlake
Splintered Bones	Carolyn Haines	Sarah Booth Delaney
Split Image	Judy Mercer	Ariel Gold
A Spoonful of Poison	M. C. Beaton	Agatha Raisin
The Sporting Club	Sinclair Browning	Trade Ellis
A Spy for the Redeemer	Candace M. Robb	Lucie D'Arby Wilton
The Spy in Question	Amanda Kyle Williams	Madison McGuire
Square in the Face	April Henry	Claire Montrose
The Squire's Tale	Margaret Frazer	Sister Frevisse
The St. Patrick's Day Murder	Lee Harris	Christine Bennett
St. Patrick's Day Murder	Leslie Meier	Lucy Stone
Stabbing Stephanie	Evan Marshall	Jane Stuart
Stable Cat	Garrison Allen	Penelope Warren
Stage Fright	Gillian Linscott	Nell Bray
Stalemate	Iris Johansen	Eve Duncan
Stalking Death	Kate Flora	Thea Kozak
Stalking the Goddess Ship	Marsha Mildon	Cal Meredith
Stalking the Puzzle Lady	Parnell Hall	Cora Felton & Sherry Carter
Star Spangled Murder	Leslie Meier	Lucy Stone
State Fair	Earlene Fowler	Albenia "Benni" Harper
Statue of Limitations	Tamar Myers	Abigail "Abby" Timberlake
Steeped in Murder	Linda French	Teodora "Teddy" Morelli
The Step Between	Penny Mickelbury	Carole Ann Gibson
Steps to the Altar	Earlene Fowler	Albenia "Benni" Harper
Sticks & Scones	Diane Mott Davidson	Goldy Bear (Schulz)
Stiff Critique	Jaqueline Girdner	Kate Jasper
A Stiff Risotto	Lou Jane Temple	Heaven Lee
Still Water	Sally Gunning	Connie Bartholomew
Still Waters	Kerry Tucker	Libby Kincaid
Still Waters	Pat Welch	Helen Black
A Stitch in Time	Monica Ferris	Betsy Devonshire
Stolen Honey	Nancy Means Wright	Ruth Willmarth
Stolen Smoke	Margaret Coel	Vicky Holden
Stone Angel a.k.a. Flight of the Stone Angel	Carol O'Connell	Sgt. Kathleen Mallory

Title of Book	Author	Character
Stone Butterfly	James Doss	Daisy Perika
Stone Cold	Marilyn Todd	Claudia Seferius
Stone Cold Red Hot	Cath Staincliffe	Sal Kilkenny
The Stone Monkey	Jeffrey Wilds Deaver	Amelia Sachs
Stone Quarry	S. J. Rozan	Lydia Chin
Stork Raving Mad (2010)	Donna Andrews	Meg Langslow
Storm Front	Linda Kay Silva	Delta Stevens
Storm Rising	Linda Kay Silva	Delta Stevens
Storm Shelter	Linda Kay Silva	Delta Stevens
Storm Track	Margaret Maron	Deborah Knott
Stormy Weather	Paula L. Woods	Charlotte Justice
The Story Teller	Margaret Coel	Vicky Holden
Straight As an Arrow	Celestine Sibley	Kate Mulcay a.k.a. Katy Kincaid
A Strange and Bitter Crop	E. L. Wyrick	Tammi Randall
The Strange Attractor a.k.a. The Catalyst	Desmond Cory	Dr. Kate Coyle
Strange Bedfellows	Paula L. Woods	Charlotte Justice
Strange Brew	Kathy Hogan Trocheck	Julia "Callahan" Garrity
The Strange Files of Fremont Jones	Dianne Day	Caroline "Fremont" Jones
Strangers in Death	J. D. Robb	Lt. Eve Dallas
Strangers in the Night	Peg Tyre	Kate Murray
Strangle A Loaf of Italian Bread	Denise Dietz	Ellie Bernstein
Stranglehold	Jennifer Rowe	Verity "Birdie" Birdwood
Strawberry Tattoo	Lauren Henderson	Sam Jones
Strawgirl	Abigail Padgett	Barbara "Bo" Bradley
A Streetcar Named Expire	Mary Daheim	Judith McMonigle (Flynn)
Strip Poker	Nancy Bartholomew	Sierra Lavotini
Strong As Death	Sharan Newman	Catherine Le Vendeur
Stronger Than Death	Manda Scott	Dr. Kellen Stewart
Stud Rites	Susan Conant	Holly Winter
A Studied Death	Betsy Struthers	Rosalie Cairns
Styx and Stones	Carola Dunn	Daisy Dalrymple
The Subtle Serpent	Peter Tremayne	Sister Fidelma
Sudden Death	Jackie Manthorne	Harriet Hubbley
A Sudden Death at the Norfolk Cafe	Winona Sullivan	Sr. Cecille Buddenbrooks
A Sudden Fearful Death	Anne Perry	Hester Latterly (Monk)
The Sudoku Puzzle Murders	Parnell Hall	Cora Felton & Sherry Carter
Suffer Little Children	Peter Tremayne	Sister Fidelma
The Suffocating Night	Andrew Taylor	Jill Francis
Sugar and Spite	G. A. McKevett	Savannah Reid
The Sugar House	Laura Lippman	Tess Monaghan
A Suggestion of Death	Marianne Wesson	Cinda Hayes
Suitable for Framing	Edna Buchanan	Britt Montero
Summer Garden Murder	Ann Ripley	Louise Eldridge
Summer Will End	Dorian Yeager	Elizabeth "Liz" Will
The Sunken Treaure	Marian J. A. Jackson	Abigail Danforth
Sunrise	Chassie West	Leigh Ann Warren
Sunset and Santiago	Gloria White	Ronnie Ventana
A Sunset Touch	Marjorie Eccles	Abigail Moon
Sunshine and Shadow	Earlene Fowler	Albenia "Benni" Harper
The Superintendent's Daughter	Marjorie Eccles	Abigail Moon
A Superior Death	Nevada Barr	Anna Pigeon
Survivor in Death	J. D. Robb	Lt. Eve Dallas
Suspect a.k.a. Deadline	Jennifer Rowe	Tessa Vance
Suspicion of Betrayal	Barbara Parker	Gail Connor

Title of Book	Author	Character
Suspicion of Deceit	Barbara Parker	Gail Connor
Suspicion of Guilt	Barbara Parker	Gail Connor
Suspicion of Innocence	Barbara Parker	Gail Connor
Suspicion of Madness	Barbara Parker	Gail Connor
Suspicion of Malice	Barbara Parker	Gail Connor
Suspicion of Rage	Barbara Parker	Gail Connor
Suspicion of Vengeance	Barbara Parker	Gail Connor
Suture Self	Mary Daheim	Judith McMonigle (Flynn)
Swan for the Money	Donna Andrews	Meg Langslow
Sweet Cherry Wine	Carol Schmidt	Laney Samms
Sweet Dreams, Irene	Jan Burke	Irene Kelly
Sweet Georgia	Ruth Birmingham	Sunny Childs
Sweet Revenge	Diane Mott Davidson	Goldy Bear (Schulz)
Sweet Sixteen	Michael Molloy	Sarah Keane
Sweet Venom	Betty Rowlands	Melissa Craig
Swimming Cat Cove	Lauren Wright Douglas	Allison O'Neil
Switching the Odds	Phyllis Knight	Lil Ritchie
Sympathy for the Devil	Jerrilyn Farmer	Madelyn Bean
T		
The Tail of the Tip-Off	Rita Mae Brown	Mary "Harry" Haristeen & Mrs. Murphy
A Tail of Two Murders	Melissa Cleary	Jackie Walsh
Tailspin	Catherine Coulter	Lacey Savich
A Taint in the Blood	Dana Stabenow	Kate Shugak
Take a Number	Janet Dawson	Jeri Howard
Taken by Storm	Linda Kay Silva	Delta Stevens
Taken to the Cleaners	Dolores Johnson	Mandy Dyer
Taking the Wrap	Dolores Johnson	Mandy Dyer
Take-Out Double a.k.a. Death Takes a Hand	Susan Moody	Cassandra "Cassie" Swann
Takes One to Know One	Kate Allen	Alison Kaine
Talked to Death	Louise Shaffer	Angie DaVito
Talking Rain	Linda French	Teodora "Teddy" Morelli
Tall, Dead, and Handsome	Annie Griffin	Hannah Malloy, Kiki Goldstein
Tang Is Not Juice	Vinnie Hansen	Carol Sabala
A Tangled Knot of Murder	C. F. Roe	Dr. Jean Montrose
Tangled Roots	Taffy Cannon	Nan Robinson
The Target	Catherine Coulter	Lacey Savich
Target for Murder	J. F. Trainor	Angela "Angie" Biwaban
Tarnished Icon	Stuart Kaminsky	Elena Timafeyeva
A Taste for Burning	Jo Bannister	Liz Graham
A Taste for Murder	Claudia Bishop	Sarah "Quill" Quilliam
Taste of Evil	Patricia and Clayton Matthews	Casey Farrel
Tea Time for the Traditionally Built	Alexander McCall Smith	Precious Ramotswe
The Tears of the Giraffe	Alexander McCall Smith	Precious Ramotswe
Tea-Totally Dead	Jaqueline Girdner	Kate Jasper
The Teddy Bear Murders	Janet Harward	Josephine Blake
Tell Me What You Like	Kate Allen	Alison Kaine
Tell No Tales	Eleanor Taylor Bland	Marti MacAlister
Telling Lies	Wendy Hornsby	Maggie MacGowen
The Telltale Turkey Caper	Georgette Livingston	Dr. Jennifer Gray
Ten Big Ones	Janet Evanovich	Stephanie Plum
Ten Little Bloodhounds	Virginia Lanier	Jo Beth Sidden
Ten Little Medicine Men	Bill Pomidor	Dr. Calista "Cal" Marley
Ten Lords A-Leaping	Ruth Dudley Edwards	Baroness "Jack" Troutbeck

Title of Book	Author	Character
The Tenacious Terrier Caper	Georgette Livingston	Dr. Jennifer Gray
Tenoclock Scholar	John Miles	Johnnie Baker
Tensleep	Sarah Andrews	Emily "Em" Hansen
The Tentmaker	Michelle Blake	Rev. Lily Connor
Tequila Mockingbird	Paul Bishop	Fey Croaker
Termination Dust	Sue Henry	Jessie Arnold
The Thai Amulet	Lyn Hamilton	Lara McClintoch
Thai Die	Monica Ferris	Betsy Devonshire
The Thanksgiving Day Murder	Lee Harris	Christine Bennett
That Way Murder Lies	Ann Granger	Meredith "Merry" Mitchell
Them Bones	Carolyn Haines	Sarah Booth Delaney
There Goes the Bride	M. C. Beaton	Agatha Raisin
There Was a Little Girl	Susan Rogers Cooper	E. J. Pugh
Thicker than Water	Rett MacPherson	Victory "Torie" O'Shea
Thin Ice	Joyce Holms	Fizz Fitzpatrick
Think on Death	David Willis McCullough	Rev. Ziza Todd
Think Twice (2010)	Lisa Scottoline	Mary DiNunzio
Third Choice	Margot Dalton	Jackie Kaminsky
Third Time Fatal	Roger Ormerod	Phillipa Lowe
This Business Is Murder	Joyce Christmas	Elizabeth Anne "Betty" Trenka
This Dog for Hire	Carol Lea Benjamin	Rachel Kaminsky Alexander
This Enemy Town	Marcia Talley	Hannah Ives
This Little Piggy Went to Murder	Ellen Hart	Sophie Greenway
This Old Murder	Valerie Wolzien	Josie Pigeon
This Old Souse	Mary Daheim	Judith McMonigle (Flynn)
The Thorne Maze	Karen Harper	Queen Elizabeth I
Thou Shalt Not Grill	Tamar Myers	Magdalena Yoder
Thread of the Spider	Val Davis	Nicolette "Nick" Scott
Three Bedrooms, One Corpse	Charlaine Harris	Aurora "Roe" Teagarden
Three Is a Crowd	D. B. Borton	Catherine "Cat" Caliban
Three to Get Deadly	Janet Evanovich	Stephanie Plum
Three Sisters	James Doss	Daisy Perika
Through a Gold Eagle	Miriam Monfredo	Glynis Tryon
Through the Darkness	Marcia Talley	Hannah Ives
Throw Darts at a Cheesecake	Denise Dietz	Ellie Bernstein
The Thunder Keeper	Margaret Coel	Vicky Holden
Thyme of Death	Susan Wittig Albert	China Bayles
A Ticket to Die For	David J. Walker	Kirsten
The Tidal Poole	Karen Harper	Queen Elizabeth I
Tiger's Palette	Jacqueline Fiedler	Caroline Canfield
Tigers Burning	Crabbe Evers	Petronella "Petey" Biggers
Tight as a Tick	Toni L. P. Kelner	Laura Fleming
Tiles and Tribulations	Tamar Myers	Abigail "Abby" Timberlake
Till the Old Men Die	Janet Dawson	Jeri Howard
Timber City Masks	Kieran York	Royce Madison
Time and Trouble	Gillian Roberts	Billie August, Emma Howe
Time Bomb	Nancy Herndon	Elena Jarvis
Time of Death	Teri Holbrook	Gale Grayson
Time of Death	Shirley Kennett	P. J. Gray
Time of Hope	Susan B. Kelly	Alison Hope
The Time of the Cricket	William Blankenship	Kay Williams
The Time of the Wolf	William Blankenship	Kay Williams
Tip a Canoe	Peter Abresch	Dodee Swisher
Tippy-Toe Murder	Leslie Meier	Lucy Stone
The Titian Committee	Iain Pears	Flavia di Stefano
Toast Mortem (2010)	Claudia Bishop	Sarah "Quill" Quilliam

Title of Book	Author	Character
Toasting Tina	Evan Marshall	Jane Stuart
To Catch a Cook	Joanne Pence	Angelina "Angie" Amalfi
To Davy Jones Below	Carola Dunn	Daisy Dalrymple
To Dream of the Dead	Phil Rickman	Rev. Merrily Watkins
To Live and Die in Dixie	Kathy Hogan Trocheck	Julia "Callahan" Garrity
To Make a Killing	Jean Bedford	Anna Southwood
To Perish in Penzance	Jeanne M. Dams	Dorothy Martin
To Play the Fool	Laurie R. King	Kate Martinelli a.k.a K. C.
To Ruin a Queen	Fiona Buckley	Ursula Blanchard
To Shield the Queen a.k.a. The Robsart Mystery	Fiona Buckley	Ursula Blanchard
To the Nines	Janet Evanovich	Stephanie Plum
To Wear the White Cloak	Sharan Newman	Catherine Le Vendeur
A Toast Before Dying	Grace F. Edwards	Mali Anderson
Tombstone Courage	J. A. Jance	Joanna Brady
Tomorrow's Promise	Lee Roddy	Laurel Bartlett
A Ton of Trouble	Lynne Murray	Josephine Fuller
Too Late for An Angel	Mignon F. Ballard	August Goodnight
Too Many Blondes	Lauren Henderson	Sam Jones
Too Many Cooks	Joanne Pence	Angelina "Angie" Amalfi
Too Many Crooks Spoil the Broth	Tamar Myers	Magdalena Yoder
Too Rich	Melissa Chan	Francesca Miles
Too Soon For Flowers	Margaret Miles	Charlotte Willett
Tool & Die	Sarah Graves	Jacobia Tiptee
The Torment of Others	Val McDermid	Carol Jordan
A Torrid Piece of Murder a.k.a. Fatal Fever	C. F. Roe	Dr. Jean Montrose
Tortoise Soup	Jessica Speart	Rachel Porter
The Total Zone	Martina Navratilova, Liz Nickles	Jordan Myles
Touch Me Not	Betty Rowlands	Sukey Reynolds
A Touch of Mortality	Ann Granger	Merry Mitchell
Touch of Terror	Patricia and Clayton Matthews	Casey Farrel
A Touch of the Grape	Claudia Bishop	Sarah "Quill" Quilliam
Tough Cookie	Diane Mott Davidson	Goldy Bear (Schulz)
Towers of Silence	Cath Staincliffe	Sal Kilkenny
Trace	Patricia D. Cornwell	Dr. Kay Scarpetta
Track of the Cat	Nevada Barr	Anna Pigeon
Track of the Scorpion	Val Davis	Nicolette "Nick" Scott
Tracking Bear	Aimee and David Thurlo	Ella Clah
Tracking Time	Leslie Glass	April Woo
Traggedy Ann	Sinclair Browning	Trade Ellis
Trail of Murder	Christine Andreae	Lee Squires
The Traitor's Tale	Margaret Frazer	Sister Frevisse
Tramp	Marne Davis Kellogg	Lilly Bennett
Trap Door	Sarah Graves	Jacobia Tiptee
The Tree People	Naomi Stokes	Jordan Tidewater
Trial and Retribution	Lynda La Plante	Pat North
Trial and Retribution II	Lynda La Plante	Pat North
Trial and Retribution III	Lynda La Plante	Pat North
Trial and Retribution IV	Lynda La Plante	Pat North
Trial and Retribution V	Lynda La Plante	Pat North
Trial and Retribution VI	Lynda La Plante	Pat North
Trick of Light a.k.a. Trick Shot	David Hunt	Kay Farrow
Trick or Treat Murder	Leslie Meier	Lucy Stone
Triple Witch	Sarah Graves	Jacobia Tiptee

Title of Book	Author	Character
Unequally Yoked	Marilyn Meredith	Tempe Crabtree
The Unexpected Corpse	B. J. Oliphant	Shirley McClintock
Unfinished Business	Barbara Seranella	Munch Mancini
Unfit to Practice	Perri O'Shaughnessy	Nina Reilly
Unhinged	Sarah Graves	Jacobia Tiptee
Unholy Angels	Kate Gallison	Mother Lavinia Grey
Unholy Ghosts	D. M. Greenwood	Rev. Theodora Braithwaite
Unleashed	Laurien Berenson	Melanie Travis
The Unlucky Collie Caper (NA)	Georgette Livingston	Dr. Jennifer Gray
Unlucky in Law	Perri O'Shaughnessy	Nina Reilly
Unnatural Causes	Leah Ruth Robinson	Dr. Evelyn Sutcliffe
Unnatural Exposure	Patricia D. Cornwell	Dr. Kay Scarpetta
Unnatural Instinct	Robert W. Walker	Dr. Jessica Coran
Unpaid Dues	Barbara Seranella	Munch Mancini
Unquestioned Loyalty	J. Dayne Lamb	Teal Stewart
Unraveled Sleeve	Monica Ferris	Betsy Devonshire
Unsafe Harbor	Jessica Speart	Rachel Porter
Unsafe Keeping	Carol Cail	Maxey Burnell
An Unthymely Death (s.s. 2003)	Susan Wittig Albert	China Bayles
Until Death	Polly Whitney	Mary "Ike" Tygart
Until Death Do Us Part	Christine McGuire	Kathryn Mackay
Until It Hurts	Polly Whitney	Mary "Ike" Tygart
Until Judgment Day	Christine McGuire	Kathryn Mackay
Until Justice Is Done	Christine McGuire	Kathryn Mackay
Until Our Last Embrace	Joyce and Jim Levene	Sharyn Howard
Until Proven Guilty	Christine McGuire	Kathryn Mackay
Until the Bough Breaks	Christine McGuire	Kathryn Mackay
Until the Day They Die	Christine McGuire	Kathryn Mackay
Until the End	Kaye Davis	Maris Middleton
Until the End of Time	Polly Whitney	Mary "Ike" Tygart
Until the Final Verdict	Christine McGuire	Kathryn Mackay
Until We Meet Again	Christine McGuire	Kathryn Mackay
Untimely Graves	Marjorie Eccles	Abigail Moon
Unwanted Company	Barbara Seranella	Munch Mancini
Unwilling Accomplice	Barbara Seranella	Munch Mancini
Up in Smoke	Charlene Weir	Susan Donavan Wren
Up Jumps the Devil	Margaret Maron	Deborah Knott
Up Next	Nancy Star	May Morrison
Used to Kill	Lillian O'Donnell	Gwen Ramadge
V		
Vacations Can Be Murder	Connie Shelton	Charlie Parker
Valentine Murder	Leslie Meier	Lucy Stone
The Valentine's Day Murder	Lee Harris	Christine Bennett
Valley of the Shadow	Peter Tremayne	Sister Fidelma
The Vanished Child	Sarah Smith	Perdita Halley
The Vanished Man	Jeffrey Wilds Deaver	Amelia Sachs
Vanishing Act	Barbara Block	Robin Light
Vanishing Act	Thomas Perry	Jane Whitefield
A Veiled Antiquity	Rett MacPherson	"Torie" O'Shea
Vendetta Defense	Lisa Scottoline	"Bennie" Rosato Law Firm
Vendetta's Victim	Alex Matthews	Cassidy McCabe
Vengeance in Death	J. D. Robb	Lt. Eve Dallas
Verdict in Blood	Gail Bowen	Joanne "Jo" Kilbourn
The Verdict on Winter	Eileen Dewhurst	Phyllida Moon
The Verge Practice	Barry Maitland	Sgt. Kathy Kolla
A Very Eligible Corpse	Annie Griffin	Hannah Malloy, Kiki Goldstein

Title of Book	Author	Character
Vi Agra Falls	Mary Daheim	Judith McMonigle (Flynn)
Vial Murders	Marsha Landreth	Dr. Samantha Turner
The Victim in Victoria Station	Jeanne M. Dams	Dorothy Martin
A Vintage Murder	Janet L. Smith	Annie MacPherson
The Violence Beat	Eve K. Sandstrom	Nell Matthews
Virgin Territory	Marilyn Todd	Claudia Seferius
Virtual Memories	Natalie Buske Thomas	Serena Wilcox
Virtual Stranger	Emer Gillespie	Karen McDade
Vision of Death	Patricia and Clayton Matthews	Casey Farrel
Visions of Sugarplums	Janet Evanovich	Stephanie Plum
Voices in the Sand	Anne Underwood Grant	Sydney Teague
Voices in the Wardrobe	Marlys Millhiser	Charlie Green
A Vow of Adoration	Veronica Black	Sister Joan
A Vow of Chastity	Veronica Black	Sister Joan
A Vow of Compassion	Veronica Black	Sister Joan
A Vow of Devotion	Veronica Black	Sister Joan
A Vow of Fidelity	Veronica Black	Sister Joan
A Vow of Obedience	Veronica Black	Sister Joan
A Vow of Penance	Veronica Black	Sister Joan
A Vow of Poverty	Veronica Black	Sister Joan
A Vow of Sanctity	Veronica Black	Sister Joan
A Vow of Silence	Veronica Black	Sister Joan
Vulture	Alex Keegan	Caz Flood
W		
Wait for the Dark	Ann Crowleigh	Clare & Mirinda Cliveley
Wake of the Hornet	Val Davis	Nicolette "Nick" Scott
Wake Up to Murder	Steve Allen	Jayne Meadows
Walk a Crooked Mile	Catherine Dain	Freddie O'Neal
Walk in the Darkness	Jon Land	Danielle Barnea
Walking Dead Man	Mary Kittredge	Edwina Crusoe
The Walls of Jericho	Jon Land	Danielle Barnea
The Wandering Arm	Sharan Newman	Catherine Le Vendeur
The Wandering Soul Murders	Gail Bowen	Joanne "Jo" Kilbourn
Wanted Dude or Alive	Kate Morgan	Dewey James
Wanton's Web	Alex Matthews	Cassidy McCabe
Warning Signs	Stephen White	Lauren Crowder
Wash, Fold, and Die	Dolores Johnson	Mandy Dyer
Watchdog	Laurien Berenson	Melanie Travis
Watching Out	Ann Granger	Fran Varaday
Water Like a Stone	Deborah Crombie	Gemma James
Wavewalker	Stella Duffy	Saz Martin
Way of the Traitor	Laura Joh Rowland	Reiko Ichiro
We Know Where You Live	Jean Taylor	Maggie Garrett
Weathering the Storm	Linda Kay Silva	Delta Stevens
Wed and Buried	Mary Daheim	Judith McMonigle (Flynn)
Wed And Buried	Toni L. P. Kelner	Laura Fleming
Wedding Day Murder	Leslie Meier	Lucy Stone
The Wedding Game	Susan Holtzer	Anneke Haagen
Wedding's Widow	Alex Matthews	Cassidy McCabe
Weigh Dead	Jean Hager	Tess Darcy
Weighed in the Balance	Anne Perry	Hester Latterly (Monk)
We'll Always Have Parrots	Donna Andrews	Meg Landslow
What Are You Wearing to Die?	Patricia Houck Sprinkle	MacLaren Yarbrough
What Big Giver Stole the Chopped Liver	Sharon Kahn	Ruby Rothman
What Evil Lurks	James R. McCahery	Lavinia London

Title of Book	Author	Character
What Lies Within (2010)	S. D. Tooley	Samantha "Sam" Casey
What's a Girl Gotta Do?	Sparkle Hayter	Robin Hudson
Whatever Doesn't Kill You	Gillian Roberts	Billie August, Emma Howe
Whatever Happened to Jennifer Steele?	Jean Ruryk	Catherine "Cat" Wilde
When Day Breaks	Mary Jane Clark	Eliza Blake
When Death Comes Stealing	Valerie Wilson Wesley	Tamara Hayle
When Shadows Fall	Patricia Rushford	Helen Bradley
When the Dead Speak	S. D. Tooley	Samantha "Sam" Casey
When the Fax Lady Sings	Leslie O'Kane	Molly Masters
When Wallflowers Die	Sandra West Prowell	Phoebe Seigel
When Will the Dead Lady Sing?	Patricia Houck Sprinkle	MacLaren Yarbrough
Where Did We Lose Harriet?	Patricia Houck Sprinkle	MacLaren Yarbrough
Where Evil Sleeps	Valerie Wilson Wesley	Tamara Hayle
Where Memories Lie	Deborah Crombie	Gemma James
Where Old Bones Lie	Ann Granger	Merry Mitchell
Where Roses Fade	Andrew Taylor	Jill Francis
Where the Bodies Are Buried	Janet Dawson	Jeri Howard
Where There's a Will	Elizabeth Daniels Squire	Peaches Dann
Where to Choose	Penny Mickelbury	Carole Ann Gibson
Whiplash (2010)	Catherine Coulter	Lacey Savich
Whisker of Evil	Rita Mae Brown	Mary "Harry" Haristeen
Whiskey Jack	J. F. Trainor	Angela "Angie" Biwaban
Whisper to the Blood	Dana Stabenow	Kate Shugak
A Whisper to the Living	Stuart Kaminsky	Elena Timofeyeva
Whisper...He Might Hear You	William Appel	Kate Berman
Whispers in the Dark	Eleanor Taylor Bland	Marti MacAlister
The White Elephant Caper	Georgette Livingston	Dr. Jennifer Gray
White Harvest	Louis Charbonneau	Kathy McNeely
White Lies	Anna Salter	Dr. Michael Stone
White Shell Woman	James Doss	Daisy Perika
White Thunder	Aimee and David Thurlo	Ella Clah
Who Invited the Dead Man?	Patricia Houck Sprinkle	MacLaren Yarbrough
Who Killed Blanche DuBois?	Carole Bugge	Claire Rawlings
Who Killed Dorian Gray?	Carole Bugge	Claire Rawlings
Who Killed Marilyn Monroe?	Liz Evans	Grace Smith
Who Killed Mona Lisa?	Carole Bugge	Claire Rawlings
Who Killed the Queen of Clubs?	Patricia Houck Sprinkle	MacLaren Yarbrough
Who Killed What's-Her-Name?	Elizabeth Daniels Squire	Peaches Dann
Who Left That Body in the Rain?	Patricia Houck Sprinkle	MacLaren Yarbrough
Who Let That Killer in the House?	Patricia Houck Sprinkle	MacLaren Yarbrough
Who Was Sylvia?	Carol Cail	Maxey Burnell
Who's Afraid of Virginia Ham?	Phyllis Richman	Chas Wheatley
Who's Sorry Now	Jill Churchill	Lily Brewster
Whose Death Is It, Anyway?	Elizabeth Daniels Squire	Peaches Dann
Why Kill the Magistrate?	Patricia Houck Sprinkle	MacLaren Yarbrough
Wicked Craving (2010)	G. A. McKevett	Savannah Reid
Wicked Fix	Sarah Graves	Jacobia Tiptee
The Wicked Flea	Susan Conant	Holly Winter
A Wicked Way to Burn	Margaret Miles	Charlotte Willett
Wicked Witch Murder	Leslie Meier	Lucy Stone
A Wide and Capable Revenge	Thomas McCall	Nora Callum
Widowmaker	William Appel	Kate Berman
The Widow's Revenge	James Doss	Daisy Perika
The Widow's Tale	Margaret Frazer	Sister Frevisse
Widows' Watch	Nancy Herndon	Elena Jarvis

Title of Book	Author	Character
The Wrong Dog	Carol Lea Benjamin	Rachel Kaminsky Alexander
Wrongful Death	Catherine Arnold	Karen Perry-Mondori
A Wrongful Death	Kate Wilhelm	Barbara Holloway
The Wyndham Case	Jill Paton Walsh	Imogen Quy
X		
The Xibalba Murders	Lyn Hamilton	Lara McClintoch
Y		
The Year 2000 Killers	Wanda Wardell Morrone	Lorelei Muldoon
Yesterday's Shadows	Lee Roddy	Laurel Bartlett
The Yom Kippur Murder	Lee Harris	Christine Bennett
You Bet Your Life	Christine T. Jorgensen	Stella the Stargazer a.k.a. Jane Smith
You Have the Right to Remain Puzzled	Parnell Hall	Cora Felton & Sherry Carter
You Only Die Twice	Edna Buchanan	Britt Montero
Z		
Zapped	Carol Higgins Clark	Regan Reilly
Zen and the Art of Murder	Desmond Cory	Kate Coyle
Zen and the City of Angles	Desmond Cory	Kate Coyle
Zen Attitude	Sujata Massey	Rei Shimura

Mystery Women Chronology 1860-1999

Year in which female character made first published appearance in a novel or collection of short stories. The chronological listing of female sleuths refers to first significant appearance. An asterisk (*) indicates that the character made at least three appearances in books that are clearly mysteries and that were published before December 31, 2001. © Indicates copyright date, used when publication date was unavailable. U.K. indicates the date was published in the United Kingdom; U.S. indicates the date of publication in the United States; CAN indicates the date of publication in Canada; AUS indicates the date of publication in Australia.

Volume 1

1861: Mrs. Paschal

1864: Mrs. G.

1875: Valeria Woodville

1884: Madeline Payne

1894: Loveday Brooke

1895: Caroline "Cad" Mettie

1897: Amelia Butterworth*; Dorcas Dene

1898: Hagar Stanley

1899: Lois Cayley; Madame Katherine Koluchy

1900: Dora Myrl*; Hilda Wade

1903: Madame Sara

1905: Mary J. "Polly" Burton; Henrietta Van Raffles

1906: Frances Baird

1910: Lady Molly Robertson-Kirk

1911: Letitia "Tish" Carberry

1912: Judith Lee

1913: Constance Dunlap ©; Ruth Fielding*

1914: Madelyn Mack; Mercedes Quero*

1915: Molly Morganthau*; Violet Strange

1917: Millicent Newberry*; Evelyn Temple; Olga von Kopf

1922: Prudence "Tuppence" Beresford*

1923: Rosie Bright; Sylvia Shale

1924: Fidelity Dove

1925: Eileen "Bundle" Brent; Sophie Lang; Blue Jean Billy Race; Madame Rosika Storey*

1926: Juliet Jackson*

1927: Meg Garret*; Leslie Maughan (U.S.); Jane Ollerby

1928: Angela Bredon; Lynn MacDonald*

1929: Dame Adela Beatrice Lestrange Bradley*; Four Square Jane; Sarah Keate*; Maud Silver* (U.S.)

1930: Nancy Drew*; Ellen Gilchrist Soames; Gwynn Leith Keats; Gail McGurk*; Jane Marple*; Kate Marsh*; Polack Annie; Harriet Vane*; Louisa Woolfe*; Daphne Wrayne*

1931: Fah Lo Suee*; Solange Fontaine; Prudence Whitby ; Hildegarde Withers*

1932: Hilda Adams*; Avis Bryden*; Angeline Tredennick; Mrs. Caywood "Julia" Weston

1933: Amanda Fitton Campion; Lizzie Collins*; Olga Knaresbrook; Della Street; Mrs. Elizabeth Warrender*

1934: Nora Charles; Clarice Claremont; Susan Dare; Peggy Fairfield; Anne Layton; Ariadne Oliver*; Alice Penny; Matilda Townsend*

1935: Jane Amanda Edwards*; Penny Mercer*; Matilda Perks; Palmyra Pym*

1936: Iris Pattison Duluth*; Baroness Clara Linz (U.S.); Anne Holt McNeill*; Dr. Joan Marvin; Georgia Cavendish Strangeways; Ethel Thomas*

1937: Adelaide Adams; Theolinda "Dol" Bonner; Carey Brent*; Patricia "Pat" Preston Cordry*; Grace Latham*; Anne "Davvie" Davenport McLean*; Daisy Jane Mott; Lucy Mott (U.S.); Tamara Valeshoff

1938: Agatha Troy Alleyn; Mary Carner*; Kay Cornish*; Valerie Dundas; Coco Hastings; Carole Trevor; Lace White*

1939: Hilea Bailey*; Janet "Janie" Allen Barron*; Bertha Cool*; Helene Brand Justus*; Sue MacVeigh*; Emma Marsh*; Rachel and Jennifer Murdoch*; Anne Seymour Webb; Susan Yates*

1940: Ethel Abbott; Amanda and Lutie Beagle; Margot Blair*; Jane Carberry*; Elsie Mae Hunt*; Pamela "Pam" North*; Miss Mabie Otis*; Katherine "Peter" Piper*; Haila Rogers Troy*; Sister Ursula; Agatha Welch

1941: Jean Holly Abbott*; Eleanora Burke; Gypsy Rose Lee; Sarah O'Brien; Andrea Reid Ramsay; Hannah Van Doren*; Kitty McLeod Whitney*

1942: Arabella "Arab" Blake*; Louise "Liz" Boykin Parrott*; Grace Pomeroy

1943: Christine Andersen; Georgine Wyeth McKinnon; Doris "Dodo" Trent and Nell Witter*

1944: Kit Marsden Acton*; Judy Ashbane; Maria Black*; Lorna Donahue; Vicky Gaines; Lady Lapin Hastings*; Abbie Harris*; Bessie Petty and Beulah Pond*

1945: Nora Hughes Blaine; Amy Brewster*; Dr. Mary Finney*; Jenny Gillette Lewis*; Katherine Forrester Vigneras

1946: Elizabeth; Eve MacWilliams; Maggie Slone; Tessie Venable

1947: Hortense Clinton*; Gale Gallagher; Suzanne "Suzy" Marshall; Lucy Pym; Terry Terence*; Julia Tyler*

1948: Jane Hamish Brown*; Eve Gill*

1949: Miriam Birdseye* and Natasha Nevkorina*; Emily Murdoch Bryce*; Janice Cameron and Lily Wu*; Marka de Lancey*

1950: Sumuru*; Ma Tellford*; Hilda Trenton

1951: Petunia Best; Liane "Lee" Craufurd*; Shirley Leighton Harper*; Laura Scudamore, The Sinister Widow*; Ginger Tintagel; Sarah Vanessa*

1952: Ann McIntosh*

1953: Nell Bartlett; Norma "Nicky" Lee*

1954: Sally Dean; Sally Strang*

1955: Miss Flora Hogg*; Mavis Seidlitz*; English translations of Souer Angele*

1956: Eileen Burke*; Sally Merton Heldar*; Marion Kerrison; Julia Probyn*; Daye Smith*

1957: Mrs. Annie Norris*; Honey West*

1958: Mother Paul*; Elizabeth "Liz" Doane

1959: Arabella Frant; Madame Maigret; Kate Starte; Marla Trent

1960: Forsythia Brown*; Kate Harris; Emmy Tibbett* (U.S.)

1962: Myra Savage (U.S.)

1963: Hillary Brand*; June Beattie Grant

1964: Telzey Amberdon*; Maxene Dangerfield*; Charmian Daniels*(U.S.); Kate Fansler*; Mary Morgan Kelly*; Sue Carstairs Maddox; Selena Mead

1965: Modesty Blaise*; Jane Boardman; Amanda Curzon*; Emma Greaves*; Anna Zordan*

1966: Sibyl Sue Blue; Mrs Elma Craggs (U.S.); Lee Crosley*; April Dancer*; Emily Pollifax*; Effie Schlupe*

1967: Madame Dominique Aubry (U.S.); Felicia Dawlish; Eve Drum*; Julia Homberg*; Freya Matthews; Emma Peel*; Sylvia Plotkin*; Regina; Charity Ross; Paola Smith; Lucilla Edith Cavell Teatime*

1968: Julie Barnes of Mod Squad*; Angel Brown*; Bernarda "Bunty" Felse* (U.S.) Dominique Frayne; Tracy Larrimore*; Amanda Nightingale*; Stevie O'Dowda; Christie Opara*; Miss Emily Seeton*; Dr. Grace Severance*; Katy Touchfeather

1969: Lisa Clark*; Gail Rogers Mitchell; Jennifer Norrington* (U.K.); Claudine St. Cyr*; Kate Theobald*

1970: Tessa Crichton* (U.K.); Kiss Darling*; Millicent Hetherege; Hon. Constance Morrison-Burke*; Deirdre O'Connor; Sheila Roath; Charity Tucker*

1971: Cherry Delight*; Donna Bella*; Cynthia Godwin; Lucy Ramsdale*; Helga Rolfe*(U.K.); Kitty Telefair*

1972: Lucy Beck*; Arlette Van Der Valk Davidson*; Laurie Grant*; Cordelia Gray (U.K.); Jacqueline Kirby*; Octavia "Tavy" Martin (U.S.); Norah Mulcahaney*; Hilary Quayle*

1973: Vicky Bliss*; Thea Crawford; Helen Blye Horowitz*; Cleopatra Jones; Melinda Pink*; Baroness Penelope St. John-Orsini*

1974: Shauna Bishop*; Vera Castang; Catherine Alexander Douglas*; Rosa Epton* (U.S.); Ann Fielding Hales; Susan Silverman*; Kate Weatherly*

1975: Pepper Anderson*; Claire Reynolds Atwell*; Helen Bullock*; Constance Cobble; Amelia Peabody Emerson*; Angela Harpe*; Ms Squad; Dr. Nora North*; Molly Owens*; Minnie Santangelo; Bea Wentworth*

1976: Jannine Austin*; Edwina Charles* (U.K.); Julie Hayes*; Hannah Land; Natasha O'Brien; Lexey Jane Pelazoni; Anna Peters*; Rebecca Rosenthal; Jaime Sommers (The Bionic Woman); Morgan Studevant

1977: Mici Anhalt*; Jana Blake; Charlie's Angels*; Betty Crighton Jones*; Sharon McCone*; Jemima Shore*; Persis Willum*

1978: Marilyn Ambers*; Kay Barth*; Tory Baxter*; Margaret Binton*; Dulcie Bligh; Darby Castle; Virginia Freer*; Helen Keremos*; Hildy Pace*; Maxine Reynolds*; Delia Riordan*; Sarah Saber; Helen Marsh Shandy; Terry Spring*

1979: Adrienne Bishop; Janna Brill*; Cody* (U.K.); Maggie Courtney*; Charlotte Eliot; Margo Franklin*; Carol Gates*; Alison B. Gordon*; Kate Graham; Anna Jugedinski*; Sarah Kelling*; Valerie Lambert*; Ann Lang; Pauline Lyons*; Megan Marshall; Charlotte Ellison Pitt*; Maggie Rome*; Penelope Spring*; Julia Sullivan; Nell Willard

Volume 2

1980: T. T. Baldwin*; Juliet Bravo* a.k.a. Jean Darblay; Ginny Fistoulari*; Karen Kovacs*; Clarissa Lovelace*; Joan Stock*; Amy Tupper; Alicia Von Helsing; Janet Wadman (Rhys)*; Delilah West*

1981: Cathy McVeigh Carter*; Sr. Mary Theresa "Emtee" Dempsey*; Fiona Fitzgerald*; Davina Graham* (U.S.); Lt. Sigrid Harald*; Dittany Henbit; Viera Kolarova; Julia Larmore, Selena Jardine, and perhaps Hilary Tamar*; Anna Lee* (U.S.); Jill Smith*; Lizzie Thomas* (U.S.); Lettie Winterbottom*

1982: Charity Day; Sarah Deane*; Maggie Elliott*; Sgt. Carollee Fleetwood; Tamara Hoyland* (U.S.); Helen Markham; Kinsey Millhone*; Eugenia Potter*; Rebecca Schwartz*; Nila Wade*; V. I. Warshawski*

1983: Mona Moore Dunbar; Norma Gold*; Jennifer Grey*; Judy Hill*; Roz Howard*; Cass Jameson*; Kyra Keaton; Elena Olivarez*; Julie Tendler Oliver; Jocelyn O'Roarke*; Bridget O'Toole*; Dolly Rawlins (U.K.); Fiona Kimber-Hutchinson Samson* (U.S.); Harriet Unwin*; Rosie Vicente*; Elizabeth Lamb Worthington*

1984: Gillian Adams*; Lauren Adler; Rev. Claire Aldington*; Sarah Cable*; Jenny Cain*; Agnes Carmichael* (U.S.); Iris Cooper*; Kate Delafield*; Vejay Haskell*; Rachel Hennings; Sgt. Hilary Lloyd (U.S.); Elizabeth MacPherson*; Dr. Tina May*; Patience "Pay" McKenna*; Mary Frances "M. F" Mulrooney; Pam Nilsen*; Sr. Mary Helen O'Connor and Kate Murphy*; Amelia Trowbridge Patton (U.S.); Andrea Perkins*; Deb Ralston*; Clio Rees (Marsh)*; Eleanor Roosevelt*; Abigail "Sandy" Sanderson*; Ellie Simon (Haskell)*; Ms Michael Tree*

1985: Belle Appleman; Liz Archer a.k.a. Angel Eyes*; Kate Baeier* (U.S.); Susan Bright*; Sabina Carpenter; Liz Connors*; Serendipity "Sarah" Dahlquist; Donna Miro and Lorna Doria; Geraldine Farrar; Jessica Fletcher*; Fiora Flynn*; Paula Glenning*; Glad Gold; Ellie Gordon*; Celia Grant* (U.S.); Marion Larch*; Isabel Macintosh*; Stoner McTavish*; Michelle Merrill*; Cassandra Mitchell*; Rain Morgan*; Theresa "Terri" Morrison; J. D. Mulroy; Rita Gardella O'Dea; Deirdre O'Hara* (CAN); Celia Prentisse; Maggie Ryan*; Rachel Sabin; Lucy Shannon; Gertrude Stein and Alice B. Toklas; Kate Trevorne; Alexandra "Alex" Winter; Matilda Worthing*

1986: Jane Britland; Rosie Caesare; Sarah Calloway*; Doran Fairweather*; Theresa Fortunato; Cynthia Frost; Judith Hayes (U.S.); Calista Jacobs*; Gwen Jones*; Rina Lazarus (Decker)*; Denise Lemoyne; Claire Malloy*; Tish McWhinny*; Susan Melville*; Debbie Miles*; Kate Miskin; Ella Nidech; Molly Palmer-Jones*; Molly Rafferty*; Joan Spencer*; Joanna Stark*; Penny Wananwake* (U.S.)

1987: Finny Aletter; Jane Bailey*; Maggie Bennett*; Mavis Bignell* (U.S.); Dr. Marissa Blumenthal; Carlotta Carlyle*; Marlene Ciampi (Karp)*; Lisa Davis; A. J. Egan; Lindsay Gordon*; Lonia Guiu (U.S.); Meg Halloran*; Arly Hanks*; Jennifer Heath*; Nikki Holden; Bonnie Indermill*; Willa Jansson*; Charlotte Kent*; Raina Lambert*; Annie Laurance (Darling)*; Constance Leidl*; Daisy Marlow; Alvira Meehan*; Melita Pargeter* (U.S.); Amanda Pepper*; Caitlin Reese*; Countess Aline Griffith Romanones*; Quin St. James*; Sara Spooner; Dee Street* (U.K.); Dixie Flannigan Struthers*; Kate Byrd Teague; Anna Tyree*; Dee Vaughn*; Emma Victor*; Jane Winfield (Hall)*

1988: Samantha Adams*; Carol Ashton*; Angela Benbow and Caledonia Wingate*; Kori Price Brichter*; Sydney Bryant*; Angel Cantini; Laura Di Palma*; Trixie Dolan and Evangeline Sinclair* (U.S.); Lydia Fairchild*; Kit Franklyn*; Ingrid Langley Gilliard* (U.S.); Rachel Gold*; Neil Hamel*; Barbara Havers*; Susan Henshaw*; Sara Joslyn; Meg Lacey; Loretta Lawson* (U.S.); Kate Maddox*; Daphne Matthews*; Georgia Lee Maxwell; Nina McFall*; Mom*; Karen Orr; Claire Parker* (U.S.); Marvia Plum*; Lady Margaret Priam*; Catherine Sayler*; Aline Scott*; Hana Shaner; Veronica Sheffield; Veronica Slate*; Sabina Swift; Tina Tamiko; Ann Tate; Sally Tepper; Sheila Travis*; Jane Tregar; Claudia Valentine* (AUS.); Gillian Verdean*; Evelyn Wade

1989: Beth Austin*; Margaret Barlow*; Bertha Barstow; Martha "Moz" Brant*; Rhea Buerklin; Emma Chizzit*; Kat Colorado*; Katharine Craig; Sandrine Casette Curry*; Dr. Janet Eldine (U.S.); Nina Fischman*; Phryne Fisher* (AUS); Anne Fitzhugh; Sgt. Molly Flanagan; Sarah Fortune*; Clara Dawson Gamadge*; Peg Goodenough; Blanche Hampton*; Kate Henry* (U.S.); Lady Jane Hildreth* (U.S.); Maggie Hill and Claire Conrad; Zee Madeiras Jackson; Harriet Jeffries*; Jane Jeffry*; Helena Justina*; Jennifer Terry Kaine*; Mavis Lashley*; Jane Lawless*; Darina Lisle* (U.K.); LuEllen*; Sheila Malory*; Dawn Markey; Chris Martin* (U.K.); Jennie McKay*; Rosie Monaghan (AUS); Cassie Newton; Rita Noonan; Abby Novack (McKenzie)*; Lee Ofsted*; Peggy O'Neill*; Kieran O'Shaughnessy*; Carrie Porter; Georgina Powers* (U.K.); Anabel Reed (Smith)*; Amanda Roberts*; Rune*; Emma Shaw (U.S.); Lisa Thomas (AUS); Diane Tregarde*; Helen West; Leslie Wetzon and Xenia Smith*; Johanna "Jo" Wilder; Grace Willis; Francesca Wilson* (U.S.); Miriam Winchester

Volume 3

The following is a preliminary expectation of sleuths to be covered in the final volume of the series. Whether or not a character has made three or more appearances is based upon information through November 2001. A third book may have been published subsequent to December 2008. New series were added regularly as work on Volume 3 continued.

1990: Irene Adler*; Gabrielle "Gabe" Amato; Connie Bartholomew*; Goldy Bear (Schulz)*; Mildred Bennett*; Helen Black*; Claire Breslinsky*; Paris Chandler; Edwina Crusoe*; Lark Dailey (Dodge)*; Abigail Danforth*; Poppy Dillworth*; Flavia Di Stefano*; Brigid Donovan*; Faith Sibley Fairchild*; Charlotte Graham*; Mary Minor "Harry" Haristeen*; Alison Hope*; Jerusha "Jeri" Howard*; Dewey James*; Jessica "Jesse" James*; Jazz Jasper*; Sister Joan*; Joanne "Jo" Kilbourn* (CAN); Michelle "Micky" Knight*; Skip Langdon*; Hester Latterly*; Lavinia London; Philipa Lowe* (U.K.); Annie MacPherson*; Cat Marsala*; Shirley McClintock*; Madison McGuire*; Jayne Meadows*; Alice Nestleton*; Chicago Nordejoong*; Patricia "Pat" Pratt*; Gwenn Ramadge*; Lucia Ramos; Cassandra Reilly*; Kay Scarpetta*; Aurora "Roe" Teagarden*; Nicky Titus*; Nikki Trakos; Holly Winter*

1991: Jessie Arnold*; Sophia "Sophy" Bancroft; Dr. Kate Berman; Petronella "Petey" Biggers*; Verity "Birdie" Birdwood*; Julie Blake*; Nell Bray*; Hollis Carpenter; Midge Cohen; Dr. Kate Coyle*; Melissa Craig*; Lauren Crowder*; Molly DeWitt*; Phrynne Fisher*; Jan Gallagher*; Simona Griffo*; Dr. Bernadette "Bernie" Hebert; Barbara Holloway*; Lil Hubbert*; Kate Jasper*; Virginia Kelly*; Libby Kincaid*; Willow King*; Amanda Knight; Lauren Laurano*; Whitney Logan*; Devon MacDonald*; Wanda Mallory*; Judith McMonigle (Flynn)*; Kathy McNeely; Francesca Miles*; Robin Miller*; Meredith "Merry" Mitchell*; Lane Montana; Kate Mulcay (one earlier book in 1958 as Kate Kincaid)*; Kathleen "Kit" Powell; Danielle "Dani" Ross*; Cynthia Chenery "C. C." Scott; Anna Southwood (AUS)*; Delta Stevens*; Blaine Stewart*; Lucy Stone*; Jane Tennison* in U.K.; Rev. Ziza Todd; Ginny Trask; Ronnie Ventana*; Liz Wareham; Fanny Zindel

1992: Kristin Ashe*; Temple Barr*; China Bayles*; Molly Bearpaw*; Becky Belski; Christine Bennett*; Eleanor "Ellie" Bernstein*; Constable Judy Best*; Elizabeth Blair*; Joanna Blalock*; Nora Bonesteel*; Victoria "Vic" Bowering*; Rev. Theodora Braithwaite*; Smokey Brandon*; Harriet Bushrow*; Rosalie Cairns*; Claire Camden*; Beth Marie Cartwright*; Dr. Jessica Coran*; Karen Crist*; Victoria Cross; Jane Da Silva*; Molly De Witt*; Mary DiNunzio*Catherine Edison; Elizabeth Elliot*; Casey Farrel*; Sister Frevisse*; Leslie Frost; Nell Fury*; Julia "Callahan" Garrity*; Liz Graham*; Charlie Greene*; Liz Gresham*; Perdita Halley*; Blanche Hampton*; Laura Ireland; Alison Kaine*; Sarah Keane*; Lucy Kingsley*; Kate Kinsella in U.S.*; Deborah Knott*; Emma Lord*; Marti MacAlister*; Maggie MacGowen*; Caroline Masters*; Christina McCall*; Annie McGrogan; Laura Michaels*; Kate Millholland*; Britt Montero*; Dr. Jean Montrose in U. S.*; Freddie O'Neal*; Maddy Phillips*; E.J. (Eloise Janine) Pugh*; Agatha Raisin*; Regan Reilly*; Lil Ritchie; Maxene St. Clair*; Charlotte Sams; Beth Seibelli (Cole)*; Claire Sharples*; Kate Shugak*; Diana Speed; Lee Squires*; Jane Tennison*; Elena Timofeyeva*; Glynis Tryon*; Dr. Samantha Turner*; Amanda Valentine*; Jackie Walsh*; Aunt Dimity Westwood and Lori Shepherd*; Blanche White*; Hannah Wolfe*; Susan Donavan Wren*

1993: Laura Ackroyd*; Angelina Amalfi*; Angela Biwaban*; Barbara "Bo" Bradley*; Joanna Brady*; Kate Brannigan*; Sr. Cecile Buddenbrooke*; Caley

Burke*; Maxey Burnell*; Cat Caliban*; Nora Callum; Cliveley Sisters; Nancy Clue and Cherry Aimless*; Henrietta "Henrie" O'Dwyer Collins*; Nancy Cook; Flavia Di Stefano*; Jessica Drake*; Kay Engels; Laura Fleming*; Insp. Liz Graham*; Amanda Hazard*; Martine "Marty" Hopkins*; Jo Hughes*; Leah Hunter*; Kate Ivory*; Gemma James*; Hepzipah Jeffries*; Claire Jenner (Claiborne)*; Tyler Jones*; Irene Kelly*; "Kimmey" Kruse; Barrett Lake*; Catherine Le Vendeur*; Wynsome "Wyn" Lewis*; Kathryn Mackay*; Kate MacLean; Royce Madison; Casey/Kate Martinelli*; Dr. Lauren Maxwell*; Dr. Anna McColl (U.K.)*; Alix Nicholson; Jane Perry*; Anna Pigeon*; Dr. Amy Prescott*; Gin Prettifield; Imogen Quy*; Nan Robinson*; Laney Samms*; Phoebe Siegel*; Cecily Sinclair*; Sydney Sloane*; Teal Stewart*; Sgt Stone*; Catherine Swinbrooke*; Alex Tanner*; Iris Thorne*; Elizabeth Anne "Betty" Trenka*; Robin Vaughn*; Madame Victoire Vernet; Dr. Anne Vernon; Lucy D'Arby Wilton (Archer)*; April Woo*; Eve Wylie (U.S.)*

1994: Kathryn "Kate" Ardleigh*; Cat Austen*; Kate Austen*; Johnnie Baker; Thea Barlow*; Nora Bonesteel*; Dr. Liz Broward; Charlotte Carter; Brooke Cassidy (Devlin)*; Molly Cates*; Olivia Chapman; Emily Charters*; Lydia Chin*; Gail Connor*; Candi and Simone Covington*; Fey Croaker*; Daisy Dalrymple*; Peaches Dann*; Tess Darcy*; Queenie Davilov; Angie DaVito; Patricia Delaney*; Louise Eldridge*; Eve Elliott*; Lynn Evans; Phoebe Fairfax (CAN)*; Jo Farewell; Sister Fidelma*; Caz Flood (U.K.)*; Merry Folger*; Margo Fortier*; Vicki Garcia; Angela Gennaro*; Sophie Greenway*; Mackenzie Griffin*; Anneke Haagen*; Marina Haines; Em Hansen*; Benni Harper*; Matilda Haycastle*; Tamara Hayle*; Karen Hightower a.k.a. Bast*; Samantha Holt*; Sara Howard; Harriet Hubbley (CAN)*; Robin Hudson*; Jo Hughes (U.S.)*; Sal Kilkenny* (U.K.); Michelle "Mickey" Knight*; Sgt. Kathy Kolla* (U.K.); Thea Kozak*; Robin Light*; Margaret Loftus; Dottie Loudermilk*; Joanna MacKenzie*; Gianna "Anna" Maglione*; Sgt Kathleen Mallory*; Saz Martin*; Angela Matelli*; Dr. Gail McCarthy*; Nuala Anne McGrail*; Elizabeth "Tenny" Mendoza; Tori Miracle*; Kate Murray; Jordan Myles*; Deirdre "Didi" Nightingale*; Kathleen O'Shaunessey; in some books spelled O'Shaughnessy*; Veronica Pace*; Lorraine Page*; Daisy Perika*; Stephanie Plum*; Laura Principal*; Sarah "Quill" Quillam*; Carmen Ramirez; Tammi Randall*; Mary Russell (Holmes)*; Desiree "Dez" Shapiro*; Emily Silver; Liz Sullivan*; Jane Smith a.k.a. Stella the Stargazer*; Emily Stone*; Cassandra Swann*; Baroness Jake Troutbeck;*; Alix Thorssen*; Mary "Ike" Tygart*; Leigh Ann Warren*; Penelope Warren*; Catherine "Cat" Wilde*; Elizabeth "Liz" Will; Jolie Wyatt*; Magdalena Yoder*; Wilhelmina "Helma" Zukas*

1995: Hannah Barlow*; Ginger Barnes*; Lilly Bennett*; Sonora Blair*; Mariah Bolt; Sister Agnes Bourdillon; Bel Carson*; Dr. Elizabeth Chase*; Ella Clah*; Cheryl Crane*; Eve Dallas*; Angie Da Vito; Jane Day*; Kay Engels; Colleen Fitzgerald; Jill Francis*; Maggie Garrett; Ariel Gold*; Natalie Gold*; Jennifer Gray*; Gale Grayson*; Mother Lavinia Grey*; Mackenzie Griffin*; Elizabeth Halperin; Kate Harrod*; Sharon Hays*; Helen Hewitt (U.K.); Holly-Jean Ho*; Vicky Holden*; Liz James*; Elena Jarvis*; Caroline "Fremont" Jones*; Samantha "Sam" Jones*; Carol Jordan (GB)*; Sara Kingsley; Fran Tremaine Kirk*; Dee Laguerre; Dr. Calista "Cal" Marley*; Dorothy Martin*; Tally McGinniss*; Cal Meredith; Ophelia Meredith; Lydia Miller; Michelle "Mitch" Mitchell*; Jordan Myles*; Megan O'Malley; Phyllida Moon*;

Charolotte "Charlie" Parker*; Joanna Piercy*; the Quilliam sisters*; Garner Quinn*; Savannah Reid*; Nina Reilly*; Schuyler Ridgway*; Sophie Rivers*; Benedetta "Bennie" Rosato*; Dr. Meredith "Mere" Sanger*; Claudia Seferius*; Jo Beth Sidden*; Margo Simon*; Marguerite Smith*; Dr. Sylvia Strange*; Judith Thornton*; Jordan Tidewater; Melanie Travis*; Jane Turner; Jane Whitefield*; Kate Wilkinson*; Kay Williams; Francesca "Fran" Wilson* (U.S.); (1993 in U.K.)

1996: Rachel Kaminsky Alexander*; Margit Andersson; Cat Austen*; Jane Austen*; Hollis Ball* (U.K.); Lily Bard*; Tory Bauer; Vicky Bauer*; Jane Bee*; Josephine Blake*; Lindsay Chamberlain*; Alexandra Cooper*; Ruby Crane*; Ruby Dark; Venus Diamond*; Starletta Duvall*; Suze Figuera*; Fizz Fitzgerald*; Lucy Freers; Theresa Galloway*; Sen. Eleanor Gorzack; Dr. P. J. Gray*; Beth Hartley*; Dido Hoare*; Mrs. Emma Hudson*; Cassidy James*; Texana Jones*; Lady Aoi; Julia Lambros*; Renee LaRoche; Heaven Lee*; Lt. Tory Lennox, USCG; Molly Masters*; Cassidy McCabe*; Dr. Anne Menlo; Abigail Moon*; Kali O'Brien*; Alison O'Neil; Dr. Andi Pauling*; Karen Perry-Mondori*; Josie Pigeon*; Caro Radcliffe; Emma Rhodes*; Benedetta "Benny" Rosato*; Nicolette "Nick" Scott*; Barbara Simons; Guadalupe "Lupe" Solano*; Dr. Kellen Stewart*; the Tate Sisters (Patricia Anne Hollowell and Mary Alice Crane)*; *; Bert and Nan Tatum*; Abby Timberlake*; Hannah Trevor*; Captain Rita Trible; Lucy Trimble; Lucy Wayles*; Fiona Wooten "Biggie" Weatherford*; Molly West; Ruth Willmarth*

1997: Mali Anderson*; Lady Susanna Appleton*; Kate Banning*; Danielle Barnea*; Miriam Bartimaeus; Elizabeth "Lisbee" Billings; Ursula Blanchard*; Helen Bradley* Dr. Celeste Braun*; Temperance "Tempe" Brennan*; Filomena "Fil" Buscarsela*; Dr. Clare Burtonall*; Sister Rose Callahan*; Letty Campbell*; Jane Candiotti*; Carrie Carlin*; Kate Cavanaugh*; Rachel Crowne; Meg Darcy*; Maggie Dillitz*; Delilah Doolittle*; Lady Alix Dunraven*; Mandy Dyer*; Kay Farrow; Lucy Freers; Josephine "Jo" Fuller*; ; P. J. Gray*; Judy Hammer and Virginia West*; Nanette Hayes*; Brett Higgins*; Marti Hirsch*; Rosie Holland; Stevie Houston*; Liu Hulan*; Casey Jones*; Jackie Kaminsky*; Loretta Kovacs*; Merry Kramer;* Gloria Lamerino*; Rosie Lavine; Munch Mancini*; Nell Matthews*; Haley McAlister; Lara McClintoch*; Sutton McPhee*; Maris Middleton*; Brenda Midnight*; Tess Monaghan*; Ruthie Kantor Morris; Lorelei Muldoon; Pat North*; Tru North*; Victory "Torie" O'Shea*; Martha Patterson*; Karen Pelletier*; Charlie Plato*; Rachel Porter*; Maggy Renard; Sukey Reynolds*; Amelia Sachs*; Lacey Savich*; Dr. Susan Shader; Rei Shimura*; Grace Smith*; Helen Sorby*; Dr. Michael Stone*; Dr. Evelyn Sutcliffe* (one book in a different form published earlier); Tory Travers*; Rose Trevelyan*; Fran Varaday*; Francesca Vierling*; Connor Westphal*; Chas Wheatley*; MacLaren Yarbrough*

1998: Billie August; Allida "Allie" Babcock*; Holly Barker*; Janet Barkin*; Laurel Bartlett*; Alma Bashears*; Madeline Bean*; Grace Beckmann* Kat Bronsky; Nikki Chase*; Wyanet "Wy" Chouinard*; Eliza Blake*; Kathryn Bogert*; Caroline Canfield; Laura Chastain*; Sunny Childs*; Kathryn "Casey" Collins; Regan Culver*; Robyn Devara*; Venus Diamond*; Matty Donahue; Eve Duncan*; Dixie Flannigan*; Carole Ann Gibson*; Meg Gillis; Susan Given; Hester Gorse*; Ann Hardaway*; Cinda Hayes*; Honey Huckleberry*;

Lexy Hyatt*; Reiko Ichiro* as a principal character); Kirsten*; Devonie Lace-Matthews*; Sierra Lavotini*; Magdalena "Maggie" Maguire*; Trish Maguire*; Hannah Malloy and Kiki Goldstein*; Jennifer Marsh*; Emily "Blue" McCarron; Karen McDade; Portia McTeague; Adele Monsarrat*; Kellie Montgomery*; Teddy Morelli*; Cordelia Morgan*; Taylor Morgan*; May Morrison; Zen Moses; Jane Nichols; Rachel O'Connor*; Kendall O'Dell*; Maureen O'Donnell*; Laura Owen*; Lily Pascale*; Molly Piper; Rose Piper; Kate Power*; Narcissa Powers and Judah Daniel*; Precious Ramotswe*; Sunny Randall*; Caroline Rhodes*; Ruby Rothman*; Trudy Roundtree*; Dodee Swisher*; Sydney Teague*; Jacobia Tiptree*; Rev. Merrily Watkins;* Serena Wilcox*; Charlotte Willett*

1999: Bel Bickhoff Barrett*; Sarah Decker Brandt*; Lily Brewster*; Olivia Brown; Margaret Campbell*; Wilhelmina "Willa" Carson*; Samantha Casey*; Denise Cleever*; Rev. Lily Connor*' Tempe Crabtree*; Sarah Booth Delaney*; Betsy Devonshire*; Tracy Eaton; Queen Elizabeth I*; Trade Ellis; Cora Felton and Sherry Carter*; Jane Ferguson and Hillary Scarborough*; Augusta Goodnight*; Belle Graham*; Lindy Graham-Haggerty*; Annabelle Hardy-Maratos*; Sally Harrington*; Sharyn Howard*; Hannah Ives*; Jolene Jackson; Hilda Johansson*; Charlotte Justice *; Zoe Kergulin; Leigh Koslow*; Magdalene la Batarde*; Meg Langslow*; Aimee Leduc*; Gilda Liberty*; Victoria "Vicky" Lucci*; Matty Madrid; Stevie Marriner*; Genevieve Masefield*; Camilla McPhee*; Claire Montrose*; Phoebe Mullins; Jake O'Hara*; Julian Palmer *; Jimi Plain; Claire Rawlings* Carol Sabala*; Marla Shore*; Bretta Solomon*; Jane Stuart*; Zöe Szabo; Torrey Tunet*; Anna Turnipseed*; Tessa Vance; Claire Watkins*;

Resources and Readings for Volumes I, 2, and 3

Although I read extensively on the political, economic, literary, and social period from 1860-2009, special credit should be given to the following books for their treatment of the subject and for the identification of authors and sleuths previously unknown to me.

Aburdene, Patricia and John Naisbitt. *Megatrends for Women*. Villard, 1992.

Allen, Frederick Lewis. *Only Yesterday, An Informal History of the 1920's*. Harper & Row, 1931.

Anderson, Bonnie S. and Judith P. Zinsser, *A History of Their Own*. Harper & Row, 1988.

Barnes, Melvyn. *Murder in Print, A Guide to Two Centuries of Crime Fiction*. Barn Owl Books, 1986.

Berkin, Carol Ruth and Mary Beth Norton. *Women of America*. Houghton Mifflin, 1979.

Billman, Carol. *The Secret of the Stratmeyer Syndicate*. Ungar, 1986.

Boardman, Fon Wyman, Jr. *America And the Jazz Age, A History of the 1920's*. Walck, 1968.

Burchill, Julie. *Girls on Film*. Pantheon, 1986.

Caprio, Betsy. *The Mystery of Nancy Drew*. Source Books, 1992.

Cawelti, John G. Adventure, *Mystery, and Romance*. University of Chicago Press, 1976.

Chafe, William H. *The American Woman, Her Changing Social, Economic, and Political Roles*, 1920-1970. Oxford University Press, 1972.

Clark, Homer H, Jr. *The Law of Domestic Relations*. West, 1968.

Collins, Gail: *When Everything Changed, The Amazing Journey of American Women from 1960 to the Present*, Little, Brown, & Co, 2009

Collins, Gail: *American Women: 400 Years of Dolls, Drudges, Helpmates, and Heroines;* Morrow, 2003; reprinted by8 Harper Perennial, 2007

Cook, Michael L. *Murder by Mail*. Bowling Green State University Popular Press, 1983.

Coser, Lewis A., Charles Kadushin, and Walter W. Powell. *BOOKS, The Culture and Commerce of Publishing*. Basic Books, 1982.

Craig, Patricia and Mary Cadogan. *The Lady Investigates, Women Detectives and Spies in Fiction*. St. Martin's Press, 1981.

Current, Richard N., T. Harry Williams, Alan Brinkley, and Frank Friedel. *American History: A Survey*, Seventh Edition, Knopf, 1987.

Dooley, Roger. *From Scarface to Scarlet, American Films in the 1930's*. Harcourt Brace, 1981.

East, Andy. *Cold War File*. Scarecrow Press, 1983.

Edwards, Julia. *Women of the World, The Great Foreign Correspondents*. Houghton Mifflin, 1988.

Eisenstadt v. Baird. 405 U.S. 438 (1972).

Evans, Sara M. *Born for Liberty*. The Free Press (Macmillan), 1989.

Freeman, Lucy. Editor. *The Murder Mystique.* Ungar, 1982.

Freidan, Betty. *The Feminine Mystique.* W. W. Norton, 1963.

Glendon, Mary Ann. *Matrimonial Property: A Comparative Study of Law and Social Change.* 49 Tulane Law Review 21 (1974).

Gold, Annalee. *75 Years of Fashion.* Fairchild, 1975.

Gorham, Deborah. *The Victorian Girl and the Feminine Ideal.* Indiana University Press, 1982.

Grannis, Chandler B. *What Happens in Book Publishing.* Columbia University Press, 1957.

Greene, Suzanne Ellery. *Books for Pleasure, Popular Fiction, 1914-45.* Bowling Green State University Popular Press, 1974.

Greer, Germaine. *The Female Eunuch.* McGraw Hill, 1970.

Griswold v. Connecticut. 381 U.S. 479 (1965).

Grun, Bernard. *Timetables of History. Second Edition,* Touchstone, 1982; Third Edition, 1991.

Hackett, Alice Payne and James Henry Burke. *80 Years of Best Sellers*: 1895-1975. R.R. Bowker, 1977.

Haskell, Molly. *From Reverence to Rape, The Treatment of Women in the Movies.* Holt, Rinehart and Winston, 1974.

Haycraft, Howard. *The Art of the Mystery Story.* Carroll & Graf, 1983 (first published in 1946).

Haycraft, Howard. *Murder for Pleasure.* Carroll & Graf, 1984 (first published in 1941).

Heising, Willetta. *Detecting Men.* Purple Moon Press, 1998.

Heising, Willetta. *Detecting Women,* Edition 3. Purple Moon Press, 1999

Henderson, Lesley. Editor. *Twentieth Century Crime & Mystery Writers,* Third Edition. St. James Press, 1991.

Holcombe, Lee. *Victorian Ladies at Work.* Archon Books, 1973.

Hoppenstand, Gary. Editor. *The Dime Novel Detective.* Bowling Green State University Press, 1982.

Horn, Maurice. Editor. *The World Encyclopedia of Comics.* Avon, 1976.

Howell, Reet. Editor. Her Story in Sport; A Historical Anthology of Women in Sports. Leisure Press, 1982.

Hubin, Allen J. *Crime Fiction, 1749-1980: A Comprehensive Bibliography.* Garland, 1984; and its *1981-1985 Supplement,* Garland, 1988.

Hubin, Allen J. *Crime Fiction, II, A Comprehensive Bibliography, 1749-1990.* Garland, 1994.

Hubin, Allen J. *Crime Fiction III, A Comprehensive Bibliography, 1749-1995.* Locus Press on CD-Rom, 1999.

Hubin, Allen J. *Crime Fiction IV, A Comprehensive Bibliogaphy, 1749-2000.*Locus Press on CD-Rom, 2003

Inge, Thomas. Editor. *American Popular Culture.* Greenwood Press, 1978.

Kael, Pauline. *5001 Nights at the Movies.* Holt, Rinehart, and Winston, 1982.

Kerker, Linda and Jane De Hart Matthews. *Women's America*, Oxford University Press. 1982.

Kraditor, Aileen S. *The Ideas of the Woman Suffrage Movement: 1890-1920*. Columbia University Press, 1965.

Landrum, Larry, Pat Browne, and Ray B. Browne. *Dimensions of Detective Fiction*. Popular Press, 1976.

Maida, Patricia D. *Mother of Detective Fiction*. Bowling Green Popular Press, 1989.

Maio, Kathleen. *Feminist in the Dark: Reviewing the Movies*. The Crossing Press, 1988.

Mason, Bobbie Ann. *The Girl Sleuth: A Feminist Guide to the Bobbsey Twins, Nancy Drew and Their Sisters*. Feminist Press, 1975.

Matthews, Glenna. *Just a Housewife*. Oxford University Press, 1987.

McDowell, Barbara and Hana Unlauf. Editors. *The Good Housekeeping Woman's Almanac*. Newspaper Enterprise Association, 1977.

McLaughlin, Steve D., Barbara D. Melber, John O. G. Billy, Denise M. Zimmerle, Linda D. Winges, and Terry R. Johnson, *The Changing Lives of American Women*. University of North Carolina Press, 1988.

McLeish, Kenneth and Valerie: *Bloomsbury Good Reading Guide to Murder Crime Fiction and Thrillers*; Bloomsbury, 1990

Moe, Karine and Shandy, Dianna: *Glass Ceilings & 100-Hour Couples*, University of Georgia Press, 2009

Morello, Karen Berger. *The Invisible Bar, The Woman Lawyer in America*. Random House, 1986.

Mott, Fran Luther. *Golden Multitudes*. Macmillan, 1947.

Newsweek; *Hear Her Roar,*November 2, 2009

Nichols, Victoria and Thompson, Susan: *Silk Stalkings, When Women Write of Murder*; Black Lizard, 1988

Osborne, Eric. *Victorian Detective Fiction*. Bodley Head, 1966, a catalogue of the collection made by Dorothy Glover and Graham Greene.

Ousby, Ian. *Bloodhounds of Heaven, The Detective in English Fiction from Godwin to Doyle*. Harvard University Press, 1976.

Peterson, Audrey. *Victorian Masters of Mystery*. Ungar, 1984.

Pruett, Lorine. *Women Workers Through the Depression*. Macmillan, 1934.

Queen, Ellery. *In the Queen's Parlor, and Other Leaves from the Editor's Notebook*. Simon & Schuster, 1957.

Queen, Ellery. Editor. *101 Years Entertainment, The Great Detective Stories, 1841-1941*. Little, Brown, 1941.

Reddy, Maureen T.: *Sisters in Crime; Feminism and the Crime Novel*; Continuum, 1988

Rehak, Melanie: *Girl Sleuth:Nancy Drew and the Women Who Created Her;* Harcourt, 2005

Reilly, John M. Editor. *Twentieth Century Crime & Mystery Writers, First Edition*. St. Martin's Press, 1980.

Reilly, John M. Editor. *Twentieth Century Crime & Mystery Writers*, Second Editon. St. Martin's Press, 1985.

Roberts, Gary G., Gary Hoppenstand and Ray B. Browne. *Old Sleuth's Freaky Female Detectives* (From the Dime Novels. Bowling Green State University Popular Press, 1990.

Rodell, Marie F. *Mystery Fiction, Theory and Technique*. Revised Edition, Hermitage House, 1952.

Roe v. Wade. 410 U.S. 113 (1973).

Rogers, Katharine M. *The Troublesome Helpmate*. University of Washington Press, 1966.

Routley, Eric. *Puritan Pleasures of the Detective Story*. Gollancz, 1972.

Sayers, Dorothy Editor (See introduction) to the anthology, *The Omnibus of Crime*. Harcourt Brace, 1929.

Slung, Michelle; Editor. *Crime on Her Mind*. Pantheon, 1975.

Solomon, Barbara Miller. *In the Company of Educated Women*. Yale University Press, 1985.

Smuts, Robert. *Women and Work in America*. Schocken, 1971.

Steedman, Carolyn. *Policing the Victorian Community*. Routledge & Kegan Paul, 1984.

Swanson, Jean and Dean James. *By a Woman's Hand*. Berkley, 1994.

Symons, Julian. *Mortal Consequences*. Harper & Row, 1972.

Taylor, Joan Kennedy. *Reclaiming the Mainstream*. Prometheus, 1988.

Terrace, Vincent. *The Complete Encyclopedia of Television Programs 1947-79*. A. S. Barnes & Company, 1979

Time Magazine; *Special Report on the State of the American Woman;* October 26, 2009

Tobias, Sheila and Lisa Anderson. *What Really Happened to Rosie the Riveter? Demobilization and the Female Labor Force, 1944-47*. MSS Modular Publications. Date unavailable.

Vicinius, Martha. *Independent Women*. University of Chicago Press, 1985.

Van Dover, J. Kenneth. *Murder in the Millions*. Ungar, 1984.

Ware, Susan. *Holding Their Own, American Women in the 1930's*. Twayne, 1982.

Weiss, Daniel Evans. *The Great Divide: How Females and Males Really Differ*. Poseidon, 1991.

Winks, Robin W. *Modus Operandi*. Godine, 1982.

Wrong, E. M.,Editor (See introduction) to the anthology, *Crime and Detection*. Oxford University Press, 1926.

I wish to thank Jon Breen for his corrections to my listings on Dorothy Sayers and E. M. Wrong.

About the Author

Colleen A. Barnett was born in Green Bay, Wisconsin, the daughter of a trial attorney and his wife. She earned bachelor's and master's degrees in Political Science from the University of Wisconsin in Madison. She dropped out of law school after three semesters to marry fellow student John Barnett. When they moved to his home town Boscobel, Wisconsin, where he joined his father in the practice of law, she remained at home to raise their family of seven children. By the time their youngest child was in grade school, older children were entering college and that was expensive.

Colleen began work as a volunteer coordinator for the Grant County Department of Social Services, rising to supervisor of the resource unit. Later, she took early retirement with John's encouragement to re-enter the University of Wisconsin Law School where she received her law degree cum laude.

Later she was employed as an attorney and mediator, and as a lecturer in Political Science at the University of Wisconsin-Richland Center. She retired at age 75 to focus on the revisions of the first three volumes of *Mystery Women.* Her future plans include spending more time with her children, grandchildren, and great-grandchildren and reading for pleasure.

After John's death, Colleen moved to St. Paul, Minnesota where her two daughters live. She is a member of the Twin Cities Sisters in Crime.